Alcohol and Drug Problems in Women

Research Advances in
Alcohol and Drug Problems

Volume 5

RESEARCH ADVANCES IN ALCOHOL AND DRUG PROBLEMS

A Continuation Order Plan is available for this series. A continuation order will bring delivery of each new volume immediately upon publication. Volumes are billed only upon actual shipment. For further information please contact the publisher.

Alcohol and Drug Problems in Women

Research Advances in Alcohol and Drug Problems

Volume 5

Edited by

Oriana Josseau Kalant

Addiction Research Foundation
Toronto, Ontario, Canada

PLENUM PRESS · NEW YORK AND LONDON

The Library of Congress cataloged the first volume of this title as follows:

Research advances in alcohol & drug problems. v. 1–

New York [etc.] J. Wiley, 1974–
v. 24 cm. annual.
"A Wiley biomedical health publication."
ISSN 0093-9714

1. Alcoholism–Periodicals. 2. Narcotic habit–Periodicals.
RC565.R37   616.8'6'005   73-18088

Library of Congress Catalog Card Number 73-18088
ISBN 0-306-40394-3

© 1980 Plenum Press, New York
A Division of Plenum Publishing Corporation
227 West 17th Street, New York, N.Y. 10011

Printed in the United States of America

ADVISORY PANEL

Contributors

HELEN M. ANNIS, Addiction Research Foundation, Toronto, Ontario

DAVID S. BELL, Alanbrook Clinic, Mosman, New South Wales, Australia

WILFRED E. BOOTHROYD, Addiction Research Foundation, Toronto, Ontario

THEODORE J. CICERO, Departments of Psychiatry and Anatomy and Neurobiology, Washington University School of Medicine, St. Louis, Missouri

KEVIN O'BRIEN FEHR, Addiction Research Foundation, Toronto, Ontario

ROBERTA G. FERRENCE, Addiction Research Foundation, Toronto, Ontario

LORETTA P. FINNEGAN, Department of Pediatrics, Thomas Jefferson University, Philadelphia, Pennsylvania

ELLEN R. GRITZ, Veterans Administration Medical Center Brentwood; and Department of Psychiatry, University of California, Los Angeles, California

ORIANA JOSSEAU KALANT, Addiction Research Foundation, Toronto, Ontario

HARRY GENE LEVINE, Social Research Group, School of Public Health, University of California, Berkeley, California. Present address: Department of Sociology, Queens College, City University of New York, Flushing, New York

CAROLYN B. LIBAN, Addiction Research Foundation, Toronto, Ontario

CATHERINE A. MARTIN, Department of Psychiatry, University of Kentucky College of Medicine, Lexington, Kentucky

WILLIAM R. MARTIN, Department of Pharmacology, University of Kentucky College of Medicine, Lexington, Kentucky

NANCY K. MELLO, Alcohol and Drug Abuse Research Center, McLean Hospital, Belmont, Massachusetts

ROBERT E. POPHAM, Addiction Research Foundation, Toronto, Ontario

LEE N. ROBINS, Department of Psychiatry, Washington University School of Medicine, St. Louis, Missouri

HENRY L. ROSETT, Departments of Psychiatry and Obstetrics and Gynecology, Boston University School of Medicine, Boston, Massachusetts

WOLFGANG SCHMIDT, Addiction Research Foundation, Toronto, Ontario

ELIZABETH M. SMITH, Department of Psychiatry, Washington University School of Medicine, St. Louis, Missouri

RICHARD P. SWINSON, Department of Psychiatry, University of Toronto, Toronto, Ontario

PAUL C. WHITEHEAD, Department of Sociology, University of Western Ontario; and Addiction Research Foundation, London, Ontario

PATRICIA WILKINSON, Health Commission of Victoria, South Melbourne, Victoria, Australia

Foreword

Over the last decade the world has experienced a growing interest in problems associated with the nonmedical use of drugs. This interest has corresponded to a real growth in the extent, diversity, and social impact of the use of alcohol and drugs in many societies. As a result, the amount of research and writing on the subject of drug problems has greatly increased, and it has become very difficult for one individual to keep up with all the relevant literature. There is thus an acute need in the field for critical reviews that assess current developments, and the present series is intended to fill this need. The series is not to be an "annual review" in the usual sense. The aim is not to cover all the work reported during the preceding year in relation to a fixed selection of topics. Rather, it is to present each year evaluative papers on topics in which enough recent progress has been made to alter the general scope in a particular area.

Owing to the multidisciplinary nature of problems of drug use and dependence, the papers published in each volume will be drawn from several disciplines. However, some volumes may be devoted to one particular problem, with individual reviews and papers examining various aspects of it.

The composition of the editorial board and the international advisory board reflects these objectives. The editors are members of the senior scientific staff of the Addiction Research Foundation of Ontario. Their own areas of special interest include the fields of biochemistry, pharmacology, psychiatry, anthropology, sociology, and jurisprudence. The members of the international advisory panel, representing seven countries in Europe, North and South America, and Australia, are well known, and their interests range over the relevant disciplines. On the basis of their knowledge of the relevant fields and their reading of the literature in various languages, they propose to the editors each year a list of the subjects that are most appropriate for review, as well as the names of investigators in different parts of the world who might be best qualified to write the reviews. Obviously no publication can guarantee that it will fill the needs of all its readers with respect to sorting out fact from conjecture, the important from the trivial, or the permanent from the transitory. Nevertheless, we hope that this series will provide a lead in the desired direction and will stimulate the type of interdisciplinary inquiry that is most required.

The Editors

Toronto

Preface

In the preface to each of the previous volumes in this series, reference has been made to the possibility that from time to time an entire volume might be devoted to reviews on different aspects of a single theme, rather than to individual reviews on unrelated subjects.

The present volume, devoted entirely to a comparison of alcohol and drug problems in women and men, is the first such "theme volume" in the series. It deals with a subject that has received rapidly growing attention in recent years, from scientists, therapists, administrators, and the general public. Undoubtedly, much of this interest has arisen as a consequence of statements and activities of members of the women's movement in North America, who have had a salutary effect on general awareness of a long-neglected problem.

At the same time, however, there has been a relatively slow response of researchers to the many gaps in scientific knowledge in this area. The present volume represents, in our view, a major contribution to the correction of this deficiency. The various reviews provide a drawing together and assessment of much knowledge that was buried in reports devoted to other topics, as well as much original research in certain areas, and suggestions for future work in many others. We believe it may well constitute a landmark in the field.

The idea for this volume was proposed by Dr. Oriana Josseau Kalant, a member of the advisory panel, who demonstrated eloquently the need for, and the feasibility of, a thoroughly scientific objective review of this topic, free of ideological debate and rhetoric. She was invited to act as special editor of this volume and has carried the editorial load almost singlehandedly. The editorial board records its appreciation of her outstanding work and awaits with interest the response of the readers to this first theme volume. Volume 6 will be of the previous type, with timely reviews on a variety of subjects.

The Editors

Acknowledgments

It is a pleasure to acknowledge the support provided by all the members of the Editorial Board of the *Research Advances in Alcohol and Drug Problems* series, particularly Robert E. Popham and Wolfgang Schmidt, during the preparation of this volume. The Editor was greatly helped by their suggestions and criticisms, as well as by those offered by Ruth Cooperstock, P. James Giffin, Joseph R. Gusfield, Jerome Jaffe, and Robin Room. Special thanks are due to Harold Kalant, who enthusiastically supported this project from its very inception and later gave most generously of his vast expertise, of his judgment, and of his time. I regret that the requirements of anonymity prevent me from thanking individually the reviewers of all the chapters, for their generous and significant contributions to the quality of the work.

I am grateful for the dedicated and enthusiastic cooperation of Sylvia Lambert and Lise M. Anglin, who provided invaluable editorial assistance, including copy editing, preparation of indexes, initial proofreading, and verification of references. In this last task, they were generously assisted by the staff of the Addiction Research Foundation Library, under the direction of Anne W. Johnston.

Vivian Ackerman, Senior Production Editor at Plenum Publishing Corporation, showed great understanding, cooperation, and patience, for which I am most thankful.

Finally, special thanks are due to my secretary, Deborah J. Lindholm, for her truly outstanding commitment to this project and for the high quality of her work.

O. J. K.

Contents

15. SEX DIFFERENCES IN THE EFFECTS OF ALCOHOL AND OTHER PSYCHOACTIVE DRUGS ON ENDOCRINE FUNCTION: CLINICAL AND EXPERIMENTAL EVIDENCE   545

Theodore J. Cicero

16. THE EFFECTS OF ALCOHOL ON THE FETUS AND OFFSPRING   595

Henry L. Rosett

17. THE EFFECTS OF OPIATES, SEDATIVE–HYPNOTICS, AMPHETAMINES, CANNABIS, AND OTHER PSYCHOACTIVE DRUGS ON THE FETUS AND NEWBORN   653

Loretta P. Finnegan and Kevin O'Brien Fehr

INDEX   725

Sex Differences in Alcohol and Drug Problems—Some Highlights

ORIANA JOSSEAU KALANT

1. INTRODUCTION

The women's movement of the past decade and, more specifically, the International Women's Year in 1975 are unquestionably the main reasons for the publication of this volume. Toward the end of 1975, women on the staff of the Addiction Research Foundation formed a group to look into various areas of specific concern to women, including the status of research into alcohol and drug problems in women and, more generally, into sex differences in these areas. Very quickly, a question arose concerning the feasibility of dedicating one volume of this series to the topic. The problem, quite simply, was whether the amount of knowledge on women's problems was sufficient to justify the project. Some felt that such an enterprise was probably premature, while others thought that the timing was optimal. Some preliminary research into the pertinent literature settled the matter clearly in the affirmative. There were unquestionably sufficient data well worth a critical examination, despite the fact that in the experimental areas of the field, the subjects of choice have most frequently been males, ranging from rats to college students. Accordingly, the Editorial Board of the Research Advances Series approved the project.

The preliminary exploration of the literature, however, made at least two problems clearly evident. First, since this was in effect a "nonfield" in many respects, it was difficult to think of suitable contributors on a number of topics. There were experts, for example, on the social history of alcohol use, on the epidemiology of alcohol and drug use, on the effects of drugs on the endocrine system and so on, but none who, to

ORIANA JOSSEAU KALANT ● Addiction Research Foundation, Toronto, Ontario.

our knowledge, had specifically explored these questions in relation to sex differences. Singular exceptions to this general situation were the fields of psychiatry and obviously of obstetrics and gynecology and of pediatrics, where specific attention had been paid to the problems of women and newborns for some time. A related problem was that whatever knowledge existed in the literature was extremely difficult to retrieve for review and examination because it was not indexed according to the relevant terms. To this day, most books in the field of alcohol and drug use do not include words such as *male/female, men/women,* or *sex differences* in their subject indexes. This situation is extremely frustrating because we all know that many articles and books do in fact include data and sometimes commentary on the subject. The task, then, of preparing critical reviews for this volume has been much more onerous than usual, and therefore our contributors deserve very special thanks.

Even though this series consists essentially of critical reviews of the *literature,* this particular volume, for obvious reasons, contains a number of chapters that are, in addition, original research papers in the sense that they include the examination and discussion of primary data. Good examples are Chapter 4, in which the recent epidemiology of sex differences in psychoactive drug use is examined; Chapter 10 dealing with sex differences in the mortality of alcoholics; Chapter 11 on sex differences in the treatment of alcoholism; and the section on sex differences in the cessation of smoking in Chapter 14. These contributions break new ground in areas that have, until recently, been badly neglected. Even more importantly, they promise to be very fruitful in promoting the understanding of all drug use, not only that of women alone.

Short of rewriting the whole field of drug use and drug problems from the point of view of women, a reasonable selection of the most relevant areas had to be made. We feel that the table of contents reflects the state of the field fairly well, though it does not represent total coverage. No doubt that will be realized in future volumes of this series and in many other publications.

Three major and to some degree overlapping themes have been dealt with in depth. They are the comparative epidemiology of alcohol and drug use in men and women, sex differences in the use of alcohol and in alcohol-related problems, and the effects of alcohol and drug use on pregnancy and the newborn. The reasons for this approach are rather simple and clear. First, it was considered essential to have a thorough examination of the rates of use of alcohol and other drugs by men and women and of the changes, if any in such rates over time, in order to know with reasonable accuracy the magnitude of potential problems in men and women and the direction of trends. Chapters 3, 4, 5, and 12 deal directly with these issues, but several other chapters also touch upon them. Second, it was considered important to delineate, as accurately as possible, the sex differences in the antecedents of alcohol and drug use, the patterns of use, the factors that affect them, and the consequences of heavy or problem use. Such knowledge is obviously essential for the planning and the effective operation of programs for prevention and treatment. Most chapters deal with these issues from various points of view. Finally, Chapters 16 and 17 explore the effects of alcohol and of most other psychoactive drugs on the fetus and the offspring.

The remarks that follow are not intended to summarize the findings and conclusions of the contributors to this volume. The authors have done so themselves most aptly. Rather, they are the editor's personal view of and commentary on the most salient highlights of these chapters and a statement of the major research questions in need of further exploration.

2. HISTORY

It is customary to begin reviews of the literature with a paragraph or two on the historical background of the subject at hand. This procedure presumably adds the dignity of scholarship to what otherwise would be a matter-of-fact review of current knowledge. The chronological jump between these initial paragraphs and the body of the work varies greatly in length in different reviews. In the case of many articles and books on cannabis and opiates, it usually leaps a couple of millennia. More frequently, it is a question of only a few decades. The gap depends simply on the time span between the first record of the use of a drug and current knowledge about it. There is nothing intrinsically objectionable in this practice, except that it provides only an illusion of history instead of a meaningful and enlightening historical perspective. Two distinct but related historical questions are important in this context. One is that of the historical evolution of the use of a drug, its origin and spread, the changes in pattern of its use, the recognition of its consequences, and the professional and social response to it. The second question concerns the analysis of broader social, economic, and other historical influences on the attitudes of societies, which set the stage and determine the level of acceptance or rejection of alcohol and drug use.

In Chapter 12, Bell traces the evolution of patterns of consumption of a number of the more widely used psychoactive drugs and shows the common pattern that women are the predominant users of licit, medically prescribed agents, while men account for the bulk of illicit use. This theme is approached and confirmed from a different perspective in the chapter on the epidemiology of psychoactive drug use, by Ferrence and Whitehead. Bell emphasizes the role of medical practioners, therefore, in the creation and the propagation of dependence on these drugs among women. As he points out, this approach offers at the same time a focus for preventive education that may have different applicabilities to the two sexes. In contrast, legal controls of illicit drug use have often succeeded only in changing the pattern of use from one drug to another. As Bell points out, reliance on legal measures alone is unlikely to solve the basic problems, and other individual and social approaches are also necessary.

In Chapter 2, Levine provides us with the second type of historical perspective. His examination of the evolution of social attitudes toward drinking in American society from the 18th century to the end of the 19th century is most interesting and rewarding. It makes clear that women played a key role in the shaping of such attitudes, particularly toward the second half of the 19th century, through the organization of the Woman's Christian Temperance Union (WCTU). But even more importantly, Levine correlates the social and economic changes that took place through the 19th century with the evolution of attitudes toward the use of alcohol. During the 18th century, when the whole family was the economic production unit of a predominantly agricultural society, drunkenness and its consequences were objected to, but not any or all use of alcohol. Women apparently drank with their men. In the 19th century, through industrialization and urbanization, the character of family life changed substantially. The men went out to work in industry or the marketplace, and the women were left in charge of children and home. Thus sex roles became much more clearly differentiated than they had been before, and women began to be perceived, and probably began to perceive themselves, as the embodiment of virtue and of moral standards. Alcohol was seen increasingly as a threat to this new, idealized family life. Eventually, the aims of the temperance and of the women's suffrage movements overlapped to a considerable extent. On the one hand, women's suffrage was seen as a way to attain legislation designed to curtail drinking, and on the other, the need to curtail drinking was seen as an issue that might win women's suffrage.

Levine's essay does not, alas, cover the 20th century. However, it is clear that the aims of the present women's movement, especially in North America, are rather different in this respect. It has sought to gain access for women to all work and recreational places that were previously the exclusive territory of men. These include, among others, bars and clubs where drinking is a primary activity. In other words, the militant women of the 19th century wanted to achieve equality by making men behave toward drinking as women did, while the militant women of today seem to want to achieve equality in this respect by behaving as men do. In summary, then, in the 18th century men and women worked and drank together. During the 19th century, and probably during a good deal of the 20th, men went out to work and drink while most women stayed at home. More recently, men, and increasingly women, go out both to work and to drink. It should be emphasized that these attitudes refer essentially to drinking patterns as opposed to the amounts drunk. Several chapters in this book clearly show that on average, women tend to drink significantly less than men.

Obviously, the historical approach is the only one available for learning about alcohol- and drug-using behavior in the past, and especially about sex differences related to it. Levine's chapter is an excellent example of how fruitful these studies can be, not only in tracing changes in drug-seeking behavior over time, but also in delineating the social, religious, and economic factors that modulate it. Such knowledge and historical perspective ought to be of great help in the design of methods of coping with the hazardous use of drugs, including alcohol. Levine's essay covers social factors affecting the use of one drug during one century in one country. How tremendously interesting it would be to have comparable studies of other countries or cultures, other times, and other drugs.

We should not expect such knowledge as that reviewed by Bell and Levine to give us definitive answers about the causes of drug use and abuse or about the best methods of controlling them. We can, however, expect historical research to raise important questions that we might otherwise not think of asking. To what extent, for example, have patterns and amounts of alcohol and drug consumption by men and women varied among different eras, cultures, and races? If they vary greatly, one may conclude that they are determined primarily by transitory social and economic factors. If, on the other hand, constant features are found in all times and places, then logically, one may postulate either basic biological determinants or sex differences in social roles that are so fundamental as to transcend all social and cultural barriers. This possibility is illustrated by the sex difference in the use of licit and illicit drugs noted by Bell (see Chapter 12). An unpublished literature survey by Jerome H. Jaffe (personal communication, 1979) led him to state:

Patterns of both nonmedical and medical use vary widely from culture to culture, and from time to time within a culture, but amidst this great variability, two findings appear repeatedly. For almost every drug and in almost every society, nonmedical drug use appears to be more common among men. With almost equal consistency (at least over the last century), the consumers of drugs ostensibly used for medical purposes are more likely to be women.

This is obviously so fundamental a concept that it requires thorough documentation and analysis in many studies. How did the rapid introduction into clinical practice of many new analgesics and sedatives at the turn of the century affect *total* patterns of drug and alcohol use by men and women? How did periods of prohibition, such as that of alcohol in North America and of cannabis in North Africa, influence the drug-consuming behavior of the two sexes? What were the consequences of periods of major social upheaval such as wars, colonial occupation, or rapid industrialization on sex differences in overall drug use?

Some aspects of these problems can be answered by modern techniques in contemporary populations. However, intensive examination of the changes occurring in a generation or less, within a single society, may miss significant factors that operate only over much longer cycles. Moreover, as the world becomes culturally more homogeneous, the opportunity of finding instructive differences may diminish. In these circumstances, the historical approach can yield otherwise inaccessible knowledge.

3. EPIDEMIOLOGY

Despite the evidence that women use alcohol, tobacco, and illicit drugs at much lower rates than men, the belief has become widespread during the last decade or so that women are rapidly catching up with men, particularly with respect to alcohol and tobacco use. Up to now, this belief has been based primarily on qualitative observations and impressions of the changes occurring in the drug-seeking behavior of both sexes in our society. It was felt, therefore, that an in-depth study of sex differences in rates of alcohol and drug use, based on sophisticated epidemiological techniques, was badly needed. The implications of the conclusions reached are of both theoretical and practical importance. Theoretically, solid knowledge of the similarities and the differences in rates of drug use by men and women can help us understand the dynamics governing this behavior. The practical implications are considerable, since they affect the responses of government, the medical profession, and other agencies to the needs of those individuals of both sexes who carry the use of psychoactive drugs to dangerous levels.

Ferrence (Chapter 3), Ferrence and Whitehead (Chapter 4), and Robins and Smith (Chapter 5) provide us with the most thorough and comprehensive examination of the data available to date. Many of the conclusions they draw are rather surprising. This is so because these authors show clearly how complex the problem is and therefore how easy it is to draw simplistic conclusions and, as a corollary, how false and misleading many of our present notions are.

One of the surprises to the nonepidemiologist is the nature and limitations of the methods available to determine accurately the rates of use of various drugs and, perhaps more importantly, the rates of hazardous use. The authors mentioned above discuss critically the limitations of these techniques and are therefore duly cautious in drawing conclusions. There is no need to repeat their analyses here. Attention should be called, however, to the unevenness of the methods available for assessing the rates of use of various drugs. For legal drugs, particularly alcohol and tobacco, there are several methods of estimating use, including surveys of total and specific populations, examination of rates of sales, and derivation of indices of hazardous use based on statistics such as driving accidents and morbidity and mortality rates associated with heavy use. These types of data are not generally available for most other licit and illicit drugs.

In the case of illicit drugs, objective data on total production and on levels of consumption in the whole population are inaccessible for obvious reasons, and we must rely on surveys and on very indirect indices, such as changes in rates of seizures by police, or on rates of death by overdose, to know if any changes in consumption are occurring. With respect to the licit and illicit nonmedical use of psychoactive drugs other than alcohol and tobacco, we do not have clearly defined consequences of heavy use that are sufficiently specific to those drugs to be used as indicators of hazardous use. Nor do we have cheap and simple methods of measuring the levels of some of these drugs in the blood, to ascertain correlations between levels of use and various specific hazards. In summary, the scope and depth of our knowledge about alcohol and tobacco use are far greater than about most other drugs. This observation should be kept in mind when comparing drug use by men and women, particularly with respect to levels of use, because it is apparent that the kinds of drugs used by the two sexes differ.

As noted above, the view is widely held that the behavior of men and women is becoming increasingly similar. Bell (Chapter 12) expresses this view most eloquently when he says:

> In the past, and until fairly recently, behavioral differences between male and female seemed to provide an absolute contrast across an enormous range of activities, including drug dependence, but they are now disappearing at such a rate that one may well wonder if any will be left in time beyond the one undisputed and essential difference.

It should be remarked parenthetically that the allegedly increased similarity of behavior is assumed tacitly to depend primarily on women's adopting the characteristic behaviors of men, rather than the opposite or a mixture of the two. In the context of drug use, this supposition means that we assume drug consumption to be increasing at such a rate that women are already, or soon will be, consuming drugs at rates comparable to those of men. With a few exceptions, the analysis of the evidence presented in this volume does not support this belief.

As discussed by Ferrence (Chapter 3), two current hypotheses concerning changes in alcohol consumption are that the rates of problem drinking by the two sexes are converging and that the typical woman alcoholic is a middle-aged housewife who drinks in secret. These two suppositions lead in turn to the belief that there are many more concealed women than men alcoholics and that the treatment facilities available to the women are therefore quantitatively and qualitatively more inadequate than those for men. However, this belief is not borne out by the available evidence. The distinction between rate of alcohol use and rates of heavy or problem drinking should be kept clearly in mind. The data analyzed by Ferrence show that although the sex ratio of drinking among the young now suggests convergence, the rates of heavy drinking among the young as well as among adults do not. Ferrence concludes that there are no convergence trends between men and women and that, overall, the sex ratio is about three to one, that is, three male heavy drinkers for every female heavy drinker. The validity of this conclusion is strengthened by the fact that it is based on a thorough analysis of four different indices ranging from liver cirrhosis mortality data to rates of public intoxication. It is hard to conceive of uniform and consistent bias among such diverse indices. None of this means that the rate of drinking is not increasing among women. Drinking rates have been increasing gradually among both men and women during the past few decades, but there is no clear evidence that the sex differential has decreased or that the rate of problem drinking among women is increasing more rapidly than among men.

Additional evidence on sex differences in the prevalence and incidence of alcohol use and alcohol problems is derived from the longitudinal studies critically examined by Robins and Smith (Chapter 5). These authors point out, however, that

> Follow-up studies of alcohol and drug use in women are few, and none has provided a sufficiently large representative sample of women with considerable use of alcohol and drugs to give us much confidence in our conclusions about the prevalence, incidence, course, predictors, or consequences of drug and alcohol involvement by women.

In other words, very large population samples would have to be selected to include sufficient female representation. The very existence of this methodological problem essentially confirms the conclusion drawn in Chapter 3, that men have more drinking problems than women. Robins and Smith also conclude, however, that the longitudinal studies available "also suggest that differences are narrowing and may disappear in time." The evidence on which this suggestion of convergence is based is that sex differences in the middle and upper classes, as well as among the young, are smaller than in the lower classes or among older people. It is suggested that these patterns may spread to the lower classes and to older people in time. The only tenable conclusion for the time being is that convergence in drinking patterns and problems in the two sexes is a future possibility rather than a present fact.

Ferrence also deals with the second hypothesis, concerning the "hidden, middle-aged, suburban alcoholic housewife." She examines the sex distribution of treatment populations, the demographics of women alcoholics, and the evidence concerning the supposedly greater stigma attached to alcoholism in women. On the basis of this evidence, Ferrence concludes that there is no hard evidence to substantiate this hypothesis. The middle-aged suburban housewife does not represent the majority of female alcoholics, and women alcoholics are not more hidden than alcoholic men.

The sex ratios corresponding to the use of licit and illicit drugs, exclusive of alcohol, are presented by Ferrence and Whitehead in Chapter 4. The drugs included for analysis are tobacco, marijuana, hallucinogens, sedatives, tranquilizers, stimulants, cocaine, and inhalants. Medical versus nonmedical use has been analyzed separately for sedatives, tranquilizers, and stimulants. The study is based on epidemiological surveys of the general population carried out in Canada and the United States over the past decade. Data for three distinct periods during the decade are presented separately in order to establish trends. The reader is referred to Chapter 4 for a detailed discussion of the methodological problems that such an analysis entails.

Again, as in the case of alcohol, the data do not substantiate the prevalent belief that the rates of drug use by men and women are becoming increasingly alike. The sex ratios are consistently above 1 for the use of illicit drugs and for the nonmedical use of licit drugs, and consistently below 1 for the medical use of licit drugs. In other words, men use illicit drugs and licit drugs nonmedically at significantly higher rates than women, while the latter use licit drugs medically at significantly higher rates than men. The differences are less marked among youth than among adults but tend to appear clearly as the young mature into adulthood. Ferrence and Whitehead conclude that there is no evidence of convergence and that for most drugs, the patterns of use of men and women are if anything diverging. The major exceptions to this generalization appear to be in relation to cannabis use by adults and tobacco smoking by the young, both of which show some indication of a decline in the male:female ratio over time. The reduction of the sex gap in cigarette smoking, as Gritz's review points out, is due both to a decrease in the percentage of men currently smoking and to an increase in the percentage of women. Moreover, the percentage of new smokers among teenage girls is higher than among boys. Nevertheless, Gritz's statistics for the period 1964–1975 in the United States show that there were still substantially more male than female smokers at the end of the decade and that there had been the same absolute increase in the percentage of men and women who had quit smoking. Therefore, the apparent narrowing of the sex gap in the young may be an instance of trend artifacts discussed by Ferrence and Whitehead in Chapter 4.

It is possible, as Ferrence and Whitehead note, that the period examined is too short to show convergence trends. It should be emphasized, however, that the decade from the late 1960s to the late 1970s saw enormous changes in the social behavior of women, so that if any changes in drug use related to other changes in the status and the self-perception of women should occur, they would have been telescoped during this period. At any rate, the belief that drug-seeking behavior is rapidly becoming the same for men and women is not supported by the facts so far.

It should be emphasized that the chapter on alcohol deals basically with alcohol problems, heavy use, abuse, or alcoholism rather than with any and all alcohol use by the two sexes. On the other hand, the chapter on all other psychoactive drugs presents data on overall rates of use. The distinction is important because women generally tend to use both alcohol and other drugs more moderately than men, and the proportion of heavy users is correspondingly smaller. It is likely, therefore, that the sex ratios would be considerably higher if only heavy drug use or dependence had been considered. Sophisticated research on the epidemiology of heavy or problem drug use by men and women is evidently needed.

These findings have subtle theoretical and practical implications. First, the epidemiology of alcohol and drug use should be actively monitored and investigated in the years to come in order to establish objectively whether the sex differences that prevail at present will remain the same or change in the future. Such a determination is of crucial importance. If the differences were to remain despite substantial changes in the social and economic status of women—a possibility that may be anticipated at the moment—then the explanation for the differences might be sought at least partly in inherent biological factors distinguishing men from women. If, on the other hand, the differences become less evident as women approach social and economic equality with men, sociological rather than biological factors must be invoked as an explanation. Either way, the findings should have a serious impact on prevention and treatment strategies, because sociological factors are more changeable and more easily subjected to deliberate manipulation than biological factors. If societal norms, for example, are mainly or at least significantly responsible for the lower rate of alcohol and drug problems in women, men could be socialized into accepting the same norms that women do, as the WCTU propounded during the 19th century. On the other hand, a congenital biological determinant of the differences would make such efforts comparatively futile. For the present, however, the established differences should be kept in mind when dealing with the availability of treatment facilities.

There is yet another possibility that should be carefully studied. Though the evidence clearly shows that men drink, smoke, and use illicit drugs more than women, while the latter use prescription drugs more than men, conceivably there is no real sex difference in need for drugs and actual total drug use. Indeed, alcohol on the one hand and the sedatives and tranquilizers on the other have closely similar psychopharmacological effects, are often used for the same purposes, and often give rise to cross-addictions in both men and women. Before the advent of barbiturates and later of tranquilizers, women also used prescription opiates at higher rates than men. In Chapter 12, Bell expresses a similar thought when he says:

> Men appear to consume drugs . . . more extensively than women. . . . While this has certainly been so in the case of illicit drugs . . . when sales of prescription and over-the-counter drugs are also taken into consideration . . . the existence of any real difference between the overall male and female consumption of the drugs of dependence is doubtful.

It would be most interesting to see whether this hypothesis can be tested by means of modern epidemiological techniques, paying attention not only to the overall prevalence of use according to pharmacological groupings but also to the quantities used.

The sex differences in ratios of alcohol and drug use described in this volume represent the results of a most valuable large-scale spontaneous experiment, which might enable us to explore in further depth than has been done up to now the many and complex factors that determine alcohol and drug use. One obvious advantage of this approach is that racial and cultural differences are eliminated as possible variables, since we can study men and women within the same culture.

4. PRECURSORS OF ALCOHOL AND DRUG DEPENDENCE

A tacit assumption in the preceding paragraphs is that dependence on any drug, including alcohol and tobacco, is basically the same phenomenon. But because the development, intensity, consequences, prevalence, and social circumstances of heavy drug use obviously differ among drugs, the degree of attention paid to precursors of problem use also differs widely. There is a vast literature on the antecedents of alcoholism and of heroin addiction but comparatively little equivalent knowledge about the problem use of most other drugs. The amount of attention paid to alcohol problems is quite understandable because of the very high prevalence of alcohol use. But the intense research interest in heroin addiction is somewhat baffling, considering that the prevalence of heroin use is much lower than that of barbiturates and tranquilizers, for example. At any rate, our knowledge of the antecedents of problem drug use is quite uneven, and that fact is reflected in this volume.

Given the marked differences in alcohol use by men and women, a comparison of the precursors of heavy use in both sexes is of high interest because it may give clues as to the causes. The role of a genetic factor in the etiology of alcoholism has been receiving increasing attention in recent years, and the results of this research, discussed by Swinson in Chapter 6, are most important. There is no question that, as Swinson puts it, "Alcoholism is undoubtedly a familial disorder." But whether the possible correlation between the frequency of alcoholism in parents and children is genetically or environmentally determined, and whether or not this possible correlation applies to both sons and daughters of alcoholics, has not yet been definitively established. Evidence for Scandinavian males based on studies of twins, half siblings, and adoptees born to alcoholic parents strongly supports the notion that a genetic factor is involved. Studies in females are too few to permit any firm conclusions at this time, but those that do exist suggest that there may be a sex difference in this respect. The limited evidence available leads Swinson to conclude that the genetic influence appears to be a potent etiological factor in males, while "environmental factors may play a larger part in the etiology of alcoholism in women than in men." It is obvious, therefore, that far more research is needed to clarify this apparent sex difference. At present, this research particularly requires more well-designed studies in women.

A related question, which does not appear to have been considered at all, is that of the possible role of genetic factors in the etiology of dependence on drugs other than alcohol. Evidently, not "alcoholism" per se but rather some biological predisposition to develop this behavior is what is inherited. Considering the similarities in the pharmacological actions of alcohol and a number of other drugs, including their capacity to produce dependence, it is cogent to ask whether or not a genetic factor is involved not only in alcoholism but in drug dependence in general. It is conceivable, for example, that both men and women can inherit a predisposition to become dependent on depressant drugs but that sex-related social factors determine the particular sex choice of alcohol versus other drugs. Indeed, most alcoholics and other drug-dependent people are not exclusive users of a single drug; rather, they are multiple-drug users, with one or another drug predominating. If it turned out to be the case that there is a genetic factor in the etiology of dependence on depressants other than alcohol, the apparent sex difference in the etiological role of genetic factors would be minimized. This is an important and exciting field for future research.

Another biological factor that may have a bearing on sex differences in the development and maintenance of patterns of problem drinking is the menstrual cycle. Investigators have only recently begun to explore this field. In Chapter 7, Mello discusses the possible interactions of endocrine, physiological, behavioral, and affective factors in the development and maintenance of problem drinking in women. The various stages of the menstrual cycle have long been known to produce changes in affect. More recently, they have also been shown to cause variation in the blood alcohol levels following intake of the same amount of alcohol. It is possible, as Mello argues, that these two factors may combine to affect drinking patterns and their reinforcement. Of particular interest in this respect is her concept that dysphoric effects of alcohol are implicated in the reinforcement of sustained chronic drinking. This possibility evidently is directly relevant to the situation in women, since some phases of the menstrual cycle are known to be correlated with dysphoria. In this context, it would be most important to gather empirical data on the actual correlation between fluctuations in the blood alcohol level reached after the same doses of alcohol during the menstrual cycle, fluctuations of mood, and fluctuations, if any, in drinking behavior. The latter have not been determined as yet. If consistent correlations were found, then it would be important to follow up the same women, to and after the menopause, to see whether the possible fluctuations level off once the cyclic hormonal changes disappear. Again, nature provides us with a spontaneous experiment for studying the effect of various hormonal factors in drinking behavior that otherwise cannot be studied experimentally in humans. If our knowledge of the role of female sex hormones in drinking behavior is rudimentary, our knowledge of how these factors affect other drug use is nil. The field is wide open for scientific exploration.

In addition to the genetic and endocrine factors considered above, it is obvious that events and influences in the individual's life history may be precursors of alcoholism. Indeed, there is a very large literature on the subject, which Boothroyd reviews in Chapter 8 with specific emphasis on women. In general, the picture of family experiences and family upbringing that emerges is indicative of similar disturbances in the early histories of both male and female alcoholics. Yet the expression of maladjustment is different in the two sexes. There is a greater tendency to neuroticism and depression in the women, even preceding the onset of heavy drinking, while in men there is a higher tendency to sociopathy. It may be noted in passing that the same sex difference in psychopathology applies to people dependent on other drugs and indeed to the population at large. A currently popular notion that alcoholism in women may be related to the confusion of gender identity caused by the changing social roles of women is not supported by Boothroyd's examination. He states, "No studies known to this reviewer convincingly relate 'sex role confusion' to alcoholism *per se*."

This apparent nonspecificity of antecedents of alcoholism raises an interesting possibility. Given the same primary familial disturbance or pathogenetic influence, perhaps the eventual expression of maladjusted behavior may assume predominantly different forms in the two sexes for either social or biological reasons or a combination of the two. These reasons may apply not only to the sex difference in neuroticism versus sociopathy but also to the predilection for alcohol versus other drugs. Obviously, this speculation requires formulation of more specific questions before it can be tested. In the same sense, Boothroyd points out the need for detailed longitudinal studies to deal not only with the antecedents but also with the determinants of the successful versus the nonsuccessful outcome of treatment interventions. He asks whether there may be a typology "that would be of more value than simply for classificatory and statistical purposes." An obvious value of such a typology would be the more effective matching of individual patients to specific therapies. This question, also raised by Annis and Liban in Chapter 11, will be discussed further below.

5. MORBIDITY AND MORTALITY

It is a fact that women outlive men. But whether this sex difference is congenitally or environmentally determined is not yet known. It is also a fact that the heavy use of alcohol, tobacco, and other drugs increases morbidity and mortality in both men and women. As Schmidt and Popham suggest in Chapter 10, a study of this fact may help to elucidate the comparative roles of biological and environmental factors in the well-known sex difference in longevity. It should be noted, however, that possible sex differences in the morbidity and the mortality of alcoholics and other heavy drug users have not yet been definitively established, because until recently, little attention has been paid to this question. Tobacco is an exception in the sense that from the beginning, studies on the correlation between smoking and the prevalence of various illnesses included analyses of the data separately for men and women. Tobacco is also an exception because the relationship between smoking and disease has been examined in the entire population over the whole continuous range of consumption from zero to the heaviest, rather than in selected subpopulations of heavy users, as has been the case with alcohol. This means that we have a better index of drug-related morbidity and mortality in tobacco smokers than in users of alcohol and other drugs, and a much better picture of sex differences.

The literature on sex differences in the morbidity of alcoholics is reviewed by Wilkinson in Chapter 9. In Chapter 10, Schmidt and Popham present an analysis by sex of the causes of mortality in alcoholics. Their sample, based on deaths recorded among alcoholic patients of both sexes admitted to the clinics of the Addiction Research Foundation over a period of 20 years, is larger than the combined total of all previous samples ever reported in the literature. The conclusions reached by Wilkinson on the one hand and by Schmidt and Popham on the other coincide in a number of respects but differ in others. This discrepancy is understandable, given the relatively scanty amount of information available, the differences in the type of data dealt with, and the enormous complexity of the problem.

The major diseases in which alcohol is etiologically involved affect the cardiovascular, respiratory, and central nervous systems and the liver. The importance of alcohol as a causal factor is also clear in the case of accidental injury and death and in cancer of the upper digestive and upper respiratory tracts. On the basis of a review of both mortality and morbidity studies, Wilkinson concludes that overall, the prevalence of physical illness is higher in alcoholic women than in alcoholic men. Schmidt and Popham report that mortality rates are a little higher among female than among male alcoholics in the younger age groups, and they remark that this finding is in agreement with several morbidity studies, "that female alcoholics are more prone to medical complications than male [alcoholics]." They find, however, that "In late middle age and old age, the excess shifts to the male to such an extent that the ratio for the sample as a whole (0.825) favors the female." When cause-specific morbidity is considered, Wilkinson concludes that men have higher rates of heart and lung disease, while women have higher rates of some conditions affecting the central nervous system, such as the

Wernicke–Korsakoff syndrome and dementia, and of liver disease, including hepatitis and cirrhosis. The reader is referred to Wilkinson's paper for an excellent critical discussion of these problems.

The findings of Schmidt and Popham are in agreement with Wilkinson's conclusions with regard to mortality due to cardiovascular and respiratory illness but seemingly not with regard to liver disease. Their results show that the mortality rates from liver cirrhosis overall are not higher in women than in men, but roughly the same. This apparent discrepancy may be explained by a possible difference in age composition in the populations considered in the two papers. Below age 50, Schmidt and Popham find that the rates are somewhat higher among women, but from age 50 on, interestingly, the rates are lower in women. This finding suggests that the menopause may play a role in the etiology of alcoholic liver disease. Indeed, clinicians of an earlier generation were convinced that women and feminoid men were more likely to develop alcoholic cirrhosis than more android males. Evidently, more experimental, clinical, and epidemiological research would help to provide an answer for these intriguing sex differences. But beyond that, the elucidation of the role of both male and female sex hormones in the development and course of alcoholic liver cirrhosis might throw some light on the etiology of this disease.

Schmidt and Popham raise a further point that transcends the specific field of alcoholism. From a comparison of the sex ratios in mortality due to different causes among the general population and among alcoholics, they open the possibility of an important method for establishing the comparative roles that constitutional and environmental factors play in pathogenesis and longevity. Indeed, they suggest that "given the hazardous character of the life style typical of both male and female alcoholics . . . the difference observed [in longevity] approximates the minimum achievable through the equalization of external factors." Their data show that most of the sex difference in liver disease in the general population is abolished in alcoholics, indicating a major pathogenetic role of alcohol itself. In contrast, an important sex difference remains in lung and cardiovascular disease, indicating a substantial role of constitutional or genetic factors. This development clearly shows the potential value of the study of sex differences to the understanding of a host of human problems.

Evidence for a causal relationship between cigarette smoking and cardiovascular and respiratory diseases is most convincing following the studies of the past two or three decades. Sex differences in the morbidity and mortality of cigarette smokers are reviewed by Gritz in Chapter 14. Coronary heart disease, the most common cause of death in developed countries, is much lower in women than in men. But, as Gritz points out, the prevalence of heart disease in women increases in proportion to their rate of cigarette smoking, so that the sex difference diminishes. A question of particular importance to women of childbearing age is the finding that the risk of heart disease increases dramatically in women who both smoke and use oral contraceptives. The latter alone do not increase this risk. This finding illustrates the now well-recognized fact that some factor in cigarette smoke in combination with progesterone acts synergistically to cause cardiovascular pathology.

Cigarette smoking is also implicated in the etiology of respiratory diseases such as chronic bronchitis, emphysema, and lung cancer. Here again, as Gritz points out, the prevalence of these conditions is higher in men than in women, but when rates of smoking in both sexes are taken into account, the sex difference diminishes significantly. The clear implication is that some factor related to smoking *per se* plays a primary causal role.

Thorough studies of sex differences in morbidity and mortality of chronic users of other drugs do not appear to have been made. We know, of course, that much morbidity, including tolerance and dependence as well as physical and mental complications due to the chronic use of various drugs, occurs in both men and women. Martin and Martin (Chapter 13) state, "The medical complications of narcotic addiction are the same in males and females." But we know very little about sex differences in propensity, prevalence, gravity, and outcomes. This is, therefore, another potentially fruitful field of research because such knowledge might throw light on the etiology of various conditions, such as, for example, the various types of mental pathology induced by amphetamines and cocaine. This is suggested by the well-documented interrelationship between endocrine and neurotransmitter function.

6. ENDOCRINE SYSTEM

In Chapter 15, Cicero provides a thorough and systematic review of the literature on the effects of psychoactive drugs on endocrine function. This review covers the effects of alcohol, opiates, cannabis, and a miscellaneous group of drugs, including amphetamines, LSD, and other stimulants, on the hypothalamic–pituitary–gonadal, –adrenal, and –thyroidal axes, as well as on prolactin, growth hormone, oxytocin, and vasopressin. Experimental studies in humans and animals of both sexes are included where available.

All of the drugs studied can exert marked effects on all of the neuroendocrine axes examined. These are clearly evident in animal experiments, but the effects have been more equivocal in humans, probably because the studies have been incomplete and the drug doses have been substantially lower. The effects vary not only with the drugs but also with the test system; for example, most of the drug-induced changes in luteinizing hormone–releasing hormone are decreases, while the release of adrenocorticotrophic hormone is increased in many instances, and prolactin release is disinhibited. The most important effects of the drugs studied appear to be exerted centrally on the releasing factors, but some drugs (e.g., ethanol) have important direct effects on the peripheral target organs.

Cicero's review indicates clearly and dramatically the remarkably uneven coverage of this important subject in the research literature. A great deal of work has been done on alcohol and opiate narcotics, yet extremely little has been done on other drugs, even though some of these, such as barbiturates and benzodiazepines, are very widely used. There is quite uneven coverage by system, with much more recent work on the hypothalamic–pituitary–gonadal axis and least on the hypothalamic–pituitary–thyroidal system. But most strikingly of all, this chapter illustrates the gross and uneven degree of disparity of knowledge available on males and on females of all species. For example, studies on ethanol and the gonadal system are confined almost exclusively to the male, while there is a fairly good balance in studies of narcotics and cannabis. In fact, the whole picture of present knowledge is a patchwork or quilt made up of different kinds of cloth and riddled with holes.

It would be easy to provide facile explanations of the imbalance of knowledge about the two sexes, such as an assumed lack of interest in studies of females by preponderantly male researchers. However, the randomness of the research efforts suggests that there are other reasons. In experimental studies, variation caused by the estrous or menstrual cycle introduces a major complication that many investigators have sought to avoid. Experiments with males require fewer subjects and are easier to interpret because there are fewer variables involved. Moreover, experimental drug studies in women of childbearing age present serious ethical problems because of the risk of adverse effects on the possible fetus. Another factor is that endocrine problems related to alcohol and drug use, so far, are less frequent and less visible in women than in men, and there is a natural tendency to direct the most effort to the most conspicuous problems. In addition, as Cicero points out, the nature of drug-induced endocrine problems is such that the consequences may be more dramatic in men. Impotence and feminization, for example, are much more likely to call attention than missed periods or infertility.

However, there remains the problem that researchers are subject to habit and that many experiments are done only in males for no well-thought-out reason. It seems astonishing, for example, that despite the obvious importance of alcoholism in both sexes, far less research on the reproductive endocrinology of the female has been done with alcohol than with opiates. This lack is difficult to justify when in North America, there are *at least* 30 women alcoholics to each woman narcotic addict. There is probably an even greater ratio of heavy tobacco smokers to narcotic addicts, and earlier menopause in smokers, as described by Gritz, suggests that tobacco may have important neuroendocrine effects. Yet this area does not appear to have been studied.

As Cicero has pointed out, there are large gaps in knowledge in this field that clearly need to be filled. One may add that there is also need of a review of priorities and experimental rationales, to redress the gross deficiency in research on drug effects on the endocrine system of females.

7. TREATMENT

With the possible exception of caffeine, alcohol and tobacco are the two most commonly used dependence-producing drugs that involve serious risks to health. In both cases, the risk is directly related to levels of use. Alcoholism, the compulsive heavy use of alcohol, has been conceptualized as a disease for several decades. It is understandable, therefore, that interventions designed and propounded to cure or control the condition are referred to as *treatments*. Although the compulsive heavy use of tobacco does not rate the label of *disease*, methods to "treat" heavy smokers have also been designed because of the acknowledgment that many heavy smokers who would like to quit cannot do so unaided. One may add in passing that the behavioral characteristics of compulsive heavy users of both alcohol and tobacco are so similar (as are the "treatment" approaches) that heavy smoking deserves a specific name. The French have logically recognized the need by coining the word *tabagisme*. English should have an equivalent: *tobacconism?*

It is commonly stated in the current treatment literature that women alcoholics and smokers are more difficult to treat and less successful than men at giving up drinking and smoking. The evidence on which these beliefs are based is reviewed for alcohol by Annis and Liban in Chapter 11 and by Gritz for tobacco in Chapter 14.

According to Annis and Liban, such statements concerning women alcoholics are based not on a critical examination of all the evidence available but on a repetition of conclusions drawn from half a dozen studies. On the basis of a much more extensive series, including 23 reported studies, Annis and Liban conclude that the evidence does not support the contention that women alcoholics fare more poorly than men under treatment conditions. There were no significant differences between women and men in 15 studies; women did better than men in 5 studies, and worse than men in 3.

Much the same situation applies to the possible sex differential in cessation of smoking following treatment. The belief that women do more poorly than men cannot be substantiated by a systematic comparison of published outcomes in men and women. Gritz found that out of more than 1000 articles dealing with cessation of smoking, only 30 provided separate data for men and women, and only 9 dealt with women alone. A statistical analysis of the sex differences, both at the end of treatment and for long-term abstinence, led her to conclude that most studies show no significant differences between the sexes. Those that showed significantly higher abstinence rates for men tended to include the largest samples. Gritz concludes that the evidence for better treatment outcomes in men "can be considered suggestive," though it is clearly not proved.

It is legitimate to conclude that overall, the limited evidence available on the treatment outcomes of male and female alcoholics and smokers fails to support the contention that women are harder to treat than men. Systematic research on this matter is obviously needed, however. It is interesting to remark in passing—and this has nothing to do with male–female differences—that in the treatment field, "alcoholics" and "smokers" are equated, suggesting that all or most smokers are ill, while only heavy, as opposed to light and moderate, drinkers are. Although this distinction at first appears arbitrary, it probably is not, because cigarette smoking seems to be a more compulsive behavior than drinking. In other words, there appears to be a larger proportion of the population of drinkers who drink rarely, occasionally, or lightly than the proportion of cigarette smokers who do so. This is probably related to the different patterns of use of the two drugs and thereby to different rates of reinforcement. Because cigarettes, as opposed to alcoholic beverages, are easily portable and can be used in many more situations of daily life than alcohol, the risk of producing heavy dependence is much greater than in the case of alcohol. Perhaps this has a bearing on treatment approaches that relate to both these drugs.

Comparisons by sex of treatment outcomes in persons addicted to other drugs do not appear to have been made. Martin and Martin in Chapter 13 and Finnegan and Fehr in Chapter 17 discuss in detail various aspects of the medical management of the pregnant opiate addict and of the neonate at delivery and postpartum, mainly in relation to the withdrawal syndrome. However, the overall question of the treatment of pregnant women who are dependent on alcohol, tobacco, or other drugs, compared with nonpregnant dependent women, does not appear to have been investigated. It would be most interesting and useful to make systematic comparisons of drug-dependent pregnant women and matched nonpregnant controls, with respect to rates of spontaneous quitting and of quitting after treatment. It seems reasonable to assume that the pregnant woman is more highly motivated than the nonpregnant woman to cease drug taking because of the highly publicized adverse effects of drugs on the fetus and because of the high concern that most women have for the health of their offspring. A comparison of outcomes in the two groups would therefore contribute significantly to assessing the role of one important factor in cessation of drug use: motivation.

The question of the possible role of other sex differences in prognostic factors bearing on treatment outcomes is examined in detail by Annis and Liban in relation to alcoholism. They conclude that at present, the evidence is suggestive but too limited to permit clear-cut conclusions. Further investigation of this issue is considered necessary because "some factors indicative of good prognosis may vary between the sexes, while others may transcend sex differences" and because "such differences may well have implications for the planning of treatment services." The same considerations obviously apply to cigarette smoking and all other types of drug dependence.

There is not just one treatment modality for drug dependence but a variety of approaches, ranging from psychotherapy to pharmacotherapy. Generally speaking, the success rates among alcoholics, smokers, and other drug-dependent persons are comparatively modest. These two facts, combined with the variability of individual prognostic factors, lend particular importance and relevance to the question raised by Annis and Liban: Are different treatment techniques specifically suitable for different subgroups of patients rather than for all alcoholics? Future research directed toward this question is potentially highly rewarding. Patient populations are not homogeneous, but at present, they are assigned to one or another treatment program fortuitously rather than according to a specific rationale. It is possible, therefore, that if, as Annis and Liban point out, studies were carried out to determine which treatment modalities are most suitable for which patients, the success rates might be much higher than they are at present. This is an exciting concept well worth further investigation. It would apply not only to possible differential therapeutic approaches for men and women but also to subgroups of men and women. It could well be that the suitability of various treatment approaches may have more to do with the individual's history of drug use, personality, family history, and other individual factors than with gender. It is also possible, at least theoretically, that sex-oriented treatment modalities may be more effective than integrated ones, because men and women, for whatever reasons, may cope with their problems in different ways. For the time being, however, these questions remain unanswered because most research has not addressed itself to the issue of patient /treatment match, or to the question of possible sex differences, since most research has been done only in men. For obvious reasons, this important hypothesis evidently transcends the field of alcoholism— and for that matter of all drug dependence—and is applicable in thera- peutic approaches to all behavioral and affective disorders. Much re- search effort should be spent on this question in the years to come.

The epidemiological data on sex differences in problem drinking among men and women and the apparent lack of sex differences in treatment outcomes evidently have not only theoretical but also impor- tant practical implications. The quantity and type of therapeutic facilities for men and women should ideally be based on the best estimates of the rates of problem drinking in the two sexes and on empirical evidence concerning the relative efficacy of different treatment strategies. As reviewed in this book, there is a reasonable and steadily growing amount of information on the first point, but quite inadequate information on the second. Therefore, if special facilities and programs for the treatment of women alcoholics are set up essentially on ideological grounds, it would be highly desirable for their outcomes to be compared objectively and scientifically with those of conventional treatment programs for women, so as to permit a rational selection of treatment methods in the future.

8. PREGNANCY

If the heavy use of psychoactive drugs has a number of deleterious effects on the health of men and women of all ages, it is not surprising that it also affects adversely the development of the fetus, which in many respects is so much more vulnerable. Because they are not autonomous but at the mercy of the internal environment created by the mother, in statistical terms fetuses of drug-using mothers are more frequently and more heavily exposed to drugs than children prior to the time when they decide on their own to self-administer drugs. It is therefore surprising that intense and active interest in this area of research is comparatively new and that consequently our knowledge is incomplete at best.

In Chapter 16, Rosett synthesizes the evidence with respect to alcohol, and Finnegan and Fehr do the same thing for all other psychoac- tive drugs in Chapter 17. In addition, Martin and Martin discuss the effects of opiates on the fetus and the offspring in Chapter 13, and Gritz discusses those of tobacco in Chapter 14. Altogether, these reviews provide a most comprehensive analysis of the topic, so that there is not much to add to these authors' presentations. A few observations, however, seem pertinent.

It is, on the surface, rather remarkable that the detrimental effects of alcohol on the fetus—the most extreme of which is known as the fetal alcohol syndrome (FAS)—have only recently become a topic of high clinical and research interest. Rosett's review makes clear that the deleterious effects of maternal drinking on the fetus had been described and scientifically demonstrated 80 years ago. Yet the possibility of a causal association was ignored in the English-language literature until its rediscovery by the Seattle group in 1970. It was apparently well recognized that the offspring of alcoholic mothers were often sickly and defective, but this effect was generally attributed to maternal malnutrition and other attributes of the mother's life-style. The wide acceptance of this view apparently resulted from an uncritical acceptance of the voice of authority. The history of this subject demonstrates the fallibility of opinion, no matter how eminent, in the absence of solid facts.

The review by Finnegan and Fehr of the effects of other psychoactive drugs on the fetus shows numerous resemblances to the FAS. Growth retardation, certain structural anomalies, and postnatal behavioral deficits are common to many of these drugs. Though features of the drug users' life-styles undoubtedly contribute to the causation of these ill effects, the evidence, both clinical and experimental, is strongly suggestive of direct drug toxicity. It might be most informative to make a systematic comparison of the findings in offspring of heavy users of all psychoactive drugs, including alcohol and tobacco, to see whether the FAS is really a specific entity or part of a broader fetal psychoactive drug syndrome. It would also be interesting to know whether male and female offspring are affected equally or differently. Besides its intrinsic clinical interest, such a study might help to clarify pathogenetic mechanisms.

While drug toxicity to the fetus has received a great deal of attention recently, the review of endocrine effects by Cicero suggests that these drugs have a broader range of important effects on the reproductive function of the female. The limited evidence available indicates the potential importance of thorough epidemiological studies of the levels of both licit and illicit drug use by both pregnant and nonpregnant women, as well as the correlation of drug use with the frequency of reduced fertility, spontaneous abortions, miscarriages, morbidity during pregnancy, and postpartum maternal behavior.

9. CONCLUDING REMARKS

From the foregoing overview, and even more from the individual reviews, it is obvious that there is a gross disparity in knowledge concerning the drug use and the drug problems of men and women.

Since women constitute at least half of the population, it is clearly important, even on practical grounds alone, to know as much as possible about their problems, especially since some of these affect their offspring of both sexes.

Apart from this immediate reason, it is also clear from the examples discussed above that comparative studies of drug problems in the two sexes, including similarities as well as differences, can yield valuable scientific insights that may be inaccessible otherwise. The topics covered in this volume, although comprehensive, by no means exhaust the possibilities. Comparative reviews on the cross-cultural social history of the use of alcohol and other drugs, on criminal behavior related to drug use, on drug-related suicide and overdose rates, and on the development of tolerance and physical dependence are a few examples that come readily to mind. All these could yield further knowledge and stimulate new areas of investigation.

Clearly, the reviews in this volume constitute an important step forward. The true measure of their value, however, will be the extent to which they succeed in generating research to answer the questions that they raise.

2

Temperance and Women in 19th-Century United States

HARRY GENE LEVINE

1. INTRODUCTION

The temperance movement during the 19th century developed and promulgated most of the basics of the modern definition of social problems resulting from alcohol consumption. Women participated in the movement, first under the control and leadership of men and later in their own organizations. Suffragists and women's rights activists supported the temperance cause believing that the liquor traffic was a serious problem for women. In addition, temperance literature and speeches gave a prominent place to women: they were presented as victims of the liquor trade and as moral agents who could help develop the reform. This paper examines both aspects of the interface between women and temperance in the United States in the 19th century: women as participants and woman as symbol and issue.

The relationship of women to the antialcohol cause should be understood in the context of two related social–historical facts. The first was the development, in the early 19th century, of a new popular and medical view of alcohol as a dangerous and destructive substance —as a demon. Antialcohol sentiment was a popular ideology defined in terms of middle-class values and concerns and addressing real problems in the life situation of many men and women. The second social–historical fact was the change in the structure of social life, in ideas about it, and particularly in the family, that occurred roughly during the first three decades of the 19th century. A distinctive market-oriented family pattern

HARRY GENE LEVINE ● Social Research Group, School of Public Health, University of California, Berkeley, California. Present address: Department of Sociology, Queens College, City University of New York, Flushing, New York.

and ideal emerged at that time that featured men going out "into the world" to work while women stayed behind to raise children and create the "proper" home. This family arrangement, as an ideal, was central to temperance thought, and, over the course of the 19th century, the antialcohol crusade was waged, in part, on behalf of that family.

The first part of this chapter describes the new drinking patterns and attitudes in 19th-century America and outlines the ideology of the temperance movement. The second part discusses the major ways women were portrayed in temperance literature—primarily as victims and as moral agents. The third part traces women's participation in the temperance movement during the century and examines the attempt by some women to forge a distinctly women's position on the liquor question.

2. THE EMERGENCE OF THE MODERN DEFINITION OF THE LIQUOR PROBLEM

Attitudes and Practices

Americans in the 17th and 18th centuries did not believe alcohol to be a dangerous drug, capable of destroying an individual, wrecking a family, or ruining a society. It was considered a tonic and a medicine and was called the Good Creature of God, even by Puritans. Alcoholic beverages were consumed at almost any occasion, including funerals, the ordination of ministers, weddings, and other church-related functions, at any time of the day or night, by men, women, and children of all classes. Liquor production, particularly rum manufacture, was very important to the economy of the colonies, especially New England. Cultural, historical, and economic forces converged to make alcoholic beverages highly regarded. During the 18th century, the per capita consumption was probably higher than for most of the 19th and 20th centuries (Rorabaugh, 1976a,b; Krout, 1925; Dorchester, 1888; Field, 1897).

Drunkenness was a frequent and obvious fact of life. From the earliest settlements, there were complaints about excessive drinking and drunkenness, but these must be understood within the positive cultural climate regarding drunkenness. Holidays and other celebrations usually included considerable drinking and drunkenness. For example, George Washington's agreement with his gardener included "four dollars at Christmas with which he may be drunk for four days and nights; two dollars at Easter to effect the same purpose" (quoted in Kobler, 1973, p. 18). In his thorough study of early American drinking patterns, William

J. Rorabaugh (1976a) concluded that "to most colonial Americans ine-briation was of no particular importance. William Byrd, for example, noted with equal indifference intoxication among members of the Gov-ernor's Council and his own servants." According to Rorabaugh, Byrd's attitude was typical of Americans at the time, for whom "drunkenness was a natural, harmless consequence of drinking." Those members of the colonial political and religious elite who did worry about drunkenness were always careful not to blame alcohol. In colonial thought and especially in Puritan writings, drunkenness, not liquor, was the issue. Drunkenness involved wilful human behavior: it was sin and vice. Men and women had the opportunity and knowledge to act otherwise. To choose sin—that is, drunkenness—was an example and an indication of human depravity (Rorabaugh, 1976a; Krout, 1925; Mather, 1673; Lender, 1973; Levine, 1978).

The 50-year period from 1776 to 1826 marked a transition in Amer-ican thought about liquor. At the beginning of the period, alcohol was considered the Good Creature of God by virtually everyone; at the end, a significant and rapidly growing minority had concluded that distilled liquor was quite literally a "demon" and a "destroyer." Within another 20 years, several million Americans had pledged to give up the use of alcoholic beverages entirely. Although physicians played a major role in defining many of the essential antiliquor ideas, these ideas were not primarily the result of scientific or medical discoveries. They were, rather, the result of transformations in social thought and in the structure and organization of social and economic life. Changes in drinking patterns were part of those changes, and they, in turn, provided fuel and evidence for the new image of alcohol as demon (Krout, 1925; Gusfield, 1963; Cherrington, 1920; Wilkerson, 1966; Levine, 1978).

According to Rorabaugh (1976a), during the first three and a half decades of the 19th century, consumption rose among most Americans. However, he suggested that a decline began to appear among the upper and the upper middle classes. The new abstemious pattern, or at least the much less frequent use of alcohol, quickly spread after 1830 to a broad cross-section of the middle class and even to certain sections of the working class. For the rest of the 19th century (and the 20th as well), consumption remained significantly below the 18th- and early-19th-cen-tury levels (Rorabaugh, 1976a,b). (See Table 1.) The strongest support for total abstinence came from native-born middle-class and upper-middle-class Protestants. As Gusfield (1963) has pointed out, alcoholic beverages became taboo to the middle class and to those aspiring to the middle class, especially women. Drinking alcohol was excluded more and more from everyday life and became associated with nonfamily and nonwork activities.

Table 1. Alcoholic Beverage Consumption, with Absolute
Alcohol for Each Beverage, per Capita of Drinking Age
(15+) Population, in Gallons[a]

Year	Spirits		Wine		Cider		Beer		Total
	Bev.	Abs. Alc.	Bev.	Abs. Alc.	Bev.	Abs. Alc.	Bev.	Abs. Alc.	Abs. Alc.
1790	5.1	2.3	.6	.1	34.	3.4	—	—	5.8
1795	5.9	2.7	.6	.1	34.	3.4	—	—	6.2
1800	7.2	3.3	.6	.1	32.	3.2	—	—	6.6
1805	8.2	3.7	.6	.1	30.	3.0	—	—	6.8
1810	8.7	3.9	.4	.1	30.	3.0	1.3	.1	7.1
1815	8.3	3.7	.4	.1	30.	3.0	—	—	6.8
1820	8.7	3.9	.4	.1	28.	2.8	—	—	6.8
1825	9.2	4.1	.4	.1	28.	2.8	—	—	7.0
1830	9.5	4.3	.5	.1	27.	2.7	—	—	7.1
1835	7.6	3.4	.5	.1	15.	1.5	—	—	5.0
1840	5.5	2.5	.5	.1	4.	.4	2.3	.1	3.1
1845	3.7	1.6	.3	.1	—	—	2.4	.1	1.8
1850	3.6	1.6	.3	.1	—	—	2.7	.1	1.8
1855	3.7	1.7	.3	.1	—	—	4.6	.2	2.0
1860	3.9	1.7	.5	.1	—	—	6.4	.3	2.1
1865	3.5	1.6	.5	.1	—	—	5.8	.3	2.0
1870	3.1	1.4	.5	.1	—	—	8.6	.4	1.9
1875	2.8	1.2	.8	.1	—	—	10.1	.5	1.8
1880	2.4	1.1	1.0	.2	—	—	11.1	.6	1.9
1885	2.2	1.0	.8	.1	—	—	18.0	.9	2.0
1890	2.2	1.0	.6	.1	—	—	20.6	1.0	2.1
1895	1.8	.8	.6	.1	—	—	23.4	1.2	2.1
1900	1.8	.8	.6	.1	—	—	23.6	1.2	2.1
1905	1.9	.9	.7	.1	—	—	25.9	1.3	2.3
1910	2.1	.9	.9	.2	—	—	29.2	1.5	2.6
1915	1.8	.8	.7	.1	—	—	29.7	1.5	2.4
1920	2.1	.9	—	—	—	—	—	—	.9
1925	2.0	.9	—	—	—	—	—	—	.9
1930	2.0	.9	—	—	—	—	—	—	.9
1935	1.5	.7	.4	.1	—	—	15.0	.7	1.5
1940	1.3	.6	.9	.2	—	—	17.2	.8	1.6
1945	1.5	.7	1.1	.2	—	—	24.2	1.1	2.0
1950	1.5	.7	1.1	.2	—	—	24.1	1.1	2.0
1955	1.6	.7	1.3	.2	—	—	22.8	1.0	1.9
1960	1.9	.8	1.3	.2	—	—	22.1	1.0	2.0
1965	2.1	1.0	1.3	.2	—	—	22.8	1.0	2.2
1970	2.5	1.1	1.8	.3	—	—	25.7	1.2	2.6

[a] From Rorabaugh (1976b).

One important change in drinking patterns, especially among the middle class, was a drinking style Rorabaugh has called "individual binge drinking." The increasing disreputableness of having even one drink meant that having entered the realm of tabooed activity, the drinker might as well keep going. Further, as the pace of rapidly developing capitalist society came to demand more and more organization and discipline in one's daily life, "drinking time" came to be a time to release the impulses and desires ordinarily held in check. Thus, if a respectable middle-class man was to go to a prostitute, get in a fight, beat his wife, or do anything he might not ordinarily do, he was likely to drink or get drunk before doing it. To get drunk was to abandon respectability and self-control. Further, the middle- and upper-class domination of political and economic life restricted drinking time for the working class as well. For workers laboring 12 hours or more, one or two nights a week were set aside for play—which in most cases meant getting drunk. Drunkenness was socially structured as a time for letting go and forgetting the hard labor of the rest of the week. For both the middle and the working classes, then, to get drunk was to enter a time and space in which one did not worry about self-control and self-discipline (Rorabaugh, 1976a; Gusfield, 1963; Krout, 1925; Dorchester, 1888).

One of the significant differences between the colonial era and the 19th century was the status accorded the tavern—the main drinking-related social institution. In the colonial period, the tavern had been an important part of social and community life; in the 19th century, the tavern was stigmatized, was identified with the lower classes and immigrants, and became an essentially male preserve. The saloon was where middle-class men went slumming and where men of all classes went to get away from their families. The 19th century featured the full flowering of a heavy-drinking subculture, isolated and stigmatized by the more respectable elements of the community (Rorabaugh, 1976a; Krout, 1925; Ade, 1931).

The Temperance Movement

Beginning with Dr. Benjamin Rush's pamphlet "An Inquiry into the Effects of Ardent Spirits," first published in 1785 and reprinted many times (Rush, 1934), the temperance movement was the leader and the main articulator of antialcohol sentiment. Rush's case against distilled liquor provided fuel for a growing concern about drinking and drunkenness on the part of wealthy and powerful Americans who were beginning to worry about the effects of liquor on morality, order, and workers' discipline. Major Protestant denominations issued statements discouraging their members from using distilled liquor, and some churches required abstinence. Temperance societies were formed in many parts of the country, but before 1826, these were primarily elite organizations, split on the question of whether they should encourage moderation in all drinks or abstinence from spirits and moderation in beer and wine. By 1826, with the formation of the American Temperance Society, *Temperance* meant abstinence from distilled liquor, and by 1836, the temperance crusade had become a mass movement committed to total abstinence from all alcoholic beverages. A new medical and popular understanding of the effects of alcohol on the mind and body had arrived (Krout, 1925; Cherrington, 1920; Dorchester, 1888).

The temperance movement was well organized and the largest enduring secular mass movement in 19th-century America: doctors, lawyers, ministers, judges, elected officials, businessmen, merchants, laborers, and farmers, and their wives, mothers, sisters, and daughters, supported the campaign to rid the nation of alcohol. Temperance forces combined the pressure of their own formidable organizations with the weight of all of the major Protestant denominations, a sizable contingent of Catholics, labor groups, farm groups, and numerous civic and professional associations. Temperance supporters turned out an enormous quantity of literature, including pamphlets, articles, books, novels, short stories, plays, poetry, and songs. Major newspapers and magazines editorially supported the temperance line. The power and impact of temperance ideology was perhaps best illustrated by the fruit of the efforts of Edward C. Delaven, a wealthy merchant from Albany, New York. Delaven secured the signatures of the following presidents of the United States to a statement condemning the use of distilled liquor: Madison, John Quincy Adams, Jackson, Van Buren, Tyler, Polk, Taylor, Fillmore, Pierce, Lincoln, and Johnson (Cherrington, 1920, pp. 114–115). The temperance position was respectable, respected, and not to be taken lightly.

Temperance ideology was in part a product of changes in popular thought about alcohol, and the temperance movement in turn shaped and changed popular opinion. The belief that liquor was the Good Creature did not die out, of course, and it was continually reinforced by the perspectives of immigrants from different cultural traditions. But the image of liquor as the merrymaker and cure-all tonic existed under the shadow of the Demon Rum. Nineteenth-century Americans, especially middle-class Protestants, lived in a society in which a whole series of assumptions and images about alcohol as a powerful and destructive substance made sense. People had at their disposal, in everyday terms, a symbol system in which alcohol was pernicious and evil. When contemporary writers talk about American ambivalence toward alcohol, what they are attempting to describe is the coexistence of two different gestalts of the relationship of alcohol to social life. In one picture, alcohol is medicine; in the other, it is poison. Both are plausible, and both at times fit the facts. In one gestalt, alcohol makes people merry and sociable; in the other, it brings out destructive impulses and destroys moral sensibilities. Since the early 19th century, both images have been part of the popular culture and imagination of the American people. The temperance movement developed the most articulate and elaborate version of the image of alcohol as destroyer. And temperance ideology offered the fullest use of alcohol as an explanation for social problems.*

The essentials of the temperance position were simple and were repeated innumerable times in literature and speeches:

a. Liquor weakened or eliminated the restraints drinkers had over their behavior; it let loose or increased the appetites, passions, and desires, while reducing moral sensibilities.

b. Alcohol was powerfully addicting. Drunkards, it was said, were the victims of the action of the substance alcohol, which had transformed their bodily needs so that their desires for alcohol were uncontrollable. Though it was recognized that not all drinkers became addicted, it was generally argued that the risk of addiction was so great as to make drinking very dangerous. In addition, the drinker risked contracting a number of diseases. Thus, people who advocated moderate drinking, and even those who practiced it privately, were thought to be encouraging sickness and intemperance, and probably destroying themselves as well.

c. Alcohol was regarded as causing a large percentage of America's social problems, especially crime, poverty, and broken homes. Liquor robbed the drinker of the self-discipline, fortitude, and rationality necessary to advance in the world and prosper. Drunken husbands and fathers abandoned their responsibilities and their families. And those morally weakened by drink, or addicted to it, often turned to crime or violence.

d. The solution, therefore, was that everyone should give up drinking, and the central strategy question of the movement was how a sober society should be brought about. In general, temperance strategy rotated around educational approaches, what was usually called *moral suasion,* and around legal restriction policies, especially prohibition. After the 1860s, prohibition was accepted and endorsed by the major organizations

---

* While I have a considerably more positive view of the concept *ambivalence* than he does, the best discussion of the use of it in writing on alcohol problems is by Room (1976).

as the ultimate goal of the movement. However, temperance groups were not single-mindedly concerned with prohibition, and Frances Willard's policy of "do everything" dominated the era. It was only in the 20th century that antialcohol forces became concerned exclusively with legal restriction and prohibition.

Economic and Family Life

The 50-year period during which the major transformation in popular attitudes about alcohol occurred (roughly 1785–1835) was also a period of massive transformation in American society. Changes in the period included the weakening or destruction of many of the social and political structures of colonial society; the weakening of traditional forms of social control, and the decline of working-class respect for authority and hierarchy; the rise of the cities; the increasing domination of economic life by the market; and the growth of an urban middle class. In short, the period witnessed the growth and the first flowering of entrepreneurial capitalism. The rise of the market as the master economic institution made possible the triumph of an ideology that asserted the uniqueness of the nation in terms of its liberties and opportunities, especially freedom from limitations on individual opportunity—on the chance to make of oneself what one wanted. In 19th-century America, that belief system was centered above all on the cult of the "self-made man," on the pursuit of individual material success and advancement—getting ahead financially. It was a small capitalist and entrepreneurial dream focused on the opportunity to make money in the market through shrewdness and disciplined rationality (Mills, 1951; Hartz, 1955; Hofstatder, 1955; Wylie, 1966).

This wider transformation included the reconstruction and reorganization of family life and of assumptions about the nature and roles of men and women. In the 17th and 18th centuries, the family was the basic unit of economic production. While changes came gradually and occurred in some places earlier than in others, by roughly the 1820s there was an identifiable urban-based middle class with a fundamentally different organization of family life. Oriented around the market, and around men going out of the home "to work," this new family was not primarily a production unit. The woman now became supervisor and arranger of the home and of home life, and the ideal of the home was elevated to the realm of the sacred. Child rearing was likewise redefined as a task for which women were uniquely qualified by virtue of their more gentle and spiritual nature. Writers of both sexes published a new kind of literature devoted to affairs of the home and the "True Woman." Child-rearing literature provided mothers with a checklist of do's and don'ts about raising self-guiding, moral individuals. Books and magazines for women instructed them about the proper attitudes to assume vis-à-vis their breadwinning husbands, how to arrange and maintain the proper home, and how to be ladies. The Cult of True Womanhood (Welter, 1973) was the woman's equivalent of the self-made man. For while the self-made man had to be strong, pragmatic, and disciplined to deal with the rigors of the market (the world), the True Woman preserved in her person and in her home the purer, moral side of human society, uncontaminated by the baseness of worldly affairs (Welter, 1973; Lerner, 1969; Easton, 1976; Wishy, 1968; Smith, 1970; Cott, 1977; Sunley, 1961; Smith-Rosenberg, 1975).

In short, by about 1830 a radical bifurcation of sex roles or spheres was developing among the middle class. Just as women were clearly inferior to men in power and responsibility, they were believed to be superior in their own assigned and limited realm. Whether the emergence of the new sex role and family arrangements marked an increase in women's oppression is a debated point. What is not at issue is the quality of the oppression. Alexis de Tocqueville, traveling in the United States in the 1830s, at the time when this family style was becoming common, observed that "the independence of woman is irrevocably lost in the bonds of matrimony . . . [she] lives in the home of her husband as if it were a cloister" (1961, p. 240).

3. WOMAN AS ISSUE AND SYMBOL IN TEMPERANCE LITERATURE

This section discusses three ways that women were portrayed in temperance literature and speeches: as drunkards, as victims, and as natural moral reformers.

The Woman as Drunkard

During the 19th century, the restrictions against women's getting drunk were so strong among Protestant middle class supporters of the temperance cause that the *topic* of women's intemperance was itself almost taboo. For example, in 1832 one speaker observed:

> I have before adverted to the practice of furnishing wine and other liquor, for the entertainment of our friends. And I firmly believe, that many a man, and many a child, have been ruined by so doing, (and if I *dared* to, I would whisper, some women too) (Scott, 1832, p. 10)

There was a coyness about this admission which appeared throughout the century. Speakers and writers did, in fact, occasionally address the issue of women drunkards. The president of the New York State temperance society pointed out that "females were seldom the subjects, although they were so frequently the victims of the vice of intemperance." However, he added:

> Would to Heaven I could be permitted to say it is always thus! But truth compels me to declare that this monster has sometimes succeeded in degrading the fairest and the loveliest of the creation to the level of the brutes. (New York State Society for the Promotion of Temperance, 1832, p. 10)

In 1887, famous temperance lecturer John B. Gough made much the same point:

> Woman too, more often sinned against, is yet sometimes the sinner by means of intoxicants. Every holy instinct and every womanly shame have been thus destroyed. (p. 278)

In short, temperance literature did mention women's drinking and becoming drunkards. It did not, however, dwell on the subject.

Temperance ideology was organized thematically and conceptually around the issue of men, especially middle-class men, becoming drunkards. It was not similarly organized around women's drinking. In part, this orientation reflected the realities of middle-class life: the opportunities for men to drink were much greater, and the penalties for women who drank heavily were often extreme. One man discussed this issue in his autobiography, which he called *Eleven Years a Drunkard*. Placed in a cell once next to a group of drunken women, he reflected on the relative opportunities for reform of men and women:

> Hopeless indeed seems the condition of fallen women. Men can reform; society welcomes them back to the path of virtue; a veil is cast over their conduct, and their vows of amendment are accepted, and their promises to reform are hailed with great delight. But, alas, for poor women who have been tempted to sin by rum, for them there are no calls to come home, no sheltering arm, no acceptance of confessions and promises to amend. (Doner, 1877)

The topic of women drinking and becoming drunkards violated the optimistic caste of temperance thought. The unease about and the relative rareness of extended discussion of women's drunkenness suggest the heavy investment that middle-class men had in the image of women as pure and virtuous—too many examples of drunken women, especially middle-class ones, could undermine the whole model of the middle-class family. It was, however, less threatening to admit to drunkenness among poor and working-class women and among immigrants. Still, the central problem was always defined as drinking by men.*

The Woman as Victim

While women were rarely portrayed as drunkards, the victimization of women by liquor and the liquor traffic was an obvious fact of life for many 19th-century women and men. Temperance writers graphically described the problems. For example, a book about the women's crusade in Portland, Oregon, was prefaced with an extended quote from an article in *Scribner's* magazine:

> For years and years, and weary, suffering years, multiplied into decades, have the women of America waited to see the traffic destroyed which annually sends sixty thousand of their sons, brothers, fathers and husbands into the drunkard's grave. They have been impoverished, disgraced, tortured in mind and body, beaten, murdered. Under the influence of maddening liquors the hands that were pledged to provide for and protect them, have withdrawn from them the means of life, or smitten them in the dust. Sons whom they have nursed upon their bosoms with tenderest love and countless prayers, have grown into beasts of whom they are afraid, or have sunk into helpless and pitiful slavery. They have been compelled to bear children to men whose habits had unfitted them for parentage—children not only tainted by disease, but endowed with debased appetites. They have seen themselves and their precious families thrust into social degradation and cut off forever from all desirable life by the vice of the men they loved. What the women of this country have suffered from drunkenness, no mind, however sympathetic, can measure, and no pen, however graphic, can describe. It has been the unfathomable black gulf into which the infatuated multitudes of men have thrown their fortunes, their health, and their industry, and out of which have came only—in fire and stench—dishonor, disease, crime, misery, despair and death. It is the abomination of abominations, the curse of curses, the hell of hells! (Victor, 1874, p. 5)

The issues raised here were the classic ones and were repeated countless times in temperance literature: (1) the destruction or death of male family members; (2) the loss of financial support by the men, resulting in disgrace, poverty, and death; (3) the diseased appetites of the fathers being passed along to the children; and (4) the indescribable shame and misery of wives and children, including being beaten and tortured.

In *Memories of the Crusade* (1890), Mother Stewart, one of the

---

*While it is far beyond the bounds of this chapter, there is interesting and important work to be done on the image of women as drunkards in the 19th century as discussed in temperance and other documents. For a discussion of current thought see Gomberg (1976).

leaders of the women's antiliquor crusade that swept Ohio and other states in 1874, reported many such cases:

> Coming home from my work one day during the Crusade, I found a lady with a little girl at my house. She at once told me her story, so common, so old, as to have ceased to excite attention. . . . As her story ran, she had married with fair prospects of a happy future; no indication of the terrible habit even then fastened upon her husband. Her father, a man of wealth, gave her a nice farm, and there they started on life's journey together. But as the years went on the old, old story of the drunkard's wife became hers; and, as she thought, in exaggerated degree. She had, finally, through his abuse, become afraid for her life,—had gathered a few articles of clothing, and taking her child by the hand, through the assistance of a friend she secretly stole away, reached the railroad and fled, leaving the husband—now the terror of her life—in peaceable possession of her home. But whither should she turn her steps? She had heard of Mother Stewart as the friend of the drunkard's wife, and she had come to her in hope of refuge and safety. She would do anything, would go out to domestic service if only she could find shelter for herself and child. Reason was so nearly dethroned, and the fear that the husband would come and rob her of her child—the only possession she had—that if the bell rang, or she heard a step on the veranda, she would clutch the child and hasten to place of hiding. (pp. 469/470)

It was a tale of failure within the middle class: the son and daughter, who appeared to have the good life set out for them, fell into terrible ruin because their father took to drink. And Stewart noted that it was a "story, so common, so old, so as to have ceased to excite attention."

Fictional stories and novels were especially appropriate vehicles for illustrating the awful consequences of drink for family life and for women. Temperance fiction was devoted to the theme of the ruin of the man and the destructive consequences for his wife and children. The temperance story was a staple of 19th-century American fiction (Brown, 1959). The theme, however, was not limited to temperance writers. For example, Herman Melville used a version of the classic tale of ruin in the case of the blacksmith in his novel *Moby Dick:*

> He had been an artisan of famed excellence, and with plenty to do; owned a house and garden; embraced a youthful, daughter-like, loving wife, and three blithe, ruddy children; every Sunday went to a cheerful-looking church, planted in a grove. But one night, under cover of darkness, and further concealed in a most cunning disguisement, a desperate burglar slid into his happy home, and robbed them all of everything. And darker yet to tell, the blacksmith himself did ignorantly conduct this burglar into his family's heart. It was the Bottle Conjuror! Upon the opening of that fatal cork, forth flew the fiend, and shrivelled up his home. . . .
>
> Why tell the whole? The blows of the basement hammer every day grew more and more between; and each blow everyday grew fainter than the last; the wife sat frozen at the window, with tearless eyes, glitteringly gazing into the weeping faces of her children; the bellows fell; the forge choked up with

cinders; the house was sold; the mother dived down into the church-yard grass; her children twice followed her thither; and the houseless, familyless old man staggered off. (1851/1956, p. 370)

Again, the point is not that Melville was a temperance writer but rather that the story of destruction by the bottle was a fact of popular consciousness extending far beyond temperance literature.

The violence of drunken men toward women was also a common theme in the pictures and drawings that were sometimes used to illustrate a text or a point. A typical scene was entitled "The Home of the Intemperate" and usually showed a wild-eyed man beating or about to beat his wife or children (for example, the frontispiece to Stebbins, 1876). Although temperance supporters differed on the issue of the naturally violent tendencies of men, the main focus of temperance ideology was to blame alcohol, and not the men, for their violence against women and children. John B. Gough (1887) put the case very well:

> I know when we hear of wife-beating and all that kind of thing, we say "Men are brutes." They are *not* brutes. I have worked among them for forty years, and have never found a brute among them. Yet I have found "hard cases." But I attribute most of it to the influence of drink. A man will not beat his wife if he is sober. (p. 162)

Gough also told of being approached by "a lady of aristocratic bearing":

> "You have had great experience," she said, "but have you ever known or heard of a son striking his mother?" "More than once," I said, "but never unless that son was influenced by drink; indeed, I cannot believe that any young man, in his sober senses, would strike his mother." She seemed relieved to know that hers was not a solitary case, and she informed me that she had a son who had been dissipated for years. (p. 185)

The most comprehensive documentation by a temperance person (and perhaps by anyone in the 19th century) of the extent of alcohol-related family violence was Samuel Chipman's study first published in 1834. Chipman visited the keepers of the jails, asylums, and poorhouses of every county in New York State and some neighboring states as well. At each site, he received a signed statement from the manager of the institution classifying the inmates as "temperate," "intemperate," or "doubtful." In addition, many of the supervisors signed short statements describing specific cases or patterns. Consider the following excerpts from some of the county reports:

> *Albany County:* Of the intemperate, at least twenty have been committed for abuse to their families.
> *Alleghany County:* Of the intemperate, three for whipping their wives—one charged with poisoning his wife—two for arson—one for abuse to his parents.
> *Broome County:* One of the intemperate was committed for whipping his wife; and two on charge of rape.

Columbia County: Fourteen were sent here for whipping their wives, or otherwise abusing their families; one of the fourteen was committed seven times for this offense.

Jefferson County: Of the intemperate, twenty-six were intoxicated when committed. One was committed on charge of arson, and nine for whipping their wives.

Niagara County: Of the intemperate a considerable number have been committed repeatedly; one man has lain in jail for two-thirds of the time for three years past, for abuse to his family when intoxicated; when sober, is a kind husband and father.

Orange County: Of the intemperate, thirteen for riots—one, a man, for assault and battery on a female—four for whipping their wives, one of them whipped his wife with a dog! One under sentence for killing his wife when drunk—most of them were brought here while intoxicated.

Schenectady County: Of the intemperate, one was a woman for abuse to her husband, and sixteen men for abuse to their wives.

Chester County, Pennsylvania: Seven for assault and battery—three for whipping their wives, and one sober woman for whipping her drunken husband.

In the conclusion to his report, Chipman noted that "in no poor house that I have visited, have I failed of finding the wife or the widow, and the children of the drunkard." Further, he pointed out that "in almost every jail were husbands confined for whipping their wives, or for otherwise abusing their families." Finally, he pointed out that the extent of the problem was only hinted at by his findings: "When we reflect that but a very small proportion of these brutes in human form are thus punished, the amount of misery and domestic suffering arising from this source exceeds the powers of the human mind to compute" (p. 30).

In temperance ideology, and in middle-class moral thought in general, the home and women were engaged in a battle against the liquor business and the demonic substance. Husbands and fathers were destroyed as breadwinners, leaving women poverty-stricken. Liquor so brutalized men and destroyed their moral sensibilities that they beat their wives and daughters.

There were further massive psychological and emotional costs for women. Perhaps these came out most strongly around the issue of loss of children, mainly of sons. During the 19th century, motherhood was the most sacred and revered part of the woman's role, and one area where women had some autonomy. Temperance ideology was addressed to the problem of women who had defined their whole meaning and purpose around their homemaking and child-rearing functions: such women lost everything because of drink. In *Women and Temperance* (1883), Frances Willard quoted a letter that she had received from a widow whose son had finally obtained a job after a long period of unemployment. He had had drinking problems, but he wanted to reform.

However, after receiving his first paycheck, he set out to buy something for his mother and instead:

> After a few hours he came, with unsteady feet, brain heated and bewildered; the face that God had made so fair swollen, flushed, disfigured; the beautiful eyes, that were to have watched for his mother's home coming, bloodshot and wild in their brightness. This was on Saturday night. On God's holy day he stole out, and drank again to quench the thirst that it but enkindles anew. To-day when the mother pleaded, when her hand would have held him back, keeping him within home's shelter, the lips she used to kiss so lovingly cursed the day that he was born, cursed the mother that gave him birth, the mother who would die to save him now, and went out again on the road that leads to death. (pp. 388–389)

The mother concluded, "my weak and wandering boy, who but for rum's traffic would be . . . an ornament to society, a power for good in the land." A temperance hymn titled "How My Boy Went Down" (Coleman, 1971, p. 74) captures well the feelings around this issue:

> It was not on the field of battle,
> It was not with a ship at sea;
> But a fate far worse than either,
> That stole him away from me.
> 'Twas the death in the tempting wine-cup,
> That the reason and senses drown
> He drank the alluring poison,
> And thus my boy went down.
> He went down from the heights of manhood,
> To the depths of disgrace and sin,
> Down to a worthless being, From the hope of what might have been.
> For the brand of a beast besotted,
> He bartered his manhood's crown, Thro' the gate of a sinful pleasure,
> My poor weak boy went down.
> It is only the same old story,
> Many mothers so often tell,
> With voices full of sadness,
> Like the tone of a funer'l bell;
> But I never once tho't when I heard it,
> I should know what it meant my self,
> I thought he'd be true to mother,
> As well as to himself.

The chorus of the song was both a cry of despair and a call to action:

> Oh! can nothing destroy this great evil,
> No bar in its pathway be thrown,
> To save from the terrible maelstrom,
> The thousands of boys going down.

Again the theme is the juxtaposition of drink and sin with home and mother.

In temperance ideology, alcohol destroyed fathers, husbands, and sons, and in so doing, it caused incredible suffering to women and their families. In *Ten Nights in a Bar-Room,* T. S. Arthur's best-selling temperance novel (1854/1966), there is Mrs. Morgan, who endures extreme poverty because her husband spends all his money on drink, and whose daughter dies after being hit accidentally with a beer mug. There is Mrs. Slade, the wife of the saloon owner, who worries constantly about the awful consequences of her husband's business, and who, after her son kills her husband, goes insane and has to be locked away. And most dramatically, there is Mrs. Hammond whose son, Willy, a bright and handsome youth, has got into the drinking and gambling habit. Willy is shot in a bar fight and Mrs. Hammond rushes to hold him:

> "I will save you, my son," she murmured in the ears of the young man. "Your mother will protect you. Oh! if you had never left her side, nothing on earth could have done you harm." (p. 89)

Unfortunately, Willy dies in his mother's arms. The shock is too much for Mrs. Hammond, who "fell, lifeless, across the body of her dead son."

Beyond the effects of the substance on the bodies and minds of men, temperance reformers pointed out that women were victimized by the functioning of the liquor business. Especially during the last quarter of the century, the liquor industry was seen as an evil power within American politics, buying votes and corrupting democracy. However, the most important aspect of the liquor business in the eyes of members of the temperance movement was the saloon. No issue or symbol captured so well the range of issues involved in the "liquor problem."

The saloon was, above all else, the antihome, the bastion of maleness, the place where men escaped from their wives and their family responsibilities. The radical split between home and society and between men and women meant that some territorial and symbolic areas were exclusively male. The worlds of work and business were such domains, but they were deeply embedded in middle-class business culture. The saloon offered escape from the cares and worries of work and home, a place of "time out" from responsibility. As Leslie Fiedler (1969) has suggested,

> The saloon was, of course, for a long time felt as the anti-type of home, at least in Protestant America . . . it was a refuge for escaping males nearly as archetypal as the wilderness and the sea. Ever since Rip Van Winkle the image of a bust with the boys had stood for flight from the shrew. (p. 259)

The saloon was rightfully perceived by temperance supporters as a competitor of the home and a direct attack on the morality and values that the home was thought to represent. The nude portraits hung over many bars were an insult and a threat to Christian women, as was the prostitution that was sometimes available in adjoining hotel rooms. Enshrined and sanctified in the home, women were quite literally disrobed in the saloon. It was no accident that the first mass action by women was an attack on the saloon. And when an independent women's temperance organization was successfully launched, its leader continually defined the liquor problem as the problem of "Home Protection." Frances Willard put the matter very simply at a speech before a Centennial Temperance Meeting (National Temperance Society, 1886) in 1885: "Ours is a great and sacred cause of the home versus the saloon. Our people are bound to discover that this country cannot support both institutions. One must go up into safety, the other down into outlawry" (p. 600). The saloon ruined men by making them intoxicated and making them drunkards, by destroying self-discipline and moral character, by fostering immoral and misogynous attitudes, by tempting children (in particular, boys), by encouraging gambling and prostitution, and by making drinking seem attractive and sociable, thus masking the terrible consequences of drink in the moral world of home and family.

The Woman as Moral Agent

An address delivered by Dr. William Scott before the Ladies Temperance Society of Sandy Hill, New York, in 1832, contained themes that were repeated throughout the 19th century. Dr. Scott offered his audience a list of the reasons why "it is the duty of women to join temperance societies" and work for total abstinence:

1. Because they were generally temperate themselves.
2. Because they controlled the fashions of the day, especially those related to the entertainment of company.
3. Because the sphere of life in which they move and the duties they were called on to perform rendered them more susceptible to feelings of humanity.
4. Because they had great influence over men.
5. Because they could do more than men to prevent the formation of intemperate habits in the young.
6. And last but not least, because the heaviest calamities occasioned by intemperance fell on them.

The assumptions about the natural "sphere of life" of women and their greater openness to "feelings of humanity" that underlie these arguments were only then attaining widespread acceptance and legitimacy. But they continued to hold sway throughout the century. Frances Willard, the charismatic leader of the Woman's Christian Temperance Union (WCTU), argued that by shaping and instructing children and husband, women contributed to the temperance cause and to building the nation. Among the middle class, it was widely assumed that, as Willard put it, "maternity is [a woman's] mission." Katherine Beecher (1972), the author of probably the most important domestic advice and homemaking manual, lectured women about their power:

> Now the Christian woman in the family and the school is the most complete autocrat that is known, as the care of the helpless little ones, the guidance of their intellect, and the formation of all their habits, are given to her supreme control. . . . There is a moral power given to woman in the family state much more controlling and abiding than the inferior physical power conferred on man. And the more men are trained to refinement, honor, and benevolence, the more this moral power of women is increased. (pp. 150–151)

Temperance ideas were built on, and were elaborations of, this sort of essentially conservative middle-class vision. For example, the WCTU's Secretary of the Department of Hereditary Tendencies noted in her 1882 report:

> The special and temporary privilege of the mother during that impressible period in which a new life lies under her molding hand, and draws its vitality from hers, reflects every impulse of soul and body, receives every impression made upon her. The latest thought of the latest thinkers intensifies belief in the potent influences of this impressible period. . . . How often does the heart-broken mother of a drinking son wish she could only put within [him] her loathing of his vices, her longing for his salvation. There was had she but known it, a time in which she could have done just this; in which she could have fashioned his soul and body as an artist forms a statue, or a painter a picture. (WCTU, 1882, pp. ii–iii)

Acting within her "proper" sphere, the mother had the power to reform her children.

Beginning around 1830, when temperance became a mass movement, encouragements for women to participate in temperance reform were generally couched in terms of their family duties, acting perhaps as foot soldiers in the crusade under the leadership and guidance of men. Women were certainly not to be leaders. In the 1850s, that idea was challenged, and by the 1870s, it had been overthrown.

There was a contradiction within middle-class moral ideology that women's rights activists had exploited since the founding meetings of the women's rights movement in Seneca Falls, New York, in 1848. Part of the justification for assigning women to the home, and excluding them from economic and political life, was to protect women's greater moral sensibilities. However, since the greater morality and virtue of women were rhetorically nearly universally acknowledged, that "fact" could be used to support women's right to participate in political and economic activities. Precisely because women were more moral than men, they should be included in political affairs in order to raise the moral level. In the last quarter of the century, the WCTU used that argument to justify women's participation in a whole range of reformist, political, and economic activities. Frances Willard (1892) made the point well in one of her presidential addresses:

> The Kansas people argue that if you were told that there existed in some ideal country two great selections of a race, the members of one often gross, often vicious, often given to loud talking, to swearing, to drinking, spitting, chewing, not infrequently corrupt; those of the other branch mild, kind, quiet, pure, devout, with none of the habitual vices of the first of the named state. If you were told that one of these branches was alone to elect rulers and to govern, you would at once say: "Tell us where this happy country is that basks in the rule of such a God-like people." "Stop a minute" says your informant. "It is the creatures I described first, it is the men who rule, the others are only women, poor silly fools, imperfect men, I assure you, nothing more." (p. 17)

After the Civil War, temperance men came to accept, and many to endorse heartily, women's participation and leadership in the movement. Senator Henry Blair (1888) believed that temperance's fight for a better world necessarily included woman's suffrage: "The complete enfranchisement of woman is the primal condition and basic fact which will mark the era of the dominance of reason and conscience in the affairs of the race" (p. 399). Blair argued for woman's suffrage on the grounds both that women were morally superior and that the temperance cause demanded it:

> There can be no doubt that the spiritual fiber of woman's organization is of a higher type than that of man. She is more closely allied with the moral and religious elements or forces in the universe. . . . The war for abstinence is a war for woman and home. It is woman's war. Man may help her. But she fights it, if it be fought, and she wins it, if it be won. . . . I believe the suffrage of woman is indispensable to the success of the temperance reform. (pp. 398–399)

The Prohibition Party, founded in 1869, made equal suffrage part of its original program. In 1880, the platform read: "We also demand as a right that women, having in other respects the privileges of citizens, shall be clothed with the ballot for their protection" (Colvin, 1926, p. 127). The justifications for women's active participation in the temperance cause and for the vote never got very far from women as victims or as moral superiors.

4. WOMEN IN THE TEMPERANCE REFORM

From the beginning of the antiliquor cause, women participated in various activities and even sponsored some events, but it was always understood, and often stated, that they were the followers of men and that their natural and proper place was in the home with the members of the family. Eventually, women began to challenge men's domination of temperance societies, and some activists from the newly formed women's rights movement attempted to carve out a distinctly women's position on the liquor problem. This activity coincided with some occasional spontaneous uprisings by women against the saloon. Finally, there was the formation and development of the Woman's Christian Temperance Union into a strong, independent women's organization. Under the leadership of Frances Willard, the WCTU argued and agitated for women's participation in a range of political and reform activities on the grounds that women must be involved in such activities precisely because according to middle-class mores, they were responsible for protecting morality and the home.

Within the Traditional Sphere

Women's participation in various reform activities began during the second great awakening, as the religious revivals of the first three decades of the 19th century were called. One historian of the period (Keller, 1942) has pointed out that it was a time of many "female societies," whose activities included collecting money, sewing clothing, operating schools for poor children, and distributing educational and religious material. Further, all this activity was new to women. The editor of a religious newspaper observed in 1818,

> It is a peculiar honor to our age, that, as a sex, women have discovered, and extensively entered, the path, in which their peculiar glory is to be found. No preceding period has seen them in such numbers, with such unanimity, with such zeal, engaged in the great work of doing good. (quoted in Keller, 1942, p. 234)

Church-sponsored and related activities were the primary recipients of women's energies. Although the temperance movement had an organizational life independent of the church and a worldly focus for its work, the ties with religion were close enough for temperance to gain greatly from women's participation.

Although women were allowed and even encouraged to engage in Christian reform work, this did not mean that they were to abandon their subordinate position to men. In 1832, for example, the president of one state temperance society encouraged the American woman to "lend her influence and her example to the cause of entire abstinence." However, he explained that "We do not ask her to declaim against this vice in public assemblies, or to visit its most loathsome haunts . . . but we beseech her to let her influence be felt in the family circle, with her relatives, and among her most intimate friends" (New York State Society for the Promotion of Temperance, 1832, p. 11). And like other organizations, temperance groups depended on women to do the mundane and lowly tasks: "lick envelopes, raise money through fairs" and so on (Welter, 1973, p. 137).

Women did organize their own temperance societies and tried to carry out their assignment of acting as moral exemplars. The following description prefaced an address delivered before a women's temperance group in 1832:

> The Ladies Temperance Society of Sandy-Hill, was formed in November, 1830, and has now 169 members. Their constitution prohibits the use of wine, ale, or strong beer, and all kinds of distilled liquor; unless they are prescribed as a medicine by a temperate physician. In consequence of their example, these liquors are now excluded from a great proportion of the houses in the village: very few females use them at all, or tolerate their use. (Scott, 1832)

That is, women aided the temperance reform by example and by influence within their sphere. Ten years later, a group identified as "The Ladies of Geneva," New York, published a speech by a Mr. Grosvenor (1842) that had been delivered at a meeting they had organized. The women arranged for the publication of the address because they were "convinced that in no way they can better promote the cause of TEMPERANCE, by arousing the minds of the Female sex to their high duties and responsibilities." The speaker argued that when a women "maintains her true position and revolves in her proper sphere, harmony and good order everywhere prevail." Further, he said that while the "civil and political" world belonged to men, "the social and domestic world is principally set apart to her." Within her realm, however, a woman could do great good. The first task was not to drink alcohol, to keep it out of the house, and to encourage men in the family not to drink. But the speaker had another task for women as well. Women were to "yield to dictates of self-preservation and the impulses of their generous natures, and come to the rescue" of the drunkards in their families. Women were to contribute to the temperance cause by devoting themselves to saving their relatives:

> Our own village furnishes many instances . . . in which, after all the ordinary expedients had entirely failed, and the victim abandoned in despair, he has finally been saved by her, whose affection is almost as undying as the immortality of the soul whose bitterness she alone can relieve. (p. 10)

This conception of the woman's role in the temperance cause as the savior of the drunkard had a long life and many notable advocates, as feminist journalist Ida Husted Harper observed at the very end of the century:

> The belief has by no means died out that it is a woman's sacred duty to marry a dissolute man in order to reform him, although the number of victims

sacrificed on this altar is growing somewhat less. So broad, just and progressive a man as Robert Ingersoll used to describe in one of his lectures, with that vivid word painting for which he was famous, the beautiful devotion of the drunkard's wife, who met her husband's curses with sweet words, kissed his bloated lips, bathed his burning face, and staggering under his blows, dragged her bruised limbs about in an effort to care for him tenderly until he was able to go out and get drunk again. Then all the men in the audience would applaud, while the women would weep and consecrate themselves anew. (quoted in Kraditor, 1965, p. 88)

During the 1840s, women worked in conjunction with male temperance groups, especially the Washingtonians, forming the Martha Washingtonians, and with the Sons of Temperance, forming the Daughters of Temperance. They helped the men by taking on such tasks as providing lunch for a temperance picnic or collecting signatures for antiliquor petitions.

The Feminist Challenge

The major challenge to the conventional view of women's role as followers and servants of men came from outside the temperance movement. In the 1830s, women participating in the antislavery crusade started questioning and rejecting ideas about women's "proper" place. Most shocking of all, they spoke in public—a violation of what many men and women felt were natural laws. Early women's antislavery crusaders' meetings were broken up by mobs of men. In 1837, the Congregational churches of Massachusetts's general association issued a statement condemning women who "assume the place and tone of a man as a public reformer" and said that when a woman does such things "she yields the power which God has given her for protection, and her character becomes unnatural." In 1840, the U.S. Anti-Slavery Society sent eight women delegates to London to the World's Anti-Slavery Convention. After fierce debate, the women were barred as delegates on the grounds that if "promiscuous female representation" were allowed, then "all order would be at an end" (Catt and Shuler, 1970, pp. 15–17; Flexner, 1975; O'Neill, 1969a). Two of the women present at the convention, Lucretia Mott and Elizabeth Cady Stanton, became more committed to women's issues as a result of their experience, and in 1848, they issued a call for a Woman's Rights Convention to be held in Seneca Falls, New York. In a formal sense, that convention marked the beginning of the women's rights movement and the drive for women's suffrage (Stanton, Anthony, and Gage, 1881).

Many of the women and men who gathered around the issue of women's rights had been supporters of the temperance cause. Elizabeth Cady Stanton (1898) had done temperance work before she had been married; Amelia Bloomer (1975) (for whom the "bloomer" pantaloons were named) ran a newspaper, *The Lily,* which began as a temperance paper but which soon gave a prominent place to feminist issues. Soon after the Seneca Falls convention, Susan Brownell Anthony, who had organized Daughters of Temperance groups in New York, met Elizabeth Cady Stanton. The two quickly became fast friends and formed a partnership that was to contribute enormously to the development of the women's rights and suffrage movements. Stanton was the writer and theoretician, Anthony the organizer (Flexner, 1975; O'Neill, 1969a; Gurko, 1976).

In 1852, the Sons of Temperance held a convention in Albany, New York. Susan B. Anthony, Mary C. Vaughn, and a number of others were sent as representatives of the Daughters of Temperance. The women's credentials were accepted, but when Susan Anthony tried to speak on a motion, she was told that "the sisters were not invited there to speak, but to listen and learn" (Cherrington, 1925–1930, Vol. 5, p. 1967). The women left the meeting and with some sympathetic temperance men organized their own meeting in an Albany church. Mary Vaughn was selected as president and addressed the group:

> We have met to consider what we, as women, can do and may do, to forward the temperance reform. . . . We are aware that this proceeding of ours, this calling together of a body of women to deliberate publicly upon plans to carry out a specified reform, will rub rather harshly upon the mould of prejudice, which has gathered thick upon the common mind.

Vaughn spoke out strongly against the conventional image of woman's role:

> We account it no reason why we should desist, when conscience, an awakened sense of duty, and aroused heart-sympathies, would lead us to show ourselves something different than an impersonation of the vague idea which has been named, Woman, and with which woman has long striven to identify herself. A creature all softness and sensibility, who must necessarily enjoy and suffer in the extreme . . . bearing happiness meekly, and sorrow with fortitude; gentle, mild, submissive, forbearing under all circumstances . . . a mere adjunct of man, the chief object of whose creation was to adorn and beautify his existence, or to minister to some form of his selfishness. This is nearly the masculine idea of womanhood, and poor womanhood strives to personify it. But not all women. This is an age of iconoclasms; and daring hands are raised to sweep from its pedestal, and dash to fragments, this false image of woman.

Lydia Fowler also addressed the group and read letters from Stanton and Bloomer. The meeting decided that women should form their own temperance organization and appointed a committee headed by Susan Anthony to prepare for a "Women's State Temperance Convention" (quoted in Stanton et al., 1881, pp. 476–480).

Three months later, on April 20, 1852, the convention opened, with more than 500 women present. During the two days of meetings, there was extended discussion about the role women should play in temperance reform and what sorts of actions were especially appropriate. They officially created "The Woman's New York State Temperance Society" and elected Elizabeth Cady Stanton as president. The strongest and most controversial issue discussed was a proposal by Stanton that "no woman remain in the relation of wife with the confirmed drunkard." Amelia Bloomer (quoted in Stanton et al., 1881) spoke out strongly in favor of Stanton's suggestion:

> We believe the teachings which have been given to the drunkard's wife touching her duty—the commendable examples of angelic wives which she has been exhorted to follow, have done much to continue and aggravate the vices and crimes of society growing out of intemperance. Drunkenness is a good ground for divorce, and every woman who is tied to a confirmed drunkard should sunder the ties; and if she do it not otherwise the law should compel it—especially if she have children. (p. 483)

In making such a proposal, Stanton and her allies were attempting to mark out a distinctly women's program on the temperance issue. They were pushing, in a strong and concrete fashion, the idea that the victimization of women by the liquor traffic was related to women's domination by men in the family. Stanton's radical proposal was an attempt to legitimize divorce for the woman married to a drunkard and, moreover, to place a positive moral value on divorce—to say that under some circumstances, a woman has a responsibility to herself, to her children, and to society to break up a family. Needless to say, her proposal was widely condemned. The *Troy Journal,* for example, was horrified at the idea of "a virtuous woman severing the tie that bound her to a confirmed drunkard," calling it the destruction of a "divine institution" and also claiming that Stanton's ideas were "reviling Christianity" (Stanton et al., 1881, pp. 483–485; Cherrington, 1925–1930, Vol. 5, p. 1967).

In June of the same year, the New York State Temperance Society, a men's organization and long one of the important leaders in the temperance movement, held a convention. They issued a call to "temperance societies of every name" to send delegates, and Bloomer, Anthony, and Smith were sent as delegates from the women's society. When Susan Anthony tried to speak, there was an uproar, she was not allowed to finish, and a vote was taken. Though none of the delegates had yet been accredited, all men's votes were counted and none of the women's. Again the women left with sympathetic men and organized their own meeting, which was much better attended than the original. For the rest of the year, Susan Anthony and a number of other women organized societies affiliated with the Woman's State Temperance Society and held meetings on a tour through many New York cities and towns.

A year later, "The First Annual Meeting of the Woman's State Temperance Society" was held. This convention climaxed a year of hard work, and, in her opening presidential address, Elizabeth Cady Stanton took the opportunity to raise some fundamental issues involving women's participation in the temperance cause. She confronted the issue of woman's rights and temperance:

> It has been objected to our Society that we do not confine ourselves to the subject of temperance, but talk too much about woman's rights. . . . We have been obliged to preach woman's rights, because many, instead of listening to what we had to say on temperance, have questioned the right of a woman to speak on any subject. (quoted in Stanton et al., 1881, p. 495)

That so many people did not believe that a woman "has a right to stand on an even pedestal with man, [and] look him in the face as an equal," said Stanton, meant that a women's temperance organization must necessarily speak about women's rights:

> Let it be clearly understood, then, that we are a woman's rights society; that we believe it is woman's duty to speak whenever she feels the impression to do so, that it is her right to be present in all the councils of Church and State. (p. 495)

While this position was radical, it did not, by itself, constitute a distinctly women's perspective on the liquor question. Stanton did outline such a position, which was a brief critique of the whole orientation of temperance ideology. Her point was that the set of problems for women that were shown up so well in the case of the drunkard's wife involved "social relations" considerably larger and deeper than the liquor business:

> Those temperance men or women whose whole work consists in denouncing rum-sellers, appealing to legislatures, eulogizing Neal Dow, and shouting Maine Law are superficial reformers, mere surface workers.

Stanton argued that if one truly examined the problems of the drunkard's wife, one saw much more then the liquor traffic:

> In discussing the question of temperance, all lecturers, from the beginning have made mention of the drunkards' wives and children, of widows' groans and orphans' tears; shall these classes of sufferers be introduced but as themes for rhetorical flourish, as pathetic touches of the speaker's eloquence; shall we passively shed tears over their condition, or by giving them their rights, bravely open to them the doors of escape from a wretched and degraded life? Is it not legitimate in this to discuss the social degradation, the

legal liabilities of the drunkard's wife? If in showing her wrongs, we prove
the right of all womankind to the elective franchise; to a fair representation
in the government; to the right in criminal cases to be tried by peers of her
own choosing, shall it be said that we transcend the bounds of our
subject? . . . If in proving to you that justice and mercy demand a legal
separation from drunkards, . . . who shall say that the discussion of this
question does not lead us legitimately into the consideration of the important
subject of divorce?

In short, for Stanton and like-minded feminists, a distinctly woman's
perspective on the liquor question necessarily raised the issue of women's
oppression (Stanton et al., 1881, pp. 493–497).

That first convention marked the high point of the organizational
convergence of temperance and women's rights; it also marked the end.
On one hand, Stanton's analysis put the issue of women's rights above
the issue of temperance; that had been Stanton's position all along and
it never changed. On the other hand, many temperance supporters,
especially the ministers, were so strongly committed to keeping women
out of public and political life, or at least under male control, that almost
any form of independent women's activity was unacceptable. A month
earlier, a meeting in New York called to arrange for the World's
Temperance Convention had split up over the issue of women's participation. After being excluded from the convention, the ten women
delegates and their male allies left to form their own "Whole World's
Temperance Convention." The two conventions met simultaneously
several months later. When Antoinette Brown tried to attend the all-male
convention, the usual uproar resulted. Brown was allowed to speak for
ten minutes while men screamed and cursed her the whole while. Writing
about the event many years later, Stanton, Anthony, and Gage noted
that the World's Temperance Convention "may be called our Waterloo
in the [Temperance] reform." The resistance of most temperance men
was too strong for them (Stanton et al., 1881, pp. 499–513; Cherrington,
1925–1930, vol. 5; Catt and Shuler, 1970).

For the rest of the century, those at the center of the campaign for
women's rights and suffrage were sympathetic to the antiliquor cause.
Susan Anthony, Amelia Bloomer, and others included the abolition of
the liquor traffic in their program for social change and for the betterment
of women. Some of their demands, such as the important one for the
vote, for employment opportunities, for equal wages, and for provisions
for divorce, became part of women's temperance as defined by Frances
Willard and the WCTU. But that did not happen until more than 25 years
later.

Uprisings

Occasionally, women's anger and frustration found very direct forms of expression. The saloon smashings of Carry Nation (Asbury, 1929) at the end of the century are among the most well known of such antiliquor statements. What is less well known is that Nation was not the first woman to physically attack the symbols and appliances of the liquor trade; indeed, there were probably a number of such instances in the 19th century. Stanton et al. (1881) described some women's actions in New York:

> The repeal of the License Law of 1846, filled the temperance hosts throughout the State with alarm, and roused many women to the assertion of their rights. . . . [Some women] took the power in their own hands, visiting saloons, breaking windows, glasses, bottles, and emptying demijohns and barrels into the streets. Coming like whirlwinds of vengeance, drunkards and rum-sellers stood paralyzed before them. Though women were sometimes arrested for these high-handed proceedings, a strong public sentiment justified their acts, and forced the liquor dealers to withdraw their complaints. (pp. 474–475)

The authors described an 1853 case that had been written up in *The Lily* involving "the pious mother of a fine family of children and a highly respectable member of the Episcopal Church":

> Mrs. Margaret Freeland, of Syracuse, was recently arrested upon a warrant issued on complaint of Emanuel Rosendale, a rum-seller, charging her with forcing an entrance to his house, and with stones and clubs smashing his doors and windows, breaking his tumblers and bottles, and turning over his whisky barrels and spilling their contents. Great excitement was produced by this novel case. It seems that the husband of Mrs. Freeland was a drunkard—that he was in the habit of abusing his wife, turning her out of doors, etc., and this was carried so far that the police frequently found it necessary to interfere to put a stop to his ill-treatment of his family. Rosendale, the complainant, furnished Freeland with the liquor which turned him into a demon. Mrs. Freeland had frequently told him of her sufferings and besought him to refrain from giving her husband the poison. . . . He disregarded her entreaties and spurned her from his door. Driven to desperation she armed herself, broke into the house, drove out the base-hearted landlord and proceeded upon the work of destruction. (Stanton et al., 1881, p. 475)

Another newspaper pointed out that the saloon owner had withdrawn his charges against the woman when he realized that public opinion supported her:

> The rum-seller cowered in the face of public feeling. This case shows that public feeling will justify a woman whose person or family is outraged by a rum-seller, for entering his grocery or tavern and destroying his liquor. (Stanton et al., 1881, p. 475)

This kind of incident could not have been very common, and *The Lily* did point out that it was a "novel case." A similar incident, this one involving a number of women, was reported by Stewart (1890) in her memoirs:

> In 1865, a very great excitement was caused by the murder of a worthy young man as he was quietly passing a saloon on the street; a shot aimed at some party in the saloon found a lodgment in the young man in the street, with fatal results. The victim was the son and only support of an aged and feeble widow. There was no law to reach the case, but a large number of respectable ladies of the town, after some secret counsels, accompanied by the bereaved mother, proceeded to the saloon and with axes and other weapons knocked in the heads of barrels and casks, and demolished bottles and fixtures. (p. 208)

Another case was reported in a letter to the *New York Tribune* in 1869. A group of women in Perrysville, Ohio, opposed the opening of a saloon in town. When the proprietor would not sell out to them, the women smashed all his liquor supplies. The author of the letter described the strong antiliquor sentiment among women and predicted the coming of a new crusade:

> The people in this part of Ohio honestly think that the next war in this country will be between women and whiskey; and though there may not be much blood shed, you may rest assured rum will flow freely in the gutter. As the women here have taken the matter in hand once before, we claim to have fought the Bunker Hill of the new Revolution. (Quoted in Earhart, 1944, p. 140)

The Woman's Christian Temperance Union and Frances Willard

In 1873, Dio Lewis, a homeopathic physician and lecturer on health and exercise for women, added to his scheduled talk a temperance lecture about his mother's confrontation with saloon owners in New York many years earlier. Lewis's father had been a habitual drunkard, and Mrs. Lewis organized a group of women in town to try to persuade saloon owners, by argument and prayer, to give up their destructive business. In his lectures, Lewis encouraged women to follow his mother's example and to take to saloons with prayer. His plan was attempted a few times without much success until in December, he arrived in Hillsboro, Ohio. Inspired by his speech, a band of women, under the leadership of the daughter of the former governor, determined to conduct a women's praying crusade against the saloons. The women proceeded to the drugstores and saloons in town, and laying their Bibles on the bar, began gently to sing and pray. They returned day after day and held vigils outside when they were locked out of these places.

Word of their efforts spread. Women's praying bands were formed in towns throughout Ohio and from Maine to California. The crusades were the first mass-action sit-ins by women in American history. And the crusaders were successful: drugstore owners signed pledges not to sell liquor, and saloon owners closed up. Over the winter and spring of 1874, thousands of saloons and drugstores were stopped from selling liquor. Usually, preliminary meetings were called by wealthier or higher-status individuals and by "the best Christian women" of the town, in order to get as many people as possible committed to crusading. With the support of a number of respectable men, the women would enter an establishment, read from the Bible, pray, sing, sometimes kneeling on a filthy floor, and announce their intention of convincing the saloon owner to close up his business. Although crusaders were always determined to conduct themselves as peaceable Christian ladies, they were not always treated kindly. In some places, they had beer slops dumped on them; they were sometimes thrown in the mud; they were even occasionally assaulted and beaten; when they were arrested, they refused to post bond and continued their daily crusades. Whenever a saloon owner capitulated, there was a public ritual that involved smashing the barrels of liquor remaining in stock and breaking the bottles. The crusade was exhausted by the summer of 1874, but it succeeded in mobilizing a great many women who previously had been afraid or unable to express themselves in public.

In the fall of 1874, a group of the leaders and organizers of the crusaders—and some sympathizers, notably Frances Willard—gathered to form an organization of women to continue the work of the crusade. The WCTU became the most important and influential women's organization in 19th-century America. Although all-male or mixed temperance societies had more members, for about 25 years the WCTU was probably the most active temperance organization. It provided much of the spirit of the antiliquor cause, and it spread its example around the world, organizing WCTUs in a number of other nations.

Under the leadership of Annie Wittenmeyer, the first president, and with Frances Willard as corresponding secretary, the WCTU developed state and local unions and a variety of committees directing work in a number of reform activities. Wittenmeyer, a religious woman, was against women seeking the vote, and during her presidency, the WCTU maintained the religious spirit of the praying bands. Frances Willard clearly chafed under Wittenmeyer's direction, but she devoted herself to developing the union, traveling around the country, giving speeches, and helping local groups organize. By the time she finally won the presidency in 1879, with the help of a feminist-oriented faction, she had helped to build the WCTU into a strong organization capable of mobilizing women in social and political action.

Willard had attended the original planning meeting for the WCTU looking for a cause or a movement to which to devote herself. She had worked previously in women's education as a teacher and as a president of a women's college in Evanston, Illinois, and she had also participated in some women's suffrage activities. Her vision of society and of social reform was organized around broad moral principles derived primarily from Christian middle-class culture. In addition, Willard had an uncommon commitment to the problems and issues of women, especially their economic and political dependence on and subservience to men. She seems not to have had very strong antiliquor feelings before coming to the WCTU, and she saw the organization as a vehicle for realizing her ambitions for herself and for other women.

Willard was a brilliant organizer and a magnetic speaker. During her career as educator and reformer, she developed her poise on a platform without losing what middle-class critics would judge to be her "ladylike" grace and presence. As Mary Earhart (1944), her biographer, noted, she was regarded quite differently from women speakers like Anthony, who were sometimes "pelted with eggs and tomatoes": "Probably no other characteristic was so frequently commented upon by the press as her lady-like dignity. . . . People did not throw things at Frances Willard" (p. 122). For 20 years as national president of the WCTU, Willard used her knowledge and skills to advance the temperance cause and the women's movement and also to define a woman's position on the liquor problem.

Willard coined a number of slogans as a way of capturing and presenting her key ideas. One of the most important was "The Do Everything Policy," a slogan with many applications, which is what Willard intended. It was first of all the answer to the question of what should be done to fight the liquor problem. The temperance movement should be involved in all social and reform activities, said Willard. But perhaps more importantly, the slogan was an answer to the question of what women should do as reformers, or how much women should do in the temperance crusade and in the political realm in general. Within the context of Victorian middle-class culture, Willard's answer was radical, for it meant that women should do everything men do. Willard's genius was in couching an essentially feminist political agenda for women in the thoroughly respectable framework of Christian temperance work and in presenting it in such a way as to attract women who ordinarily would have shied away from such an activist role. By urging "Do Everything" as a program for the temperance movement, she was also allowing that women's temperance must, of course, do everything.

Further, by organizing the national WCTU into more than 30 departments, each with a superintendent and a license to "do everything," she made it possible for women to engage in a wide range of public and political activities. The slogan was also a challenge to the social style of timid womanhood. Willard ridiculed, albeit gently, those who felt it inappropriate for women to agitate for social reform, and she took considerable pride in the WCTU's achievements in getting women to assert themselves politically. In a speech at the founding meetings of the National Council of Women, she explained how an institutional structure can counter some of the effects of socialized passivity:

> The highest power of organization for women is that it brings them out; it translates them from the passive into the active voice; the dear, modest, clinging things didn't think they could do anything, and, lo and behold! they found out they could. They come to you with a quiver of the lip, and look at you so hopeful and expectant, and wonder if they could do something; and a year or two after, you hear them with a deep voice and perfect equipoise telling their dearest thought to a great audience, or you see them in the silent charities, carrying out their noblest purpose toward humanity. (Willard, p. 592)

During the last quarter of the century, the WCTU got women, especially middle-class women, out of their homes; gave them power and responsibility; let them use and further develop skills as writers, editors, and organizers; encouraged them to become public speakers and to travel; and in general provided them with a variety of ways to escape from some of the isolation, loneliness, and stagnation of their socially assigned roles. As Mother Stewart (1890) put it, "Our work has been a wonderful training school for the women, teaching them self-reliance, and developing ability to pray and speak in public assemblies, to lead meetings with parliamentary precision, as well as womanly grace" (p. 397).

Another major slogan of Willard's was "Home Protection." She used it in a number of ways but chiefly as the justification for women's suffrage, at least on liquor issues. The invention and use of the notion "Home Protection" is a supreme example of the way Willard employed the images and symbols of middle-class culture in order to agitate for women's rights. Within the Protestant middle-class culture, the "home" achieved an extraordinary level of sentimental value and weight. Above all, the "home" was the nest and the natural sphere of "mother." Willard's argument was the fullest exploitation of the ideological contradiction of assigning women as the home's protectors and then denying them access to political channels. Because the home was threatened by forces outside it, most notably by the liquor traffic, women had to leave the home in order to protect it; especially, they had to vote. In 1879, when she was president of the Illinois WCTU but not yet of the national organization, Willard prepared a pamphlet that she titled "Home Protection Manual: Containing an Argument for the Temperance Ballot for Women, and How to Obtain It as a Means for Home Protection." Willard explained the program:

> "Home Protection" is the general name given to a movement already endorsed by the WCTU Unions of eight states, the object of which is to secure for all women above the age of twenty-one years the ballot as one means for the protection of their homes from the devastation caused by the legalized traffic in strong drink.

Willard carefully pointed out the continuities between the original crusade and her program for women's voting:

> The "Home Protection Crusade" for woman's temperance ballot is the natural successor of the Temperance Crusade of 1873–74, and simply changes its objective point. . . . In giving prominence to this branch of work, we are but transferring the crusade from the saloon to the sources whence the saloon derives its guaranties and safeguards. Surely this does not change our work from sacred to secular! Surely, that is a short-sighted view which says: "It was womanly to plead with saloon-keepers not to sell; but it is unwomanly to plead with law makers not to legalize the sale and give us power to prevent it." (Willard, 1879)

Willard's reformist agenda even extended into the family. She wanted a transformed and more egalitarian family life. Despite her feminist goals, however, her program was in many ways a conservative one: she wanted the family reshaped within the contours of middle-class, Victorian, Christian ideals. The double standard was to be replaced by what she called "The white life for two"; men were to be raised to the moral standards and behavior of Christian women:

> To meet the new creation, how grandly men themselves are growing; how considerate and brotherly, how pure in word and deed! The world has not yet known half the amplitude of character and life to which men will attain when they and women live in the same world. (Willard, 1905, p. 64)

Willard wanted to reduce the distance between the male and female worlds, and she understood that the egalitarianism she sought was at odds with rigid sex roles. She even suggested that men become involved in the home and in child care, a very unusual suggestion even for radical feminists (see DuBois, 1975).

> Man in the home will have a larger place in the proportion that woman, in the constantly more homelike world, gains larger standing room. Motherhood will not be less, but fatherhood a hundredfold more magnified. To say this is to declare the approaching beatitude of men. For when to the splendor of their intellectual powers and the magnificence of their courage shall be added the unselfish devotion that comes of "child-ward care," we shall see characters more Christ-like than the world has ever known save in its calendar of saints. (Willard, 1905, p. 72)

The program of family reform was so important to Willard that it had to be safeguarded by even more than prohibition and women's suffrage. Unlike Elizabeth Stanton, who regarded the problems of the drunkard's wife as one good reason for liberalizing divorce, Willard saw the drunken husband as the *only* reason for divorce: "I believe in uniform national marriage laws, in divorce for one cause only, in legal separation on account of drunkenness" (1905, p. 95). In certain ways, then, Willard never abandoned some of the fundamental ideas of women's roles as articulated in the earliest days of the temperance crusade: except for drunkards, women were still to make reform by reforming their men.

> The advancement, improvement and the safety of the nation depend upon the perfect home, and earth's noblest thing is the woman perfected in the wife, the mother who rules that home. The husband's character and work, the child's love and life, are dependent upon her; what she is they will be. The history of the home life of our famous men demonstrates that it was a woman's love, encouragement and help that inspired them to the noblest purposes, and through her influence they became a power for good. A man may build a palace, but he can never make of it a home. The spirituality and love of a woman alone can accomplish this. By right divine these are a woman's special and unrivaled privileges. (1897, p. 240)

Frances Willard represented one form of the classic 19th-century American reformer: concerned with society as a whole, working in many fields, intensely moral and motivated by a vision of the good society. Within the temperance movement, the strongest alliance Willard and the WCTU made was with the Prohibition Party. Founded a few years before the WCTU, the Prohibition Party was organized around the same middle-class moral vision that had been at the heart of the pre-Civil War Republican Party (Colvin, 1926; Foner, 1970). Most temperance supporters were Republicans and unwilling to join the new party. Willard herself broke a deep emotional tie with the Republicans only in 1884, when the platform committee refused to consider Prohibition seriously. Like others committed to the Prohibition Party, she saw it as a political vehicle for organizing a new American constituency committed to a broad moral and political program (Willard, 1889, pp. 382–409; Colvin, 1926, pp. 276–292). Willard's vision continued to grow, and, by the early 1890s, she was publicly calling herself a socialist. Much to the chagrin of some WCTU members, she was willing to grant that sometimes poverty caused drunkenness as well as the reverse. While her socialism was not very well thought out, it did include considerable compassion for the plight of poor and working-class people and support for their struggles. On these political points at least, Willard was more liberal or radical than many, perhaps most, of the WCTU women.

During the period of Willard's presidency (1879–1898) the WCTU had a position and power in the temperance movement, and in American society, that it would never have again. The temperance campaign turned in the 20th century into the prohibition movement; under the direction of the Anti-Saloon League, everything became secondary to the pursuit of legal restriction. The do-everything era of Willard yielded to the single-minded drive for prohibition. The WCTU remained important but secondary to the league; it helped the league and worked with it. After Willard, the WCTU in most respects abandoned its position of leadership within women's politics and within temperance reform (Gusfield, 1954, 1963; Mezvinsky, 1959; Unger, 1933).

5. CONCLUSION

It is important to keep in mind the difference between the 17th and 18th centuries and the 19th century in respect to most of the issues discussed here. During the colonial period, women were not viewed as victims of the liquor business nor as moral superiors whose natural sphere was the home and whose mission was to reform their men. While women probably drank less than men, they drank regularly without shame or guilt. Indeed, women ran taverns—a quite respectable way to earn a living (Dexter, 1924; Earle, 1895; Spruill, 1938). Except for what Krout (1925) has called "voices in the wilderness," there was not much antidrunkenness sentiment in the 17th and 18th centuries; and there was no antialcohol reform despite the fact that consumption was higher than for most of the 19th century. There was an earthy and Elizabethan-like spirit to much of colonial society. Similarly, in colonial cities, there was only a small mercantile middle class with a modern family arrangement. It was in the early years of the 19th century that the market-oriented family became more common and invested with a moral weight that it did not have in the 18th century. Thus, while temperance ideas and what I have called the middle-class family pattern had roots in the 17th and 18th centuries, both emerged together historically, and, by about the mid-1830s, both had become dramatic new social facts.

Temperance Movement
Woman as Moral agent
Guardian of virtue
" " Middle class
famil[y]

Harry Gene Levine

From its takeoff as a mass movement in the late 1820s, the temperance movement was concerned with defending the middle-class family. For example, temperance literature did not usually deal with family farms where six or seven or more children worked with and under their mother and father or where other relatives cooperated in productive enterprises. The family as described in temperance speeches, pamphlets, stories, and novels was urban, set in a town, village, or small city. The family was small and nucleated: one, two, or at most a few children. The husband earned a living as a clerk, a mechanic, or a businessman of some sort; whatever his class background, he was a "self-made man" who supported his family by hard work. The wife was economically dependent on the husband; usually there was no other family to draw on, no network of kin who could be used for support and help. Husband, wife, and offspring were alone in society. Should the husband slip, all went down.

Part of the reason that temperance worked as popular ideology and endured as a mass movement was that it spoke to real concerns. Women were indeed dependent on their husbands; the economic opportunities for women were extremely limited. If family networks were not as weak or nonexistent as temperance writers suggested, the feelings of aloneness were certainly strong and real. And while this family pattern was presented in terms of the values and lifestyle of the middle class, the working class too was increasingly faced with much the same situation: nucleation, isolation, and economic dependency of women on men.

The world of 19th-century temperance is a familiar one to us today, despite the obvious and important differences. The ideas and social arrangements that first appeared as major social forms around 1830 are still part of our social landscape. We still live within a cultural milieu that includes two gestalts of the relationship of alcohol to social life. We recognize both the Good Creature of God and the Demon Rum; alcohol is for people today both merrymaker and destroyer. The popular image of alcohol as demon and destroyer was the unique and extraordinary contribution of the 19th century; and it is a view of alcohol as evil within a quite particular set of ideals and social arrangements. I have called that configuration middle-class culture and ideology and have tried to show, by letting the participants speak, some of the contours of that world.

Part of the difficulty in examining the ideas of the temperance movement is not that they are so far away and so different, but that they are so close. From the early 19th century up to the present time, the standard argument with the temperance line has been that although basically temperance people are right in asserting that alcohol causes many problems, their position exaggerates the extent of the problem. However, the reasons for the exaggerations are rarely seriously explored. Irrationality, which is a description, is used as a catch-all explanation:

temperance reformers thought all those crazy things because they were crazy. This sort of explanation is especially prevalent with regard to women (e.g., Sinclair, 1964).

It is important to recognize that, in a number of ways, women had good reason to regard alcohol as an enormous evil. In 19th-century American society, the place of liquor in the structure and organization of social life was such that it appeared as part of a number of troubling situations. In many towns and cities, the saloon *was* the antithesis of the home. It was a male institution, and it was not simply a place where men went but a part of the system of privileges and freedoms that men enjoyed and that women did not. To attack the saloon was to attack both a symbol of male power and privilege and also an institution that contributed to the system: a meeting and socializing place. Further, the ingestion of alcohol was often part of a kind of "time out" (MacAndrew and Edgerton, 1969) in which drinkers felt freed from some normal restraints. Drinking and drunken men did gamble away their money and visit prostitutes, and they did come home and assault their wives and children, as Samuel Chipman and Mother Stewart documented. Men did become drunkards, spend their money on drink, work much less or stop altogether, and abandon their wives and families.

Further, there is no doubt that for many men and women during the 19th century the program of total abstinence offered by the temperance movement as a path to a successful middle-class life did work. When one "bought into" the temperance line, one also bought a commitment to a set of rules, values and ideals, especially regarding work, family life, and personal habits. Largely because of the class and constituency most attracted to temperance groups, temperance men were more likely to be church-going, middle-class, steady, family men. But like Alcoholics Anonymous today, in the 19th century the temperance movement pro-vided a supportive environment for men to give up drinking and recommit themselves to a sober, industrious, and self-controlled lifestyle (Levine, 1978).

Finally, toward the end of the century, and during the first two decades of the 20th century, the liquor industry supported and helped finance the fight against women's suffrage. The liquor industry quite rightly viewed women's suffrage as a powerful threat and fought it every way they could (Catt and Schuler, 1970; U.S. Senate Committee on the Judiciary, 1919; Flexner, 1975; Kraditor, 1971).

For all these reasons—because of the saloon, because of the way men behaved when drinking and drunk, and because of the positions taken by the industry—women's participation in temperance and support for the antialcohol crusade was rational and appropriate, and in some ways extremely shrewd. Frances Willard's strategy was to advance the cause of women by using the liquor issue as a politically effective way to get past various prejudices and culturally legitimated justifications for women's traditional role. Within the structure of 19th-century Victorian society, "do everything" as a slogan for women was quite radical. By focusing on the problems for women presented by liquor and the saloon, temperance women were able to raise and confront issues relating to the economic and political aspects of women's oppression.

On the other hand, there was something fundamentally bizarre and wrong-headed about the temperance crusade. Alcohol is not an extraordinary evil; for most people for most of civilization, it has been a small blessing—part of the holy portion of life. Nineteenth-century middle-class Americans, and especially temperance people, continued to view alcohol as sacred, but they included it in the darker realms. Frances Willard personified alcohol in one of her earlier speeches:

> Permit me now to introduce a different character, who comes to the court of King Majority as chief ambassador from the empire of his Satanic Majesty. Behold! I show you the skeleton at our patriotic banquet. It has a skull with straightened forehead and sickening smile; but bedecked with wreaths of vine, clusters of grape, and heads of golden grain—King Alcohol, present at court in radiant disguise. With foaming beer-mug at his lips, he drinks the health of King Majority. (Willard, 1879, p. 6)

This representation was done with intentional flair—Willard was playing with images, but her point was serious: alcohol is of the devil. She quoted at length from a minister whose pamphlet she urged "be ordered in large quantities." His argument, a standard temperance one, was that enormous evil resulted from liquor consumption. As in most temperance writings and speeches, alcohol was used as a scapegoat explanation, that is, a manufactured object was assigned responsibility for problems that had their causes elsewhere:

> . . . that it is the chief source of the crime, pauperism and destruction by riot which burden society with oppressive taxes; that it wages constant war upon the purity and peace of the home, corrupting the sexes in their relation to each other, trampling upon the rights of women and children; defiling and sundering the most sacred relations of life; that it is the greatest cause of personal sorrow, domestic unhappiness, public vice, and waste of life and substance. (quoted by Willard, 1879, p. 24)

Alcohol was not "the greatest cause" or "chief source" of poverty, crime, or broken families. The structure of political and economic life — for example, the operations of the economy and the labor market—were the key elements. The temperance movement demonized alcohol; they invested it with magical destructive powers; they made it a scapegoat. While it is impossible to go into the issue here, one of the major reasons for the widespread acceptance of antiliquor sentiment among middle-class men and women was the utility and credibility of alcohol consumption as an explanation for a wide range of social problems, especially poverty, crime, violence, and broken homes. Alcohol use as an explanation of social problems challenged little that was important to the middle class; the temperance analysis involved no fundamental changes in the organization of social, political, and economic life.

There were, in the 19th century, two distinct ways in which, for example, the case of the drunkard's wife could be construed—located in an idea system of problem identification and explanation. The first, which was part of temperance ideology from its beginnings, was to use the plight of the drunkard's wife and her children—beaten, poverty-stricken, suffering terrible shame—to show the evils of alcohol and the necessity of total abstinence and prohibition. This was the main temperance line throughout the 19th century: it recognized women's plight and explained it by attributing it to liquor.

The second way of regarding the drunkard's wife was as an extreme case illustrative of the problems of women. Women whose husbands were not drunkards often encountered the same problems of being ill-treated and abandoned. Elizabeth Stanton objected to the mention of "drunkards' wives and children and of widows' groans and orphans' tears" when "introduced but as themes for rhetorical eloquence." For Stanton there was an inactiveness in the sentimentalization of woman as victim—it did not take women's problems seriously: "shall we passively shed tears over their condition, or by giving them their rights bravely open to them the doors of escape from a wretched and degraded life?" (quoted in Stanton et al., 1881, p. 426).

The first way, the identification of alcohol as the chief issue in the case of the wife of the drunkard, was a basic temperance point. One unique contribution of women to the temperance reform—possibly the most important theoretical one—was identifying the problems of the drunkard's wife as part of the condition of women in the family and society. Many temperance men presented the first position. Perhaps only Elizabeth Stanton and a handful of others clearly held up the second as an alternative. Frances Willard and the WCTU employed both modes of analysis and explanation and attempted to forge a synthesis.

The WCTU program was a contradictory combination of Victorian middle-class moral vision, on one hand, and feminist goals and analysis, on the other. At its best it drew on the liberationist tradition in middle-class ideology and combined feminism with other social issues in a critique of oppression and domination. "There are three sets of slaves that we women are working to emancipate," Willard explained. "They are white slaves, that is degraded women; wage slaves, that is the working classes; and whiskey slaves, that is the product furnished by brewers and distillers'' (1892, p. 37). At its worst, it put forward scapegoat explanations and sentimental solutions for social problems. "Were I asked to define in a sentence the thought and purpose of the Woman's Christian Temperance Union," said Willard, "I would reply: 'It is to make the whole world homelike' '' (1905, p. 78). The issue of domestication and liberation formed the two poles in the debate among women in 19th-century America. In the WCTU under Willard, they were both represented for a while—which was the main reason that the WCTU was the largest and most important women's organization in 19th-century America, and one reason that it was able to spread its example to a number of other nations.

REFERENCES

Ade, G., 1931, *The Old-Time Saloon: Not Wet—Not Dry, Just History,* Ray Long and Richard R. Smith, New York.

American Quarterly Temperance Magazine No. II, 1833, Review of Dr. Scott's address. Published by the Executive Committee of the New York State Temperance Society, Albany.

Arthur, T. S., 1966, *Ten Nights in a Bar-Room,* Odyssey, New York. (First published in 1854.)

Asbury, H., 1929, *Carrie Nation,* Knopf, New York.

Beecher, C., 1972, An address to the Christian women of America, in: *The Oven Birds: American Women on Womanhood* (G. Parker, ed.), pp. 147–163, Doubleday, New York.

Benson, M. S., 1935, *Women in Eighteenth-Century America: A Study of Opinion and Social Usage,* Columbia University Press, New York.

Blair, H. W., 1888, *The Temperance Movement: or, The Conflict between Man and Alcohol,* William E. Smythe, Boston.

Blocker, J. S., Jr., 1976, *Retreat from Reform: The Prohibition Movement in the United States, 1890–1913,* Greenwood, Westport, Conn.

Bloomer, D. C., 1975, *Life and Writings of Amelia Bloomer* (1895), Schocken, New York.

Brown, H. R., 1959, *The Sentimental Novel in America, 1789–1860,* Pageant, New York.

Calhoun, A. W., 1960, *A Social History of the American Family,* 3 vols. (1917), Barnes & Noble, New York.

Catt, C. C., and Shuler, N. R., 1970, *Woman Suffrage and Politics: The Inner Story of the Suffrage Movement,* University of Washington Press, Seattle.

Cherrington, E. H., 1920, *The Evolution of Prohibition in the U.S.A.,* American Issue Press, Westerville, Ohio.

Cherrington, E. H., Johnson, W. E., and Stoddard, C. F., 1925–1930, *Standard Encyclopedia of the Alcohol Problem,* 6 vols., American Issue Press, Westerville, Ohio.

Chipman, S., 1845, *The Temperance Lecturer: Being Facts Gathered from a Personal Examination of All the Jails and Poor-Houses of the State of New York,* Albany, N.Y.

Clark, N. H., 1976, *Deliver Us from Evil: An Interpretation of American Prohibition,* Norton, New York.

Coleman, E. G., 1971, *The Temperance Songbook,* American Heritage Press, New York.

Colvin, D. L., 1926, *Prohibition in the United States,* George H. Doran, New York.

Cott, N. F., 1977, *The Bonds of Womanhood: "Woman's Sphere" in New England, 1780-1835,* Yale University Press, New Haven, Conn.

Dexter, E. A., 1924, *Colonial Women of Affairs: Women in Business and the Professions in America Before 1776,* Houghton Mifflin, Boston.

Doner, T., 1877, *Eleven Years a Drunkard,* Ill.

Dorchester, D., D.D., 1888, *The Liquor Problem in All Ages,* Phillips & Hunt, New York.

DuBois, E., 1975, The radicalism of the woman suffrage movement: Notes toward the reconstruction of nineteenth-century feminism, *Feminist Studies* 3(1):63–71.

Dulles, F. R., 1940, *America Learns to Play: A History of Popular Recreation, 1607–1940,* Appleton, New York.

Earhart, M., 1944, *Frances Willard: From Prayers to Politics,* University of Chicago Press, Chicago.

Earle, A. M., 1895, *Colonial Dames and Good Wives,* Macmillan, New York.

Easton, B., April 1976, Industrialization and femininity: A case study of nineteenth century New England, *Soc. Prob.* 23:389–401.

Fiedler, L., 1969, *Love and Death in the American Novel,* Dell, New York.

Field, E., 1897, *The Colonial Tavern,* Preston & Rounds, Providence, R.I.

Flandrau, T. H., 1842, *Address Delivered at a Meeting of the Female Washingtonian and Other Temperance Societies of the City of Utica, May 9, 1842,* Woodland & Donaldson, Utica, N.Y.

Flexner, E., 1975, *Century of Struggle: The Woman's Rights Movement in the United States,* Harvard University Press, Cambridge, Mass.

Foner, E., 1970, *Free Soil, Free Labor, Free Men: The Ideology of the Republican Party Before the Civil War,* Oxford University Press, New York.

Gomberg, E. S., 1976, Alcoholism in women, in: *Social Aspects of Alcoholism* (B. Kissin and H. Begleiter, eds.), pp. 117–166, Plenum, New York.

Gordon, E. P., 1924, *Women Torch-Bearers: The Story of the Woman's Christian Temperance Union,* National Woman's Christian Temperance Union Publishing House, Evanston, Ill.

Gough, J. B., 1870, *Autobiography and Personal Recollections,* Francis Dewing, San Francisco.

Gough, J. B., 1887, *Platform Echoes,* A. D. Worthington, Hartford, Conn.

Grosvenor, G. J., 1842, *An Address on the Importance of Female Influence to the Temperance Reformation,* Ira Merrell, Geneva, N.Y.

Gurko, M., 1976, *The Ladies of Seneca Falls: The Birth of the Woman's Rights Movement,* Schocken, New York.

Gusfield, J. R., 1954, *Organizational Change: A Study of the Woman's Christian Temperance Union,* Ph.D. dissertation, University of Chicago.

Gusfield, J. R., 1963, *Symbolic Crusade: Status Politics and the American Temperance Movement,* University of Illinois Press, Urbana.

Hartman, M. S. and Banner, L. W. (eds.), 1974, *Clio's Consciousness Raised: New Perspectives on the History of Women,* Harper & Row, New York.

Hartz, L., 1955, *The Liberal Tradition in America,* Harcourt, Brace & World, New York.

Hofstadter, R., 1955, *The Age of Reform: From Bryan to F.D.R.,* Vintage, New York.

Jensen, R., 1973, Family, career, and reform: Women leaders of the progressive era, in: *The American Family in Social–Historical Perspective* (M. Gordon, ed.), pp. 267–280, St. Martin's Press, New York.

Keller, C. R., 1942, *The Second Great Awakening in Connecticut,* Yale University Press, New Haven, Conn.

Kobler, J., 1973, *Ardent Spirits: The Rise and Fall of Prohibition,* Putnam, New York.

Kraditor, A. S., 1965, *The Ideas of the Woman Suffrage Movement, 1890–1920,* Columbia University Press, New York.

Krout, J. A., 1925, *The Origins of Prohibition,* Knopf, New York.

Lender, M., 1973, Drunkenness as an offense in early New England: A study of "Puritan" attitudes, *Q. J. Stud. Alcohol* **34**:353–366.

Lerner, G., 1969, The lady and the mill girl: Changes in the status of women in the age of Jackson, *Midcont. Am. Stud. J.* **10**:5–15.

Levine, H. G., 1978, The discovery of addiction: Changing conceptions of habitual drunkenness in America, *J. Stud. Alcohol* **39**:143–174.

MacAndrew, C., and Edgerton, R. B., 1969, *Drunken Comportment: A Social Explanation,* Aldine, Chicago.

Mather, I., 1673, *Wo to Drunkards,* Cambridge, Mass. (2d ed., 1712).

Melville, H., 1956, *Moby Dick,* Houghton Mifflin, Boston. (First published in 1851.)

Mezvinsky, N., 1959, *The White-Ribbon Reform 1874–1920,* Ph.D. dissertation, University of Wisconsin.

Mills, C. W., 1951, *White Collar: The American Middle Classes,* Oxford University Press, New York.

National Temperance Society, 1886, *One Hundred Years of Temperance: A Memorial Volume of the Centennial Temperance Conference Held in Philadelphia, Pennsylvania, September, 1885,* New York.

New York State Society for the Promotion of Temperance, 1832, *Annual Report,* Albany, N.Y.

O'Neill, W. L., 1969a, *Everyone Was Brave: The Rise and Fall of Feminism in America,* Quadrangle Books, Chicago.

O'Neill, W. L., 1969b, *The Woman Movement: Feminism in the United States and England,* Quadrangle Books, Chicago.

Parker, G. (ed.), 1972, *The Oven Birds: American Women on Womanhood, 1820–1920,* Doubleday & Co., Garden City, N.Y.

Paulson, R. E., 1973, *Women's Suffrage and Prohibition: A Comparative Study of Equality and Social Control,* Scott, Foresman, Glenview, Ill.

Riegel, R. E., 1963, *American Feminists,* University of Kansas Press, Lawrence.

Room, R., 1976, Ambivalence as a sociological explanation: The case of the cultural explanations of alcohol problems, *Am. Sociol. Rev.* **41**(December):1047–1065.

Rorabaugh, W. J., 1976a, *The Alcoholic Republic; America, 1790–1840,* Ph.D. dissertation, University of California, Berkeley. (Published by Oxford University Press, 1979.)

Rorabaugh, W. J., 1976b, Estimated U.S. Alcoholic Beverage Consumption, 1790–1860, *J. Stud. Alcohol* **37**:357–364.

Rose, Mrs. H., 1858, *Nora Wilmot: A Tale of Temperance and Woman's Rights,* Osgood & Pearce, Columbus, Ind.

Rush, B., 1934, An inquiry into the effects of ardent spirits . . . (8th ed., 1814), in: *A New Deal in Liquor: A Plea for Dilution* (Y. A. Henderson, ed.), Doubleday, New York.

Scott, Dr. W. K., 1832, *An Address Delivered before the Ladies' Temperance Society of Sandy-Hil on Saturday Evening, April 21, 1832,* Sandy-Hill, N.Y.

Sibley, F., 1888, *Templar at Work: What Good Templary Is, What It Does, and How to Do It* (2nd ed.), Right Worthy Grand Lodge, Independent Order of Good Templars, Mauston, Wisconsin.

Sinclair, A., 1964, *Era of Excess: A Social History of the Prohibition Movement,* Harper & Row, New York.

Sinclair, A., 1965, *The Emancipation of the American Woman,* Harper & Row, New York.

Smith, P., 1970, *Daughters of the Promised Land: Women in American History,* Little, Brown, Boston.

Smith-Rosenberg, C., 1975, The female world of love and ritual: Relations between women in nineteenth-century America, *Signs: J. Women in Culture and Society* 1:1.

Spruill, J. C., 1938, *Women's Life & Work in the Southern Colonies,* University of North Carolina Press, Chapel Hill.

Stanton, E. C., 1898, *Eighty Years & More: Reminiscences 1815–1897,* (republished by Schocken, New York, 1971).

Stanton, E. C., Anthony, S. B., and Gage, M. H. (eds.), 1881, *History of Woman Suffrage, Vol. 1, 1848–1861,* Fowler & Wells, New York.

Stebbins, J. E., and Brown, T. A. H., 1876, *Fifty Years History of the Temperance Cause,* J. P. Fitch, Hartford, Conn.

Stewart, Mother, 1890, *Memories of the Crusade: A Thrilling Account of the Great Uprising of the Women of Ohio in 1873 against the Liquor Crime,* H. J. Smith, Chicago.

Sunley, R., 1961, Early nineteenth century American literature on childrearing in: *Childhood in Contemporary Cultures* (M. Mead and M. Wolfstein, eds.), University of Chicago Press, Chicago.

Thompson, E. J. T., 1906, *Hillsboro Crusade Sketches and Family Records,* Jennings and Graham, Cincinnati.

Timberlake, J. H., 1963, *Prohibition and the Progressive Movement 1900–1920,* Harvard University Press, Cambridge, Mass.

Tocqueville, A. de, 1961, *Democracy in America,* Vol. 2, Schocken, New York.

Unger, S., 1933, *A History of the Woman's Christian Temperance Union,* Ph.D. dissertation, Ohio State University.

U.S.Senate Committee on the Judiciary, Senator Overman, Chairman, 65th Congress, 1919, *Brewing and Liquor Interests and German Propaganda,* Government Printing Office, Washington, D.C.

Victor, Mrs. F. F., 1874, *The Women's War with Whisky, or Crusading in Portland,* Portland, Ore.

Welter, B., 1973, The cult of true womanhood: 1820–1960, in: *The American Family in Social–Historical Perspective* (M. Gordon, ed.) pp. 224–250, St. Martin's, New York.

Whitaker, F. M., 1971, *A History of the Ohio Woman's Christian Temperance Union, 1874–1920,* Ph.D. dissertation, Ohio State University.

Wilkerson, A. E., 1966, *A History of the Concept of Alcoholism as a Disease,* D.S.W. dissertation, University of Pennsylvania.

Willard, F. E., 1879, *Home Protection Manual,* The Independent, New York.

Willard, F. E., 1883, *Woman and Temperance: Or, The Work and Workers of the Woman's Christian Temperance Union* (republished by Arno Press, New York, 1972).

Willard, F. E., 1889, *Glimpses of Fifty Years: The Autobiography of an American Woman,* Woman's Temperance Publication Association, Chicago.

Willard, F., 1892, *Annual Address before the Nineteenth National W.C.T.U. Convention,* Chicago.

Willard, F. E., 1893, *Address before the Second Biennial Convention of the World's Woman's Christian Temperance Union,* Woman's Temperance Publishing Association, Chicago.

Willard, F. E., 1897, *Occupations for Women,* The Success Company, Cooper Union, New York.

Willard, F. E., 1905, *What Frances E. Willard Said* (Anna A. Gordon, ed.), Fleming H. Revell, New York.

Wishy, B., 1968, *The Child and the Republic: The Dawn of Modern American Child Nurture,* University of Pennsylvania Press, Philadelphia.

Wittenmeyer, A., 1878, *History of the Woman's Temperance Crusade,* Office of the Christian Woman, Philadelphia.

Woman's Christian Temperance Union, 1882, *Minutes of the National Woman's Christian Temperance Union at the Ninth Annual Meeting,* Chicago, Ill.

Woman's Christian Temperance Union, 1884, *Minutes of the National Woman's Christian Temperance Union at the Eleventh Annual Meeting,* Chicago, Ill.

Wylie, I. G., 1966, *The Self-Made Man in America: The Myth of Rags to Riches,* Free Press, New York.

3

Sex Differences in the Prevalence of Problem Drinking

ROBERTA G. FERRENCE

1. INTRODUCTION

"If the many hidden alcoholics among women came out into the open and sought treatment, there would be a one to one ratio with male alcoholics . . . public education is needed to enable women to escape from the double stigma of being both alcoholic and morally degenerate and to seek help with a clear conscience" (*The Journal,* Jan. 1, 1979).

These comments are typical of many current reports about the prevalence of alcoholism among women. It is said that there have been great and disproportionate increases in drinking and heavy drinking among women (e.g., Fraser, 1973; Gunther, 1975; Korcok, 1978; Naegele, 1979) and that large numbers of middle-aged women in suburbia spend their days imbibing secretly: the so-called "closet drinkers" suffering from the "empty-nest syndrome" (e.g., Curlee, 1969; Wanberg and Knapp, 1970).

Two main themes can be identified in these reports. The first is convergence, that is, that rates of drinking and alcoholism are increasing faster among women than among men, so that drinking patterns of men and women are becoming alike. The second is the stereotype of the female alcoholic as a middle-aged suburban housewife who keeps her bottle hidden in a cookie jar. Unfortunately, these perceptions of female drinking patterns are rarely documented. Much of the supporting evidence is anecdotal and often issues from those involved in the treatment of alcoholics. Since these perceptions have major implications for the identification and treatment of women who are problem drinkers, as well

---

ROBERTA G. FERRENCE • Addiction Research Foundation, Toronto, Ontario.

as for more general preventive measures, it is important to determine their validity.

This chapter deals with a review of various types of data that relate to the perceptions of women drinkers that have been described, and with the examination of the relationship between social changes and current trends in drinking behavior. A brief outline of appropriate recommendations for developing public policy, programs, and future research is also included.

This examination of existing data cannot provide definitive conclusions about sex differences in problem drinking. The lack of certain types of longitudinal and repeated cross-sectional data for substantial periods, as well as the inadequacy of information regarding possible sex differences in self-reports of consumption and in the diagnosis of problem drinking and related health and social problems, clearly makes it unwise to attempt this. However, there are certain steps that can be taken. The first is to look at the kinds of evidence that might tell us something about differential reporting for women and men. The second is to examine critically the best data that are currently available. The third is to engage in some informed speculation on the basis of relevant theory. One of the pitfalls of a purely empirical approach is that the most plausible and perhaps correct hypothesis may be rejected because the data are somewhat inadequate.

2. THE EPIDEMIOLOGICAL PERSPECTIVE

Sources of Information

Throughout this review, there will be heavy reliance on data that describe the general population rather than particular segments of it. Even when nonrepresentative groups are used, they are mainly from those studies that report cases for a large geographical area. This approach is epidemiological in the sense that epidemiology seeks to determine the distribution and causes of diseases or health-related behaviors in populations (MacMahon and Pugh, 1970). The use of such an approach is advantageous because it attempts to overcome the biases due to selective factors associated with the study of clinical populations. Its use is even more critical when one is dealing with sex differences, because men and women have different patterns of help-seeking, they use facilities in different proportions, and those who seek help probably represent different subgroups of the larger population of problem drinkers (Mechanic, 1978).

The epidemiological approach is most useful when the same populations of users and heavy users are examined at regular intervals over long periods of time. Unfortunately, there is a scarcity of data of this kind, particularly for heavy users. Large longitudinal or repeated cross-sectional surveys are very costly, particularly if detailed data on drinking patterns are sought. Retrospective studies, which ideally compare drinking histories of alcoholics with those of nonalcoholic controls, are less costly but are subject to the major methodological problems that are associated with retrospective reporting of drinking behavior (de Lint and Schmidt, 1976). Because few surveys provide usable data on sex differences, it is necessary to supplement them with population estimates based on death rates for liver cirrhosis to measure long-term trends. Possible types of error in death rate data are discussed later in this paper.

Throughout this analysis, we have had to rely on rates of prevalence of various measures of problem drinking. Prevalence data are particularly useful for determining the size of the population that might require services, but they are less sensitive than incidence data to changes that occur over time. Future longitudinal research on drinking patterns should attempt to measure the rate at which new drinkers and new heavy drinkers occur in the general population (cf. Hunt, 1977).

Possible Sources of Sex Bias

Homiller (1978) has described a number of potential sources of sex bias in alcohol research. Those that relate to the issues raised in this paper involve the use of cirrhosis mortality data and the findings of surveys of alcohol consumption. Specifically, Homiller suggested the possibility that both types of data yield falsely low estimates of alcoholism in women, because of the apparently greater stigma attached to alcoholism in women and the failure of previous research to take account of differences between women and men with regard to autopsy rates, susceptibility to cirrhosis, body weight, and the social consequences of drinking.

A few studies have investigated the possibility of differential reporting among men and women. Cahalan and Treiman (1976) asked heavy drinkers how likely they were to conceal their drinking and found no differences between men and women. Garrett and Bahr (1974) compared self-rating with quantity–frequency measures of drinking status for several populations of drinkers and found that men consistently underrated their drinking, whereas women perceived their drinking accurately or were as likely to rate themselves more heavily as less heavily. There is other evidence that women do indeed have different norms for heavy drinking (Pool, 1978), and these correspond to society's expectations that women drink less than men. Wechsler et al. (1972) found a high correlation between blood alcohol levels and self-report data. This finding lends more credibility to the kind of data usually collected in surveys of use.

Barr et al. (1974, 1975, 1976, 1977) asked high school students to indicate the accuracy of their own responses to questions about their use of alcohol and other drugs. The scale ranged from "fairly accurate" to "should be disregarded." The answer "should be disregarded" was given nearly twice as frequently by males as by females in all grades surveyed. This sex difference in reported inaccuracy increased progressively beyond grade 8, mainly because of a greater reduction in inaccuracy among female students. For grade 12 students, reported unreliability was more than three times as common among males as among females. Since similar age trends occur for the consumption of alcohol and other drugs, we can speculate that both are the result of an increasing differentiation in behavior among males and females that occurs with maturity. If these results are valid and generalizable, adult women may be much less likely than males to underreport their consumption of alcohol and other drugs.

There is considerable evidence that household surveys underestimate total consumption by as much as 50% when compared to sales data (Pernanen, 1974; Johnson et al., 1977). However, the magnitude of underreporting by respondents may be much less than believed. Heavy consumers are less likely to be included in such surveys because they are more often institutionalized, incarcerated, or homeless. Also, they may be unable to be interviewed because they refuse, are not at home, or are intoxicated. Since women are more likely to live in a home, and to be at home, those who are heavy drinkers may be more likely to be included in such surveys than men who drink heavily.

Fitzgerald and Mulford (1978) compared sales records and survey data to examine the way in which underreporting by survey respondents varied by level of consumption. Although respondents understated their consumption quite substantially, they did so uniformly, thereby preserving the rank order of actual levels of consumption. Thus, what evidence there is, though it is by no means conclusive, suggests that women are more likely than men to be included in household surveys and are at least as likely as men to report their consumption accurately.

Most studies of consumption have failed to take into account sex differences in body weight and composition. On average, women weigh considerably less than men and have a higher proportion of body fat and a correspondingly lower proportion of body water. Since alcohol is distributed throughout the body water, the average woman has a significantly smaller volume of distribution for alcohol than the average man. Therefore, the same absolute amount of alcohol would produce a considerably higher concentration in the woman. Since intoxication and its various consequences depend on the concentration of alcohol attained in the blood and tissues, it has been argued that the definitions of hazardous intake and of alcoholism should be based on lower daily intakes for women than for men, in order to avoid underestimates among women. To what extent this factor should be used to weigh the sex-specific rates of consumption has not yet been established. We do not know, for example, whether or not the average sex difference in body weight for the general population applies to the population of heavy drinkers. Moreover, North American men have a higher average body weight than those in countries such as Italy, yet no one has suggested that Italian men become alcoholics faster or at lower levels of consumption than men in North America [Schmidt, personal communication (1979)]. There are differences in the rate of metabolism of alcohol between women and men (Jones and Jones, 1976), and these may conceivably affect the amount of damage that occurs. Finally, women may drink more slowly than men so that their blood alcohol levels may not rise as quickly or as far as those of men (Orford et al., 1974).

Studies of clinical populations of male and female alcoholics indicate that about 96% consume at levels above 15 cl of absolute alcohol per day (Popham and Schmidt, 1976). Moreover, the mean annual consumption by alcoholics appears to be about the same in widely different countries, despite differences in average body size. Since alcoholics show a substantial range of consumption, from 15 to 40 cl per day [Schmidt, personal communication (1979)], one would expect that individuals would be distributed within this range according to their body weights and that there would be a preponderance of women at the lower end of the range and of men at the upper end. If this assumption is correct, estimates of the proportion of alcoholics in a population that are based on those drinkers who consume at least 15 cl of absolute alcohol per day would not exclude a significant proportion of women who are clinically recognizable alcoholics. At present, there is no clear justification for correcting estimates of consumption and alcoholism on the basis of sex differences in average body weight and composition. Nevertheless, both corrected and uncorrected estimates are included in this chapter.

Another problem occurs with the scales used in indexes that measure alcohol-related problems. Many are geared toward the measurement of problems associated with activities that men are more likely to engage in than women, such as those pertaining to their jobs, driving, and drinking in public establishments. This difference does not affect consumption data but may account for the fact that in some studies, the excess of males over females is greater among "problem drinkers" than among "heavy drinkers" (Liban and Smart, 1980).

Most indexes include a number of problems that are not subject to sex bias. Symptoms of problem drinking such as blackouts or missing meals should occur equally among heavy drinkers of both sexes unless there are sex-linked physiological factors that affect them. In fact, there are a number of symptoms of problem drinking that occur with equal frequency among male and female heavy drinkers (Johnson et al., 1977). For consequences that one would expect to show sex differences, such as job-related problems, one can control for employment status. Johnson et al. (1977) did control in this way and found no difference in the percentage of employed male and female heavy drinkers who had been fired or threatened with dismissal. Thus, scales of problem drinking should really be viewed as measures of particular problems or sets of problems, rather than as comprehensive measures of alcoholism.

The preceding discussion raises a number of methodological issues regarding the measurement of sex differences in problem drinking. There are serious deficiencies in our knowledge of these issues, but to date, there is no compelling evidence to suggest a major underreporting of consumption and of problems among women.

3. THE CONVERGENCE HYPOTHESIS

What evidence is there to support the contention that there is convergence in drinking patterns and, in particular, that heavy drinking is increasing more rapidly among women than among men? The evidence may be examined in relation to such measures as general levels of alcohol use, levels of frequent or heavy use, health problems, and other alcohol-related problems.

With respect to these measures, there are two types of data: those derived from studies of the general population and those derived from clinical or other special populations. Ideally, the first type of study uses randomly selected samples that are representative of the general population under study, and some surveys have indeed used random samples. Others involving selected populations such as high school students probably have general validity because they are distinguished by criteria unrelated to the use of alcohol. For samples of the general population, we can examine rates and sex ratios of general use, frequent and heavy use, problem drinking, and alcohol-related mortality.

Studies of special populations involve persons with alcohol-related problems who are identified by medical, social, or criminal justice facilities. These are dealt with separately because they are likely to differ in many respects from natural populations of problem drinkers and because patterns of admission, referral, and apprehension are important factors in determining the proportions of women and men identified (Mechanic, 1978). Included here are studies of hospital patients, clients of alcohol treatment facilities, and persons identified by other medical and social service facilities. In addition, there are persons charged with alcohol-related offenses, such as public drunkenness and impaired driving.

Much of the analysis reported in this chapter is based on sex ratios of rates of use or problems. These ratios are calculated by dividing the rate for males by the rate for females and multiplying by 100. Although ratios are somewhat less stable than rates, they serve the purpose of standardizing different types of data so that comparisons can be made easily. The use of 100 rather than 1 as the standard ratio makes it easier to discern small changes in ratios over time. This format is commonly used for mortality data.

General Population Studies

Surveys of Alcohol Use. Studies of the use of alcohol in the general population have produced a range of data. The most common measure is "any use in the past year," but some studies have gathered more detailed information on quantity and frequency of use. In order to clarify trends in different levels of use, we will examine three general categories of use: period prevalence (usually any use in the past year), daily use, and "heavy" use, which refers to the highest levels of use measured by various indexes. The "heavy" use category includes those drinking at levels that are associated with physical damage and with significant levels of problems as measured by various scales. Surveys of high school students constitute the main source of data for young people; surveys of the general population provide data for adults, and some of these include young people. Annual prevalence rates of alcohol use range from about 50% to 90%, and sex ratios of these rates range from about 100 to 150. In general, rates of use are higher among young people than among adults, and sex ratios are about the same or somewhat lower.

Students and Young People. Blane and Hewitt (1977) described general trends in the prevalence of alcohol use among high school students. On the basis of their analysis of 65 surveys, they reported that the mean percentage difference in prevalence rates for males and females was 17.8 for the period prior to 1966 and 7.2 for the period 1966–1975. An examination of individual studies that were carried out at three or more points in time between 1968 and 1978 (Barr et al., 1974, 1975, 1976, 1977; Smart et al., 1974; Blackford, 1977; Johnston et al., 1977, 1979; Smart and Goodstadt, 1977a; Hollander and Macurdy, 1978) shows that there has been a slight decline in sex ratios during that period in some studies but not in others (Table 1). Most of the annual changes are not significant, but there appears to be a downward linear trend over time. Sex ratios were consistently less than 140 in the late 1960s and early 1970s, and many were under 110; current sex ratios range from 100 to 128. The mean percentage difference between male and female prevalence rates reported between 1976 and 1978 in one national study of high school seniors in the United States was 5.0 (Johnston et al., 1977, 1979), which is slightly lower than the difference of 7.2 reported by Blane and Hewitt (1977) for the period 1966–1975.

Sex ratios of use tend to be lower among students in the highest grades, and highest among those in grades 7 and 8 (Table 2). Trends for specific grades are less uniform but do reflect the overall pattern of convergence.

Some, but not all, surveys show a slight decline in sex ratios for monthly and weekly use of alcohol among high school students over the past 10 years; trends in daily use are unclear (Digital Resources Corporation, 1971; Hays, 1971, 1972, 1974; Barr et al., 1974, 1975, 1976, 1977; Smart et al., 1974; Rachal et al., 1975; Blackford, 1977; Johnston et al., 1977, 1979; Smart and Goodstadt 1977a; Hollander and Macurdy, 1978). Sex ratios of weekly and monthly use fall between 100 and 200, whereas those for daily drinking range from 200 to 300. In three specific studies of weekly prevalence, sex ratios decreased within the past decade from 181 to 116 (Blackford, 1977), 176 to 127 (Hays, 1971, 1972, 1974), and 130 to 106 (Hollander and Macurdy, 1978). For daily drinking, Johnston et al. (1977, 1979) reported a decrease that is not statistically significant from 287 in 1975 to 259 in 1978, and Barr et al. (1974, 1975, 1976, 1977) reported decreases for beer and wine (333 to 315 and 250 to 200, respectively) but an increase for spirits (240 to 340). Rachal et al. (1975) reported a sex ratio of 240 in 1974 for their category of heavy drinking, which refers to drinking at least weekly, typically in large amounts. This is the only national study that includes all grades. Smart and Goodstadt (1977a) reported a sex ratio of 200 among students who consumed six or more drinks per week in 1977 in the Province of Ontario, which represents about one-third of the Canadian population.

Levels of use that are likely to cause damage are rarely measured among populations of students. Johnston et al. (1977, 1979) reported longitudinal data for the number of times five or more drinks were consumed at a sitting during the previous two weeks by high school seniors. In each of the four years studied (1975–1978), about half of the males and more than one-quarter of the females had consumed this much at least once in the two weeks. Sex ratios increased from about 120 for "once" to more than 400 for "10 or more times." At the highest level, about 4% of males and 1% of females reported drinking five or more

Table 1. Annual Prevalence (%) and Sex Ratios[a] (M:F) of Alcohol Use over Time among Students and Youth in Canada and the United States between 1968 and 1978[b]

Year	Tor[c]			Van[d]			US(S)			Fla[e]			Cal			US(Y)[f]		
	M	F	SR	M	F	SR	M	F	SR	M	F	SR	M	F	SR	M	F	SR
1968	52	40	128										68	63	109			
1969													76	70	109			
1970	56	50	114	63	58	108							76	72	105			
1971													79	75	106			
1972	73	68	107										82	79	104	27	21	129
1973										54	39	138	85	84	102			
1974	75	71	105	73	68	107	77	69	111	57	42	138	87	86	101	39	29	134
1975										57	42	136	87	86	101			
1976										55	40	136	86	85	101	36	29	124
1977	79	74	107							55	43	128	88	88	101	37	25	148
1978				80	76	106												

[a] Sex ratios calculated before rates are rounded off.
[b] Tor (Toronto) Grades 7, 9, 11, 13: Smart et al. (1974); Smart and Goodstadt (1977a).
Van (Vancouver) Grades 8–12: Hollander and Macurdy (1978).
US(S) (United States) Grades 7–12: Rachal et al. (1975).
Fla (Florida) Grades 6–12: Barr et al. (1974, 1975, 1976, 1977).
Cal (San Mateo, Calif.) Grades 9–12: Blackford (1977).
US(Y) (United States) ages 12–17: Abelson et al. (1977).
[c] Past 6 months, 1968, 1970, 1972, 1974; past 12 months in Ontario, 1977.
[d] Past and present use.
[e] Beer only.
[f] 1972, past week; 1974, 1976, 1977, past month.

Table 2. Sex Ratios of the Annual Prevalence of Alcohol Use over Time among Students in Grades 7 and 12 in Selected Surveys between 1968 and 1978[a]

| | Grade 7 or 8 | | | | | Grade 12 | | | | | |
| | Fla[b] | | | | | Fla[b] | | | | | |
Year	B	W	L	Cal	Tex	B	W	L	Cal	Tex	US
1968									127		
1969				136					129		
1970				117					93		
1971				128	114				117	119	
1972				120					106		
1973	139	123	135	108	113	145	103	130	106	110	
1974	175	109	140	103		135	102	115	93		
1975	160	117	181	109		152	104	127	95		107
1976	110	105	130	112		124	95	121	99		106
1977	141	100	211	113		129	89	114	99		107
1978											105

[a] Fla (Florida): Barr et al. (1974, 1975, 1976, 1977).
Cal (San Mateo, Calif.): Blackford (1977).
Tex (Houston, Texas): Hays (1971, 1972, 1974).
US (United States): Johnston et al. (1977, 1979).
[b] B = beer; W = wine; L = liquor.

drinks daily for the previous two weeks (Table 3). These surveys are carried out in the spring of each year; since they coincide with examination time, reported rates of heavy use may be somewhat higher than during the rest of the year. However, changes in sex ratios over time are unlikely to be affected by the time of year, and there is no discernible trend over the four-year period. Abelson [personal communication (1979)] reported similar findings for youths aged 12–17 in the United States in 1977. The sex ratio for five or more drinks on an average day was 439.

Lee and Shimmel (1976) examined the drinking patterns of high school students in various areas of New York State in 1975. Sex ratios for "usually drink five or more" were 209 for beer, 156 for wine, and 179 for liquor. Sex ratios were similarly high for "drinking in school" (195) and "passed out during past year" (179) but were close to 100 for "drunk three or more times" (111) and "experienced blackouts" (93). Wechsler and McFadden (1976) and Hollander and Macurdy (1978) reported similarly low sex ratios for occasional intoxication. The low sex ratio for blackouts is not consistent with Lee and Shimmel's other findings and may be a result of differing perceptions of a blackout by males and females.

This review of high school surveys indicates that female students are almost as likely as male students to drink at least occasionally and to

Table 3. Prevalence and Sex Ratios of "Heavy" Use of Alcohol among Students and Youth in Selected Surveys

Year	Source	Area	Measure of use	% Male	% Female	Sex ratio[a] (M:F)
Single Surveys						
1974	Rachal et al. (1975)	United States (Gr. 7–12)	Moderate/heavy and heavy	31	18	140
				15	6	240
1975	Cahalan and Treiman (1976)	San Francisco (Ages 12–17)	Frequent drinker	2	1	200
1976	Hetherington et al. (1978)	Saskatchewan	Moderate/heavy and heavy	22	12	183
				1	<1	200
1977	Smart and Goodstadt (1977a)	Ontario (Gr. 7, 9, 11, 13)	6+ per week	1	<1	350
1977	Abelson (1979)	United States (Ages 12–17)	Daily in past month 5+ on average day	8	2	439
Repeated surveys						
1973	Barr et al. (1974)	Florida	Daily (beer)	4	1	333
1974	Barr et al. (1974)	Florida	Daily (beer)	4	1	364
1975	Barr et al. (1975)	Florida	Daily (beer)	4	1	433
1976	Barr et al. (1976)	Florida	Daily (beer)	3	1	350
1977	Barr et al. (1977)	Florida	Daily (beer)	4	1	315
1975	Johnston et al. (1977)	United States (Grade 12)	Daily/past month	9	3	287
1976	Johnston et al. (1977)	United States (Grade 12)	Daily/past month	8	3	300
1977	Johnston et al. (1977)	United States (Grade 12)	Daily/past month	9	4	239

[a] Sex ratios calculated before rates are rounded off.

(Continued)

Table 3. (Continued)

Year	Source	Area	Measure of use	% Male	% Female	Sex ratio[a] (M:F)
1978	Johnston et al. (1977, 1979)	United States (Grade 12)	Daily/past month	8	3	259
1975	Johnston et al. (1979)	United States (Grade 12)	5+ drinks, 10+ times in past two weeks	4	1	467
1976	Johnston et al. (1979)	United States (Grade 12)	5+ drinks, 10+ times in past two weeks	3	1	412
1977	Johnston et al. (1979)	United States (Grade 12)	5+ drinks, 10+ times in past two weeks	4	1	450
1978	Johnston et al. (1979)	United States (Grade 12)	5+ drinks, 10+ times in past two weeks	4	1	411

become intoxicated once in a while. Although there has been a slight decline in the sex ratio for all users over the years, the change is not dramatic since sex ratios for this group have been close to 100 for a long time (cf. Chappell and Goldberg, 1953).

As frequency of drinking increases, sex ratios increase sharply. Even for weekly drinking, rates are from 30% to more than 200% higher for males than for females. Daily drinking is two to three times higher for males, and frequent heavy drinking is more than four times as high. Since most categories of drinking are open-ended at the top, sex ratios for reported rates are lower than they would be if all possible intervals were included.

Although there appears to be some convergence in sex-specific rates of occasional and weekly drinking over the past 10 years, there is some evidence that this trend may not continue. The youngest cohorts in the San Mateo study (Blackford, 1977) were drinking less than previous cohorts did, and sex ratios had increased slightly. In 1974, rates of use reached their peak and sex ratios reached their lowest point for students in grades 7 and 8. In 1976 and 1977, rates of use decreased and sex ratios increased (Table 2). The data for daily and heavy drinking are not extensive enough to provide a basis for firm conclusions; nevertheless, there is no evidence of a trend between 1973 and 1978 (Table 3).

Adults. There are enough repeated cross-sectional surveys among adults to permit examination of trends in the prevalence of alcohol use (Table 4). National data for Canada and the United States are available for several years since the beginning of World War II, although most were collected during the past decade. Rates of annual prevalence of use are higher for both women and men in Canada than in the United States. However, sex ratios of use are fairly similar (about 120) for samples in surveys that are essentially the same, for example, the Canadian and American Gallup Polls.

There has been a gradual increase in the prevalence of use by both sexes over the past 30 years, but there is no clear trend toward convergence in use. Since most national surveys use samples of about 1000–1500, confidence intervals are sufficiently large that rates of use can vary by about 4%. For this reason, sex ratios could vary by as much as 20 points, solely as a result of random error. Variations in the time of year that a survey is conducted and in the population base used to calculate the rates could account for additional variability in sex ratios. Thus, with the exception of a somewhat higher sex ratio in 1939 in the United States (156), sex ratios for annual prevalence of use have not varied by more than 20 points within any series of surveys that have been carried out. Furthermore, similar sex ratios are found at widely

Table 4. Prevalence (%) and Sex Ratios (M:F) of Alcohol Use among Adults in Canada and the United States[a,b]

| | Surveys: U.S. | | | | | | | | | | | | Surveys: Canada | | | | | | | | |
| | U.S. Gallup (AIPO) | | | RAC[c] | | | NIAAA NIDA | | | ADP | | | Can. Gallup (CIPO) | | | H & W Canada | | | Ontario | | |
Year	M	F	SR	M	F	SR	M	F	SR	M	F	SR	M	F	SR	M	F	SR	M	F	SR
1939	70	45	156																		
1945	75	59	127																		
1958	67	45	149										70	60	117						
1960	69	54	128										76	62	123						
1962													76	62	123						
1964	70	56	125																		
1965										77	60	128									
1966	69	61	114																		
1967																					
1968	71	58	121																		
1969													74	61	121				86	75	115
1970																					
1971							70	58	121												

Year																				
1972	76	62	123	65	42	155	72	54	133												
1973							75	58	129												
1974				67	51	131	74	53	140				82	68	121						
1975							76	58	131	73	55	133									
1976				67	51	131				74	61	121				86	77	112			
1977	77	65	118	67	50	134				79	63	120				73	67	109			
1978													83	73	114	79	68	116	86	75	114
1979																76	67	114	87	77	114

[a] AIPO: American Institute of Public Opinion, Gallup, 1966; Gallup, January 1966, February 1968, May 1974, April 1977.
RAC: Response Analysis Corporation: Abelson et al. (1977).
NIAAA/NIDA: National Institute on Alcohol Abuse and Alcoholism; National Institute on Drug Abuse; Johnson et al. (1977); NORC General Social Survey (1977).
ADP: American Drinking Practices: Cahalan et al. (1969).
CIPO: Canadian Institute of Public Opinion, 1958, 1960, 1962, 1969, 1974, 1978.
H & W CANADA: Health and Welfare Canada, MacGregor (1978, 1979a,b).
ONTARIO: de Lint et al. (1970); Smart and Goodstadt (1976, 1977b).
With the exception of RAC data, measures of use are fairly comparable (e.g., Do you use? Do you ever drink? Drink at least once a year?). Population base may vary over time.
[b] Sex ratios are calculated before rates are rounded off.
[c] 1972: past week; 1974, 1976, 1977: past month.

spaced intervals, so that the possibility of there being a significant linear trend is greatly reduced.

The widely held belief that convergence is occurring seems to stem in part from the disproportionate increase in use among women that occurred between 1974 and 1978 in Canada and the United States as reported by the Gallup Poll in each country. The advantage of using a series of surveys (Table 4) is that changes of this type can be compared with changes that occurred in previous years. Comparable disproportionate increases in use among males occurred in the United States in the late 1960s and in Canada in the late 1950s, and the sex ratios before those changes were similar to those reported currently. If sex ratios continue to decline into the 1980s, a case could be made for convergence.

This analysis of prevalence data for adults does not support the convergence hypothesis for the postwar period in North America. Higher sex ratios may have characterized the use of alcohol prior to this period, and subsequent surveys will be needed to indicate whether or not the convergence in rates of use that appears to have occurred among young people will persist into adulthood.

A number of surveys report prevalence rates for the daily use of alcohol or an equivalent weekly volume (Table 5). In this category of use, rates are much lower than those for annual prevalence, and sex ratios are very much higher. Rates of daily use range from 10% to 17% for men and from 2% to 5% for women. Sex ratios range from about 250 to more than 400. Rates of use of six or more drinks per week (in other studies, eight or more) are somewhat higher, ranging from 17% to 34% for men to between 4% and 16% for women. The sex ratios are within the range of those for daily use. The use, in some cases, of drinkers rather than the entire population as the base for calculation produces higher rates of use and accounts for at least some of the variation. The variability of these data and the short time period surveyed make it impossible to assess trends over time. However, the very high sex ratios obtained suggest that daily drinking will continue to be clearly differentiated by sex for some time to come.

A recent national survey of adults in 32 large urban centers in Canada (Data Laboratories, 1977) provides information on frequency of use and changes in level of use, compared with five years earlier (i.e., 1972). Eighteen percent of males and eleven percent of females said that they drank "frequently" or "very frequently." Since women appear to have different norms than men for defining levels of use (Pool, 1978), it is likely that these figures are somewhat inflated for women. Slightly more women than men (23% versus 21%) stated that they drank less than they did five years earlier. More men than women reported that they drank more than they did five years before (22% versus 20%). These

Table 5. Prevalence and Sex Ratios of "Daily" Use of Alcoholic Beverages by Adults in Selected Surveys in Canada and the United States

Year	Source	Area	Measure of use		% Male	% Female	Sex ratio[a] (M:F)
1971	Warheit et al. (1976)	Florida (whites)		Daily	31	20	155
1975	Edwards et al. (1975)	Chicago		Daily	13	5	260
1976	MacGregor (1978)	Canada	8+	per week	29	11	273
	Smart and Goodstadt (1976)	Ontario	6+	per week	23	11	210
1977	Abelson (1979)	United States		Daily	10	4	253
	Smart and Goodstadt (1977b)	Ontario		Daily	17	4	400
1978	Gillies (1978)	Durham County, Ontario		Daily	10	2	429
1979	MacGregor (1979a)	Canada	6+	per week	34	11	315
	MacGregor (1979b)	Canada	6+	per week	40	16	247

[a] Sex ratios are calculated before rates are rounded off.

small changes, if statistically significant, could represent the effects of either maturation or widespread concurrent changes in the total population. In any case, these data do not support the convergence hypothesis.

For the purposes of this analysis, the best measure of heavy or hazardous use would be based on average consumption or blood alcohol concentration (cf. Johnson et al., 1977). These measures would give us a clearer picture of use likely to be hazardous to health, would control for sex differences in body weight and composition, and would make it easier to distinguish among different levels of heavy use. Unfortunately, such measures are rarely used, and the available data are based on two types of measures: either the average number of drinks consumed per day or over a particular period of time, or some type of quantity-frequency index (Cahalan et al., 1969).

Rates of heavy use among adults vary considerably depending on the particular measure employed but are similar to those for daily drinking (Table 6). Sex ratios are all in excess of 200 and several exceed 400. The highest sex ratios are for the most extreme categories of heavy drinking (e.g., high volume/high maximum; four or more drinks per day).

Two series of repeated cross-sectional data permit an examination of trends over time (Table 7). MacGregor (1978, 1979a,b) and Johnson et al. (1977) reported remarkably similar rates of "heavy" drinking (about 14 or more drinks per week) in Canada and the United States in the 1970s. Rates range from 15% to 22% for males and from 3% to 6% for females. Sex ratios range from 300 to 600 with a median of 444. In an earlier national study in the United States, Cahalan et al. (1969) reported similar rates and a similar sex ratio for 1965 (Table 6). For the period between 1971 and 1976, there is a statistically significant upward linear trend for males in the United States but not for females (Johnson et al., 1977). The Canadian data show no clear trend, but a longer time series would obviously be more informative.

A few studies include sex-specific data on average alcohol consumption in the general population. Such measures are particularly useful because they can be used to estimate the proportion of persons in the population who are drinking at levels likely to be hazardous to their health. To some extent, this approach circumvents the problem of underreporting by heavy drinkers. Empirical evidence indicates that the proportion of heavy drinkers in a population is roughly proportional to the square of the mean consumption for that population (Bruun et al., 1975). More precise estimates can be calculated by applying the Ledermann formula (cf. Hyland and Scott, 1969). This means that as average consumption increases, hazardous consumption increases at a much higher rate.

Johnson et al. (1977) used a blood alcohol concentration (BAC) index to facilitate comparisons between men and women. This measure gives

Table 6. Prevalence and Sex Ratios of "Heavy" Use of Alcohol among Adults in Selected Surveys in Canada and the United States

Year	Source	Area	Measure of use[a]	% Male[b]	% Female[b]	Sex ratio[c] (M:F)
1962	Knupfer (1967)	San Francisco	Heavy (QF)	29	13	223
			Very heavy (QF)	14	4	350
1965	Cahalan et al. (1969)	United States	Hi volume/hi maximum (VV)	19	3	633
1971	Cutler and Storm (1973)	British Columbia	Heavy (QFV)	40	18	225
			Hi volume/hi maximum (VV)	29	7	386
1973	Schaps and Rubin (1973)	Pennsylvania	4+ per day	13	3	457
1974	Chambers and Griffey (1975)	United States	Heavy	20	5	363
	Whitehead (1974)	Saskatchewan	Heavy	12	6	218
1975	Cahalan and Treiman (1976)	San Francisco	Frequent heavier (QF)	11[d]	4[d]	275
	Edwards et al. (1975)	Chicago	Get high 2+ per week	6	2	300
	Wechsler et al. (1978)	Boston	Heavy (QFV)	38	12	319
	Barnes and Russell (1978)	New York State	Heavy (QFV)	39	11	355
1976	MacGregor (1978)	Canada	4+ per day/past week	7	1	744
1977	Abelson (personal communication, 1979)	United States	5+ on average day	13	3	443
1978	Gillies (1978)	Durham County, Ontario	10 cl + per day/past week	10	3	357

[a] In most cases, *heavy use* means "drink almost daily with 5+ on occasion or drink weekly with 5+ usually." QF = quantity/frequency index; VV = volume/variability index; QFV = volume/variability index. (See Cahalan et al., 1969, for a description of these indexes.)
[b] Some rates are based on drinkers only; others on entire sample.
[c] Sex ratios are calculated before rates are rounded off.
[d] Age 18–59.

Table 7. Prevalence and Sex Ratios of "Heavy" Use of Alcohol among Adults in Repeated Cross-Sectional Surveys in Canada and the United States

Year	Source	Area	Measure of use	% Male	% Female	Sex ratio[a] (M:F)
1976	MacGregor (1978)	Canada	15 drinks+/past week	15	3	432
1978	MacGregor (1979a)	Canada	14 drinks+/past week	20	4	547
1979	MacGregor (1979b)	Canada	14 drinks+/past week	19	4	455
1965	Cahalan et al. (1969)	United States	Heavy (QFV)	21	5	420
1971	Johnson et al. (1977)	United States	Heavy (QF)[b]	15	5	300
1972	Johnson et al. (1977)	United States	Heavy (QF)[b]	15	4	375
1973	Johnson et al. (1977)	United States	Heavy (QF)[b]	22	6	367
1973	Johnson et al. (1977)	United States	Heavy (QF)[b]	19	4	475
1974	Johnson et al. (1977)	United States	Heavy (QF)[b]	18	5	360
1975	Johnson et al. (1977)	United States	Heavy (QF)[b]	20	4	500
1976	Johnson et al. (1977)	United States	Heavy (QF)[b]	18	3	600

[a] Sex ratios are calculated before rates are rounded off.
[b] Drink almost daily with 5+ on occasion or drink weekly with 5+ usually (14+ drinks per week on average).

the maximum BAC that people could have if they drank their average daily consumption in 1–2 hr. The mean BAC score for a national sample surveyed in the United States in 1975 was .023 per day for men and .012 for women. The sex ratio for these scores, based on drinkers and nondrinkers is 192. When the means are used to calculate approximate levels of hazardous consumption (10 cl and over), the sex ratio increases to 264. There is evidence that sex differences with regard to the prevalence of heavy drinking may be even greater than expected on the basis of average consumption (Skog, 1977). Thus, this more objective estimate of hazardous drinking probably provides the best conservative estimate of sex differences in problem drinking in the general population. Sex ratios for clinically recognizable alcoholics may be somewhat higher because their average consumption is probably greater than the mean for all those drinking at hazardous levels.

In summary, heavy drinking, as defined by these reports, is consistently and substantially greater among men than among women even when sex differences in body weight and composition are controlled. Available data provide no evidence to support convergence, and one set of data suggests the possibility of divergence.

Surveys of Problem Drinking. A number of surveys that examine patterns of alcohol use also attempt to determine rates of problem drinking or alcohol dependence. Unfortunately, most of these do not provide comparable data because of differences in the type and severity of the problems included in the measures used. Rates of problem drinking average about 18% for men and 7% for women (Table 8). Since some of these studies use rather broad definitions of problem drinkers, their rates of problem drinking may include a significant proportion of persons whose problems with alcohol are relatively minor. Johnson et al. (1977) suggested that the rate of "serious problem drinking" lies between 10% and 15% for men and 3% and 5% for women. Young people are less likely than adults to engage in very heavy drinking but are more likely to suffer acute behavioral consequences from it when they do (Cahalan and Treiman, 1976).

With regard to the specific problems that are included in different studies, sex ratios are lowest (but still above 100) for "physicians' warnings about drinking" and for subjective reports (e.g., "felt guilty about drinking"; "did something I felt sorry about"). Higher sex ratios are associated with alcohol-related offenses and frequent intoxication. In one study of young people, females had a slightly higher rate of undesirable "consequences" than males but a much lower rate of heavy drinking (Cahalan and Treiman, 1976). This finding suggests that women are more likely than men to experience problems, or at least to perceive certain events as undesirable, even when their rates of heavy drinking are lower.

Table 8. Prevalence and Sex Ratios of Problem Drinking among Adults and Young People in Selected Surveys

Year	Source	Area	Measure of use	% Male	% Female	Sex ratio[a] (M:F)
Adults						
1960	Bailey et al. (1965)	New York City	Problems/excessive drinking	32	9	356
1963	Mulford (1964)	United States	1+ troubles	16	2	800
1964	Knupfer (1967)	San Francisco	Dependence	12	3	363
			1+ social consequences	4	1	600
			1+ problems	43	21	205
1967	Cahalan (1970)	United States	Severe problems	15	4	375
1973	Johnson et al. (1977)	United States	Problem drinker[b]	11	3	362
1974	Johnson et al. (1977)	United States	Problem drinker[b]	6	2	264
1975	Johnson et al. (1977)	United States	Problem drinker[b]	10	3	288
1975	Cahalan and Treiman (1976)	San Francisco	Heavy intake/binge	22	11	207
			High tangible consequences	12	7	180
1978	Liban and Smart (1979)	Durham County, Ontario	3+ problems	20	8	268
			3+ dependency symptoms	25	10	261
Youth						
1974	Rachal et al. (1975)	United States (Gr. 7–12)	Drunkenness × 4/yr or 2+ negative consequences	34	23	147
1975	Cahalan and Treiman (1976)	San Francisco (Ages 12–17)	Heavy intake/binge	10	6	167
			High tangible consequences	13	15	87

[a] Sex ratios calculated before rates are rounded off.
[b] Score of 8+ on 16-item symptom list: frequently = 2; sometimes = 1.

Mortality Data. There are a variety of ways in which alcohol damages the human body. However, the one that is best correlated with the heavy consumption of alcohol is liver cirrhosis (Schmidt and de Lint, 1972). This association makes cirrhosis mortality a most useful indicator for determining trends in heavy use. A close parallel is provided by the relationship between lung cancer and smoking. Heart disease accounts for a larger proportion of smoking-related deaths than lung cancer (U.S. Health, Education and Welfare, 1979), but rates of tobacco consumption are more highly correlated with those of lung cancer mortality than with any other disease, making lung cancer the better indicator of trends in smoking behavior.

An examination of age and sex-specific death rates for liver cirrhosis in Canada between 1946 and 1976 (Statistics Canada, 1945–1977) indicates that rates for males are substantially higher than those for females in the same age group and that this disparity has persisted over time (Table 9). Rates increase sharply with age, but sex ratios increase only slightly with age and, in some years, decline in the older age groups.

Since cirrhosis can be due to factors other than alcohol, it would be useful to look at rates of cirrhosis associated with excessive drinking. Rather than restricting our analysis to death rates for cirrhosis with mention of alcohol, which apparently leads to an underestimation of actual mortality due to this cause, we can estimate these rates by using a rate of nonattributable cirrhosis, or "dry floor," of 4.1 per thousand (Brenner, 1959, 1960). This is the rate of cirrhosis for the general population that is estimated to be unrelated to the use of alcohol.

This method of estimating alcoholic cirrhosis produces rates that are substantially higher than those reported for alcoholic cirrhosis, support-

Table 9. Death Rates and Sex Ratios (M:F) of Liver Cirrhosis in Canada for Four Age Groups between 1946 and 1976[a]

| | Age group | | | | | | | | | | | |
| | 30–39 | | | 40–49 | | | 50–59 | | | 60+ | | |
Year	M	F	SR	M	F	SR	M	F	SR	M	F	SR
1946	1.5	1.3	115	4.9	2.6	188	12.0	5.5	218	26.5	15.6	170
1951	1.9	1.5	127	6.6	3.4	194	15.6	8.6	181	25.4	16.3	156
1956	2.2	1.7	129	10.0	5.9	169	19.9	10.5	189	33.1	14.6	227
1961	3.3	2.1	157	10.0	5.7	175	22.7	10.7	212	38.0	18.4	207
1966	4.5	3.1	145	13.2	7.1	186	27.4	13.4	204	37.9	19.0	199
1971	5.3	3.0	177	22.6	8.6	263	39.8	17.4	229	48.0	23.1	208
1976	7.3	3.3	220	28.4	10.8	263	53.1	20.0	265	64.8	24.8	261

[a] Two-year centered moving average of rates per 100,000 population per annum (Statistics Canada, 1945–1977).

ing the contention that there is underreporting (Table 10). The divergence in sex ratios that characterizes total rates of cirrhosis over time is decreased, which suggests that much of this divergence is due to the increasing proportion of cirrhosis deaths over time that are attributable to alcohol, rather than to a disproportionate increase in rates of cirrhosis among men. The similarity of the sex ratios for both the estimated and the reported rates of alcoholic cirrhosis indicates that although only about half of these cases are reported, underreporting is no greater for women than for men.

To substantiate this conclusion further, we can also take advantage of the longitudinal nature of these data. It has been argued that rates of alcoholic cirrhosis among women are probably underreported because of the special stigma associated with alcoholism among women and that this is the explanation for much of the sex difference in mortality rates (Homiller, 1978; Working Group on Women Alcoholics, 1977). However, if this hypothesis were true, one would expect that over time, the change in social values would cause the stigma to show some signs of decreasing, that is, that certifying physicians in the 1970s would be less likely to underreport cirrhosis among women than physicians in, say, the early 1960s. If there had been a decrease in underreporting for women, even without any disproportionate increase in mortality, sex ratios should have declined, even if only slightly. No such decline has occurred.

Another way of examining the issue of underreporting and stigma is to look at trends in death rates for other diseases. Cirrhosis, lung cancer, and suicide are comparable as causes of death because each is associated with the heavy use of a substance that is consumed voluntarily, and death tends to occur in middle or late middle age. When we compare death rates for these three causes in Canada in 1950 and 1976 (Statistics Canada, 1945–1977), we find that both lung cancer and suicide rates show a higher annual rate of change for women than for men (Table 11). This trend is associated with disproportionate increases in smoking among women (Health and Welfare Canada, 1977) and probably with higher rates of licit drug use that are associated with suicide among women (Cooperstock and Sims, 1971; Mellinger et al., 1974).

Age-specific rates as a substitute for trend data can also be used to examine trends over time. The results can be misleading if the behavior or the disease studied is characteristic of a particular age group and a "maturing-out" process occurs. For example, heavy drinking among college students does not persist in a majority of cases into the adult years (Fillmore, 1974). However, since deaths from cirrhosis and lung cancer usually result from excessive drinking or smoking over a number of years, a comparison of age-specific rates for these two causes of death is quite appropriate.

Table 10. Death Rates and Sex Ratios (M:F) of Cirrhosis and Alcoholic Cirrhosis and Estimated Death Rates and Sex Ratios of Alcoholic Cirrhosis in Canada between 1950 and 1977[a]

Year	Total rates of cirrhosis			Estimated rates of alcoholic cirrhosis using nonattributable rate of 4.1			Reported rates of alcoholic cirrhosis		
	Male	Female	Sex ratio	Male	Female	Sex ratio	Male	Female	Sex ratio
1950	9.9	5.9	168	5.8	1.8	322	na[b]	na[b]	—
1955	11.8	5.8	203	7.7	1.7	453	na[b]	na[b]	—
1960	15.2	8.2	185	11.1	4.1	271	na[b]	na[b]	—
1965	16.6	8.6	193	12.5	4.5	278	5.5	2.1	262
1972	26.4	12.4	213	22.3	8.3	269	12.1	4.5	269
1977	30.4	12.6	242	26.3	8.5	309	15.7	5.5	287

[a] Rates per 100,000 population per annum aged 25 and over (Statistics Canada, 1945–1977). Sex ratios are calculated before rates are rounded off.
[b] Not available for these years.

Table 11. Death Rates and Sex Ratios (M:F) of Cirrhosis, Lung Cancer, and Suicide in Canada in 1950 and 1976 and Percentage Increases for That Period[a]

Cause of death	Death rate[b]						Average annual percentage increase 1950–1976	
	1950			1976				
	Male	Female	Sex ratio	Male	Female	Sex ratio	Male	Female
Cirrhosis	9.9	5.9	168	31.2	13.0	241	8.3	3.0
Lung cancer	27.3	5.5	496	100.2	21.5	466	10.3	11.2
Suicide	19.7	5.8	340	25.5	10.6	240	1.1	3.2

[a] Statistics Canada (1945–1977).
[b] Annual rate per 100,000, age 25+.

If there were disproportionate increases among women in heavy drinking and heavy smoking over time, we should find a gradual decline in sex ratios for each younger age group. This trend is very apparent in the case of death rates from lung cancer, but there is little change in sex ratios with age for death rates from cirrhosis (Table 12). The slightly lower sex ratio for the youngest age group is due to the somewhat higher proportion of cirrhosis that is unrelated to the use of alcohol. This small difference is found consistently over the past 30 years (Table 9).

In this analysis, we have used several different approaches to examine trends in cirrhosis death rates and evidence of underreporting for women. There is no suggestion that either convergence or underreporting is occurring. It could be argued that the increases in drinking among women are so recent that they are unlikely to be reflected in death rates. While it is true that cirrhosis can take as long as 20 years to cause death, it can also develop in as few as 5 years. Many of the deaths experienced by 30- to 40-year-olds have probably occurred following a shorter period of morbidity. Sex ratios for this younger age group are not converging.

Changes in rates of cirrhosis mortality for a particular cohort can occur within as few as three years of an increase of heavy drinking by those individuals (Brenner, 1975). This is true because the rate of heavy drinking in a population increases gradually over time as more and more drinkers increase their consumption to the point at which damage occurs. Thus, even an increase in heavy drinking that occurred within the past 10 years should have some effect on mortality rates. To date, there has been no recorded effect.

Data for other types of alcohol-related mortality also fail to show a trend toward convergence over time (Table 13). Death rates for alcoholism, alcoholic psychosis, and alcohol poisoning showed substantial increases between 1969 and 1977 that are similar to those for cirrhosis (Statistics Canada, 1945–1977); sex ratios stayed the same or increased.

Table 12. Death Rates and Sex Ratios of Liver Cirrhosis and Lung Cancer for Four Age Groups in Canada, 1976[a]

Age group	Liver cirrhosis[b]			Lung cancer		
	Male	Female	Sex ratio (M:F)	Male	Female	Sex ratio (M:F)
30–39	7.3	3.3	220	2.5	1.3	192
40–49	28.4	10.8	263	25.7	9.5	271
50–59	53.1	20.0	265	113.4	29.5	384
60+	64.8	24.8	261	349.1	56.7	616

[a] Annual rates per 100,000 population (Statistics Canada, 1945–1977).
[b] Two-year centered moving average.

Table 13. Death Rates and Sex Ratios (M:F) of Alcohol-Related Conditions in
Canada in 1969 and 1977[a]

| | 1969 | | | 1977 | | |
Cause of death	Male	Female	Sex ratio	Male	Female	Sex ratio
Liver cirrhosis	10.0	5.6	179	16.7	7.2	233
Alcoholic cirrhosis	3.4	1.6	212	8.6	3.0	276
Alcoholism	2.0	0.6	338	4.6	1.2	391
Alcoholic psychosis	0.3	0.1	429	0.3	0.1	467
Alcohol poisoning	1.5	0.9	168[b]	1.9	1.2	160[b]

[a] Annual rates per 100,000 population (Statistics Canada, 1945–1977).
[b] Sex ratios are lower because this category includes alcohol in combination with other drugs.

(The number of deaths resulting from alcoholic psychosis is so small that sex ratios are somewhat unstable.)

On the basis of this review, there is no convincing evidence that women have rates of consumption or problems that approach those of men. Because there are few good longitudinal studies of heavy consumption, it is difficult to assess whether or not the gap is narrowing in the long run. Data for cirrhosis and other alcohol-related causes of death do not support such a conclusion at this time. If patterns of heavy use are converging, the effects should be reflected in the sex ratios for deaths from this disease at some point in the near future.

Special Population Studies

Morbidity Data.   Data for hospital admissions and separations (discharges, transfers, etc.) of cases with alcohol-related diagnoses provide an alternative method of examining trends in sex differences. Diagnostic evidence is gathered from live patients and the conclusions are drawn by practicing physicians. Any new trends are likely to be picked up more quickly than when mortality data are used.

The pattern for these morbidity cases is almost identical to that for mortality cases (Table 14). Sex ratios for hospital separation rates of liver cirrhosis in Canada were stable at slightly above 200 from 1972 to 1975, whereas the total number of cases increased by about 10% in that three-year period (Statistics Canada, 1972–1975). Hospital separation rates for cases of alcoholism rose substantially, while sex ratios decreased slightly but remained above 400. Sex ratios for alcoholic psychosis exhibited a similar pattern, but there was a much smaller increase in rates.

Admissions to psychiatric institutions and separations provide a different but less complete picture of sex differences in alcohol-related morbidity (Statistics Canada, 1979). Sex ratios were above 400 for cases of alcoholism and above 300 for cases of alcoholic psychosis in Canada

Table 14. Rates and Sex Ratios of Hospital Separations for Alcohol-Related Conditions in Canada, 1972 to 1975[a]

	Liver cirrhosis			Alcoholism			Alcoholic psychosis		
	Male	Female	Sex ratio	Male	Female	Sex ratio	Male	Female	Sex ratio
1972	124.1	59.3	209	339.0	72.1	470	48.0	9.5	505
1973	134.5	61.1	220	405.5	91.9	441	48.9	10.4	470
1974	134.3	63.8	211	441.2	99.8	442	54.2	11.5	471
1975	128.7	58.3	221	419.1	100.8	416	48.5	11.7	415

[a] Annual rates per 100,000 population, age 25+ and sex ratios (Statistics Canada, 1972–1975).

in 1976 (Table 15). If sex ratios were decreasing, one would expect first admissions (new cases) to have lower sex ratios than readmissions (existing cases). This situation does not occur generally for psychiatric institutions but does appear to be true for cases of alcoholism admitted to hospitals for addicts.

It is not clear why only one facility would show this pattern, but it may be that such programs are considered more suitable for women now than they were previously. Women are more likely than men to be cross-addicted (Curlee, 1970), and the lower sex ratios in the hospitals for addicts may be due to an increasing interest in patients who are cross-addicted or to an actual increase in the proportion of women alcoholics who are cross-addicted.

In Canada, sex ratios are highest for alcohol-related admissions to public mental hospitals and lowest for alcohol-related admissions to public psychiatric units. In fact, sex ratios for the latter are similar to those for most estimates of problem drinking in the general population. The differences in sex ratios among the four types of institutions largely reflect general referral patterns rather than those specific to alcoholic patients. For example, sex ratios for admissions with alcohol disorders to psychiatric facilities in the United States in 1970 ranged from 254 for private mental hospitals to 568 for public mental hospitals (National Institute of Mental Health, 1971). However, when sex differences in total admissions are controlled, the sex ratios for alcohol-related admissions to these institutions were 367 and 374, respectively. There is still some variation among all types of facilities even when such controls are employed, but it is substantially less than it would be otherwise.

Surveys of Alcohol-Related Morbidity.   Official statistics on alcohol-related admissions and separations are widely available for large medical institutions. On the other hand, statistics on patients of private physicians and clients of general social agencies, and those that provide services specifically to problem drinkers are not often routinely kept; when they are, there is usually no consistent centralized collection of these data. To obtain a more comprehensive picture of the population with alcohol-related problems that uses these services, it is frequently necessary to survey the relevant services and, in some cases, to set up internal systems for collecting appropriate data. Such surveys are usually carried out in order to assess the number of persons in treatment in a particular geographic area.

Few surveys of this type have been carried out to date. Those that have vary considerably in the range of sources used and in the definition of cases applied. Some include only those agencies and institutions that are geared specifically to clients with alcohol-related problems. Others

Table 15. Rates and Sex Ratios of Admissions and Separations of Cases of Alcoholism and Alcoholic Psychosis to Psychiatric Institutions in Canada by Type of Institution in 1976[a]

Alcoholism	First admissions			Readmissions			Discharges		
	Male	Female	Sex ratio	Male	Female	Sex ratio	Male	Female	Sex ratio
Public mental hospital	15.2	2.4	621	17.0	3.1	548	33.3	5.9	564
Public psychiatric unit	12.2	3.9	313	12.4	4.4	282	25.8	9.0	287
Psychiatric hospital	5.6	1.1	496	9.7	2.5	388	15.5	3.9	397
Hospital for addicts	37.5	7.4	510	21.7	2.7	804	59.4	9.9	600
Total (includes other)	70.9	14.9	476	61.2	12.7	482	135.0	28.7	470

Alcoholic psychosis	First admissions			Readmissions			Discharges		
	Male	Female	Sex ratio	Male	Female	Sex ratio	Male	Female	Sex ratio
Public mental hospital	1.6	0.3	462	2.3	0.4	536	3.7	0.9	411
Public psychiatric unit	2.4	0.7	320	1.6	0.6	267	4.2	1.6	263
Psychiatric hospital	0.3	0.1[b]	436	0.2	0.1	164	0.6	0.2	295
Hospital for addicts	<0.05[b]	<0.05[b]	259	<0.05[b]	0.00	—	<0.05[b]	<0.05[b]	465
Total (includes other)	4.5	1.2	386	4.4	1.2	373	8.9	2.7	333

[a]Annual rate per 100,000 population (Statistics Canada, 1979); sex ratios calculated before rates rounded off.
[b]Fewer than 10 cases.

cover an array of social and medical services, which have varying proportions of problem drinkers among their clientele.

There is considerable variation in sex ratios according to the type of service covered in the survey. The lowest, between 200 and 400, are associated with outpatient and short-term residential facilities for alcoholics (Reid, 1977) and with physicians' general practices (Keller and Efron, 1955; Edwards et al., 1973; Murdock et al., 1979). The highest, over 1000, characterize cases seen by the police (Keller and Efron, 1955) or by detoxication centers (Reid, 1977). Sex ratios for cases seen by hospitals and general social agencies are about 400 (Edwards et al., 1973; Murdock et al., 1979).

Sex ratios for cases collected from several sources in a particular geographic area also vary greatly, in large part because of the type of facility included. For example, Reid's (1977) study of treatment facilities for alcoholics in Ontario, Canada, reports a sex ratio of 502 for all clients in the province. However, the ratios for each of the 10 areas studied range from 227 to 3233 because the proportion of females ranged from 3% to 31%. When sex ratios are high, small variations in the proportion of females produce major differences in the ratios.

It is almost impossible to compare studies carried out at different points in time. Because of changes in the mix of agencies and in referral patterns, recorded changes in sex ratios are difficult to interpret. While such changes might be fairly representative of changes in the composition of the treated population, they would not necessarily reflect trends in the prevalence of drinking problems in the community.

No satisfactory longitudinal studies have been carried out that have applied the same methods. What we can conclude is that sex ratios for the total treated population of problem drinkers exceed those for estimates of prevalence. However, if we narrow our focus to those portions of treated populations that are probably most representative of the larger community, and presumably of the untreated population, the gap between estimates of morbidity based on surveys of facilities and those based on household surveys narrows considerably and may even disappear. For example, facilities such as detoxication centers that cater largely to homeless male alcoholics have very small proportions of females among their clientele. On the other hand, sex ratios for patients with alcohol problems seen by family physicians (Keller and Efron, 1955; Ferrence et al., 1977) and in outpatient facilities (National Institute of Mental Health, 1971; Reid, 1977) are clearly within the range of estimates for the general population, that is, between 200 and 300.

Alcohol-Related Offenses.   Public drunkenness is probably the most stigmatized nonviolent behavior associated with the use of alcohol. Rates of charges for drunkenness in both Canada and the United States peaked in the mid-1960s at about 8 per 1000 population and have since declined to about 3 per 1000, which is well below the rate for the early 1950s (Kelley, 1976; Statistics Canada, 1951–1972). Sex ratios are almost identical in both countries and have remained remarkably stable over the past 30 years. Sex ratios at the beginning of this period were about 1400. They declined slightly to about 1000 as rates increased but have since returned to about 1400 as rates have declined.

Canadian national data are available only up to 1972. However, charges laid under provincial statutes in Canada are largely alcohol-related (about 80%), and these are available for an additional five years. These involve a variety of behaviors that breach the Liquor Acts, including underage drinking and drinking in an unlicensed public place. Sex ratios for charges laid under provincial statutes in Ontario between 1973 and 1977 are stable at about 1400 for adults and 230 for juveniles (Provincial Secretariat for Justice, 1978).

The impairment of drivers by alcohol provides a very different measure of alcohol-related problems in the general driving population. Two types of studies provide useful data: those that measure impairment in random roadside spot checks or among those who come to the attention of police, and those that report impairment among persons involved in fatal and nonfatal traffic collisions.

Studies that use police reports of impairment have been criticized because of the potential for bias that arises when personal judgments are made by police officers (Zylman, 1974). Although there is no evidence that such bias occurs systematically (Whitehead, 1977), the use of instruments that measure the level of alcohol in the blood has the additional advantages that differences in body weight and composition are controlled for and a range of consumption levels can be ascertained.

The prevalence of drinking and driving has been measured in two major roadside surveys (Smith et al., 1976; Damkot et al., 1977). Sex ratios increased with increasing BAC in both surveys and were about 200 for BAC readings of .10 and over, the level at which drivers are usually charged (Table 16). Unfortunately, there are no longitudinal data for this measure.

Statistics for impaired driving charges show a very low proportion of females (Table 16). The proportion increased from 6% to 8% in the United States between 1960 and 1975 and from 2% to 4% in Canada between 1966 and 1976 (Kelley, 1976; Statistics Canada, 1969, 1974, 1978). Even though these are large proportional increases, they represent rather small absolute increases. Sex ratios for these data are extremely high, in part because they are based on the actual number of charges rather than some measure of the population at risk. Thus, the decline in sex ratios over time, 1600 to 1100 in the United States and 4168 to 2358

Table 16. Prevalence and Sex Ratios of Drinking and Driving and Alcohol-Related Collisions in Canada and the United States

Year	Source	Area	Measure	% Males	% Females	Sex ratio[a] (M:F)
Roadside surveys						
1974	Smith et al. (1976)	Canada	BAC			
			<.02	78	89	**88**
			.02–.04	10	6	**172**
			.05–.09	8	4	**214**
			.10+	4	2	**191**
1974	Damkot et al. (1977)	Vermont	BAC			
			<.01	47	66	**71**
			.01–.04	26	16	**159**
			.05–.09	16	13	**126**
			.10+	11	5	**237**
Alcohol–related collisions						
1973	TIRF (1975)	Canada	Impaired/total driver fatalities:			
			All ages	40	19	**211**
			Age 16–19	45	11	**409**
			Impaired/total driver fatalities:			

1976	Simpson et al. (1978)	Canada	All ages	42	18	**233**
			Alcohol-related/total collisions:			
1968–1969	Whitehead (1977)	London, Canada	Age 16–20, 24	4	2	**186**
1969–1970	Whitehead (1977)	London, Canada	Age 16–20, 24	4	1	**495**
1970–1971	Whitehead (1977)	London, Canada	Age 16–20, 24	5	1	**516**
1971–1972	Whitehead (1977)	London, Canada	Age 16–20, 24	9	2	**572**
1972–1973	Whitehead (1977)	London, Canada	Age 16–20, 24	9	2	**457**
1973–1974	Whitehead (1977)	London, Canada	Age 16–20, 24	9	3	**343**
1974–1975	Whitehead (1977)	London, Canada	Age 16–20, 24	11	3	**334**

				% of all charged		
				Male	Female	
Impaired driving						
1960	Kelley (1976)	United States	Offences charged (DUI)	94	6	**1600**
1975	Kelley (1976)	United States	Offences charged (DUI)	92	8	**1100**
1966	Statistics Canada (1969)	Canada	Offences charged (DWI)	98	2	**4168**
1971	Statistics Canada (1974)	Canada	Offences charged (DWI)	97	3	**3553**
1976	Statistics Canada (1978)	Canada	Offences charged (DWI)	96	4	**2358**
1971	Statistics Canada (1974)	Canada	Refused breath test	98	2	**4002**
1976	Statistics Canada (1978)	Canada	Refused breath test	96	4	**2642**

a Sex ratios calculated before rates are rounded off.

in Canada, was at least partly due to the increase in numbers of women driving and driving at times when they are more likely to be apprehended. Warren (1979) has estimated that the sex ratio for this risk was about 270 for Canada in 1974.

Two Canadian studies of alcohol-related fatal collisions carried out in 1973 (Traffic Injury Research Foundation, 1975) and 1976 (Simpson et al., 1978) show sex ratios of 211 and 233, respectively, for the proportion of impaired drivers among total driver fatalities (Table 16). Whitehead (1977) examined the prevalence of alcohol-related collisions among young drivers aged 16 to 20 and 24 in London, Canada, between 1968 and 1975. There was a substantial increase in the proportion of collisions that were alcohol-related following the lowering of the drinking age in mid-1971. There appears to have been a decline in sex ratios after this point, but a longer time series would provide more conclusive evidence. The sex ratio for 1974–1975 was still above 300.

These data on drinking and driving and alcohol-related collisions suggest that males are at least twice as likely as females to drive while impaired. The higher sex ratios for charges laid are probably due to sex differences in the distribution of BACs over the legal limit, that is, the average BAC for male impaired drivers would be higher than for female impaired drivers, and therefore, a greater proportion of male impaired drivers would come to the attention of police because of erratic driving, collisions, or other infractions. There probably has been some disproportionate increase over time in the proportion of women who drive while impaired, but numbers for women are still quite low compared with those for men.

Two sets of data can be used to examine the possibility that there is underreporting of women who drive while impaired. Data on fatal crashes in Canada in 1973 indicate that women drivers were almost as likely as men to be tested for BAC (74.4% versus 78.5%). This finding is somewhat surprising since men are twice as likely as women to be impaired (Traffic Injury Research Foundation, 1975). Vingilis (1979) examined sex and age differences in the screening of drivers for impairment in Toronto, Canada. She found that women and younger drivers were overrepresented among those stopped for testing compared to those actually charged with impairment. To explain this finding, she suggested that young police officers may find it less threatening to ask young drivers and females than to ask older male drivers to submit to breath tests and that women and young people have less tolerance for alcohol and may actually be more impaired. Both of these studies concluded that women who are impaired are not significantly less likely to be detected by official screening processes.

This completes the examination of data collected in studies of special populations. The results are less than conclusive. Three of the five indicators we have looked at show some evidence of convergence, but the issue is complicated by the short time period for morbidity data and the lack of complete information on risk factors for impaired driving.

The apparent decline in sex ratios for hospital separations of cases of alcoholism and alcoholic psychosis is not supported by a lower sex ratio for first admissions of such cases to psychiatric institutions, compared with readmissions. Furthermore, sex ratios for morbidity cases are not very different from those for mortality cases, which is not what one would expect if sex ratios were actually declining.

4. THE "HIDDEN" FEMALE ALCOHOLIC

The second theme identified at the outset of this review has to do with the notion that the female alcoholic is "hidden." Presumably, what is meant is that (1) women alcoholics are underrepresented in the treatment population because there are few facilities geared to the needs of women; (2) women alcoholics are less visible because they are less likely to work outside the home; and (3) women alcoholics are both ignored and protected by family and physicians because of the greater stigma associated with the heavy use of alcohol by women. Each of these three statements will be dealt with in an attempt to assess the validity of the contention that the female alcoholic is "hidden."

Women Alcoholics Are Underrepresented in the Treatment Population

In the previous discussion of surveys of alcohol-related morbidity, we found a very broad range of sex ratios among clients of different types of services. There is no doubt that women problem drinkers are underrepresented in some agencies, particularly those such as detoxication centers that are geared specifically to alcohol problems. However, sex differences in patterns of service utilization by problem drinkers seem to reflect general help-seeking patterns. Traditionally, women have made more use than males of physicians and some kinds of social agencies for a variety of medical and social problems. They have been much less likely to use other types of facilities, such as those that provide shelter and care for homeless persons. However, as Mulford (1977) has pointed out, "The 'double-standard' hypothesis would lead us to expect relatively more women to enter treatment. Indeed, women in treatment report having made more prior efforts to quit [drinking] than have the men."

There are few data regarding the comparative efficacy of programs geared specifically to alcoholics and those provided to persons with a range of problems. In fact, the success rate for most types of alcoholism treatment is not particularly encouraging (Emrich, 1975; Armor et al., 1976; Schuckit and Cahalan, 1976). Thus, even though women are clearly underrepresented in some alcohol-specific programs, we do not know that a *much* smaller proportion of them are treated at all or that they receive less effective treatment. Sex ratios for alcoholic clients of physicians, hospitals for alcoholics, social agencies, outpatient clinics, and short-term residential programs range from 250 to 400 (Reid, 1977; Ferrence et al., 1977; Murdock et al., 1979), a range that is clearly within the ballpark for sex ratios of heavy use and alcohol-related problems for the general population. In a study that compared treated alcoholics with their untreated alcoholic relatives, Woodruff et al. (1973) found that women alcoholics were more likely to be seen by a psychiatrist than their male counterparts.

The fact that sex ratios for treated populations are in some cases higher than those for the general population should not be interpreted to mean that most men are being treated whereas most women are not. In fact, the vast majority of alcoholics of both sexes receive no treatment. For example, among respondents classified as having a serious dependence on alcohol in Durham County, Ontario, only one in nine had ever received formal treatment (Liban and Smart, 1979). Although the sample was small, there is no evidence that females were less likely to have received treatment than males.

We can conclude that women are to some extent "hidden" with regard to their representation in the treatment sector. However, it is largely because they make less use of certain highly visible programs that are geared specifically to alcoholics rather than because they are grossly underrepresented in the treatment sector as a whole. It is also questionable whether increases in the number of traditional alcohol treatment facilities for women would have a sizable impact on the number of women in treatment (Marshman, 1978).

Women Alcoholics Are Less Visible

The notion persists that women alcoholics are "hidden" because most of them are housewives, who can successfully hide their drinking because they have less exposure to the outside world. In a recent article, Pinder and Boyle (1977) commented on this issue:

> It is the housewife as a secret drinker who has intrigued the public. Phrases such as "the drinker in the pantry" and "behind lace curtains" contribute to

the tendency to ignore the fact that 33 per cent of married women are employed full time in the labor force and may be as subject to alcoholism as their sisters who are home-makers. (p. 29)

Research evidence does not support the stereotype of the typical female alcoholic as a middle-aged suburban housewife. Not only are the majority of women not housewives (Labour Canada, 1976), but rates of problem drinking among housewives are actually lower than expected on the basis of their representation in the population. In fact, it is younger women, lower-class women, employed and unemployed women, and single, divorced, and separated women who have the highest rates of problem drinking (Knupfer, 1967; Cahalan and Cisin, 1976; Johnson et al., 1977; Liban and Smart, 1979).

Women who are not in the labor force are less likely to drink heavily (Whitehead, 1974; Johnson et al., 1977) and are much less likely to encounter problems if they drink at all (Johnson et al., 1977). Even among populations of alcoholics, married women are underrepresented (Mulford, 1977), and they are less likely than unmarried women to experience severe symptoms (Bromet and Moos, 1976). No differences were found between married and unmarried women in mean scores for drinking alone or drinking at home. (Seventy percent of married women in this study did not work outside the home.)

Mulford (1977) has argued that according to the "hidden housewife hypothesis," one would expect the alcoholic process to be prolonged, not shortened, among housewives. His findings show no difference between housewives and other women in the interval between onset of heavy drinking and entry into a treatment program. Further, he suggested that the stereotype of the female alcoholic as a "hidden housewife" may be just as invalid as the image of the male alcoholic as a skid-row derelict.

The claim that women hide their drinking more than men is also open to question. The general belief is that heavy drinking is more deviant for women so that they must cover it up (Garzon, 1974). Other than the apparent logic of this behavior, there is no clear evidence that women who are problem drinkers do indeed cover up their drinking more than men. Most of the findings (cf. Gomberg, 1976) are based on clinical impressions or on samples of alcoholics who may be atypical. In a representative sample, Johnson et al. (1977) found no sex differences in the percentage of heavier drinkers who "sneak drinks" or "hide a bottle." Perhaps society has seized on the housewife as the stereotype of the female alcoholic because she seems most vulnerable and because the contrast between our image of the housewife and the alcoholic is the most dramatic.

Women Alcoholics Are Ignored and Protected

There is little documented evidence to support the notion that women alcoholics are ignored and protected because of the greater stigma associated with alcoholism among women. Women's problems may tend to be taken less seriously than those of men, but it can also be argued that men's drinking is more likely to be ignored because heavy drinking is less deviant for men. The widespread belief that the majority of husbands of alcoholic women leave them, whereas relatively few women leave their alcoholic husbands (Fraser, 1973), suggests that women may actually be *less* protected when they drink heavily. Perhaps our stereotype of the male as protective has affected our thinking in this area. Further investigation of this issue is clearly indicated.

The question of stigma is one that has been relatively unexplored. Although it is commonly believed that alcoholism carries a greater stigma for women than for men, there is no conclusive evidence to prove that it does. Stafford and Petway (1977) tested this assumption and found no basis for its validity. In recent years, a number of public figures, both male and female, have openly discussed their problems with alcohol, and there has been no apparent stigmatization of the women involved. There has been a failure to distinguish between the condition of alcoholism and drunk-and-disorderly behavior. When alcoholism is viewed as a medical problem requiring treatment, it seems unlikely that greater stigma would accrue to women who are heavy drinkers. However, attitudes toward drunkenness in women are harsher than those toward men (Gomberg, 1976; Stafford and Petway, 1977). Of course, such attitudes are not restricted to alcohol-related behaviors because women are generally expected to act with more decorum than men. Even if attitudes toward women problem drinkers were more negative than those toward men, it does not follow that those involved in referrals for treatment, in diagnosis, or in certification of death would underreport female cases. Mental illness is stigmatized in our society, yet no one suggests that, as a result, large numbers of cases are covered up or not referred for treatment.

In this discussion of the "hidden" female alcoholic, we have found little evidence to support the notion that there are a disproportionate number of undetected women problem drinkers. They may be less visible in public because they are less likely to appear intoxicated, to get into fights, or to engage in loud behavior. But these differences reflect general sex differences in socially prescribed norms for behavior rather than those relating solely to drinking. Women problem drinkers are probably no more "hidden" than men from those who are involved in their private lives, their family, friends, physicians, and employers.

It is apparent that the vast majority of women and men who drink heavily or experience at least some problems with alcohol are undetected by official agents such as social and medical professionals and the police. Room (1977) has pointed out that

> . . . the search for the "hidden alcoholic" and the increasing emphasis on case-finding and "secondary prevention" are doomed to failure if these efforts are predicated on the existence of a large hidden population many times greater than the number in clinics but resembling clinical populations in every way except that they are not hospitalized. (p. 82)

Even for those who are "found," there is no evidence that women are underrepresented compared to men, when those factors that bring people into contact with treatment and social control agents are taken into account.

5. FUTURE TRENDS

It is often argued that the combined effects of the women's movement and other social changes are producing increased stress for women that will lead them to engage in heavier drinking. There appears to be little solid evidence to support this argument. Beckman (1978) has commented on this subject:

> The consciousness raising caused by the women's movement is likely only to cause a type of sex role conflict (between a feminine personality and new demands for masculine attitudes and behaviors) that appears unrelated to alcoholism in women. Although the women's movement may be associated with increased alcoholism among women, the causal mechanism involved does not appear to be sex role conflict. (p. 417)

Even if women are exposed to greater stress than men, there is no reason to believe that alcohol would be the favored method of coping. As Bowker (1977) has pointed out, "The weakness of the 'empty nest' theory of female alcoholism . . . is precisely that it is males, not females, who are most likely to use alcohol to cope with depression and anxiety. Women prefer prescription psychotherapeutic drugs."

There may well be increases in rates of alcoholism among women in the future, but there is no clear reason to believe that they will be greater than those for men. Affluence and the increasing integration of drinking patterns are two of the main influences on increases in consumption (Brenner, 1975; Bruun et al., 1975) and may not affect females more than males. To date, few women have entered those nontraditional occupations that provide high incomes, greater freedom, and increased exposure to alcohol (Labour Canada, 1976). The proportion of women among executives, traveling salespersons, truck drivers, bartenders, or owners of small businesses is still very small. Women continue to be heavily concentrated in clerical and service positions, where they are closely supervised, and in professions such as teaching, nursing, and social work, where they are expected to maintain personal standards that are higher than those of the rest of the community. Women who have been housewives and are returning to work are less likely to enter nontraditional fields. Furthermore, sex differentials in income are not decreasing significantly (Ontario Ministry of Labour, 1978), while at the same time, the proportion of single parents, who are mostly women, is increasing. If one accepts the role of economic factors in drinking (e.g., Brenner, 1975), women are unlikely to make disproportionate gains in consumption in the immediate future. The tendency for employers to give percentage increases in wages only widens the gap and may wipe out whatever gains women make.

6. IMPLICATIONS FOR PUBLIC POLICY, PROGRAMMING, AND RESEARCH

The trends and patterns discussed previously have a number of important implications for programs, public policy, and future research. The raised consciousness regarding women's status in society has understandably influenced the attitudes of women in the field of addictions. Current demands for increased facilities and programs for women are a response both to this raised consciousness and to the conclusion that compared with men, women are underserviced, at least by alcohol-specific facilities.

In arguing for women's share of the funding pie, it is important to retain credibility. By claiming that women alcoholics are increasing disproportionately and approaching the numbers of male alcoholics, there is a risk of losing credibility if this turns out not to be the case. This approach is probably not the best one and may, in fact, be quite unnecessary.

With increasing financial constraints, it is not realistic to advocate the unending expansion of treatment facilities that will be needed to cope with the increasing numbers of female alcoholics. Instead of rushing to provide equivalent facilities for women, it would be wise to examine how to get the greatest impact from what will inevitably be limited resources.

Historically, the concern of alcohol researchers and clinicians has been the social consequences of heavy drinking; currently, there is increasing concern about health problems. The ultimate value of the epidemiological approach is that it identifies a complete range of persons at risk for various types of problems. This approach would enable policymakers to take as their focus of concern all of those women, whether light, moderate, or heavy drinkers, who may be at risk of damaging themselves or their children. For this reason, we should give greater attention to primary prevention programs aimed at reducing consumption among women in general and among those of childbearing age in particular. Attempting to broaden the treatment net alone will restrict the impact of such programs to a small percentage of those women who are heavy drinkers and will totally exclude those at risk because of more moderate consumption. Adopting broader strategies that encompass a much larger proportion of female drinkers is likely to be much more effective in meeting public health objectives for women.

In specific terms, the following recommendations are likely to have the greatest impact on alcohol-related problems among women:

a. The adoption of a general public health orientation to prevention. Appropriate policies include a halt to further liberalization of alcohol control measures and tying the price of alcohol to levels of disposable income (Addiction Research Foundation, 1978). Such general measures applied to the whole population would obviously have impact on women as well as men.

b. A concurrent public education program that focuses on appropriate levels of risk for women and hazards such as the fetal alcohol syndrome that are peculiar to women.

c. Changes in the existing treatment network to improve accessibility to women. (See Homiller, 1977, for examples of appropriate changes.)

Prerequisite to the implementation of some of these policies is the accomplishment of a series of research objectives relating to women and alcohol (cf. Homiller, 1977). The most important of these are as follows:

a. To establish female norms for hazardous levels of consumption.
b. To determine sex-specific rates of heavy consumption and to delineate trends over time. This goal would involve an evaluation of the significance of different types of bias that can affect reported rates for males and females when various measures are used.
c. To identify the type and magnitude of alcohol-related problems that are specific to women.
d. To identify help-seeking patterns among women with alcohol-related problems.
e. To identify the most appropriate methods for directing public education toward women.

In order to generate new hypotheses, one must look at female alcoholism within several contexts. Problem drinking among women should be viewed as part of the total range of drinking behavior among women; within the context of alcoholism among both women and men; as one of a variety of types of deviant behavior such as psychiatric illness; and as one of a range of drug-using behaviors such as smoking.

Some of this research is in progress; much more is required. Because interest in alcoholism among women has become widespread only recently, we are really in a better position than in the past to take advantage of improvements in research techniques and theoretical advances to increase our understanding of this problem and to develop effective strategies for prevention and control.

7. SUMMARY AND CONCLUSIONS

The purpose of this chapter was to test two current hypotheses concerning the prevalence of problem drinking among women. The "convergence hypothesis" and the "hidden housewife hypothesis" have been examined through the use of several types of data and have been analyzed for the purpose of determining their validity. On the basis of this investigation, there is no clear justification at present to conclude either that sex differences in problem drinking are disappearing or that the housewife who drinks in secret is typical of women problem drinkers in general.

To test the convergence hypothesis, an analysis was made of four types of data. Sex ratios were calculated for several measures of alcohol use, alcohol-related mortality and morbidity, and alcohol-related offenses. Changes in these sex ratios over time were examined for evidence of convergence (Table 17). Two major conclusions can be drawn from these analyses:

a. The best estimate of the sex ratio for problem drinking is between 250 and 350, or about 300 in Canada and the United States.

Despite the fact that sex ratios for different measures of problem drinking range from 168 to over 1700, there is remarkable concurrence among sex ratios for four of the best independent sources of data. The sex ratio for an estimate of heavy drinking based on average BAC scores of a U.S. national sample in 1975 was 264 (Johnson et al., 1977). The sex ratio for an estimate of alcoholic cirrhosis mortality in Canada in 1977 was 309 (Statistics Canada, 1945–1977). The sex ratio for frequent symptoms of problem drinking in the United States in 1975 was 288 (Johnson et al., 1977). Finally, the sex ratios for clinical populations of problem drinkers seen at outpatient and short-term residential facilities and at a hospital for alcoholics in Ontario, Canada, in 1976 ranged from 260 to 330 (Marshman, 1978; Skinner and Shaffner, 1978). Since the first

Table 17. Summary of Current Sex Ratios and Trends for Measures of Drinking and Alcohol-Related Problems[a]

Measure	Current average sex ratio (M:F)		Trend to convergence (time period in years)	
	Adults	Youth	Adults	Youth
Use				
Annual use	119	103	No (35)	Yes (11)
Daily use	298	283	No (8)	No (6)
Heavy use	556	436	No (18)	No (4)
Heavy use (estimated from BAC)	289	—	—	—
Problem drinking	245	[b]	No (19)	—
Mortality				
Cirrhosis	242	—	No (28)	—
Alcoholic cirrhosis	287	—	No (13)	—
Alcoholism	391	—	No (9)	—
Alcoholic psychosis	467	—	No (9)	—
Alcohol poisoning	168	—	No (9)	—
Morbidity				
Liver cirrhosis	221	—	No (4)	—
Alcoholism	416	—	Possibly (4)	—
Alcoholic psychosis	415	—	Possibly (4)	—
Offenses				
Impaired driving	1729	—	Yes (16)	—
Public drunkenness	1400	—	No (30)	—

[a] Sex ratios for some mortality data and for offenses includes persons under age 25.
[b] Insufficient data.

two sex ratios incorporate controls for sex bias in reporting, their similarity to the third and fourth sex ratios attests to the validity of using problem scales and certain clinical populations as sources of information about sex differences in problem drinking.

Sex ratios for death rates, medical treatment of alcoholism, and alcoholic psychosis are somewhat higher, at about 400. These higher ratios are not necessarily due to underreporting of women in those disease categories. It is more likely that they represent valid differences in the prevalence of clinically recognizable alcoholism. Since problem drinking, heavy drinking, and alcoholic cirrhosis can occur at levels of consumption that are lower than those associated with clinical alcoholism, these categories would include a larger segment of that part of the consumption curve that is closer to the mean and, hence, a larger proportion of women. Sex ratios for alcohol-related offenses are predictably high because they reflect sex differences that characterize most types of criminal behavior.

b. There is no clear evidence to support the contention that rates of problem drinking for women and men have converged, or even that sex ratios are decreasing.

Sex ratios for the best estimators of trends—namely, "heavy use," "problem drinking," and deaths from alcoholic cirrhosis—have not changed since the first period of data collection in the early 1960s. The lack of any discernible trend in sex ratios for rates of annual use and of total cirrhosis mortality among adults suggests that the period of stability for sex ratios in problem drinking may extend back as far as the early postwar period and perhaps further. The similarity of sex ratios for both cirrhosis mortality and morbidity rates throughout the present decade adds support to this conclusion.

There has been a slight decrease in sex ratios of annual use among youth. This statistic of course does not measure problem drinking and has not been accompanied by a similar change in sex ratios for heavy use, although data for the latter are somewhat skimpy. The trend in annual use ratios may be the result of larger social processes, but it may also reflect specific changes in drinking patterns brought about by the lowering of the legal drinking age in many parts of North America in the early 1970s. One would expect that the legalization of drinking by 18- to 21-year-olds would have a greater impact on females than on males, because females are less inclined to engage in deviant behavior. A more detailed analysis is required to test this alternative explanation.

Sex ratios for different levels of use among adults and youth are remarkably similar, considering the differences in patterns of use among the two groups (Harford and Mills, 1978). At this point, we do not know whether or not the slightly lower sex ratios for young people will persist when the latter reach adulthood.

Sex ratios for other measures of alcohol-related mortality have not decreased in recent years. The pattern for morbidity data is less clear, chiefly because of the short period for which comparable data are available. The apparent decrease in sex ratios for hospital separations of cases of alcoholism and alcoholic psychosis is hard to accept when sex ratios for deaths from these causes have remained unchanged.

There has been no decrease in sex ratios of charges for public drunkenness over the long run, but there has been a reduction in those for impaired driving, although they remain very high. As stated previously, we do not know the extent to which increased driving among women accounts for this change.

We tested the notion that the female alcoholic is typically a housewife who drinks in secret, is protected by those close to her, and is therefore unlikely to seek treatment voluntarily or to come to the attention of official caregivers. Our conclusions do not support this stereotype.

Housewives are, in fact, underrepresented among women who are problem drinkers. There is no clear evidence that women are protected more than men when they drink heavily. Women are not underrepresented to any significant extent in most types of treatment facilities, although they are less likely to be represented in detoxication and long-term residential settings. Finally, there is no justification at present for concluding that alcoholism among women is stigmatized to the extent that they are less likely than men to seek treatment.

Since the data do not support either the "convergence" or the "hidden housewife" hypotheses, we might well ask why these notions have become so ingrained in our thinking about women and alcohol problems. There are a number of factors that could lead one to believe that these hypotheses are correct.

a. The *number* of women problem drinkers has increased. In addition to general increases in the population, changes in the structure of the population due to variations in the birthrate and in sex-specific mortality have led to an increase in the proportion of older women and of young people in the population. This means that the proportion of female problem drinkers in the older age groups has probably increased. The disproportionate increase in the younger age group also adds to the number of women in the population who are problem drinkers because sex ratios for heavy drinking are lower among young people than among adults. It should be stressed that these changes occur independently of any changes in age and sex-specific *rates* of problem drinking. Furthermore, the increase in the number of male problem drinkers can be greater than that for females, even when sex ratios for problem drinking are stable or decreasing.

b. Sex ratios for heavy use are lower among young people than among adults. This finding often leads to the assumption that these youthful patterns will persist into adulthood, even though there is evidence that use, in fact, decreases with age among a substantial proportion of the population and that it decreases among more women than men (Mulford, 1964).

c. Some convergence has occurred in other areas of drug-using behavior, such as in rates of smoking among men and women (Chapter 4, this volume), international differences in alcoholic beverage preference (Bruun et al., 1975), and regional differences in alcohol consumption patterns (Whitehead, 1975). In fact, a previous article on alcoholism among women and young people (Whitehead and Ferrence, 1976) also concluded that some convergence was occurring. However, many of the data used in the present chapter were not available at the time, and those that were used were not subjected to as intensive an analysis.

Convergence, however, does not appear to be as ubiquitous as one might believe. For example, there has been no convergence in sex ratios for the use of most illicit drugs (Ferrence and Whitehead, 1980). A plausible interpretation of these differences is that convergence occurs when there is increased contact between diverse groups and when there are no social norms that proscribe such behavior for one sex group and not the other. Thus, drinking in general is apparently almost as acceptable for young women as for young men, whereas heavy drinking is not.

d. There may have been an increase in the proportion of women entering treatment. It is difficult to compare current admission rates with those in the past because of changes in the mix of facilities. However, even within facilities, sex ratios appear to be decreasing. Certainly, the absolute numbers of women as well as of men have increased, and this fact alone could give the impression of a disproportionate increase in alcoholism among women. It is interesting to note that reports of convergence among clinical populations are not limited to the present decade but occurred at least a generation ago (e.g., Block, 1952).

e. It is a well-known psychological phenomenon that people tend to overestimate the proportion of persons in a group who belong to a visible minority, particularly when their presence is unexpected. Thus, people perceive greater numbers of women or blacks in groups that are predominantly male or white. Women alcoholics may appear to constitute a larger proportion of all alcoholics simply because they are a highly visible minority. Therefore, small absolute increases may be perceived as disproportionately large. This selective perception is probably strongest among representatives of the media, who are most interested in rare events. The same phenomenon also applies to the housewife who is a problem drinker. Housewives are probably viewed as even more conventional than other women, so that when they become alcoholic, they very likely evoke an even greater interest from others and are that much more visible, even when their numbers are small.

f. There has been more discussion both in public and in the media about problem drinking in recent years. The presentation of information about heavy drinking among women, and among housewives in particular, may give the impression that such problems did not exist to any significant extent in the past.

g. The women's movement of the 1970s has also increased the visibility of women by focusing our attention on them. As evidence of this increased concern about women, we can note that there have been warnings to women that they will pay a price for their increased emancipation in the form of higher death rates from stress-related conditions, such as heart disease, ulcer, and hypertension. Despite largely undocumented claims to the contrary, the death rates for women and men from these and most other causes have continued to diverge throughout the 1970s, even with disproportionate increases in rates of lung cancer among women. Throughout history, women have been subject to "scare tactics" during periods of social change with respect to their status. In the last century, they were warned that their reproductive organs would wither away if they espoused the cause of suffrage (Ehrenreich, 1979). In more recent years, the working mother has been held responsible for juvenile deliquency and marital breakdown. Some of the present concern about alcoholism and other health problems among women is very probably part of a social reaction to a revision in the status of women.

Recent increases in the visibility of women parallel those that occurred during World War II when large numbers of women entered the labor force. Lisansky (1958) noted a number of unsubstantiated reports during the first post-war decade that described alarming increases in alcoholism among women.

On the other hand, there are a number of reasons to expect rates of problem drinking among women to be substantially lower than those among men, even if supporting data were not available. At the risk of having this review classified with those that "combine elegant epidemiology with crude journalism" (Kreitman, 1979, p. 6), I will engage in some "informed speculation on the basis of relevant theory."

The most obvious reason is that there are positive norms for heavy drinking among men, but not among women. Heavy drinking is considered appropriate masculine behavior. This is different than saying that heavy drinking is stigmatized more for women than for men and relies less on the concept that human beings naturally engage in excessive behavior unless strong social sanctions prevent them from doing so.

Women have less opportunity to drink as often or as heavily as men do, and this prevents more of them from gradually increasing their consumption to the point where damage occurs. Compared with men, women have less disposable income, they encounter fewer social occasions that include the use of alcohol, they work at jobs that are more closely supervised, and they are less likely to be in groups, activities, or locations that are commonly associated with drinking, such as the military, veterans' associations, pool halls, conventions, and fraternities.

Women are more likely to have family and friends with whom they can share their concerns, and they are more willing to use these systems of social support when problems do occur. Furthermore, they tend to use drugs other than alcohol to deal with crises.

Physiological factors may have some bearing on sex differences in heavy use. Many women drink less or not at all during pregnancy, and this behavior may become more pronounced with increasing knowledge about fetal damage. It is quite possible that such temporary abstinence or reduced drinking may affect their subsequent patterns of use. Women have traditionally been more health conscious than men, and this may also affect their drinking behavior.

Most of these factors are associated with definitions of appropriate sex roles that are widely held in our society. Although it seems reasonable to suppose that current changes in the status of women will ultimately lead to greater similarity between men and women in drinking patterns as well as in other behaviors, this hypothesis does not necessarily follow. Women's incomes may increase disproportionately to those of men in the future, but there is no reason to believe that women will adopt positive norms for heavy drinking. The women's movement seeks improvement in the physical and mental health of women, so that one could just as easily predict that informal sanctions against heavy drinking will increase. Women may be more likely to drink heavily in the company of men than in the company of other women, so that increased social interaction with other women could actually lead to lower levels of consumption. Much of this is speculation, but it is presented to suggest that improvements in the status of women will not necessarily lead to increases in problem drinking and could conceivably result in a reduction in alcohol-related damage among women. Obviously, much further research is required to delineate the relationship between sex roles and drinking patterns. The results of these efforts would be valuable not only for explaining sex differences in problem drinking but also for establishing the etiology of problem drinking in general.

Acknowledgments

The author wishes to acknowledge the helpful assistance of Lise Anglin, Deborah J. Lindholm, and other staff members of the Social and Biological Studies Division of the Addiction Research Foundation. Wolfgang Schmidt, Robert E. Popham, and Harold Kalant acted as consultants on this project. The clarity and strength of many of the arguments presented here are due in large measure to their counsel. Paul C. Whitehead reviewed the manuscript and offered many valuable suggestions.

Some of the data included in this chapter were made available by the Drug Abuse Epidemiology Data Center (DAEDAC) at Texas Christian University, Fort Worth. I am indebted to the staff of Statistics Canada, the Health Promotion Branch of Health and Welfare Canada, the National Institute on Alcohol Abuse and Alcoholism (NIAAA), and the Response Analysis Corporation for their advice and assistance in acquiring data.

Oriana J. Kalant, editor of this volume, displayed great optimism and fortitude in her efforts to foster this chapter. I am grateful for her support and for the many valuable consultations in which she generously contributed both her technical expertise and her sound judgment.

REFERENCES

Abelson, H. I., Fishburne, P. M., and Cisin, I., 1977, *National Survey on Drug Abuse,* Vol. 1, *Main Findings,* National Institute on Drug Abuse, Rockville, Md.

Addiction Research Foundation, 1978, A strategy for the prevention of alcohol problems, Addiction Research Foundation, Toronto.

Armor, D. J., Polich, J. M., and Stanbul, H. B., 1976, Alcoholism and Treatment, Rand Corporation, Santa Monica, Calif.

Bailey, M. B., Haberman, P. W., and Alksne, H., 1965, The epidemiology of alcoholism in an urban residential area, *Q. J. Stud. Alcohol* **26**:19–40.

Barnes, G. M., and Russell, M., 1978, Drinking patterns in Western New York State, *J. Stud. Alcohol,* **39**:1148–1157.

Barr, C. L., Fountain, A. W., and Klock, J. A., 1974, Student drug and alcohol opinionnaire and usage survey, Grades 6, 7, 8, 9, 10, 11, 12: June 1973 to January 1974. Test and Measurements Unit, Curriculum Division, Duval County School Board, Jacksonville, Fla.

Barr, C. L., Fountain, A. W., and Klock, J. A., 1975, Student drug and alcohol opinionnaire and usage survey, Grades 6, 7, 8, 9, 10, 11, 12. January 1975. Tests and Measurements Unit, Curriculum Division, Duval County School Board, Jacksonville, Fla.

Barr, C. L., Fountain, A. W., Benham, C. J., and Winesett, H., 1976, Student drug and alcohol opinionnaire and usage survey, Grades 6, 7, 8, 9, 10, 11, and 12. Tests and Measurements Unit, Curriculum Division, Duval County School Board, Jacksonville, Fla.

Barr, C. L., Fountain, A. W., and Staats, W. D., 1977, Student drug and alcohol opinionnaire and usage survey, Grades 6, 7, 8, 9, 10, 11 and 12. Supervisor of Instructional Material, Duval County School Board, Jacksonville, Fla.

Beckman, L. J., 1978, Sex-role conflict in alcoholic women: Myth or reality, *J. Abnorm. Psychol.* **87**:408–417.

Blackford, L. St. Clair, 1977, Summary report—surveys of student drug use, San Mateo County, Calif.

Blane, H. T., and Hewitt, L. E., 1977, *Alcohol and Youth. An Analysis of the Literature, 1960–75,* University of Pittsburgh, for National Institute on Alcohol Abuse and Alcoholism.

Block, M. A., 1952, Alcoholism: The physician's duty, *GP* **6**:53–58.

Bowker, L. H., 1977, *Drug Use among American Women, Old and Young: Sexual Oppression and Other Themes,* R. and E. Research Associates, San Francisco.

Brenner, B., 1959, Estimating the prevalence of alcoholism: Toward a modification of the Jellinek formula, *Q. J. Stud. Alcohol* **20**:255–260.

Brenner, B., 1960, Estimating the prevalence of alcoholism from vital rates, *Q. J. Stud. Alcohol* **21**:140–141.

Brenner, M. H., 1975, Trends in alcohol consumption and associated illnesses. Some effects of economic changes, *Am. J. Public Health* **65**:1279–1292.

Bromet, E., and Moos, R., 1976, Sex and marital status in relation to the characteristics of alcoholics, *J. Stud. Alcohol* **37**:1302–1312.

Bruun, K., Edwards, G., Lumio, M., Mäkelä, M., Pan, L., Popham, R. E., Room, R., Schmidt, W., Skog, O.-J., Sulkunen, P., and Österberg, E., 1975, *Alcohol Control Policies in Public Health Perspective,* Vol. 25, The Finnish Foundation for Alcohol Studies, Finland.

Cahalan, D., 1970, *Problem Drinkers,* Jossey-Bass, New York.

Cahalan, D., and Cisin, I. H., 1976, Drinking behavior and drinking problems in the United States, in: *The Biology of Alcoholism,* Vol. 4 (B. Kissin and H. Begleiter, eds.), pp. 77–116, Plenum, New York.

Cahalan, D., and Treiman, B., 1976, *Drinking Behavior, Attitudes, and Problems in San Francisco,* report prepared for Bureau of Alcoholism, Department of Public Health, City and County of San Francisco.

Cahalan, D., Cisin, I. H., and Crossley, H. M., 1969, *American Drinking Practices. A National Study of Drinking Behavior and Attitudes,* College and University Press, New Haven, Conn.

Canadian Institute of Public Opinion, 1958, 1960, 1962, 1969, 1974, 1978, "Do you ever have occasion to use any alcoholic beverage such as liquor, wine or beer or are you a total abstainer?" The Gallup Poll of Canada, Canadian Institute of Public Opinion, Toronto.

Chambers, C. D. and Griffey, M. S., 1975, Use of legal substances within the general population: The sex and age variables, *Addict. Dis.* **2:**7–19.

Chappell, M. N., and Goldberg, H. D., 1953, *Use of Alcoholic Beverages by High School Students in Nassau County Related to Parental Permissiveness,* The Mrs. John S. Sheppard Foundation, New York.

Cooperstock, R., and Sims, M., 1971, Mood-modifying drugs prescribed in a Canadian city: Hidden problems, *Am. J. Public Health,* **61:**1007–1016.

Curlee, J., 1969, Alcoholism and the "empty nest," *Bull. Menninger Clin.,* **33:**165–171.

Curlee, J., 1970, A comparison of male and female patients at an alcoholism treatment center, *J. Psychol.* **74:**239–247.

Cutler, R., and Storm, T., 1973, *Drinking Practices in Three British Columbia Cities,* Vol. 1, *General Population Surveys,* The Alcoholism Foundation of British Columbia, Vancouver.

Damkot, D. K., Toussie, S. R., Akley, N. R., Geller, H. A., and Whitmore, D. G., 1977, *On-the-Road Driving Behavior and Breath Alcohol Concentration,* prepared for Department of Transportation, National Highway Traffic Safety Administration Contract No. HS-364-3-757.

Data Laboratories, 1977, *Report of a Survey on Alcohol Consumption and Liquor Laws,* survey conducted for *Weekend Magazine,* Canada.

de Lint, J., and Schmidt, W., 1976, Alcoholism and mortality, in: *The Biology of Alcoholism,* Vol. 4 (B. Kissin and H. Begleiter, eds.), pp. 275–305, Plenum, New York.

de Lint, J., Schmidt, W., and Pernanen, K., 1970, *The Ontario Drinking Survey: A Preliminary Report,* Addiction Research Foundation, Toronto.

Digital Resources Corporation, 1971, *A Model for Criminal Justice System Planning and Control,* Vol. 3, *School Surveys,* Long Beach, Calif.

Edwards, G., Hawker, N., Henseman, C., Peto, J., and Williamson, V., 1973, Alcoholics known or unknown to agencies: Epidemiological studies in a London suburb, *Br. J. Psychiatry* **123:**169–183.

Edwards, H. M., Johnston, M. E., and Simon, W., 1975, *The Incidence and Prevalence of Drug Use among Adults in Illinois,* Department of Mental Health, Institute for Juvenile Research, Chicago.

Ehrenreich, B., 1979, Is success dangerous to your health?, *Ms.* (May):51.

Emrick, C. D., 1975, A review of psychologically oriented treatments of alcoholism. II. The relative effectiveness of treatment versus no treatment, *J. Stud. Alcohol* **36:**88–108.

Ferrence, R. G., Adamtau, L. L., Murdock, W., and Brook, R. C., 1977, *Services for Alcoholics: A Study of Primary Care Physicians in the Lake Erie Region,* Substudy No. 887, Addiction Research Foundation, Toronto.

Fillmore, K. M., 1974, Drinking and problem drinking in early adulthood and middle age; An exploratory 20-year follow-up study, *Q. J. Stud. Alcohol* **35:**819–840.

Fitzgerald, J. L., and Mulford, H. A., 1978, Distribution of alcohol consumption and problem drinking. Comparison of sales records and survey data, *J. Stud. Alcohol* **39:**879–893.

Fraser, J., 1973, The female alcoholic, *Addictions* **20**:64–80.

Gallup, G., 1966, *Gallup Political Index; Political, Social and Economic Trends,* American Institute of Public Opinion, Princeton, N.J.

Gallup, G., 1966, 1968, 1974, 1977, "Do you ever drink?" The Gallup Poll, unpublished data, The Roper Center, New Haven, Conn.

Garrett, G. R., and Bahr, H. M., 1974, Comparison of self-rating and quantity-frequency measures of drinking, *Q. J. Stud. Alcohol* **35**:1293–1306.

Garzon, S., 1974, *Alcoholism and Women, Alcohol Health and Research World* (Summer). U.S. Department of Health, Education and Welfare, Washington, D.C.

Gillies, M., 1978, *The Durham Region Survey: Alcohol Use Characteristics of the Survey Sample,* Substudy No. 997, Addiction Research Foundation, Toronto.

Gomberg, E. S., 1976, Alcoholism in women, in: *The Biology of Alcoholism,* Vol. 4, *Social Aspects of Alcoholism* (B. Kissin and H. Begleiter, eds.), pp. 117–166, Plenum, New York.

Gunther, M., 1975, Female alcoholism: The drinker in the pantry, *Today's Health* **53**: 15–18.

Harford, T. C., and Mills, G. S., 1978, Age-related trends in alcohol consumption, *J. Stud. Alcohol* **39**:207–210.

Hays, J. R., 1971, The incidence of drug abuse among secondary school students in Houston. I. *St. Joseph Hosp. Med-Surg. J.* **6**(1,2).

Hays, J. R., 1972, The incidence of drug abuse among secondary school students in Houston, 1971. II. *St. Joseph Hosp. Med-Surg. J.* **7**:146–152.

Hays, J. R., 1974, The incidence of drug abuse among secondary school students in Houston, 1973, *St. Joseph Hosp. Med-Surg. J.* **9**:12–17.

Health and Welfare Canada, 1977, Smoking habits of Canadians, 1975, Technical Report Series (No. 7, December), Health and Welfare Canada, Ottawa.

Hetherington, R. W., Dickinson, J., Cipywnyk, D., and Hay, D., 1978, Drinking behaviour among Saskatchewan adolescents, *Can. J. Public Health* **69**:315–324.

Hollander, M. J., and Macurdy, E. A., 1978, *Alcohol and Drug Use among Vancouver Secondary School Students: 1970, 1974 and 1978,* Alcohol and Drug Commission, Ministry of Health, British Columbia.

Homiller, J. D., 1977, *Women and Alcohol: A Guide for State and Local Decision Makers,* Alcohol and Drug Problems Association of North America, Washington, D.C.

Homiller, J. D., 1978, Sex bias in alcoholism research, *Focus Alcohol Drug Issues* **1**:11, 28, 29.

Hunt, L. G., 1977, Incidence of first use of a drug: Significance and interpretations, *Addict. Dis.* **3**:177–186.

Hyland, J., and Scott, S., 1969, *Alcohol Consumption Tables: An Application of the Ledermann Equation to a Wide Range of Consumption Averages,* Addiction Research Foundation, Toronto.

Johnson, P., Armor, D. J., Polich, S., and Stambul, H., 1977, *U.S. Adult Drinking Practices: Time Trends, Social Correlates and Sex Roles,* prepared for the National Institute on Alcohol Abuse and Alcoholism, Santa Monica, Calif.

Johnston, L. D., Bachman, J. G., and O'Malley, P. M., 1977, *Drug Use among American High School Students 1975–1977,* National Institute on Drug Abuse, Rockville, Maryland.

Johnston, L. D., Bachman, J. G., and O'Malley, P. M., 1979, *Drugs in the Class of 1978: Behavior, Attitude and Recent National Trends,* National Institute on Drug Abuse, Washington, D.C.

Jones, B. M., and Jones, M. K., 1976, Women and alcohol: Intoxication, metabolism and the menstrual cycle, in: *Alcoholism Problems in Women and Children* (M. Greenblatt and M. A. Schuckit, eds.), pp. 103–136, Grune & Stratton, New York.

The Journal, 1979, Male, female alcoholism ratio probably equal, Jan. 1, Addiction Research Foundation, Toronto.

Keller, M., and Efron, V., 1955, The prevalence of alcoholism, *Q. J. Stud. Alcohol* **16:**619–644.

Kelley, C. M., 1976, *Crime in the United States,* Superintendent of Documents, U.S. Government Printing Office, Washington, D.C.

Knupfer, G., 1967, V. The epidemiology of problem drinking, *Am. J. Public Health,* **57:**973–986.

Korcok, M., 1978, Women—alcohol and other drugs, *Focus* **1:**4.

Kreitman, N., 1979, *Preventive Enthusiasm and Scientific Caution,* presented at the 10th Congress of the International Association for Suicide Prevention, June, Ottawa.

Labour Canada, 1976, *Women in the Labour Force: Facts and Figures,* Part 1. Labour Force Survey Catalogue No. L38-30/1976, Labour Canada, Ottawa.

Lee, E., and Shimmel, E., 1976, *A Study of the Drinking Behavior of 26,000 New York State Pupils: A Comparative Study of Four Populations,* Hunter College, New York, N.Y.

Liban, C., and Smart, R. G., 1980, Generational and other differences between males and females in problem drinking and its treatment, *Drug Alcohol Depend.* **5:**207–222.

Lisansky, E. S., 1958, The woman alcoholic, *Ann. Am. Acad. Polit. Soc. Sci.* **315:**73–81.

MacGregor, B., 1978, *Alcohol Consumption in Canada—Some Preliminary Findings of a National Survey in Nov.–Dec., 1976* (ERD-78-152), Health and Welfare Canada, Ottawa.

MacGregor, B., 1979a, An assessment of the visibility of Phase 111A of the Dialogue on Drinking Campaign, unpublished survey, November 1978, Health and Welfare Canada, Ottawa.

MacGregor, B., 1979b, Unpublished data, Health and Welfare Canada, Ottawa.

MacMahon, B., and Pugh, T. F., 1970, *Epidemiology: Principles and Methods,* Little, Brown, Boston, Mass.

Marshman, J., 1978, *The Treatment of Alcoholics: An Ontario Perspective, The Report of the Task Force on Treatment Services for Alcoholics,* Addiction Research Foundation, Toronto.

Mechanic, D., 1978, Sex, illness, illness behavior, and the use of health services, *Soc. Sci. Med.* **12B:**207–214.

Mellinger, G. D., Balter, M. B., Parry, H. J., Manheimer, D. I., and Cisin, I. H., 1974, An overview of psychotherapeutic drug use in the United States, in: *Drug Use: Epidemiological and Sociological Approaches* (E. Josephson and E. E. Carroll, eds.), pp. 333–366, Hemisphere Publishing, Washington, D.C.

Mulford, H. A., 1964, Drinking and deviant drinking, U.S.A., 1963, *Q. J. Stud. Alcohol* **25:**634–650.

Mulford, H. A., 1977, Women and men problem drinkers, *J. Stud. Alcohol* **38:**1624–1639.

Murdock, W., Ferrence, R. G., and Rush, B. R., 1980, *Services for Alcoholics: A Study of Medical and Social Service Facilities in the Lake Erie Region,* Addiction Research Foundation, Toronto.

Naegele, B. E., 1979, *Prevalence of Alcoholism among Canadian Women: "The Iceberg Phenomenon,"* prepared for the School of Addiction Studies, Addiction Research Foundation, Toronto, Ontario.

National Institute of Mental Health, 1971, *Admissions to Psychiatric Facilities for Alcohol-Related Disorders in the United States in 1970,* Rockville, Md.

National Opinion Research Center, 1977, General Social Survey (unpublished data), Roper Center, New Haven, Conn.

Ontario Ministry of Labour, 1978, *Women in the Labour Force, "Fact and Fiction,"* Factsheet No. I, Women's Bureau, Toronto.

Orford, J., Waller, S., and Peto, J., 1974, Drinking behavior and attitudes and their correlates among university students in England, *Q. J. Stud. Alcohol* **35**:1316–1374.

Pernanen, K., 1974, Validity of survey data on alcohol use, in: *Research Advances in Alcohol and Drug Problems,* Vol. 1 (R. J. Gibbins, Y. Israel, H. Kalant, R. E. Popham, W. Schmidt, and R. G. Smart, eds.), pp. 355–374, Wiley, New York.

Pinder, L., and Boyle, B., 1977, Double jeopardy employees, *Addictions* **24**(3): 19–35.

Pool, J. S., 1978, *An Assessment of the Visibility of Phase 2B of the Dialogue on Drinking Campaign,* prepared for the Evaluation Division of the Research Bureau Non-Medical Use of Drugs Directorate, Health and Welfare Canada.

Popham, R. E., and Schmidt, W., 1976, Some factors affecting the likelihood of moderate drinking by treated alcoholics, *J. Stud. Alcohol* **37**:868–882.

Provincial Secretariat for Justice, 1978, *Justice Statistics Ontario,* Toronto.

Rachal, J. V., Williams, J. R., Brehm, M. L., Cavanaugh, B., Moore, R. P., and Eckerman, W. C., 1975, *A National Study of Adolescent Drinking Behavior, Attitudes and Correlates* (Report No. PB-246-002; NIAAA/NCALI-75/27), U.S. National Technical Information Service, Springfield, Va.

Reid, A. E., 1977, *Alcoholism and Drug Treatment in Ontario: A Review of Current Programs,* University of Manitoba, Winnipeg.

Room, R., 1977, Measurement and distribution of drinking patterns and problems in general populations, in: *Alcohol-Related Disabilities* (G. Edwards, M. M. Gross, M. Kellar, J. Moser, and R. Room, eds.), pp. 61–87, WHO Offset Publication No. 32, World Health Organization, Geneva.

Schaps, E., and Rubin, E., 1973, *A Study of the Prevalence and Intensity of Drug and Alcohol Use in the Commonwealth of Pennsylvania,* Harrisburg, Pennsylvania, The Governor's Council on Drug and Alcohol Use in the Commonwealth of Pennsylvania.

Schmidt, W., and de Lint, J., 1972, Causes of deaths of alcoholics, *Q. J. Stud. Alcohol* **33**:171–185.

Schuckit, M. A., and Cahalan, D., 1976, Evaluation of alcohol treatment programs, in: *Alcohol and Alcohol Problems* (W. Filstead, J. J. Rossi, and M. Keller, eds.), pp. 229–266, Ballinger, Cambridge, Mass.

Simpson, H. M., Warren, R. A., Pagé-Valin, L., and Collard, D., 1978, *Analysis of Fatal Traffic Crashes in Canada, 1976, Focus: The Impaired Driver,* Traffic Injury Research Foundation of Canada, Ottawa.

Skinner, H. A., and Shaffner, K. R., 1978, *Sex Differences and Addiction: A Comparison of Male and Female Clients at the Clinical Institute,* Substudy No. 983, Addiction Research Foundation, Toronto.

Skog, O.-J., 1977, Does the same distributional model for alcohol consumption apply to both male and female populations? SIFA Mimeograph Series, No. 10, National Institute for Alcohol Research, Oslo.

Smart, R. G., and Goodstadt, M. S., 1976, *Alcohol and Drug Use among Ontario Adults: Report of a Household Survey, 1976,* Substudy No. 798, Addiction Research Foundation, Toronto.

Smart, R. G., and Goodstadt, M. S., 1977a, *Alcohol and Drug Use among Ontario Students in 1977: Preliminary Findings,* Substudy No. 889, Addiction Research Foundation, Toronto, Canada.

Smart, R. G., and Goodstadt, M. S., 1977b, Alcohol and drug use among Ontario adults, Unpublished data, Addiction Research Foundation, Toronto, Canada.

Smart, R., Fejer, D., Smith, D., and White, J., 1974, *Trends in Drug Use among Metropolitan Toronto High School Students: 1968–1974,* published by the Addiction Research Foundation of Ontario, Toronto, Canada.

Smith, G. A., Wolynetz, M. S., and Wiggins, T. R. I., 1976, *Drinking Drivers in Canada: A National Roadside Survey of the Blood Alcohol Concentrations in Nighttime Canadian Drivers,* Road and Motor Vehicle Safety Branch, Transport Canada, Ottawa.

Stafford, R. A., and Petway, J. M., 1977, Stigmatization of men and women problem drinkers and their spouses, *J. Stud. Alcohol* **38**:2109–2121.

Statistics Canada, 1945–1977, *Causes of Death: Provinces by Sex and Canada by Sex and Age,* Catalogue No. 84-203; Vital Statistics Catalogue No. 84-202, Statistics Canada, Ottawa.

Statistics Canada, 1951–1972, *Statistics of Criminal and Other Offences,* Catalogue No. 85-205, Statistics Canada, Ottawa.

Statistics Canada, 1969, 1974, 1978, 1979, *Canada Year Book,* Statistics Canada, Ottawa.

Statistics Canada, 1972–1975, *Hospital Morbidity 1972, 1973, 1974 and 1975,* Catalogue No. 82-206, Statistics Canada, Ottawa.

Statistics Canada, 1979, *Mental Health Statistics,* Vol. 1, *Institutional Admissions and Separations,* Health Division, Statistics Canada, Ottawa.

Traffic Injury Research Foundation, 1975, *Analysis of Fatal Traffic Crashes in Canada, 1973, Focus: The Impaired Driver,* Traffic Injury Research Foundation of Canada, Ottawa.

U.S. Department of Health, Education and Welfare, 1979, *Smoking and Health: A Report of the Surgeon General,* DHEW Publication No. (PHS) 79-500066, Rockville, Maryland.

Vingilis, E., 1979, *Sex and Age Characteristics of Suspected Impaired Drivers,* Substudy No. 1039, Addiction Research Foundation, Toronto.

Wanberg, K. W., and Knapp, J., 1970, Differences in drinking symptoms and behavior of men and women alcoholics, *Br. J. Addict.* **64**:347–355.

Warheit, G. J., Arey, S. A., and Swanson, E., 1976, Patterns of drug use: An epidemiologic overview, *J. Drug Issues* **6**:2232–2237.

Warren, R., 1979, *Why Are Women Safer Drivers?* Traffic Injury Research Foundation, Ottawa.

Wechsler, H., and McFadden, M., 1976, Sex differences in adolescent alcohol and drug use: A disappearing phenomenon, *J. Stud. Alcohol* **37**:1291–1301.

Wechsler, H., Thum, D., Demone, H. W., and Dwinnell, J., 1972, Social characteristics and blood alcohol level: Measurements of subgroup differences, *Q. J. Stud. Alcohol* **33**:132–147.

Wechsler, H., Demone, H. W., and Gottlieb, N., 1978, Drinking patterns of Greater Boston adults: Subgroup differences on the QFV Index, *J. Stud. Alcohol* **39** (7).

Whitehead, P. C., 1974, *Drinking Practices and Attitudes in Saskatchewan,* prepared for AWARE, the Saskatchewan Program for Responsible Use of Alcohol, London, Canada.

Whitehead, P. C., 1975, *Trends in the Consumption of Alcoholic Beverages in Canada: Provincial Patterns and Differences among Types of Beverages,* Addiction Research Foundation, London, Ontario.

Whitehead, P. C., 1977, *Alcohol and Young Drivers: Impact and Implications of Lowering the Drinking Age,* Health Protection Branch, Department of National Health and Welfare, Ottawa, Monograph Series, No. 1, (November).

Whitehead, P. C., and Ferrence, R. G., 1976, Women and children last: Implications of trends in consumption for women and young people, in: *Alcoholism Problems in Women and Children* (M. Greenblatt and M. A. Schuckit, eds.), pp. 163–192, Grune & Stratton, New York.

Woodruff, R. A., Guze, S. B., and Clayton, P. J., 1973, Alcoholics who see a psychiatrist compared with those who do not, *Q. J. Stud. Alcohol* **34**:1162–1171.

Working Group on Women Alcoholics for the Addiction Research Foundation Task Force on Treatment Services, 1977, *Women with Alcohol Problems and Their Treatment Needs in Ontario,* Addiction Research Foundation, Toronto.

Zylman, R., 1974, Fatal crashes among Michigan youth following reduction of legal drinking age, *Q. J. Stud. Alc.* **35**:283–286.

4

Sex Differences in Psychoactive Drug Use

Recent Epidemiology

ROBERTA G. FERRENCE AND PAUL C. WHITEHEAD

1. INTRODUCTION

The study of sex differences in the use of psychoactive drugs is particularly appropriate and timely for several reasons. Prior to the late 1960s, epidemiological studies of the incidence of drug-using behaviors were few in number. The socially significant increase in the use of illicit drugs during the late 1960s and early 1970s stimulated the collection of a sizable body of data on drug use throughout North America. These data offer an opportunity for retrospective analyses of drug-using behaviors.

Recently, there has been a growing interest in sex differences relative to a number of different types of behavior, and this interest is undoubtedly tied to elevated consciousness about the status of women in our society. Concurrent with changes in perception have been marked changes in some types of behavior that can best be described as a convergence of patterns for males and females. The reduction and in some cases the near disappearance of the well-known "double standard" during the present decade, particularly among young people, has been documented in a number of areas such as drinking behavior (Blackford, 1977) and sexual behavior (*Playboy Magazine,* 1976).

Until the late 1960s, the nonmedical use of psychoactive drugs was

ROBERTA G. FERRENCE ● Addiction Research Foundation, Toronto, Ontario.   PAUL C. WHITEHEAD ● Department of Sociology, University of Western Ontario, London, Ontario; and Addiction Research Foundation, London, Ontario.

much less widespread than it has been during the past decade. Studies carried out at that time tended to focus on smaller, clinical populations of heavy drug users who were not representative of the general population (e.g., Olson, 1964; Ellinwood et al., 1966). Researchers were restricted to relatively small surveys because the technology required to carry out large epidemiological surveys was less developed. However, illicit drug use was undoubtedly considered more deviant than at present, and this attitude may be the more important factor in explaining the emphasis on the psychological characteristics of drug users. For example, in studies of addict populations, female drug addicts are variously described as more nonconformist than males (Maglin, 1974), more attention-seeking (Ellinwood et al., 1966), and more deviant (Chein et al., 1965).

Recent studies based on samples from the general population provide a more accurate picture of sex differences in drug use. However, in these studies, the tendency has been to collect demographic and socioeconomic data rather than to attempt to describe psychological profiles of users.

In the study of patterns of drug use during the past decade, there are a number of theoretical frameworks that can be used to generate hypotheses about the nature of relationships that can be expected. There are three principal advantages to starting with hypotheses. First, it focuses the analysis and allows for the generation of criteria that can be used in deciding what data constitute an appropriate test. Second, the fact that the hypotheses are generated from broader theoretical frameworks means that it is possible to have greater confidence in those hypotheses that are affirmed, and it makes us less quick to reject a hypothesis that is supported by only some of the data. Third, it helps to distinguish between changes that are real and those that may be the product of fairly random fluctuations or sampling error.

Four different though somewhat overlapping models seem particularly useful in the study of sex differences. These involve the theoretical concepts of deviance, the diffusion of innovation, the social network, and socioeconomic status.

Deviance Model

What we call a *deviance model* is based primarily on socialization experiences as they are manifested in sex roles. Such a model attempts to account for sex differences in rates of drug-using behavior in terms of what are generally considered socially acceptable types and levels of behavior for males and females.

Studies of crime have repeatedly demonstrated that males show higher rates of law-violating behavior than females. Sutherland and

Cressey (1966) have summarized much of this research by pointing out that:

> . . . the crime rate for men is greatly in excess of the rate for women—in all nations, all communities within a nation, all age groups, all periods of history for which organized statistics are available, and for all types of crime except for those peculiar to women, such as infanticide and abortion.

The exact mechanisms that may account for these empirical regularities have yet to be specified. In spite of some claims that appear to be to the contrary (cf. Smart, 1976), the magnitude of the difference is too great to be explained in terms of differential treatment in the administration of justice (see, for example, Harris, 1977).

Males and females, even as brothers and sisters, share many experiences, such as parents and neighborhoods, but these experiences are filtered through social mores dominated by strongly held definitions of the roles that are appropriate for males and females. Hence, they experience different patterns of supervision, different emphases in socialization, different opportunities for deviant and nondeviant behavior, and, ultimately, different rates of unlawful behavior. On this basis, we would expect females to have much lower rates of illicit drug use than males and to use these drugs less often and in smaller quantities. Rates of licit drug use would vary, depending on historical patterns of use. For example, we might expect drugs, such as tobacco, that were first used widely by males to have higher sex ratios of use than drugs such as tranquilizers, which were introduced more recently and were initially used by both sexes with much less differentiation.

Once the use of a drug has become widespread, the stigma associated with its use decreases. One would therefore expect rates of use to be relatively more differentiated by sex when a drug is first used than when it has been in use for some time. Because older people acquired their patterns of use when a particular drug was first introduced and have probably persisted in these patterns, we would expect sex ratios of use to be more pronounced among older persons than among younger ones for all but the most recently introduced drugs.

The use of opiates provides a good illustration of the deviance model. The U.S. Harrison Act, passed in 1914, made the possession of opiates illegal except on a doctor's prescription. This marked the point at which sex ratios for the use of these drugs passed from well below 100 to well above it (Cuskey et al., 1972). Women presumably were less inclined than men to behave illegally in regard to opiate use.

Thus, on the basis of the deviance model, we would expect substantial differences in the way the use of licit and illicit drugs is distributed among men and women.

Diffusion of Innovation

The diffusion of innovation model has been used to describe the adoption of innovations as diverse as agricultural practices, children's games, contraceptive techniques, fluoridation, and the prescribing habits of physicians (Katz et al., 1963; Rogers, 1962; Bell and Champion, 1976). In general terms, the invention or discovery of a product, substance, or method is followed by a period of diffusion characterized by an exponential increase in use. The final phase occurs when use peaks and then levels off (continuance) or declines (discontinuance). Adoption is more likely to occur if use is supported by existing values. This process can be graphically represented by an S curve that represents cumulative use over time. Innovations with a high rate of adoption such as drugs tend to have a low rate of discontinuance. Thus, the effect of introducing a new drug is usually additive rather than substitutive relative to total drug use (Whitehead, 1974, 1976). This model is analogous to the epidemic model for infectious diseases, but it is more appropriate to describe the use of drugs, which is largely voluntary and is spread by a somewhat different mechanism than infectious diseases (cf. Hunt, 1977).

Early adopters tend to be those with high social status, a high level of education, more exposure to mass media, more contact with agents of change, and greater social participation (Bell and Champion, 1976). On the basis of this description, we would expect males to adopt the use of most drugs earlier than females, and college students before other members of the population. The adoption of specific drugs would, of course, vary according to the nature of the agent of change and the nature of the channels of interpersonal communication. Thus, we would expect early adopters of marijuana, for example, to be higher-class male university students in cosmopolitan centers, and we would expect early adopters of tranquilizers to be middle-aged and older women, who are more likely than other segments of the population to have contact with physicians.

"Late adopters" are generally lower in social status and tend to secure new ideas from peers via interpersonal channels (Bell and Champion, 1976). Thus, women, those persons with lower education or of lower social class, the very old, and the very young would tend to become users at a later stage of diffusion, if at all.

The use of cigarettes, for instance, was widely adopted in the early 1920s by males, who were introduced to them by soldiers returning from Europe after the war. However, use among women did not become widespread until World War II (Green and Nemzer, 1973; Schuman, 1977), when large numbers of women were employed in factories, had more money, and had greater access to users. In general, we would expect to find that those drugs that were widely adopted by one sex, at an earlier period in history than by the other, would tend to peak at an earlier point and to decline sooner as well, if discontinuance ultimately occurred.

Social Network Model

The social network model does not constitute a coherent theory of sex differences in drug use; rather, it represents a framework that ties together various observed regularities in the social behaviors of acquiring and using drugs. It is a first cousin of Sutherland's theory of differential association (Sutherland and Cressey, 1966). Much of the literature relevant to this model is reviewed by Bowker (1977). Males are seen as the "agent of contagion" or "carriers" of patterns of drug use to females (Freeland and Campbell, 1973; Bowker, 1977). Males initiate females into drug use and generally acquire most drugs for them and dispense most drugs to them. Certain drugs such as tobacco can be legally and easily obtained, and there is no clear evidence that distributors of cigarettes encourage use among one sex more than the other, although males used to be more often the target of advertising and promotion campaigns involving free cigarettes. (The promotion of other forms of tobacco is aimed almost solely at males.) The majority of other licit psychoactive drugs are legally available only by prescription through physicians (mostly male), and there is evidence that women are more likely than men to receive these drugs for the same presenting symptoms (Dunnell and Cartwright, 1972). An exception to this pattern occurs in the use of stimulant drugs by athletes, when male physicians and coaches dispense drugs to a predominantly male group. Women users are also more likely to have female reference groups that discuss health, health problems, and medication (Linn and Davis, 1971). Thus, while men are the primary distributors of licit drugs to women, other women provide peer-group support and information.

The distribution of illicit drugs is also largely controlled by males. In fact, Bowker (1977) contended that "access to (and control of) the illegal drug distribution system . . . is the primary factor in higher male rates of the use of certain kinds of drugs." There is considerable evidence to support this statement. Males are much more likely to buy their own drugs (Bowker, 1977); to acquire them from people they do not know well (Nielson and Hirabayashi, 1975); to grow their own marijuana (Nielson and Hirabayashi, 1975); to be introduced to drugs by other males, usually in small all-male groups; to introduce them to females in larger mixed groups (Goldstein, 1966; Wolfson et al., 1971; Freeland and Campbell, 1973; Bowker, 1977); and in the case of intravenous use of heroin, to "shoot" alone and to "shoot" females (Howard and Borges, 1970).

Illicit drug use among males is largely influenced by peer-group relationships, whereas females begin and continue drug use in the context of dating relationships (Freeland and Campbell, 1973). Bowker (1977) found that male college students were much more likely than females to use drugs as a means of facilitating sexual relations. He contended that because women are usually given drugs by men rather than purchasing them, they feel more obligated to continue in the relationship and to engage in sexual activity.

The "extramedical" use of licit drugs appears to follow a similar pattern. Parry et al. (1973b) suggested that men who distribute drugs to others are most likely to give them to their wives or women friends, whereas females tend to distribute them to female friends or family members.

Many of the data we have reviewed that focus on factors in the social network of drug users indicate that female drug use is generally restricted to situations involving fairly intimate relationships with men; for example, doctor and patient, boyfriend and girlfriend, and probably husband and wife. Males, on the other hand, engage in the use of drugs in a much wider variety of settings.

Socioeconomic Model

Men and women differ in socioeconomic status, and it is likely that this difference is reflected in the type and level of drug use in which they engage. Although there are no major sex differences in the average level of education achieved, women are less likely than men to earn income, and the incomes of employed women are considerably lower than those of men (Ontario Ministry of Labour, 1978).

On the basis of this information, we would expect women and men at the same level of personal income to have comparable rates of drug use. Unfortunately, sex-specific data on drug use are not reported by level of personal income, and family income is not an appropriate measure for comparison. However, if socioeconomic status is related to drug use, we would expect women who earn incomes to have higher levels of drug use than women who have no direct earnings, and we would expect employed women with higher incomes to have higher rates of use than those with lower incomes. Sex differences in rates of use would probably increase with age because income levels rise faster for males than for females.

There are likely to be differences that are specific to certain types of drugs because of the different costs associated with acquiring them. The use of expensive drugs, such as heroin, would be more highly differentiated by sex than the use of less costly drugs, such as marijuana. Cigarettes are cheaper yet, and prescription drugs are generally inexpensive compared with most illicit drugs and are often covered by drug plans. Furthermore, it would be easier for married women without independent incomes to obtain money from their husbands to buy licit than illicit drugs.

2. METHODOLOGICAL ISSUES AFFECTING SEX DIFFERENCES IN DRUG USE

There are many problems involved in acquiring data on the use of drugs (Whitehead and Smart, 1972; Petzel et al., 1973; Mercer and Smart, 1974; Sadava, 1975; Single et al., 1975; Smart, 1975, 1978; Hubbard et al., 1976; Richards and Blevens, 1977; White and Fallis, 1977a). However, with few exceptions (e.g., Parry et al., 1970–1971), the effect of these difficulties on reported sex differences in rates of drug use has received little attention. In most cases, a sex distribution of some variable related to methodology—for example, accuracy of response—is presented, but the implications are not discussed.

Two major sources of potential error with regard to sex differences involve sampling procedures and the reporting process.

Biases in Sampling

It is commonly known that household samples of the general population underrepresent males, particularly young males, because they are relatively mobile and are more likely to live away from home, to have no fixed address, to be institutionalized, to live in places that are less accessible to interviewers, to have no telephones, and to spend less time at home. Since the use of drugs is most common among young men (except for a few licit drugs) and because drug users in particular are even more likely to be inaccessible, surveys of the general population concerning drug-using behavior probably underrepresent male users more than female users. Such underrepresentation is more likely to affect rates of heavy use and rates of less frequently used drugs, such as heroin. There would be less effect on rates of use of more conventional drugs, such as tobacco, because the use of these drugs would not be a major reason for reduced accessibility and because use is distributed more evenly and more widely in the population.

The conditions that lead to underrepresentation would very likely be more prevalent at some times rather than at others (cf. Hubbard et al., 1976). For instance, during the diffusion phase of drug use, males, who are in a higher-status category, would tend to be the early adopters. The use of drugs is also most deviant in this phase, so the males involved would very likely be those who are least accessible to interviewers. Thus, it is likely that reported rates of male use during the early diffusion phase would diverge more from actual rates of use than at a later time when drug use is more widespread. Because this divergence would be in the direction of lower rates of use, the rate of increase of drug use would appear to be steeper than it actually is. Reported rates of use for females would appear to rise more gradually than those for males because the diffusion phase for females would be occurring at a time when the use of the particular drug had become more acceptable and the female users, who are generally easier to locate than males, would be more representative of the general population. Such bias has the effect of distorting the details of the portrait of changes in rates of drug-using behavior, but it does not markedly alter the general picture, especially with regard to sex differences. Reported sex ratios of use would simply be a little lower than they really are when a new drug is introduced.

Attempts have also been made to produce estimates of use based on clinical and other special populations (Greenwood, 1971; Dupont and Piemme, 1973; Richman and Dunham, 1976). However, with respect to sex differences, such estimates are probably just as biased, and the bias would be less consistent, because of the differential rates of use of various types of facilities by males and females. For example, estimates using medical clinics might overrepresent females, whereas those based on rates of arrest would tend to underrepresent them.

Samples of high school students are probably most representative of the total population of the earliest grades studied (i.e., grades 6–9). Johnston et al. (1977) estimated that 15–20% of students drop out before they graduate. It is generally believed that males drop out at a higher rate than females, although one study (Wechsler and McFadden, 1976) found no sex differences in this rate. In addition, students in technical courses, who are mostly males, are more likely to leave after grade 10.*

"Dropouts" also have considerably higher rates of drug use (Utah Governor's Citizen Advisory Committee, 1969). Even though some drug use may begin after dropping out, most regular users have already established their pattern of use before they leave school (Annis and Watson, 1975). Thus, high school students become less and less repre-

---

* In parts of Canada where grade 13 is available, students in this grade are probably of higher socioeconomic status on the average, so that their patterns of sex differences would be more characteristic of higher socioeconomic categories. Commercial programs, in contrast to academic programs, extend to only grade 12.

sentative of young people as grade increases, and this process may be more pronounced for males.

An additional sampling problem is caused by differential rates of absenteeism among student drug users and nonusers. Single et al. (1975) found that absenteeism for users was three times that for nonusers. If heavy users are more likely to be male and more likely to be absent than light users, observed sex ratios of use among high school students would be lower than actual sex ratios.

A further sampling problem is that males are less likely to indicate their sex on a questionnaire (Blackford, 1972). If such males are not representative of other male students in their drug use, bias may be introduced.

In summary, sampling problems tend to lead to underrepresentation of males in general and male drug users in particular. This fact would have the effect of lowering reported sex ratios of illicit drugs and possibly licit drugs.

Biases in Reporting

Biases in reporting are of particular concern in research on drug-using behavior because of the extensive use of self-report methods for the collection of data. The problems include those that are typical of self-report techniques, though they are magnified by the fact that most of the behaviors are deviant, in varying degrees.

Errors involving problems of recall in surveys of drug-using behaviors may differentially affect males and females. Single et al. (1975) studied inconsistencies in self-reported drug use and found that those respondents who have inconsistent responses at two points in time are most likely to be infrequent users of licit drugs who have not used the drug recently. Although this finding would affect sex differences in rates of use for those drugs that are used experimentally by proportionately more of one sex, usually females, than the other, the problem is much reduced because the majority of studies have asked about recent use or use during a specified previous time period rather than "ever used." Furthermore, if the stereotype that females are generally more conscientious than males is valid, they would be more likely to respond accurately to questions about previous use, and this effect would tend to minimize underreporting due to infrequent use.

Deliberate underreporting or overreporting of drug use could stem from several sources. In many social groups, any use of illicit drugs is considered deviant, as is heavy use of licit drugs. If there is concern about stigma, one would predict that underreporting would occur. If the respondent attaches status to such "deviant" behaviors, theoretically overreporting would occur. Reviews of studies that tested for reliability or validity (Whitehead and Smart, 1972; Smart, 1975) indicate that underreporting is the most frequent source of inaccuracy, probably because status would more likely be gained by overreporting use to peers rather than to researchers. Barr et al. (1974, 1975, 1976, 1977) found that self-reports of inaccurate responses by high school students were between 7% and 9% for males and 4–6% for females. However, it is not clear which drugs were reported most inaccurately by which sex group.

Since males are less restricted in their behavior than females and more often rewarded by their peers for deviant behavior, one would predict that underreporting would be greatest for illicit drug use among females. Conversely, one would expect males to underreport the use of licit drugs, particularly those such as tranquilizers that are used mostly by women. Cooperstock (1977) has found this to be the case for licit drug use. Parry et al. (1970–1971) examined the validity of responses among users of licit psychotropic drugs and found that about 29% of males gave invalid responses compared with 18% of females. They also suggested that underreporting among males is related to higher rates of use by females and the accompanying negative attitudes that males have toward these drugs. Thus, the legal status of the drug, the general level of use, and the sex ratio of rates of use can all affect the amount of stigma attached to drug use.

Attempts to measure this phenomenon of underreporting have led to the inclusion of bogus drugs in surveys of drug use. The names of these drugs usually sound like some of the more exotic hallucinogens that are used mostly by males. Reported rates of use tend to be very low— usually less than 1% (Whitehead and Smart, 1972)—and Kopplin et al. (1977) report no sex differences. Whitehead and Smart (1972) and Petzel et al. (1973) have indicated that heavy users of drugs, who are predominantly male, are more likely to report use of a bogus drug. However, as Single et al. (1975) pointed out, this may be unintentional overreporting by users who feel they have "tried everything."

Other studies have investigated the effects of anonymity and personal contact on the reported use of drugs (King, 1970). While neither of these variables is a significant source of error, underreporting tends to occur during personal interviews in response to questions regarding current use and heavy use. Since males are more likely than females to be heavy users of most drugs, there is probably an effect on the sex ratio for heavy but not all drug use. However, since most surveys are carried out by mail or telephone or by administering questionnaires to groups, only a few studies would be affected.

A more general problem involves the failure to report negative findings (cf. Block, 1976). Some studies of drug use do not report male and female data separately. Relying solely on published reports of sex differences could result, therefore, in higher sex ratios than are actually the case. It is partly for this reason that we have in many cases gone back to the original data in order to examine sex differences, whether or not such information figured prominently in the published reports.

We have discussed some of the ways in which methodological problems in surveys of drug use can affect sex differences in reported rates. Because of the lack of any systematic attempt to measure these effects in various populations, it is difficult to estimate the extent to which they affect reported sex differences. However, it is likely that sex ratios for reported rates of use are most accurate when a particular drug is used with equal frequency by males and females. In such a case, intentional error should be at a minimum because it would probably be equally acceptable for either sex to use the drug. As sex ratios diverge from 100, the sex with the lower rate of use tends to underreport use. However, this source of bias is probably minor, as other measures of use of licit drugs—for example, those based on prescription records (Sims, 1973)—show sex ratios of use that are very similar to those found in self-report studies (e.g., Parry, 1968).

Sampling biases are probably more serious, particularly when we are dealing with household surveys of the use of lesser-used illicit drugs such as heroin (Glenn, 1977). Since the least accessible "floating" group probably represents a sizable proportion of all users, it is unlikely that this sampling bias that underrepresents males would be balanced by such a large reporting bias on the part of females. However, the reported pattern of use for these drugs involves a predominance of males. Underrepresentation of males may artificially reduce the already large preponderance of males, but this possibility again involves distortion rather than a grossly false image of the situation.

In summary, sampling biases that lead to underrepresentation of males would tend to lower sex ratios, particularly for illicit drugs. However, reporting biases would tend to result in slightly higher sex ratios for illicit drugs and slightly lower sex ratios for the medical use of licit drugs. Our estimate of the net effect of these factors is that reported sex ratios for illicit drug use and nonmedical use of licit drugs are somewhat low, whereas those for the medical use of licit drugs and for tobacco are probably close to those for actual use because the reporting and sampling biases tend to cancel each other out.

Our concern is with fairly large changes in rates of use, with changes over time within the same population, and with sex ratios of rates, which means that consistent under- or overreporting by both sexes is controlled (cf. Johnston, 1977). Thus, within this context, the very real limitations of much of the data on drug use are somewhat minimized.

3. METHODS

This analysis is restricted to studies of drug use in Canada and the United States largely because most of the surveys with adequate sample size and appropriate methodology were carried out on this continent. Some excellent work has been done in other countries, but we feel that limiting our efforts to North America produces a more uniform data base without unduly reducing the quantity of available information.

Our concern is with sex differences in the nonmedical use of psychoactive drugs other than alcohol, which is dealt with in another chapter. The substances in question include illicit drugs, such as marijuana, heroin, cocaine, and the hallucinogens; licit but nonprescription substances such as tobacco and solvents*; and prescription drugs such as the tranquilizers, sedatives, and stimulants, which are sometimes obtained from nonmedical sources. *Tobacco use* refers to cigarette smoking unless otherwise specified.

The adequacy of information is highly variable from drug to drug. For instance, studies of cigarette smoking are fairly extensive and generally of good quality. Marijuana use has been fairly well studied but less comprehensively. Reports of heroin and cocaine use are subject to many methodological problems, although reasonable estimates can be made through the use of a variety of techniques (Rittenhouse, 1977), and error generally occurs in a direction that underestimates use.

Studies of the use of licit psychoactive drugs, such as tranquilizers, sedatives, and stimulants pose different sorts of problems. The distinction between licit and illicit sources of supply is seldom made, though of crucial importance. Drugs that are obtained from physicians can be used for medical or nonmedical reasons; even medical use can be as prescribed or not. At best, only one of these factors is taken into account in any particular study, and then, not always the same one.

To limit ourselves to those studies that clearly differentiate between medical and nonmedical use (e.g., Bakal et al., 1976; Smart et al., 1977) would have severely restricted our analysis. In fact, few studies made this distinction before 1974. What we have done instead is to include various types of use and to indicate their differences in context.

All surveys of drug-using behavior have collected information on the sex of the respondents; however, rates of drug use by sex have been

---

*With the exception of alcohol.

reported irregularly, and rates of drug use by sex and age (or grade) have been reported infrequently. This is partly a reflection of the relatively low degree of interest in sex differences a decade ago. It also reflects the fact that many of the surveys have involved relatively small samples (200–500 respondents being typical), so that breakdowns by age and sex become meaningless because of the small number of cases in most categories. This problem also occurs with larger samples (over 1000) for the less frequently used drugs.

Almost 2000 studies of drug use in Canada and the United States are available for analysis [Drug Abuse Epidemiology Data Center (DAE-DAC), personal communication (1978)]. In order to focus on the data that are of the highest quality and are most useful for testing hypotheses, we have not included most of these studies. All clinical investigations and studies with fewer than 500 respondents were set aside. Surveys that had obviously biased samples (for example, those conducted in private schools or among psychology students) were also omitted, as were studies with low rates of response. This process of elimination reduced the total number of surveys to about 90. Thus, we embarked on our analysis with a group of studies that we felt met our criteria for sample size, representativeness in the case of national samples, and high response rates. In spite of this sifting and paring, there are still wide variations in the measures of drug-using behavior employed (lifetime prevalence, period prevalence, and point prevalence are all used, but seldom in the same study) and with the categories of drug use (e.g., LSD, hallucinogens, psychedelics) in the remaining studies. The use of varying terminology has meant that in some cases, we have had to omit data that are not comparable; in others, we have had to report rates of use that are not representative of an entire class of drugs. For example, for high school students, we report rates of use of barbiturates rather than all sedatives because this is the category used by most researchers studying that particular population. As much as possible, we have resolved these problems by controlling for measure of use and by comparing studies with similar categories of drug use. This approach means, of course, that the number of studies that is appropriate to the test of any hypothesis is small and varies from one hypothesis to another. [See Rittenhouse (1978) for a detailed examination of the comparability of drug use data with particular emphasis on the measurement of patterns of use and other variables.]

Many of the better large-scale surveys carried out in various communities and areas of North America are single cross-sectional studies or surveys that were carried out at two very close points in time, for example, 1971 and 1972. Because of the variability in methodology between studies and the problems of comparing data from different regions, we have restricted our use of these types of studies to questions that do not involve examining changes over time.

To study trends in rates of use for males and females or changes in sex ratios over time, we have focused on two types of data. First are the general population surveys of youth and adults that have been conducted nationally at intervals in both the United States and Canada (e.g., Gallup Poll; Health and Welfare Canada; U.S. Department of Health, Education, and Welfare). These studies are of high quality and are limited only in that they do not include all the drugs of interest, but they do focus on the most commonly used drugs. Second, we have examined a number of high school surveys that were repeated at three or more points in time (e.g., Bakal et al., 1974, 1976; Blackford, 1977). There are some differences in methodology across communities, but basically, the same methodology was used in each community over time. Both types of survey provide sex-specific data for school grades.

Surveys of college students have not been included in our analysis for a number of reasons: college students are not representative of their age group; virtually all the studies are limited to a particular region, or more often, a specific university; and few provide useful longitudinal data. Other surveys of the general population and of high school students that report results by sex, but not by age or grade, are useful in only some instances.

Our intention is to provide an overall picture of patterns of the nonmedical use of drugs in the general population. There is considerable evidence that such use occurs among residents of institutions, such as psychiatric hospitals, nursing homes, and penal institutions (Whitehead et al., 1973; Botterell, 1975). However, since our concern is with sex differences rather than the total extent of drug use, the inclusion of data for populations that are distributed much differently by sex could seriously bias our interpretation. Therefore, we have not included them.

4. RESULTS

Three sets of questions need to be answered about sex differences in the use of psychoactive drugs. First, do sex differences exist for the use of some or all drugs? Second, is there any evidence that sex differences (or their absence) have changed? Third, if changes have taken place, how might one account for them, and what are the implications for the future?

To answer these general questions, we first examine sex-specific data on drug use from various sources and describe sex-specific rates of drug use and changes in these rates and in sex ratios of use over time.

Second, we present and test a series of hypotheses derived from the models of drug use described previously.

Our analysis is heavily based on sex ratios: the sex ratio for a particular drug is the percentage of male users divided by the percentage of female users multiplied by 100. Equal rates of use for males and females result in a sex ratio of 100. Sex ratios above 100 indicate a preponderance of males, whereas those below 100 result from an excess of females.

Sex ratios are a simple standardized measure that facilitates comparisons among different sets of data. In some of our analyses, we have used median sex ratios. This approach is advantageous because it reduces the influence of highly deviant values and because sex ratios do not constitute true interval data.

Sex ratios are less stable than actual rates of use, so that it is necessary to be cautious in interpreting changes over time and across studies. This fact is particularly important because many of the rates are based on relatively small study samples (1000–1500), and age and sex-specific rates of use of the least-used drugs can involve a small number of users.

Abelson and Fishburne (1976) give 95% confidence limits for rates of use of various drugs among youth aged 12–17 ($N = 986$). For a drug with a low rate of use, such as cocaine, the rate is 3.4% with limits of 2.2 and 5.1. Even for a widely used drug such as marijuana, with a rate of 22.4%, the limits are 19.3 and 25.8. Since the confidence interval would be even larger for sex-specific rates, one can appreciate the amount of variation in sex ratios that could be entirely random. For this reason, we have placed the greatest emphasis on those trends that involve large differences in sex ratios or those that have persisted for several years.

Changes in Rates and Sex Ratios of Drug Use

Data on rates and sex ratios of use indicate that sex differences in drug use do exist and that for many drugs, these differences are quite substantial. In certain years, for certain drugs, sex ratios may approximate 100. However, an examination of trends over time usually indicates that this parity is part of a larger pattern in which sex ratios are increasing or decreasing.

In general terms, the highest sex ratios are for the illicit "hard" drugs—heroin, cocaine, and the hallucinogens—and the inhalants, which can be legally obtained. Sex ratios for marijuana use are slightly lower. In all these cases, sex ratios are higher for adults than for young people.

The licit drugs—sedatives, stimulants, and tranquilizers—have high sex ratios for nonmedical use and much lower sex ratios for any use or for specifically medical use. The difference is much greater among adults than among youth. Tobacco is currently used about equally by young persons of both sexes, but rates are higher among adult males than among adult females.

Students.   Three sets of studies of students in high school and the late elementary grades allow us to appreciate changes in rates of use and sex ratios among young people over time. The San Mateo surveys (Blackford, 1977) extend from 1968 to 1977; the Toronto and Ontario surveys (Smart et al., 1975; Smart et al., 1977) were conducted in 1968, 1970, 1972, 1974, and 1977; and surveys were conducted in Alberta in 1971, 1974, and 1976 (Bakal et al., 1974, 1976). Other data sets have been excluded in this analysis because of limited time spans or very different measures of use.

These data are not exactly comparable, but since we are examining changes in reported rates of use or sex ratios, this potential problem is minimized.

Tobacco.   Rates of tobacco use peaked about 1973 and decreased slightly by 1977, but the sex ratio decreased more markedly from an excess of male to a clear excess of female smokers. By 1977, the sex ratio was below 90. Rates of use are currently still high, ranging from 30% to over 50% of students.

Illicit Use of Tranquilizers.   Illicit use of tranquilizers was generally below 10% during the entire period, and rates were lowest in 1976 (7.1%) and 1977 (5.0%). During the period 1968–1974, sex ratios were low (57–80), but they were highest in 1976 (99) and 1977 (111).

Illicit Use of Stimulants.   There was sizable variation in rates of illicit use of stimulants across studies, but rates of use tended to decrease somewhat over time. Sex ratios generally indicated a modest preponderance of females (85–95) and a decrease between 1968, when there was a clear preponderance of males, and 1977, when the sex ratio was close to 100.

Illicit Use of Barbiturates.   The illicit use of barbiturates peaked about 1971 or 1972 and decreased after that time. At their peak, the rates of use tended to be between 15% and 18%; they have since declined to between 6% and 9%. Sex ratios have generally been lowest and below 100 since the peak year, but the pattern is not uniform. Most of the sex ratios were between 90 and 100, but a few were higher, on the order of 120 and 145.

Marijuana.   Rates of marijuana use do not appear to have peaked in any of the series of surveys, but the rates of increase were largest in the early 1970s and far smaller (1% or 2% per year) in the mid to late 1970s. In California, rates of use in 1976 and 1977 were about 46%, while in the Canadian cities, they were approximately 25%. Sex ratios were consistently above 100 in all the surveys, but there are marked differences between San Mateo and the Canadian communities. In San Mateo, the sex ratios ranged from 107 to 117 between 1969 and 1977. In the Canadian cities, the range was between 126 and 141 for the same period. The highest observed rate in Canada (25% in 1977) was still lower than the lowest rate in San Mateo (32% in 1968 and 1969), so it is not possible to ascertain whether the sex ratios would have been more similar in a circumstance of equal rates of use.

LSD.   Rates of use of LSD peaked in 1974 in San Mateo (13.4%) and in 1970 in Toronto (8.5%)—probably also in Alberta—and by 1977, both sets of rates were less than 10% (9.9% in San Mateo and 6.2% in Toronto).

Sex ratios generally decreased between 1968 and 1972–1973, when they were between 120 and 130 in all three communities. In San Mateo, they decreased further during the 1970s to about 10%. In the Canadian cities, they fell to between 130 and 140 from 1970 to 1977.

Cocaine.   Very limited data are available and they suggest low rates of use (under 5%) and high sex ratios (160–190).

Heroin.   Rates of heroin use were uniformly under 4%, and most sex ratios were between 135 and 160, with no clear trend over time.

*Inhalants.**   Rates of glue sniffing were consistently less than 6%. Sex ratios declined to about 100 in the early 1970s and rose somewhat in the late 1970s.

The relationships between age (or grade) and rates of drug use and sex ratios are a relevant consideration because there is so much variation across age categories. The characteristic pattern for rates of use is that they increase with grade in school. This can be observed over a period of years and across a number of surveys conducted in different communities (Tables 1–9). Two minor exceptions to this dominant pattern occur. First, rates of solvent or glue sniffing tend to be highest in the lower rather than the higher grades. Second, rates of use are frequently a bit lower in grade 12 than in grade 11, very likely because of the higher rates of dropouts among students heavily involved in drug use in the later grades.

Sex ratios display the reverse pattern. An examination of grades 7, 10, and 12 reveals that the highest sex ratios tend to occur in grades 7 and 12, while grade 10 has the lowest ratios for most drugs.

---

* The term *inhalants* is used in U.S. student surveys. Canadian researchers invariably use the term *glue*. This difference is probably largely a semantic one, since most inhalant use at the time of the studies involved glue sniffing.

Table 1. Rates of *Any* Tobacco Use and Sex Ratios (SR) over Time for Students in Selected Areas[a]

	Grade 7						Grade 10		
Year	Tex[c]	Alta[c]	Cal[b]	Fla[d]	Sask[e]	NS[c]	Tex[c]	Alta[c]	Cal[b]
1968									54.9
									(98)
1969			41.7		6.4	33.3			52.8
			(110)		(103)	(125)			(90)
1970	22.1		36.1			48.5	42.0		54.2
	(119)		(112)			(143)	(116)		(90)
1971	25.3	29.9	38.8				45.5	49.1	53.7
	(120)	(119)	(115)				(104)	(103)	(91)
1972			39.9						56.3
			(113)						(93)
1973	27.0		48.3	25.8			45.8		60.0
	(101)		(109)	(102)			(108)		(96)
1974		28.4	48.6	18.9				49.8	58.6
		(74)	(98)	(105)				(88)	(92)
1975			46.1						59.2
			(99)						(92)
1976		37.7	42.9	23.4				59.0	59.3
		(100)	(97)	(83)				(106)	(84)
1977			40.8	21.1					57.2
			(99)	(117)					(81)

Rates and Sex Ratios of *Regular* Use of Tobacco

Year	Tex[g]	Alta[e]	Cal[f]	Fla[f]	Sask[f]		Tex[g]	Alta[e]	Cal[f]
1968									
1969					8.7				
					(129)				
1970	10.1						25.9		27.7
	(122)						(118)		(97)
1971	12.3	8.3					29.0	28.1	28.5
	(109)	(191)					(115)	(119)	(89)
1972									29.1
									(91)
1973	15.4		10.0	10.8			29.0		27.1
	(81)		(107)	(112)			(104)		(94)
1974		7.5	9.6	7.7				31.8	26.9
		(100)	(92)	(90)				(89)	(80)
1975			7.9						26.6
			(90)						(77)
1976		5.5	7.0	9.9				26.7	27.1
		(173)	(109)	(81)				(123)	(64)
1977			5.7	9.1					24.4
			(84)	(92)					(59)

[a] Houston, Texas (Hays, 1971, 1972, 1974); rural Alberta (Bakal et al., 1974, 1976); San Mateo County, California (Blackford, 1977); Duval County, Florida (Barr et al., 1974, 1975, 1976, 1977); Saskatoon, Saskatchewan (Mathews and Piper, 1975); the United States (Johnston et al., 1977); and Halifax, Nova Scotia (Whitehead, 1971).

Grade 10			Grade 12						
Fla[d]	Sask[e]	NS[c]	Tex[c]	Alta[c]	Cal[b]	Fla[d]	Sask[e]	US[e]	NS[c]
					56.7 (106)				
					57.8 (101)				53.3 (149)
		55.4 (105)	43.4 (147)		52.6 (98)				58.8 (104)
	60.3 (118)		43.6 (115)	50.4 (98)	53.4 (99)				
	55.2 (108)				54.8 (99)				
39.1 (94)			46.6 (104)		57.0 (101)	37.5 (129)	66.2 (114)		
34.4 (77)				47.3 (96)	57.6 (98)	35.0 (127)			
					55.9 (96)			36.7 (104)	
38.6 (72)				49.8 (98)	54.5 (84)	38.3 (84)		38.8 (96)	
37.0 (84)					55.5 (87)	40.1 (106)		38.4 (92)	

Fla[f]	Sask[f]		Tex[g]	Alta[e]	Cal[f]	Fla[f]	Sask[f]	US[g]
			28.5 (166)		30.8 (100)			
	36.2 (124)		32.1 (134)	33.2 (104)	30.7 (102)			
	31.6 (112)				31.5 (98)			
26.6 (97)			32.0 (115)		31.1 (94)	27.7 (138)	36.9 (131)	
22.5 (94)				35.9 (104)	30.8 (84)	26.6 (136)		
					28.3 (78)			17.9 (122)
27.0 (79)				28.9 (103)	28.2 (70)	29.4 (76)		19.0 (111)
26.8 (93)					28.4 (66)	31.4 (123)		19.3 (104)

[b] Past 12 months.   [e] Monthly.
[c] Past 6 months.   [f] Weekly.
[d] Current.   [g] Daily.

Table 2. Rates of *Any* Tranquilizer Use and Sex Ratios (SR) over Time for Students in Selected Areas[a]

Year	Grade 7			Grade 10			Grade 12			
	Alta[c]	Fla[d]	NS[c]	Alta[c]	Fla[d]	NS[c]	Alta[c]	Fla[d]	NS[c]	US[b]
1968										
1969			2.4[g]						8.4	
			(182)						(133)	
1970			4.7[g]			8.0			10.1	
			(520)			(39)			(109)	
1971	5.1			9.8			11.2			
	(71)			(57)			(31)			
1972										
1973		4.3			10.6			21.7		
		(98)			(67)			(30)		
1974	3.1	2.9		12.5	8.9		11.6	7.2		
	(94)	(63)		(50)	(84)		(55)	(112)		
1975		3.0			8.5			7.9		10.6
		(90)			(42)			(89)		(90)
1976	3.8	1.9[g]		9.5	9.1		9.0	6.7		10.3
	(138)	(85)		(91)	(88)		(127)	(94)		(85)
1977		1.9[g]			9.2			7.1		10.8
		(147)			(74)			(103)		(89)

Rates and Sex Ratios of *Regular* Use of Tranquilizers

Year	Alta[e]	Fla[f]	Alta[e]	Fla[f]	Alta[c]	Fla[d]
1968						
1969						
1970						
1971	1.2[g]		2.3		3.7	
	(21)		(28)		(26)	
1972						
1973		0.9[g]		2.1		2.2
		(100)		(128)		(83)
1974	0.4[g]	1.7[g]	3.0	1.0[g]	2.1	1.2[g]
	(100)	(167)	(26)	(375)	(32)	(33)
1975		0.2[g]		1.7[g]		0.9[g]
		—		(62)		(350)
1976	1.0[g]	0.3[g]	2.6	1.4[g]	1.5[g]	0.7[g]
	(138)	(100)	(86)	(65)	(114)	(117)
1977		0.4[g]		1.2[g]		1.2[g]
		—		(109)		(200)

[a] Rural Alberta (Bakal et al., 1974, 1976); Duval County, Florida (Barr et al., 1974, 1975, 1976, 1977); Halifax, Nova Scotia (Whitehead, 1971); and the United States (Johnston et al., 1977).
[b] Past 12 months.   [e] Monthly.
[c] Past 6 months.   [f] Weekly.
[d] Current.   [g] Fewer than 20 cases.

General Population.   National studies of general populations provide an opportunity to examine changes in rates and sex ratios of drug-using behavior over time and across age categories. Most such studies collect information on period prevalence, that is, incidence of use in a recent period. The chief exception is for the use of marijuana, which is usually expressed in terms of lifetime prevalence ("ever used").

Unfortunately, most national surveys do not inquire about the use of all drugs or do not publish sex-specific data. An exception is the national survey of the nonmedical use of psychoactive drugs by Abelson et al. (1977). There are a number of surveys of the use of licit drugs, but it is difficult to make comparisons because of variations in types of use reported. For example, some ask about any use, others about nonmedical use only, and others about medical use. The type of drug used within each category may vary for males and females. This is particularly true of stimulant use, which ranges from diet pills, used primarily by females, to "speed," used mostly by males. Since tobacco and marijuana are the only drugs for which several sets of comparable data are available for analysis, our conclusions relative to the use of other drugs in the general population are somewhat tentative.

Tobacco.   In 1969, the American Gallup Poll surveyed adults 21 years of age and over and found that 41% of respondents had ever used tobacco (45.6% of the men and 36.4% of the women: a sex ratio of 125). Surveys conducted in 1972 and 1974 produced almost identical results (American Institute of Public Opinion, 1969a, 1972, 1974).

Current use, as measured in another national survey (U.S. Department of Health, Education and Welfare, Public Health Service, 1973, 1976), declined from about 45% in 1964 to 34% in 1975. Rates of use decreased for both sexes, but the drop was greater for males. Sex ratios fell from 165 to 136.

Abelson and associates (1973, 1975, 1976, 1977; Social Research Group, 1978) measured current use among U.S. adults 18 and over. Rates were slightly higher (39–41%) and sex ratios slightly lower (119–133) than in the U.S. Department of Health, Education, and Welfare study, and rates and sex ratios remained fairly stable over the six-year period. These differences are probably due to the inclusion of 18- to 20-year-olds (Abelson and Atkinson, 1975).

National studies conducted in Canada indicate similar patterns in the use of tobacco. The total rate of daily smoking was 48.1% in 1963 and 47.7% in 1974 for use in the past week (Canadian Institute of Public Opinion, 1963). The sex ratio decreased slightly from 147 to 137. In one repeated cross-sectional study, rates decreased from 45.5% in 1965 to 38.8% in 1975 (Health and Welfare Canada, 1976, 1977). Among males, 57.9% smoked in 1965. Their number decreased to 45.6% in 1975. Rates

Table 3. Rates of *Any* Stimulant Use and Sex Ratios (SR) over Time for Students in Selected Areas[a]

Year	Grade 7						Grade 10		
	Tex[d]	Alta[d]	Cal[c]	Fla[e]	NS[d]	NEng[b]	Tex[d]	Alta[d]	Cal[c]
1968									16.0
									(98)
1969			5.5		3.0[k]				19.6
			(86)		(140)				(95)
1970	5.0		3.3		5.0[k]	2.0	15.7		21.5
	(104)		(132)		(233)	(122)	(104)		(76)
1971	4.1	3.7	5.6			1.6[k]	19.1	7.8	23.2
	(145)	(97)	(90)			(68)	(101)	(94)	(73)
1972			5.7						25.1
			(85)						(83)
1973	5.0		3.2	2.1[k]			20.6		20.9
	(85)		(133)	(100)			(134)		(95)
1974		2.8	3.4	1.4[k]				7.3	18.9
		(167)	(100)	(80)				(84)	(88)
1975			2.8	2.5[k]					16.5
			(96)	(257)					(75)
1976			2.3	1.5[k]					14.5
			(130)	(100)					(88)
1977			2.5	2.1[k]					13.2
			(123)	(133)					(88)

Rates and Sex Ratios of *Regular* Use of Stimulants

Year	Tex[g]	Alta[f]	Cal[g,i]	Fla[g,j]	Tex[g]	Alta[f]	Cal[g,i]
1968							
1969							
1970	2.6[k]				7.1		3.2
	(148)				(114)		(68)
1971	2.1[k]	0.7[k]			9.4	1.6[k]	3.5
	(163)	(44)			(95)	(88)	(75)
1972							4.1
							(80)
1973	2.8[k]		0.6	0.4[k]	11.2		3.3
	(112)		(200)	(14)	(133)		(89)
1974		0.6[k]	0.5	0.6[k]		1.1[k]	2.7
		(100)	(125)	(63)		(150)	(80)
1975			0.5	0.5[k]			2.3
			(80)	(400)			(84)
1976			0.4	0.4[k]			2.0
			(205)	(60)			(90)
1977			0.3	1.1[k]			1.8
			(150)	(250)			(71)

[a] Houston, Texas (Hays, 1971, 1972, 1974); rural Alberta (Bakal et al., 1974, 1976); San Mateo County, California (Blackford, 1977); Duval County, Florida (Barr et al., 1974, 1975, 1976, 1977); Halifax, Nova Scotia (Whitehead, 1971); the United States (Johnston et al., 1977); and New England (Rosenberg et al., 1974).

Grade 10			Grade 12						
Fla[e]	NS[d]	NEng[b]	Tex[d]	Alta[d]	Cal[c]	Fla[e]	NS[d]	US[h]	NEng[b]
					18.3 (127)				
					22.8 (129)		7.0[k] (147)		
	4.8[k] (146)	10.7 (66)	16.7 (201)		19.5 (93)		10.1[k] (277)		19.2 (102)
		15.6 (101)	22.1 (118)	6.1 (63)	24.8 (117)				25.8 (95)
					25.1 (106)				
11.3 (109)			20.2 (122)		21.0 (101)	12.8 (142)			
9.3 (133)				6.8 (109)	23.0 (93)	12.2 (122)			
9.8 (82)					21.8 (95)	11.7 (97)		16.2 (95)	
11.2 (120)					18.5 (99)	11.9 (65)		15.8 (103)	
10.7 (83)					20.8 (99)	12.7 (147)		16.3 (98)	

Fla[g,j]	Tex[g]	Alta[f]	Cal[g,i]	Fla[g,j]
	8.0 (256)		3.1 (126)	
	9.2 (158)	1.9[k] (153)	5.0 (130)	
			5.2 (110)	
1.9[k] (153)	10.1 (118)		4.3 (107)	2.3[k] (147)
2.0[k] (242)		1.1[k] (250)	4.3 (70)	1.5[k] (158)
0.9[k] —			4.1 (86)	0.9[k] (350)
0.9[k] (58)			3.6 (85)	1.2[k] (156)
1.8[k] (147)			3.0 (82)	1.9[k] (138)

[b] Ever used.
[c] Past 12 months.
[d] Past 6 months.
[e] Current.
[f] Monthly.
[g] Weekly.
[h] Daily.
[i] Amphetamines.
[j] Speed.
[k] Fewer than 20 cases.

Table 4. Rates of *Any* Barbiturate Use and Sex Ratios (SR) over Time for Students in Selected Areas[a]

Year	Grade 7					Grade 10		
	Tex[c]	Alta[c]	Cal[b]	Fla[d]	NS[c]	Tex[c]	Alta[c]	Cal[b]
1968								
1969					1.5[g]			
					(71)			
1970	3.6[g]		3.2		5.1[g]	11.7		18.5
	(129)		(106)		(166)	(104)		(81)
1971	4.0[g]	2.7		5.6		6.2	5.2	18.0
	(139)	(122)		(107)		(103)	(119)	(88)
1972			5.0					16.6
			(106)					(93)
1973	4.3[g]		5.0	3.4		18.9		14.8
	(81)		(111)	(127)		(158)		(99)
1974		1.6[g]	4.9	2.4[g]			5.9	14.3
		(136)	(106)	(71)			(90)	(105)
1975			3.6	1.9[g]				12.8
			(112)	(54)				(77)
1976		1.5[g]	3.0	1.3[g]			5.4	13.6
		(164)	(122)	(213)			(132)	(80)
1977			2.6	1.3[g]				10.8
			(206)	(189)				(77)

Rates and Sex Ratios of *Regular* Use of Barbiturates

Year	Tex[f]	Alta[e]	Cal[f]	Fla[f]		Tex[f]	Alta[e]	Cal[f]
1968								
1969								
1970	2.3[g]					4.3[g]		2.7
	(114)					(146)		(77)
1971	2.4[g]	0.8[g]				8.2	1.4[g]	2.4
	(182)	(129)				(125)	(56)	(109)
1972								2.4
								(147)
1973	2.0[g]		0.6[g]	0.7[g]		10.4		1.8
	(90)		(267)	(63)		(200)		(177)
1974		0.2[g]	0.6[g]	0.4[g]			1.6[g]	1.7
		(67)	(140)	(167)			(113)	(136)
1975			0.4[g]	0.3[g]				1.4[g]
			(60)	(150)				(145)
1976		0.1[g]	0.3[g]	0.3[g]			1.0[g]	1.3[g]
		—	(500)	—			(133)	(86)
1977			0.3[g]	0.5[g]				1.2[g]
			(150)	—				(100)

[a] Houston, Texas (Hays, 1971, 1972, 1974); rural Alberta (Bakal et al., 1974, 1976); San Mateo County, California (Blackford, 1977); Duval County, Florida (Barr et al., 1974, 1975, 1976, 1977); the United States (Johnston et al., 1977); and Halifax, Nova Scotia (Whitehead, 1971).

Grade 10		Grade 12					
Fla[d]	NS[c]	Tex[c]	Alta[c]	Cal[b]	Fla[d]	NS[c]	US[b]
						3.5[g]	
						(438)	
	4.0[g]	11.4		14.2		5.3[g]	
	(61)	(373)		(104)		(231)	
		4.3[g]	5.0	16.8			
		(372)	(194)	(123)			
				14.8			
				(109)			
11.9		17.8		12.7	12.0		
(127)		(122)		(123)	(138)		
10.3			4.4	14.7	11.6		
(124)			(159)	(100)	(167)		
6.8				13.6	10.5		11.7
(57)				(93)	(141)		(122)
7.7			4.5[g]	12.0	7.3		10.7
(126)			(358)	(103)	(143)		(115)
7.0				12.9	8.6		10.8
(130)				(99)	(139)		(128)

Fla[f]		Tex[f]	Alta[e]	Cal[f]	Fla[f]
		4.6[g]		2.0	
		(338)		(160)	
		3.3[g]	1.5[g]	3.0	
		(16)	(383)	(168)	
				2.1	
				(200)	
2.4[g]		8.1		2.0	1.6[g]
(140)		(87)		(225)	(256)
1.9[g]			1.1[g]	1.3[g]	1.3[g]
(147)			(144)	(100)	(178)
0.7[g]				1.6[g]	0.6[g]
(30)				(138)	(175)
1.0[g]			0.9[g]	1.6[g]	1.4[g]
(280)			—	(220)	(367)
0.8[g]				1.4[g]	1.6[g]
(167)				(170)	(146)

[b] Past 12 months. [e] Monthly.
[c] Past 6 months. [f] Weekly.
[d] Current. [g] Fewer than 20 cases.

Table 5. Rates of *Any* Marijuana Use and Sex Ratios (SR) over Time for Students in Selected Areas[a]

	Grade 7							Grade 10	
Year	Tex[d]	Alta[d]	Cal[c]	Fla[e]	Md[b]	NS[d]	NEng	Tex[d]	Alta[d]
1968									
1969			10.8 (102)		3.0[i] (127)	1.5[i] (38)			
1970	4.3 (183)		8.5 (136)			7.4[i] (227)	6.3 (131)	22.7 (114)	
1971	5.9 (125)	4.3 (153)	15.1 (140)				10.3 (119)	27.7 (137)	16.7 (115)
1972			15.2 (130)		4.2[i] (246)				
1973	7.8 (79)		17.5 (133)	9.4 (131)				33.6 (167)	
1974		4.0 (220)	20.4 (126)	8.8 (136)					26.1 (125)
1975			19.0 (126)	8.3 (191)					
1976		7.7 (108)	18.7 (139)	9.6 (167)					32.2 (130)
1977			19.1 (149)	9.3 (147)					

Rates and Sex Ratios of *Regular* Use of Marijuana

Year	Tex[g]	Alta[f]	Cal[g]	Fla[g]	Md[g]			Tex[g]	Alta[f]
1968									
1969					0.0[i] (—)				
1970	2.3 (114)							12.9 (112)	
1971	3.0 (216)	1.5 (222)						18.6 (171)	6.9 (121)
1972					0.8[i]				
1973	3.8 (90)		2.8 (143)	2.6 (117)				21.8 (205)	
1974		1.4 (440)	3.2 (174)	2.3 (200)					
1975			2.9 (138)	1.6 (357)					11.1 (123)
1976		1.7 (113)	3.1 (177)	2.8 (75)					
1977			3.0 (200)	3.4 (86)					13.4 (164)

[a] Houston, Texas (Hays, 1971, 1972, 1974); rural Alberta (Bakal et al., 1974, 1976); San Mateo County, California (Blackford, 1977); Duval County, Florida (Barr et al., 1974, 1975, 1976, 1977); Montgomery County, Maryland (Montgomery County, 1972); Halifax (Whitehead, 1971); New England (Rosenberg et al., 1974); and the United States (Johnston et al., 1977).

Grade 10					Grade 12							
Cal[c]	Fla[e]	Md[b]	NS[d]	NEng[d]	Tex[d]	Alta[d]	Cal[c]	Fla[e]	Md[b]	US[c]	NS[d]	NEng[d]
30.2							38.3					
(115)							(140)					
38.6		14.9					44.1		24.0		13.4	
(117)		(103)					(132)		(134)		(239)	
43.5		12.5[i]		34.3	32.8		47.7				26.4	48.0
(107)		(117)		(94)	(213)		(115)				(192)	(119)
48.9				43.3	35.7	23.0	53.5					55.2
(103)				(124)	(141)	(125)	(121)					(117)
50.5		36.3					56.8		44.4			
(105)		(124)					(115)		(129)			
54.0	36.4				42.5		59.2	38.5				
(108)	(127)				(135)		(106)	(159)				
56.0	32.2					32.3	60.1	35.8				
(105)	(127)					(164)	(106)	(154)				
54.2	36.0						59.6	40.9		40.0		
(109)	(114)						(115)	(130)		(131)		
56.0	40.4					34.5	58.6	45.1		44.5		
(106)	(124)					(140)	(109)	(141)		(134)		
57.3	42.2						63.0	51.9		47.6		
(107)	(111)						(105)	(130)		(127)		

Cal[g]	Fla[e]	Md[g]			Tex[g]	Alta[f]	Cal[g]	Fla[g]	Md[g]	US[h]
		6.1							6.8	
		(109)							(123)	
16.6					20.0		18.7			
(137)					(259)		(144)			
20.1					23.7	9.7	25.2			
(136)					(188)	(144)	(172)			
22.3		14.1			29.5		25.9		15.8	
(134)		(120)			(150)		(156)		(156)	
23.4	19.0						26.4	21.7		
(148)	(149)						(159)	(165)		
24.2	15.2					15.3	28.5	17.4		
(120)	(142)					(218)	(150)	(225)		
21.5	18.9						25.8	18.8		6.2
(127)	(158)						(147)	(179)		(208)
21.8	21.8					16.8	25.7	23.1		8.0
(127)	(155)					(166)	(141)	(166)		(220)
22.0	21.1						29.3	25.7		9.3
(127)	(126)						(142)	(213)		(221)

[b] Ever used. [f] Monthly.
[c] Past 12 months. [g] Weekly.
[d] Past 6 months. [h] Daily.
[e] Current. [i] Fewer than 20 cases.

Table 6. Rates of *Any* LSD Use and Sex Ratios (SR) over Time for Students in Selected Areas[a]

	Grade 7						Grade 10		
Year	Tex[d,i]	Alta[d]	Cal[c]	Fla[e]	NS[d]	NEng[b]	Tex[d,i]	Alta[d]	Cal[c]
1968									9.7 (134)
1969			2.5 (133)		0.4[j] (100)				14.9 (132)
1970	1.8[j] (133)		1.2[j] (156)		4.7[j] (210)	0.6[j] (100)	11.0 (128)		16.0 (113)
1971	7.2 (106)	2.8 (133)	2.5 (117)			0.5[j] —	8.3 (113)	10.2 (126)	14.9 (118)
1972			2.6 (108)						16.1 (121)
1973	2.2[j] (258)		3.4 (143)	2.0[j] (129)			11.7 (224)		17.3 (120)
1974		1.3[j] (333)	4.0 (114)	1.4[j] (80)				6.8 (108)	16.7 (125)
1975			3.1 (88)	1.4[j] (300)					15.7 (94)
1976			2.8 (167)	1.2[j] (243)					14.0 (101)
1977			2.2 (153)	1.9[j] (208)					11.8 (118)

Rates and Sex Ratios of *Regular* Use of LSD

Year	Tex[g,i]	Alta[f]	Cal[g]	Fla[g]		Tex[g,i]	Alta[f]	Cal[g]
1968								
1969						3.5[j] (109)		1.9 (164)
1970	2.4[j] (100)					4.9[j] (111)	3.0 (205)	2.1 (193)
1971	1.0[j] (300)	0.7[j] (114)						1.9 (164)
1972						5.7[j] (190)		1.9 (164)
1973	1.1[j] (200)		0.5[j] (150)	0.5[j] (80)				1.4[j] (440)
1974		0.3[j] —	0.5[j] (400)	0.5[j] (100)			1.6[j] (45)	1.6[j] (210)
1975			0.4[j] (40)	0.3[j] —				1.4[j] (180)
1976			0.4[j] (300)	0.1[j] —				1.0 (111)
1977			0.3[j] (150)	0.4[j] —				1.0[j] (122)

[a] Houston, Texas (Hays, 1971, 1972, 1974); rural Alberta (Bakal et al., 1974, 1976); San Mateo County, California (Blackford, 1977); Duval County, Florida (Barr et al., 1974, 1975, 1976, 1977); Halifax, Nova Scotia (Whitehead, 1971); the United States (Johnston et al., 1977); and New England (Rosenberg et al., 1974).

	Grade 10			Grade 12						
Fla[e]	NS[d]	NEng[b]		Tex[d,i]	Alta[d]	Cal[c]	Fla[e]	NS[d]	US[h]	NEng[b]
						13.0 (177)				
						17.1 (205)			4.3[j] (330)	
	5.5[j] (122)	8.3 (90)		10.7 (304)		14.7 (146)		13.2[j] (211)		12.8 (194)
		11.7 (146)		7.0 (256)	8.3 (143)	16.6 (171)				20.2 (119)
						17.5 (155)				
8.8 (136)				11.6 (123)		16.7 (149)		9.2 (210)		
7.5 (178)					8.2 (368)	18.2 (124)		9.4 (212)		
5.1[j] (84)						17.9 (122)		7.1 (131)	11.2 (152)	
4.5[j] (210)						15.7 (132)		4.7[j] (102)	9.4 (168)	
2.3[j] (318)						16.7 (121)		3.4[j] (127)	8.8 (166)	

Fla[g]				Tex[g,i]	Alta[f]	Cal[g]	Fla[g]
				4.8[j] (405)		1.8 (260)	
				4.3[j] (608)	1.4[j] —	2.2 (340)	
						2.0 (233)	
1.9[j] (280)				3.5[j] (146)		1.8 (260)	1.9[j] (322)
1.4[j] (367)					1.3[j] (767)	1.5[j] (164)	1.1[j] (267)
0.8[j] (88)						1.9[j] (185)	1.1[j] (50)
0.8[j] (700)						1.7[j] (127)	0.9[j] (467)
0.4[j] —						1.7[j] (209)	0.6[j] (300)

[b] Ever used.
[c] Past 12 months.
[d] Past 6 months.
[e] Current.
[f] Monthly.
[g] Weekly.
[h] Daily.
[i] Hallucinogens.
[j] Fewer than 20 cases.

Table 7. Rates of *Any* Cocaine Use and Sex Ratios (SR) over Time for Students in Selected Areas[a]

Year	Grade 7				Grade 10	
	Tex[d]	Alta[d]	Fla[e]	NEng[b]	Tex[d]	Alta[d]
1968						
1969						
1970	2.5[h]			0.5[h]	4.6[h]	
	(233)			(200)	(88)	
1971	2.5[h]			0.9[h]	8.2	
	(272)			(200)	(167)	
1972						
1973	(2.3)[h]		1.5[h]		9.8	
	(73)		(164)		(315)	
1974			1.8[h]			
			(52)			
1975			2.4[h]			
			(235)			
1976		3.8[h]	1.9[h]			6.1
		(138)	(640)			(169)
1977			1.0[h]			
			—			

Rates and Sex Ratios of *Regular* Use of Cocaine

Year	Tex[g]	Alta[f]	Fla[g]		Tex[g]	Alta[f]
1968						
1969						
1970	1.6[h]				2.1[h]	
	(107)				(86)	
1971	0.8[h]				4.3[h]	
	(220)				(146)	
1972						
1973	0.6[h]		0.1[h]		5.4[h]	
	(140)		—		(529)	
1974			0.5[h]			
			(233)			
1975			0.3[h]			
			—			
1976		1.8[h]	0.3[h]			1.7[h]
		(125)	(67)			(162)
1977			0.1[h]			
			—			

[a] Houston, Texas (Hays, 1971, 1972, 1974); rural Alberta (Bakal et al., 197 1976); Duval County, Florida (Barr et al., 1974, 1975, 1976, 1977); the Unit States (Johnston et al., 1977); New England (Rosenberg et al., 1974).

Grade 10		Grade 12				
Fla[e]	NEng[b]	Tex[d]	Alta[d]	Fla[e]	US[c]	NEng[b]
	3.4[h]	5.2[h]				4.2[h]
	(91)	(285)				(300)
	4.9	8.7				9.5
	(151)	(239)				(98)
6.8		9.3		9.7		
(170)		(123)		(181)		
6.1				11.0		
(267)				(265)		
5.6				9.6	5.6	
(113)				(189)	(192)	
6.0			3.9[h]	7.5	6.0	
(231)			(756)	(166)	(170)	
4.7				8.8	7.2	
(135)				(361)	(190)	
Fla[g]		Tex[g]	Alta[f]	Fla[g]		
		1.9[h]				
		(640)				
		2.6[h]				
		(333)				
1.1[h]		3.2[h]		1.6[h]		
—		(152)		(244)		
1.4[h]				1.3[h]		
(250)				(178)		
0.6[h]				1.1[h]		
(140)				(200)		
0.8[h]			0.4[h]	1.4[h]		
(700)			—	(833)		
0.8[h]				1.6[h]		
(167)				(933)		

[b] Ever used.   [e] Current.   [h] Fewer than 20 cases.
[c] Past 12 months.   [f] Monthly.
[d] Past 6 months.   [g] Weekly.

Table 8. Rates of *Any* Heroin Use and Sex Ratios (SR) over Time for Students in Selected Areas[a]

Year	Grade 7				Grade 10	
	Cal[c]	NS[d,g]	Fla[e]	NEng[b]	Cal[c]	NS[d,g]
1968						
1969		0.6[h]				
		(200)				
1970		3.5[h]		0.3[h]		3.7[h]
		(367)		—		(51)
1971				0.2[h]	3.0	
				—	(195)	
1972					3.3	
					(154)	
1973			1.0[h]		3.1	
			(122)		(195)	
1974			0.9[h]		3.4	
			(500)		(139)	
1975			1.1[h]		3.0	
			(214)		(119)	
1976	1.6[h]		0.6[h]		2.2	
	(220)		—		(175)	
1977	1.9		0.8[h]		2.6	
	(171)		(400)		(113)	

Rates and Sex Ratios of *Regular* Use of Heroin

Year	Cal[f]	Cal[f]
1968		
1969		
1970		
1971		1.0[h]
		(280)
1972		0.9[h]
		(200)
1973		0.8[h]
		(300)
1974		1.1[h]
		(200)
1975		0.9[h]
		(200)
1976	0.4	0.6[h]
	(300)	(500)
1977	0.3	0.8[h]
	(200)	(150)

[a] San Mateo County, California (Blackford, 1977); Halifax, Nova Scotia (Whitehead, 1971); Duval County, Florida (Barr et al., 1974, 1975, 1976, 1977); and New England (Rosenberg et al., 1974).

Grade 10		Grade 12			
Fla[e]	NEng[b]	Cal[c]	NS[d,g]	Fla[e]	NEng[b]
			1.9[h] (95)		
	1.8[h] (133)		1.6[h] (192)		3.9[h] (420)
	2.8[h] (143)	4.3 (227)			5.4[h] (300)
		3.7 (170)			
3.6 (196)		3.6 (154)		2.7[h] (260)	
2.1[h] (320)		3.5 (156)		3.1[h] (244)	
1.0[h] (54)		3.6 (148)		2.7[h] (194)	
1.6[h] (82)		3.0 (181)		2.1[h] (600)	
2.0[h] (208)		3.5 (141)		1.4[h] (833)	

Fla[f]		Cal[f]		Fla[f]	
		1.3 (333)			
		0.9[h] (200)			
1.5[h] (400)		1.2[h] (243)		1.6[h] (357)	
0.7[h] (250)		1.2[h] (140)		1.0[h] (217)	
0.3[h]		1.0[h] (233)		0.7[h] (100)	
— (40)		1.0[h] (138)		1.1[h] (600)	
0.4[h]		1.3[h] (257)		0.5[h] (833)	
0.7[h] (250)					

[b] Ever used.
[c] Past 12 months.
[d] Past 6 months.
[e] Current.
[f] Weekly.
[g] Opiates.
[h] Fewer than 20 cases.

Table 9. Rates of *Any* Inhalant Use and Sex Ratios (SR) over Time for Students in Selected Areas[a]

	Grade 7					Grade 10		
Year	Tex[c,g]	Alta[c,h]	Fla[d,g]	NS[c,h]	NEng[c,h]	Tex[c,g]	Alta[c,h]	Fla[d,g]
1968								
1969				3.7[i] (78)				
1970	5.1 (137)			7.3[i] (143)	5.6 (363)	6.0 (153)		
1971	1.8[i] (112)	7.2 (165)			12.0 (144)	11.4 (119)	3.6 (209)	
1972								
1973	3.7[i] (106)		5.2 (126)			7.2 (186)		5.3 (152)
1974		8.0 (94)	5.0 (186)				3.3 (164)	3.6[i] (145)
1975			7.2 (103)					3.5[i] (64)
1976		6.0 (114)	6.5 (108)				4.0 (229)	4.4[i] (156)
1977			6.6 (152)					4.8 (88)

Rates and Sex Ratios of *Regular* Use of Inhalants

Year	Tex[f,g]	Alta[e,h]	Fla[f,g]			Tex[f,g]	Alta[e,h]	Fla[f,g]
1968								
1969								
1970	3.2[i] (205)					1.7[i] (240)		
1971	2.2[i] (175)	1.2[i] (229)				3.4[i] (143)	1.0[i] (217)	
1972								
1973	1.9[i] (171)		0.8[i] (200)			3.0[i] (173)		1.5[i] (263)
1974		1.0[i] (111)	0.8[i] (100)				1.2[i] (243)	0.8[i] (167)
1975			1.0[i] (100)					0.4[i] (60)
1976		0.7[i] (367)	0.5[i] (233)				0.7[i] (100)	0.6[i] (450)
1977			0.8[i] (—)					0.5[i] (400)

[a] Houston, Texas (Hays, 1971, 1972, 1974); rural Alberta (Bakal et al., 1974, 1976); Duval County, Florida (Barr et al., 1974, 1975, 1976, 1977); the United States (Johnston et al., 1977); Halifax, Nova Scotia (Whitehead, 1971); and New England (Rosenberg et al., 1974).

Grade 10		Grade 12					
NS[c,h]	NEng[c,h]	Tex[c,g]	Alta[c,h]	Fla[d,g]	NS[c,h]	NEng[c,h]	US[b]
					0.0		
					—		
5.2^i	9.3	5.3			6.4^i	7.1	
(41)	(108)	(226)			(195)	(154)	
	10.2	15.0	2.6^i			9.7	
	(145)	(211)	(240)			(223)	
		3.5^i		3.4^i			
		(289)		(158)			
			2.5^i	2.2^i			
			(257)	(139)			
				3.6^i			
				(118)			
			1.8^i	2.1^i			3.0
			—	(356)			(190)
				1.5^i			3.7
				(500)			(213)

		Tex[f,g]	Alta[e,h]	Fla[f,g]			
		1.9^i					
		(236)					
		0.9^i	0.7^i				
		(200)	(333)				
		1.6^i		1.1^i			
		(244)		(425)			
			0.7^i	0.6^i			
			(333)	(100)			
				0.2^i			
				—			
			0.2^i	0.5^i			
			—	(233)			
				0.4^i			
				(60)			

[b] Past 12 months.   [e] Monthly.   [h] Glue.
[c] Past 6 months.   [f] Weekly.   [i] Fewer than 20 cases.
[d] Current.   [g] Solvents.

for females have remained at about 32% since 1965. The result is a decrease in the sex ratio from 175 in 1965 to 143 in 1975.

The prevalence of smoking among adults decreases with age, but the decrease is substantial (about 50%) only for those beyond middle age (Table 10). Sex ratios tend to increase with age, and again, the ratios are highest for the oldest age category. For example, sex ratios for current use range from 107 to 160 in the younger and middle age groups and from 169 to 285 in the oldest group. Young people also have relatively low rates of smoking, but sex ratios are closer to those for younger adults.

Marijuana.   Marijuana is the most widely used illicit drug and is second only to tobacco in rates of use for those drugs considered in this study. Abelson and associates (1973, 1975, 1976, 1977; Social Research Group, 1978) examined the use of marijuana in the United States for most years between 1971 and 1977. Total rates of lifetime prevalence among adults increased from 15% in 1971 to 25% in 1977. Among males, rates went from 21% in 1971 to 30% in 1977. Among females, 10% reported ever having used marijuana in 1971 and 19% did so in 1977. Sex ratios are high among adults and have shown some decline: 210 in 1971; 157 in 1977.

Rates of use during the past month are roughly one-third of rates for lifetime prevalence and display the same pattern: 7–11% among males; 3–6% among females, with sex ratios of 233 in 1971 and 182 in 1977.

The Gallup Poll in the United States (American Institute of Public Opinion, 1969b) found that in 1969, 4.8% of respondents aged 21 and over had ever used marijuana (6.5% of males and 3.1% of females). In 1973, the rate increased to 9.6% (13.6% for males and 5.9% for females). During this four-year period, the sex ratio increased from 210 to 231.

The Canadian Gallup Poll (Canadian Institute of Public Opinion, 1973), in a study of adults 18 years of age and over in 1973, found that 12% of respondents had ever used marijuana (15% of males and 9% of females, a sex ratio of 167). The total rate of use was exactly the same as that found seven months earlier in the comparable American Gallup Poll. However, the sex ratio for the United States sample was somewhat higher at 207. Sixteen months later, rates of use in Canada had risen to 18.9% for males and 9.9% for females, with a sex ratio of 191 (Canadian Institute of Public Opinion, 1974a).

Sixteen months later, rates of use in Canada had risen to 18.9% for males and 9.9% for females, with a sex ratio of 191 (Canadian Institute of Public Opinion, 1974a).

A national study of cannabis use among adults (18 years and older) was conducted in Canada in January 1978 (Rootman and Fralick, 1978).

Three measures of use were employed, and the sex ratio increased with increasing levels of use.

Lifetime prevalence of marijuana use in this Canadian study was 19.5% for males and 13.0% for females, a sex ratio of 150. Use in the past year was lower at 9.4%, with a higher sex ratio of 183.

An examination of rates of use and sex ratios across age categories reveals marked differences (Table 11). The highest rates of lifetime prevalence of marijuana use are usually found in the younger group of adults, 40–50% in recent years. However, rates of use for youth aged 18–20 are not much less, and in one case are higher. Even those under 18 years of age have higher rates (now almost 30%) than adults aged 25–45, who have rates of use of about 15%. Rates of use among those over the age of 45 are very low in comparison: 2.7% in 1974.

Sex ratios tend to increase with age and are very high—above 250—among those over the age of 25. There are too few users in the oldest age category to produce reliable sex ratios. Sex ratios are lowest among adolescents, in one year as low as 100. However, while sex ratios for adults have declined slightly over time, those for adolescents appear to be increasing.

Sedatives.   In 1967, rates of sedative use and frequent sedative use during the past year increased with age from roughly 4% among younger respondents to 6% among respondents in the mid-age category to 9% among older respondents (Table 12). In 1975, Abelson and Fishburne (1976) found that the rate of lifetime prevalence for nonmedical use only was highest (12%) among the younger respondents (18–25 years of age) and fairly low (2.8% and 2.4%) among persons aged less than 18 and over 25 years. The pattern was similar in 1977 (Abelson et al., 1977), but use increased for the 18–25 age group.

Sex ratios of the combined medical and nonmedical use of sedatives during the past year and of frequent use were generally low, often around 50. However, lifetime prevalence of nonmedical sedative use had higher sex ratios, and these tended to increase with age. Between 1975 and 1977, these sex ratios increased for all age categories.

Stimulants.   Several studies of stimulant use have been conducted, but as in the case of other drugs, different reporting periods were involved and some studies combined both medical and nonmedical use. Thus, comparisons within studies across categories of age are the most appropriate ones available (Table 13).

In 1967, Manheimer et al. (1968) found that frequent use among younger and mid-age respondents was fairly similar: about 8%. Among older respondents, the rate was only 2.6%. The sex ratios were all low, but highest among mid-age respondents (67) followed by youngest re-

Table 10. Rates of *Regular* Cigarette Use and Sex Ratios (SR) over Time for Youth and Adults in Selected National Surveys in Canada and the United States[a]

	Youth				Younger					Middle	
Year	HEW[b]	Ab[b]	AIPO[c]	H+W[d]	HEW[b]	NORC[b,e]	Ab[b]	CIPO[c]	AIPO[c]	H+W[d]	HEW[b]
1959											
1960											
1961											
1962											
1963								56.2 (140)			
1964					54.5 (160)						48.2 (149)
1965				27.0 (187)						51.5 (152)	
1966					55.6 (126)					51.8 (138)	50.1 (135)
1967											
1968	13.5 (170)										
1969									50.6 (125)		
1970	15.8 (151)			30.5 (143)	42.4 (154)					47.7 (130)	42.2 (120)
1971		15.0 (114)									
1972	15.1 (124)	17.0 (100)	52.5 (148)	31.7 (123)					49.7 (124)	46.6 (130)	
1973											
1974	16.1 (103)	25.0 (113)	50.7 (88)	30.1 (116)				55.6 (112)	47.1 (108)	46.2 (128)	
1975		23.4 (81)		28.5 (108)	37.6 (121)					43.3 (126)	39.3 (126)
1976											
1977		22.3 (105)				47.2 (159)	47.3 (107)				

[a] Hammond and Garfinkel (1961): 30–54, 55+; Canadian Institute of Public Opinion (1963): 20–29, 30–49, 50+; (1974b): 20–29, 30–59, 60+: American Institute of Public Opinion (1969a, 1972, 1974): less than 21, 21–25, 26–55, 56+; U.S. Department of Health, Education, Public Health Service and Welfare (1976): 12–18, 21–24, 25–54, 55+; National Opinion Research Center (1977): 21–25, 26–55, 56+; Health and Welfare Canada (1976, 1977): 15–19, 20–24, 25–44, 45+; Abelson et al. (1973, 1975, 1976, 1977): 12–17, 18–25, 26+.

	Adults										
	Middle						Older				
NORC[b,e]	Ab[b]	CIPO[c]	AIPO[c]	H+W[d]	H+G[d]	HEW[b]	NORC[b,e]	CIPO[c]	AIPO[c]	H+W[d]	H+G[d]
					44.4 (151)						25.2 (257)
					43.2 (148)						23.6 (249)
		52.1 (139)						37.1 (196)			
						27.3 (285)					
			48.2 (172)		(268)					20.6 (363)	
			48.1 (164)		26.0 (280)					20.3 (389)	
		46.4 (122)							25.3 (148)		
			44.6 (149)			23.5 (181)				21.0 (299)	
		47.6 (119)	43.5 (147)					27.0 (128)		20.4 (292)	
		53.6 (142)	46.0 (123)	41.5 (145)				39.8 (184)	28.4 (135)	19.8 (274)	
				40.9 (138)		22.4 (169)				20.1 (271)	
46.5 (142)	38.7[f] (142)						31.5 (181)				

[b] Current.
[c] Weekly.
[d] Daily.
[e] Includes all forms of tobacco.
[f] Age 26+.

Table 11. Rates of Any Marijuana Use[a] and Sex Ratios (SR) over Time for Four Age Categories in Selected National Surveys[b]

	Youth				Younger			Adults Middle			Older	
Year	Ab	Jos	AIPO	CIPO	Ab	AIPO	CIPO	Ab	AIPO	CIPO	AIPO	CIPO
1969						17.8 (147)			4.5 (395)		1.6 (158)	
1970												
1971	14.0 (100)	15.6 (121)										
1972	14.0 (115)	15.3 (150)										
1973			42.2 (120)			39.4 (215)			10.5 (253)		1.5 (400)	
1974	23.0 (114)			34.5 (135)			41.3 (185)			11.8 (267)		2.7 (61)
1975	22.4 (137)				52.9 (141)			12.9 (271)				
1976												
1977	28.0 (143)				59.9 (120)			15.3 (198)				

[a] All rates are for lifetime prevalence (ever used).
[b] Abelson and associates (1973, 1975, 1976, 1977): 12–17, 18–25, 26+; Josephson (1974): less than 19; American Institute of Public Opinion (1969b): 21–25, 26–45, 46+; (1973): 18–20, 21–25, 26–45, 46+; Canadian Institute of Public Opinion (1974a): 18–20, 21–25, 26–45, 46+.

Table 12. Rates of Sedative Use and Sex Ratios (SR) over Time for Four Age
Categories in Selected Surveys[a]

| | Youth | Adults | | | | | | | |
| | | Younger | | | Middle | | | Older | |
Year	U.S.[b,e]	U.S.[b,e]	San F[c]	Cal[d]	U.S.[b,e]	San F[c]	Cal[d]	San F[c]	Cal[d]
1967			4.5	3.3		6.0	5.6	8.0	10.0
			(29)	(103)		(50)	(51)	(52)	(76)
1975	2.8	11.9			2.4				
	(67)	(140)			(150)				
1977	3.1	18.4			2.5				
	(138)	(175)			(342)				

[a] Abelson et al. (1977), U.S., 1975, 1977: 12–17, 18–25, 25+; Mellinger et al. (1971), California, 1967: 18–29, 30–44, 45+; Manheimer et al. (1968), San Francisco, 1967: 21–29, 30–49, 50+.
[b] Ever used. [c] Used in past year. [d] Frequent use. [e] Nonmedical use only.

spondents (35) and lowest among oldest respondents (20). Mellinger et al. (1971) examined use in the past year for 1967 and found that rates of use decreased with age: 23.5% among 18- to 29-year-olds; 9.0% among 30- to 44-year-olds; and 4.0% among those 45 years of age and over. They found the sex ratios to be 104 among the younger respondents, 29 among mid-age respondents, and 33 among the oldest respondents.

Parry et al. (1973a) studied the use of stimulants during the past year in 1970. They found the rates of use to be low, 5.5%, 6.5%, and 3.0% from younger to older age categories. Similarly the sex ratios were very low, 10, 18, and 33, respectively.

Abelson and associates (1976, 1977; Social Research Group, 1978) found the rates of lifetime prevalence of nonmedical use to be only about 5% for both 12- to 17-year-olds and those 26 years of age and older. Those aged 18–25 had much higher rates (16% and 21% in 1975 and 1977). In contrast to the sex ratios for rates of medical and nonmedical use combined, the sex ratios of nonmedical use showed a preponderance of males: about 100 for the 12- to 17-year-olds; about 160 for younger people; and 200 or more for those over 25 years of age.

Tranquilizers. In 1967, Manheimer et al. (1968) found the lowest rates of frequent use of tranquilizers among younger respondents (6.7%) and the highest rates among mid-age respondents (11.7%). Sex ratios were lowest (13) among the youngest respondents and still low (approximately 55) among the rest (Table 14).

Mellinger et al. (1971) studied rates of use in the past year in 1967. The highest rate was found among middle-aged respondents (12.0%) and the lowest among older respondents (8.8%). Sex ratios ranged from 47 (younger) to 71 (middle-aged).

Table 13 Rates of Stimulant Use and Sex Ratios (SR) over Time for Four Age Categories in Selected Surveys[a]

	Youth		Younger			Adults						
						Middle				Older		
Year	U.S.[b,e]	U.S.[b,e]	San F[c]	U.S.[c]	Cal[d]	U.S.[b,e]	San F[c]	U.S.[c]	Cal[d]	San F[c]	U.S.[c]	Cal[d]
1967			23.5 (104)		7.6 (35)		9.0 (29)		7.9 (68)	4.0 (33)		2.6 (20)
1970				5.5 (10)				6.5 (18)			3.0 (33)	
1975	4.4 (100)	16.6 (162)				5.6 (200)						
1977	4.9 (94)	21.2 (163)				4.7 (243)						

[a] Abelson et al. (1977), U.S., 1975, 1977: 12–17, 18–25, 26+; Mellinger et al. (1971), San Francisco, 1967: 18–29, 30–44, 45+; Parry et al. (1973a), U.S., 1970: 18–29, 30–44, 45+; Manheimer et al. (1968), California, 1967: 21–29, 30–49, 50+.
[b] Ever used.
[c] Used in past year.
[d] Frequent use.
[e] Nonmedical use.

Table 14. Rates of Tranquilizer Use and Sex Ratios (SR) over Time for Four Age Categories in Selected Surveys[a]

| | Youth | Adults | | | | | | | | | |
| | | Younger | | | | Middle | | | | Older | |
Year	U.S.[b,e]	U.S.[b,e]	San F[c]	U.S.[c]	Cal[d]	U.S.[b,e]	San F[c]	U.S.[c]	Cal[d]	San F[c]	Cal[d]
1967			11.0 (47)		6.7 (13)		12.0 (71)		11.7 (52)	8.8 (59)	9.3 (57)
1970				8.5 (42)				14.0 (33)		16.8 (43)	
1975	3.3 (75)	9.1 (157)				2.7 (150)					
1977	3.6 (161)	12.9 (156)				2.6 (286)					

[a] Abelson et al. (1977), U.S., 1975, 1977: 12–17, 18–25, 26+; Mellinger et al. (1971), San Francisco, 1967: 18–29, 30–44, 45+; Parry et al. (1973a), U.S., 1970: 18–29, 30–44, 45+; Manheimer et al. (1968), California, 1967: 21–29, 30–49, 50+.
[b] Ever used. [c] Used in past year. [d] Frequent use. [e] Nonmedical use only.

The study of use during the past year in 1970 conducted by Parry et al. (1973a) indicates that the lowest rates were found among younger respondents (8.5%) and higher rates among middle-aged (14.0%) and older respondents (16.8%). Again, sex ratios were fairly low (33–43).

Abelson and associates (1976, 1977; Social Research Group, 1978) found rates of lifetime prevalence of the nonmedical use of tranquilizers in 1975 and 1977 to be 9–13% among younger respondents and about 3% among those aged 12–17 and 26 years and over. Sex ratios were high, usually above 150, and were increasing.

Other Drugs. There is only one source of national data about the use of illicit drugs other than marijuana by the general population (Abelson and associates, 1973, 1975, 1976, 1977; Social Research Group, 1978). Unfortunately, total rates of lifetime prevalence are the only data available for all four years of the study, and these are unsatisfactory for establishing trends. Furthermore, sex-specific data are available only for 1977. However, annual prevalence is given for 1974 and 1975, so that we can infer something about current patterns of use.

The use of heroin does not appear to be increasing among any age group and may, in fact, be decreasing. Lifetime prevalence is increasing among both youth and adults, but use may have peaked, as annual prevalence is not increasing.

The use of inhalants follows a similar pattern. Hallucinogens are being used more by adults, but use seems to have peaked among youth.

These data are difficult to analyze because of the cohort effect—in this case, the movement of users from the youth to the adult age group. This effect is particularly troublesome when one is looking at lifetime prevalence and may produce a quite false picture of current use.

Sex ratios for 1977 exceeded 200 for the use of cocaine and heroin by both youths and adults (Social Research Group, 1978). Sex ratios were equally high for the use of hallucinogens and inhalants by adults but were somewhat lower among young persons for hallucinogens (163) and very much lower for inhalants (116).

The data for hallucinogens and inhalants may appear to be somewhat different from those presented for students because of differences in the particular drugs included in these categories both over time and across age categories (for example, psilocybin rather than LSD and vasodilators such as isobutyl nitrite rather than glue).

Summary. Based on these studies and this analysis, a number of general observations can be made about the nature of changes in rates of use and sex ratios over time. The following apply to students:

a. At least for the time series covered, rates of use for drugs other than tobacco, marijuana, and cocaine peaked prior to 1974 or 1975, and rates of use in 1976 and 1977 were below the peak rates and in most cases lower than the rates that prevailed around the turn of the decade.

b. Total rates of tobacco use among students in grades 7–12 have remained remarkably stable during the past decade, although rates of smoking peaked and decreased among males while they increased among females. However, there is some indication from the San Mateo studies (Blackford, 1977) that rates of use among the youngest females (grades 7 and 8) have peaked and are beginning to decline.

The sex ratio has decreased from over 100, where it still is for many categories of adults, to well under 100. These trends are exaggerated when smoking is considered in terms of regular use rather than any use in the past 6 or 12 months.

c. Rates of marijuana use have not peaked, but rates of increase among students in grades 7 and 12 were not as great in the period since 1975 as they were in the earlier part of the decade.

Sex ratios of marijuana use almost always exceed 100 but do not appear to be changing in any consistent fashion. In San Mateo, they were 20–25 points lower than in the Canadian communities.

d. Rates of illicit use of stimulants, tranquilizers, barbiturates, and LSD have all peaked and are decreasing. However, sex ratios of these drugs do not display any clear trends. There is sizable year-to-year variation in sex ratios within the communities studied. However, these are dwarfed by the variation across communities in studies conducted in the same year.

e. The use of cocaine is probably increasing, although data from different studies are not consistent. Sex ratios are high and so variable that no trends are apparent.

f. Opiates have consistently low rates of use. Sex ratios are relatively unstable, probably because of low rates of use, and remain relatively high compared with sex ratios for other drugs.

g. As with heroin, rates of glue and solvent sniffing are low and fairly stable. Sex ratios are somewhat lower than those for heroin but just as unstable.

The study of changes in patterns of drug use among adults is assisted in the case of tobacco by the existence of national surveys conducted since the early 1960s. Data for other drugs are available beginning in the late 1960s, but they were not collected as regularly.

a. Between the early 1960s and the early 1970s, smoking decreased by close to 25%. Between 1970 and 1975, total rates of use decreased at a slower rate, and the sex ratios continued to decrease. Unlike the sex ratios for students, the sex ratio for tobacco use by adults remains well above 100, usually between 120 and 145.

Between the mid-1960s and the mid-1970s, men in all age categories reduced their rates of smoking. Rates among women between the ages of 21 and 54 also decreased; however, they did not decrease as sharply as those of men. Further, older women (55 and over) increased their rates of tobacco use. This finding does not indicate a trend among older women but represents a cohort effect. Women in previous cohorts for that age group had lower rates of use because they reached adulthood before the time that smoking became widespread among women, that is, before World War II (cf. Green and Nemzer, 1973).

b. Rates of marijuana use increased between 1969 and 1974, and the sex ratios remained high, usually between 170 and 250. There is some indication that sex ratios are declining among adults; future surveys are needed to confirm this.

c. Rates of the nonmedical use of licit psychoactive drugs are increasing among young adults but not among other age categories. Sedative and tranquilizer use exhibits similar patterns, with illicit use highest among young adults and licit use highest among older adults. However, stimulant use of all kinds is highest among the younger group. Sex ratios are stable for stimulants but may be increasing for sedatives and tranquilizers.

Testing Hypotheses of Drug Use

A consideration of the four models of changes in sex differences in drug-using behavior discussed earlier produces a number of testable hypotheses. Three of these hypotheses relate to both the deviance and the social network model:

a. Sex ratios of drug use are inversely related to the legality or legal status of the drug.
b. Sex ratios of prescription drug use are inversely related to the legality of the use of the drug.
c. Sex ratios of regular drug use are in the same direction as those for general rates of use, but the pattern is more pronounced.

Three others relate specifically to the deviance model*:

a. Sex ratios of drug use are inversely related to rates of use.
b. Sex ratios of drug use become increasingly pronounced with age.
c. Sex ratios of drug use are directly related to perceived risk to health.

* We are unable to test the following hypothesis because we lack appropriate data: Sex ratios of drug use are inversely related to the length of time a drug has been in widespread use.

Two testable hypotheses are suggested by the diffusion of innovation model:

a. Rates of drug use among early adopters peak earlier than rates of use among late adopters.
b. Cohorts of users who begin use later in the diffusion phase are less differentiated by sex than those who begin use earlier, in terms of the time at which peak use occurs.

Four additional hypotheses derive from the social network model:

a. Rates of illicit drug use peak earlier among males than among females.
b. Males begin drug use at an earlier age than females (i.e., sex ratios of drug use are higher in early adolescence than in late adolescence).
c. Sex ratios of drug use are inversely related to the perceived availability of drugs.
d. Sex ratios of drug use are inversely related to the extent to which females have access to male carriers.

The economic model produces three testable hypotheses:

a. Sex ratios are directly related to the cost of drugs.
b. Rates of drug use for females are higher for employed females than for those not earning any income.
c. Rates of drug use for employed females vary directly with income.

In order to examine the models of sex differences in drug use that we have described, we will test each hypothesis using sets of appropriate data. In each case, we look at sex differences that relate to the dimension we are examining and, where possible, at changes in sex differences over time.

Sex Ratios of Drug Use Are Inversely Related to the Legality or Legal Status of the Drug.   Nine drugs for which sex-specific rates are commonly reported were ranked according to their legal status as specified by current drug legislation (Table 15). Data from 10 different studies of drug use were used to test the hypothesis (Chambers, 1971; New Hampshire Governor's Committee, 1972; Hays, 1974; Bakal et al., 1976; Kandel et al., 1976; White and Fallis, 1977b; Johnston et al., 1977; Blackford, 1977; Barr et al., 1977; Smart et al., 1977). The criteria for inclusion of a study in the analysis were first, that at least six of the nine drugs be included (only one study reported use for fewer than eight drugs), and second, that the sample of users for each drug be sufficiently large to provide reasonably stable sex ratios. When both licit and illicit use of prescription

Table 15. Median Sex Ratios of Drug Use and Rank Orders of Drugs

Drug category	Median sex ratios[a]	Rank order				
		Sex ratios	Legal status	Risk to health	Availability	Cost
Cocaine	178	9	1.5	6	2.5	9
Heroin	158	8	1.5	8	1	8
Hallucinogens	144	7	4	7	2.5	7
Inhalants	141	6	9	—	—	3
Marijuana	129	5	3	3	7	6
Barbiturates	100	4	5.5	4.5	4	3
Stimulants	95	3	5.5	4.5	5	3
Tobacco	92	2	8	1	8	3
Tranquilizers	83	1	7	2	6	3
Spearman's rho (r_s)			-0.59 $-0.92^{b,c}$	0.83^c	-0.76^c	0.87^c

[a] Based on data from the following studies: Chambers (1971); New Hampshire Governor's Committe (1972); Hays (1974); Kandel et al. (1976); Bakal et al. (1976); Smart et al. (1977); Blackford (1977); Ba et al. (1977); Johnston et al. (1977); White and Fallis (1977b).
[b] Calculated excluding inhalants.
[c] $p < .01$.

or controlled drugs was reported, we used the sex ratio for licit use because this is the legal status of the drug and therefore the pertinent information for the test of this hypothesis.

Sex ratios of drug use for each study were ranked for all nine drugs. The median sex ratio for each drug was calculated, and these ratios were also ranked. The ranks of the legal statuses of the drugs and the median sex ratio for each were correlated using Spearman's coefficient of rank-order correlation (r_s).

When all nine drugs are included, we obtain a negative correlation that does not quite achieve statistical significance ($r_s = -.592$). However, one of the drugs, solvents, does not fit the pattern at all.

The use of solvents is atypical in many ways. For instance, use tends to be greatest in early adolescence, with a marked decrease toward later adolescence. In the 1960s, patterns of inhalation mostly involved the fumes from model airplane glue and occasionally gasoline. Over time, other types of solvents have been included, such as metallic spray paint. Thus, the "drug" in question is hardly a unitary phenomenon. Finally, these substances are technically legal but are dispensed with caution by storekeepers. Thus, a young girl would probably have more difficulty buying airplane glue than a young boy.

When solvents are excluded from the analysis, the correlation for the remaining eight types of drugs increases dramatically to $r_s = -.917$ ($p < .01$).

Our findings are supported by Bowker's (1977) secondary analysis of data obtained by Chambers in a study of drug use in New York State (Chambers, 1971). Bowker's analysis of data for the proportion of male users of a drug and the proportion of drugs obtained illegally yielded a Spearman's rank-order correlation of −.77.

Sex Ratios of Prescription Drug Use Are Inversely Related to the Legality of the Use of the Drug. To test this hypothesis, studies that differentiate between licit and illicit use of prescription drugs were examined. (Among studies, this terminology varies and includes medical and nonmedical use and prescription and nonprescription sources of supply. Even though these terms are not exactly equivalent, they probably reflect similar forms of drug-using behavior.) Only seven studies collected data in this manner, and most of them are fairly recent (Russell and Hollander, 1974; Abelson and Atkinson, 1975; Macro Systems, 1975; Abelson and Fishburne, 1976; Bakal et al., 1976; Smart et al., 1977; White and Fallis, 1977b). This fact probably reflects the growing awareness on the part of researchers of the nonmedical use of these drugs. Sex ratios for both licit and illicit use were calculated, and the median sex ratios for adults and youth were compared for each category of drug.

Median sex ratios for the licit use of prescription drugs among adults range from 23 for amphetamines to 71 for sedatives. The corresponding median sex ratios for illicit use are 229 and 200. Similar disparities occur for tranquilizers and other stimulants. Among young people, the same pattern is observed, but the differences are less striking. Median sex ratios for licit and illicit use are 78 and 105 for the use of tranquilizers, 101 and 122 for barbiturate use, and 116 and 118 for stimulants.

Sex Ratios of Regular Drug Use Are in the Same Direction as Those for General Rates of Use, but the Pattern Is More Pronounced. To test this hypothesis, we examined data from a survey of approximately 20,000 high school students that was conducted over a 10-year period (Blackford, 1977). The analysis involved two steps. First, we determined the proportion of pairs of data that fit the hypothesis. For this study, any use during the past year represented general use, and use 50 or more times in the past year represented regular use. Thus, examples of data that support the hypothesis would be sex ratios of 112 and 135 for general and regular use of a drug that is used more by males, and sex ratios of 90 and 74, respectively, for a drug that is used more by females. Theoretically, the inversion of sex ratios of any use and heavy use occurs at 100.

The second step was to determine the relationship between sex ratios for any use and sex ratios for regular use. To do this, we calculated rank-order correlations between the deviation of the sex ratio for any use from 100 and the difference between the sex ratios for regular use and for any use.

The proportion of pairs of sex ratios that support the hypothesis was quite high for four of the drugs studied (marijuana, 100%; LSD, 89%; heroin, 87%; tobacco, 76%) and somewhat lower for the other two drugs examined (amphetamines, 57%; barbiturates, 40%). Three of the four drugs that fit the hypothesis fairly well are drugs that are used more by males. All the sex ratios for the use of heroin and marijuana fall above 100, and most of those for LSD do the same. Thus, sex ratios for drugs that are used more by males do conform very closely to the hypothesis. There is less support for drugs that are used more by females, although with tobacco, most of the sex ratios below 100 clearly fit the hypothesis.

There are at least two possible explanations for this finding. On the one hand, the inversion of sex ratios for any and regular use may occur well below the sex ratio of 100; that is, any use by females may have to become much greater than male use for regular use by females to become less deviant. On the other hand, the inversion process may be sufficiently variable so that many of those sex ratios that are close to 100 may only seem to deviate from the hypothesis. For example, sex ratios of 98 and 102, 95 and 98, or 104 and 101, for any and regular use, do not conform to the hypothesis. However, there is no reason to expect inversion to occur at precisely 100, and these pairs of sex ratios may not differ significantly, in either the statistical or the substantive sense.

When we examine pairs of sex ratios that do not conform to the hypothesis, we find that a high proportion are, in fact, very close to 100. In 9 of the 10 deviant pairs for tobacco, both sex ratios fall between 90 and 110. In more than half of the deviant pairs for amphetamines and barbiturates, at least one sex ratio falls within that range. Thus, slight variability in the point of inversion appears to explain a good part of the lack of conformity to the hypothesis.

When we looked for a lower point at which inversion might have occurred for the use of amphetamines and barbiturates, we found that sex ratios for barbiturate use do not invert even at ratios well below 100. This finding suggests that general and regular use of barbiturates may be of two different types, with females accounting for much of the general use and males for more of the regular use. There is no such clear pattern for the use of amphetamines, perhaps because amphetamine use is not a unitary phenomenon and can refer to speed (oral or intravenous), pep pills, and diet pills, each of which has a different pattern of use for males and females.

Our analysis of the relationship between sex ratios of general use and regular use produced a range of positive correlations for the various drugs. The correlation coefficients (r_s) are .53 for tobacco ($p < .01$), .43 for LSD ($p < .05$), .31 for heroin, .23 for barbiturates, .17 for amphetamines, and .11 for marijuana. Not all of these relationships are statistically significant, but all are in the predicted direction. This analysis is not crucial to our test of the hypothesis but adds specificity to it. Thus, not only do sex ratios for regular use follow a pattern that is similar to that of sex ratios for any use, but that pattern is more pronounced; it becomes even more pronounced as the sex ratios get farther away from 100.

Sex Ratios of Drug Use Vary Inversely with Rates of Use.   Our data afford two separate tests of this hypothesis. First, we examined the relationship between sex ratios and rates of use for particular drugs using cross-sectional data collected over at least five years in two separate studies (Barr et al., 1974, 1975, 1976, 1977; Blackford, 1977). Second, we looked at the relationship between median sex ratios and rates of use for nine different drugs in three separate studies (Barr et al., 1977; Blackford, 1977; Smart et al., 1977).

We were able to examine the relationship across time in 15 cases. Of the 15 correlations (Spearman's rank-order correlation), 12 were in the predicted direction, although none reached statistical significance. When we examined the relationship across drugs, the association was much stronger. Spearman's rho range from $-.70$ ($p < .05$) to $-.83$ ($p < .01$) in the three studies we used.

These findings support the hypothesis that rates of use of particular drugs are inversely related to sex ratios of use and suggest that the greater the degree of deviance associated with the use of a drug, as represented by increasingly lower rates of use, the higher the sex ratios of use.

Our analysis of use across time for particular drugs is complicated by the fact that rates of use often change very little over a few years, so that the rank orders are much less stable than they are across drugs. This instability in part explains our less consistent findings. However, a visual examination of the data indicates that in many cases, the relationship holds only for the period when rates are rising. In some cases, when use peaks and falls, sex ratios continue to decline or level off. Thus, a reformulation of our hypothesis may be indicated. It would incorporate the assumption that once use has become fairly widespread, and presumably less deviant, any subsequent decline in use would not increase the perceived deviance associated with use.

The hypothesis we have tested appears to be most valid in very general terms and probably over longer periods of time than those examined here. It is less useful for making more precise predictions in the short term.

Sex Ratios of Drug Use Become Increasingly Pronounced with Age.   The sex ratios of drug use among adults (18 and over) in several studies were ranked and correlated with ranks of the age groups used in each study. Separate calculations were done for each study. Only those surveys with sex ratios for at least five age groups are included in our analysis.

Sex ratios of drug use are positively related to age for tobacco. The median value of Spearman's rho for nine sets of data for tobacco use is .70 ($p < .05$) (Hammond and Garfinkel, 1964; Lanphier and Phillips, 1971a; American Institute of Public Opinion, 1974; Canadian Institute of Public Opinion, 1974b; Seltzer et al., 1974; U.S. Department of Health, Education and Welfare, Public Health Service, 1976; Health and Welfare Canada, 1976, 1977; National Opinion Research Center, 1977).

Sex ratios for other drugs are based on relatively small samples, so that the sample size for specific age groups is often below 20. However, results from the few studies that examine the use of other drugs by age (Manheimer et al., 1968, 1971; Lanphier and Phillips, 1971a; American Institute of Public Opinion, 1973; Canadian Institute of Public Opinion, 1974a) suggest that sex ratios for the use of tranquilizers and marijuana are positively related to age, whereas those for sedatives and stimulants are negatively related.

These findings suggest that sex ratios for the use of some drugs do become more pronounced with age.

Sex Ratios of Drug Use Are Directly Related to Perceived Risk to Health.   Johnston et al. (1977) asked high school seniors how much they thought people risk harming themselves if they use various drugs once or twice. (Tranquilizers and inhalants were not included.) To test this hypothesis, we ranked the proportions of respondents who perceived this risk to be great. We have omitted the data for tobacco reported by Johnston et al. because they did not ask about experimental use. On the basis of the ranks assigned to other drugs, we estimated that using tranquilizers and tobacco once or twice would rank lowest in order of perceived risk.

When we correlated the ranks for perceived risk to health with those for median sex ratios from several different studies, we found that the rank-order correlation (r_s) is .83 ($p < .01$). This strong positive correlation clearly supports the hypothesis that sex ratios for drug use are associated with perceived risk to health (Table 15).

Rates of Drug Use among Early Adopters Peak Earlier than Rates of Use among Late Adopters.   To test this hypothesis, we determined the year of peak use for several different drugs among adults and youth in a variety of studies (Canadian Institute of Public Opinion, 1963, 1974b; American Institute of Public Opinion, 1969a, 1972, 1974; U.S. Department of Health, Education, and Welfare, Public Health Service, 1973, 1976; Bakal et al., 1974, 1976; Barr et al., 1974, 1975, 1976, 1977; Smart et al., 1975; Abelson et al., 1973, 1975, 1976; Health and Welfare Canada, 1976, 1977; Blackford, 1977).

Because the use of at least one drug (marijuana) is still increasing, we can include only those drugs for which use has plateaued or entered the discontinuance phase. Further, we have to omit studies in which the apparent peak year of use occurred during the first or final year of the study, because we have no way of knowing whether they were the correct years of peak use. We have also eliminated studies in which lifetime prevalence was the measure of use, because this measure is not sufficiently specific to pinpoint the year of peak use.

To determine which sex category was the early adopter and which the late adopter for each drug, we looked at rates of use for males and females for the earliest surveys conducted, mostly in the late 1960s. For surveys that were repeated several times, we used data from the first year of the series.

Most drugs are adopted first by males. Heroin, cocaine, LSD, tobacco, and inhalants had higher rates of early use among males in all the studies examined. Early rates of use of tranquilizers are consistently higher among females. However, patterns of use of stimulants and sedatives are less consistent.

Among adults, females have higher rates of stimulant and sedative use in the early studies. Among youth, females appear to use them first in some studies and males in others. These discrepancies are probably due to two factors. First, local variations in the proportion of total stimulant use accounted for by different forms of stimulants probably explain much of the difference in patterns of use among adults and youth. The second factor has to do with the type of data collected. In studies of adult use, there is probably a higher proportion of medical use included, both because of the wording of questions and because actual medical use is higher. Even though data for stimulant and sedative use represent less unitary phenomena than data for other drugs, we would expect that the uncertainty about which sex adopts these drugs first would also be evident with regard to peaks in use.

Of the eight drug categories that manifested peaks in use, four indicated clear sex differences in the year of peak use (Table 16). Tobacco, inhalants, and cocaine peaked earlier among males; tranquilizers peaked earlier among females. Sedatives, stimulants, and heroin peaked slightly earlier among male youth, but differences were small. Hallucinogen use was not differentiated by sex among youth. Sufficient data for adults are not available for any of the illicit drugs.

These results show a fairly consistent relationship between the early adoption of a drug and the time of peak use. The use of tobacco, heroin, cocaine, tranquilizers, and inhalants conforms to the hypothesis. The lack of clear sex differentiation in the early use of sedatives and stimulants is reflected in the pattern of peak use. Hallucinogens are used earlier by males, but peak in the same year for young males and females.

Table 16. Peak Year of Drug Use for Males and Females

Population Drug	Number of studies	Median peak year		Mean difference (yr)	Sex that peaked first
		M	F		
Adults					
Inhalants	—	Not peaked	Not peaked	—	—
Tobacco	5[a,b,c,d,e]	1965	1972	5.0	M
Prescribed psychotherapeutic drugs (nonmedical use)	1[a]	1975	1972	3.0	F
Hallucinogens	—	No data	No data	—	—
Marijuana	—	Not peaked	Not peaked	—	—
Heroin	—	No data	No data	—	—
Cocaine	—	No data	No data	—	—
Youth					
Inhalants	3[f,g,h]	1971	1974	1.7	M
Tobacco	6[b,d,e,g,h,i]	1972	1974	2.5	M
Tranquilizers	3[f,g,h]	1973	1972	1.7	F
Sedatives	4[f,g,h,i]	1971–1972	1972–1973	0.8	M
Stimulants	4[f,g,h,i]	1971	1971–1972	0.2	M
Hallucinogens	4[f,g,h,i]	1972–1973	1972–1973	0.0	—
Marijuana	—	Not peaked	Not peaked	—	—
Heroin	3[g,h,i]	1972	1972	0.3	—
Cocaine	—	Not peaked	Not peaked	—	—

[a] Abelson et al. (1973, 1975, 1976).
[b] Health and Welfare Canada (1976, 1977).
[c] Canadian Institute of Public Opinion (1963, 1974b).
[d] U.S. Department of Health, Education, and Welfare, Public Health Service (1973, 1976).
[e] American Institute of Public Opinion (1969a, 1972, 1974).
[f] Bakal et al. (1974, 1976).
[g] Barr et al. (1974, 1975, 1976, 1977).
[h] Smart et al. (1975).
[i] Blackford (1977).

Cohorts of Users Who Begin Use Later in the Diffusion Phase Are Less Differentiated by Sex than Those Who Begin Use Earlier, in Terms of the Time at Which Peak Use Occurs. To test this hypothesis, we compared sex differences in the median peak years of drug use for youth and adults. Young people constitute a more recent cohort of users than adults, so that this comparison is an appropriate test of the hypothesis.

When we compared the mean difference in years between median peak years of use for tobacco and for licit psychotherapeutic drugs (sedatives, stimulants, and tranquilizers), the only drugs for which data on adults were available, we found that in both cases, the mean difference was at least twice as large for adults as it is for youth (Table 16). For tobacco, the mean differences were 5.0 years for adults and 2.5 years for young people. Sex differences in the peak year of use for licit psychotherapeutic drugs were 3.0 years for adults and 0.9 years for youth (the latter calculated by averaging data for the three drugs).

The findings consistently support the hypothesis that later cohorts of drug users are less differentiated by sex in terms of the year of peak use, and regardless of which sex peaks first.

Rates of Illicit Drug Use Peak Earlier among Males than among Females.   To test this hypothesis, we used the same data employed to relate sex differences in the year of peak use to sex differences in the time of adoption of the drug. Since the use of marijuana and cocaine has not yet peaked, we are limited to an examination of data for two drugs, heroin and the hallucinogens, and then only among students.

Among this group, the use of heroin peaked earlier among males; however, there was no apparent difference in the peak year of use for hallucinogens.

A clearer test of this hypothesis would involve more precise data for youth (calculated in terms of months rather than years) as well as data for adults. These results are not conclusive but do provide some support for our hypothesis.

Males Begin Drug Use at an Earlier Age than Females (i.e., Sex Ratios of Drug Use are Higher in Early Adolescence than in Late Adolescence).   Several types of data are available to test this hypothesis. These include average age of first use, percentage using by a certain age, and sex ratios of use for several age categories.

First use of tobacco was examined in a large survey of adults (Sterling and Weinkam, 1976). For whites, the average age of first use was 17.9 years for males and 21.5 years for females. Among blacks, the corresponding ages were 19.1 years and 21.7 years.

A study of tobacco use among Canadian schoolchildren (Hanley and Robinson, 1976) showed sizable sex differences in age of first use. For example, among 18-year-old students, 26% of males and 8% of females smoked their first cigarette by the age of 10. Sex differences were greatest for those who started at the youngest ages, such as 6 or 7, and were much reduced by the age of 15 or 16. An examination of successive cohorts of users in this survey indicates that sex differences are decreasing over time.

Among New England university students who used marijuana (Wolk, 1968), 35% of males and 25% of females began using marijuana before they went to college.

Johnston et al. (1977) examined the first use of eight psychoactive drugs among high school seniors in 1977. With the exception of tranquilizers, rates of use among males were much higher and sex ratios were all at least 200 for those using first in the earliest grade category, grade 6 or below. The sex ratios of first use for most drugs, including tranquilizers, declined with increasing grade of first use. However, for heroin and hallucinogens, they remained fairly high across grades.

The data we have presented provide considerable support for the hypothesis that males start using drugs earlier than females.

Sex Ratios of Drug Use Are Inversely Related to the Perceived Availability of Drugs.   Johnston et al. (1977) asked high school seniors how difficult they thought it would be to obtain a variety of different drugs. (Inhalants and tobacco were not included.) To test this hypothesis, we ranked the proportions of respondents who perceived the drugs to be fairly easy or very easy to get. We added tobacco to this list and estimated that it would be perceived as more available than any of the other drugs (cf. Smart, 1977).

To examine the relationship between perceived availability and sex ratios of use, we calculated Spearman's rank-order correlation. A fairly strong negative correlation ($r_s = -.76; p < .01$) describes the relationship between these two variables, and this result provides considerable support for the hypothesis (Table 15).

Sex Ratios of Drug Use Are Inversely Related to the Extent to Which Females Have Access to Male Carriers.   To test this hypothesis, we have used sex ratios for those drugs that females tend to acquire from males. Because no specific data are available on the access females have to male carriers we have examined sex ratios for use during different stages of the life cycle to operationalize this hypothesis. Females would probably have the greatest access to male carriers of illicit drugs during high school and college, when dating is frequent; there would be less access during the earlier years of school and even less during adulthood, when most women are married.

For licit psychoactive drugs, one would expect the lowest sex ratios to occur during the adult years, when women have greater contact with physicians. Younger women have less contact and very young females have the least (U.S. Department of Health, Education, and Welfare, 1975). Therefore, we would expect sex ratios to be higher among younger women and highest among very young women.

Sex ratios for use among three groups were examined. Grade 7 students represent the youngest group studied in most surveys. Grade 12 students are usually involved in dating and probably represent a point of high access to male carriers for illicit drug use. (College data are not used because these students are not representative of their age group.) Sex ratios for adults represent the third age category.

Sex ratios for five drugs were calculated for each of the three groups, where possible, and ranked according to observed and expected order (Table 17). Two illicit drugs and three licit drugs were included. Sufficient

Table 17. Observed (O) and Expected (E) Rank Orders of Median Sex Ratios[a] of Drug Use for Three Stages of the Life Cycle

	Marijuana			LSD			Sedatives			Tranquilizers			Stimulants		
	Sex ratio	O	E	Sex ratio	O	E	Sex ratio	O	E	Sex ratio	O	E	Sex ratio	O	E
Grade 7	147	2	2	153	2	2	122	3	3	94[b]	3	3	123	3	3
Grade 12	122	1	1	127	1	1	121	2	2	91	2	2	98	2	2
Adults	186	3	3	NA			69	1	1	54	1	1	21	1	1

[a] Based on 1975–1977 data (Barr et al., 1975, 1976, 1977; Bakal et al., 1976; Abelson and Fishburne, 1976; Blackford, 1977; Johnston et al., 1977).
[b] Based on 1972–1974 data (Barr et al., 1974; Bakal et al., 1976).

data are available only for marijuana and partly for LSD, of the illicit drugs, and sedatives, tranquilizers, and stimulants among the licit drugs.

For each of the five drugs studied, the observed and expected rank orders of the median sex ratios are identical. These results uniformly support the hypothesis that female access to male carriers is associated with sex differences in rates of drug use.

Sex Ratios of Drug Use Are Directly Related to the Cost of Drugs. Nine categories of drugs were ranked according to the estimated cost to the user of obtaining one dose of the drug (Table 15). Because costs have varied over time and across geographic locations, we have used approximate costs for the years 1972–1977, when most of the studies used to test this hypothesis were conducted. Since five of the drugs (tobacco, tranquilizers, barbiturates, stimulants, and glue) are very inexpensive (less than 10 cents per dose) and fall within such a narrow range, we have assigned them tied ranks. These data are correlated with ranks of median sex ratios of use based on the 10 studies of drug use among young people used to test the hypothesis. (Insufficient data were available to test separately for adults.)

Our analysis of these data produced a Spearman rank-order correlation of .87 ($p < .01$). This high positive correlation supports the hypothesis that sex ratios of drug use are directly associated with the cost of drugs.

Rates of Drug Use for Females Are Higher for Employed Females than for Those Not Earning Any Income. Only a few studies have examined the relationship between employment status and rates of drug use. Although most of these data are reported separately for males and females, very few control for age or socioeconomic status. Conflicting reports in the literature probably reflect the effect of these confounding variables as well as variations in measures of use.

Chambers and Inciardi (1971) found that working women in New York State are several times more likely to use illicit drugs, such as heroin, cocaine, and LSD, but are less than half as likely to use licit drugs such as sedatives, tranquilizers, and stimulants. Marijuana use is higher among employed women, but the difference is less dramatic. Guse et al. (1976) also reported lower rates of use of licit psychoactive drugs among women who are employed. Manheimer et al. (1968) reported higher rates of frequent use of stimulants and sedatives for women in the labor force and higher rates of tranquilizer use for those not in the labor force. Among 18- to 34-year-old women, marijuana use is highest among the unemployed and lowest among housewives; rates for employed women fall in between. Parry et al. (1973a) found that annual rates of use of minor tranquilizers and sedatives were highest among both upper- and lower-class housewives (27% and 24%) and lowest among upper-class working women and upper-middle-class housewives (16% and 15%). However, rates of heavy use vary inversely with social class.

Studies of smoking behavior indicate that women who do not work rank lowest in the use of tobacco (Green and Nemzer, 1973; U.S. Department of Health, Education, and Welfare, Public Health Service, 1976), although rates of use for employed and nonemployed women appear to be converging (Green and Nemzer, 1973). However, Sterling and Weinkam (1976) failed to find significant differences in rates of tobacco use among females who currently smoke or among those who had ever smoked. Among young women 18–35 years of age, there is little difference in rate of use of cigarettes between employed women and housewives. However, housewives are more likely to be heavy smokers (U.S. Department of Health, Education, and Welfare, 1977).

These findings suggest that employed women have higher rates of illicit drug use, whereas unemployed women who are housewives have higher rates of tranquilizer use. However, this finding and the higher rate of marijuana use among unemployed women may be partly a function of age. More specific data than those available to us are required to test this hypothesis.

Rates of Drug Use for Employed Females Vary Directly with Income. Very little attention has been paid to the relationship between drug use and income, except for the use of alcohol, which does not concern us here. In a national study of prescription drug use, Parry (1968) found that the use of tranquilizers and stimulants among females increases with income. However, sedative use is more stable across income levels. Schuman (1977) examined rates of tobacco use among men and women separately for different levels of income and found that smoking is directly related to income among women, but not among men.

These limited data tend to support the hypothesis, but further evidence would be advantageous.

5. DISCUSSION AND CONCLUSIONS

The basic questions with which we started are: Do sex differences exist in the use of various drugs? If so, is there evidence that they have changed or are changing over time? The answers have theoretical implications.

Median sex ratios for the use of different drugs among youth and adults are represented graphically for three periods of time (Figs. 1 and 2). The period prior to 1972 corresponds to the diffusion phase of the use of certain illicit drugs that has been referred to as the *drug crisis* of the late 1960s and early 1970s. The second period (1972–1974) represents a time of peak use for many illicit and some licit drugs, and the most recent interval (1975–1978) is characterized by mixed patterns, with the use of some drugs rising and others falling. Sufficient data are not available for all drugs, but those sex ratios displayed are derived from several different studies (Horn et al., 1959; Canadian Institute of Public Opinion, 1963, 1973, 1974a,b; Parry, 1968; Laforest, 1969; Stennett et al., 1969; American Institute of Public Opinion, 1969a,b; 1972, 1973, 1974; Annis et al., 1971; Clarke and Levine, 1971; Digital Resources Corporation, 1971;

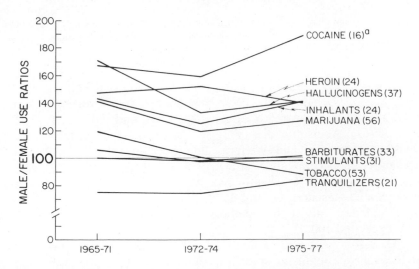

Fig. 1. Median sex ratios for the nonmedical use of drugs among students and youth for three periods of time. Parenthetical values indicate the number of data sets used.

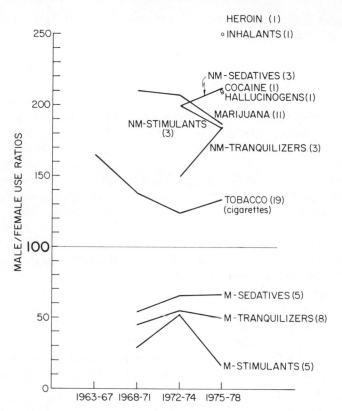

Fig. 2. Median sex ratios for the use of drugs among adults in selected national surveys for three periods of time. Sex ratio for heroin exceeds 300. Parenthetical values indicate the number of data sets used. NM, Nonmedical use; M, medical use.

Hager et al., 1971; Johnson et al., 1971; Lanphier and Phillips, 1971a,b; Russell, 1971; Schaps et al., 1971; New Hampshire Governor's Commission, 1972; Lavenhar and Sheffet, 1973; Love and Killorn, 1973; Parry et al., 1973a; Abelson et al., 1973, 1975, 1976, 1977; U.S. Department of Health, Education, and Welfare, Public Health Service, 1973, 1976; Epstein et al., 1976; Kandel et al., 1976; Sorosiak et al., 1976; Wechsler and McFadden, 1976; Health and Welfare Canada, 1976, 1977; Pool, 1977; Social Research Group, 1978; Rootman and Fralick, 1978). Data were included only if the numbers for sex-specific use of a particular drug exceeded 100.

Data for youth and students have been combined (Figure 1). Most of the surveys involved students, and the addition of youth from the general population simply provided additional data but did not change the results significantly. Medical and nonmedical use is displayed separately for adults (Figure 2). Whereas surveys of students generally specify nonmedical use only and inquire about the use of several illicit drugs, surveys of adults tend to focus on the use of licit drugs and do not always specify nonmedical use. While some of the studies used to denote medical use may include some nonmedical use, none clearly separated the two types, and we feel that they primarily involved medical use.

These data clearly indicate that there are major sex differences in the use of most drugs and that these differences persist over time. Sex differences for drug use are more extreme for adults than for youth. Median sex ratios among adults range from 17 to over 200; among youth, the range is less: 74 to 189. This finding suggests that sex differences are a somewhat less important factor in determining levels of drug use among young people. It is difficult to tell whether this pattern will persist among the current cohort of young people as they mature. However, the fact that sex ratios among adults and youth separately have not become noticeably less differentiated over time, except those for marijuana, suggests that sex ratios for youth will become more like those of adults as they mature.

When specific drugs are examined, we find that sex ratios for illicit drugs are invariably above 100 and are considerably higher than those for licit drugs. Sex ratios for the specifically nonmedical use of licit drugs are similar to those for illicit drugs. Over the past decade, the rank order of sex ratios for the use of various drugs has remained roughly the same.

Not only are there sizable sex differences in the use of most drugs among both youth and adults, but there is also no evidence that patterns of drug use are converging. In fact, in the majority of cases, they are diverging. One apparent exception is the decrease in the sex ratio for marijuana use among adults. However, the fact that the sex ratio has increased slightly among youth strongly suggests that this is simply a cohort effect that has resulted from the entrance of a younger cohort of marijuana users with a lower sex ratio into the adult group. The decrease in the sex ratio for heroin use is small and probably not very meaningful.

These findings contrast sharply with some prevalent beliefs. It is widely held that patterns of drug-using behavior among women and men are becoming more alike; that rates of use of most drugs are increasing rapidly; and that rates of use are increasing faster among women than among men. Rates of use of only two drugs, marijuana and cocaine, appear to be increasing, but the magnitude of the increase in rates of use is unclear because most of the data are reported in terms of lifetime prevalence; furthermore, sex ratios for their use are not decreasing.

Two factors may somewhat mitigate our conclusions. In our analysis, we are dealing with only a very limited period of time. If data were available for periods of 25 or 50 years, these results might be different. Second, had we been able to use data that were consistent for the specific drugs included, for the measures of frequency of use and type of use employed, our findings might have differed.

To examine this latter possibility, we have calculated median sex ratios using data from Blackford (1977), the only researcher who has continuously collected data over the three time periods. These data have limitations: first, because they apply only to high school students in an affluent area of California; second, because they are available only for six drugs and are missing early data for two years; and third, because the medians are based on few sex ratios. However, they do allow us to control for several important factors and provide an alternate picture of changes in sex ratios of drug use over time (Fig. 3).

These data bear considerable resemblance to those for the larger group of young people. Although most of the sex ratios are somewhat lower in this study, the rank order of sex ratios for use are similar, and illicit drugs have higher sex ratios than licit drugs. There are some variations in trends over time, but there is no evidence to support the convergence hypothesis. There does appear to be a slight trend toward a reduction in sex ratios over time for the use of LSD and barbiturates, as well as for the use of tobacco, which also appears in our more general analysis of drug use. However, these decreases are not large, and therefore, it is difficult to determine their significance.

In both the aggregated and single study data we have examined, the

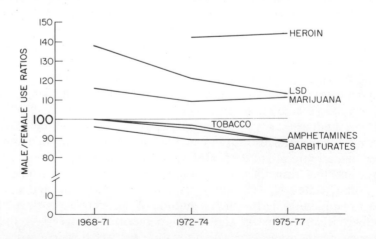

Fig. 3. Median sex ratios for the use of drugs among junior and senior high school students in San Mateo County, California, for three periods of time.

only trend that is fairly consistent is a decrease in the sex ratios for tobacco use among youth. It is well known that rates of use of tobacco are decreasing among males but not among females. In fact, the younger females appear to be increasing their use. The reversal of this trend among the youngest females in the San Mateo study during 1976 and 1977 suggests that sex ratios for tobacco use may begin to increase again shortly, or at least to level off.

We have limited our analysis to studies of drug use in Canada and the United States. However, a cross-national study of the use of minor tranquilizers and sedatives in nine Western European countries (Balter et al., 1974) produced similar results. The rates of use of these drugs are remarkably similar across countries, ranging from 13% to 21% for women and 7% to 12% for males, and sex ratios of use fall between 42 and 77, with five of the nine falling between 50 and 60. Rates for the United States using comparable data occur well within the range of rates, while the sex ratio is at the bottom of the range. (A critical examination of this study by Cooperstock, 1975, did not produce any evidence that sex ratios are at all biased.)

These findings indicate the pervasive nature of sex differences in patterns of drug use and suggest that the most useful explanations of differences are those derived from the kinds of broad theoretical frameworks we have used.

We have applied four theoretical models to drug-using behavior. A series of hypotheses derived from these models has been tested through the use of data from various studies. Within the limits of the data we have employed, 12 of the 15 hypotheses tested receive considerable support, and the remaining three receive some support but results are less persuasive because of a lack of good data.

In some cases where no useful data were available for adults, we have used data for students to test our hypotheses. Theoretically, this procedure affects the generalizability of our results; however, given the pervasive nature of sex differences, it is highly unlikely that the relationships we have found would not characterize adults as well. What is most likely is that they would be even stronger among those in older age groups.

We will consider each model in turn, discussing its implications for our research and attempt to provide a more integrated approach to explaining sex differences in drug use.

Associations between sex ratios and other variables, of course, are not necessarily causal; that is, a change in one of these variables for a particular drug does not necessarily produce a change in sex ratios for the use of that drug. A more definitive examination of these relationships is beyond the scope of this chapter and is suggested as a priority for future research. However, there are examples of quasi experiments that support a causal relationship. For example, the change in the legal status of opium in the United States preceded the reversal of sex differences in patterns of use. This fact does not exclude the possibility that changing patterns of use may also have had an effect on the introduction of legislation. However, the magnitude of the change and the speed with which it occurred suggest that the relationship was predominantly in the other direction.

The four hypotheses that stem from the deviance model are supported by our data, suggesting that the traditional stereotypes of sex-role behavior do characterize the use of drugs. Males have higher rates of illicit drug use and nonmedical use of licit drugs and are more likely than females to engage in the regular use of drugs. Females, on the other hand, have lower rates of use of most drugs, generally use them less often, and are much less likely to use illicit drugs. They are also more likely than males to use those drugs with the least perceived risk to health. Thus, females are more conservative in their use of drugs and engage in less deviant behavior when they acquire and use drugs.

The implications of these findings are considerable. They suggest that the decriminalization or legalization of the use of any drug that is currently illegal could produce disproportionately higher rates of use among females. Thus, we would expect that changes in legislation affecting marijuana would result in a general increase in use by both sexes, as well as a disproportionate increase in use by women. On the other hand, the increasing evidence that a broad range of drugs is implicated in various types of damage associated with reproduction (genetic, prenatal, and postnatal damage) may raise the perceived risk to health of the use of a variety of drugs, especially among young women, and might result in a relative decrease in their use.

The diffusion of innovation model is supported insofar as we were able to test it. A more definitive test would involve an analysis of rates of drug use among males and females over time using more sophisticated statistical techniques than those employed here. However, this analysis would have to be done with data collected over several years using the same methods. At present, the only sets of data that could even be considered for such an analysis are the national data on smoking (U.S. Department of Health, Education and Welfare, Public Health Service, 1976; Health and Welfare, Canada, 1976, 1977) and the San Mateo, California High School Drug Surveys (Blackford, 1977). Even these sets of data would be enhanced by additional years of data collection.

On the basis of our more limited analysis, males had higher initial rates of use of all drugs examined except tranquilizers; their use of these drugs tended to peak earlier than use among females for those drugs that appear to have completed the diffusion phase, again with the exception of tranquilizers. As we predicted, male college students had the highest rates of marijuana use in the early years: 51% in 1970; 66% in 1971 (*Playboy Magazine,* 1976). Adult women had the highest rates of tranquilizer use (Manheimer et al., 1968).

The advantage of the diffusion model is that it enables one to distinguish between trends toward convergence and sex-specific cycles of use that may appear to be converging at certain times. Thus, an examination of the data for tobacco use when sex ratios were still above 100 would suggest convergence. However, rates have recently begun to diverge, indicating a later peak in use for females, and there is some evidence that rates among young women are about to decline (Blackford, 1977). These trends can only be explained by using the diffusion model, and they contradict predictions that undifferentiated use by sex is the "logical conclusion" of declining sex ratios (cf. Nielson and Hirabayashi, 1975; Bossé and Rose, 1976).

This is not to suggest that over the long run, convergence may not be occurring as well. However, we feel that it is important to separate the effects of the diffusion process from any coexisting trend toward convergence.

A different aspect of the diffusion process concerns the discontinuance of drug use. Studies of the incidence of smoking among men and women indicate that a higher proportion of males than females have quit smoking (Horn et al., 1959; Hammond and Garfinkel, 1961; Green and Nemzer, 1973; Srole and Fischer, 1973; Wynder et al., 1974; Kelson et al., 1975; Health and Welfare Canada, 1976; U.S. Department of Health, Education, and Welfare, Public Health Service, 1976; Hanley and Robinson, 1976; Schuman, 1977), and the inference is often made that women have more difficulty quitting and are not as "serious" about doing it. In terms of diffusion theory, we would expect cessation of smoking among women to lag behind that for men by about five years. An examination of national data from the United States indicates that the proportion of former smokers among females of those who have ever smoked lags about four years behind the proportion for males (Schuman, 1977).

The diffusion of innovation model is more descriptive than explanatory. There is a need for mechanisms to explain the lag effect. In the case of smoking cessation, there are several likely factors: rates of smoking-related illness have historically been much lower among women because most of the harmful effects of smoking are long-term. Thus, women would perceive themselves as being at lower risk (Schuman, 1977) and their physicians would probably have similar attitudes. In many respects, they are also objectively at lower risk. Women have always smoked less than men and are more likely to smoke filter cigarettes and those lower in tar and nicotine. They also inhale less (Schuman, 1977). Furthermore, they have no socially acceptable alternatives such as pipes or cigars to turn to.

The increasing rates of lung cancer and heart disease among women, the evidence that smoking has a harmful effect on the fetus, and the recently discovered hazards associated with smoking and contraceptive pills are undoubtedly raising the level of perceived risk associated with smoking among women.

We have used tobacco as an example in our discussion of the diffusion of innovation model because its patterns of use are well documented and because it provides the clearest example of the diffusion process. There are no comparable data for the use of other drugs among adults, and as Blackford (1977) has noted, the lag effect among high school students tends to be one year at most. Thus, there is clearly a need for further research in this area relative to the use of the other drugs.

The social network model views drug use as a social phenomenon that involves the introduction of new users to drugs by those who have already begun use. Males, who control the production and distribution of drugs, influence the extent to which females obtain and consume drugs and the circumstances in which this occurs. The most usual context for initiation occurs within a dating relationship or a medical consultation. This model accounts for both the higher rates of the use of most drugs by males and the gap in time between use by males and females.

The social network model is strongly supported by our tests of six of the seven hypotheses. Some of the results are based on fairly indirect tests of the model, for example, the finding that the legal status of drugs is inversely related to sex ratios for their use. Others are more direct, such as those that examine access to male "carriers" and perceived availability.

The social network model of drug use has certain implications for social policy and research. Changes in the legal status of any drug could have a significant bearing on the access females have to drugs. A change in the status of marijuana, for example, could reduce female dependence on males for acquiring this drug. More controls on prescription drugs, such as the restrictions imposed on amphetamines, or simply a voluntary effort on the part of physicians to prescribe fewer drugs, could potentially reduce rates of use of those drugs among women more than among men. Certain social changes, such as the increase in females entering the medical profession or changes in traditional dating patterns and male and female peer-group relationships, could also affect the availability of drugs to women.

The socioeconomic model views drugs as a commodity and sex

differences in drug use as a product of sex differences in socioeconomic access to this commodity. The low cost of many drugs suggests that demand for them is relatively inelastic, that is, only major increases in cost would affect patterns of purchase.

We were limited in the type of data available to test this model, but we can conclude that there is a relationship between cost and sex ratios for use. If we assume that this association is causal, we can predict that unless the fairly constant disparity between incomes for men and women decreases, there will be little change in sex ratios for the use of those drugs that are costly and also in sex ratios for the frequent use of all drugs except those covered by prescription plans.

On the other hand, the continuing influx of women into the labor force will result in an increase in their disposable income. This effect could result in higher rates of use among women, although most of these women belong to age groups that have relatively low rates of use of the more costly drugs.

At a more general level, any increases or decreases in the cost of particular drugs relative to disposable income could potentially alter patterns of drug use among females because their demand for all drugs is more elastic than that of males because their average disposable income is much lower. Research geared specifically to examining sex differences in economic behavior would assist in clarifying these issues.

Each of the four models of sex differences in drug-using behavior contributes to an increased understanding of the variation in patterns of drug use between women and men. However, it would be advantageous to provide a more integrated explanation of sex differences in drug use.

The diffusion of innovation model accounts for many of the differences we have found and is particularly useful for explaining changes over time. However, it does not account for the fact that rates of use of some drugs are consistently higher among males than among females; nor does it explain why females at different ages and at different points of time adopt the use of drugs at varying lengths of time after males adopt them.

The other three models are most useful in explaining these phenomena and can each be used to provide a different perspective of the same behavior. For example, trends in smoking behavior can be explained by the use of all four models.

We have already discussed the diffusion and the discontinuance of smoking. During World War I, smoking had become acceptable for men but was considered quite deviant for women. When women went to work during World War II, sex stereotypes had decreased somewhat so that smoking became a less deviant behavior. Women also had more discretionary spending power and could acquire cigarettes directly. Thus, the increasing adoption of a drug decreases the deviance associated with its use and may also reduce the cost to a level that is more within the range of women. When use becomes less deviant, it becomes easier to bypass the traditional patterns of obtaining drugs from males.

We are suggesting that each of the four models we have introduced and tested is appropriate for interpreting sex differences in drug-using behavior and that the most complete explanation is achieved by using all four.

Our analysis of sex differences in psychoactive drug use has confirmed much previous research, but it has also produced some surprises. Sex differences in the use of certain drugs are declining, but we must disagree with Wechsler and McFadden (1976), who concluded that sex differences are a "disappearing phenomenon." Neither is there much evidence that rates of drug use are increasing faster among women than among men. In cases where this appears to be happening, the trend is probably temporary and due to the time lag for rates of use among women. The relative nature of any increase should be emphasized. For example, the largest part of the decrease in sex ratios for tobacco use is due to the fall in rates of use by males rather than the increase in use by females.

The slight increase in sex ratios for use among young people that has occurred since 1974 may in fact indicate a reversal of a trend toward declining sex ratios. It is premature to do more than speculate; however, we can suggest that current economic difficulties and an apparent trend among young people toward conservatism in areas such as dress and political behavior may indeed be associated with such a reversal.

This is not to suggest that we should be complacent about current trends in drug use among women. Most of the drugs we have studied are not associated with severe acute effects. However, much further research is required to determine the nature of long-term effects and less obvious kinds of damage. Alcohol has been used for centuries, but the widespread acceptance of the notion that drinking causes fetal damage did not occur until the 1970s. Rate of use for most other drugs are much lower than those for alcohol. With increasing rates of use, there will very likely be discoveries of damaging effects that are now unknown or are only the subject of speculation. Women are at greater risk than men for a variety of types of damage because of their reproductive capacity, and they may be at increased risk in other ways, such as having lower average body weight. Moreover, peak use for most drugs occurs during the reproductive years.

The use of marijuana has become very widespread and in one national study of high school seniors (Johnston et al., 1977) has a higher rate of daily use among males than alcohol. Even if sex ratios for the use of marijuana do not decrease appreciably, the increasing rates of use and of frequent use may pose threats to the health of women at some point in the future.

Continued research on the effects of psychoactive drugs and inter-action among these drugs on women as well as on men is essential if future damage is to be prevented. Equally important, however, is the continuation and expansion of highly focused research on patterns of drug use among women and men. The flurry of one-shot studies that constituted the response to the drug crisis of a decade ago is largely past. The greatest need at this point is for more precise monitoring of drug use through the use of repeated cross-sectional surveys (cf. Abelson et al. 1977; Blackford, 1977; Johnston et al., 1977). Longitudinal surveys that study drug-using behavior among successive cohorts of users, such as those by Josephson and associates and Johnston and associates, also provide valuable information about trends. There is a need for larger and more frequent adult studies similar to those conducted for tobacco use. These should include measures of period prevalence that are comparable to other studies, as well as reliable measures of frequency of use.

Efforts should be made to measure total psychoactive drug use. The tendency to ask about the use of only a single type of drug in a larger category—for example, barbiturates or LSD—may result in an under-estimate of use for that category of drugs. Some studies ask only about prescription psychoactives and ignore over-the-counter medication. There is also considerable evidence that combination drugs, in which tranquilizers or sedatives are combined with other drugs, form a very sizable proportion of total psychoactive drug use (Cooperstock, 1974; Rosenbaum, 1977). These kinds of drugs are less relevant to this study because they are less likely to be used nonmedically; however, further investigation of their use is advisable.

Only recently have efforts been made to distinguish between the medical and nonmedical use of licit drugs (Abelson and Fishburne, 1976; Abelson et al., 1977; Smart et al., 1977). We have indicated the large discrepancies between sex ratios for these two types of use and recom-mend even more detailed examinations of types of use and greater consistency of measures. Recent studies have used either reported type of use (medical, nonmedical) or source of drug (physician, other), which are two quite different measures. There may also be a need to distinguish between recreational use and self-medication with illegally acquired prescription drugs.

Alcohol is sometimes excluded in studies of drug use. Its similarity in terms of broad epidemiological patterns of use (Whitehead, 1975), its physiological effect, and its role as a potentiator of other drugs suggest that it, too, should be included in studies of other drugs. As well, its possible role as an alternative "coping" substance for men (Parry, 1968) means that the addition of this widely used drug could provide a much more accurate picture of the distribution of psychoactive drug use among women and men.

ACKNOWLEDGMENTS

The authors wish to acknowledge the valuable assistance provided by Jan Gorman, Senior Research Assistant with the Lake Erie Region of the Addiction Research Foundation, in connection with organizing data for this paper. We are deeply indebted to her.

Most of the U.S. data utilized in this chapter were made available by the Drug Abuse Epidemiology Data Center (DAEDAC) located at the Institute of Behavioral Research, Texas Christian University, Fort Worth. DAEDAC is supported by the National Institute on Drug Abuse. Most of the Canadian data were made available by Nancy Jennings from the computerized substance abuse data files of the Machine Readable Archives (MRA), a division of the Public Archives of Canada, 395 Wellington Street, Ottawa.

Oriana Kalant, editor of this volume, has won our admiration and respect for the assistance, encouragement, and patience that she displayed toward us during each phase of this project.

REFERENCES

Abelson, H., and Atkinson, R., 1975, *Public Experience with Psychoactive Substances: A Nationwide Study of Adults and Youth,* Response Analysis Corporation, Princeton, N.J.

Abelson, H., and Fishburne, P., 1976, *Non-Medical Use of Psychoactive Substances; 1975/ 6 Nationwide Study among Youth and Adults,* Response Analysis Corporation, Princeton, N.J.

Abelson, H., Cohen, R., Schrayer, D., and Rappeport, M., 1973, *Drug Experience, Attitudes, and Related Behavior among Adolescents and Adults,* Response Analysis Corporation, Princeton, N.J.

Abelson, H., Fishburne, P., and Cisin, I., 1977, *The National Survey on Drug Abuse: 1977,* Vol. 1, *Main Findings,* National Institute on Drug Abuse, Department of Health, Education, an Welfare, Rockville, Md.

American Institute of Public Opinion, 1969a, Use of Cigarettes, July 1969, Gallup Poll, unpublished data, Roper Center, New Haven, Conn.

American Institute of Public Opinion, 1969b, Use of Marijuana, September 1969, Gallup Poll, unpublished data, Roper Center, New Haven, Conn.

American Institute of Public Opinion, 1972, Use of Cigarettes, April 1972, Gallup Poll, unpublished data, Roper Center, New Haven, Conn.

American Institute of Public Opinion, 1973, Use of Marijuana, January 1973, Gallup Poll, unpublished data, Roper Center, New Haven, Conn.

American Institute of Public Opinion, 1974, Use of Cigarettes, May 1974, Gallup Poll, unpublished data, Roper Center, New Haven, Conn.

Annis, H. M., Klug, R., and Blackwell, D., 1971, *Drug Use among High School Students in Timmins,* Addiction Research Foundation Substudy No. 434, Toronto.

Annis, H., and Watson, C., 1975, Drug use and school dropout: A longitudinal study, *Can. Counsellor* **9:**155–162.

Bakal, D. A., Milstein, S. L., and Rootman, I., 1974, *Trends in Drug Use among Rural Students in Alberta: 1971–1974,* Report, Non-Medical Use of Drugs Directorate, Health and Welfare Canada, Ottawa.

Bakal, D. A., Rootman, I., and Campbell, D., 1976, *Drug Use in Rural Alberta: 1976,* Report, Non-Medical Use of Drugs Directorate, Health and Welfare Canada, Ottawa.

Balter, M. B., Levine, J., and Manheimer, D. I., 1974, Cross-national study of the extent of antianxiety/sedative drug use, *N. Engl. J. Med.* **290:**769–774.

Barr, C. L., Fountain, A. W., and Klock, J. A., 1974, *Student Drug and Alcohol Opinionnaire and Usage Survey, Grades 6, 7, 8, 9, 10, 11, 12. June 1973 to January, 1974,* Test and Measurements Unit, Curriculum Division, Duval County School Board, Jacksonville, Fla.

Barr, C. L., Fountain, A. W., and J. A. Klock, 1975, *Student Drug and Alcohol Opinionnaire and Usage Survey, Grades 6, 7, 8, 9, 10, 11, 12. January 1975,* Tests and Measurements Unit, Curriculum Division, Duval County School Board, Jacksonville, Fla.

Barr, C. L., Fountain, A. W., Benham, C. J., and Winesett, H., 1976, *Student Drug and Alcohol Opinionnaire and Usage Survey, Grades 6, 7, 8, 9, 10, 11, and 12,* Duval County School Board, Jacksonville, Fla.

Barr, C. L., Fountain, A. W., and Staats, W. D., 1977, *Student Drug and Alcohol Opinionnaire and Usage Survey, Grades 6, 7, 8, 9 10, 11, and 12,* Duval County School Board, Supervisor of Instructional Media, Jacksonville, Fla.

Bell, D. S., and Champion, R. A., 1976, *Monitoring Drug Use in New South Wales,* Part 3, *Division of Health Service Research,* Health Commission of New South Wales, Sydney, Australia.

Blackford, L. St. Clair, 1972. Surveillance of levels of drug use in a student population, *Drug Forum* **1:**307–313.

Blackford, L. St. Clair, 1977, *Summary Report—Surveys of Student Drug Use, San Mateo County, California: Alcohol–Amphetamines–Barbiturates, Heroin, LSD, Marijuana, Tobacco,* Department of Public Health and Welfare, San Mateo County, Calif.

Block, J. H., 1976, Issues, problems and pitfalls in assessing sex differences: A critical review of The Psychology of Sex Differences, *Merrill-Palmer Q.* **22:**283–308.

Bossé, R. and Rose, C. L., 1976, Smoking cessation and sex role convergence, *J. Health Soc. Behav.* **17:**53–61.

Botterell, E. H., 1975, *The Provision of Medical and Health Care Services to Inmates in Federal Penitentiaries.* The Second Report of the National Health Services Advisory Committee to the Commissioner of Penitentiaries, Office of the Solicitor-General, Ottawa.

Bowker, L. H., 1977, *Drug Use among American Women, Old and Young: Sexual Oppression and Other Themes,* R. and E. Research Associates, San Francisco.

Canadian Institute of Public Opinion, 1963, Use of Cigarettes, August 1963, The Gallup Poll of Canada, unpublished data, Roper Center, New Haven, Conn.

Canadian Institute of Public Opinion, 1973, Twelve Percent of Adults Have Tried Marijuana, The Gallup Report, August 1, The Gallup Poll of Canada, Toronto.

Canadian Institute of Public Opinion, 1974a, Marijuana Use Among Adults, December 1974, The Gallup Poll of Canada, unpublished data, Roper Center, New Haven, Conn.

Canadian Institute of Public Opinion, 1974b, Use of Cigarettes, March 1974, The Gallup Poll of Canada, unpublished data, Roper Center, New Haven, Conn.

Chambers, C. D., 1971, *An Assessment of Drug Use in the General Population, Special Report No 1: Drug Use in New York State,* New York State Addiction Control Commission, New York.

Chambers, C. D., and Inciardi, J. A., 1971, *An Assessment of Drug Use in the General Population, Special Report No. 2: Drug Use in New York State, Drug Use in New York City, Drug Use in Selected Geographical Regions of New York State,* New York State Addiction Control Commission, New York.

Chein, I., Gerard D., Lee, R., and Rosenfeld, E., 1965, *The Road to H,* pp. 299–320, Basic Books, New York.

Clarke, J. W., and Levine, E. L., 1971, Marijuana use, social discontent and political alienation: A study of high school youth, *Am. Pol. Sci. Rev.* **65:**120–130.

Cooperstock, R., 1974, Some factors involved in the increased prescribing of psychotropic drugs in: *Social Aspects of the Medical Use of Psychotropic Drugs* (R. Cooperstock, ed.), Addiction Research Foundation, Toronto.

Cooperstock, R., 1975, *A Critical Examination of Two Studies of Psychoactive Drug Consumption,* Addiction Research Foundation Substudy 716, Toronto.

Cooperstock, R., 1977, *The Epidemiology of Psychotropic Drug Use in Canada Today,* Addiction Research Foundation Substudy 906, Toronto.

Cuskey, W. R., Premkumar, T., and Sigel, L., 1972, Survey of opiate addiction among females in the United States between 1850 and 1970, *Public Health Rev.* **1:**5–39.

Digital Resources Corporation, 1971, School surveys, in: *Model for Criminal Justice System Planning and Control,* Vol. 3, Long Beach, Calif.

Dunnell, K., and Cartwright, A., 1972, *Medicine Takers, Prescribers and Hoarders,* Routledge and Kegan Paul, London.

Dupont, R. L., and Piemme, T. E., 1973, Estimation of the number of narcotic addicts in an urban area, *Med. Ann. D.C.* **42:**323–326.

Ellinwood, E. H., Smith, W. G., and Vaillant, G. E., 1966, Narcotic addiction in males and females: A Comparison, *Int. J. Addict.* **1:**33–45.

Epstein, M. H., Crenshaw, C. S., Albert, V. M., and Friedman, A. S., 1976, High School drug survey, Washington County, Georgia, *J. Med. Assoc. Ga.* **65:**407–410.

Freeland, J. B., and Campbell, R. S., 1973, The social context of first marijuana use, *Int. J. Addict.* **8:**317–324.

Glenn, W. A., 1977, Problems related to survey sampling, in: *The Epidemiology of Drug Abuse: Current Issues* (L. G. Richards and L. B. Blevins, eds.), National Institute on Drug Abuse, Rockville, Md.

Goldstein, R., 1966, *1 in 7: Drugs on Campus,* Walker, New York.

Green, D. E., and Nemzer, D. E., 1973, Changes in cigarette smoking by women—An analysis, 1966 and 1970, *Health Services Rep.* **88:**631–636.

Greenwood, J. A., 1971, *Estimating the Number of Narcotic Addicts,* Report SCID-TR-3, October, Bureau of Narcotics and Dangerous Drugs, Government Printing Office, Washington, D.C.

Guse, L., Morier, G., and Ludwig, J., 1976, *Winnipeg Survey of Prescription Drug (Mood-Altering) Use among Women,* Technical Report, NMUDD, Manitoba Alcoholism Foundation, October 30.

Hager, D. L., Stewart, C. S., and Vener, A., 1971, Patterns of adolescent drug use in Middle America, *J. Counselling Psychol.* **18:**292.

Hammond, E. C., and Garfinkel, L., 1961, Smoking habits of men and women, *J. Natl. Cancer Inst.* **27**:419–422.

Hammond, E. C., and Garfinkel, L., 1964, Changes in cigarette smoking, *J. Natl. Cancer Inst.* **33**:49–64.

Hanley, J. A., and Robinson, J. C., 1976, Cigarette smoking and the young: A national survey, *Can. Med. Assoc. J.* **114**:511–517.

Harris, A. R., 1977, Sex and theories of deviance: Toward a functional theory of deviant type-scripts, *Am. Sociol. Rev.* **42**:3–16.

Hays, J. R., 1971, The incidence of drug abuse among secondary school students in Houston, I, *St. Joseph Hosp. Med.-Surg. J.* **6**:52–72.

Hays, J. R., 1972, The incidence of drug abuse among secondary school students in Houston, 1971, II, *St. Joseph Hosp. Med.-Surg. J.* **7**:146–152.

Hays, J. R., 1974, The incidence of drug abuse among secondary school students in Houston, 1973, *St. Joseph Hosp. Med.-Surg. J.* **9**:12–17.

Health and Welfare Canada, 1976, *Smoking Habits of Canadians, 1965–1974.* Technical Report Series, No. 1, January, Non-Medical Use of Drugs Directorate, Ottawa.

Health and Welfare Canada, 1977, *Smoking Habits of Canadians, 1975,* Technical Report Series, No. 7, December, Non-Medical Use of Drugs Directorate, Ottawa.

Horn, D., Courts, F. A., Taylor, R. M., and Solomon, E. S., 1959, Cigarette smoking among high school students, *Am. J. Public Health* **49**:1497–1511.

Howard, J., and Borges, P., 1970, Needle sharing in the Haight: social and psychological functions, *J. Health Soc. Behav.* **11**:220–230.

Hubbard, R. L., Eckerman, W. C., and Rachal, J. V., 1976, *Methods of Validating Self-Reports of Drug Use: A Critical Review,* Proceedings of the American Statistical Association, Social Statistics Division.

Hunt, L. G., 1977, Prevalence of active heroin use in the United States, in: *The Epidemiology of Heroin and Other Narcotics* (J. D. Rittenhouse, ed.), National Institute on Drug Abuse Research Monograph 16, National Institute on Drug Abuse, Rockville, Md.

Johnson, K. G., Donnelly, J. H., Scheble, R., Wine, R., and Weitman, M., 1971, Survey of adolescent drug use. I. Sex and grade distribution, *Am. J. Public Health* **61**:2418–2432.

Johnston, L. D., 1977, Survey data as contributors to estimation, in: *The Epidemiology of Heroin and Other Narcotics* (J. D. Rittenhouse, ed.), NIDA Research Monograph 16, November, pp. 103–108, Department of Health, Education and Welfare (National Institute on Drug Abuse), Rockville, Md.

Johnston, L. D., Bachman, J. G., and O'Malley, P. M., 1977, *Drug Use among American High School Students: 1975–1977,* National Institute on Drug Abuse, Rockville, Md.

Josephson, E., 1974, Adolescent marijuana use, 1971–1972: Findings from two national surveys, *Addict. Dis.* **1**:55–72.

Kandel, D., Single, E., and Kessler, R. C., 1976, The epidemiology of drug use among New York State high school students: Distribution, trends, and change in rates of use, *Am. J. Public Health* **66**:41–53.

Katz, G., Levin, M. L., and Hamilton, H., 1963, Traditions of research on the diffusion of innovation, *Am. Sociol. Rev.* **28**:237–252.

Kelson, S. R., Pullella, J. L. and Otterland, A., 1975, The growing epidemic: A survey of smoking habits and attitudes toward smoking among students in Grades 7 through 12 in Toledo and Lucas County (Ohio) public schools—1964 and 1971, *Am. J. Public Health* **65**:923–938.

King, F. W., 1970, Anonymous versus identifiable questionnaires in drug usage surveys, *Am. Psychol.* **25**:982–985.

Kopplin, D. A., Greenfield, T. K., and Wong, H. Z., 1977, Changing patterns of substance use on campus: A four-year follow-up study, *Int. J. Addict.* **12:**73–94.

Laforest, L., 1969, *The Incidence of Drug Use among High School and College Students of the Montreal Island Area,* Office de la Prevention et du Traitement de l'Alcolisme et des Autres Toxicomanies, Quebec.

Lanphier, C. M., and Phillips, S. B., 1971a, The Non-Medical Use of Drugs and Associated Attitudes: A National Household Survey, unpublished, Commission of Inquiry into the Non-Medical Use of Drugs Research Project, Ottawa, Canada.

Lanphier, C. M., and Phillips, S., 1971b, Secondary School Students and Non-Medical Drug Use: A Study of Students Enrolled in Grades 7 through 13, a report submitted to Commission of Inquiry into the Non-Medical Use of Drugs, Survey Research Centre, Institute for Behavioral Research, York University, Toronto.

Lavenhar, M. A., and Sheffet, A., 1973, Recent trends in non-medical use of drugs reported by students in two suburban New Jersey communities, *Prev. Med.* **2:**490–509.

Linn, L. S., and Davis, M. S., 1971, The use of psychotherapeutic drugs by middle-aged women, *J. Health Soc. Behav.* **12:**331–340.

Love, A., and Killorn, L. H., 1973, *Drug Use among Adolescents in Prince Edward Island,* Addiction Research Foundation of Prince Edward Island, Charlottetown.

Macro Systems, 1975, *Alcohol and Other Drug Use and Abuse in the State of Michigan: Final Report,* Department of Public Health, Office of Substance Abuse Services, Lansing, Michigan.

Maglin, A., 1974, Sex role differences in heroin addiction, *Soc. Casework* **55:** 160–167.

Manheimer, D. I., Mellinger, G. D., and Balter, M. B., 1968, Psychotherapeutic drugs — use among adults in California, *Cal. Med.* **109:**445–451.

Manheimer, D. I., Mellinger, G. D., and Balter, M. B., 1971, *Use of Marijuana in an Urban Cross-Section of Adults, Communication and Drug Abuse,* Proceedings of the Second Rutgers Symposium on Drug Abuse.

Mathews, V. L., and Piper, G. W., 1975, *The Saskatoon Smoking Survey: Five-Year Trends,* A Report to the Department of National Health and Welfare, Ottawa, December.

Mellinger, G. D., Balter, M. B., and Manheimer, D. I., 1971, Patterns of psychotherapeutic drug use among adults in San Francisco, *Arch. Gen. Psychiatry* **25:**385–394.

Mercer, G. W., and Smart, R. G., 1974, The epidemiology of psychoactive and hallucinogenic drug use, in: *Research Advances in Alcohol and Drug Problems,* Vol. 1 (R. J. Gibbins, Y. Israel, H. Kalant, R. E. Popham, W. Schmidt, and R. G. Smart, eds.), Wiley, Toronto.

Montgomery County (Maryland) Public Schools, 1972, *Teenager Attitudes towards the Use of Drugs, Alcohol and Cigarettes: Findings of a Survey Conducted in January, 1972, among Students in Grades 7 through 12 of the Montgomery County, Maryland, Public Schools,* Rockville, Md., Montgomery Public Schools, August 31.

National Opinion Research Center, 1977, Use of Cigarettes, 1977, General Social Survey, unpublished data, Roper Center, New Haven, Conn.

New Hampshire Governor's Committee on Drug Abuse, 1972, *Report, Governor's Committee on Drug Abuse Data Collection,* Concord, N.H.

Nielson, M., and Hirabayashi, G., 1975, *Women and Soft Drug Use: The Changing Adolescent Scene, Non-Medical Use of Drugs Directorate Health and Welfare Canada, Ottawa.*

Olson, R., 1964, MMPI sex differences in narcotic addicts, *J. Genet. Psychol.* **71:**257–266.

Ontario Ministry of Labor, 1978, *Women in the Labor Force: "Fact and Fiction,"* *Factsheet No. 1,* Women's Bureau, Toronto.

Parry, H. J., 1968, Use of psychotropic drugs by U.S. adults, *Public Health Rep.* **83**:799–810.

Parry, H. J., Balter, M. B., and Cisin, I. H., 1970–1971, Primary levels of underreporting psychotropic drug use, *Public Opinion Q.* **34**:582–592.

Parry, H. J., Balter, M. B., Mellinger, G. D., Cisin, I. H., and Manheimer, D. I., 1973a, National patterns of psychotherapeutic drug use, *Arch. Gen. Psychiatr.* **28**:769–783.

Parry, H. J., McSpadden, E. L., Cisin, I. H., Balter, M. B., Manheimer, D. I., and Mellinger, G. D., 1973b, *Acquisition and Distribution of Prescription Psychotherapeutic Drugs through Non-medical Channels,* paper presented to the Annual Conference of the American Association for Public Opinion Research, Asheville, N.C., May.

Petzel, T. P., Johnson, J. E., and McKillip, J., 1973, Response bias in drug surveys, *J. Consult. Clin. Psychol.* **40**:437–439.

Playboy Magazine, 1976, What's really happening on campus? *Playboy* **23**(10):128.

Pool, J. S., 1977, *Consumption of Prescribed Drugs in Canada,* Non-Medical Use of Drugs Directorate ERD-77-113, Health and Welfare Canada, Ottawa.

Richards, L. G., and Blevens, L. B. (eds.), 1977, *The Epidemiology of Drug Abuse: Current Issues,* NIDA Research Monograph 10, National Institute on Drug Abuse, Rockville, Md.

Richman, A., and Dunham, H. W., 1976, A sociological theory of the diffusion and social setting of opiate addiction, *Drug Alcohol Depend.* **1**:383–389.

Rittenhouse, J. D. (ed.), 1977, *The Epidemiology of Heroin and Other Narcotics,* National Institute on Drug Abuse, Research Monograph Series 16, Rockville, Md.

Rittenhouse, J. D. (ed.), 1978, *Report of the Task Force on Comparability in Survey Research on Drugs,* National Institute on Drug Abuse, Rockville, Md.

Rogers, E. M., 1962, *Diffusion of Innovations,* Free Press, New York.

Rootman, I., and Fralick, P., 1978, *Cannabis Use in Canada: 1966–1978,* Non-Medical Use of Drugs Directorate ERD-78-146, Health and Welfare Canada, Ottawa.

Rosenbaum, P. D., 1977, *The Legal Abuse of Prescription Drugs: Evidence of a Continuing Problem,* Addiction Research Foundation, Substudy No. 881, Toronto.

Rosenberg, J. S., Kasl, S. V., and Berberian, R. M., 1974, Sex differences in adolescent drug use: Recent trends, *Addict. Dis.* **1**:73–96.

Russell, J. S., 1971, *Drug Use among Vancouver Secondary School Students,* Narcotic Addiction Foundation of British Columbia, Vancouver.

Russell, J. S., and Hollander, M. J., 1974, *Drug Use among Vancouver Secondary School Students: 1970 and 1974,* Narcotic Addiction Foundation of British Columbia, Vancouver.

Sadava, S. W., 1975, Research approaches in illicit drug use: A critical review, *Genet. Psychol. Monogr.* **91**:3–59.

Schaps, E., Sanders, C., and Hughes, P., 1971, *District 214 Drug Survey: An Interim Report,* University of Chicago, Department of Psychiatry, Chicago.

Schuman, L. M., 1977, Patterns of smoking behavior, in: *Research on Smoking Behavior,* Research Monograph Series 17 (M. E. Jarvik, J. W. Cullen, E. R. Gritz, T. M. Vogt, and L. J. West, eds.), pp. 36–66, National Institute on Drug Abuse, Department of Health, Education and Welfare, Rockville, Md.

Seltzer, C. C., Friedman, G. D., and Siegelaub, A. B., 1974, Smoking and drug consumption in white, black and oriental men and women, *Am. J. Public Health* **64**:466–473.

Sims, M., 1973, Drug overdoses in a Canadian city, *Am. J. Public Health* **63**:215–226.

Single, E., Kandel, D., and Johnson, B. D., 1975, The reliability and validity of drug use responses in a large scale longitudinal survey, *J. Drug Issues* **5**:426–443.

Smart, C., 1976, *Women, Crime and Criminology: A Feminist Critique,* Routledge and Kegan Paul, London.

Smart, R. G., 1975, Recent studies of the validity and reliability of self-reported drug use, 1970–1974, *Can. J. Criminol. Corrections* **17**:326–333.

Smart, R. G., 1977, Perceived availability and the use of drugs, *Bull. Narc.* **29**(4):59–63.

Smart, R. G., 1978, *The Methodology for Drug Use Surveys of Non-student Youth*, Addiction Research Foundation Substudy 981, Toronto.

Smart, R. G., Fejer, D., Smith, D., and White, J. W., 1975, *Trends in Drug Use among Metropolitan Toronto High School Students: 1968–1974*, Addiction Research Foundation, Toronto.

Smart, R. G., Goodstadt, M. S., and Sone, I. J., 1977, *Alcohol and Drug Use among Ontario Students in 1977*, Addiction Research Foundation, Toronto.

Social Research Group, The George Washington University, 1978, *Supplemental Tables. Population Projections based on the National Survey on Drug Abuse: 1977*, National Institute on Drug Abuse, Department of Health, Education and Welfare, Washington.

Sorosiak, F. M., Thomas, L. E., and Balet, F. N., 1976, Adolescent drug use: An analysis, *Psychol. Rep.* **38**:211–221.

Srole, L., and Fischer, A. K., 1973, The social epidemiology of smoking behavior 1973 and 1970: The midtown Manhattan study, *Soc. Sci. Med.* **7**:341–358.

Stennett, R. G., Feenstra, H. J., and Aharan, C. H., 1969, *Tobacco, Alcohol and Drug Use Reported by Secondary School Students (Preliminary Report)*, A joint project of the Addiction Research Foundation and the Board of Education for the City of London, March.

Sterling, T. D., and Weinkam, J. J., 1976, Smoking characteristics by type of employment, *J. Occup. Med.* **18**:743–754.

Sutherland, E. H., and Cressey, D. R., 1966, *Principles of Criminology* (7th ed.), Lippincott, Philadelphia.

U.S. Department of Health, Education and Welfare, 1975, *Physician Visits: Volume and Interval since Last Visit, United States–1971*, Vital and Health Statistics (Series 10, No. 97), National Center for Health Statistics, Rockville, Md.

U.S. Department of Health, Education and Welfare, Public Health Service, 1973, *Adult Use of Tobacco, 1970*, National Clearinghouse for Smoking and Health, DHEW Publication No. (HSM) 73-8727.

U.S. Department of Health, Education and Welfare, 1977, *Cigarette Smoking among Teenagers and Young Women*, DHEW Publication No. (NIH) 77-1203, National Cancer Institute, Atlanta and Bethesda.

U.S. Department of Health, Education and Welfare, Public Health Service, 1976, *Adult Use of Tobacco–1975*. Center for Disease Control and National Cancer Institute, June, Atlanta and Bethesda.

Utah Governor's Citizen Advisory Committee on Drugs, 1969, *Drug Use among High School Dropouts in the State of Utah*, Advisory Committee Report on Drug Abuse.

Wechsler, H., and McFadden, M., 1976, Sex differences in adolescent alcohol and drug use: A disappearing phenomenon, *J. Stud. Alcohol* **37**:1291–1301.

White, J., and Fallis, A., 1977a, *The Extent of Drug Use among Canadian Students in 1976*, Report prepared for Non-Medical Use of Drugs Directorate, ERD-77-96, Health and Welfare, Canada, Ottawa.

White, J., and Fallis, A., 1977b, *The Extent of Drug Use and Alcohol Related Problems in an Ontario School System*, Non-Medical Use of Drugs Directorate, Health and Welfare Canada, InfoResults Limited, Weston, Ontario.

Whitehead, P. C., 1971, The epidemiology of drug use in a Canadian city at two points in time: Halifax, 1969–1970, *Br. J. Addict.* **66**:301–314.

Whitehead, P. C., 1974, Multi-drug use: Supplementary perspectives, *Int. J. Addict.* **9**:185–204.

Whitehead, P. C., 1975, The time to combine: Epidemiological similarities of the use and abuse of alcohol and other drugs, *Am. J. Drug Alcohol Abuse* **2:**255–261.

Whitehead, P. C., 1976, An epidemiological description of the development of drug dependence: Environmental factors and prevention, *Am. J. Drug Alcohol Abuse* **3:**323–338.

Whitehead, P. C., Johnson, F. G., and Ferrence, R. G., 1973, Measuring the incidence of self-injury: Some methodological and design considerations, *Am. J. Orthopsychiatry* **43:**142–148.

Whitehead, P. C., and Smart, R. G., 1972, Validity and reliability of self-reported drug use, *Can. J. Criminol. Corrections* **14:**83–89.

Wolfson, E. A., Lavenhar, M. A., Blum, R., Quinones, M. A., Einstein, S., and Louria, D. B., 1971, Survey of drug abuse in six New Jersey high schools: 1-Methodology and general finding in: *Proceedings of the First International Conference on Student Drug Surveys, Newark, 1971* (S. Einstein and S. Allen, eds.), Baywood Publishing, Farmingdale, N.Y.

Wolk, D. J., 1968, Marijuana on the campus: A study at one university, *J. Am. Coll. Health Assoc.* **17:**144–149.

Wynder, E. L., Covery, L. S., and Mabuchi, K., 1974, Current smoking habits by selected background variables: Their effect on future disease trends, *Am. J. Epidemiol.* **100:**168–177.

5

Longitudinal Studies of Alcohol and Drug Problems
Sex Differences

LEE N. ROBINS AND ELIZABETH M. SMITH

1. INTRODUCTION

The literature on the etiology and natural history of alcoholism and drug addiction in women is limited. Longitudinal studies are particularly useful for addressing these questions, but the majority of longitudinal studies of alcohol and drug use are confined to males (McCord and McCord, 1960; Robins et al., 1974, 1975; Vaillant, 1973; Glueck and Glueck, 1968). Women are typically scarce in drug and alcohol treatment populations. When treatment samples are followed up, the few women may be dropped prior to follow-up or may be followed but not analyzed separately because of their small numbers. Follow-ups of general population samples are also usually restricted to men because of the large samples that would be required to identify enough female alcoholics or drug addicts to make their study worthwhile. Where follow-up studies of women exist, information is often restricted to *use* of alcohol and drugs rather than addiction or problem use, both because of the scarcity of women with substance abuse problems and because many of the available studies are restricted to adolescents, who have not had time to develop problems. The relative lack of longitudinal studies of women's drug and alcohol abuse and the small samples of women heavily involved with drugs or alcohol in the few existing studies mean that we know even less

LEE N. ROBINS and ELIZABETH M. SMITH ● Department of Psychiatry, Washington University School of Medicine, St. Louis, Missouri. This work was supported in part by USPHS Grants DA 00013, MH 18864, AA 03539, DA 00259.

about both the causes of women's substance abuse and its natural history than we do about men's.

In the following section we review those longitudinal studies that report on the use and abuse of alcohol and illicit drugs by females. Longitudinal studies are defined as those studies in which data collected at at least two points in time in the life of the same individual are linked. A number of studies that have repeatedly measured drug abuse over time in general populations or in school populations (Garfield and Garfield, 1973; Blackford, 1974; Abelson and Atkinson, 1975) are omitted because they have not linked data at the two points at the individual level, although they have discovered trends of use and abuse over time in institutions or communities. We omit follow-up studies that included women but failed to report results separately by sex (Haastrup, 1973; Brill and Christie, 1974; Smith and Fogg, 1975). We also omit follow-up studies reporting results by sex when they report only treatment outcomes, death rates, and the incidence of fetal alcohol syndrome in the offspring because these topics are covered in other chapters. Finally, a number of longitudinal studies that promise to provide important new data about substance abusc in women have had to be omitted because the results are not yet available (Josephson, 1976; Johnston et al., 1977; Rachal et al., 1975).

Available Longitudinal Studies of Women's Drinking or Drug Problems

Longitudinal Studies of Normal Children and Adolescents. Many longitudinal studies of alcohol and drugs are confined to young populations and cover a brief span of time. These studies typically select populations of high school and college students and follow them for periods of one to five years. They generally focus on alcohol and marijuana, the most common drugs. Most include a count of "ever used"; some also measure number of times drugs have been used or the number of times the person has had a drink. There is usually little information on drinking or drug *problems,* as befits studies in which the modal case is an abstainer or a very occasional user.

Jessor and Jessor (1975, 1977; Jessor, 1976) followed 483 high school students (188 males and 244 females) yearly for four years. A 75% random sample of students, stratified by sex and grade level, was drawn in grades 7, 8, and 9 from the three junior high schools in a western community during the spring of 1969. Each selected student was contacted by letter and asked to participate in a four-year study of personality and social and behavioral development. Parents of the students were also contacted by letter to obtain signed permission for their children's participation. Parental permission was granted for 712 students, and of these, 589 took part in the Year 1 testing. This constituted 52% of the original sample of 1,126. There was an 82% retention of the Year 1 participants from year to year, achieving finally a sample of 38% of the original random sample with information in all four years. The sample was relatively homogeneous, primarily white Protestant and middle and upper middle class.

The Jessors' college study (1977) selected males and females who were college freshmen at a large university in the same community that was the site of the high school study. A 10% random sample stratified by sex was drawn from the enrolment roster for 1969's entering freshman class in the college of arts and sciences. Students selected were invited by letter to participate in the study. A total of 276 students (55% of the males and 54% of the females in the original sample) took part in the initial testing. By the fourth year, 226, or 83%, of the original participants were still in the study. The college sample was similar to the high school sample in terms of demographic characteristics.

In both samples, annual data collection was by questionnaire. Initiation into drinking, marijuana, and sexual behavior over the prior year was studied within a framework of the social psychology of problem behavior seen as a function of personality, perceived social environment, and behavioral variables.

Kandel's group (Kandel, 1973, 1975; Single et al., 1974; Kandel et al., 1976a,b; Margulies et al., 1977) obtained data from a random sample of the adolescent population attending public secondary schools in New York State in the fall of 1971. In the spring of 1972, five to six months later, students were contacted again. Usable questionnaires were obtained from 8206 adolescents at Time 1 (a response rate of 81%) and 7250 at Time 2 (a response rate of 75%). The questionnaires were confidential and names were not signed, but a self-generated code was used that was supposed to produce the identical number at both time periods, making it possible to study changes in individuals. Unfortunately, the same number was not always produced. In all, 66% (5468) of all students answering at Time 1 could be matched to themselves at Time 2 so that changes in behavior could be studied.

Data were also obtained from the mothers, fathers, and best friends of a subsample. These data were collected through structured self-administered questionnaires and included information about parents' and friends' drug and alcohol use.

Zucker and DeVoe (1973) surveyed students in the only public high school in a Middle Atlantic community to obtain information on drinking behavior. A subsample of girls and boys who were freshmen and sophomores at the time of the survey was selected for follow-up two years later. The follow-up sample was selected to ensure an adequate dispersion on a heavy to light to nondrinking continuum. Information was obtained by questionnaire regarding amount of alcohol consumption and problem drinking, antisocial behavior, perceptions of parents' child-rearing practices, and assessment of personality and family characteristics. Parents also completed questionnaires on child-rearing practices, personality variables, and their own alcohol consumption and drinking problems. Interviews were achieved with 75 girls and 104 boys and their parents. The refusal rate is not specified, nor is the size of the original sample.

Kellam et al. (1978) studied 705 seventeen-year-olds who had first been studied when in grade 1, 10 years before. All first-graders in a lower-income black neighborhood in Chicago, a total of 1241 students, had been assessed regarding their social adaptational status and psychological well-being twice during the first grade. Teachers assessed social adaptational status in standardized interviews, and clinicians and mothers rated the children's psychological well-being. IQ tests and measures of readiness for learning to read administered by the school were also available.

Follow-up was achieved with 75% of the original sample whose mothers had been interviewed. At follow-up, the subjects completed a questionnaire administered in groups regarding alcohol and illicit drug use, the frequency of their use in the past two months, and history of ever using. The questionnaire was read aloud to the adolescents to overcome reading difficulties.

Ginsberg and Greenley (1978) surveyed college students in all classes regarding marijuana use by a mailed questionnaire sent to a random sample of students registered at the University of Wisconsin in the fall of 1971. An 82% response rate was obtained (1502 respondents). In 1974, the 319 respondents who had been freshmen or sophomores at the time of the original survey and who were still in school were mailed a follow-up questionnaire. Of these, 86% responded, yielding a sample of 274. Information was obtained regarding marijuana use during the past year as well as social and demographic information.

Follow-Up of General Adult Populations. Cahalan et al. (1969; Cahalan, 1970) followed a national probability sample of 1359 adults (751 males and 608 females) three years after they had been originally interviewed in 1964–1965 regarding their drinking practices. Subjects were aged 21 to 59 years at first interview. While the first interview covered quantity and frequency of beer, wine, and hard liquor consumed during the last year, drinking *problems* were inquired about only in the second interview and only for those drinking in the past year. Thus those ex-problem drinkers who had become teetotalers were not identified. Household interviews were conducted with 81% of the survivors initially interviewed. Since the first interview achieved a 90% response rate, this represents a 73% follow-up rate for those initially selected for interview.

Follow-Up from Childhood or Adolescence into Adulthood. While follow-up studies of adolescents and adults can inquire into drinking and drug histories at both Time 1, when the study begins, and at follow-up, studies that begin with children and follow them into adolescence or adulthood can ask about drinking or drugs only at the second point in time, since at the first point the subjects have not yet entered the age of risk.

Two longitudinal projects from the Institute of Human Development at the University of California that followed children at intervals from infancy through adulthood (Jones, 1968, 1971; Block and Hahn, 1971) learned about drinking problems at the final contact, when the subjects were in their 30s or 40s. The Berkeley Guidance Study selected every third child born in Berkeley during 1928–1929 from birth registry records. A total of 248 infants and their families were selected for the study, which focused on personality development and parent–child relationships and included an extensive program of tests and measurements. One hundred thirty-nine subjects were followed through age 18 and were again seen 12 years later as 30-year-old adults.

The Oakland Growth Study began in 1932 and selected 212 white, middle-class children in the fifth grade who were planning to attend a junior high school connected with the University of California. The subjects were followed through high school and at several periods in adulthood by interview, personality, projective, interest, and attitude tests. Approximately 100 subjects were reinterviewed during their early 40s.

The adult follow-ups of these two studies were merged, and information about drinking was obtained when they were adults, not only regarding current drinking behavior, but retrospectively. Among the topics covered were age and circumstance of first drink; present consumption patterns; reasons for drinking; changes in drinking habits; drinking patterns of parents, spouse, children, and friends; and attitudes toward drinking. The subjects were classified into one of five amount/frequency/problem categories: problem drinkers, heavy drinkers, moderate drinkers, and nondrinkers and abstainers. Associations were then sought between this categorization and personality characteristics in three age periods: junior high, senior high school, and adulthood, as assessed by raters using Q-sort techniques.

The number of subjects followed varies in different reports of the studies. Block and Hahn's sample (1971) included 84 males and 87 females, and Jones's study (1968, 1971) included 66 males, of whom 52 could be classified according to drinking pattern, and 45 females.

Terman (1959) and Oden (1968) followed 1528 children, selected in 1921–1922 from California public schools, who had IQ scores (intelligence ratings) that placed them in the top 1% of the school population. These subjects were followed at intervals by interview for those remaining in California, by written questionnaires, and by correspondence with relatives over a 40-year period. Information on their drinking problems as well as their adult psychiatric status, death and suicide rates, health, marital history, occupation, interests, and attitudes was obtained. Complete follow-up data were reported on 664 males and 524 females regarding their self-reported drinking behavior at a median age of 49 years. No information was available on youthful drinking behavior.

Brunswick (1978) followed a sample of 664 black Harlem youth, initially aged 12–17 years, for a period of 6–8 years. The restudy sample numbered 535 (277 males and 259 females), 80% of the original sample. The sample was representative of young adults in a community at high risk for drug and alcohol use. In addition to in-person interviews, medical records were also obtained. The first interview focused largely on health problems and did not ask specifically about alcohol and drugs. These were systematically inquired about in the second interview.

Two studies followed adolescents into adulthood and obtained drinking information at both time periods, although the data obtained in adolescence were rather incomplete in the first. Robins (1966; Robins et al., 1962) followed both male and female patients of a municipal child psychiatric clinic and matched control subjects 30 years after the patients had been seen. The 503 white patients (138 female and 365 male with IQs above 80 who survived to age 25) and 100 students selected from public school records and matched to patients for census tract of childhood residence, age, sex, race, and IQ constituted the study population. Both groups were interviewed at a median age of 43 with regard to adult drinking behavior as well as other psychiatric and social problems. Adult and childhood information was also collected from police and institutional records. The mean age of the patients at the time they were seen in the clinic was 13 years. Most had been referred by the juvenile court and by community agencies. Childhood data on drinking for the patients came from their clinic records and were also obtained retrospectively for both patients and controls by interview at follow-up.

Fillmore (1974, 1975; Fillmore et al., 1978) followed 109 men and 97 women 20 years after they had been studied as college students by Straus and Bacon (1953). Initial information on drinking behavior was obtained by an extensive self-administered questionnaire mailed to college students aged 16–25 years, between 1949 and 1952. Approximately 12,000 students from 27 colleges and universities submitted their names for future follow-up, and a stratified sample was chosen from this pool of volunteers. The subjects were primarily white and were described at Time 1 as upper middle to upper class. When the subjects were in their late 30s and early 40s, follow-up information about drinking behavior was obtained by a mailed self-administered questionnaire (66%) and a telephone interview (34%).

Follow-Up Studies of Persons with Drinking and Drug Problems at Time 1. The studies we have discussed thus far are all studies that began with persons unselected with respect to drug and alcohol problems. There have also been a number of follow-up studies of clinical populations of alcoholics and drug addicts, although the majority do not include females or do not analyze the data separately for the sexes.

Among the notable exceptions is O'Donnell's (1969) follow-up of drug addicts who were hospitalized at Lexington prior to 1960. A sample of 266 white, primarily rural patients who resided in Kentucky at the time of admission was selected by a stratified random procedure. At follow-up, information was obtained or interviews completed on all but 4 of the subjects. In no case was information obtained from fewer than two sources in addition to the hospital record. The sample of 54 women and 212 men were followed after discharge for a maximum of 22 years and a mean of 10 years for females and 11.6 years for males. Information on alcohol and drugs was obtained both while they were in Lexington (Time 1) and again at follow-up (Time 2).

Croughan (1978) carried out a prospective follow-up study by interview of 100 women who were consecutive first admissions to Lexington during 1971–1972 and reinterviewed them five years later. For each of 86% of the women, a control male admitted to Lexington during the same time period and matched to the woman for age, race, and area of residence was selected. Information on alcohol and drug use was obtained at both Time 1 and Time 2.

Paulus and Halliday (1967) followed up 153 patients who had been treated at the Narcotic Addiction Foundation, one to five years after their initial contact. Structured interviews were used to obtain follow-up information. Drinking information is reported only at follow-up.

Martin et al. (1978) followed 66 convicted female felons initially selected from all women under supervision in one district of a state probation and parole office during July and August of 1969. Information was obtained from interviews with subjects both in 1969 and six years later, from family members, and from criminal records of the FBI and the highway patrol. A diagnosis of alcoholism was made for 31 of the felons (47%) and a diagnosis of drug dependence was made for 17 (26%).

Duvall et al. (1963) followed 283 males and 170 females discharged from Lexington Hospital in 1952 or 1953 five years after discharge by personal interviews.

Richman (1966; Richman et al., 1971, 1972) followed two groups of drug addicts through the New York City addict case register. The first group included 369 males and 131 females who were a representative sample of heroin addict admissions to a drug treatment center during 1959–1963. A search of the case register for their names was carried out after 5–10 years. The second group included 130 males and 47 females who had been in prison in 1954–1955 and diagnosed as drug addicts. He searched for their names in the case register 10 years later.

Sells and Simpson (1976) provided information on large and diverse samples of male and female patients in nine types of treatment programs at 46 federally funded drug treatment centers, a total of 13,607 out of 16,686 patients admitted between June 1972 and March 1973. Their purpose was to compare the kinds of clients seen in different types of treatment and the effectiveness of different treatments.

Schuckit and Winokur (1972) followed 45 women three years after they had been admitted to two psychiatric hospitals with a diagnosis of alcoholism. Information was obtained on all patients. The sample was chosen to include 20 depressive alcoholics, 21 primary alcoholics, and 4 sociopathic alcoholics.

Studies Proposed or in Progress.   Two proposed studies have been described:

Fillmore and Marden (1977) reported on a large-scale prospective study to be carried out by Carpenter and Lester of the Rutgers Center of Alcohol Studies, involving a total of 600 subjects (300 male and 300 female) and including two special risk groups (children of alcoholic parents and children attending a mental health clinic) and one random sample of children. Measurements included physiological, psychological, sociological, and behavioral variables. These plans have recently been expanded to involve 5700 persons in 16 cohorts 13–22 years of age at entry into the study. This project will attempt to discover prognostic factors in alcohol problems.

Goodwin (1977) is planning to follow into adulthood a group of Danish children who were part of a pre- and postnatal study. Records of parental hospitalization for alcoholism are available for 250 boys and 226 girls whose adult outcomes will be compared with those of a control group from the same original study.

Johnston et al. (1977) have begun a five-year follow-up study of drug and alcohol use among a national sample of successive cohorts of high school seniors. At present, data are available only for the intake year.

There are plans to follow a subsample for five years with respect to drug and alcohol use through self-administered mailed questionnaires.

Smith and Cloninger will be extending the follow-up by Schuckit and Winokur (1972) by following the same women 10 years after their diagnosis to learn more about the natural history of alcoholism in women.

2. PATTERNS OF DRUG AND ALCOHOL USE

Longitudinal studies allow us to compare the patterns of drug and alcohol use between men and women with respect to their prevalence and incidence, their course, and the likelihood of receiving treatment.

Prevalence

Prevalence data can be obtained from cross-sectional as easily as from longitudinal studies. When prevalence figures are provided by longitudinal studies, they can apply either to Time 1, Time 2, or both periods. If a longitudinal study provides only Time 1 prevalences for an adult sample of the general population, its prevalence data are identical with those one would get from a cross-sectional study, since Time 1 of a longitudinal study is simply a cross-sectional study that gives baseline figures for predicting later outcomes or measuring change over time. If a study of a general adult population sample selected at Time 1 provides prevalence figures only after follow-up at Time 2, a bias may be introduced because of selective loss of cases over the follow-up interval, and thus prevalence estimates may be inferior to those provided by cross-sectional studies.

On the other hand, a longitudinal study *can* provide better prevalence figures at Time 2 than a cross-sectional study if the sample at Time 1 was not a general adult sample, but rather a sample of children or adolescents chosen *prior* to the onset of drug or alcohol problems, and if at Time 2 there is a high recovery rate. When samples are selected *before* any of the sample has developed alcohol or drug problems, and when virtually all are successfully followed up, the longitudinal study avoids one bias to which cross-sectional studies are subject: missing cases who died young and those who at the time of the study are in jail, hospitals, or living as transients. In the Terman study following gifted children into their 40s and 50s (Terman, 1959; Oden, 1968), for instance, considerably more alcoholics were identified than one might have expected to find in a house-to-house survey of upper-middle-class adults. By choosing cases in childhood and maintaining contact with them over the years, the researchers obtained information about those dead or hospitalized and perhaps got franker information from those still in households than they might have received if the interviewers had had no previous contact with them.

Longitudinal studies of drug and alcohol use have been carried out both in general population samples and in special population samples, such as addicts who come to treatment. Only general population samples provide prevalence figures of interest. In treatment samples, prevalence at Time 1 of the substance for which treatment is being obtained depends on whether Time 1 is defined as the moment of first contact with the program, when prevalence is close to 100%, or early in treatment, when it may be close to zero. At Time 2, prevalence varies with the length of the interval since Time 1, the success of the intervening treatment, and whether opportunity to use the substance has been curtailed by hospitalization or imprisonment. Thus, the figures obtained fluctuate widely with special circumstances and are of little generalizability.

In every general population sample followed with respect to alcohol use or problems, women have been found to have a lower rate than men. The results are not so uniform for illicit drug use, but when *frequent* or *problem* drug use is measured, again the less problematic status of women is found. Indeed, one of the difficulties that has beset follow-up studies of women's drug and alcohol abuse has been the rarity of such problems. Fillmore et al., for instance (1978), reported having had to reduce criteria for problem drinking in college in order to obtain a sample of problem drinkers that was balanced by sex.

While women apparently have fewer drinking and drug problems than men, it is difficult to find out just what the prevalence rate for women is. Definitions vary from study to study with respect to what constitutes drinking or drug use, what constitute problems, and over how long a period prevalence is being measured. Some studies report "ever drank," some report "drinking in the last year," others report "more than nonexperimental, currently."

Despite these difficulties, it is clear that rates of alcohol use for both females and males are now very high before the end of high school, and well before the age at which alcohol can be legally purchased. For instance, Kandel et al. (1976a) found that 84% of boys and 80% of girls had used alcohol in high school, while the Jessors (1977) found that 76% of boys and 73% of girls in their sample of high school students (grades 10–12) had used alcohol. Among 12th-grade students, 83% of boys and 79% of girls had tried drinking. Use continued to increase with age. By the end of college, 98% of men and 93% of women had used alcohol. Lower figures than "almost all" are obtained only when the criterion is set at "more than occasional use." Using this definition, Fillmore (1974) found that only about half of men and women had been drinkers in college around 1950, and there was no difference between the sexes. This low figure reflects both her relatively strict definition and the fact that the study was initiated at a time when drinking among the young may have been less universal than it is now.

Marijuana use is less common than drinking, but rates are also high among the young in recent studies, and sex differences tend to be smaller in some studies than for alcohol. Ginsberg and Greenley (1978), for example, found no sex differences in the frequency with which marijuana use begins in college. The rate of marijuana use reported in young people fluctuates widely, from less than a third of the boys in Kandel's et al. (1976a) high school study to 80% of boys in Harlem (Brunswick, 1978). For girls, Kandel et al. (1976a) and Jessor and Jessor (1977) found similar rates in high school (28% for Kandel and about one-third for Jessor). But rates climbed for Jessor's female high school seniors to 50%, and by the end of college, they had risen to 62%. Rates vary with the date of the study (since marijuana use has been increasing over time) and with the age of the respondents (since college-age respondents use more alcohol and drugs than do high-school-age respondents). Region and social class appear to matter less than one might expect. There is remarkably little difference, for instance, between rates for the Jessors' (1977) college students and rates for blacks of about the same age in Harlem (Brunswick, 1978), few of whom came from a group in which college attendance is common.

General population studies usually focus exclusively on alcohol and/ or marijuana because use of other illicit drugs is so rare. (The Jessors provided information about "hard" drugs but did not give use rates by sex.) When heroin use rates are provided, they vary markedly. In Chicago's Woodlawn (Kellam et al., 1978), an all-black area, rates of ever having used heroin for adolescents of both sexes at about age 17 were only 2%, whereas in Harlem, rates were 16% for black males and 10% for black females in their early twenties. This discrepancy points to the importance of sample age differences. Many longitudinal studies of drug use have been carried out in very young samples. As a result, the age at follow-up often falls within the period of risk of first use of the drugs. This means that slight differences in the mean ages or the age distributions of the samples can produce enormous variations in rates. The Harlem sample was only a little older than the Woodlawn sample. However, first heroin use has been reported to occur most often around ages 18–20, just *past* the age of the Woodlawn sample. We are, then, at a loss to know whether there are real differences in drug use practices in the two locales or whether the figures shortly converged as the Woodlawn sample entered the age of greatest risk.

We have reported thus far only on rates of use. Rates of *problem* use are difficult to compare between studies because each study chooses its own criteria for what constitutes problem or excessive substance use. Terman (1959) and Oden (1968), who followed children with IQs in the top 1% of the population, found that almost 3% of their very intelligent men and 1% of their very intelligent women qualified as alcoholic on the basis of having been hospitalized for treatment for an alcohol problem. Most other studies of "alcohol abuse" require no evidence of problems but instead use high frequency of use as their criterion. Kellam, for instance, gave rates for drinking 40 times or more in a lifetime, while Brunswick gave rates for drinking 3 or more times a week. Such criteria yield very high rates of "alcohol problems," with Brunswick reporting that in Harlem 47% of young black men and 26% of young black women had used alcohol this frequently, rates similar to those reported by Cahalan (1970) for "any problem" with alcohol in a national sample, in which 43% of men and 21% of women reported having had at least one drinking-related problem during the three-year follow-up period.

The Jessors (1977) used frequency of drunkenness plus number of adverse consequences of drinking as criteria for alcohol problems in their follow-up study of the emergence of drinking and other deviant behaviors over the high school and college years. These criteria produced figures similar to those of Brunswick: 39% for males in high school and 36% for males in college, and somewhat less (31% and 26%) for females.

The studies we have cited all produced similar estimates of problem drinking rates despite having used different criteria. It is tempting but probably incorrect to interpret these similar figures as showing that despite different approaches, the "truth about drinking problems will out." A more likely explanation is that researchers who are interested in predicting problem drinking all choose a cutoff point that selects a large minority of that sample as "positive" to facilitate statistical analysis. It is nonetheless true that despite these varying ways of counting and measuring alcohol problems, male rates are always considerably higher than female rates.

Lack of comparability because of differing ways of measuring apply to longitudinal studies of the use of illicit drugs as well as alcohol. Kellam's and Brunswick's were the only longitudinal studies found that attempted to specify a *problem* level for marijuana, defined again by frequency of use rather than by ill effects of use. Kellam reported almost three times as many boys as girls having used marijuana 40 or more times. Brunswick, on the other hand, found relatively little difference by sex in either marijuana or heroin use. Defining frequent use of marijuana as use three times a week or more, she found 25% of males and 21% of females to have used this much, and with respect to problems with heroin, males exceeded females by only 8% to 6%.

Incidence

While longitudinal studies offer no great advantage with respect to prevalence, they should be particularly useful in ascertaining incidence — the number of new cases that emerge within a specified time interval, such as the interval between Time 1 and Time 2. In fact, only a few existing longitudinal studies can provide this information because most have obtained drug and alcohol information at only one point in time. At this point, they asked about lifetime incidence, that is, whether use or problems ever occurred, and if so, when they began, questions that could have been asked equally well in cross-sectional studies. Among the exceptions are Kandel's (Margulies et al., 1977) study of high school students who answered questions about drugs and alcohol twice, with a five- to six-month interval between; the Jessors' study of high school and college students who responded yearly for four years for alcohol and three times for marijuana use in high school and four times in college; Croughan's study of heroin addicts, which investigated alcohol addiction at periods five years apart; and Fillmore's study of college drinkers requestioned about drinking 20 years later.

In Kandel's study (Margulies et al., 1977), 30% of the high school students who had been nondrinkers at Time 1 drank within the next five to six months. Among the Jessors' few college entrants who had not yet had a drink (4% of men and 12% of women), approximately half became drinkers over the four years of the study, whether males or females. Among the Jessors' high school students, more than half of whom had never had a drink in the first year of the study, again about half of those abstinent at entry into the study began drinking over the next four years (55% of the boys; 61% of the girls). In Fillmore's (1974) study, 73% of those never having drunk when they answered the questionnaire in college had drunk by the time they answered the questionnaire sent them 20 years later (71% of the males and 74% of the females).

The Jessors also provided incidence rates for marijuana use. Among college entrants who had never used marijuana, initiations in college were considerably more common for men than women, 57% versus 19%, so that by the end of college, men who had ever used exceeded women who had ever used, reversing the sex difference at entry. In high school, rates of initiation over the two years after first assessment among nonusers were similar for boys and girls, with rather low rates for both: 21% for boys, 24% for girls.

Unfortunately, none of these studies provides incidence figures for *problems* with alcohol or drugs. Thus, we cannot yet confirm or interpret the cross-sectional findings of a later onset of alcohol problems and narcotic addiction in women than in men.

Prevalence and Incidence in Samples from Special Populations

We obviously cannot measure the prevalence or incidence of the use of a substance in a population selected for the abuse of that substance—by definition, prevalence is 100%, and the incidence of new cases is 0%. Nor can one derive general population estimates of prevalence or incidence from follow-ups of populations chosen for deviant behaviors (e.g., delinquents) or special assets (high IQ or college attendance). But it is possible to use longitudinal studies of such special samples to compare the sexes with respect to the use of substances other than the one qualifying the subject for inclusion in a drug-abusing sample, and it may be interesting to note whether sex differences similar to those in the general population also occur in special populations selected on grounds other than drug abuse.

In Sells and Simpson's (1976) study of drug patients being treated mainly for narcotic addiction, although the use of other illicit drugs did not differ by sex, male drug patients had used more alcohol and had had more alcohol problems in the two months prior to entering treatment than had women patients. O'Donnell's (1969) follow-up of Kentucky narcotics addicts admitted to Lexington also showed much higher rates of alcoholism at some time prior to follow-up among males than females (85% versus 44%). Croughan's (1978) five-year follow-up of drug patients at Lexington again showed more alcohol problems in the posttreatment period for males than females (38% versus 21%). Like Sells and Simpson, Croughan found no difference by sex in the use of illicit drugs. Similarly, in a follow-up study of child guidance clinic patients, Robins (1966) found more alcohol problems in adulthood for male than for female patients.

Croughan's study was distinctive in that it studied incidence as well as prevalence. He found that the higher rate of alcoholism in male than female patients at follow-up was not merely a continuation of a higher rate of alcoholism existent before the onset of heroin addiction. Among men who had *not* had alcohol problems prior to their entering treatment, one out of four became diagnosable as alcoholic during the follow-up period, as compared with only one out of six females who had not been alcoholic when they entered treatment.

Thus, studies of special populations clearly confirm general population studies with respect to the relative immunity of women from alcohol problems. They also confirm the studies of adolescents, which show much less striking sex differences in the use of illicit drugs than in alcohol problems. They have not yet told us about sex differences in risks of having *problems* with illict drugs.

Increasing Similarity of Male and Female Rates

There is general agreement that women are becoming more like men with respect to moderate drinking, cigarette use, and occasional drug use. One piece of evidence is that the difference between men and women is less in the upper and middle classes than in the lower class, where women are much more often teetotalers than are men (Cahalan, 1970). Whether one argues that drug use patterns of the middle class "filter down" or that the class structure will continue to change in the direction of a shrinking blue-collar sector relative to the white-collar sector, middle-class patterns can be expected to become more widespread.

Another indication of convergence is that among younger people, sex differences are much less striking than are differences between older women and men. Again, whether innovation by the young spreads to their elders or whether there will merely be attrition of patterns now found among the elderly as the older generation dies off, male and female rates are likely to become more alike.

The finding that more women are drinking and smoking and that college women use marijuana about as much as college men (Jessor and Jessor, 1977) does not tell us whether the female advantage in lower rates of *problems* with drugs and alcohol will also disappear over time. However, findings from Brunswick (1978) and Robins et al. (1962) suggest that if drug and alcohol use become as common among women as among men, then problem rates may well equalize. Brunswick found no male–female difference in problem rates when she looked only at drinkers and drug users. The difference in rates depended on the greater number of women who abstain entirely. Similarly, Robins found that *among heavy drinkers,* there were no differences in alcoholism rates for men and women. The sex difference in the sample as a whole depended on the fact that fewer women than men became heavy drinkers. Thus, one would expect that as heavy drinking becomes less distinctively male, women will lose their current relative immunity from substance dependence.

The Course of Alcohol and Drug Use and Problems

Kandel (1973, 1975) has shown that licit and illicit drug use form a Guttman scale for high school students. Their drug use typically begins with beer and wine and progresses from there to hard liquor and cigarettes, next to marijuana, thereafter to "pills," and finally to heroin. Since the scale applies to both girls and boys, it seems likely that all female users of hard drugs have used alcohol and soft drugs previously, just as men have. Kandel also found that the interval between use of a precursor drug and moving on to the next drug was about the same for girls as for boys, again suggesting that the sequential use of alcohol and drugs follows approximately the same pattern for men and women.

Whether men's and women's ages of risk for beginning various drugs are the same could be discovered through longitudinal studies, but this question has not yet been clearly answered. Certainly the fact that supplies of illicit drugs on the street wax and wane and that the relative popularity of various illicit drugs fluctuates means that ages of risk will also differ from one period to the next. One study of first male marijuana use by age and calendar year (O'Donnell et al., 1976) has attempted to separate ages of vulnerability from "epidemic" years. This study showed that the increased popularity of illicit drugs in the late 1960s was reflected in a jump in initiation rates around 1968, but this jump occurred only for men within a limited span of ages—especially those aged 18–21 at that time. Alcohol, which had been easily available and continuously popular throughout the lifetime of these young men, showed no such "epidemic" year, and changes in rates of first use simply reflected age of risk, with use rising above 50% by age 16 and above 90% by age 20 in every birth cohort.

Brunswick, working with a sample in their late teens and early 20s, showed that for most drugs, rates of "ever used" continued to increase for women up to about age 23 and then leveled off, suggesting that age 23 was near the end of the risk period for initiations. For men, onset was earlier and new cases increased little over the age span studied. These findings suggest that women's age of risk continues later than men's. While the upper range of her study is too low to ensure that more cases of women will not be added later, the fact that new cases slacken off in the early 20s suggests that most first use of drugs and alcohol occur before age 25 if it occurs at all.

Problem use, of course, may not appear for some time after use begins. Unfortunately, however, no longitudinal study has yet definitively answered the question about how late in life women's first alcohol or drug problems can appear.

Both longitudinal and retrospective studies of men have showed that the earlier drinking begins, the more likely it is to lead to alcohol problems. This finding is now reported for women as well by Brunswick. However, Brunswick also agreed with a number of retrospective studies of female alcoholics that show onset of alcoholism and drug abuse for women to be somewhat later than for men. Brunswick found that women started each drug investigated at an age approximately one year greater than the age at which men started the same drug. If delayed onset is general for women across all drug types, this finding helps to explain why female heroin addicts tend to come to treatment later (Sells and Simpson, 1976): having started later, they would have been addicts for a shorter time at the same age. However, Brunswick found, in addition, that female heroin users had used the drug for longer before coming to treatment than had men treated for heroin use. Of her female addicts, 72% had used heroin for four years or more before coming to treatment, while for men, only 25% had been using heroin for such a long time at entry into treatment.

It is clear from longitudinal studies that drug and alcohol problems often terminate spontaneously. The differences between the sexes in rates of recovery do not appear to be very great. Fillmore (1974, 1975) found that only a quarter of men and a third of women who had been problem drinkers in college were still problem drinkers at follow-up. Her elaborate attempts to identify patterns of drinking in college that would predict drinking problems in middle age 20 years later were not very successful for either sex (Fillmore et al, 1978). The mass of drinking behavior and drinking attitude descriptors collected in college accounted for only 11% of the variance for women and 14% for men. The poor ability to predict from college age to middle age could be due either to great instability in drinking problems over time or to poor measurement— in either or both periods. It is impossible to choose between these alternatives in a single study. However, Cahalan (1970) also found a sharp drop-off in problems, particularly for women. He reported that alcohol problems for women drop off sharply by age 50, whereas for some men they continue into the 70s.

These results in samples from general populations are echoed in the relatively high rates of recovery reported for problem drinkers who enter treatment. While this topic is covered more fully in another chapter, it is worth noting that Schuckit and Winokur's (1972) follow-up of women treated for alcoholism three years earlier showed one-third free of alcohol problems for at least two years at reinterview, and of this group, almost half had become social drinkers, not needing to abstain in order to achieve their freedom from problems. Like Fillmore, Schuckit and Winokur were not able to identify drinking patterns of female alcoholics that could efficiently predict outcome.

Recovery rates in the Schuckit and Winokur study are not as high as the spontaneous recovery rates in Fillmore's study. Presumably, this discrepancy is explained by the greater severity of problems among those problem drinkers who came to treatment. Nonetheless, rates of spontaneous recovery from problem drinking are sufficiently high, even among those in treatment, so that judging treatment effectiveness requires comparison with an untreated control group, followed for the same interval, who initally were equally severely affected.

The fact that drinking problems do drop off spontaneously with aging among both women and men shows that the typical findings of cross-sectional studies that older men and women have relatively low rates of problem drinking cannot be entirely explained either by the change in social mores, with heavy drinking more severely disapproved in the era during which the older generation's drinking patterns were being set than currently, or by the high mortality rate of drug and alcohol abusers, which implies that those who survive into old age have usually been only briefly addicted if at all. These historical changes and health hazards must in part explain the relatively low level of alcohol and drug problems in older people, but longitudinal studies discover a role for the aging process itself as well.

Rates of problem drinking appear to converge as men and women age. In part this convergence is due to the later onset of problems for women and the fact that so many young men's drinking problems dissipate in their 30s. Fillmore noted a large difference between the sexes in rates of drinking problems in college, with 44% of men versus 19% of women having drinking problems. At follow-up, the men's rates had declined markedly to 19%, whereas the women's rates were still low. This constancy of women's rates was maintained despite the high turnover rates for them discussed above: those recovering were replaced by new problem drinkers.

Use of Multiple Psychoactive Substances

Every study of drugs in men shows a strong association between the use of illicit drugs and heavy drinking. Zucker and DeVoe (1973) found that the use of alcohol and drugs is even more highly correlated among girls than among boys. However, studies of female heroin addicts show them less involved with alcohol than male addicts. O'Donnell (1969) found that female heroin addicts were less often heavy drinkers before treatment than male heroin addicts, and Croughan (1978) found that female heroin addicts are less often dependent on alcohol after treatment than males, even after controlling for their pretreatment alcoholism.

Studies comparing the sexes with respect to the variety of psychoactive drugs used are few, but Brunswick (1978) has reported that women use a somewhat less varied collection of drugs than men do. For instance, Brunswick found that women who used any drugs were twice as likely as men to use only a single illicit drug, and women rarely used two drugs simultaneously. Thus, male users appear not only more likely than female users to use with high frequency, but they also seem to use a greater variety of drugs.

Coming to Treatment

Obviously, the seriousness of the problems encountered by drug and alcohol users is an important factor in whether or not they will come to treatment, but other factors also play a role. The best predictor of coming to heroin treatment found by Brunswick (1978) was simply the length of heroin use. If heroin use continues long enough, perhaps all users eventually come to treatment. However, Brunswick's results also suggest that men may have easier access to treatment than women do. While there were equal numbers of men and women with heroin problems in her Harlem sample, more than twice as many men (9%) as women (4%) had come to treatment for heroin, and as we noted earlier, women who did come to treatment had been using heroin longer than men. One wonders whether the lower treatment rate for women resulted because their problems were less severe, or whether drug treatment facilities, designed primarily for men because there are so many more male than female addicts, fail to attract women to treatment. (Treatment is so rare for alcohol problems and problems with drugs other than heroin, that we can compare men's and women's access to treatment only for heroin.)

Another possible reason for a low treatment rate for women might be a higher rate of spontaneous remission. Perhaps more women than men addicted to heroin recover on their own during the three or four years that usually elapse between onset of addiction and entry into treatment. It would indeed be interesting to learn to what extent sex differences in coming to treatment are responsive to differences in need, as reflected in severity and duration of addiction, and to what extent there is a difference in men and women's access to treatment. Prospective longitudinal studies of men and women identified in cross-sectional studies as having drug or alcohol problems would seem an efficient way to answer these questions. If women actually do receive less treatment for alcohol and drugs than men, given equally severe and persistent disorders, it would be valuable to learn what barriers to treatment they experience.

3. PREDICTORS OF DRUG AND ALCOHOL USE AND PROBLEMS

While accurate prevalence and incidence rates of drug and alcohol use and problems require representative samples of the population of interest, the search for predictors of use and problem use may avail itself of a variety of samples. Special samples and biased samples can help to identify predictors, even though an accurate estimate of the *size* of the contribution of these predictors to the overall level of problems requires a representative sample.

Follow-up studies are particularly valuable in the search for predictors of onset of problems or change in their rates when the predictor is measured *before* the onset or change occurs or fails to occur. As long as the outcome is measured independently of knowledge of that earlier measure, there is no danger of the bias that is likely to occur in a cross-sectional study when the prior history is obtained retrospectively.

Demographic Predictors of Drinking and Drug Use Problems

Only a few longitudinal studies have been able to look at demographic variables as predictors of alcohol and drug problems because only a few have utilized samples with a wide range of social background variables. Among studies that do provide demographic correlates of drug or alcohol use are Cahalan's (1970) and Brunswick's (1978). The Brunswick study, although limited to one race and one geographic area and a rather narrow age range (six years), does cover a range of occupations, education, region of birth, marital status, income, and parenthood. These variables could be related to marijuana and heroin use. There was no opportunity to find predictors of alcohol use, since virtually the entire sample were alcohol users. Brunswick found little relationship between demographic variables and drug use. The only significant demographic differences were that older females were more likely to use marijuana, and that for both sexes, but especially among women, high school dropouts more often became heroin users. More than two-thirds (71%) of female heroin users and 55% of male heroin users had not finished high school.

Studying drinking problems in a national sample, Cahalan found more demographic differences. For instance, he showed youthfulness to be associated with heavy drinking for both men and women, and among women, he found blacks more often heavy drinkers than whites, although there was no difference by race among men. In addition, religious background was a predictor for both men and women, with Catholics drinking more than Protestants or Jews. With regard to occupational status, operatives (i.e., semiskilled) of both sexes had relatively high rates of heavy drinking, and women who were either themselves service workers or married to service workers also had a high rate of heavy drinking, although this occupational status was not associated with high rates for men. Among both men and women, the college-educated had low rates of heavy drinking. Among women, marital status was strikingly related to heavy drinking, with more of those divorced and separated drinking heavily than those married. No relationship between marital status and drinking level was found for men. Men and women living in large cities had higher heavy drinking rates than those residing elsewhere, and city size affected women more than men. Cahalan's findings are consistent with the view that poverty, urbanization, and lack of ties to abstinence religions foster heavy drinking in both women and men. Among women, it is the young, urban, low-status, divorced Catholic who should be at greatest risk.

Family and Peer Predictors of Drinking and Drug Problems

All longitudinal studies that have investigated the relationship between parents' and children's substance use agree that for both sexes, use of drugs or alcohol by parents increases the chance of their use by children. This finding is reported by Kandel (1973) and Margulies et al. (1977), by Zucker and DeVoe (1973), by Cahalan et al. (1969), and by Robins (1966). O'Donnell (1969) has shown that heroin use in women is often preceded by their husband's or boyfriend's use, and Kellam et al. (1978) agreed that the boyfriends of adolescent drug-using girls in Chicago often had been responsible for introducing the girls to drugs. Thus, it is the male of the pair who is usually the first user, whether among adults or among adolescents. The importance of introduction by a member of the peer group is echoed in the finding of Margulies et al. (1977) that girls are even more influenced by peers' use of "spirits" than are boys and in the Jessors' (1976, 1977) finding that girls were more susceptible to the influence of their friends' drug use than boys. They also found parents' use more influential for girls than for boys, though less important than peer influence.

These findings suggest that in initiation into the use of alcohol and drugs, girls are more often conforming to interpersonal role models, whereas boys are more often engaging in the behavior as part of a complex of mildly deviant activities. For both boys and girls, interpersonal influences seem more important than psychological factors in predicting experimentation.

In addition to the parents' drinking and drug behaviors, certain of their attitudes and characteristics have also been found to predict drinking among their children. Zucker and DeVoe (1973), for instance, found that heavily drinking and problem drinking sons had had rejecting mothers, while heavily drinking daughters had had distant mothers. The role of the mother's negative personality in predicting heavy drinking was clearer for sons than for daughters. When sons were heavy drinkers, mothers disproportionately were described as rejecting, punitive, and absent. When daughters were heavy drinkers, mothers were disproportionately described as unaffectionate and punishing, but on the other hand, also as interceding more. The sons, however, tended to perceive fathers more negatively than mothers, while daughters were negative regarding both parents.

Jones (1968, 1971) also attempted to find an association between parental personality characteristics and alcoholism in their children. Her findings for women remain extremely tentative because her sample yielded only three female alcoholics. The mothers of both male and female alcoholics were described as sour, disagreeable, and dissatisfied. The mothers of male alcoholics were additionally described as uninterested, and not cheerful. For female alcoholics, a high level of family conflict and father's alcoholism were also reported.

Personal Determinants of Onset of Problems with Alcohol and Drugs

Follow-up studies of male drinking problems have provided a rather clear picture of childhood behavioral predictors. Before they ever began drinking, men who were to become heavy or problem drinkers tended to be more impulsive, rebellious, and deviant than their peers. In many ways, they resembled the boys who would become delinquent, and indeed, male delinquents and problem drinkers are overlapping populations. For women, the prodromal pattern is much less clear. In some studies, women show the same pattern as men. For instance, the Jessors (1977) found that alcohol problems for girls as well as for boys were associated with an increased tolerance for deviance, low achievement, and high independence. Looking at alcoholism in women who had previously been heroin addicts, O'Donnell (1969) noted that women who developed alcohol problems had been even more involved in deviant subcultures before their addiction than had men. Robins et al.'s (1962) study of child guidance clinic patients showed that antisocial behavior in childhood predicted alcoholism for both sexes. Zucker and DeVoe (1973) also showed that adolescent girls and boys who became heavy drinkers had been more antisocial than other adolescents.

In contrast to these findings, for girls but not for boys, an association has been found between neurotic or depressive symptoms and later drinking patterns. Jones (1968, 1971), for instance, in her follow-up of the Oakland Growth Study of children, noted that while alcoholic men tended to have been rebellious, impulsive, and undercontrolled as children, women who became alcoholic had been more submissive, depressed, and withdrawn than other girls. Block and Hahn's sample (1971) overlapped with Jones's sample but included some children from the Berkeley Guidance Study as well. By Q-sort analysis of childhood records, they found that women who were problem and heavy drinkers had been described as hyperfeminine, repressed, and fearful in childhood and early adolescence and were excessively dependent on their families and peers.

Kellam et al. (1978) used information collected in first grade to predict alcohol and drug use at age 17. They found for both boys and girls that a high IQ predicted a heavier use of alcohol at age 17, a finding not previously reported. This finding would probably conflict with others' findings of an association between early deviance and delinquency as a predictor of alcohol problems, since delinquents generally have slightly low IQs.

While personality predictors of alcohol problems in men are reasonably clear-cut, personality predictors of their illicit drug use are much less so. While male high school marijuana users were reported to be more deviance-prone by Jessor and Jessor (1977), there is also evidence from Kellam et al. (1978) that adolescent male drug use is predicted by greater-than-average maturity in first grade, but also by aggression. These mixed messages with regard to personal antecedents of drug use seem consistent with Johnston's finding (1974) that male drug users in their last year of high school come from both ends of the spectrum, from those who are deviant and from those who are unusually good students.

These opposite predictors of drug use have been found for women as well. Evidence for coming from the deviant end of the spectrum can be found in several studies: Zucker and DeVoe (1973) found that girls who became drug users tended to have been antisocial and rebellious and to have made low grades. In the Jessors' studies, deviance-proneness is less closely associated with marijuana use for girls than for boys, but it does weakly predict drug use for girls. For both boys and girls, they found drug use to be predicted by a low value on achievement, a high tolerance for deviance, a high value for independence, alienation and social criticism, not being religious, having had previous sexual experience, having had alcohol problems, and making poor grades. On the other hand, Kellam et al. (1978) did not find that aggression predicted drug use for girls as it did for boys. Indeed, for girls, he found no correlation between either aggressiveness or shyness and later drug use; rather, he found that girls who had been relatively free of adjustment problems in first grade were somewhat more likely to use drugs at 17, suggesting a correlation with the positive end of the adjustment spectrum.

These contradictory results may stem in part from confusing drug and alcohol use with drug or alcohol problems. If drug and alcohol *problems* were studied, one might expect to find a more clear-cut relationship between early deviance and/or psychiatric symptoms. At present, however, it is not clear what kinds of behavior predict future drug involvement for either males or females.

Even with respect to alcohol abuse, it is difficult at present to draw firm conclusions from these studies about personality factors predicting unusually early or problem use by women. There seems to be some tendency for women to share the patterns found in men, for whom poor school achievement and early deviance are associated with later use of alcohol. On the other hand, there is more evidence for women than for men that being depressed and withdrawn may also be a route to the abuse of alcohol. If the latter finding turns out to be a general one, it would be consonant with the finding that alcoholism in women is more often secondary to depression than is alcoholism in men (Winokur and Clayton, 1968). It would also help to explain the finding that onset of alcoholism is often later for women than for men. Antisocial behaviors, with which alcoholism appears to be more strongly associated in men than in women, peak in late adolescence and early adulthood, declining thereafter (Robins, 1966), while depression and neurotic illnesses peak in middle age (Hagnell, 1966). To the extent that women's alcoholism is more often associated with the latter problems and less often with antisocial behavior, one would expect later onset.

4. CONSEQUENCES OF ALCOHOL AND DRUG ABUSE

Social Consequences

There are some suggestions from the treatment literature that women's lives may be less disrupted by alcohol and drugs than are men's. For instance, according to O'Donnell (1969), Croughan (1978), and Duvall et al. (1963), after drug treatment, more men than women serve time in correctional institutions, and Paulus and Halliday (1967) reported better family relationships after treatment for women than for men. A follow-up of female criminals by Martin et al. (1978) showed that for women, a history of drug dependence at the time of incarceration predicted recidivism (75% had further arrests versus 33% who were not drug-dependent), but a history of alcoholism did not do so (38% of the alcoholics were rearrested versus 56% of nonalcoholics). Thus, drugs but not alcohol seem to have important predictive value for whether serious antisocial behavior in young women will or will not continue over the next six years. The lack of effect of alcoholism on women's recidivism contrasts strikingly with results found for male criminals, for whom alcoholism is indeed a predictor of recidivism (Guze, 1976).

If these results had come only from the treatment literature, we might have taken them as evidence that treatment is more effective for women than for men. That the social consequences of alcoholism also seem less severe in a general population sample and in a prisoner population requires us to consider other explanations. These results may simply show that women are at lower risk of institutionalization and family disruption regardless of whether they are alcohol abusers or not. In the general population, incarceration rates are much higher for men than for women, and the difference is too great to be explained entirely by men's higher rate of alcoholism and drug abuse. Further, women tend to maintain ties with the extended family more than men do. Any follow-up study comparing men and women, whether drug and alcohol abusers or not, can be expected to show lower rates of incarceration and closer family relationships during the follow-up interval for women than for men. To answer the question of whether the social impact of addiction to alcohol or drugs is truly less for women than for men, one would need to obtain *expected* rates of outcomes for each sex by simultaneously following comparison groups of men and women with similar histories prior to the onset of drug and alcohol problems.

Marital rates of heroin addicts also differ by sex, as shown by O'Donnell (1969), Croughan (1978), and Brunswick (1978). Each found that among heroin addicts, women had a much higher marriage rate than did men. This finding may show only that marriage tends to precede heroin addiction for women and follow it for men. The fact that many addicted women were introduced to heroin by their husbands suggests that they might not have become addicts had they not married. In addition, women have a later onset of heroin use and a younger age at marriage than do men. Given these three factors, the chances that marriage will precede addiction is considerably greater for women than men. We still do not know whether preexisting addiction is less likely to deter future marriage for women than for men. To answer this question, we need a follow-up study of later marriage by men and women still single at the time they became addicted to alcohol or drugs.

Since more female than male addicts marry, not surprisingly, they also more often have children than do male addicts. Brunswick found that three-quarters of heroin-using women had one or more children, whereas only half of the men did. This finding may also be explained by the later onset of heroin use in women than in men, rather than by heroin's causing less family disruption for women. Indeed, Jones et al. (1974) have pointed out that a large proportion of the children of female alcoholics are reared by others, showing that alcoholic women do not function well as mothers. Many children of female heroin addicts must also end in foster homes, judging by the fact that the mothers of 7% of a consecutive series of children in foster care in New York City had used narcotics for two or more years (Fanshel, 1975). According to recent reports associating maternal alcohol and drug abuse with children's prematurity, low IQ, fetal alcohol syndrome, withdrawal symptoms in infants born to mothers addicted to narcotics, and child abuse, addicted mothers may do as much or more damage to their offspring than addicted fathers.

A look at the employment records of female addicts shows that addicted women may have even more difficulty holding a job than addicted men. Brunswick (1978) reported that almost all of the female heroin users studied were staying home or doing nothing. Very few of them were in school or at work, even fewer than among male heroin users. Thus, the advantages of drug- and alcohol-dependent women in social adjustment as compared with men seem to be only in those areas that can be explained by their later age of onset or by differences in sex roles found in society at large.

The studies we have discussed have concentrated on heroin addiction and alcoholism, both of which are clearly associated with poor functioning in women. There is no evidence, however, that mild drug use has adverse social consequences for either sex. Kellam et al. (1978) found that his young drug users of both sexes were more socially involved than the remainder of his population, although they were also more involved in antisocial behavior. Clearly the degree of use is crucial in assessing the social consequences of women's drug and alcohol use.

Deaths

As compared with the general population, alcoholics and heroin addicts have greatly increased death rates (see Chapter 10). The increase is even more striking for women than for men, since women addicts' death rates are reported to be higher than men's, while in the general population women's rates are much lower than men's. Unfortunately, studies comparing addicts' death rates by sex seem not to have taken into account the fact that since onset of alcoholism and addiction is later in women than in men, female addicts are probably on the average somewhat older than male addicts. That age differences consequent on later onset for women may explain the apparent excess of female deaths among addicts is suggested by Croughan's (1978) study, in which male heroin addicts were matched to female addicts for age at treatment. He found identical death rates for men and women during the follow-up period. While there may be no higher rate of deaths for female than male addicts, addiction does seem to wipe out the advantage women enjoy in national mortality statistics.

5. CONCLUSIONS

Longitudinal studies confirm the cross-sectional observation that men have more drinking and drug problems than women, but they also suggest that differences are narrowing and may disappear in time. Thus, they add support to the view that research into the prevention and treatment of women's alcohol and drug abuse must increase to confront a growing problem.

Research thus far has shown childhood and adolescent behavior and family backgrounds somewhat less highly correlated with substance abuse for women than for men. We have pointed to two possible explanations derived from longitudinal studies for this observation: first, it may be because women begin drinking and using drugs later in life than men, and second, in women, substance abuse may more often be secondary to depressive disorders, for which childhood predictors are scarce. In any case, it is easier to predict drinking problems from childhood and adolescent factors for men than it is for women. Thus, it is unlikely that we will soon be able to identify young girls at sufficiently high risk for alcoholism or drug dependence to make efforts at prevention economically attractive.

Despite the discovery of some differences between men and women in the frequency and course of their drug and alcohol problems, the findings from longitudinal studies are more impressive for the similarites they find between the sexes than for the differences. For both sexes, substance abuse appears to be associated with early deviance, coming from deviant families, and associating with user peers. The order in which drugs are used is similar in men and women, and heavy use leads to similar rates of problems.

This chapter has attempted to summarize what we now know from longitudinal studies about sex differences in alcohol and drug use and abuse. If the findings seem uncertain, that uncertainty truly reflects the state of our knowledge. Follow-up studies of alcohol and drug use in women are few, and none has provided a sufficiently large representative sample of women with considerable use of alcohol and drugs to give us much confidence in our conclusions about the prevalence, incidence, course, predictors, or consequences of drug and alcohol involvement of women. An exploration of the interaction between fewer opportunities for women to use enough of such substances to put them at risk of dependence, their greater acceptance of norms supporting moderation or abstinence, and possible lower vulnerability will be necessary before we begin to understand why women have fewer alcohol and drug problems than men and to what extent this advantage is likely to persist.

REFERENCES

Abelson, H., and Atkinson, R., 1975, *Public Experience with Psychoactive Substances,* Part 1, *Main Findings,* Response Analysis Corporation, Princeton, N.J.

Blackford, L., 1974, *Trends in Levels of Use Shown in Seven Annual Surveys 1968–1974, Junior and Senior High School Students,* San Mateo County Department of Public Health and Welfare, San Mateo, Calif.

Block, J., and Hahn, N., 1971, *Lives through Time,* Bancroft Books, Berkeley, Calif.

Brill, N., and Christie, R., 1974, Marijuana use and psychosocial adaptation, *Arch. Gen. Psychiatry,* **31:**713–719.

Brunswick, A., 1978, Black youth and drug use behavior, mimeograph.

Cahalan, D., 1970, *Problem Drinkers: A National Survey,* Jossey-Bass, San Francisco.

Cahalan, D., Cisin, I., and Crossley, H., 1969, *American Drinking Practices: A National Study of Drinking Behavior and Attitudes* (Rutgers Center for Alcohol Studies, Monograph No. 6), College and University Press, New Haven, Conn.

Croughan, J., 1978, Drug dependence, unpublished paper, Department of Psychiatry, Washington University School of Medicine, St. Louis.

Drug Treatment in New York City and Washington, D.C.: Follow Up Studies, 1977, NIDA Services Research Monograph Series, U.S. Government Printing Office, Washington, D.C. (DHEW Publication No. (ADM)77-506.)

Duvall, H., Locke, B., and Brill, L., 1963, Follow-up study of narcotic drug addicts five years after hospitalization, *Public Health Rep.* **3:**78–185.

Fanshel, D., 1975, Parental failure and consequences for children: The drug-abusing mothers whose children are in foster care, *Am. J. Public Health* **65:**604–612.

Fillmore, K., 1974, Drinking and problem drinking in early adulthood and middle age, *J. Stud. Alcohol* **35:**819–840.

Fillmore, K., 1975, Relationships between specific drinking problems in early adulthood and middle age, *J. Stud. Alcohol* **36:**882–907.

Fillmore, K., and Marden, P., 1977, Longitudinal research at the Rutgers Center of Alcohol Studies, *Alcoholism: Clinical and Experimental Research,* **1**(3): 251–257.

Fillmore, K., Bacon, S., and Hyman, M., 1978, The 25 year longitudinal panel study of drinking by students in college, 1949–1951, progress report, February 1978, The Rutgers Center for Alcohol Studies, New Brunswick, N.J.

Garfield, M., and Garfield, E., 1973, A longitudinal study of drugs on a campus, *Int. J. Addict.* **84:**599–611.

Ginsberg, I., and Greenley, J., 1978, Competing theories of marijuana use: A longitudinal study, *J. Health Soc. Behav.* **19:**22–34.

Glueck, S., and Glueck, E., 1968, *Delinquents and Non-Delinquents in Perspective,* Howard University Press, Cambridge, Mass.

Goodwin, D., 1977, Genetic and experimental antecedents of alcoholism: A prospective study, *Alcoholism: Clinical and Experimental Research* **1**(3): 259–265.

Guze, S., 1976, *Criminality and Psychiatric Disorders,* Oxford University Press, New York.

Haastrup, S., 1973, *Young Drug Abusers,* Munksgaard, Copenhagen.

Hagnell, O., 1966, *A Prospective Study of the Incidence of Mental Disorder,* Scandinavian University Books, Stockholm.

Jessor, R., 1976, Predicting time of onset of marijuana use: A developmental study of high school youth, *J. Consult. Clin. Psychol.* **44:**125–134.

Jessor, R., and Jessor, S., 1975, Adolescent development and the onset of drinking: A longitudinal study, *J. Stud. Alcohol* **36:**27–51.

Jessor, R., and Jessor, S., 1977, *Problem Behavior and Psychosocial Development: A Longitudinal Study of Youth,* Academic Press, New York.

Johnston, L., 1974, Drug use during and after high school: Results of a national longitudinal study, *Am. J. Public Health* **64**(supp.):29–37.

Johnston, L., Bachman, J., and O'Malley, P., 1977, *Drug Use among American High School Students 1975–1977,* National Institute on Drug Abuse, Rockville, Md.

Jones, K., Smith, D., Streissguth, A., and Myrianthopoulos, N., 1974, Outcome in offspring of chronic alcoholic women, *Lancet* **1:**1076–1078.

Jones, M. C., 1968, Personality correlates and antecedents of drinking patterns in adult males, *J. Consult. Clin. Psychol.* **32:**2–12.

Jones, M. C., 1971, Personality antecedents and correlates of drinking patterns in women, *J. Consult. Clin. Psychol.* **36:**61–69.

Josephson, E., 1976, Antecedents and consequences of teenage drug behavior, paper presented at Conference on Strategies of Longitudinal Research in Drug Use, April 1976, Puerto Rico.

Kandel, D., 1973, Interpersonal influences on adolescent drug use, paper presented at Conference on the Epidemiology of Drug Use, February 1973, Puerto Rico.

Kandel, D., 1975, Stages in adolescent involvement in drug use, *Science* **190:**912–914.

Kandel, D., Kessler, R., and Margulies, R., 1976a, *Adolescent Initiation into Stages of Drug Use: A Sequential Analysis,* paper presented at Conference on Strategies of Longitudinal Research in Drug Use, April 1976, Puerto Rico.

Kandel, D., Single, E., and Kessler, R., 1976b, The epidemiology of drug use among New York State high school students: Distribution, trends and change in rates of use, *Am. J. Public Health* **66:**43–53.

Kellam, S., Ensminger, M., Simon, M., Turner, R., and Zaidi, Q., 1978, *Mental Health in First Grade and Teenage Drug Use,* Social Psychiatry Study Center, Department of Psychiatry, University of Chicago, Chicago.

Margulies, R., Kessler, R., and Kandel, D., 1977, A longitudinal study of onset of drinking among high school students, *J. Stud. Alcohol* **38:**897–912.

Martin, R., Cloninger, C., Guze, S., 1978, Female criminality and the prediction of recidivism, *Arch. Gen. Psychiatry* **35:**207–214.

McCord, W., and McCord, J., 1960, *Origins of Alcoholism,* Stanford University Press, Stanford, Calif.

Oden, M., 1968, The fulfillment of promise: 40-year follow-up of the Terman gifted group, *Genet. Psychol. Monogr.* **77:**3–93.

O'Donnell, J., 1969, *Narcotic Addicts in Kentucky,* U.S. Public Health Service, Chevy Chase, Md.

O'Donnell, J., Voss, H., Clayton, R., Slatin, G., and Room, R. (Feb.) 1976, *Young Men and Drugs: A Nationwide Survey,* NIDA Monograph (Series No. 5), U.S. Government Printing Office, Washington, D.C.

Paulus, I., and Halliday, R., 1967, Rehabilitation and the narcotic addict: Results of a comparative Methadone withdrawal program, *Can. Med. Assoc. J.* **96:**655–659.

Rachal, J., Williams, J., Brehm, M., Cavanaugh, B., Moore, R., and Eckerman, W., 1975, A national study of adolescent drinking behavior, attitudes and correlates, Prepared for National Institute on Alcohol Abuse and Alcoholism, U.S. National Technical Information Service, Springfield, Va.

Richman, A., 1966, Follow-up of criminal narcotic addicts, *Can. Psychiatr. Assoc. J.* **11**(2):107–115.

Richman, A., Clark, J., Bergner, L., and Patrick, S., 1971, Follow-up of 500 heroin users by means of a case register, Draft of paper presented at the Thirty-Third Annual Scientific Meeting, Committee on Problems of Drug Dependence, National Academy of Sciences-National Research Council (Feb. 1971).

Richman, A., Perkins, M., Bihari, B., and Fishman, M., 1972, Entry into methadone maintenance programs: A follow-up study of New York City heroin users detoxified in 1961–1963, *Am. J. Pub. Health* **62**(7):1002–1007.

Robins, L., 1966, *Deviant Children Grown Up: A Sociological and Psychiatric Study of Sociopathic Personality,* Williams & Wilkins, Baltimore.

Robins, L., Bates, W., and O'Neal, P., 1962, Adult drinking patterns of former problem children, in: *Society, Culture and Drinking Patterns* (D. Pittman and C. Synder, eds.), pp. 395–412, Wiley, New York.

Robins, L., Davis, D., and Nurco, D., 1974, How permanent was Vietnam drug addiction, *Am. J. Public Health* **64**:38–43.

Robins, L., Helzer, J., and Davis, D., 1975, Narcotic use in Southeast Asia and afterward, *Arch. Gen. Psychiatry* **32**:955–961.

Schuckit, M., and Winokur, G., 1972, A short term follow-up of women alcoholics, *Dis. Nerv. Syst.* **33**:672–678.

Sells, S., and Simpson, D., 1976, *Studies of the Effectiveness of Treatments for Drug Abuse,* Ballinger, Cambridge, Mass.

Single, E., Kandel, D., and Faust, R., 1974, Patterns of multiple drug use in high school, *J. Health Soc. Behav.* **15**:344–357.

Smith, G., and Fogg, C., 1975, Teenage drug use: A search for causes and consequences, in: *Predicting Adolescent Drug Abuse: A Review of Issues, Methods and Correlates* (D. Lettieri, ed.), National Institute on Drug Abuse, Rockville, Md.

Straus, R., and Bacon, S., 1953, *Drinking in College,* Yale University Press, New Haven, Conn.

Terman, L., 1959, *Genetic Studies of Genius,* Vol. 5, *The Gifted Group at Mid-Life,* Stanford University Press, Stanford, Calif.

Vaillant, G., 1973, A 20 year follow-up of New York narcotic addicts, *Arch. Gen. Psychiatry* **29**:237–241.

Winokur, G., and Clayton, P., 1968, Family history studies, IV, Comparison of male and female alcoholics, *Q. J. Stud. Alcohol* **29**:885–891.

Zucker, R., and DeVoe, C., 1973, Life history characteristics associated with problem drinking and antisocial behavior in adolescent girls: A comparison with male findings, in: *Life History Research in Psychopathology,* Vol. 4 (M. Roff, R. Wirt, and G. Winokur, eds.), University of Minneapolis Press, Minneapolis.

6

Sex Differences in the Inheritance of Alcoholism

RICHARD P. SWINSON

1. INTRODUCTION

Alcoholism is undoubtedly a familial disorder. The findings of much research have been summarized by Goodwin (1971), who stated that "without exception, every family study of alcoholism, irrespective of country of origin, has shown much higher rates of alcoholism among the relatives of alcoholics than apparently occurs in the general population." In general, the lifetime expectancy of alcoholism in male first-degree relatives of alcoholics is between 30% and 50%. The female first-degree relatives of alcoholics develop alcoholism in 3–8% of cases. These rates are considerably higher than those for the relatives of nonalcoholics.

The finding that a disorder follows a familial pattern of distribution poses the question of the precise etiology of the disorder. Disorders may run in families because of early learning experiences provided by the rearing parents or because of the genetic endowment that the child receives from the parents at conception. There may also be an interaction between these two factors, a conclusion reached by a number of contributors to *Nature and Nurture in Alcoholism* (Seixas et al., 1972), which provides an overview of the two sides of the familial nature of alcoholism. The purpose of this review is twofold: first, to examine the evidence for the proposition that alcoholism is genetically determined, and second, to compare the relative effects of any genetic factors in the two sexes.

In human subjects, it is, of course, not possible deliberately to

RICHARD P. SWINSON • Department of Psychiatry, University of Toronto, Toronto, Ontario.

control either the genetic or the environmental effects on an individual as can be done in animals. From the finding that rats can be bred with high or low addiction potential (Nichols, 1972), it can be extrapolated that something similar might occur in man. Because of the impossibility of carrying out direct genetic or environmental experiments in man, however, the research methodology necessary to investigate the relative importance of the various factors involved is indirect except in those instances where a "natural experiment" has taken place.

These indirect methods of assessing the relative importance of genetic and environmental factors are well established. *Twin studies* provide an indication of the proportionate effect of the two factors. Dizygous (DZ) twins have a different genetic endowment, in part, but share a common early environment unless they are physically separated. Monozygous (MZ) twins, however, share both a common genetic endowment and a common environment. Disorders that are genetically determined show higher concordance rates in MZ than DZ pairs, and disorders with a large environmental component show little or no difference between the concordance rates for the two types of twin pairs.

Adoption constitutes one of the "natural experiments" that occur in the life experience of some children. Adoption studies provide a way of examining what happens when the biological child of a parent (or parents) with a target disorder is reared in an environment determined by adoptive parents who do not have the target disorder. If the target disorder is environmentally produced, it should not occur at a higher rate in the adopted children than in the biological children of the adopting parents. The adopted children should also show a lower rate of the disorder than their biological parents and other children of the same parents who are reared in the original family setting. Conversely, if the etiology of the target disorder is largely genetically determined, moving the child to a nonaffected family, even early in its life, will not change the likelihood of the adopted child developing the disorder. Thus, cohorts of adopted children who reach the age of risk for the condition will develop the condition with the same frequency as their biological parents and their nonadopted siblings. It will be appreciated that there are many difficulties in carrying out such studies; these are detailed below.

Half-sibling studies provide another way in which the effects of genetic and environmental influences can be separated. In adoption studies, a child born to two persons, one of whom at least is affected by the condition under investigation, is then reared by two other persons, neither of whom, ideally, has the same condition. In half-sibling studies a group of subjects who suffer from a target condition is identified. Those subjects with half-siblings are then examined. Half-siblings share one common parent but have received a different genetic endowment from the other parent. Half-siblings may or may not be reared together; where they are reared apart, similar comparisons can be made to those in adoption studies. If the shared parent suffers from the target disorder, whatever genetic endowment there is in the disorder will be shared by the half-siblings. Alternatively, if the target disorder occurs in a parent who is not the shared parent, then any genetic effects will be evident only in the half-sibling of that parent. In yet another situation, a child may be born to parents neither of whom has the target condition but may then be taken to live with another adult who has the condition. In this way, the effects of living in the environment of the condition can be assessed in the absence of any genetic endowment from the condition.

Genetic marker studies provide another indirect way of assessing the hereditary component of a disorder. Some disorders are found in association with a characteristic that is known to be genetically determined. For example, peptic ulcers in particular sites in the upper alimentary tract are associated with particular blood groups. McConnell (1966) has reported that prepyloric ulcers and concomitant gastric and duodenal ulcers are associated with blood group O, whereas chronic ulcers in the middle third of the stomach have no blood group association. Thus, there is a genetically determined component in the etiology of prepyloric ulceration.

A large number of studies have been reported in the area of alcoholism that involve genetic markers. These have investigated four different markers: blood groups, the secretion of ABH blood group substance in the saliva, taste sensitivity to phenylthiocarbamide (PTC), and color vision. All of these characteristics are gentically determined although they can be altered by environmental factors. Thus, a finding of an association between a disorder and a genetic marker has to be examined closely if one is to ascertain whether or not the process of the disorder might have affected the characteristic that is being used as an independent variable.

The last area that is considered in this review is the association between alcoholism and other psychiatric disorders. For a number of reasons, the evidence in this area is not as definite as that in the other types of indirect genetic studies. First, there is the problem of the definition of the independent variable to be used as a marker. There is no argument about whether or not a subject is of blood group A, O, B, or AB because the tests for determining the classification are standardized and open to minimal interpretive error. However, when an investigation uses "depression," for example, as the starting point of a study on the association of a psychiatric disorder (in this case, affective disorder) with alcoholism, then the investigators face the problem of defining *depression*. It is not within the scope of this review to consider the problems of psychiatric diagnosis in any detail. A discussion can be found in *Psychiatric Diagnosis* by Woodruff et al. (1974). It will be appreciated that to investigate the concurrence of two disorders, neither of which is accurately defined and both of which are susceptible to marked observer interpretive bias, leads to considerably reduced experimental reliability.

In considering the experimental definitions of alcoholism, many researchers in the area of genetic investigations have failed to state their criteria for the diagnosis of alcoholism. Others have failed to obtain opinions other than their own in reaching their diagnoses. All of the results that are discussed below have to be considered in the light of the definition of alcoholism applied by each investigator. It is certainly not possible to assume that there is uniformity across the different groups of subjects studied. The second main task of the review, as already stated, is to compare the results of genetic research in female and male alcoholics. Since there has been little work specifically with females, the comparisons will be few. Investigators have either tended to control for sex as a variable by investigating males only or have not reported their data separately for the two sexes.

2. TWIN STUDIES

Males

Two large twin studies have been reported, both from Scandinavia. Kaij (1960) made use of the twin birth registers and the Temperance Board records to study 174 pairs of male twins born in Sweden between 1890 and 1939. The pairs were included in the study if either twin had a record of convictions for drunkenness or other alcohol abuse. All the probands and their twins were interviewed personally.

In the 48 monozygous (MZ) twin pairs, a concordance rate of drinking problems of 54.2% was found. In the 126 dizygous (DZ) pairs, the concordance rate was 35%. A recalculation of the data by Slater and Cowie (1971) revealed that the concordance rate of DZ pairs was 32% higher than expected and for MZ pairs 114% higher than expected. The difference between the MZ and DZ pairs' concordance rates indicated that there was a genetic factor involved in the etiology of the reported alcohol abuse.

A study in Finland by Partanen et al. (1966) examined 902 male twins born between 1920 and 1929. The aim of the study was to compare the effects of genetic and environmental influences on variations in the use of alcoholic beverages. For each pair, the drinking behavior, zygosity, environmental factors, and psychological and physiological traits were examined. Zygosity (that is, whether each pair was DZ or MZ) was checked by serological comparisons, by taste sensitivity to phenylthio-carbamide (PTC), and also by an anthropological scale of 10 factors. Subjects were interviewed personally by the investigators.

The conclusions of the study were that abstinence, normal drinking, and heavy drinking all showed evidence of heritability, which was deduced from the finding of higher MZ concordance than DZ concordance. The specific drinking patterns that showed evidence of heritability included the frequency and the amount of alcohol consumption.

The social consequences of drinking were also examined, but since the concordance rates for the MZ and DZ pairs did not differ statistically, there was no evidence that hereditary factors were of importance in producing the social consequences of alcoholism. Most other studies of the genetics of alcoholism define the disorder and select the subjects on the basis of such social consequences of alcohol intake as public drunkenness, arrests, job loss, and marital breakdown. It would be expected that if a genetic factor is involved in the etiology of alcoholism then the complex behaviors that make up the syndrome of alcoholism would, as in Partanen et al.'s study, show high concordance rates in MZ twin pairs. However, unless the individual twins of any given pair were subject to very different environmental conditions, it would also be expected that the social consequences would be similar for the members of each pair. This study has been severely criticized by Popham et al. (1967), who believed that the basic question asked by Partanen and his colleagues is unanswerable by the method used since it does not supply a means of separating the proportionate effects of the environment and genetics in the group studied.

Females

There have been no reports of twin studies in female alcoholics.

3. ADOPTION STUDIES

The advantage of adoption studies, as explained above, lies in the possiblity of investigating the development of a subject who has the genetic endowment of a target population and environmental exposure to a rearing family without the target condition. As a result, the effects of genetic and environmental factors on the developing child can be partially separated.

Such studies are exceedingly difficult to carry out because it is rare to identify children born to alcoholic parents who are fostered or adopted at an early age and who are also available for follow-up at the age of risk for alcoholism. There have been a number of studies reported. These are considered in two sections. The first section consists of a single joint study of both sexes, and the second consists of a series of recent Scandinavian studies.

Joint Male–Female Study

The pioneer study in this area was performed by Roe and Burk (1944). Twenty-seven children were identified whose fathers were excessive drinkers exhibiting the social consequences of alcoholism. The mothers of the children were also found to exhibit a great deal of psychopathology. Only 4 of the 27 mothers were considered psychologically normal. The other 23 were excessive drinkers, sexual deviants, or negligent toward their children.

The children under study were placed in other families with nonalcoholic parents before they reached the age of 5 years. They were compared with a control group of illegitimate or orphaned children who, as far as was known, did not have an alcoholic parent. No evidence of paternity was obtained for either group. At follow-up, the subjects were between 22 and 40 years old; the "alcoholic" subjects had a mean age of 32 years and the controls 28 years. The drinking behavior of the two groups was found to be remarkably similar. In neither group was there any evidence of alcohol abuse. Regular alcohol use was reported by 7% of the "alcoholic group" and 9% of the controls; occasional alcohol use was reported by 63% and 55%, respectively; and abstinence by 30% and 36%, respectively. The "alcoholic group" did show a nonstatistically significant increase in adjustment problems. It was concluded that there was no evidence of hereditary effects in the development of excessive drinking in the subjects studied.

Unfortunately, this pioneer study was methodologically unsound, especially because of lack of data on paternity and lack of knowledge about the parents of the control group. The children were reared by their biological parents for lengthy periods, a factor that would confound the results, and the adoptive families for the two groups differed. Finally, the age of the subjects at follow-up was relatively young with respect to the period of risk for the development of alcoholism.

Scandinavian Studies

Goodwin and his colleagues have reported on a series of studies on the offspring of alcoholics since 1973 (Goodwin et al., 1973, 1974, 1977a,b), and a separate study has been conducted by Bohman (1978).

Scandinavian countries offer many advantages over other countries for researchers carrying out adoption studies. First, the population is very stable, with little immigration or emigration; and second, comprehensive records are available that cover data on adoption, psychiatric illness, and excessive drinking. Goodwin and his colleagues were able to obtain information on a total of 5483 nonfamily adoptions that occurred in Copenhagen between 1924 and 1947. Bohman's data were derived from 2324 nonfamily adoptions in Stockholm between 1930 and 1949.

Danish Adoption Studies

Males. In the first study, Goodwin et al. (1973) investigated the alcohol problems of 55 adopted males, each having a biological parent who had been hospitalized primarily for alcoholism. In 85% of the cases, the alcoholic parent was the father. All the probands had been separated from their biological parents within six weeks of birth and had been adopted into an unrelated family.

Two control groups were also chosen on the basis of the same adoption circumstances. One group consisted of 50 adoptees whose parents had no history of hospitalization for any psychiatric disorder; the second group of 28 controls had a biological parent who was hospitalized for a psychiatric disorder other than alcoholism.

The adoptive parents of the probands did not differ significantly from those of the control subjects in terms of economic status and psychopathology. The probands and the controls were not significantly different from each other on demographic characteristics apart from an increased rate of divorce in the proband group.

The two control groups were combined into a single group of 78 subjects. A comparison of psychopathology exclusive of alcoholism in the two groups revealed a nonsignificant increase in anxiety and depression in the control group. However, 40% of the probands had received psychiatric treatment, compared with 24% of the controls ($p < 0.01$), and 15% of the probands had been hospitalized for psychiatric reasons, compared with 3% of the controls ($p < 0.05$). Eight probands had been hospitalized for psychiatric disorders, and by the criteria used for the diagnosis of alcoholism, six were considered alcoholic. Neither of the two hospitalized controls was alcoholic.

The two groups were also compared in terms of their specific drinking problems. Five statistically significant variables were found, all of which had higher rates in the proband group. The variables were hallucinations during alcohol withdrawal, loss of control over alcohol intake, repeated morning drinking, treatment for drinking problems, and exhibiting a drinking pattern that satisfied the authors' criteria for alcoholism. Judgments about the presence of drinking problems were made by a psychiatrist who was blind to the grouping of the subjects.

The findings demonstrated that children born to an alcoholic parent are four times more likely to develop alcohol-related problems than children of nonalcoholic parents, even when separation from the biological parent occurs within six weeks of birth. This study added a lot of weight to the argument that genetic factors are of importance in the development of alcoholism.

A second study by the same group (Goodwin et al., 1974) examined the brothers of the alcoholic proband group in the above study. Of the original probands, 20 had a total of 35 brothers who were reared by the probands' biological parents; 6 were full siblings, 4 were maternal half-siblings, and 25 were paternal half-siblings. The nonadopted sons were older than those adopted and were less likely to have married. The adopted sons were reared in better socioeconomic conditions than their nonadopted brothers.

As was expected, a greater rate of psychopathology in their parents was reported by the nonadopted sons than by the adopted sons. Interestingly though, only one-half of the nonadopted sons reported having an alcoholic parent despite the fact that one parent in each family had been identified independently as suffering from alcoholism. This observation casts doubt on the validity of family alcoholism rates that are derived from uncorroborated reports of a single family member.

The findings overall failed to reveal any statistically significant differences between the two groups of sons. The drinking patterns and problems of the groups differed only insofar as the adopted sons showed a higher incidence of amnesia after drinking than the nonadopted sons (40%:13%). A total of 25% of the adopted sons and 17% of their nonadopted sibs were diagnosed as being alcoholic.

The effect of the severity of parental alcoholism on the two groups was examined. It was found that this factor was predictive of the severity of alcoholism in the offspring. This finding held true for both the adopted and the nonadopted sons regardless of the length of time the offspring had been reared in the home of the alcoholic parent.

If environmental factors were responsible for a major part of the etiology of alcoholism, it would be expected that exposure to an alcoholic home environment, with its disruptions and modeling of excessive drinking, would lead to an increase in the rate of alcoholism in those children reared in such an environment compared with children reared in an outside environment. The finding that there was essentially no difference between the two groups studied lends further support to the contention that genetic factors are implicated in the etiology of alcoholism or, at least, of severe alcoholism in males.

Females. The same group of researchers that reported on the above studies in males also investigated the adopted daughters of alcoholic parents (Goodwin et al., 1977a,b).

The pool of subjects from which the male probands were derived served as the source for the 65 women in the proband group in the first study of the daughters of alcoholics (Goodwin et al., 1977a). A total of 65 controls with nonalcoholic biological parents were also selected. Because of refusals and other factors, the final groups consisted of 49 probands and 47 controls.

Demographically, the two groups did not differ. As far as could be ascertained from interviewing the subjects, the foster home experiences of the two groups also did not differ significantly. No differences were found when the psychopathology of the two groups of adoptees was compared. The only significant finding on comparing the drinking problems of the probands and the controls was that, as in the male probands reported above, the occurrence of amnesia following drinking was markedly increased in the proband group (22%:6%). Of the probands, 2% were considered to have had drinking problems, and an additional 2% were diagnosed as alcoholic. In the control group, no problem drinkers were identified, but 4% were diagnosed as alcoholic. For both groups, the frequency of drinking problems was about four times that expected in a normal control group.

The failure to find any difference between the rates of excessive drinking in the adopted female children of alcoholic parents and the adopted female children of nonalcoholic parents contrasts with the findings on the male children. A number of factors might have influenced these findings. For example, the sample size, 49 subjects, was very small, and many of the subjects had not reached the age of maximum risk. The mean age for both groups was 35 years, so that it would be interesting to observe the future development of drinking problems as the groups age.

One further flaw in the study, recognized by the investigators, stems from the fact that although it was known that the control-group subjects did not have a parent who had been admitted to a hospital because of drinking problems, nonetheless it was not known whether the putative biological fathers were the actual fathers or whether the parents had a drinking problem for which they had not been hospitalized. Obviously, then, this control group was not an ideal one for purposes of a genetic study.

Environmental factors may play a larger part in the etiology of alcoholism in women than in men. The two control women who were diagnosed as suffering from alcoholism had alcoholic foster fathers. In the previous studies, none of the male adopted sons of alcoholics had an alcoholic adoptive parent. Thus, in males, the genetic influence appears to be a potent etiological factor, but the same conclusion cannot be drawn for female adoptees.

The fourth study conducted on the Danish sample was a comparison of the alcoholics' daughters who were given up for adoption with the daughters who were raised by their biological alcoholic parents; 49 adopted daughters and 108 nonadopted daughters were available for study. Demographic comparisons revealed that the adopted daughters were older (37 years) than the nonadopted daughters (32 years). More of the adopted daughters had divorced.

The nonadopted daughters had generally been raised in less advantageous conditions than the adopted subjects. The nonadopted daughters experienced significantly more family breakdown and more parental psychopathology in the form of paternal alcoholism or antisocial behavior and maternal depression.

The frequency of psychopathology in the two groups of subjects was compared. The two groups experienced similar rates of depression and anxiety, but the adopted daughters had received psychiatric treatment more often than the nonadopted daughters. In view of the finding that the nonadopted daughters had been reared in homes that had high rates of psychopathology, it might be expected that the nonadopted group would receive more psychiatric treatment than the adopted group. It is possible, in families where there is a high level of psychopathology, that the psychological disturbance of any individual may not be noticed as being deviant. Alternatively, if an individual's psychopathology is recognized, that person may not be regarded as needing help from a professional.

The drinking patterns of the two groups were very similar. Again, it was found that the adopted daughters demonstrated a higher frequency of alcoholic amnesia than those in the nonadopted group. A total of 2% of the adopted daughters and 3% of the nonadopted daughters were diagnosed as alcoholic. An additional 2% of each group were regarded as having drinking problems. The rates of alcoholism in both groups were four times higher than the expected rates for the normal population.

Depression was diagnosed in 14% of the adopted daughters and in 27% of the nonadopted daughters. These frequencies were not significantly different. A comparison was made with a nonadopted control group of women whose parents were not alocholic. Of these 37 women, 7% suffered from depression. Comparisons of the frequencies of depression in the three groups revealed that the daughters of alcoholics reared with their alcoholic parents had significantly increased rates of depression over the normal control group. The other differences were not statistically significant.

Overall, the findings in the studies of the daughters of alcoholics indicate that there is an increase in drinking problems and depression over that expected in a normal control population. However, these findings are not significantly different from those in the adopted daughters of nonalcoholics. Environmental factors, thus, may play a larger part in determining alcoholism in women than they do in men.

Swedish Adoption Study.   Another Scandinavian study, done in two parts, has been reported by Bohman (1978). In the initial investigation, 2324 people were identified who had been born in Stockholm between 1930 and 1949 and who had been adopted by parents outside their biological families. The criterion for early adoption was much lengthier than that in the studies already quoted in that Bohman accepted adoption at up to three years of age as being "early," whereas the Danish studies only accepted adoptions at up to 6 weeks as "early." All the adoptions were of illegitimate children. The Excise Board (alcohol abuse) Register and the Criminal Register were searched for entries related to the adopted children and their biological parents. The biological fathers and mothers of the adopted children were greatly overrepresented on both registers compared with the frequency of registration in the general population. The adopted males did not appear to have any increase in registration on either the alcohol or criminality registers. The adopted females, however, were overrepresented on both registers when compared with a normal population.

Bohman examined the offspring of the parents who were registered on either the alcohol register or the criminal register with regard to the frequency of the registration of the offspring on the same registers. The findings for the males are summarized in Table 1. It can be seen that alcohol abuse in either parent was associated with an increase in alcohol abuse in their male offspring and also with an increase in alcohol abuse in combination with criminality. Criminality alone in either parent was not associated with an increase in either criminality or alcohol abuse in male offspring.

No increase in registration in either register was found for the female

Table 1. Parental versus Adopted Male Offspring Registration for Alcoholism and Criminality[a]

		Father alcoholic	Mother alcoholic	Father criminal	Mother criminal
Male adoptees	Alcohol abuse	+	+	−	−
	Criminality	+	+	−	−

[a] +, Increased over expected; −, not increased.

offspring when the same circumstances were considered, but the numbers were too small to allow definite conclusions to be drawn. These findings confirm evidence of genetic influence in the etiology of alcoholism in male children of alcoholic parents. The findings for female children also parallel those in the Danish studies.

In the second part of the study, 390 probands were selected on the basis of the severity of the parents' alcohol abuse or criminality. (Bohman said he examined 380 probands, but actually the total of the eight groups examined equals 390.) Those probands whose parents exhibited marked alcohol problems or criminality were selected.

There were slightly fewer probands from severely affected mothers because there were very few mothers whose problems were as severe as the fathers' problems. Controls were selected from adoptees whose parents did not appear on either the alcohol abuse or the criminality register. The results reflected the findings of the initial study (see Table 1). In the case of adopted men, having either parent registered for severe alcohol abuse was associated with an increased frequency of alcohol abuse in the adoptees. A total of 20% of the male probands and 6% of the male controls appeared on the alcohol abuse register. Having an alcoholic or criminal father was not associated with an increase in criminality in the male adoptees. Having an alcoholic mother was associated with an increase in alcohol abuse and an increase in criminality: 33.4% of the probands and 19% of the controls were registered for alcohol abuse.

No significant differences were found between the rates of alcoholism and criminality in the female probands and the female controls. In both groups, 3% of the subjects were registered for alcohol abuse. This rate is higher than that expected in a normal population control group and is comparable to the frequency of 2% alcoholism rates found in the Danish studies of female adoptees of alcoholic parents.

In examining the relationship between criminality in the parents and alcohol abuse in the female offspring, it was found that there was a tendency toward increased frequency of alcohol abuse in the proband group. A total of 2% of the probands and none of the controls were registered for alcohol abuse. The figures are too small to allow any firm conclusions to be drawn.

In examining the effects of late versus early placement of the male offspring in his sample, Bohman found that this variable appeared to have no effect on the rates of registration for either alcohol abuse or criminality for the control group. In the proband group, there was a statistically nonsignificant increase in the registration of males on the alcohol abuse register for those who were placed after their first birthday compared with those placed in the first year of life.

For the male offspring of alcoholic or criminal parents, there appeared to be a genetic endowment in the development of alcoholism but not in the development of criminality. For the female offspring, the results were inconclusive, largely because of the sample size, but no evidence was found to support the hypothesis of a genetic endowment for the development of either alcoholism or criminality.

This study, which used a large sample for the first part, confirms the findings of the Danish studies regarding the discrepancies between the results in the male and female offspring of alcoholics. The control study was restricted to a very small sample size in which the ages of the subjects were not stated. These factors make the interpretation of the findings somewhat tentative.

Summary of Adoption Studies

The conclusion from all the recent studies on the development of alcoholism in male adoptees is that being born of an alcoholic parent has a great influence on the likelihood of subsequent development of alcoholism in the offspring. Further, it appears that this influence, which is exerted genetically rather than environmentally, is fairly specific to the development of alcohol abuse rather than merely reflective of widespread psychopathology or criminality.

For female offspring, the conclusions are less clear. The number of probands in each study has been small and their age at the time of examination has tended to be rather young with respect to the risk of development of alcoholism; these conditions may well have introduced a bias against the chances of discovering alcoholic female subjects. The finding of a fourfold increase in the incidence of alcoholism in the adopted daughters of alcoholic parents was matched by a similar finding in the adopted daughters of nonalcoholics. The adopted offspring of alcoholic parents consistently report increased frequencies of specific drinking behaviors and symptoms related to excess alcohol intake, particularly for the occurrence of alcoholic amnesia. In identifying alcohol abuse problems in males and females, both parents and offspring, it has been assumed that alcoholism in the two sexes has the same constellation of signs and symptoms. This assumption may have led to a male model of alcoholism's being taken as the investigative model for both sexes. In order to elucidate the possible genetic endowment of alcoholism in females, it would be necessary to obtain data from a large group of females at risk of developing alcoholism and to compare, prospectively, the development of the disorder with that in a group of males. After this procedure, futher adoption studies using a larger sample size of females could be undertaken.

At the present time, the evidence for a genetic factor in the development of alcoholism in female adoptees is inconclusive.

4. HALF-SIBLING STUDIES

As noted in the introduction, half-sibling studies provide an alternative method of examining the effects of genetic factors in the etiology of a disorder. Schuckit et al. (1972) used this method in a study of 69 alcoholic probands.

The probands were selected on the basis of a diagnosis of primary alcoholism and having at least one half-sibling. Alcoholism was defined by its social consequences.

The proband group consisted of 60 males and 9 females with a mean age of 40 years. Interviews were conducted with a total of 90 relatives. Of the biological fathers of the probands, 35% were found to be alcoholic, as were 32% of the full brothers and 31% of the half-brothers. Of the biological mothers, 5% were alcoholic, as were 8% of the full sisters and 6% of the half-sisters.

The half-siblings, by definition, shared only one parent with the proband alcoholic. Although there was no stipulation concerning the sex of the shared parent, in 54 of the 69 cases it was the mother. Of the biological mothers shared with the probands, 9% were alcoholic. Of the biological fathers shared with the probands, 18% were alcoholic.

The effect of having an alcoholic biological parent on the drinking patterns of half-siblings was examined. Of those half-siblings who were alcoholic, 62% had at least one alcoholic biological parent. Of those half-siblings who were *not* alcoholic, 20% had an alcoholic biological parent. This difference is highly significant statistically ($p < 0.005$). Living with an alcoholic parent or with an alcoholic surrogate parent occurred with equal frequency in the alcoholic and nonalcoholic half-siblings. A comparison of the effect of having an alcoholic biological parent, or a nonalcoholic parent combined with being raised by an alcoholic parental figure or without such a parental figure, showed that the most powerful factor in determining the development of alcoholism in the offspring was being the biological child of an alcoholic. To quote the authors: "The only consistent predictor of alcoholism in half-siblings was the presence of an alcoholic biological parent."

The data for males and females were not analyzed separately. As noted above, only nine female probands were included. There is certainly a need to replicate the study for both male and female subjects.

5.   GENETIC MARKER STUDIES

Blood Groups

There have been many studies of the distribution of ABO blood group types in alcoholics. Achte (1958) found that the blood group proportions of 212 alcoholics did not differ from those of 1383 healthy controls. This finding was confirmed by Buckwalter et al. (1964), Camps et al. (1967, 1969), Hill et al. (1975), Reid et al. (1968), Swinson and Madden (1973), and Winokur et al. (1976).

Conversely, Nordmo (1959) found a highly significant increase in the proportion of blood group A subjects in a study of 939 alcoholics. Billington (1956) and Speiser (1958) reported an association of blood group A with portal cirrhosis.

Given the current state of the development of population genetics, and particularly the difficulties of obtaining true controls for blood group studies, it can only be concluded that there is no definite evidence for an association between alcoholism and ABO blood group distribution. Comparative studies of the distribution for male and female alcoholics have not revealed any sex differences in the ABO blood group proportions (Hill et al., 1975; Swinson, 1970).

Other serological markers have been investigated to a very small extent. Hill et al. (1975) found that nonalcoholic family members of alcoholic probands showed a significantly increased frequency of the homozygous recessive gene ss of the MNSs system when compared with the alcoholic probands. This finding was not confirmed by Winokur and his co-workers (1976).

ABH Secretor Status

The secretion or nonsecretion of ABH blood group substance in the saliva is an example of a genetic polymorphism in which there are only two phases, secretion and nonsecretion. Three of the available studies of ABH secretion or nonsecretion in alcoholics (Camps et al., 1967, 1969; Swinson and Madden, 1973) reported on European populations where the expected prevalence of nonsecretors is 22.7% (Race and Sanger, 1968).

Camps and Dodd (1967) and Camps et al. (1969) reported on the secretor status of the alcoholics in whom they had investigated ABO blood groups. They found that the incidence of nonsecretion was 32% in the whole group of alcoholics and 39.2% among those of blood group A

($p < 0.01$). In normal populations, the incidence of nonsecretion does not differ in the different ABO blood groups.

Swinson and Madden (1973) also examined the secretor status of 222 alcoholics. Of these, 141 (63.51%) were found to be secretors and 81 (36.49%) nonsecretors. The proportions of secretors and nonsecretors were again found to vary between the different ABO blood group types.

As can be seen from Table 2, the secretor–nonsecretor proportions in blood group O approximate the expected frequencies, but in blood group A, there is a marked increase in the proportion of nonsecretors to about twice that expected.

The calculation of significance for blood group samples taken from heterogeneous populations cannot reliably be performed by simple chi-squares. Using Woolf's (1954) method to examine blood group A and blood group O alcoholics, it was found that the change in proportion in group A was statistically significant at $p < 0.005$ ($X^2 = 13.88$, 3 df), but for group O the change did not reach significant levels ($X^2 = 0.598$, 3 df). The changes in groups B and AB failed to reach significant levels, although the sample size for both was so small as to render the conclusion doubtful, whatever the result.

There were no differences between the results for men and women in the above study, but Camps and Dodd (1967) found that the male alcoholics had a nonsecretor status in 35% of cases, whereas the female alcoholics were nonsecretors in only 28.8% of cases. In their study of 100 cirrhotics, Reid et al. (1968) did not confirm the above findings, but their sample size was small.

The finding of an excess of nonsecretors among alcoholics in a single blood group is difficult to explain. Although secretion–nonsecretion is a genetically determined characteristic, it might be altered by excess alcohol intake. However, it is extremely unlikely that alcohol would so affect only those alcoholics of blood group A. An alternative explanation is that nonsecretors of blood group A become alcoholic more often than people of other blood groups and secretor status. The above studies are in need of replication in large-sample studies.

Phenylthiocarbamide (PTC) Taste Sensitivity

PTC taste sensitivity is bimodally distributed. PTC has an unpleasant bitter taste that can be detected at low concentrations by "tasters" and only at high concentrations by "nontasters." Subjects are usually tested to determine the taste threshold for PTC by using 14 varying concentrations in water (Harris and Kalmus, 1949). Solution 4, containing 187 mg/ liter of PTC, is the antimodal point. Normal populations contain approximately 30% nontasters (Kitchin et al., 1959).

Table 2. Percentage of ABH Secretors and NonSecretors in 222 Alcoholics

	Group O $N = 107$	Group A $N = 76$	Groups B and AB $N = 39$	Total $N = 222$
Secretors	71.96	52.64	61.53	63.51
Nonsecretors	28.04	47.36	38.47	36.49

Lester (1966) quoted Peeples (1962) as finding an increase in nontasters in a group of 52 alcoholics compared with 72 controls. The method of administering the test was not described. Although Harris and Kalmus (1949) described a reliable method of PTC taste-testing, a number of investigators have used an alternative method that has the advantage of being quickly administered but the major disadvantage of being unreliable. In the simple method, subjects are asked to taste a piece of filter paper impregnated with a single concentration of PTC solution. This method, as noted, is unreliable to start with but was made even less reliable by one group of investigators (Reid et al., 1968) who used a solution of PTC that did not correspond to the accepted antimodal concentration. The fact that Reid and his colleagues found no difference between 100 cirrhotics and 100 controls in their PTC taste sensitivity cannot be interpreted, given the experimental conditions of the study.

Swinson (1972a) compared 146 alcoholic patients (188 male, 28 female) with 256 controls from the same geographic area (Kitchin et al., 1959). The Harris and Kalmus method was used. The results showed that there was a highly significant difference between the distribution of the PTC taste thresholds of the alcoholics and controls across the 14 solutions ($p < 0.0001$). The proportions of tasters and nontasters among the alcoholics were, however, not significantly different from those in the control population: 26.04% of the alcoholics and 29.4% of the controls were classified as nontasters.

These two findings can be explained by the occurrence of a loss of taste sensitivity in the "taster" alcoholics. Such a loss might occur as a result of age, tobacco consumption, or alcohol consumption. There is no evidence of a genetically based difference between alcoholics and nonalcoholics in PTC taste-testing. There are no comparative data for male and female alcoholics.

Color Vision Defects

Color-vision defects occur as genetic polymorphisms that are sex-linked. Thus, males have much higher frequencies of the defects than females, and females act as heterozygous carriers of the defects. Although color-vision defects are largely genetically determined, they can also be acquired as a result of a wide variety of pathological processes (François and Verriest, 1957, 1961).

Interest in the color vision of cirrhotics was initiated by a report from Santiago, Chile (Cruz-Coke, 1964). Cruz-Coke reported on his findings in a study of 400 men and 400 women. A total of 58 of the males and 12 of the females had cirrhosis. Of the cirrhotic men, 16 (27.5%) had defective color vision, as did 4 (33.3%) of the cirrhotic women when tested with the Hardy Rand Rittler (HRR) 1947 pseudoisochromatic plates (Hardy et al., 1947). These findings were highly significant statistically ($p < 0.0001$). Unable to demonstrate an association between color blindness and any biochemical factor affecting his subjects at the time of testing, Cruz-Coke concluded that a genetic factor was responsible for the results found.

Since this first report, there have been many other investigations, the results of which have fallen into three groups:

a. Those showing no association between cirrhosis or alcoholism and color-vision defects (Gorrell, 1967; Thuline, 1967; Reid et al., 1968).

b. Those showing a transient association between alcoholism and color-vision defects that was not confirmed on retesting (Fialkow et al., 1966; Smith, 1972).

c. Those showing a consistent association between alcoholism and color-vision defects (Cruz-Coke, 1965, 1966; Cruz-Coke and Varela, 1965, 1966; Carta et al., 1967; Dittrich and Nebauer, 1967; Saraux et al., 1966; Varela et al., 1969; Sassoon et al., 1970; Swinson, 1972b; Ugarte et al., 1970).

A detailed discussion of the methodology involved in the above studies is available in a paper by Swinson (1972). Many basic variables have been left uncontrolled in many of the investigations of color-vision defects, so that the conclusions drawn from the research invite a great deal of criticism. The variables include (1) the target population; (2) the fitness of the subjects at the time of testing; (3) the type of color-vision tests used; and (4) the interpretation of the findings of any testing method in the hands of different investigators.

(1) Target populations have varied from those labeled alcoholic to those diagnosed as cirrhotic. Those diagnosed as alcoholic have included subjects requiring hospital admission because of alcohol-related problems, those who were self-selected at Alcoholics Anonymous, and those in whom there was a history of alcohol use which interfered with employment, family relations or social adjustment to the point where the patient was unable to function satisfactorily. There is no evidence that the groups of subjects are strictly comparable.

(2) Certain color-vision tests require that the subject be able to

comprehend detailed instructions and perform complex tasks. In order to be certain that an alcoholic is functioning at an optimal level, it is necessary to know that he is not intoxicated. In one of the studies by Cruz-Coke and Varela (1965), 100 subjects were selected randomly from an outpatient clinic and were found to have a statistically significant (p < 0.001) increase in color-vision defects in a single episode of testing with a single test. Such findings have to be interpreted in the light of the results of the work of Fialkow et al. (1966) and of Smith (1972). In both of these studies, alcoholics were tested within a few days of admission to the hospital. Fialkow and his colleagues tested 24 male and 22 female subjects and found that 40% of the males and 41% of the females had color-vision defects on two separate tests. The color-defective subjects were 19 in number, 9 of whom were available for retesting later during their inpatient stay. Of the 9, 7 had regained normal color vision and 1 had changed from being classified as demonstrating a severe deutan defect to showing only a mild unclassifiable defect.

Smith (1972) investigated 205 alcoholic patients with the Ishihara plates. Initially, 65 males (37.8) and 13 females (39%) were classified as color-vision defective. On retesting 10 days later, only 17 males (9.89%) and 5 females (15%) were still classified as color defective. It was concluded in both studies that the defects found were secondary to some biochemical or metabolic disorder consequent on alcoholism or cirrhosis of the liver. It should be noted also that the frequency of color-vision defects in females was as high as that in males, which argues strongly against a sex-linked genetic etiology for the defects.

(3) The type of test used has varied very widely in this area of study. Some investigators have used single pseudoisochromatic plate tests (Cruz-Coke, 1964, 1965; Cruz-Coke and Varela, 1965; Gorrell, 1967; Reid et al., 1968; Sassoon et al., 1970; Smith, 1972; Ugarte et al., 1970); others have used two tests (Cruz-Coke, 1966; Fialkow et al., 1966; Thuline, 1967); and still others three tests (Cruz-Coke and Varela, 1966; Swinson, 1972b). Kalmus (1965) has pointed out that no single method or single test of color vision is infallible in detecting abnormal color vision, and thus, a great deal of doubt is thrown on the validity of the results of those investigators who relied on a single test.

The method of using the tests has also been subject to much variability. Although the pseudoisochromatic plates are simple to administer, they are designed to be used in light of particular characteristics; this safeguard has not always been observed, and the findings are therefore of doubtful value.

(4) The interpretation of the test results has also been open to question. For example, Gorrell (1967), who used only the Ishihara plates, interpreted some of his results as being indicative of minor color-vision

defects that, in fact, are not detectable by the method used. In a family study of 65 male alcoholics and their first-degree relatives, Varela et al. (1969) made use of a single test, the Farnsworth Munsell 100-hue test. Despite the fact that the test identifies reduced hue discrimination and is not diagnostic (Cox, 1960), it was used by Varela and his colleagues to make a diagnostic classification of the subjects' color vision.

From the above, it is apparent that this area of study is in a state of great confusion with little firm evidence available. As stated above, some investigators have found no association between color-vision defects and alcoholism, whereas others have found an association that disappears on retesting. Still other authors, notably from Chile, have found a consistent association between color-vision defects and cirrhosis or alcoholism. It is these findings that raise the possiblity that color-vision defects are genetic markers in alcoholism. Cruz-Coke and his colleagues, in a series of investigations since 1965, have found consistently increased rates of color-vision defects among alcoholics. These results were reviewed by Cruz-Coke in 1970. The original report of Cruz-Coke (1965) was of color-vision defects in 25 of 77 cirrhotic patients. Later Cruz-Coke and Varela (1966) found that 18% of male alcoholics exhibited the same defect. Further work by the same team (Varela et al., 1969) demonstrated that the Farnsworth Munsell 100-hue test revealed significantly more blue–yellow axis defects in alcoholics and their female first-degree relatives than in a control group. As a result of their findings, it was suggested by the Chilean workers that alcoholism might be part of an X-linked genetic polymorphism. It was further concluded that there was an advantage to the heterozygotes, who must be female, and the advantage was thought to lie in the direction of increased "fertility or viability."

Swinson (1972a) also found an association between alcoholism and color-vision defects but drew very different conclusions from his findings. A total of 149 alcoholics (121 male and 28 female) were examined by means of three tests at least 10 days after complete withdrawal from alcohol and all medication. All subjects were diagnosed as suffering from alcoholism by three physicians independently. The color-vision tests used were the Ishihara plates, the Dvorine plates, and the Crawford anomaloscope. The findings are shown in Table 3.

Two conclusions can be drawn from these results. First, the proportion of subjects identified as color defective is dependent on the test employed, and second, there are no differences between males and females in the percentages of color-defective alcoholics.

Kalmus (1965) stated that the anomaloscope is the most satisfactory instrument for determining whether or not a subject has normal color vision and further stated that the anomaloscopic method is superior to the 100-hue test in this regard. The types of defect detected on the

Table 3. Percentage of Color-Vision Defects Found among 149
Alcoholics on Three Tests[a]

Test	% of defective males (N = 121)	% of defective females (N = 28)
Ishihara	6.61	Nil
Dvorine	14.81	14.28
Anomaloscope	26.92	33.33

[a] From Swinson (1972a).

anomaloscope testing were determined and their distribution compared with the distribution of the same defects within a normal population (Pickford, 1951). There was a statistically significant difference ($p <$ 0.025) between the controls and the alcoholics, which suggests that the defects detected in the alcoholic population are not the same as those that are genetically determined in the normal population.

The specific types of color-vision defects found in acquired disorders have been examined by François and Verriest (1957, 1961). The most common acquired defects, amounting to 58% of the total, are in the blue–yellow axis. The findings by Swinson and by the Chilean team are compatible with the results of the François and Verriest investigations.

Summary of Color-Vision Studies

It can be concluded that sensitive color-vision tests reveal a statistically significant increase in frequency of color-vision defects in alcoholics. Although investigators from Chile have concluded that evidence for a genetic linkage between alcoholism and color-vision defects exists, other investigators have not been able to replicate their findings. In the present state of the research, it appears safest to regard the color-vision defects as being due to an acquired lesion rather than to a genetically based condition.

There is no evidence to suggest that female alcoholics differ from the normal female population with respect to genetically determined color-vision defects.

Alcohol Dehydrogenase Variations and Pc 1 Duarte Polymorphism

Alcohol is metabolized in the liver by the action of alcohol dehydrogenase (ADH). It has been found that human ADH is not a single enzyme; it provides yet another instance of genetic polymorphism. Harada et al. (1978) have produced evidence of the nature of this polymorphism, which exists in two of the isoenzymes of ADH, namely,

ADH_2 and ADH_3. It has not yet been shown that there is any difference between normals and alcoholics with regard to ADH.

The metabolism of alcohol has been examined in a group of nonalcoholic men who had an alcoholic first-degree relative. Schuckit and Rayses (1979) administered 0.5 ml/kg body weight of ethanol to 20 experimental subjects and to 20 matched controls. On measuring the levels of acetaldehyde produced by the breakdown of ethyl alcohol, it was found that the experimental subjects produced significantly higher levels of acetaldehyde than the controls ($p < 0.004$).

This finding is of great interest since it indicates the possibility of a metabolic difference between controls and a healthy young group at risk for the development of alcoholism, which precedes pathological drinking. The finding is a preliminary one that awaits replication and, as with so much of the genetic research in alcoholism, should be extended to include female subjects.

In a very recent study, Comings (1979) reported on the distribution of a mutant brain-specific protein that he has termed *Pc 1 Duarte*. This protein is said to represent the first polymorphism of a human protein that is specific to nerve tissue and prominent in the caudate and putamen areas of the brain.

In a control series of subjects, whose brains were examined postmortem, it was found that 31.6% carried the mutant gene. Small groups of subjects suffering from a variety of neurological and psychiatric disorders were also examined. Statistically significant increases in the occurrence of the *Pc 1 Duarte* mutation were found in patients suffering from depressive diseases and alcoholism. The total number of alcoholics whose brain specimens were examined was 13, of which 8 were found to be homozygous for the gene and one heterozygous, a total frequency of 69%.

While of great interest, this finding remains preliminary and based on only a small number of subjects. The sex distribution of the alcoholic subjects was not detailed.

6.   THE RELATIONSHIP BETWEEN ALCOHOLISM AND OTHER PSYCHIATRIC DISORDERS

As noted above in the adoption studies, not only alcoholism but also other psychiatric disorders run in the same families in excess of what is expected. Those disorders reported most commonly in association with alcoholism are affective (mood) and personality disorders. There are also occasional reports of alcoholism's being associated with schizophrenia and with rarer conditions such as anorexia nervosa.

Alcoholism and Affective Disorders

The affective or mood disorders are conditions in which there is a marked and persistent change in the pervasive mood of the sufferer. The mood may become one of intense sadness in depressive states or one of intense happiness or elation in hypomanic or manic states.

Coincidental with the mood change in depression are many other symptoms, such as loss of appetite, loss of interest, loss of libido, and suicidal ideation. In mania, the subjects are generally overactive, over-talkative, grandiose, and lacking judgment.

Until recently, it has been customary to classify depressive states into endogenous or reactive types, which may or may not be of psychotic intensity, and to classify mania as a phase of manic–depressive psychosis, one of the functional psychoses. This classification has proved to have many defects and is being replaced by a classificatory system derived by Winokur and his colleagues over the past few years (Winokur, 1973).

Winokur has divided affective disorders into three basic types: bereavement (as a model for reactive depression), secondary depression, and primary affective disorder.

Secondary depression is a depressive episode occurring in a person who has a preexisting physical illness or psychiatric illness other than primary affective disorder. Thus, depression occurring in a schizophrenic or someone with lupus erythematosus would be classified as secondary depression.

Primary affective disorder consists of an episode of depression or mania in a person who has had no previous psychiatric illness or who has a history of earlier depressive or manic episodes. Primary affective disorder is further classified into bipolar affective disease and depressive disease. In bipolar affective disease, there may be a picture and history of mania alone or of mania and depression. Patients who present solely with depression but in whom there is a family history of mania are also classified as suffering from bipolar affective disease.

Depressive disease, or unipolar depression, is subdivided yet again into pure depressive disease and depressive spectrum disease. Pure depressive disease is characterized by the late onset of depressive illness in male probands in Winokur's studies. The male and female first-degree relatives are at equal risk of developing depression, and there is no alcoholism or sociopathy associated with the illness in the probands' families. Depressive spectrum disease is characterized by early onset depression in a female, a high risk of depressive illness in first-degree relatives, and an association with sociopathy and alcoholism in the relatives. Table 4 is adapted from Winokur's paper (p. 91).

In an examination of the frequency of alcoholism in male relatives of depressed probands, the only significant finding was that early onset females had significantly ($p < 0.05$) more alcoholic male relatives than did late onset male probands. It was also found, when the sex of the proband was controlled, that early onset probands had more alcoholic relatives than late onset probands ($p < 0.01$).

In a review of the area, Gershon and his colleagues (1977) noted, however, that Shields (1975), using data from Berlin collected in 1938, was unable to confirm the differences between early onset and late onset probands and suggested therefore that Winokur's findings might reflect cultural rather than genetic influences. Gershon et al. (1977) quoted a number of studies that have failed to replicate Winokur's findings and concluded that alcoholism in familes with affective disorder may arise from cultural factors or from independent genetic factors producing alcoholism. They further concluded that "the presence of alcoholism in the relatives of patients with specific types of affective disorders does not necessarily suggest that these types of affective disorders are genetically distinct" (p. 115).

7. CONCLUSIONS

This paper has reviewed the evidence for the presence or absence of genetic factors in the etiology of alcoholism and for any differences between the two sexes in this regard. The conclusions are considered for each sex separately.

Males

Twin studies offer support for the genetic hypothesis in the etiology of alcoholism although the results of the two reported studies conflict. Kaij's study (1960) demonstrates that the social consequences of alcoholism appear to be genetically transmitted, whereas Partanen and his colleagues (1966) found that only drinking behaviors, and not the social consequences of drinking, were genetically determined. It would be of value to examine another large group of twins with respect to both their drinking behaviors and the social effects of their drinking.

The adoption studies carried out with male subjects offer at this time the strongest evidence that there is a genetic factor operating in alcohol-

Table 4. Risk for Alcoholism and Depression in First-Degree Family Members of Depressive Probands

	Risk for depression (%)	Risk for alcoholism (%)
Female probands		
Early onset:		
1st-degree male relatives	13	10
1st-degree female relatives	23	0.4
Late onset:		
1st-degree male relatives	7	6
1st-degree female relatives	15	0
Male probands		4
Early onset:		
1st-degree male relatives	20	
1st-degree female relatives	18	3
Late onset		
1st-degree male relatives	12	3
1st-degree female relatives	9	0.5

ism. The studies have been well performed with precise attention to drinking behaviors and the consequences of drinking. The environmental conditions relating to the rearing of the probands have been controlled as well as possible. Factors that would add to the value of the studies include obtaining larger samples and increasing the length of follow-up so that more of the probands enter the age of greatest risk for the development of alcoholism.

It would seem unwarranted to generalize from the findings of the Scandinavian studies since it cannot as yet be concluded that alcoholics in other cultures would necessarily demonstrate similar genetically determined patterns of transmission. Although opportunities to perform such research in other countries are very limited, it is necessary that an independent study be done in a society dissimilar to the Scandinavian societies before a general conclusion can be drawn.

Half-sibling studies have supported the findings of other genetic research, but as yet, the data are very limited and replication studies are needed.

Genetic marker studies have been largely inconclusive. There is no firm evidence that blood groups or PTC taste sensitivity are associated with alcoholism. The findings regarding ABH secretion have been consistent within alcoholic populations in the United Kingdom but have not yet been replicated for other populations, nor have they been confirmed in large groups of subjects. The color-vision defects found in alcoholics are in all likelihood due to acquired lesions. It remains to be demonstrated that a genetically determined pattern of color-vision defects occurs at a statistically significantly increased rate in alcoholics who are not physically or mentally impaired at the time of testing. If such a result were to ensue from reliable test procedures, it would then be appropriate to carry out studies of the families of alcoholics to determine their patterns of color-vision defects.

That alcoholism and other psychiatric disorders commonly occur together is certain. To demonstrate, however, that they coexist because of a genetic linkage is much more difficult. The research of Winokur and his colleagues into the familial association of alcoholism and affective disorders has had considerable impact on the ways in which affective disorders are regarded. These studies provide an internally consistent model that has clinical acceptability. However, as noted above, data collected from other populations have not supported the conclusions regarding the genetic etiology of affective disorders that Winokur's group have found in North American subjects.

Females

One of the major differences between male and female alcoholics is simply that males have been studied much more. The females studied have been those diagnosed as alcoholic on the basis of symptomatology derived largely from knowledge of alcoholism in men. Such females may or may not be typical of the "average" female alcoholic. Possibly, they are the most disordered of the female alcoholic population, particularly when they have been selected on the basis of public drunkenness, job loss, or legal infractions.

Evidence of the inheritance of alcoholism in women is lacking. There are no twin studies of female alcoholics, and both half-sibling and genetic marker studies are noncontributory. The only area of research that has attempted to examine the genetics of alcoholism in females is that involving adoption studies.

Goodwin and his colleagues and Bohman have cast light on a largely neglected area. The finding that alcoholism occurs four times as frequently as expected in the adopted-away biological daughters of alcoholic parents is of great interest, but similar results in the control populations of two separate studies negate the possiblity of forming definite conclusions about genetic influences. One can only wait for further evidence to be derived from the same subjects as they age or from a new and larger sample of subjects.

The association of affective disorders with alcoholism in women has been interpreted in opposing fashions by different groups of researchers. The methodology of the work in this area is of a high standard, and the conclusions drawn have been consistent with the findings. Further research in populations of societies elsewhere than North America must take place, therefore, before definite conclusions can be stated regarding the validity of alcoholism as part of depressive spectrum disorder.

In summary, although there is sufficient evidence to say that alcoholism in men has an etiological basis that is influenced by genetic factors, it is not yet possible to say the same for female alcoholics.

One last point remains to be considered. That is, if alcoholism is inherited, then what is it that is transmitted genetically? In addressing this question, Goodwin (1979) has suggested that genetic and nongenetic factors might interact in the following way in the etiology of alcoholism:

1. The potential alcoholic must be able to drink large amounts of alcohol.
2. The experience of euphoria after alcohol intake varies and is possibly genetically determined.
3. The euphoria and dysphoria produced by alcohol intake might be genetically determined, causing those who experience the greatest alcohol-induced affective change to repeat the intake of alcohol.
4. The effects of alcohol in the genetically susceptible individuals described above may be massively reinforcing.
5. Because of stimulus generalization, alcohol intake may come to be associated with a wide range of circumstances and internal states, thus predicting relapse in susceptible individuals.

Other explanations of what factors might be inherited include the possibility that complex behavioral sequences might be genetically determined, as suggested by Wilson (1975). Since this area of research is still in its infancy, we shall have to await further investigation to clear up the present uncertainties.

ACKNOWLEDGMENTS

The author would like to express his appreciation to Ms. Margaret Marchitto for her secretarial assistance, to Dr. A. Munro for his helpful and constructive criticism, and to Dr. Oriana J. Kalant for the application of her editorial expertise and considerable patience.

REFERENCES

Achte, K., 1958, Correlation of ABO blood groups with alcoholism, *Duodecim* 74:20–22.
Billington, B. F., 1956, Note on distribution of blood groups in bronchiectasis and portal cirrhosis, *Aust. Ann. Med.* 5:20–22.
Bohman, M., 1978, Some genetic aspects of alcoholism and criminality, *Arch. Gen. Psychiatry* 35:269–276.
Buckwalter, J. A., Pollock, C. B., Hasleton, G., Krohn, J.A., Nance, M. J., Ferguson, J.

L., Bondi, R. L., Jacobsen, J. J., and Lubin, A. H., 1964, The Iowa blood type disease research project, *J. Iowa St. Med. Soc.* **54:**58–66.

Cadoret, R. J., Woolson, R., and Winokur, G., 1977, The relationship of age of onset in unipolar affective disorder to risk of alcoholism and depression in parents, *J. Psychiatr. Res.* **13:**137–142.

Camps, F. E., and Dodd, B. E., 1967, Increase in the incidence of nonsecretors of ABH blood group substance among alcoholic patients, *Br. Med. J.* **1:**30–31.

Camps, F. E., Dodd, B. E., and Lincoln, R. J., 1969, Frequencies of secretors and non-secretors of ABH substance among 1,000 alcoholic patients *Br. Med. J.* **4:**457–459.

Carta, E., Vincinguerra, E., and Barrea, E., 1967, A study of colour sense in patients with disease of the liver, *Ann. Ottalmol. Clin. Ocul.* **93:**350.

Comings, D. E., 1979, Pc 1 Duarte, a common polymorphism of a human brain protein, and its relationship to depressive disease and multiple sclerosis, *Nature* **277:**28–32.

Cox, J., 1960, Colour vision defects acquired in disease of the eye, *Br. J. Physiol. Opt.* **13:**25.

Cruz-Coke, R., 1964, Colour blindness and cirrhosis of the liver, *Lancet* **2:**1064–1065.

Cruz-Coke, R., 1965, Colour blindness and cirrhosis of the liver, *Lancet* **1:**1131.

Cruz-Coke, R., 1966, Asociación entre la oportunidad para la selección natural, los defectos de visión de colores y el alcoholismo crónico, en diversas poblaciones humanas, *Archos. Biol. Chile* **3:**31–26.

Cruz-Coke, R., 1970, *Colour Blindness: An Evolutionary Approach,* C. C Thomas, Springfield, Ill.

Cruz-Coke, R., and Varela, A., 1965, Inheritance of alcoholism: Its association with colour blindness, *Lancet* **2:**1348.

Cruz-Coke, R., and Varela, A., 1966, Inheritance of alcoholism: Its association with colour blindness, *Lancet* **2:**1282, 1284.

Dittrich, H., and Nebauer, O., 1967, Störungen des Farbsehens bei Leberkrankheiten, *Muench. Med. Wochenschr.* **109:**2690.

Fialkow, P., Thuline, H., and Fenster, F., 1966, Lack of association between cirrhosis and the common types of colour blindness, *N. Engl. J. Med.* **275:**584–587.

François, J., and Verriest, G., 1957, Les dyschromatopsies acquises, *Ann. Ocul.* **190:**713–746, 812–859, 893–943.

François, J., and Verriest, G., 1961, On acquired deficiency of colour vision, *Vision Res.* **1:**201–219.

Gershon, E. S., Targum, S. D., Kessler, L. R., Mazure, C. M., and Bunney, W. E., Jr., 1977, Genetic studies and biological strategies in the affective disorders, *Prog. Med. Genet.* **2:**101–164.

Goodwin, D. W., 1971, Is alcoholism hereditary? *Arch. Gen. Psychiatry* **25:**545–549.

Goodwin, D. W., 1979, Alcoholism and heredity, *Arch. Gen. Psychiatry* **36:**57–61.

Goodwin, D. W., Schulsinger, F., Hermansen, L., Guze, S. B., and Winokur, G., 1973, Alcohol problems in adoptees raised apart from alcoholic biological parents, *Arch. Gen. Psychiatry* **28:**238–243.

Goodwin, D. W., Schulsinger, F., Møller, N., Hermansen, L., Winokur, G., and Guze, S. B., 1974, Drinking problems in adopted and nonadopted sons of alcoholics, *Arch. Gen. Psychiatry* **31:**164–169.

Goodwin, D. W., Schulsinger, F., Knop, J., Mednick, S., and Guze, S. B., 1977a, Alcoholism and depression in adopted-out daughters of alcoholics, *Arch. Gen. Psychiatry* **34:**751–755.

Goodwin, D. W., Schulsinger, F., Knop, J., Mednick, S., and Guze, S. B., 1977b, Psychopathology in adopted and nonadopted daughters of alcoholics, *Arch. Gen. Psychiatry* **34:**1005–1009.

Gorrell, G. J., 1967, A study of defective human colour vision with the Ishihara test plates, *Ann. Hum. Genet.* **31**:39–43.

Harada, S., Agarwal, D. P., and Goedde, H. W., 1978, Human liver alcohol dehydrogenase isoenzyme variations, *Hum. Genet.* **40**:215–220.

Hardy, L. H., Rand, G., and Rittler, M. C., 1947, Screening test for defective red-green vision: Test based on 18 pseudoisochromatic plates from American Optical Company's compilation, *Arch. Ophthalmol.* **38**:442–449.

Harris, H., and Kalmus, H., 1949, The measurement of taste sensitivity to phenylthiourea (P.T.C.), *Ann. Hum. Genet.* **15**:24–31.

Hill, S. Y., Goodwin, D. W., Cadoret, R., Osterland, C. K., and Doner, S. M., 1975, Association and linkage between alcoholism and eleven serological markers, *J. Stud. Alcohol* **36**(7):981–992.

Kaij, L., 1960, *Alcoholism in Twins: Studies on the Etiology and Sequels of Abuse of Alcohol*, Almqvist and Wiksell, Stockholm.

Kalmus, H., 1965, *Diagnosis and Genetics of Defective Colour Vision*, Pergamon, New York.

Kitchin, F. D., Howel-Evans, W., Clarke, C. A., McConnell, R. B., and Sheppard, P. M., 1959, P.T.C. test response and thyroid disease, *Br. Med. J.* **1**:1069–1074.

Lester, D., 1966, Self-selection of alcohol by animals, human variation and the etiology of alcoholism, *Quart. J. Stud. Alc.* **27**:395–438.

McConnell, R. B., 1966, *The Genetics of Gastro-Intestinal Disorder*, Oxford University Press, London.

Nichols, J. R., 1972, The children of addicts: What do they inherit? *Ann. N.Y. Acad. Sci.* **197**:60–65.

Nordmo, S. H., 1959, Blood groups in schizophrenia, alcoholism and mental deficiency, *Am. J. Psychiatry* **116**:460–461.

Partanen, J., Bruun, K., and Markkanen, T., 1966, Inheritance of drinking behavior: A study on intelligence, personality and use of alcohol of adult twins, Study No. 14, The Finnish Foundation for Alcohol Studies, Helsinki.

Peeples, E. E., 1962, *Taste Sensitivity to Phenylthiocarbamide in Alcoholics*, Master's thesis, Stetson University, De Land, Fl.

Pickford, R. W., 1951, *Individual Differences in Colour Vision*, Routledge and Kegan Paul, London.

Popham, R. E., de Lint, J. E. E., and Schmidt, W., 1967, Review of Partanen, Bruun, and Markkanen, 1966, *Alkoholpolitik* **3**:146–149.

Race, R. R., and Sanger, R., 1968, *Blood Groups in Man* (5th ed.), Blackwell, Oxford, England.

Reid, N. C. R. W., Brunt, P. W., Biais, W. B., Maddrey, W. C., Alonso, B. A., and Iber, F. L., 1968, Genetic characteristics and cirrhosis: A controlled study of 200 patients, *Br. Med. J.* **2**:463–465.

Roe, A., and Burk, B., 1944, The adult adjustment of children of alcoholic parents raised in foster homes, *Q. J. Stud. Alcohol* **5**:378–393.

Saraux, H., Labet, R., and Biais, W. B., 1966, Aspects actuels de la névrite optique de l'éthylique, *Ann. Ocul.* **199**:943.

Sassoon, H. F., Wise, J. B., and Watson, J. J., 1970, Alcoholism and colour vision: Are there family links?, *Lancet* **2**:367.

Schuckit, M. A., Goodwin, D. A., and Winokur, G., 1972, A study of alcoholism in half-siblings, *Am. J. Psychiatry* **128**:1132–1136.

Schuckit, M. A., and Rayses, V., 1979, Ethanol ingestion: Differences in blood acetaldehyde concentrations in relatives of alcoholics and controls, *Science* **203**: 54–55.

Seixas, F. A., Omenn, G. S., Burk, E. D., and Eggleton, S., 1972, Nature and nurture in alcoholism, *Ann. N.Y. Acad. Sci.* **197**:5–7.

Shields, J., 1975, Some recent developments in psychiatric genetics, *Arch. Psychiatr. Nervenkr.* **220**:347–360.

Slater, E., and Cowie, V., 1971, *The Genetics of Mental Disorders,* Oxford University Press, London.

Smith, J. W., 1972, Color vision in alcoholics, *Ann. N.Y. Acad. Sci.* **197**:143–147.

Speiser, P., 1958, Krankheiten und Blutgruppen, *Krebsarzt* **4**:208–218.

Swinson, R. P., 1970, *A Study of Genetic Polymorphism in an Alcoholic Population,* unpublished M.D. thesis, University of Liverpool, United Kingdom.

Swinson, R. P., 1972a, Colour vision defects in alcoholism, *Br. J. Physiol. Opt.* **27**:43–50.

Swinson, R. P., 1972b, Genetic polymorphism and alcoholism, *Ann. N.Y. Acad. Sci.* **197**:129–133.

Swinson, R. P., and Madden, J. S., 1973, ABO blood groups and ABH substance secretion in alcoholics, *Q. J. Stud. Alcohol* **34**:64–70.

Thuline, H. C., 1967, Inheritance of alcoholism, *Lancet* **1**:274.

Ugarte, G., Cruz-Coke, R., Rivera, L., Altschiller, H., and Mardones, J., 1970, Relationship of colour blindness to alcoholic liver damage, *Pharmacology* **4**:308.

Van Valkenburg, C., Lowry, M., Winokur, G., and Cadoret, R., 1977, Depression spectrum disease versus pure depressive disease, *J. Nerv. Ment. Dis.* **165**:341–347.

Varela, A., Rivera, L., Mardones, J., and Cruz-Coke, R., 1969, Colour vision defects in non-alcoholic relations of alcoholic patients, *Br. J. Addict.* **64**:67–73.

Wilson, E. O., 1975, *Sociobiology: The New Synthesis,* Harvard University Press, Cambridge, Mass.

Winokur, G., 1972, Types of depressive illness, *Br. J. Psychiatry* **120**:265–266.

Winokur, G., 1973, The types of affective disorders, *J. Nerv. Ment. Dis.* **156**:82–96.

Winokur, G., Tanna, V., Elston, R., and Go, R., 1976, Lack of association of genetic traits with alcoholism: C3, Ss and ABO systems, *J. Stud. Alcohol* **37**:1313–1315.

Woodruff, R. A., Goodwin, D. W., and Guze, S. B., 1974, *Psychiatric Diagnosis,* Oxford University Press, New York.

Woolf, B., 1954, On estimating the relation between blood groups and disease, *Ann. Genet.* **19**:251–253.

7

Some Behavioral and Biological Aspects of Alcohol Problems in Women

NANCY K. MELLO

1. INTRODUCTION AND OVERVIEW

It is generally acknowledged that relatively little is known about alcoholism and problem drinking in women. The origins, expression, and consequences of alcohol abuse for women remain obscure. Although these issues have not been resolved for alcohol problems generally, most of the existing information about alcohol abuse has come from clinical studies of men. The question of possible sex-related differences has seldom been raised explicitly (Edwards et al., 1973; Mulford, 1977; Wanberg and Horn, 1970).

In the past few years, there have been several reviews of the literature on the female alcoholic (Beckman, 1975, 1976; Bourne and Light, 1979; Corrigan, 1974; Gomberg, 1976; Lindbeck, 1972; Schuckit, 1972; Schuckit and Morrissey, 1976; Wilsnack, 1976). Unfortunately, this number of reviews does not reflect an expansion of information about alcoholism in women. Each review has examined essentially the same sparse series of papers, although from somewhat different perspectives, and with different emphases. The goal of this essay is not to reanalyze the small collection of studies already critically reviewed by others but to discuss some biological and behavioral factors that may possibly influence the expression of alcohol problems in women. Whether or not the myriad factors implicated in the development of alcohol problems apply equally to women and to men is not known.

The term *alcohol problems* is used to refer both to problem drinking and to chronic alcoholism, since these presumably represent points on a

---

NANCY K. MELLO • Alcohol and Drug Abuse Research Center, McLean Hospital, Belmont, Massachusetts.

hypothetical continuum of alcohol abuse. Alcoholism is traditionally defined by the occurrence of withdrawal signs and symptoms after cessation of drinking (Victor and Adams, 1953; Mello and Mendelson, 1977). However, the quantity of alcohol and the minimum time necessary for the development of physiological dependence on alcohol is unknown and cannot be examined directly except through retrospective self-reports (Mello and Mendelson, 1977). The recurrent polemics surrounding the definition of alcohol abuse and alcoholism have been discussed extensively elsewhere (Mello and Mendelson, 1975, 1978; Mendelson and Mello, 1979) and will not be repeated here.

Changing Views of Alcohol Problems in Women

It once appeared that fewer women developed alcohol problems than men, and various sex-related social and cultural factors were thought to act as protective barriers. Now, alcohol problems in women are becoming more visible (Greenblatt and Schuckit, 1976), and a number of social factors have contributed to an apparent change in the risk factors. Similar trends have been noted for cardiovascular disease, once thought to be an almost exclusive province of men (Moriyama et al., 1971). The well-documented association between alcohol abuse and excessive cigarette smoking (Griffiths et al., 1976) and recent evidence of increased risk for myocardial infarction in women who smoke (Slone et al., 1978) indicate another dimension of potential vulnerability for female alcohol abusers.

Within the past decade, there have been many interacting changes in social attitudes toward alcoholism (Mello, 1978a). Increasing acceptance of alcoholism as a medical illness has helped to reduce the stigma associated with drinking problems, and consequently, more problem drinkers are seeking treatment. Whatever social factors may once have facilitated denial of alcohol problems or militated against their development in women, these no longer appear to be as effective. The notion that women are constitutionally (i.e., psychologically or biologically) protected from alcoholism is no longer taken seriously (cf. Gomberg, 1976).

The alternative hypothesis, that factors unique to women in some sense cause alcoholism, has been a topic of some debate (Schuckit and Morrissey, 1976). Against a background of anecdote and speculation, certain stereotypes of the "woman alcoholic" have emerged and tend to persist. Objective studies to confirm or refute these stereotypes have not been conducted. In a comprehensive review of the literature on alcoholism in women, Schuckit and Morrissey (1976) concluded that it is not possible to generalize about the female alcoholic and argue that existing evidence does not support the hypothesis that factors presumably unique to women are causally related to the development of alcoholism. Schuckit and Morrissey suggested that the course and development of alcohol problems appear to be more influenced by social class and socioeconomic status than by sex differences. They concluded that there may be as many differences between female alcoholics, as a function of social class and socioeconomic status, as between male and female alcoholics. The numerous inconsistencies in the literature are attributed to a failure to compare male and female alcoholics in the context of differences between men and women in the general population. Schuckit and Morrissey argued for the importance of controlling for underlying psychiatric disorders, socioeconomic status, occupational status, and marital status in any effort to compare female and male alcoholics.

Reasonable as this conclusion appears to be, it is apparent that women do have certain unique characteristics that differentiate them from men. The periodic hormonal changes associated with the menstrual cycle are an obvious sex difference. The relationship between mood changes and neuroendocrine fluctuations associated with the menstrual cycle is a provocative and as yet unresolved question. It is not known if affective or hormonal changes associated with phases of the menstrual cycle significantly modulate the expression of drinking problems in women.

One objective of this review is to examine the often fragmentary evidence concerning correlations between mood changes and the menstrual cycle and to consider the possible relation of such covariance to alcohol use in women. The notion that affective and hormonal changes associated with phases of the menstrual cycle may be one factor that contributes to the exacerbation or perpetuation of problem drinking in women will be explored. This hypothesis does *not* imply that such fluctuations uniquely dispose women to alcohol problems. Rather, the question is whether or not certain uniquely female factors such as menstrual-cycle–related fluctuations in mood may modulate drinking patterns in female alcohol abusers through time.

The factors that maintain alcohol abuse are poorly understood, and the role of mood in modulating drinking patterns has not been established unequivocally (Mello and Mendelson, 1978). Once a pattern of excessive drinking has become established, it is possible that the constellation of factors that combine to perpetuate alcohol abuse may differ between men and women. Since a better understanding of the way in which excessive alcohol use and abuse of drugs are maintained may suggest improved ways to modify this behavior, the identification of possible maintenance variables is of great importance. However, the following objection may be advanced against the idea that complex changes associated with the biology of the menstrual cycle could influence drinking patterns in women.

The hypothesis that female alcohol abusers may differ in some respects from male alcohol abusers often becomes hopelessly confused and enmeshed in the crosscurrents of the women's liberation movement. Those who define social equality in terms of a denial of sex differences may tend to view examination of possible differences between male and female alcoholics as perniciously sexist. Alternatively, it can be argued that the time-honored tradition of ignoring alcohol problems in women, and assuming that any sex-related differences are inconsequential, also reflects a sexist view with more profound and potentially adverse implications. Assumptions about drinking problems in men are often applied indiscriminately to women. However, if the proximal determinants and consequences of alcohol abuse are somewhat different for women than for men, then women may benefit from different treatment emphases. As alcohol problems in women have become more generally recognized, many have argued for separate treatment and rehabilitation programs (Sandmaier, 1977). One implication of a call for separate treatment programs is a need to deal with separate problems. The extent to which there are sufficiently separate problems to demand separate treatment resources remains an empirical question that is difficult to extricate from women's efforts to obtain nonsexist treatment generally. Ambivalence about the role of women and challenges to sex-role stereotyping have both increased in recent years. Women's striving for equivalent opportunities necessarily conflicts with a tradition of "special consideration" and the complex matrix of constraints and privileges that such terms have come to represent.

Changing Concepts of Substance Abuse

In addition to some gradual change in attitudes toward women, there has also been a change in attitudes about drug abuse generally. There is increasing attention to the *similarities* between drug abuse problems. The traditional assumption that alcoholism is separate and different from opiate addiction or barbiturate addiction has usually resulted in separate research and treatment efforts. Now, the empirical reality of polydrug use (Benvenuto et al., 1975; Bourne, 1975) challenges the idea that drug-related disorders can be defined by any single drug. It appears unlikely that alcohol problems will exist independently of other drug problems in the future (cf. Freed, 1973). Moreover, it is increasingly recognized that various drug abuse patterns may have certain common characteristics that transcend the pharmacological distinctions between drugs. In addition to the tolerance and physical dependence that define pharmacological addiction to opiates, alcohol, and barbiturates, there may be other similarities in drug use patterns and behavioral consequences.

At a time when there is a commendable effort to try to identify commonalities among various forms of substance abuse—for example, alcoholism, heroin addiction, tobacco smoking, and obesity (Committee on Substance Abuse and Habitual Behavior, 1977)—discussion of possible differences within one form of substance abuse, alcoholism, on the basis of sex seems almost regressive. Still, the way in which both drug use and drug effects may be modulated by phases of the menstrual cycle is a testable and as yet unanswered question. The eventual heuristic value of this question can only be evaluated once the current diffuse and often conflicting speculations are balanced by objective data.

The remainder of this essay selectively reviews five areas and discusses their possible relevance to alcohol problems in women. A section on the origins of alcohol abuse examines the current status of information about the determinants of alcohol problems in men and the implications for further studies in women. The sections on mood, the menstrual cycle and alcohol explore the evidence that dysphoric mood changes, alcohol consumption, and certain effects of alcohol each may covary with phases of the menstrual cycle. However, any interpretation of an apparent covariance between dysphoria and drinking is greatly complicated by the accumulating evidence that alcohol is not necessarily effective in alleviating dysphoria and anxiety.

A final section discusses recent studies of the behavioral consequences of alcohol intoxication in men and the little that is known about alcohol effects in women. The paradoxical finding that alcohol often increases anxiety and depression in male alcoholics and heavy social drinkers is difficult to reconcile with common expectancies. However, this inconsistency points to an important area for further study if we are to better understand how alcohol's effects maintain drinking behavior and to identify its reinforcing consequences. Since alcohol intoxication results in both "positive" and "negative" consequences, it will be important to determine the contribution of each to the maintenance of alcohol abuse, in men and in women. The emerging data indicate a need for reappraisal of the traditional, rather simplistic concepts about why alcohol abuse recurs. This essay will attempt to integrate these seemingly disparate topics, to identify major gaps in information about alcohol problems in women, and to suggest some possible areas for further study.

2. ORIGINS OF ALCOHOL ABUSE

Alcohol abuse can take many forms, and no single factor has been found to predict or explain why some people develop alcohol problems and others do not. Many factors within the individual and the environment influence whether or not alcohol problems occur and whether or not these remain constant through time. Alcoholism is a complex disorder that is multiply determined by an interaction of behavioral, biological, and sociocultural variables (Mello and Mendelson, 1975). Our understanding of the relative contributions of these variables to the development of alcohol problems is a continually evolving process.

A number of individual-specific and sociocultural variables are often alleged to account for the development of alcohol abuse problems. A brief summary of the current status of some factors alleged to favor the development of alcoholism in men are compared with the status of current information about these factors in women.

Individual-Specific Variables

Personality.   Personality type has not been shown to predict reliably who will develop alcohol problems. It is now generally agreed that male alcohol addicts and problem drinkers are as diverse and heterogeneous a group as persons with any other behavior disorder (cf. Mello and Mendelson, 1975, 1978). An analysis of various psychometric studies of women alcoholics led Beckman (1976) to conclude that there is no unique constellation of traits that defines the "typical" female alcoholic. Beckman pointed out that it is not clear how women alcoholics differ from male alcoholics or from women who have other emotional and psychological problems.

Psychopathology.   There is both positive and negative evidence concerning the contribution of psychiatric disorders to the development of alcohol problems. However, alcohol abuse can no longer be dismissed as simply a symptom of a major psychotic or neurotic condition. Alcohol abuse and alcoholism may coexist with many psychiatric disorders, and the critical determinants of each condition are unknown (Mello and Mendelson, 1975).

Depression is often associated with alcohol problems, and it does appear that women develop depression prior to the expression of severe alcohol problems more often than men (Schuckit, 1973). Schuckit has suggested that alcoholism and affective disorders are related illnesses in women, since these problems are associated with higher rates of dysphoria and suicide and often occur in the same woman in a family with a high incidence of alcoholism and affective disorders.

The interweaving of alcohol abuse and depression, and depression and alcohol abuse, is far too complex to attribute primacy to either condition. However, there is compelling evidence that more women than men become depressed (Weissman and Klerman, 1977). From this perspective, self-medication for the alleviation of depression would be an understandable point of entry into a pattern of problem drinking. Accumulating clinical evidence now indicates that alcohol intoxication in fact may increase depression and anxiety in male social drinkers and alcoholics (Mello and Mendelson, 1978), and the implications of these data for understanding how alcohol abuse is controlled and maintained are discussed in Section 6 of this review.

Genetic Factors. Although many people develop alcohol problems independently of a family history of alcoholism, there is now convincing evidence for the importance of genetic factors in the genesis of this complex illness (Goodwin et al., 1973, 1974; Schuckit et al., 1972). Discrimination between the relative contribution of familial learning factors and genetic variables was accomplished by examining people who were separated from their biological parents soon after birth and were raised by nonrelatives. It was found that the rate of alcoholism in a group of men with an alcoholic biological parent was almost four times that of a control group of adoptees (Goodwin et al., 1973).

There is considerable evidence that alcoholic women are more likely to have alcoholic fathers than nonalcoholic women (Beckman, 1976). Clinical impressions and self-report data suggest that female alcoholics tend to reject their parents, and especially their mothers (Beckman, 1976). Female alcoholics often marry alcoholic men or choose cold, domineering husbands and drink as their fathers drank (Beckman, 1976). Schuckit and Morrissey (1976) pointed out that these associated factors do not adequately distinguish between genetic and environmental influences in the development of alcohol problems.

The current status of data on sex differences in the inheritance of alcoholism is reviewed in Chapter 6 of this volume. Goodwin and co-workers (1977) have recently studied the daughters of alcoholics, comparing women raised by foster parents with women raised by their alcoholic biological parents and with a control group of adopted women whose biological parents were not alcoholic. Of the women studied, 90% were abstainers or very light drinkers, whereas 40% of the Danish male adoptees studied were heavy drinkers. Only 4% of the women in both comparison groups were alcoholic or had serious problems with alcohol. Since the sample was relatively small, Goodwin and co-workers reported that these data do not permit any definitive conclusions. However, they suggest that alcoholism in women may have a partial genetic basis. Depression was equivalent in control women and daughters of alcoholics.

However, daughters raised by their alcoholic parents showed significantly more depression than controls. Goodwin and co-workers (1977)
suggested that social factors may contribute to the estimated low prevalence of alcoholism among Danish women (.1–1%). Goodwin also
postulated that a relative alcohol intolerance may be more frequent
among women than among men and that this intolerance may partially
account for the lower incidence of alcohol problems in women.

Alcohol Metabolism. Thus far, no unique aspect of alcohol metabolism has been found to account for the development of alcohol abuse in
some individuals but not in others. Conflicting results have been obtained
in studies comparing Caucasian males with Indian or Eskimo males with
respect to rate of alcohol metabolism. Differences in body structure and
composition (i.e., proportions of lipid, protein, and water), dietary status,
drinking patterns, and body weight all may influence rates of alcohol
metabolism. No differences in alcohol metabolism were reported in a
carefully controlled comparison of Indian and Caucasian subjects (Bennion and Li, 1976). Although alcohol consumption can induce a significant
increase in the rate of alcohol metabolism (Mendelson et al., 1965), there
were no significant differences in the rate of alcohol metabolism between
normal male controls and alcohol addicts after a three-week period of
abstinence (Mendelson, 1968).

There is no evidence of *sex differences* in the rate of alcohol
metabolism (Dubowski, 1976; Jones and Jones, 1976b). Possible sex
differences in alcohol absorption have recently been examined. Since
females have a greater proportion of adipose tissue than males, it would
be expected that peak blood alcohol levels would be higher in women
following an equivalent dose of alcohol (mg/kg). This pattern has in fact
been reported by Dubowski (1976) and by Jones and Jones (1976a). It
also appears that the highest peak blood alcohol levels (following equivalent doses of alcohol) occur at ovulation and during the premenstruum
(Jones and Jones, 1976a,b). Jones and Jones (1976b) suggested that
variations in hormonal levels of estrogen and progesterone during the
menstrual cycle may account for these variations in peak blood alcohol
level. Moreover, oral contraceptives appeared to reduce the rate of
alcohol metabolism in comparisons made with control women with
normal menstrual cycles (Jones and Jones, 1976b). The implications of
possible variations in the effects of alcohol with menstrual cycle phases
for alcohol self-administration behavior are considered more fully in
Sections 4 and 5 of this chapter.

Sociocultural Variables

Social Influences on Development. Studies of alcoholic men have
been unable to identify a clear pattern of social developmental factors

that place certain individuals at high risk for the development of alcohol problems. Longitudinal studies suggest that the same childhood patterns of early school problems, delinquency, drug use, and broken homes predict adult drinking patterns for ghetto-reared blacks and whites (Robins and Guze, 1971). Although the economically disadvantaged appear to have more alcohol problems, it is important to realize that none of these factors permits reliable prediction of the development of problem drinking. Moreover, no particular pattern of child rearing has been shown to facilitate or to protect against the development of alcohol abuse across cultures (Bacon, 1973). No single cultural attitude has been shown to be universally effective in promoting or impeding alcohol abuse.

The influence of parental role models does not appear to be as powerful a determinant of alcohol abuse as was once believed. It has been shown that exposure to an alcoholic parent figure does not necessarily increase the risk of development of alcoholism in male children (Goodwin et al., 1974; Schuckit et al., 1972). Whatever adverse learning and experiential factors result from growing up with an alcoholic parent figure, alcoholism in the biological parent appears to predict the development of alcoholism in the children with far greater reliability than any of the environmental factors studied.

Similarly, there is somewhat equivocal evidence concerning the role of sociocultural factors in the development and maintenance of patterns of alcohol abuse and alcoholism. It is clear that alcoholism is not equally distributed across all strata of society. The largest proportion of heavy drinkers are persons of lower economic status who live in urban areas (Cahalan et al., 1969). A higher rate of severe drinking problems is reported to exist among ghetto-reared black men (Bourne, 1973; Robins and Guze, 1971) and American Indian and Eskimo populations (Alcohol and Health, 1971). Other ethnic groups—for example, Chinese, Jews, Greeks, Italians, Portuguese, Spaniards, and southern French—are reported to have a relatively low incidence of alcohol problems (Alcohol and Health, 1971). Social attitudes toward drinking and the explicitness of social controls appear to contribute to these observed differences.

Wilsnack (1976) has argued that drinking problems in women reflect conflicts and tensions related to sex role. It is generally acknowledged that traditional sex roles are currently in transition. However, social norms concerning drinking still differ for men and women. It is generally the case that drinking has been considered more acceptable for men than for women, and drunkenness in women has prompted greater disapproval (Wilsnack, 1976). The effect of increased earnings on female drinking patterns remains to be determined. Indices of alcoholism and alcohol use have been found to be associated with disposable income relative to the price of alcohol (Popham et al., 1975).

Wilsnack (1976) argued that one cause of alcoholism in women may be the conflict between conscious and culturally expected femininity and stylistic and unconscious masculinity. This sex-role conflict may lead to doubts about adequacy as a woman, and alcohol may be used to "restore feelings of female adequacy and womanliness" (Wilsnack, 1976). However, Wilsnack acknowledged that sex-role conflicts do not always lead to alcoholism. The sex-role flexibility associated with the women's liberation movement may shift motivation for drinking toward social and convivial goals and tension reduction (Wilsnack, 1976). These several hypotheses have been developed primarily on the basis of data from projective tests such as the Thematic Apperception Test, which presumably measures "unconscious" masculine and feminine tendencies. Although these hypotheses are provocative, the construct validity of projective test assessments of unconscious feelings and attitudes remains open to question.

Beckman (1976) and Schuckit and Morrissey (1976) concluded that existing evidence concerning sex-role changes and their relationship to alcohol problems is contradictory. Furthermore, Beckman (1976) has also argued that if feelings and conflicts associated with femininity are critical for the woman alcoholic, then it is not reasonable to attempt to compare personality characteristics of men and women alcoholics. A better question would appear to be, "How do alcoholic women differ from normal women?"

Conclusions

No single sociocultural factor or characteristic that is unique to the individual has been identified that can predict or account for the development of alcohol problems in men or women. Alcohol problems can develop in anyone, and the essential conditions appear to be ingestion of sufficient alcohol over sufficient time. The minimum amount of alcohol required for the development of withdrawal signs and symptoms is not known, and the factors that influence individual susceptibility to, or resistance to, alcohol addiction are unclear (Mello and Mendelson, 1977).

Given the diversity of individuals with alcohol abuse problems, it may prove more productive to study factors that periodically initiate and maintain excessive drinking episodes rather than to focus exclusively on a search for distant origins. A better understanding of how alcoholism is maintained could permit more effective manipulation of critical maintenance variables that control drinking behavior. Identification of the relevant factors could lead to the development of more effective forms of intervention. This assumption is implicit in the following discussion of possible relationships between the behavioral effects of alcohol and variations in perceived mood associated with the menstrual cycle. Since conclusive studies to establish the degree of covariance between these variables have yet to be conducted, discussion of factors that may modulate drinking patterns in women can only suggest areas for future inquiry.

3. MOOD AND THE MENSTRUAL CYCLE

There is abundant clinical evidence that dysphoric mood states in women are correlated with certain phases of the menstrual cycle. An association between mood fluctuations and menstrual cycle phases has been a consistent finding despite a wide diversity of methods and subjects (Smith, 1975; Steiner and Carroll, 1977). Among the symptoms believed to be correlated with phases of the menstrual cycle are irritability, anxiety, depression, tension, disturbed sleep, lethargy, impaired concentration, headaches, constipation, bloating, backaches, breast tenderness, weight changes, and changes in sexual feelings and activity (Moos, 1969; Smith, 1975; Wilcoxon et al., 1976). It is generally agreed that dysmenorrhea is not necessarily associated with dysphoric changes in feeling state (Smith, 1975; Moos, 1969). Moreover, these symptoms may not occur in all women, at every cycle, and are not all specific to women or to the menstrual cycle process. However, it is the periodic recurrence of a constellation of such symptoms, in concert with menstrual cycle phases, that invites consideration of the possible implications for women with alcohol problems.

The relationship between mood and phases of the menstrual cycle has usually been studied through retrospective or concurrent self-reports and thematic analysis of brief samples of unstructured verbal material (cf. Parlee, 1973, for review). Self-report studies have consistently shown an association between fluctuations in affect and phases of the menstrual cycles. Increased dysphoria and anxiety during the premenstrual and early menstrual phase has been a frequent finding (Golub, 1976a; Dalton, 1964, 1969; Ivey and Bardwick, 1968; Janowsky et al., 1973; May, 1976; Moos, 1969; Silbergeld et al., 1971; Patkai et al., 1974; cf. Smith, 1975, for review). A brief description of some illustrative studies follows.

Ivey and Bardwick (1968) examined mood changes in college students at ovulation and two or three days before the onset of menstruation, over two menstrual cycles. Five-minute verbal samples describing any memorable life experience were recorded on four occasions. Samples were scored for thematic content on the Gottschalk Verbal Anxiety Scale. On the basis of these scores, 21 of the 26 subjects studied were found to be more anxious at the premenstrual phase and more self-confident and self-satisfied at the period of ovulation.

Moos (1969) obtained mood ratings from 15 married women at nine different points in two consecutive menstrual cycles. Anxiety and aggressive feelings peaked during menstruation, declined rapidly with the cessation of menstrual flow, then built up gradually toward a secondary peak and subsequent fall about the 20th day of the normal cycle.

The importance of repeated observations of subjects during the menstrual cycle, rather than reliance on retrospective descriptions, has been clearly shown (May, 1976). May obtained mood report ratings from 30 adult women during the premenstrual period, during menstruation, and at mid-cycle over the course of two menstrual cycles. Of this sample, 50% showed an increase in depression just before menstruation, whereas 40% showed the most depression while actually menstruating. There was no significant relation between physical complaints and emotional complaints. Retrospective reports of mood changes were unrelated to changes actually reported at the three phases of the menstrual cycle. Many women who in fact reported maximal tension during menstruation had previously described the premenstrual phase as associated with the most depression and anxiety (May, 1976).

Despite the apparent consistency with which menstrual cycle phases have been related to depression and anxiety, several investigators have objected that a series of methodological problems limit the generality of the findings obtained (Bardwick, 1975; Parlee, 1973, 1974; Sommer, 1973; Wilcoxon et al., 1976). These problems include (1) the subjects' awareness of the objective of the study, which could result in the report of opinions rather than actual feelings; (2) the use of retrospective questionnaires, which may elicit stereotyped responses and may or may not reflect actual fluctuations in mood and behavior; (3) the lack of an adequate baseline period of observation prior to the onset of the critical premenstrual period; (4) inconsistent definitions of the specific menstrual cycle phases; (5) the lack of an adequate control group; (6) reliance on group averages without reporting the range of variability among subjects.

The notion that self-reports of premenstrual depression may reflect social expectancies (Parlee, 1973, 1974) has received some support from the studies of Ruble and co-workers (Ruble, 1977; Brooks et al., 1977). Women who thought that they were premenstrual reported more stereotypically appropriate symptoms than women who believed that they were at mid-cycle, even though both groups were actually six or seven days premenstrual (Ruble, 1977). A female control group, given no information about their cycle status, fell between the two groups in symptom reports but were somewhat more similar to the group who believed that they were premenstrual.

Interviews following symptom reports established that all but 3 of the 44 women studied believed what they were told about their menstrual cycle phase. These data were interpreted to show that psychosocial factors can influence reports of menstruation-related symptoms and lead to an exaggeration of symptom reports (Ruble, 1977). Although this ingenious study is an advance over studies that merely demonstrate that strong beliefs and attitudes about menstrual cycles exist, there was no attempt to assess the concordance of reports given in response to false cycle information with self-reports during actual phases of the menstrual cycle. Possible differences in customary reactions to the premenstrual period among the three groups of women were not examined, so the possible effect of differences in premenstrual experience cannot be evaluated. It has been shown that retrospective self-reports may not correspond to self-reports during menstrual cycle phases (May, 1976), and it is apparent that valid and reliable self-reports are difficult to obtain.

The issue of an adequate control group in self-report studies of mood in relation to menstrual cycle phases has rarely been considered. Recently, Wilcoxon et al. (1976) compared women and men with respect to self-reports of somatic changes, moods, stressful events, and pleasant activities over 35 consecutive days. The sample consisted of 11 women taking oral contraceptives, 11 women with natural cycles, and a control group of 11 men. Male controls were randomly assigned to a pseudocycle, and data were analyzed to compare the three subject groups across three phases of the menstrual cycle.

Men and women did not differ in frequency of reports of negative affect, impaired concentration, and stressful events over the 35-day · period. However, both female samples reported an increase in each of these three variables as a function of the menstrual cycle. The presence or absence of contraceptive medication appeared to determine which phase of the menstrual cycle was associated with the most symptoms. In women whose progesterone and estrogen levels were maintained at a stable high level throughout the cycle (except during menstruation), a significantly higher degree of negative affect, anxiety, dysphoria, and happy–sad changes occurred during the premenstrual phase. In women who did not use contraceptive medication, the menstrual period was associated with the highest degree of negative affect. It is of interest that the magnitude of variance in these variables was greatest for women on contraceptive medication. Somatic complaints relating to water retention and pain were clearly related to the menstrual cycle, although oral contraceptive medication tended to reduce the frequency of these complaints.

Further analysis indicated that the four negative mood factors (negative affect, impaired concentration, happy–sad, and anxiety–dysphoria) each had a significantly greater association with stressful events than with the phase of the menstrual cycle. The authors concluded that the experience of negative affect by women "cannot be understood apart from the kinds of activities and challenges that women face in their environments" (p. 412). Wilcoxon et al. (1976) interpreted these data to indicate that there is not a "uniform, monolithic effect of either the menstrual cycle or associated bodily changes upon women's moods and activities" (p. 413).

These several studies illustrate the recurrent disagreement about which menstrual cycle phase is primarily associated with dysphoric mood states and anxiety. Dalton (1969) has described the most vulnerable period as the four days immediately prior to menstruation and the first four days of menstruation. Dalton also indicated that some women may experience dysphoric symptoms for a day or two at ovulation; then symptoms remit and occur again at the premenstruum. There is recent evidence that patterns of emotional and physical variation during the menstrual cycle may differ in women with different durations of menstrual flow (Erickson, 1980). Eighteen women with short menstrual periods (five days or less) were compared with 8 women with long menstrual periods (six days or more) with respect to frequency of positive and negative emotional states, cognitive difficulties, and physical complaints. The women were unaware of the purpose of the study and completed a diary response sheet every day at the same time for a six-week period. Data were analyzed for each of five menstrual cycle phases—early menstrual, early follicular, estimated ovulatory, mid-luteal, and premenstruum—defined on the basis of each subject's report of menstruation onset. Usually, phases from at least two menstrual cycles could be identified. It was found that women with relatively short menstrual periods conformed to the common pattern of negative affective states during the premenstruum and also at the beginning of the early follicular phase following menstruation. In contrast, women with long menstrual periods experienced the most negative states during the ovulatory and mid-luteal phase. The premenstrual and follicular phases were associated with positive affective states in women with long menstrual periods. Women with short menstrual periods experienced the most positive feeling states during the ovulatory and mid-luteal phase. The two groups did not differ in the overall level of negative affective responses or physical complaints (Erickson, 1980).

Consideration of patterns of positive as well as negative affective states represents a significant departure from the usual self-report study, in which the negative affective changes associated with the premenstruum are emphasized (cf. Golub, 1976a). Reports of increased feelings of well-being during the premenstruum in women with long menstrual periods conflict with mood patterns usually reported and are interpreted by Erickson (1980) as inconsistent with the hypothesis that women experience discomfort because they have been taught that they should feel premenstrual tension and anxiety (cf. Ruble, 1977).

Clinical Implications of Mood Disorders Associated with the Menstrual Cycle

The clinical implications of dysphoria associated with the menstrual cycle have been well documented (cf. Smith, 1975, for review). An association between the premenstruum and admissions to mental hospitals and psychiatric wards has been consistently shown (Smith, 1975). Moreover, several clinical studies have reported an exacerbation of psychotic disorders, especially depression, at the premenstrual phase of the menstrual cycle (cf. Smith, 1975; Steiner and Carroll, 1977). Efforts to relate phases of the menstrual cycle to violence, suicide, and accidents have resulted in inconsistent findings (cf. Smith, 1975, Parlee, 1973). For example, no significant relationship between attempted suicide and phase of the menstrual cycle was established in a study of 107 emergency ward admissions for attempted suicide (Birtchnell and Floyd, 1974). It is usually concluded that marked differences in methodology and ambiguities in definition of phase of the menstrual cycle limit the generality of those studies that show a significant association between attempted suicide and menstrual phases (Smith, 1975; Parlee, 1973).

Although many women experience cyclic changes in depression and anxiety, as well as elation, in association with the menstrual cycle, the extent to which these affective changes are modulated by concomitant variations in neuroendocrine hormone activity is unknown. The covariance between mood, neuroendocrine hormone secretory patterns, and menstrual cycle phases remains to be determined. Cyclic changes in estrogen and progesterone levels have long been thought to contribute to characteristic changes in behavior, although this hypothesis has not been directly confirmed (cf. Bardwick, 1975; Parlee, 1973; Smith, 1975; Steiner and Carroll, 1977, for review). Treatment of premenstrual depression with progesterone, as well as tranquilizers, lithium, and vitamins, has not yielded unequivocal positive results. Steiner and Carroll (1977) concluded that none of these treatments has been shown to be effective in controlled clinical trials.

It is apparent that there is no simple relationship between neuroendocrine hormone levels and mood. Erickson (1980) pointed out that women with short menstrual periods reported more positive emotional states at the ovulatory and mid-luteal phases, which are associated with relatively high estrogen secretion. Negative feeling states were reported at both the premenstrual and early follicular phase, when estrogen levels are characteristically low. In contrast, women with long menstrual periods

reported more positive feeling states during the premenstrual and follicular phases, which are characterized by low levels of estrogen, and more
negative mood states during the ovulatory and mid-luteal phases, which
are associated with high levels of estrogen and progesterone (Erickson,
1980).

The hypothesis that changes in hormone level influence mood
disturbances related to the menstrual cycle has been indirectly assessed
by comparing women with natural menstrual cycles and women taking
oral contraceptives. For the most part, such comparisons have yielded
somewhat inconclusive results. Although oral contraceptive medication
may reduce cyclic affective fluctuations in some women (Silbergeld et
al., 1971; Paige, 1971), it may increase depression in some others. No
consistent relationship between oral contraceptives and depression has
been established (Weissman and Klerman, 1977).

Summary

The existing evidence supports the common clinical impression that
some women experience anxiety and dysphoria in association with
certain phases of the menstrual cycle. The temporal pattern of positive
and negative fluctuations in affect appears to differ in women with long
and short menstrual cycles. This may account for some of the inconsistencies in the clinical literature. The premenstrual period is most commonly associated with dysphoria and lability of affect, but the menstrual
period and the ovulatory period may also be associated with increased
anxiety and depression. How these subjective changes and feeling states
are influenced or modulated by concurrent changes in neuroendocrine
secretory patterns is unknown. How various forms of self-medication
behavior, including alcohol use, may be influenced by perceived changes
in mood also remains to be determined.

4.   MENSTRUAL CYCLES AND ALCOHOL CONSUMPTION

The belief that alcohol use is initiated to cope with anxiety, depression, and dysphoria is too commonplace and pervasive to require
documentation. Since dysphoria and anxiety are believed to be associated
with alcohol use, and also with premenstrual tension and menstruation,
it is logical to speculate that menstrual cycle changes may be related to
patterns of alcohol use in women. Podolsky (1963) was one of the first to
state this hypothesis explicitly on the basis of clinical observations of
seven female patients with alcohol problems. Each patient reported that
her alcohol consumption was heaviest during the premenstrual period.

Each patient suffered from severe premenstrual tension and deliberately used alcohol to decrease or modulate the unpleasant symptoms associated with the premenstruum. Podolsky (1963) commented that:

> In general, such women drink in order to alleviate the symptoms of premenstrual tension. The tempo of drinking is increased during the premenstruum. Alcohol is utilized partly to relieve tension, but for the most part to allow the acting out and verbalization of passivity demands. (p. 818)

Belfer, Shader, and co-workers confirmed the clinical impression that alcohol use is related to menstrual tension in a study of female alcoholics (Belfer and Shader, 1976; Belfer et al., 1971). Self-reports of the relation of menstrual tension and/or menopause to drinking patterns were obtained from 34 alcoholic women and 10 nonalcoholic women who accompanied their alcoholic husbands to an alcohol clinic. These groups were also compared on a series of psychometric personality inventories. Over 50% of the alcoholic women related drinking to the menstrual cycle and especially to the premenstrual period. Belfer and co-workers (1971) stated that:

> this association was made in the absence of obvious disturbances in sexual or menstrual function and in lieu of any difference in the scores of women who experienced maximal vs. minimal task interference, physical discomfort or psychological discomfort during their menstrual cycle. (p. 543)

Psychometric data revealed no significant differences between women who did and did not relate drinking to menstrual cycle changes in either the pre- or postmenopausal group. However, the alcoholic women were significantly more anxious and depressed than the nonalcoholic control group, based on a variety of psychometric measures and clinical impressions. Belfer and co-workers emphasized the importance of distinguishing between anxiety and depression as a concomitant of a physiological process, rather than as a primary precipitant of alcoholism, since the latter could be determined only by prospective studies (Belfer and Shader, 1976; Belfer et al., 1971).

Despite the apparent importance of examining the relationship between alcohol use patterns and the menstrual cycle in women, there have been no empirical studies of the temporal concordance among drinking, mood, and neuroendocrine changes associated with menstruation in female alcoholics or problem drinkers. In fact, only one empirical study of alcohol use by alcoholic women has been published (Tracey and Nathan, 1976). Unfortunately, menstrual cycle status during the experimental drinking period was not reported, and the issue of variations in drinking patterns during the menstrual cycle was not explored (Tracey and Nathan, 1976).

5.   MENSTRUAL CYCLES AND ALCOHOL EFFECTS

Recent studies have shown sex differences in the response to a single acute dose of alcohol in normal nonalcoholic men and women (Jones and Jones, 1976a,b). Moreover, there is suggestive evidence that certain behavioral and biological effects of alcohol may also be modulated by phases of the menstrual cycle.

Biological Effects of Alcohol

It has been consistently shown that women develop higher blood alcohol levels than men after an equivalent dose of alcohol (Jones and Jones, 1976a,b; Dubowski, 1976). Acute alcohol doses of 0.33, 0.66, and 1.32 ml/kg each produced higher blood alcohol levels in women than in male controls (Jones and Jones, 1976a,b). Women also absorbed alcohol faster and reached a peak blood alcohol level sooner than male controls (Jones and Jones, 1976b).

These findings are striking since females drank slightly less alcohol than males, calculated on a ml/kg basis. Jones and Jones (1976b) also pointed out that females have less water per body unit than males, and since alcohol is distributed throughout the body water, it is not surprising that the same dose of alcohol would result in a higher peak blood alcohol level in females than in males.

Blood alcohol levels also differed as a function of the phase of the menstrual cycle. Female subjects were studied throughout the course of a single menstrual period and were tested at two of three possible periods of the menstrual cycle, the menstrual flow period (Days 1–3); the intermenstrual period (Days 13–18); or the premenstrual period (Days 21–28). Male subjects were tested approximately every two weeks to maintain a comparable intertest interval. Females tested during the premenstrual period developed significantly higher peak blood alcohol levels and absorbed alcohol more rapidly than females tested during the menstruum or the intermenstrual period. Although there was a tendency for peak blood alcohol levels, absorption rates, and elimination rates to increase from the beginning to the end of the menstrual cycle, these differences were not statistically significant (Jones and Jones, 1976a,b).

Jones and Jones (1976a) suggested that higher peak blood alcohol levels during the premenstrual phase may be related to more rapid alcohol absorption. It might be expected that water retention during the premenstruum might result in lower blood alcohol levels after a fixed dose of alcohol than at other times. However, the degree of water retention in relationship to the total body water–lipid pool would be the primary determinant of ethanol dilution in body water compartments.

In order to examine more closely the apparent relationship between phase of the menstrual cycle and peak blood alcohol level, a single subject was given one dose of alcohol (0.66 ml/kg) every day through one complete menstrual cycle. Blood alcohol levels were extremely variable, but the highest peaks occurred during the premenstrual period and near the estimated time of ovulation (Jones and Jones, 1976a). These observations on a single subject were subsequently replicated in three women tested individually through a complete menstrual cycle. Subjects were given a moderate dose of alcohol (0.66 ml/kg) at the same time each day. Although there was great variation in blood alcohol levels, the highest peak blood alcohol levels again occurred during the premenstrual period and at about the time of ovulation (Jones and Jones, 1976b). In contrast to the variability shown by females, males tended to have very consistent peak blood alcohol levels from test session to test session following the same dose of alcohol (Jones and Jones, 1976b).

These differences in peak blood alcohol levels following equivalent doses of alcohol suggest that women may have difficulty predicting their intoxication levels at certain phases of the menstrual cycles. Jones and Jones (1976b) discussed the possible influence of unpredictable alcohol effects on drinking patterns in women and suggested that this unpredictability could attenuate spontaneous alcohol consumption. Alternatively, if women become more intoxicated than men at an equivalent dose of alcohol, and if intoxication is further enhanced during the premenstrual phase, women may perceive alcohol as maximally effective at that time. Clinical observations indicate that alcoholic women sometimes relate increases in drinking to the premenstrual period (Podolsky, 1963; Belfer et al., 1971; Belfer and Shader, 1976). Any variation in drinking patterns as a function of the phases of the menstrual cycle could reflect enhanced dysphoria or increased intoxication or both.

Jones and Jones (1976a,b) have speculated about the possible role of estrogen and progesterone in the increased blood alcohol levels observed. They argued for the importance of investigating the relationship between menstrual cycles, endocrinological changes, and blood alcohol variables in order to clarify further the way in which women react to alcohol. Since oral contraceptives result in a slower metabolism of some drugs, Jones and Jones (1976b) have suggested that oral contraceptives containing synthetic estrogen might also result in slower alcohol metabolism. Ethanol metabolism was examined in 11 women taking oral contraceptives and 11 female controls. The two groups of women attained almost identical peak blood alcohol levels following a standard dose of alcohol (0.66 ml/kg). However, women on oral contraceptive medication metabolized ethanol significantly more slowly than control women as determined by each of three metabolic measures. Consequently, women taking oral contraceptives remained intoxicated longer than women not taking oral contraceptives. There were no significant differences between these two groups in the rate of alcohol metabolism as a function of the phase of the menstrual cycle (Jones and Jones, 1976b).

A male control group was also studied on three successive occasions at intervals of approximately two weeks. The disappearance rate of alcohol was comparable in men and in women who were not using oral contraceptives, even though these women consistently attained higher peak blood alcohol levels than men. There were no significant differences in the rates of alcohol metabolism between men and women. However, control women metabolized alcohol slightly faster than men, and men metabolized alcohol slightly faster than women on oral contraceptives (Jones and Jones, 1976b, 1977). Dubowski (1976) has also reported that the rate of alcohol elimination in men and women does not differ significantly.

Behavioral Effects of Alcohol

The behavioral effects of a standard dose of alcohol on cognitive task performance were compared in 20 female and 10 male subjects (Jones and Jones, 1976a). Accuracy of performance on a free recall verbal memory task was equivalent during a prealcoholic baseline. Alcohol (.66 ml/kg) impaired immediate recall equally in both groups, but females were significantly more impaired than males on a delayed-recall task. Moreover, delayed recall by females was equally impaired on both the ascending and descending limbs of the blood alcohol curve. It is usually found that subjects are more impaired on the ascending than on the descending blood alcohol curve on tasks that measure reaction time, immediate memory, and other aspects of cognitive performance (Jones, 1973; Jones and Vega, 1972).

Subsequent studies of the effects of alcohol on a reaction time task yielded somewhat equivocal results that appeared to be confounded by practice effects (Jones and Jones, 1977). Female subjects were more impaired than males following a standard dose of alcohol (0.52 g/kg). Comparisons between women with normal menstrual cycles and women taking oral contraceptives showed variations that the investigators described as related to menstrual cycle phases. Women with normal menstrual cycles showed significant performance impairment during the menstrual and intermenstrual phase, whereas women taking oral contraceptives were most impaired during the premenstruum (Jones and Jones, 1977). These behavioral variations appear to be inconsistent with the menstrual-cycle–related changes in relative blood alcohol levels described by these investigators (Jones and Jones, 1976a,b). For example, it is surprising that the premenstrual period, purportedly associated with the highest blood alcohol levels, was not consistently accompanied by the greatest deficits in performance. Although women on oral contraceptive medication were reported to metabolize alcohol more slowly than other women, these women were least impaired on the reaction time task. Jones and Jones did not comment on these issues (Jones and Jones, 1976a,b, 1977). Final interpretation of these data awaits replication and resolution of the apparent inconsistencies between behavioral and biological findings.

Performance, Mood, and the Menstrual Cycle

Sex differences in alcohol-induced impairment of performance appeared to be related to phases of the menstrual cycle for measures of reaction time, and unrelated to phases of the menstrual cycle for measures of delayed recall (Jones and Jones, 1976a,b, 1977). These data raise a question about the possible interactions between performance and the menstrual cycle, and it is of interest to examine the relevant findings obtained in drug-free women.

The notion that increased depression and anxiety associated with certain phases of the menstrual cycle could impair cognitive performance has been the subject of considerable adverse speculation about the performance capacities of women. Data concerning menstrual-cycle–related behavioral changes are sometimes presented to portray women as helpless victims of hormones (Tiger, 1970) and thereby support a male supremacy position by implication. One unfortunate result of this tendency has been that some scientists who are concerned about sex discrimination have developed an opposite and equally unfortunate reaction, that is, to attempt to deny that menstrual cycles are related to changes in feeling state for some women. Neither a sexist overinterpretation nor denial of an evident reality is in the best interest of understanding the hormonal regulatory mechanisms that may affect behavior.

Curiously, the underlying assumption that mood may change performance is rarely made explicit and is almost never questioned. Depression or elation may impair or enhance performance, and these are testable hypotheses. The rather convoluted extension of this question— "Do women perform poorly during certain phases of the menstrual cycle?"—appears to assume that negative mood and performance covary. Golub (1976b) has shown that negative mood states do not necessarily impair performance. Fifty women over the age of 30 were given simultaneous measures of mood and cognitive function four days before the onset of menstruation and during the intermenstrual period. These women described themselves as significantly more depressed and anxious, and they showed significantly higher scores on anxiety and depression measures, during the premenstrual period. However, there were no significant differences in test performance during the premenstrual period and the intermenstruum on simple and complex cognitive function tests (Golub, 1976b). Overall academic performance also does not differ in women with premenstrual symptoms and women who do not report such symptoms (Schuckit et al., 1975). In fact, women who reported premenstrual symptoms achieved a slightly higher college grade-point average than symptom-free women (Schuckit et al., 1975).

In a comprehensive review of the effect of menstrual cycles on cognitive and perceptual motor behavior, Sommer (1973) concluded that studies utilizing objective performance measures generally fail to demonstrate menstrual-cycle–related changes. For example, two groups of women were given equivalent forms of the Watson–Glazer Critical Thinking Appraisal Test at weekly intervals and were asked to indicate their phase of the menstrual cycle (premenstrual, menstrual, follicular, and luteal) following test administration. Women using an oral contraceptive performed at a significantly higher level than women who did not use an oral contraceptive, and neither age, general intelligence, nor socioeconomic factors appeared to account for this difference. However, there were no variations in performance on the Watson–Glazer test as a function of phase of the menstrual cycle (Sommer, 1972).

Several studies have shown variations in sensory acuity as a function of the menstrual cycle (Sommer, 1973). Changes in threshold for olfactory or temperature stimuli have been reported, but Sommer pointed out that these studies require little active performance by the subject as compared to cognitive and perceptual motor tasks. An increase in visual threshold during the premenstrual period has also been reported (Ward et al., 1978). There appears to be a dissociation between performance on tasks requiring detection of a visual signal and tasks requiring discrimination of evenly spaced dots from paired dots, presented tachistoscopically (Ward et al., 1978). During the premenstrual period, visual detection was impaired and visual discrimination was facilitated in 12 women (Ward et al., 1978). Although the explanation for these findings is unclear, corneal edema associated with water retention during the premenstruum could impair visual detection and simultaneously enhance discrimination by reducing sensitivity to irrelevant stimuli. It was concluded that the mechanisms involved in producing sensory threshold changes during the menstrual cycle are unknown (Ward et al., 1978). An unusual feature of this study was that menstrual cycle phase was precisely defined by radioimmunoassay of plasma levels of estradiol, progesterone, luteinizing hormone, and follicle-stimulating hormone.

Summary

Certain biological effects of alcohol appear to differ between men and women and to covary with phases of the menstrual cycle. Following an equivalent dose of alcohol, women absorbed alcohol faster and reached a higher peak blood alcohol than male controls. There were no significant sex differences in the rate of alcohol elimination. Blood alcohol levels in women were also higher at ovulation and during the premenstruum than at other phases of the menstrual cycle. Associated changes in subjective perception of intoxication were not examined. However, women were more impaired than men on delayed recall following alcohol administration, but these impairments were unrelated to phases of the menstrual cycle. Women were also more impaired than men on a reaction time task, and variations in performance appeared to be related to menstrual cycle phases. In normal, drug-free women, performance on cognitive tasks has not been shown to vary as a function of the menstrual cycle. However, there is evidence that sensory acuity may vary as a function of the menstrual cycle.

Although the replicability and generality of these provocative findings on sex-specific and menstrual-cycle–related differences in the effects of alcohol remain to be determined, they illustrate the need for many controls in studies of drug effects in women. Not only is it important to obtain extensive baseline measures under drug-free conditions, but it may also be necessary to compare drug effects across several phases of the menstrual cycle, depending on the type of task performance required.

6. MOOD AND ALCOHOL INTOXICATION

It is usually assumed that drinking episodes begin in response to a stressful experience or to diminish feelings of anxiety and depression. Moreover, it is generally believed that alcohol is effective in modulating dysphoric feelings and that this is one basis for the perpetuation of alcohol abuse. Clinical examination of drinking patterns in alcoholics and the behavioral effects of alcohol intoxication indicate that neither of these commonplace assumptions is entirely accurate. The relevant studies have been done with men, and the generality of these findings for women remains to be determined.

It has been especially difficult to objectively examine factors that precede, and perhaps precipitate, a drinking episode. Some alcoholics report planning for a drinking spree to coincide with a slack period at work, much as others plan for a vacation. Affluent alcoholics may drink daily without interruption, rather than only in response to a crisis (Tamerin et al., 1971). Observations during long-term inpatient studies of drinking patterns indicate that stressful occurrences on the ward may result in an abrupt cessation of drinking by some alcoholic individuals (Mello, 1972). It is unlikely that factors related to stress, anxiety, and dysphoria can account completely for episodic alcohol abuse. The belief that alcohol produces positive, euphorigenic effects and that these gratifications sustain drinking also has not been supported by clinical studies (Mello and Mendelson, 1978). Contrary to common expectancy, the effects of alcohol intoxication on mood are not invariably positive.

Mood is an imprecise term used here to convey a range of feeling states from depression, anxiety, and despondency to relaxation, contentment, and euphoria. The use of so vague and all-inclusive a term as *mood* is justified in part by the numerous difficulties involved in adequately measuring any subjective state. The basic problem is how to ensure that the measures of mood employed in fact reflect the subjective experience of the individual. Changes in mood can be assessed only by reports of subjective states, and it is necessary to assume that verbal behavior reflects an individual's subjective feelings. However, objective reference criteria are difficult to establish, and verbal behavior may be greatly influenced by the expectancies and cooperativeness of the respondent. Examination of the effects of alcohol on mood states is a further complication of an already complicated and difficult topic. Most investigators have relied on a combination of standard psychometric instruments, global clinical impressions, observations of social behavior, and verbal behavior during a clinical interview. To the extent that these various measures are correlated, the investigator enjoys greater confidence in the validity of the observations.

Despite these methodological limitations and cautionary qualifications, there has been a remarkable consistency in results from clinical studies of the effects of alcohol intoxication on mood (cf. Mello and Mendelson, 1978). Chronic alcohol intoxication invariably produces an increase in depression, anxiety, and dysphoria in alcoholic men (Mayfield, 1968; McNamee et al., 1968; Mello and Mendelson, 1972; Mendelson, 1964; Nagarajan et al., 1973; Nathan et al., 1970, 1971a,b; Persky et al., 1977; Tamerin and Mendelson, 1969; Tamerin et al., 1970; Wolin and Mello, 1973). Usually, the severity of dysphoria and anxiety tends to increase in alcoholics as heavy drinking continues (Alterman et al., 1975). Moreover, social drinkers also report increased anxiety and depression after the ingestion of six to eight ounces of alcohol (Warren and Raynes, 1972; Williams, 1966). Dose-related increases in anxiety were reported by normal men and women given low acute doses of alcohol (0.5, 0.8, and 1.2 g/kg) and a placebo under double-blind conditions (Logue et al., 1978).

In contrast, four alcoholic women reported a decrease in depression, anger, fatigue, and confusion during a 12-day drinking period when blood alcohol levels were often above 100 mg/100 ml (Tracey and Nathan, 1976). The observed differences between alcoholic men and alcoholic women were attributed to the more controlled drinking patterns seen in women (Tracey and Nathan, 1976).

The degree of dysphoria induced by alcohol appears to be related to the dose of alcohol consumed. In social drinkers, dysphoria has not been reported after consumption of two or three ounces of alcohol; rather, six to eight ounces is required to produce these negative effects. The alcoholic individual has greater alcohol tolerance, and therefore, larger quantities of alcohol are necessary to produce an increase in depression and anxiety.

Since alcohol intoxication often increases feelings of despondency and anxiety, perhaps it is not surprising that aggressive behavior is another frequent accompaniment of alcohol abuse (Mendelson and Mello, 1974; Tamerin and Mendelson, 1969; Taylor and Gammon, 1975; Tinklenberg, 1973). The efficacy of alcohol as a tension reducer has also been repeatedly challenged (Cappell and Herman, 1972; Steffen et al., 1974). Moreover, alcohol intoxication appears to have adverse effects on sexual arousal in both men (Briddell and Wilson, 1976; Farkas and Rosen, 1975; Rubin and Henson, 1976; Wilson and Lawson, 1976b) and women (Wilson and Lawson, 1976a).

These findings challenge the traditional assumption that the subjective effects of alcohol intoxication are primarily positive and indicate that alcohol does not reliably provide euphoria, relaxation, relief from tension, or the enhancement of social conviviality commonly expected. The euphoria sometimes seen during social drinking (cf. Smith et al., 1975) is commonly believed to contribute to recurrent alcohol use and abuse. It has also been assumed that alcohol abuse involves a magnification and perpetuation of the several satisfactions of social drinking. In fact, alcohol abuse may distort the simplest pleasures of intoxication and transform the anticipated rewards of social drinking into their antithesis. The joyous bacchanal of ancient legend was spared the scrutiny of behavioral scientists, but the image of festive intoxication has persisted. It is curious that these long-accepted beliefs have been challenged only within the past 15 years by observations of alcoholic individuals *during* intoxication. As direct observations of the effects of alcohol intoxication replace inferences based on self-reports obtained during sobriety, many traditional beliefs are reevaluated and gradually replaced with new and different concepts.

In view of the numerous seemingly adverse consequences of alcohol intoxication, the persistence of excessive alcohol use is perplexing. It is not clear why the dysphoric effects of alcohol intoxication have so little effect on drinking behavior. An awareness of the several medical, social, economic, and legal problems often associated with chronic alcohol abuse is seldom an effective deterrent to drinking. It is usually argued that the *immediate* rather than the *delayed* consequences of alcohol abuse are more effective in controlling drinking behavior. However, since some of the immediate consequences of drinking also appear to be aversive, this temporal distinction may also require some reappraisal. Clearly, it is misleading to assume that there are only "positive" effects of intoxication.

There are no satisfactory explanations for the repetition of excessive drinking and alcohol withdrawal episodes or for the persistence of alcohol abuse in view of its immediate and delayed adverse consequences. The hypotheses that alcoholics continue to drink to avoid the discomfort of withdrawal signs and symptoms or because they have "lost control" of drinking have not been supported by recent clinical research (cf. Mello, 1975; Mello and Mendelson, 1978, for review).

The Role of Aversive Consequences in Drug Self-Administration

Many drugs of abuse have now been shown to increase anxiety and depression during intoxication (Mello, 1978b). These data have led to the hypothesis that "aversive" consequences may be one important factor in the control of drug self-administration behavior (Mello, 1977, 1978b). In thinking about the way in which drugs come to control behavior leading to their self-administration, it is important to examine all the consequences of drug use. The basic assumption is that drug self-administration is controlled or maintained by its consequences, one of which appears to be dysphoric changes in mood.

It is of interest to recall that an initial drug experience often has a variety of aversive emotional and somatic consequences for the naive drug user (cf. Mello, 1977, 1978b). Alcohol addicts tend to have a clear recollection of their "first drink" (Kuehnle et al., 1974). However, clinical impressions suggest that the first drink was not memorable because of its relaxing, euphorigenic, tension-reducing, and self-actualizing effects for the drinker (Kuehnle et al., 1974; Catanzaro, 1968). It is more likely that the future alcoholic drank to the point of intoxication, with associated despondency, nausea, and vomiting. Yet, despite these "aversive" consequences of initial drug use, many individuals persist in alcohol administration to the point of abuse and addiction. The process by which an aversive drug experience becomes translated into a repetitive drug use pattern is not understood. It could be postulated that with the development of drug tolerance, these seemingly unpleasant somatic and emotional effects undergo a transition to a state of relative tranquility and well-being. Alternatively, it could be postulated that the initial dysphoria, nausea, and vomiting experienced by the naive drinker remain an integral part of the reinforcing properties of subsequent alcohol abuse. It is now evident that alcohol abuse, as well as other forms of drug abuse, continue *despite* the recurrence of these seemingly aversive consequences during intoxication (Mello, 1978b).

It is possible that these clinical data merely reflect a discrepancy between social expectancies and the observed effects of alcohol and other drugs. However, there is also evidence that seemingly aversive consequences maintain self-administration behavior in primate models under certain conditions. One example is the repetitive self-administration of an electric shock. The aversive properties of electric shock have been amply documented, and avoidance of electric shock has been a consistent finding. However, it has also been found that the same electric shock that can maintain escape and avoidance behavior may, under certain conditions, be self-administered by the same monkey. This phenomenon, called *response-produced shock,* developed from the observations of Kelleher and co-workers in 1963 (Kelleher et al., 1963) and has now been observed in many laboratories across several species (Morse and Kelleher, 1970). Under certain conditions, monkeys will continue to self-administer electric shock for months and even for years. These data are cloquent testimony to the capacity of "aversive" events to control behavior leading to their self-administration. Morse et al. (1977) have recently reviewed data on the control behavior by noxious stimuli and have discussed the generality of this phenomenon.

A second example of aversive control of behavior is the self-administration of narcotic antagonist drugs by opiate-dependent monkeys. Narcotic antagonists induce withdrawal signs in opiate-dependent monkeys, and it has been consistently observed that opiate-dependent monkeys work to escape and avoid the infusion of narcotic antagonists (Downs and Woods, 1975; Hoffmeister and Wuttke, 1973). There are two reports that injections of a narcotic antagonist can maintain self-administration in monkeys that are physiologically dependent on morphine (Goldberg et al., 1972; Woods et al., 1975). Monkeys continued to work for antagonist infusions despite the occurrence of withdrawal signs (Goldberg et al., 1972).

Since consequences that appear to be aversive do maintain behavior leading to their self-administration, more careful attention to the role of "aversive" consequences in human drug self-administration seems indicated. Morse and Kelleher (1977) have criticized the common tendency to think about reinforcers in terms of the alleged properties of events rather than in terms of the functional relations between events and behavior. They emphasized that the defining characteristics of reinforcers and of punishers are how they change behavior. It is important to recognize that the same event may have either reinforcing or punishing consequences, that is, increase or decrease behavior leading to its presentation, depending on the conditions under which it is presented. Defining stimulus events in terms of their behavioral effects, rather than in terms of *a priori* assumptions about their alleged properties, is a radical departure from most traditional formulations. However, defining reinforcement in terms of its behavioral effect can accommodate experimental data on response-produced shock and antagonist self-administration, as well as clinical evidence of the aversive consequences of alcohol abuse during intoxication. It is possible that increased anxiety and dysphoria associated with alcohol intoxication are one part of the total stimulus complex that maintains alcohol abuse. Exclusive attention to the alleged positive and rewarding consequences of alcohol intoxication does not appear to account adequately for the clinical findings (Mello, 1977, 1978b).

Summary

The factors that initiate and maintain alcohol and drug abuse are poorly understood. Traditional explanations structured in terms of hedonism or euphoric consequences of intoxication do not appear to account for alcohol abuse. Recent clinical data and primate models indicate that self-administration behavior is maintained by seemingly "aversive" consequences in a variety of situations. Chronic abuse of alcohol and other drugs is often associated with increases in dysphoria and anxiety rather than with the anticipated "positive" effects. However, these data have been obtained in studies of alcoholic men. Four alcoholic women have shown the expected pattern of decreased depression and anxiety during a period of chronic intoxication. The generality and determinants of these findings in women remain to be established. Further research on these issues is urgently needed.

7. SUMMARY AND CONCLUSIONS

Some behavioral and biological factors have been examined that are unique to women and which may influence temporal patterns of problem drinking. It has been suggested that drinking patterns may be directly influenced by the mood changes associated with phases of the menstrual cycle. Aside from clinical reports, and inferences drawn from research on the covariance between menstrual cycle phases and mood, there is no direct evidence that bears on this issue. However, identification of factors that contribute to the maintenance of alcohol abuse is of central importance for understanding and modification of problem drinking. This question is not specific to alcoholism; it is relevant to all forms of substance abuse. Drinking and drug abuse problems may develop for many reasons. Once established, there may be similarities in the way abuse patterns are maintained that transcend the specific pharmacological properties of the drug.

The alleviation of depression and anxiety is one of the most commonly reported reasons for excessive drinking. Although the effectiveness of alcohol as an antidepressant appears to depend on the drinker's expectancies rather than on any intrinsic pharmacological actions, nonetheless the anticipation of relief from depression and anxiety probably is an important factor in the initiation of drinking episodes. This expectancy about alcohol's effects may be an important facet of problem drinking in women for several reasons. Depressive disorders occur more frequently in women than in men, and these sex differences cannot be explained away as an artifact of case finding or reporting style (Weissman and Klerman, 1977). Depression antecedent to the development of problem drinking is a frequent clinical observation in women (Schuckit, 1973; Schuckit and Morrissey, 1976). Moreover, periodic increases in depression and anxiety in association with phases of the menstrual cycle are often reported (Smith, 1975; Steiner and Carroll, 1977; Moos, 1969; Dalton, 1964, 1969), and there is some clinical evidence that psychotic disorders may become more severe at the premenstruum. Although the pattern of positive and negative fluctuations in affect across the menstrual cycle may vary among women with different durations of menstrual flow (Erickson, 1979), there does appear to be a predictable covariance between menstrual cycle phases and feelings of relative well-being or dysphoria. The possible contribution of neuroendocrine hormones to cyclic changes in affective states remains to be determined (cf. Bardwick, 1975; Steiner and Carroll, 1977) and is an important aspect of the entire question of biological factors in depression.

Given that many women experience recurrent episodes of dysphoria and anxiety in association with the menstrual cycle, the way in which such mood variations influence alcohol consumption and alcohol abuse would appear to be an important unanswered question. The intriguing observation that equivalent doses of alcohol produce higher blood alcohol levels at the premenstruum and at ovulation (Jones and Jones, 1976a,b) further suggests the possible importance of the menstrual cycle in modulating the biological and behavioral effects of alcohol.

There is no obvious reason to assume that the wealth of information about alcoholic men can be completely generalized to alcoholic women. Over the past 15 years, clinical research on alcoholic men has greatly changed our conceptions about the behavioral and biological effects of alcohol (cf. Mello, 1978a; Mello and Mendelson, 1978) and has identified new and important areas for further investigation. Once direct observations of drinking patterns and the immediate effects of alcohol were made, the inaccuracies and distortions of retrospective self-report data obtained during sobriety became strikingly apparent. Unfortunately, a comparable clinical research effort to study alcoholic women has not been undertaken, and with few exceptions (Tracey and Nathan, 1976), behavioral data are largely based on retrospective self-reports and psychometric measures obtained during sobriety.

One of the most curious findings to emerge from behavioral studies of alcohol effects in men is that chronic intoxication increases rather than alleviates depression, anxiety, and dysphoria (cf. Mello and Mendelson, 1978). Yet, these aversive consequences of intoxication are seldom recalled during sobriety; rather, the anticipated positive effects are believed to have occurred. Moreover, the degree of despondency and anxiety induced by alcohol appears to increase as larger doses of alcohol are consumed. These findings contradict the assumption that drinking is maintained by its immediate positive effects, despite the predictable long-term adverse social, legal, and medical consequences. Rather, alcohol abuse often distorts many of the simplest alcohol-related pleasures. The implications of these data are far-reaching and indicate the need for a reevaluation of many common assumptions about the behavioral effects of alcohol intoxication. The possible role of seemingly aversive consequences in maintaining alcohol and other substance abuse has seldom been seriously considered (cf. Mello, 1978b). However, an increased understanding of the way in which drinking behavior is maintained demands a more empirical approach to the problem. The enigmas of alcohol abuse may eventually be clarified once the behavioral and biological effects of alcohol are examined in terms of their actual consequences, rather than assumed to conform to common expectancies and beliefs.

This essay has examined only a few of the unanswered questions about the biological and behavioral effects of alcohol in women. The role of factors that maintain alcohol abuse has been emphasized, because this appears to be a fundamental issue in understanding alcoholism and other forms of drug abuse. However, it is apparent that more information is needed about virtually every aspect of alcohol problems in women.

ACKNOWLEDGMENTS

Preparation of this review was supported by Grant No. DA 4 RG 010 and DA 01 676 from the National Institute of Drug Abuse, ADAMHA, and by Grant No. AA 04368 from the National Institute of Alcohol Abuse and Alcoholism. I thank Marjorie Donohoe for excellent assistance in the preparation of this manuscript.

REFERENCES

Alcohol and Health, First Special Report to the U.S. Congress, 1971, U.S. Government Printing Office (DHEW Publ. No. (HSM) 72-9099), Washington, D.C., p. 121.

Alterman, A. I., Gottheil, E., and Crawford, H. D., 1975, Mood changes in an alcoholism treatment program based on drinking decisions, *Am. J. Psychiatry* **132**:1032–1037.

Bacon, M. K., 1973, Cross-cultural studies of drinking, in: *Alcoholism: Progress in Research and Treatment* (P. G. Bourne and R. Fox, eds.), pp. 171–174, Academic, New York.

Bardwick, J. M., 1975, Psychological correlates of the menstrual cycle and oral contraceptive medication, in: *Hormones, Behavior, and Psychopathology* (E. J. Sacher, ed.), pp. 95–103, Raven Press, New York.

Beckman, L. J., 1975, Women alcoholics: A review of social and psychological studies, *J. Stud. Alcohol* **36**:797–824.

Beckman, L. J., 1976, Alcohol problems and women: An overview, in: *Alcoholism Problems in Women and Children* (M. Greenblatt and M. A. Schuckit, eds.), pp. 65–96, Grune & Stratton, New York.

Belfer, M. L., and Shader, R. I., 1976, Premenstrual factors as determinants of alcoholism in women, in: *Alcoholism Problems in Women and Children* (M. Greenblatt and M. A. Schuckit, eds.), pp. 97–102, Grune & Stratton, New York.

Belfer, M. L., Shader, R. I., Carroll, M., and Hermatz, J. S., 1971, Alcoholism in women, *Arch. Gen. Psychiatry* **25**:540–544.

Bennion, L. J., and Li, T. K., 1976, Alcohol metabolism in American Indians and whites: Lack of racial differences in metabolic rate and liver alcohol dehydrogenase, *N. Engl. J. Med.* **294**:9–13.

Benvenuto, J. A., Lau, J., and Cohen, R., 1975, Patterns of nonopiate/polydrug abuse: Findings of a national collaborative research project, in: *Problems of Drug Dependence*, Proceedings of the 37th Annual Scientific Meeting, Committee on Problems of Drug Dependence, National Academy of Sciences—National Research Council, pp. 234–254, Washington, D.C.

Birtchnell, J., and Floyd, S., 1974, Attempted suicide and the menstrual cycle—A negative conclusion, *J. Psychosom. Res.* **18**:361–369.

Bourne, P. G., 1973, Alcoholism in the urban Negro population, in: *Alcoholism: Progress in Research and Treatment* (P. G. Bourne and R. Fox, eds.), pp. 211–226, Academic, New York.

Bourne, P. G., 1975, Polydrug abuse—Status report on the federal effort, in: *Developments in the Field of Drug Abuse: National Drug Abuse Conference* (E. Senay, V. Shorty, and H. Alksen, eds.), pp. 197–207, Schenkman, Cambridge, Mass.

Bourne P., and Light, E., 1979, Alcohol problems in blacks and women, in: *Diagnosis and Treatment of Alcoholism* (J. H. Mendelson and N. K. Mello, eds.), McGraw-Hill, New York, pp. 83–123.

Briddell, D. W., and Wilson, G. T., 1976, Effects of alcohol and expectancy set on male sexual arousal, *J. Abnorm. Psychol.* **85**:225–234.

Brooks, J., Ruble, D., and Clark, A., 1977, College women's attitudes and expectancies concerning menstrual-related changes, *Psychosom. Med.* **39**:288–298.

Cahalan, D., Cisin, I. H., and Crossley, H. M., 1969, *American Drinking Practices: A*

National Study of Drinking Behavior and Attitudes, Monograph No. 6, Rutgers Center of Alcohol Studies, New Brunswick, N.J.

Cappell, H., and Herman, P. C., 1972, Alcohol and tension reduction: A review, *Q. J. Stud. Alcohol* **33**:33–64.

Catanzaro, R. J., 1968, The disease: Alcoholism, in: *Alcoholism, The Total Treatment Approach* (R. J. Catanzaro, ed.), pp. 5–25, Thomas, Springfield, Ill.

Committee on Substance Abuse and Habitual Behavior—Assembly of Behavioral and Social Sciences, 1977, *Common Process in Habitual Substance Use: A Research Agenda,* p. 39, National Academy of Sciences, Washington, D.C.

Corrigan, E. M., 1974, Woman and problem drinking: Notes on beliefs and facts, *Addict. Dis.* **1**:215–222.

Dalton, K., 1964, *The Premenstrual Syndrome,* Thomas, Springfield, Ill.

Dalton, K., 1969, *The Menstrual Cycle,* Pantheon, New York.

Downs, D. A., and Woods, J. H., 1975, Fixed-ratio escape and avoidance–escape from naloxone in morphine-dependent monkeys: Effects of naloxone dose and morphine pretreatment, *J. Exp. Anal. Behav.* **23**:415–427.

Dubowski, K. M., 1976, Human pharmacokinetics of ethanol, I, Peak blood concentrations and elimination in male and female subjects, *Alcohol Tech. Rep.* **5**:55–72.

Edwards, G. E., Hensman, C., and Peto, J., 1973, A comparison of female and male motivation for drinking, *Int. J. Addict.* **8**:577–587.

Erickson, B. E., 1980, Emotional, cognitive and physical variations during the menstrual cycle, II, Differences among women, *Psychosom. Med.* (in press).

Farkas, G. M., and Rosen, R. C., 1975, Effect of alcohol on elicited male sexual response, *J. Stud. Alcohol* **37**:265–272.

Freed, E. X., 1973, Drug abuse by alcoholics: A review, *Int. J. Addict.* **8**:451–473.

Goldberg, S. R., Hoffmeister, F., and Schlichting, U. U., 1972, Morphine antagonists: Modification of behavioral effects by morphine dependence, in: *Drug Addiction,* Vol. 1, *Experimental Pharmacology* (J. M. Singh, L. Miller, and H. Lal, eds.), pp. 31–48, Futura, Mt. Kisco, N.Y.

Golub, S., 1976a, The magnitude of premenstrual anxiety and depression, *Psychosom. Med.* **38**:4–12.

Golub, S., 1976b, The effect of premenstrual anxiety and depression on cognitive function, *J. Pers. Soc. Psychol.* **34**:99–104.

Gomberg, E. S., 1976, The female alcoholic, in: *Alcoholism* (R. E. Tarter and A. A. Sugerman, eds.), pp. 603–636, Addison-Wesley, Reading, Mass.

Goodwin, D. W., Schulsinger, F., Hermansen, L., Guze, S. B., and Winokur, G., 1973, Alcohol problems in adoptees raised apart from alcoholic biological parents, *Arch. Gen. Psychiatry* **28**:238–243.

Goodwin, D. W., Schulsinger, F., Moller, N., Hermansen, L., Winokur, G., and Guze, S. B., 1974, Drinking problems in adopted and nonadopted sons of alcoholics, *Arch. Gen. Psychiatry* **31**:164–169.

Goodwin, D. W., Schulsinger, F., Knop, J., Mednick, S., and Guze, S. B., 1977, Alcoholism and depression in adopted-out daughters of alcoholics, *Arch. Gen. Psychiatry* **34**:751–755.

Greenblatt, M., and Schuckit, M. A. (eds.), 1976, *Alcoholism Problems in Women and Children,* Grune & Stratton, New York.

Griffiths, R. R., Bigelow, G. E., and Liebson, I., 1976, Facilitation of human tobacco self-administration by ethanol: A behavioral analysis, *J. Exp. Anal. Behav.* **25**:279–292.

Hoffmeister, F., and Wuttke, W., 1973, Negative reinforcing properties of morphine antagonists in naive rhesus monkeys, *Psychopharmacologia* **33**:247–258.

Ivey, M. E., and Bardwick, M. J., 1968, Patterns of affective fluctuation in the menstrual cycle, *Psychosom. Med.* **30**:336–345.

Janowsky, D. S., Berens, S. C., and Davis, J. M., 1973, Correlations between mood, weight and electrolytes during the menstrual cycle: A renin–angiotensin–aldosterone hypothesis of premenstrual tension, *Psychosom. Med.* **35**:143–154.

Jones, B. M., 1973, Memory impairment on the ascending and descending limbs of the blood alcohol curve, *J. Abnorm. Psychol.* **82**:24–32.

Jones, B. M., and Jones, M. K., 1976a, Alcohol effects in women during the menstrual cycle, *Ann. N.Y. Acad. Sci.* **273**:567–587.

Jones, B. M., and Jones, M. K., 1976b, Women and alcohol: Intoxication, metabolism and the menstrual cycle, in: *Alcoholism Problems in Women and Children* (M. Greenblatt and M. A. Schuckit, eds.), pp. 103–136, Grune & Stratton, New York.

Jones, B. M., and Jones, M. K., 1977, Interaction of alcohol, oral contraceptives and the menstrual cycle with stimulus-response compatibility, in: *Currents in Alcoholism* (F. A. Seixas, ed.), pp. 457–477, Grune & Stratton, New York.

Jones, B. M., and Vega, A., 1972, Cognitive performance measured on the ascending and descending limb of the blood alcohol curve, *Psychopharmacologia* **23**:99–114.

Kelleher, R. T., Riddle, W. C., and Cook, L., 1963, Persistent behavior maintained by unavoidable shocks, *J. Exp. Anal. Behav.* **6**:507–517.

Kuehnle, J. C., Anderson, W. H., and Chandler, E., 1974, Report on first drinking experience in addictive and nonaddictive drinkers, *Arch. Gen. Psychiatry* **31**:521–523.

Lindbeck, V. L., 1972, The woman alcoholic: A review of the literature, *Int. J. Addict.* **7**:567–580.

Logue, P. E., Gentry, D., Linnoila, M., and Ervin, C. W., 1978, The effect of alcohol consumption on state anxiety changes in male and female nonalcoholics, *Am. J. Psychiatry* **135**:1079–1081.

May, R. R., 1976, Mood shifts and the menstrual cycle, *J. Psychosom. Res.* **20**:125–130.

Mayfield, D., 1968, Psychoparmacology of alcohol, I, Affective change with intoxication, drinking behavior and affective state, *J. Nerv. Ment. Dis.* **146**:314–321.

McNamee, H. B., Mello, N. K., and Mendelson, J. H., 1968, Experimental analysis of drinking patterns of alcoholics: Concurrent psychiatric observations, *Am. J. Psychiatry* **124**:1063–1069.

Mello, N. K., 1972, Behavioral studies of alcoholism, in: *The Biology of Alcoholism,* Vol. 2, *Physiology and Behavior* (B. Kissin and H. Begleiter, eds.), pp. 219–291, Plenum, New York.

Mello, N. K., 1975, A semantic aspect of alcoholism, in: *Biological and Behavioural Approaches to Drug Dependence* (H. D. Cappell and A. E. LeBlanc, eds.), pp. 73–87, Addiction Research Foundation, Toronto.

Mello, N. K., 1977, Stimulus self-administration: Some implications for the prediction of drug abuse liability, in: *Predicting Dependence Liability of Stimulant and Depressant Drugs* (T. Thompson and K. R. Unna, eds.), pp. 243–260, University Park Press, Baltimore.

Mello, N. K., 1978a, Alcoholism and the Behavioral Pharmacology of Alcohol: 1967–1977, in: *Psychopharmacology, A Generation of Progress* (M. A. Lipton, A. DiMascio, and K. F. Killam, eds.), pp. 1619–1637, Raven Press, New York.

Mello, N. K., 1978b, Control of drug self-administration: The role of aversive consequences, in: *Phencyclidine (PCP) Abuse: An Appraisal* (R. C. Peterson and R. C. Stillman, eds.), pp. 93–127, NIDA Monograph Series, Rockville, Md.

Mello, N. K., and Mendelson, J. H., 1972, Drinking patterns during work contingent and non-contingent alcohol acquisition, *Psychosom. Med.* **34**:139–164.

Mello, N. K., and Mendelson, J. H., 1975, Alcoholism: A biobehavioral disorder, in: *American Handbook of Psychiatry,* Vol. 4, *Organic Conditions and Psychosomatic Medicine* (M. Reiser, ed.), pp. 371–403, Basic Books, New York.

Mello, N. K., and Mendelson, J. H., 1977, Clinical aspects of alcohol dependence, in:

Drug Addiction I, Handbook of Experimental Pharmacology, Vol. 45/I (W. R. Martin, ed.), pp. 613–666, Springer-Verlag, Berlin.

Mello, N. K., and Mendelson, J. H., 1978, Alcohol and human behavior, in: *Handbook of Psychopharmacology,* Vol. 12, *Drugs of Abuse* (L. L. Iversen, S. D. Iversen, and S. H. Snyder, eds.), pp. 235–317, Plenum, New York.

Mendelson, J. H. (ed.), 1964, Experimentally induced chronic intoxication and withdrawal in alcoholics, *Q. J. Stud. Alcohol,* Supplement 2.

Mendelson, J. H., 1968, Ethanol-1-C¹⁴ metabolism in alcoholics and nonalcoholics, *Science* 159:319–320.

Mendelson, J. H., and Mello, N. K., 1974, Alcohol, aggression and androgens, in: *Aggression, Proceedings A.R.N.M.D.* (S. H. Frazier, ed.), pp. 225–247, Williams & Wilkins, Baltimore.

Mendelson, J. H., and Mello, N. K. (eds.), 1979, *The Diagnosis of Alcoholism: Diagnosis and Treatment of Alcoholism,* McGraw-Hill, New York, p. 405.

Mendelson, J. H., Stein, S., and Mello, N. K., 1965, Effects of experimentally induced intoxication on metabolism of ethanol-1-C¹⁴ in alcoholic subjects, *Metabolism* 14:1255–1266.

Moos, R. H., 1969, Typology of menstrual cycle symptoms, *Am. J. Obstet. Gynecol.* 103:390–401.

Moriyama, I. M., Krueger, D. E., and Stamler, J., 1971, *Cardiovascular Diseases in the United States,* Harvard University Press, Cambridge, Mass.

Morse, W. H., and Kelleher, R. T., 1970, Schedules as fundamental determinants of behavior, in: *The Theory of Reinforcement Schedules* (W. N. Schoenfeld, ed.), pp. 139–185, Appleton-Century-Crofts, New York.

Morse, W. H., and Kelleher, R. T., 1977, Determinants of reinforcement and punishment, in: *Operant Behavior,* Vol. 2 (W. K. Honig and J. E. R. Staddon, eds.), pp. 174–200, Prentice-Hall, Englewood Cliffs, N.J.

Morse, W. H., McKearney, J. W., and Kelleher, R. T., 1977, Control of behavior by noxious stimuli, in: *Handbook of Psychopharmacology,* Vol. 7 (L. L. Iversen, S. D. Iversen, and S. H. Snyder, eds.), pp. 151–180, Plenum, New York.

Mulford, H. A., 1977, Women and men problem drinkers, *J. Stud. Alcohol* 38:1624–1639.

Nagarajan, M., Gross, M. M., Kissin, B., and Best, S., 1973, Affective changes during six days of experimental alcoholization and subsequent withdrawal, in: *Alcohol Intoxication and Withdrawal: Experimental Studies, Advances in Experimental Medicine and Biology,* Vol. 35 (M. M. Gross, ed.), pp. 351–363, Plenum, New York.

Nathan, P. E., Titler, N. A., Lowenstein, L. M., Solomon, P., and Rossi, A. M., 1970, Behavioral analysis of chronic alcoholism: Interaction of alcohol and human contact, *Arch. Gen. Psychiatry* 22:419–430.

Nathan, P. E., O'Brien, J. S., and Lowenstein, L. M., 1971a, Operant studies of chronic alcoholism: Interaction of alcohol and alcoholics, in: *Biological Aspects of Alcohol* (M. K. Roach, W. M. McIsaac, and P. J. Creaven, eds.), pp. 341–370, University of Texas Press, Austin.

Nathan, P. E., O'Brien, J. S., and Norton, D., 1971b, Comparative studies of the interpersonal and affective behavior of alcoholics and nonalcoholics during prolonged experimental drinking, in: *Recent Advances in Studies of Alcoholism* (N. K. Mello and J. H. Mendelson, eds.), pp. 619–646, U.S. Government Printing Office [(HSM) 71-9045], Washington, D.C.

Paige, K. E., 1971, Effects of oral contraceptives on affective fluctuations associated with the menstrual cycle, *Psychosom. Med.* 33:515–537.

Parlee, M. B., 1973, The premenstrual syndrome, *Psychol. Bull.* 80:454–465.

Parlee, M. B., 1974, Stereotypic beliefs about menstruation: A methodological note on the

Moos Menstrual Distress Questionnaire and some new data, *Psychosom. Med.* **36**:229–240.

Patkai, P., Johannson, G., and Post, B., 1974, Mood, alertness and sympathetic-adrenal medullary activity during the menstrual cycle, *Psychosom. Med.* **36**:503–512.

Persky, H., O'Brien, C. P., Fine, E., Howard, W. J., Khan, M. A., and Beck, R. W., 1977, The effect of alcohol and smoking on testosterone function and aggression in chronic alcoholics, *Am. J. Psychiatry* **134**:612–625.

Podolsky, E., 1963, The woman alcoholic and premenstrual tension, *J. Am. Med. Wom. Assoc.* **18**:816–818.

Popham, R. E., Schmidt, W., and de Lint, J., 1975, The prevention of alcoholism: Epidemiological studies of the effects of government control measures, *Br. J. Addict.* **70**:125–144.

Robins, L. N., and Guze, S. B., 1971, Drinking practices and problems in urban ghetto populations, in: *Recent Advances in Studies of Alcoholism* (N. K. Mello and J. H. Mendelson, eds.), pp. 825–842, U.S. Government Printing Office [(HSM) 71-9045], Washington, D.C.

Rubin, H. B., and Henson, D. E., 1976, Effects of alcohol on male sexual responding, *Psychopharmacologia* **47**:123–134.

Ruble, D., 1977, Premenstrual symptoms: A reinterpretation, *Science* **197**:291–292.

Sandmaier, M., 1977, Alcohol programs for women: Issues, strategies and resources, pp. 1–26, National Clearinghouse for Alcohol Information, National Institute on Alcohol Abuse and Alcoholism, Washington, D.C.

Schuckit, M. A., 1972, The alcoholic woman: A literature review, *Psychiatr. Med.* **3**:37–43.

Schuckit, M. A., 1973, Depression and alcoholism in women, *Proceedings,* First Annual Alcoholism Conference of the National Institute on Alcohol Abuse and Alcoholism, June 1971, U.S. Government Printing Office, Washington, D.C.

Schuckit, M. A., and Morrissey, E. R., 1976, Alcoholism in women: Some clinical and social perspectives with an emphasis on possible subtypes, in: *Alcoholism Problems in Women and Children* (M. Greenblatt and M. A. Schuckit, eds.), pp. 5–35, Grune & Stratton, New York.

Schuckit, M. A., Goodwin, D. A., and Winokur, G., 1972, A study of alcoholism in half siblings, *Am. J. Psychiatry* **128**:1132–1136.

Schuckit, M. A., Daly, V., Herrman, G., and Hineman, S., 1975, Premenstrual symptoms and depression in a university population, *Dis. Nerv. Syst.* **36**:516–517.

Silbergeld, S., Brast, N., and Noble, E. P., 1971, The menstrual cycle: A double-blind study of symptoms, mood and behavior, and biochemical variables using Enovid and placebo, *Psychosom. Med.* **33**:411–428.

Slone, D., Shapiro, S., Rosenberg, L., Kaufman, D. W., Hartz, S. C., Rossi, A. C., Stolley, P. D., and Miettinen, O. S., 1978, Relation of cigarette smoking to myocardial infarction in young women, *N. Engl. J. Med.* **298**:1273–1276.

Smith, S. L., 1975, Mood and the menstrual cycle, in: *Topics in Psychoneuroendocrinology* (E. J. Sachar, ed.), pp. 19–58, Grune & Stratton, New York.

Smith, R. C., Parker, E., and Noble, E. P., 1975, Alcohol and affect in dyadic social interaction, *Psychosom. Med.* **37**:25–40.

Sommer, B., 1972, Menstrual cycle changes and intellectual performance, *Psychosom. Med.* **34**:263–269.

Sommer, B., 1973, The effect of menstruation on cognitive and perceptual motor behavior: A review, *Psychosom. Med.* **35**:515–534.

Steffen, J. J., Nathan, P. E., and Taylor, H. A., 1974, Tension-reducing effects of alcohol: Further evidence and some methodological considerations, *J. Abnorm. Psychol.* **83**:542–547.

Steiner, M., and Carroll, B. J., 1977, The psychobiology of premenstrual dysphoria: Review of theories and treatments, *Psychoneuroendocrinology* **2**:321–335.

Tamerin, J. S., and Mendelson, J. H., 1969, The psychodynamics of chronic inebriation: Observations of alcoholics during the process of drinking in an experimental group setting, *Am. J. Psychiatry* **125**:886–899.

Tamerin, J. S., Weiner, S., and Mendelson, J. H., 1970, Alcoholics' expectancies and recall of experiences during intoxication, *Am. J. Psychiatry* **126**:1697–1704.

Tamerin, J. S., Newmann, C. P., and Marshall, M. H., 1971, The upper-class alcoholic: A syndrome in itself, *Psychosomatics* **12**:200–204.

Taylor, S. P., and Gammon, C. B., 1975, Effects of type and dose of alcohol on human physical aggression, *J. Pers. Soc. Psychol.* **32**:169–175.

Tiger, L. 1970, The possible biological origins of sexual discrimination, *Impact Sci. Soc.* **20**:29–44.

Tinklenberg, J. R.,1973, Alcohol and violence, in: *Alcoholism: Progress in Research and Treatment* (P. G. Bourne and R. Fox, eds.), pp. 195–210, Academic Press, New York.

Tracey, D. A., and Nathan, P. E., 1976, Behavioral analysis of chronic alcoholism in four women, *J. Consult. Clin. Psychol.* **44**:832–842.

Victor, M., and Adams, R. D., 1953, The effect of alcohol on the nervous system, *Res. Publ. Assoc. Res. Nerv. Ment. Dis.* **32**:526–573.

Wanberg, K. W., and Horn, J. L., 1970, Alcoholism symptom patterns of men and women: A comparative study, *Q. J. Stud. Alcohol* **31**:40–61.

Ward, M. M., Stone, S. C., and Sandman, C. A., 1978, Visual perception in women during the menstrual cycle, *Physiol. Behav.* **20**:239–243.

Warren. G. H., and Raynes, A. E., 1972, Mood changes during three conditions of alcohol intake, *Q. J. Stud. Alcohol* **33**:979–989.

Weissman, M. M., and Klerman, G. L., 1977, Sex differences and the epidemiology of depression, *Arch. Gen. Psychiatry* **34**:98–111.

Wilcoxon, L. A., Schrader, S. L., and Sherif, C. W., 1976, Daily self-reports on activities, life events, moods and somatic changes during the menstrual cycle, *Psychosom. Med.* **38**:399–417.

Williams, A. F., 1966, Social drinking, anxiety and depression, *J. Pers. Soc. Psychol.* **3**:689–693.

Wilsnack, S. C., 1976, The impact of sex roles and women's alcohol use and abuse, in: *Alcoholism Problems in Women and Children* (M. Greenblatt and M. A. Schuckit, eds.), pp. 37–64, Grune & Stratton, New York.

Wilson, G. T., and Lawson, D. M., 1976a, Effects of alcohol on sexual arousal in women, *J. Abnorm. Psychol.* **85**:489–497.

Wilson, G. T., and Lawson, D. M., 1976b, Expectancies, alcohol and sexual arousal in male social drinkers, *J. Abnorm. Psychol.* **85**:587–594.

Wolin, S. J., and Mello, N. K., 1973, The effects of alcohol on dreams and hallucinations in alcohol addicts, *Ann. N.Y. Acad. Sci.* **215**:266–302.

Woods, J. H., Downs, D. A., and Carney, J., 1975, Behavioral functions of narcotic antagonists: Response-drug contingencies, *Fed. Proc.* **34**:1777–1784.

8

Nature and Development of Alcoholism in Women

WILFRED E. BOOTHROYD

1. INTRODUCTION

Up until the past decade, there has been a paucity of studies on alcoholism in women. Recently, a growing body of literature on this topic has emanated from a variety of disciplinary backgrounds. In this chapter, an attempt is made to summarize the important findings to date. Familial factors, environmental influences, development of drinking patterns, and more theoretical considerations of personality and psychopathology are described. The final section reports the emerging recognition of a relationship between alcoholism and affective disorders in women.

2. FAMILIAL FACTORS

The family background of both male and female alcoholics has been the subject of a considerable number of studies. Wall (1937) found that female alcoholics in a hospital setting had had no particularly strong ties to either parent or to any of their siblings compared with the strong mother attachment reported by 37% of male alcoholics. The family background of these patients was described as "not unusual" though there was a considerable amount of parental discord. Van Amberg (1943) reported that in 16% of his 50 female alcoholics there was an "unusually strong" father–daughter relationship. Of the fathers, 40% were alcoholic, seriously neurotic, or psychotic. As a group, the mothers were better adjusted. However, 14% were alcoholic and mentally ill, as were siblings

WILFRED E. BOOTHROYD • Addiction Research Foundation, Toronto, Ontario.

of 28% of the patients. Lisansky (1957) found that 42% of her 46 female alcoholic outpatients came from broken homes, as did almost the same proportion of the male outpatient alcoholics. In almost all cases, it was the father who was the absent parent. Approximately the same percentage of patients reported problem drinking by one or both parents. The female patients had a higher percentage of strict and controlling mothers than fathers, while the reverse was true for the male alcoholics. Wood and Duffy (1966) found a similarly high proportion of rigid, distant, perfectionistic mothers of their group of 69 well-educated alcoholic women, half of whose fathers were alcoholic and rebelled against their dominant wives only when drunk. None of these patients had parents who were happily married. The daughters were unable to satisfy the expectations of the controlling mothers and perceived themselves as more like their affectionate but weak and ineffective fathers. This series tends to confirm Lolli's (1953) impression that the usual parental combination for women alcoholics is a domineering mother and a weak, or absent, father. Kinsey (1968) reported similar findings from his study of 46 alcoholic women of low socioeconomic status in a state hospital. They too described strong, controlling mothers and weak, indulgent fathers, most of whom were alcoholic, psychotic, or absent. Happy parental marriages were totally absent. They also reported that the parents, especially the mother, preferred other siblings to them. A deep sense of personal inadequacy developed in these women, who used alcohol in an attempt to counteract these feelings.

Female alcoholics tend to have more "heavy drinking" mothers (and, incidentally, spouses) (Bromet and Moos, 1976) than male alcoholics. Also, alcoholic women, compared with nonalcoholic women, are more likely to have alcoholic parents, especially fathers (Sherfey, 1955; Cramer and Blacker, 1966; Driscoll and Barr, 1972). Two-thirds of the female patients of Johnson et al. (1966) had alcoholic relatives, including one third with alcoholic parents. As would be expected, more male relatives than female relatives (of all alcoholics) have a history of alcoholism, but this incidence is higher than in the relatives of the general population. Whether or not the female relatives show a similarly increased incidence is not clear, the available evidence being contradictory (Amark, 1951; Winokur and Clayton, 1968; Winokur et al., 1970).

Alcoholics of both sexes report a higher than expected occurrence of psychiatric illness, especially affective disorders, among their female relatives. This finding is even more marked for female alcoholics than for males (Winokur and Clayton, 1968; Winokur et al., 1970, 1971). The affective disorder frequently has the characteristics of a unipolar depression. These authors considered the possibility that an X-linked recessive gene may be implicated in alcoholism, at least as one significant factor. While the evidence is slim, this possibility can hardly be denied.

Much of the literature postulates or implies a causal relationship between parental alcoholism (and, in a few cases, problem drinking in more distant family members) and the subsequent development of alcohol abuse among the offspring. Not unexpectedly, the old problem of heredity versus environment comes to the fore. Fortunately, this difficulty, while of great interest in the field of prevention, does not interfere with most practical issues in the understanding of the nature and the individual development of alcoholism as a phenomenon. It is important to distinguish between whatever is different in the familial backgrounds of male and female alcoholics only to the degree that such knowledge can contribute in practical ways to programs of treatment and/or prevention. Contradictory findings among authors are less disturbing than the tendency on the part of a number of investigators to jump to general conclusions by overinterpreting a very limited set of data. For example, insufficient attention has been paid to the fact that norms of family relationships, including sex-role expectations, vary considerably from one social class or culture to another, as does the impact of these conditions on the personality development of family members, particularly the children.

3. PERSONAL ENVIRONMENTAL INFLUENCES

Early parental deprivation is much more frequently reported by alcoholic populations than at large (de Lint, 1964). In alcoholics, this early life trauma is more often associated with female patients than with males (Fort, 1949; de Lint, 1964; Basquin and Osouf, 1965; Sclare, 1970; Rathod and Thompson, 1971). Female alcoholics tend to reject their parents, especially their mothers (Kinsey, 1966; Driscoll and Barr, 1972; Beckman, 1975). Women who experienced broken homes before the age of 10 are significantly more likely to become heavy drinkers than are men with the same early life history. This widely recognized sex difference is difficult to explain on theoretical grounds. De Lint (1964) suggested a possible connection with the tendency toward "nonaffiliation" found by Schachter (1959) in his study of female alcoholics. The complexity of the matter is illustrated by Smart's (1963) finding that female (but not male) alcoholic later-borns are statistically overrepresented.

That this unsatisfactory relationship to parents during the formative years contributes to the development of a sense of personal inadequacy and a lack of self-worth can be reasonably assumed (Kinsey, 1968). One manifestation may take the form of psychosexual immaturity (Wood and Duffy, 1966; Wilsnack, 1973c). Few alcoholic women have happy marriages even before their recourse to heavy drinking. This finding is very striking in some series, as, for example, in Fort and Porterfield's (1961) sample of 34 female alcoholic patients who reported 31 divorces in a total of 52 marriages. The evidence with regard to the personality types of husbands chosen by women who become alcoholic is inconclusive. Kinsey (1968) found that there was a strong tendency for his patients to have married men who were domineering and cruel, including second marriages by his widowed or divorced patients. Wood and Duffy (1966) had earlier reported the same tendency. The causative role of the existence of a grossly unhappy marital relationship in the development of subsequent alcoholism has been argued. Perhaps both are the results of the unhappy childhoods so frequently reported by these patients.

Women alcoholics give histories of greater emotional trauma in their past lives than do men (Podolsky, 1963; Rathod and Thomson, 1971) and have a greater tendency to relate the onset of their heavy drinking to an identified stressful event or situation. Recurrent episodes of heavy drinking, whether short-lived benders or bouts lasting for several weeks, are reported to be reactive to particularly difficult circumstances within their families or their immediate circle of peers (Curlee, 1970; Franck and Rosen, 1949; Lisansky, 1957; Lolli, 1953; Wilsnack, 1973a; Hoffmann and Noem, 1975b). Such women have been reasonably described as "reactive alcoholics" (Gomberg, 1974).

In more general terms, Basquin and Osouf (1965) were impressed with the importance of social, professional, and personal isolation in the backgrounds of the female alcoholics they studied in France. On the physical side, Wilsnack (1973) found that alcoholic women have suffered from more gynecological disorders than women generally.

There is a fairly wide variation in the number of alcoholic spouses of alcoholics as reported in several studies. Lisansky (1957) found that one-third of her outpatient alcoholic women and over half of the inpatients had husbands who were problem drinkers. This finding contrasted sharply with the outpatient men, of whom only 9% had alcoholic wives. Wood and Duffy (1966), on the other hand, found that of their 69 relatively well-educated (all were at least high school graduates) women patients, although their marriages were almost without exception "emotionally unrewarding," only 4 had husbands who were alcoholic. One-third of Kinsey's (1968) 46 lower-class female patients were married to men who were described as "inebriates," the proportion rising to 80% in subsequent marriages. In a further series (Rosenbaum, 1958), half of the husbands were well-defined alcoholics, and another quarter were excessive or heavy social drinkers. In Sclare's (1970) study, 16% of the 50 females had alcoholic husbands, but none of the control group of 50 males were married to an alcoholic wife. The proportion of female to male patients with alcoholic spouses in Bromet and Moos's (1976) study was about three to one.

Although it is outside the scope of this review, it is worth noting in passing that there is a considerable literature on the wives of alcoholic men. The observations and theories range from moralistic pronouncements with a discernible "male chauvinist" slant on the one hand, to an equal, but opposite, "hurt little woman" bias on the other. There has been very little study (except statistical) devoted to the husbands of alcoholic women.

4. DRINKING PATTERNS

For the past several decades at least, men in our culture have consumed more alcohol than have women (Cahalan and Cisin, 1968; Cahalan et al., 1969; Forslund and Gustafson, 1970; Wechsler et al., 1972). A larger percentage of male college students than female students formerly drank socially (Slater, 1952; Straus and Bacon, 1953; Maddox and McCall, 1964). Recently, however, the difference has decreased and by now may have disappeared (San Mateo County, 1971; Wechsler and Thum, 1973; Wechsler and Thum, 1974; U.S. National Institute on Alcohol Abuse and Alcoholism—USNIAAA, 1975). This reduction is particularly noticeable among adolescents (San Mateo County, 1971). Wechsler and McFadden (1976) found that in two Massachusetts schools, girls in grades 9–12 were drinking more wine and distilled spirits than were the boys (and were using more amphetamines, barbiturates, and multiple drugs). Delinquent girls were found to drink more frequently and more excessively than delinquent boys (Widseth and Mayer, 1971). Of these girls, about a third usually drank alone, a pattern almost never seen in delinquent boys.

The change in the direction of increased drinking for middle-class women apparently began in the 1940s (Jellinek, 1947). At the same time, they began to smoke more. "The tea party became the cocktail party." Social mores were changing, and the trend increased in strength as groups in which drinking was common came to expect conformity on the part of hopeful "joiners." In such social situations, status was assigned partly on the basis of drinking behavior. Women who wanted to drink less were subjected to a variety of influences to keep to a fairly narrow set of limits, as to both lower levels and upper levels of consumption, set by powerful group norms (Trice, 1956). However, the change did not occur at the same rate, nor to the same degree, in all social classes. Dollard (1945) found that the proportion of women who drank increased progressively from the lower middle class to the lower lower class. Lawrence and Maxwell (1962), on the other hand, found that in their Status IV, corresponding to Dollard's lower lower class, only about 20% of the women drank at all, compared with about 60% at higher social levels. This discrepancy may be accounted for by a variation in geographic location, the lapse in time, or a difference in local cultural mores in the populations studied. Generalization is tempting but dangerous even when one is dealing with data that are "statistically significant." Nevertheless, it would appear that these findings, isolated though they are, do support the popular impression that there has been a marked change in the drinking practices of women, at least in the Western world.

Pari passu with this change in behavior, there has been a marked alteration in society's attitude toward drinking by women, though it still does not have the same acceptance as is accorded alcohol use by men. Men and women generally, including male and female alcoholics, agree that it is "worse" for women than for men to be intoxicated (Lawrence and Maxwell, 1962; Knupfer, 1964; Curlee, 1967). This is true in other cultures as well as our own (Horton, 1943; Child et al., 1965). Child et al. stated, "Under the generally prevailing conditions of human life, temporary incapacity of a woman is more threatening than is temporary incapacity of a man. For example, care of a field can be postponed for a day, but care of a child cannot" (p. 60).

In the past, women have been more likely than men to be protected from the consequences of their abuse of alcohol (Senseman, 1966). A diagnosis of alcoholism was rarely made, women usually being seen as "emotionally disturbed" in circumstances that in a male would be unhesitatingly described as alcoholic (Curlee, 1970). Physicians regard women alcoholics as "sicker" (Johnson, 1965) and are more likely to prescribe medication as a part or all of the necessary treatment (Fraser, 1973) than they are for women patients generally (Broverman et al., 1970).

Many studies have indicated that women as a whole, including those who subsequently become alcoholic, begin drinking at a later age than men (Curran, 1937; Wall, 1937; Lisansky, 1957; Glatt, 1961; Winokur and Clayton, 1968; Wanberg and Horn, 1970; Rimmer et al., 1971; Garrett and Bahr, 1973a; Bromet and Moos, 1976). Homeless women, on the other hand, report drinking at an earlier age than homeless men (Moorhead, 1958; Garrett and Bahr, 1973b).

The transition from social drinking to early problem drinking to alcoholism evidently occurs over a shorter space of time in women than in men (Glatt, 1961a; Winokur and Clayton, 1968; Curlee, 1970; Efron et al., 1974) though at a later age (Wall, 1937; Lisansky, 1957; Wanberg and Horn, 1970; Rimmer et al., 1971). In this connection, it is interesting to note the ominous signs of impending loss of control as described in retrospect by women alcoholics themselves. Johnson et al. (1966) asked their subjects to recall their own experiences with particular reference to this item. Three changes in behavior were identified: gulping drinks, arriving at a party already under the influence, and minimizing the amount consumed. These subjects believed that they drank for reasons that were different from those of social drinkers, namely, as a conscious attempt to combat feelings of inferiority and loneliness.

The general tendency of problem drinkers, at a certain stage in their progress toward alcoholism, to attempt to conceal their drinking and their liquor supply seems to be particularly marked in women (Johnson et al., 1966). Less frequent absence from work is part of this pattern of hiding the problem from friends and associates. The concealment techniques may be remarkably effective. Johnson et al. asked their subjects for the names of persons who could be contacted for their assessment of the problem as it affected each subject. It is of great interest that the contacts, both professional and social, varied widely in their descriptions of the alcoholic's behavior, her personality, and the impact of the excessive drinking. Some close associates who were thought by the subjects to be aware of the situation did not realize that the women had a drinking problem.

With regard to patterns of alcoholic drinking, some authors have found that women are less likely than men to engage in drinking bouts (Rimmer et al., 1971; Schuckit et al., 1971), but other observers (Madden and Jones, 1972; Wanberg and Horn, 1973) have reported that on the whole, male alcoholics tend to drink more continuously and females more sporadically. In total quantity, women alcoholics drink less beer and wine (Lisansky, 1957; Sclare, 1970; Wanberg and Knapp, 1970) and possibly hard liquor (Bromet and Moos, 1976).

At least until very recently, women have tended to drink alone more than men, and drinking alone was not only confined to those women whose drinking is referred to as the *alcoholic housewife syndrome.* Lisansky (1957) found that over half of her outpatient women drank alone, compared with one-fifth of the men. All of Wood and Duffy's (1966) middle-class patients drank at home alone and rarely went to bars, as did the women alcoholics studied by Sclare (1970) in Glasgow. The same strong tendency was reported by Wanberg and Knapp (1970) in Colorado, and similar findings were reported by other authors (Rosenbaum, 1958; Senseman, 1966; Pemberton, 1967; Bromet and Moos, 1976). Garrett and Bahr (1973a) found less difference among homeless men and women in New York City, where one-half of the women and one-third of the men drank alone. The heavy drinkers in this population showed a more marked divergence: two-thirds of the women compared with one-quarter of the men engaged primarily in solitary drinking. One obvious reason for this sex difference in drinking patterns is that until recently, women spent more time alone and at home than men. Now that more women are at work outside the home, it will be interesting to find out if the above generalization still holds.

Women alcoholics in the United States are more likely to depend on psychotropic drugs than are men (Curlee, 1970), though this is apparently not true in Great Britain (Sclare, 1970; Rathod and Thomson, 1971). Women in general use mood-modifying drugs more than men, and physicians are more likely to prescribe such medication for their female than for their male patients (Cooperstock, 1971, 1978).

5. PERSONALITY

Most workers have found that the social and recreational adjustment of the women who were later to become alcoholic tended strongly toward isolation and neuroticism (Lolli 1953; Lisansky, 1957; Rosenbaum, 1958; Wood and Duffy, 1966; Zelen et al., 1966; Winokur and Clayton, 1968). This view is well summarized by Fort and Porterfield (1961) when they stated that "In view of the greater restrictions on female drunkenness, it is possible that women are not liable to become alcoholics unless they are handicapped by neuroticism . . . or are under the impact of strong emotional stimuli" (p. 291). One study (Van Amberg, 1943), however, showed that most women alcoholics had normal premorbid personality characteristics and social adjustment, with the possible exception (a major one) of psychosexual development. In the same study, no premorbid differences were found for women who developed a psychotic disturbance in the course of their alcoholic illness in a comparison with those who did not. The similarities between the two groups included type, onset, and duration of their illness and apparent etiological factors, including precipitating life situations. The value of this study, like most others in this area of concern, is limited by the retrospective nature of the reports by patients, families, and professional workers.

Jones (1971) reported increasing data based on the longitudinal Oakland Growth Study. Forty-five women, varying from abstainers to problem drinkers, were divided into categories according to the amount they drank. Unfortunately, the numbers were so small in each category, particularly at the two extremes, that interpretations based on the findings must be considered highly tentative. The suggestion is, however, that "adult alcohol-related behavior is to some extent an expression of personality tendencies which are exhibited before drinking patterns have become established" (p. 61). Interestingly, this study indicated that both problem drinkers and nondrinkers had personalities characterized by inadequate coping devices. Other attributes determined the behavioral response in terms of use of alcohol. Heavy drinkers, moderate drinkers, and light drinkers showed certain constellations of specific personality traits, which were also to a limited degree characteristic of each category. The importance of being able to identify populations at risk, if such predictability is confirmed by further work, would probably justify the high cost in time and money that such long-term longitudinal studies involve.

Epidemiological studies have shown that in general, more women than men are treated for psychiatric illness, including both neuroses and psychoses (Gove and Tudor, 1973). [The opposite ratio applies to such behavior deviations as alcoholism, drug dependency and delinquency (Gomberg, 1974).] It is therefore not surprising that there appears to be more concomitant psychiatric illness among female alcoholics than among males, although unfortunately, few of the studies that so report are adequately controlled. There is a higher incidence of depression and suicide attempts (Van Amberg, 1943; Kinsey, 1966; Wood and Duffy, 1966; Winokur and Clayton, 1968; Winokur et al., 1970, 1971; Sclare, 1970; Rimmer et al., 1971; Rathod and Thomson, 1971) and of anxiety and neuroticism (Zelen et al., 1966; Belfer et al., 1971; Parker, 1972) among alcoholic women than among alcoholic men. Belfer et al. (1971) also found that female alcoholics are significantly more anxious and depressed than nonalcoholic women, which is hardly surprising. Glatt (1961b), however, found no significant difference in rates of suicide attempts between male alcoholics and female alcoholics.

Hoffmann and Wefring (1972) studied a large number of male and female chronic alcoholics in hospital, using the Brief Psychiatric Rating Scale. Female alcoholics scored significantly higher than males in anxiety, guilt feelings, tension, depressed mood, hostility, and neuroticism, but lower on blunted affect and lack of improvement. There was no difference in scores on 20 other factors. Bromet and Moos (1976) raised the possibility that reports of sex differences in these categories may be related to differences between married female alcoholics and married male alcoholics in the presence of current anxiety or a sense of well-being. Married alcoholics of both sexes had better scores on these variables than the unmarried (including separated, divorced, and widowed). However, the married men reported less depression and more self-confidence than the married women (or than the unmarried alcoholics of either sex).

How do alcoholic women see themselves compared to nonalcoholic women? In a well-controlled study of 200 female subjects, one-half of whom were alcoholics, McLachlan et al. (1979) used a social competence scale to measure the degree of difference. The alcoholic women saw themselves as less effective in goal achievement and less socially competent. They were more dissatisfied about their purpose in life and less worthy as "citizens." An anxiety scale revealed more overt and covert anxiety than in the controls.

Alcoholism is frequently referred to as a form of "chronic suicide," the view being that alcoholics are consciously or otherwise drinking themselves to death. While this interpretation is occasionally warranted in thoroughly studied individual cases, there is insufficient evidence to justify application to the majority of heavy drinkers. In a careful in-depth study of women who have attempted suicide, Maris (1971) came to a quite different—in fact, opposite—conclusion. In a word, this view is that most suicide attempts, sometimes dubbed *parasuicides,* are in fact meant to be self-preservative rather than self-destructive. To oversimplify the complex psychopathology involved, the self-immolation represents a plea to society for acknowledgment, recognition, and release from stigmatization. It is not unreasonable to extrapolate this concept to what is usually considered the self-destructive nature of alcoholism. This is a consideration which should be of particular importance to therapists.

In terms of sex differences, the results of personality studies have been in conflict, perhaps related to the particular assessment scale that was being used. (For a good, brief summary of these results, see Beckman, 1975). Even if it can be shown that a supportable generalization can be made with reference to women alcoholics (for example, in the area of "internalization" versus "externalization"), there remains sufficient individual variation to justify careful assessment of each individual patient as a step toward the establishment of a therapeutic approach for that particular personality.

6. BASIC PSYCHOPATHOLOGY

A number of attempts have been made to identify the underlying psychopathology in female alcoholics. Investigations have been carried out on groups of subjects who varied widely in their social and clinical characteristics and in the treatment settings from which they were selected. Curran's (1937) patients were very ill and in a state hospital. Wood and Duffy (1966) studied "invisible" alcoholics from the upper middle class attending a private clinic. Kinsey (1968) personally interviewed patients who were actively involved in Alcoholics Anonymous. There is general agreement that all of these groups of women had developed "a deep sense of personal inadequacy and lack of preparation for adult roles" (Kinsey, 1968, p. 1466). This sense of inadequacy, in turn, was attributable to early family life experience, frequently in the form of identification with an alcoholic parent (usually the father) and an unloving mother to whom there was a strong, but highly ambivalent, attachment. A common feature was overdependence on one or both parents and failure to achieve a capacity for mature interdependent relationships.

On a phenomenological basis, this generalization receives support from the studies of Lolli (1953), Lisansky (1957), Zelen et al. (1966), and Jones (1971), to which reference has already been made. Blane (1968) stated,

> ... the central, perhaps inevitable, feature in women with alcoholic problems is a concern, even a preoccupation, about being inadequate and inept, surrounded by an aura of futility that bespeaks her utter helplessness to change herself. The profound conviction of her inadequacy is one aspect of this complex that is diamond-hard in its indestructibility. (p. 112)

This is an extreme statement, apparently based on observations of women who were depressed as well as alcoholic, and is unwarranted in its generalization.

However, the frequent presence of distorted self-concepts and poor self-esteem as contributing factors to the development and maintenance of alcoholic patterns of drinking has been convincingly demonstrated by several authors (Armstrong and Hoyt, 1963; Vanderpool, 1969; Berg, 1971). This is, of course, true for men as well as women.

The most popular theory with regard to the psychosocial etiology of alcoholism is that there is a close relationship between heavy drinking and the presence of unsatisfied dependency needs (McCord and McCord, 1962). The main evidence comes from the demonstration in male alcoholics of maternal deprivation and lack of oral gratification in childhood. The resultant frustration is repressed and appears in the form of pathological dependence on the contents of the bottle. On theoretical grounds, there is no reason to suppose that this may not be as true for women as for men, though traditionally it has been assumed that women accept a dependency relationship with less conflict, a notion that is now much less common as women's "liberation" is more widely accepted.

Alternative etiological factors have been suggested. McClelland et al. (1972) felt that the most important motivational factor in drinking by men is the satisfaction of power needs. These authors suggested that the assumed excess of personal power concerns in men as compared with women may be at least part of the reason that in almost all cultures men drink more than women. The tacit assumption here is that women also drink to develop more feelings of power. However, in Wilsnack's (1973b) studies of the psychological effects of social drinking on her female subjects, there was no indication that the consumption of moderate amounts of alcohol gratified dependency needs or increased feelings of power. On the other hand, feelings of "womanliness" were greatly enhanced, thus giving support to earlier suggestions that alcoholic women have major concerns in the area of feminine identification and sex-role confusion—not unexpected outcomes of the early life parental conflicts already noted. Wilsnack's findings suggest that one factor that predisposes women to alcoholism is "disturbed feminine identification" at an unconscious level—in brief, that alcohol is used to combat a prevailing sense of inadequacy as a woman by enhancing feelings of femininity. Heavy drinking leads to consequences that are regarded by society, her friends, and herself as "unwomanly," and thus a vicious cycle is established. This is a persuasive formulation that is quite consistent with Kinsey's (1966, 1968) earlier findings that alcohol is used by women alcoholics for "its ability to modify undesirable attributes of self" and enables the woman "to be the type of person she wants to be" (p. 1466).

The psychosexual development of women alcoholics has received a considerable amount of attention. A number of clinical accounts report a high incidence of heterosexual inadequacy, homosexuality, and frigidity (Karpman, 1948; Levine, 1955; Sherfey, 1955; Calef, 1967; Kuttner and Lorencz, 1970). However, the erstwhile notion that sexual promiscuity is characteristic of alcoholic women has been proved false by a number of studies (Levine, 1955; Glatt, 1961b; Wood and Duffy, 1966; Schuckit, 1972b). Many investigators (Curran, 1937; Wall, 1937; Lisansky, 1957; Rosenbaum, 1958; Kinsey, 1966; Curlee, 1967) have noted the presence of disturbed self-images and sex-role ambiguity in their subjects. In Curran's (1937) study of 65 women alcoholics who were psychotic, he noted that their hallucinations suggested a marked sense of inferiority in the sexual area. Most of the hallucinated threats involved damage to the woman's body, particularly her genitalia. Homosexual concerns, however, were less prominent than in the hallucinations of male alcoholics. Parker (1972) undertook a psychometric investigation comparing women who were alcoholic with those who were moderate drinkers. He found a positive relationship between the degree of deviant drinking and the woman's rejection of the perceived feminine sex role, intensity of emotional response, and neurotic behavior. Zucker (1968), on the other hand, found no difference in masculine and feminine sex-role identity, either overt or fantasized, in adolescent girls who drank and those who did not. This finding contrasted with the "hypermasculine façade" found in adolescent boys who were heavy drinkers. Zucker rightfully warned against facile interpretation of these data as applicable to older age groups. Several other studies (Berner and Solms, 1953; Blane, 1968; Mogar et al., 1970; Wilsnack, 1973a), in addition to some of those already mentioned, have strongly suggested that psychosexual concerns may play a major role in the production of emotional tension that becomes so intolerable that relief is sought in the excessive use of alcohol.

The main criticism that can be leveled at many of these investigations is that the actual findings hardly justify the author's interpretations. The relevant literature is replete with expressions such as "masculine identification" or "inadequate feminine identity," which, though impressive, lack common understanding or definition. However defined, when these characteristics are not demonstrable at a conscious level, it is not difficult to adduce their "existence" at levels that are variously described as "less conscious," "preconscious," or "subconscious." A further temptation to which it is easy to succumb is to ascribe uncritically a behavioral manifestation (the excessive use of alcohol) to the demonstrated presence of problems in the psychosexual area of the subjects' personalities. No studies known to this reviewer convincingly relate "sex-role confusion" to alcoholism *per se* as opposed to neuroticism, affective disturbances, or personality disorders. The reported data, when examined apart from the inferences drawn therefrom, suggest little difference between, for example, the sex-role preference of alcoholic women as a group and that of women who are not alcoholics (Kinsey, 1966; Belfer et al., 1971; Parker, 1972; Wilsnack, 1973a; Gomberg, 1974). Each individual case requires careful study to determine whether the heavy drinking is a response to anxiety arising from intrapersonal conflicts. It would be reasonable to suspect that in some individual women, the conflict arises, to greater or lesser degree, from psychosexual ambivalence. Much time and skill would be required to make such a psychodynamic formulation, and still more to develop a practical therapeutic plan.

The literature contains some interesting controversy surrounding the "greater pathology" concept. Karpman (1948) states flatly that "alcoholic women are much more abnormal than alcoholic men," and explains this assertion on the basis of the repression to which women are subject and the difficulties that they encounter in seeking a conflictual resolution that is "within the limits of conventional social acceptance of their sex."

As part of a larger study on female alcoholism, Johnson (1965) interviewed 40% (randomly selected) of the physicians in an urban community to ascertain their views on alcoholism generally, and particularly on alcoholism in women. Two-thirds of the physicians felt that women alcoholics behaved differently from men alcoholics. One difference was where they drank (at home), and another was their sensitivity about acknowledging their illness to others. The physicians also felt that their women alcoholic patients were "sicker" in that they manifested more personality disorders and tended to drink in response to crisis situations. (This latter impression was denied by a sample of the women alcoholics, who stated that they drank in order to gain more confidence in coping with their everyday problems.)

There has been a brisk and largely antipathetic reaction to the suggestion that women show greater psychopathology. Kinsey (1966) challenged the proponents of this view on grounds of lack of convincing and supportable evidence. It is becoming increasingly clear that the clinical experience that gave rise to the greater pathology concept was related to a combination of the "double standard" of expectations for the behavior of women compared with men, along with the fact that only the most disturbed female alcoholics emerge for treatment, undoubtedly because of the greater stigma that society attaches to women who are problem drinkers or even drink alcohol at all. Discussion of this controversial topic in the literature suggests a considerable degree of confusion as to what is to be included under the term *pathology*. Many of the phenomena correspond to "signs and symptoms" in the medical sense and, as such, are manifestations of the underlying condition rather than causal factors. In this sense, they may be considered secondary pathology in that they may play an important role in the maintenance of the vicious cycle of psychological tension and drinking that is characteristic of alcoholic behavior and response.

Apart altogether from the search for etiological factors in female alcoholism *per se* is the approach of those investigators (Johnson et al., 1966; Pemberton, 1967; Wilsnack, 1973b,c; Bedell, 1974; Johnson, 1974) who have simply asked women of various social strata when and why they drink. Responses included: to gain social acceptance, to escape tension, to relieve loneliness, and to overcome feelings of inferiority.

Beckman (1975) reasonably contended that:

> . . . considering the heterogeneity in characteristics of women alcoholics, it is possible that no general theory of alcoholism in women is viable. However, no such conclusion can be reached until theories developed about the origin of alcoholism in women have been tested. (p. 804)

And to that a hearty Amen from this reviewer.

7. RELATIONSHIP TO AFFECTIVE ILLNESS

Winokur and Pitts (1965) were among the first of several authors to relate alcoholism in women to affective illness, both in the patients themselves and in their relatives, particularly women relatives (Pitts and Winokur, 1966; Winokur and Clayton, 1968). These authors have shown that many more women alcoholics than men have concomitant depression or a history of affective illness and also report a significantly higher occurrence of suicidal thoughts and delusions. The female alcoholics have more psychiatrically ill parents and second-degree relatives than their male counterparts, especially in the area of affective disorders. This evidence strongly suggests that a number of alcoholics, particularly female, should be seen as having affective disorders as their primary diagnoses.

This theme was further developed by Schuckit et al. (1969) in a careful study of 70 female alcoholics. Of this number, just over one-half (39) were considered "primary" alcoholics, in that the alcoholism occurred in the absence of other concurrent psychiatric illness. Of the remainder, the majority (19) gave a history of affective disorder antedating the development of alcoholism. A smaller number (12) fell into a variety of other psychiatric diagnoses. It was noted that primary alcoholics were somewhat older and had been alcoholic much longer than those with alcoholism secondary to affective disorder. The latter gave a history of many more suicidal attempts (though it is to be noted that women generally have a higher suicide rate than men). The age of onset for alcoholism was the same. Though the rate of psychiatric illness (including alcoholism) in close relatives of the two groups was equal, there was an interesting and important difference in the type of disturbance suffered by the ill first-degree relatives: the male relatives of both groups tended to be alcoholic; the female relatives tended to have the same psychiatric diagnosis as the subjects—alcoholism in the case of the primary alcoholics and affective disturbance in the case of the primary affective disorders. Belfer et al. (1971) found that half of the alcoholic women they studied had had a prior diagnosis of depressive reaction.

Amark (1951) had already found that psychogenic psychoses were more likely to occur in the relatives of alcoholics generally than in the general population and that of these psychogenic illnesses, depression was the most common. Woodruff et al. (1973) studied demographic and personal history data on a group of male and female alcoholics with depression, alcoholics without depression, and patients with unipolar depression without alcoholism. Comparisons among the groupings revealed that in many ways alcoholics with depression resembled alcoholics without depression more than they resembled depressed patients who were not alcoholics. Of interest here was a coincidental finding that 37% of the male alcoholics and 22% of the female alcoholics, with or without depression, also received a diagnosis of sociopathy.

Comparing male and female alcoholics on a similar parameter, Winokur et al. (1970, 1971) found again that females were significantly more likely to have a diagnosis of primary affective disorder than males, for whom sociopathy was more likely to be diagnosed. Schuckit et al. (1969) compared sociopathic alcoholism to primary alcoholism. The former was found in 8% of female alcoholics and in 25% of the men, reversing the sex distribution of affective disorder alcoholics. In general, sociopathic alcoholics had an earlier age of onset and were younger when first treated. There was a history of more antisocial behavior, more marital problems, and more personality disorders than in primary alcoholics, and the prognosis was more guarded.

These authors have also listed the features that characterize affective disorder alcoholics as compared with primary alcoholics. The former had a history of depressive episodes before they became problem drinkers. Alcoholism began at a later age, but treatment was instituted somewhat earlier and the prognosis was considerably better. The incidence of medical complications was lower but that of suicide attempts higher than for primary alcoholics. Affective disorder alcoholics constituted 25% of the female alcoholics but only 4% of the males (Schuckit et al., 1969; Winokur et al., 1970; Schuckit, 1973).

8.   PERSPECTIVE

The nature of alcoholism has been, and still is, a matter for vigorous debate. The effort to conceptualize alcoholism as an illness had its first great proponent in the person of Dr. E. M. Jellinek. Support came from a considerable number of other physicians and gave rise to the "medical model." Research and clinical studies, some of which have been reported above, were devoted to the "etiology of the illness." However, the more closely investigators looked at the phenomena characterizing the development of alcoholism, in women as well as in men, the more apparent it became that the medical model was appropriate mainly for some of the physical and psychiatric complications. The literature strongly suggests that problem drinking is more of a behavior disturbance, with a wide variety of causes, manifestations and outcomes, the only common factor being the excessive imbibition of alcohol. It seems unlikely, therefore, that research into the nature and development of the problem will lead to a breakthrough or to a "mystery revealed" such as may well happen in, for example, cancer.

Does this mean that from now on we should stop doing careful systematic studies of how and why women and men drink to excess and confine ourselves to anecdotal and descriptive accounts with individual application only? The answer is surely in the negative. Systematic study following scientific principles still has an important role in the furtherance of the body of knowledge we require if we are to develop more effective and efficient programs of both prevention and "treatment." For example, we need to know much more about the reasons, complex though they may be, for "normal" social drinking, an area of study that has been largely ignored. Then we need to find out what "goes wrong" in those persons, especially women for purposes of the focus of this volume, for whom the harm resulting from alcohol use begins to outweigh the benefits. May this happen as a masked manifestation of subclinical depression? What about the possible presence of an X-linked recessive gene? Shall we be able to predict from early life experience who is going to be particularly vulnerable? If alcohol abuse is a vocational hazard for men in certain occupations, how may we prevent producing the same proportion of victims among women as they enter the same work world? In short, we must bring to bear on the problem the developing insights of sociology, psychology, physiology, and even anthropology, ethnology, and genetics to test the few theories that have so far been propounded concerning the origin of alcoholism in women.

Were it not for the stupendous cost, longitudinal investigation would be an important part of the answer to the need for predictability. More practical would be careful prospective or even retrospective studies of successful intervention. Why did a certain therapeutic approach work for this woman but not for that? Is there a typology that would be of more value than simply for classificatory and statistical purposes? Would it be wise to consider alcohology a specialty and female alcohology a subspecialty, with all that this division would imply in terms of professionalism and possible elitism?

These are among the ponderings that engage the mind of the reader as the available literature is perused. Although in the studies reported to date, more questions have been raised than answered, much has been learned "about" as well as about "how to and how not to," and given a reasonable balance between empiricism and theory development, the prospects for ongoing progress are encouraging.

REFERENCES*

Amark, C. A., 1951, A study in alcoholism. Clinical, social–psychiatric and genetic investigations, *Acta Psychiatr. Neurol. Scan. Suppl.* **70:**1–283.

Anonymous, 1944, The moral, mental and physical background of female inebriates, *Br. J. Inebriety* **42:**3–20.

Anonymous, 1962, Hur Bekampa Det Kvinnliga Alkoholmissbrudet? (How to combat alcohol misuse in women?), *Soc. Meddel.* 379–381, 408.

Anonymous, 1970, Besorgniserregende Zunahme des Frauenalkoholismus. (Alarming increase of alcoholism among women), *Ther. Ggw.* **109:**130–131.

Anonymous, 1973, Alcoholism in women, *J. Am. Med. Assoc.* **225:**988.

Anonymous, 1974, Alcoholism and women, *Alcohol Health. Res. World* (Summer), 2–7.

Anonymous, 1975, (Questions and Answers). Libido of female alcoholics, *Med. Aspects Hum. Sex.* **9,**99.

Anonymous, 1976, Women alcoholics in New Jersey, *Alcohol Tech. Rep.* **5:**64–69.

Anonymous, 1977, Causes of female alcoholism, *Intellect* **105:**213.

Anonymous, 1977, Sexes equal in alcohol, drug use, *Science News* **111:**277–278.

Anonymous, 1977, Women don't inherit alcoholism, *Med. World News* **18:**34–35.

Argeriou, M., 1975, Daily alcohol consumption patterns in Boston: Some findings and a partial test of the Tuesday hypothesis, *J. Stud. Alcohol* **36:**1578–1583.

Argeriou, M., and Paulino, D., 1976, Women arrested for drunken driving in Boston: Social characteristics and circumstances of arrest, *J. Stud. Alcohol* **37:**648–658.

Armstrong, R. G., and Hoyt, D. B., 1963, Personality structure of male alcoholics as reflected in the IES test, *Q. J. Stud. Alcohol* **24:**239–248.

---

* The list of references contains a number of articles and books that are not referred to directly in the text but have been retained as they are all relevant to the subject of this chapter.

Bacon, M. F., 1965, Male pride and the alcoholic wife, *Md. State Med. J.* **14**:69–70.

Bahn, A. K., Anderson, C. L., and Norman, V. B., 1963, Outpatient psychiatric clinic services to alcoholics, 1959, *Q. J. Stud. Alcohol* **24**:213–226.

Bahr, H. M., and Garrett, G. R., 1971a, Drinking and homelessness, in: *Disaffiliation among Urban Women* (H. M. Bahr and G. R. Garrett, eds.), pp. 182–223, Columbia University Bureau of Applied Social Research, New York.

Bahr, H. M., and Garrett, G. R., 1971b, Drinking patterns of homeless women, in: *Disaffiliation among Urban Women* (H. M. Bahr and G. R. Garrett, eds.), pp. 261–308, Columbia University Bureau of Applied Social Research, New York.

Bahr, H. M., and Garrett, G. R., 1976, *Women Alone: The Disaffiliation of Urban Females,* D. C. Heath and Company, Toronto.

Bailey, M. B., Haberman, P. W., and Alksne, H., 1965, The epidemiology of alcoholism in an urban residential area. *Q. J. Stud. Alcohol.* **26**:19–40.

Bardwick, J. M., 1972, *Readings on the Psychology of Women,* Harper & Row, New York.

Basquin, M., and Osouf, C., 1965, Étude de 50 cas d'ethylisme feminin. Constatations sociologiques, cliniques et etiologiques. (A study of 50 female alcoholics, sociological, clinical and etiological observations.), *Rev. Alcool.* **11**:173–180.

Batchelor, I. R. C., 1954, Alcoholism and attempted suicide, *J. Ment. Sci.* **100**:451–461.

Bateman, N. I., and Petersen, D. M., 1971, Variables related to outcome of treatment for hospitalized alcoholics, *Int. J. Addict.* **6**:215–224.

Bateman, N. I., and Petersen, D. M., 1972, Factors related to outcome of treatment for hospitalized white male and female alcoholics, *J. Drug Issues* **2**:66–74.

Battegay, R., and Ladewig, D., 1970, Gruppentherapie und Gruppenarbeit mit Suechtigen Frauen. (Group therapy and work with addicted women.) *Br. J. Addict.* **65**:89–98.

Becker, D., and Kronus, S., 1977, Sex and drinking patterns: An old relationship revisited in a new way, *Social Problems* **24**:482–497.

Becker, W., 1971, Frauen-alkoholismus: Eine Gefahrdung Dieser Zeit. (Alcoholism in women: A contemporary hazard), *Ther. Ggw.* **110**:400–410.

Beckman, L. J., 1975, Women alcoholics: A review of social and psychological studies, *J. Stud. Alcohol* **36**:797–824.

Beckman, L. J., 1978, Self-esteem of women alcoholics, *J. Stud. Alcohol* **39**:491–498.

Bedell, J. W., 1974, The alcoholic housewife in the American culture, *Alcoholism Digest* **3**:4–8.

Belfer, M. L., Shader, R. I., Carroll, M., and Harmatz, J. S., 1971, Alcoholism in women, *Arch. Gen. Psychiatry* **25**:540–544.

Benincasa-Stagni, E., and Citterio, C., 1960, Psicogenesi e Sociogenesi Dell'Alcoolismo Femminile. (Psychogenesis and sociogenesis of alcoholism in women.), *Neuropsichiatria* **27**:331–412.

Berezin, F. C., and Roth, N. R., 1950, Some factors affecting the drinking practices of 383 college women in a coeducational institution, *Q. J. Stud. Alcohol* **11**:212–221.

Berg, N. L., 1971, Effects of alcohol intoxication on self-concept; Studies of alcoholics and controls in laboratory conditions, *Q. J. Stud. Alcohol* **32**:442–453.

Berner, P., and Solms, W., 1953, Alkoholismus bei Frauen. (Alcoholism in women.) *Wien. Z. Nervenheilkd Deren Grenzbeg.* **6**:275–301.

Birchmore, D. F., and Walderman, R. L., 1975, The woman alcoholic: A review. *Ont. Psychol.* **7**:10–16.

Blane, H. T., 1968, *The Personality of the Alcoholic,* Harper & Row, New York.

Bleuler, M., 1971, Alkoholismus mit verändertem Gesicht. (The changing face of alcoholism.), *Fürsorger* **39**:7–8.

Bochnik, H. J., Burchard, J., and Dieck, C., 1959, Alkoholmissbrauch bei Frauen:

Klinische Erfahrungen zwischen 1936 und 1957. (Alcohol misuse by women: Clinical experience between 1936 and 1957.), *Nervenarzt* **30**:433–442.

Borowitz, G. H., 1964, Some ego aspects of alcoholism, *Br. J. Med. Psychol.* **37**:257–263.

Bowker, L. H., 1977, Drug use among American women, old and young, R. & E. Research Assoc., San Francisco, 66 pp.

Brenner, B., 1967, Alcoholism and fatal accidents, *Q. J. Stud. Alcohol* **28**:517–528.

Bromet, E., and Moos, R., 1976, Sex and marital status in relation to the characteristics of alcoholics, *J. Stud. Alcohol* **37**:1302–1312.

Broverman, I. K., Broverman, D. M., Clarkson, F. E., Rosenkrantz, P. S., and Vogel, S. R., 1970, Sex-role stereotypes and clinical judgments of mental health. *J. Consult. Clin. Psychol.* **34**:1–7.

Brown, B. S., Kozel, N. J., Meyers, M. B., and Dupont, R. L., 1973, Use of alcohol by addict and nonaddict populations, *Am. J. Psychiatry* **130**:599–601.

Browne-Mayers, A. M., Seelye, E. E., and Sillman, L., 1976, Psychosocial study of hospitalized middle-class alcoholic women, *Ann. N.Y. Acad. Sci.* **273**:593–604.

Brunswick, A. F., and Tarica, C., 1974, Drinking and heatlh: A study of urban black adolescents, *Addict. Dis.* **1**:21–42.

Brusa, G., and Pittaluga, E., 1965, Indagine Sulla Personalita Nell'Alcoolismo Femminile. (Investigation of the personality in female alcoholics.), *Riv. Patol. Nerv. Ment.* **86**:513–530.

Burtle, V., Whitlock, D., and Franks, V., 1974, Modification of low self-esteem in women alcoholics: A behavior treatment approach, *Psychotherapy* **11**:36–40.

Burton, C. K., 1973, *Female Alcoholism*. Research Department, The Alcoholism Foundation of British Columbia, Vancouver, 18 pp.

Busch, H., Kormendy, E., and Feuerlein, W., 1973, Partners of female alcoholics, *Br. J. Addict.* **68**:179–184.

Cahalan, D., and Cisin, I. H., 1968, American drinking practices: Summary of findings from a national probability sample, I, Extent of drinking by population subgroups, *Q. J. Stud. Alcohol* **29**:130–151.

Cahalan, D., Cisin, I. H., and Crossley, H. M., 1969, American drinking practices; A national study of drinking behavior and attitudes, Rutgers Center of Alcohol Studies, Monogr. No. 6, New Brunswick, N.J.

Calef, V., 1967, Alcoholism and ornithophobia in women, *Psychoanal. Q.* **36**:584–587.

Calicchia, J. P., and Barresi, R. M., 1975, Alcoholism and alienation, *J. Clin. Psychol.* **31**:770–775.

Canter, F. M., 1970, Alcoholism, tension-increase and existence, *Psychotherapy* **7**:75–78.

Carlson, R., 1971, Sex differences in ego functioning: Exploratory studies of agency and communion, *J. Consult. Clin. Psychol.* **37**:267–277.

Chambers, C. D., and Griffey, M. S., 1975, Use of legal substances within the general population: The sex and age variables, *Addict. Dis.* **2**:7–19.

Chase, M., 1956, The homeless woman alcoholic, *Proc. 1st Inst. Skid-Row Alc.,* pp. 75–82.

Chesler, P. B., 1973, A word about mental health and women, *Ment. Hyg.* **57**:5–7.

Child, I. L., Barry, H., III, and Bacon, M. K., 1965, A cross-cultural study of drinking, III, Sex differences, *Q. J. Stud. Alcohol Suppl.* **3**:49–61.

Christenson, S. J., and Swanson, A. Q., 1974, Women and drug use: An annotated bibliography, *J. Psychedelic Drugs* **6**:371–414.

Ciotola, P. V., and Peterson, J. F., 1976, Personality characteristics of alcoholics and drug addicts in a merged treatment program, *J. Stud. Alcohol* **37**:1229–1235.

Clarke, S. K., 1974, Self-esteem in men and women alcoholics, *Q. J. Stud. Alcohol* **35**:1380–1381.

Cloninger, C. R., and Guze, S. B., 1970, Female criminals: Their personal, familial, and social backgrounds. The relation of these to the diagnosis of sociopathy and hysteria, *Arch. Gen. Psychiatry* **23**:554–558.

Committee on Labor and Public Welfare, U.S. Senate 1976, Hearing before the Subcommittee on Alcoholism and Narcotics, Alcohol Abuse among Women: Special Problems and Unmet Needs, a selective annotated bibliography.

Cook, S., and Gregory, D., 1975, Description of services provided for women at alcoholism treatment facilities in the state of Oklahoma for fiscal year 1974, *Alcohol Tech. Rep.* **4**:10–11.

Cooke, G., Wehmer, G., and Gruber J., 1975, Training paraprofessionals in the treatment of alcoholism: Effects on knowledge, attitudes and therapeutic techniques, *J. Stud. Alcohol* **36**:938–948.

Cooperstock, R., 1971, Sex differences in the use of mood-modifying drugs: An explanatory model, *J. Health Soc. Behav.* **12**:238–244.

Cooperstock, R., 1978, Sex differences in psychotropic drug use, *Soc. Sci. Med.* **12**(3b):179–186.

Cooperstock, R., 1979, A review of women's psychotropic drug use, *Can. J. Psychiatry* **24**:29–34.

Corrigan, E. M., 1974, Women and problem drinking: Notes on beliefs and facts, *Addict. Dis.* **1**:215–222.

Cox, D. F., and Bauer, R. A., 1964, Self-confidence and persuasibility in women, *Publ. Opin. Q.* **28**:463–466.

Cramer, M. J., and Blacker, E., 1963, "Early" and "late" problem drinkers among female prisoners, *J. Health Hum Behav.* **4**:282–290.

Cramer, M. J., and Blacker, E., 1966, Social class and drinking experience of female drunkenness offenders, *J. Health Hum Behav.* **7**:276–283.

Craddick, R. A., Leipold, V., and Leipold, W. D., 1976, Effect of role empathy on human figures drawn by women alcoholics, *J. Stud. Alcohol* **37**:90–97.

Cullen, K. J., and Woodings, T., 1975, Alcohol, tobacco and analgesics—Busselton, 1972, *Med. J. Aust.* **2**:211–214.

Curlee, J., 1967, Alcoholic women: Some considerations for further research, *Bull. Menninger Clin.* **31**:154–163.

Curlee, J., 1968, Women alcoholics, *Fed. Probat.* **32**:16–20.

Curlee, J., 1969, Alcoholism and the "empty nest," *Bull. Menninger Clin.* **33**:165–171.

Curlee, J., 1970, A comparison of male and female patients at an alcoholism treatment center, *J. Psychol.* **74**:239–247.

Curlee, J., 1971, Sex differences in patient attitudes toward alcoholism treatment, *Q. J. Stud. Alcohol* **32**:643–650.

Curran, F. J., 1937, Personality studies in alcoholic women, *J. Nerv. Ment. Dis.* **86**:645–667.

Cuskey, W. R., Premkumar, T., and Edington, B., 1973, Female drug abuse—The third dimension, *Publ. Health Rev.* **2**:341–352.

Dahlgren, L., 1971, Alkoholism hos Kvinnor. (Alcoholism in Women.) *Lakartidningen* **63**:3485–3492.

Davis, H. G., 1966, Variables associated with recovery in male and female alcoholics following hospitalization, Ph.D. dissertation, Texas Technological College.

de Lint, J. E. E., 1964, Alcoholism, birth rank and parental deprivation, *Am. J. Psychiatr.* **120**:1062–1065.

Demone, H. W., Jr., 1963, Experiments in referral to alcoholism clinics, *Q. J. Stud. Alcohol* **24**:495–502.

Der Heydt, H., 1962, Frauenalkoholismus—Eine soziale Gefahr? Hinweise auf mögliche Gründe. (Alcoholism among women—A social danger? Suggestions as to possible causes.), *Sozialistische Arbeitswissenschaft* **11**:68–72.

Deshaies, G., 1963, L'alcoolisme de la femme. (Alcoholism in women.) *Rev. Alcool.* **9**:235–247.

Deshaies, G., 1965, Aspects psychiques de l'alcoolisme chez la femme. (Psychological aspects of alcoholism in women.) *Vie Med.* **46**:1739–1747.

Dion, K. L., 1975, Women's reactions to discrimination from members of the same or opposite sex, *J. Res. Pers.* **9**:294.

Dollard, J., 1945, Drinking mores of the social classes, in: *Alcohol, Science and Society.* Quarterly Journal of Studies on Alcohol, Inc., New Haven, pp. 94–101.

Dowsling, J., and MacLennan, A., eds., 1978, *The chemically dependent woman. Rx: Recognition, referral, rehabilitation.* Addiction Research Foundation, Toronto.

Driscoll, G. Z., and Barr, H. L., 1972, Comparative study of drug dependent and alcoholic women, in: *Alcohol and Drug Problems Association of North America, Selected Papers of the Twenty Third Annual Meeting.* Washington, D.C., Alcohol and Drug Problems Association of North America, pp. 9–20.

Durand, D. E., 1975, Effects of drinking on the power and affiliation needs of middle-aged females, *J. Clin. Psychol.* **31**:549–553.

Edwards, G., Hensman, C., and Peto, J., 1972, Drinking in a London suburb, III, Comparisons of drinking troubles among men and women. *Q. J. Stud. Alcohol Suppl.* **6**:120–128.

Edwards, G., Hensman, C., and Peto, J., 1973, A comparison of female and male motivation for drinking, *Int. J. Addict.* **8**:577–587.

Efron, V., Keller, M., and Gurioli, C., 1974, *Statistics on Consumption of Alcohol and on Alcoholism,* Rutgers Center of Alcohol Studies, New Brunswick, N.J.

Epps, P., 1957, Women in prison on "attempted suicide" charges, *Lancet* **2**:182–184.

Favreau, O., 1975, Research on sex differences in behaviour; Some reinterpretations, *McGill J. Educ.* **10**(1):20–32.

Fillmore, K. M., 1970, *Abstinence, drinking and problem drinking among adolescents as related to apparent parental drinking practices*, M.A. thesis, University of Massachusetts.

Fillmore, K. M., 1975, Relationships between specific drinking problems in early adulthood and middle age; An exploratory 20-year follow-up study, *J. Stud. Alcohol* **36**:882–907.

Fleming, M., 1974, Hostility in recovering alcoholic women compared to non-alcoholic women, and the effect of psychodrama on the former in reducing hostility, Ph.D. dissertation, United States International University.

Follin, S., and Pivet, S., 1956, Quelques aspects particuliers de l'alcoolisme féminin. (Some special aspects of alcoholism in women.) *Rev. Neurol.* **94**:646–649.

Forslund, M. A., and Gustafson, T. J., 1970, Influence of peers and parents and sex differences in drinking by high-school students, *Q. J. Stud. Alcohol* **31**:868–875.

Fort, T. F., 1949, *A Preliminary Study of Social Factors in the Alcoholism of Women,* Texas Christian University thesis.

Fort, T., and Porterfield, A. L., 1961, Some backgrounds and types of alcoholism among women, *J. Health Hum Behav.* **2**:283–292.

Franck, K., and Rosen, E., 1949, A projective test of masculinity–femininity, *J. Consult. Clin. Psychol.* **13**:247–256.

Fraser, J., 1973, The female alcoholic, *Addictions* **20**:64–80.

Frezza, U., and Zantoni, G., 1972, Incidenza dei deliri di gelosia in soggetti di sesso femminile affetti da alcoolismo cronico. (Incidence of jealous delirium in female alcoholics.) *Alcoholism* **8**:101–106.

Gallant, D. M., Rich, A., Bey, E., and Terranova, L., 1970, Group psychotherapy with married couples: A successful technique in New Orleans alcoholism clinic patients, *J. La. State Med. Soc.* **122**:41–44.

Garai, J. E., 1970a, Sex differences in breakdown of mental health, *Genet. Psychol. Monogr.* **81**:131–132.

Garai, J. E., 1970b, Sex differences in identity and intimacy, *Genet. Psychol. Monogr.* **81**:133–134.

Garrett, G. R., 1970, *Problem Drinking among Women: A Research Review.* Columbia University, Bureau of Applied Social Research, New York.

Garrett, G. R., 1971, *Drinking behavior of homeless women.* Ph.D. dissertation, Washington State University.

Garrett, G. R., and Bahr, H. M., 1973a, Homeless women, in: *Skid Row: An Introduction to Disaffiliation* (H. M. Bahr, ed.), Oxford University Press, New York, pp. 152–197.

Garrett, G. R., and Bahr, H. M., 1973b, Women on skid row, *Q. J. Stud. Alcohol* **34**:1228–1243.

Garrett, G. R., and Bahr, H. M., 1974, Comparison of self-rating and quantity–frequency measures of drinking, *Q. J. Stud. Alcohol* **35**:1294–1306.

George, A., 1976, *Occupational Health Hazards to Women: A Synoptic View.* Advisory Council on the Status of Women, Ottawa, p. 128.

Gillies, H., 1976, Homicide in the west of Scotland, *Br. J. Psychiatry* **128**:105–127.

Glassco, K., 1975, Drinking habits of seniors in a southern university, *J. Alcohol Drug Educ.* **21**:25–29.

Glatt, M. M., 1957, Women in prison on "attempted suicide" charges, *Lancet* **2**:387–388.

Glatt, M. M., 1961a, Drinking habits of English (middle class) alcoholics, *Acta Psychiatr. Scand.* **37**:88–113.

Glatt, M. M., 1961b, Treatment results in an English mental hospital alcoholic unit, *Acta Psychiatr. Scand.* **37**:143–168.

Gleser, G. C., and Sacks, M., 1973, Ego defenses and reaction to stress; A validation study of the defense mechanism inventory, *J. Consult. Clin. Psychol.* **40**:181–187.

Gomberg, E. S., 1974, Women and alcoholism, in: *Women in Therapy: New Psychotherapies for a Changing Society* (V. Franks and V. Burtle, eds.), Brunne/Mazel, New York, pp. 169–190.

Gomberg, E. S., 1976, Alcoholism in women, in: *The Biology of Alcoholism,* Vol. 4, *Social Aspects of Alcoholism* (B, Kissin and H. Begleiter, eds.), Plenum, New York, pp. 117–166.

Gove, W. R., and Tudor, J. F., 1973, Adult sex roles and mental illness, *Am. J. Sociol.* **78**:812–835.

Greenblatt, M., and Schuckit, M. A., 1976, *Alcoholism Problems in Women and Children.* Grune & Stratton, New York.

Gundel, K., 1972, *Vergleich der Soziogenese des weiblichen und männlichen Alkoholismus anhand einer Sekundaranalyse klinischer Daten.* (Comparison of the sociogenesis of women and men alcoholics based on a secondary analysis of clinical data.) Ph.D. dissertation, Ludwig-Maximilians-Universität, Munchen, p. 243.

Gustafson, K., 1974, Den nya kvinnan—Dricker hon som en karl? (The new woman—does she drink like a man?) *Alkohol och Narkotika* **68**:22–27.

Haberman, P. W., 1970, Denial of drinking in a household survey, *Q. J. Stud. Alcohol* **31**:710–717.

Haberman, P. W., and Sheinberg, J., 1967, Implicative drinking reported in a household survey: A corroborative note on subgroup differences, *Q. J. Stud. Alcohol* **28**:538–543.

Hanson, D. J., 1974, Drinking attitudes and behaviors among college students. *J. Alcohol Drug Educ.* **19**:6–14.

Hart, L., 1974, Attitudes among a group of female alcoholics towards alcoholism, *Br. J. Addict.* **69**:311–314.

Hatcher, E. M., Jones, M. K., and Jones, B. M., 1977, Cognitive deficits in alcoholic women, *Alcoholism: Clin. Exper. Res.* **1**:371–377.

Hausmann, C., Albert, R., and Kayser, H., 1968, Suizidversuch: Psychiatrische Untersuchung bei 820 Frauen. (Suicide attempt: Psychiatric study of 820 women.) *Dtsch. Med. Wochenschr.* **93**:1883–1887.

Hecht, C. A., Grine, R. J., and Rothrock, S. E., 1948, The drinking and dating habits of 336 college women in a coeducational institution, *Q. J. Stud. Alcohol* **9**:252–258.

Helson, R., 1972, The changing image of the career women, *J. Soc. Issues* **28**:33–46.

Hemmi, T., and Yabuki, Y., 1964 (On female drug and alcohol addicts.), *Acta Criminol. Med. Leg. Jap.* **30**:13.

Herjanic, M., Henn, F. A., and Vanderpearl, R. H., 1977, Forensic psychiatry: Female offenders, *Am. J. Psychiatry* **134**:556–558.

Hewitt, C. C., 1943, A personality study of alcoholic addiction, *Q. J. Stud. Alcohol* **4**:368–386.

Hilgard, J. R., and Newman, M. F., 1963, Parental loss by death in childhood as an etiological factor among schizophrenic and alcoholic patients compared with a nonpatient community sample, *J. Nerv. Ment. Dis.* **137**:14–28.

Hirsh, J., 1962, Women and alcoholism, in: *Problems in Addiction: Alcoholism and Narcotics* (W. C. Bier, ed.), Fordham University Press, New York, pp. 108–115.

Hoffmann, H., and Bonyuge, E. R., 1977, Personalities of female alcoholics who became counselors, *Psychol. Rep.* **41**:37–38.

Hoffmann, H., and Jackson, D. M., 1974, Differential personality inventory for male and female alcoholics, *Psychol. Rep.* **34**:21–22.

Hoffmann, H., and Noem, A. A., 1975a, Sex differences in a state hospital population of alcoholics on admission and treatment variables, *Psychol. Rep.* **37**:145–146.

Hoffmann, H., and Noem, A. A., 1975b, Social background variables, referral sources and life events of male and female alcoholics, *Psychol. Rep.* **37**:1087–1092.

Hoffmann, H., and Wefring, L. R., 1972, Sex and age differences in psychiatric symptoms of alcoholics, *Psychol. Rep.* **30**:887–889.

Homiller, J. D., 1977, *Women and Alcohol: A Guide for State and Local Decision Makers,* Alcohol and Drug Problems Association of North America, Washington.

Horn, J. L., and Wanberg, K. W., 1973, Females are different: On the diagnosis of alcoholism in women, *Proc. 1st Annual Alcoholism Conference NIAAA,* 332–352.

Horton, D., 1943, The function of alcohol in primitive societies: A cross-cultural study, *Q. J. Stud. Alcohol* **4**:199–320.

Howell, M. C., 1974, What medical schools teach about women, *N. Engl. J. Med.* **291**:304–307.

Huba, G. J., Segal, B., and Singer, J. L., 1977a, Consistency of day dreaming styles across samples of college male and female drug and alcohol users, *J. Abnorm. Psychol.* **86**:99–102.

Huba, G. J., Segal, B., and Singer, J. L., 1977b, Organization of needs in male and female drug and alcohol users, *J. Consult. Clin. Psychol.* **45**:34–44.

Humphrey, J. A., French, L., Niswander, G. D., and Casey, T. M., 1974, The process of suicide: The sequence of disruptive events in the lives of suicide victims, *Dis. Nerv. Syst.* **35**:275–277.

Jacob, A. G., and Lavoie, C., 1971, A study of some of the characteristics of a group of women alcoholics, in: *Selected Papers Presented at the General Sessions Twenty-Second Annual Meeting, Sept. 12–17, Hartford, Conn.* (R. Brock, ed.), The Alcohol and Drug Problems Association of America, Washington, pp. 25–32.

Jacobson, G. R., 1976, Field dependence among male and female alcoholics, II, Norms for the rod-and-frame test, *Percept. Mot. Skills* **43**:399–402.

James, I. P., Scott-Orr, D. N., and Curnow, D. H., 1963, Blood alcohol levels following attempted suicide, *Q. J. Stud. Alcohol* **24**:14–22.

James, J. E., 1975, Symptoms of alcoholism in women: A preliminary survey of A.A. members, *J. Stud. Alcohol* **36**:1564–1569.

James, J. E., and Goldman, M., 1971, Behavior trends of wives of alcoholics, *Q. J. Stud. Alcohol* **32**:373–381.

Jansen, D. G., 1974, Use of the personal orientation inventory with state hospital alcoholics, *J. Clin. Psychol.* **30**:310–311.

Jansen, D. G., and Hoffmann, H., 1973, Demographic and MMPI characteristics of male and female state hospital alcoholic patients, *Psychol. Rep.* **33**:561–562.

Jellinek, E. M., 1947, *Recent Trends in Alcoholism and Alcohol Consumption,* Hillhouse Press, New Haven.

Jessor, R., Carman, R. S., and Grossman, P. H., 1968, Expectations of need satisfaction and drinking patterns of college students, *Q. J. Stud. Alcohol* **29**:101–116.

Johnson, C. F., 1974, Does maternal alcoholism affect offspring? *Clin. Pediatr.* **13**:633–634.

Johnson, M. W., 1965, Physicians' views on alcoholism with special reference to alcoholism in women, *Nebr. Med. J.* **50**:378–384.

Johnson, M. W., De Vries, J. C., and Houghton, M. I., 1966, The female alcoholic, *Nurs. Res.* **15**:343–347.

Jones, B. M., 1975, Alcohol and women: Intoxication levels and memory impairment as related to the menstrual cycle, *Alcohol Tech. Rep.* **4**:4–10.

Jones, B. M., and Jones, M. K., 1976a, Alcohol effects in women during the menstrual cycle, *Ann. N.Y. Acad. Sci.* **273**:576–587.

Jones, B. M., and Jones, M. K., 1976b, Male and female intoxication levels for three alcohol doses or do women really get higher than men? *Alcohol Tech. Rep.* **5**:11–14.

Jones, M. C., 1971, Personality antecedents and correlates of drinking patterns in women, *J. Consult. Clin. Psychol.* **36**:61–69.

Jung, J., 1977, Drinking motives and behavior in social drinkers, *J. Stud. Alcohol* **38**:944–952.

Karp, S. A., Poster, D. C., and Goodman, A., 1963, Differentiation in alcoholic women, *J. Pers.* **31**:386–393.

Karpman, B., 1948, *The Alcoholic Woman,* Linacre Press, Washington.

Kastler-Maitron, and Burckard, E., 1955, Quelques considérations sur l'alcoolisme chronique chez la femme. (Some considerations on chronic alcoholism in women.), *Cah. Psychiatr.* **10**:31–44.

Kattan, L., Horwitz, J., Caballero, E., Cordua, M., and Marambio, C., 1973a, Caracteristicas del alcoholismo en la mujer y evaluación del resultado de su tratamiento en Chile. (Characteristics of alcoholism in women and evaluation of its treatment in Chile.), *Acta Psiquiat. Psicol. Am. Lat.* **19**:194–204.

Kattan, L., Horwitz, J., Caballero, E., Cordua, M., and Marambio, C., 1973b, Evaluación de los resultados del tratamiento del alcoholismo en la mujer: Indicadores de valor pronóstico. (Evaluation of results of alcoholism treatment in women: indicators of prognostic value.), *Acta Psiquiat. Psicol. Am. Lat.* **19**:265–279.

Kesselman, J. R., 1976, Female alcoholics, *New Dawn* **1**:68–71.

Keyserlingk, H., 1962, Ueber den Alkoholismus bei Frauen. (On alcoholism in women.) *Psychiat. Neurol. Med. Psychol.* **14**:268–272.

Kielholz, P., 1970, Alcohol and depression, *Br. J. Addict.* **65**:187–193.

Kinsey, B. A., 1966, *The Female Alcoholic: A Social Psychological Study,* Charles C Thomas, Springfield, Ill.

Kinsey, B. A., 1968, Psychological factors in alcoholic women from a state hospital sample, *Am. J. Psychiatry* **124**:1463–1466.

Klatsky, A. L., Friedman, G. D., Siegelaub, A. B., and Gerard, M. J., 1977, Alcohol consumption among white, black, or oriental men and women: Kaiser-Permanente Multiphasic Health Examination data. *Am. J. Epidemiol.* **105**:311–323.

Kneist, W., and Petermann, A., 1964, Rauch- und Trinkgewohnheiten 14-bis 18 jähriger Wungen und Mädchen. (Smoking and drinking habits of 14- to 18-year-old boys and girls.), *Z. Gesamte Hyg.* **10**:737:748.

Knupfer, G., 1964, Female drinking patterns, Paper presented at the Fifteenth Annual Meeting of the North American Association of Alcoholism Programs, Washington, D.C., September 1964.

Kuller, L., Lilienfeld, A., and Fisher, R., 1966, Sudden and unexpected deaths in young adults: An epidemiological study, *J. Am. Med. Assoc.* **198**:248–252.

Kuttner, R. E., and Lorencz, A. B., 1970, Promiscuity and Prostitution in urbanized Indian communities, *Ment. Hyg.* **54**:79–91.

Lawrence, J. J., and Maxwell, M. A., 1962, Drinking and socioeconomic status, in: *Society, Culture, and Drinking Patterns* (D. J. Pittman and C. R. Snyder, eds.), Wiley, New York, pp. 141–145.

Lecoq, R., and Fronquet, P., 1955, À propos de l'alcoolisme féminin. (Concerning alcoholism among women.), *Gaz. Hôp. Civ. Mil.* **127**:477–483.

Leczycka, K., 1972, Klinika alkoholizmu u kobiet. (Clinic for female alcoholism.), *Probl. Alkoholizmu* **7**:5–7.

Lemere, F., O'Hollaren, P., and Maxwell, M. A., 1956, Sex ratio of alcoholic patients treated over a 20-year period, *Q. J. Stud. Alcohol* **17**:437–442.

Lengrand, J. -P., 1964, Contributions a l'étude de l'alcoolisme féminin dans le Nord. (Contributions to the study of female alcoholism in the North of France.), *Bailleul*, 87 pp.

Lester, B. K., 1975, Alcoholism and women, *Alcohol Tech. Rep.* **4**:1–3.

Levi-Minzi, S., Mareggiati, M., and Tagliavini, S., 1965, In tema di alcoolismo femminile. (On the theme of alcoholism in women.) *Rass. Stud. Psichiat.* **54**:403–427.

Levine, J., 1955, The sexual adjustment of alcoholics. A clinical study of a selected sample, *Q. J. Stud. Alcohol* **16**:675–680.

Levy, S. J., and Doyle, K. M., 1974, Attitudes toward women in a drug abuse treatment program, *J. Drug Issues* **4**:428–434.

Lindbeck, V. L., 1972, The woman alcoholic: A review of the literature, *Int. J. Addict.* **7**:567–580.

Lisansky, E. S., 1957, Alcoholism in women: Social and psychological concomitants, I, Social history data, *Q. J. Stud. Alcohol* **18**:588–623.

Lisansky, E. S., 1958, The woman alcoholic, *Ann. Am. Acad. Polit. Soc. Sci.* **315**:73–81.

Litmanovitch, A. A., 1960, Osobennosti techeniya i lecheniya khronicheskogo alkogolizma u zhenschchin. (Peculiarities in the course and treatment of chronic alcoholism in women.) *Zh. Nevropatol. Psikhiatr. im. S.S. Korsakova* **60**:1515–1517.

Lolli, G., 1953, Alcoholism in women, *Conn. Rev. Alcoholism* **5**:9–11.

Louria, D. B., Kidwell, A. P., Lavenhar, M. A., Thind, I. S., and Najem, R. G., 1976, Primary and secondary prevention among adults: An analysis with comments on screening and health education, *Prev. Med.* **5**:549–572.

Lukianowicz, N., 1973, Suicidal behavior: An attempt to modify the environment, *Psychiatr. Clin.* **6**:171–190.

Luzader, C., 1976, The homeless alcoholic woman, *Addictions*, **5**(3):14–15.

Madden, J. S., and Jones, D., 1972, Bout and continuous drinking in alcoholism, *Br. J. Addict.* **67**:245–250.

Maddox, G. L., and McCall, B. C., 1964, *Drinking among teenagers: A sociological interpretation of alcohol use by high-school students*, Rutgers Center of Alcohol Studies, Monogr. No. 4, New Brunswick, N.J.

Malzberg, B., 1944, The expectation of an alcoholic mental disorder in New York state, 1920, 1930, and 1940, *Q. J. Stud. Alcohol* **4**:523–534.

Mangano, M. G., 1965, Some social aspects of alcoholism among women, in: *Selected Papers presented at the 11th European Institute on the Prevention and Treatment of Alcoholism*. International Council on Alcohol and Alcoholism, Oslo.

Maris, R. W., 1971, Deviance as therapy: The paradox of the self-destructive female, *J. Health Soc. Behav.* **12**:113–124.

Markham, J., 1957, Casework treatment of an alcoholic woman with severe underlying pathology, *Q. J. Stud. Alcohol* **18**:475–491.

Marvin, M. W., 1976, Alcohol problems in Canada: A summary of current knowledge. Tech. Rep. Series No. 2. Non-Medical Use of Drugs Directorate, Research Bureau, Ottawa.

Masi, F. A., 1977, The employed woman alcoholic, *Labor-Management Alc. J.* **6**:39–43.

Massam, A., 1973, Female drinking on increase, *The Journal* **2**(10):1.

Massot, Hamel, and Deliry, 1965, Alcoolisme féminin: Donnés statistiques et psycho-pathologiques. (Alcoholism in women: Statistical and psychopathological data.) *J. Med. Lyon* **37**:265–269.

Mayer, J., and Green, M., 1967, Group therapy of alcoholic women ex-prisoners, *Q. J. Stud. Alcohol* **28**:493–504.

Mayer, J., Myerson, D. J., Needham, M. A., and Fox, M. M., 1966, The treatment of the female alcoholic: The former prisoner, *Am. J. Orthopsychiatry* **36**:248–249.

McClelland, D. C., Davis, W. M., Kalin R., and Wanner, E., 1972, *The Drinking Man*, Free Press, New York.

McCord, W., and McCord, J., 1962, A longitudinal study of the personality of alcoholics, in: *Society, Culture, and Drinking Practices*. (D. J. Pittman and C. R. Snyder, eds.), Wiley, New York, pp. 413–430.

McCord, W., McCord, J., and Gudeman, J., 1960, *Origins of Alcoholism*, Stanford University Press, Stanford, Calif.

McLachlan, J. F. C., 1974, A hostility scale for form R of the MMPI, *J. Clin. Psychol.* **30**:369–371.

McLachlan, J. F. C., 1975, Classification of alcoholics by an MMPI actuarial system, *J. Clin. Psychol.* **31**:145–147.

McLachlan, J. F. C., Walderman, R. L., Birchmore, D. F., and Marsden, L. R., 1979, Self-evaluation, role satisfaction and anxiety in the woman alcoholic, *Int. J. Addict.* **14**(6):809–832.

Medhus, A., 1974, Morbidity among female alcoholics, *Scand. J. Soc. Med.* **2**:5–11.

Medhus, A., 1975a, Conviction for drunkenness—A late symptom among female alcoholics, *Scand. J. Soc. Med.* **3**:23–27.

Medhus, A., 1975b, Criminality among female alcoholics, *Scand. J. Soc. Med.* **3**:45–49.

Medhus, A., 1976, Female alcoholics: Correlation between sociomedical variables, *Br. J. Addict.* **71**:109–113.

Midenet, M., Midenet, J., and Desbois, G., 1973, L'alcoolisme de la femme de 50 ans. (Alcoholism in fifty-year-old women.) *Lyon Med.* **229**:479–483.

Mogar, R. E., Wilson, W. M., and Helm, S. T., 1970, Personality subtypes of male and female alcoholic patients, *Int. J. Addict.* **5**:99–113.

Moore, R. A., 1971, The prevalence of alcoholism in a community general hospital, *Am. J. Psychiatry* **128**:638–639.

Moorhead, H. H., 1958, Study of alcoholism with onset forty-five years or older, *Bull. N.Y. Acad. Med.* **34**:99–108.

Morgan, H. G., Barton, J., Pottle, S., Pocock, H., and Burns-Cox, C. J., 1976, Deliberate self-harm: A follow-up study of 279 patients, *Br. J. Psychiatry* **128**:361–368.

Mulford, H. A., 1977, Women and men problem drinkers: Sex differences in patients served by Iowa's community alcoholism centers, *J. Stud. Alcohol* **38**:1624–1639.

Munkelt, P., and Lienert, G. A., 1964, Blutalkoholspiegel und psychophysische Konstitution. (Blood alcohol level and psychophysical constitution.), *Arzneim.-forsch.* **14**:573–575.

Munkelt, P., Lienert, G. A., Frahm, M., and Soehring, K., 1962, Geschlechtsspezifische Wirkungsunterschiede der Kombination von Alkohol und Meprobamat auf psychisch stabile und labile Versuchspersonen. (Sex-specific differences in effect of alcohol combined with meprobamate on psychologically stable and labile subjects.), *Arzneim.-forsch.* **12**:1059–1065.

Murcia-Valcarcel, E., 1969, L'alcoolisme chez la femme. (Alcoholism in women.), *Rev. Alcool.* **15**:285–298.

Myerson, D. J., 1957, Psychiatric aspects: The women of Skid Row, *Proc. 2nd Inst. Homeless and Institutional Alc.*, pp. 3–16.

Myerson, D. J., 1959, Clinical observations on a group of alcoholic prisoners: With special reference to women, *Q. J. Stud. Alcohol* **20**:555–572.

Myerson, D. J., 1966, A therapeutic appraisal of certain married alcoholic women, *Int. Psychiatr. Clin.* **3**:143–157.

Myerson, D. J., MacKay, J., Wallens, A., and Neilberg, N., 1961, A report of a rehabilitation program for alcoholic women prisoners, *Q. J. Stud. Alcohol* **Suppl.** **1**:151–157.

Nachin, C., Lengrand, J. P., Crépin, D., and Blanchard, M., 1965, Sur le traitement de l'alcoolisme féminin en milieu psychiatrique. (On the treatment of female alcoholism in a psychiatric milieu.), *Lille Méd* **10**:302–305.

Nellis, M., 1976, *Drugs, Alcohol and Women: A National Forum Source Book*, National Research and Communications Associates, Washington.

Nobel, D., 1949, Psychodynamics of alcoholism in a woman, *Psychiatry* **12**:413–425.

Obitz, F. W., and Swanson, M. K., 1976, Control orientation in women alcoholics, *Q. J. Stud. Alcohol* **37**:694–697.

Orford, J., Waller, S., and Peto, J., 1974, Drinking behaviour and attitudes and their correlates among university students in England, I, Principal components in the drinking domain; II, Personality and social influence; III, Sex differences, *Q. J. Stud. Alcohol* **35**:1316–1374.

Orford, J., Guthrie, S., Nicholls, P., Oppenheimer, E., Egert, S., and Hensman C., 1975, Self-reported coping behavior of wives of alcoholics and its association with drinking outcome, *J. Stud. Alcohol* **36**:1254–1267.

Paolino, T. J., Jr., McCrady, B., Diamond, S., and Longabaugh, R., 1976, Psychological disturbances in spouses of alcoholics: An empirical assessment, *J. Stud. Alcohol* **37**:1600–1608.

Parker, F. B., 1972, Sex-role adjustment in women alcoholics, *Q. J. Stud. Alcohol* **33**:647–657.

Parker, F. B., 1975, Sex-role adjustment and drinking disposition of women college students, *J. Stud. Alcohol* **36**:1570–1573.

Parr, D., 1957, Alcoholism in general practice, *Br. J. Addict.* **54**:25–39, 41–46.

Patel, A. R., Roy, M., and Wilson, G. M., 1972, Self-poisoning and alcohol, *Lancet* **2**:1099–1103.

Pemberton, D. A., 1967, A comparison of the outcome of treatment in female and male alcoholics. *Br. J. Psychiatry* **112**:367–373.

Pescor, M. J., 1944, A comparative statistical study of male and female drug addicts, *Am. J. Psychiatry* **100**:771–774.

Pishkin, V., and Throme, F., 1977, A factorial structure of the dimensions of femininity in alcoholic, schizophrenic and normal populations, *J. Clin. Psychol.* **33**:10–17.

Pitts, F. N., Jr., and Winokur, G., 1966, Affective disorder, VII, Alcoholism and affective disorder, *J. Psychiatr. Res.* **4**:37–50.

Podolsky, E., 1963, The woman alcoholic and premenstrual tension, *J. Am Med. Women's Assoc.* **18**:816–818.

Polivy, J., and Herman, C. P., 1976, Effects of alcohol on eating behavior: Influence of mood and perceived intoxication, *J. Abnorm. Psychol.* **85**:601–606.

Priest, R. G., 1976, The homeless person and the psychiatric services: An Edinburgh survey, *Br. J. Psychiatry* **128**:128–136.

Proctor, R. C., 1956, A new therapeutic approach to certain cases of alcoholism, *South. Med. J.* **49**:73–75.

Rathod, N. H., and Thomson, I. G., 1971, Women alcoholics: A clinical study, *Q. J. Stud. Alcohol* **32**:45–52.

Regan, M. M., Jr., 1976, Personality differences between acute and chronic female alcohol abusers, *Alcohol Tech. Rep.* **5**:7–10.

Riemenschneider, H., 1971, Veränderung des Persönlichkeitsbildes alkoholkranker Frauen während der Entziehungsbehandlung. (Changes in the personality profile of women alcoholics during withdrawal treatment.), *Suchtgefahren* **17**:16–18.

Riley, J. W., Jr., Marden, C. F., and Lifshitz, M., 1948, The motivational pattern of drinking: Based on the verbal responses of a cross-section sample of users of alcoholic beverages, *Q. J. Stud. Alcohol* **9**:353–362.

Rimmer, J., 1974, Psychiatric illness in husbands of alcoholics, *Q. J. Stud. Alcohol* **35**:281–283.

Rimmer, J., Pitts, F. M., Jr., Reich, T., and Winokur, G., 1971, Alcoholism, II, Sex, socioeconomic status and race in two hospitalized samples, *Q. J. Stud. Alcohol* **32**:942–952.

Robinson, D., 1976, *From Drinking to Alcoholism: A Sociological Commentary,* Wiley, New York.

Rosenbaum, B., 1958, Married women alcoholics at the Washingtonian Hospital, *Q. J. Stud. Alcohol* **19**:79–89.

Rosenberg, C. M., and Amodeo, M., 1974, Long-term patients seen in an alcoholism clinic, *Q. J. Stud. Alcohol* **35**:660–666.

Rotter, J. B., 1966, Generalized expectancies for internal versus external control of reinforcement, *Psychol. Monogr.* **80**:1–28.

Sandmaier, M., 1977, *Alcohol Abuse and Women: A Guide to Getting Help,* U.S. Government Printing Office, Washington.

San Mateo County (Calif.), Dept. of Public Health and Welfare, 1971, Student Drug Use Surveys, 1968–1971, San Mateo.

Santamaria, J. N., 1972, The social implications of alcoholism, *Med. J. Aust.* **59**:523–528.

Schachter, S., 1959, *The Psychology of Affiliation,* Stanford University Press, Stanford, Calif.

Schmidt, W., and de Lint, J., 1969, Mortality experiences of male and female alcoholic patients, *Q. J. Stud. Alcohol* **30**:112–118.

Schuckit, M. A., 1972a, The alcoholic woman: A literature review, *Psychiatry Med.* **3**:37–43.

Schuckit, M. A., 1972b, Sexual disturbance in the woman alcoholic, *Med. Aspects Hum. Sex.* **6**:44, 48–49, 53, 57, 60–61, 65.

Schuckit, M. A., 1973, Depression and alcoholism in women, in: *Proceedings of the First Annual Alcoholism Conference of the National Institute on Alcohol Abuse and Alcoholism, June 1971,* Washington, D.C., DHEW, pp. 355–363.

Schuckit, M. A., and Gunderson, E., 1975, Alcoholism in Navy and Marine Corps women: A first look, *Mil. Med.* **140**:268–271.

Schuckit, M. A., and Winokur, G., 1972, A short term follow-up of women alcoholics, *Dis. Nerv. Syst.* **33**:672–678.

Schuckit, M., Pitts, F. N., Jr., Reich, T., King, L. J., and Winokur, G., 1969, Alcoholism, I, Two types of alcoholism in women, *Arch. Gen. Psychiatry* **20**:301–306.

Schuckit, M. A., Rimmer, J., Reich, T., Winokur, G., 1971, The bender alcoholic, *Br. J. Psychiatry* **119**:183–184.

Sclare, A. B., 1970, The female alcoholic, *Br. J. Addict.* **65**:99–107.

Sclare, A. B., 1975, The woman alcoholic, *J. Alcohol.* **10**: 134–137.

Sclare, A. B., 1977, Alcohol problems in women, in: *Alcoholism and Drug Dependence: A multidisciplinary Approach* (J. S. Madden, R. Walker, and W. H. Kenyon, eds.), Plenum, New York, pp. 181–187.

Scott, E. M., and Manaugh, T. S., 1976, Femininity of alcoholic women's preferences on Edwards Personal Preference Schedule, *Psychol. Rep.* **38**:847–852.

Segal, B., Rhenberg, G., and Sterling, S., 1975, Self-concept and drug and alcohol use in female college students, *J. Alcohol Drug Educ.* **20**:17–22.

Senseman, L. A., 1966, The housewife's secret illness: How to recognize the female alcoholic, *R.I. Med. J.* **49**:40–42.

Shainess, N., 1970, Is there a separate feminine psychology? *N.Y. State J. Med.* **70**:3007–3009.

Sherfey, J. M., 1955, Psychopathology and character structure in chronic alcoholism, in: *Etiology of Chronic Alcoholism* (O. Diethelm, ed.), Thomas, Springfield, Ill.

Silber, A., Gottschalk, W., and Sarnoff, C., 1960, Alcoholism in pregnancy, *Psychiatr. Q.* **34**:461–471.

Slater, A. D., 1952, A study of the use of alcoholic beverages among high-school students in Utah, *Q. J. Stud. Alcohol* **13**:78–86.

Smart, R. G., 1963, The relationship between birth order and alcoholism among women, *Ont. Psychol. Assoc. Q.* **16**:10–16.

Sorosiak, F. M., Thomas, L. E., and Balet, F. N., 1976, Adolescent drug use: An analysis, *Psychol. Rep.* **38**:211–221.

Stafford, R. A., and Petway, J. M., 1977, Stigmatization of men and women problem drinkers and their spouses: Differential perception and leveling of sex differences, *J. Stud. Alcohol* **38**:2109–2121.

Straus, R., and Bacon, S. D., 1953, *Drinking in College,* Yale University Press, New Haven, Conn.

Suffet, F., and Brotman, R., 1976, Female drug use: Some observations, *Int. J. Addict.* **11**:19–33.

Sugerman, A. A., Sheldon, J. B., and Roth, C., 1975, Defense mechanisms in men and women alcoholics, *J. Stud. Alcohol* **36**:422–424.

Tamerin, J. S., 1976, Sex differences in alcoholics: A comparison of male and female alcoholics' self and spouse perceptions, *Am. J. Drug Alcohol Abuse* **3**:457–472.

Tamerin, J. S., Tolor, A., De Wolfe, J., Packer, L., and Neumann, C. P., 1974, Spouses' perceptions of their alcoholic partners: A retrospective view of alcoholics by themselves and their spouses, *Proceedings of the Third Annual Alcoholism Conference NIAAA,* pp. 33–49.

Thomas, D. A., 1971, *A study of selected factors on successfully and unsuccessfully treated alcoholic women,* Ph.D. thesis, Michigan State University, Department of Clinical Psychology.

Topper, M. D., 1974, Drinking patterns, culture change, sociability and Navajo "adolescents," *Addict. Dis.* **1**:97–116.

Tracey, D. A., 1975, *An experimental analysis of the behavior of female alcoholics*, Ph.D. dissertation, Rutgers University.

Tracey, D. A., and Nathan, P. E., 1976, Behavioral analysis of chronic alcoholism in four women, *J. Consult. Clin. Psychol.* **44**:832–842.

Trice, H. M., 1956, Alcoholism: Group factors in etiology and therapy, *Hum. Org.* **15**:33–40.

Ullman, A. D., 1957, Sex differences in the first drinking experience, *Q. J. Stud. Alcohol* **18**:229–239.

Ullman, A. D., 1962, First drinking experience as related to age and sex, in: *Society, Culture, and Drinking Patterns* (D. Pittman and C. Snyder, eds.), pp. 259–266, Wiley, New York.

U.S. Department of Health, Education and Welfare, 1971, Extent and patterns of use and abuse of alcohol, in: *The First Special Report to the U.S. Congress on Alcohol and Health,* U.S. Government Printing Office, Washington, pp. 21–36.

U.S. National Institute on Alcohol Abuse and Alcoholism, 1975, Alcohol and health; Second special report to the Congress. DHEW Publ. No. ADM-75-212, U.S. Government Printing Office, Washington, D.C.

U.S. National Institute on Alcohol Abuse and Alcoholism, 1977, *Women in treatment for alcoholism: A profile,* Bethesda, MD, 10 pp.

Van Amberg, R. J., 1943, A study of 50 women patients hospitalized for alcohol addiction, *Dis. Nerv. Syst.* **4**:246–251.

Vanderpool, J. A., 1969, Alcoholism and the self-concept, *Q. J. Stud. Alcohol* **30**:59–77.

Wall, J. H., 1937, A study of alcoholism in women, *Am. J. Psychiatry* **93**:943–955.

Waller, S., and Lorch, B. D., 1977, First drinking experiences and present drinking patterns: A male–female comparison, *Am. J. Drug Alcohol Abuse* **4**:109–121.

Wanberg, K. W., and Horn, J. L., 1970, Alcoholism symptom patterns of men and women: A comparative study, *Q. J. Stud. Alcohol* **31**:40–61.

Wanberg, K. W., and Horn, J. L., 1973, Alcoholism syndromes related to sociological classifications, *Int. J. Addict.* **8**:99–120.

Wanberg, K. W., and Knapp, J., 1970, Differences in drinking symptoms and behavior of men and women alcoholics, *Br. J. Addict.* **64**:347–355.

Ward, J. S., 1974, The environment of alcoholism in Australia, *Aust. J. Alcoholism Drug Dep.* **1**:79–83.

Wechsler, H., and McFadden, M., 1976, Sex differences in adolescent alcohol and drug use: A disappearing phenomenon, *J. Stud. Alcohol* **37**:1291–1301.

Wechsler, H., and Thum, D., 1973, Teen-age drinking, drug use, and social correlates, *Q. J. Stud. Alcohol* **34**:1220–1227.

Wechsler, H., and Thum, D., 1974, Drug use among teen-agers: Patterns of present and anticipated use, *Int. J. Addict.* **8**:905–916.

Wechsler, H., Thum, D., Demone, H. W., Jr., and Dwinnell, J., 1972, Social characteristics and blood alcohol level. Measurements of subgroup differences, *Q. J. Stud. Alcohol* **33**:132–147.

Whitlock, F. A., and Lowrey, J. M., 1967, Drug-dependence in psychiatric patients, *Med. J. Aust.* **1**:1157–1166.

Widseth, J. C., and Mayer, J., 1971, Drinking behavior and attitudes toward alcohol in delinquent girls, *Int. J. Addict.* **6**:453–461.

Wilkinson, P., Santamaria, J. N., Rankin, J. G., and Martin, D., 1969, Epidemiology of alcoholism: Social data and drinking patterns of a sample of Australian alcoholics, *Med. J. Aust.* **1**:1020–1025.

Wilsnack, S. C., 1973a, Femininity by the bottle, *Psychology Today* **6**:39–43, 96.

Wilsnack, S. C., 1973b, The needs of the female drinker: Dependency, power, or what? in: *Psychological and Social Factors in Drinking and Treatment and Treatment Evaluation*, Proceedings of the Second Annual Conference of the National Institute on Alcohol Abuse and Alcoholism, National Institute of Mental Health, Rockville, Md., pp. 65–83.

Wilsnack, S. C., 1973c, Sex role identity in female alcoholism, *J. Abnorm. Psychol.* **82**:253–261.

Wilson, G. T., and Lawson, D. M., 1976, Effects of alcohol on sexual arousal in women, *J. Abnorm. Psychol.* **85**:489–497.

Winokur, G., and Clayton, P., 1967, Family history studies, II, Sex differences and alcoholism in Primary Affective Illness, *Br. J. Psychiatry* **113**:973–979.

Winokur, G., and Clayton, P. J., 1968, Family history studies, IV, Comparison of male and female alcoholics, *Q. J. Stud. Alcohol* **29**:885–891.

Winokur, G., and Pitts, F. N., Jr., 1965, Affective disorder, VI, A family history study of prevalences, sex differences and possible genetic factors, *J. Psychiatr. Res.* **3**:113–123.

Winokur, G., Reich, T., Rimmer, J., and Pitts, F. N., Jr., 1970, Alcoholism, III, Diagnosis and familial psychiatric illness in 259 alcoholic probands, *Arch. Gen. Psychiatry* **23**:104–111.

Winokur, G., Rimmer, J., and Reich, T., 1971, Alcoholism, IV, Is there more than one type of alcoholism? *Br. J. Psychiatry* **118**:525–531.

Wood, H. P., and Duffy, E. L., 1966, Psychological factors in alcoholic women, *Am. J. Psychiatry* **123**:341–345.

Woodruff, R. A., Jr., Guze, S. B., Clayton, P. J., and Carr, D., 1973, Alcoholism and depression, *Arch. Gen. Psychiatry* **28**:97–100.

Woodside, M., 1961, Women drinkers admitted to Holloway prison during February 1960: A pilot survey, *Br. J. Criminol.* **1**:221–235.

Zeichner, A. M., 1951, Alcoholism as a defense against social isolation, *Case Rep. Clin. Psychol.* **2**:51–59.

Zelen, S. L., Fox, J., Gould, E., and Olson, R. W., 1966, Sex-contingent differences between male and female alcoholics, *J. Clin. Psychol.* **22**:160–165.

Zucker, R. A., 1968, Sex-role identity patterns and drinking behavior of adolescents, *Q. J. Stud. Alcohol* **29**:868–884.

9

Sex Differences in Morbidity of Alcoholics

PATRICIA WILKINSON

1. INTRODUCTION

It is now well accepted that alcoholics suffer more physical illness and die sooner than nonalcoholics. A number of mortality studies (Table 1) have shown that death rates are increased and life expectancy is reduced among alcoholics when they are compared with the general population. The ratio of the observed frequency (f_o) of deaths among alcoholics to the expected frequency (f_e) of deaths in the population at large is consistently increased in samples of alcoholics studied in different parts of the world. They vary from a f_o/f_e of about four in a South African series to one of 2.0 in Canada.

Much of the excess mortality is the result of accidents, violence, and suicide (Brenner, 1967; Schmidt and de Lint, 1969). These deaths have tended to occur particularly in younger alcoholics who were not obviously physically deteriorated, and they have been attributed primarily to predisposing social and psychological factors. Nevertheless, a significant proportion of deaths in all series could be attributed to physical disease: mortality rates notably in excess of those for the general population being found for diseases of the liver, for the circulatory and respiratory systems, and for neoplasms.

This excess mortality among alcoholics resulting from physical disease suggests an increased incidence of antecedent physical morbidity, a suggestion supported by studies of morbidity among alcoholics. Lindgren (1957) (quoted by Medhus, 1974) and Lokander (1962) demonstrated an increased rate of absenteeism due to sickness among male Swedish

PATRICIA WILKINSON • Health Commission of Victoria, South Melbourne, Victoria, Australia.

Table 1. Excess Mortality Observed in Alcoholics

Investigator	Number in sample		Country	Observed/expected deaths (f_o/f_e)
	Males	Females		
Tashiro and Lipscomb (1963)	1431	261	U.S.	2.5
Sundby (1967)	1722		Norway	2.1
Brenner (1967)	1343 patients[a]		U.S.	3.0
Schmidt and de Lint (1969)	5395	1119	Canada	2.0
Gillis (1969)	707	95	South Africa	about 4
Lindelius and Salum (1972)	1026		Sweden	3.6
Pell and D'Alonzo (1973)	842	57	U.S.	3.2
Nicholls et al. (1974)	678	257	England	2.7

[a] Numbers of men and women in sample not indicated.

employees known to have alcohol problems. While some of this excess sickness was due to mental disorders, physical morbidity from diseases of the respiratory, circulatory, and digestive systems was conspicuous. Pell and D'Alonzo (1968, 1970) likewise found indications of increased physical morbidity among alcoholic employees in North America.

Most of these earlier observations on alcohol-related mortality and morbidity were carried out on male alcoholics (Lindelius and Salum, 1972; Lindgren, 1957; Lokander, 1962; Sundby, 1967). Where women were included, their numbers tended to be very small, usually too few for them to be considered separately from the men.

A notable exception was a study by Texon (1950). This was the first in which the prevalence of alcohol-related illness was reported in males and females separately. Texon reviewed the clinical findings in 500 consecutive patients, 382 men and 118 women, admitted to an alcohol treatment service in a New York general hospital, and he compared the spectra of physical illness in the two sexes. He did not find any remarkable differences between males and females in either overall or cause-specific morbidity.

Only recently has sustained interest been aroused in the possible differences in alcohol-related illness in the two sexes. In her introduction to a review of the literature on women alcoholics, Lindbeck (1972) commented, "the woman alcoholic has been a stepchild in the field of research." She was discussing sociological and psychological data, but her remark is appropriate to the area of medical research as well.

Although there is now an increasing clinical interest, and an impression that women alcoholics may be more illness-prone than men (Ashley et al., 1977; Wilkinson et al., 1971b), documentation of differences in morbidity between male and female alcoholics is still scanty, and not easy to interpret.

There are several reasons for the gaps in existing knowledge. Alcoholism is less common among women than among men (Dahlgren, 1975). Because uncontrolled drinking is disapproved of more in women (Lindbeck, 1972; Popham, 1959; Sclare, 1970), female alcoholics are less ready to admit their problems, and physicians are more reluctant to make a diagnosis of alcoholism. The relationship between physical illness and the underlying condition may thus go unrecognized, and the female alcoholic is then likely to be treated by a different agency from the male. As well, until recently, the care and treatment of both male and female alcoholics were the responsibility of the psychiatrist rather than the physician. As Seixas commented in 1975,

> The tendency . . . has been not only for the people in the health sciences to neglect alcoholism as contributing to physical pathology, but for the people treating alcoholism to neglect the alcohol-related physical pathology as something separate, too late or trivial in the face of the major change in life style necessary to produce a contented abstinent individual from a discontented heavy drinker.

Incentives and opportunities were thus limited for those interested and skilled in the recognition of physical disease to study the natural history of alcoholism and its physical concomitants in sufficiently large numbers of men and women side by side.

During the last two decades, however, there has been increasing interest in and concern about the physical problems of alcoholism. Treatment of the alcoholic has become more the province of the physician. More agencies have been provided where both male and female alcoholics are treated and where physical as well as psychological and social manifestations can be observed and investigated. There has been a change of attitude, too, toward the woman alcoholic, so that she is less ashamed to admit her problem and to seek help (Dahlgren, 1975; Sclare, 1970). There are also indications that the number of women alcoholics is increasing, not just because they are more willing to present for treatment, but because the condition is becoming commoner among women (Lindbeck, 1972; Oltman and Friedman, 1965). As a result of this increase in interest and opportunity, much more has been observed and documented about physical morbidity in alcoholism in both sexes, and differences in experience between males and females have begun to appear.

Possible Reasons for Sex Differences in Morbidity in Alcoholics

A number of factors, not all of them related to alcohol consumption, may contribute to the differences in physical morbidity found between male and female alcoholics.

a. The prevalence of illness in a series under study may differ between the sexes because their exposure to alcohol has differed. One or other sex may have consumed larger amounts of alcohol, may have drunk for longer, or may have preferred a different kind of beverage. It is generally agreed that, compared with their male counterparts, female alcoholics are, as a group, more disturbed psychologically and pass more rapidly through the various stages of uncontrolled drinking (Beckman, 1975; Schmidt and de Lint, 1969; Sclare, 1970). Even so, in most countries, women alcoholics are thought to start drinking heavily at a later age than men (Ashley et al., 1977; Dahlgren, 1975; Lindbeck, 1972; Wilkinson et al., 1969b). In a Canadian series, Ashley et al. (1977) found that women alcoholics began to drink hazardously about five years later than men. In Australia, the lag in the onset of heavy drinking was even longer (Wilkinson et al., 1969b). Women alcoholics also tend to drink less (Ashley et al., 1977; Sclare, 1970; Wilkinson et al., 1969b) but often prefer wine. This beverage has been thought to be especially toxic, particularly to the liver, by some workers (Mackay, 1966; Schmidt and Bronetto, 1962; Whitlock, 1974), although not by others (de Lint, 1977).

b. Differences in factors related to the alcoholic lifestyle may contribute to observed differences in morbidity. Alcoholics are more likely to neglect themselves, to eat poorly, and to misuse other drugs of dependence, especially tranquilizers and sedatives (Ashley et al., 1977; Curlee, 1970; Lindelius et al., 1974; Wilkinson et al., 1971a). Differences in diet or in exposure to such drugs may contribute to differences in alcohol-related morbidity between the two sexes.

c. Sex differences in morbidity in the general population may be reflected in alcoholic subgroups and must be taken into account when comparing male and female alcoholics. Nonalcoholic men and women have different morbidity experiences for certain diseases. For instance, men run a greater risk of developing chronic bronchitis than women do, and this susceptibility is unrelated to tobacco (Tager and Speizer, 1976). Because of the existence of such differences, male and female alcoholics cannot always be compared directly. The appropriate nonalcoholic "standard" of morbidity must be set for each sex before one makes comparisons of morbidity findings between alcoholics of the two sexes. This setting of "standards" is made for the two sexes in mortality studies when f_o/f_e is calculated separately for each sex and compared, rather than comparing crude mortality rates in men and women.

d. Alcohol itself may affect morbidity and mortality differently in the two sexes. It may do this in two ways. Because of a sex-related difference in susceptibility to the effects of alcohol, there may be an increased incidence of disease in one sex or the other. In other words, the disease may *develop* more rapidly. As a result, prevalence of disease is increased, and life expectancy is diminished. The alcohol may also accelerate the course of a disease, so that it *progresses* more rapidly. This more rapid progression will result in a poorer prognosis for the disease and a shortened life expectancy, but no increase in actual prevalence. The prevalence of such a disease may even be decreased.

2. SEX DIFFERENCES IN GENERAL MORBIDITY

Evidence from Mortality Studies

It is not intended to discuss mortality studies in alcoholics in detail here, since this is done in Chapter 10. However, it is necessary to highlight those studies that, by contrasting death rates and life expectancy in males and females, indicate the likelihood of differences in physical morbidity between the two sexes.

The major epidemiological studies that have included large enough numbers of women to allow comparison of death rates between male and female alcoholics are listed in Table 2. The largest of these studies was that of Schmidt and de Lint (1969), but all were of sufficient size to allow comparisons of general mortality rates between the sexes. All investigators found that f_o/f_e was greater for women than it was for men. The alcoholic lifestyle tended to equalize the quite different mortality experiences of men and women in the general population and to obliterate the better life expectancy normally enjoyed by women. The risk of earlier

Table 2. Excess Mortality Compared in Male and Female Alcoholics

Investigator	Country	Number in sample		f_o/f_e	
		Males	Females	Males	Females
Gillis (1969)	South Africa	707	95	3.9	4.5
Schmidt and de Lint (1969)	Canada	5395	1119	2.03	3.2
Lindelius et al. (1974)	Sweden	139	118	2	4
Nicholls et al (1974)	England	678	257	2.65	3.07
Dahlgren and Myrhed (1977)	Sweden	100	100	3.0	5.6

death as a consequence of heavy drinking was thus increased more for alcoholic women than it was for men.

In the studies of Dahlgren and Myrhed (1977), Lindelius et al. (1974), and Schmidt and de Lint (1969), a significant part of this excess mortality among women resulted from accidents, poisoning, violence, and suicide. These tended to occur among the younger women, who were probably physically fairly healthy. Nevertheless, there is evidence in all five series to suggest that some, though not all, of the excess mortality that women alcoholics experience is the result of physical illness.

Two other mortality studies are worthy of note. In the first, Fitzgerald et al. (1971) followed a series of alcoholics treated at a rural American state hospital. At the end of four years, they found that 11% of 392 men and 19% of 139 women had died. Details of cause of death were not reported. These findings suggest considerable excess mortality and, with it, excess antecedent morbidity among the women. In the second study, Medhus (1975) examined a group of 83 women who had received compulsory treatment for alcoholism in Malmö and found that f_o/f_e for all causes of death was "fully 7." No males were studied in comparison. The most nearly comparable sample of male Swedish alcoholics on whom mortality data are available is that of Lindelius and Salum (1972), in which f_o/f_e was 3.6. The women in Medhus's series were socially disadvantaged and psychologically disturbed, and this fact was reflected in a very high death rate from accidents, violence, and suicide, particularly among the younger women. Nevertheless, comparison of death rates in the two series, male and female, would suggest that the women, particularly those in the older age groups, may have suffered greater excess mortality from physical disease as well.

It is not possible to deduce how much this sex difference may be related to alcohol exposure and how much to other deleterious factors in the alcoholic lifestyle, such as poor diet, neglect, or drug misuse. It is reasonable, however, to postulate that the alcoholic woman may be more prone than her male counterpart to some physical illnesses that ultimately prove fatal.

Evidence from Morbidity Studies

The impression from the above studies of mortality in alcoholics that women alcoholics may be more susceptible to physical illness was first supported by two Australian studies. Wilkinson et al. (1969b) obtained details of alcohol consumption from 220 patients presenting to an alcoholism clinic attached to a general teaching hospital in Melbourne. There were 179 men and 41 women in the series who were drinking hazardously when they presented. The women had drunk less and for a shorter period of time before they were first examined. The men had drunk a mean of 220 ± 100 g alcohol per day for a mean of 15.8 ± 8.4 years, while the women had consumed a mean of 155 ± 55 g alcohol per day for 11.7 ± 8.0 years. The majority of the women, like the men, were beer drinkers. Despite their lower exposure to alcohol, it was found that physical illness was more prevalent among the women patients. Proportionately more women than men were referred from within the hospital with medical problems. Since the women had drunk less alcohol than the men for a shorter time, their increased morbidity could hardly be explained on grounds that they were more advanced alcoholics. Furthermore, the results of a survey into the drinking habits of people outside the hospital indicated that the ratio of male to female alcoholics in the series was similar to that in the community. These findings were taken to suggest that, as a sex, women might be predisposed to the physical consequences of alcoholism, rather than that the women in the series were a biased selection.

A subsequent study from the same clinic examined the prevalence of physical disease in a larger series of patients, 821 men and 179 women, and related this prevalence to their sex and exposure to alcohol (Wilkinson et al., 1971b). In this series, the women had again on average drunk less than the men, and for a shorter period of time. The men's consumption averaged 265 ± 110 g per day for 18.8 ± 8.1 years, compared with the women, whose mean consumption was 170 ± 65 g per day for 12.6 ± 11.2 years. More than two-thirds of the patients had evidence at presentation of some disability, either symptomatic or asymptomatic. The proportions were similar in the two sexes despite the shorter history of exposure to alcohol among the women. In this series of patients, there was little difference between the sexes in the source of referral. Nearly similar proportions of physically ill men and women were referred from within the hospital and outside. When they were first examined, 86.7% of the men and 90% of the women referred from within the hospital had evidence of physical disease, as did 62.3% of the men and 57.5% of the women who were referred from outside agencies. The proportion of male to female alcoholics in this second series was again similar to that in the community. It was considered unlikely, therefore, that the relatively greater susceptiblity to illness that the women showed was due either to greater exposure to alcohol or to some bias in their selection. While these findings suggest that women alcoholics are more illness-prone, it is not clear whether proneness to illness is the result of increased susceptibility to alcohol or to some associated factor or factors in their lifestyle. Nor is it clear whether they develop alcohol-related diseases more frequently, or whether morbidity progresses more rapidly, or both.

In an attempt to clarify these relationships further, Ashley et al. (1977) have studied a large series of Canadian alcoholics of both sexes and have compared demographic and social data, information on the use of tobacco and drugs of dependence, and physical disease profiles in the two sexes. The series comprised 736 men and 135 women. All were patients who had been admitted to the Medical Unit of the Addiction Research Foundation of Ontario, who had remained long enough to be examined, and who were not on "skid row" at the time of admission. Skid-row patients were excluded, because Canadian skid-row men had been shown in a separate study (Ashley et al., 1976) to comprise a distinct entity with a different profile of physical illness from non-skid-row alcoholic men, and because the skid-row patients were almost exclusively male. The ratio of males to females in Ashley's series was similar to that found in a survey of alcoholism in an adjacent community, and the authors felt that bias in the selection of patients for admission was unlikely. Findings were similar to those in the Australian study. Women had again drunk less alcohol for a shorter time, a mean of 227.6 ± 103.5 g for 14.1 ± 8.5 years compared with 316 ± 119.7 g for 20.2 ± 9.3 years for the men. Despite highly significant differences in amount and duration of exposure to alcohol, the prevalence of most disease entities was similar in the two sexes. The authors suggested that this finding supported the likelihood that the development of physical morbidity is accelerated in females compared with males. Whether this acceleration is an effect of alcohol itself or a result of some other factor associated with the alcoholic lifestyle remains unclear. Smoking habits did not differ between the two sexes, but significantly more women (26.7%) than men (18.3%) used drugs of dependence (predominantly tranquilizers and barbiturates) abnormally.

Three further studies also suggest that physical disease may develop more frequently or more rapidly in women alcoholics than in men. In 1959, Observer and Maxwell compared the patterns of absence from work because of sickness in 32 male and 16 female employees with drinking problems, with those of a control group of employees matched for age, sex, and occupational level. Both male and female problem drinkers had more episodes of sickness and took more time off work than did the controls. When the two sexes were compared, it was found that the difference between control and problem groups was greater among the women, for numbers of sickness episodes. The increase in total time off work was not, however, as marked in the women.

In 1970, Sclare compared the records of 50 male and 50 female alcoholics randomly selected from those of patients admitted to the psychiatry department of a Scottish hospital. A total of 24 females and 26 males had evidence of physical impairment other than brain damage.

The females tended to consume smaller amounts of alcohol, and significantly more came for treatment with a duration of alcoholism of five years or less, again suggesting that alcohol-related physical illness may develop more rapidly in females than in males.

In 1974, when reporting the demographic and socioeconomic characteristics of a sample of alcoholic patients admitted to four London hospitals for treatment, Edwards et al. commented briefly on the prevalence of physical disease in their series. Their findings are summarized in Table 3. While there was little difference in the prevalence of illness between men and women taken as a whole, illness of any kind and alcohol-related illness were found more frequently in younger women compared with younger men. The authors did not elaborate on the nature of the illnesses encountered in those patients.

3. SEX DIFFERENCES IN CAUSE-SPECIFIC MORBIDITY

When death and illness rates from different causes are examined individually, it is found that female susceptibility to alcohol-related illness is not increased consistently for all diseases. It appears that women may be particularly vulnerable to certain complications, notably cirrhosis and anemia, but less prone to heart disease. As well as the studies already discussed, which have encompassed the overall picture of sex differences in alcohol-related mortality and morbidity, there have been a number of investigations concerned with particular disease entities. Liver disease in the alcoholic has aroused the most interest and has probably been studied the most extensively.

Alcoholic Liver Disease

Alcoholic Hepatitis and Cirrhosis.   The first indication that the natural history of cirrhosis of the alcoholic might differ between the two

Table 3. Prevalence of Physical Disease in Sample of 935 Patients Admitted to Four English Hospitals for Treatment of Alcoholism[a]

	% with any illness	% with alcohol-related illness
678 men		
All ages	16	3
Under 35 years	11	0
257 women		
All ages	14	3
Under 35 years	21	6

[a] After Edwards et al. (1974).

sexes was given by Spain in 1945. He reviewed a total of 250 consecutive necropsies in which portal cirrhosis had been found. There were 190 males and 60 females in the series, a ratio of 3:1, which was less than the presumed ratio of male to female alcoholics in the community. The average age at death of the women was some five and a half years less than that of the men. Spain also noted that the women were more likely to die from the cirrhosis itself, compared with the men, rather than from unrelated causes. On the basis of these findings, he suggested that cirrhosis occurred more frequently and carried a worse prognosis in women than it did in men.

Two epidemiological studies of mortality among alcoholics, which were large enough to compare deaths from separate causes in the two sexes, showed relatively more deaths from cirrhosis among alcoholic women than among alcoholic men. Tashiro and Lipscomb (1963) found that 11 out of a total of 1341 male alcoholics (0.76%) died of cirrhosis in the five years that they followed them, but 6 out of 261 women (2.3%) died during the same time. Schmidt and de Lint (1969) in their study of 5395 alcoholic men and 1119 alcoholic women, calculated f_o/f_e for the two sexes separately for several major causes of death. They found that f_o/f_e for cirrhosis was 11.0 for men but 25.0 for women. The mortality study of Nicholls et al. (1974) of 678 men and 257 women did not identify deaths from cirrhosis separately. They were included in deaths from "diseases of digestive system," for which f_o/f_e was 3.83 for men and 7.79 for women. The authors observed, however, that these excess rates were largely due to cirrhosis since deaths from other diseases of the digestive system did not depart significantly from normal expectations.

Viel et al. (1968) attempted to compare the prevalence of cirrhosis in nonalcoholics and alcoholics of both sexes by studying the necropsy findings in 1348 Chileans who had died from violence. They related the histopathological appearances in the liver to information obtained from relatives about drinking habits in life. They found cirrhosis very infrequently among abstainers and normal drinkers. Among heavy drinkers and alcoholics, they found it much more often, increasing with increasing age. The total number of females identified as heavy drinkers was small, but the prevalence of cirrhosis discovered among them was more than twice that among the alcoholic men (Table 4).

Findings have varied in studies of morbidity among unselected samples of alcoholic patients. Texon (1950) and Sclare (1970) found no sex difference in the prevalence of cirrhosis among the patients they studied. Wilkinson et al. (1971b), however, found clinical and histological evidence of cirrhosis in 69 out of 821 men (8.4%), but 29 out of 179 women (16.6%), in a series of Australian alcoholics presenting for treatment of their alcoholism. When the first 70 of these cases were

Table 4. Prevalence of Cirrhosis Discovered at Necropsy among
Nonalcoholic and Alcoholic Chileans Dying from Violence[a]

	Total patients	Number with cirrhosis	% with cirrhosis
Nonalcoholics			
Male	571	7	1.2
Female	239	3	1.3
Alcoholics			
Male	508	36	7.1
Female	30	5	16.7

[a] Calculated from Viel et al. (1968).

studied in more detail (1969a), it was found that the cirrhotic women had on average drunk significantly less and for a shorter period of time than the men. Ashley et al. (1977) found a comparable prevalence of cirrhosis among Canadian men and women (4.4%:3.0%) treated for alcoholism but also found that the women had a somewhat shorter exposure to alcohol (Table 5). Levels of drinking are not given for the cirrhotic patients separately, but the women alcoholics in the series as a whole drank significantly less than the men ($p < .01$).

It is now generally accepted that alcoholic hepatitis is the precursor of cirrhosis in the alcoholic (Schaffner and Popper, 1970). Several investigators have recently examined the incidence of hepatitis as well as cirrhosis in male and female alcoholic patients. Brunt et al. (1974) reviewed a series of 258 patients with various forms of alcoholic liver disease and found relatively more women with hepatitis than with cirrhosis or fatty liver. Bhathal et al. (1975) reviewed liver biopsies obtained from 100 patients attending a clinic for the management of alcoholism and found that 8 out of 23 women (35%) had alcoholic hepatitis ± cirrhosis compared with 22 out of 77 men (28%). Krasner et al. (1977) surveyed 293 patients with biopsy-proven alcoholic liver disease and found that women had a significantly higher incidence of

Table 5. Average Duration of Hazardous Drinking
in Men and Women with Alcoholic Cirrhosis

Investigator	Years of hazardous drinking	
	Men	Women
Wilkinson et al. (1969a)	20.0 ± 9.5	13.5 ± 8.4[a]
Ashley et al. (1977)	19.3 ± 8.0	17.4 ± 8.9

[a] $p < .01$.

hepatitis with or without superimposed cirrhosis than men. Biopsies from 70 out of 215 men (32.6%) compared with 35 out of 79 women (44.9%) showed the lesion of alcoholic hepatitis ± cirrhosis.

Krasner also found that the long-term prognosis for women in their series was worse than that for men, whether they continued to drink or not. This finding of a worsened prognosis as well as an increased incidence of alcoholic cirrhosis and its precursor in women accords with Spain's (1945) observations but conflicts with more recent findings. Garceau et al. (1964) found a better survival among women with cirrhosis, both alcoholic and nonalcoholic, compared with men. Powell and Klatskin (1968) found no difference in survival between males and females with alcoholic cirrhosis. Rankin et al. (1970) found that although alcoholic women were more prone to develop cirrhosis, once the disease was established the prognosis was no worse than it was in men if other factors were comparable. Basile (1977) has also challenged Krasner's findings. While agreeing about a higher incidence of serious forms of alcoholic hepatitis in women, he stated that he did not see a significant sex-related difference in the long-term prognosis of alcoholic liver disease.

Increased prevalence of alcoholic hepatitis and cirrhosis was found in women despite a shorter exposure to hazardous levels of drinking (Table 5) and lower mean levels of alcohol consumption (Krasner et al., 1977; Wilkinson et al., 1969a). A series of epidemiological investigations into the relationship between the level of alcohol consumption and cirrhosis morbidity in France (Caroli and Péquignot, 1958; Péquignot, 1974; Péquignot et al., 1974) also indicate an increased susceptibility to alcoholic cirrhosis among women. Péquignot (1974) has found that in both sexes, there is a threshold of alcohol consumption above which the risk of developing cirrhosis is dose-related. The threshold of alcohol intake for women is considerably lower than for men, 20–40 g ethanol per day, compared with 60 g per day, and above this threshold, the risk increases more rapidly for women (Péquignot et al., 1974).

This difference in susceptibility was previously attributed to differences in diet (Caroli and Péquignot, 1958; Spain, 1945), but more recently, a constitutional difference between the sexes has been postulated (Krasner et al., 1977; Péquignot et al., 1974; Wilkinson et al., 1969a). Krasner et al. (1977) have suggested that this difference may be related to differences in either the metabolism of alcohol or immunological responses between the sexes. Nonalcoholic liver disease, particularly the autoimmune variety, is commoner among women and frequently carries a worse prognosis (Mistilis, 1968). Krasner found a significantly higher incidence of serum autoantibodies among the women alcoholics in his series and suggested that, in women, alcohol might exert a more damaging effect by triggering a more vigorous and relentless immune destruction of hepatocytes.

Fatty Liver.   In contradistinction to alcoholic hepatitis and cirrhosis, there is evidence that fatty liver may be more common among men than among women (Table 6). Texon (1950) reported finding clinical evidence of fatty liver in relatively more males than females in his series of 500 alcoholic patients. In their histopathological studies of liver biopsies from two series of alcoholic patients, Bhathal et al. (1975) and Krasner et al. (1977) both found that fatty liver occurred more frequently among men than among women. Ashley et al. (1977) also found fatty liver significantly more often among men than among women in their large series of Canadian alcoholic patients. These authors have considered several possible mechanisms to account for this difference. First, they suggested that the abnormal use of drugs of dependence that they found to be more common in their women alcoholics might be a factor, since barbiturates decrease the capacity of the liver to accumulate fat (Lieber, 1975). Second, they speculated whether differences in dietary fat intake between the sexes might be contributory. Third, they postulated that decreases in testosterone levels in the blood, which can result in men from prolonged excessive use of alcohol (Rubin et al., 1976; van Thiel and Lester, 1974), might favor the accumulation of liver fat.

Hepatoma.   Hepatoma is a not uncommon complication of cirrhosis, both alcoholic and nonalcoholic (Stone et al., 1968). It occurs more frequently in alcoholic cirrhosis, and much more frequently in men than in women. This increased frequency among male cirrhotics has been attributed to the higher incidence of alcoholism in men. Krasner et al. (1976), however, found in reviewing 279 patients who had died of liver disease that among those with alcoholic cirrhosis, deaths from hepatoma were commoner among men than among women. In a further study on 293 patients, all with histologically proven alcoholic liver disease of various kinds, these workers (Krasner et al., 1977) found that hepatoma occurred in 6.1% of 215 men, but in only 1.3% of 78 women. The pathogenesis of this difference is not understood, but if men with alcoholic cirrhosis do survive for longer than women, this longer survival may account to some extent for the greater incidence of hepatoma in males.

Peptic Ulcer Disease

It is not universally agreed that alcoholism predisposes to peptic ulcer disease. Although there is a widespread clinical impression that peptic ulcers are seen more frequently and at a younger age among alcoholics, it is difficult to find evidence to confirm this impression.

Table 6. Prevalence of Fatty Liver in Alcoholic Men and Women

Investigator	Sample	Country	% Prevalence of fatty liver	
			Male	Female
Texon (1950)	Clinical diagnosis in 382 men and 118 women treated for alcoholism	U.S.	76.4	61.9
Bhathal et al. (1975)	Histopathological diagnosis in 77 men and 23 women treated for alcoholism	Australia	71.4	52.2
Krasner et al. (1977)	Histopathological diagnosis in 215 men and 78 women with alcoholic liver disease	England	21.4[a]	10.3
Ashley et al. (1977)	Clinical or histopathological diagnosis in 736 men and 135 women treated for alcoholism	Canada	47.7[b]	27.4

[a] $p < .05$.
[b] $p < .01$.

Hagnell and Wretmark (1957), in a study of 130 Swedish male alcoholics, found a prevalence of peptic ulceration of 18.5% compared with 8.1% in a random sample of males taken from the general population. Bingham (1960), however, found a prevalence of only 5.3% in 430 alcoholics surveyed for evidence of peptic ulceration.

Several studies have compared the prevalence of radiologically or surgically proven ulcer disease in alcoholic men and women. Again, the results vary considerably (Table 7), but alcoholic men appear more prone to the condition, as do nonalcoholic men (Truelove and Reynell, 1972; Sturdevant, 1976). This finding may be related to the fact that until recently, smoking, which delays healing in peptic ulcer disease (Doll et al., 1958), was commoner in men, both alcoholic and nonalcoholic, than in their female counterparts.

In the most recent study (Ashley et al., 1977), in which the male predominance was least, gastrointestinal hemorrhages and ulcer surgery were first recorded in the women after a significantly shorter duration of hazardous drinking compared with men. It is possible that the early morbidity among the women in this series was related to their levels of smoking, which were as high as those of the men, as well as to their alcohol consumption.

Alcoholic Pancreatitis

Alcoholic pancreatitis has been recognized as a definite entity in which alcohol is a direct causative factor (Marks and Bank, 1963; Sarles et al., 1965). It appears to be more common in men than in women. Marks and Bank (1963), Sarles et al. (1965), and Edlund et al. (1968) all emphasized that it is typically a male disease. In several large series of patients with alcoholic pancreatitis in which the sex of the patients was noted, men greatly outnumber women (Table 8). However, in two series of patients receiving treatment for alcoholism in whom the overall prevalence of pancreatitis was reported (Ashley et al., 1977; Wilkinson et al., 1971b), the sex difference, while maintained, was much less striking. Wilkinson et al. found that 2.2% of 821 men and 1.1% of 179 women had evidence of pancreatitis, past or present, in their series of alcoholic patients, while Ashley et al. found a history of the condition in 0.8% of 736 men and 0.7% of 135 women on admission.

Reasons for this male preponderance are not obvious. Nutrition is not an important etiological factor (Marks and Bank, 1963, Sarles et al., 1965). Sarles et al. (1965) did not think that the nature of the alcoholic beverage played any role, but both Marks and Bank (1963) and Edlund et al. (1968) commented on the preference of many of their patients for strong liquor. Spirits are drunk more often by male alcoholics than by

Table 7. Prevalence of Peptic Ulcer Disease in Alcoholic Men and Women

Investigator	Sample	Country	% Prevalence of peptic ulcer	
			Men	Women
Texon (1950)	382 men and 118 women receiving treatment for alcoholism	U.S.	5.8	0
Edwards et al. (1967)	242 men and 51 women attending AA	England	10.0	7.0
Barchha et al. (1968)	64 men and 18 women alcoholics receiving treatment in general hospital	U.S.	21.8	11.1
Wilkinson et al. (1971b)	821 men and 179 women receiving treatment for alcoholism	Australia	7.9	4.0
Wilkins (1974)	229 men and 51 women identified as alcoholics in general practice survey	England	14.0	4.0
Ashley et al. (1977)	736 men and 135 women receiving treatment for alcoholism	Canada	4.1	3.7

Table 8. Sex Distribution of Patients with Alcoholic Pancreatitis

Investigator	Sample	Country	Number of patients in series	
			Male	Female
Howard (1960)	94 alcoholic patients treated for alcoholic pancreatitis or sequelae	U.S.	67	27
Marks and Bank (1963)	148 cases of pancreatitis associated with moderate or heavy alcohol intake	South Africa	140	8
Sarles et al. (1965)	100 cases of calcifying pancreatitis; alcohol intake > 50 g/day in all but six	France	93	7
Edlund et al. (1968)	60 cases with acute pancreatitis and a history of alcoholism	Sweden	59	1
James et al. (1974)	45 cases of chronic pancreatitis with a history of alcoholism	England	39	6

females, and it is possible that this greater consumption of spirits could contribute to the greater incidence of pancreatitis among alcoholic men.

Anemia

Anemia is a common complication of alcoholism. It can be attributed to a variety of factors, including poor diet, liver disease, gastrointestinal hemorrhage, alcohol-induced malabsorption, and a direct toxic effect of alcohol on the bone marrow (Straus, 1973). Because of the increased demands that menstruation, pregnancy, and the use of oral contraceptives make on hematopoiesis (Hillman, 1974), both iron- and folate-deficient anemias are likely to be more common in the female alcoholic.

In his study of 50 male and 50 female alcoholics, randomly chosen, Sclare (1970) found that 12 women but only 4 men had an iron-deficiency anemia. Ashley et al. (1977) found evidence of a "mixed" anemia in 13.3% of the 135 female alcoholics in their series, but in only 4.2% of the 736 men. These anemias were first documented in the women after a significantly shorter period of hazardous drinking, 11.7 ± 7.2 years as opposed to 23.5 ± 9.1 years in the men.

Wu et al. (1975) studied peripheral blood and bone marrow appearance, and they measured serum, erythrocyte, and liver folate levels in 84 patients, 56 men and 28 women, who had been drinking more than 80 g of alcohol per day. They found that 6 (10.7%) of the men and 5 (17.9%) of the women had clinical macrocytic anemia. The women also had generally lower mean serum, red cell, and liver folate levels than the men. As well, both sexes showed evidence of toxic depression of erythropoiesis. It was not possible to determine whether this latter effect differed in severity in the two sexes. The authors attributed the differences they found between the sexes to differences in diet between the men and the women. They did not discuss the possiblity of differences in absorption of folate between the sexes.

Metabolic Disturbances

Excessive ingestion of alcohol stresses and deranges a number of metabolic pathways (Lieber and de Carli, 1977) and produces a variety of metabolic abnormalities. There are indications that there may be a sex difference in at least two alcohol-induced disorders of metabolism.

Hyperuricemia.   Oxidation of excessive amounts of alcohol results in the production of large amounts of lactic acid, which in turn reduces the capacity of the kidney to excrete uric acid (Lieber et al., 1962). The resulting hyperuricemia is reversed when alcohol is withdrawn. Recently, this secondary disturbance of urate metabolism has been shown to be more severe in women alcoholics than in men. In a normal population, the serum uric acid levels of premenopausal women are lower than those of men. In a large series of alcoholics who had recently been drinking, Olin et al. (1973) found that the distribution of serum uric acid levels was similar in the two sexes. The investigators attributed this finding to a higher incidence of folate deficiency among the women. They postulated that in addition to the alcohol-induced hyperuricemia, a secondary "anabolic" uricemia developed when red cell production increased, in response to the withdrawal of alcohol and an improvement in diet.

Alcoholic Ketoacidosis. Excessive ingestion of alcohol can produce severe ketoacidosis in some alcoholic patients who are not diabetic. In the first four series reported, women outnumbered men (Table 9), and this finding led Cooperman et al. (1974) to speculate that a hormonal mechanism might explain the difference. They suggested that circulating estrogens might increase the precursor supply of fatty acids and so enable ketonemia to develop more rapidly in women. This sex difference has been disputed by Fulop and Hoberman (1975), who did not find a preponderance of women among the cases they studied. Their series included six "mild" diabetics, who did not require specific hypoglycemic therapy, but who did exhibit postprandial hyperglycemia or mildly reduced glucose tolerance.

Cardiovascular Disease

Heart disease accounts for a large proportion of illness (Pell and D'Alonzo, 1968; Texon, 1950) and deaths (Nicholls et al., 1974; Schmidt and de Lint, 1972) among alcoholics, as it does in the general population, but the difference in death rates between the sexes is less in alcoholics

Table 9. Male and Female Patients with
Nondiabetic Alcoholic Ketosis

	Patients with alcoholic ketosis	
Investigator	Men	Women
Dillon et al. (1940)	2	5
Jenkins et al. (1971)	0	3
Levy et al. (1973)	3	2
Cooperman et al. (1974)	0	6
Fulop and Hoberman (1975)	11[a]	4[a]
	4[b]	2[b]

[a] Nondiabetics.
[b] "Mild" diabetics.

(Nicholls et al., 1974; Schmidt and de Lint, 1972). There is considerable overlap between the clinical entities of heart disease described in alcoholics, but two conditions can be recognized clearly on which data have been reported separately and compared in the two sexes. These are alcoholic cardiomyopathy and hypertension.

Alcoholic Cardiomyopathy. Clinical reports of alcoholic cardiomyopathy, a thiamine-resistant disease of heart muscle due directly to the toxic effects of alcohol on the heart muscle (Burch and De Pasquale, 1969), have consistently shown a predominantly male distribution (Brigden and Robinson, 1964; Evans, 1959; McDonald et al., 1971). Evans's series contained only men; Brigden's contained 49 men and 1 woman; and McDonald et al. reported on 47 men and 1 woman. The male predominance was at first assumed to be explained by the sex difference in the prevalence of alcoholism until Regan (1971) commented on the male predominance and suggested that it might indicate a constitutional difference between the sexes.

Depressed myocardial function can be recognized in alcoholics by means of special electromechanical techniques before clinical cardiomyopathy has developed (Spodick et al., 1972). Wu et al. (1976) measured myocardial contractility and intraventricular conduction in 22 male and 14 female alcoholics comparable for age and drinking history. They assessed myocardial contractility from the ratio of the preejection period to the left ventricular ejection time (PEP/LVET) and measured intraventricular conduction by means of high fidelity electrocardiography. PEP/LVET was found to be increased in alcoholics of both sexes, when compared with normal controls, indicating reduced contractility, but the increase was significant only in the males. Furthermore, the difference in PEP/LVET between male and female alcoholics was highly significant. Intraventricular conduction time was also prolonged significantly in the male alcoholics compared with both normal males and the alcoholic females. The authors postulated a constitutional sex difference in the susceptibility of heart muscle to the effects of alcohol.

Hypertension. Several studies have shown an association between heavy alcohol consumption and raised blood pressure in males (Mathews, 1976) and females (Klatsky et al., 1977). Most reported series of hypertensive patients drawn from the general population contain more women than men (Sokolow and Harris, 1961), although the men tend to have a worse prognosis. However, when alcoholic populations are studied, the prevalence of raised blood pressure is similar among males (Table 10). This hypertension is frequently labile, subsiding on withdrawal of alcohol but recurring if drinking is resumed (Pell and D'Alonzo, 1968; Wilkinson et al., 1971b). It is not understood how alcohol produces this rise in blood pressure or whether it has any serious sequelae.

Table 10. Prevalence of Hypertension in
Alcoholic Men and Women

Investigator	% Prevalence of hypertension in alcoholic patients	
	Men	Women
Texon (1950)	6.0	5.1
Wilkinson et al. (1971b)	16.8	17.1
Ashley et al. (1977)	8.7	6.7

Chronic Respiratory Disease

Chronic nontuberculous lung disease with mucus hypersecretion, airway obstruction, and impairment of diffusion is commoner in alcoholics than in the general population (Banner, 1973; Emirgil et al., 1974; Rankin et al., 1969), possibly because alcoholics are more likely to be tobacco smokers than nonalcoholics (Rankin et al., 1969), since smoking has been shown to play a part in the development of respiratory disease in the general population (Anderson and Ferris, 1962).

Women alcoholics have been found to be less prone to chronic lung disease than men. Wilkinson et al. (1971b) reported chronic bronchitis in 18.3% of 821 men and 12.6% of 179 women, while Ashley et al. (1977) found evidence of chronic obstructive lung disease in 12.1% of 736 men compared with 5.9% of 135 women ($p < .05$). This sex difference cannot be explained on the basis of a difference in tobacco consumption, since the great majority of alcoholics of both sexes are heavy smokers (Ashley et al., 1977; Maletzky and Klotter, 1974). It appears rather to reflect the greater susceptibility of men to developing chronic bronchitis, with mucus hypersecretion, at all levels of cigarette smoking (Tager and Speizer, 1976).

A recent study by Emirgil and Sobol (1977) is therefore of considerable interest. These authors measured pulmonary function in 44 former alcoholics, 25 men and 19 women. A high prevalence (64%) of obstructive pulmonary disease, as measured by expiratory flow rates, unrelated to smoking habits was found in both sexes. This prevalence was unexpectedly greater among the women (77%) and was present not only in the women who were smokers but in 3 out of 4 women who had never smoked. The authors suggested that alcohol *per se* may have played a part in the pathogenesis of the obstructive change. Burch and De Pasquale (1966) first suggested that alcohol itself, by virtue of its excretion through the lungs, might have an injurious effect, and it is possible that this effect is more severe in the female.

Diseases of the Nervous System

Alcoholic Withdrawal Syndrome.   The syndrome of tremor, sweating, and anxiety, progressing to extreme agitation, confusion, frank hallucinosis, and sometimes fits, associated with the abrupt withdrawal of alcohol, is said to be commoner in male alcoholics, but it is not easy to find documented evidence to support this assumption. Gross et al. (1974) stated that "men appear to be a higher risk group than women," and Dahlgren (1975) wrote, "experience has shown that women are more prone to develop Korsakoff's psychosis with polyneuritis, men more often DT." Wilkinson et al. (1971b), however, found evidence of alcohol withdrawal in 44 (5.4%) of men and 11 (6.1%) of women out of a total of 821 men and 179 women, when they were first examined. Sclare (1970) also found no significant difference between the male and female incidence of delirium tremens in the 50 men and 50 women he reviewed. Of these patients, 16 men and 15 women had a history of the condition. Ashley et al. (1977), on the other hand, reported the occurrence of acute brain syndrome on admission to the hospital in 12 (1.6%) of 736 men but only in 1 (0.7%) of 137 women presenting for treatment of alcoholism. In this series, acute brain syndrome was first manifest after the same mean period of exposure to alcohol in the two sexes. Also, 25 of the 139 men (36.0%) but only 11 of the 118 women (9.3%) treated in a Swedish psychiatric unit during the years 1962–1966 (Lindelius et al., 1974) had experienced at least one episode of delirium tremens.

It has been suggested that the development of acute withdrawal symptoms may be related to the pattern and level of intake (Gross et al., 1974) and also to the consumption of spirits (Neilsen, 1965). This possibility may explain the increased frequency among men, who tend to drink more heavily than women and who more frequently consume spirits.

Wernicke–Korsakoff Syndrome.   The Wernicke–Korsakoff syndrome, in which patients who are otherwise alert exhibit both retrograde and anterograde amnesia and sometimes ophthalmoplegia, is found in a proportion of chronic alcoholics. It is a result of midbrain damage consequent on thiamine depletion (Victor et al., 1971). It appears to be more common among women alcoholics than among men. Dahlgren (1975) has commented that women are more prone to it, but without giving further details. Rosenbaum and Merritt (1939) reviewed all cases of alcoholic Korsakoff's syndrome admitted to a North American general hospital over a period of three years. They found 34 men and 16 women with the condition, a male:female ratio of 2.1:1, considerably lower than that obtained among alcoholics in the population at the time. In the very detailed study made by Victor et al. (1971) of 245 cases of Wernicke–Korsakoff syndrome, the ratio of males:females was 1.7:1. All but six of their patients were alcoholics, and the authors commented that this sex ratio was "considerably less than the 4:1 ratio that has been noted for alcoholism in general." The greater incidence of this condition in women alcoholics has been attributed to the greater frequency with which women alcoholics neglect their diet (Victor and Adams, 1961).

Alcoholic Dementia. Dementia consequent on cerebral atrophy has now been described as an entity occurring independently of, although not infrequently associated with, the Wernicke–Korsakoff syndrome in alcoholics (Horvath, 1975). Horvath has reported in some detail a group of 100 demented alcoholics drawn from a series of 1100 Australian patients receiving treatment for alcoholism. There were 65 men and 35 women in his series, that is, 6.6% and 21%, respectively, of the male and female alcoholics in the total sample. Not only was dementia three times more common among the women, but it was also apparent after a shorter and smaller exposure to alcohol. The demented alcoholic men had drunk a mean of 300 g of alcohol per day for 20.8 years, whereas the women had drunk a mean of only 180 g per day for 15.8 years.

In his series of 50 male and 50 female alcoholics, Sclare (1970) reported 2 men and 1 woman with early dementia. Ashley et al. (1977) reported approximately equal proportions of men and women—3.7% and 3.0%, respectively—in their series of 871 alcoholic patients. The women, however, had drunk excessively for a shorter period than the men, for a mean of 19.5 ± 7.7 years, compared with 24.0 ± 9.4 years, a suggestive though not significant difference.

Horvath (1975) suggested that malnutrition might be one factor, but not the only one, in the pathogenesis of this disorder and in the increased frequency found among women alcoholics.

Marchiafava–Bignami's Disease. This extremely uncommon degenerative condition of the central nervous system, in which there is characteristic demyelination of the corpus callosum, was at first thought to be confined to male alcoholics. It was originally reported as occurring solely in men of Italian stock who drank crude red wine. More recently, rare cases have been reported in women. The pathogenesis of the disorder is not understood. Gross nutritional deficiencies, consumption of rough wines, and chronic methanol poisoning have all been implicated (Dreyfus, 1974; Poser, 1973).

Alcoholic Choreoathetosis. In 1970, Mullin et al. reported 12 patients, 6 men and 6 women, with a transient choreoathetotic movement disorder affecting mainly the upper half of the body during the early stages of treatment for chronic alcoholism. This condition was not associated with familial chorea, gross liver disease, vitamin deficiencies, or the use of phenothiazines. The authors commented on the high female prevalence and drew attention to its resemblance to the disturbance that is sometimes seen with chronic phenothiazine intoxication and that is also more common in women.

Alcoholic Peripheral Neuropathy. The neuropathy of alcoholism is attributed mainly to a nutritional deficiency of B vitamins, although its pathogenesis is not fully understood and the possibility of a toxic effect of alcohol on the neuron has also been considered (Mayer and Garcia-Mullin, 1972). Alcoholic neuropathy was believed to be more frequent among women alcoholics (Dahlgren, 1975; Victor and Adams, 1961), but this sex difference appears to have become less obvious in recent years (Hornabrook, 1961). In an Australian series of 1,000 alcoholic patients (Wilkinson et al., 1971b), peripheral neuropathy was relatively more common among women, occurring in 25.1% of them compared with 17.7% of the men. In a more recent series in Canada (Ashley et al., 1977), the condition occurred relatively more often among the men, in 4.6% of cases compared with 2.2% of the women. There was little difference in this series between the sexes in the duration of drinking before the first recorded occurrence of the disorder.

The greater frequency recorded in women has been attributed to inadequate food intake associated with an unremitting pattern of drinking found more commonly among women alcoholics (Victor and Adams, 1961; Victor et al., 1971).

Alcoholic Neuropathic Arthropathy. This condition, although it is strictly a disorder of the skeletal system, is included here as it is a complication of severe alcoholic neuropathy.

In 1973, Thornhill et al. reported 10 alcoholics suffering from destructive bone and joint changes in the feet associated with alcoholic neuropathy. In addition, there was painless ulceration of the plantar surfaces of the toes and feet. All the patients were males, even though the authors did see and treat female alcoholics in their practice.

Cancer

Alcoholics are especially prone to cancer, particularly of the mouth, pharynx, larynx, esophagus, and liver (Kissin and Kaley, 1974). The development of hepatoma in alcoholic patients with cirrhosis of the liver has already been discussed.

Despite the increased frequency of these cancers among alcoholics, they are still not very common. There are no studies large enough of alcoholic patients alone to compare the incidence of cancers of the head, neck, and esophagus between the sexes. Some knowledge can be gleaned from incidence studies in the general population, where levels of drinking in affected patients have been reported.

A strong correlation with both heavy drinking and heavy smoking has been shown for carcinomas of the mouth, larynx, and pharynx (Flamant et al., 1964; Kissin et al., 1973; Wynder et al., 1957a). In most epidemiological studies, the incidence rates for these carcinomas are much higher in men, higher than would at first seem explicable by the higher male prevalence of either smoking or drinking. Vincent and Marchetta (1963) have suggested that exposure to alcohol may augment the carcinogenic effects of tobacco, and Wynder et al. (1957a) have calculated that if the risks accrued from smoking and drinking were removed, the remaining risks to males and females might at least be similar. The development of carcinoma of the esophagus is related more directly to alcohol consumption and less to smoking (Flamant et al., 1964; Tuyns, 1970; Wynder and Bross, 1961). Again, in most parts of the Western world, the incidence is considerably higher in men than in women (Audigier et al., 1975; Flamant et al., 1964). Iron deficiency, particularly where it has led to the development of Plummer–Vinson syndrome, appears to predispose to carcinomas of the hypopharynx and esophagus (Wynder et al., 1957a), and in countries where iron deficiency is endemic, these carcinomas are commoner among women than among men in the general population (Kmet and Mahboubi, 1972; Wynder et al., 1957b). Wynder and Bross (1961) have suggested that because they are more prone to iron deficiency, women may actually have greater inherent chance of developing esophageal carcinoma. Such a predisposition would certainly exist for alcoholic women, too, compared with their male counterparts, since they not infrequently develop iron deficiency in association with heavy drinking (Straus, 1973).

4. SUMMARY AND CONCLUSIONS

A wide variety of physical disturbances are known to be associated with excessive alcohol consumption. For some of these conditions, no data are available to indicate whether or not their development differs between the two sexes. In other conditions, there is evidence to suggest some difference, but it is tantalizingly sparse and difficult to evaluate. With yet other conditions, more definite sex differences in incidence have been identified and studies have been undertaken to explore the underlying causes. In some cases, the differences have been related to differences in the lifestyle of male and female alcoholics. In other disorders, intriguing possibilities are being raised of inherent differences between the sexes in the body's response to alcohol.

The evidence that alcohol affects the female liver differently and more adversely than the male liver is now fairly compelling. This is a constitutional difference, but the exact mechanisms underlying it are not yet clear. Differences in the hepatic metabolism of alcohol, related to hormonal differences (Krasner et al., 1977; Wilkinson et al., 1969a) and differences in immunological responses in women, have been suggested (Krasner et al., 1977). Alcohol is able to induce hepatic microsomal enzymes (Kalant et al., 1976), and it is possible that differences in this ability are of significance in the development of liver damage. In future studies that focus on the cellular and subcellular responses of the liver to alcohol, it will be important to record and consider the sex of the subject, human or animal, when interpreting the results.

There seems to be ample evidence in the detailed work of Victor et al. (1971) that the Wernicke–Korsakoff syndrome is commoner in women and that it is related to thiamine deficiency. Horvath's (1975) observations on alcoholic dementia strongly suggest that female alcoholics experience a greater incidence of this condition as well. More epidemiological studies are needed to add to Horvath's findings if we are to discover how much the condition is a direct consequence of alcohol excess and how much the result of malnutrition or some other factor. With the advent of computerized axial tomography and newer methods of psychometric testing, these studies should be easier to carry out.

Evidence that there are sex-related differences in the response of the myocardium and the lung to alcohol is more recent and more fragmentary. Both myocardial disease and chronic lung disease have long been observed to occur more frequently in male than in female alcoholics, but the effects of smoking have so obscured all other etiological influences that it has been difficult to pinpoint the effects of alcohol *per se*. It will be valuable to separate these effects and compare them in the two sexes, for this procedure may throw light on basic mechanisms of cardiac and respiratory pathology in both the alcoholic and the nonalcoholic. Both epidemiological studies and detailed measurements of myocardial and pulmonary function are needed to confirm and extend the exciting findings of Wu et al. (1976) and Emirgil and Sobol (1977).

The recent work of Ashley et al. (1977), Olin et al. (1973), and Wu et al. (1975) indicates fairly conclusively that folate deficiency is a commoner problem among alcoholic women than it is among alcoholic men. This prevalence must be consequent in some part on sex-related differences in dietary intake and requirements of folate, but whether there may also be an alcohol-induced difference in folate absorption has yet to be determined.

The evidence for sex-related differences in several other alcohol-induced disorders is more tenuous. Epidemiological studies are needed to substantiate the impression that alcohol-induced hypertension may be commoner among men, as well as metabolic studies to unravel the mechanisms of its production.

The data on alcoholic pancreatitis are confused and confusing. Careful documentation is needed of the prevalence of heavy drinking among series of patients with pancreatitis—and, conversely, of the occurrence of pancreatitis among patients being treated for alcoholism—to establish whether the condition is truly commoner in the male alcoholic. Dietary and smoking habits as well as alcohol consumption may be important predisposing factors in the development of pancreatitis in the alcoholic, and information must be collected about them as well when studies are undertaken. Work in this field may well be hampered by the relative inaccessibility of the pancreas and the difficulties attendant on the accurate measurement of pancreatic function, until newer investigative techniques are developed.

The findings with regard to the prevalence of peptic ulceration and cancers of the upper gastrointestinal tract among alcoholics are confused, too. There is no clear evidence that the observed predisposition of males to these conditions is a function of the effect of alcohol *per se*. Other etiological factors, in particular heredity and analgesic ingestion in the case of peptic ulceration, and cigarette smoking in both conditions, may be overriding and must certainly be taken into account when interpreting any epidemiological studies.

Data on some of the rarer alcohol-related diseases that have been included in this review are very sparse, and any sex differences among them are clearly of questionable significance. These diseases include such entities as alcoholic ketosis and the rarer degenerative diseases of the nervous system. They have been mentioned, nevertheless, for completeness and in the hope of stimulating documentation of further cases. Such documentation, however sporadic, may contribute to a better understanding of the occurrence and pathogenesis of these diseases.

Epidemiological and clinical studies must include details of all aspects of drinking habits. Accurate records of the length, degree, and periodicity of alcohol exposure, as well as the beverage consumed, are of paramount importance. Where possible, intake should be related to body weight, since men are often significantly heavier than women. The levels of alcohol reached in the blood, as well as the amounts of alcohol consumed, may be important in the development of alcohol-related disease, particularly of the central nervous system. It has been suggested that a preference for strong liquor may result in high blood levels of alcohol and may explain the higher incidence in males of delirium tremens (Neilsen, 1965) and pancreatitis (Edlund, 1968). There is also some evidence that in women, higher blood alcohol levels are reached per gram dose of alcohol per kilogram of body weight (Jones and Jones, 1976), so that monitoring of the blood alcohol levels reached in series of patients of both sexes could contribute to the understanding of the diseases that may develop.

Other features in the alcoholic's lifestyle must also be recorded in any study that attempts to explore sex-related differences in morbidity in the alcoholic. Excessive use of other drugs of dependence, particularly tobacco, analgesics, and barbiturates, is common among alcoholics. For cultural reasons, their consumption may vary markedly in the two sexes. These substances have their own deleterious effects on body tissues, which may complicate and obscure the effects of alcohol. Their use by alcoholic patients under study must therefore be quantified carefully.

Nutritional factors are now considered less important than previously in the pathogenesis of alcoholic liver disease, but their possible role in the development of other alcohol-related diseases cannot be ignored. The prolonged use of drugs such as oral contraceptives that impose particular nutritional and metabolic demands must also be considered. Where malnutrition is suspected of playing a part in the development of morbidity in the alcoholic, comparison between the sexes of the absorption and utilization of various dietary factors, particularly the B vitamins, may be fruitful.

Even with careful and comprehensive documentation, findings must be interpreted cautiously. Criteria for the definition and diagnosis of both alcoholism and its many complications can vary widely. They can differ not just between series of patients but within them as well, particularly between males and females of a series. Women alcoholics tend to remain hidden for longer than men, even though their condition often progresses more rapidly, both psychologically and physically. As a result, the true cause of their ill health may remain unrecognized until it reaches a more advanced stage, thus obscuring the true prevalence of their alcohol-related diseases. Because their alcoholism is concealed or unrecognized and because they change their names when they marry, women alcoholics are often more difficult to follow for long periods than men. This difficulty may affect the frequency with which they are reported to develop late complications, such as brain damage and cancers.

It would seem important, however, despite all likely problems with methodology and interpretation, to continue to explore any possible sex differences in alcohol-related disease. Ashley et al. (1977) have emphasized the need for further studies in view of the rising incidence of female alcoholism. Such studies might help clarify the pathogenesis not only of alcohol-related illness but of a number of diseases of the nonalcoholic as well.

ACKNOWLEDGMENTS

I am indebted to Robyn Sanders for her careful typing and retyping of the manuscript and to my family for their patient support during the preparation of this chapter.

REFERENCES

Anderson, D. O., and Ferris, B. G., Jr., 1962, Role of tobacco smoking in the causation of chronic respiratory disease, *N. Engl. J. Med.* **267**:787–794.

Ashley, M. J., Olin, J. S., Le Riche, W. H., Kornaczewski, A., Schmidt, W., and Rankin, J. G., 1976, Skid row alcoholism: A distinct sociomedical entity, *Arch. Intern. Med.* **136**:272–278.

Ashley, M. J., Olin, J. S., Le Riche, W. H., Kornaczewski, A., Schmidt, W., and Rankin, J. G., 1977, Morbidity in alcoholics. Evidence for accelerated development of physical disease in women, *Arch. Intern. Med.* **137**:883–887.

Audigier, J. C., Tuyns, A. J., and Lambert, R., 1975, Epidemiology of oesophageal cancer in France: Increasing mortality and persistent correlation with alcoholism, *Digestion* **13**:209–219.

Banner, A. S., 1973, Pulmonary function in chronic alcoholism, *Am. Rev. Respir. Dis.* **108**:851–857.

Barchha, R., Stewart, M. A., and Guze, S. B., 1968, The prevalence of alcoholism among general hospital ward patients, *Am. J. Psychiatry* **125**:681–684.

Basile, A., 1977, Alcoholic liver disease (letter), *Br. Med. J.* **2**:319.

Beckman, L. J., 1975, Women alcoholics: A review of social and psychological studies, *J. Stud. Alcohol* **36**:797–824.

Bhathal, P. S., Wilkinson, P., Clifton, S., Rankin, J. G., and Santamaria, J. N., 1975, The spectrum of liver disease in alcoholism, *Aust. N.Z. J. Med.* **5**:49–57.

Bingham, J. R., 1960, Precipitating factors in peptic ulcer, *Can. Med. Assoc. J.* **83**:205–211.

Brenner, B., 1967, Alcoholism and fatal accidents, *J. Stud. Alcohol* **28**:517–528.

Brigden, W., and Robinson, J., 1964, Alcoholic heart disease, *Br. Med. J.* **2**:1283–1289.

Brunt, P. W., Kew, M. C., Scheuer, P. J., and Sherlock, S., 1974, Studies in alcoholic liver disease in Britain, I, Clinical and pathological patterns related to natural history, *Gut* **15**:52–58.

Burch, G. E., and De Pasquale, N., 1966, Alcoholic lung disease: An hypothesis, *Am. Heart J.* **73**:147–148.

Burch, G. E., and De Pasquale, N. P., 1969, Alcoholic cardiomyopathy, *Am. J. Cardiol.* **23**:723–731.

Caroli, J., and Péquignot, G., 1958, Enquête sur les circonstances diététiques de la cirrhose alcoolique en France, *Proceedings of World Congress on Gastroenterology* **1**:661–665.

Cooperman, M. T., Davidoff, F., Spark, R., and Pallotta, J., 1974, Clinical studies of alcoholic ketoacidosis, *Diabetes* **23**:433–439.

Curlee, J., 1970, A comparison of male and female patients at an alcoholism treatment centre, *J. Psychol.* **74**:239–247.

Dahlgren, L., 1975, Special problems in female alcoholism, *Br. J. Addict.* **70**:18–24.

Dahlgren, L. and Myrhed, M., 1977, Alcoholic females, II, Causes of death with reference to sex difference, *Acta Psychiatr. Scand.* **56**:81–91.

de Lint, J., 1977, Critical examination of data bearing on the type of alcoholic beverage consumed in relation to health and other effects, *Br. J. Addict.* **72**:189–197.

Dillon, E. S., Dyer, W. W., and Smelo, L. S., 1940, Ketone acidosis in nondiabetic adults, *Med. Clin. North Am.* **24**:1813–1822.

Doll, R., Jones, F. A., and Pygott, F., 1958, Effect of smoking on the production and maintenance of gastric and duodenal ulcers, *Lancet* 1:657–662.

Dreyfus, P. M., 1974, Diseases of the nervous system in chronic alcoholics, in: *The Biology of Alcoholism III* (B. Kissin and H. Begleiter, eds.), pp. 265–290, Plenum New York.

Edlund, Y., Norbäck, B., and Risholm, L., 1968, Acute pancreatitis, etiology and prevention of recurrence: Follow-up study of 188 patients, *Rev. Surg.* 25:153–157.

Edwards, G., Hensman, C., Hawker, A., and Williamson, V., 1967, Alcoholics Anonymous: The anatomy of a self-help group, *Soc. Psychiatry* 1:195–204.

Edwards, G., Kyle, E., and Nicholls, P., 1974, Alcoholics admitted to four hospitals in England, I, Social class and the interaction of alcoholics with the treatment system, *Q. J. Stud. Alcohol* 35:499–522.

Emirgil, C., and Sobol, B. J., 1977, Pulmonary function in former alcoholics, *Chest* 72:45–51.

Emirgil, C., Sobol, B. J., Heyman, B., and Shibutani, K., 1974, Pulmonary function in alcoholics, *Am. J. Med.* 57:69–77.

Evans, W., 1959, The electrocardiogram of alcoholic cardiomyopathy, *Br. Heart J.* 21:445–456.

Fitzgerald, B. J., Pasewark, R. A., and Clark, R., 1971, Four-year follow-up of alcoholics treated at a rural state hospital, *Q. J. Stud. Alcohol* 32:636–642.

Flamant, R., Lasserre, O., Lazar, R., Leguerinais, J., Denoix, P., and Schwartz, D., 1964, Differences in sex ratio according to cancer site and possible relationship with use of tobacco and alcohol: Review of 65,000 cases, *J. Natl. Cancer Inst.* 32:1309–1316.

Fulop, M., and Hoberman, H., 1975, Alcoholic ketosis, *Diabetes* 24:785–790.

Garceau, A. J., and the Boston Inter-Hospital Liver Group, 1964, The natural history of cirrhosis, II, The influence of alcohol and prior hepatitis on pathology and prognosis, *N. Engl. J. Med.* 271:1173–1179.

Gillis, L. S., 1969, The mortality rate and causes of death of treated chronic alcoholics, *S. Afr. Med. J.* 43:230–232.

Gross, M. M., Lewis, E., and Hastey, J., 1974, Acute alcohol withdrawal syndrome, in: *The Biology of Alcoholism III* (B. Kissin and H. Begleiter, eds.), pp. 191–263, Plenum, New York.

Hagnell, O., and Wretmark, G., 1957, Peptic ulcer and alcoholism: A statistical study in frequency behaviour, personality traits and family occurrence, *J. Psychosom. Res.* 2:35–44.

Hillman, R. W., 1974, Alcoholism and malnutrition, in: *The Biology of Alcoholism III* (B. Kissin and H. Begleiter, eds.), pp. 513–586, Plenum, New York.

Hornabrook, R. W., 1961, Alcoholic neuropathy, *Am. J. Clin. Nutr.* 9:398–403.

Horvath, T. B., 1975, Clinical spectrum and epidemiological features of alcoholic dementia, in: *Alcohol, Drugs and Brain Damage, Proceedings of a Symposium: Effects of Chronic Use of Alcohol and Other Psychoactive Drugs on Cerebral Function* (J. G. Rankin, ed.), pp. 1–16, Addiction Research Foundation, Toronto.

Howard, J. M., 1960, Alcoholic pancreatitis, in: *Surgical Diseases of the Pancreas* (J. M. Howard and G. L. Jordan, eds.) pp. 190–202, Lippincott, Philadelphia.

James, O., Agnew, J. E., and Bouchier, I. A. D., 1974, Chronic pancreatitis in England: A changing picture? *Br. Med. J.* 2:34–38.

Jenkins, D. W., Eckel, R. E., and Craig, J. W., 1971, Alcoholic ketoacidosis, *J. Am. Med. Assoc.* 217:177–183.

Jones, B. M., and Jones, M. K., 1976, Male and female intoxication levels for three alcohol doses or do women really get higher than men? *Alc. Tech. Rep.* 5:11–14 (abstracted in *J. Stud. Alcohol* 1977, 38:692).

Kalant, H., Khanna, J. M., Lin, G. Y., and Chung, S., 1976, Ethanol—A direct inducer of drug metabolism, *Biochem. Pharmacol.* **25**:337–342.

Kissin, B., and Kaley, M. M., 1974, Alcohol and cancer, in: *The Biology of Alcoholism III* (B. Kissin and H. Begleiter, eds.), pp. 481–511, Plenum, New York.

Kissin, B., Kaley, M. M., Su, W. H., and Lerner, R., 1973, Head and neck cancer in alcoholics: The relationship to drinking, smoking and dietary patterns, *J. Am. Med. Assoc.* **224**:1174–1175.

Klatsky, A. L., Friedman, G. D., Siegelaub, A. B., and Gérard, M. J., 1977, Alcohol consumption and blood pressure, *N. Engl. J. Med.* **296**:1194–1200.

Kmet, J., and Mahboubi, E., 1972, Esophageal cancer in the Caspian littoral of Iran: Initial studies, *Science* **175**:846–853.

Krasner, N., Johnson, P., Bomford, A., Eddleston, A. L. W. F., and Williams, R., 1976, Hepatoma in chronic liver disease (abstract), *Gut* **17**:390.

Krasner, N., Davis, M., Portmann, B., and Williams, R., 1977, Changing pattern of alcoholic liver disease in Great Britain: relation to sex and signs of autoimmunity, *Br. Med. J.* **1**:1497–1500.

Levy, L. J., Duga, J., Girgis, M., and Gordon, E. E., 1973, Ketoacidosis associated with alcoholism in nondiabetic subjects, *Ann. Intern. Med.* **78**:213–219.

Lieber, C. S., 1975, Liver disease and alcohol: Fatty liver, alcoholic hepatitis, cirrhosis, and their interrelationships, *Ann. N.Y. Acad. Sci.* **252**:63–84.

Lieber, C. S., and de Carli, L. M., 1977, Metabolic effects of alcohol on the liver, in: *Metabolic Aspects of Alcoholism* (C. S. Lieber, ed.), pp. 31–79, University Park Press, Baltimore.

Lieber, C. S., Jones, D. P., Losowsky, M. S., and Davidson, C. S., 1962, Interrelation of uric acid and ethanol metabolism in man, *J. Clin. Invest.* **41**:1863–1870.

Lindbeck, V. L., 1972, The woman alcoholic: A review of the literature, *Int. J. Addict.* **7**:567–580.

Lindelius, R., and Salum, I., 1972, Mortality, in: *Delirium Tremens and Certain Other Acute Sequels of Alcohol Abuse* (I. Salum, ed.), *Acta Psychiatr. Scand. Suppl.* **235**:86–100.

Lindelius, R., Salum, I., and Agren, G., 1974, Mortality among male and female alcoholic patients treated in a psychiatric unit, *Acta Psychiatr. Scand.* **50**:612–618.

Lindgren, G., 1957, Alkohol och arbete. *Sven. Läkartidn.* **48**:3613. Quoted in A. Medhus, 1974, Morbidity among female alcoholics, *Scand. J. Soc. Med.* **2**:5–11.

Lokander, S., 1962, Sick absence in a Swedish company: A sociomedical study, *Acta Med. Scand. Suppl.* **377**:1–172.

Mackay, I. R. 1966, The effects of alcohol on the gastrointestinal tract, *Med. J. Aust.* **2**:372–376.

Maletzky, B. M., and Klotter, J., 1974, Smoking and alcoholism, *Am. J. Psychiatry* **131**:445–447.

Marks, I. N., and Bank, S., 1963, The etiology, clinical features and diagnosis of pancreatitis in the South Western Cape: A review of 243 cases, *S. Afr. Med. J.* **37**:1039–1053.

Mathews, J. D., 1976, Alcohol use, hypertension and coronary heart disease, *Clin. Sci. Molec. Med.* **51**(Suppl. 3):661–663.

Mayer, R. F., and Garcia-Mullin, R., 1972, Peripheral nerve and muscle disorders associated with alcoholism, in: *The Biology of Alcoholism II* (B. Kissin and H. Begleiter, eds.), pp. 21–56, Plenum, New York.

McDonald, C. D., Burch, G. E., and Walsh, J. J., 1971, Alcoholic cardiomyopathy managed with prolonged bed rest, *Ann. Intern. Med.* **74**:681–691.

Medhus, A., 1974, Morbidity among female alcoholics, *Scand. J. Soc. Med.* **2**:5–11.

Medhus, A., 1975, Mortality among female alcoholics, *Scand. J. Soc. Med.* **3**:111–115.

Mistilis, S. P., 1968, Liver disease in pregnancy with particular emphasis on the cholestatic syndromes, *Aust. Ann. Med.* **17**:248–260.

Mullin, P. J., Kershaw, P. W., and Bolt, J. M., 1970, Choreoathetotic movement disorder in alcoholism, *Br. Med. J.* **4**:278–281.

Neilsen, J., 1965, Delirium tremens in Copenhagen, *Acta Psychiatr. Scand. Suppl.* **187**:1–92.

Nicholls, P., Edwards, G., and Kyle, E., 1974, Alcoholics admitted to four hospitals in England: General and cause-specific mortality, *Q. J. Stud. Alcohol* **35**:841–855.

Observer and Maxwell, M. A., 1959, A study of absenteeism, accidents, and sickness payments in problem drinkers in one industry, *Q. J. Stud. Alcohol* **20**:302–312.

Olin, J. S., Devenyi, P., and Weldon, K. L., 1973, Uric acid in alcoholics, *Q. J. Stud. Alcohol* **34**:1202–1207.

Oltman, J. E., and Friedman, S., 1965, Trends in admissions to a state hospital, 1942–1964, *Arch. Gen. Psychiatry* **13**:544–551.

Pell, S., and D'Alonzo, C. A., 1968, The prevalence of chronic disease among problem drinkers, *Arch. Environ. Health* **16**:679–684.

Pell, S., and D'Alonzo, C. A., 1970, Sickness absenteeism of alcoholics, *J. Occup. Med.* **12**:198–210.

Pell, S., and D'Alonzo, C. A., 1973, A five-year mortality study of alcoholics, *J. Occup. Med.* **15**:120–125.

Péquignot, G., 1974, Les problèmes nutritionnels de la société industrielle, *Vie Méd. Canad. Franç.* **3**:216–225.

Péquignot, G., Chabert, C., Eydoux, H., and Courcoul, M.-A., 1974, Augmentation au risque de cirrhose en fonction de la ration d'alcool, *Rev. Alcohol.* **20**:191–202.

Popham, R. E., 1959, Some social and cultural aspects of alcoholism, *Can. Psychiatr. Assoc. J.* **4**:222–229.

Poser, C. M., 1973, Demyelination in the central nervous system in chronic alcoholism: Central pontine myelinolysis and Marchiafava–Bignami's disease, *Ann. N.Y. Acad. Sci.* **215**:373–381.

Powell, W. J., Jr., and Klatskin, G., 1968, Duration of survival in patients with Laennec's cirrhosis: Influence of alcohol withdrawal and possible effects of recent changes in general management of the disease, *Am. J. Med.* **44**:406–420.

Rankin, J. G., Hale, G. S., Wilkinson, P., O'Day, D. M., Santamaria, J. N., and Babarczy, G., 1969, Relationship between smoking and pulmonary disease in alcoholism, *Med. J. Aust.* **1**:730–733.

Rankin, J. G., Wilkinson, P., and Santamaria, J. N., 1970, Factors influencing the prognosis of the alcoholic patient with cirrhosis, *Aust. Ann. Med.* **3**:232–239.

Regan, T. J., 1971, Ethyl alcohol and the heart, *Circulation* **44**:957–963.

Rosenbaum, M., and Merritt, H. H., 1939, Korsakoff's syndrome, *Arch. Neurol. Psychiatry* **41**:978–983.

Rubin, E., Lieber, C. S., Altman, K., Gordon, G. G., and Southren, A. L., 1976, Prolonged ethanol consumption increases testosterone metabolism in the liver, *Science* **191**:563–564.

Sarles, H., Sarles, J.-C., Camatte, R., Muratore, R., Gaini, M., Guien, C., Pastor, J., and Le Roy, F., 1965, Observations on 205 confirmed cases of acute pancreatitis, recurring pancreatitis and chronic pancreatitis, *Gut* **6**:545–559.

Schaffner, F. M. D., and Popper, H., 1970, Alcoholic hepatitis in the spectrum of ethanol-induced liver injury, *Scand. J. Gastroenterol. Suppl.* **7**:69–78.

Schmidt, W., and Bronetto, J., 1962, Death from liver cirrhosis and specific alcohol beverage consumption: an ecological study, *Am. J. Public Health* **52**:1473–1482.

Schmidt, W., and de Lint, J., 1969, Mortality experiences of male and female alcoholic patients, *Q. J. Stud. Alcohol* **30**:112–118.

Schmidt, W., and de Lint, J., 1972, Causes of death of alcoholics, *Q. J. Stud. Alcohol* **33**:171–185.

Sclare, A. B., 1970, The female alcoholic, *Br. J. Addict.* **65**:99–107.

Seixas, F., 1975, Medical consequences of alcoholism (preface), *Ann. N.Y. Acad. Sci.* **252**:5–8.

Sokolow, M., and Harris, R. E., 1961, The natural history of hypertensive disease, in: *Hypertension: Recent Advances* (A. N. Brest and J. H. Moyer, eds.), pp. 3–19, Kimpton, London.

Spain, D. M., 1945, Portal cirrhosis of the liver, a review of 250 necropsies with reference to sex differences, *Am. J. Clin. Pathol.* **15**:215–219.

Spodick, D. H., Pigott, V. M., and Chirife, R., 1972, Preclinical cardiac malfunction in chronic alcoholism: Comparison with matched normal controls and with alcoholic cardiomyopathy, *N. Engl. J. Med.* **287**:677–680.

Stone, W. D., Islam, N. R. K., and Paton, A., 1968, The natural history of cirrhosis, *Q. J. Med.* **37**:119–132.

Straus, D. J., 1973, Hematologic aspects of alcoholism, *Semin. Hematol.* **10**:183–194.

Sturdevant, R. A. L., 1976, Epidemiology of peptic ulcer: Report of a conference, *Am. J. Epidemiol.* **104**:9–14.

Sundby, P., 1967, *Alcoholism and Mortality,* The National Institute for Alcoholic Research, Publication no. 6, pp. 207, Universitetsforlaget, Oslo.

Tager, I. B., and Speizer, F. E., 1976, Risk estimates for chronic bronchitis in smokers: A study of male–female differences, *Ann. Rev. Respir. Dis.* **113**:619–625.

Tashiro, M., and Lipscomb, W. R., 1963, Mortality experience of alcoholics, *Q. J. Stud. Alcohol* **24**:203–212.

Texon, M., 1950, Medical aspects of an alcoholic service in a general hospital: Report of 500 cases *Q. J. Stud. Alcohol* **11**:205–211.

Thornhill, H. L., Richter, R. W., Shelton, M. L., and Johnson, C. A., 1973, Neuropathic arthropathy (Charcot forefeet) in alcoholics, *Orthop. Clin. North Am.* **4**:7–20.

Truelove, S. C., and Reynell, P. C., 1972, Peptic ulcer, in: *Diseases of the Digestive System,* pp. 156–187, Blackwell, Oxford, England.

Tuyns, A. J., 1970, Cancer of the oesophagus: Further evidence of the relation to drinking habits in France, *Int. J. Cancer* **5**:152–156.

van Thiel, D. H., and Lester, R., 1974, Sex and alcohol, *N. Engl. J. Med.* **291**:251–253.

Victor, M., and Adams, R. D., 1961, On the etiology of the alcoholic neurologic diseases with special reference to the role of nutrition, *Am. J. Clin. Nutr.* **9**:379–397.

Victor, M., Adams, R. D., and Collins, G. H., 1971, *The Wernicke–Korsakoff Syndrome,* Blackwell Scientific Publications, Oxford, England.

Viel, B., Donoso, S., Salcedo, D., and Varela, A., 1968, Alcoholic drinking habit and hepatic damage, *J. Chronic Dis.* **21**:157–166.

Vincent, R. G., and Marchetta, F., 1963, The relationship of the use of tobacco and alcohol to cancer of the oral cavity, pharynx or larynx, *Am. J. Surg.* **106**:501–505.

Whitlock, F. A., 1974, Liver cirrhosis, alcoholism and alcohol consumption, *Q. J. Stud. Alcohol* **35**:586–605.

Wilkins, R. H., 1974, in: *The Hidden Alcoholic in General Practice,* pp. 122–123, Elek Science, London.

Wilkinson, P., Santamaria, J. N., and Rankin, J. G., 1969a, Epidemiology of alcoholic cirrhosis, *Aust. Ann. Med.* **18**:222–226.

Wilkinson, P., Santamaria, J. N., Rankin, J. G., and Martin, D., 1969b, Epidemiology of alcoholism: Social data and drinking patterns of a sample of Australian alcoholics, *Med. J. Aust.* **1**:1020–1025.

Wilkinson, P., Kornaczewski, A., Rankin, J. G., and Santamaria, J. N., 1971a, Bromureide dependence in alcoholics, *Med. J. Aust.* **2**:479–482.

Wilkinson, P., Kornaczewski, A., Rankin, J. G., and Santamaria, J. N., 1971b, Physical disease in alcoholism: Initial survey of 1,000 patients, *Med. J. Aust.* **1**:1217–1223.

Wu, A., Chanarin, I., Slavin, G., and Levi, A. J., 1975, Folate deficiency in the alcoholic — Its relationship to clinical and haematological abnormalities, liver disease and folate stores, *Br. J. Haematol.* **29**:469–478.

Wu, C. F., Sudhaker, M., Ghazanfar, J., Ahmed, S. S., and Regan, T. J., 1976, Preclinical cardiomyopathy in chronic alcoholics: A sex difference, *Am Heart J.* **91**:281–286.

Wynder, E. L., and Bross, I. J., 1961, A study of etiological factors in cancer of the esophagus, *Cancer* **14**:389–413.

Wynder, E. L., Bross, I. J., and Feldman, R. M., 1957a, A study of etiological factors in cancer of the mouth, *Cancer* **10**:1300–1323.

Wynder, E. L., Hultberg, S., Jacobsson, F., and Bross, I. J., 1957b, Environmental factors in cancer of upper alimentary tract: A Swedish study with special reference to Plummer-Vinson (Paterson–Kelly) syndrome, *Cancer* **10**:470–487.

10

Sex Differences in Mortality
A Comparison of Male and Female Alcoholics

WOLFGANG SCHMIDT and ROBERT E. POPHAM

1. INTRODUCTION

For more than a century, the almost invariable observation of students of longevity has been that the female of the species outlives the male. Because the difference appears to be nearly universal in the animal world (Hamilton, 1948), a biological explanation has been favored. However, in the case of man, pronounced variation in the sex mortality ratio over short periods in the same population (see, for example, Krasner et al., 1977) indicates that attribution to constitutional factors alone is an oversimplification. It is indeed most probable that there is a genetically determined difference in longevity, but variations in the magnitude of this difference through time are likely to be due to environmental factors.

Essentially two approaches to determining the contribution of environmental influences are evident in the literature. In the first, the objective is to parcel out the contribution to the trend in the mortality sex ratio of *specific* causes of death and then to examine the effects of cigarette smoking and various other external factors. The small relevant literature has been well reviewed by Retherford (1975), and his own analysis is the most comprehensive recent example. Using data from three countries for the period 1910–1965, he confirmed the observation of superior female longevity and showed that the sharp increase in the sex ratio in the present century has been attributable mainly to cigarette

WOLFGANG SCHMIDT and ROBERT E. POPHAM ● Addiction Research Foundation, Toronto, Ontario.

smoking: over the period, the increase in smoking among men has been very much greater than among women.

In a much earlier and more restricted version of this approach, Bandel (1930) examined the relationship between the trend in the mortality sex ratio and that in per capita alcohol consumption. His principal finding is summarized in Fig. 1. Evidently the correlation was remarkably high. The author noted that biological factors probably predispose to a difference in mortality between the sexes. However, he concluded that changes in the level of alcohol consumption offered a reasonable explanation of the *variation* in excess male mortality through time.

The findings of these two studies are not necessarily contradictory but are dependent on a historical difference in smoking and drinking habits. Bandel's data for Bavaria applied to a period when regular cigarette smoking was rare; alcohol consumption, in contrast, was high and largely confined to males. In both studies, a less favorable mortality picture was found for males. However, whereas variation in the male excess is largely due to cigarette smoking in this century, drinking behavior appears to have been the relevant factor in the last century. It stands to reason that the importance of either or both of these behaviors varies regionally as well as temporally. The important point in the present context is that both drinking and smoking can have a significant impact on the mortality sex differential.

The second, and theoretically most general, approach seeks to select

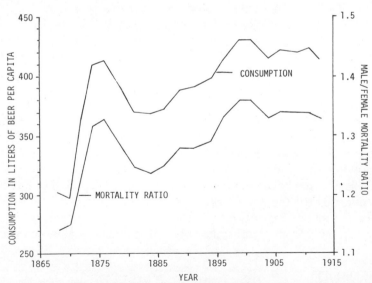

Fig. 1. Apparent consumption of beer and excess mortality of males over females in Bavaria, 1867–1913. Consumption is based on sales of beer in liters per capita to those aged 20 and older; mortality ratios are based on the death rates in the population aged 40–69 years.

a group of persons for whom the differences between the sexes in environmental hazards to health are minimal. In the one example of which we are aware, Madigan (1957) compared the mortality experience, over the period 1900–1954, of male and female members of Roman Catholic teaching orders and found that the sex difference and changes in this difference through time were similar to those which occurred in the general population over the period. He assumed that a low level of "socio-cultural stress and strain" was characteristic of the life situations of both sexes and, therefore, that the difference found could be attributed to constitutional factors. However, he failed to consider the possibility that differences between men and women in exposure to environmental hazards applied as well to the religious orders—albeit, perhaps, at a lower level—as to the general population. For example, the brothers and sisters may have differed in their drinking and smoking habits in the same direction as do men and women in the general population. In any event, a genetic explanation for variation in the mortality sex ratio over a period of only some 50 years seems hardly credible.

The present authors' study can be conceptualized as a further example of the second approach in that it seeks to minimize the differences in environmental hazards affecting the two sexes. But, in contrast to Madigan's approach, the selection of alcoholics implies that the hazards involved are at a very high level relative to those prevailing in the general population. This is particularly so in the case of two important etiological variables: smoking and drinking. It is reasonable to postulate that the two sexes in the sample did not differ significantly in these two behaviors. All were voluntary admissions to a treatment center for alcoholism and were, virtually by definition, persons whose tendency was to drink the maximum that can be sustained chronically. As for smoking, a previous study indicated that the two sexes differed little in this clinical population of alcoholics (Dreher and Fraser, 1967–1968). Under these circumstances, one would expect that the general mortality differential between the sexes would be much reduced, and indeed, a sex ratio of one might be predicted for those causes of death in which alcohol and tobacco use are the primary etiological factors. In short, the sample offers a way to control for certain of the principal environmental hazards by maximizing them in both sexes. To the extent that differences between the sexes nevertheless persist, the explanation is more likely to be found in constitutional factors.

2. METHOD

The case material of this study comprised all admissions from 1951 to 1970, inclusive, to the Toronto clinical services for alcoholics of the

Addiction Research Foundation. There were 9889 males and 2158 females with a diagnosis of alcoholism and a confirmed history of frequent regular consumption of large amounts of alcohol.

As a first step, an attempt was made to identify those patients who were alive after 31 December, 1971, through a check of the records of various institutions (e.g., employment registries, hospitals, jails) and by contacting the patients themselves or persons who could provide information about them. For those who could not be so identified, a search was made of death records in Ontario for the period 1951–1971. Also, in a number of cases, confirmation of death came from the population registers of other Canadian provinces and some foreign countries. We found that 1823 men and 296 women had died during the study period.

It was not possible to establish in every instance whether a patient was alive or dead at the end of 1971. For example, a few patients who had left the country or appeared in the clinic records under an assumed name could not be located. For the present purpose, all such patients were assumed to be alive. Therefore, the number of confirmed deaths is probably slightly less than the actual number.

The follow-up period ranged from a maximum of 21 years (those admitted at the beginning of 1951) to a minimum of 1 year (those admitted at the end of 1970). The calculation of age-specific person-years of exposure to the risk of death is best explained in an example: a 43-year-old patient who was admitted in 1961 and died in 1971 was taken to have contributed over the study period, one and a half person-years to the age class 40–44,* five person-years to the age class 45–49, and four years to the age class 50–54.

Expected frequencies were calculated on the basis of the mortality of the Ontario population as reported in the official vital statistics. General and cause-specific mortality expectancies were first tabulated for each calendar year separately and then combined into a single expectancy for five-year age groups. To ensure comparability of the mortality data for the sample with those for the general population, the cause of death entered on the death certificate by the provincial registrar was used, although in some instances independent information suggested a different primary cause.†

---

* Exposure to the risk of death during the admission year could vary from 1 to 12 months, depending on the date of admission. To simplify calculation, a half-year of exposure was uniformly assigned in the case of this year.

† For additional information on the method employed and previous reports on the mortality experience of smaller samples of the same clinical population of alcoholics, see de Lint and Schmidt (1970) and Schmidt and de Lint (1969, 1970, 1972, 1973). It is perhaps

3. GENERAL MORTALITY BY AGE AND SEX

The person-year distribution by age and sex for the alcoholic sample is provided in Table 1. The expected numbers of deaths were calculated on the basis of the age-specific death rates for the general population. Overall, the ratios of observed over expected deaths indicate considerable excess mortality in both male and female alcoholics. The excess is highest in the younger age groups and decreases with age. By age 70, the mortality rates differ little from those of the general population. The comparison also indicates that up to age 60, the excess mortality of female alcoholics is markedly greater than that of male alcoholics. The result is a mortality ratio of the total female sample of 3.04 as against 1.90 for the male. This difference does not necessarily imply that female alcoholics have a higher mortality rate than male alcoholics. As pointed out earlier, females in the general population have a much lower mortality than males, which results in lower expected values for the female sample. Accordingly, to determine whether or not male and female alcoholics differ from one another in mortality experience requires a different type of comparison. This is shown in Table 2. When observed female deaths are compared with an expectancy based on the male alcoholic death rate, the picture is reversed: female alcoholics have significantly fewer deaths than expected. However, this difference is not consistent across all age groups. Up to about age 50, female alcoholics have higher death rates than male alcoholics. This is the age range in which a majority of clinic patients fall at point of first admission. The differences are thus in agreement with the observation in several morbidity studies (Ashley et al., 1977; Wilkinson et al., 1971) that female alcoholics are more prone to medical complications than male. At the same time, it is noteworthy that when the full life span is taken into account—something rarely practicable in clinical studies—the unfavorable position of the female alcoholic no longer holds. In late middle age and in old age, the excess shifts to the male to such an extent that the ratio for the sample as a whole (0.825) favors the female.

Finally, it is of interest to compare the sample ratio with the comparable figure for the general population. Clearly, the female–male difference (0.54) is much more pronounced than in the alcoholic sample.

---

noteworthy that the few previous studies of the mortality experience of male and female alcoholics are not relevant in the present context. These have been mainly concerned with comparisons of the mortality rates of each sex with those of the general population (Dahlgren and Myrhed, 1977a; Lindelius et al., 1974; Tashiro and Lipscomb, 1963). In any case, the numbers of alcoholic female deaths reported in such studies have been too small to permit valid conclusions respecting cause-specific differences.

Table 1. Observed (f_o) and Expected (f_e) Deaths from All Causes among Alcoholics[a]

Age	Males				Females			
	Person years	Number of deaths		f_o/f_e	Person years	Number of deaths		f_o/f_e
		f_o	f_e			f_o	f_e	
15–29	3,212.5	16	4.49	3.56	915.5	4	0.55	7.25
30–34	6,258.0	36	9.35	3.85	1,400.0	12	1.20	10.00
35–39	10,760.5	113	22.90	4.94	2,321.0	25	3.04	8.21
40–44	14,009.0	195	47.76	4.08	3,101.0	51	6.40	7.96
45–49	14,518.5	253	85.80	2.95	2,049.5	54	10.25	5.27
50–54	13,270.5	294	130.96	2.24	2,740.0	40	14.15	2.83
55–59	10,728.5	341	173.72	1.96	2,096.5	55	16.80	3.27
60–64	6,795.0	243	172.10	1.41	1,170.0	20	14.76	1.36
65–69	3,639.5	186	141.45	1.31	615.5	16	11.94	1.34
70 and older	2,449.0	146	172.37	0.85	396.5	19	18.23	1.04
Total	85,641	1823	960.90	1.90[b]	17,805	296	97.32	3.04[b]

[a] f_e is based on the death rates in the population of Ontario.

[b] $p < .01$. Rare events, such as deaths within a given period, follow the Poisson distribution in which the variance is equal to the mean. A 0.01 level of confidence in the significance of a difference is obtained when the observed frequency differs from the expected frequency by at least three standard deviations. A difference of two standard deviations indicates a 0.05 level of confidence.

Table 2. Observed (f_o) and Expected (f_{em})[a] Deaths from All Causes among Female Alcoholics

Age	f_o	f_{em}	f_o/f_{em}	General population mortality sex ratio[b]
15–29	4	4.37	0.92	0.42
30–34	12	8.15	1.47	0.57
35–39	25	24.84	1.01	0.62
40–44	51	43.10	1.18	0.61
45–49	54	53.28	1.01	0.57
50–54	40	61.47	0.65	0.52
55–59	55	66.45	0.83	0.50
60–64	20	41.65	0.48	0.50
65–69	16	31.62	0.51	0.50
70 & older	19	23.44	0.81	0.62
Total	296	358.37	0.83[c]	0.54

[a] f_{em} is based on the death rates in the male alcoholic sample in the Ontario population.

[b] Standardized over five-year age groups to be comparable to the sex ratios in the alcoholic sample.

[c] $p < .01$.

The shared alcoholic lifestyle evidently tends to equalize an otherwise very different mortality experience.

4. MALE AND FEMALE MORTALITY BY CAUSE

In Table 3, the mortality experience of the sample is shown by cause. Expected values are based on the age-standardized death rates for the sex group in the general population of Ontario. In both male and female alcoholics, heart disease was by far the leading cause of death, accounting for 31.5% of the male deaths and 20.3% of the female deaths. Cirrhosis is second, accounting for 8.4% of male and 10.8% of female deaths. Suicide in men (7.1% of all male deaths) and accidental poisoning in women (9.1% of all female deaths) ranked third. In these causes, both sexes exceeded expectancies significantly. Generally, the mortality experience of the sample is similar to that commonly found among alcoholics and other heavy drinkers: considerable excess mortality from cancer of the lung, head, and neck and from heart disease, pneumonia, cirrhosis, gastric ulcer, and traumatic causes (Schmidt and Popham, 1975–1976). In addition, the relatively large size of the sample revealed excesses in certain comparatively rare causes, namely, epilepsy and bronchitis. In other single-cause categories, the numbers are small and therefore statistically unstable. However, there are noteworthy excesses in three combined categories: (1) nutritional, metabolic, and blood disease; (2) other diseases of the respiratory system; and (3) diseases of the digestive tract. Generally speaking, the same causes, in nearly the same proportions, contribute to the excess mortality in male and female alcoholics (illustrated in Fig. 2). The ratios of observed over expected values tend to be higher for the females, but, as previously indicated, this difference does not necessarily mean that female alcoholics have a higher mortality from these causes than males. In fact, in most cases, it simply reflects the lower mortality of females in the general population.

In Table 4, the two sex groups are compared directly in the manner described above (Table 2). The sex ratio in mortality for the general population is standardized to be comparable to the observed–expected ratio for the alcoholic sample. Attention is confined in this table to the causes of death known to be associated with the alcoholic lifestyle, for all of which considerable excess mortality is displayed in Table 3. Generally, previous studies have implicated three etiological factors in the excess mortality of alcoholics: heavy drinking, heavy smoking, and the combined effect of these two behaviors (Schmidt and Popham, 1975–1976). It would seem that, where alcohol ingestion is the predominating factor, the ratio of observed over expected approaches one as in

Table 3. Observed (f_o) and Expected $(f_e)^a$ Deaths by Cause among Alcoholics

	Males			Females		
	Number of deaths			Number of deaths		
Causes of death	f_o	f_e	f_o/f_e	f_o	f_e	f_o/f_e
All causes	1823	960.89	1.90^b	296	97.33	3.04^b
Malig. neoplasm of upper digestive and upper respiratory tract	52	13.51	3.85^b	5	0.72	6.97^b
Malig. neoplasm of trachea, bronchus, and lung	89	53.18	1.67^b	4	1.46	2.74^c
All other malig. neoplasms	99	125.42	0.79^c	28	28.99	0.97
Diabetes	17	11.85	1.44	1	2.09	0.48
Nutritional, metabolic, and blood diseases	19	8.86	2.15^b	2	1.31	1.53
Alcoholism	84	5.18	16.21^b	15	0.35	43.48^b
Vascular lesions of central nervous system	83	69.31	1.20	21	10.34	2.03^b
Epilepsy	14	1.15	12.19^b	2	0.17	11.91^b
All other diseases of nervous system and sense organs	6	7.05	0.85	2	1.11	1.80
Rheumatic heart disease	17	11.34	1.50	2	2.42	0.83
Arteriosclerotic and degenerative heart disease	575	400.38	1.44^b	60	24.55	2.44^b
All other diseases of circulatory system	38	43.84	0.87	10	5.22	1.92
Pneumonia	60	21.49	2.79^b	8	2.06	3.88^b
Bronchitis	24	10.73	2.24^b	1	0.33	3.07
All other diseases of respiratory system	24	16.83	1.43	6	1.05	5.74^b
Peptic ulcer	26	9.30	2.80^b	1	0.49	2.02
Cirrhosis	153	16.85	9.08^b	32	1.86	17.25^b
All other diseases of digestive system	35	15.23	2.30^b	7	2.33	3.01^b
Diseases of genitourinary system	11	13.60	0.81	4	1.81	2.21
Motor vehicle accidents	42	28.83	1.46^c	4	2.17	1.84
Accidental poisoning	59	3.93	15.01^b	27	0.48	56.37^b
Accidental falls	56	8.30	6.75^b	8	0.74	10.86^b
Accidents caused by fire	35	3.57	9.81^b	12	0.35	34.48^b
All other accidents	48	21.54	2.23^b	6	0.59	10.20^b
Suicide	129	22.34	5.77^b	21	1.74	12.06^b
Homicide	7	1.46	4.80^b	3	0.24	12.61^b
All other causes^d	21	15.69	1.34	4	2.05	1.95

^{a} f_e is based on the age-standardized death rates in the population of Ontario.
^{b} $p < 0.01$.
^{c} $p < 0.05$.
^{d} Infective and parasitic diseases (11 male, 0 female); diseases of skin, bones, and muscles (3 male, 0 female); congenital malformations (2 male, 0 female); ill-defined symptoms and senility (5 male, 4 female).

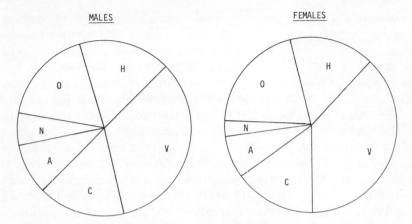

Fig. 2. Proportionate contribution of major causes of death to the excess mortality of alcoholics. Calculated on the basis of the data in Table 3. H, arteriosclerosis and degenerative heart disease; V, violent causes; C, cirrhosis; A, alcoholism; N, malignant neoplasms; O, all other causes.

Table 4. Observed (f_o) and Expected (f_{em})[a] Deaths by Cause among Female Alcoholics

Causes of death	f_o	f_{em}	f_o/f_{em}	General population mortality sex ratio[b]
All causes	296	358.56	0.83[c]	0.54
Cancers of upper digestive and upper respiratory tracts	5	10.15	0.49	0.28
Cancers of trachea, bronchus, and lung	4	16.49	0.24[c]	0.15
Alcoholism	15	17.52	0.86	0.33
Vascular lesions of the central nervous system	21	15.67	1.34	0.83
Arteriosclerotic and degenerative heart disease	60	109.16	0.55[c]	0.33
Pneumonia	8	11.64	0.69	0.52
Cirrhosis	32	30.66	1.04	0.56
Accidents, poisonings, and violence	81	79.01	1.03	0.34

[a] f_{em} is based on the death rates in the male alcoholic sample.
[b] See Table 2, footnote b.
[c] $p < 0.01$.

the case of alcoholism, cirrhosis, and violent causes. Where smoking is primary—notably lung cancer—the ratio is small, and where a combined effect may occur, the ratio is intermediate, as in the case of cancers of the head and neck, heart disease, and pneumonia. The ratio for deaths due to vascular lesions of the central nervous system is an exception to this pattern. The death rate for female alcoholics is higher than for male. A difference in the same direction has been reported in the massive study by Hammond (1966) of the effects of smoking, and, indeed, it was the only cause of death for which the excess mortality of smokers over nonsmokers was greater for the females than for the males. Given that male alcoholics in the present sample do not differ significantly from the general male population in the death rate from this cause (Table 3), it would appear that a sex-specific effect of smoking rather than of drinking explains the elevated death rate among female alcoholics.

Sex-linked susceptibilities to such alcohol- or smoking-related causes of death as cirrhosis and lung cancer have also been suggested in the literature. In the case of cancer of the lung, female smokers appear to have lower death rates than male smokers. While it has never been possible to control fully for duration, amount, and other relevant aspects of smoking, the likelihood of a real difference in susceptibility is increased by the finding that, among nonsmokers, men have a higher rate of death from this cause (Hammond, 1966). In the present sample, the females likewise had very significantly fewer deaths than expected. The sample is of particular interest because male and female subsamples of these alcoholics have been found to differ little in their smoking histories; and, indeed, the mean consumption of cigarettes, at the time of interview, was distinctly higher for the female subsample (Dreher and Fraser, 1967–1968).

It is also instructive to consider the difference in the case of lung cancer within the context of sex differences or their absence in mortality from other cancers. In Table 5, a breakdown of the mortality data showing the distribution of deaths by site of cancer is provided. In the alcoholic sample, the sex ratio for deaths due to cancer of the mouth or throat (0.28)—where smoking rather than drinking is probably the more important factor—is very similar to that for lung cancer (0.24), and both differ little from the comparable ratios in the general population (0.26 and 0.15, respectively). On the other hand, the sex ratio for cancer of the esophagus—where there is convincing evidence of a strong independent alcohol effect (Schmidt and Popham, 1975–1976)—approaches one (0.96) in the alcoholic sample in contrast to 0.33 in the general population. These differences are consistent with the pattern suggested earlier: male and female alcoholics differ little in alcohol-related mortality, but where smoking is the dominant factor, female alcoholics have

Table 5. Observed (f_o) and Expected (f_e)[a] Deaths from Cancer among Alcoholics

Site of cancer	Males			Females			Females		General population mortality sex ratio[c]
	Number of deaths			Number of deaths			Number of deaths		
	f_o	f_e	f_o/f_e	f_o	f_e	f_o/f_e	f_{em}	f_o/f_{em}	
All cancers	240	192.10	1.25[d]	37	31.17	1.19	45.08	0.82	0.87
Buccal cavity, pharynx, and larynx	36	8.49	4.24[d]	2	0.41	4.88	7.02	0.28[e]	0.26
Esophagus	16	5.02	3.19[d]	3	0.31	9.77[e]	3.13	0.96	0.33
Trachea, bronchus, and lung	89	53.18	1.67[d]	4	1.46	2.74	16.49	0.24[d]	0.15
Lower digestive tract	48	47.96	1.00	4	6.43	0.62	8.90	0.45	0.73
Breast and uterus	—	0.28	—	13	11.55	1.13	—	—	—
Prostate	11	10.10	1.09	—	—	—	—	—	—
All other sites	40	67.08	0.60[d]	11	11.01	1.00	7.73	1.42	0.86

[a] f_e is based on the age-standardized death rates in the population of Ontario.
[b] f_{em} = expected deaths for female alcoholics based on the death rates in the male alcoholic sample.
[c] See Table 2, footnote b.
[d] $p < 0.01$.
[e] $p < 0.05$.

lower rates of death. Among the cancers for which there is no evidence to implicate either smoking or drinking, neither male nor female alcoholics exceed the general population expectations in their death rates.

Among alcohol-related diseases, cirrhosis of the liver has been reported to involve a sex-linked susceptibility. For example, Péquignot et al. (1974) found that the potentially cirrhogenic level of intake was substantially less in females than in males. Wilkinson et al. (1969), in a study of a clinical sample of alcoholics, concluded that cirrhotic female patients have usually drunk less over a shorter period than their male counterparts. And in a recent survey of hospitalized patients with alcoholic liver disease (Krasner et al., 1977), the five-year survival rate for women with hepatitis or cirrhosis was substantially lower than for men. The results of the present study appear to be at variance with these observations: the sex ratio of 1.05 (Table 4) indicates that male and female alcoholics are remarkably similar in mortality from cirrhosis. However, in previous studies of severe liver disease in females, the patients have been mainly under 50 years of age. As shown in Table 6, a higher incidence is also found in this age group in the present sample. On the other hand, the sex difference disappears when the death rates for the older age groups are included. The importance of alcohol in deaths due to violence and accidents is well known. It is therefore not surprising that in contrast to the sex ratio in the general population, male and female alcoholics differ very little in their death rates from all violent causes combined. However, as indicated in Table 7, there are notable differences in the specific mode of death. Females are underrepresented in fatal motor vehicle accidents, probably because of lower exposure. The sex ratio in the sample differs little from that in the general population. In contrast, female alcoholics have a considerably higher rate of death from accidental poisoning, and in this respect, the ratio differs markedly from that for the general population. Most of these deaths were a consequence of the combined effect of alcohol and another psychoactive drug, usually a barbiturate. This finding is consistent with Devenyi

Table 6. Observed (f_o) and Expected (f_{em}) Deaths from Cirrhosis among Female Alcoholics

Age	f_o	f_{em}	f_o/f_{em}	Gen. pop. mortality sex ratio[b]
Under 50	18	14.44	1.25	0.69
50 and older	14	16.22	0.86	0.50
Total	32	30.66	1.04	0.56

[a] f_{em} is based on the death rates in the male alcoholic sample.
[b] See Table 2, footnote b.

Table 7. Observed (f_o) and Expected (f_e)[a] Deaths from Violent Causes among Alcoholics and f_{em}[b] for Female Alcoholics

Cause of death	Males			Females			Females		General population mortality sex ratio[c]
	Number of deaths			Number of deaths			Number of deaths		
	f_o	f_e	f_o/f_e	f_o	f_e	f_o/f_e	f_{em}	f_o/f_{em}	
All violent causes	376	89.98	4.18[a]	81	6.30	12.85[a]	79.01	1.03	0.34
Transportation accidents	51	35.37	1.44[e]	5	2.27	2.20	10.76	0.47	0.31
Accidental poisoning	59	3.93	15.01[a]	27	0.48	56.37[a]	12.52	2.16[a]	0.58
Suicide	129	22.34	5.77[a]	21	1.74	12.06[a]	27.16	0.77	0.38
Accidental falls	56	8.30	6.75[a]	8	0.74	10.86[a]	11.28	0.71	0.46
Accidents caused by fire	35	3.57	9.81[a]	12	0.35	34.48[a]	7.16	1.68	0.48
Other accidents	39	15.01	2.60[a]	5	0.49	10.31[a]	8.70	0.58	0.16
Homicide	7	1.46	4.80[a]	3	0.24	12.61[a]	1.43	2.10	0.78

[a] f_e is based on the age-standardized death rates in the population of Ontario.
[b] f_{em} = expected deaths for female alcoholics based on the death rates in the male alcoholic sample.
[c] See Table 2, footnote b.
[a] $p < 0.01$.
[e] $p < 0.05$.

and Wilson's (1971) finding of a higher rate of barbiturate abuse among females in a subsample of the alcoholic population in the present study.

The rate of suicidal death is lower (though not significantly) in female alcoholics. However, it is likely that some deaths reported under the rubric of accidental poisoning were, in fact, suicides and that the proportion so masked is greater for females than for males. This possibility is suggested by the distribution of mode of suicide shown in Table 8. Clearly, women alcoholics favor poisoning; the preference of males is for violent means. It may be, therefore, that a better approximation to the true sex ratio for both accidental poisoning and suicide is obtained by combining the two cause categories. The result is a ratio of 1.20, which does not differ significantly from 1.

For the remaining violent causes, male and female alcoholics have much higher death rates than their counterparts in the general population, but they do not differ significantly from one another (see Table 7).

5.   THE AGE FACTOR

We have shown earlier (Table 2) that the sex differentials in the overall mortality of alcoholics favor males at ages below 50 and females at older ages. In Table 9, age-specific sex ratios are shown for five leading causes of death. Evidently, the age pattern mentioned is also reflected in deaths from most of the causes listed in the table. Only in the case of violent deaths do we find a reversal: females over the age of 50 have higher rates than males. Thus, up to middle age, female alcoholics have a higher risk of dying from chronic degenerative disease. This finding brings to mind Lolli's impression that female alcoholics pass more rapidly through the various stages of uncontrolled drinking (Lolli,

Table 8. Mode of Suicide of Male and Female Alcoholics

Mode of suicide	Males		Females	
	Number	%	Number	%
Poisoning by solid and liquid substances	33	25.6	14	66.7
Poisoning by gases	19	14.7	—	—
Hanging	25	19.4	—	—
Drowning	1	0.8	3	14.3
Shooting	38	29.5	1	4.8
Cutting and piercing	4	3.1	—	—
Jumping from high places	6	4.7	3	14.3
Jumping before vehicles	3	2.3	—	—

Table 9. Mortality Sex Ratios in the Alcoholic
Sample[a] and in the Population of Ontario[b] by
Age and Cause of Death

| Cause of death | Mortality sex ratio | | | |
| | Alcoholics | | General population | |
	15–49	50+	15–49	50+
All causes	1.09	0.67	0.58	0.53
Cancer	2.06	0.58	1.43	0.76
Heart disease	0.70	0.53	0.20	0.38
Cirrhosis	1.25	0.86	0.69	0.50
Alcoholism	1.37	0.25	0.32	0.34
Violent deaths	0.89	1.24	0.31	0.37

[a] Female mortality rates divided by male rates.
[b] Standardized over five-year age groups to be comparable to
the sex ratios in the alcoholic sample.

1953). After middle age, the risk of death from violent causes is greater. Most of the latter are suicides or are due to an overdose of drugs and alcohol, a finding that suggests that severe emotional problems are comparatively common at this point in the drinking history.

6. TRENDS IN MORTALITY SEX RATIOS IN THE GENERAL POPULATION

Summary measures of the sex mortality differential in general populations have shown an increasing disparity, favoring females. If we separate the contribution to this trend in overall mortality of various causes of death (Fig. 3), it becomes apparent that the net effect is the result of both increases and decreases in the sex ratios: changes in the mortality from some causes have lessened the disparity, and others have increased it. The graph shows that the sex ratios of the primarily alcohol-related deaths—cirrhosis, alcoholism, and cancer of the esophagus—are increasing, while the ratios for the primarily smoking-related deaths, which comprise cancers of the lung, mouth, and throat, are decreasing. The rate of decline in these ratios is more pronounced in the case of cancer of the lung and bronchus, which are causes with a relatively pure tobacco etiology, than in cancers of the mouth and throat. In the latter, both smoking and drinking are etiologically relevant (Schmidt and Popham, 1975–1976).

A narrowing gap between the sexes in the rate of death from smoking-related causes has been reported for many parts of the Western

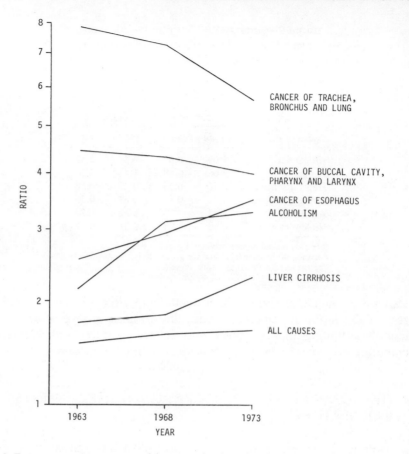

Fig. 3. Two-year moving averages of the ratio of male to female death rates for selected causes in the population aged 20 and older, Ontario 1963, 1968, and 1973. Based on data in *Ontario Vital Statistics.*

world and is generally attributed to the fact that, since World War II, women have smoked more and more like men. The increase in the sex ratios of the alcohol-related causes is unexpected in the light of several reports that point to a decline in sex differences in alcoholism prevalence over the recent past (Dahlgren and Myhred, 1977b; Working Group on Women Alcoholics, 1977). The explanation for this apparent contradiction may lie in the type of data on which these findings are based. Thus, the claim of a decline in the sex ratio is based chiefly on changes in sex-specific rates of clinical admission for alcoholism. The increase in the sex ratio, found in our data (Figure 2), refers to deaths from alcohol-related disease, which typically occur only after many years of heavy drinking. It is possible, therefore, that the increase in the prevalence of heavy drinking among women is too recent to be reflected in mortality data. Support for this explanation can be found in earlier trends in the sex ratio of lung cancer deaths. The ratio increased over many years prior to the decline shown in the graph. The reason for the recent reversal is that the tendency of women to smoke like men dates back to World War II years. Hence, sufficient time has elapsed for the smoking trend to be reflected in mortality statistics. If the time lag hypothesis is valid, we would expect a downward turn in the mortality sex ratios from alcohol-related causes in the not-too-distant future.

7. CONCLUDING COMMENTS

As is now very well known, there are marked differences in the mortality experience of men and women in general populations. One important question is the extent to which the differences persist when the two sex groups share a common lifestyle of extremely hazardous character. An alcoholic sample is peculiarly well suited to an examination of this question since two prominent elements in the lifestyle of the alcoholic—heavy drinking and heavy smoking—have been shown to have a significant impact on the mortality sex differential. Given similarity in these two behaviors alone, one would expect a notable reduction in the difference in mortality rates. Specifically, the ratio would be expected to approach one in the case of those causes of death in which alcohol and tobacco use are the primary etiological factors.

With respect to the overall mortality picture, the expectation was confirmed: there was a significant reduction in the difference between the two sexes. In the alcoholic sample, there were 83 female deaths per 100 male deaths in contrast to a ratio in the general population of 54 per 100 (Table 2). This tendency to equalization held also for the contribution to the overall death rates of the major causes of death (illustrated in Fig. 4). Male and female alcoholics are clearly much more alike than their counterparts in the general population.

The expectation was also confirmed in the case of death rates from causes with a primary alcohol etiology, such as cirrhosis and violent causes. On the other hand, a substantial sex difference remained in mortality from diseases in which smoking is implicated. There were four male deaths from lung cancer for every female death among the alcoholics (Table 4). Likewise, a considerable difference remained in the death rates from heart disease. The differences in mortality from these two causes account for nearly the whole of the difference in overall mortality between the male and the female alcoholics. The two sexes have been shown to be similar in amount and duration of smoking. Accordingly,

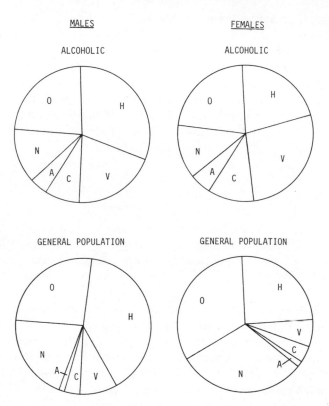

Fig. 4. Contribution of major causes of death to mortality of alcoholics and to mortality in a comparable segment of the general population of Ontario. H, arteriosclerosis and degenerative heart disease; V, violent causes; C, cirrhosis; A, alcoholism; N, malignant neoplasms; O, all other causes.

while other environmental influences cannot be ruled out, it is difficult to escape the conclusion that the heart and lung of the female are inherently less vulnerable, and that lesser vulnerability is responsible for the residual difference in mortality in the alcoholic sample. Indeed, given the hazardous character of the lifestyle typical of both male and female alcoholics, it might be hypothesized that the difference observed in the present sample approximates the minimum achievable through the equalization of external factors.

ACKNOWLEDGMENTS

The authors wish to thank Mrs. Joan Moreau and Mr. Stephen Israelstam for their dependable assistance in the often onerous tasks of compiling, checking, and analyzing the primary data.

REFERENCES

Ashley, M. J., Olin, J. S., le Riche, W. H., Kornaczewski, A., Schmidt, W., and Rankin, J. G., 1977, Mortality in alcoholics: Evidence for accelerated development of physcial disease in women, *Arch. Intern. Med.* **137**:883–887.

Bandel, R., 1930, Die spezifische Männersterblichkeit als Masstab der Alkoholsterblichkeit, in: *Ergebnisse der Sozialen Hygiene und Gesundheitsfürsorge, Bd. II,* pp. 424–492, Georg Thieme Verlag, Leipzig.

Dahlgren, L., and Myrhed, M., 1977a, Alcoholic Females, II, Causes of death with reference to sex difference, *Acta Psychiatr. Scand.* **56**:81–91.

Dahlgren, L., and Myrhed, M., 1977b, Female Alcoholics I, Ways of admission of the alcoholic patient: A study with special reference to the female alcoholic, *Acta Psychiatr. Scand.* **56**:39–49.

de Lint, J., and Schmidt, W., 1970, Mortality from liver cirrhosis and other causes in alcoholics: A follow-up study of patients with and without a history of enlarged fatty liver, *Q. J. Stud. Alcohol* **31**:705–709.

Devenyi, P., and Wilson, M., 1971, Abuse of barbiturates in an alcoholic population, *Can. Med. Assoc. J.* **104**:219–221.

Dreher, K. F., and Fraser, J. G., 1967–1968, Smoking habits of alcoholic outpatients, *Int. J. Addict.* **2**:259–270; **3**:65–80.

Hamilton, J. B., 1948, The role of testicular secretions as indicated by the effects of castration in man and by studies of pathological conditions and the short lifespan associated with maleness, *Recent Progress in Hormone Research* **3**:257–322.

Hammond, E. D., 1966, Smoking in relation to the death rates of one million men and women, in: *Epidemiological Approaches to the Study of Cancer and Other Chronic Diseases, National Cancer Institute Monograph 19* (W. Haenszel, ed), pp. 127–204, U. S. Deptartment of Health, Education and Welfare, National Cancer Institute, Bethesda, Md.

Krasner, N., Davis, M., Portmann, B., and Williams, R., 1977, Changing pattern of alcoholic liver disease in Great Britain: Relation to sex and signs of autoimmunity, *Br. Med. J.* **1**:1497–1500.

Lindelius, R., Salum, I., and Agren, G., 1974, Mortality among male and female alcoholic patients treated in a psychiatric unit, *Acta Psychiatr. Scand.* **50**:612–618.

Lolli, G., 1953, Alcoholism in women, *Conn. Rev. Alcsm.* **5**:9–11.

Madigan, F. C., 1957, Are sex mortality differentials biologically caused? *Milbank Memorial Fund Quart.* **35**:202–223.

Péquignot, G., Chabert, C., Eydoux, H., and Courcoul, M.-A., 1974, Augmentation du risque de cirrhose en fonction de la ration d'alcool, *Rev. Alcool.* **20**:191–202.

Retherford, R. D., 1975, *The Changing Sex Differential in Mortality: Studies in Population and Urban Demography No. 1,* University of California, Greenwood Press, Berkeley, p. 139.

Schmidt, W., and de Lint, J., 1969, Mortality experiences of male and female alcoholic patients, *Q. J. Stud. Alcohol* **30**:112–118.

Schmidt, W., and de Lint, J., 1970, Social class and the mortality of clinically treated alcoholics, *Br. J. Addict.* **64**:327–331.

Schmidt, W., and de Lint, J., 1972, Causes of death of alcoholics, *Q. J. Stud. Alcohol* **33**:171–185.

Schmidt, W., and de Lint, J., 1973, The mortality of alcoholic people, *Alcohol Heath and Research World,* Experimental Issue (Summer, 1973): 16–20.

Schmidt, W., and Popham, R. E., 1975–1976, Heavy alcohol consumption and physical health problems: A review of the epidemiological evidence, *Drug Alcohol Depend. (Lausanne)* **1**:27–50.

Stolnitz, G. J., 1956, A century of international mortality studies. II, *Popul. Stud.* **10**:17–42.

Tashiro, M., and Lipscomb, W. R., 1963, Mortality experiences of alcoholics, *Q. J. Stud. Alcohol* **24**:203–212.

Wilkinson, P., Santamaria, J. N., and Rankin, J. G., 1969, Epidemiology of alcoholic cirrhosis, *Aust. Ann. Med.* **18**:222–226.

Wilkinson, P., Kornaczewski, A., Rankin, J. G., and Santamaria, J. N., 1971, Physical disease in alcoholism: Initial survey of 1,000 patients, *Med. J. Aust.* **1**:1217–1223.

Working Group on Women Alcoholics, 1977, *Women and Alcohol Problems and Their Treatment Needs in Ontario*, Report prepared for the Addiction Research Foundation Task Force on Alcoholism Treatment Services, Toronto, p. 87.

11

Alcoholism in Women

Treatment Modalities and Outcomes

HELEN M. ANNIS and CAROLYN B. LIBAN

1. INTRODUCTION

The literature on the treatment of the female alcoholic is dominated by
rhetoric, hypothesis, and speculation supplemented by the occasional
clinical observation and descriptive case history. Numerous concerned
professionals have commented on the dearth of serious empirical investigation devoted to the area (Lisansky, 1958; Hirsh, 1962; Curlee, 1967;
Lindbeck, 1972; Corrigan, 1974; Gomberg, 1974; Birchmore and Walderman, 1975; Litman, 1975; Beckman, 1976; Carver, 1977). Lindbeck
(1972) summarized the situation by noting that the female alcoholic has
been a stepchild in the field of research. It has begun to be acknowledged
that this lack of scientific knowledge about the treatment of the female
alcoholic constitutes a serious blind spot in the field of alcohol studies.

Traditionally, women have represented a relatively small proportion
of the patients seeking treatment for alcoholism problems (Keller and
Efron, 1955; Lemere et al., 1956). More recently, there is evidence that
the ratio of female to male alcoholic patients in many treatment facilities
has decreased substantially (Cahn, 1970; Corrigan, 1974; Gomberg, 1974;
Health and Welfare Canada, 1976), with some facilities reporting ratios
of less than 1:3 (Rimmer et al., 1971; Bateman and Petersen, 1972;
Ferrence et al., 1977; Kammeier, 1977; Moore, 1977). Perhaps because
of their smaller numbers in most treatment settings, treatment research
has tended to exclude women entirely from study. In those instances in

---

HELEN M. ANNIS and CAROLYN B. LIBAN • Addiction Research Foundation, Toronto,
Ontario.

which women have been included within largely male patient samples, investigators have generally not examined their data for possible sex differences.

The relative absence of research interest in the treatment of the female alcoholic is documented in several review articles on outcome studies of psychotherapy with alcoholics. Hill and Blane (1967) noted that of 49 studies published between 1952 and 1963, approximately half failed to specify the sex composition of their samples. Two more recent reviews by Baekeland et al. (1975) and May and Kuller (1975) showed that women were excluded from the majority of outcome evaluation reports: among 35 inpatient alcoholism treatment studies reviewed by Baekeland et al. (1975), only 8 included female patients. The most comprehensive analysis of the sex composition of treatment evaluation studies is presented by Costello (1975) and Costello et al. (1977). Of 80 articles reporting one-year outcome results published between 1951 and 1975, 9 studies (11.2%) failed to specify the sex of the sample, 42 (52.5%) employed a male-only sample, no study (0%) employed a female-only sample, and the remaining 29 studies (36.2%) employed a mixed male and female sample. However, only 10 of the studies (12.5% of the total) reported treatment outcome results separately for male and female alcoholics.

The paucity of research evidence on the progress of the female alcoholic in treatment has contributed to the development of a sizable body of myth and speculation. It has become a cliché in the area to claim that female alcoholics are harder to treat and have a poorer prognosis than male alcoholics.* What is the strength of the evidence for this claim? Do female alcoholics admitted to existing treatment facilities in fact have poorer outcomes than male alcoholics? Reviews of the literature that have dealt with this issue (Corrigan, 1974; Gomberg, 1974, 1976a,b; Beckman, 1975; Birchmore and Walderman, 1975) have done so only in passing and have tended to quote the same half dozen studies. No detailed critical appraisal attempting to deal with all published literature bearing on this issue has yet appeared. A major purpose of the present chapter is to examine available empirical findings on the treatment of female alcoholics, mainly in comparison with male alcoholics.

Outcome studies on psychotherapy with alcoholics have been

* The belief that women have a poorer prognosis than men has led to a call for a variety of solutions involving the provision of separate facilities and programming for female alcoholics, the fostering of women's self-help groups, androgynous therapy, and feminist counseling. No empirical investigations have yet been reported on the relative effectiveness of such strategies with the female alcoholic compared with more traditional programming.

searched for sex-related data presentation. For some purposes, a small number of published treatment reports dealing with female-only samples is included. The review is limited to research published between 1950 and early 1978 and includes only English-language reports.

2. DO FEMALE ALCOHOLICS HAVE POORER TREATMENT OUTCOME THAN MALE ALCOHOLICS?

Table 1 summarizes treatment modality and design features for a total of 23 studies presenting male and female outcome information on follow-up periods varying between six months and six years. Ten of these studies (Hoff and McKeown, 1953; Glatt, 1955; Selzer and Holloway, 1957; Fox and Smith, 1959; Blake, 1967; Bell and Levinson, 1971; Browne-Mayers et al., 1976; Crawford, 1976; Glover and McCue, 1977; Ruggels et al., 1977) did not analyze for sex differences in outcome rates but did provide sufficient information within the reports to allow us to perform the necessary statistical tests. Considerable evidence suggests that patients lost to follow-up are a serious source of sampling bias (Hill and Blane, 1967; Baekeland et al., 1975) and that such patients are best considered treatment failures (Wolff and Holland, 1964; Gerard and Saenger, 1966; Miller et al., 1970; Dunne, 1973; Vannicelli et al., 1976; Moos and Bliss, 1978). This can be a particularly important consideration in examining sex differences in outcome if more patients of one sex than of the other are lost to follow-up. Consequently, for all studies providing a sex breakdown within the unsuccessful follow-up group, we included those lost to follow-up in our calculation of the sex difference outcome statistic. Only 2 among the 23 studies reviewed (Glatt, 1961; Fitzgerald et al., 1971) performed significance tests for sex differences by including cases lost to follow-up within the unimproved groups. Our reanalysis of the remaining reports changed the conclusion with regard to the existence of sex differences in only one case (Pemberton, 1967).

Of the 23 studies reviewed, 15 (65%) showed no significant difference in remission rates for male and female alcoholics following treatment (Davies et al., 1956; Selzer and Holloway, 1957; Gerard and Saenger, 1966; Blake, 1967; Pemberton, 1967; Ritson, 1968; Bell and Levinson 1971; Fitzgerald et al., 1971; Bateman and Petersen, 1972; Gillies et al., 1974; Blaney et al. 1975; Browne-Mayers et al., 1976; Crawford, 1976; Glover and McCue, 1977; McLachlan, 1978). Five studies (22%) provided evidence of significantly higher improvement rates among female alcoholics (Fox and Smith, 1959; Davis, 1966; Dahlgren, 1975; Kammeier, 1977; Ruggels et al., 1977), while three studies (13%) were found to support the hypothesis of better prognosis following treatment for male

Table 1. Sex Differences in Treatment Outcome

Author	Country	Sample	Treatment setting	Treatment modality
Bateman and Petersen (1972)	United States	M (N = 381) F (N = 136)	Inpatient (state hospital alcohol rehabilitation center)	Psychiatric team approach, medical care, milieu therap group therapy
Bell and Levinson (1971)	Canada	M (N = 120) F (N = 34)	Inpatient→out patient (hospital)	Group therapy, individual counseling, family therapy, didactic instruction, physiotherapy, relaxation training, AA Discussion groups on OP bas plus contacts by a "clinica secretarv"
Blake (1967)	Scotland	M (N = 45) F (N = 14)	Inpatient (hospital)	Group I—Relaxation trainin, —Motivation training —Aversion therapy Group II—Aversion therapy
Blaney et al. (1975)	Ireland	M (N = 228) F (N = 23)	Inpatient (general psychiatric hospital and a specialized alcoholism unit)	Group I—Alcohol withdraw Group II—Alcohol withdraw — Group therapy —Education —Disulfiram, AA
Browne-Mayers et al. (1976)	United States	M (N = 74) F (N = 62)	Inpatient (psychiatric hospital)	Individual and group therapy AA, family therapy, occupational and recreatio therapy, aftercare planning
Crawford (1976)	New Zealand	M (N = 262) F (N = 51)	Inpatient (hospital)	Individual, group, family, an milieu therapy AA and disulfiram encourage
Dahlgren (1975)	Sweden	M–F (N not specified)	Inpatient (hospital)	Not specified
Davies et al. (1956)	England	M (N = 39) F (N = 11)	Inpatient→out- patient (hospital)	Disulfiram, psychotherapy, A social work
Davis (1966)	United States	M (N = 86) F (N = 45)	Inpatient (psychiatric hospital)	AA-oriented counseling prog
Fitzgerald et al. (1971)	United States	M (N = 392) F (N = 139)	Inpatient (state psychiatric hospital)	Alcohol education, occupatio therapy, group therapy, individual counseling,AA

| Length of program | Follow-up | | | Outcome | |
	Interval	Rate	Sex of patients lost to follow up	Measure	Sex difference
4 weeks	6 months	72%	Unspecified	Drinking behavior (abstinent [no drinks since discharge]/ drinking)	Not significant
IP: 4 weeks OP: 1 year	1–1½ years	95%	Specified	Global index of drinking, physical health, and mental status (sig. improved/moderately improved/unchanged)	Not significant
3–4 weeks	1 year	85%	Specified	Drinking behavior (abstinent/improved/ relapsed/no information)	Not significant
Not specified	6 months	87%	Unspecified	Drinking behavior (favorable/intermediate/ unfavorable)	Not significant
17 weeks	3 years	Unknown	Unspecified	Drinking behavior (abstinent/nonabstinent)	Not significant
12 weeks	2 years	71%	Specified	Drinking behavior (abstinent/improved/ unimproved)	Not significant
Not specified	1 year	Unknown	Unspecified	Unspecified	Women showed better results (insufficient information provided to test for significance)
IP: 8–13 weeks OP: several months	2 years	98%	Specified	Drinking behavior (abstinent [with few slips]/drinking with good adjustment/ unimproved)	Not significant
Variable ($\bar{x}$ = 6 weeks)	1½ years	76%	Unspecified	Drinking behavior (abstinent since discharge/presently abstinent/improved/ unimproved)	Women significantly more improved than men
16 weeks	4 years	62%	Specified	Combined index of drinking and vocational and family adjustment (good adj. without drinking/good adj. with drinking/poor adj. with drinking)	Not significant

(Continued)

Table 1. (*Continued*)

Author	Country	Sample	Treatment setting	Treatment modality
Fox and Smith (1959)	United States	M (N = 214) F (N = 37)	Inpatient→out patient (clinic)	Group therapy, religious counseling, occupational an recreational therapy, drug therapy OP group meetings and drug therapy
Gerard and Saenger (1966)	United States	M1 ≃ 1664 F ≃ 133	Outpatient (clinics)	Varied between clinics: grou and individual therapy, medication, drug therapy, physical and occupational therapy, marital therapy, milieu and pastoral therap "team" approach
Gillies et al. (1974)	Canada	M–F (N = 968) (N not specified by sex)	Inpatient (1 medical unit and 1 hospital) Outpatient (clinics)	Individual therapy, individual interviews with various sta medication and drug thera all units Group therapy, marital thera at the majority of units Family therapy, marital grou therapy at some of units
Glatt (1955)	England	M (N = 70) F (N = 24)	Inpatient (psychiatric hospital)	Eclectic group therapy, milie therapy, occupational ther Antabuse, AA
Glatt (1961)	England	(a) M (N = 70) F (N = 24) (b) M (N = 150) F (N = 42)	Inpatient (psychiatric hospital)	Eclectic group therapy, milie therapy, occupational ther Antabuse, AA
Glover and McCue (1977)	Scotland	M (N = 58) F (N = 27)	Inpatient (psychiatric hospital)	Group I—Electrical aversio therapy Group II—"Conventional" methods
Hoff and McKeown (1953)	United States	M (N = 692) F (N = 100)	Inpatient→out patient (hospital)	Sedatives, group therapy TE OP individual therapy
Kammeier (1977)	United States	M (N = 402) F (N = 188)	Inpatient	Individual and family counsel group therapy, AA

Length of program	Follow-up			Outcome	
	Interval	Rate	Sex of patients lost to follow up	Measure	Sex difference
1–13 weeks several onths	1–1½ years	Unknown	Unspecified	Drinking behavior plus program attendance (good progress [sober and attending group meetings regularly]/ some progress/no progress or lost to contact)	Women significantly more improved than men
able (median 4 weeks)	1 year	76%	Unspecified	Drinking behavior (abstinent/controlled/ problem drinkers)	Not significant
able pically 3 onths)	1 year	70%	Unspecified	Alcohol involvement scale—score change between intake and follow-up (abstinent/ much improved/ somewhat improved/not improved)	Not significant
weeks	½–2 years	82%	Specified	Drinking behavior (recovered/improved/ unimproved)	Not significant
				Home adjustment	Not significant
				Social adjustment	Not significant
				Subjective adjustment	Not significant
				Work adjustment	Males significantly more improved than females
weeks	2–3½ years	81%	Specified	Drinking behavior (recovered/improved/	Males significantly more improved than females
	6 months– 3½ years	78%	Specified	unimproved/ unimproved)	Males significantly more improved than females
eks	½–4 years ($\bar{x}$ = 13 months)	88%	Unspecified	Drinking behavior (abstinent/controlled/ unimproved)	Not significant
1–2+ weeks 1 year	2 months– 2½ years	86%	Specified	Drinking behavior (abstinent/improved/ unimproved)	Males significantly more improved than females
weeks	2 years	63%	Specified	Drinking behavior (abstinent/improved/ unimproved)	Not significant
				Relationships with others	Significant
				Participation in community affairs	Significant
				Physical health	Significant
				Enjoyment of life	Significant
				Accept and give help	Significant

(Continued)

Table 1. (*Continued*)

Author	Country	Sample	Treatment setting	Treatment modality
McLachlan (1978)	Canada	M ($N = 416$) F ($N = 125$)	Inpatient→outpatient (hospital)	Group therapy, individual counseling, family therapy didactic instruction, physiotherapy, relaxation training, AA Discussion groups on OP ba plus contacts by a "clinica secretary"
Pemberton (1967)	Scotland	M ($N = 50$) F ($N = 50$)	Inpatient→outpatient (hospital)	Group I—"Intensive" progr; electrical aversion therapy psychotherapy, LSD thera Group II—"Routine" progra supportive psychotherapy, drug therapy, Antabuse
Ritson (1968)	Scotland	M ($N = 84$) F ($N = 16$)	Inpatient→outpatient Outpatient only	Group I—IP: Vitamins, tranquilizers, group therap milieu therapy —OP: group therapy Group II—Individual therapy group therapy, Antabuse encouraged
Ruggels et al. (1977)	United States	M non-DWI ($N = 1018$) F non-DWI ($N = 234$)	Inpatient and outpatient	Emergency/detoxication care inpatient hospital care, intermediate care, outpatie (group and individual counseling/therapy), consultation, education, adjunctive services (occupational therapy and family counseling), medica supervision, Antabuse ther
Selzer and Holloway (1957)	United States	M ($N = 73$) F ($N = 25$)	Inpatient (state psychiatric hospital)	Psychiatric interviews, occupational and recreatio therapy, AA

| Length of program | Follow-up | | | Outcome | |
	Interval	Rate	Sex of patients lost to follow up	Measure	Sex difference
4 weeks 1 year	1–1½ years	96%	Specified	Drinking behavior (abstinent/ relapsed–recovered/ significantly improved/ unimproved)	Not significant
specified	2 months–2 years (x̄ = 1¼ years	89%	Specified	Drinking behavior (successful [abstinent or drinking moderately]/ unsuccessful)	Not significant (based on reanalysis of results with unknown Ss included in unsuccessful group)
Not ecified 1 year	6 months 1 year	99% 96%	Unspecified Unspecified	Drinking behavior (abstinent/improved/ unchanged)	Not significant
					Not significant
able (range 2–18 onths)	1½ years	57%	Specified	Drinking behavior (Q–F index and Impairment index: recovered/ nonrecovered)	Females significantly more improved than males
eek–28 onths dian = 2.5 onths)	6 years	85%	Specified	Drinking behavior (abstinent/drinking) Combined index of drinking behavior and adjustment (abstinent/drank with good adjustment/drank with poor adjustment/ frequently intoxicated)	Not significant Not significant

alcoholics (Hoff and McKeown, 1953; Glatt, 1955, 1961). A description of the treatment modalities, follow-up measures, and design features of each study within the three discrepant outcome groups is presented below. This presentation is followed by a discussion of the methodological adequacy of the various studies and the type of conclusions that seem warranted.

Studies Showing No Sex Difference in Treatment Outcome

Bateman and Petersen (1972) followed up 381 male and 136 female alcoholics who had completed the full treatment program involving a 28-day hospital stay at a state alcoholic rehabilitation center in the southern United States. The program stressed a psychiatric team approach with medical care, milieu therapy, group therapy, and posthospital planning. Patients were followed up primarily through a mailed questionnaire six months after hospital discharge and were rated on the basis of their responses as either "abstinent" for the entire postdischarge period or "drinking" if they had taken any alcoholic beverages at all over the preceding six months. On the basis of this stringent, dichotomous outcome criterion, 30% of the males who responded to the follow-up questionnaire and 22% of the females claimed total abstinence; this difference was not statistically significant. Unfortunately, only a modest follow-up rate (72%) was achieved and no information is provided on the sex composition of nonresponders. Consequently, it is possible that differential follow-up rates between the sexes may be a biasing factor in this outcome result.

Bell and Levinson (1971) reported on a one-year follow-up of 120 male and 34 female alcoholics seen at the Donwood Institute, a specialized public hospital in Toronto. The four-week inpatient component of this program employed a wide variety of therapeutic modalities including intensive group psychotherapy, individual counseling, family therapy, physiotherapy, recreational therapy, didactic instruction, and encouragement of Alcoholics Anonymous (AA) involvement. A special emphasis was placed on the "Continuing Therapy Program," which ran for a minimum of one year following discharge from the inpatient program. During this period, attendance at AA meetings was encouraged, weekly contact was maintained with each patient by his/her assigned lay worker (called a *clinical secretary*), and patients were encouraged to attend weekly two-hour discussion groups with fellow program graduates. Follow-up interviews, conducted approximately one year following discharge from inpatient status, assessed change along multiple improvement rating scales in the areas of alcohol dependence, physical health, and mental functioning. Only scores on the combined, global improvement index, however, were presented. Overall improvement rates for males (68%) and females (65%) did not differ.

A recent larger-scale follow-up study of patients at the Donwood Institute has been reported by McLachlan (1978). The components of the treatment program involved were essentially the same as described above in the earlier study at this institute by Bell and Levinson (1971). Four cohorts of patients totaling 416 males and 125 females were followed up by personal interview over periods ranging from 12 to 18 months subsequent to discharge. As in the Bell and Levinson (1971) study, a follow-up return rate of 96% was achieved. The excellence of the follow-up rates in these studies is undoubtedly attributable to the very active continuing therapy program (see above) in operation during the year subsequent to hospital discharge, whereby at least weekly contact was maintained with each patient. To date, reports on this study have been restricted to follow-up results for drinking behavior subsequent to hospital discharge. Remission categories were defined as "total abstinence" over the entire follow-up period, "relapsed–recovered" (no more than two months of drinking and at least one month sobriety prior to follow-up), "drinking reduced" (decrease in alcohol consumption to at least half of baseline), and "unimproved." On the basis of these clearly defined outcome categories, no differences in remission rates between male and female patients were indicated.

Blake (1967) reported one year follow-up data for 45 male alcoholics and 14 female alcoholics treated in an inpatient hospital setting over a three- to four-week period by electrical aversion therapy alone or by relaxation–aversion therapy. No significant sex difference in outcome was observed: 64% of the females and 53% of the males were abstinent or much improved one year after discharge.

Blaney et al. (1975) studied a sample of 228 male and 23 female alcoholic patients who were admitted in 1968 to two treatment facilities in Northern Ireland. One of these facilities was a general psychiatric hospital with no specialized alcohol unit, in which treatment was mainly directed toward alcohol withdrawal. The other facility was a specialized alcoholism treatment unit where, in addition to the management of alcohol withdrawal, the treatment regime included group therapy, educational techniques, disulfiram, and AA involvement. At six months following discharge, there was no significant difference in the incidence of favorable or improved drinking outcome between male and female patients seen in either of the two programs.

Browne-Mayers et al. (1976) reported a three-year follow-up study of 62 female alcoholics and 74 male alcoholics admitted to a coeducational alcoholism service within a psychiatric hospital in New York. A traditional multimodal treatment program was offered including individual and group therapy, AA, family therapy, nursing care plans, recreational and occupational therapy, after-care planning, and regular follow-up activity. The average duration of hospitalization was 17 weeks. The majority of the patients were married and drawn from the professional and business executive classes. Over 50% of the women had some college education and most were employed or involved in volunteer or community service activity. Three-quarters of the women reported that stress within the family setting contributed to their drinking problem. The authors note that on follow-up three years following discharge, slightly more men than women were abstinent. However, an analysis of the outcome figures reported in the study indicated no significant difference in the improvement rates of the male and female samples.

Crawford (1976) followed up 262 male and 51 female alcoholics over a two-year period following discharge from a 12-week inpatient hospital program in New Zealand. The program stressed education and the development of insight through individual, group, family, and milieu therapy. Residents were also encouraged to use disulfiram and participate in AA. Corroborating information was sought for self-reports on drinking behavior. A follow-up rate of approximately 70% was achieved at the two-year interval, with those not contacted at follow-up assumed to have relapsed. A total of 44% of the males and 57% of the females were abstinent or improved at follow-up. A chi-square test applied by the present authors to the results presented in the Crawford report showed no significant difference between the sexes in outcome.

Davies et al. (1956) presented two-year outcome information for 39 male and 11 female consecutive alcoholic admissions at the Maudsley Hospital between 1949 and 1951. The inpatient program typically involved a stay of two to three months in hospital with an emphasis on disulfiram therapy, psychotherapy, AA, and long-term social work. After discharge, patients were expected to maintain regular contact on an outpatient basis at a special follow-up clinic. It was found that 54% of the females compared with 31% of the males remained abstinent, with few if any "slips" over the two-year follow-up period. The very small numbers involved dictate caution in the interpretation of these results. Nevertheless, it would appear that female alcoholics fared at least as well as males in this treatment program.

Fitzgerald et al. (1971) conducted a four-year follow-up of 392 male and 139 female alcoholics who had been admitted to a 16-week specialized inpatient alcohol program in a state hospital in Wyoming. The program stressed education about alcohol, group therapy, occupational therapy, individual counseling, and participation in AA community meetings. Drug therapy was not used. The sobriety status of the patients at follow-up was based on self-report questionnaires as well as on anecdotal information from relatives, community residents, AA, police, and clergy. A combined outcome index was employed based on drinking behavior as well as vocational and family adjustment. No essential difference in posthospital adjustment was observed for male and female patients in any of the four follow-up years. During the fourth year after discharge, 45% of the males and 43% of the females were abstinent or drinking moderately while maintaining vocational and familial responsibilities. No significant difference was indicated between male and female patients' longitudinal sobriety history following treatment.

Gerard and Saenger (1966) reported a large-scale follow-up of 797 male and female alcoholics admitted to eight publicly supported outpatient clinics within state alcoholism programs in the United States. Approximately one-sixth of the study population was female. Treatment offered varied widely between clinics but tended to involve group and individual therapy, tranquilizers and antidepressant medication, drug therapy (e.g., Antabuse), physical and occupational therapy, marital therapy, and pastoral counseling. About half of the clients are reported as arriving for fewer than five appointments, but no information is provided on the relative dropout rates of male and female clients. Clinic personnel who had been involved in the treatment program contacted each patient for a follow-up interview. Sex differences are reported only on the drinking outcome criterion. The same proportion of men and women were found to be abstinent or controlled drinkers one year following treatment.

Gillies et al. (1974) reported a one-year follow-up of 968 male and female alcoholics admitted to two inpatient hospitals and four outpatient clinics of the Addiction Research Foundation in Ontario. Individual therapy was the predominant mode of treatment offered in all units, though many patients also received group therapy or marital or family counseling. Tranquilizers and antidepressant medication were frequently prescribed for the patients, and the use of Antabuse was encouraged. Length of patient contact varied widely in all units but seldom exceeded three months. On the basis of change scores between intake and follow-up on the Alcoholic Involvement Scale, patients were classified as "abstinent" for the total 12-month follow-up period, "much improved," "somewhat improved," and "not improved." No significant difference was indicated in the percentage of male and female patients falling within the various improvement categories.

In a study at Stratheden Hospital, Fife, Scotland, Glover and McCue

(1977) compared the outcome of a program of electrical aversion therapy with conventional methods on a sample of 58 male and 27 female inpatients. On follow-up six months to four years following treatment, the females tended to show somewhat better outcomes than the males in both the experimental electrical aversion condition (78% of females improved compared with 58% of males) and in the conventional therapy comparison condition (43% of females improved compared with 28% of males). However, these sex differences in drinking outcome did not reach statistical significance, possibly because of the small sample sizes involved. In any case, the extreme variability of the follow-up periods and the absence of information on the comparability of follow-up intervals across sex render interpretation of these findings difficult.

Pemberton (1967) reported an outcome evaluation of 50 consecutive female and 50 consecutive male admissions to a hospital-based specialized alcohol unit in Scotland. The program fell into two categories: (1) the "intensive" treatment regime involving the use of either electrical aversion therapy or psychotherapy with an abreactive agent (CO_2 or LSD); and (2) the "routine" treatment package involving supportive psychotherapy, often with the use of drug therapy or Antabuse. On the basis of follow-up interviews conducted with patients and family members 8–24 months following hospital discharge, patients were classified as "successful" (abstinent or drinking moderately) or "unsuccessful." The author concluded that the outcome in males (18 "successful") was better than that in females (10 "successful"). It should be noted that this widely cited conclusion is justified statistically only by excluding nonrespondents from the analysis. If patients lost to follow-up are categorized as unsuccessful, no significant sex difference in treatment outcome is indicated by the results of Pemberton's study. There was some suggestion that females responded better to the "intensive" treatment regime, whereas males responded equally well to the "routine" program. Given the very small number of successful cases involved, however, any generalization is extremely risky.

Ritson (1968) evaluated the progress of 84 male alcoholics and 14 female alcoholics at six-month and one-year intervals following their admission to a specialized alcoholism unit in Scotland. Patients were admitted to either (1) an outpatient program or (2) an inpatient hospital program followed by outpatient care. The inpatient program stressed milieu therapy, vitamin therapy, group psychotherapy, and the use of tranquilizers, while the outpatient unit focused on individual therapy and the use of Antabuse. No significant differences were found between male and female abstinence or improvement rates at 6 and 12 months or between success rates within the inpatient and outpatient programs.

Selzer and Holloway (1957) conducted a six-year follow-up study of 73 male and 25 female alcoholics admitted to a Michigan State Psychiatric Hospital during 1948 and early 1949. Length of stay in the program varied from a few days to 28 months, with a median length of 2–5 months. In addition to periodic interviews with the ward psychiatrist, the program consisted primarily of occupational and recreational therapy and voluntary attendance at AA meetings. Follow-up interviews with both the patients and their families failed to indicate any sex differences in response to treatment. Among the male patient sample, 19% had remained abstinent over the six-year follow-up interval, compared with 16% of the females. On a combined index of current adjustment, 36% of the males and 32% of the females were found to be either abstinent or drinking moderately with good adjustment.

Studies Finding Better Treatment Outcome among Male Alcoholics

An early pioneering effort by Glatt (1955) reported on the effects of a two- to three-month inpatient program within a psychiatric hospital involving an emphasis on milieu therapy, eclectic group therapy, occupational therapy, some use of drugs (Antabuse and apomorphine) and the encouragement of AA attendance. Outcome results, six months to two years following hospital discharge, are presented for 70 male and 24 female consecutive alcoholic admissions. The author reported that males more frequently showed improvement in drinking on follow-up (67%) than females (58%). However, a supplementary analysis indicated that the reported sex difference in drinking outcome was not statistically significant. Follow-up results by sex are also presented in the areas of "work adjustment," "home adjustment," "social adjustment," and "subjective adjustment." Unfortunately, no operational definition of these terms is offered. No difference between male and female alcoholics on follow-up were found in terms of "home," "social," or "subjective adjustment," but males did show a much greater improvement in "work adjustment" compared with females. The meaning of this isolated, statistically significant sex difference in outcome is not entirely clear since it is unlikely that many of the female alcoholics studied were employed.

The early study by Glatt (1955) was based on a follow-up interval of six months to two years. Glatt (1961) reported on an extended follow-up of the same cohort of 94 patients over a two- to three-and-a-half year interval following discharge. Whereas no significant sex difference was indicated in drinking improvement rates within the first two years, in the third year following discharge, males had significantly better outcome than females; 73% of the males compared with 42% of the females were found to be "recovered" or "distinctly improved" over the longer follow-up period. It is interesting to note that this difference is primarily due to the deteriorating condition within the female sample over time. However, given the very small size of the female sample ($N = 24$), this trend must be interpreted with caution.

Hoff and McKeown (1953) studied 692 male and 100 female alcoholics admitted to a specialized alcoholism service at the Medical College of Virginia Hospital in Richmond. The program typically involved a one- to two-week hospital stay with group therapy followed by outpatient individual therapy with optional use of tetraethylthiuram (TETD) for approximately one year. On follow-up two months to two and a half years after admission, 71% of the males and 54% of the females were rated as abstinent or improved. This difference was significant. Males who had taken TETD were also shown to be more likely to be abstinent or improved on follow-up (79%) than females (67%). Males who had not taken TETD also showed more improvement than females, although the difference in this case was not found to be significant.

Studies Finding Better Treatment Outcome among Female Alcoholics

In a study at the Karolinska Hospital, Sweden, Dahlgren (1975) reported that women who accepted aftercare following hospitalization adhered more faithfully to the program and showed somewhat better results after one year than men. Unfortunately, no information is provided on the treatment modalities involved, the sample sizes, the follow-up rates, or the outcome criteria employed.

Davis (1966) followed up 86 male alcoholics and 45 female alcoholics admitted to a state psychiatric hospital in Texas having a specialized AA-oriented alcoholism program with a full-time addictions counselor. Length of stay in the program was variable, with a mean of 41 days. All patients volunteered for participation in the study and were followed up one and one half years following discharge. On an index of severity of drinking, females showed a significantly higher rate of improvement following treatment than their male counterparts. It was concluded that female alcoholics are better therapeutic risks for an AA-oriented program than are male alcoholics.

A widely quoted study in the field is that by Fox and Smith (1959), who reported on a one-year follow-up of 214 male and 37 female consecutive alcoholic admissions to a state clinic in Georgia. Patients in the sample had stayed one week to three months in the clinic's inpatient program followed by up to several months in the outpatient program.

Group therapy, religious counseling, and occupational and recreational therapy, as well as drug therapy, comprised the inpatient program, while regular group meetings and drug therapy were stressed in the aftercare outpatient program. Outcome was assessed on a combined criterion involving drinking behavior after discharge from inpatient status and adherence to the aftercare outpatient regime. Patients categorized as having "good progress" had been completely sober or had had only a few slips since discharge and were participating regularly in the outpatient program. On this complex criterion, women were found to have a significantly better outcome than men; 51% of the females showed "good progress" compared with 26% of the males. Unfortunately, it is not possible to determine, on the basis of the information presented, whether more males than females were lost to follow-up. This factor could introduce a serious bias in the interpretation of the significant sex difference in treatment outcome. What is clear is that more females than males complied with the requirements for attendance at the outpatient group meetings that formed an integral part of the outcome improvement criterion.

Kammeier (1977) reported on a two-year follow-up of 402 male and 188 female alcoholics admitted to the Hazelden Foundation, a private residential treatment facility in Center City, Minnesota. Treatment, administered by a multidisciplinary staff, focused on the steps of the AA program and included individual and family counseling, group therapy, lectures and films, spiritual counseling, psychological evaluation, and bibliotherapy. Two years after discharge, mailed follow-up questionnaires were returned by 63% of the sample (64% of the males and 61% of the females). No differences were observed in the reported drinking frequency of men and women over the two-year follow-up interval. Significant differences between the sexes in other areas of adjustment, however, were found. More women than men reported improvement in relationships with others (spouse, parents, friends, "Higher Power"), in participation in community affairs, in physical health, in enjoyment of life, and in their ability to give and receive help from others.

Ruggels et al. (1977) reported on the large-scale follow-up study of eight selected Alcoholism Treatment Centers (ATCs) funded by the National Institute of Alcohol Abuse and Alcoholism (NIAAA) in the United States. Because of its national scope, diversity of patients and treatments, and range of outcome measures, this is the most comprehensive alcoholism treatment evaluation undertaken to date. The community-based centers (ATCs) provided emergency–detoxification care, inpatient care (hospital), intermediate care (quarterway house, halfway house, partial hospitalization), and outpatient care, as well as consultation and education programs. Assignment to the different treatment settings was reportedly made on the basis of "perceived need" by the counselor and on "client preference." Within the outpatient program, clients who had experienced little prior treatment were generally offered individual counseling–therapy, while those who had a history of repeated treatment contacts were assigned to group therapy. The 18-month follow-up sample was composed of 1018 male non-driving-while-intoxicated (non DWI) patients and 234 female non-DWI patients who had entered treatment at one of the eight centers. Of this sample, 57% (55% males, 65% females) were successfully contacted for the follow-up interview; this was the lowest follow-up rate of the studies reviewed. Some evidence is presented (Armor et al., 1976) suggesting that the low follow-up rate may not have introduced a serious bias into the 18-month NIAAA results, although other authors (Emrick and Stilson, 1977) have questioned both the appropriateness and the interpretation of the evidence presented. Sufficient information was provided in the Ruggels et al. (1977) supplementary report to permit us to test for sex differences in remission rates. Employing either our regular analytic procedure, which included patients lost to follow-up within the unimproved groups, or an alternative analytic strategy whereby computations were based only on patients interviewed at follow-up, female non-DWI patients showed significantly higher remission rates than male non-DWI patients.

Discussion

One conclusion seems clear. Women alcoholics admitted to the majority of treatment programs reviewed did not evidence a significantly poorer response to treatment than men. Within the small number of studies reporting sex differences in favor of either men or women, no pattern emerges suggestive of any relationship between sex and treatment variables. Programs showing better prognosis for males as well as those showing better prognosis for females involved fairly traditional multimodal inpatient programs frequently followed by group or individual outpatient counseling.

From the methodological and conceptual viewpoints, the available evidence on the issue of sex differences in treatment outcome leaves much to be desired. The nature of the available evidence does not permit an assessment of the possible role played by type of treatment in outcome of male and female alcoholics. With very few exceptions (e.g., Blake, 1967; Glover and McCue, 1977), conventional hospital-based inpatient or clinic outpatient programs were studied. The results, therefore, are necessarily restricted to an examination of male and female progress within traditional treatment packages.

The majority of reports involved simple follow-up studies with no randomized control groups or comparisons across treatment groups.

Consequently, no conclusions can be drawn on the extent to which observed changes within each sex are attributable to treatment or would have occurred in the absence of specific treatment. Little is now known about possible differences in the natural course of outcome for male and female alcoholics.

Most studies reviewed were based on consecutive admissions to a facility over a given period of time. However, in a third of the studies, the sample was restricted to fewer than 25 alcoholic women. Such small sample sizes raise questions of their representativeness of all alcoholics seen within these facilities. In any case, given the extreme heterogeneity of the alcoholic population, the generalizability of any one study's results to the general male and female alcoholic population is certainly limited.

Drinking behavior was the only criterion employed in the majority of studies, although a few studies used a combined index of drinking behavior together with other areas of adjustment (Selzer and Holloway, 1957; Fox and Smith, 1959; Bell and Levinson, 1971; Fitzgerald et al., 1971). Only two studies (Glatt, 1955; Kammeier, 1977) reported results on multiple outcome criteria. About one-half of the studies failed to define adequately the rules applied for the assignment of patients to the various outcome improvement categories, so that the reliability of the outcome ratings in many reports is questionable. Differential interviewer bias in assessing change between the sexes cannot be ruled out in most studies, nor can the possible operation of sex differences in self-report reliability on drinking behavior. In no study reporting a significant sex difference was a corroborating source of information routinely sought to supplement the self-report data.

The use of inadequate follow-up procedures is a particularly troublesome aspect of several of the studies that showed significant sex differences in treatment outcome. In all three of the studies in which males were found to have better prognosis than females, extreme variability is evident in the length of the follow-up periods employed (Hoff and McKeown, 1953: two months to two and a half years; Glatt, 1955: six months to two years; Glatt, 1961: two years to three and a half years). No information is provided in any of these studies on the comparability of the follow-up interval between the sexes. Therefore, it is impossible to assess the influence this factor may have had on the outcome results.

One of the most serious methodological problems in the literature reviewed was the failure of investigators to assess outcome against pretreatment baseline measures. In none of the studies with significant sex differences in treatment outcome was remission defined in terms of actual change from pretreatment levels of drinking. Among the remaining studies with nonsignificant results, only four established adequate baseline measures at intake (Blake, 1967; Bell and Levinson, 1971; Gillies et al., 1974; McLachlan, 1978). In the absence of documentation of drinking patterns within male and female samples prior to treatment, any post-treatment differences may not be attributable to differential remission rates between the sexes but may merely reflect differences in the original severity of drinking patterns.

Typically, the studies made no attempt to research relatively homogeneous subgroups of alcoholics of either sex. This shortcoming may well account for the large number of nonsignificant findings (cf. Glaser, 1976). With highly heterogeneous subject pools, the outcome variance can be expected to be large and may have obscured significant treatment effects within the sexes.

Finally, a serious problem with existing evidence on sex difference in treatment outcome is the lack of attention to differences in the characteristics of the male and female samples being compared. Two recent studies have found that pretreatment patient characteristics can account for about 70% of the explained variance in treatment outcome (Ruggels et al., 1975; Vogler et al., 1975). Studies comparing populations of male and female alcoholics have consistently reported differences on demographic characteristics, family histories, and drinking patterns (Sherfey, 1955; Lisansky, 1957; Curlee, 1967; Winokur and Clayton, 1968; Winokur et al., 1970; Core-Shell Staff, 1978). Yet, very few of the studies on sex difference in treatment outcome reported even simple demographic characteristics for the male and female samples. Given the powerful prognostic significance of such factors, the discrepant findings among the studies reviewed on relative male and female remission rates are most likely attributable to pretreatment characteristics of the samples studied.

3.   DO PROGNOSTIC FACTORS IN TREATMENT OUTCOME DIFFER FOR MALE AND FEMALE ALCOHOLICS?

The great majority of studies documenting the dominant role played by patient prognostic factors in treatment outcome have focused on the male alcoholic. Study samples typically have been restricted to males, or a small number of females have been included in largely male samples with only a combined analysis reported. To date, relatively little attention has been paid to the possibility that there may be important sex differences in prognostic factors in treatment outcome. Given the differing roles and expectations of males and females in our society, the factors indicative of good prognosis may differ between the sexes.

Prognostic Factors for Female Alcoholics

A total of only 13 studies was found with a minimum six-month follow-up period that examined the treatment outcome of female alcoholics in terms of one or more prognostic characteristics. The factors examined and the direction of the relationships to treatment outcome are presented in Table 2. All positive and negative entries in Table 2 refer to statistically significant relationships. In several cases, significance tests were not reported in the original articles, but sufficient information was presented to allow us to perform the necessary statistical tests.

Demographic and Socioeconomic Factors. In the majority of studies, age was unrelated to the treatment outcome in female alcoholics (Davis, 1966; Pemberton, 1967; Thomas, 1971; Schuckit and Winokur, 1972; Ruggels et al., 1977); one study (Bateman and Petersen 1972), however, showed that female alcoholics 45 years of age or older were more likely to be abstinent on follow-up. Mixed results were reported on the relationship of education to treatment outcome. Three studies reported no significant relationship (Davis, 1966; Thomas, 1971; Schuckit and Winokur, 1972); one study (Ruggels et al., 1977) showed females with grade-12 education or higher to have better outcomes, while another (Bateman and Petersen, 1972) reported a negative relationship between years of education and abstinence on follow-up. Similar conflicting results are reported for occupational level. Two studies (Davis, 1966; Thomas, 1971) showed no significant relationship between occupational level and outcome for female alcoholics, while another (Bateman and Petersen, 1972) showed that females with lower-status occupations had significantly higher rates of abstinence on follow-up. Women who classified themselves as "housewives" were found to have remission rates approximately twice as high as any other occupational category (Gerard and Saenger, 1966). Income (Thomas, 1971; Ruggels et al., 1977), employment stability (Bromet and Moos, 1977), and residential stability (Ruggels et al., 1977) have been found to be unrelated to outcome in female alcoholics, whereas full-time employment at the time of admission to treatment (Bateman and Petersen, 1972; Ruggels et al., 1977) and low socioeconomic status (Bateman and Petersen, 1972) have been found to relate positively to treatment outcome. Finally, one study (Bromet and Moos, 1977) reported that female alcoholics who were living with their spouses had better posttreatment outcomes. Although the majority of studies (Glatt, 1961; Davis, 1966; Pemberton, 1967; Bateman and Petersen, 1972; Crawford, 1976; Ruggels et al., 1977) failed to show any significant relationship between current marital status and treatment outcome, most showed a trend toward greater improvement among

Table 2. Prognostic Factors in Treatment Outcome of Women Alcoholics

Variable	Prognostic relationship	Investigator (year)
Demographic, socioeconomic factors		
Age	+	Bateman and Petersen (1972)
	Unrelated	Davis (1966)
	Unrelated	Pemberton (1967)
	Unrelated	Ruggels et al. (1977)
	Unrelated	Schuckit and Winokur (1972)
	Unrelated	Thomas (1971)
Education	−	Bateman and Petersen (1972)
	+	Ruggels et al. (1977)
	Unrelated	Davis (1966)
	Unrelated	Schuckit and Winokur (1972)
	Unrelated	Thomas (1971)
Occupational level	−	Bateman and Petersen (1972)
	+	Bromet and Moos (1977)
	Unrelated	Davis (1966)
	Unrelated	Thomas (1971)
(housewife)	+	Gerard and Saenger (1966)
Income	Unrelated	Ruggels et al. (1977)
	Unrelated	Thomas (1971)
Socioeconomic status	−	Bateman and Petersen (1972)
Employed on admission	+	Bateman and Petersen (1972)
	+	Ruggels et al. (1977)
Employment stability	Unrelated	Bromet and Moos (1977)
Residential stability	Unrelated	Ruggels et al. (1977)
Currently married	+	Bromet and Moos (1977)
	Unrelated	Bateman and Petersen (1972)
	Unrelated	Crawford (1976)
	Unrelated	Davis (1966)
	Unrelated	Glatt (1961)
	Unrelated	Pemberton (1967)
	Unrelated	Ruggels et al. (1977)
Familial and marital factors		
Alcoholism in parents	−	Thomas (1971)
	Unrelated	Schuckit and Winokur (1972)
Alcoholism in siblings	−	Schuckit and Winokur (1972)
	Unrelated	Thomas (1971)
Alcoholism in spouse	Unrelated	Bateman and Petersen (1972)
	Unrelated	Thomas (1971)
Mental illness in primary relatives	−	Schuckit and Winokur (1972)
	Unrelated	Thomas (1971)
Marital stability	Unrelated	Bateman and Petersen (1972)
	Unrelated	Crawford (1976)
	Unrelated	Davis (1966)
	Unrelated	Glatt (1961)

(Continued)

Table 2. (*Continued*)

Variable	Prognostic relationship	Investigator (year)
	Unrelated	Pemberton (1967)
	Unrelated	Ruggels et al. (1977)
	Unrelated	Schuckit and Winokur (1972)
	Unrelated	Thomas (1971)
Marital problems	Unrelated	Thomas (1971)
Attitude of spouse	Unrelated	Bateman and Petersen (1972)
	Unrelated	Pemberton (1967)
Number of children	Unrelated	Bateman and Petersen (1972)
Extent of contact with family	Unrelated	Bateman and Petersen (1972)
Social relationships		
Membership in club or organization	+	Bateman and Petersen (1972)
Religious involvement	Unrelated	Bateman and Petersen (1972)
Number of close friends	Unrelated	Bateman and Petersen (1972)
	Unrelated	Schuckit and Winokur (1972)
Quarrels with others	Unrelated	Ruggels et al. (1977)
History of alcohol and drug use		
Age at first drink	−	Bateman and Petersen (1972)
	Unrelated	Schuckit and Winokur (1972)
	Unrelated	Thomas (1971)
Age at regular, excessive, or uncontrolled drinking	+	Schuckit and Winokur (1972)
	Unrelated	Bateman and Petersen (1972)
	Unrelated	Davis (1966)
	Unrelated	Pemberton (1967)
	Unrelated	Thomas (1971)
Length of drinking history	−	Schuckit and Winokur (1972)
	Unrelated	Bateman and Petersen (1972)
	Unrelated	Pemberton (1967)
	Unrelated	Ruggels et al. (1977)
	Unrelated	Thomas (1971)
Choice of alcoholic beverage	Unrelated	Bateman and Petersen (1972)
	Unrelated	Thomas (1971)
Drinking pattern	Unrelated	Bateman and Petersen (1972)
Amount of daily alcohol consumption	+	Bateman and Petersen (1972)
	Unrelated	Schuckit and Winokur (1972)
Frequency of alcohol use	Unrelated	Ruggels et al. (1977)
	Unrelated	Schuckit and Winokur (1972)
Arrests	Unrelated	Davis (1966)
	Unrelated	Schuckit and Winokur (1972)
Type and phase of alcoholism	Unrelated	Bateman and Petersen (1972)
Drinking milieu	Unrelated	Thomas (1971)
Abuse of other drugs	−	Thomas (1971)
AA attendance	Unrelated	Bateman and Petersen (1972)
	Unrelated	Ruggels et al. (1977)
Impairment index	Unrelated	Ruggels et al. (1977)

(Continued)

Table 2. (*Continued*)

Variable	Prognostic relationship	Investigator (year)
Quantity–frequency index	Unrelated	Ruggels et al. (1977)
Physical complications		
Gastritis	−	Schuckit and Winokur (1972)
Alcohol-related illnesses	−	Thomas (1971)
Cerebral organic impairment	Unrelated	Pemberton (1967)
Delirium tremens, other medical complications	Unrelated	Pemberton (1967)
Blackouts, hallucinosis	Unrelated	Schuckit and Winokur (1972)
Diagnosis		
Underlying neurosis	+	Pemberton (1967)
Affective disorder	Unrelated	Schuckit and Winokur (1972)
Psychopathy	−	Glatt (1961)
Psychosis, neurosis, character disorder, normal	Unrelated	Thomas (1971)
Anxiety symptoms, phobias, conversion symptoms, impulsivity, vagrancy, pathological lying	Unrelated	Schuckit and Winokur (1972)
Personality test scores		
Deviation from normal profile (MMPI)	Unrelated	Thomas (1971)
Introversion (MPI)	+	Pemberton (1967)
Neuroticism (MPI)	Unrelated	Pemberton (1967)
Group dependency (16 PF)	+	Davis (1966)
	Unrelated	Pemberton (1967)
Integrated threat of civil authority (fear anxiety profile)	−	Davis (1966)
Self-rating of		
Alcohol as a major problem area	+	Davis (1966)
	+	Davis (1966)
Others trying to help	−	Davis (1966)
Wanting a drink		
Intellectual functioning		
Revised Army Beta Test	+	Bateman and Petersen (1972)
Raven's Matrices	Unrelated	Pemberton (1967)
Vocabulary (Wide Range)	Unrelated	Davis (1966)
Vocabulary (Mill Hill)	Unrelated	Pemberton (1967)
Pretreatment factors		
Abstinence prior to treatment	Unrelated	Bateman and Petersen (1972)
	Unrelated	Ruggels et al. (1977)
Voluntary admission	+	Davis (1966)
Traumatic precipitating events	Unrelated	Thomas (1971)
Previous treatment admissions	Unrelated	Davis (1966)
	Unrelated	Pemberton (1967)
	Unrelated	Ruggels et al. (1977)

(*Continued*)

Table 2. (Continued)

Variable	Prognostic relationship	Investigator (year)
AA referral to treatment	+	Thomas (1971)
Referral due to suicide threat or attempt	+	Schuckit and Winokur (1972)
Referral due to inability to stop drinking	−	Schuckit and Winokur (1972)
Institutionalization in past month	Unrelated	Ruggels et al. (1977)
Treatment factors		
Use of protective drug (TETD)	+	Hoff and McKeown (1953)
Private hospital (vs. state hospital)	Unrelated	Schuckit and Winokur (1972)
"Intensive" treatment (vs. routine treatment)	+	Pemberton (1967)
Aversive conditioning therapy (vs. conventional methods)	Unrelated	Glover and McCue (1977)
Program completion	+	Fitzgerald et al. (1971)
	Unrelated	Crawford (1976)
Length of stay in hospital	Unrelated	Davis (1966)
	Unrelated	Ruggels et al. (1977)
Number of outpatient visits	Unrelated	Ruggels et al. (1977)
Use of services (inpatient, hospital, outpatient, emergency/detoxication)	Unrelated	Ruggels et al. (1977)
Sex of therapist	Unrelated	Ruggels et al. (1977)

married female alcoholics (Glatt, 1961; Pemberton, 1967; Crawford, 1976; Ruggels et al., 1977).

Familial Factors.   The incidence of marital problems (Thomas, 1971), the attitude of the spouse (Pemberton, 1967; Bateman and Petersen, 1972), the number of children (Bateman and Petersen, 1972), the extent of contact with the family (Bateman and Petersen, 1972), marital stability (Glatt, 1961; Davis, 1966; Pemberton, 1967; Thomas, 1971; Bateman and Petersen, 1972; Schuckit and Winokur, 1972; Crawford, 1976; Ruggels et al., 1977), and alcoholism in the spouse (Thomas, 1971; Bateman and Petersen, 1972) have all been found to be unrelated to treatment outcome for the female alcoholic. Alcoholism in parents (Thomas, 1971), alcoholism in siblings (Schuckit and Winokur, 1972), and mental illness in primary relatives (Schuckit and Winokur, 1972) have been linked to poor treatment outcome, although the results across studies have not always been statistically significant (Thomas, 1971; Schuckit and Winokur, 1972).

Social Relationships.   Religious involvement (Bateman and Petersen, 1972), the number of close friends (Bateman and Petersen, 1972; Schuckit and Winokur, 1972), and the incidence of quarrels with others (Ruggels et al., 1977) have failed to show any prognostic significance for the female alcoholic. Membership in a single club or organization, however, has been found to be significantly related to abstinence on follow-up (Bateman and Petersen, 1972). Interestingly, the number of club memberships has been found to bear a curvilinear relationship to outcome, with no memberships and multiple memberships being associated with lower rates of abstinence (Bateman and Petersen, 1972).

History of Alcohol and Drug Use.   Abuse of drugs other than alcohol has been shown to relate to poor treatment outcome for the female alcoholic (Thomas, 1971). In addition, several factors related to the female alcoholic's history of alcohol use have also been found to relate to poor treatment prognosis in at least one study; these include older age at first drink (Bateman and Petersen, 1972); engagement in regular, excessive, or uncontrolled drinking at a relatively young age (Schuckit and Winokur, 1972); and a lengthy drinking history (Schuckit and Winokur, 1972), although one or more of these factors has failed to reach significance in other investigations (Davis, 1966; Pemberton 1967; Thomas, 1971; Bateman and Petersen, 1972; Schuckit and Winokur, 1972; Ruggels et al., 1977). Most other alcohol-related variables have shown no prognostic significance for the female alcoholic; these include choice of alcoholic beverage (Thomas, 1971; Bateman and Petersen, 1972), drinking pattern (Bateman and Petersen, 1972), frequency of alcohol use (Schuckit and Winokur, 1972; Ruggels et al., 1977), arrests (Davis, 1966; Schuckit and Winokur, 1972), type and phase of alcoholism (Bateman and Petersen, 1972), drinking milieu (Thomas, 1971), prior AA attendance (Bateman and Petersen, 1972; Ruggels et al., 1977), an alcohol impairment index (Ruggels et al., 1977), and a quantity–frequency measure of alcohol intake (Ruggels et al., 1977).

Physical Complications.   A number of presenting alcohol-related physical complications have been linked to poor response by female alcoholics in traditional treatment programs. Gastritis (Schuckit and Winokur, 1972), cirrhosis of the liver, peripheral neuritis, and perigastritis (Thomas, 1971) have been found to be associated with lower remission rates. Trends indicative of poorer response to treatment have also been reported for cerebral organic impairment (Pemberton, 1967) and delirium tremens (Pemberton, 1967), although these relationships failed to reach statistical significance with the small female alcoholic samples employed.

Psychiatric Diagnosis.   The presence of an underlying neurosis (Pemberton, 1967) has been found to relate positively to outcome, while the existence of psychopathy (Glatt, 1961) has been shown to bear a strong negative relationship to treatment outcome among female alcoholics. Most other diagnostic categories have failed to show prognostic significance (Thomas, 1971; Schuckit and Winokur, 1972).

Personality Test Scores.   Scores on a variety of personality tests administered on admission to treatment have been found to be predictive of successful outcome on follow-up. Significant prognostic indicators include high introversion (Maudsley Personality Inventory) (Pemberton, 1967), high group dependency (16 Personality Factor Questionnaire) (Davis, 1966), low integrated threat of civil authority (Fear Anxiety Profile) (Davis, 1966), high level of intellectual functioning (Revised Army Beta Test) (Bateman and Petersen, 1972), and self-ratings revealing alcohol as a major problem area, the perception of others as trying to help, and the negation of the desire for alcohol (Davis, 1966).

Pretreatment Factors.   A number of factors associated with conditions surrounding the treatment admission have been found to be significant prognostic variables. Referral by AA to treatment (Thomas, 1971), referral due to a suicide threat or attempt (Schuckit and Winokur, 1972), and voluntary admission status (Davis, 1966) have been shown to be predictive of successful outcome, while referral due to inability to stop drinking has been found to relate to poor outcome among female alcoholics. No significant prognostic relationship has been shown for abstinence prior to treatment (Bateman and Petersen, 1972; Ruggels et al., 1977), traumatic precipitating events (Thomas, 1971), previous treatment admissions (Davis, 1966; Pemberton, 1967; Ruggels et al., 1977), or institutionalization in the previous month (Ruggels et al., 1977).

Treatment Factors.   Very few variables associated with the treatment regime have been found to relate significantly to outcome in the female alcoholic. Use of a protective drug (TETD) (Hoff and McKeown, 1953) has been shown to be predictive of improved outcome, although it should be noted that no drug study adequately controlling for patient motivation has yet been reported. One study (Pemberton, 1967) suggested that female alcoholics may respond better to "intensive" treatment programs; unfortunately, the type of treatment and the amount of therapy have been seriously confounded in all reported work to date. There is some indication that the female alcoholic who completes a treatment program is more likely to have an improved outcome (Fitzgerald et al., 1971), although this relationship has not always been found to be significant (Crawford, 1976). Most treatment variables have shown no significant prognostic relationship; these include treatment in a private versus a state hospital (Schuckit and Winokur, 1972), aversive conditioning versus conventional therapies (Glover and McCue, 1977), length of stay in the hospital (Davis, 1966; Ruggels et al., 1977), number of outpatient visits (Ruggels et al., 1977), and the use of a wide variety of treatment services (Ruggels et al., 1977).

A final treatment variable to be considered is the sex of the therapist. It is claimed in some quarters that the female alcoholic may make better progress in therapy with a female therapist (Birchmore and Walderman,

1975; Calobrisi, 1976). Only one empirical investigation has been published bearing directly on this issue (Ruggels et al., 1977). As part of the recent follow-up study of NIAAA-funded Alcoholism Treatment Centers in the United States, the relationship of sex of therapist to treatment outcome was examined. Remission rates for both male and female alcoholics were found to remain unaffected by the sex of the therapist. Unfortunately, no information is presented on the training or the orientation of the therapists involved. It is not known whether more of the female than the male therapists were sympathetic to nonsexist counseling techniques or to feminist theories of emotional distress among women. Therefore, the more specific proposition that outcome results for female alcoholics may be superior with female therapists of a nonsexist or feminist orientation remains untested.

Comparison of Prognostic Factors with Male Alcoholic Samples

Of the 13 studies reviewed above that examined prognostic factors in treatment outcome among female alcoholics, 11 (Hoff and McKeown, 1953; Glatt, 1961; Davis, 1966; Gerard and Saenger, 1966; Pemberton, 1967; Fitzgerald et al., 1971; Bateman and Petersen, 1972; Crawford, 1976; Bromet and Moos, 1977; Glover and McCue, 1977; Ruggels et al., 1977) included male alcoholic comparison groups drawn from the same clinic settings. Table 3 presents a summary of the direction of prognostic relationships for male and female alcoholics in these studies. As in Table 2, significance tests were not reported in several of the original articles, but sufficient information was presented to allow us to perform the necessary statistical tests.

What can be concluded from this evidence? Do prognostic factors operate in different ways for male and female alcoholic patients? The answer would appear to be mixed. While there is considerable agreement in prognostic factors between the sexes reported in some studies (Hoff and McKeown, 1953; Glatt, 1961; Fitzgerald et al., 1971; Bromet and Moos, 1977), differences in significant prognostic characteristics are reported in other studies (Davis, 1966; Bateman and Petersen, 1972). Considering the differences and similarities in role demands and expectations of males and females in our society, it seems likely that some factors indicative of good prognosis may vary between the sexes, while others may transcend sex differences.

However, because of a number of methodological limitations in the studies reviewed, the evidence at this time can be considered, at best, only suggestive. Given the small sample sizes involved in several of the studies, very large prognostic effects would have been necessary to show statistical significance. Interpretation of nonsignificant results is further complicated by the failure in many cases to report the spread or variability on the different prognostic factors within the male and female alcoholic samples studied. A nonsignificant finding for the importance of social stability in outcome for female alcoholics, for example, may relate to the highly restrictive range of values on this variable represented in the sample of female alcoholics studied. Other discrepancies between study findings and factors associated with improvement may be due to differences in measurement reliability, study design, or sample selection factors related to the particular pretreatment characteristics of the populations studied. Finally, the possible interaction of patient-by-treatment effects must be considered; certain patient characteristics may be differentially related to improvement depending on the nature of the treatment program involved. Results to date are too limited to assess adequately the extent to which such considerations may account for discrepant findings on the significance of prognostic factors for male and female alcoholics between studies, or for differences observed between the sexes within studies. Further work is needed to validate the existence of possible sex differences in prognostic factors, since such differences may well have implications for the planning of treatment services.

4. NEW DIRECTIONS

What can one conclude about effective treatment modalities for the female alcoholic? To date, almost nothing. More surprising, given the relative intensity of the research effort devoted to her male counterpart, is the fact that very little more is known about effective treatment techniques for the male alcoholic. The paucity of existing knowledge of effective treatment programming in the alcoholism field is highlighted by two recent review articles (Baekeland et al., 1975; Emrick, 1975); major determinants of treatment outcome have been found repeatedly to be strongly linked to the presenting characteristics of patients and to be largely independent of the kind of treatment offered. The present review of the treatment of the female alcoholic is consistent with this conclusion. What is needed to advance knowledge in the alcoholism treatment field in general, and in the treatment of the female alcoholic in particular, is not more of the same kind of research effort but a change in the nature of the research question being addressed.

Patient Specificity

The question being addressed in most treatment research undertaken to date lacks specificity. Largely neglected has been the systematic study of individual differences in response to various types of treatment. Among the important individual differences to be considered is the sex of the client. There is considerable evidence that alcoholics can also be

Table 3. Sex Differences in Prognostic Factors in Treatment Outcome

Variable	Prognostic relationship		Investigator (year)
	Males	Females	
Demographic socioeconomic factors			
Age	+	+	Bateman and Petersen (1972)
	Unrelated	Unrelated	Davis (1966)
	Unrelated	Unrelated	Pemberton (1967)
	+	Unrelated	Ruggels et al. (1977)
Education	Unrelated	−	Bateman and Petersen (1972)
	Unrelated	Unrelated	Davis (1966)
	+	+	Ruggels et al. (1977)
Occupational level (housewife)	Unrelated	−	Bateman and Petersen (1972)
	Unrelated	Unrelated	Davis (1966)
	Unrelated	+	Gerard and Saenger (1966)
Socioeconomic status	Unrelated	−	Bateman and Petersen (1972)
	Unrelated	Unrelated	Ruggels et al. (1977)
Employed on admission	Unrelated	+	Bateman and Petersen (1972)
	Unrelated	+	Ruggels et al. (1977)
Currently married	Unrelated	Unrelated	Bateman and Petersen (1972)
	+	+	Bromet and Moos (1977)
	+	Unrelated	Crawford (1976)
	Unrelated	Unrelated	Davis (1966)
	Unrelated	Unrelated	Glatt (1961)
	Unrelated	Unrelated	Pemberton (1967)
	+	Unrelated	Ruggels et al. (1977)
Residential stability	+	Unrelated	Ruggels et al. (1977)
Employment stability	+	Unrelated	Bromet and Moos (1977)
Familial and marital factors			
Alcoholism in spouse	Unrelated	Unrelated	Bateman and Petersen (1972)
Marital stability	Unrelated	Unrelated	Bateman and Petersen (1972)
	+	+	Bromet and Moos (1977)
	+	Unrelated	Crawford (1976)
	+	Unrelated	Davis (1966)
	Unrelated	Unrelated	Glatt (1961)
	Unrelated	Unrelated	Pemberton (1967)
	+	Unrelated	Ruggels et al. (1977)
Attitude of spouse	Unrelated	Unrelated	Bateman and Petersen (1972)
Number of children	Unrelated	Unrelated	Bateman and Petersen (1972)
Extent of contact with family	−	Unrelated	Bateman and Petersen (1972)
Social relationships			
Membership in club or organization	Unrelated	+	Bateman and Petersen (1972)
Religious involvement	Unrelated	Unrelated	Bateman and Petersen (1972)
Number of close friends	Unrelated	Unrelated	Bateman and Petersen (1972)
Quarrels with others	Unrelated	Unrelated	Ruggels et al. (1977)
History of alcohol use			
Age at first drink	Unrelated	−	Bateman and Petersen (1972)

Table 3. (*Continued*)

Variable	Prognostic relationship		Investigator (year)
	Males	Females	
Age at regular, excessive, or			
uncontrolled drinking	Unrelated	Unrelated	Bateman and Petersen (1972)
	Unrelated	Unrelated	Davis (1966)
	Unrelated	Unrelated	Pemberton (1967)
Length of drinking history	Unrelated	Unrelated	Bateman and Petersen (1972)
	Unrelated	Unrelated	Pemberton (1967)
	Unrelated	Unrelated	Ruggels et al. (1977)
Choice of alcoholic beverage	Unrelated	Unrelated	Bateman and Petersen (1972)
Drinking pattern	Unrelated	Unrelated	Bateman and Petersen (1972)
Amount of daily alcohol	Unrelated	+	Bateman and Petersen (1972)
consumption			
Impairment index	Unrelated	Unrelated	Ruggels et al (1977)
Quantity–frequency index	–	Unrelated	Ruggels et al. (1977)
Arrests	Unrelated	Unrelated	Davis (1966)
Type and phase of alcoholism	Unrelated	Unrelated	Bateman and Petersen (1972)
Number of days drinking in			
past month	Unrelated	Unrelated	Ruggels et al. (1977)
AA attendance	+	Unrelated	Bateman and Petersen (1972)
	Unrelated	Unrelated	Ruggels et al. (1977)
Physical complications			
Cerebral organic impairment	Unrelated	Unrelated	Pemberton (1967)
Delirium tremens, other medical			
complications	Unrelated	Unrelated	Pemberton (1967)
Diagnosis			
Underlying neurosis	+	+	Pemberton (1967)
Psychopathy	–	–	Glatt (1961)
Personality test scores			
Introversion (MPI)	Unrelated	+	Pemberton (1967)
Neuroticism (MPI)	Unrelated	Unrelated	Pemberton (1967)
Group dependency (16 PF)	Unrelated	+	Davis (1966)
	Unrelated	Unrelated	Pemberton (1967)
Integrated threat of civil			
authority (fear anxiety profile)	Unrelated	–	Davis (1966)
Dread of marital rejection			
(fear anxiety profile)	–	Unrelated	Davis (1966)
Dread of civil authority			
(fear anxiety profile)	–	Unrelated	Davis (1966)
Repression of threat of			
assault (fear anxiety profile)	+	Unrelated	Davis (1966)
Self-rating of wanting a drink	Unrelated	–	Davis (1966)
Self-rating of alcohol as a			
major problem area	Unrelated	+	Davis (1966)
Self-rating of others trying			
to help	Unrelated	+	Davis (1966)
Self-rating of problem has			
affected family	+	Unrelated	Davis (1966)

(*Continued*)

Table 3. (Continued)

Variable	Prognostic relationship		Investigator (year)
	Males	Females	
Intellectual functioning:			
Revised Army Beta Test	Unrelated	+	Bateman and Petersen (1972)
Raven's Matrices	+	Unrelated	Pemberton (1967)
Wide Range Vocabulary	Unrelated	Unrelated	Davis (1966)
Mill Hill Vocabulary Scale	Unrelated	Unrelated	Pemberton (1967)
Pretreatment factors			
Abstinence prior to treatment	+	Unrelated	Bateman and Petersen (1972)
	Unrelated	Unrelated	Ruggels et al. (1977)
Voluntary admission	Unrelated	+	Davis (1966)
Previous treatment admissions	+	Unrelated	Davis (1966)
	Unrelated	Unrelated	Pemberton (1967)
	−	Unrelated	Ruggels et al (1977)
Institutionalization in prior month	Unrelated	Unrelated	Ruggels et al. (1977)
Treatment factors:			
Use of protective drug	+	+	Hoff and McKeown (1953)
"Intensive" treatment (vs. routine treatment)			
	Unrelated	+	Pemberton (1967)
Aversive conditioning therapy (vs. conventional methods)	+	Unrelated	Glover and McCue (1977)
Program completion	+	Unrelated	Crawford (1976)
	+	+	Fitzgerald et al. (1971)
Length of stay in hospital	Unrelated	Unrelated	Davis (1966)
	Unrelated	Unrelated	Ruggels et al. (1977)
Outpatient visits	Unrelated	Unrelated	Ruggels et al. (1977)
Use of services:			
Inpatient	Unrelated	Unrelated	Ruggels et al. (1977)
Hospital	Unrelated	Unrelated	Ruggels et al. (1977)
Outpatient	Unrelated	Unrelated	Ruggels et al. (1977)
Emergency/detoxication	−	Unrelated	Ruggels et al. (1977)
Sex of therapist	Unrelated	Unrelated	Ruggels et al. (1977)

reliably differentiated into a number of subtypes on the basis of physiological variables (Mendelson and Mello, 1973), clinical history (Winokur et al., 1971; Rimmer et al., 1972), psychological test scores (Reilly and Sugerman, 1967; Stein et al., 1971; Evenson et al., 1973; Skinner et al., 1974), demographic and social stability variables (Gillis and Keet, 1969; Trice et al., 1969; Evenson et al., 1973), and the situational determinants of drinking (Marlatt, 1975). Promising dimensions for study among female alcoholics have been suggested by several authors (Schuckit et al., 1969; Gomberg, 1974, 1976b; Schuckit and Morrissey, 1976). Studies to date that have pooled results across all female alcoholic patients may have obscured the existence of significant improvement within subgroups.

Recognition of the heterogeneity within the female alcoholic population, and the study of salient differences in relation to treatment response, is critical to advancement of knowledge on the treatment of the female alcoholic.

Treatment Specificity

Since the female alcoholic population is not homogeneous, it is most unlikely that a single form of treatment will be equally efficacious for all. Nevertheless, conventional programming has almost invariably offered the same basic treatment package to all male and female alcoholic admissions. Not only has the sex of the patient failed to play a major role in the nature of the services rendered (Sue, 1976; Ruggels et al., 1977), but little attempt has been made to develop treatment techniques to meet the specific presenting problems and needs of the individual patient, whether male or female. The lack of treatment specificity in the alcoholism field has been commented on by several investigators (Pattison, 1966; Annis, 1973; Glaser, 1977; Kissin, 1977). Compared with men, the different pattern of development of alcoholism in women (Schuckit, 1972; Beckman, 1975; Ashley et al., 1977), the different reasons given by women for seeking treatment (Lisansky, 1957; Curlee, 1970; Sclare, 1970), and the different degree of acceptability of certain forms of treatment to women (Curlee, 1971) suggest that certain treatment modalities may have wider applicability in meeting the needs of female compared with male alcoholics. For example, it has been suggested (Lolli, 1953) that given the apparently greater role played by situational precipitating events in the onset of problem drinking in women, environmental intervention strategies may be particularly appropriate. Since disruption of familial relationships is frequently a major concern among female alcoholics, family intervention techniques have been proposed (Pattison, 1965; Meeks and Kelly, 1970; Esser, 1971; Dinaburg et al., 1977). Depending on the individual female alcoholic's presenting characteristics, it is likely that certain treatment intervention strategies will prove more efficacious than others.

Patient–Treatment Match

Although evidence to date is meager (cf. Ogborne, 1978), a number of empirical studies do suggest the importance of matching specific kinds of patients to specific treatment interventions to maximize success (Wallerstein, 1957; Karp et al., 1970; Kissin et al., 1970; Tomsovic and Edwards, 1970; Vogler et al., 1970; Pittman and Tate, 1972; Sobell and Sobell, 1972; Bromet et al., 1977). Nevertheless, as several investigators have noted (Pattison, 1966, 1974; Baekeland et al., 1975; Baekeland and

Lundwall, 1977; Glaser, 1977; Kissin, 1977; Tuchfeld, 1977), relatively little research attention has yet been focused on the question of patient–treatment match. How do differing presenting characteristics among female alcoholics interact with specific treatment intervention strategies in determining long-term outcome? Serious pursuit of this question will entail (1) the application of reliable patient assessment procedures and (2) the development of better-specified treatment interventions than typically are found within conventional alcoholism services. Rather than offering the same basic package of help to all, a range of clearly defined, alternative treatment strategies is needed, designed to meet the specific needs of the populations being served. Research addressed to specific patient–treatment combinations should significantly expand our knowledge of the therapeutic modalities most suited to different types of female alcoholics.

REFERENCES

Annis, H., 1973, Directions in treatment research, *Addictions* **20**:50–59.

Armor, D. J., Polich, J. M., and Stambul, H. B., 1976, *Alcoholism and Treatment*, prepared for the U.S. National Institute on Alcohol Abuse and Alcoholism, Rand Corp., Santa Monica, Calif.

Ashley, M. J., Olin, J. S., Le Riche, W. H., Kornaczewski, A., Schmidt, W., and Rankin, J. G., 1977, Morbidity in alcoholics: Evidence for accelerated development of physical disease in women, *Arch. Intern. Med.* **137**:883–887.

Baekeland, F., and Lundwall, L. K., 1977, Engaging the alcoholic in treatment and keeping him there, in: *The Biology of Alcoholism,* Vol. 5, *Treatment and Rehabilitation of the Chronic Alcoholic* (B. Kissin and H. Begleiter, eds.), pp. 161–195, Plenum, New York.

Baekeland, F., Lundwall, L., and Kissin, B., 1975, Methods for the treatment of chronic alcoholism: A critical appraisal, in: *Research Advances in Alcohol and Drug Problems,* Vol. 2 (R. J. Gibbins, Y. Israel, H. Kalant, R. E. Popham, W. Schmidt, and R. G. Smart, eds.), pp. 247–327, Wiley, Toronto.

Bateman, N. I., and Petersen, D. M., 1972, Factors related to outcome of treatment for hospitalized white male and female alcoholics, *J. Drug Issues* **2**:66–74.

Beckman, L. J., 1975, Women alcoholics: A review of social and psychological studies, *J. Stud. Alcohol* **36**:797–824.

Beckman, L. J., 1976, Alcoholism problems and women: An overview, in: *Alcoholism Problems in Women and Children* (M. Greenblatt and M. Schuckit, eds.), pp. 65–95, Grune & Stratton, New York.

Bell, R. G., and Levinson, T., 1971, An evaluation of The Donwood Institute treatment program, *Ont. Med. Rev.* **38**:219–226.

Birchmore, D. F., and Walderman, R. L., 1975, The woman alcoholic: A review, *Ont. Psychologist* **7**:10–16.

Blake, B. G., 1967, A follow-up of alcoholics treated by behaviour therapy, *Behav. Res. Ther.* **5**:89–94.

Blaney, R., Radford, I. S., and MacKenzie, G., 1975, A Belfast study of the prediction of outcome in the treatment of alcoholism, *Br. J. Addict.* **70**:41–50.

Bromet, E., and Moos, R. H., 1977, Environmental resources and the posttreatment functioning of alcoholic patients, *J. Health Soc. Behav.* **18**:326–338.

Bromet, E., Moos, R., Bliss, F., and Wuthmann, C., 1977, Posttreatment functioning of alcoholic patients: Its relation to program participation, *J. Consult. Clin. Psychol.* **45**:829–842.

Browne-Mayers, A. N., Seelye, E. E., and Sillman, L., 1976, Psychosocial study of hospitalized middle-class alcoholic women, in: *Work in Progress on Alcoholism* (F. A. Seixas and S. Eggleston, eds.), pp. 593–604, Annals of the New York Academy of Sciences, New York.

Cahn, S., 1970 *The Treatment of Alcoholics: An Evaluative Study,* Oxford University Press, New York.

Calobrisi, A., 1976, Treatment programs for alcoholic women, in: *Alcoholism Problems in Women and Children* (M. Greenblatt and M. Schuckit, eds.), pp. 155–162, Grune & Stratton, New York.

Carver, V., 1977, The female alcoholic in treatment, *Can. Psychological Rev. Psychol. Can.* **18**:96–103.

Core-Shell Staff, 1978, The phase II pilot test of the Core-Shell treatment system, Addiction Research Foundation of Ontario, Substudy #962, p. 115.

Corrigan, E. M., 1974, Women and problem drinking: Notes on beliefs and facts, *Addict. Dis.* **1**:215–222.

Costello, R. M., 1975, Alcoholism treatment and evaluation: In search of methods, *Int. J. Addict.* **10**:251–275.

Costello, R. M., Biever, P., and Baillargeon, J. G., 1977, Alcoholism treatment programming: Historical trends and modern approaches, *Alcoholism: Clin. Exper. Res.* **1**:311–318.

Crawford, R. J. M., 1976, Treatment success in alcoholism, *N. Z. Med. J.* **84**:93–96.

Curlee, J., 1967, Alcoholic women: Some considerations for further research, *Bull. Menninger Clin.* **31**:154–163.

Curlee, J., 1970, A comparison of male and female patients at an alcoholism treatment center, *J. Psychology* **74**:239–247.

Curlee, J., 1971, Sex differences in patient attitudes toward alcoholism treatment, *Q. J. Stud. Alcohol* **32**:643–650.

Dahlgren, L., 1975, Special problems in female alcoholism, *Br. J. Addict.* **70** (Suppl. No. 1):18–24.

Davies, D. L., Shepherd, M., and Myers, E., 1956, The two-years' prognosis of 50 alcohol addicts after treatment in hospital, *Q. J. Stud. Alcohol* **17**:485–502.

Davis, H. G., 1966, *Variables associated with recovery in male and female alcoholics following hospitalization,* Doctoral dissertation, Texas Technological College.

Dinaburg, D., Glick, I. D., and Feigenbaum, E., 1977, Marital therapy of women alcoholics, *J. Stud. Alcohol* **38**:1247–1258.

Dunne, J. A., 1973, Counseling alcoholic employees in a municipal police department, *Q. J. Stud. Alcohol* **34**:423–434.

Emrick, C. D., 1975, A review of psychologically oriented treatment of alcoholism, II, The relative effectiveness of different treatment approaches and the effectiveness of treatment versus no treatment, *J. Stud. Alcohol* **36**:88–108.

Emrick, C. D., and Stilson, D. W., 1977, The "Rand Report": Some comments and a response, *J. Stud. Alcohol* **38**:152–163.

Esser, P. H., 1971, Evaluation of family therapy with alcoholics, *Br. J. Addict.* **66**:251–255.

Evenson, R. C., Altman, H., Sletten, I. W., and Knowles, R. R., 1973, Factors in the description and grouping of alcoholics, *Am. J. Psychiatry* **130**:49–54.

Ferrence, R. G., Adamtau, L. L., Murdock, W. and Brook, R. C., 1977, Services for alcoholics: A study of primary care physicians in the Lake Erie Region, Addiction Research Foundation, Substudy No. 887, Toronto.

Fitzgerald, B. J., Pasewark, R. A., and Clark, R., 1971, Four-year follow-up of alcoholics treated at a rural state hospital, *Q. J. Stud. Alcohol* **32**:636–642.

Fox, V., and Smith, M. A., 1959, Evaluation of a chemopsychotherapeutic program for the rehabilitation of alcoholics, *Q. J. Stud. Alcohol* **20**:767–780.

Gerard, D. L., and Saenger, G., 1966, *Out-Patient Treatment of Alcoholism*, University of Toronto Press, Toronto.

Gillies, M., Laverty, S. G., Smart, R. G., and Aharan, C. H., 1974, Outcome in treated alcoholics: Patient and treatment characteristics in a one year follow-up study, *J. Alcoholism* **9**:125–134.

Gillis, L. S., and Keet, M., 1969, Prognostic factors and treatment results in hospitalized alcoholics, *Q. J. Stud. Alcohol* **30**:426–437.

Glaser, F. B., 1976, Selecting patients for treatment: An heuristic model. Unpublished manuscript, Addiction Research Foundation of Ontario.

Glaser, F. B., 1977, Comment on "Alcoholism: A controlled trial of 'treatment' and 'advice,' " *J. Stud. Alcohol* **38**:1819–1827.

Glatt, M. M., 1955, A treatment centre for alcoholics in a public mental hospital: Its establishment and its working, *Br. J. Addict.* **52**:55–92.

Glatt, M. M., 1961, Treatment results in an English mental hospital alcoholic unit, *Acta Psychiatr. Scand.* **37**:143–168.

Glover, J. H., and McCue, P. A., 1977, Electrical aversion therapy with alcoholics: A comparative follow-up study, *Br. J. Psychiatry* **130**:279–286.

Gomberg, E. S., 1974, Women and alcoholism, in: *Women in Therapy* (V. Franks and V. Burtle, eds.), pp. 169–190, Brunner/Mazel, New York.

Gomberg, E. S., 1976a, Alcoholism in women, in: *Social Aspects of Alcoholism* (B. Kissin and H. Begleiter, eds.), pp. 117–166, Plenum, New York.

Gomberg, E. S., 1976b, The female alcoholic, in: *Alcoholism: Interdisciplinary Approaches to an Enduring Problem* (R. E. Tarter and A. A. Sugerman, eds.), pp. 603–636, Addison-Wesley, Don Mills, Reading, Mass.

Health and Welfare Canada, May 1976, *Alcohol Problems in Canada: A Summary of Current Knowledge*, Technical Report Series No. 2, Non-Medical Use of Drugs Directorate, Ottawa.

Hill, M. J., and Blane, H. T., 1967, Evaluation of psychotherapy with alcoholics: A critical review, *Q. J. Stud. Alcohol* **28**:76–104.

Hirsh, J., 1962, Women and alcoholism, in: *Problems in Addiction: Alcohol and Drug Addiction* (W. Bier, ed.), pp. 108–115, Fordham University Press, New York.

Hoff, E. C., and McKeown, C. E., 1953, An evaluation of the use of tetraethylthiuram disulfide in the treatment of 560 cases of alcohol addiction, *Am J. Psychiatry* **109**:670–673.

Kammeier, M. L., 1977, Alcoholism is the common denominator, *Hazelden Papers,* No. 2, Center City, Minn.

Karp, S. A., Kissin, B., and Hustmyer, F. E., Jr., 1970, Field dependence as a predictor of alcoholic therapy dropouts, *J. Nerv. Ment. Dis.* **150**:77–83.

Keller, M., and Efron, V., 1955, Prevalence of alcoholism, *Q. J. Stud. Alcohol* **16**:619–644.

Kissin, B., 1977, Comment on "Alcoholism: A controlled trial of 'treatment' and 'advice,' " *J. Stud. Alcohol* **38**:1804–1808.

Kissin, B., Platz, A., and Su, W. H., 1970, Social and psychological factors in the treatment of chronic alcoholism, *J. Psychiatr. Res.* **8**:13–27.

Lemere, F., O'Hollaren, P., and Maxwell, M. A., 1956, Sex ratio of alcoholic patients treated over a 20-year period, *Q. J. Stud. Alcohol* **17**:437–442.

Lindbeck, V. L., 1972, The woman alcoholic: A review of the literature, *Int. J. Addict.* **7**:567–580.

Lisansky, E. S., 1957, Alcoholism in women: Social and psychological concomitants, I, Social history data, *Q. J. Stud. Alcohol* **18**:588–623.

Lisansky, E. S., 1958, The woman alcoholic, *Ann. Am. Acad. Pol. Soc. Sci.* **315**:73–81.

Litman, G., 1975, Women and alcohol: Facts and myths, *New Behav.* 126–129.

Lolli, G., 1953, Alcoholism in women, *Conn. Rev. Alcoholism* **5**:9–11.

Marlatt, G. A., 1975, The drinking profile: A questionnaire for the behavioral assessment of alcoholism, in: *Behavior Therapy Assessment: Diagnosis and Evaluation* (E. J. Marsh and L. G. Terdal, eds.), Springer, New York.

May, S. J., and Kuller, L. H., 1975, Methodological approaches in the evaluation of alcoholism treatment: A critical review, *Prevent. Med.* **4**:464–481.

McLachlan, J., 1978, Sex differences in recovery rates after one year, Research Note No. 9, The Donwood Institute, Toronto.

Meeks, D. E., and Kelly, C., 1970, Family therapy with the families of recovered alcoholics, *Q. J. Stud. Alcohol* **31**:399–413.

Mendelson, J. H., and Mello, N. K., 1973, Alcohol-induced hyperlipidemia and beta lipoproteins *Science* **180**:1372–1374.

Miller, B. A., Pokorny, A. D., Valles, J., and Cleveland, S. E., 1970, Biased sampling in alcoholism treatment research, *Q. J. Stud. Alcohol* **31**:97–107.

Moore, R. A., 1977, Ten years of inpatient programs for alcoholic patients, *Am. J. Psychiatry* **134**:542–545.

Moos, R., and Bliss, F., 1978, Difficulty of follow-up and outcome of alcoholism treatment, *J. Stud. Alcohol* **39**:473–490.

Ogborne, A. C., 1978, Patient characteristics as predictors of treatment outcomes for alcohol and drug abusers, in: *Research Advances in Alcohol and Drug Problems,* Vol. 4 (Y. Israel, F. D. Glaser, H. Kalant, R. E. Popham, W. Schmidt, and R. G. Smart, eds.), pp. 177–223, Plenum, New York.

Pattison, E. M., 1965, Treatment of alcoholic families with nurse home visits, *Fam. Process* **4**:75–94.

Pattison, E. M., 1966, A critique of alcoholism treatment concepts: With special reference to abstinence, *Q. J. Stud. Alcohol* **27**:49–71.

Pattison, E. M., 1974, Rehabilitation of the chronic alcoholic, in: *The Biology of Alcoholism,* Vol. 3, *Clinical Pathology* (B. Kissin and H. Begleiter, eds.), pp. 587–658, Plenum, New York.

Pemberton, D. A., 1967, A comparison of the outcome of treatment in female and male alcoholics, *Br. J. Psychiatry* **113**:367–373.

Pittman, D. J., and Tate, R. L., 1972, A comparison of two treatment programs for alcoholics, *Int. J. Soc. Psychiatry* **18**:183–193.

Reilly, D. H., and Sugerman, A. A., 1967, Conceptual complexity and psychological differentiation in alcoholics, *J. Nerv. Ment. Dis.* **144**:14–17.

Rimmer, J., Pitts, F. N., Jr., Reich, T., and Winokur, G., 1971, Alcoholism, II, Sex, socioeconomic status and race in two hospitalized samples, *Q. J. Stud. Alcohol* **32**:942–952.

Rimmer, J., Reich, T., and Winokur, G., 1972, Alcoholism vs diagnosis and clinical variation among alcoholics, *Q. J. Stud. Alcohol* **33**:658–666.

Ritson, B., 1968, The prognosis of alcohol addicts treated by a specialized unit, *Br. J. Psychiatry* **114**:1019–1029.

Ruggels, W. L., Armor, D. J., Polich, J. M., Mothershead, A., and Stephen, M., 1975, *A Follow-Up Study of Clients at Selected Alcoholism Treatment Centers Funded by NIAAA, Final Report,* Stanford Research Institute, Menlo Park, Calif.

Ruggels, W. L., Mothershead, A., Pyszka, R., Loebel, M., and Lotridge, J., 1977, *A Follow-Up Study of Clients at Selected Alcoholism Treatment Centers Funded by NIAAA* (Supplemental Report), Stanford Research Institute, Menlo Park, Calif.

Schuckit, M., 1972, The alcoholic woman: A literature review, *Psychiatr. Med.* **3**:37–43.

Schuckit, M. A., and Morrissey, E. R., 1976, Alcoholism in women: Some clinical and social perspectives with an emphasis on possible subtypes, in: *Alcoholism Problems in Women and Children* (M. Greenblatt and M. Schuckit, eds.), pp. 5–35, Grune & Stratton, New York.

Schuckit, M. A., and Winokur, G., 1972, A short term follow up of women alcoholics, *Dis. Nerv. Syst.* **33**:672–678.

Schuckit, M., Pitts, F. N., Jr., Reich, T., King, L. J., and Winokur, G., 1969, Alcoholism, I, Two types of alcoholism in women, *Arch. Gen. Psychiatry* **20**:301–306.

Sclare, A. B., 1970, The female alcoholic, *Br. J. Addict.* **65**:99–107.

Selzer, M. L., and Holloway, W. H., 1957, A follow-up of alcoholics committed to a state hospital, *Q. J. Stud. Alcohol* **18**:98–120.

Sherfey, M. J., 1955, Psychopathology and character structure in chronic alcoholism, in: *Etiology of Chronic Alcoholism* (O. Diethelm, ed.), pp. 16–42, Thomas, Springfield, Ill.

Skinner, H. A., Jackson, D. N., and Hoffmann, H., 1974, Alcoholic personality types: Identification and correlates, *J. Abnorm. Psychol.* **83**:658–666.

Sobell, M. B., and Sobell, L. C., 1972, Individualized Behaviour Therapy for Alcoholics: Rationale, Procedures, Preliminary Results and Appendix, California Mental Health Research Monograph No. 13, California Department of Mental Hygiene, Sacramento.

Stein, K. B., Rozynko, V., and Pugh, L. A., 1971, The heterogeneity of personality among alcoholics, *Br. J. Soc. Clin. Psychol.* **10**:253–259.

Sue, S., 1976, Clients' demographic characteristics and therapeutic treatment: Differences that make a difference, *J. Consult. Clin. Psychol.* **44**:864.

Thomas, D. A., 1971, *A study of selected factors on successfully and unsuccessfully treated alcoholic women*, Doctoral dissertation, Michigan State University.

Tomsovic, M., and Edwards, R. V., 1970, Lysergide treatment of schizophrenic and nonschizophrenic alcoholics: A controlled evaluation, *Q. J. Stud. Alcohol* **31**:932–949.

Trice, H. M., Roman, P. M., and Belasco, J. A., 1969, Selection for treatment: A predictive evaluation of an alcoholism treatment regimen, *Int. J. Addict.* **4**:303–317.

Tuchfeld, B. S., 1977, Comment on "Alcoholism: A controlled trial of 'treatment' and 'advice,' " *J. Stud. Alcohol* **38**:1808–1813.

Vannicelli, M., Pfau, B., and Ryback, R. S., 1976, Data attrition in follow-up studies of alcoholics, *J. Stud. Alcohol* **37**:1325–1330.

Vogler, R. E., Lunde, S. E., Johnson, G. R., and Martin, P. L., 1970, Electrical aversion conditioning with chronic alcoholics, *J. Consult. Clin. Psychol.* **34**:302–307.

Vogler, R. E., Compton, J. V., and Weissbach, T. A., 1975, Integrated behavior change techniques for alcoholics, *J. Consult. Clin. Psychol.* **43**:233–243.

Wallerstein, R. S., 1957, *Hospital Treatment of Alcoholism: A Comparative, Experimental Study*, Menninger Clinic Monograph Series No. 11, Basic Books, New York.

Winokur, G., and Clayton, P. J., 1968, Family history studies, IV, Comparison of male and female alcoholics, *Q. J. Stud. Alcohol* **29**:885–891.

Winokur, G., Reich, T., Rimmer, J., and Pitts, F. N., Jr., 1970, Alcoholism, III, Diagnosis and familial psychiatric illness in 259 alcoholic probands, *Arch. Gen. Psychiatry* **23**:104–111.

Winokur, G., Rimmer, J., and Reich, T., 1971, Alcoholism, IV, Is there more than one type of alcoholism? *Br. J. Psychiatry* **118**:525–531.

Wolff, S., and Holland, L., 1964, A questionnaire follow-up of alcoholic patients, *Q. J. Stud. Alcohol* **25**:108–118.

12

Dependence on Psychotropic Drugs and Analgesics in Men and Women

DAVID S. BELL

1. INTRODUCTION

The consideration of dependence by women on drugs poses two contrasting problems. In regard to the drugs, we need to seek what is common in a field where differences are striking, but in regard to their use by females, we seek to define differences from the male in a field where uniformity is increasing.

Unlike the distinctive contrasts between the drugs, female and male drug dependence present little in the way of differences, apart from the statistics of incidence and prevalence, which in a rapidly changing world are particularly ephemeral and in any case are to be considered elsewhere in this book. Not that this uniformity has always been the case, far from it. In the past, and until fairly recently, behavioral differences between male and female seemed to provide an absolute contrast across an enormous range of activities including drug dependence. These differences are now disappearing at such a rate that one may well wonder if any will be left in time beyond the one undisputed and essential difference.

If the material to be presented is to be more than a mass of heterogeneous and disjointed facts, the unifying influence of a theoretical structure has to be imposed on it. In this chapter, it will be derived from a concept of the nature of drug dependence rather than of the nature of women.

The scope of this chapter includes all drugs of dependence except alcohol, tobacco, and the opiates. The term *psychotropic drugs* is used in

DAVID S. BELL • Alanbrook Clinic, Mosman, New South Wales, Australia.

the title simply for brevity, referring as it does to the minor tranquilizers, sedatives, hypnotics, and stimulants. Henceforth, the minor tranquilizers and hypnotics will be subsumed together with the barbiturates under the classification of *hypnotic sedatives* and will be separated from the *stimulants,* which in the main refer to the amphetamines and cocaine. The *analgesics* are the nonopiate pain-relieving substances such as aspirin, phenacetin, paracetamol, and related substances, alone or in compound preparations. *Marijuana* refers to the various forms in which cannabis may be used, including the more concentrated preparations such as hashish and the resin oil. The *hallucinogens,* in practice, include mainly lysergic acid diethylamide 25 (LSD), but they also include a great range of substances in less common use, such as mescaline, atropine and related chemicals, certain analogs of amphetamine, mushrooms, cacti, and other plants such as nutmeg. A sixth group of drugs, not specifically mentioned in the title to this chapter but to be considered, are the *inhalants.*

2.   THE RELATIONSHIP BETWEEN DRUG USE AND DEPENDENCE

Drugs of dependence are remarkably diverse with respect not only to their chemical constitution but also to their range of effects, subjective and objective (May, 1953). This is clearly the case for the range of drugs discussed in this chapter. The one feature that all of these drugs have in common is the capacity to generate a subjective pleasurable effect. Perhaps less evident is the fact that all users of a drug, whether dependent or not, and possibly even whether animal or insect (Bejerot, 1977), seek this identical effect. That continued unremitting excessive use such as the binge may generate unpleasure in time, or even intense suffering, does not gainsay that the use was initiated to obtain the pleasure.

The community of interest of all drug users is illustrated graphically in the observation that for drugs of dependence, licit or illicit, throughout a variety of population groups, consumption follows a unimodal distribution along a smooth curve with log normal characteristics that reveals no clear points of differentiation between light, moderate, and heavy users (Smart and Whitehead, 1973). Changes in the shape of the normal distribution curve under various conditions indicate that all users— whether dependent or not, abusers, misusers, or the social and gregarious—are affected similarly by external influences bearing on availability and supply of the drug and that they covary so closely that they cannot be distinguished statistically (Smart, 1977). These findings provide no basis for assuming fundamentally different motivating forces in dependent and nondependent users.

From these facts may be derived the conclusion *that drug dependence is indivisible from drug use,* differing in degree rather than in kind, both having as their basis the seeking of drug-induced pleasure or relief. Although the motivation for drug use would seem to be of the essence, it is perhaps the least studied aspect of drug dependence. As an example, in a recent text on the "basic aspects" of drug abuse (Pradhan and Dutta, 1977), only part of one paragraph touches on the motivation for drug use (Cohen, 1977b). This is equally true of most other popular books on drugs (e.g., Ray, 1978). Few have even commented on this major gap in our knowledge (Bell, 1974; Orcutt, 1975).

To a large extent, this gap is due to the difficulty of examining experimentally the nature of the drug-induced reward. There is a large body of literature on drug self-administration studies in experimental animals (Kelleher et al., 1976; Thompson and Unna, 1977; Griffiths and Bigelow, 1978; Kalant, 1978). These studies have permitted many conclusions about factors that influence the onset, duration, intensity, and loss of drug-taking behavior under experimental conditions. However, they have not yet shed much light on the actual nature of the rewarding effect that reinforces this behavior. For this, we must still rely mainly on descriptions provided by drug users themselves.

The Drug-Induced Sensation

All types of users, pathological or not, describe drugs as providing, among other things, a sense of security and as erasing anxieties and concern and at times generating a sense of personal power. The word used most commonly, and the one that seems most aptly to describe the sought-after drug-induced sensation, is *confidence* or some equivalent term. For example, amphetamine addicts have explained the drug-induced effect in terms of its giving them the sense of being the most intelligent or the most powerful person in the world, or of being capable of doing anything they cared to try (Bell and Trethowan, 1961a), or of narrowing the gap between their actual and their ideal self-images (Teasdale and Hinkson, 1971). Depressants as well as stimulants convey to the user similar feelings of great physical or intellectual power and lack of concern. This feeling may be described as superconfidence and is observable among those intoxicated on commonly used drugs such as alcohol. To some users of marijuana, "Nothing seemed impossible to accomplish" (Chopra, 1969).

The psychoanalytic literature provides a useful formulation that places the sense of confidence sought by the drug addict in the context of specific mechanisms of psychological malfunction (Fenichel, 1955), but the same concepts of immature behavior are equally relevant to the nonpathological use of drugs. The psychoanalytic term "the oceanic sense of unlimited omnipotence," in its delightful extravagance of redundancy, conveys aptly the grossly immature and unrealistic nature of the sensation of superconfidence. Furthermore, in drawing a direct parallel to infantile behavior, the term brings attention to many other significant similarities, such as the paradoxical juxtaposition of helplessness with the sense of unlimited power. The cyclic fluctuation of the drug user from the elation of intoxication to the despair of withdrawal bears comparison to the extremes experienced by the infant, fluctuating between similar extremes of satiation and hunger (Radó, 1933). Although all users do not allow themselves to plumb the same depths of helplessness during intoxication or of despair during withdrawal, the differences are more a matter of degree than of quality.

The remarkable value of the sense of confidence engendered by the drug would seem to arise from the relief it provides from fear and insecurity, and it suggests that these are the most widespread and continually pressing forms of psychological pain experienced by man and woman alike. That this should be so is not necessarily self-evident, nor is the fact that the fear and insecurity are particularly pressing accompaniments of interpersonal relationships, but on reflection, it is readily realized that fear and insecurity are based on reality (Bell, 1974). Of all the potential sources of danger, pain, and distress for the human being, other human beings are the most threatening. No doubt the fear of other human beings has had survival value in the evolutionary context. We are the survivors of a long evolutionary process in which the living are the successors of those who have been the most efficient in exterminating other variants of the species. The danger of extermination remains no less real in modern times, which have seen modern technology applied to the task of genocide, but in addition, everyday life situations continuously pose a great range of other threats and dangers from fellow human beings to the life, happiness, and prosperity of the individual. Conceivably, this threat contributes to the widespread use of drugs, which provide occasional and controlled relief from this pressing need to beware our fellow man.

Everyday experience with alcohol and tobacco, as well as with the other drugs considered in this chapter, presents innumerable examples of their use to relieve the concerns of commonplace relationships with others. When the concerns are severe enough to warrant the description of "social anxiety," the use of any of these drugs may become exaggerated enough to be considered pathological (Kraft, 1968). The many examples of alcoholics drinking to overcome their problems in relating to others (McGuire et al., 1966; Simmons, 1968; Tamerin and Mendelson, 1969; Weiner et al., 1971) are matched by dependence on the other drugs to be discussed in this chapter. Insofar as women undertake tasks different from men, their concerns differ and their confidence is tested in different circumstances, explaining differences in detail between men and women for nonpathological as well as pathological use. Hence the probable reason that in women alcoholism often begins shortly after childbirth or drunkenness in relation to dinnertime (Browne, 1965).

The Precipitants of Drug Dependence

A passing event that prompts consumption on one occasion has to be distinguished from one that introduces a long-lasting situation. Childbirth, for example, has more significance than a passing event because it initiates the new and demanding adult role of parenthood (Browne, 1965). Life events that introduce new interpersonal strains, either through the imposition of new roles on the individual or through the loss of someone else, have been observed to precede the onset of dependence on stimulants (Bell, 1971a), and a variety of observations suggest that a similar sequence of events probably occurs in the case of dependence on other drugs as well. The comparison extends further still. The precipitants of amphetamine dependence correspond to the first 14 events in a rating scale of 43 readjustment life events that appeared to be significant precipitants of physical illness (Holmes and Rahe, 1967) and also to the critical life events that can precipitate various psychiatric disorders (Brown and Birley, 1968; Maddison and Viola, 1968; Paykel et al., 1969).

Among the most dramatic precipitants are sexual life events (Bell, 1971a). Of 34 cases in which a salient life event could be identified as a precipitant of amphetamine dependence, 11 involved sexual relationships. All the subjects concerned were sexually maladjusted, having been either frigid, impotent, or overtly perverse before the drug use or dependence began. A consideration of the nature of the subjective experience of sexuality for each individual gives some idea of how stressful to them were the new adult sexual roles into which they had been introduced by the sexual experience. Three of them commenced their addiction within a short period of their first experience of heterosexual coitus. In the course of the act itself, they first realized the sense of revulsion or fear that heterosexuality conveyed to them and in consequence were brought face to face with the inadequacies and conflicts that made them unable to cope with the role of adult heterosexuality. These subjects found that they did not enjoy heterosexual coitus but that they did enjoy homosexual intercourse or homosexual fantasies during heterosexual intercourse.

Insofar as women undertake or become forced into roles that differ from those of men, the life events that influence women to turn to drugs for the sensation of confidence differ from those characteristic for men. In the field of sexuality, prostitution is more often the role of women than of men, and the observations of the relationship between the onset of drug dependence and the adoption of prostitution (Maerov, 1965) are mainly pertinent to women. Similarly so for the differences to be found in the other category of precipitants, the loss of an emotionally significant relationship with another person, which may arise as the result of either rejection or separation. The loss of a spouse through death is far more often the fate of women than of men. Maddison and Viola (1968) found that in the year following bereavement, more than one widow in three increased her consumption of drugs, markedly so in 6% of cases. As with sexuality, the original relationship is usually found to have been disturbed and grossly ambivalent. This type of "object loss" is, of course, a common antecedent of psychiatric disorder (Adamson and Schmale, 1965).

The Drug Effect Sought in Dependence

Not only does the sensation of confidence engendered by the drug place in perspective the motivating need for all drug use, normal and abnormal, but it also has relevance to the consequences common to the use of all drugs of dependence. In the normal course of events, confidence is a pleasurable feeling state that accompanies the success of effort directed toward the tasks necessary for survival and reproduction. It may be that the feeling of pleasure is the ultimate reward sought by the individual rather than the material success itself. For this reason, the essential benefit of pleasure also produces its greatest danger. Even while failing at the task of survival, the individual responds to the signal of success and so may continue in harmful or even fatal activity. The drug provides the reward without effort or performance (Radó, 1963), so much so that in drug dependence, the effort for survival or procreation may cease altogether. Perhaps no more explanation than this is needed to understand the "amotivational syndrome" seen after the chronic use of marijuana (McGlothlin and West, 1968), particularly when it is acknowledged that a similar state is seen in dependence on a variety of other drugs as well, such as alcohol, barbiturates, narcotics, and inhalants. Equally understandable is the appearance of behavior inimical to survival or procreation, such as serious self-neglect leading to illness and death, loss of libido, and the gross neglect of offspring, which are common accompaniments of drug dependence.

Of course, not all users are lured into this disastrous state. The ease of obtaining the pleasurable drug effects attracts many to sporadic use, particularly for the socially convivial and gregarious occasion. Most sporadic users do not manifest an overall preference for drug-induced illusion, still maintaining interest in the satisfactions to be gained from reality-oriented activity and performance. The choice of the user between the alternatives of the illusion or the reality of confidence is the operational nub of drug dependence. Choice of the illusion suggests that the person who becomes dependent on drugs gains greater satisfaction from the illusion than from reality, either because the illusion is superlative or because the possibilities of satisfaction from reality are so limited.

The first of these explanations requires that the drug-induced sensation enjoyed by the drug-dependent person be far superior to that experienced by other users, so much so that all other sources of gratification pall into insignificance. Individuals go to such lengths to obtain the drug-induced pleasure that their deeds appear to support this notion. A related argument is based on the belief that the experience is qualitatively different to the extent that it is irresistible. Without arguing that the drug-induced pleasure is necessarily more gratifying, some have postulated the existence of some vague and undefined biochemical abnormality that places the drug-dependent individual at the mercy of a drug-induced effect qualitatively different from that experienced by those who use the drug in a more restrained manner. Instead of making a choice between illusion or reality, the drug-dependent person is seen as the victim of an overpowering desire for the drug. The victim hypothesis does not necessarily attempt to place in perspective the subjective experience of drug use, incongruent periods of moderate use, or the motivation of the "victim."

Many observations exist to refute the possibility that those who become dependent on drugs enjoy effects that are superior or qualitatively different from those experienced by other users (Bell, 1970). Epidemiological evidence, as noted above, shows that the users in a community cannot be differentiated statistically and that they respond uniformly to generalized social influences. Turning from the community to the individual, a variety of facts further controvert the idea of unique drug effects as the basis of dependence. An inherited biochemical abnormality or a qualitatively different sensation are refuted by every user who can at some time use in moderation and who at other stages in a lifetime "suffers" from drug dependence. Equally difficult to explain is the readiness with which the drug-dependent individual may shift to the use of another drug, chemically dissimilar and physiologically distinct in its actions, so long as the substitute has the one property in common with all drugs of dependence, the capacity to produce the desired sensation.

The alternative possibility is that the drug-induced illusion of confidence is preferred by the drug-dependent because the possibilities of satisfaction from reality are so limited. The discussion about the precipitants of drug dependence has noted the evidence that the affected individuals were maladjusted and psychologically disturbed before the drug use began. This evidence is consistent with the broad trend of evidence, which establishes that individuals who use drugs more than others have one consistent feature in common, deviancy. Their family backgrounds have a higher prevalence of psychiatric disorder and parental separation, they have a higher prevalence of psychiatric disorder and parental deprivation, and they are more likely to have been truants and delinquents, to have failed at school and work, to have committed crimes, and to be sexually deviant or perverse. In a survey of a general population sample, the use of a three-point deviancy scale established a quantitative relationship between antisocial behavior and drug use (Bell and Champion, 1979); the moderately deviant used drugs to a greater degree than the nondeviant, but the difference was much more marked between the moderately and the highly deviant groups.

Deviance and Dependence

No doubt maladjustment militates against an individual's chances of success at work, play, and love, handicaps interpersonal relationships, and, in the competitive field of survival or reproduction, considerably limits the possibilities of satisfaction from reality. From an existential viewpoint, the drug-dependent lack the ability to create euphoria from the everyday activities of life (Greaves, 1974). Above all, maladjustment of this nature breeds insecurity and fear, the very reverse of the sense of confidence at the core of the drug experience. The fact that the drug provides the illusion of confidence explains why drug use substitutes for coping behavior among deviant individuals, in whom the essence of deviancy would seem to be that they lack the resources to cope as the result of constitutional or environmental disorder.

If allowance be made for the extent to which social pressures have channeled the deviance of women to paths that differ from those of men, apparent differences are readily resolved. For that matter, cultural and social influences explain the differences that have existed between the sexes for the whole range of drug use. The drugs to be discussed in this chapter include all those that have in the past been preferred more by women than by men, in particular the mood-modifying prescription drugs (Cooperstock, 1971). The higher rate of use of prescription drugs by women corresponds to the higher rates for women of neurotic illness, symptoms of mental and physical discomfort, and help seeking (Cooperstock, 1976). The same relationship is also relevant to the higher rates of use by women of over-the-counter drugs such as the analgesics. The significant pressures would seem to have been those encouraging men to be the more assertive and aggressive and at the same time relatively stoical, whereas women have been permitted greater freedom to express feelings and to acknowledge emotional difficulties (Cooperstock, 1971). In consequence, the deviancy of men has tended to be expressed in aggressive and assertive antisocial behavior, in contrast to the preferred mode of women, that is, illness and attempted suicide.

Men appear to consume drugs, and particularly those considered elsewhere in this book, more extensively than women (Fejer and Smart, 1972). While this has certainly been so in the case of the illicit drugs, including those that are the subject of this chapter, when sales of the prescription and over-the-counter drugs are also taken into consideration (Chambers and Hunt, 1977a), the existence of any real difference between the overall male and female consumption of the drugs of dependence is doubtful. Once again, it may be seen that social and cultural pressures have served to create the apparent difference, the tendency for men to express their deviance in antisocial behavior being closely related to their greater use of illicit drugs (Bell and Champion, 1979).

All of these differences are said to be fast disappearing in those communities where women are escaping from traditional social restrictions, and particularly in the section that is least hampered by past indoctrination, the radical young (Suffet and Brotman, 1976). As drug use increases more rapidly among women than among men (Chambers and Hunt, 1977b), the sex differential for the use of all drugs by secondary-school children was fast disappearing between 1969 and 1971 in the Netherlands (Buikhuisen and Timmerman, 1972) and between 1967 and 1972 in Denmark (Boolsen, 1975) and was described as a "disappearing phenomenon" in Massachusetts in 1974 (Wechsler and McFadden, 1976). In regard to some drugs such as tobacco, between 1969 and 1977 young women in Australia had not only achieved equality of consumption but appeared to be on the way to reversing the previous difference (Champion et al., 1978). These changes appear to correspond not only with the trend for females to adopt male roles throughout the broad range of social activities but also with the tendency for females to become aggressive and assertive in the antisocial sphere as well and to commit property offenses and acts of violence (File, 1976).

Accordingly, over the past decade the characteristics of drug use by women have been those of a group in transition. Before the transition accelerated, those women who ignored the prescribed barriers were fewer in numbers than the men who committed antisocial acts and were also more disturbed psychologically than their male counterparts (Gossop, 1976). Being the advance guard of a group in transition, they possessed characteristics in common with both groups. The women who adopted the use of illicit drugs still retained the general tendency of women to seek medical aid more than men, making up a disproportionately high number among those who sought help in hospital casualty departments and among those who attempted suicide (Ghodse, 1977). They also appeared in a disproportionately high number among the drug dependents who obtained psychiatric inpatient care (Whitlock and Lowrey, 1967), yet a comparison of male and female inpatients revealed little of significant difference between the two groups (Klinge et al., 1976). In a population of female prisoners, the addicts had had more contact as adults with psychiatric outpatient services and more thoughts of suicide and had made more attempts at suicide than the nonaddicts (Climent et al., 1974). At the same time, the female users of illicit drugs, in comparison with women using licit drugs, had a higher rate of criminal convictions, in particular for violent crime (Noble et al., 1972).

Psychotropic Drug Use: Treatment and Dependence

The circumstances in which psychotropic drugs are prescribed are remarkably similar to the antecedents of dependence. The individuals seeking the prescription are maladjusted, the maladjustment reduces their ability to cope with a disturbing life event, and they seek relief through a drug effect that will give them a sensation of having adjusted. The inadequacy of this maneuver is largely ignored, not only by the maladjusted but also seemingly by those who prescribe for them.

The assumption that the "therapeutic" use of psychotropic drugs is beneficial is made so firmly that few have dared to question it. Bayer (1973) pointed out that it is doubtful whether the psychotropic drugs correct or prevent pathological disorder. No proof exists to show that they provide any therapeutic benefit at all, unless a pleasurable effect is taken as synonymous with a therapeutic alleviation of distress. That the *feeling* of benefit cannot be assumed to be beneficial should be obvious from a comparison with the experience of the drug-dependent, but nevertheless this would seem to be the sole basis on which the psychotropics have been judged by patient and physician alike. As noted above, in this case the patient is more likely to be female than male.

All psychotropic drugs are also potentially drugs of dependence. The assumption that they provide undeniable and extensive benefit has not been objectively substantiated. Deedes (1970) questioned whether the issue is "not how we prevent these drugs from being misused, but whether we really need some of them at all." This question could be taken further, to whether we need any of them at all, not because of the danger that some users may become dependent but because the production of this drug-induced state is an undesirable way of coping with problems and of producing confidence. As they are used mainly by women, the impact of this use on their children will probably become in time a matter of great concern to society.

The Dynamics of the Adoption of Drug Use

To complete the background of the use of the drugs of dependence, and particularly those that are the subject of this chapter, certain characteristics remain to be considered. Drugs such as the sedatives and the analgesics not only are used more by women, but are used more by those with lower socioeconomic status (Gibson et al., 1977; Parry et al., 1973) and increasing age (Chapman, 1976). This relationship with class and age is found to exist in the case of males as well, and with all drugs that have a long-established and relatively stable pattern of use. Quite the opposite is the case for those drugs that have been introduced recently, in which case the young of higher socioeconomic status and with higher education predominate among the users. These characteristics of drug users conform to the features of the diffusion process for most social phenomena (Boolsen, 1975), which are adopted first by the more cosmopolitan and then follow an orderly process of diffusion through the friendship network of the community, to be adopted last of all by those of lower socioeconomic status and least education (Rogers and Shoemaker, 1971).

The early adopters of a new illicit drug are usually male. Later, as the use of a particular drug becomes more widespread, the sex differential is said to diminish (Boolsen, 1975). This is the stage, known as *late majority adoption* (Rogers and Shoemaker, 1971), that many communities reached in the 1970s, in which females still had a lower prevalence of use for certain drugs, but their use was said to be increasing more rapidly than that of men. A specific example of this phenomenon, the adoption of tobacco use by females in Australia, has been outlined by Bell and Champion (1977). However, it must be noted that tobacco is a licit drug, and it is not yet clear that a similar disappearance or reversal of the sex differential will occur with most illicit drugs.

In the case of those drugs that are used predominantly by women, the history of their early adoption is now lost in the obscure past. Conceivably, for the reasons that Cooperstock (1971) has stated, they have always been preferred by women, and only lately have men turned to them in comparable numbers—in which case, the dynamics of adoption are the reverse of those outlined for tobacco by Bell and Champion (1977), the men being the late adopters. This would certainly seem to have been the case for at least one class of drugs to be considered, the bromureides. Regardless of the status of men as adopters of the drugs preferred by women, the females have entered the phase of late adoption in which the extent of use has reached a plateau and become stable and the late adopters, with a higher prevalence of lower class and increasing age, predominate.

The Influence of Female Drug Use

For those who take the narrow view of modern drug use, the phenomena are not related to everyday life, and the recent upsurge of illicit drug use is inexplicable. This viewpoint is adopted by many in an effort to avoid taking personal responsibility for what they represent as a totally foreign intrusion into the fabric of their lives. In general, the women who smoke tobacco or use prescribed mood-changing drugs regularly reject as outrageous, in company with men who drink alcohol and use tobacco regularly, the suggestion that their attitudes and activities are the major influence responsible for the use of illicit drugs by the young. Nevertheless, the observed facts establish a relationship between the use of stimulants by the mother and marijuana by the child, or the use of barbiturates by the mother and drugs such as the narcotics by the child (Kandel, 1974).

To the use of drugs by women may be added the broader consideration of the influence of women's attitudes on the use of drugs. Maternal use of all types of drugs of dependence affect not only the use of drugs by their children but also the opposite extreme of total abstention from use (Bell et al., 1976), at least insofar as alcohol is concerned. The influence of the parents shows evidence of sex patterning of the actual drugs used (Annis, 1974), daughters tending more toward the pattern of their mothers than of their fathers, but as a rule the children generalize the principles of drug use they learn from their parents to other drug categories introduced to them by their peers. The use of drugs by the young fits the "cultural deviance" model of behavior, in which the family develops in the children the potential for deviance that is realized once the delinquent acts appear in their peer culture (Kandel, 1974).

In addition to influencing their children, women may influence their spouses to drink alcohol to excess (Bell, 1971b) or to use other drugs. The wife and mother may seek through covert encouragement of drug use (Schwartzman, 1975)—similar to the black-sheep mechanism producing delinquent behavior (Johnson and Burke, 1955)—to obtain vicarious gratification from the antisocial behavior of the child (Little and Pearson, 1966) or the psychological advantage to be gained from the perpetuation of the spouse's immature behavior patterns (Seldin, 1972).

3. THE HYPNOTIC SEDATIVES

The sedatives are outstandingly the drugs of dependence used predominantly by women, at least in Western communities. This group of drugs includes the barbiturates, the bromides and bromureides (Andrews, 1965), the vast range of minor tranquilizers including the benzodiazepines, and the more recently introduced sedatives such as methaqualone.

The term *hypnotic* indicates that the drug produces sleep. To do so, it produces a preliminary sedating or soothing effect, which in fact is the action sought by the majority of users, particularly in daytime use. This soothing effect is identical with that described as tranquilizing, and for this reason, the distinctions are abandoned in this chapter. In practice, these substances have proved to be completely interchangeable in use, misuse, abuse, treatment, and dependence.

All of these substances have been introduced in relatively recent times, but the extent of their use is still outmatched by that of the ancient sedative, alcohol. Alcohol shares many biochemical and physiological properties with the modern sedatives, in particular the production of a relatively stereotyped withdrawal syndrome that includes epileptic convulsions and a delirious phase. Furthermore, alcohol is synergistic with any of the sedatives and is so used in particular by those who are dependent. A nationwide survey of the United States established that between 1970 and 1974, almost all users of barbiturates also used alcohol regularly, 10% of them heavily, and that this pattern was even more marked among the users of minor tranquilizers, 15% of whom were heavy drinkers (Chambers and Hunt, 1977b). The close relationship was emphasized when the term *drug dependence* was first introduced and the sedatives and alcohol were grouped together in the "drug dependence of barbiturate–alcohol type" (Eddy et al., 1965).

The opiates have also been used since ancient times for their sedating action, but sufficient distinctions in structure and action exist to make a valid separation between them and the sedatives.

Bromides

Historically, the bromides were the first of the sedatives to be introduced in modern times. The problems they have created, together with the reactions of the community, have been typical of the sedatives in general. Initially, they were used mainly for the treatment of epilepsy and for this purpose achieved widespread use in the late 19th century.

Their action depends on the presence in the body of an inorganic bromide ion, which because of its slow elimination gradually accumulates during regular use. Because of this fact, the extent of bromide use could be established by relatively simple biochemical tests well before comparable instruments were available for other drugs of dependence. In consequence, the essential features of bromide dependence were established many decades ago.

The combination of the bromide radical with acyl derivatives of urea produced the bromureides early in this century. Being more potent sedatives than the simple bromides, they replaced them in general use. As long ago as 1907, the observation was made that they could produce toxic symptoms similar to those caused by the inorganic bromides. This effect was denied indirectly, inadequately, and erroneously by studies that seemed to establish that only a negligible proportion of the bromureides was broken down in the tissues of rabbits to release inorganic bromide. Andrews (1965) documented the facts, which show that in the history of the bromides, this error is typical of how "many incorrect ideas had lingered on long after evidence disproving them had been published." Perhaps because of this tendency, the bromureides have in many nations enjoyed unrestricted over-the-counter sales. In consequence, their use has grown to be a problem of major proportions in many nations before being recognized and subjected to control through the restriction of sale by prescription only. The experience in Australia may serve as a typical example of the macrocosm.

Apart from their use as an anticonvulsant at the turn of the century, the bromides were employed for routine sedation in many Australian lunatic asylums. In the general population, the use of the bromides spread much more extensively among women than among men. The prejudice of the Australian men against these drugs is illustrated by a common and completely unsubstantiated belief among the infantrymen of World War II that bromides were placed secretly in their rations to inhibit their sexual drive. Over-the-counter sales of bromureides expanded steadily in the years that followed World War II. Psychiatrists in particular became concerned about the incidence of bromide dependence among their patients (Evans, 1955) and began to press for restriction of their sale, only to be effectively countered by the manufacturers with the assertion that the benefit conferred on the majority through the free availability far outweighed any harm experienced by a small minority, who were in any case predisposed to disorder and merely succumbing to the inevitable. A similar argument has been used, with appropriate modification, to advocate free availability for every drug of dependence, once the problems they create begin to be brought to public attention.

As sales mounted, the size of the problem increased progressively

(Andrews, 1965). Toward its peak, before restrictions were introduced, raised serum bromide levels were found in 9% of admissions to a psychiatric unit (Kessell, 1969), particularly among middle-aged females, in whom the prevalence was as high as 25%. Bromureide dependence was found in association with alcoholism among females (Wilkinson et al., 1969) and appeared to be increasing rapidly among male alcoholics as well (Wilkinson et al., 1971). The indications were that had unrestricted use continued, men would have followed women into the phase of majority adoption of the bromureides.

In 1971, the availability was restricted to prescription only in the State of Victoria, following which the incidence of raised serum bromide levels among admissions to psychiatric units there dropped remarkably (Andrews et al., 1974). The other states of Australia that followed this lead enjoyed the same results. Similar experiences have been reported from other countries (Andrews, 1965), and some, such as West Germany, are still in the process of attempting to contain the problem (Poser and Poser, 1975).

Barbiturates

The initial spread of barbiturate use began slowly following the discovery of the sedative action of barbital in 1903 and the introduction of phenobarbital in 1912. In a course parallel to that described for the bromureides, barbiturate use increased rapidly in the years that followed World War II. Describing the growth of the problem in the United States, Fort (1964) remarked on a widespread refusal to believe that they produced dependence: "Despite conclusive evidence to the contrary, many physicians in the United States appear to think and act as though barbiturates are completely harmless drugs that can be prescribed in unlimited quantities." Although he failed to comment on the disproportionately high use by women, he referred to the drug's most famous victim, Marilyn Monroe, and quoted advertising statements that made it clear that the manufacturers knew who were their best customers: "When you prescribe a single morning dose . . . she will stick to her diet more willingly. She will feel better all day long" . . . "In obstetrics, gynecology, well tolerated for use during complete pregnancy cycle." In any event, the problem of barbiturate use was allowed to escalate until 1973, when strict controls were introduced in the United States (Falco, 1976).

Women dependent on barbiturates have the characteristic background of deviance to be expected with any drug of dependence. Whitlock (1970) found an inordinately high incidence of psychiatric illness and disturbed marriages, an "almost universal disturbance of sexual life," and "lifelong patterns of personality disorder." Most of these women used other drugs as well, such as alcohol and analgesics.

Gradually, it became evident that a serious danger the barbiturates posed was the effectiveness with which they could be used for suicide. The extent of this danger in Australia was clearly established once their use was reduced; the rise in reported suicide rates during the period 1960–1967 and the subsequent decline paralleled changes in the availability of sedatives, in particular of the barbiturates (Oliver and Hetzel, 1972). The decline followed a government restriction not of the quantities that the physician could prescribe in general but only of those quantities that could be obtained through the government-subsidized Pharmaceutical Benefits Scheme. In other words, some individuals apparently could be prevented from committing suicide by presenting them with the hurdle of a relatively trivial expense.

Thalidomide

The barbiturates were succeeded by sedatives with equally impressive records, perhaps none more so than thalidomide. Thalidomide had its own unique significance for women, the induction of fetal malformations. The groundwork was laid by the increasing awareness among physicians of the part that the barbiturates were playing in successful suicide attempts and accidental poisonings. Thalidomide was promoted as a safe hypnotic on the basis that even enormous doses were not fatal. Ironically, one famous advertisement depicted a small child whose safety could have depended, it was claimed, on its prescription.

The havoc thalidomide created in such a short time resulted from a special combination of factors. As already noted, a new drug is more likely to be adopted at first by the young. In this case, the young with young children of their own seemed to be particularly suited for the prescription of a sedative that could not harm the young child who might by accident gain access to the pill container. The combination of being prone to early adoption of a new idea and belonging to the susceptible age group applied particularly to the wives of young physicians. The change from the barbiturates to apparently less toxic sedatives such as thalidomide was promoted deliberately in medical training and was adopted first by the younger physicians (Cooperstock and Sims, 1971). This circumstance seems to explain the unduly high proportion of children with thalidomide-induced malformations borne by the wives of young, recently graduated physicians.

One boon was that the disastrous effect on the fetus was exposed to public attention much more rapidly, despite the notorious efforts of the manufacturers to conceal the first news, than possibly any other newly discovered harmful side effect of a drug of this type. The experience also illustrates an important principle enunciated by Rogers and Shoemaker (1971) about the adoption of a new idea: to take up an innovation early in its diffusion promises great benefits to the adopter but is potentially risky should the new idea prove to be a failure. Not only with the drugs of dependence but generally in regard to all innovations, failure is more frequent than success.

Benzodiazepines

From the point of view of rapid adoption and widespread use, diazepam undoubtedly represents the greatest success story of any modern sedative. True to what is almost a ritual on the introduction of a new drug of dependence, a host of articles attested to its freedom from addicting properties (Maletzky and Klotter, 1976). The fact that none of those making this claim advanced substantial evidence of merit did not deter the readers from accepting their assertions. The initial uncritical acceptance is always succeeded by a cold awakening to reality, and every sedative ever used has invariably been found to produce drug dependence. As reluctantly as always, this conclusion is being reached about diazepam and all other benzodiazepines in use.

In a study of diazepam users, Maletzky and Klotter (1976) uncovered an interesting aspect of this phenomenon of denial. The physicians who had regarded the subjects in this study as dependent on an unspecified drug often modified their opinion when they were informed that the drug involved was diazepam, commenting with relief that "it was only Valium" and hence could not be dangerous. Raters who had relatively little preknowledge "of diazepam's presumed safety" rated significantly higher addiction levels for almost all subjects than did the physicians. Maletzky and Klotter found that the individual more likely to become dependent on diazepam "would certainly seem to possess some past drug or alcohol history, at least a psychiatric history, and to be more commonly a woman."

The benzodiazepines have certainly proved to be less dangerous than the barbiturates and other sedatives when used in a suicide attempt. Apart from this one advantage, no significant feature exists to differentiate diazepam from most other sedatives, and the use of these drugs by women forms part of the broad general trend toward the increasing use of drugs of dependence in the community.

And Many Others Too Numerous to Mention

Most of the drugs that remain to be considered belong to the category of the minor tranquilizers, which are the most commonly used of the psychoactive drugs prescribed for adults. In a random household survey of metropolitan Toronto in 1971, Fejer and Smart (1973) found that more than three times as many females as males held prescriptions for these drugs and that the proportion increased steadily with increasing age.

Perhaps no greater impact was made by any minor tranquilizer than by the first to be introduced, meprobamate. Promoted with forceful advertising and publicity in the United States, the drug was elevated to the position of the magical cure-all (Greenblatt and Shader, 1971). Once again, the meager results of uncontrolled studies presenting favorable results were accepted widely and uncritically and produced an attitude of unjustified optimism. In time, the drug was established to be no better than, the barbiturates.

Exactly the same sequence of forceful advertising, promotion on the grounds of safety, and subsequent disillusionment was seen with methaqualone. Its early uncritical acceptance by the medical profession was followed by the rapid spread of nonmedical use in Germany, Japan, and the United Kingdom. This well-documented sequence was ignored in the United States, only to be repeated there in 1972, followed by severe restrictions on the sale of methaqualone in 1973 (Falco, 1976). Where methaqualone was prescribed extensively by physicians, its use became widespread among women. In the United Kingdom, the combination of methaqualone with diphenhydramine, known as Mandrax®, was widely accepted by the medical profession and prescribed extensively, partly replacing the barbiturates and being used mainly by women. In other countries such as West Germany, the nonmedical use predominated at an early stage, in which case it became particularly prevalent among young males (Falco, 1976). Following the successful control of an outbreak of heroin use that peaked in 1961 and began to decline in 1963 (Kato, 1972), the epidemic of methaqualone abuse in Japan reached a peak in 1964. In that case, the problem was primarily one of illicit use and affected males predominantly, with a male:female ratio of 3:1.

Similarly, an outbreak of illicit intravenous barbiturate use in the United Kingdom succeeded the measures that helped to curb the heroin problem there. This type of barbiturate use arose in a male population considerably more antisocial than the females who predominated in the endemic form of oral barbiturate use; among the intravenous users of drugs, those using barbiturates showed even more hostility than those using the narcotics or amphetamines (Gossop and Roy, 1976).

The fact that so many sedatives have been received with uncritical enthusiasm has been used to illustrate the attitude of denial widespread in society in relation to drugs of dependence. The experience with chlormethiazole illustrates a different approach. Because of past experience with so many other drugs with a similar action, from the very outset there has been an awareness of the risk that it could produce dependence (Reilly, 1976). This risk was highlighted by the fact that it soon became recognized as an effective agent for the management of the symptoms of withdrawal from alcohol and other drugs. In consequence, the drug has been used responsibly and cautiously, and the recorded cases of dependence have remained few and far between (Reilly, 1976). To date, this experience demonstrates that responsible prescribing can contain a potential drug problem, but any relaxation of caution could easily allow this drug to follow the same course as the others. This example, like the voluntary withdrawal of methamphetamine from sale by pharmacists in Britain (Alarcón, 1972) and the imposition of penal sanctions against physicians who prescribed it irresponsibly in Washington, D.C. (Greene and DuPont, 1973), illustrates the efficacy of such controls against abuse of drugs derived from licit sources.

Sedatives are used particularly extensively in the hospital. Many patients are introduced to them when they enter a general hospital for treatment. At one general hospital in Australia, it was found that 33% of males and 41% of females had used sedatives at home, but in the hospital, the use increased to encompass 75% of males and 80% of females (Johns et al., 1971). Even in this environment of uniform and almost coercive promotion, females still maintained a slight lead over the males. Deliberate action has been taken in some hospitals to counter this influence, for example, the abolition of routine night sedation rounds coupled with an attitude-changing educational program for staff conducted in small discussion groups (Sheerin, 1973). If night sedation has to be used, the drug of choice advocated at present is nitrazepam.

4. ANALGESICS

The principal nonopiate pain-relieving substances are aspirin, phenacetin, paracetamol, and salicylamide. They may be supplied in powder or tablet form, singly or in compound preparations of two or more, or together with other substances such as the stimulant caffeine or the opiate-derived analgesic codeine. Being used widely for the relief of pain due to minor and common disorders, in many countries they are freely available and may be sold by any retailer who cares to stock them. Following much the same pattern as the sedatives, the analgesics have been used traditionally by women. Similarly, the prevalence of regular and excessive use correlates with increasing age and lower social class. As long ago as 1907, an article in a popular magazine observed that "What the 'drink habit' is among men in Australia, the 'headache powder' is among women" (New South Wales Joint Parliamentary

Committee on Drugs, 1978). In a large Australian city, the overall prevalence of daily aspirin ingestion was found to be 7.9% for males and 14.7% for females, and as high as 25.8% of women in the lowest social grades (Gillies and Skyring, 1972).

Analgesic consumption among patients with psychiatric disorders is significantly higher than among other patients or the healthy in those populations in which significant overall consumption takes place (Abrahams et al., 1970). Similarly, where both analgesic and barbiturate use are significant, more females than males are dependent on both, and the prevalence is highest in the psychiatric inpatient group. Murray et al. (1970) suggested that the prevalence of daily analgesic ingestion among females admitted to a psychiatric hospital in Scotland could have been as high as 33%. They commented that:

> Psychiatrists are largely unaware, both of the frequency and dangers of analgesic abuse in their patients, and should be on the alert for the syndrome in middle-aged women with chronic neurosis, inadequate personality or reactive depression, especially if known to abuse other drugs or have headaches.

The fact that the analgesics produce a pleasurable sensation is recognized reluctantly, perhaps even more reluctantly than the similar dependence-producing essence of the tobacco effect. This denial produces a vacuum, which, being abhorred by nature, is filled with pseudoknowledge, the concept of the "habit." Convoluted reasoning professes to explain that the habit may arise simply from repeated use. As a habit is virtually no more than repeated use, this reasoning can be boiled down to the tautological assertion that repeated use leads to repeated use. Of course, it fails to explain why the use was initiated. Certainly it fails to explain why some take to the habit and others do not, or why the predilection to this type of habit correlates with deviancy and with the use of other licit and illicit drugs (Estes and Johnson, 1971). Another convolution is added to place the hypothesized mechanism of the habit at a further remove from the individual's motivation, that is, to propose that the use is initiated by the prompting of social, cultural, and peer pressures. The distant issue of how these pressures arose can then be left at peace, apparently far removed from individual psychology, with the optimistic hope that the developing science of sociology will eventually unravel the mysteries.

Though this assertion is denied by many observers, in the author's experience the analgesics share with all other drugs of dependence the ability to produce an unrealistic sense of confidence together with the associated unrealistic relief from anxiety. Those who use large quantities commonly describe the sensation that they seek and actually experience in the identical terms used in relation to other drugs of dependence, for example, as a "high."

The tardy recognition of ill effects extended not only to the production of dependence but also to a variety of harmful side effects. As an example, phenacetin had been in use for about 75 years before it was suspected to play a part in the production of "chronic interstitial nephritis," a disease soon to be renamed *analgesic nephropathy*. Several studies have shown an inordinately high incidence of this kidney disorder among women. A series reported by Jacobs and Morris (1962) included 38 women and 4 men, while Burry (1966) reported a female:male ratio of nearly 3:1. Once the true etiology of this condition was recognized, previous beliefs had to be revised radically. Up to then, the high incidence among women had been explained as being the result of "infection," and the fact that it was more prevalent in hot climates, where the urine is more concentrated and the kidney subjected to a higher local concentration of the toxic substances, remained unexplained (Nanra et al., 1970). Gastric ulcer attributable to high intake of analgesics is also reported to be more common among women than among men, by a ratio of about 1.5:1 (Douglas and Johnston, 1961).

Once the nephrotoxic effect of phenacetin was recognized, it soon became apparent that most, if not all, other analgesics were suspect (Kincaid-Smith, 1967). It became clear that aspirin is the major nephrotoxic agent and that phenacetin and paracetamol play only secondary or synergistic roles (Nanra, 1976). The advanced stage of the disease is now established to be the result of a minimum cumulative intake of 2 kg of aspirin or phenacetin and is associated with a variety of other disorders as well (Murray, 1973), in particular gastric and hemotological manifestations, ischemic heart disease, and premature aging (Nanra, 1976).

As can be expected of a drug of dependence, many users, though warned of the inevitable consequences, do not desist. Simply viewed in this light, the persistent user with analgesic nephropathy has an obvious similarity to the smoker who persists despite severe bronchitis or ischemic heart disease, the alcoholic with hepatic cirrhosis, and the heroin addict suffering from the effects of intravenous administration. The comparison extends further to include the inordinately high prevalence of the features of deviance. Murray (1972) followed 39 patients with analgesic nephropathy for periods ranging from 7 to 120 months and found that 19 continued their analgesic use despite the obvious danger. The persistent users were found to be more disturbed than the rest of the group and to be of lower social class. They had a higher incidence of alcoholism and analgesic abuse in their family histories, of parental deprivation, and of psychiatric disease or attempted suicide, and they were more prone to abuse other drugs and to smoke excessively. They were subject to chronic family stress. Personality disorders were common in both groups but were more severe among the persistent users.

As was the case with the bromides, no better example of the problem can be found than the experience with analgesics in Australia. In this regard, an interesting sidelight is thrown on the discussion of the essence of the drug-induced sensation. The brand of analgesic that has dominated the market has been promoted with an advertisement that has remained unaltered over many decades, quite unique in a sphere where success usually depends on frequent change of the message. Apparently, no better message was necessary. This advertisement depicted a young and attractive woman sitting astride the one word, spelled out in letters much larger than the rest of the message, *CONFIDENCE*.

A lesson frequently learned with the sedatives has been that forceful promotion probably explains the wide-scale adoption of a specific legally available drug in a community. Certainly, the analgesics have been advertised to an exceptional degree in Australia (Kincaid-Smith, 1969), and their use is correspondingly higher than in comparable nations, for example, 160% more than that in Western Europe (New South Wales Joint Parliamentary Committee on Drugs, 1978).

The incidence of their ill effects is correspondingly high. Based on the consumption of phenacetin alone in a country town, Purnell and Burry (1967) estimated that at least 4% of the population had already suffered appreciable kidney damage. Of course, the figures can now be seen to be an underestimate of the problem, concentrating as they did on phenacetin and neglecting the more toxic aspirin. A comparison of autopsy rates indicated that the incidence of between 3% and 12% for papillary necrosis in various hospital surveys throughout Australia was 50 times as high as that found in the United States (Kincaid-Smith, 1969). Billington (1965) established that there had been a steady increase in the rate of peptic ulcer among women in Australia since 1943, which had not occurred in other parts of the world. In a prospective study of 170 peptic ulcer patients (92 males, 78 females) between 1960 and 1966, Duggan and Chapman (1970) found that women outnumbered men 1.3:1 in the gastric ulcer group, while the ratio was 1:2 for duodenal ulcer. There was a high correlation between gastric ulcer and heavy use of aspirin in the females, but not in the males.

The correlation of excessive use with age and lower social class has been noted a number of times. In Australia, the consumption of alcohol is higher among aboriginal males than in any other group, and aboriginal females would seem to have the highest rates of analgesic consumption (Kamien, 1975). As is to be expected, the consumption among members of a trade union was found to be higher than in a middle-class group

(Gibson et al., 1977), but in one particular trade union, the highest rates of drug consumption, including that of the analgesics, were found in the one branch where the most dissatisfaction existed, where "occupational mental stress was more evident" (Ferguson, 1973), and where industrial action in the form of strikes occurred most frequently.

As a result of the preoccupation with phenacetin, the first step taken to control the problem in Australia was to exclude it from some proprietary analgesic compound preparations. At first, it was believed that this action had produced a drop in the rates of renal mortality and morbidity (Burry et al., 1974), but this belief is now seriously disputed (Nanra, 1976). The publicity given to the ill effects of the analgesics may have contributed to a slight decline in overall use from 1973 to 1974 among schoolchildren in one city, but this effect was found only among the light and moderate users. What is more material to the problem of dependence is that the rate of heavy use has continued to increase, and particularly so among the females (Irwin, 1976). Over a longer period (1970–1976), a definite decline in the use of analgesics seems to have taken place among high school students in a different city in Australia, and in this case, the decrease was greatest among females, so much so that at the end of this period, the rates for females equaled those for males (Perry, 1977). This pattern suggests that the female group, having led the way in the adoption of analgesics, is leading the way in their discontinuance.

A similar sequence of events has occurred in Canada, Sweden, Switzerland, the United Kingdom, the United States, and various other countries (Prescott, 1976). In Japan, the cycle of methaqualone dependence was treated as vigorously as the cycle of heroin use that had preceded it, and with much the same results; that is, once the problem was successfully controlled, it was succeeded by another—in this case, of analgesic use, which began to increase in 1967 (Kato, 1972). The problem of analgesic abuse in northeast Scotland (Prescott, 1966) would seem to have continued unabated over the years (Murray, 1973). The occasional information that penetrates the Iron Curtain from the Communist world indicates that similar problems exist on both sides (Vondráček et al., 1968).

5. INHALANTS

The distinction between the inhalants and other drugs of dependence has many arbitrary features. Of course, this arbitrary distinction is not peculiar to the inhalants. The arbitrary distinction between alcohol and certain sedatives and the even more tenuous distinction between sedatives, hypnotics, and minor tranquilizers has already been noted. Most drugs of dependence may be taken by inhalation. Herodotus, who lived in the fifth century B.C., described how the Scythians enclosed themselves in a carefully sealed tent and threw hemp "seeds" onto red-hot stones. They were said to enjoy it so much that they "howled with pleasure" (Moss, 1970). Of course, inhalation is still the preferred route of administration for marijuana, in preference to eating it or using it intravenously. In many communities, the amphetamine problem began with the excessive use of the Benzedrine inhaler (Kalant, 1966; Bell, 1967). The smoking of opium is an ancient practice, and cocaine and heroin may be inhaled in the powder form.

Most of the examples noted above are excluded by restricting the term *inhalant* to those drugs that are volatile at room temperature. Although the amphetamine in the Benzedrine inhaler is volatile in this preparation, it is not categorized as an inhalant, and in fact, the addicts who used it soon learned that they can obtain a larger dose by dissolving and drinking the contents of the inhaler. Even those substances that are correctly classified as inhalants are sometimes taken by another route. Ether may be drunk as well as inhaled. The first known ether addict, James Graham, a famous London quack in his time, inhaled it for many years before his death in 1794, and inhalation has been preferred by most of those who have followed him in its use. However, almost a century after its introduction, a notorious outbreak of ether use in Northern Ireland involved drinking rather than inhalation (Nagle, 1968).

In terms of their chemical constitution, the inhalants are diverse and difficult to classify. All are generalized central nervous system depressants. Those that depend for their effect on an intoxicating action are related chemically and pharmacologically to alcohol, ether, and chloroform and may be classified as sedatives (Cohen, 1977a). Some inhalants produce the depressant action at least partly through the induction of cerebral anoxia.

The oldest known example of the inhalation of a gas belongs to this category. The prophetic messages of the Oracle of Delphi were produced by seating a priestess over a fissure in a rock from which natural carbon dioxide gas emanated, inducing in her a trancelike state (Cohen, 1977a). Nitrous oxide depends in part at least for its action on the production of anoxia, and it would seem that the desired effect resulting from the inhalation of the inert Freons, the propellant of aerosol sprays, is entirely dependent on the production of cerebral anoxemia. A great range of potential inhalants are used in modern life. They are used so extensively that the usual methods for restricting the availability of a drug cannot apply to them. Examples are petroleum and some of its by-products, plastic cement, lacquer thinners, and other industrial solvents. Airplane glue has been particularly popular, and many juvenile users have been described simply as glue sniffers.

The use of commercial solvents as intoxicants probably began in California during the late 1950s (Cohen, 1977a). The use has spread to all other similar industrialized communities since then, but perhaps none more so than Japan, where the use of organic solvents began to increase in 1968, not long after their problem with analgesics began and shortly after they had contained their previous drug problem with methaqualone (Kato, 1972).

In the main, the inhalants appear to have been used by males, and in recent years by the juvenile delinquent male. Cohen (1977b) cited a mean age of 14 years and a male-to-female ratio of 10:1. However, Smart and Fejer (1975) reported, on the basis of biennial surveys in Toronto schools between 1968 and 1974, that sniffing of glue and various solvents had almost equal prevalence among boys and girls. The difference in findings may reflect different criteria for inclusion, specifically the matter of occasional or experimental versus regular use. The regular users tend to be the underprivileged, for example, the Mexican-Americans in certain communities of the United States. The sniffing of gasoline fumes by aboriginal children in isolated communities of northern Australia (Tomlinson, 1975) is comparable to the experience among native children in northern Manitoba (Jager, 1975).

As is to be expected, the use of inhalants correlates with deviancy and in particular with antisocial behavior. The users of inhalants come from deviant families and are deviant themselves (Cohen, 1977a). As one example of antisocial deviance, all 12 cases in a series devoted to lighter fluid sniffing had been arrested for delinquent behavior at some time before they began to use the drug (Ackerly and Gibson, 1964). Among a group of heroin addicts, those who had sniffed glue were more deviant, had abused twice as many substances, and had a higher rate of attempted suicide than those without a history of glue use (D'Amanda et al., 1977), who were themselves in any case a markedly deviant group.

6. STIMULANTS

The use of naturally occurring stimulants has a long history. The best known, cocaine, is to be found in the leaf of the coca bush, natural to South America. The coca habit is believed to have had its origin among the tribes of the central Amazon, long before it became entrenched in the Andes. By the time the Inca civilization had reached full development in the tenth century, the coca bush was considered a divine plant, and the use of its leaf was limited to members of the Inca aristocracy (Gutierrez-Noriega and Von Hagen, 1950). The disruption of the Inca culture by the Spaniards removed this cultural control, and the use of coca was even encouraged by the new rulers, particularly among those working in the mines. Today, there is much use of coca in South America, despite attempts at control. Its use may be compared with that of tobacco, alcohol, and betel nut in other societies and is subject to much the same cultural controls, which discourage women from its use. In the Andean region, women are not expected to use it except when involved in hard physical labor (Goddard et al., 1969). Another similarity to the use of other drugs is that its use is associated with malnutrition, poor work performance, and poor personal hygiene (Buck et al., 1970).

Another naturally occurring stimulant is obtained from the kat plant, cultivated in parts of East Africa and the Arabian Peninsula. It is consumed by chewing or by making an infusion of the tender parts of the plant in as fresh a state as possible, a serious and perhaps fortunate limitation on its distribution. Its effects are identical with those of amphetamine but are less marked because of the limited dose that can be absorbed (Eddy et al., 1965). Nevertheless, the social consequences of its use are serious (Kalant, 1966). The betel nut, which is used extensively in the Western Pacific region and Southeast Asia, would also seem to be a mild stimulant (Lewin, 1964), producing not only dependence but also the typical stimulant psychosis after prolonged excessive use (Burton-Bradley, 1966). As with the coca leaf, cultural influences militate to a great extent against the use of these drugs by women.

Amphetamine was first synthesized in 1887 but was not used therapeutically until 1932, when Benzedrine was introduced as an inhalant. In 1935, its use was extended to narcolepsy, one of the very few applications that has proved in time to be valid. The list of diseases for which it was recommended in succeeding years (Bett et al., 1955) suggests that it could well have been the modern panacea. In World War II, it was used extensively to counter fatigue among the servicemen of combatant nations on both sides. This application was to set the stage for enormous expansion in use during the postwar years, especially in Japan.

The stimulant action of amphetamine can be used to counteract fatigue in individuals engaged in tasks requiring vigilance and judgment for prolonged periods (Hauty and Payne, 1958). This is the basis of its wartime use and of its periods of popularity among students studying and sitting for examinations and among athletes. Before the introduction of tricyclic antidepressants, amphetamine was used extensively for the treatment of depression. Employed for this supposed action and for its anorectic action in the management of obesity, amphetamine was prescribed widely, particularly for women (Chambers and Hunt, 1977b; Kiloh and Brandon, 1962). In point of fact, for the treatment of depression amphetamine proved to be no better than a placebo (Hare et al., 1962), and its value in the treatment of obesity is most doubtful (Bell, 1969). In retrospect, it may be realized that its supposed actions were immaterial; amphetamine was being prescribed by physicians to people who were in actual fact using it as a drug of dependence. Patients circulated from doctor to doctor on the "pep-pill merry-go-round" (Graham-Bonnalie, 1961), obtaining the drug with the pretext of slimming. In many parts of the world, the popularity of "antiobesity" clinics using amphetamines (Seevers, 1965), and catering principally to women, increased steeply. Not surprisingly in these circumstances, the prescribing of amphetamine varied widely from practice to practice (Hood and Wade, 1968), but the resistance of the insightful practitioner was not sufficient to prevent the use from becoming extensive.

Two patterns of use in the community may occur, much the same as has already been illustrated for the sedatives. Women predominate among the users where the legal use by prescription is widespread, but illicit use features the young antisocial male instead. The pattern may change from the one to the other within a short period. In the United Kingdom, the combination of a sedative and a stimulant in the notorious "purple hearts" proved to be particularly popular among adolescents (Connell, 1965). Rather than counteract the action of each other, the combination of the two enhanced their euphoriant effects as well as other actions (Legge and Steinberg, 1962). Once again in the history of drug dependence, the rapid growth of a new problem was clearly to be seen but was virtually ignored, this time by the Brain Committee (Interdepartmental Committee, 1961, 1965), which had the specific task before it of evaluating new problems and of recommending action to contain them. In consequence, "the flood gates remained open" (Benjamin, 1968) until amphetamine (the common form being in combination with a barbiturate) use became so flagrant that popular concern forced the House of Commons to introduce severe emergency measures in 1964. By this time, the predominance of females noted by Kiloh and Brandon (1962) had altered to a predominance of males, illustrated by the attendance at a special drug-dependence clinic (Gardner and Connell, 1972). As is to be expected, they had a high incidence of family, personal, and interpersonal disorder (Brook et al., 1974).

In Sweden, the intravenous use of amphetamines (including phenmetrazine, another anorexiant agent) for their euphoriant effect became widespread among the young from 1965 onward. The users had a high incidence of background disorder, psychiatric problems, and antisocial activities (Herulf, 1969). In Japan, the problem created by amphetamine use began at the end of World War II, when stockpiles of the drug accumulated by the armed forces were made available to the public. The first steps to restrict its availability were taken in 1948, and as successive measures became more stringent, use of the drug became increasingly restricted to young antisocial males who came from lower-class groups and had shown evidence of antisocial behavior before starting their drug use (Hemmi, 1969).

However, in both Sweden and Japan, those females who were involved in this pattern of drug use tended to be heavily involved. In Stockholm between 1965 and 1968, men arrested for criminal offenses outnumbered arrested women by approximately 7:1, but in the 20- to 29-year age groups, known amphetamine abusers constituted a much higher percentage of the female detainees than of the males (Bejerot, 1969). In Japan, at the peak of the problem in 1954, over 55,000 drug offenders were arrested, and it was estimated that about 2 million persons were involved (Brill and Hirose, 1969). The proportion of female to male drug offenders was far higher for amphetamine (1:3) than for drug offenses in general (1:10). Furthermore, the female drug offenders sent to correctional institutions tended to be more recalcitrant, aggressive, and difficult than the male cases.

Surprisingly few deaths related to amphetamine use have been recorded in the medical literature (Kalant and Kalant, 1976). Nevertheless, of those reviewed, 16 out of 47 occurred in women. A clear difference is seen, however, in the causes of death in males and females. Amphetamine in high doses can produce a psychotic state indistinguishable from paranoid schizophrenia (Bell, 1965). This occurrence was first reported by Young and Scoville (1938) and was thoroughly documented by Connell (1958), Kalant (1966), and Ellinwood and Petrie (1976). The psychotomimetic action of the drug was finally established by experimental reproduction of the psychosis in human volunteers (Bell, 1973; Griffith et al., 1972). A similar psychosis is produced by other stimulants such as cocaine, kat, and betel nut, and even by fenfluramine (Dare and Goldney, 1976), an amphetamine derivative with little stimulant effect that is used for its anorexiant action. When psychotic, the user becomes a danger to himself and to other users, being alert and coordinated, and thus competent to attack his imagined persecutors (Bell, 1967). Not surprisingly, therefore, among 26 amphetamine-related deaths in Ontario in 1972–1973, two-thirds of the deaths were due to violence, accident, or suicide. However, this was true of 15 of 19 deaths in males but only 3 of 7 deaths in females (Kalant and Kalant, 1976). Similar findings have been reported from Japan (Masaki, 1956), Sweden (Rylander, 1969), and the United States (Griffith, 1966; Smith, 1972).

7. MARIJUANA AND HALLUCINOGENS

In the worldwide trend of increasing drug use, marijuana has experienced a substantial upsurge. An overview reveals two different patterns in the East, where marijuana use entered the phase of late adoption long ago (Chopra, 1969), and the West, where it entered the phase of early majority adoption only in the last decade or two. But even in the East, where the level of its use has been stable for many centuries, the current upsurge in drug use has increased the use of marijuana. In India during the last century, its use was relatively low and almost totally confined to men, only 0.5–1.0% of the population using it regularly and only 0.025% to excess (Kalant, 1972). Since the appearance of hippie visitors in Nepal, marijuana use has become a problem in the local community as well as among the visitors (Sharma, 1975). The pattern of the problem is characteristic for a drug of dependence; the chronic users have a poor work record, poor social and family relationships, a lack of interest in sex, and a general loss of initiative and efficiency. These are also the characteristics of chronic users in other areas where use has been endemic for a long time, unaffected by recent trends, for example, in Egypt (Soueif, 1967, 1971, 1975).

In those communities where marijuana has been introduced recently, the adoption has followed the pattern to be expected of an innovation (Rogers and Shoemaker, 1971). If these early adopters are compared with others of their own class and educational status, they are found to be deviant, with a higher rate of family disorder and personal psychological problems than the nonusers (Harmatz et al., 1972; Kosviner et al., 1974; Linn, 1972). Studies restricted to female college students show that they, like the males, use other drugs, such as alcohol and tobacco, more extensively than the nonusers (Rouse and Ewing, 1973; Steffenhagen et al., 1972). As the use of marijuana spreads from these cosmopolitan, middle-class, and better-educated adopters to the majority adopters, users of lower social class with antisocial characteristics become increasingly represented, particularly among the heavy users (Bell and Champion, 1979). In time, it can be expected that the preponderance of the young among the users will be replaced by the association of increasing use with increasing age.

Being an illicit drug, in the early stages of adoption marijuana is used more among males than among females, but in the young student populations where females have obtained "equality" with males, women tend to approach parity with men in its use. In these societies, marijuana occupies an intermediate position between the socially accepted drugs such as the sedatives and the socially unacceptable such as heroin, with the consequence that, as the stage of majority adoption is reached among the young in the industrialized nations, the prevalence of females using this drug approaches that of the males much more closely than is the case for the other illicit drugs such as heroin (Prather and Fidell, 1978). In this respect, marijuana occupies a position rather similar to that described for the stimulants in Japan at the peak of their consumption and before the introduction of the severe restrictions that gradually narrowed the use down to the antisocial male population.

Other hallucinogens in current illicit use show essentially the same features of sex difference in frequency and evolution of use. Hallucinogens occur widely in the plant kingdom (Schultes, 1969, 1970). Perhaps the oldest known to man is the mushroom *Amanita muscaria,* or fly agaric (Wasson, 1970). The use of hallucinogens in Central America would seem to have been an equally ancient practice (Hofmann, 1971). The first of these to be studied was peyote, the cactus *Anhalonium lewinii,* containing the alkaloid mescaline, the effects of which were described so graphically by Huxley (1954). A third important type of hallucinogen, ololiuqui, contains *d*-lysergic acid amide, as do the ergot alkaloids. A large variety of other plant materials containing hallucinogenic alkaloids are found in the Amazon basin (Schultes, 1969, 1970). Almost all of these materials became deeply embedded in religious belief and practices, including shamanic rites. Their use became subject to taboos, and women were generally not permitted to take part (see, for example, the description of the *epéna* rites by Seitz, 1967).

In the Western world, lysergic acid diethylamide (LSD), an ergot alkaloid first synthesized in 1938, has far exceeded all others in the spread of its nonmedical use. Following a course similar to that of most of the drugs discussed in this chapter, it was first tested as a therapeutic agent but was rapidly taken up by users intent on purely hedonistic purposes. A variety of other synthetic substances have since entered into similar use (Hoffer and Osmond, 1967; Shulgin, 1963), but none has won the same degree of acceptance.

Since the hallucinogens never became well established as therapeutic agents but passed almost immediately into illicit use, it is not surprising that chronic users are preponderantly male and have an inordinately high rate of background family disorder, psychological illness, and antisocial behavior (Barron et al., 1970; Smart and Fejer, 1969; Smart and Jones, 1970). Smart and Fejer (1975) found a consistently higher percentage of male students than of female students who had used LSD in their Toronto school surveys in 1968–1974, and the difference was still present in 1977 (Smart and Goodstadt).

8. SEXUAL EFFECTS

To conclude a chapter on drug use by women with the effects on sexual behavior may well be condemned as sexist. Certainly, sexuality is not central to a theme that involves one sex alone. Nevertheless, many of the drugs that have been discussed enjoy the reputation of possessing aphrodisiac properties, a reputation that has no doubt encouraged their use among females as well as among males. In fact, the outstanding examples—methaqualone, the stimulants, marijuana, and LSD—have had a higher proportion of female users than other illicit drugs known to reduce libido, such as heroin. Whether the reputation is actually warranted remains an open question.

The only group of drugs whose sexual effects have been adequately documented are the stimulants. For all the other substances, the reputation is only hearsay. Methaqualone was nicknamed the "love drug," apparently because of its capacity to produce disinhibition, paresthetic effects, and tingling sensations (Falco, 1976). In the United Kingdom, Mandrax® was known as "randy Mandies" for the same reason. Being a depressant substance, its effect is probably no more than the notorious action of that model of depressants, alcohol, which also produces disinhibition and thereby increases desire, if at the expense of adequate performance.

Leary (1970) claimed that "LSD is the most powerful aphrodisiac ever discovered by man" and that "sexual ecstasy is the most basic reason for the current LSD boom." He claimed that of all those he had given LSD, the religious "experienced the most intense sexual reaction. And in two religious groups that prize chastity and celibacy there have been wholesale defections of monks and nuns who left their religious orders to get married" (p. 112). For a while, many sought this ecstasy in experimentation, apparently only to find it a myth.

The stimulants produce through sympathetic stimulation an effect on some males of prolonging the erection and delaying emission. A similar effect of increasing sexual desire, but delaying orgasm for many hours, may occur with women (Bell and Trethowan, 1961b). Both partners may take the drug to prolong heterosexual intercourse for periods up to or exceeding 10 hours.

Only some enjoy the sexually stimulant effect of the stimulants. In the group of amphetamine addicts studied by Bell and Trethowan (1961a), the responses ranged from the cases of heightened desire mentioned above to the other extreme of impotence. In some, perverse trends became overt or exaggerated, and others reported no change. When the preexisting sexual adjustment of the individual was taken into account, the final effect of the drug seemed to be consistent with the formulation that amphetamine increased the libidinal drive but that the disturbance of the precarious equilibrium in these disturbed individuals resulted in the breaking down of defenses and the appearance of regression in some. Only in some of the cases where inhibition of sexuality existed prior to the drug use did little or no change take place; in other words, the inhibition continued to repress the sexual effects of the drug. Where change did take place in the sexually inhibited, it was in the direction of regression. These observations have been confirmed by subsequent accounts (Greaves, 1972; Rylander, 1969; Scher, 1966). Gossop et al. (1974) found that those who used these drugs intravenously suffered more disruption of sexual functioning than oral users did, and that females were more affected than the males.

Marijuana has also had a long-standing reputation as an aphrodisiac. On closer examination, the sum total of the effects resembles those found with the stimulants; that is, some users report an increase in sexual drive, some report a decrease, the manifestations of perverse sexuality increase, and some users eventually become impotent (Chopra, 1969). The disturbance of a precarious equilibrium between conflicting sexual drives may be mistaken for an aphrodisiac effect.

9.   SUMMARY AND CONCLUSIONS

Drugs of many different pharmacological types are capable of giving rise to problems of dependence. The motives underlying their use are correspondingly varied, but the chief effect common to all of them is the ability to give rise to feelings of pleasure or relief that create an unrealistically heightened self-confidence in the user. Men and women who use these drugs derive essentially the same reinforcing effect, but they differ significantly with respect to the specific circumstances precipitating drug use. The effects of drugs, especially the stimulants, on sexuality are applicable to both males and females, but the initiation of heavy drug use subsequent to childbirth or to loss of spouse is of particular relevance to women in this context. Women make greater use of licit drugs, originally obtained on medical prescription, while men predominate among users of illicit drugs or of licit drugs diverted to illicit channels. Consequently, there is a stronger association between deviancy and drug use among males; however, those females who do become regular users of illicit drugs tend to show an even higher degree of deviancy than the males.

Consequently, when societies adopt new forms of psychoactive drug use, two different patterns are evident. For licit drugs, women users predominate in the early stages and use by men may or may not increase at a later stage. For illicit drugs, early use is chiefly by deviant males, but if the drug gains wide social acceptance, the association with deviancy diminishes and the sex differential among users tends to diminish.

Numerous studies indicate high correlations between maternal use of various psychotropic drugs and the use of licit or illicit drugs by their children. This observation deserves closer study, because it may indicate an important influence in the shaping of attitudes toward drug use.

Among the hypnotics, sedatives and minor tranquilizers, bromides, barbiturates, thalidomide, and benzodiazepines all illustrate the pattern of predominant use by women, originating in widespread uncritical prescribing by physicians, or too-easy availability from over-the-counter sale. Chlormethiazole, a drug with similar properties, has not been abused because physicians have been alerted to the risk in time and have prescribed it in responsible fashion. Methaqualone has followed both patterns in different countries: in Britain, it has been used mainly by women on prescription, while in Germany and Japan it rapidly became a street drug, used chiefly by deviant young males. In Japan, it illustrated another type pattern, that of adoption as a new drug fad to replace opiates when use of the latter was stamped out by vigorous control measures.

Nonnarcotic analgesics, despite general denial of this view, are also capable of producing rewarding mood changes in regular users. Women predominate heavily among such users; Australian studies indicate female:male ratio of 2:1 or 3:1. There is a corresponding excess of women among victims of analgesic nephropathy (renal papillary necrosis) and gastric ulcer. Heavy use of these drugs is correlated with deviance, preceding personality disorder, and use of other psychoactive drugs. Moreover, when the methaqualone epidemic in Japan was stamped out, it was apparently replaced by a wave of analgesic abuse.

The stimulants illustrate the same dichotomy of use patterns as methaqualone. Prescription use has been commoner among middle-aged females, while street use has occurred chiefly among young deviant males. Since large doses of these drugs can lead to a temporary paranoid psychosis, violence is a common accompaniment of such use, and stimulant-related deaths among males are mainly due to violence or mishap.

Marijuana illustrates very well the transition from the early stage of almost exclusively male use by deviant groups to the later stage of growing use among females when a high level of social acceptance is reached. However, it has not yet, and may never, reach the late stage of greater use by females than by males among certain age groups, as has happened with tobacco. In contrast, LSD and other hallucinogens have remained principally a male prerogative, and the drugs have never attained broad social acceptance in Occidental society. Oddly enough, among other societies, in which natural hallucinogens have served ritual or religious rather than deviant purposes, their use is also largely confined to males, because the inferior status of women denies them the right to participate.

Recognition of these patterns places the onus on the medical profession and on governments to apply the lessons learned from past experience, rather than to deny them. Responsible and judicious prescription of psychoactive drugs may be one of the most important means of preventing drug dependence among women.

REFERENCES

Abrahams, M. J., Armstrong, J., and Whitlock, F. A., 1970, Drug dependence in Brisbane, *Med. J. Aust.* **2**:397–404.

Ackerly, W. C., and Gibson, G., 1964, Lighter fluid "sniffing," *Am. J. Psychiatry* **120**:1056–1061.

Adamson, J. D., and Schmale, A. H., 1965, Object loss, giving up, and the onset of psychiatric disease, *Psychosom. Med.* **27**:557–576.

Alarcón, R. de, 1972, An epidemiological evaluation of a public health measure aimed at reducing the availability of methylamphetamine, *Psychol. Med.* **2**:293–300.

Andrews, S., 1965, Blood bromide levels in psychiatric patients taking bromureides, *Med. J. Aust.* **1**:646–652.

Andrews, S., Francis, I., and Oey, H. G., 1974, Incidence of bromureide use by psychiatric patients before and after introduction of restrictive legislation, *Med. J. Aust.* **1**:18–19.

Annis, H. M., 1974, Patterns of intra-familial drug use, *Br. J. Addic.* **69**:361–369.

Barron, S. P., Lowinger, P., and Ebner, E., 1970, A clinical examination of chronic LSD use in the community, *Compr. Psychiatry* **11**:69–79.

Bayer, I., 1973, The abuse of psychotropic drugs, *Bull. Narc.* **25**(3):11–25.

Bejerot, N., 1969, Intravenous drug abuse in the arrest population in Stockholm: Frequency studies, in: *Abuse of Central Stimulants* (F. Sjöqvist and M. Tottie, eds.), pp. 235–249, Almqvist and Wiksell, Stockholm.

Bejerot, N., 1977, The nature of addiction, in: *Drug Dependence* (M. M. Glatt, ed.), pp. 69–96, M. T. P. Press, Lancaster.

Bell, D. S., 1965, Comparison of amphetamine psychosis and schizophrenia, *Br. J. Psychiatry* **111**:701–707.

Bell, D. S., 1967, Addiction to stimulants, *Med. J. Aust.* **1**:41–45.

Bell, D. S., 1969, Double-blind trial of anorectic agents, *Med. J. Aust.* **1**:599–600.

Bell, D. S., 1970, Drug addiction, *Bull. Narc.* **22**(2):21–32.

Bell, D. S., 1971a, The precipitants of amphetamine addiction, *Br. J. Psychiatry* **119**:171–177.

Bell, D. S., 1971b, Social background of the use and abuse of alcohol and drugs: Clinical aspects, in: *29th International Congress on Alcoholism and Drug Dependence* (L. G. Kiloh and D. S. Bell, eds), pp. 69–77, Butterworths, Australia.

Bell, D. S., 1973, The experimental reproduction of amphetamine psychosis, *Arch. Gen. Psychiatry* **29**:35–40.

Bell, D. S., 1974, Man and his mind-changers: Health, illness and deviancy, *Aust. J. Alcohol. Drug Depend.* **1**:8–11.

Bell, D. S., and Champion, R. A., 1977, The dynamics of trends in drug use in Australia, *Bull. Narc.* **29**(3):21–31.

Bell, D. S., and Champion, R. A., 1979, Deviance, delinquency and drug use, *Br. J. Psychiatry* **134**:269–276.

Bell, D. S., Champion, R. A., and Rowe, A. J. E., 1976, Monitoring alcohol use among young people in New South Wales 1971 to 1973, *Aust. J. Alcohol. Drug Depend.* **3**:51–54.

Bell, D. S., and Trethowan, W.H., 1961a, Amphetamine addiction, *J. Nerv. Ment. Dis.* **133**:489–496.

Bell, D. S., and Trethowan, W. H., 1961b, Amphetamine addiction and disturbed sexuality, *Arch. Gen. Psychiatry* **4**:74–78.

Benjamin, I., 1968, The control of drug use in the United Kingdom, in: *The Pharmacological and Epidemiological Aspects of Adolescent Drug Dependence* (C. W. M. Wilson, ed.), pp. 355–358, Pergamon, Oxford.

Bett, W. R., Howells, L. H., and MacDonald, A. D., 1955, *Amphetamine in Clinical Medicine: Actions and Uses,* Livingstone, Edinburgh.

Billington, B. P., 1965, Observations from New South Wales on the changing incidence of gastric ulcer in Australia, *Gut* **6**:121–133.

Boolsen, M. W., 1975, Drugs in Denmark, *Int. J. Addic.* **10**:503–512.

Brill, H., and Hirose, T., 1969, The rise and fall of a methamphetamine epidemic: Japan 1945–55, *Semin. Psychiatry* **1**:179–194.

Brook, R., Kaplun, J., and Whitehead, P. C., 1974, Personality characteristics of adolescent amphetamine users as measured by the MMPI, *Br. J. Addic.* **69**:61–66.

Brown, G. W., and Birley, J. L. T., 1968, Crisis and life changes and the onset of schizophrenia, *J. Health Soc. Behav.* **9**:203–214.

Browne, W. J., 1965, The alcoholic bout as an acting out, *Psychoanal. Q.* **34**:420–437.

Buck, A. A., Sasaki, T. T., Hewitt, J. J., and MacRae, A. A., 1970, Coca chewing and health: An epidemiologic study among residents of a Peruvian village, *Bull. Narc.* **22**(4):23–32.

Buikhuisen, W., and Timmerman, H., 1972, The development of drug-taking among secondary school children in the Netherlands, *Bull. Narc.* **24**(3):7–16.

Burry, A. F., 1966, A profile of renal disease in Queensland: results of an autopsy survey, *Med. J. Aust.* **1**:826–834.

Burry, A. F., Axelsen, R. A., and Trolove, P., 1974, Analgesic nephropathy: Its present contribution to the renal mortality and morbidity profile, *Med. J. Aust.* **1**:31–40.

Burton-Bradley, B. G., 1966, Papua and New Guinea transcultural psychiatry: Some implications of betel chewing, *Med. J. Aust.* **2**:744–746.

Chambers, C. D., and Hunt, L. G., 1977b, Drug use patterns in pregnant women, in: *Drug Abuse in Pregnancy and Neonatal Effects* (J. L. Rementería, ed.), pp. 73–81, Mosby, St. Louis.

Chambers, C. D., and Hunt, L. G., 1977a, Epidemiology of drug abuse, in: *Drug Abuse* (S. N. Pradhan and S. N. Dutta, eds.), pp. 11–29, Mosby, St. Louis.

Champion, R. A., Egger, G. J., and Trebilco, P., 1978, Monitoring drug and alcohol use and attitudes among school students in New South Wales: 1977 results, *Aust. J. Alcohol. Drug Depend.* **5:**59–64.

Chapman, S. F., 1976, Psychotropic drug use in the elderly, *Med. J. Aust.* **2:**62–64.

Chopra, G. S., 1969, Man and marijuana, *Int. J. Addict.* **4:**215–247.

Climent, C. E., Raynes, A., Rollins, A., and Plutchik, R., 1974, Epidemiological studies of female prisoners, II, Biological, psychological, and social correlates of drug addiction, *Int. J. Addict.* **9:**345–350.

Cohen, S., 1977a, Abuse of inhalants, in: *Drug Abuse* (S. N. Pradham and S. N. Dutta, eds.), pp. 290–302, Mosby, St. Louis.

Cohen, S., 1977b, Profiles of drug abusers, in: *Drug Abuse* (S. N. Pradham and S. N. Dutta, eds.), pp. 30–36, Mosby, St. Louis.

Connell, P. H., 1958, *Amphetamine Psychosis,* Maudsley Monograph No. 5, pp. 133, Chapman and Hall, London.

Connell, P. H., 1965, Adolescent drug taking, *Proc. Roy. Soc. Med.* **58:**409–412.

Cooperstock, R., 1971, Sex differences in the use of mood-modifying drugs: An explanatory model, *J. Health Soc. Behav.* **12:**238–244.

Cooperstock, R., 1976, Psychotropic drug use among women, *Can. Med. Assoc. J.* **115:**760–763.

Cooperstock, R., and Sims, M., 1971, Mood-modifying drugs prescribed in a Canadian city: Hidden problems, *Am. J. Public Health* **61:**1007–1016.

D'Amanda, C., Plumb, M. M., and Taintor, Z., 1977, Heroin addicts with a history of glue sniffing: A deviant group within a deviant group, *Int. J. Addict.* **12:**255–270.

Dare, G. L., and Goldney, R. D., 1976, Fenfluramine abuse, *Med. J. Aust.* **2:**537, 540.

Deedes, W. F., 1970, Politics of drug dependence, in: *ABC of Drug Addiction,* pp. 26–30, Wright, Bristol.

Douglas, R. A., and Johnston, E. D., 1961, Aspirin and chronic gastric ulcer, *Med. J. Aust.* **2:**893–897.

Duggan, J. M., and Chapman, B. L., 1970, The incidence of aspirin ingestion in patients with peptic ulcer, *Med. J. Aust.* **1:**797–800.

Eddy, N. B., Halbach, H., Isbell, H., and Seevers, M. H., 1965, Drug dependence: Its significance and characteristics, *Bull. WHO* **32:**721–733.

Ellinwood, E. H., Jr., and Petrie, W. M., 1976, Psychiatric syndromes produced by nonmedical use of drugs, in: *Research Advances in Alcohol and Drug Problems,* Vol. 3 (R. J. Gibbins et al., eds.), pp. 177–221, Wiley, New York.

Estes, J. W., and Johnson, M., 1971, Relationships among medical and nonmedical uses of pharmacologically active agents, *Clin. Pharmacol. Therap.* **12:**883–888.

Evans, J. L., 1955, Bromide intoxication, *Med. J. Aust.* **1:**498–504.

Falco, M., 1976, Methaqualone misuse: Foreign experience and United States drug control policy, *Int. J. Addict.* **11:**597–610.

Fejer, D., and Smart, R. G., 1972, Drug use, anxiety and psychological problems among adolescents, *Ont. Psychol.* **4:**10–21.

Fejer, D., and Smart, R. G., 1973, The use of psychoactive drugs by adults, *Can. Psychiatr. Assoc. J.* **18:**313–320.

Fenichel, O., 1955, *The Psychoanalytic Theory of Neurosis,* Routledge and Kegan Paul, London.

Ferguson, D., 1973, Smoking, drinking and non-narcotic analgesic habits in an occupational group, *Med. J. Aust.* **1:**1271–1274.

File, K. N., 1976, Sex roles and street roles, *Int. J. Addict.* **11:**263–268.

Fort, J., 1964, The problem of barbiturates in the United States of America, *Bull. Narc.* **16**(1):17–35.

Gardner, R., and Connell, P. H., 1972, Amphetamine and other nonopioid drug users attending a special drug dependence clinic, Br. Med. J. 2:322–326.

Ghodse, A. H., 1977, Drug dependent individuals dealt with by London casualty departments, Br. J. Psychiatry 131:273–280.

Gibson, J., Johansen, A., Rawson, G., and Webster, I., 1977, Drinking, smoking and drug-taking patterns in a predominantly lower socioeconomic status sample, Med. J. Aust. 2:459–461.

Gillies, M. A., and Skyring, A. P., 1972, The pattern and prevalence of aspirin ingestion as determined by interview of 2,921 inhabitants of Sydney, Med. J. Aust. 1:974–979.

Goddard, D., Goddard, S. N. de, and Whithead, P. C., 1969, Social factors associated with coca use in the Andean region, Int. J. Addict. 4:577–590.

Gossop, M., 1976, Drug dependence and self-esteem, Int. J. Addict. 11:741–753.

Gossop, M. R., and Roy, A., 1976, Hostility in drug dependent individuals: Its relation to specific drugs, and oral or intravenous use, Br. J. Psychiatry 128:188–193.

Gossop, M. R., Stern, R., and Connell, P. H., 1974, Drug dependence and sexual dysfunction: A comparison of intravenous users of narcotics and oral users of amphetamines, Br. J. Psychiatry 124:431–434.

Graham-Bonnalie, F. E., 1961, Pep pill merry-go-round, Br. Med. J. 2:112.

Greaves, G., 1972, Sexual disturbances among chronic amphetamine users, J. Nerv. Ment. Dis. 155:363–365.

Greaves, G., 1974, Toward an existential theory of drug dependence, J. Nerv. Ment. Dis. 159:263–274.

Greenblatt, D. J., and Shader, R. I., 1971, Meprobamate: A study of irrational drug use, Am. J. Psychiatry 127:1297–1303.

Greene, M. H., and DuPont, R. L., 1973, Amphetamines in the district of Columbia, I, Identification and resolution of an abuse epidemic, J. Am. Med. Assoc. 226:1437–1440.

Griffith, J., 1966, A study of illicit amphetamine drug traffic in Oklahoma City, Am. J. Psychiatry 123:560–569.

Griffith, J. D., Cavanaugh, J., Held, J., and Oates, J. A., 1972, Dextroamphetamine: Evaluation of psychotomimetic properties in man, Arch. Gen. Psychiatry 26:97–100.

Griffiths, R. R., and Bigelow, G. E., 1978, Commonalities in human and infrahuman drug self-administration, in: The Bases of Addiction (J. Fishman, ed.), pp. 157–174, Dahlem Konferenzen, Berlin.

Gutierrez-Noriega, C., and Von Hagen, V. W., 1950, The strange case of the coca leaf, Sci. Monthly 70:81–89.

Hare, E. H., Dominian, J., and Sharpe, L., 1962, Phenelzine and dexamphetamine in depressive illness, Br. Med. J. 1:9–16.

Harmatz, J. S., Shader, R. I., and Salzman, C., 1972, Marihuana users and nonusers, Arch. Gen. Psychiatry 26:108–112.

Hauty, G. T., and Payne, R. B., 1958, Problems resulting from the use of habituating drugs in industry, II, Effects of analeptic and depressant drugs upon psychological behaviour, Am. J. Public Health 48:571–577.

Hemmi, T., 1969, How we have handled the problem of drug abuse in Japan, in: Abuse of Central Stimulants (F. Sjöqvist and M. Tottie, eds.), pp. 147–153, Almqvist and Wiksell, Stockholm.

Herulf, B., 1969, Narcotic consumption among school children in Stockholm, in: Abuse of Central Stimulants (F. Sjöqvist and M. Tottie, eds.), pp. 215–225, Almqvist and Wiksell, Stockholm.

Hoffer, A., and Osmond, H., 1967, The Hallucinogens, Academic, New York.

Hofmann, A., 1971, Teonanáctl and ololiuqui, two ancient magic drugs of Mexico, Bull. Narc. 23(1):3–14.

Holmes, T. H., and Rahe, R. H., 1967, The social readjustment rating scale, *J. Psychosom. Res.* **11**:213–218.

Hood, H., and Wade, O. L., 1968, Use of amphetamines in general practice, *Lancet* **2**:96–97.

Huxley, A., 1954, *The Doors of Perception,* Chatto and Windus, London.

Interdepartmental Committee on Drug Addiction, 1961, Report; 1965, Second Report, HMSO, London.

Irwin, R. P., 1976, Minor analgesic use among high-school students, *Med. J. Aust.* **2**:522–527.

Jacobs, L. A., and Morris, J. G., 1962, Renal papillary necrosis and the abuse of phenacetin, *Med. J. Aust.* **2**:531–538.

Jager, M., 1975, Native children sniffing gasoline, *Aust. J. Alcohol. Drug Depend.* **2**:78.

Johns, M. W., Hepburn, M., and Goodyear, M. D. E., 1971, Use of hypnotic drugs by hospital patients, *Med. J. Aust.* **2**:1323–1327.

Johnson, A. M., and Burke, E. C., 1955, Parental permissiveness and fostering in child rearing and their relationship to juvenile delinquency, *Proc. Staff Meetings Mayo Clinic* **30**:557–565.

Kalant, H. (rapporteur), 1978, Behavioral aspects of addiction—Group report, in: *The Bases of Addiction* (J. Fishman, ed.), pp. 463–496, Dahlem Konferenzen, Berlin.

Kalant, O. J., 1966, *The Amphetamines: Toxicity and Addiction,* University of Toronto Press, Toronto (Second edition, 1973.)

Kalant, O. J., 1972, Report of the Indian hemp drugs commission, 1893–94: A critical review, *Int. J. Addict.* **7**:77–96.

Kalant, O. J., and Kalant, H., 1976, Death in amphetamine users: Causes and estimates of mortality, in: *Research Advances in Alcohol and Drug Problems,* Vol. 3 (R. J. Gibbins et al., eds.), pp. 317–357, Wiley, New York.

Kamien, M., 1975, A survey of drug use in a part-aboriginal community, *Med. J. Aust.* **1**:261–264.

Kandel, D., 1974, Interpersonal influences on adolescent illegal drug use, in: *Drug Use* (E. Josephson and E. E. Carroll, eds.), pp. 207–240, Wiley, New York.

Kato, M., 1972, Epidemiology of drug dependence in Japan, in: *Drug Abuse* (C. J. D. Zarafonetis, ed.), pp. 67–70, Lea and Febiger, Philadelphia.

Kelleher, R. T., Goldberg, S. R., and Krasnegor, N. (eds.), 1976, *Control of Drug Taking Behavior by Schedules of Reinforcement,* Williams & Wilkins, Baltimore.

Kessell, A., 1969, Serum bromide levels in a mental health unit, *Med. J. Aust.* **1**:1073–1077.

Kiloh, L. G., and Brandon, S., 1962, Habituation and addiction to amphetamines, *Br. Med. J.* **2**:40–43.

Kincaid-Smith, P., 1967, Analgesic nephropathy in perspective, *Med. J. Aust.* **2**:320–321.

Kincaid-Smith, P., 1969, Analgesic nephropathy: A common form of renal disease in Australia, *Med. J. Aust.* **2**:1131–1135.

Klinge, V., Vaziri, H., and Lennos, K., 1976, Comparison of psychiatric inpatient male and female adolescent drug abusers, *Int. J. Addict.* **11**:309–323.

Kosviner, A., Hawks, D., and Webb, M. G. T., 1974, Cannabis use amongst British university students, I, Prevalence rates and differences between students who have tried cannabis and those who have never tried it, *Br. J. Addict.* **69**:35–60.

Kraft, T., 1968, Social anxiety and drug addiction, *Br. J. Soc. Psychiatry* **2**:192–195.

Leary, T., 1970, *The Politics of Ecstasy,* MacGibbon and Kee, London.

Legge, D., and Steinberg, H., 1962, Actions of a mixture of amphetamine and a barbiturate in man, *Br. J. Pharmacol.* **18**:490–500.

Lewin, L., 1964, *Phantastica: Narcotic and Stimulating Drugs,* pp. 236–242, Routledge and Kegan Paul, London.

Linn, L. S., 1972, Psychopathology and experience with marijuana, *Br. J. Addict.* **67**:55–64.
Little, R. B., and Pearson, M. M., 1966, The management of pathologic interdependency in drug addiction, *Am. J. Psychiatry* **123**:554–560.
Maddison, D., and Viola, A., 1968, The health of widows in the year following bereavement, *J. Psychosom. Res.* **12**:297–306.
Maerov, A. S., 1965, Prostitution: A survey and review of 20 cases, *Psychiatr. Q.* **39**:675–701.
Maletzky, B. M., and Klotter, J., 1976, Addiction to diazepam, *Int. J. Addict.* **11**:95–115.
Masaki, T., 1956, The amphetamine problem in Japan, *WHO Tech. Rep. Ser.* **102**:14–21.
May, E. L., 1953, The chemistry of drugs of addiction, *Am. J. Med.* **14**:540–545.
McGlothlin, W. H., and West, L. J., 1968, The marihuana problem: An overview, *Am. J. Psychiatry* **125**:370–378.
McGuire, M. T., Stein, S., and Mendelson, J. H., 1966, Comparative psychosocial studies of alcoholic and nonalcoholic subjects undergoing experimentally induced ethanol intoxication, *Psychosom. Med.* **28**:13–26.
Moss, G. C., 1970, Legalize marijuana? *Med. J. Aust.* **2**:252.
Murray, R. M., 1972, Persistent analgesic abuse in analgesic nephropathy, *J. Psychosom. Res.* **16**:57–62.
Murray, R. M., 1973, Dependence on analgesics in analgesic nephropathy, *Br. J. Addict.* **68**:265–272.
Murray, R. M., Timbury, G. C., and Linton, A. L., 1970, Analgesic abuse in psychiatric patients, *Lancet* **1**:1303–1305.
Nagle, D. R., 1968, Anesthetic addiction and drunkenness: A contemporary and historical survey, *Int. J. Addict.* **3**:25–39.
Nanra, R. S., 1976, Analgesic nephropathy, *Med. J. Aust.* **1**:745–748.
Nanra, R. S., Hicks, J. D., McNamara, J. H., Lie, J. T., Leslie, D. W., Jackson, B., and Kincaid-Smith, P., 1970, Seasonal variation in the post-mortem incidence of renal papillary necrosis, *Med. J. Aust.* **1**:293–296.
New South Wales Joint Parliamentary Committee on Drugs, 1978, Progress report, Parliament of New South Wales, Sydney.
Noble, P., Hart, T., and Nation, R., 1972, Correlates and outcome of illicit drug use by adolescent girls, *Br. J. Psychiatry* **120**:497–504.
Oliver, R. G., and Hetzel, B. S., 1972, Rise and fall of suicide rates in Australia: Relation to sedative availability, *Med. J. Aust.* **2**:919–923.
Orcutt, J. D., 1975, Social determinants of alcohol and marijuana effects: A systematic theory, *Int. J. Addict.* **10**:1021–1033.
Paykel, E. S., Myers, J. K., Dienelt, M. N., Klerman, G. L., Lindenthal, J. J., and Pepper, M. P., 1969, Life events and depression, *Arch. Gen. Psychiatry* **21**:753–760.
Parry, H. J., Balter, M. B., Mellinger, G. D., Gisin, I. H., and Manheimer, D. I., 1973, National patterns of psychotherapeutic drug use, *Arch. Gen. Psychiatry* **28**:769–783.
Perry, N. R. F., 1977, The changing pattern of minor analgesic consumption amongst high school students in Hobart, *Med. J. Aust.* **2**:365–367.
Poser, W., and Poser, S., 1975, Bromide abuse, *Med. J. Aust.* **1**:218–219.
Pradhan, S. N., and Dutta, S. N., 1977, *Drug Abuse: Clinical and Basic Aspects,* Mosby, St. Louis.
Prather, J. E., and Fidell, L. S., 1978, Drug use and abuse among women: An overview, *Int. J. Addict.* **13**:863–885.
Prescott, L. F., 1966, Analgesic abuse and renal disease in North-East Scotland, *Lancet* **2**:1143–1145.
Prescott, L. F., 1976, Analgesic nephropathy—The international experience, *Aust. N. Z. J. Med.* **6**(Suppl. i):44–48.

Purnell, J., and Burry, A. F., 1967, Analgesic consumption in a country town, *Med. J. Aust.* **2**:389–391.

Radó, S., 1933, The psychoanalysis of pharmacothymia (drug addiction), *Psychoanal. Q.* **2**:1–23.

Radó, S., 1963, Fighting narcotic bondage and other forms of narcotic disorders, *Compr. Psychiatry* **4**:160.

Ray, O., 1978, *Drugs, Society, and Human Behaviour*, Mosby, St. Louis.

Reilly, T. M., 1976, Physiological dependence on, and symptoms of withdrawal from, chlormethiazole, *Br. J. Psychiatry* **128**:375.

Rogers, E. M., and Shoemaker, F. F., 1971, *Communication of Innovations,* Free Press, New York.

Rouse, B. A., and Ewing, J. A., 1973, Marijuana and other drug use by women college students: Associated risk taking and coping activities, *Am. J. Psychiatry* **130**:486–490.

Rylander, G., 1969, Clinical and medico-criminological aspects of addiction to central stimulating drugs, in: *Abuse of Central Stimulants* (F. Sjöqvist and M. Tottie, eds.), pp. 251–273, Almqvist and Wiksell, Stockholm.

Scher, J., 1966, Patterns and profiles of addiction and drug abuse, *Arch. Gen. Psychiatry* **15**:539–551.

Schultes, R. E., 1969, The plant kingdom and hallucinogens, II, *Bull. Narc.* **21**(4):15–27.

Schultes, R. E., 1970, The plant kingdom and hallucinogens, III, *Bull. Narc.* **22**(1):25–53.

Schwartzman, J., 1975, The addict, abstinence, and the family, *Am. J. Psychiatry* **132**:154–157.

Seevers, M. H., 1965, Abuse of barbiturates and amphetamines, *Postgrad. Med.* **37**:45–51.

Seitz, G. J., 1967, Epéna, the intoxicating snuff powder of the Waika Indians and the Tucano medicine man, Agostino, in: *Ethnopharmacologic Search for Psychoactive Drugs* (D. H. Efron, B. Holmstedt, and N. S. Kline, eds.), pp. 315–338, U.S. Department of Health, Education and Welfare, Washington, D.C.

Seldin, N. E., 1972, The family of the addict: A review of the literature, *Int. J. Addict.* **7**:97–107.

Sharma, B. P., 1975, Cannabis and its users in Nepal, *Br. J. Psychiatry* **127**:550–552.

Sheerin, E., 1973, A programme which led to reduction in night sedation in a major hospital, *Med. J. Aust.* **2**:678–681.

Shulgin, A. T., 1963, Psychotomimetic agents related to mescaline, *Experientia* **29**:127–128.

Simmons, O. G., 1968, The sociocultural integration of alcohol use: A Peruvian study, *Q. J. Stud. Alcohol* **29**:152–171.

Smart, R. G., 1977, Social policy and the prevention of drug abuse: perspectives on the unimodal approach, in: *Drug Dependence* (M. M. Glatt, ed.), pp. 263–279, M.T.P. Press, Lancaster.

Smart, R. G., and Fejer, D., 1969, Illicit LSD users: Their social backgrounds, drug use and psychopathology, *J. Health Soc. Behav.* **10**:297–308.

Smart, R. G., and Fejer, D., 1975, Six years of cross-sectional surveys of student drug use in Toronto, *Bull. Narc.* **27**(2):11–22.

Smart, R. G., and Goodstadt, M., 1977, Alcohol and drug use among Ontario students in 1977: Preliminary findings, Addiction Research Foundation Report, Toronto.

Smart, R. G., and Jones, D., 1970, Illicit LSD users: Their personality characteristics and psychopathology, *J. Abnorm. Psychol.* **75**:286–292.

Smart, R. G., and Whitehead, P. C., 1973, The prevention of drug abuse by lowering *per capita* consumption: Distribution of consumption in samples of Canadian adults and British university students, *Bull. Narc.* **25**(4):49–54.

Smith, R. C., 1972, Speed and violence: Compulsive methamphetamine abuse and criminality in the Haight-Ashbury district, in: *Drug Abuse: Proceedings of the International Conference* pp. 435–448, Lea and Febiger, Philadelphia.

Soueif, M. I., 1967, Hashish consumption in Egypt, with special reference to psychosocial aspects, *Bull. Narc.* **19**(2):1–12.

Soueif, M. I., 1971, The use of cannabis in Egypt: A behavioural study, *Bull. Narc.* **23**(4):17–28.

Soueif, M. I., 1975, Chronic cannabis users: Further analysis of objective test results, *Bull. Narc.* **27**:1–26.

Steffenhagen, R. A., McAree, C. P., and Nixon, H. L., 1972, Drug use among college females: Socio-demographic and social psychological correlates, *Int. J. Addict.* **7**:285–293.

Suffet, F., and Brotman, R., 1976, Female drug use: Some observations, *Int. J. Addict.* **11**:19–33.

Tamerin, J. S., and Mendelson, J. H., 1969, The psychodynamics of chronic inebriation: Observations of alcoholics during the process of drinking in an experimental group setting, *Am. J. Psychiatry* **125**:886–899.

Teasdale, J. D., and Hinkson, J., 1971, Stimulant drugs: Perceived effect on the interpersonal behavior of dependent subjects, *Int. J. Addict.* **6**:407–417.

Thompson, T., and Unna, K. R. (eds.), 1977, Prediction of abuse liability of stimulant and depressant drugs, National Academy of Sciences and National Research Council (USA), Washington, D.C.

Tomlinson, J., 1975, Petrol sniffing in the Northern Territory, *Aust. J. Alcohol. Drug Depend.* **2**:74–77.

Vondráček, V., Prokupek, J., Fischer, R., and Ahrenbergová, M., 1968, Recent patterns of addiction in Czechoslovakia, *Br. J. Psychiatry* **114**:285–292.

Wasson, R. G., 1970, Soma of the Aryans: An ancient hallucinogen? *Bull. Narc.* **22**:(3):25–30.

Wechsler, H., and McFadden, M., 1976, Sex differences in adolescent alcohol and drug use: A disappearing phenomenon, *J. Stud. Alcohol* **37**:1291–1301.

Weiner, S., Tamerin, J. S., Steinglass, P., and Mendelson, J. H., 1971, Familial patterns in chronic alcoholism: A study of a father and son during experimental intoxication, *Am. J. Psychiatry* **127**:1646–1651.

Whitlock, F. A., 1970, The syndrome of barbiturate dependence, *Med. J. Aust.* **2**:391–396.

Whitlock, F. A., and Lowrey, J. M., 1967, Drug-dependence in psychiatric patients, *Med. J. Aust.* **1**:1157–1166.

Wilkinson, P., Horvath, T. B., Santamaria, J. N., and Rankin, J. G., 1969, Bromism in association with alcoholism: A report of five cases, *Med. J. Aust.* **1**:1352–1355.

Wilkinson, P., Kornaczewski, A., Rankin, J. G., and Santamaria, J. N., 1971, Bromureide dependence in alcoholics, *Med. J. Aust.* **2**:479–482.

Young, D., and Scoville, W. B., 1938, Paranoid psychosis in narcolepsy and the possible danger of Benzedrine treatment, *Med. Clin. North Am.* **22**:637–645.

13

Opiate Dependence in Women

CATHERINE A. MARTIN and WILLIAM R. MARTIN

1. INTRODUCTION

Opiate addiction and dependence in women have received scant attention by both medical and scientific investigators. This neglect may be partly attributed to the relatively small extent of the problem. Most statistics indicate that women comprise approximately 20–25% of the addict population. Although on a percentage basis the incidence of narcotic addiction in women is relatively small, the total number of women addicts in the United States probably exceeds 100,000. Well-controlled clinical studies of the effects of both acutely and chronically administered narcotics have been conducted mainly at the National Institute of Drug Abuse Addiction Research Center at Lexington, Kentucky. This facility was unique in that research subjects were prisoners and the drug milieu could be carefully controlled. Male subjects were employed exclusively in these studies, principally because of economics and because the highly trained scientific supporting personnel were males. It remains to be seen whether valid data on the effects of chronically administered narcotics can be acquired in female as well as male human subjects in other circumstances.

Because of a lack of hard data, many important aspects of narcotic addiction in women remain obscure. Nevertheless, there are substantive reasons to believe that the actions of narcotics in females and males are similar. Several examples illustrate this point. The potency of new analgesics are commonly experimentally assessed in several types of clinical pain, postpartum pain, and postoperative pain, as well as pain in

CATHERINE A. MARTIN and WILLIAM R. MARTIN • Departments of Psychiatry and Pharmacology, University of Kentucky College of Medicine, Lexington, Kentucky.

patients with neoplastic disease (Houde et al., 1965). Studies of analgesics in postpartum pain obviously have been conducted exclusively with females, while studies in postoperative pain and cancer pain have been conducted with both males and females. There has been excellent concordance in both potency estimates and absolute potencies when standard drugs such as morphine or codeine have been compared with experimental drugs for the different populations studied. Further, there has been excellent concordance between potency estimates of analgesic activity and the potency of narcotic analgesics to suppress abstinence in male narcotic dependent addicts (Jasinski, 1977; Martin, 1966). The question of sex differences in pain and analgesics has been discussed by Beecher (1959) and Houde et al. (1965). Although narcotic dependence has been most studied in male humans, it has also been intensively studied in female chronic spinal dogs (Gilbert and Martin, 1976; Martin et al., 1976; Wikler and Frank, 1948). All of the major signs and most minor signs of abstinence seen in male humans have been seen in female dogs.

There are a number of especially important issues concerning addiction in females as well as male–female differences that can be profitably studied and resolved. The difference in incidence in drug abuse between males and females needs to be established. Although it is most commonly believed that the reason for the sex difference is cultural and social, endocrine differences may also be of importance. There is also reason to believe that the chronic use of narcotics may produce long-persisting biological changes, not only in the abuser, but also in offspring, which may have psychiatric implications.

2. EPIDEMIOLOGY AND DEMOGRAPHY

Prior to the passage of the Harrison Narcotic Act in 1914, the use of narcotics appears to have been higher in women than in men in the United States. In several surveys conducted from 1878 to 1915, there were 1.4–2.0 times as many women as men using narcotics excessively (Terry and Pellens, 1928/1970). Throughout the history of the U.S. Public Health Service Hospitals at Lexington and later Fort Worth, the number of male patients admitted was several times greater than the number of females admitted. Of all admissions from 1935 through 1964 (87,809), 83% were male and 17% were female (Ball et al., 1966). An analysis of records of federal prisoners from 1936–1937 showed that 4.5 times as many men as women were committed for violation of narcotics laws as compared with 18 times as many men for other crimes (Kolb, 1938).

Simpson et al. (1976) analyzed 27,440 admissions to federally funded community drug treatment programs. Of these, 25% were women. There was considerable variation in percentages between different ethnic groups, ranging from 31% for white females to 16% for Puerto Rican and Mexican-American females. Of all black admissions, 24% were females.

Prior to the passage of the Pure Food and Drug Act (1906) and the Harrison Narcotic Act (1914), opium was available in over-the-counter nostrums that were widely used to treat a variety of discomforts. Kolb (1938) believed that the sexes had "the same inherent impulses to enhance pleasure and relieve pain by artificial means." He felt that women used opium to relieve "physical and mental distress," while men took it in large measure for the thrill, thus accounting for the preponderance of women users. However, when the use of narcotics was made a criminal offense, the proportion of women dropped because of their fear of and respect for the law.

It is still generally held that the relatively low abuse rate of narcotics among women is culturally determined, although a biological basis cannot be excluded.

3. PERSONALITY AND ANTISOCIAL BEHAVIOR

Although the incidence and prevalence of addiction in males appears to be higher than in females, the reasons for this difference are not readily apparent. Ellinwood et al. (1966) interviewed 81 males and 30 female addicts. Approximately 20% of both groups stated that they had begun using narcotics for medical reasons; 67% had begun out of curiosity, for pleasure or kicks, or to be part of a gang; and about 10% were introduced by members of their family. By history, their sources of narcotics were similar—mostly from fellow addicts and illicit sources. The Minnesota Multiphasic Personality Inventory (MMPI) profiles of male and female are similar (Olson, 1964), showing a significant and pathological elevation on the psychopathic deviate scale. The profiles of the males of this study resembled the "undifferentiated psychopath" profile described by Hill (1962) and Hill et al. (1962), while the profiles of the females most resembled his "neurotic psychopath" profile, with significantly higher elevations on the "depression" and "paranoia" scales.

A number of authors have identified a subgroup of addicts who had an elevation on the schizophrenia (Sc) scale of the MMPI (Hill, 1962; Hill et al., 1962) or who were clinically diagnosed as schizophrenic or schizoid (Kolb, 1925). Ellinwood et al. (1966) found that male addicts were somewhat more commonly diagnosed as sociopathic and having personality disorders, whereas females were more often diagnosed as neurotic or psychotic. The prevalence of homosexuality and frigidity may be somewhat higher in female addicts than in the general female population (Ellinwood et al., 1966; Marmor, 1976). Female addicts may have experienced a broken home more frequently and at an earlier age (6 years old or younger) than male addicts (Ellinwood et al., 1966; O'Donnell, 1969).

In light of Olson's (1964) findings on MMPIs in male and female narcotic addicts, one useful framework for comparing male and female narcotic addicts is that of Woodruff et al. (1974), "Diagnostic Criteria for Antisocial Personality Disorders." Five of these criteria are:

a. *School problems as manifested by truancy, suspension, expulsion, or fighting that leads to trouble with teachers or principals.* The majority of female and male addicts were high school dropouts (Ellinwood et al., 1966; O'Donnell, 1969) and had a high rate of truancy.

b. *Trouble with the police as manifested by two or more arrests for nontraffic offenses, four or more arrests for moving traffic offenses, or a felony conviction.* Twice as many male as female addicts had gone to a reform school (Ellinwood et al., 1966). Reports vary as to the percentage of narcotic offenses for male and female addicts. Ellinwood et al. (1966) stated that although less than 10% of the male and female addicts studied used drug sales for support, narcotic convictions were reported in one-half of the males and one-third of the females. O'Donnell (1969) found that 33% of male addicts and 15% of female addicts committed drug offenses after onset of addiction. While on drugs, men frequently committed property crimes to support their drug habits, while women relied on prostitution (Ellinwood et al., 1966). D'Orban (1973) followed 66 incarcerated female addicts after their release. Data on their delinquency and narcotic addiction were obtained from criminal records and not self-reports. Four years after their release from prison, one-third (36%) were off narcotics; one-sixth (15%) had died, two from septicemia, seven from overdoses, and one from suicide; 62% had been arrested for drug offenses and stealing. Male addicts averaged greater than twice (2.7 years) as many years in prison as female addicts (1.1 years) (Ellinwood et al., 1966). The percentage of male addicts with arrests and sentences before and after addiction is higher than that of female addicts. There appears to be a greater increase in arrests and imprisonment following addiction in males than in females (See Table 1). D'Orban (1974) found that the number of previous convictions was the only variable significantly related to continued narcotic abuse defined as notification of narcotic use to the Home Office Drugs Branch.

Table 1. Percentage of Arrests and Sentences before and after Addiction, by Sex[a]

	Arrests before addiction	Sentences before addiction	Arrests after addiction	Sentences after addiction
Female	2%	0%	22%	7%
Male	28%	15%	53%	41%

[a] Compiled from data published by O'Donnell (1969).

c. *Poor work history as manifested by being fired, quitting without another job to go to, or frequent job changes.* Male addicts were employed more often than female addicts (Ellinwood et al., 1966). Since many female addicts were housewives or students (O'Donnell, 1969), the application of this criterion is somewhat ambiguous for females. From 1961 to 1967, there was a decrease in the number of female addicts legally employed and an increase in the number using illegal activities as a primary means of support (Cuskey et al., 1971). During the year following termination of formal education and six months prior to hospitalization, 16–21% of the female addicts reported legal occupations, 44–45% reported illegal activities, and 35% were dependents; 70% had not had a job one year prior to admission, and 33% had had no regular job in six years (Chambers et al., 1970).

d. *Marital difficulties as manifested by deserting the family, two or more divorces, frequent separation due to marital discord, recurrent infidelity, recurrent physical attacks on spouse, or being suspected of battering a child.* Of male addicts, 40% (compared with 17% of Kentucky males) and of female addicts, 51% (compared with 16% of Kentucky females) had been married more than once. Two-thirds of the addicts' marriages that terminated ended by divorce or separation (O'Donnell, 1969).

e. *Sexual problems as manifested by prostitution, pimping, more than one episode of venereal disease, or flagrant promiscuity.* Nearly half of the female addicts had been involved in prostitution, and the majority (79%) of these used it at some time as their primary means of support. Over half (52%) of the female addicts reporting prostitution were arrested for it (Chambers et al., 1970).

Although the diagnostic criteria for antisocial personality disorder have not been applied in a controlled fashion to the study of the female addict, there is an indication that many female addicts fulfill the criteria. Based on existing psychometric data, it seems probable that many female addicts may have a personality disorder or an antisocial personality. The prevalence of antisocial behavior among females and female addicts appears to be less than among males.

4. THE EFFECTS OF NARCOTICS ON PITUITARY FUNCTION AND HORMONES

Most of the reports of the effects of narcotic analgesics on endocrine function in females have been about animals. Studies in humans have been conducted largely on males. However, there is reason to believe that similar changes, based on animal studies, would be observed in females. For this reason, the effects of narcotics on endocrine function in man and animals will be briefly described for some hormones.

Pang et al. (1974) found that low doses of morphine (10 mg/kg) increased plasma levels of luteinizing hormone (LH) in female rats, while higher doses (60 mg/kg) decreased plasma levels. Intermediate doses had no consistent effect. Morphine (5–20 mg/kg) depressed serum LH levels in male rats (Bruni et al., 1977). Inspection of the data of Cicero et al. (1977) reveals an early but nonsignificant increase in serum LH levels produced by morphine, which was antagonized by naloxone. Naloxone in its own right increased serum LH levels. Paradoxically, met-enkephalin administered intraperitoneally also increased serum LH levels, and this effect was also antagonized by naloxone (Bruni et al., 1977).

Tolerance developed to morphine's depressant effect on serum LH levels in male rats when the drug was administered chronically by the pellet implantation technique (Cicero et al., 1977). Neither morphine nor met-enkephalin altered serum follicle-stimulating hormone (FSH) levels in male rats. Naloxone in the dose of 0.2 mg/kg did not alter serum FSH, while doses of 2 and 5 mg/kg increased it (Bruni et al., 1977).

Single doses of morphine (20 mg/kg and 50 mg/kg) inhibited ovulation in the female rat (Barraclough and Sawyer, 1955; Packman and Rothchild, 1976; Pang et al., 1974). When morphine was administered chronically, a breakthrough of ovulation occurred (Barraclough and Sawyer, 1955). Morphine's inhibitory effect on ovulation was antagonized by naloxone (Packman and Rothchild, 1976).

Chronic administration of heroin and methadone to male addicts depresses gonadotropins and testosterone levels (Martin et al., 1973; Mendelson and Mello, 1975; Mendelson et al., 1975a,b). On the other hand, Cushman (1971) did not find any marked disparity between plasma levels of LH in methadone-maintained patients and normal subjects. Martin et al. (1977), however, found that the mean plasma levels of LH and testosterone of abstinent male narcotic addicts and alcoholics were

50–100% higher than those of control subjects. This finding may explain these apparently disparate observations, in that narcotics may depress the addicts' elevated levels of LH and testosterone to the normal range.

Narcotic analgesics enhanced the release of prolactin, possibly through an inhibition of dopaminergic processes (Sachar, 1978). A therapeutic dose of morphine (10 mg) administered preoperatively caused a rise in serum prolactin levels but not of growth hormone (GH), thyroid-stimulating hormone (TSH), or cortisol (Tolis et al., 1975). Tolis et al. found that apomorphine, a presumed dopamine agonist, abolished the morphine-induced prolactin rise. Lal et al. (1977) found that apomorphine increased serum prolactin levels in male rats pretreated with morphine. The finding that the endogenous polypeptides, the enkephalins and β endorphin, share certain pharmacologic properties in common with narcotic analgesics has stimulated study of their physiological effects. Studies to date have for the most part been conducted in male rats, and the findings have been variable. Thus, leucine-enkephalin produced no consistent effect on serum prolactin levels (Lien et al., 1976), while met-enkephalin produced a modest but not consistent increase (Bruni et al., 1977; Lien et al., 1976).

Morphine has the ability, depending on dose and the animal under study, to both stimulate and inhibit the release of ACTH (Sloan, 1971). Extensive studies have been conducted in man. Single doses of morphine have little or only a modest depressant effect on the excretion of 17-ketosteroids. Eosinophil counts are decreased (Eisenman et al., 1954, 1958, 1961, 1969; Fraser et al., 1957; McDonald et al., 1959). These findings suggest that single doses of morphine may depress adrenal function in men and women. Although the early studies with chronic administration of morphine suggested that adrenal function was suppressed (Eisenman et al., 1958), subsequent studies with chronic morphine and methadone indicate that there is little change in 17-OH corticosteroid excretion (Eisenman et al., 1969) or plasma cortisol levels (Mendelson et al., 1975b).

In patients receiving nitrous oxide and 1–2 mg/kg of morphine, there was no change in the GH rise to the stress of general surgery in comparison with a halothane control group. It was also found that 4 mg/kg of morphine alone obliterated the GH rise (Reier et al., 1973). Morphine in female humans in a 10-mg dose did not have an effect on serum GH concentration (Tolis et al., 1975). However, in male rats, morphine in doses of 0.3–20 mg/kg and met-enkephalin in a 5-mg dose increased serum GH concentration (Bruni et al., 1977; Rivier et al., 1977; Simon et al., 1975). This effect was reversed by naloxone (Bruni et al., 1977). Naloxone in doses from 0.2 to 5 mg/kg reduced serum GH concentration (Bruni et al., 1977).

5.   EFFECTS OF NARCOTICS ON THE REPRODUCTIVE SYSTEM AND PREGNANCY

In view of the profound effects of narcotics on endocrine function and the fact that 80–85% of female addicts are of childbearing age (Liu-Fu, 1967), narcotic effects on reproduction are obviously important. There are several general questions that need to be answered: (1) Does acute or sporadic use of narcotics alter the fertility of either males or females? (2) Does either low dose or high dose chronic narcotic use alter fertility and fetal development? The latter question is of some importance and concern in methadone-maintained patients. Unfortunately, at this time only anecdotal answers can be given to these questions.

Many female addicts, most of whom reported normal menstrual cycles prior to addiction, were of the opinion that heroin causes infertility and cessation of menstruation when taken in large doses for prolonged periods (Gaulden et al., 1964; Perlmutter, 1967; Stoffer, 1968). On close questioning, 65–67% reported abnormal cycles of 35 days or longer (Gaulden et al., 1964; Wikler, 1975). They stated that their periods returned to normal when drug ingestion ceased, whether they were in treatment or not (Gaulden et al., 1964; Thomas et al., 1977). Wallach et al. (1969) found that the menstrual cycles of females in methadone maintenance programs frequently became normal. Some female addicts dependent on methadone had amenorrhea, often failed to exhibit cyclical changes in serum FSH, and lacked mid-cycle peaks in serum gonadotropins and luteal increments in serum progesterone (Santen and Bilic, 1973; Santen et al., 1975).

It is now well established that narcotic-maintained females can become pregnant and that males can be potent as previously mentioned. Wallach et al. (1969) followed 95 women, whose ages ranged from 24 to 38 years, in a methadone maintenance program. The maintenance dose was from 60 to 120 mg of methadone. Of these women, 13 became pregnant. Blinick (1971) reported 20 deliveries and probably at least 33 pregnancies in 188 women in methadone maintenance therapy. Stoffer (1968) studied 100 street addicts whose primary drug of abuse was heroin. Of these, 63% stated that they were infertile while abusing heroin; however, there were 77 pregnancies in 39 of these patients.

Rosenthal et al. (1964) expressed concern about the severe pregnancy wastage among female addicts. They stated that 16 of 102 women delivering a live child reported previously aborting 1 or 2 times, with a total of 35 abortions in 102 women. Reddy et al. (1971) reported that 11 of 40 addicted mothers of infants whom he followed had lost at least one previous pregnancy, and 2 had had multiple spontaneous abortions. Of heroin addict deliveries reported by Stern (1966), 7% were stillbirths.

Rementería and Nunag (1973) also reported a stillbirth rate of 6.4% in heroin addicts. They suggested that simultaneous fetal and maternal narcotic withdrawal and labor may expose the infant to an insufficient supply of oxygen and may be a factor in this high stillbirth rate.

Methadone maintenance programs have provided an especially favorable circumstance for assessing the effect of chronic narcotic use on pregnancy. They are claimed to provide relief from many stresses in the addict's life, such as malnutrition and lack of continuing medical surveillance (Blinick, 1971). Possibly they select for addicts with decreased multiple-drug abuse, alcoholism, and schizophrenia (Wallach et al., 1969).

Finnegan (1976) analyzed the neonatal death statistics of 303 infants born to heroin- or methadone-dependent mothers. She found the death rate to be highest (10%) in infants born to mothers who were methadone-dependent and who received inadequate prenatal care; intermediate (4.8%) in infants born to heroin-dependent mothers with no prenatal care; and lowest (2.5%) in infants born to methadone-dependent mothers with adequate prenatal care. A comparison of the data on the incidence of pathological pregnancy among women in methadone maintenance programs, and street addicts, with those of the general population is presented in Table 2. As can be seen, spontaneous and induced abortions as well as stillbirths are higher in heroin addicts than in either the general population or females in methadone maintenance programs; however, the differences are not statistically significant. The data do not suggest a unique causal relationship between heroin or methadone use and fetal wastage. The female narcotic addicts' antepartum course is difficult to assess as their participation in prenatal care is infrequent. Stern (1966) found that the average number of obstetric clinic visits prior to delivery was less than one, with only one-third of the expectant mothers visiting once and one-sixth visiting more than once. Perlmutter (1967) reported that 76% of the pregnant addicts who presented for delivery had made no prenatal visits. Of 22 patients, 4 had a total of 14 visits. However, Zelson et al. (1973) have found an increase in the number of pregnant addicts attending prenatal clinics in recent years. From 1960 to 1969, fewer than 20% attended prenatal clinics. However, from 1971 to 1972, 47% of the heroin addicts and 42% of the methadone-dependent mothers attended prenatal clinics.

Several female addicts reported that their use of heroin increased during pregnancy. Very few heroin addicts who were withdrawn during pregnancy were able to remain drug-free (Stern, 1966). Of cases where the last dose was known, it was taken within a few hours of admission (Krause et al., 1958; Stern, 1966). On the other hand, Wallach et al. (1969) reported that methadone maintained expectant mothers needed no change in their maintenance dose. These impressions are not necessarily

Table 2. Incidence of Pathological Pregnancies in General (1968) and in Narcotic Dependent Female Population

	Stillbirths	Abortions			Ectopic pregnancies
		Spontaneous	Induced	Total	
General population (Hellman and Pritchard, 1971)	$\frac{5.5 \times 10^4}{3.47 \times 10^6}$	$\frac{6 \times 10^5}{3.47 \times 10^6}$	—	—	$1/100\text{–}1/450^a$
Methadone maintenance (Blinick et al., 1973)	$\frac{5}{105}$	$\frac{4}{105}$	$\frac{15}{105}$	$\frac{19}{105}$	$\frac{1}{105}$
Heroin addicts (Stoffer, 1968)	—	$\frac{23}{77}$	$\frac{14}{77}$	$\frac{37}{77}$	—
Heroin addicts (Stern, 1966)	$\frac{5}{70}$	—	—	—	—
Narcotic addicts (Rementería and Nunag, 1973)	$\frac{3}{46}$	—	—	—	—

[a] Estimated on the basis of small samples.

disparate. It must be remembered that methadone, heroin, and morphine are agonists (Martin, 1967), and the brain has a limited number of opioid receptors. Street doses of heroin probably occupy only a modest portion of the opioid receptors, while maintenance doses of methadone employed in the patients of Wallach et al. (1969) probably nearly saturated the opioid receptors (Martin and Sloan, 1977; Martin et al., 1972).

Medical complications seen in pregnant females on admission for delivery include multiple abcesses, cellulitis, venous thrombosis, serum hepatitis (Stern, 1966), bacterial endocarditis, tetanus, malaria, venereal diseases (Hill and Desmond 1963), and infected ulcerating veins (Krause et al. 1958). Perlmutter (1967) found that 23% of addicts admitted for delivery had positive serologies and had not received treatment. He speculated that this finding was a consequence of the high rate of prostitution among female addicts.

Stern (1966) reported that obstetrical complications (41%) are common in female addicts. He found that 16% had toxemia, 9% abruptia placenta, and 9% postpartum hemorrhage. Other complications included retained placenta, ruptured marginal sinus, cephalopelvic disproportion (Stern, 1966), and severe nausea and vomiting following Caesarean section (Krause et al., 1958). Breech presentation is more frequent in addicts than in nonaddicts. Perlmutter (1967) postulated that breech presentation is secondary to the increased frequency of prematurity of infants born to pregnant addicts.

6. TERATOGENICITY, CONGENITAL DEFECTS, AND PROTRACTED CHANGES

It is difficult to determine the etiology of congenital defects of infants born to addict mothers because of frequent polydrug use, the impurity of the drugs taken, the variable dose and frequency of drug ingestion, and the fact that prenatal care is frequently poor. For this reason, animal studies must be employed to obtain controlled data.

Chronically, morphine (up to 70 mg/kg/day) was given prior to and throughout gestation of female rats (Myers, 1931). The rats became pregnant and bore litters of "healthy appearing young in average number." Morphine in very large single doses (100–500 mg/kg) administered to mice on the eighth or ninth day following impregnation did not alter the number of implantation sites but did increase fetal resorption (Harpel and Gautieri, 1968). There was also a decrease in fetal weight and size as well as an increased incidence of exencephaly and axial skeletal fusions. Some of these changes, such as decreased size and weight and axial skeletal fusions, can be attributed in part to the transient decrease in food consumption caused by morphine. Morphine also produces placental vasoconstriction, which is antagonized by nalorphine (Gautieri and Ciuchta, 1962). Since anoxia on Days 8 or 9 of pregnancy can produce exencephaly and skeletal fusions, the effect of very large doses of morphine could also have been a consequence of morphine vasoconstrictor effect on the placenta with resulting fetal hypoxia (Harpel and Gautieri, 1968).

Friedler (1974a, b) and Friedler and Cochin (1972) have conducted a series of studies on the long-term effects of morphine dependence on developmental processes. In the first studies, female rats made dependent on morphine were withdrawn and mated five days after the last dose of morphine. The offspring grew less rapidly than controls and exhibited tolerance to morphine. Although rats born to nonaddict females and postaddict males did not have impaired growth, the offspring of either postaddict male or postaddict female mice or both were significantly smaller than controls, and these differences persisted through the F_2 generations. The chronic administration of narcotics during the course of gestation may also alter fetal development. Taeusch et al. (1973) observed that pregnant rabbits receiving repeated intravenous injections of heroin at the end of gestation had offspring with decreased body weight.

Zelson and Green (1977) found that 48% of 665 infants born to drug-addicted mothers weighed under 2500 g and that 44% of these were small for their gestational age. Infants born to mothers using methadone had a higher birth weight than those born to street addicts. In a study assessing the role of prenatal care on fetal development, Finnegan (1976) found that the highest (48%) percentage of infants weighing less than 2500 g were those born to mothers who were heroin-dependent and received no prenatal care; intermediate (36%) were those born to methadone-dependent mothers with inadequate prenatal care; and lowest (17%) were those born to methadone-dependent mothers with adequate prenatal care. Naeye et al. (1973) reported that over half of pregnant heroin addicts or their infants had evidence of infection. Infants born to heroin addicts with infection had gestational ages significantly lower than those born to heroin addicts without infection. Thus, several factors may alter fetal development in narcotic addicts, including drugs, prenatal care, and intercurrent infections. Although there is little evidence that gross fetal abnormalities are a consequence of chronic narcotic administration, the possibility that subtle developmental and metabolic abnormalities can be produced cannot be excluded and is deserving of additional investigation.

7. DIAGNOSIS AND TREATMENT OF THE NARCOTIC-DEPENDENT FEMALE AND NEONATE

Signs of abstinence in female addicts and neonates have not been studied under controlled conditions as they have been in males (Himmelsbach, 1937; Martin and Jasinski, 1969). There is, however, little reason to believe that the abstinence syndromes in males and females are different. On the other hand, there is reason to believe that abstinence in the neonate may differ in some respects from that in the adult. For this reason, signs of abstinence for the adult and the neonate are discussed separately here.

Diagnosis of narcotic dependence in the female and the male addict is made on the basis of clinical judgment and findings as well as laboratory data. A number of signs, such as needle tracks, phlebitis, ulcers, constricted pupils, and signs of abstinence, may lead the clinician to suspect narcotic dependence. The medical complications of narcotic addiction are the same in males and females (Sapira, 1968). Further, many addicts have pathological liver function tests, such as elevated transaminases, which are usually indicative of a chronic anicteric serum hepatitis (Gorodetzky et al., 1968). The problem of hepatitis in addicts has been recently reviewed (Cherubin, 1977). A careful psychiatric history will disclose that many addict patients have been involved in several types of sociopathic behavior in addition to drug abuse (see Section 3 above). Finally, a urine specimen obtained on admission should be analyzed for the presence of drugs. Chronic heroin users have morphine in their urine. The urine test should also alert the physician to the possibility of polydrug abuse and multiple dependencies. The most common associated dependencies are on alcohol (whose presence can be demonstrated by analyzing a blood sample) and sedative–hypnotic drugs. If the patient has used large quantities of amphetamine, she may have a postwithdrawal depression (Griffith, 1977), which may be confused with or exacerbate a postpartum psychosis or blues. The types of urine-testing procedures and their limitations and advantages have been reviewed by Gorodetzky (1977).

Signs of acute abstinence seen in patients dependent on heroin, morphine, methadone, and other narcotics include yawning, lacrimation, rhinorrhea, piloerection (gooseflesh), sweating, restlessness, twitching of muscles, jerks of the limbs, insomnia, hypertension, tachycardia, tachypnea, fever, mydriasis, loose stools, diarrhea, and vomiting. The earliest symptoms of abstinence are feelings of weakness and restlessness. These symptoms are followed by nausea, abdominal cramps, irritability, malaise, joint and muscle pain, and loss of appetite. The signs and symptoms can be quantified and the severity of the abstinence reaction can be objectively measured (Jasinski, 1977). Stern (1966) and Krause et al. (1958) have described the following postpartum symptoms in abstinent heroin addicts: sweating, yawning, eye blinking, tremor, abdominal and joint pain, nervousness, insomnia, and severe anxiety with crying.

Physical dependence in the newborn is a common sequel of maternal addiction. Reports of withdrawal signs have been observed in 67–91% of infants born to mothers addicted to narcotics (Hill and Desmond, 1963; Zelson et al., 1971). There was little change in the incidence of neonatal withdrawal in infants born at the New York Medical College, Metropolitan Hospital Center, over a 10-year period (Zelson et al., 1971).

Signs of narcotic withdrawal in the neonate in approximately decreasing frequency are irritability, hypertonicity, hyperactivity, tremor, excessive need to suck, excessive crying, high-pitched cry, respiratory distress, respiratory grunts, jerks, seizures, poor sleep, hyperactivity, yawning, hypoglycemia, elevated temperature, nasal congestion, and sneezing (Cobrinik et al., 1959; Hill and Desmond, 1963; Lewis and Stothers, 1973; Reddy et al., 1971; Wikler, 1975; Zelson et al., 1971). Other symptoms described include swift changes in color, hyperactive reflexes, and vasomotor instability. The convulsions and respiratory distress that can occur in such infants are rarely, if ever, seen in adults. Early and mild signs of abstinence include tremors, irritability, hyperactivity, vomiting, stuffy nose, yawning, poor food intake, high-pitched shrill crying, diarrhea, and modest elevation of body temperature. When the degree of dependence is great, the more severe signs of abstinence are twitching, convulsions, depressed respiration, cyanosis, lacrimation, hyperhidrosis, and severe fever (101–108°F).

The majority of neonates (63%) show withdrawal signs within the first 24 hours of life. The qualitative characteristics, time course, and intensity of the narcotic analgesic (heroin, morphine, and methadone) abstinence syndrome in the newborn have not been systematically studied under well-controlled conditions as they have in the adult male (Himmelsbach, 1937; Isbell et al., 1948; Martin and Fraser, 1961; Martin and Jasinski, 1969; Martin et al., 1973). The intensity of the abstinence syndrome is probably related to quantity of narcotic ingested. Zelson et al. (1971) found a direct correlation between length of addiction and quantity of narcotic ingested by the mother (as assessed by history and the incidence of withdrawal signs). A total of 63% of the infants showed withdrawal signs if their mother used 1–5 bags, 75% with 6–10 bags, and 76% with 11 or more bags of heroin; 55% of the infants showed withdrawal signs if the mothers were addicted for less than one year, 73% for one to four years, and 75% for five years or more.

Conflicting conclusions have been yielded by reports comparing withdrawal syndromes of infants born to heroin or methadone addicts.

Wallach et al. (1969) reported that infants born to methadone addicts had minimal withdrawal signs, whereas Reddy et al. (1971) reported that the withdrawal syndrome of infants born to methadone-dependent users was more serious than that of infants born to heroin addicts. They found that 76% of the infants born to heroin addicts and 91% of the infants born to methadone addicts showed withdrawal signs. The withdrawal signs and their course were similar. However, the infants born to mothers addicted to methadone showed a significantly higher number of more severe withdrawal signs. Kron et al. (1976) found that in infants of narcotic addicts, nutritive sucking as measured by sucking rate and nutrient consumption was half that of normal infants. Infants born to street addicts had a higher suck ratio, nutrient consumption, and percentage of time spent sucking than infants born to mothers attending methadone clinics. Despite their nursing difficulties, Apgar scores of infants born to addict mothers were frequently normal (Reddy et al., 1971); however, pathological scores were sometimes seen (Zelson et al., 1973). Infants born to street addicts tended to have slightly higher scores than those born to mothers in maintenance programs (Kron et al., 1976). The somewhat higher Apgar scores seen in infants born to street addicts as opposed to mothers in methadone maintenance programs are probably related to the levels of maternal dependence.

Wilson et al. (1973) have described "subacute withdrawal." They found that 82% of the infants born to heroin addicts, who had withdrawal symptoms in the nursery, also had symptoms three to six months after discharge. Signs described by the infants' foster mothers were restlessness, agitation, tremors, brief sleep periods, excessive milk intake, colic, and vomiting; those described by physicians were irritability, exaggerated rooting reflexes and oral activity, wide-amplitude tremors, spontaneous startles, vasomotor instability, hyperacusis, and poor socialization. This syndrome may be related to the protracted abstinence described in adult postaddicts (Martin and Sloan, 1977; Martin et al., 1973).

The treatment of the dependent postpartum addict and the neonate is problematic. Certainly, maternal signs of abstinence should be relieved and maintenance therapy instituted. This treatment should minimize the use of street drugs, hustling, and discharge against medical advice. The issue of the nursing of infants by methadone-maintained mothers is controversial. Kreek et al. (1974) studied a patient maintained on 50 mg of methadone a day. Methadone milk levels ranged from 0.03 μg/ml to 0.12 μg/ml. On the basis of these data, Kreek et al. argued that the quantity of methadone present in mothers' milk is unlikely to produce an adverse clinical effect. Blinick et al. (1973) found that the breast milk of mothers maintained on 80–100 mg of methadone a day contained 0.17–5.6 μg/ml. This could mean that the infants were ingesting up to 1 mg/kg of methadone per day. The significance is not known, as the pharmacokinetics of methadone in the infant are yet to be determined. Because of these considerations and the fact that addicts are frequently polydrug abusers, caution should be used in advising addict mothers to nurse.

The prognosis for the withdrawing addict mother must be guarded. Around one-fourth (20–28%) leave against medical advice, and some of these leave even while they are being treated for withdrawal (Krause et al., 1958; Stern, 1966). Methadone has been used for maternal withdrawal (Krause et al., 1958; Stern, 1966). Although Stern (1966) recommended the additional use of chlorpromazine, Fraser and Isbell (1956) found that chlorpromazine did not markedly alter the morphine abstinence syndrome in males.

Numerous drugs have been recommended for treating neonatal withdrawal, including phenobarbital, methadone, chlorpromazine, chloral hydrate, paregoric, and diazepam (Cobrinik et al., 1959; Hill and Desmond, 1963; Wikler, 1975). Kron et al. (1976) reported that paregoric-treated infants born to addict mothers sucked more vigorously than those treated with phenobarbital and diazepam or than untreated infants. Constipation and lethargy may be a consequence of the use of paregoric (Hill and Desmond, 1963). Diazepam has caused respiratory arrest in some infants, even at low dosages (Finnegan et al. 1975). Barbiturates decreased signs of central nervous system irritability such as myoclonic jerks and produced sedation but did not appear to decrease other signs of abstinence (Cobrinik et al. 1959; Vinchow and Hackel, 1960; Wikler, 1975).

8. SUMMARY AND CONCLUSIONS

Narcotic addiction is less prevalent in women than in men. The personality characteristics of many female addicts are in most respects similar to those of male addicts. They exhibit sociopathic behavior and may well have antisocial personalities. Determining the relative importance of social and biological factors might give insight into the etiology of drug abuse. The etiology of the behavior and personality characteristics has not been established, and various authorities have speculated about genetic, environmental, neurochemical, and neuroendocrine disorders (Martin, 1977). As a group, female addicts appear to be somewhat more neurotic and less psychopathic than male addicts.

Single doses of narcotics have a profound effect on endocrine function, although the long-term effect of these changes is not known. The effects of the chronic use of narcotics, either on the street or as maintenance therapy, are not well understood. Certain findings suggest that with chronic administration of narcotics, partial tolerance develops to their endocrine effects. Female addicts can become pregnant and male addicts may be potent while ingesting large doses of narcotics chronically. Existing data suggest that chronic narcotic use probably does not markedly affect pregnancy. In any event, the effects of narcotics are probably small compared with the impact of self-neglect and poor medical care received by the pregnant addict.

Narcotics readily cross the placenta. Chronic use of narcotics thus makes both the mother and the fetus dependent. For this reason, efforts should be made to diagnose maternal narcotic dependence. Physical findings, a psychiatric history, and laboratory tests are helpful. Abstinence causes maternal discomfort and impedes fetal nursing and maturation.

The long-term effects of maternal chronic narcotic use on the development of the infant and child have not been adequately studied. Studies in mice and rats suggest that chronic narcotic dependence can affect infant maturation. The implication of these findings for human maturation should be explored further.

REFERENCES

Ball, J. C., Bates, W. M., and O'Donnell, J. A., 1966, Characteristics of hospitalized narcotic addicts, in: *Health, Education, and Welfare Indicators,* U.S. Government Printing Office, Washington, D.C.

Barraclough, C. A., and Sawyer, C. H., 1955, Inhibition of the release of pituitary ovulatory hormone in the rat by morphine, *Endocrinology* 57:329–337.

Beecher, H. K., 1959, *Measurement of Subjective Responses,* Oxford University Press, London and New York.

Blinick, G., 1971, Fertility of narcotic addicts and effects of addiction on the offspring, *Soc. Biology,* 18(Suppl):S34–S39.

Blinick, G., Jerez, E., and Wallach, R., 1973, Methadone maintenance, pregnancy and progeny, *J. Am. Med. Assoc.* 225:477–479.

Bruni, J. F., Van Vugt, D., Marshall, S., and Meites, J., 1977, Effects of naloxone, morphine and methionine enkephalin on serum prolactin, luteinizing hormone, follicle stimulating hormone, thyroid stimulating hormone and growth hormone, *Life Sci.* 21:461–466.

Chambers, C. D., Hinesley, R. K., and Moldestad, M., 1970, Narcotic addiction in females: a race comparison, *Int. J. Addict.,* 5:257–278.

Cherubin, C. E., 1977, Hepatic complications, in: *Drug Abuse, Clinical and Basic Aspects,* (S. N. Pradhan and S. N. Dutta, eds.), pp. 344–354, C. V. Mosby, Saint Louis.

Cicero, T. J., Bell, R. D., Meyer, E. R., and Schweitzer, J., 1977, Narcotics and the hypothalamic–pituitary–gonadal axis: Acute effects on leutinizing hormone, testosterone and androgen-dependent systems, *J. Pharmacol. Exp. Ther.* 201:76–83.

Cobrinik, R. W., Hood, R. T., and Chusid, E., 1959, The effect of maternal narcotic addiction in the newborn infant: Review of the literature and report of 22 cases, *Pediatrics* 24:288–304.

Cushman, P., 1971, *Some Endocrinological Aspects of Heroin Addiction and Methadone Maintenance Therapy, Proceedings,* Third National Conference on Methadone Treatment, Publication 2172 (November, 1970), Public Health Service (1971) pp. 144–149.

Cuskey, W. R., Moffett, A. D., and Clifford, H. B., 1971, Comparison of female opiate addicts admitted to Lexington Hospital in 1961 and 1967, *Health Services and Mental Health Administration Health Reports* **86:**332–339.

d'Orban, P. T., 1973, Female narcotic addicts: A follow-up study of criminal and addiction careers, *Br. Med. J.* **14:**345–347.

d'Orban, P. T., 1974, A follow-up study of female narcotic addict variables related to outcome, *Br. J. Psychiatry* **124:**28–33.

Eisenman, A. J., Fraser, H. F., and Isbell, H., 1954, Effects of ACTH and gonadotropin during a cycle of morphine addiction, *Fed. Proc.* **1954:**203.

Eisenman, A. J., Fraser, H. F., Sloan, J. W., and Isbell, H., 1958, Urinary 17-ketosteroid excretion during a cycle of addiction to morphine, *J. Pharmacol. Exp. Ther.* **124:**305–311.

Eisenman, A. J., Fraser, H. F., and Brook, J. W., 1961, Urinary excretion and plasma levels of 17-hydroxycorticosteroids during a cycle of addiction to morphine, *J. Pharmacol. Exp. Ther.* **132:**226–231.

Eisenman, A. J., Sloan, J. W., Martin, W. R., Jasinski, D. R., and Brooks, J. W., 1969, Catecholamine and 17-hydroxycorticosteroid excretion during a cycle of morphine dependence in man, *J. Psychiatr. Res.* **7:**19–28.

Ellinwood, E. H., Jr., Smith, W. G., and Vaillant, G. E., 1966, Narcotic addiction in males and females: A comparison, *Int. J. Addict.* **1**(2):33–45.

Finnegan, L., 1976, Clinical effects of pharmacologic agents on pregnancy, the fetus, and the neonate, *Ann. N. Y. Acad. Sci.* **281:**74–89.

Finnegan, L. P., Connaughton, J. F., and Schut, J., 1975, Infants of drug-dependent women: Practical approaches for management, in: *Problems of Drug Dependence, Proceedings of the Thirty-Seventh Annual Scientific Meeting, Committee on Problems of Drug Dependence,* 489–517, National Academy of Sciences, Washington, D.C.

Fraser, H. F., and Isbell, H., 1956, Chlorpromazine and reserpine, *Am. Med. Assoc. Arch. Neurol. Psychiatry* **76:**257–262.

Fraser, H. F., Eisenman, A. J., and Brooks, J. W., 1957, Urinary excretion of 5 HIAA and corticoids after morphine, meperidine, nalorphine, reserpine and chlorpromazine, *Fed. Proc.* **16:**298.

Friedler, G., 1974a, Effect of pregestational morphine administration to mice on behavior of their offspring, *Pharmacologist* **16:**203.

Friedler, G., 1974b, Morphine administration to male mice: Effects on subsequent progeny, *Fed. Proc.* **33:**515.

Friedler, G., and Cochin, J., 1972, Growth retardation in offspring of female rats treated with morphine prior to conception, *Science* **175:**654–656.

Gaulden, E. C., Littlefield, D. C., Putoff, O. E., and Seivert, A. L., 1964, Menstrual abnormalities associated with heroin addiction, *Am. J. Obstet. Gynecol.* **90**(2):155–159.

Gautieri, R. E., and Ciuchta, H. P., 1962, Effect of certain drugs on perfused human placenta. I. Narcotic analgesics, serotonin and relaxin, *J. Pharm. Sci.* **51:**55–58.

Gilbert, P. E., and Martin, W. R., 1976, The effects of morphine- and nalorphine-like drugs in the nondependent, morphine-dependent and cyclazocine-dependent chronic spinal dog, *J. Pharmacol. Exp. Ther.* **198:**66–82.

Gorodetzky, C. W., 1977, Detection of drugs of abuse in biological fluids, in: *Drug Addiction II* (W. R. Martin, ed.), pp. 319–409, Springer-Verlag, Heidelberg.

Gorodetzky, C. W., Sapira, J. D., Jasinski, D. R., and Martin, W. R., 1968, Liver disease in narcotic addicts I. Role of the drug, *Clin. Pharmacol. Ther.* **9:**720.

Griffith, J. D., 1977, Amphetamine dependence: Clinical features, in: *Drug Addiction II* (W. R. Martin ed.), pp. 277–304, Springer-Verlag, Heidelberg.

Harpel, H. S., and Gautieri, R. F., 1968, Morphine-induced fetal malformations I, exencephaly and axial skeletal fusions, *J. Pharm. Sci.* **57**:1590–1597.

Hellman, L. M., and Pritchard, J. A., 1971, *Williams Obstetrics Fourteenth Edition,* pp. 1–18, 535, Appleton-Century-Crofts, New York.

Hill, H. E., 1962, The social deviant and initial addiction to narcotics and alcohol, *Q. J. Stud. Alcohol* **23**:562–582.

Hill, H. E., Haertzen, C. A., and Davis, H., 1962, An MMPI factor analytic study of alcoholics, narcotic addicts and criminals, *Q. J. Stud. Alcohol* **23**: 411–431.

Hill, R. M., and Desmond, M. M., 1963, Management of the narcotic withdrawal syndrome in the neonate, *Pediatr. Clin. North Am.* **10**:67–86.

Himmelsbach, C. K., 1937, *Rossium Treatment of Drug Addiction,* Public Health Reports (Wash.) Suppl. 125.

Houde, R. W., Wallenstein, S. L., and Beaver, W. T., 1965, Clinical measurement of pain, *Med. Chem.* **5**:75–122.

Isbell, H., Wikler, A., Eisenman, A. J., and Frank, K., 1947, Effect of single doses of 10820 (4,4-diphenyl-6-dimethylamino-heptanone-3) in man, *Fed. Proc.* **6**:341.

Isbell, H., Eisenman, A. J., Wikler, A., and Frank, K., 1948, The effects of single doses of 6-dimethylamino-4-4 diphenyl-3-3 heptanone (amidone, methadon or "10820") on human subjects, *J. Pharmacol. Exp. Ther.* **92**:83–89.

Jasinski, D. R., 1977, Assessment of the abuse potentiality of morphine-like drugs (methods used in man), in: *Drug Addiction I* (W. R. Martin, ed.), pp. 197–258, Springer-Verlag, Heidelberg.

Kolb, L., 1925, Types and characteristics of drug addicts, *Ment. Hyg.* **9**:300–313.

Kolb, L., 1938, Drug addiction among women, *American Prison Association,* **1938**:349–357.

Krause, S. O., Murray, P. M., Holmes, J. B., and Burch, R. E., 1958, Heroin addiction among pregnant women and their newborn babies, *Am. J. Obstet. Gynecol.* **75**:754–758.

Kreek, M. J., Schechter, A., Gutjahr, C. L., Bowen, D., Field, F., Queenan, J., and Merkatz, I., 1974, Analyses of methadone and other drugs in maternal and neonatal body fluids: Use in evaluation of symptoms in a neonate of mother maintained on methadone, *Am. J. Drug Alcohol Abuse* **1**:409–419.

Kron, E. K., Litt, M., Phoenix, M., and Finnegan, L., 1976, Neonatal narcotic abstinence: Effects of pharmacotherapeutic agents and maternal drug usage on nutritive sucking behavior, *J. Pediatr.* **88**:637–641.

Lal, H., Brown, W., Drawbaugh, R., Hynes, M., and Brown, G., 1977, Enhanced prolactin inhibition following chronic treatment with haloperidol and morphine, *Life Sci.* **20**:101–105.

Lewis, B. W., and Stothers, J. K., 1973, Congenital narcotic addiction, *Postgrad. Med. J.* **49**:83–85.

Lien, E. L., Fenichel, R. L., Garsky, V., Sarantakis, D., and Grant, N. H., 1976, Enkephalin-stimulated prolactin release, *Life Sci.* **19**:837–840.

Liu-Fu, J. S., 1967, *Neonatal Narcotic Addiction,* U.S. Department of Health, Education and Welfare, Welfare Administration, Children's Bureau, U.S. Government Printing Office, Washington, D.C.

Marmor, J., 1976, Frigidity, dyspareunia and vaginismus, in: *Modern Synopsis of Comprehensive Textbook of Psychiatry II* (A. M. Freedman, H. I. Kaplan, and B. J. Sadock, eds.), pp. 763–765, Williams & Wilkins, Baltimore.

Martin, W. R., 1966, Assessment of the dependence producing potentiality of narcotic analgesics, in: *International Encyclopedia of Pharmacology and Therapeutics,* Vol. 1 (L. Lasagna, ed.), pp. 155–180, Pergamon, New York.

Martin, W. R., 1967, Opioid antagonists, *Pharmacol. Rev.* **19**:463–521.

Martin, W. R., 1977, General problems of drug abuse and drug dependence, in: *Drug Addiction I* (W. R. Martin, ed.), pp. 1–35, Springer-Verlag, Heidelberg.

Martin, W. R., and Fraser, H. F., 1961, A comparative study of physiological and subjective effects of heroin and morphine administered intravenously in postaddicts, *J. Pharmacol. Exp. Ther.* **133**:388–399.

Martin, W. R., and Jasinski, D. R., 1969, Physiological parameters of morphine dependence in man—Tolerance, early abstinence, protracted abstinence, *J. Psychiatr. Res.* **7**:9–17.

Martin, W. R., and Sloan, J. W., 1977, Neuropharmacology and neurochemistry of subjective effects: Analgesia, tolerance and dependence produced by narcotic analgesics, in: *Drug Addiction I* (W. R. Martin, ed.), pp. 43–158, Springer-Verlag, Heidelberg.

Martin, W. R., Gorodetzky, C. W., and Thompson, W. O., 1972, Receptor dualism, some kinetic implications, in: *Agonist and Antagonist Actions of Narcotic Analgesic Drugs* (H. W. Kosterlitz, H. O. J. Collier, and J. E. Villarreal, eds.) pp. 30–44, Macmillan, New York.

Martin, W. R., Jasinski, D. R., Haertzen, C. A., Kay, D. C., Jones, B. E., Mansky, P. A., and Carpenter, R. W., 1973, Methadone—a re-evaluation, *Arch. Gen. Psychiatry* **28**:286–295.

Martin, W. R., Eades, C. G., Thompson, J. A., Huppler, R. E., and Gilbert, P. E., 1976, The effects of morphine- and nalorphine-like drugs in the non-dependent and morphine-dependent chronic spinal dog, *J. Pharmacol. Exp. Ther.* **197**:517–532.

Martin, W. R., Hewett, B. B., Baker, A. J., and Haertzen, C. A., 1977, Aspects of the psychopathology and pathophysiology of addiction, *Drug Alcohol Depend.* **2**:185–202.

McDonald, R. K., Evans, F. T., Weise, V. K., and Patrick, R. W., 1959, Effect of morphine and nalorphine on plasma hydrocortisione levels in man, *J. Pharmacol. Exp. Ther.* **125**:241–247.

Mendelson, J. H., and Mello, N. K., 1975, Plasma testosterone levels during chronic heroin use and protracted abstinence, a study of Hong Kong addicts, *Clin. Pharmacol. Ther.* **17**:529–533.

Mendelson, J. H., Mendelson, J. E., and Patch, V. D., 1975a, Plasma testosterone levels in heroin addiction and during methadone maintenance, *J. Pharmacol. Exp. Ther.* **192**:211–217.

Mendelson, J. H., Meyer, R. E., Ellingboe, J., Mirin, S. M., and McDougle, M., 1975b, Effects of heroin and methadone on plasma cortisol and testosterone, *J. Pharmacol. Exp. Ther.* **195**:296–302.

Myers, H. B., 1931, The effect of chronic morphine poisoning upon growth: The oestrous cycle and fertility of the white rat, *J. Pharmacol. Exp. Ther.* **41**:317–323.

Naeye, R. L., Blanc, W., LeBlanc, W., Khatamee, M. A., 1973, Fetal complications of maternal heroin addiction: Abnormal growth, infection and episodes of stress, *J. Pediatr.* **83**:1055–1061.

O'Donnell, J. A., 1969, *Narcotic Addicts in Kentucky*, Public Health Service, Publication No. 1881.

Olson, R. W., 1964, MMPI sex differences in narcotic addicts, *J. Gen. Psychol.* **71**:257–266.

Packman, P. M., and Rothchild, J. A., 1976, Morphine inhibition of ovulation: Reversal by naloxone, *Endocrinology* **99**:7–10.

Pang, C. N., Zimmermann, E., and Sawyer, C., 1974, Effects of morphine on the proestrous surge of luteinizing hormone in the rat, *Anat. Rec.* **178**:434.

Perlmutter, J. F., 1967, Drug addiction in pregnant women, *Am. J. Obstet. Gynecol.* **99**:569–572.

Reddy, A. M., Harper, R. G., and Stern, G., 1971, Observations on heroin and methadone withdrawal in the newborn, *Pediatrics* **48**:353–358.

Reier, C. E., George, J. M., and Kilman, J. W., 1973, Cortisol and growth hormone response to surgical stress during morphine anesthesia, *Anesth. Analg.* **52**:1003–1009.

Rementería, J. L., and Nunag, N. N., 1973, Narcotic withdrawal in pregnancy stillbirth incidence with a case report, *Am. J. Obstet. Gynecol.* **116**:1152–1156.

Rivier, C., Vale W., Ling, N., Brown, M., and Guillemin, R., 1977, Stimulation *in vivo* of the secretion of prolactin and growth hormone by β endorphine, *Endocrinology* **100:**238–241.

Rosenthal, T., Patrick, S. W., and Krug, D. C., 1964, Congenital neonatal narcotics addiction: A natural history, *Am. J. Public Health* **54:**1252–1262.

Sachar, E. J., 1978, Neuroendocrine Responses to Psychotropic Drugs, in: *Psychopharmacology: A Generation of Progress* (M. A. Lipton, A. DiMascio, and K. F. Killam, eds.), Raven, New York.

Santen, R. J., and Bilic, N., 1973, *Proceedings of the 55th Annual Meeting of the Endocrine Society*, A-112.

Santen, R. J., Sofsky, J., Bilic, N., and Lippert, R., 1975, Mechanism of action of narcotics in the production of menstrual dysfunction in women, *Fertil. Steril.* **26:**538–548.

Sapira, J. D., 1968, The narcotic addict as a medical patient, *Am. J. Med.* **45:**555–588.

Simon, M., George, R., and Garcia, J., 1975, Acute morphine effects on regional brain amines, growth hormone and cortisterone, *Eur. J. Pharmacol.* **34:**21–26.

Simpson, D. D., Savage, L. J., Joe, G. W., Demaree, R. G., and Sells, S. B., 1976, DARP Data book, *Statistics on Characteristics of Drug Users in Treatment during 1969–1974*. Institute of Behavioral Research Report 76-4, Texas Christian University, Fort Worth.

Sloan, J. W., 1971, Corticosteroid hormones, in: *Narcotic Drugs Biochemical Pharmacology* (D. H. Clovet, ed.), pp. 262–282, Plenum, New York.

Stern, R., 1966, The pregnant addict: A study of 66 case histories, 1950–1959, *Am. J. Obstet. Gynecol.* **94:**253–257.

Stoffer, S. S., 1968, A gynecologic study of drug addicts, *Am. J. Obstet. Gynecol.* **101:**779–783.

Taeusch, H. W., Carson, S. H., Wang, N. S., and Avery, M. E., 1973, Heroin induction of lung maturation and growth retardation in fetal rabbits. *J. Pediatr.* **82:**869–875.

Terry, C. E., and Pellens, M., 1928, *The Opium Problem*, Patterson Smith, Montclair, New Jersey, Bureau of Social Hygiene, Inc. (Reprinted 1970.)

Thomas, J. A., Shahid-Salles, K. S., and Donovan, M. P., 1977, Effects of narcotics on the reproductive system, *Adv. Sex Horm. Res.* **3:**169–195.

Tolis, G., Hickey, J., and Guyda, H., 1975, Effects of morphine on serum growth hormone, cortisol, prolactin and thyroid stimulating hormone in man, *J. Clin. Endocrinol. Metab.* **41:**797–800.

Vinchow, A., and Hackel A., 1960, Neonatal narcotic addiction, *GP* **22:**90–93.

Wallach, R., Jerez, E., and Blinik, G., 1969, Pregnancy and menstrual function in narcotic addicts treated with methadone, the methadone maintenance treatment program, *Am. J. Obstet. Gynecol.* **105:**1226–1229.

Wikler, A., 1975, Drug dependence, in: *Clinical Neurology* (B. Baker and L. H. Baker, eds.), pp. 1–61, Harper & Row, Hagerstown, Md.

Wikler, A., and Frank, K., 1948, Hindlimb reflexes of chronic spinal dogs during cycles of addiction to morphine and methadon, *J. Pharmacol. Exp. Ther.* **94:**382–400.

Wilson, G. S., Desmond, M. M., and Verniaud, W. M., 1973, Early development of infants of heroin-addicted mothers, *Am. J. Dis. Child.* **126:**457–462.

Woodruff, R. A., Goodwin, D. W., and Guze, S. B., 1974, *Psychiatric Diagnosis,* Oxford University Press, New York.

Zelson, C., and Green, M., 1977, Progeny and drug abuse, in: *Drug Abuse Clinical and Basic Aspects* (S. N. Pradhan and S. N. Dutta, eds.), pp. 430–451, C. V. Mosby, St. Louis.

Zelson, C., Rubio, E., and Wasserman, E., 1971, Neonatal narcotic addiction: 10 year observation, *Pediatrics* **48:**178–189.

Zelson, C., Lee, S. J., and Casalino, M., 1973, Neonatal narcotic addiction comparative effects of maternal intake of heroin and methadone, *N. Engl. J. Med.* **289:**1216–1220.

14

Problems Related to the Use of Tobacco by Women

ELLEN R. GRITZ

1. INTRODUCTION

The use of tobacco by women is as old as the history of tobacco itself, long antedating its "discovery" by 15th- and 16th-century explorers of the Americas. In Western society today, women are fast approaching men in the rate of initiation and prevalence of tobacco use. After several centuries of fluctuating use patterns, this trend began in the 1920s under the strong influence of radically altered social and cultural patterns. The health risks and attendant early mortality introduced by smoking, which were formerly primarily restricted to the male sex, are now appearing among females. Additional interactive risk factors that occur only in women, such as oral contraceptive use, further complicate the potential health risks of smoking in that sex. Of concern to all involved with the public health problem posed by tobacco use, primarily cigarette smoking, is the poor record of attempts at cessation of smoking. While the epidemiological literature points to a growing discontinuance pattern in the U.S. population as a whole, the results of treatment programs aiming at cessation of smoking are disappointing, especially for the long term. There are many suggestions from both nationwide surveys and cessation studies that a smaller proportion of women than men are quitting. The interpretation of this finding is complicated by several demographic variables, such as history of cigarette use, socioeconomic status, and age.

The aim of this chapter is to provide an analysis of tobacco use among women, with comparative reference to men in the principal areas

ELLEN R. GRITZ • Veterans Administration Medical Center Brentwood; and Department of Psychiatry, University of California, Los Angeles, California.

just outlined. These include anthropological and historical trends, epidemiological surveys, psychological and physiological factors, health risks, pregnancy, and smoking cessation.

2. ANTHROPOLOGICAL AND HISTORICAL SURVEY OF TOBACCO USE

> The gods and spirits, it is widely held, crave tobacco smoke so intensely that they are unable to resist it. . . . Just as the tobacco shaman of the Warao requires tobacco smoke with tremendous physiological and psychological urgency, and is literally sick without it, so the gods await their gift of tobacco smoke with the craving of the addict, and will enter into mutually beneficial relationships with man so long as he is able to provide the drug. . . . No wonder that in the indigenous world tobacco was considered too sacred for secular or purely hedonistic use. (Wilbert, 1975, pp. 455–457)

Cross-Cultural Survey

The use of tobacco in the New World most likely antedates Columbus by thousands of years and was traditionally largely confined to magicoreligious purposes (Wilbert, 1975; Furst, 1976). In pre-European times, domesticated tobacco had a broad distribution in the Americas. Of the two principal cultivated species of tobacco, *Nicotiana rustica* and *Nicotiana tabacum,* the former achieved a far wider geographical dispersion, perhaps as much because of its considerably higher nicotine content as because of its ease of cultivation. The latter species is our common commercial tobacco. The higher nicotine content of *N. rustica* may be significant because of its use as a ritual narcostimulant, especially in South America. Since the advent of the European explorers, the use and cultivation of tobacco have continued to spread throughout the Americas, "so that today there is virtually no native population, from Canada to Patagonia, that does not know or use tobacco" (Wilbert, 1975, p. 441). The discussion of the ritual use of tobacco that follows derives from Wilbert's excellent summary.

In modern times, tobacco is ingested by smoking (cigarettes, cigars, or pipes), chewing, snuffing, drinking, and licking. Drinking tobacco is probably the most ancient form of use. It is prepared in liquid form by boiling or steeping in water or by maceration in spittle. It is then drunk, taken through the nose, or licked from fingers or a stick dipped in the liquid. The concentrated form is so potent that toxic effects of nicotine (e.g., pallor and tremor) are usually apparent after only two or three doses. Repeated ingestion of large doses induces extreme nausea, vomiting, a comatose state, and intensive dream visions. Both male and female shamans use tobacco in this fashion, as do individuals during certain rituals such as initiations. Among the Jivaro Indians of the Montaña region in South America, there is a four-day tobacco feast that has as its purpose the initiation of the girl into adulthood via intervention of the tobacco spirit. Through dance, chanting, and the imbibing of large quantities of tobacco water, a trance state is achieved, during which she converses with the Earth Mother and receives a promise of fertility and long life.

Space does not permit extensive illustration of the ritual use of tobacco, but in all modes of ingestion, it figured prominently in ceremonies surrounding important social or milestone life events, healing, divining, and purification. It was used by men, women, and even children in some cultures. Tobacco was taken by itself or in combination with hallucinogens such as *Coca datura, Banisteriopsis caapi (yahuasca),* or the cactus *Trichocereus pachanoi.* In summary, prior to the epoch of European exploration, tobacco was employed in South American cultures and in the Caribbean primarily as a psychotropic but also as a medicinal and hygienic agent. In the centuries following the exploratory voyages, the geographical diffusion of tobacco has been associated with a secularization and "profanation" of its use.

In North America, tobacco use was similarly associated originally with shamanistic practice, which was open to both men and women. Pipe and tobacco were frequently part of the ritual paraphernalia of the shaman. The sharing of a pipe with members of the community was considered crucial to the success of healing in a curing rite of the Paviotso tribe (Park, 1938).

Tobacco is an integral part of the folk medicine of many cultures and has been described, to cite only a few examples, for the cultures of the New World Indians (DeLucas, 1968), Asia (Laufer, 1924b), and the Ohio Valley in the United States (Thompson, 1960). The curative powers ascribed to tobacco range from topical application for boils to ingestion to counteract cholera and reduce the swelling associated with dropsy. The popularity of tobacco in this context is most ironic in light of the fact that it is considered a health menace today.

Enterprising sailors caused the use of tobacco to spread around the world in 200 years by introducing it to local populations who were eager to sample and cultivate it. Special implements were designed to optimize absorption, such as the water pipe in Asia and the bamboo tube pipe of New Guinea (Laufer, 1924b; Lewis, 1924). In all of these cultures, men, women, and often children ingested tobacco. Although there were variations in the mode of ingestion associated with each sex, no sex-associated prohibitions of tobacco use have been reported. A most curious form of intake known as *reverse smoking* is chiefly found among elderly women of lower socioeconomic groups in the Caribbean region, although it has been described among males in Sardinia and India as well (Haneveld, 1965; Quigley et al., 1966). The cigarette is held between the teeth, with lit end inside the mouth, and lips sealed around the rod. Moisture from the lips produces a ring around the cigarette, which slows its burning time; butts are frequently smoked to the end and ashes swallowed. The origin and purpose of this custom are unidentified, but it may be considered a means of maximizing smoke intake and therefore nicotine effects. Since this practice is not popular among the young, it may die out in the near future. As another example of local tobacco practices popular among women, the aged "grannies" of southern Appalachia commonly smoke pipes (Thompson, 1960).

This review should serve to underscore the widespread popularity of tobacco in every culture that has been exposed to it. Although modes of ingestion may differ widely, they have the common purpose of optimizing the delivery of nicotine, the principal alkaloid, to the bloodstream and the brain. The attribution of supernatural forces to tobacco and its magicoreligious use further suggest the importance of central nervous system effects leading to altered states of consciousness, perhaps in conjunction with botanical hallucinogens. Men and women shared in the ritual and, later, secular use of tobacco in most or all cultures. It is of particular interest to review the history of tobacco use in Western society because this society's level of permissiveness toward use by women has fluctuated widely.

Historical Survey: Western Culture

Tobacco was first sampled by the early explorers, Columbus, Verrazzano, and Cartier. The seeds of the plant were brought to France and cultivated by Andrew de Thevet in 1556 or 1557. A few years later, in 1565, John Hawkins brought tobacco to England, and Sir Walter Raleigh and Thomas Hariot were instrumental in popularizing its use by providing the native Virginia clay pipe (Morison, 1971). Elizabethan England eagerly adopted tobacco, even though Queen Elizabeth herself and her successor, King James I, opposed its use. Both men and women used tobacco; the pipe was more popular in England and snuff in Ireland, Scotland, and Spain (Laufer, 1924a). The use of tobacco rapidly spread to all of western Europe, and, indeed, around the world, despite the efforts of various kings and popes to halt it.

Tobacco seems to have been adopted as a prophylactic and therapeutic agent for the plague in the mid-17th century; men, women, and children used it for this purpose, either by smoking or chewing (Laufer, 1924a). Tobacco chewing never became popular in Europe and was later regarded as a distinctly American, filthy custom (Robert, 1952).

United States: Colonial Times to World War II. With the exception of the Puritans, many of the early colonists adopted the Indian customs of smoking if they were not already familiar with them from Europe. New England colonial women reputedly smoked while kneading their bread, cooking, and lying in bed, and western frontier women were said to puff on pipes while nursing (Heimann, 1960). The wives of Presidents Andrew Jackson and Zachary Taylor both smoked pipes (Robert, 1952). Tobacco was also snuffed, dipped, and chewed. Chewing was the main form of tobacco use between 1800 and 1850 in the United States but was primarily practiced by men. There are some fascinating descriptions of snuff dipping, also referred to as *digging,* among women of both upper and lower classes (Lander, 1885; Robert, 1952). The following is a 19th-century account of this practice:

> The female snuff-dipper takes a short stick, and wetting it with her saliva, dips it into her snuff-box, and then rubs the gathered dust all around her mouth, and into the interstices of her teeth, where she allows it to remain until its strength has been fully absorbed. Others hold the stick thus loaded with snuff in the cheek, a la quid of tobacco, and suck it with a decided relish, while engaged in their ordinary avocations; while others simply fill the mouth with the snuff, and imitate, to all intents and purposes, the chewing propensities of the men. (Robert, 1952, p. 102)

With the trend toward urbanization, and the accompanying shift in the role of the female, tobacco use seems to have dropped off among women before the Civil War. Cigarettes (i.e., "small cigars") were introduced around this time and were initially termed effeminate because of their weaker quality (Robert, 1952; Heimann, 1960). They did become popular with some urban ladies, but cigarette smoking developed slowly and was inspired mainly by the British.

Between the Civil War and World War I, tobacco use was confined mainly to adult males, but there were still many groups of women using it. Mountain women smoked pipes, bohemian ladies smoked small cigars, "genteel maidens" smoked cigarettes, and New England factory girls used snuff (Robert, 1952). It is also likely that many women of all classes used tobacco surreptitiously.

One of the violently antitobacco authors of the late 19th century (who also happened to be a woman) described the widespread use of snuff in all classes in southern society and even among upper-class women in New York City (Lander, 1885). The antitobacco crusade apparently had its heyday prior to the Civil War, but some staunch advocates continued their battles relentlessly (Robert, 1952). Lander (1885) went so far as to claim, "Tobacco is the relentless foe of woman. It withdraws man from her society, and makes him glory in his isolation, thus greatly marring, if not positively undermining, the relation between the sexes" (p. 178).

Nevertheless, smoking gradually increased in popularity, while the practice of tobacco chewing peaked around 1890, declining thereafter because of stricter laws regarding spitting. Cigarette smoke became more inhalable with the introduction of flue curing (Virginia type or Bright tobacco). The development of the "blended" cigarette in 1913, a mixture of air-cured Burley and Turkish tobacco and the flue-cured Virginia, provided ease of inhalation with pleasing flavor and aroma. The stage was set for wide-scale adoption of cigarettes by women (Wagner, 1971).

The years between 1915 and 1930 determined the course of smoking for women in America. Irene and Vernon Castle, popularizers of such dances as the tango, the Castle walk, and the turkey trot, also popularized the use of the automobile among young people. This soon became the setting for much of the liberal behavior of the day: smoking, drinking, and petting (Lewine, 1970). Rebellion, romance, and emancipation became the theme of cigarette advertising from 1919 on. Women gained the vote and the exuberant liberalism of the "flapper" in the Roaring Twenties. Finally, in 1927–1929 George Washington Hill, of the American Tobacco Company, in his cigarette advertising campaign openly confronted the American public with the fact that American women were smoking (Robert, 1952; Lewine, 1970). He solicited testimonials for his cigarettes from famous American actresses and European opera singers, as well as from the famous aviatrix Amelia Earhart. His famous slogan, "Reach for a Lucky instead of a sweet," brought down the wrath of the confectioners, some of whom retaliated by refusing to sell cigarettes, and the confectionery industry filed a complaint with the Federal Trade Commission. The FTC issued a warning that cigarettes were not to be sold as weight-reducing devices. Other forms of advertisement were immediately developed. Whether as a result of the bold advertising campaigns or as part of the tenor of the times, women began to smoke openly in cities and towns in this decade. In 1930, the estimated percentage of female smokers of 18 years and over was 2% of the adult population. This figure rose steadily to a peak of 39% in 1961 (Burbank, 1972).

Antitobacco forces continued to wage their battle in intermittent bursts. During the period between 1885 and 1909, tobacco was alleged to put mustaches on women and to cause insanity. In the 1920s, additional medical problems were cited, and women were fired from jobs and expelled from schools for smoking publicly. An attempt was made to pass a bill prohibiting women from smoking in public in the District of Columbia. By 1929, however, the opposition had largely subsided, and women were permitted to smoke in some colleges, such as Bryn Mawr, although certain schools, among them the Women's Medical College of Pennsylvania and Swarthmore College, had not yet permitted open smoking (Robert, 1952; Boucot, 1968).

By the 1940s, one-fifth of American women and almost two-thirds of American men smoked (Burbank, 1972). During World War II, the demand for cigarettes for the troops was so great that some women apparently switched temporarily to pipes (Robert, 1952). This chronology brings us to the beginnings of systematic surveys of the smoking habits of the adult population, to which we now turn.

3. CURRENT PATTERNS OF TOBACCO USE IN THE UNITED STATES

In this section, recent patterns of tobacco use among women are summarized for the United States. The most recent report of the Royal College of Physicians (1977) discusses epidemiological data for the United Kingdom. Epidemiological surveys have been conducted in the United States since 1955, when Haenszel et al. (1956) adopted the Current Population Survey of the U.S. Bureau of the Census. A second current population survey was similarly conducted in 1966 by the Bureau of the Census (Ahmed and Gleeson, 1970). Utilizing a private opinion survey service, the National Clearinghouse for Smoking and Health (NCSH) made national surveys of the adult population in 1964, 1966, 1970, and 1975. Finally, nationwide surveys of teenage (ages 12–18) smoking patterns have been carried out every two years since 1968 by the NCSH (U.S. Department of Health, Education, and Welfare—USDHEW, 1976b).

Initiation and Recruitment

The initiation of smoking in the teenage or preteenage years is social in origin. It is a response to modeling pressures related to peer and parental behaviors as well as media influences that associate smoking with popularity, maturity, and sexuality (USDHEW, 1976b; Salber et al., 1963; Bewley et al., 1974). Other social factors bearing a relationship to smoking recruitment include social class, performance in school, and alcohol ingestion (Salber and Abelin, 1967; McKennell and Thomas, 1967; Russell, 1971). That is, more smoking occurs in the lower socioeconomic classes, among low-achieving students, and in those who drink more alcohol. Perhaps the most important finding of the 1968–1974 surveys is that the smoking habits of teenage girls are changing drastically (see Figs. 1 and 2; USDHEW, 1976b). They are catching up to their male counterparts with alarming speed. There has been a dramatic increase in the number of girl smokers, across age groups and as a function of time. While teenage boys show increased recruitment to smoking as they become older, the percentage of smokers did not change within each age group between surveys. In parallel fashion, diminishing proportions of teenagers in each age group, and in each survey, remained nonsmokers. Girls showed a continuous decrease in "never-smokers," but boys

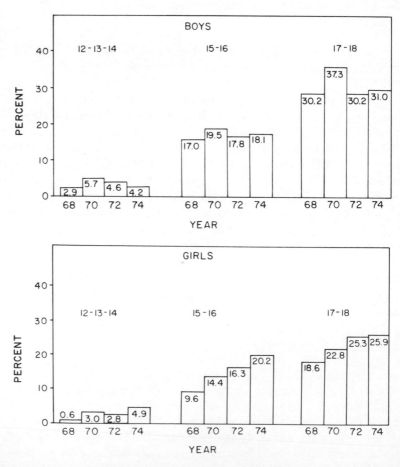

Fig. 1. Percentage of current regular smokers—teenage, 1968–1974. *Source:* U.S. Department of Health, Education, and Welfare, Public Health Service. Patterns and prevalence of teenage cigarette smoking: 1968, 1970, 1972, and 1974. DHEW Publication No. (CDC) 75-8701.

exhibited stable onset patterns, similar to those of current smoking prevalence. The overall change in regular smoking in teenagers, which has increased eight times over from 4% in 1968 to 32% in 1974, is almost entirely due to increased smoking among teenage girls.

The changing patterns of smoking in teenage girls and young women were further explored in an extensive research project conducted in 1975 for the American Cancer Society (ACS) by a survey opinion corporation (USDHEW, 1977). Teenage girls between 13 and 17 years of age and young women between 18 and 35 years of age were found to have similar smoking habits. While the major increase in incidence of smoking is in

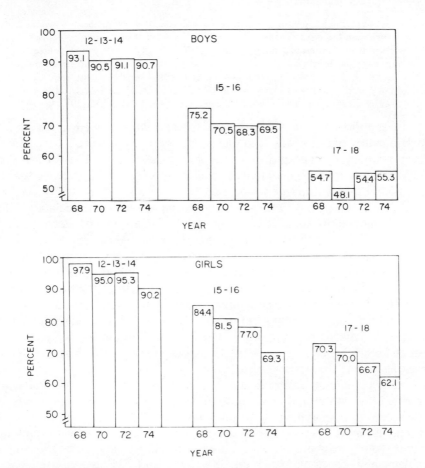

Fig. 2. Teenage cigarette smoking—never smoked or experimented only, 1968–1974. *Source:* U.S. Department of Health, Education, and Welfare, Public Health Service. Patterns and prevalence of teenage cigarette smoking: 1968, 1970, 1972, and 1974. DHEW Publication No. (CDC) 75-8701.

the teenage group—the proportion of young women smokers rising only 2% in 10 years—there has been a sharp increment in the proportion of heavy smokers in both groups. Only 10% of teenage girl smokers smoked at least a pack a day in 1969, compared with 39% in 1975; among young women smokers, the figures increased from 51% in 1965 to 61% in 1975. The smoking habits of teenage boys did not similarly increase.

The dynamics cited for this intensification of smoking behaviors include a ubiquitous smoking environment, the demise of antismoking commercials on television, the evolution of social norms, and a corresponding set of new values that encourage freedom of behavior and rebelliousness. The authors state,

> In general, the teen-age girls have been more influenced by the new youth values than the boys. These "New Values," originally generated by college youth in the sixties and now permeating the majority of all young people, represent the breakdown of previous moral norms and are characterized by the rejection of authority, emphasis on emotional rather than the rational, freer sexual morality, a strong accent on self and self-fulfillment, the acceptance of illegal drugs and a more informal life style. (USDHEW, 1977, p. 9)

In support of these factors, the researchers supplied a wealth of questionnaire data, which can be only briefly highlighted here. In a comparison of teenage girl smokers with nonsmokers, the former are found to be more self-confident, socially and sexually experienced, and rebellious against authority. The smokers are also more likely to use alcohol and marijuana. The peer and parental factors associated with teenage smoking in the NCSH surveys (USDHEW, 1976b) were verified and expanded: two-thirds of the teenage girl smokers reported that at least 50% of their friends smoked, compared with one-third of teenage girl nonsmokers; almost three-fourths of the smoking girls have boyfriends who smoke, compared with about one-fourth of the nonsmokers. The NCSH surveys reported a much smaller likelihood that a teenager will smoke if no one smokes in the household than if a parent or a sibling smokes. Furthermore, smoking is even more common in single- or no-parent homes, a finding very likely associated with the higher rate of smoking among divorced adults.

Young women smokers in the ACS study were found to be similar to teenage girls with regard to smoking friends. Interesting findings emerged with regard to employment status and the women's movement in the 18 to 35-year group. It has been hypothesized that the increase in heavy smoking among young women is related to increased employment. (For both smokers and nonsmokers, about 38% work and 62% are housewives.) However, it was found that in the age range 18–35, housewives smoke more heavily than employed women. Of the housewives who smoke, 66%—and only 53% of the working women—smoke a pack a day or more.

Finally, identification with the women's movement was equally common among smokers and nonsmokers (approximately 70%).

The overall conclusion to be drawn from these analyses of smoking in teenage and young adult women is that cigarette smoking habits are more and more approaching those of similarly aged males. Parallel trends exist in the United Kingdom (McKennell and Thomas, 1967; Russell, 1971; Royal College of Physicians, 1977) and probably in other Western nations as well. The social forces identified with these trends are less associated with any formal identification with a movement specific to females, such as the women's movement, than with a value system encompassing changing social norms for all youth. The precise relationships of the shift in smoking patterns to other demographic variables, such as education, family income, and marital status, will probably be in a state of flux in the recent future and will bear watching. These relationships have been carefully worked out for the adult population but are admittedly less clear for women than for men, undoubtedly because of the greater evolution in the social role of the female in the second half of this century. It is at this point that an examination of recent adult smoking patterns in the United States becomes pertinent.

Prevalence

In the adult population, there has been a gradual decline between 1964 and 1975 in the percentage of males who are current smokers, but there has been very little change among women (Schuman, 1978) (see Table 1). Up to 1970, men were initiating smoking at a constant rate but discontinuing at an accelerated rate, thus lowering the percentage of current smokers. Women, on the other hand, were increasing in rate of

Table 1. Distribution of Classes of Cigarette Smokers Aged 21 Years and Over According to Sex: Four Surveys of the National Clearinghouse for Smoking and Health

Year of Survey	Percentages by class of smoker and sex							
	Never		Ever[a]		Former[a]		Current[a]	
	Male	Female	Male	Female	Male	Female	Male	Female
1964	24.9	61.1	75.1	38.9	22.2	7.4	52.9	31.5
1966	24.5	56.8	75.5	43.2	23.6	9.5	51.9	33.7
1970	25.1	54.7	74.9	45.3	32.6	14.8	42.3	30.5
1975	31.5	56.6	68.5	43.4	29.2	14.5	39.3	28.9

[a] The percentage under "Ever" is the sum of those under "Former" and "Current" for the same sex and year.

initiation as well as in rate of discontinuance, but the balance was such that current smoking prevalence remained relatively constant. In 1975, the pattern had changed: though slightly fewer males had ceased smoking, even fewer males had started, so that the proportion of current smokers had dropped. Among women, there was a slight decrease in those beginning to smoke and virtually no change in the percentage of former smokers, resulting in a slight decline in the proportion of current smokers. Smoking discontinuance patterns are further discussed in the section dealing with cessation.

A graphic presentation of smoking prevalence by age and sex (Fig. 3) reveals the previously mentioned recent increase (1970–1975) in smoking among young women in the age group 21–24. However, smoking declined among women 25–54 years of age. Schuman (1978) pointed out that the apparent increase in smoking among women in the 55- to 64-year age

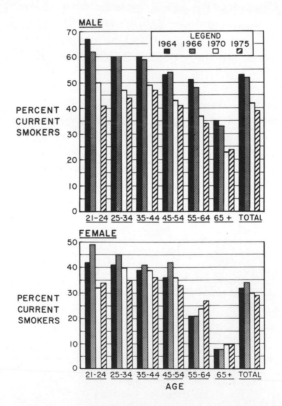

Fig. 3. Proportion of smokers in the adult population, according to age, 1964–1975, *Source:* U.S. Department of Health, Education, and Welfare, Public Health Service. Adult use of tobacco: 1975. Center for Disease Control and National Cancer Institute, June 1976.

range is a cohort effect, a residual of the actual increase in smoking in the 45- to 54-year age range reported in 1966. It was in this age group that the greatest increase in smokers occurred in the time period between 1955 and 1966, although the age of smoking onset was decreasing for all age groups of women (Ahmed and Gleeson, 1970; Schuman, 1978).

Demographic Factors

There are a number of other demographic factors on which men and women differ with relation to smoking patterns. These are summarized only for the most current national survey (USDHEW, 1976a).

Marital Status. Approximately the same percentage of married and single males smoked (38%), but slightly more single (31%) than married women (28%) smoked. Among the divorced or separated, a staggering 60% of males and 50% of females smoked. On the other hand, only 19% of widowed women smoked, a finding that is very likely associated with the lower smoking rates of older women in general.

Socioeconomic Status. The variables of educational level, occupational class, and family income are all considered aspects of socioeconomic status (SES). For both men and women, number of years of *education* was inversely related to prevalence of smoking, except in the group that only attended grade school, which had fewer smokers. Since the latter group had lower purchasing power, there may have been an interaction between education and income.

The *occupational data* reveal opposite trends for men and women. Smoking prevalence was lowest among male white-collar workers (36%) compared with all other occupational classes (47%), while more female white-collar workers (34%) smoked than all other groups (32%). In the category of professional–technical workers, however, only 26% of women and 31% of men were current smokers. Of the 40% of women working outside the home, 33% smoked, compared with 27% of housewives.

A survey of smoking habits in health professionals conducted in 1975 revealed noticeably lower prevalence rates for physicians, dentists, and pharmacists than for the overall population of adult males: in 1975, 21%, 23%, and 28% of members of these professions, respectively, smoked, compared with 39% of adult males (USDHEW 1976c). Nurses, on the other hand, smoked more than other working female adults (39% versus 34%). A survey of psychologists at California State University and Colleges reported parallel findings (Dicken and Bryson, 1978). Women psychologists were significantly more likely to smoke than male colleagues. Also, rate of smoking in male psychologists (28%) was slightly higher than in male health professionals and was approximately the same for women psychologists (38%) as for nurses. Since current smoking prevalence was substantially lower among the category of professional women in general, this finding raises the question of what specific factors may increase smoking among certain groups of female professionals. Issues of power, competitiveness, and striving for equality in status have been cited (Dicken and Bryson, 1978).

The relationship of smoking prevalence to *family income* was similar to that of occupation. Among men, smoking prevalence was inversely related to income: 35% of men in families with incomes of $20,000 or more and 46% of men with incomes of $7500–$10,000 smoked. However, there was a direct relationship between income and smoking prevalence in women: 34% of women in families with incomes over $20,000 smoked, compared with 26% in the $5000–$7500 bracket. The family income analysis is complicated by the inability to separate one-income from two-income homes and by the relationship between smoking and marital status, which is not parceled out here.

Thus, two of the three socioeconomic variables point to the same finding, that female smoking was more prevalent with higher SES, while men showed the opposite trend. Since a college education is probably a prerequisite to a job classified as professional, the low smoking rates for men and women in that category accorded with the education analysis. This statement is subject to the qualification regarding subgroups of professionals discussed above and to the changing smoking patterns among teenage and young adult women.

Tobacco Consumption

There are several other variables from the NCSH surveys related to the smoking practices of men and women that deserve mention (Schuman, 1978; USDHEW, 1976a). Beginning with an average of 17.7 cigarettes per day in 1955, intake in men remained constant at approximately 22 cigarettes per day in the 1964–1975 surveys. Female intake, which was 13.0 cigarettes per day in 1955, remained at approximately 18 between 1966 and 1970 and had risen slightly to 18.8 in 1975. Both men and women, however, reported a continuous decrease in depth of inhalation; yet in 1975, 65.2% of men and 44.1% of women still reported inhaling cigarettes either deeply or partly into the chest. Regarding type of cigarette smoked, the 1975 survey reported that more women than men smoked filter-tip cigarettes (all types), 90.6% versus 79.3%. Women seem to be innovators in changing smoking practices. Sixty-one percent of women and only 10% of men reported changing brands at least once, and women led the trend in adopting king-size filter-tip and 100-mm cigarettes. On the other hand, women seemed to be almost exclusively cigarette smokers. Cigars and pipes were currently used by 18% and 25%

of men, respectively, but by only 0.5% of women. Only 1% of women used snuff and chewing tobacco, versus 3% and 5% of men, respectively. The "liberation" of the American female with regard to cigarette smoking has not spread to other forms of tobacco use except among very limited populations.

In this section, an attempt has been made to summarize recent trends in smoking among teenage and adult Americans. The demographic and temporal relationships are complex and point to different trends in incidence and prevalence among men and women. The principal finding of increased smoking in the female population is due to a number of converging factors in the social, political, economic, and psychological realms.

4. PHYSIOLOGICAL AND PSYCHOLOGICAL FACTORS IN SMOKING

The Physiological Response to Nicotine

Nicotine is the only active alkaloid in tobacco and is responsible for a host of profound pharmacological changes attendant on smoking. Human and animal research in this area is reviewed in a former contribution to this series of volumes and in several other works (Russell, 1976; Larson and Silvette, 1975; Gritz and Jarvik, 1978; Volle and Koelle, 1975). Only the briefest summary is presented here.

In man, nicotine has direct effects on the central and autonomic nervous systems and indirectly on almost every organ in the body. It has biphasic, dose-dependent stimulant and depressant actions in the autonomic nervous system, mimicking the neurotransmitter acetylcholine at neuromuscular junctions, in autonomic ganglia, and at postganglionic autonomic effectors. It is likely to have similar actions in the central nervous system, although the stimulant effect predominates. In the brain, nicotine is thought to act both at the level of the cerebral cortex and on subcortical structures, and it has been shown to produce electroencephalographic changes with acute and chronic administration and on withdrawal. Nicotinic stimulation of the reticular activating system, critical in regulating arousal, and of the hippocampus, which is implicated in learning, has been of particular interest. Effects on mood have yet to be clearly elucidated. Other central nervous system actions of nicotine include the production of tremor and convulsions, respiratory excitation, vomiting, cardiovascular responses, and antidiuresis. Major organ systems affected by smoking via central and/or peripheral pathways are the cardiovascular, respiratory, gastrointestinal, and musculoskeletal.

The neuroendocrine response is also quite important; for example, nicotine stimulates both adrenal medullary and adrenal cortical activity, resulting in the release of catecholamines and corticosteroids. One consequence of the release of the catecholamine epinephrine is an increase in free fatty acids in the blood, and a second is elevation of heart rate and blood pressure. There is some suggestion that males show greater neuroendocrine stress reactions (increased adrenal activity and catecholamine secretion) than females (Frankenhaeuser, 1977; Frankenhaeuser et al., 1978). In these same studies, females reported more discomfort and dissatisfaction concerning their behavior in a stressful situation than did males, even though achievement was equal. These findings may be relevant to the relationship between personality dynamics and smoking behavior in the two sexes, since women more frequently report smoking while experiencing negative affect than do men (see section below). Perhaps smoking serves as a pharmacological prompting mechanism to further mobilize stress reactions for women (Frankenhaeuser, 1978). This hypothesis deserves exploration.

Psychological Factors

There is an enormous literature on personality factors in smoking, which is well summarized in several sources (Smith, 1970; Larson and Silvette, 1975; USDHEW, 1964). Personality measures generally suggest that smokers are more extroverted and antisocial than nonsmokers and may be more impulsive, externally oriented, and "oral" than nonsmokers. The mental health of smokers has been compared with that of nonsmokers with little consensus. There are numerous findings of both equivalent adjustment and poorer mental health in smokers, but none of superior status.

Do personality dynamics in smoking differ for males and females? Several studies suggest that men and women "use" cigarettes differently. Frankenhaueser (1978) has identified a situational component relating to arousal. Men tend to crave cigarettes more in low-arousal situations associated with boredom and fatigue. Women, however, show the greatest desire to smoke in stressful situations. These observations have been related to physiological measures of stress response previously mentioned.

Psychotherapists working with heavy smokers have observed that women smoke to suppress anger, reduce negative affect, and defend against loneliness or rejection; men smoke in response to frustration in relationships with supervisors and wives involving issues of passivity and dependence (Bozzetti, 1972; Tamerin, 1972). Studies of college students yield similar observations; Ikard and Tomkins (1973) reported that significantly more women than men demonstrated solely negative-affect smoking. Female smokers showed significantly more preoccupation over power themes than did male smokers (Fisher, 1976). This effect may be linked to issues surrounding anger over a relative lack of power, competition, and status (cf. Dicken and Bryson, 1978).

Some therapists maintain that teaching people ways to handle negative affect is essential to "curing" smoking (Bozzetti, 1972; Tamerin, 1972; also see Ikard and Tomkins, 1973). Bozzetti and Tamerin, who worked with "hard-core" smokers, recommended intensive analysis of the dynamics of smoking behavior over a relatively long treatment period (10–12 weeks). They stressed dealing with the important issues of fear of failure, fear of loss of control, and the affective significance of giving up smoking. Given the extensive range of situations in which any heavy smoker lights a cigarette—a behavior occurring approximately every 48 minutes for a pack-a-day smoker during a 16-hr day—it is difficult to imagine that the reduction of negative affect could constitute the critical difference between male and female smoking habits and ease of smoking cessation. Yet, on the other hand, a physiological "stress response-mobilization hypothesis" was tentatively offered that might account for increased smoking by women in such situations. Learning alternate means to handle negative feelings may reduce the "desire" to smoke and ease quitting. Again, the possibility should not be ruled out until more data, both clinical and experimental, have been examined.

A Social–Psychological Perspective

An examination of historical, socioeconomic, and political trends adds a further dimension to the analysis of individual dynamics in smoking. The initial section of this chapter reviewed anthropological and historical patterns of tobacco use in women and left no doubt that social forces are extremely important in shaping usage.

The political changes in the 20th century that have given women the vote, that have seen them provide over 40% of the current U.S. labor force, and that have given them economic buying power and growing equality in the educational and professional sphere have similarly made available to them the same stimuli (rewards and punishments) to which men are exposed. Included among these are consumption of alcohol and a variety of "recreational" pharmacological agents, exposure to a host of formerly "male" diseases, and the use of tobacco. The relationship of tobacco use to disease is the subject of the next section of this chapter. American industry has not been loath to capitalize on the emerging female market. Indeed, several brands of cigarettes are aimed specifically at the female sex and are advertised by cleverly devised visual composites and verbal slogans ("You've come a long way, baby"). It was noted previously that women are innovative in trying different brands and styles of cigarettes. Perhaps women are more aware of advertisements suggesting changes in consumer behavior. Thus, social, economic, and political forces are all working in the direction of promoting smoking among females.

It may be expected that unless the public health and antismoking movements are successful in reversing the current trends, smoking will continue to increase among women until rates are close to or identical to those of men. Demographic factors may interact in such a way as to skew or reverse certain relationships (e.g., income), but on the whole, there is no reason to expect a divergence in usage patterns in the future. As the lifestyles of men and women increase in similarity, it will be interesting to reexamine gender differences in the personality dynamics of smoking.

Nicotine as a Reinforcer

Nicotine has been considered by many a drug of dependence. This argument is complicated by semantic issues surrounding definition of the words *dependence, addiction,* and *abstinence syndrome.* Abstinence from nicotine, which is a stimulant, does not produce the classic withdrawal syndromes associated with opiate or barbiturate use. Many individuals claim to be able to quit suddenly without any dysphoria even after regular heavy intake. The issue is puzzling, as there are also widely documented reports of severe dysphoria and physiological changes after cessation of smoking (see Section 7 for references). The psychiatric establishment has recently decided that the continued use of tobacco by individuals who wish to give it up but are unable to, or who are suffering severe physical illness in conjunction with its use, will be termed a *tobacco use syndrome.* This terminology appears in the third edition of the *Diagnostic and Statistical Manual of Mental Disorders* (Jaffe and Jarvik, 1978).

The thrust of this discussion is to underline the powerful reinforcing actions of nicotine. A number of investigators have attempted to demonstrate nicotine titration, or self-regulation, in smokers (see reviews by Russell, 1976; Gritz and Jarvik, 1978). To date, nicotine has been shown to affect, but not entirely control, smoking intake. The principal explanation has been the role of secondary reinforcing factors associated with cigarette or tobacco use, such as lighting and handling and oral, visual, and social stimulus connections. This field of study is extremely active at the present time.

To return to the theme of smoking patterns in men and women, the powerful reinforcing effects of nicotine suggest that its intake would be regulated by pharmacological and physiological principles of action that, on the whole, do not differ in men and women. History of use, dose, tolerance, and sensitivity may affect the potential for nicotine to act as a reinforcer, but the epidemiological data suggest that factors such as history of use and dose are becoming more similar for the two sexes. There is as yet no evidence supporting differential sensitivity, tolerance, or withdrawal difficulty. In conclusion, it is maintained that the primary reason people smoke is to achieve an optimal blood and tissue level of nicotine, and that this level should not differ systematically for men and women.

5. SMOKING AND DISEASE

Gender Differences in Mortality and Morbidity

As introduction and proviso to the discussion of smoking-related disease, some commentary on morbidity and mortality rates in men and women is warranted. In 20th-century America, mortality rates for men have been higher than for women at all ages. Furthermore, mortality sex ratios for the 15 most common causes of death show an excess of deaths among males in 14 of the categories (Lewis and Lewis, 1977). These data show an increase in relative death rates in men between 1950 and 1969, 20 years marked by important progress in medical care. It is remarkable that women utilize health care services, on the whole, more than men despite the former group's lower mortality and morbidity rates for selected chronic conditions. In their excellent discussion of these findings and the implications of "sexual equality" for health status and health care, Lewis and Lewis maintained that sex-related differences on these dimensions are more related to socially influenced behaviors and roles than to genetics. Women are societally conditioned to be more concerned with health than men—as patients, as arrangers of health care for families, and as role models for them. Will the change in sex roles bring decreased use of health services among women? Will mortality ratios for major diseases reach unity as women increase unhealthy behaviors such as smoking, concomitant with increases in stress? These issues remain to be clarified, although the trend in smoking-related diseases is clearly to close the gap between the sexes.

The effect of excessive stress on physical and mental health is generally considered a negative one. It has been particularly implicated in coronary heart disease. It is important to bear in mind that at the same time that the smoking habits of the sexes are becoming increasingly similar, sex-role changes in our society are subjecting women to greater stress. This is occurring in many areas: educational and occupational competition; upward striving in managerial positions; greater physical mobility; and changing marital patterns that can give women the dual role of child caretaker and full-time member of the labor force. One must be careful when examining the results of retrospective studies to be cognizant of the variety of factors that may be operative beyond the controlled variables.

The relationship between smoking and disease to be presented below is firmly established, but the interactive effects of the psychological and sociocultural variables just mentioned are not often simultaneously considered. They should not be omitted from consideration in light of the evolution in sex roles in our society.

The Report of the Advisory Committee to the Surgeon General entitled "Smoking and Health" (USDHEW, 1964) was the first formal documentation of the relationship between cigarette smoking and disease in the United States (cf. Royal College of Physicians, 1962). This report established a causal association between cigarette smoking and lung cancer and chronic bronchitis, and a strong association with chronic bronchopulmonary disease, cardiovascular disease, and other conditions. Since then, a number of reports from this office, a recent summary prepared by the Royal College of Physicians entitled "Smoking or Health" (1977), and a voluminous literature have continued to support and extend these findings. The greater incidence of smoking-related disease among men is attributed to their greater likelihood of being smokers and to their heavier use of tobacco compared with that of women. For all of the smoking-related diseases, as use of tobacco among women increases, so does the rate of these diseases. In each disease category, discontinuance of smoking reduces the risk of developing the specific condition. The findings are summarized here for cardiovascular disease, bronchopulmonary conditions, and smoking-related cancers.

Cardiovascular Disease

More people die from coronary heart disease (CHD) in developed countries than from any other single cause, and women are much less prone to develop such disease, particularly below the age of 50. The mortality–sex ratio (M/F) for heart disease in the United States in 1969 was 1.95 (Lewis and Lewis, 1977). In a study of British physicians, 52% of the excess mortality in male smokers was attributable to CHD plus other cardiovascular conditions (Royal College of Physicians, 1977); similar findings have been reported elsewhere (Holbrook, 1977). Epidemiological studies from a number of countries repeatedly establish cigarette smoking as a major risk factor for CHD as well as for peripheral vascular disease. The possible mechanisms whereby nicotine and carbon monoxide (the major implicated agents) may contribute to pathogenesis involve increased cardiac work load, cardiac arrhythmias, and thrombosis for nicotine and diminution of the oxygen-carrying capacity of the blood and passage of cholesterol through arterial walls for carbon monoxide (Royal College of Physicians, 1977).

As more women have become regular smokers and have increased the number of cigarettes smoked per day, their rate of cardiovascular disease has begun to rise dramatically. A number of studies have shown sample populations of women suffering myocardial infarction (MI) to be composed of a greater proportion of smokers than in the general population (Royal College of Physicians, 1977). The use of oral contraceptives has often been cited as an interactive risk factor contributing to MI. However, a recent study (Slone et al., 1978) of myocardial infarction in women under 50 who were neither users of oral contraceptives nor subject to any other risk factor revealed a significantly higher proportion of smokers among the cases than among the controls (89% versus 55%, estimated relative risk = 6.8, $p < .001$). The authors stated that in this group of women below age 50, thought not to be at high risk, 76% of the myocardial infarctions were estimated to be attributable to smoking. Among the heaviest smokers (more than 35 cigarettes/day,) the rate was 20 times higher than in nonsmokers. The findings are sobering, but their reliability remains to be demonstrated in further clinical studies. A possible confounding factor exists as a result of excluding from the case group only those women who had used oral contraceptives in the month preceding hospital admission; one wonders what the history of the case population was for their entire reproductive period.

By now, the use of oral contraceptives as an interactive factor with cigarette smoking in contributing to coronary heart disease has been well documented (Mann et al., 1976; Jain, 1976; Jick et al., 1978). Oral contraceptive use alone does not constitute a significant risk factor for CHD, but combined with smoking, the relative risk is about 12:1 compared with the risk to those who neither smoke nor take oral contraceptives. Depending on number of cigarettes smoked per day, the relative risk can rise to 15:1 in heavy smokers (Jain, 1976). Jick et al. (1978) calculated that the absolute risk for myocardial infarction in women who both smoke and use oral contraceptives is approximately 1 per 8400 annually in the age group 27–37 and that it rises to 1 in 250 in the age group 44–45. These authors cautioned against the use of these drugs in older women with histories predisposing to MI, especially if they smoke.

Another recent report concerning vascular disease proposes a synergistic relationship between smoking and current oral contraceptive use in

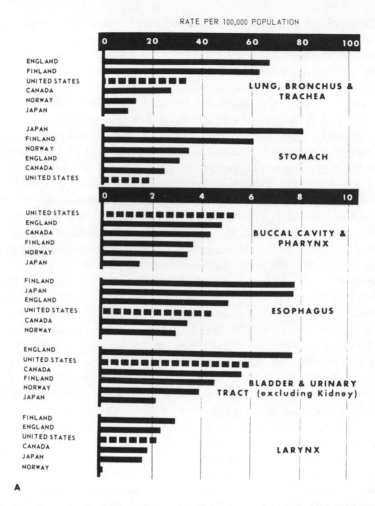

Fig. 4. Age-adjusted mortality rates for cancer of six sites in six selected countries: (A) males; (B) females. *Source:* U.S. Department of Health, Education, and Welfare, 1964, Public Health Service. Smoking and health: Report to the Advisory Committee to the Surgeon General of the Public Health Service. PHS Publication No. 1103.

increasing the risk of subarachnoid hemorrhage (Petitti and Wingerd, 1978). Although the number of cases was small, there were a large number of matched controls for each case, and the statistical results were significant. The relationship, which is similar in nature to the increased risk of MI in women who both smoke and use oral contraceptives, awaits confirmation in further studies.

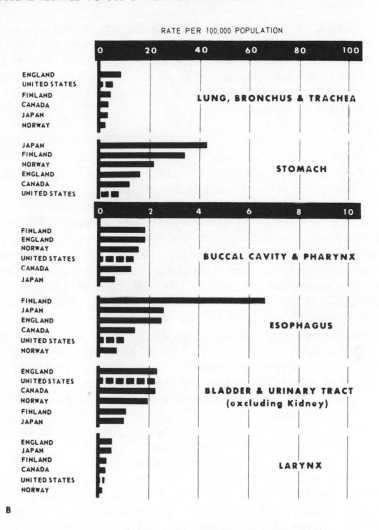

Fig. 4. (Continued)

Nonneoplastic Bronchopulmonary Diseases

This category of diseases, known collectively as chronic obstructive pulmonary disease (COPD), includes chronic bronchitis and emphysema. Cigarette smoking has been causally connected with these conditions (USDHEW, 1973; Royal College of Physicians, 1977). Higher death rates from COPD have been reported in smokers compared with nonsmokers, as have impaired pulmonary function, symptoms of pulmonary disease, and respiratory infections. These findings hold for both men and women, although rates are lower among women on the whole. When smoking habits are equated, differences in incidence are markedly reduced. Atmospheric pollution and occupational exposure to dust may interact with smoking to increase the rates of these diseases in men and women. In the United States, COPD is one of the most important causes of chronic disability (Holbrook, 1977).

Cancer

Since 1937, cancer has ranked second only to cardiovascular disease as a cause of death in the United States (USDHEW, 1964). In 1930, 118,000 people died from cancer in the United States, and in 1979, 395,000 deaths were predicted (Devesa and Schneiderman, 1977; Silverberg, 1979). From a combination of epidemiological, experimental, and pathological findings, cigarette smoking has been established as the most important cause of lung cancer and a significant factor in the development of cancer at a number of other sites (USDHEW, 1973; Royal College of Physicians, 1977; Holbrook, 1977; Williams and Horm, 1977; Silverberg, 1979). The prevalence of cancer for any one site varies according to age and nationality. Fig. 4 presents age-adjusted mortality rates from a 1962 report for cancer of six sites in six selected countries for males and females. One of the sites listed, stomach, is affected in a complex manner by a number of risk factors, including ingestion of smoked foods and alcohol; smoking has been implicated, but not established as a risk factor. Individual countries present different patterns of risk among the various sites. The remainder of this discussion is limited to smoking and cancer epidemiology within the United States.

The most clearly supported relationships between smoking and cancer occur at the sites of lung, larynx, pharynx, oral cavity, esophagus, and bladder; cancer of other urinary tract organs and of the pancreas may also be related to smoking (Williams and Horm, 1977; Holbrook, 1977; Royal College of Physicians, 1977). The relationship between smoking and lung cancer has been stated most succinctly by the U.S. Public Health Service (USDHEW, 1973):

> For both men and women, the risk of developing lung cancer is directly related to total exposure to cigarette smoke as measured by the number of cigarettes smoked per day, the total lifetime number of cigarettes smoked, the duration of smoking in years, the age of initiation of smoking, the depth of inhalation of tobacco smoke, and the "tar" and nicotine levels in the cigarettes smoked. (p. 67)

Lung cancer is almost entirely a disease of smokers, and a monotonic relationship exists between the number of cigarettes smoked per day and the increase of mortality risk compared to nonsmokers. For males who smoke a pack of cigarettes per day, the increased risk is of the order of tenfold (Royal College of Physicians, 1977). The difference in mortality rates for lung cancer between men and women is mostly attributable to the lower exposure of women to cigarette smoke. Women smoke fewer cigarettes, inhale less, smoke more filter cigarettes, and have a shorter lifetime smoking history than men (USDHEW, 1973). But the changing patterns of cigarette smoking among women are rapidly erasing the sex difference in lung cancer morbidity and mortality. Age-adjusted lung cancer death rates for 1930–1975 reflect the change in female smoking habits as well as the large increase in mortality among males (see Fig. 5). These figures are affected by the growth in population, the changes in life expectancy in the population (and relative age distribution), and the conjoint action of these two factors as well as changes in risk (Devesa

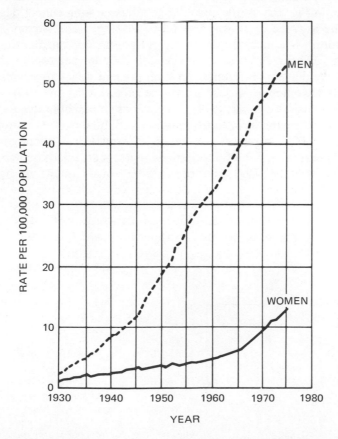

Fig. 5.   Age-adjusted lung cancer death rates, United States, 1930–1975. *Source:* Adapted from E. Silverberg, 1979, Cancer statistics, *Ca—A Journal for Clinicians* **28:**17–32.

and Schneiderman, 1977; Zdeb, 1977). For 1979, it was estimated that there would be 82,000 new cases of lung cancer reported among men and 30,000 among women in the United States; furthermore, it was estimated that 72,300 men and 25,200 women would die from lung cancer in that same year (Silverberg, 1979). Over the course of an entire lifetime, the lung is the most probable site in which men will develop cancer and the fourth most probable in women, preceded by breast, large intestine, and corpus uteri (Zdeb, 1977; Seidman et al., 1978). The overall ranking of sites changes somewhat, with different cutoff points for determining probabilities from birth. For example, if day of birth through age 65 is considered, lung cancer remains the leading male site but moves down to sixth place for women, with cervix uteri and ovary newly ranking above it (Zdeb, 1977).

The population dose–response curve for lung cancer mortality is illustrated in Fig. 6, plotting current age-adjusted lung cancer death rates against the average of 30 years of past smoking. "Postlatency cigarette consumption" is a measure of the cigarette tobacco consumption rate in the given year for 30+-year smokers, per 100,000 persons at risk. The curve shows that the difference between present lung cancer death rates in men and women is a dose–response effect reflecting differences in past tobacco use (Burbank, 1972). Lung cancer mortality rates for women have been increasing at proportionately much higher rates than for men (Holbrook, 1977). However, cessation of smoking is accompanied by gradually decreasing risk of developing lung cancer, relative to continuing smoking (USDHEW, 1973; Holbrook, 1977; Royal College of Physicians, 1977).

Smoking interacts with other risk factors for lung and other cancers, such as certain instances of industrial exposure (asbestos, uranium mining) that affect primarily men; air pollution, which affects both sexes;

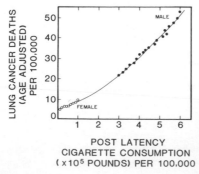

Fig. 6. The population dose–response curve. Age-adjusted lung cancer death rates for yearly postlatency cigarette consumption levels, 1950–1968. Source: F. Burbank, 1972, U.S. lung cancer death rates begin to rise proportionately more rapidly for females than for males: A dose–response effect? Journal of Chronic Diseases 25:473–479.

and alcohol use, which also affects both men and women (Royal College of Physicians, 1977; Holbrook, 1977).

Lung cancer has been discussed in detail as the prototype of a smoking-related cancer that has been the subject of intensive clinical and research studies. Evidence for other sites follows similar patterns, with independent or interactive risk factors differing for each site.

The principal constituents of cigarette smoke that may be responsible for the genesis of cancers are a number of carcinogens found in tobacco "tar" (particulate matter condensate, with nicotine and moisture extracted); these include polynuclear aromatic hydrocarbons and the N-nitrosamines. In addition, cigarette smoke contains irritant gases such as acrolein, nitrogen dioxide, formaldehyde, hydrogen sulfide, and ammonia, some of which are also cocarcinogens, and hydrocyanic acid, a respiratory enzyme poison (Holbrook, 1977; Royal College of Physicians, 1977).

Other Physical Illnesses

Smoking has been strongly implicated in peptic ulcer disease, with regard to incidence, slowing of healing, and mortality (Royal College of Physicians, 1977; Holbrook, 1977). As with other cancers, incidence and mortality rates are higher in men than in women and are associated with pattern of tobacco intake. The mechanism by which smoking contributes to ulceration has not yet been elucidated. However, a contributing factor may be the chronic depression of pancreatic alkaline secretions in heavy smokers, which could result in duodenal hyperacidity (Royal College of Physicians, 1977).

A variety of other deviations in physical functioning has been studied in relationship to adverse effects of smoking. Alterations in allergic conditions, the immune system, and ability to engage in physical exercise are just a few. The reader is referred to review sources (Royal College of Physicians, 1977; Holbrook, 1977; USDHEW, 1964, 1973).

Age of Menopause

A new finding of particular importance to women linking cigarette smoking and age of natural menopause has been reported in two large independent studies conducted by the Boston Collaborative Drug Surveillance Program (Jick et al., 1977). Examining smoking status and number of menopausal women at each year between 44 and 53 years of age, it was found that a greater proportion of current smokers were menopausal than never-smokers. When the data were age-standardized, the proportion of women who were menopausal varied directly with smoking status; that is, the smallest percentage of postmenopausal women fell into the never-smoker category, surpassed by ex-smokers, those smoking one-half pack per day, and those smoking one pack per day or more. Confounding variables such as parity, marital status, and drug use were not found to alter the results. The authors cited two possible physiological mechanisms that might account for their findings: central nervous system effects of nicotine on hormonal functions important to the menopausal process and induction of liver enzymes that may affect the metabolism of steroid hormones.

Health Attitudes and Behaviors

The extraordinarily serious health consequences of smoking have not deterred almost 30% of the adult female and 40% of the adult male population from regular smoking. Of these same current smokers, 70–80% agree that cigarette smoking is harmful, constitutes a health hazard that requires action, and causes disease and death (USDHEW, 1976a). The value placed on health compared with other positive life goals was slightly lower for smokers than for nonsmokers and was highest for ex-smokers in this same survey: out of a maximum score of 6, current smokers averaged 4.66 (M = 4.55, F = 4.81), nonsmokers averaged 4.82 (M = 4.68, F = 4.9), and ex-smokers averaged 4.89 (M = 4.78, F = 5.06). The higher scores of women support their traditional concern with health in our culture (Lewis and Lewis, 1977) but are incongruent with recent smoking trends. It is interesting that fewer current smokers (male and female) than nonsmokers and ex-smokers reported having personally known someone with CHD, lung cancer, or emphysema/chronic bronchitis. The finding may reflect some kind of psychological process of denial, as only about one-third of current smokers admitted knowing someone personally whose "health" was adversely affected by smoking compared with over 60% of nonsmokers. Clearly, mechanisms must be operating to reduce cognitive dissonance in smokers between their knowledge of health consequences and their behavior. One of these mechanisms may be to deny that the health problems of others are related to smoking. This is a fertile field for further research and action, especially where the potential for capitalizing on women's involvement with health care is concerned.

6. PREGNANCY

The woman who smokes during pregnancy not only continues to expose her own body to significant health risks but also exposes the unborn fetus. The fetus provides a prime example of recipient effects of passive smoking, since many of the chemical products of smoking are transmitted into its blood stream via the placenta. These effects are large considering the difference in body size. Of course, the level of tobacco smoke components absorbed by the fetus depends on maternal levels, placental transmission, and other complex factors. In addition to direct effects on the fetus, which include fetal growth retardation and increased perinatal mortality, smoking introduces the possibility of complications of pregnancy that may result in the loss of the fetus. Although the documentation of a significant relationship between smoking in pregnancy and the effects to be discussed is strong, the specific components of tobacco smoke accounting for any of the complications have yet to be identified. The most likely candidates are nicotine, carbon monoxide, and cyanide. An excellent review of studies published prior to 1973 appears in the "Health Consequences of Smoking" (USDHEW, 1973). The effects of maternal smoking in pregnancy are discussed in temporal order, from conception through birth and perinatal and early childhood periods.

Conception

The *sex ratio* of male to female infants born to smokers is not affected by smoking (USDHEW, 1973).

Conception through 20 Weeks' Gestational Age

Most studies of *spontaneous abortion,* usually defined as the loss of a fetus before 20 weeks' gestational age, do not differentiate between it and *miscarriage,* which is usually defined as embryonic or fetal loss before 12 weeks' gestational age. A statistically significant association of maternal smoking with spontaneous abortion was found in a number of reports prior to 1973. However, potentially confounding variables such as maternal age, parity, health status, attitude toward pregnancy, and medication use, which have been related to the occurrence of spontaneous abortion, were often not controlled for (USDHEW, 1973). Since then, two studies taking some of these factors into account have shown the same trend. A study of first pregnancies in adolescent black and white women of low socioeconomic status reported significantly more incidence of spontaneous abortion and fetal loss in smokers than in nonsmokers, which was not related to race (Hollingsworth et al., 1976). In a second study of 574 women who aborted spontaneously and of 374 controls, a highly significant association of smoking with pregnancy outcome was identified (Kline et al., 1977). Smokers had 1.8 times the likelihood of spontaneous abortion as nonsmokers. This relationship was obtained with statistical controls for age and for previous pregnancies ending in spontaneous abortion, induced abortion, and live birth; cases and controls did not differ in ethnicity, marital status, and several socioeconomic variables. It is not known whether the increased incidence of spontaneous abortion in smokers is related to the same mechanisms that lower mean birth weight. If future studies continue such controls, the association between smoking and spontaneous abortion may become firm.

Twenty Weeks' Gestational Age to Term (37 Weeks)

There are certain *complications of pregnancy* that can result in fetal death *in utero,* in preterm delivery, and in neonatal death. Meyer and Tonascia (1977) used the data from the Ontario Perinatal Mortality Study, which collected information on 51,490 single births occurring between 1960 and 1961, to trace the relationship between smoking and certain complications of pregnancy. Smoking was significantly related to an increase of bleeding during pregnancy, abruptio placentae (premature detachment of the placenta), placenta previa (development of the placenta in the lower uterine segment), and premature and prolonged rupture of the membranes. At all gestation periods, placenta previa and abruptio placentae were more likely to occur in smokers than in nonsmokers, the differences being largest early in the pregnancy. Smokers incurred a threefold greater risk of premature rupture of the membranes for births occurring before 34 weeks' gestation, and this risk remained higher through term. These conditions are responsible for an elevated incidence of fetal death, premature delivery, and neonatal death. It is important to emphasize in this context, however, that the increase in mortality associated with maternal smoking was related to the increased probability of very early delivery. In this study, the authors showed that smokers' babies were delivered preterm significantly more often than nonsmokers', but that at comparable gestational ages, survival rates of live-born babies did not differ according to smoking status. The findings of increased rate of very early delivery and of pregnancy complications obtained from this epidemiological study remain controversial and await further confirmation.

A significantly lower incidence of *hypertension* and *preeclamptic toxemia* is observed among smokers than among nonsmokers even when other risk factors are controlled (USDHEW, 1973; Andrews and McGarry, 1972; Duffus and MacGillivray, 1968). In these reports, hypertension was defined as a diastolic blood pressure of 90 mm Hg or a systolic blood pressure of 150 mm Hg on at least two occasions prior to pregnancy or week 20 thereof. Preeclampsia is a toxemia occurring at or after the 20th week of pregnancy associated with elevated diastolic blood pressure, clinical edema, and proteinurea. The decreased incidence of these conditions in smoking women has been hypothesized to be due to the muscle capillary dilation by nicotine or to the hypotensive effects of thiocyanate, the detoxification product of cyanide (Andrews and McGarry, 1972; Andrews, 1973). In order to explain the difference in incidence, it has been suggested that pregnant women who smoke and who are at risk for preeclampsia may abort, thus lowering the incidence rate of this condition. When the rates for spontaneous abortion, preeclampsia, and toxemia are taken together, there is no difference between smoking and nonsmoking pregnant women (Royal College of Physicians, 1977). Although pregnant women who smoke may have reduced incidence of these two disorders, perinatal mortality rate of infants born to women who did develop such disorders was much higher for smokers than for nonsmokers (Duffus and MacGillivray, 1968; USDHEW, 1973).

The Perinatal and Neonatal Periods

The perinatal period is usually defined as from birth through the first week of life, and the neonatal period extends to the 28th day of life. Of necessity, this discussion will overlap with the preceding topic in regard to fetal growth retardation and to perinatal mortality.

The most firmly established connection between maternal smoking and pregnancy is the effect termed *fetal growth retardation,* first reported in 1957 and then repeatedly confirmed (Simpson, 1957; USDHEW, 1973; Royal College of Physicians, 1977; Andrews and McGarry, 1972; Hollingsworth et al., 1976; Miller et al., 1976; Meyer and Tonascia, 1977). Full-term babies born to women who smoke are, on the average, 200 g lighter than babies of comparable gestational age whose mothers do not smoke. The reduction in birth weight is not an effect of gestational prematurity; rather, the babies are termed small-for-date. Furthermore, the distribution of birth weights of infants born to smokers is almost identical to that of infants born to nonsmokers except for a shift to the left (lighter mean value). Fetal growth retardation does not usually occur if a woman ceases smoking after the fourth month of pregnancy.

Yerushalmy (1971, 1972) strongly opposed the acceptance of a causal relationship between smoking and lowered birth weight, claiming that the observed excess of low-birth-weight infants among smokers reflects underlying characteristics of the mother and is not due to her smoking habits. The "statistical controversy" thus generated has been resolved by refutation of his alternative analyses on the basis of inadequate controls or lack of relevance (Goldstein, 1977).

If a woman continues to smoke throughout her pregnancy, she has nearly a twofold risk of delivering a low-birth-weight infant (less than 2500 g) compared to a nonsmoker; a direct dose–response relationship exists between number of cigarettes smoked and the incidence of low-birth-weight babies. The relationship between smoking and birth weight has been shown to hold when a variety of other possible influences have been controlled, and the relationship has been demonstrated across culture, race, and geographical setting. In summary, the USDHEW (1973) states that "evidence . . . suggests that cigarette smoking is causally associated with the delivery of small-for-date infants" (p. 106).

Fetal growth retardation may comprise more than one type of condition. While the 1973 summary (USDHEW) stated that the infants of smokers grew at an accelerated rate in the first six months of life compared with those of nonsmokers, a later report (Miller et al., 1976) identified two separate syndromes (low ponderal index and abnormally short crown–heel length for fetal age) in which postnatal weight gain and growth rates differ. Infants of smokers were not evenly distributed across both syndromes, suggesting that the relationship of smoking to fetal growth retardation may be more complex than hitherto considered.

The accelerated growth rate of small-for-date infants born to smoking mothers has been considered a response to the removal of a toxic substance (USDHEW, 1973). In this regard, a number of factors may be influential in producing the retardation effect. While none has been firmly established in a causal relationship, a combination of such alterations in fetal and maternal biochemistry and physiology during pregnancy may well act to retard fetal growth. Nicotine, carbon monoxide, and cyanide are the three most frequently mentioned compounds.

Nicotine, which crosses the placental barrier and has been measured in the amniotic fluid (Van Vunakis et al., 1974), has been shown to significantly reduce the proportion of time in which fetal breathing movements occur (Gennser et al., 1975; Manning and Feyerabend, 1976). This effect is hypothesized to be a result of fetal hypoxia following uteroplacental vasoconstriction (Manning and Feyerabend, 1976). Figure 7 shows the effect of smoking nicotine-containing tobacco cigarettes compared with smoking nicotine-free herbal cigarettes. The action of nicotine was further verified when the same reduction in fetal breathing movements was observed after chewing a specially formulated gum containing 8 mg nicotine, a dose that produced peak maternal nicotine blood levels similar to those following smoking. Nicotine has also been measured in the milk of lactating mothers (Ferguson et al., 1976). An extensive animal literature on prenatal nicotine administration is summarized in several sources (Larson and Silvette, 1975; Longo, 1977).

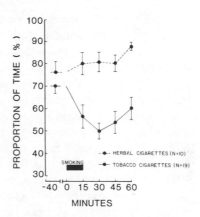

Fig. 7. The mean proportion of time (±SE) during which fetal breathing movements were present in normal pregnancies before and after smoking either tobacco cigarettes or herbal cigarettes. *Source:* F. A. Manning and C. Feyerabend, 1976, Cigarette smoking and fetal breathing movements, *British Journal of Obstetrics and Gynecology* **83:**262–270.

Carbon monoxide, a combustion product of cigarettes, binds with hemoglobin to produce elevated COHb levels in smokers compared with nonsmokers. Steady-state fetal COHb levels are a complex function of maternal COHb concentration, fetal CO production, placental diffusion, and relative hemoglobin–gas affinities. Since fetal blood has greater oxygen affinity than maternal blood, probably the most important outcome of an increase in COHb concentration in maternal and fetal blood can be a significant reduction in oxygenation of fetal tissues (Longo, 1976, 1977).

Cyanide, another component of tobacco, has been implicated in explaining reduced birth weight (Pettigrew et al., 1977; Andrews, 1973; McGarry and Andrews, 1972). Vitamin B_{12} is depleted in smokers as it is used in the detoxification of cyanide to thiocyanate. The metabolism of sulfur-containing compounds that are vital for fetal enzyme activity, growth, and development could be affected, since sulfur amino acid requirements may be increased as well. Both cyanide and thiocyanate have been measured in cord blood and are thus likely to cross the placenta.

Perinatal mortality refers to those deaths occurring within the perinatal period and includes late fetal death (stillbirth) and death occuring within the first seven days of life. The USDHEW (1973) stated that there is "a strong, probably causal association between cigarette smoking and higher fetal and infant mortality among smokers' infants" (p. 134). Because low birth weight is associated with increased infant mortality, the infants of cigarette smokers, who are lighter than those of nonsmokers at a given gestational age, have a higher mortality risk. The association between smoking and infant mortality holds when adjustment is made for other risk factors influencing mortality rates.

While the definition of perinatal mortality varies, Meyer and Tonascia (1977) were careful to define it to include "fetal deaths of at least 20 weeks' gestation and neonatal deaths during the first seven days after delivery" (p. 498) in their analysis of data from the Ontario Perinatal Mortality Study. They analyzed perinatal mortality at each period of gestational age among births to smoking and nonsmoking mothers. There was a twofold increased probability of death *in utero* between 20 and 28 weeks' gestation if the woman smoked, an increased probability from 32 weeks to term, and no significant difference beyond 38 weeks. The finding for neonatal deaths was similar (see also Andrews and McGarry, 1972). As indicated previously, these authors attributed these results to an increased risk of very early delivery among women who smoke, which is associated with poorer survival rates in general.

Thus, low birth weight and prematurity have been named as influences on perinatal mortality rates, with the latter only recently being brought to attention. The perinatal mortality studies are difficult to compare because of differences in definition of terms, treatment of abortion data, and sample population, issues that are beyond the scope of this chapter.

Later Infancy and Childhood

Passive smoking in the first year of life (when one or both parents smoke) is associated with a higher rate of pneumonia and bronchitis than found in infants of nonsmoking parents (Harlap and Davies, 1974; Colley et al., 1974). This finding may be relevant to research on the sudden infant death syndrome (SIDS), as an association between SIDS and maternal smoking has been reported (Bergman and Wiesner, 1976). Since passive smoking does raise the probability of developing respiratory tract infections, and up to half the victims of SIDS show evidence of mild infection (usually respiratory) on postmortem (Naeye, 1977), parental smoking may well be a risk factor for this syndrome.

Long-term effects of maternal smoking in pregnancy are progressively more difficult to isolate from birth onward because of the increasing influence of environmental factors. In one epidemiological study, initial differences in height between the offspring of smokers and nonsmokers were reported to persist for as long as 11 years, and some slight impairment in reading ability was also noted, but these differences were small and affected by other sociobiological factors (Butler and Goldstein, 1973; Royal College of Physicians, 1977). Evidence from smaller-scale studies is conflicting: one study supported the existence of weight and height differences at 4 and 6½ years of age (Dunn et al., 1976); a second study also reported a small height decrement for the children of smokers at birth and 1 year, but the two groups of children did not differ in height or intellectual function at 4 or 7 years (Hardy and Mellits, 1972). It is very unlikely that long-term effects, even if they do exist, can be identified in other than large-scale studies, since the interaction of other influences is so great.

Why do Women Continue to Smoke during Pregnancy?

If smoking is associated with potential detrimental effects to the fetus as well as increased risk of severe complications to the mother, why don't women quit smoking during their pregnancies? A glance at Table 2 reveals that only three systematic studies of smoking cessation interventions in pregnancy have been reported in the literature. The only one of these to report a 50% quitting rate (for those 8 women completing treatment, of an original 11) was composed of a sample of women all of whom had completed college or business–trade school (Danaher et al., 1978). This is the group most responsive to educational materials. In a study performed among British working-class women (Baric et al., 1976), the few women with any education were more likely to be among the 21% who stopped smoking during pregnancy. In this sample, sources of information regarding health risks in pregnancy were in rank order of frequency: television, posters and leaflets, husbands, family and friends, books or magazines, a doctor, and a nurse. While every woman had been exposed to the information regarding smoking and pregnancy, there were large differences in acceptance of this information. Women about to have their first baby were more likely to believe the educational materials than multiparous women. A similar observation was made by Donovan et al. (1975). Yet another factor affecting utilization of the information is the tendency of working-class women to rely more on lay referral systems (family and friends) than on medical sources or the mass media (Graham, 1976). Scientific knowledge may not be given great credibility in this group of women compared with those who are more educated or more socially mobile. Finally, Graham pointed out the role and value that smoking may play in the woman's life in terms of structuring activity periods and status. Preventing excessive weight gain has also been given as a reason to continue smoking in pregnancy (Donovan et al., 1975).

Estimates of smoking cessation among pregnant women run about one-third both in the United Kingdom and in the United States (Baric et al., 1976; USDHEW, 1977). It is estimated that another one-third cut down on smoking (USDHEW, 1977). These figures speak to the need for more powerful methods of affecting the behavior, as well as the intellectual knowledge, of pregnant smokers. They also speak to the critical

Table 2. Education: Smoking Cessation Treatment by Sex

Study	Treatment	N	End-of-treatment (%)	Six months (%)	Long term (%)
1. Guilford (1967)[a]	Five-day plan[b]: unaided / aided	75 M / 100 F / 82 M / 91 F		23 M / 12 F[e] }[e]; 27 M / 29 F[d] }[d]	
2. Peterson et al. (1968)[a]	Five-day plan	134 M and F	79 M and F		19 M / 19 F (18 mo follow-up on 121 Ss)
3. Berglund (1969)[a]	Five-day plan	895 M and F	87 M / 84 F	32 M / 27 F[e]	31 M / 23 F[d](4–18 mo)
4. Burns (1969)	M.D. advice to resp. dis. pts.	66 M / 28 F		53 M / 32 F[d](3 mo)	
5. Ochsner and Damrau (1970)	Pamphlets[b]	20 M / 33 F	85 M / 52 F }[d]		
6. Delarue (1973)	Education; small groups	472 M and F			34 M / 21 F }(12 mo)
7. Handel (1973)	Antismoking message in med. exam.	45 M / 55 F			38 M / 11 F }[d](12 mo)

	Method	N		
8. Pyszka et al. (1973)[a]	Amer. Cancer Soc. Clinics	131 M 223 F	39 M and F	28 M 20 F (18 mo)
9. Kanzler et al. (1976)	Smokenders	210 M 343 F	70 M 69 F	57 M }[a] (48 mo) 30 F }
10. Dubren (1977)[a]	TV spots	92 M 218 F	15 M }[a] 7 F }	
11. Baric et al.[c] (1976)	M.D. advice	134 F:		
	(spont. quitters)	24	83	
	(intervention)	63	14	
	(control)	47	14	
12. Donovan (1977)[c]	M.D. advice	552 F	50% reduction	
13. Danaher et al. (1978)[c]	Education; skill training group	11 F	50 (of 8 Ss finishing treatment)	50 (9 mo)

[a] Results based only on those completing treatment or contacted for follow-up.
[b] Success = 90–100% reduction in smoking.
[c] Pregnancy intervention studies.
[d] $p < .05$.
[e] $.05 < p < .10$.

importance of involving the entire social structure of the smoker, from spouse to obstetrician, in the effort to effect behavioral change.

7. SMOKING CESSATION

There is no question that smoking cessation may be termed a "problem" among women. This is not to say that it is easy for men, but there is a partially anecdotal and partially objective assertion in the treatment literature that men have greater success than women in giving up smoking. The basis for this assertion lies partially in the epidemiological analyses of cessation rates and partially in the literature describing smoking cessation clinics and experimental programs.

Estimates from Epidemiological Surveys

In the terminology of the 1955 Current Population Survey (Haenszel et al., 1956), "smoking discontinuance" was defined as nonsmoking or occasional smoking (not daily) in a former regular smoker. Discontinued smokers therefore included some abstainers as well as some who may have been only temporary abstainers. This ambiguity was avoided in the 1964–1975 NCSH surveys. A "former smoker" was defined as someone who does not now smoke, either regularly or occasionally, but who once did.

Haenszel et al. (1956) were the first to report lower discontinuance rates for women than for men in the overall urban and rural nonfarm population; the reverse held true in the farm population. In males, discontinuance rates were related to economic status; professionals, managers and proprietors, and farmers had high discontinuance rates, while factory workers evidenced low rates. In females, however, it was employment status, not occupational group, that was related to discontinuance rate; unemployed women (primarily housewives) had higher discontinuance rates than employed women. Haenszel and his colleagues reported one other crucial statistical manipulation of sex versus discontinuance rate: sex differences in discontinuance are mostly due to the shorter exposure of women to the smoking habit. When one takes into account the difference in the average length of time men and women have been smoking, and the "risk of discontinuance," " . . . the sex difference virtually disappears" (p. 47). Phrased simply, cessation must be measured with respect to varying lengths of time of the duration of smoking.

Nowhere in the reports of the national surveys that followed has such a statistical adjustment since been made. It is very possible that differential cessation rates for men and women reflect duration of smoking as well as social influences on quitting. Such a consideration should be applied to examination of subject populations in the cessation-treatment reports as well. To further complicate matters, age at initiation of smoking and other parameters, such as the number of cigarettes smoked per day and the type of cigarette (filter versus nonfilter), have changed differentially over time for the two sexes. At present, it is impossible to sort out the influence of these variables on cessation rate. The primary point to be made is that this measure is not a simple one and must be interpreted with caution.

With these reservations in mind, quitting rates reported in the national surveys conducted by the NCSH in 1964, 1966, 1970, and 1975 may be examined (Table 1; Schuman, 1978). The percentage of former smokers increased steadily in both sexes between 1964 and 1970, but the general pattern of incidence and prevalence was different for men and women. A two-year follow-up of over 500 former smokers, identified in the 1964 nationwide survey, revealed that men were significantly more likely than women to remain successful abstainers, pointing to duration of discontinuance as yet another variable of import (Eisinger, 1971). In 1975, fewer males had ceased smoking, and there was virtually no change in the percentage of former female smokers.

Demographic Factors. Cessation rates can be reported either as the percentage of former smokers among all persons surveyed (never-smoker + former smoker + current smoker), or as the percentage of those who once smoked regularly but no longer do. The former statistic, which has been used in the preceding discussion, describes the number of former smokers in relation to the entire sample. The latter limits the comparison to all smokers and is more relevant to treatment data. The latest figures will therefore be presented only in regard to the smoking population. Following up the 1955 trends in quitting associated with socioeconomic status and occupation, sex differences persist. The same general relationship of quitting rate to *occupational category* for men was still valid in 1975 and, based on employment status, was still distinct for women (USDHEW, 1976a). A total of 49% of professional males and 42% of professional females who had ever smoked were not smoking in 1975; 44% of other white-collar workers and 35% of male factory workers had given up smoking. This compares with 27% of working women other than professionals and 34% of housewives.

A 1975 survey compared smoking in health professionals with smoking in the general population, again describing the data in terms of the percentage of those who had ever regularly smoked who no longer did so (USDHEW, 1976c). Between 55% and 64% of physicians, dentists, and pharmacists were former smokers in 1975, compared with 43% of all adult males. Only 36% of nurses had quit, compared with 30% of all adult working women, or 34% of all adult females.

To sum up the occupational data by sex, more adult males have given up smoking than adult females in every occupational classification; professionals are closest when one compares quitting rates among those who have ever smoked, but male health professionals are far ahead of nurses. Finally, housewives are slightly ahead of working women in general in giving up smoking.

There is a direct relationship between *number of years of school completed* and percentage of former smokers for both men and women. Looking at ever-smokers who had quit in 1975, we find that among those with a college education or higher, 52% of males and 48% of females no longer smoked. Among all other educational categories, the figures were 40.5% for males and 31.3% for females, a finding that parallels that for occupation.

Number of Cessation Attempts

There are some interesting similarities in the attempts to quit smoking for men and women, pointed out by Schuman (1978). Both male and female current smokers seemed to have made approximately the same number of attempts to quit, more than those reported by former smokers. In addition, quitting seemed to be getting easier or more urgent for both sexes, as the percentage of former smokers who tried only once to quit rose between 1964 and 1970 from 13.0% to 22.9% in males and from 9.9% to 25.3% in females. The number of smokers who tried at least once to quit remained about the same for both sexes, around 50% for current smokers. There was also little sex difference among those who had tried two or more times to quit: about one-third of current smokers and slightly over one-fifth of former smokers in 1970, a decrease since 1966. These findings suggest that the sexes do not have disparate experiences in quitting smoking, yet the observation remains that a greater proportion of men have given up smoking than women.

Prior Years of Smoking and Estimates of Recidivism. The epidemiological data for the 1964–1975 surveys do not statistically adjust for duration of smoking, the factor Haenszel found so important in accounting for the observed sex difference in discontinuance rate. There is evidence that this factor was still operative. The 1975 survey revealed that male former smokers had smoked for an average of 19 years before quitting, and females for an average of 15 years. It is not possible to examine directly differential recidivism rates for the sexes, which have been reported (Eisinger, 1971). Among the former smokers in the 1975 survey, significantly more females (33%) had abstained for less than four years than males (25%); the same was true for under one year's abstention, 12.4% females versus 8.1% males ($p < .001$ for both comparisons). The NCSH surveys do demonstrate that the pool of ex-smokers is large, although the percentages of males and females who had given up smoking remained stable from 1970 to 1975, at approximately 43% males and 33% females.

The surveys do not distinguish between those who quit unaided and those who quit after attending formal treatment of some sort. It might be expected that the latter group contained a high proportion of individuals who had failed in the attempt to quit by their own efforts. Reports of treatment success rates should be considered in light of the population treated, one that has severe difficulty giving up smoking. This issue has not been carefully examined.

Estimates from Treatment Reports

It is beyond the scope of this chapter to review the smoking cessation literature *in toto;* the reader is referred to the excellent review by Raw in the previous volume of this series (Raw, 1978), as well as to several other works (Gritz and Jarvik, 1978; Schwartz, 1978; Lichtenstein and Danaher, 1976). These reviews do not specifically address the question of a sex difference in quitting, although Schwartz cited differential rates wherever possible.

Among the plethora of treatments that have been applied to smoking, the overall finding is that end-of-treatment cessation rates tend to be very good, while maintenance of cessation tends to be very poor. In 1971, a well-known group of researchers demonstrated that recidivism curves for heroin addiction, alcoholism, and smoking are almost identical, with long-term cessation falling off steeply from end of treatment (Hunt et al., 1971). Within three months, approximately 35% of successful quitters were still not smoking, and by one year, the figure was closer to 20%. In 1978, Raw cited virtually the same figures. There have been scattered reports of improvement in techniques of obtaining abstinence and in maintaining it, using rapid smoking (an aversive conditioning technique), hypnosis, and group therapy. The long-term cure rates of 60% or higher at six months reported in these studies have not been universally obtained (Schmahl et al., 1972; Kline, 1970; Bozzetti, 1972; Schwartz, 1978).

Are There Gender Differences in Success Rates? Prior to this report, the literature does not contain a systematic comparison of reports of cessation and maintenance rates for men and women. A chain of reports of poorer cessation among women is extant, and these tend to be cited as a supporting literature for this "fact." My examination of the question has revealed this issue to be more complex. Women clearly do not surpass men in success at quitting, but a majority of studies show no difference between sexes.

A review of the smoking cessation literature, which by now amounts to well over 1,000 articles, reveals only 30 reports of differential quitting rates for male and female smokers, and an additional 9 in which only females were studied. It is quite unfortunate that so many valuable data are lost to the literature. For the sake of brevity, smoking cessation treatments have been categorized into four major approaches: education, psychotherapy, behavior modification, and pharmacotherapy. The categorization is, by necessity, only a rough separation of treatment modalities. While there is unavoidable overlap and many clinical approaches combine methodologies, the studies were grouped by "best fit." Evaluation of the gender difference question does not rest directly on the categorization schema.

The 39 studies fell evenly across the four broad categories chosen to encompass all types of treatment: education—10 (plus 3 pregnancy intervention studies); psychotherapy, group and individual—7; behavior modification—8; and pharmacotherapy—11. Tables 2–5 present success rates for males and females at end of treatment, plus follow-up abstinence rates at 6 months and 12 months or longer. Complete abstinence from smoking was the only criterion of success specifically charted, as recidivism among those who only reduce consumption is demonstrably rapid. Two exceptions to this rule were made for programs that reported "success" in terms of 90–100% reduction (see Table 2). Several studies that used percentage of reduction in smoking were listed for completeness but were not analyzed.

Examination of the tables reveals first that recidivism still reclaims most abstinent graduates of smoking treatment programs; that on the whole, long-term success rates are still around 25%; and that pharmacotherapy seems the least effective type of treatment. On the whole, behavior therapy would seem to have a slight edge in maintaining long-term abstinence.

Since many of the studies listed in the tables did not report significance evaluations for male–female quitting rates, the chi-square statistic or Fisher exact probability test was calculated wherever sufficient data were available (for 21 studies). Because of the limited number of studies identified for analysis and the often limited sample size, the results of borderline ($p < .05 < p < .10$) and acceptable ($p < .05$) level of significance are reported for the information of the reader. The data are summarized for end of treatment and for long-term abstinence rates by category: in terms of number of studies in which reported male quitting

Table 3. Psychotherapy: Smoking Cessation Treatment Results by Sex

| Study | Treatment | N | Percentage abstinence | | |
			End-of-treatment (%)	Six months (%)	Long term (%)
1. Moses (1964)	Hypnosis, discussion	35 M 15 F	83 M 53 F }ᶜ	11 M 12 F	8 M 12 F } (12 mo)
2. Mann and Janis (1968)	Emotional role-playing	26 F			23–50 F (18 mo)[a]
3. Streltzer and Koch (1968)	Emotional role-playing	30 F	OF (4 wks post)		
4. Lichtenstein et al. (1969)	Emotional role-playing	54 F	9.2 F (4–5 wks post)		
5. Fee and Benson (1971)	Group therapy	306 M 204 F	56 M 38 F }b		16 M 9 F } b (6–12 mo)
6. Bozzetti (1972)	Group therapy	7 M 7 F	57 M 43 F		85 M 57 F } (12 mo)
7. Tamerin (1972)	Group therapy	16 F	69 F		

[a] % reduction in smoking.
[b] $p < .05$.
[c] $.05 < p < .1$.

Table 4. Behavior Modification: Smoking Cessation Treatment Results by Sex

Study	Treatment	N	End-of-treatment(%)	Percentage abstinence Six months (%)	Long term (%)
1. Keutzer (1968)	Breath holding, coverant control, negative practice, attention placebo	73 M 73 F	18 M 29 F		
2. Russell (1970)	Electric shock aversion	10 M 4 F	70 M 50 F		40 M 50 F (12 mo)
3. Chapman et al. (1971)	Shock, self-management; posttreatment therapist monitoring:				
	2 weeks:	4 M 8 F	75 M 100 F	25 M 37 F	25 M 29 F
	11 weeks:	4 M 7 F	100 M 100 F 86 F	50 M 71 F	50 M (12 mo) 57 F
4. Berecz (1972)	Electric shock aversion, imagined versus real smoking	56 M 32 F	[a]		
5. Suedfeld and Ikard (1973)	Sensory deprivation	3 M 2 F	100 M 50 F	67 M 50 F (3 mo)	
6. Delahunt and Curran (1976)	Negative practice or self-control	50 F	67	22	
	Negative practice and self-control		89	56 }	
	Control		15	0 } [d]	
	Nonspecific treatment		56	11	
7. Russell et al. (1976)	Electric shock and controls	28 M 28 F	64 M[b] 57 F[b]		
8. Tongas et al. (1976)[c]	Covert sensit., smoke aversion, group therapy, combined treatment	38 M 34 F		71 M} 39 F}[e]	62 M}[e](12 mo) 32 F} 48 M}[e](24 mo) 18 F}

[a] Percentage reduction: little for F, more for M in imagined smoking condition.
[b] Two weeks posttreatment.
[c] Results based only on those completing treatment.
[d] $p < .05$.
[e] $.05 < p < .10$.

Table 5. Pharmacotherapy: Smoking Cessation Treatment Results by Sex

Study	Treatment	N	End-of-treatment (%)	Six months (%)	Long term (%)
1. Turle, (1958)[a]	Hydroxyzine	23 F	4 F		
2. Merry and Preston (1963)[a]	Lobeline	45 M / 31 F	29 M / 32 F		0 M / 0 F (12 mo)
3. Whitehead and Davies (1964)	Methylphenidate / Diazepam	10 M / 6 F	20 M / 0 F		
4. Golledge (1965)[a]	Lobeline	19 M / 8 F	63 M / 63 F[b]		
5. Mausner et al. (1967)	Lobeline	157 M and F	[b]		
6. Ross (1967)[a]	Lobeline / Amphetamine	728 M / 745 F	40 M / 29 F }[c]		21 M / 12 F }[c] (10–57 wks)
7. Schauble et al. (1967)[a]	Lobeline / Amphetamine / Lobeline, amphetamine, and education	33 M / 35 F / 14 M / 17 F	18 M / 26 F }[c] / 57 M / 26 F		
8. Wilhelmsen (1968)	Methylscopolamine tranquilizer	291 M / 200 F		56 M / 41 F }[c] (2 mo)	
9. Wetterqvist (1971, 1974)[a]	Methylscopolamine	192 M / 98 F	50 M / 33 F }[c]		19 M }(12 mo) 9 M }(60 mo) / 12 F 5 F
10. Arvidsson (1971)[a]	Anticholinergics, groups, aversion therapy	50 M / 50 F	85 M / 85 F		48 M }[c](12 mo) / 22 F
11. West et al. (1977)[a]	Lobeline, amphetamine	255 M / 288 F	43 M / 33 F }[c]		22 M }[c](60 mo) / 13.5 F

[a] Results based only on those completing treatment or contacted for follow-up.
[b] Borderline trend, greater reduction in M.
[c] $p < .05$.

rates were significantly higher than female rates; number of studies in which males and females did not differ in quitting rates; and number of studies for which results were not reported in a form amenable to statistical evaluation.

For *end of treatment results,* in the education category (Table 2), 2 out of 10 studies supported the hypothesis of higher male quitting rates, two reported no difference, and six could not be evaluated; in the psychotherapy category (Table 3), 1 out of 7 studies supported the hypothesis of higher male quitting rates, 2 reported no difference, and 4 could not be evaluated; in the behavior modification category (Table 4), none out of 8 studies supported the hypothesis of higher male quitting rates, 5 showed no difference, and 3 could not be evaluated; in the pharmacotherapy category (Table 5), 3 out of 11 studies reported higher male quitting rates, 5 showed no difference, and 3 could not be evaluated.

For *long-term abstinence* (follow-up) *results,* in the education category, out of 10 studies, 3 showed higher male quitting rates, 2 showed no difference, and 5 were not analyzable; in the psychotherapy category, out of 7 studies, 1 showed male superiority at follow-up, 2 showed no difference, and 4 were not analyzable; in the behavior modification category, out of 8 studies, none showed higher male long-term abstinence rates, 3 showed no difference, and 5 could not be analyzed; in the pharmacotherapy category, out of 11 studies, 3 showed higher male abstinence rates, 2 showed no difference, and 6 could not be evaluated.

There are a meager three reports in the literature (listed in Table 2) of smoking cessation interventions in *pregnant women.* Of the two studies reporting abstinence figures, one showed no difference between intervention and control groups (Baric et al., 1976), and one showed 50% abstinence of those completing treatment at nine-month follow-up; this latter result is very encouraging, but it is based on a very small sample in an affluent community, where one might expect high compliance (Danaher et al., 1978).

The majority of studies show no significant difference between male and female quitting rates, either at end of treatment or at long-term follow-up. Counting only those studies in which significance of male–female differences could be evaluated, men had significantly higher quitting rates at end of treatment in 30% of the reports (6 out of 20) and at long-term follow-up in 44% of the reports (7 out of 16). Approximately half of the studies could not be evaluated at one or the other time interval, however, because of either lack of information or use of a wholly female sample. There are isolated incidents of reversals in trend (women doing better than men), but none of the differences have reached statistical significance. Those studies reporting significantly higher abstinence rates for men tended to be those with large subject samples.

Therefore, the overall evidence for this trend can be considered suggestive.

Social Support. A social support hypothesis is frequently cited in the treatment literature to explain gender differences in quitting. It is often suggested that women do differentially better in programs that provide a maximum amount of social support and tend to do worse in situations where program support is low or where outside factors militate against quitting. For example, Resnikoff et al. (1968) were able to differentiate those women (but not men) who did poorly in group-plus-medication treatment from those who did well using the Social Introversion scale of the Minnesota Multiphasic Personality Inventory. This scale measures outgoing tendencies and degree of discomfort in social situations. Women scoring high on this scale (shyer, more socially introverted) did more poorly than low-scoring women. This study provides just one example of the observation that social support seems to be of lesser consequence to men in quitting smoking, although spousal encouragement is important (Schwartz and Dubitzky, 1968). Considering the overall categories in Tables 2–5, women do more poorly in treatments characterized by less individual attention, such as education and pharmacotherapy, compared with the categories of psychotherapy and behavior modification, where contact is usually maximized in a small-group or individual–therapist setting.

A number of examples may be offered in support of this hypothesis. Guilford's 1966 study is an oft-cited demonstration that women do significantly more poorly quitting smoking on their own (unaided) than in a group (aided), while men achieve constant success rates across treatments. (It should be pointed out that quitting rates of men and women within each treatment, aided or unaided, did not differ significantly; a significant difference was found only when comparing female success rates across treatment groups.) In a similar vein, Dubren (1977) reported that twice as many women as men participated in a television stop-smoking campaign, but that many fewer women were able to stop smoking, presumably because of lack of clinic support. Both Tongas et al. (1976) and Wilhelmsen (1968) commented that housewives have greater difficulty quitting than people who are not alone all day, a finding that is not congruent with the nationwide survey of Haesnzel et al. (1956). Berglund (1969) found that the number of regular smokers and nonsmokers in the subject's environment was relevent to the quitting efforts of women but not to those of men (cf. Schwartz and Dubitzky, 1968).

Personality Dynamics. There may be other reasons related to the psychodynamics of smoking behavior that explain why women might experience greater difficulty giving up smoking than men. These were discussed in Section 4 of this chapter. While delving into psychodynamic speculation can be highly provocative, dynamic analysis is clearly not critical to quitting smoking, although it may be important in maintaining abstinence. Many of the studies in which men and women achieve similar abstinence rates do not utilize a technique of dynamic analysis. These are exemplified most clearly in the behavior modification literature and may involve aversive conditioning, self-control strategies, and nonspecific support efforts. For example, Russell et al. (1976) reported equivalent success with heavy smokers of both sexes. Subjects who received electric-shock aversion treatment were just as successful as "attention-placebo" controls, but the no-treatment controls did not fare as well. The question of whether insight is a necessary prerequisite for achieving permanent behavior change is a major battleground in the psychotherapy literature and cannot at present be resolved. It does not appear that insight, or lack of it, provides a critical difference to male–female smoking cessation efforts.

The Smoking Abstinence Syndrome.   Little attention seems to have been paid to sex differences in smoking withdrawal. As nicotine is a potent central nervous system stimulant and depressant with direct or indirect actions on cholinergic and adrenergic neurotransmission, a wide range of physiological and psychological changes might be expected to occur on cessation of chronic administration. These include decreased heart rate, decreased urinary epinephrine and norepinephrine, increased hand steadiness and skin temperature, irritability, hunger, craving, and sleep changes, all of which are consistent with a lowering of arousal level (Knapp et al., 1963; Myrsten and Elgerot, 1974; USDHEW, 1964; Horn, 1970). Among the studies reviewed for this chapter, few mentioned gender as a factor in connection with withdrawal, and none suggested that men and women differ in the severity of smoking withdrawal symptoms. Factors contributing to relapse, such as craving and nervousness, were reported to be similar for men and women (Peterson et al., 1968), and women who experienced the greatest craving during the initial five days of abstinence were most likely to be recidivists (Guilford, 1967). It is likely that the abstinence syndrome is a major factor in recidivism during the first few weeks of cessation when relapse is most common (Hunt et al., 1971) and that the number of cigarettes smoked per day is an important variable in ease of withdrawal (Burns, 1969).

It is also during this early period of abstinence that learning of substitute behaviors for smoking must occur. Whether by association with nicotine as a primary reinforcer, or by some other mechanism (e.g., a dynamic explanation involving oral satisfaction), the act of smoking becomes intimately linked with many daily behaviors. The insight therapist, the learning theorist–behavior modifier, the educator, and the pharmacotherapist all try to break the bonds between smoking and the rest of behavior, using widely differing techniques. The poor long-term success rates provide a sad tribute to the tenacity of those reinforcing bonds in all human beings, regardless of sex.

To summarize the treatment literature, neither sex is very successful in quitting smoking. There is some evidence that men have higher initial as well as long-term success rates than women, but the evidence is far from conclusive. The picture is further complicated by demographic factors such as duration of smoking, number of cigarettes smoked daily, and depth of inhalation. Social support in the cessation program and in the environment may also be relevant to the differential success rates that were reported.

A major contribution to the resolution of this question would be reexamination of the data from the vast number of studies in the literature that do not report gender differences in treatment outcome. In order to resolve the question of the existence of gender differences in treatment success, previously published data that omitted such an analysis might be reexamined by interested authors. An additional recommendation is that future studies contain breakdowns of data by sex and a statistical evaluation of differential outcome. One might then be able to make predictive hypotheses concerning outcome to be tested in further research.

8. SUMMARY AND CONCLUSIONS

Prior to the era of European exploration, tobacco was widely known and cultivated throughout the Americas. It was traditionally employed for magicoreligious purposes, but its use became secularized after worldwide distribution. Tobacco was readily accepted by both men and women in indigenous populations and was initially just as eagerly adopted by European civilization.

Migration, urbanization, and societal change were accompanied by fluctuations in sex-associated smoking patterns in the United States. Women began to take up cigarette smoking in significant numbers after 1930; epidemiological data suggest that the smoking habits of men and women are becoming progressively similar. Increased smoking in the female population is a combined function of earlier recruitment and heavier smoking practices.

Nicotine is a potent pharmacologic agent, with effects on the brain, the autonomic nervous system, and various body organs. It is postulated to act as a primary reinforcer in smoking. There have been speculations that smoking serves different psychological purposes for men and for women, primarily in the area of negative-affect reduction.

The serious nature of the health hazards associated with smoking make it imperative that a downward trend in female smoking be firmly established before women achieve the dubious distinction of having mortality rates for smoking-related disease equal to those of men. Cancer of the lung, larynx, pharynx, oral cavity, and bladder; cardiovascular disease; chronic obstructive pulmonary disease; and peptic ulcer disease—all have been causally or strongly linked to smoking. There are additional health risks that apply to women smokers alone: the use of oral contraceptives has been identified as an interactive risk factor for coronary heart disease, and smoking may lower the age of natural menopause.

The pregnant woman who smokes exposes not only her own body but also that of the developing fetus to the harmful effects of smoking. Smokers bear infants approximately 200 g lighter than nonsmokers. The mechanism of this fetal growth retardation is now unclear but has been linked to the effects of components of cigarette smoke, such as carbon monoxide, nicotine, and cyanide. The increased risk of perinatal mortality among infants born to smokers has been associated with both lowered birth weight and prematurity. Relationships are being discovered between smoking and increased incidence of spontaneous abortion and certain complications of pregnancy. The risk attendant on maternal smoking extends into the first year of life, in terms of increased risk of developing certain respiratory infections. Yet, only one third of pregnant women smokers abstain during pregnancy.

Since women in our society are more involved than men with health care services, in terms of personal utilization and the family provider role, it should be possible to appeal to those concerns with regard to smoking and illness. Professionals in the fields of medicine, public health, and behavioral science are devoting increasing efforts to promoting smoking cessation and the prevention of its onset in teenagers. The relatively low treatment success rates probably reflect a selective elimination process; that is, those who are able to quit by themselves do not need to attend formal programs. National surveys (U.S.) show that in 1975, approximately 43% of the male and 33% of the female population who had ever smoked were no longer doing so. The treatment literature contains very few studies in which success rates are reported by gender. There is a suggestion that women do more poorly in achieving abstinence as well as in maintaining it over the long run. This finding awaits further confirmation, as the majority of reports showed no gender difference in treatment success. If the finding should prove reliable, to what can it be attributed?

    a. Psychophysiological differences between males and females in the reaction to stress, for which smoking is a learned response?

    b. Format of treatment being insufficiently supportive and person-
alized?

    c. Lack of a social support system in the environment to sustain
quitting motivation and effort?

Whatever aspect of smoking behavior the scientist or clinician
should choose to study—its prevention, psychological and physiological
mechanisms, disease consequences, or cessation-directed treatment—
their efforts and cooperation are much needed. The research questions
are manifold, and the solutions, as yet, are few.

ACKNOWLEDGMENT

We acknowledge the support of this research by the American
Cancer Society, Inc., through Grant No. PDT 2K.

REFERENCES

Ahmed, P. I., and Gleeson, G. A., 1970, *Changes in Cigarette Smoking Habits between
1955 and 1966*, Public Health Service Publication No. 1000, Series 10, No. 59,
Rockville, Md.

Andrews, J., 1973, Thiocyanate and smoking in pregnancy, *J. Obstet. Gynaecol. Br.
Commonw.* **80**:810–814.

Andrews, J., and McGarry, J. M., 1972, A community study of smoking in pregnancy, *J.
Obstet. Gynaecol. Br. Commonw.* **79**:1057–1073.

Arvidsson, T., 1971, Views on smoking withdrawal: Experiences with smoking withdrawal
in Stockholm, *Socialmedicinsk Tidskr.* **2**:113–116. As reported in USDHEW, *Smoking
and Health Bulletin*, No. 71-0531.

Baric, L., MacArthur, C., and Sherwood, M., 1976, A study of health education aspects
of smoking in pregnancy, *Int. J. Health Educ.*, **19** (Suppl.):1–17.

Berecz, J., 1972, Modification of smoking behavior through self-administered punishment
of imagined behavior: A new approach to aversion therapy, *J. Consult. Clin. Psychol.*
38:244–250.

Berglund, E., 1969, *Tobacco Withdrawal Clinics: The Five-Day Plan, The Final Report*,
Norwegian Cancer Society, Oslo.

Bergman, A. B., and Wiesner, L. A., 1976, Relationship of cigarette smoking to sudden
infant death syndrome, *Pediatrics* **58**:665–668.

Bewley, B. R., Bland, J. M., and Harris, R., 1974, Factors associated with the starting of
cigarette smoking by primary school children, *Br. J. Prev. Soc. Med.* **28**:37–44.

Boucot, K. R., 1968, Smoking problems of young women in the 1920's, *Arch. Environ.
Health* **16**:596–597.

Bozzetti, L. P., 1972, Group psychotherapy with addicted smokers, *Psychother. Psychosom.* **20**:172–175.

Burbank, F., 1972, U.S. lung cancer death rates begin to rise proportionately more rapidly
for females than for males: A dose–response effect? *J. Chronic Dis.* **25**:473–479.

Burns, B. H., 1969, Chronic chest disease, personality, and success in stopping cigarette
smoking, *Br. J. Prev. Soc. Med.* **23**:23–27.

538   ELLEN R. GRITZ

Butler, N. R., and Goldstein, H., 1973, Smoking in pregnancy and subsequent child development, *Br. Med. J.* **4**:573–575.

Chapman, R. F., Smith, J. W., and Layden, T. A., 1971, Elimination of cigarette smoking by punishment and self-management training, *Behav. Res. Ther.* **9**:255–264.

Colley, J. R., Holland, W. W., and Corkhill, R. T., 1974, Influence of passive smoking and parental phlegm on pneumonia and bronchitis in early childhood, *Lancet* **2**:1031–1034.

Danaher, B. G., Shisslak, C. M., Thompson, C. B., and Ford, J. D., 1978, A smoking cessation program for pregnant women: Exploratory study, *Am. J. Public Health* **68**:896–898.

Delahunt, J., and Curran, J. P., 1976, Effectiveness of negative practice and self-control techniques in the reduction of smoking behavior, *J. Consult. Clin. Psychol.* **44**:1002–1007.

Delarue, N. C., 1973, A study in smoking withdrawal, *Can. J. Public Health* **64**:S5–S19.

DeLucas, A. C., 1968, Myths, remedies and sayings on tobacco connected with folk medicine, trans. from *Medicamenta* **26**:161–165. As cited in *Bibliography of Smoking and Health,* USDHEW, 1970.

Devesa, S. S., and Schneiderman, M. A., 1977, Increase in the number of cancer deaths in the United States, *Am. J. Epidemiol.* **106**:1–5.

Dicken, C., and Bryson, R., 1978, Psychology in action: The smoking of psychology, *Am. Psychol.* **33**:504–507.

Donovan, J. W., 1977, Randomised controlled trial of anti-smoking advice in pregnancy, *Br. J. Prev. Soc. Med.* **31**:6–12.

Donovan, J. W., Burgess, P. L., Hossack, C. M., and Yudkin, G. D., 1975, Routine advice against smoking in pregnancy, *J. R. College Gen. Pract.* **25**:264–268.

Dubren, R., 1977, Evaluation of a televised stop-smoking clinic, *Public Health Rep.* **92**:81–84.

Duffus, G. M., and MacGillivray, I., 1968, The incidence of pre-eclamptic toxemia in smokers and nonsmokers, *Lancet* **1**:994–995.

Dunn, H. G., McBurney, A. K., Ingram, S., and Hunter, C. M., 1976, Maternal cigarette smoking during pregnancy and the child's subsequent development, I, Physical growth to the age of 6-½ years, *Can. J. Public Health* **67**:499–505.

Eisinger, R. A., 1971, Psychosocial predictors of smoking recidivism, *J. Health Soc. Behav.* **12**:355–362.

Fee, W. M., and Benson, C., 1971, Group therapy: A review of 6 years' experience in a Scottish anti-smoking clinic, *Community Med.* **126**:361–364.

Ferguson, B. B., Wilson, D. J., and Schaffner, W., 1976, Determination of nicotine concentrations in human milk, *Am. J. Dis. Child.* **130**:837–839.

Fisher, J., 1976, Sex differences in smoking dynamics, *J. Health Soc. Behav.* **17**:156–163.

Frankenhaeuser, M., 1977, Sex differences in psychoneuroendocrine reactions to challenging situations, *Exp. Brain Res.* **28**:R17.

Frankenhaeuser, M., 1978, Sex differences in reactions to psychosocial stressors and psychoactive drugs, in: *Society, Stress and Disease,* Vol. 3, *The Productive and Reproductive Age—Male and Female Roles and Relationships* (L. Levi, ed.), pp. 135–140, Oxford University Press, Toronto.

Frankenhaeuser, M., Rauste von Wright, M., Collins, A., von Wright, J., Sedvall, G., and Swahn, C. G., 1978, Sex differences in psychoneuroendocrine reactions to examination stress, *Psychosom. Med.* **40**:334–343.

Furst, P. T., 1976, *Hallucinogens and Culture,* Chandler and Sharp, San Francisco.

Gennser, G., Marsal, K., and Brantmark, B., 1975, Maternal smoking and fetal breathing movements, *Am. J. Obstet. Gynecol.* **123**:861–867.

Goldstein, H., 1977, Smoking in pregnancy: Some notes on the statistical controversy, *Br. J. Prev. Soc. Med.* **31**:13–17.

Gollege, A. H., 1965, Influencing factors in anti-smoking clinics, *Med. Officer* **114**:59–61.

Graham, H., 1976, Smoking in pregnancy: The attitudes of expectant mothers, *Soc. Sci. Med.* **10**:399–405.

Gritz, E. R., and Jarvik, M. E., 1978, Nicotine and smoking, in: *Handbook of Psychopharmacology*, Vol. 2 (L. L. Iverson, S. D. Iverson, and S. H. Snyder, eds.), pp. 426–464, Plenum, New York.

Guilford, J. S., 1967, Sex differences between successful and unsuccessful abstainers from smoking, in: *Studies and Issues in Smoking Behavior* (S. V. Zagona, ed.), pp. 95–102, University of Arizona Press, Tucson.

Haenszel, W., Shimkin, M. B., and Miller, H. P., 1956, *Tobacco Smoking Patterns in the United States*, U.S. Public Health Monograph 45, Public Health Service Publication 463, Government Printing Office, Washington, D.C.

Handel, S., 1973, Change in smoking habits in a general practice, *Postgrad. Med. J.* **49**:679–681.

Haneveld, G. T., 1965, A curious smoking habit in the Caribbean region, *Trop. Geogr. Med.* **17**:186–190.

Hardy, J. B., and Mellits, E. D., 1972, Does maternal smoking during pregnancy have a long-term effect on the child? *Lancet* **2**:1332–1336.

Harlap, S., and Davies, A. M., 1974, Infant admissions to hospital and maternal smoking, *Lancet* **1**:529–532.

Heimann, R. K., 1960, *Tobacco and Americans,* McGraw-Hill, New York.

Holbrook, J. H., 1977, Tobacco and health, *Ca* **27**:344–353.

Hollingsworth, D. R., Moser, R. S., Carlson, J. W., and Thompson, K. T., 1976, Abnormal adolescent primiparous pregnancy: Association of race, human chorionic somatomammotropin production, and smoking, *Am. J. Obstet. Gynecol.* **126**:230–237.

Horn, D., 1970, *Adult Use of Tobacco, Report of the National Clearinghouse for Smoking and Health*, U.S. Public Health Service, Department of Health, Education, and Welfare, Publication No. (HSM)73-8727.

Hunt, W. A., Barnett, L. W., and Branch, L. G., 1971, Relapse rates in addiction programs, *J. Clin. Psychol.* **22**:455–456.

Ikard, F. F., and Tomkins, S., 1973, The experience of affect as a determinant of smoking behavior: A series of validity studies, *J. Abnorm. Psychol.* **81**:172–181.

Jaffe, J. H., and Jarvik, M. E., 1978, Tobacco use and tobacco use disorder, in: *Psychopharmacology: A Generation of Progress* (M. A. Lipton, A. DiMascio, and K. F. Killan, eds.), pp. 1665–1676, Raven, New York.

Jain, A. R., 1976, Cigarette smoking, use of oral contraceptives, and myocardial infarction, *Am. J. Obstet. Gynecol.* **126**:301–307.

Jick, H., Porter, J., and Morrison, A. S., 1977, Relation between smoking and age of natural menopause, *Lancet* **1**:1354–1355.

Jick, H., Dinan, B., and Rothman, K. J., 1978, Oral contraceptives and nonfatal myocardial infarction, *J. Am. Med. Assoc.* **239**:1403–1408.

Kanzler, M., Jaffe, J., and Zeidenberg, P., 1976, Long- and short-term effectiveness of a large-scale proprietary smoking cessation program—A 4-year follow-up of Smokenders participants, *J. Clin. Psychol.* **32**:661–669.

Keutzer, C. S., 1968, Behavior modification of smoking: The experimental investigation of diverse techniques, *Behav. Res. Ther.* **6**:137–157.

Kline, J., Stein, Z. A., Susser, M., and Warburton, D., 1977, Smoking: A risk factor for spontaneous abortion, *N. Engl. J. Med.* **297**:793–796.

Kline, M. V., 1970, The use of extended group hypnotherapy sessions in controlling cigarette smoking, *Int. J. Clin. Exp. Hypn.* **18**:270–281.

Knapp, P., Bliss, C. M., and Wells, H., 1963, Addictive aspects in heavy cigarette smoking, *Am. J. Psychol.* **119**:966–972.

Lander, M., 1885, *The Tobacco Problem,* Lee and Shepard, Boston.

Larson, P. S., and Silvette, H., 1975, *Tobacco: Experimental and Clinical Studies* (Supplement III), Williams & Wilkins, Baltimore.

Laufer, B., 1924a, *Introduction of Tobacco into Europe,* Field Museum of Natural History, Anthropology Leaflet No. 19, Chicago.

Laufer, B., 1924b, *Tobacco and Its Use in Asia,* Field Museum of Natural History, Anthropology Leaflet No. 18, Chicago.

Lewine, H., 1970, *Good-Bye to All That,* McGraw-Hill, New York.

Lewis, A., 1924, *Use of Tobacco in New Guinea and Neighboring Regions,* Field Museum of Natural History, Chicago.

Lewis, C. E., and Lewis, M. A., 1977, The potential impact of sexual equality on health, *N. Engl. J. Med.* **297**:863–869.

Lichtenstein, E., and Danaher, B. G., 1976, Modification of smoking behavior: A critical analysis of theory, research, and practice, in: *Progress in Behavior Modification,* Vol. 3 (M. Hersen, R. M. Eisler, and P. M. Miller, eds.), pp. 79–132, Academic, New York.

Lichtenstein, E., Keutzer, C. S., and Himes, K. H., 1969, "Emotional" role-playing and changes in smoking attitudes and behavior, *Psychol. Rep.* **25**:379–387.

Longo, L. D., 1976, Carbon monoxide: Effects of oxygenation of the fetus in utero, *Science* **194**:523–525.

Longo, L. D., 1977, Some physiologic effects of carbon monoxide and nicotine on the fetus "in utero," in: *Smoking and Heatlh,* Vol. 2, *Health Consequences, Education, Cessation Activities, and Governmental Action,* U.S. Department of Health, Education, and Welfare, Publication No. (NIH)77-1413, pp. 211–230.

Mann, J. I., Doll, R., Thorogood, M., Vessey, M. P., and Waters, W. E., 1976, Risk factors for myocardial infarction in young women, *Br. J. Prev. Soc. Med.* **30**:94–100.

Mann, L. A., and Janis, I. L., 1968, A follow-up study on the long-term effects of emotional role playing, *J. Pers. Soc. Psychol.* **8**:339–342.

Manning, F. A., and Feyerabend, C., 1976, Cigarette smoking and fetal breathing movements, *Br. J. Obstet. Gynaecol.* **83**:262–270.

Mausner, B., Mausner. J. S., and Rial, W. Y., 1967, The influence of a physician on the smoking behavior of his patients, in: *Studies and Issues in Smoking Behavior* (S. V. Zagona, ed.), pp. 103–107, University of Arizona Press, Tucson.

McGarry, J. M., and Andrews, J., Smoking in pregnancy and vitamin B_{12} metabolism, *Br. Med. J.* **2**:74–77.

McKennell, A. C., and Thomas, R. K., 1967, *Adults and Adolescents' Smoking Habits and Attitudes* (Government Social Survey), HMSO, London.

Merry, J., and Preston, G., 1963, The effect of buffered lobeline sulphate on cigarette smoking, *Practitioner* **190**:628–631.

Meyer, M. B., and Tonascia, J. A., 1977, Maternal smoking, pregnancy complications and perinatal mortality, *Am. J. Obstet. Gynecol.* **128**:494–502.

Miller, H. C., Hassanein, K., and Hensleigh, P. A., 1976, Fetal growth retardation in relation to maternal smoking and weight gain in pregnancy, *Am. J. Obstet. Gynecol.* **125**:55–60.

Morison, S. E., 1971, *The European Discovery of America, The Northern Voyages,* A.D. *500–1600,* Oxford University Press, New York.

Moses, F. M., 1964, Treating the smoking habit by discussion and hypnosis, *Dis. Nerv. Syst.* **25**:184–188.

Myrsten, A. L., and Elgerot, A., 1974, Effects of abstinence from tobacco smoking on physiological and psychological arousal level in habitual smokers, Reports from the Psychological Laboratories, No. 428, University of Stockholm, Stockholm.

Naeye, R. L., 1977, Sudden infant death syndrome: Review of recent advances, *Arch. Pathol. Lab. Med.* **101:**165–167.

Ochsner, A., and Damrau, F., 1970, Control of cigarette habit by psychological aversive conditioning: Clinical evaluation in 53 smokers, *J. Am. Geriatr. Soc.* **18:**365–369.

Park, W. Z., 1938, *Shamanism in Western North America,* Northwestern University, Evanston, Ill.

Peterson, D. I., Lonergan, L. H., Hardinge, M. G., and Teel, C. W., 1968, Results of a stop-smoking program, *Arch. Environ. Health* **16:**211–214.

Petitti, D. B,, and Wingerd, J., 1978, Use of oral contraceptives, cigarette smoking, and risk of subarachnoid hemorrhage, *Lancet* **2:**234–236.

Pettigrew, A. R., Logan, R. W., and Willocks, J., 1977, Smoking in pregnancy—Effects on birth weight and on cyanide and thiocyanate levels in mother and baby, *Br. J. Obstet. Gynaecol.* **84:**31–34.

Pyszka, R. H., Ruggels, W. L., and Janowica, L. M., 1973, *Health Behavior Change: Smoking Cessation,* Stanford Research Institute, Menlo Park, Calif., December 1973, mimeograph.

Quigley, L. F., Shklar, G., and Cobb, C. M., 1966, Reverse cigarette smoking in Caribbeans: Clinical, histologic, and cytologic observations, *J. Am. Dent. Assoc.* **72:**867–873.

Raw, M., 1978, The treatment of cigarette dependence, in: *Research Advances in Alcohol and Drug Problems,* Vol. 4 (Y. Israel, F. B. Glaser, H. Kalant, R. E. Popham, W. Schmidt, and R. G. Smart, eds.), pp. 441–485, Plenum, New York.

Resnikoff, A., Schauble, P. G., and Woody, R. H., 1968, Personality correlates of withdrawal from smoking, *J. Psychol.* **68:**117–120.

Robert, J. C., 1952, *The Story of Tobacco in America,* Knopf, New York.

Ross, C. A., 1967, Smoking withdrawal research clinics, *Am. J. Public Health* **57:**677–681.

Royal College of Physicians, 1962, *Smoking and Health,* Pitman Medical Publishing Company, Tunbridge Wells, England.

Royal College of Physicians of London, 1977, *Smoking or Health,* Pitman Medical Publishing Company, London.

Russell, M. A. H., 1970, Effect of electric aversion on cigarette smoking, *Br. Med. J.* **1:**82–86.

Russell, M. A. H., 1971, Cigarette smoking: Natural history of a dependence disorder, *Br. J. Med. Psychol.* **44:**1–16.

Russell, M. A. H., 1976, Tobacco smoking and nicotine dependence, in: *Research Advances in Alcohol and Drug Problems,* Vol. 3, (R. J. Gibbins, Y. Israel, H. Kalant, R. E. Popham, W. Schmidt, and R. G. Smart, eds.), pp. 1–47, Wiley, New York.

Russell, M. A. H., Armstrong, E., and Patel, U. A., 1976, Temporal contiguity in electric aversion therapy for cigarette smoking, *Behav. Res. Ther.* **14:**103–123.

Salber, E. J., and Abelin, T., 1967, Smoking behavior of Newton school children—5-year follow-up, *Pediatrics* **40:**363–372.

Salber, E. J., Welsh, B., and Taylor, S. V., 1963, Reasons for smoking given by secondary school children, *J. Health Hum. Behav.* **4:**118–129.

Schauble, P. G., Woody, R. H., and Resnikoff, A., 1967, Educational therapy and withdrawal from smoking, *J. Clin. Psychol.* **23:**518–519.

Schmahl, D. P., Lichtenstein, E., and Harris, D. E., 1972, Successful treatment of habitual smokers with warm smoky air and rapid smoking, *J. Consult. Clin. Psychol.* **36:**105–111.

Schuman, L. M., 1978, Patterns of smoking behavior, in: *Research on Smoking Behavior* (M. E. Jarvik, J. W. Cullen, E. R. Gritz, T. M. Vogt, and L. J. West, eds.), pp. 36–65, National Institute on Drug Abuse, Monograph No. 17, Washington, D.C.

Schwartz, J. L., 1978, Smoking cures: Ways to kick an unhealthy habit, in: *Research on Smoking Behavior* (M. E. Jarvik, J. W. Cullen, E. R. Gritz, T. M. Vogt, and L. J. West, eds.), pp, 308–336, National Institute on Drug Abuse Monograph, No. 17, Washington, D.C.

Schwartz, J. L., and Dubitsky, M., 1968, One-year follow-up results of a smoking cessation program, *Can. J. Public Health* **59**:161–165.

Seidman, H., Silverberg, B. S., and Bodden, A., 1978, Probabilities of eventually developing and dying of cancer, *Ca* **28**:33–48.

Silverberg, E., 1979, Cancer statistics, 1979, *Ca* **29**:6–21.

Simpson, W. J., 1957, A preliminary report on cigarette smoking and the incidence of prematurity, *Am. J. Obstet. Gynecol.* **73**:808–815.

Slone, D., Shapiro, S., Rosenberg, L., Kaufman, D. W., Hartz, S. C., Rossi, A. C., Stolley, P. D., and Miettinen, O. S., 1978, Relation of cigarette smoking to myocardial infarction in young women, *N. Engl. J. Med.* **298**:1273–1276.

Smith, G. M., 1970, Personality and smoking: A review of the empirical literature, in: *Learning Mechanisms in Smoking* (W. A. Hunt, ed.), pp. 42–61, Aldine, Chicago.

Streltzer, N. E., and Koch, G. V., 1968, Influence of emotional role-playing on smoking habits and attitudes, *Psychol. Rep.* **22**:817–820.

Suedfeld, P., and Ikard, F. F., 1973, Attitude manipulation in restricted environments, IV, Psychologically addicted smokers treated in sensory deprivation, *Br. J. Addict.* **68**:170–176.

Tamerin, J. S., 1972, The psychodynamics of quitting smoking in a group, *Am. J. Psychiatry* **129**:101–107.

Thompson, L. S., 1960, *A Few Notes on the Folklore of Tobacco*, Ohio Valley Folk Research Project, The Ross County Historical Society, Ohio Valley Folk Publication, Chillicothe, New Series No. 41.

Tongas, P., Goodkind, S., and Patterson, J., 1976, An investigation of effects of post-treatment maintenance on the cessation of smoking within four behavioral treatment modalities, Paper presented at the Western Psychological Association Convention, Los Angeles.

Turle, G. C., 1958, An investigation into the therapeutic action of hydroxyzine (Atarax) in the treatment of nervous disorders and the control of the tobacco habit, *J. Med. Sci.* **104**:826–833.

U.S. Department of Health, Education, and Welfare, Public Health Service, 1973, *The Health Consequences of Smoking*, DHEW Publication No. (HSM) 73-8704, Washington, D.C.

U.S. Department of Health, Education, and Welfare, 1973, *Adult Use of Tobacco: 1970*, National Clearinghouse for Smoking and Health, Bureau of Health Education, Center for Disease Control, Public Health Service, DHEW Publication No. (HSM) 73-8727, Washington, D.C.

U.S. Department of Health, Education, and Welfare, Public Health Service, 1964, *Smoking and Health*, Report of the Advisory Committee to the Surgeon General of the Public Health Service, Publication No. 1103, Washington, D.C.

U.S. Department of Health, Education, and Welfare, Public Health Service, 1976a, *Adult Use of Tobacco*: Center for Disease Control and National Cancer Institute, June 1976, Washington, D.C.

U.S. Department of Health, Education, and Welfare, Public Health Service, 1976b, *Teen-age Smoking: National Patterns of Cigarette Smoking, Ages 12 through 18, in 1972 and 1974*, DHEW Publication No. (NIH) 76-931, Washington, D.C.

U.S. Department of Health, Education, and Welfare, 1976c, *Survey of Health Professionals,*

1975, National Clearinghouse for Smoking and Health, Bureau of Health Education, Center for Disease Control, Public Health Service, pp. 1–9, Atlanta.

U.S. Department of Health, Education, and Welfare, Public Health Service, 1977, *Cigarette Smoking among Teen-agers and Young Women*, DHEW Publication No. (NIH) 77-1203, Washington, D.C.

Van Vunakis, H., Langone, J. J., and Milunsky, A., 1974, Nicotine and cotinine in the amniotic fluid of smokers in the second trimester of pregnancy, *Am. J. Obstet. Gynecol.* **120**:64–66.

Volle, R. L., and Koelle, G. B., 1975, Ganglionic stimulating and blocking agents, in: *The Pharmacological Basis of Therapeutics* (5th ed.) (L. S. Goodman and A. Gilman, eds.), pp. 565–574, Macmillan, New York.

Wagner, S., 1971, *Cigarette Country,* Praeger, New York.

West, D. W., Graham, S., Swanson, M., and Wilkinson, G., 1977, Five year follow-up of a smoking withdrawal clinic population, *Am. J. Public Health* **67**:536–544.

Wetterqvist, H., 1971, Points in the matter of giving up smoking: Smoking withdrawal in Lund, *Socialmedicinsk Tidskr.* **2**:111–112, as reported in author's abstract in U.S. Department of Health, Education, and Welfare Smoking and Health Bulletin 71-0536, Washington, D.C.

Wetterqvist, H., 1974, Experimental work in the antidotal treatment of smokers, 1966–1967, *Lakartidningen,* 1973, **70**:3591–3595, as reported in author's abstract in U.S. Department of Health, Education, and Welfare Smoking and Health Bulletin 74-0424, May 1974, Washington, D.C.

Whitehead, R. W., and Davies, J. M., 1964, A study of methylphenidate and diazepam as possible smoking deterrents, *Curr. Ther. Res.* **6**:363–367.

Wilbert, J., 1975, Magico-religious use of tobacco among South American Indians, in: *Cannabis and Culture* (V. Rubin, ed.), pp. 439–461, Mouton, The Hague.

Wilhelmsen, L., 1968, One year's experience in an anti-smoking clinic, *Scand. J. Respir. Dis.* **49**:251–259.

Williams, R. R., and Horm, J., 1977, Association of cancer sites with tobacco and alcohol consumption and socioeconomic status of patients: Interview study from the Third National Cancer Survey, *J. Natl. Cancer Inst.* **58**:525–547.

Yerushalmy, J., 1971, The relationship of parents' cigarette smoking to outcome of pregnancy—Implications as to the problem of inferring causation from observed associations, *Am. J. Epidemiol.* **93**:443–446.

Yerushalmy, J., 1972, Infants with low birthweight born before their mothers started to smoke cigarettes, *Am. J. Obstet. Gynecol.* **112**:277–284.

Zdeb, M. S., 1977, The probability of developing cancer, *Am. J. Epidemiol.* **106**:6–16.

15

Sex Differences in the Effects of Alcohol and Other Psychoactive Drugs on Endocrine Function

Clinical and Experimental Evidence

THEODORE J. CICERO

1. INTRODUCTION

General Considerations

There is relatively little information on the effects of psychoactive drugs on neuroendocrine function in humans or animals of either sex. In this brief narrative, those data that are available are reviewed. As is evident, in some areas there are few or no data on the effects of psychoactive drugs on neuroendocrine function in the female, providing little basis for a review of male–female differences in neuroendocrine responses to psychoactive drugs. Nevertheless, it is hoped a state-of-the-art analysis of the male will provide a firm basis for badly needed future studies of the female.

All of the available literature was examined for this review, but attention was focused primarily on the last five years. The principal reason is that radioimmunoassays have come into wide use in endocrine studies only recently, and thus direct examinations of drug–endocrine interactions have been possible only in the past several years. Much of the early literature, which employed bioassays or in which inferences

THEODORE J. CICERO • Departments of Psychiatry and Anatomy and Neurobiology, Washington University, School of Medicine, St. Louis, Missouri.

were drawn based on indirect evidence, has been avoided here wherever possible. Occasionally, however, when no direct measurements of endocrine parameters were available, what literature was at hand was discussed to provide as complete an overview as possible. In this review, the following psychoactive drugs have been examined: ethanol, the narcotics, marijuana, and central nervous system (CNS) stimulants, including amphetamine and LSD. The selection of drugs was limited by two considerations: first, whether there were sufficient data to warrant discussion, and, second, whether the drugs are commonly used in a nonclinical situation to alter mood.

There is a rapidly expanding body of information on the effects of psychoactive drugs on certain neuroendocrine axes in males, such as the hypothalamic–pituitary–gonadal and the hypothalamic–pituitary–adrenal axes. By contrast, we know considerably less about a number of other neuroendocrine systems (e.g., prolactin, growth hormone, and the hypothalamic–pituitary–thyroid axis), and sex differences in neuroendocrine responses to psychoactive drugs have been largely ignored. In this review, each neuroendocrine axis is discussed separately. Within each discussion, the clinical and experimental data pertaining to males are presented first, and then any available female data are contrasted with those obtained for the male. The human and animal literature has been evaluated concomitantly in each section, since findings in either area have governed developments in the other and, hence, any separation of human and animal studies would be contrived and confusing. Generally, however, an attempt has been made to describe the clinical situation observed in humans and then to follow this description with a detailed discussion of the human and animal experimental evidence.

Problems Unique to Studies in Humans

The effects of psychoactive drugs on endocrine function in humans have been inadequately studied in males and essentially ignored in females.

Drug studies of females have been avoided for two important reasons: (1) there are hourly, daily, weekly, and monthly (menstrual) cyclic variations in reproductive [e.g., estrogen, progesterone, luteinizing hormone (LH) and follicle-stimulating hormone (FSH)] and other [e.g., prolactin, cortisol, and adrenocorticotrophic hormones (ACTH)] hormones that make precise determinations of hormone status extremely difficult, particularly since there are considerable individual variations in these cyclic patterns; and (2) many women of childbearing age take oral contraceptives, which, of course, markedly alter hormonal status. Because of these factors, studies of drug–endocrine interactions in the female have been avoided. Unfortunately, even when such studies have been attempted, the cyclic nature of endocrine secretions has been overlooked so that the validity of many of the data is questionable.

Although cyclic hormone variations in the female seem to be well documented, such variations in the male have generally not been considered. However, a good deal of recent evidence suggests that many hormones in the male undergo such variations. For example, testosterone may have random, episodic, and highly individual secretion patterns, and it is certain that it has a circadian rhythm (Persky, 1977; Doering et al., 1975; Lacerda et al., 1973; West et al., 1973). In addition, there also appear to be diurnal, hourly, and random variations in the plasma level of many other hormones in the male, such as growth hormone, ACTH, cortisol, and prolactin (Sassin et al., 1972; Weitzman et al., 1971).

Clearly, studies of the effects of psychoactive drugs on endocrine function in the human must take into account the cyclic and individual nature of hormone secretions by obtaining multiple blood samples at regular intervals throughout the day or month (in the case of female reproductive studies) and by using very large subject populations. This kind of study has not been done for the most part: in many studies, sample sizes have been small; single blood samples are routine; when 24-hr blood samples have been obtained, only a single 24-hr period has been examined; and, finally, within any single study, not all relevant hormone measurements have been made, such as serum LH, FSH, and testosterone in the case of reproductive endocrinology.

There are other problems inherent in utilizing the human in drug–endocrine studies. Many variables, which may or may not be related to drug variables alone, can influence neuroendocrine status. For example, alcoholics or narcotic addicts have numerous problems other than their obvious addictions, such as psychiatric disturbances, organ pathology (e.g., liver and brain), poor nutritional status, polydrug abuse, and several other contaminating variables. Any of these variables can markedly alter endocrine profiles and hence must be controlled, which often, unfortunately, is impossible. Even if normal volunteers are employed, considerable care must be taken to assure that the subjects are healthy and that precise estimates of drug type and use patterns are obtained. This procedure has not always been rigorously carried out, and a number of these studies are therefore difficult to interpret.

The factors reviewed above explain in large part two facets of the human literature on the effects of psychoactive drugs on neuroendocrine status: the paucity of data for the female and the vast number of inconsistencies in the literature (and, consequently, the inability to generate definitive conclusions for either the male or the female human). In the following review, an attempt has been made to pull together all of the human and animal data to provide as consistent a picture as possible.

2. DRUG–ENDOCRINE STUDIES

Hypothalamic–Pituitary–Gonadal (H–P–G) Axis

Ethanol.   There is a vast amount of data on the effects of ethanol on the H–P–G axis in the male. By contrast, there are very few data on the female.

Studies in the Male.   Male alcoholics have many difficulties with their reproductive function, such as impaired libido, reduced fertility, gynecomastia, spider angiomata, testicular atrophy, and redistribution of secondary sex-linked body hair (Mendelson and Mello, 1976; Van Thiel and Lester, 1974, 1976a,b; Wright et al., 1976; Zanoboni and Zanoboni-Muciacci, 1975). Associated with the demasculinization or feminization observed in the alcoholic are pronounced reductions in serum testosterone levels and, possibly, an increase in estrogens (Lester and Van Thiel, 1977; Marks and Wright, 1977; Persky et al., 1977; Baker et al., 1976; Gordon et al., 1976; Green et al., 1976; Huttunen et al., 1976; Dotson et al., 1975; Farmer and Fabre, 1975; Pentikäinen et al., 1975; Mendelson and Mello, 1974; Ylikahri et al., 1974a,b, 1976; Chopra et al., 1973; Fabre et al., 1973; Galvão-Teles et al., 1973; Kent et al., 1973; Coppage and Cooner, 1965; Lloyd and Williams, 1948). Much research in the male alcoholic has understandably focused on the synthesis and the biological disposition of testosterone. A good deal of evidence has accumulated that suggests that the synthesis of testosterone by the testes is impaired and its catabolism by the liver enhanced in the alcoholic male (Gordon and Southren, 1977; Baker et al., 1976; Gordon et al., 1975, 1976; Rubin et al., 1976; Southren and Gordon, 1976; Dotson et al., 1975; Chopra et al., 1973). In addition to these testicular and hepatic difficulties, however, there also appears to be a defect in the hypothalamic–pituitary–luteinizing hormone (LH) axis (Gordon and Southren, 1977; Loosen and Prange, 1977; Simionescu et al., 1977; Baker et al., 1976; Distiller et al., 1976; Gordon et al., 1976; Mowat et al., 1976; Van Thiel and Lester, 1974, 1976a,b; Wright et al., 1975, 1976; Ylikahri et al., 1976; Dotson et al., 1975; Van Thiel et al., 1974b; Kent et al., 1973). That is, in most studies of the alcoholic, LH levels have generally not been significantly depressed by ethanol, and some investigators have interpreted this finding as an indication that the primary effect of ethanol must be on the peripheral aspects of the H–P–G axis. However, these data in fact suggest a profound effect on the hypothalamic–pituitary–LH axis. If testosterone levels are lowered in the male (e.g., by castration), there is an immediate sharp rise in serum LH levels of 10–20 times, which is due to a decrease in negative feedback control by testosterone (Smith and Davidson, 1974; Coyotupa et al., 1973; Davidson, 1969). Since ethanol depresses serum testosterone levels in the chronic alcoholic, one would expect to find a very large compensatory increase in serum LH levels. Increases in LH have been reported by some investigators (though certainly not all), but these are generally quite small and are considerably less than would be expected if the hypothalamic–pituitary–LH axis were functioning normally. Thus, ethanol must suppress the activity of the hypothalamic–pituitary axis.

Prompted by these observations in the chronic alcoholic, a number of investigators have attempted to generate an animal analog in the male rodent. Several investigators have found that chronic ethanol administration produces a decrease in secondary sex organ weights, atrophic testes, and markedly reduced serum testosterone levels in the male rat (Symons and Marks, 1975; Van Thiel et al., 1975a; Badr and Bartke, 1974; Fahim et al., 1970). Decreases in serum LH levels have also been noted (Symons and Marks, 1975; Van Thiel et al., 1975a), suggesting that ethanol has dual effects on both the peripheral and the central aspects of the H–P–G axis, much as has been suggested in the human (Gordon and Southren, 1977; Lester and Van Thiel, 1977; Baker et al., 1976; Gordon et al., 1976; Van Thiel et al., 1974b). There is a serious problem with these animal analogs, however, which deserves immediate attention. Specifically, there are reports that in adult male rats, fed a nutritionally adequate diet, there were only transient effects of chronic ethanol administration on the H–P–G axis, which quickly dissipated (Cicero, unpublished observations; Eskay et al., 1978). After as long as six weeks on ethanol, no deficits in LH, testosterone, the testes, or the secondary sex organs were found in these studies. A probable reason for this discrepancy is that weanling (21–30 days) rats were used in the earlier studies (Symons and Marks, 1975; Van Thiel et al., 1975a), whereas adult rats were employed in the later ones (Cicero, unpublished observations; Eskay et al., 1978). Weanling rats, exposed to ethanol-containing liquid diets, gain very little weight relative to controls. For example, in one study (Van Thiel et al., 1975a), 21-day-old rats that had been restricted to an ethanol-containing liquid diet for 40 days weighed approximately 100 g, whereas ad libitum-fed controls weighed 250 g. Although pair-fed controls (which still weighed considerably more than ethanol-treated rats) were employed and the data were corrected for these gross differences in body weight, an interaction between severe body weight reduction and ethanol consumption must be suspected in these studies. There could, of course, simply be a developmental difference in the sensitivity of the H–P–G axis to ethanol, which could explain these discordant findings, but this possibility remains to be demonstrated unequivocally.

The foregoing studies in the male human and rat chronically treated with ethanol have shed little light on ethanol-specific effects on the H–P–G axis and the mechanisms underlying ethanol's disruptive effects on reproductive endocrinology. The human alcoholic or the rat chronically exposed to ethanol is unsuitable for investigating the specific effects of ethanol for a number of reasons. First, the human alcoholic does not live in a vacuum and simply ingest ethanol into an otherwise healthy body. Alcoholics, to a greater or lesser degree, have many biomedical and psychosocial problems related or additional to their alcoholism: liver damage, other organ pathology (including brain damage), poor nutritional status, various metabolic disturbances, multidrug abuse, and psychiatric disorders. There is abundant evidence that any of these variables can influence the activity of the H–P–G axis (Blake, 1975; Euker et al., 1975; Howland et al., 1974; Bartke et al., 1973; Dunn et al., 1972). For example, individuals with liver damage, whether produced by ethanol or not, have grossly abnormal endocrine profiles (Distiller et al., 1976; Green et al., 1976; Mowat et al., 1976; Gordon et al., 1975; Galvão-Teles et al., 1973). If alcoholics are selected on the basis of liver damage, or if they are not excluded because of it, it is clear that endocrine profiles observed in these individuals may or may not reflect a change due to ethanol *per se*. An additional problem with chronic alcoholics is the difficulty in properly controlling for such facets of their drinking histories as the amounts consumed, the patterns of consumption, and the duration of the excessive use of alcohol. The use of animals would seem to circumvent many of the problems inherent in studies on the chronic alcoholic, but animal analogs also have serious limitations. The poor nutritional status frequently observed is, of course, the principal difficulty with these analogs, but there are other problems, such as controlling for the stress of bouts of intoxication interspersed with withdrawal episodes, determining the exact dose of ethanol consumed by the animals, and taking into account the temporal distribution of their intake, any of which could influence the H–P–G axis (Blake, 1975; Euker et al., 1975; Bartke et al., 1973). Finally, in chronically treated animals and humans, it is difficult to separate the primary and secondary effects of ethanol on the H–P–G axis since endocrine profiles are simply obtained at a fixed point, which gives only a global picture of the extent of damage at that time. This picture presumably reflects primary, secondary, and tertiary effects of the drug as well as the interplay of adaptive changes in compensatory feedback systems.

To avoid the problems associated with a chronic drug delivery model, a number of investigators have examined the effects of acute, single injections of ethanol on the H–P–G axis. A number of such studies in the human have generated conflicting data. For example, an acute injection of ethanol in a normal, healthy human male has been reported both to increase and to leave unchanged serum testosterone levels, and LH levels have been found to be increased, unchanged, or depressed after acute ethanol administration (Gordon and Southren, 1977; Mendelson et al., 1977; Gordon et al., 1976; Leppäluoto et al., 1975; Rowe et al., 1974; Ylikahri et al., 1974b; Toro et al., 1973). In the rodent, Cicero and his co-workers have examined the effects of single doses of ethanol on the H–P–G axis in the male rat (Cicero et al., 1978, 1979; Cicero and Badger, 1977a,b). These investigators have found increases, no change, or decreases in serum LH and testosterone levels after a single injection of ethanol, depending on the dose employed and the time of obtaining blood samples after the injection. These data indicate the importance of considering pharmacologic variables in ethanol-related studies (which are often ignored) and show that under appropriate conditions a single injection of ethanol can be used effectively to examine the drug's depressant effects on the activity of the H–P–G axis. Badr and Bartke (1974) have also found that testosterone levels were low in animals treated for a brief period of time (5 days) with ethanol, but they did not examine the effect of single injections. Nevertheless, their data tend to confirm the conclusion of Cicero et al. that acute or subacute ethanol administration can be used to examine effectively the mechanism by which ethanol disrupts the H–P–G axis and thus avoid the multiple problems associated with chronic drug delivery.

Using an acute ethanol injection paradigm, Cicero and co-workers have demonstrated that both serum LH and testosterone were depressed after a single injection of ethanol (Cicero and Badger, 1977a,b; Cicero et al., 1978). In these studies, the fall in LH seemed to precede slightly a fall in testosterone levels, suggesting a causal relationship. Moreover, the investigators found that acutely administered ethanol suppressed the castration-induced increases in serum LH levels found in the male rat 24 hr after castration. These data indicate that ethanol disrupts activity in the hypothalamic–pituitary–LH axis. Although the foregoing data could be interpreted to indicate that ethanol exerts its primary effect on the hypothalamic–pituitary–LH axis, which then leads to a secondary fall in serum testosterone levels, Cicero et al. (1979) have demonstrated that ethanol acutely alters the production of testosterone by the testes *in vivo*. In these studies, a single injection of ethanol reduced the production of testosterone stimulated by the administration of human chorionic gonadotropin (hCG). These *in vivo* effects of ethanol on testicular steroidogenesis in the rat support the concept of a testicular deficit in the chronic human alcoholic. This concept has been suggested on the basis of inference, testosterone metabolic clearance rates, and hCG-stimulated testosterone production in the nonintoxicated chronic alcoholic with liver damage (Gordon and Southren, 1977; Mendelson et al., 1977; Baker et al., 1976; Van Thiel et al., 1974a). The studies of Cicero et al. (1979), however, are the first to show that ethanol *per se* in the nonalcoholic acutely alters testicular steroidogenesis.

The data described above clearly indicate that ethanol's effects on reproductive endocrinology in the male are significant. Ethanol disrupts the hypothalamic–pituitary–LH axis, which results in a reduction in serum LH levels. This in turn leads to a reduction in stimulated-testicular steroidogenesis, which, when coupled with the pronounced reduction in the biosynthesis of testosterone induced by ethanol, combines to result in markedly depressed serum testosterone levels. If ethanol acutely accelerates the ability of the rat to metabolize testosterone, as occurs in the chronically treated human and rat (Gordon et al., 1976; Rubin et al., 1976; Fahim et al., 1970), then it might be expected that the pressures on testosterone would be even more significant.

The locus of action of ethanol within the hypothalamic–pituitary axis is a matter of speculation at this point, but a variety of evidence suggests that ethanol's effects, at least acutely, are centered at the level of the hypothalamus. This conclusion is based on the results of several studies. Cicero et al. (1978) and Leppäluoto et al. (1975) found that ethanol administered acutely to normal adult male rats failed to alter the response of the pituitary to luteinizing hormone–releasing hormone (LH–RH). In addition, Symons and Marks (1975) found that LH–RH was just as effective in releasing LH and follicle-stimulating hormone (FSH) in the male rat chronically treated with ethanol as it was in control animals. Finally, Baker et al. (1976) found that in many chronic male alcoholics, the response to LH–RH was within the normal range. This conclusion must be tempered by the fact that these same investigators (Baker et al., 1976) also found that some alcoholics did not respond appropriately to LH–RH, and Van Thiel et al. (1974a) observed that the response to clomiphene was abnormal in some, but not all, of their alcoholics. The reasons for the latter discrepancies and inconsistencies in the human literature are unclear but are probably due to uncontrolled variations inherent in the chronic alcoholic (see above). Nevertheless, the bulk of all currently available evidence suggests that ethanol *per se* does not directly interfere with the ability of LH–RH to promote the release of LH, nor does it interfere with the biosynthesis of LH in the pituitary. In addition, Cicero et al. (1979) found that LH–RH restored LH to non-drug-treated levels in the castrated animal whose LH surge had been blocked by ethanol. These data argue strongly that the locus of action of ethanol in blocking the hypothalamic–pituitary–LH axis is at the level of the hypothalamus, at least acutely. There is some confusion concerning whether or not this is also true for the chronic male alcoholic. This confusion should be resolved.

Studies in the Female.   The literature with regard to the effects of ethanol on female reproductive endocrinology and physiology is extremely limited. Apart from the fact that it has been reported that ethanol disrupts the estrous and menstrual cycle in animals and humans (Wallgren and Barry, 1971; Aron et al., 1965; Cranston, 1958), there is little direct evidence regarding ethanol's effects on female reproductive function. Whether ethanol exerts any effects on the hypothalamic–pituitary axis or at the level of the ovaries remains a fertile area for investigation. However, it seems reasonable to expect that both effects occur, given the male data reviewed above and the suggestions of Van Thiel et al. (1977) that ethanol has direct effects on the ovaries in the human female. The void in the literature pertaining to the effects of ethanol on the H–P–G axis in the female is undoubtedly due, at least in large part, to the fact that the devastating consequences of ethanol on male reproductive function are so clear and clinically noteworthy that investigations of these difficulties have seemed more pressing than studies on the female.

Narcotics.   In contrast to the effects of ethanol on the H–P–G axis, there is a considerable amount of data regarding the effects of narcotics in both the male and the female.

Studies in the Male.   Narcotic addicts, like chronic alcoholics, have pronounced difficulties with their reproductive function, although the severity of their impairments appears to be somewhat less than in the alcoholic. Nevertheless, gynecomastia, impotence, loss of libido, and an impaired function of the secondary sex organs have been observed in heroin addicts or patients maintained on methadone. As was the case with the demasculinization observed in the alcoholic, pronounced reductions in serum testosterone levels have been found in males chronically treated with narcotics (Mendelson et al., 1975a,b, 1976; Mirin et al., 1976; Cicero et al., 1975a; Azizi et al., 1973; Martin et al., 1973). The only exception seems to be the reports by Cushman (1972b, 1973) that testosterone levels were not significantly changed in methadone-maintained males, but even in these individuals, testosterone levels tended to be lower than normal. Luteinizing hormone levels have also been found to be lower or normal in narcotic-maintained individuals, suggesting a hypothalamic–pituitary–LH deficit as well as possible peripheral effects of the drugs.

In animals, Hohlweg et al. (1961) first noted that the seminal vesicles and prostates of animals chronically treated with morphine were smaller than, and histologically distinct from, the corresponding secondary sex organs taken from placebo-treated animals. These investigators also noted histological changes in the pituitary, which suggested to them that the pituitary and the gonads were both affected by morphine. These observations stood alone for a number of years until Cicero et al. (1974) found that the secondary sex organs were atrophied in male rats treated with morphine for as few as three days. These findings have subsequently been confirmed by other investigators in mice, pigeons, and man (Tokunaga et al., 1977; Vyas and Singh, 1976; Cicero et al., 1975a; Thomas and Dombrosky, 1975). The basis for the decrease in the weight and the functional activity of the secondary sex organs has been examined in detail by Cicero and co-workers. In a series of studies, they concluded that the narcotics exerted these effect solely by their ability to deplete serum testosterone (Cicero et al., 1975b, 1976a, 1977b). In subsequent studies, this group has also shown that a single acute injection of morphine promptly reduces serum testosterone levels, with the maximum depression ($>$ 90%), occurring 3–5 hr after the injection (Cicero et al., 1976b, 1977b). This testosterone-depleting activity of the narcotics appeared to be a receptor-mediated, specific narcotic effect since (1) all narcotics produced the effect; (2) the relative potency of the narcotics in depleting testosterone paralleled their pharmacologic activity in other assays (Cicero, 1977); (3) the levorotatory isomers of the narcotics were considerably more potent than the dextrorotatory isomers; and (4) naloxone shifted the morphine-dose response curve to the right in a parallel fashion (Cicero et al., 1976b, 1977b; Mirin et al., 1976). Tolerance also developed to the testosterone-depleting effects of the narcotics (Cicero et al., 1976a). Other investigators have also shown that narcotics, both acutely and chronically, depress serum testosterone levels in rats, mice, pigeons, and man (Ellingboe et al., 1978; Brambilla et al., 1977; Bruni et al., 1977; Tokunaga et al., 1977; Mendelson et al., 1976; Mirin et al., 1976; Vyas and Singh, 1976; Mendelson and Mello, 1975; Mendelson et al., 1975a,b; Cushman and Kreek, 1974; Azizi et al., 1973; Martin et al., 1973).

The mechanism by which the narcotics decrease serum testosterone levels has also been extensively examined in the male rat. Cicero et al. found that the narcotics exerted no effect on the *in vivo* or *in vitro* secretion of testosterone by the testes, nor did they inhibit the hCG-stimulated production of testosterone by the decapsulated rat testes (Cicero et al., 1977b). This lack of direct effect of the narcotics on the testes, which is in marked distinction to the effects of alcohol and marijuana, appears to point to an effect of the narcotics on the hypothalamic–pituitary axis. Three approaches have been employed to examine this issue.

First, the effects of narcotics on the secondary sex organs and serum testosterone levels of hypophysectomized (HYPOX) rats, given supplemental hCG injections, were examined (Cicero et al., 1976a). The rationale for this approach was that if the narcotics acted at the level of the testes, then they should still be effective in HYPOX animals. If, on the other hand, the narcotics influenced only the hypothalamic–pituitary axis, then they should be ineffective. The results of these studies indicated that morphine did not lower serum testosterone levels or impair the function of the secondary sex organs, suggesting that the narcotics affected the hypothalamic-pituitary aspect of the H–P–G axis.

Second, the temporal changes in LH and testosterone after a single injection of morphine were examined (Cicero et al., 1977b). In these studies, it was found that serum LH levels fell 1–2 hr prior to a fall in testosterone. These data are compatible with an interpretation that the fall in serum LH levels is a necessary prerequisite step leading to the fall in testosterone levels in view of the role of LH in regulating testicular steroidogenesis (Ahluwalia et al., 1974; DuFau et al., 1973; Moyle and Ramachandran, 1973). This speculation is strengthened, of course, by the lack of any demonstrable effect of the narcotics on the testes *in vivo* or *in vitro*.

Third, the effects of narcotics on the castration-induced increase in serum LH in the male rat were examined (Cicero et al., 1977a). In these studies, morphine markedly impaired the ability of the hypothalamic–pituitary–LH axis to respond appropriately to the stimulation produced by castration.

The three lines of evidence outlined above, and the complete absence of any effect of the narcotics on the peripheral aspects of the H–P–G axis, indicate that the narcotics exert their primary effect on the hypothalamic–pituitary–LH axis. All other effects of the narcotics—reductions in serum testosterone levels and atrophy of the secondary sex organs—appear to be secondary consequences of this primary depression of the hypothalamic–pituitary–LH axis. Other investigators have also found that acute and chronic narcotic administration depressed serum LH levels in all species examined (Ellingboe et al., 1978; Brambilla et al., 1977; Tokunaga et al., 1977; Mirin et al., 1976; Hohlweg et al., 1961).

The locus of action of the narcotics within the hypothalamic–pituitary axis appears to be at the level of the hypothalamus. This conclusion is based on several observations. First, it has been demonstrated that neither acute nor chronic narcotic administration alters the content of LH in the pituitary (Cicero et al., 1977a), indicating that the synthesis of LH is unimpaired by the narcotics. Second, the ability of LH–RH to stimulate the release and synthesis of LH in the pituitary of normal male rats *in vivo* (Cicero et al., 1977a) and man (Ellingboe et al., 1978; Mendelson et al., personal communication) has been found to be unaltered by acute doses of morphine. Third, the depression in the castration-induced increase in serum LH levels produced by the narcotics (see above) can be completely reversed by LH–RH [Cicero, unpublished observations (1978)]. Finally, in a series of *in vitro* studies, it was found that the narcotics did not inhibit the basal or LH–RH stimulated release of LH from the anterior pituitary (Cicero et al., 1977a). These observations seem to rule out any acute or chronic effects of the narcotics at the level of the pituitary and strongly indicate that they act at the hypothalamus, perhaps by inhibiting the synthesis and/or the secretion of LH–RH. The biggest challenge at present is to determine clearly just how the narcotics influence those hypothalamic factors that regulate the release of gonadotropins in the male. It would seem particularly important to examine the role of opioid peptidergic systems in regulating LH release. Such studies are of primary interest since it has been shown that the effects of narcotics on LH levels are mediated by specific opioid receptors, presumably in the hypothalamus. It seems logical, therefore, that there would exist an endogenous opioid ligand, with an affinity for this receptor, which could very well influence the elaboration of LH by the hypothalamic–pituitary axis. Additional studies, of course, will be needed to clarify those neuronal systems involved in the release of LH–RH (e.g., noradrenergic, dopaminergic, cholinergic) that are affected by the narcotics.

Studies in the Female. The fact that narcotics disrupt female reproductive function was first recognized in 1955 (Barraclough and Sawyer, 1955; Sawyer et al., 1955), several years prior to similar observations in the male. These investigators found that morphine inhibited ovulation in female rats and rabbits. Subsequently, a number of investigators have found that heroin and methadone disrupt the menstrual cycle in the human female. Santen et al. (1975), for example, found that only 30% of females maintained on methadone reported normal menses while on methadone or heroin, whereas 95% of the women retrospectively reported normal menses prior to any drug use. Of those women with menstrual dysfunction, 35% reported permanent amenorrhea on both methadone and heroin, whereas the remainder reported transient amenorrhea on either one or the other drug. It also appeared that improvement in menstrual regularity occurred with long-term methadone use, suggesting the development of tolerance. Similarly, Gaulden et al. (1964) found that 65% of women heroin users had abnormal menstrual cycles, either prolonged beyond 35 days or completely eliminated while on heroin, whereas prior to heroin use nearly 100% had had normal cycles. After cessation of heroin use, menses returned to normal for nearly all women. Finally, Stoffer (1968) also found heroin-related menstrual abnormalities in 90% of heroin addicts; 48% were still abnormal three months after cessation of heroin. Abnormalities included amenorrhea (cessation of menses), oligomenorrhea (reduced frequency of menses), hypomenorrhea (reduction in duration and flow), polymenorrhea (shortening of intervals between menses), and hypermenorrhea (increase in flow). Amenorrhea and oligomenorrhea occurred most frequently (in 63% and 10% of women, respectively).

In the last five years, coincidentally with the development of appropriate radioimmunoassays, several groups have begun to examine the endocrinological basis for the antiovulatory properties of the narcotics. Direct narcotic effects at the level of the ovaries have not been reported or systematically examined, and there does not appear to be any compelling evidence to suggest that the ovaries might be targets for the narcotics, particularly since there are no gonadal effects in the male. Nevertheless, the possibility of ovarian effects of the narcotics should be explored, since there has been some speculation regarding direct effects of ethanol and marijuana on the ovaries.

Bearing in mind this gap in the literature, it appears most reasonable to conclude at this time that the narcotics block ovulation by inhibiting the hypothalamic–pituitary–LH axis. Several investigators have confirmed the original observation of Barraclough and Sawyer that morphine can block ovulation in several species, including man (Johnson and Rosecrans, 1978; Thomas et al., 1977; Packman and Rothchild, 1976; Santen et al., 1975; George, 1971; Gaulden et al., 1964; Stoffer, 1968). This effect appears to be mediated via opiate receptors since naloxone prevents the antiovulatory effect of morphine (Packman and Rothchild, 1976). Until quite recently, most investigators have inferred that morphine blocks ovulation by inhibiting the preovulatory surge in LH that occurs in the afternoon preceding ovulation. However, this inference has only recently been rigorously supported by direct evidence. Zimmermann and his colleagues (Pang et al., 1974, 1977; Zimmermann and Pang, 1976; Pang and Zimmermann, 1975), and subsequently others (Johnson and Rosecrans, 1978; Muraki et al., 1977; Muraki and Tokunaga, 1977), demonstrated that acute morphine treatment suppressed the preovulatory surge of LH in the female, provided that the drug was given between 2 PM and 4 PM the afternoon before ovulation, coincident with the surge in LH. This effect of morphine was reversed by the narcotic antagonist naloxone (Pang et al., 1977). These investigators also demonstrated that narcotics inhibited the increase in serum LH levels induced by ovariectomy in the rat, supporting the conclusion that the narcotics act on the hypothalamic–pituitary–LH axis (Zimmermann and Pang, 1976). Santen et al. (1975) also found that mid-cycle LH and FSH peaks were absent in anovulatory women maintained on methadone. In addition, Tolis et al. (1975) found that morphine acutely depressed LH levels in normal women. Since it has been shown that narcotics do not inhibit the effects of LH–RH on the pituitary (Pang et al., 1977; Zimmermann and Pang, 1976), it appears that in the female as in the male, the locus of action of these drugs is at the level of the hypothalamus.

The literature on females reviewed above indicates that narcotics inhibit the H–P–G axis in much the same fashion as they do in the male. There are, however, several distinctions that can be drawn between the effects of the narcotics on the H–P–G axis in the male and the female. Perhaps the most significant difference relates to the doses required to inhibit its activity in the two sexes. The doses of morphine required to inhibit the secretion of LH and to block ovulation in the female rat are extremely high (> 50 mg/kg in most studies). In the male rat, on the other hand, a dose of less than 1 mg/kg reduces serum LH and testosterone levels by 50%. It is not at all clear what accounts for this massive difference in the sensitivity of the H–P–G axis to morphine. Whether there are similar differences in the human remains to be determined. Studies should be carried out to examine this striking and potentially important sex difference.

In the preceding discussion of effects in the male and the female, changes in serum follicle-stimulating hormone (FSH) were not discussed, since there has been relatively little systematic examination of morphine-induced changes in this gonadotropin. Whatever changes have been observed have been slight, and the available data are conflicting. Rennels (1961) found that chronic morphine administration led to an increase in pituitary FSH concentrations in male rats, whereas several groups have found no change in male rats or humans (Ellingboe et al., 1978; Bruni et al., 1977; Cicero et al., 1974) in FHS levels after acute or chronic narcotic treatment. In another study, however, Tokunaga et al. (1977) found an *increase* in serum FSH, and a decrease in LH (see above), in male rats following chronic exposure. To further complicate this picture, Zimmermann and Pang (1976) found a slight fall in serum FSH levels after acute narcotic treatment in female rats. On the basis of these data, it is difficult to conclude with certainty whether the narcotics influence serum FSH levels, and if so, how. It appears, however, that the magnitude of changes in FSH, when any have been found in the male or the female, would have been insufficient to produce any meaningful changes in gonadal function.

Marijuana.   There is a fairly recent but rather substantial body of literature on the effects of marijuana and its active principle tetrahydrocannabinol (THC) on the H–P–G axis of both males and females.

Studies in the Male.   In the male of every species thus far examined—mice, rats, dogs, monkeys, and pigeons—chronic THC or marijuana administration produces a pronounced atrophy of the secondary

sex organs, degenerative changes in the testes, and impaired spermatogenesis (Dixit et al., 1974, 1977; Rosenkrantz and Braude, 1976; Collu,
1976; Harmon et al., 1976; Symons et al., 1976; Vyas and Singh, 1976;
Collu et al., 1975a; Solomon and Shattuck, 1974; Ling et al., 1973;
Thompson et al., 1973). Associated with this loss in the functional and
structural integrity of the ancillary sex organs and testes, a pronounced
reduction in serum testosterone levels has been uniformly found in all
male animals (List et al., 1977; Harmon et al., 1976; Symons et al., 1976;
Vyas and Singh, 1976) and humans (Kolodny et al., 1974, 1976). Mendelson et al. (1974, 1977, 1978) have reported that THC did not lower
testosterone levels in young male hospitalized marijuana smokers. This
finding, however, is in marked contrast to the reports by Kolodny et al.
in the human male. The reasons for this discrepancy are not clear. Apart
from the conflicting evidence in man, however, there seems to be little
debate that chronic marijuana or THC administration lowers serum
testosterone levels. In addition, THC has been found to lower serum
testosterone acutely after a single injection in man (Kolodny et al., 1976;
but note Mendelson et al., 1977, 1978) and animals (Besch et al., 1977;
Smith et al., 1976), indicating that the drug itself directly alters activity
in the H–P–G axis in an animal free of possible confounding variables
(e.g., stress or severe weight reduction) that might be associated with
chronic drug administration.

There are, of course, two possible mechanisms by which marijuana
could alter the production of testosterone: by direct interference with
testicular steroidogenesis or by inhibition of the hypothalamic–pituitary–
LH axis. As is the case with ethanol, but not with the narcotics, THC
has been reported to inhibit testicular steroidogenesis *in vivo* and *in vitro*
(Burstein et al., 1978; Dalterio et al., 1977). In addition to these direct
testicular effects, there are also pronounced effects on the hypothalamic–pituitary–LH axis, since THC, both chronically and acutely, has
been found to depress serum LH levels in every species (there is again
the controversy in man, however) in which it has been measured (Collu,
1976; Symons et al., 1976; Collu et al., 1975a; Marks, 1973).

The locus of action of THC within the hypothalamic–pituitary–LH
axis is not known at this time. Symons et al. (1976) found that LH–RH
was relatively ineffective in reversing the LH-reducing properties of
chronic THC in the male rat. However, this conclusion must be viewed
cautiously, since only weanling rats were used in these studies, and their
growth and nutritional status during the period of chronic exposure to
THC were poor. It is hoped that studies of the acute effects of THC on
the response to LH–RH or chronic studies in adults will be undertaken
to determine definitively whether THC affects the pituitary in the male.
These studies are particularly critical, since it has been shown that acute

THC treatment does not alter the response of the pituitary to LH–RH in the female monkey (Ayalon et al., 1977). Hence, there is either a significant sex or species difference, or THC may indeed not affect the pituitary in the male. Obviously, this point must be resolved.

There is an additional mechanism that has been proposed to explain the demasculinization or feminization that occurs in males chronically treated with marijuana or THC, which is distinct from the hypoandrogenicity produced by the drug. Specifically, it has been proposed that THC is an estrogenlike substance. This conclusion is based on the fact that THC, at least in some studies, increased uterine weights in ovariectomized female rats (Solomon and Cocchia, 1977; Solomon et al., 1976, 1977). These findings, however, have not been confirmed by all investigators (Okey and Bondy, 1977; Dixit et al., 1975; Okey and Truant, 1975; Thompson et al., 1973), and the lack of a good dose–response relationship in these studies is somewhat disturbing. Nevertheless, there is an additional piece of evidence that could support an estrogenlike activity of THC. Specifically, it has been found that THC can compete with estrogen for uterine cytosol estrogen-binding proteins (Rawitch et al., 1977), although again there is some dispute on this point (Okey and Bondy, 1977; Okey and Truant, 1975). These binding studies by no means indicate that THC has physiological effects similar to estrogen, but they have been interpreted to support the aforementioned suggestion that THC may have estrogenic activity. There is obvious controversy in this area, but if it can be established that THC has estrogenlike effects under normal physiological conditions, the demasculinization observed in the male chronically treated with marijuana or THC could be due to both *hypo*androgenization and *hyper*estrogenization. This is an exciting possibility worthy of prompt experimental attention.

Studies in the Female.   There is only a single study of the effects of marijuana on the H–P–G axis in the female human (Kolodny et al., 1977). In this study, 26 regular users of marijuana (4 times per week) were compared with 16 age-matched controls who had never used marijuana. No significant effects of THC on LH, FSH, estrogen, or progesterone were found, but testosterone levels were significantly higher in marijuana users than in controls. These data contrast strongly with those in the animal literature. Since this is a single study, it is hoped that other data will be forthcoming, particularly as these investigators have produced many data in the male suggesting pronounced effects on reproductive endocrinology. Their claim could reflect an interesting sex difference, some procedural detail (self-report of marijuana use was relied on), or some other variable.

In contrast to the paucity of data in the human, there are ample data in animals. In the female rat or monkey chronically or acutely treated with THC, the H–P–G axis is markedly affected, much as it is in the male. In contrast to the effects of THC on the male gonads, however, there is a good deal of debate regarding direct ovarian effects of THC and possible estrogenlike or antiestrogenlike effects of THC. In the ovariectomized female rat, as briefly mentioned above, there is some indication that THC may act like estrogen, since it was found to increase uterine weights in these animals (Solomon and Cocchia, 1977; Solomon et al., 1976, 1977). On the other hand, in the normal or ovariectomized female rat, some investigators have found precisely the opposite effects, that is, *lower* uterine weights after a period of chronic administration of cannabis resin or THC (Okey and Bondy, 1977; Solomon et al., 1977; Dixit et al., 1975; Okey and Truant, 1975; Thompson et al., 1973). Solomon and co-workers have dismissed the latter studies, however, on several points, including the purity of the cannabis extract utilized and dose–response issues (Rawitch et al., 1977; Solomon and Cocchia, 1977).

The argument most strongly advanced in support of estrogenlike effects of THC is that it binds to the cytosolic estrogen-binding protein (Rawitch et al., 1977), a finding that has been interpreted to indicate that THC and estrogen share certain properties (i.e., that THC is estrogen-like). Two other equally plausible interpretations of these data seem likely. First, THC was found to have little intrinsic activity as an estrogen (e.g., in increasing uterine weight in ovariectomized animals). Hence, if THC has a high affinity for estrogen binding sites in the uterus, its net effect might be to reduce the effects of estrogen *in vivo* by competing for the same receptor and exerting only minor activity of its own. Second, both antiestrogens and estrogen-like compounds may very well have equal affinities for the cytosol binding protein. For example, in many systems, such as the binding of opiates to the opioid receptor, both agonists and antagonists have very high affinities for the same receptor. Thus, binding data alone could be used to support the position that THC is an estrogen-like or an anti-estrogen-like compound. This evidence, therefore, gives only weak support for a role for THC as an estrogen-like compound. Nevertheless, this intriguing possibility requires a good deal of further study.

Perhaps the most definitive evidence regarding the effects of THC on the ovaries comes from recent studies by Ayalon et al. (1977), who found that acute administration of a relatively low dose of THC to normal female rats resulted in a suppression of LH and, consequently, ovulation. Although LH–RH could overcome the THC-induced decrease in LH, ovulation did not readily occur, a finding that suggested a direct effect on the ovaries. Further experiments revealed that LH administration could overcome the inhibitory effects of THC on ovulation, and the concomitant increase in prostaglandins (PGE) in the ovaries, but that the dose–response curve was shifted in parallel to the right, suggesting that THC competitively inhibited the accumulation of PGE (and, hence, ovulation) in the ovaries. These studies indicate rather clearly that THC can block the effects of LH on the ovaries by competitively inhibiting the biochemical processes set in motion by the gonadotropin. Thus, while there is still some controversy on this point, the majority of the available studies suggest a direct ovarian effect of THC.

With respect to the effects of marijuana and THC on the hypothalamic–pituitary–LH axis in the female, it appears that both acute and chronic THC administration in ovariectomized and normal females effectively suppress LH and FSH levels (Besch et al., 1977; Chakravarty et al., 1975; Marks, 1973; Nir et al., 1973). Since this effect can be reversed by LH–RH, it appears that the effects of THC on the hypothalamic–pituitary–LH axis are confined to the hypothalamus (Ayalon et al., 1977). However, the latter conclusion is based only on a single study, and given the uncertainty in the male (see above), more studies should be done to establish unequivocally at what point in the hypothalamic–pituitary–LH axis THC and marijuana exert their primary effects in the female.

From the literature reviewed above, it appears that THC and marijuana affect the H–P–G axis in the female and the male almost identically. Marijuana seems to have direct gonadal effects in both sexes and also disrupts the hypothalamic–pituitary–LH axis. There seems to be no qualitative or quantitative differences between marijuana's effect on the H–P–G axis in the male or female.

Amphetamine, LSD and, Other Stimulants.   There are no data available regarding the effects of *d*- or *l*-amphetamine on reproductive endocrinology in humans or animals, but there is one report that chronic LSD administration did not alter serum LH and FSH levels in the male rat (Collu et al., 1975b). There are no other data available on the effects of stimulants on the H–P–G axis in either the male or the female.

Hypothalamic–Pituitary–Adrenal (H–P–A) Axis

Ethanol.   There have been fewer studies concerned with the effects of ethanol on the H–P–A axis than on the H–P–G axis. There are even fewer data regarding male–female differences.

In most studies, in male or female rats or rabbits, it has been found that ethanol intoxication acutely elevates corticosterone levels (Pohorecky et al., 1978; Kakihana, 1977; Sze et al., 1974; Suzuki et al., 1972; Noble, 1971; Ellis, 1962, 1965, 1966; Kalant et al., 1963; Czaja and Kalant, 1961). Ethanol also appears to elevate cortisol levels acutely in alcoholics and normal, healthy human volunteers (Stokes, 1973; Bellet et al., 1970a,b; Merry and Marks, 1969; Jenkins and Connolly, 1968;

Mendelson and Stein, 1966; Kissin et al., 1960; Perman, 1960). This adrenal response to ethanol appears to be mediated by an ethanol-induced release of ACTH from the anterior pituitary in both man and animals based on two lines of evidence: first, pituitary ACTH levels, determined by bioassay, were found to be markedly depleted by acute alcohol injections in rodents (Noble, 1971), and, second, ethanol has been found to be ineffective in promoting the release of corticosterone in hypophysectomized animals (Ellis, 1966) or the release of cortisol in humans with pituitary tumors (Jenkins and Connolly 1968). These data indicate that an intact pituitary is necessary to permit the activating effects of ethanol on the H–P–A axis. On the basis of these findings, it appears that the increase in corticosterone or cortisol output produced by ethanol is mediated by an initial release of ACTH. Whether cortico-tropin-releasing factor (CRF) levels are elevated by ethanol and, hence, the locus of action of ethanol within the hypothalamic–pituitary–ACTH axis, remains to be determined.

A major problem is inherent in studies of the effects of ethanol or other psychoactive drugs on the H–P–A axis. Specifically, it is extremely difficult to determine whether the stress produced by acute or chronic drug administration causes the observed pituitary–adrenal activation or whether the drug *per se* directly impinges on the H–P–A. In the case of ethanol, a rather strong case can be made that the stress of ethanol intoxication, rather than the drug itself, produces heightened H–P–A activity. This conclusion is based on the fact that levels of corticosterone in rats or cortisol in humans are not increased by ethanol until extremely high, intoxicating blood ethanol levels are achieved (Stokes, 1973; Mendelson et al., 1971; Bellet et al., 1970a,b; Jenkins and Connolly, 1968; Mendelson and Stein, 1966; Kissin et al., 1960; Perman, 1960). Moreover, although it has been reported that a good dose–response relationship exists between the dose of ethanol employed and the serum levels of corticosterone (Ellis, 1966), most studies have shown that a release of cortisol or corticosterone seems to occur in a more-or-less all-or-none fashion once a critical blood ethanol level has been attained (Kalant, 1975). In addition, it has also been found that both the route of administration of ethanol and the speed of attainment of the peak blood ethanol levels also influence whether an adrenal response occurs (Kalant, 1975; Suzuki et al., 1972; Merry and Marks, 1969; Kalant et al., 1963; Czaja and Kalant, 1961). These considerations may explain some discordant results in the literature (particularly when low, nonintoxicating doses of ethanol have been used), and, what is of somewhat greater importance, they suggest that the adrenal activation produced by acute ethanol administration may be a nonspecific effect of ethanol as a stressor. Indeed, a harsh appraisal could be that there is no evidence to suggest that ethanol exerts specific effects on the H–P–A axis; rather, this adrenal activation can be totally ascribed to the stress generated by acute intoxication. Perhaps future studies will ultimately tease apart ethanol-specific from stress-generated effects on the H–P–A axis.

Whether ethanol produces adrenal activation by a direct drug effect or as a nonspecific effect of stress, there are two studies that suggest that corticosterone may be necessary for the expression of withdrawal behavior in rodents. Sze et al. (1974) demonstrated in both rats and mice that adrenalectomy markedly decreased the severity of the alcohol withdrawal reaction. Similarly, Kakihana (1977) has shown that mice with high corticosterone levels had much more severe withdrawal seizures than mice with low corticosterone levels. These two studies suggest that the adrenal may actively participate in certain aspects of alcohol's effects, particularly the expression and perhaps the development of physical dependence. These are interesting observations, and future studies should be continued along the same lines and also extended to include the involvement of the adrenal in other aspects of ethanol's pharmacology (e.g., acute effects and the development of tolerance). In addition, sex differences and species generality should also be assessed.

There appear to be no sex differences in the response of the H–P–A axis to ethanol in most animals or humans. However, there may be a distinction between the male and the female in selected inbred strains of mice. Specifically, Kakihana (1977) has found a significant sex difference in the corticosterone response to ethanol in so-called long-sleep (LS) and short-sleep (SS) mice, which have been bred by McClearn and his colleagues (Heston et al., 1974; McClearn, 1973). In the LS or ethanol-susceptible male mouse, the corticosterone response to a single dose of ethanol was considerably greater than the corresponding response in SS animals. In the female, the ethanol-induced increase in corticosterone was of approximately the same magnitude in both strains. These data suggest that LS males overrespond to ethanol in relation to SS males and LS or SS females. Whether these results suggest a difference in the sensitivity to ethanol *per se* or, rather, the fact that ethanol is simply a greater stressor in LS males (see above) is not known. Nevertheless, this sex difference in responsivity of the H–P–A axis to ethanol in these two inbred strains is extremely interesting and warrants a good deal of further investigation.

Narcotics. Morphine and other narcotics acutely elevate serum corticosteroids in rats, mice, cats, and dogs (Zimmermann et al., 1977; Hellman et al., 1975; Simon et al., 1975; Borrell et al., 1974; deWied and deJong, 1974; deWied et al., 1974; French et al., 1974; Kokka and George, 1974; Morita et al., 1974; Kokka et al., 1973; Sloan, 1971; Lotti et al., 1969), but probably not in man (Hellman et al., 1975; Mendelson et al., 1975b; Cushman and Dole, 1973; Sloan, 1971). This adrenal activation may occur via a drug-induced secretion of ACTH (deWied and deJong, 1974; Morita et al., 1974; Kokka et al., 1973), but this possibility has been assessed only indirectly (see below). These effects of the narcotics on the H–P–A axis seem to be specific, receptor-mediated ones, since all narcotics appear to activate the H–P–A axis and the effects of the narcotics are competitively blocked by naloxone (George and Kokka, 1976; Kokka and George, 1974; Kokka et al., 1973). Tolerance also appears to develop to the ACTH-releasing properties of the narcotics (George and Kokka, 1976; Kokka and George, 1974). During withdrawal, there is, however, another sharp increase in serum corticosterone in animals (Sloan, 1971) and serum cortisol in humans (George and Kokka, 1976; Hellman et al., 1975). It is not known whether narcotics act at the level of the pituitary or the hypothalamus in releasing ACTH, but the evidence favors a hypothalamic site of action since the drugs are potent releasers of ACTH after discrete intracranial injections (French et al., 1974; Kokka and George, 1974; Lotti et al., 1969). There are no studies currently available in which CRF levels have been measured, so that it can only be inferred, though rather strongly, that the hypothalamus is the locus of action of the narcotics.

Narcotics activate the H–P–A axis in both males and females, with no apparent quantitative or qualitative distinction between the sexes.

The recent discovery of endogenous opioids in brain and pituitary has prompted considerable interest in what role, if any, these endogenous compounds might play in hypothalamic–pituitary function. The most significant interaction between the opioids and the hypothalamic–pituitary axis appears to take place in the H–P–A axis. Specifically, endogenous opioids, particularly β-endorphin, may be involved in the functional activity of the H–P–A axis. The latter conclusion is based on the fact that β-endorphin and ACTH are contained in the same cells in the pituitary (Bloom et al., 1977; Pelletier et al., 1977; Watson et al., 1977), may be derived from the same precursor molecule (Mains et al., 1977), and are co-released in response to the same stimuli, including CRF administration (Guillemin et al., 1977; Krieger et al., 1977). The precise nature of the role opioids play in the activation of the H–P–A axis and their participation in the stress reaction are intriguing issues worthy of considerable research interest. Sex differences in the effect of endogenous opioids on the H–P–A axis have apparently not been examined.

Marijuana.   There are very few studies of the effects of marijuana and THC on the H–P–A axis. What data are available indicate that THC, administered both acutely and chronically, elevates plasma corticosterone levels in animals (Bromley and Zimmermann, 1976; Smith et al., 1976; Kokka and Garcia, 1974; Pertwee, 1974; Barry et al., 1973; Kubena et al., 1971) but probably does not alter the activity of the H–P–A axis in humans (Kolodny, 1974, 1976; Benowitz et al., 1976). This effect in animals appears to be mediated by a release of ACTH, since THC is ineffective in promoting an increase in corticosterone in hypophysectomized rats (Barry et al., 1973; Kubena et al., 1971). These data suggest a locus of action in the hypothalamus, but the evidence at this point appears to be insufficient to permit a definitive conclusion. Tolerance appears to develop to the effects of marijuana on the H–P–A axis (Pertwee, 1974). The issue of whether THC exerts specific effects on the H–P–A axis, or whether stress plays a significant role in the effects of the drug on this axis, should also be addressed. There are no apparent sex differences in the effects of THC on the H–P–A axis, but there are simply too few data to permit meaningful conclusions.

Amphetamine, LSD, and Other Stimulants. Acute doses of a *d*- or *l*-amphetamine have been shown to decrease cortisol production in both male and female rhesus monkeys (Marantz et al., 1976). These data conflict with reports that methamphetamine increased cortisol production in humans (Rees et al., 1970; Besser et al. 1969). These differences reflect either a species difference or a difference between methamphetamine and *d*- and *l*-amphetamine. It has also been reported that acute and chronic LSD treatment elevated corticoid production and that tolerance developed to this action (Halaris et al., 1975). There are no other reports of the effects of amphetamine, LSD, or other stimulants on the H–P–A axis and, obviously, there are no reported sex differences.

Hypothalamic–Pituitary–Thyroid (H–P–T) Axis

Ethanol. There are considerably fewer data on the effects of ethanol on the H–P–T axis than on virtually any other neuroendocrine axis, even though interest in the effects of ethanol on the H–P–T axis historically predates interest in any other endocrine system. Research on the effects of ethanol on the H–P–T axis began with Richter's (1956, 1957) demonstration more than two decades ago that thyroid extracts or purified thyroid hormones decreased the preference for ethanol in rats, whereas a reduction in the activity of the thyroid led to an increase in ethanol intake. Although these observations have never been confirmed, and in fact have been directly contradicted (Hilbom, 1971; Prieto et al., 1958), these studies focused attention on possible interactions between ethanol and the H–P–T axis. However, studies of the effects of ethanol on the H–P–T axis in the intervening 30 years have not generated consistent results, and even when an interaction between ethanol and the H–P–T axis has been suggested, the magnitude has been rather slight. Perhaps the most consistent effect of ethanol on the function of the thyroid is to modestly increase the uptake of triiodothyronine (T_3) or thyroxine (T_4)

in certain target organs, particularly the liver (Ramakrishanan et al., 1976; Nomura et al., 1975; Israel et al., 1973; Bleecker et al., 1969; Augustine, 1967). The significance of ethanol-induced increases in the uptake of these hormones, and their subsequent metabolic effects, is not clear, since very high concentrations of ethanol were required to produce this effect, and many drugs increase T_4 uptake by the liver.

In terms of the function of the thyroid itself in chronic alcoholics, Goldberg (1960, 1962) reported that chronic alcoholics had a marked degree of hypothyroidism, evidenced by the low protein-bound iodine (PBI) levels in their sera compared to those of a normal population. He suggested that hypothyroidism may be a significant feature of the clinical status of the alcoholic, and he claimed a good clinical response to treatment with thyroid hormones in alcoholics (Goldberg, 1960). On the basis of the large amount of data gathered since this initial report, however, it does not appear that alcoholics have hypothyroidism (Wright et al., 1976; Augustine, 1967; Selzer and Van Houten, 1964) or that thyroid hormones have any utility in the treatment of alcoholism (Kalant et al., 1962; Satterfield and Guze, 1961).

The effects of alcohol on the uptake of ^{131}I or ^{125}I in the human by the thyroid has also received considerable attention, but again, conflicting results have been obtained. Some investigators have reported increases in iodine uptake (Murdock, 1967), others no change (Stokes, 1973), and still others have found significant decreases in the drinking alcoholic (Ramakrishanan et al., 1976; Murdock, 1967). There are very few studies available that shed any light on the issue of the effects of alcohol on the hypothalamic–pituitary aspect of the H–P–T axis. When TSH has been measured (very rarely), the levels of this anterior pituitary hormone have not been found to be significantly altered in the chronic alcoholic or after acute administration in normal healthy volunteers (Wright et al., 1976; Leppäluoto et al., 1975; Toro et al., 1973). Wright et al. (1976) found a diminished TSH response to TSH–RH in about 10% of their chronic alcoholics, whereas most other indices of thyroid function were completely normal in these subjects. The significance of this apparent refractoriness to TSH–RH stimulation in a small percentage of alcoholics is unclear, but on the basis of this study and those reviewed above, it appears that the effects of alcohol on the hypothalamic–pituitary aspect of the H–P–T axis are slight, if indeed existent at all.

In a recent study in animals, Patel et al. (1978) examined the effects of chronic ethanol ingestion (3 months with 10% ethanol as the sole source of fluid) on plasma T_3, T_4, and reverse T_3 (RT_3) in male and female rats. These investigators found that T_3, T_4, and RT_3 were lower in ethanol-treated males than in controls, whereas only T_3 and T_4, but not RT_3, were significantly lower in ethanol-treated females. It should be noted, however, that the effects of ethanol on T_3, RT_3, and T_4 were modest in either sex. Moreover, there was a trend for RT_3 to be lower in ethanol-treated females, but this difference did not attain statistical significance. Thus, the issue of whether there is a reliable sex difference in RT_3, or other thyroid hormones, cannot be clearly resolved at this time. In a more general sense, it would also be of some importance to establish definitely whether ethanol's effects on the H–P–T axis are biologically meaningful in either sex, something that still remains unclear.

Narcotics. It is well established that morphine inhibits the release of TSH, decreases the uptake of ^{131}I by the thyroid, and decreases the release of ^{131}I-labeled hormones from the thyroid in all animals and humans of either sex (Bruni et al., 1977; Martin et al., 1977; Bakke et al., 1974; George, 1973; Schreiber et al., 1968; Lomax and George, 1966). These effects occur after both acute and chronic treatment, all narcotics produce them, and naloxone antagonizes their actions (Bastomsky et al., 1977; George and Kokka, 1976; Bakke et al., 1974; George, 1973; Shenkman et al., 1972; Lomax et al., 1970; Schreiber et al., 1968). Interestingly, it has been found that tolerance does not develop to the effects of morphine on the H–P–T axis (George and Kokka, 1976; Lomax, 1970). There do not appear to be any sex-related differences in the effects of narcotics on the H–P–T axis, although females have rarely been used in such studies.

Marijuana. There have been no studies of the effects of THC on the function of the H–P–T axis in humans, and only a few in animals. These studies indicate that the release of radio-labeled iodine from the thyroid (George and Kokka, 1976; Lomax, 1970) and serum thyroxine concentrations (Nazar et al., 1977) were both depressed following acute and chronic THC treatment. In recent studies, Gordon et al. (1978) found that THC reduced basal serum TSH levels and those stimulated by ether and cold stress. The administration of TRF overcame the depressant effect of THC, pointing to a hypothalamic locus of action. Thyroxine serum levels were reported as normal in chronic human users by Kolodny et al. (1974).

Amphetamine, LSD, and Other Stimulants. There are no data available regarding the effects of CNS stimulants on the H–P–T axis.

Other Anterior Pituitary Secretions

In the following sections, what little we know about the effects of psychoactive drugs on anterior pituitary hormone secretions, other than those reviewed above, is discussed. There are only a few studies, and frequently, these have produced conflicting results. This review is necessary nonetheless to provide a current analysis of the effects of these drugs on the secretions of the anterior pituitary and, hopefully, to stimulate the reader's interest in some badly ignored research areas.

Prolactin

Ethanol.   Van Thiel et al. (1975b) have found an increase in prolactin levels in the serum of chronic alcoholics, relative to controls. Not all investigators, however, have found changes in prolactin levels in man after acute or chronic administration (Earll et al., 1976; Yen et al., 1974; Toro et al., 1973; Turkington, 1972). In the male rat, chronic ethanol administration elevates serum prolactin levels, but there are no studies using acute administration (Gordon and Southren, 1977). Ethanol *in vitro* has also been reported to increase the release of prolactin by the pituitary (Thorner et al., 1978). There appear to be no studies in the female of any species.

Narcotics.   Acute and chronic administration of morphine elevates serum prolactin levels in male and female animals and humans. Tolerance appears to develop to this effect, and on abrupt withdrawal of narcotics after chronic administration, prolactin levels are markedly reduced relative to those of controls (Lal et al., 1977). In addition to morphine, all other opiates thus far examined also increase prolactin levels in the monkey, the rodent, and man (Guidotti and Grandison, 1978; Santagostino et al., 1978; Bruni et al., 1977; Lal et al., 1977; Zimmermann and Pang, 1976; Clemens and Sawyer, 1974). These effects are antagonized by naloxone, suggesting that this is a specific, receptor-mediated narcotic effect (Bruni et al., 1977). Furthermore, as was the case for ACTH, prolactin levels are markedly elevated by endogenous opioids, suggesting that these compounds may play a normal role in the regulation of serum prolactin levels and ACTH (Santagostino et al., 1978; Bruni et al., 1977; Dupont et al., 1977b; Rivier et al., 1977; Lien et al., 1976). The locus of action of the endogenous opioids in releasing prolactin appears to be at the level of the hypothalamus, since these compounds release prolactin when applied intracranially but not in the pituitary *in vitro* (Dupont et al., 1977b; Rivier et al., 1977), except perhaps at very high concentrations (Lien et al., 1976).

There are no sex differences in the effects of morphine on prolactin; prolactin levels are elevated to the same degree by narcotics in both males and females.

Marijuana.   In the ovariectomized female monkey and rat, prolactin levels increase substantially. In several studies, it has been shown that a single acute injection of THC depressed this castration-induced increase in prolactin (Nir et al., 1973). Similarly, acute administration of THC has also been shown to depress prolactin in the normal female, although this inhibitory effect obviously is more pronounced and dramatic in the ovariectomized animal (Chakravarty et al., 1975). In the only study available in the human female, Kolodny et al. (1977) found that prolactin levels were consistently and significantly lower in chronic female marijuana users when compared with controls. These human data agree very well with the animal data just mentioned.

In contrast with these findings in the female, single doses of THC in the male rat were shown to elevate serum prolactin levels significantly in one study (Daley et al., 1974). Chronic THC administration has been studied only in the male. Prolactin levels in the pituitary were elevated in young (21 days) but not old (60 days) animals, treated for 3 weeks with THC (Collu et al., 1974, 1975a). No changes were observed in serum prolactin level in either the young or the old animals. The significance of elevated pituitary levels of prolactin and no change in serum levels after chronic THC administration is unclear. In human males, Kolodny et al. (1974, 1976) found no effects of chronic THC use on serum prolactin levels.

At the present time, the effects of acute and chronic THC administration on prolactin have been inadequately studied, and there seems to be some controversy in the literature. Nevertheless, there may be a sex difference in the effect of THC on prolactin, but more definitive studies are required.

Amphetamines, LSD, and Other Stimulants. There is only a single study available with respect to the effects of amphetamine or other stimulants on prolactin levels. In this study, prolactin levels were found to be slightly lower in male rats treated with a single dose of amphetamine (Ravitz and Moore, 1977). There are no other reports available concerning the effects of CNS stimulants on prolactin in males or females.

Growth Hormone

Ethanol. The effects of ethanol on growth hormone in humans appear to be equivocal: different investigators have found increases, decreases, or no change in growth hormone levels in human males (Leppäluoto et al., 1975; Bellet et al., 1970b). However, there seems to be good agreement that ethanol blocks the release of growth hormone stimulated by hypoglycemia or L-dopa in man (Priem et al., 1976; Riesco et al., 1974). In animals, there are only a few studies of the effects of ethanol on growth hormone, but it appears that both acute and chronic ethanol administration decrease serum growth hormone levels in the male (Ratcliffe, 1972). There are no studies related to possible male–female differences in humans or animals, and the paucity of data for the male permits few meaningful conclusions. Studies of the effects of ethanol on stimulated-growth-hormone release in animals would be of particular interest in view of comparable studies in humans suggesting a possible effect.

Narcotics. In most species, experimental manipulations that affect prolactin and growth hormone do so in opposite directions; that is, they increase prolactin and decrease growth hormone. In the case of morphine and other narcotics, however, both prolactin and growth hormone levels are significantly elevated after acute or chronic administration (Bruni et al., 1977; Cocchi et al., 1977; Shaar et al., 1977; Ferland et al., 1976; George and Kokka, 1976; Martin et al., 1975; Simon et al., 1975; Kokka et al., 1973; Cushman, 1972a). The growth hormone response to morphine is exquisitely sensitive; μg/kg doses produce marked elevations in growth hormone (Ferland et al., 1976; George and Kokka, 1976; Martin et al., 1975). In addition, all opiates elevate growth hormone, and these effects can be blocked by naloxone (George and Kokka, 1976; Martin et al., 1975; Kokka et al., 1973). In man, it has also been reported that methadone and heroin block the increase in growth hormone produced by insulin hypoglycemia (Cushman, 1972a). Comparable data are not available in females. Endogenous opioids also significantly increase growth hormone secretion, and this effect can be blocked by naloxone (Bruni et al., 1977; Cocchi et al., 1977; Dupont et al., 1977a; Rivier et al., 1977; Shaar et al., 1977). Finally, narcotics and endogenous opioids do not release growth hormone from the pituitary *in vitro,* suggesting a hypothalamic locus of action (Rivier et al., 1977).

Not only does the growth hormone response to morphine occur at very low doses, but in every study, narcotics consistently elevate growth hormone in every species. Hence, the growth hormone response to morphine seems to be a reliable and sensitive index of narcotic action. There are no sex-related differences in the response of growth hormone to exogenous or endogenous opioids.

Marijuana. Reports on the effects of THC on growth hormone in both humans and animals are contradictory in the male, and there are essentially no data available for the female. Both increases and decreases in growth hormone have been found after the administration of THC, either acutely or chronically (Collu, 1976; Benowitz et al., 1976; Collu et al., 1975a; Daley et al., 1974). Interestingly, one investigator found both an increase in growth hormone in response to chronic intraventricular injections of THC (Collu, 1976) and, in a different study a year earlier, a decrease in growth hormone secretion in response to chronic, systematically administered THC (Collu et al., 1975a). Collu offered no explanation for this inconsistency in his own work. Moreover, the remainder of the animal literature does not shed much light on this confusion, since both increases and decreases in growth hormone have been found. In the male human, it has been reported that the growth hormone response to insulin-induced hypoglycemia was significantly blunted by THC (Benowitz et al., 1976), but there are no comparable data in animals. The confusion in the literature permits no meaningful conclusions at this time about the effects of THC on growth hormone.

Amphetamine, LSD, and Other Stimulants. *d*-Amphetamine and *l*-amphetamine appear to increase serum growth hormone levels in both human males and male and female rhesus monkeys (Parkes et al., 1977; Smith et al., 1977; Kokka and Masuoka, 1976; Marantz et al., 1976; Langer et al., 1975; Rees et al., 1970; Besser et al., 1969). In contrast to this acute effect of amphetamine, chronic LSD treatment (relatively high doses) decreased growth hormone levels in prepubertal male rats (Collu et al., 1975b). There are no other studies available.

Posterior Pituitary Hormones

Oxytocin

Ethanol. The effects of ethanol on oxytocin in the female have been examined extensively, and there seems to be little doubt that ethanol inhibits its secretion (Fuchs, 1966, 1969; Wagner and Fuchs, 1968; Fuchs et al., 1967; Luukainen et al., 1967; Fuchs and Wagner, 1963), although the levels of this posterior pituitary hormone have rarely been measured (the milk-ejection response has been used as a bioassay most often). In females of every species, the milk-ejection response has been found to be markedly inhibited, in a dose-dependent fashion, by acute and chronic ethanol administration (Fuchs, 1966, 1969; Wagner and Fuchs, 1968; Fuchs et al., 1967; Luukainen et al., 1967; Fuchs and Wagner, 1963). Whether ethanol reduces oxytocin levels in the male rat has not been examined, undoubtedly because the role of oxytocin in the male is not well understood.

Narcotics. Suckling in lactating female rats elicits the milk-ejection response, which is presumably mediated by oxytocin release. In a recent study, Haldar and Sawyer (1978) found that morphine and two related narcotics, oxilorphan and butorphanol, markedly inhibited the milk-ejection response in lactating females. This effect was blocked by the narcotic antagonist naloxone. The authors conclude that oxytocin release was blocked by these drugs, since systemically administered oxytocin reversed the inhibiting effects of the narcotics. There are no other reports on the effects of narcotics on oxytocin release in males or females.

Marijuana. There are no studies available.

Amphetamine, LSD, and Other Stimulants. No data are currently available.

Antidiuretic Hormone (ADH)

Ethanol. There seems to be little question that acute ethanol administration or ingestion produces diuresis in both the male and female (Marquis et al., 1975; Kleeman, 1972; Cobo and Quintero 1969; Kozlowski et al., 1967; Raiha, 1960; Bissett and Walker, 1957; Strauss et al., 1950; Eggleton, 1942). It seems equally clear that ethanol produces this effect by inhibiting the secretion of antidiuretic hormone (ADH) via an action in the hypothalamus (Cobo and Quintero, 1969; Kozlowski et al., 1967; Raiha, 1960). Interestingly, acute tolerance appears to develop to the diuretic properties of ethanol; this effect may or may not be related to the development of tolerance to the effects of the drug on ADH release. The latter possibility has not been investigated. This interesting phenomenon deserves further exploration. There are no reported sex differences in the effects of ethanol on antidiuretic hormone in animals.

Narcotics. Morphine has been reported by several investigators to promote antidiuresis, which they concluded was due to a drug-induced release of ADH (Inturrisi and Fujimoto 1968; Schneiden and Blackmore, 1955; Giarman and Condouris, 1954; Duke et al., 1951). However, other investigators have found that the morphine analogs oxilorphan and butorphanol caused profuse polyuria in rats and humans, which they interpreted to support an inhibitory effect of the narcotics on ADH secretion (Miller, 1975; Nutt and Jasinski, 1974). The reasons for these discrepancies are unclear, but there are two possible interpretations. First, morphine could uniquely produce a release of ADH that is not mediated via opiate receptors since its analogs are inactive; or, second, the antidiuretic effect of morphine may be due to an action unrelated to ADH release, perhaps via cardiovascular or some other effects of the drug. In any event, the effects of narcotics on ADH release—or, more precisely, water retention—are unclear at present and require clarification.

Marijuana. There are two reports in the literature that indicate that acute marijuana and THC administration produce diuresis in the male rat (Biswas and Ghosh, 1975; Barry et al., 1970, 1973). Both groups concluded that this diuretic effect was mediated by a fall in serum ADH. There are no other reports of such effects, and male–female differences have not been explored. More documentation is required to establish clearly that marijuana has diuretic effects, particular since polyuria is not considered a prominent effect of cannabis use.

Amphetamine, LSD, and Other Stimulants. There are no data available with respect to the effects of amphetamine on ADH release. There is a single report that high, acute doses of LSD in male rats increased ADH release (Biswas and Ghosh, 1975), resulting in antidiuresis. No male–female differences were examined in the latter study. No other data are available on the effects of CNS stimulants on ADH release in animals.

3. SUMMARY AND GENERAL CONSIDERATIONS

Summary

On the basis of the extensive discussion of the literature presented in this review, it seems possible to draw several conclusions. To facilitate this process, in the following subsections, the factual information available on the effects of ethanol, narcotics, marijuana, and CNS stimulants on the various neuroendocrine systems examined is summarized.

Ethanol

Hypothalamic–Pituitary–Gonadal (H–P–G) Axis. Alcoholics and animals chronically treated with ethanol undergo a series of changes in reproductive function, including loss of libido, testicular atrophy, gynecomastia, and other signs and symptoms of hypogonadism. Acutely and chronically administered, ethanol depresses serum testosterone levels in the male of every species. Ethanol is a potent inhibitor of testicular steroidogenesis. It also depresses the elaboration of LH by the hypothalamic–pituitary axis, with the locus of action being the hypothalamus.

Ethanol thus induces multiple disturbances in the H–P–G axis, which combine to produce marked impairments in reproductive endocrinology and function in the male. Relatively little is known about the effects of ethanol on the H–P–G axis in females.

Hypothalamic–Pituitary–Adrenal (H–P–A) Axis. Ethanol acutely increases serum cortisol levels in humans and corticosterone levels in animals. It is uncertain whether these increases are caused by ethanol *per se* or by the stress associated with intoxication and/or withdrawal. The adrenal steroids may play a role in the expression of ethanol withdrawal behavior. Ethanol appears to exert its effects on either the pituitary or the hypothalamus, rather than on the adrenal itself. There may be a sex difference in the response of the H–P–A axis to ethanol in two inbred strains of mice (LS and SS), but in other species or humans, no prominent sex differences have been found.

Hypothalamic–Pituitary–Thyroidal (H–P–T) Axis. Ethanol acutely elevates the uptake of T_3 and T_4 by their target organs and enhances the uptake of ^{125}I by the thyroid. Its effects on TRF and TSH are not well established, and hence, the locus of action within the H–P–T axis is unknown. It has been reported that T_3, T_4, and RT_3 are lowered by chronic ethanol administration in male rodents but that RT_3 levels are only modestly affected in females. These are the only sex differences reported and they seem slight indeed.

Prolactin. It has been shown in some but not all studies that prolactin levels are modestly increased in human alcoholics. Studies of acute ethanol effects on prolactin in man and animals have produced inconsistent results. Ethanol releases prolactin from the pituitary *in vitro.* No studies have been made of sex differences in the effects of ethanol on prolactin.

Growth Hormone. Although inconsistent effects of ethanol on basal growth hormone levels have been found in man, ethanol does appear to block the stimulation of growth hormone release by hypoglycemia or L-dopa in man. It suppresses growth hormone in rodents. There are no reported sex differences.

Oxytocin. Ethanol inhibits oxytocin release in the female of every species. No studies have been carried out in males.

ADH (Vasopressin). Acute ethanol administration produces diuresis by inhibiting the secretion of vasopressin. Ethanol exerts its effects at the level of the hypothalamus. There are no reported sex differences.

Narcotics

H–P–G Axis. Narcotics have pronounced and clinically noteworthy effects on the H–P–G axis in both the male and the female of every species. There are no direct effects of narcotics on the ovaries, the testes, or the secondary sex organs. Rather, the narcotics suppress testosterone levels in the male by inhibiting the elaboration of LH by the hypothalamic–pituitary–LH axis. The anovulatory effects of these drugs, and their disruption of the menstrual cycle in women and the estrous cycle in rodents, appear also to be due to their inhibitory effects on the hypothalamic–pituitary–LH axis.

In both the male and the female, it appears that narcotics depress LH by an action on the hypothalamus, probably by inhibiting the release of LH–RH. The only apparent sex difference in the effects of narcotics on the H–P–G axis is in terms of sensitivity: doses 25–50 times greater are required to suppress LH levels in the female than in the male.

H–P–A Axis. Narcotics acutely elevate corticosteroids in rats, mice, cats, and dogs, but they probably do not alter cortisol secretion in humans. This effect appears to be mediated through specific narcotic receptors, and tolerance develops. Tolerance appears to be mediated by a suppression of ACTH, probably by virtue of an inhibition of CRF, although this possibility has not been assessed. There appears to be a close relationship between endogenous opioids and ACTH since (1) they are derived from the same precursor molecules; (2) they are contained within the same cells in the pituitary; and (3) they are co-released in response to the same stimuli. There are no sex differences in the effects of narcotics on the H–P–A axis.

H–P–T Axis. Narcotics inhibit the release of TSH and decrease the uptake of ^{131}I by the thyroid. They decrease the release of ^{131}I-labeled hormones from the thyroid. These effects appear to be mediated by specific opioid receptors, but tolerance does not appear to develop. There are no reported sex differences.

Prolactin. Narcotics elevate serum prolactin in all species of either sex. This effect is receptor-mediated. Endogenously occurring opioids also release prolactin, suggesting a normal role for these substances in prolactin release. The locus of action of narcotics appears to be at the level of the hypothalamus. There are no apparent sex differences.

Growth Hormone. Narcotics markedly elevate growth hormone levels in all species. The effect of narcotics on the release of growth hormone appears to be receptor-mediated. Endogenous opioids also significantly increase growth hormone levels. The locus of action is suprasellar. No sex-related differences have been found.

Oxytocin. Narcotics block the milk-ejection response in females, presumably by inhibiting oxytocin release. Naloxone blocks this effect. No studies have been carried out in the male.

Vasopressin. Conflicting results have been obtained. Sex differences have not been examined.

Marijuana

H–P–G Axis. Marijuana and its active extracts produce atrophic changes in the secondary sex organs and testes, and they impair spermatogenesis after their chronic administration to the male of all animal species. Testosterone levels are markedly reduced by chronic marijuana administration in the male of every species, with the possible exception of man, about which some controversy exists. Marijuana inhibits testicular steroidogenesis.

Arguments have been advanced that marijuana is either an estrogen-like or an anti-estrogen-like substance. Neither position seems strongly supported by experimental evidence as yet, but it seems that marijuana may have direct ovarian effects in the female. It markedly reduces LH secretion in both males and females. The locus of action of marijuana in the hypothalamic–pituitary–LH axis is uncertain, but the existing data suggest an action within the hypothalamus. The only existing study in the human female revealed no changes in reproductive endocrinology. This finding is in marked contrast to studies in other species. In infrahuman primates and other animal species, there are no apparent sex differences.

H–P–A Axis.   Marijuana elevates corticosterone levels in animals but probably does not produce adrenal activation in humans. The locus of action appears to be at the level of the hypothalamus. There are no apparent sex differences.

H–P–T Axis.   Marijuana suppresses the release of labeled iodine from the thyroid and markedly reduces serum thyroxine concentrations. Basal and TRF-stimulated TSH levels are also reduced by marijuana. The locus of action appears to be at the level of the hypothalamus. There are no reported sex differences.

Prolactin.   Data are too controversial to permit any conclusions for either sex.

Growth Hormone.   Data are too controversial to permit any conclusions for either sex.

Oxytocin.   There are no studies available.

Vasopressin.   Marijuana has been found to produce diuresis in the male rat, a finding that has been inferred to mean that vasopressin release has been inhibited. There are no studies in the female.

Amphetamines, LSD, and Other Stimulants

H–P–G Axis.   There are no data in humans of either sex. In one study on the male rat, chronic LSD administration did not alter LH or FSH levels. There are no other data.

H–P–A Axis.   Acute doses of *d-* or *l-*amphetamine decrease cortisol production in male and female rhesus monkeys. On the other hand, methamphetamine increases cortisol production in humans. It has also been reported that acute and chronic LSD treatment elevated corticoid production in rodents. There are no apparent sex differences, and there are obvious conflicts in the data.

H–P–T Axis.   There are no data available.

Prolactin.   In a single study, amphetamine was found to lower serum prolactin levels in male rats after an acute injection. No other data exist.

Growth Hormone.   Amphetamines increase growth hormone in both human males and male and female monkeys. Chronic LSD treatment decreased growth hormone levels in prepubertal male rats. No other data are available.

Oxytocin.   There are no data available.

Vasopressin.   LSD in male rats increased ADH release after acute doses. There are no other studies available.

General Considerations

The preceding review has focused attention on several aspects of the literature pertaining to the effects of psychoactive drugs on neuroendocrine function.

First, there has been a recent resurgence of interest in the effects of psychoactive drugs on endocrine function that is due in large part to the rapid advances in the field of endocrinology, notably the development of sensitive and specific radioimmunoassays for hormones.

Second, although there appears to be a general level of research interest in drug–endocrine interactions, there has been a very heavy emphasis on selected drugs (e.g., narcotics) and certain neuroendocrine systems (e.g., the hypothalamic–pituitary–gonadal axis) at the expense of other substances and neuroendocrine axes.

Third, studies in males have greatly outnumbered those in females, so that we know very little about sex differences in neuroendocrine responses to psychoactive drugs.

Fourth, there are relatively few studies in the human, male or female.

Fifth, what studies are available in the human permit few definitive conclusions about the effects of psychoactive drugs on neuroendocrine systems for a number of reasons: (1) drug variables, such as dose–response and time–response considerations, have been inadequately incorporated into the design of many studies; (2) drug-specific effects in humans are difficult to evaluate since so many variables that could influence neuroendocrine function are not or cannot be controlled; (3) a number of design problems with the endocrinological aspects of drug–endocrine studies in humans, such as a failure to recognize or accommodate for the cyclic nature of hormone secretions, have also greatly limited the validity of a number of studies.

As should be obvious from these conclusions, there are problems and large gaps in the literature on the effects of drugs on neuroendocrine systems in animals and humans. The purpose of this review is to give an analysis that might provide a strong basis for badly needed studies designed to overcome these problems and fill the gaps in our knowledge.

ACKNOWLEDGMENTS

A good deal of the author's research reviewed in this manuscript was supported in part by USPHS grants DA-01407, DA-00259 and AA-03242. The author is also a recipient of Research Scientist Development

Award AA-70180. The author wishes to express his gratitude to Edward R. Meyer and Roy D. Bell, who helped in the literature searches, and to Dr. Rhea Dornbush, who gave valuable insights into some of the clinical research. Finally, I owe a debt of gratitude to Dorothy Giedinghagen and Leslie Faught for the excellent typing of the manuscript.

REFERENCES

Ahluwalia, B., Williams, J., and Verma, P., 1974, *In vitro* testosterone biosynthesis in the human fetal testis, II, Stimulation by cyclic AMP and human chorionic gonadotropin (hCG), *Endocrinology* **95**:1411–1415.

Aron, E., Flanzy, M., Combescot, C., Puisas, J., Demaret, J., Reynouard-Brandt, F., and Igert, C., 1965, L'alcool est-il dans le vin l'élément qui perturbe, chez la ratte, le cycle vaginal, *Bull. Acad. Nat. Méd.* (Paris) **149**:112–120.

Augustine, J. R., 1967, Laboratory studies in acute alcoholics, *Can. Med. Assoc. J.* **96**:1367–1370.

Ayalon, D., Nir, I., Cardova, T., Bauminger, S., Puder, M., Naor, Z., Kashi, R., Zor, U., Harell A., and Lindner, H. R., 1977, Acute effects of Δ¹-tetrahydrocannabinol on the hypothalamo-pituitary-ovarian axis in the rat, *Neuroendocrinology* **23**:31–42.

Azizi, F., Vagenakis, A. G., Longcope, C., Ingbar, S. H., and Braverman, L. E., 1973, Decreased serum testosterone concentration in male heroin and methadone addicts, *Steroids* **22**:467–472.

Badr, F. M., and Bartke, A., 1974, Effect of ethyl alcohol on plasma testosterone levels in mice, *Steroids* **23**:921–928.

Baker, H. W., Burger, H. G., de Kretser, D. M., Dulmanis, A., Hartson, B., O'Connor, S., Paulsen, C. A., Purcell, N., Rennie, G. C., Seah, C. S., Taft, H. P., and Wang, C., 1976, A study of the endocrine manifestations of hepatic cirrhosis, *Q. J. Med.* **45**:145–178.

Bakke, J. L., Lawrence, N. L., and Robinson, S., 1974, The effect of morphine on pituitary–thyroid function in the rat, *Eur. J. Pharmacol.* **25**:402–406.

Barraclough, C. A., and Sawyer, C. H., 1955, Inhibition of the release of the pituitary ovulatory hormone in the rat by morphine, *Endocrinology* **57**:329–337.

Barry, H., III, Perhach, J. L., and Kubena, R. K., 1970, Δ⁹-Tetrahydrocannabinol activation of pituitary-adrenal function, *Pharmacologist* **12**:258.

Barry, H., III, Kubena, R. K., and Perhach, J. L., Jr., 1973, Pituitary–adrenal activation and related responses to delta-1-tetrahydrocannabinol, *Prog. Brain Res.* **39**:323–330.

Bartke, A., Steele, R. E., Musto, N., and Caldwell, B. V., 1973, Fluctuations in plasma testosterone levels in adult male rats and mice, *Endocrinology* **92**:1223–1228.

Bastomsky, C. H., Dent, R. R., and Tolis, G., 1977, Elevated serum concentrations of thyroxine-binding globulin and caeruloplasmin in methadone-maintained patients, *Clin. Biochem.* **10**:124–126.

Bellet, S., Roman, L., DeCastro, O. A. P., and Herrera, M., 1970a, Effect of acute ethanol intake on plasma 11-hydroxycorticosteroid levels, *Metabolism* **19**:664–667.

Bellet, S., Yoshimine, N., DeCastro, O. A. P., Roman, L., Parmar, S. S., and Sandberg, H., 1970b, Effects of alcohol ingestion on growth hormone levels: Their relation to 11-hydroxycorticoid levels and serum FFA, *Metabolism* **20**:762–769.

Benowitz, N. L., Jones, R. T., and Lerner, C. B., 1976, Depression of growth hormone and cortisol response to insulin-induced hypoglycemia after prolonged oral delta-9-tetrahydrocannabinol administration in man, *J. Clin. Endocrinol. Metab.* **42**:938–941.

Besch, N. F., Smith, C. G., Besch, P. K., and Kaufman, R. H., 1977, The effect of marihuana (delta-9-tetrahydrocannabinol) on the secretion of luteinizing hormone in the ovariectomized rhesus monkey, *Am. J. Obstet. Gynecol.* **128**:635–642.

Besser, G. M., Butler, P. W. P., Landon, J., and Rees, L., 1969, Influence of amphetamines on plasma corticosteroid and growth hormone levels in man, *Br. Med. J.* **4**:528–530.

Bisset, G. W., and Walker, J. M., 1957, The effect of nicotine, hexamethonium and ethanol on the secretion of antidiuretics and oxytocic hormones of the rat, *Br. J. Pharmacol.* **12**:461–467.

Biswas, B., and Ghosh, J. J., 1975, Delta-9-tetrahydrocannabinol and lysergic acid diethylamide: Comparative changes in the supraoptic and paraventricular neurosecretory activities in rat hypothalamus, *Anat. Anz.* **138**:324–331.

Blake, C. A., 1975, Effects of "stress" on pulsatile luteinizing hormone release in ovariectomized rats, *Proc. Soc. Exp. Biol. Med.* **148**:813–815.

Bleecker, M., Ford, D. H., and Rhines, R. K., 1969, A comparison of [131]-tri-iodothyronine accumulation and degradation in ethanol-treated and control rats, *Life Sci.* **8**:267–275.

Bloom, F., Battenberg, E., Rossier, J., Ling, N., Leppaluoto, J., Vargo, T. M., and Guillemin, R., 1977, Endorphins are located in the intermediate and anterior lobes of the pituitary gland, not in the neurohypophysis, *Life Sci.* **20**:43–47.

Borrell, J., Llorens, I., and Borrell, S., 1974, Study of the effects of morphine on adrenal corticosteroids, ascorbic acid and catecholamines in unanaesthetized and anaesthetized cats, *Hormone Res.* **5**:351–358.

Brambilla, F., Sacchetti, E., and Brunetta, M., 1977, Pituitary-gonadal function in heroin addicts, *Neuropsychobiology* **3**:160–166.

Bromley, B. L., and Zimmermann, E., 1976, Divergent release of prolactin and corticosterone following Δ^9-tetrahydrocannabinol injection in male rats, *Fed. Proc.* **35**:220.

Bromley, B. L., Gordon, J. H., and Zimmermann, E., 1977a, Δ^9-Tetrahydrocannabinol block of 5-hydroxytryptamine stimulated release of prolactin in male rats, *Soc. Neurosci. Abstr.* **3**:287.

Bromley, B., Gordon, J. H., and Zimmermann, E., 1977b, Δ^9-tetrahydrocannabinol inhibition of ether and perphenazine-induced release of prolactin in male rats, *Fed. Proc.* **36**:1026.

Bruni, J. F., Van Vugt, D., Marshall, S., and Meites, J., 1977, Effects of naloxone, morphine and methionine enkephalin on serum prolactin, luteinizing hormone, follicle stimulating hormone, thyroid stimulating hormone, and growth hormone, *Life Sci.* **21**:461–466.

Burstein, S., Hunter, S. A., Shoupe, T. S., and Taylor, P., 1978, Cannabinoid inhibition of testosterone synthesis by mouse Leydig cells, *Res. Commun. Chem. Pathol. Pharmacol.* **19**:557–560.

Burton, G., and Kaplan, H. M., 1968, Sexual behavior and adjustment of married alcoholics, *Q. J. Stud. Alcohol.* **29**:603–609.

Chakravarty, I., Sheth, A. R., and Ghosh, J. J., 1975, Effect of acute Δ^9-tetrahydrocannabinol treatment on serum luteinizing hormone and prolactin levels in adult female rats, *Fertil. Steril.* **76**:947–948.

Chopra, I. J., Tulchinsky, D., and Greenway, F. L., 1973, Estrogen–androgen imbalance in hepatic cirrhosis, *Ann. Intern. Med.* **79**:198–203.

Cicero, T. J., 1977, An *in vivo* assay for the analysis of the biological potency and structure-activity relationships of narcotics: Serum testosterone depletion in the male rat, *J. Pharmacol. Exp. Ther.* **202**:670–675.

Cicero, T. J., and Badger, T. M., 1977a, A comparative analysis of the effects of narcotics, alcohol and the barbiturates on the hypothalamic–pituitary–gonadal axis, in: *Alcohol Intoxication and Withdrawal: Studies in Alcohol Dependence* (M. M. Gross, ed.), pp. 95–115, Plenum, New York.

Cicero, T. J., and Badger, T. M., 1977b, Effects of alcohol on the hypothalamic–pituitary–gonadal axis in the male rat, *J. Pharmacol. Exp. Ther.* **201**:427–433.

Cicero, T. J., Meyer, E. R., Bell, R. D., and Wiest, W. G., 1974, Effects of morphine on the secondary sex organs and plasma testosterone levels of rats, *Res. Commun. Chem. Pathol. Pharmacol.* **7**:17–24.

Cicero, T. J., Bell, R. D., Wiest, W. G., Allison, J. H., Polakoski, K., and Robins, E., 1975a, Function of the male sex organs in heroin and methadone users, *N. Engl. J. Med.* **292**:882–887.

Cicero, T. J., Meyer, E. R., Wiest, W. G., Olney, J. W., and Bell, R. D., 1975b, Effects of chronic morphine administration on the reproductive system of the male rat, *J. Pharmacol. Exp. Ther.* **192**:542–548.

Cicero, T. J., Meyer, E. R., Bell, R. D., Koch, G. A., 1976a, Effects of morphine and methadone on serum testosterone and luteinizing hormone levels and on the secondary sex organs of the male rat, *Endocrinology* **98**:367–372.

Cicero, T. J., Wilcox, C. E., Bell, R. D., and Meyer, E. R., 1976b, Acute reductions in serum testosterone levels by narcotics in the male rat: Stereospecificity, blockade by naloxone and tolerance, *J. Pharmacol. Exp. Ther.* **198**:340–346.

Cicero, T. J., Badger, T. M., Wilcox, C. E., Bell, R. D., and Meyer, E. R., 1977a, Morphine decreases luteinizing hormone by an action on the hypothalamic–pituitary axis, *J. Pharmacol. Exp. Ther.* **203**:548–555.

Cicero, T. J., Bell, R. D., Meyer, E. R., and Schweitzer, J., 1977b, Narcotics and the hypothalamic–pituitary–gonadal axis: Acute effects on luteinizing hormone, testosterone and androgen-dependent systems, *J. Pharmacol. Exp. Ther.* **201**:76–83.

Cicero, T. J., Bernstein, D., and Badger, T. M., 1978, Acute effects of alcohol on the hypothalamic–pituitary aspect of the hypothalamic–pituitary–gonadal axis, *Alcoholism: Clin. Exp. Stud.* **2**:249–254.

Cicero, T. J., Meyer, E. R., and Bell, R. D., 1979, Effects of ethanol on the hypothalamic–pituitary–luteinizing hormone axis and testicular steroidogenesis, *J. Pharmacol. Exp. Ther.* **208**:210–215.

Clemens, J. A., and Sawyer, B. D., 1974, Evidence that methadone stimulates prolactin release by dopamine receptor blockade, *Endocr. Res. Commun.* **1**:373–378.

Cobo, E., and Quintero, C. A., 1969, Milk-ejecting and anti-diuretic activities under neurohypophyseal inhibition with alcohol and water overload, *Am. J. Obstet. Gynecol.* **105**:877–887.

Cocchi, D., Santagostino, A., Gil-Ad, I., Ferri, S., and Muller, E. E., 1977, Leu-enkephalin-stimulated growth hormone and prolactin release in the rat: Comparison with the effect of morphine, *Life Sci.* **20**:2041–2045.

Collu, R., 1976, Endocrine effects of chronic intraventricular administration of Δ^9-tetrahydrocannabinol to prepuberal and adult male rats, *Life Sci.* **18**:223–230.

Collu, R., Leboeuf, F., Letarte, J., and Ducharme, J. R., 1974, Endocrine effects of chronic administration of Δ^9-tetrahydrocannabinol to prepuberal male rats, *Pediatric Res.* **8**:94.

Collu, R., Letarte, J., Leboeuf, F., and Ducharme, J. R., 1975a, Endocrine effects of chronic administration of psychoactive drugs to prepuberal male rats, I, Δ^9-tetrahydrocannabinol, *Life Sci.* **16**:533–542.

Collu, R., Letarte, J., Leboeuf, F., and Ducharme, J. R., 1975b, Endocrine effects of chronic administration of psychoactive drugs to prepuberal male rats, II, LSD, *Can. J. Physiol. Pharmacol.* **53**:1023–1026.

Coppage, W. S., Jr., and Cooner, A. E., 1965, Testosterone in human plasma, *N. Engl. J. Med.* **273**:902–907.

Coyotupa, J., Parlow, A. F., and Kovacic, N., 1973, Serum testosterone and dihydrotestosterone levels following orchiectomy in the adult rat, *Endocrinology* **92**:1579–1581.

Cranston, E. M., 1958, Effect of tranquilizers and other agents on sexual cycle of mice, *Proc. Soc. Exp. Med. Biol.* **98**:320–322.

Cushman, P., Jr., 1972a, Growth hormone in narcotic addiction, *J. Clin. Endocrinol. Metab.* **35**:352–358.

Cushman, P., 1972b, Sexual behavior in heroin addiction and methadone maintenance, *N.Y. State J. Med.* **72**:1261–1265.

Cushman, P., 1973, Plasma testosterone in narcotic addiction, *Am. J. Med.* **55**:452–458.

Cushman, P., and Dole, V. P., 1973, Detoxification of rehabilitated methadone maintained patients, *J. Am. Med. Assoc.* **226**:747–752.

Cushman, P., Jr., and Kreek, M. J., 1974, Methadone-maintained patients. Effect of methadone on plasma testosterone, FSH, LH, and prolactin, *N.Y. State J. Med.* **74**:1970–1973.

Czaja, C., and Kalant, H., 1961, The effect of acute alcoholic intoxication on adrenal ascorbic acid and cholesterol in the rat, *Can. J. Biochem. Physiol.* **39**:327–334.

Daley, J. D., Branda, L. A., Rosenfeld, J., and Younglai, E. V., 1974, Increase of serum prolactin in male rats by (−)-trans-delta-9-tetrahydrocannabinol, *J. Endocrinol.* **63**:415–416.

Dalterio, S., Bartke, A., and Burstein, S., 1977, Cannabinoids inhibit testosterone secretion by mouse testes *in vitro, Science* **196**:1472–1473.

Davidson, J. M., 1969, Feedback control of gonadotropin secretion, in: *Frontiers in Neuroendocrinology* (W. F. Ganong and L. Martini, eds.), pp. 343–388, Oxford University Press, New York.

deWied, D., and deJong, W., 1974, Drug effects and hypothalamic–anterior pituitary function, *Annu. Rev. Pharmacol.* **14**:389–412.

deWied, D., van Ree, J. M., and deJong, W., 1974, Narcotic analgesics and the neuroendocrine control of anterior pituitary function, in: *Narcotics and the Hypothalamus* (E. Zimmermann and R. George, eds.), pp. 251–264, Raven, New York.

Distiller, L. A., Sagel, J., Dubowitz, B., Kay, G., Carr, P. J., Katz, M., and Kew, M. C., 1976, Pituitary–gonadal function in men with alcoholic cirrhosis of the liver, *Horm. Metab. Res.* **8**:461–465.

Dixit, V. P., Sharma, V. N., and Lohiya, N. K., 1974, The effect of chronically administered cannabis extract on the testicular function of mice, *Eur. J. Pharmacol.* **26**:111–114.

Dixit, V. P., Arya, M., and Lohiya, N. K., 1975, The effect of chronically administered cannabis extract on the female genital tract of mice and rats, *Endokrinologie* **66**:365–368.

Dixit, V. P., Gupta, C. L., and Agrawal, M., 1977, Testicular degeneration and necrosis induced by chronic administration of cannabis extract in dogs, *Endokrinologie* **69**:299–305.

Doering, C. H., Kraemer, H. C., Brodie, K. H., and Hamburg, D. A., 1975, A cycle of plasma testosterone in the human male, *J. Clin. Encocrinol. Metab.* **40**:492–500.

Dotson, L. E., Robertson, L. S., and Tuchfeld, B., 1975, Plasma alcohol, smoking, hormone concentrations, and self-reported aggression, *J. Stud. Alcohol* **36**:578–586.

DuFau, M. L., Watanabe, K., and Catt, K. J., 1973, Stimulation of cyclic AMP production by the rat testis during incubation with hCG *in vitro, Endocrinology* **92**:6–11.

Duke, H. N., Pickford, M., and Watt, J. A., 1951, Antidiuretic action of morphine: Its site and mode of action in hypothalamus of dog, *Q. J. Exp. Physiol.* **36**:149–158.

Dunn, J. D., Armiura, A., and Scheving, L. E., 1972, Effect of stress on circadian periodicity in serum LH and prolactin concentration, *Endocrinology* **90**:29–33.

Dupont, A., Cusan, L., Garon, M., Labrie, F., and Li, C. H., 1977a, β-endorphin stimulation of growth hormone release *in vivo, Proc. Natl. Acad. Sci. USA* **74**:358–359.

Dupont, A., Cusan, L., Labrie, F., Coy, D. H., and Li, C. H., 1977b, Stimulation of prolactin release in the rat by intraventricular injection of β-endorphin and methionine–enkephalin, *Biochem. Biophys. Res. Commun.* **75**:76–82.

Earll, J. M., Gaunt, K., Earll, L., and Djuh, Y. Y., 1976, Effect of ethyl alcohol on ionic calcium and prolactin in man, *Aviat. Space Environ. Med.* **47**:808–810.

Eggleton, M. G., 1942, Diuretic action of alcohol in man, *J. Physiol.* **101**:172–191.

Eisenman, A. J., Fraser, H. F., and Brooks, J. W., 1961, Urinary excretion and plasma levels of 17-hydroxycorticosteroids during a cycle of addiction to morphine, *J. Pharmacol. Exp. Ther.* **132**:226–231.

Eisenman, A. J., Sloan, J. W., Martin, W. R., Jasinski, D. R., and Brooks, J. W., 1969, Catecholamine and 17-hydroxycorticosteroid excretion during a cycle of morphine dependence in man, *J. Psychiatr. Res.* **7**:19–28.

Ellingboe, J., Mendelson, J. H., Holbrook, P. G., Valentine, N., and Kuehnle, J., 1978, Naltrexone effects on luteinizing hormone (LH) secretion and mood states implicate endogenous opioid mechanisms in regulation of the hypothalamic–pituitary–gonadal axis, *Fed. Proc.* **37**:275.

Ellis, F. W., 1962, Effect of ethanol on plasma corticosterone concentration in rats, *Fed. Proc.* **21**:339.

Ellis, F. W., 1965, Adrenal cortical function in experimental alcoholism in dogs, *Proc. Soc. Exp. Biol. Med.* **120**:740–744.

Ellis, F. W., 1966, Effect of ethanol on plasma corticosterone levels, *J. Pharmacol. Exp. Ther.* **153**:121–127.

Eskay, R., Majchrowicz, E., Goldman, M., and Ryback, R., 1978, Effect of chronic ethanol administration on the hypothalamic–pituitary–gonadal axis, *Fed. Proc.* **37**:478.

Euker, J. S., Meites, J., and Riegle, G. D., 1975, Effects of acute stress on serum LH and prolactin in intact, castrate and dexamethasone-treated male rats, *Endocrinology* **96**:85–92.

Fabre, L. F., Jr., Pasco, P. J., Liegel, J. M., and Farmer, R. W., 1973, Abnormal testosterone excretion in men alcoholics, *Q. J. Stud. Alcohol* **34**:57–63.

Fahim, M. S., Dement, G., Hall, D. G., and Fahim, Z., 1970, Induced alterations in the hepatic metabolism of androgens in the rat, *Am. J. Obstet. Gynecol.* **107**:1085–1091.

Farmer, R. W., and Fabre, L. F., Jr., 1975, Some endocrine aspects of alcoholism, *Adv. Exp. Med. Biol.* **56**:277–289.

Ferland, L., Labrie, F., Coy, D. H., Armiura, A., and Schally, A. V., 1976, Inhibition by six somatostatin analogs of plasma growth-hormone levels stimulated by thiomylal and morphine in the rat, *Mol. Cell. Endocrinol.* **4**:79–88.

French, E. D., Garcia, J. F., and George, R., 1974, Intracerebral morphine and naloxone effects on growth hormone and cortisol in naive and morphine dependent cats, *Proc. West. Pharmacol. Soc.* **17**:159.

Fuchs, A. R., 1966, The inhibitory effects of ethanol on the release of oxytocin during parturition in the rabbit, *J. Endocrinol.* **35**:125–134.

Fuchs, A. R., 1969, Ethanol and the inhibition of oxytocin release in lactating rats, *Acta Endocrinol. (Copenhagen)* **62**:546–554.

Fuchs, A. R., and Wagner, G., 1963, Effect of alcohol on release of oxytocin, *Nature* **198**: 92–94.

Fuchs, F., Fuchs, A. R., Poblete, V. F., and Risk, A., 1967, Effects of alcohol on threatened premature labor, *Am. J. Obstet. Gynecol.* **99**:627–637.

Galvão-Teles, A., Anderson, D. C., Burke, G. W., Marshall, J. C., Corker, C. S., Brown, R. L and Clark, M. L., 1973, Biologically active androgens and oestradiol in men with chronic liver disease, *Lancet* **1**:173–177.

Gaulden, E. C., Littlefield, D. C., Putoff, O. E., and Seivert, A. L., 1964, Menstrual abnormalities associated with heroin addiction, *Am. J. Obstet. Gynecol.* **90**:155–160.

George, R., 1971, Hypothalamus: Anterior pituitary gland, in: *Narcotic Drugs Biochemical Pharmacology* (D. H. Clouet, ed.), pp. 283–299, Plenum, New York.

George, R., 1973, Effects of narcotic analgesics on hypothalamo –pituitary–thyroid function, *Prog. Brain Res.* **39**:339–345.

George, R., and Kokka, N., 1976, The effects of narcotics on growth hormone, ACTH and TSH secretion, in: *Tissue Responses to Addictive Drugs* (D. H. Ford and D. H. Clouet, eds.), pp. 527–540, Spectrum, New York.

Giarman, N. J., and Condouris, G. A., 1954, The antidiuretic action of morphine and some of it analogs, *Arch. Int. Pharmacodyn. Ther.* **97**:28–33.

Goldberg, M., 1960, The occurrence and treatment of hypothyroidism among alcoholics, *J. Clin. Endocrinol. Metab.* **20**:609–621.

Goldberg, M., 1962, Thyroid function in chronic alcoholsim, *Lancet* **ii**:764–769.

Gordon, G. G., and Southren, A. L., 1977, Metabolic effects of alcohol on the endocrine system, in: *Metabolic Aspects of Alcoholism* (C. S. Lieber, ed.), pp. 249–302, University Park Press, Baltimore.

Gordon, G. G., Olivo, J., Rafil, F., and Southren, A. L., 1975, Conversion of androgens to estrogens in cirrhosis of the liver, *J. Clin. Endocrinol. Metab.* **40**:1018–1026.

Gordon, G. G., Altman, K., and Southren, A. L., 1976, Effect of alcohol (ethanol) administration on sex hormone metabolism in normal men, *N. Engl. J. Med.* **295**:793–797.

Gordon, J. H., Bromley, B. L., Gorski, R. A., and Zimmermann, E., 1978, Effects of Δ^9-tetrahydrocannabinol on TSH secretion, *Proc. Endocrine Society* **60**:675.

Green, J. R., Mowat, N. A., Fisher, R. A., and Anderson, D. C., 1976, Plasma oestrogens in men with chronic liver disease, *Gut* **17**:426–430.

Guidotti, A., and Grandison, L., 1978, Participation of hypothalamic endorphins in the control of prolactin release, *Adv. Biochem. Psychopharmacol.* **18**:191–198.

Guillemin, R., Vargo, T., Rossier, J., Minick, S., Ling, N., Rivier, C., Vale, W., and Bloom, F, 1977, β-endorphin and adrenocorticotropin are secreted concomitantly by the pituitary gland, *Science* **197**:1367–1369.

Halaris, A. E., Freedman, D. X., and Fang, V. S., 1975, Plasma corticoids and brain tryptophan after acute and tolerance dosage of LSD, *Life Sci.* **17**:1467–1472.

Haldar, J., and Sawyer, W. H., 1978, Inhibition of oxytocin release by morphine and its analogs, *Proc. Soc. Exp. Biol. Med.* **157**:476–480.

Harmon, J., and Aliapoulios, M. A., 1972, Gynecomastia in marihuana users (letter), *N. Engl. J. Med.* **287**:936.

Harmon, J. W., Locke, D., Aliapoulios, M. A., and Macindoe, J. H., 1976, Interference with testicular development by Δ^9-tetrahydrocannabinol, *Surg. Forum* **27**:350–352.

Hellman, L., Fukushima, D. K., Roffwarg, H., and Fishman, J., 1975, Changes in estradiol and cortisol production rates in men under the influence of narcotics, *J. Clin. Endocrinol. Metab.* **41**:1014–1019.

Heston, W. D. W., Erwin, V. G., Anderson, S. M., and Robbins, H., 1974, A comparison of the effects of alcohol on mice selectively bred for differences in ethanol sleep-time, *Life Sci.* **14**:365–370.

Hilbom, M. E., 1971, Thyroid state and voluntary alcohol consumption of albino rats, *Acta Pharmacol. Toxicol.* **29**:95–105.

Hohlweg, W., Knappe, G., and Doerner, G., 1961, Tierexperimentelle Untersuchungen über den Einfluss von Morphin auf die gonadotrope und thyreotrope Hypophysen-funktion, *Endokrinologie* **40**:152–159.

Howland, B. E., Beaton, D. B., and Jack, M. I., 1974, Changes in serum levels of gonadotropins and testosterone in the male rat in response to fasting, surgery and ether, *Experientia* **30**:1223–1225.

Huttunen, M. O., Härkönen, M., Niskanen, P., Leino, T., and Ylikahri, R., 1976, Plasma testosterone concentrations in alcoholics, *J. Stud. Alcohol* **37**:1165–1177.

Inturrisi, C. E., and Fujimoto, J. M., 1968, Studies on the antidiuretic action of morphine in the rat, *Eur. J. Pharmacol.* **2**:301–307.

Israel, Y., Videla, L., MacDonald, A., and Bernstein, J., 1973, Metabolic alterations produced in the liver by chronic ethanol administration: Comparison between the effects produced by ethanol and by thyroid hormones, *Biochem. J.* **134**:523–529.

Jenkins, J. S., and Connolly, J., 1968, Adrenocortical response to ethanol in man, *Br. Med. J.* **2**:804–805.

Johnson, J. G., and Rosecrans, J. A., 1978, Blockade of the preovulatory LH surge by methadone in rats, *Res. Commun. Chem. Pathol. Pharmacol.* **19**:435–444.

Kakihana, R., 1977, Endocrine and autonomic studies in mice selectively bred for different sensitivity to ethanol, in: *Alcohol Intoxication and Withdrawal*, Vol. 3a, *Biological Aspects of Ethanol* (M. M. Gross, ed.), pp. 83–95, Plenum, New York.

Kalant, H., 1975, Direct effects of ethanol on the nervous system, *Fed. Proc.* **34**:1930–1941.

Kalant, H., Sereny, G., and Charlebois, R., 1962, Evaluation of triiodothyronine in the treatment of acute alcohol intoxication, *N. Engl. J. Med.* **262**:1–14.

Kalant, H., Hawkins, R. D., and Czaja, C., 1963, Effect of acute alcohol intoxication on steroid output of rat adrenals *in vitro*, *Am. J. Physiol.* **204**: 849–855.

Kent, J. R., Scaramuzzi, R. J., Lauwers, W., Parlow, A. F., Hill, M., Penardi, R., and Hilliard, J., 1973, Plasma testosterone, estradiol and gonadotrophins in hepatic insufficiency, *Gastroenterology* **64**:111–115.

Kissin, B., Schenker, V., and Schenker, A. C., 1960, The acute effects of alcohol ingestion on plasma and urinary 17-hydroxycorticoids in alcoholic subjects, *Am. J. Med. Sci.* **239**:690–705.

Kleeman, C. R., 1972, Water metabolism, in: *Clinical Disorders of Fluid and Electrolyte Metabolism* (M. H. Maxwell and C. R. Kleeman, eds.), pp. 243–257, McGraw-Hill, New York.

Kleeman, C. R., and Maxwell, M. H., 1972, Regulation of body water, in: *Clinical Disorders of Fluid and Electrolyte Metabolism* (M. H. Maxwell and C. R. Kleeman, eds.), pp. 115–158, McGraw-Hill, New York.

Kokka, N., and Garcia, J. F., 1974, Effects of Δ^9-THC on growth hormone and ACTH secretion in rats, *Life Sci.* **15**:329–338.

Kokka, N., and George, R., 1974, Effects of narcotic analgesics, anesthetics, and hypo-thalamic lesions on growth hormone and adrenocorticotropic secretion in rats, in: *Narcotics and the Hypothalamus* (E. Zimmermann and R. George, eds.), pp. 137–157, Raven, New York.

Kokka, N., and Masuoka, D. T., 1976, Effects of amphetamine and apomorphine on ACTH and growth hormone secretion, *Proc. West. Pharmacol. Soc.* **19**:209–211.

Kokka, N., Garcia, J. F., and Elliott, H. W., 1973, Effects of acute and chronic administration of narcotic analgesics on growth hormone and corticotrophin (ACTH) secretion in rats, *Prog. Brain Res.* **39**:347–360.

Kolodny, R. C., Masters, W. H., Kolodner, R. M., and Toro, G., 1974, Depression of plasma testosterone levels after chronic intensive marihuana use, *N. Engl. J. Med.* **290**:872–874.

Kolodny, R. C., Lessin, P., Toro, G., Masters, W. H., and Cohen, S., 1976, Depression of plasm testosterone with acute marihuana administration, in: *The Pharmacology of Marihuana* (M. C. Braude and S. Szara, eds.), pp. 217–225, Raven, New York.

Kolodny, R. C., Bauman, J., Biggs, M. A., Webster, S. K., and Dornbush, R. L., 1977, Endocrine and sexual effects of female chronic marijuana use, paper presented at the meeting of the International Academy of Sex Research, Bloomington, Ind.

Kozlowski, S., Szczepanska, E., and Zielinski, A., 1967, The hypothalamo–hypophyseal antidiuretic system in physical exercises, *Arch. Int. Physiol. Biochim.* **75**:218–228.

Kramer, J., and Ben-David, M., 1974, Suppression of prolactin secretion by acute administration of Δ^9-THC in rats, *Proc. Soc. Exp. Biol. Med.* **147**:482–484.

Krieger, D. T., Liotta, A., and Li, C. H., 1977, Human plasma immunoreactive β-lipotropin: Correlation with basal and stimulated plasma ACTH concentrations, *Life Sci.* **21**:1771–1778.

Kubena, R. K., Perhach, J. L., and Barry, H., 1971, Corticosterone elevation mediated centrally by Δ^1-tetrahydrocannabinol in rats, *Eur. J. Pharmacol.* **14**:89–92.

Lacerda, L. de, Kowarski, A., Johanson, A. J., Athanasiou, R., and Migeon, C. J., 1973, Integrated concentration and circadian variation of plasma testosterone in normal men, *J. Clin. Endocrinol. Metab.* **36**:366–371.

Lal, H., Brown, W., Drawbaugh, R., Hynes, M., and Brown, G., 1977, Enhanced prolactin inhibition following chronic treatment with haloperidol and morphine, *Life Sci.* **20**:101–105.

Langer, G., Heinze, G., Reim, B., and Matussek, N., 1975, Growth hormone response to d-amphetamine in normal controls and in depressive patients, *Neurosci. Lett.* **1**:185–189.

Lemere, F., and Smith, J. W., 1973, Alcohol-induced sexual impotence, *Am. J. Psychiatry* **130**:212–213.

Leppäluoto, J., Rapeli, M., Varis, R., and Ranta, T., 1975, Secretion of anterior pituitary hormones in man: Effects of ethyl alcohol, *Acta Physiol. Scand.* **95**:400–406.

Lester, R., and Van Thiel, D. H., 1977, Gonadal function in chronic alcoholic men, in: *Alcohol Intoxication and Withdrawal,* Vol. 3, *Biological Aspects of Ethanol* (M. M. Gross, ed.), pp. 399–413, Plenum, New York.

Levine, J., 1955, The sexual adjustment of alcoholics, *Q. J. Stud. Alcohol* **16**:675–680.

Lien, E. L., Fenichel, R. L., Garsky, V., Sarantakis, D., and Grant, N. H., 1976, Enkephalin-stimulated prolactin release, *Life Sci.* **19**:837–840.

Ling, G. M., Thomas, J. A., Usher, D. R., and Singhal, R. L., 1973, Effects of chronically administered Δ^1-tetrahydrocannabinol on adrenal and gonadal activity of male rats, *Int. J. Clin. Pharmacol.* **7**:1–5.

List, A., Nazar, B., Nyquist, S., and Harclerode, J., 1977, The effects of Δ^9-tetrahydrocannabinol and cannabidiol on the metabolism of gonadal steroids in the rat, *Drug Metab. Dispos.* **5**:268–272.

Lloyd, C. W., and Williams, R. H., 1948, Endocrine changes associated with Laennec's cirrhosis of the liver, *Am. J. Med.* **4**:315–330.

Lomax, P., 1970, The effect of marihuana on pituitary-thyroid activity in the rat, *Agents Actions* **1:**252–257.

Lomax, P., and George, R., 1966, Thyroid activity following administration of morphine in rats with hypothalamic lesions, *Brain Res.* **2:**361–367.

Lomax, P., Kokka, N., and George, R., 1970, Thyroid activity following intracerebral injection of morphine in the rat, *Neuroendocrinology* **6:**146–152.

Loosen, P. T., and Prange, A. J., Jr., 1977, Alcohol and anterior-pituitary secretion (letter), *Lancet* **2:**985.

Lotti, V. J., Kokka, N., and George, R., 1969, Pituitary–adrenal activation following intrahypothalamic microinjection of morphine, *Neuroendocrinology* **4:**326–332.

Luukkainen, T., Vaistö, L., and Jarvinen, P. A., 1967, The effect of oral intake of ethyl alcohol on the activity of pregnant human uterus, *Acta Obstet. Gynecol. Scand.* **46:**486–493.

Mains, R. E., Eipper, B. A., and Ling, N., 1977, Common precursor to corticotropins and endorphins, *Proc. Natl. Acad. Sci. USA* **74:**3014–3018.

Marantz, R., Sachar, E. J., Weitzman, E., and Sassin, J., 1976, Cortisol and GH responses to d- and l-amphetamine in monkeys, *Endocrinology* **99:**459–465.

Marks, B. H., 1973, Δ^1-tetrahydrocannabinol and luteinizing hormone secretion, in: *Drug Effects on Neuroendocrine Regulation, Progress in Brain Research* (E. Zimmermann, ed.), pp. 331–338, Elsevier, Amsterdam.

Marks, V., and Wright, J. W., 1977, Endocrinological and metabolic effects of alcohol, *Proc. R. Soc. Med.* **70:**337–344.

Marquis, C., Marchetti, J., Burlet, C., and Boulangé, M., 1975, Sécrétion urinaire et hormone antidiurétique chez des rats soumis à une administration répétée d'éthanol, *C. R. Séances Soc. Biol.* **169:**154–161.

Martin, B. R., Dewey, W. L., Chau-Pham, T., and Prange, A. J., Jr., 1977, Interactions of thyrotropin releasing hormone and morphine sulfate in rodents, *Life Sci.* **20:**715–722.

Martin, J. B., Audet, J., and Saunders, A., 1975, Effects of somatostatin and hypothalamic ventromedial lesions on GH release induced by morphine, *Endocrinology* **96:**839–847.

Martin, W. R., Jasinski, D. R., Haertzen, C. A., Kay, D. C., Jones, B. E., Mansky, P. A., and Carpenter, R. W., 1973, Methadone—A reevaluation, *Arch. Gen. Psychiatry* **28:**286–295.

McClearn, G. E., 1973, The genetic aspects of alcoholism, in: *Alcoholism: Progress in Research and Treatment* (P. G. Bourne and R. Fox, eds.), pp. 337–358, Academic, New York.

McDonald, R. K., Evans, F. T., Weise, V. K., and Patrick, R. W., 1959, Effect of morphine and nalorphine on plasma hydrocortisone levels in man, *J. Pharmacol. Exp. Ther.* **125:**241–247.

Mendelson, J. H., and Mello, N. K., 1974, Alcohol, aggression and androgens, *Res. Publ. Assoc. Res. Nerv. Ment. Dis.* **52:**225–247.

Mendelson, J. H., and Mello, N. K., 1975, Plasma testosterone levels during chronic heroin use and protracted abstinence: A study of Hong Kong addicts, *Clin. Pharmacol. Ther.* **17:**529–533.

Mendelson, J. H., and Mello, N. K., 1976, Behavioral and biochemical interrelations in alcoholism, *Annu. Rev. Med.* **27:**321–333.

Mendelson, J. H., and Mello, N. K., 1977, Co-variance of neuroendocrine function and behavior: A potential technique for assessing drug abuse liability, in: *Predicting Dependence Liability of Stimulant and Depressant Drugs* (T. Thompson and K. R. Unna, eds.), pp. 291–302, University Park Press, Baltimore.

Mendelson, J. H., and Stein, S., 1966, Serum cortisol levels in alcoholic and nonalcoholic subjects during experimentally induced ethanol intoxication, *Psychosom. Med.* **28**:616–626.

Mendelson, J. H., Ogata, M., and Mello, N. K., 1971, Adrenal function and alcoholism, I, Serum cortisol, *Psychosom. Med.* **33**:145–157.

Mendelson, J. H., Kuehnle, J., Ellingboe, J., and Babor, T. F., 1974, Plasma testosterone levels before, during and after chronic marihuana smoking, *N. Engl. J. Med.* **291**:1051–1055.

Mendelson, J. H., Mendelson, J. E., and Patch, V. D., 1975a, Plasma testosterone levels in heroin addiction and during methadone maintenance, *J. Pharmacol. Exp. Ther.* **192**:211–217.

Mendelson, J. H., Meyer, R. E., Ellingboe, J., Mirin, S. M., and McDougle, M., 1975b, Effects of heroin and methadone on plasma cortisol and testosterone, *J. Pharmacol. Exp. Ther.* **195**:296–302.

Mendelson, J. H., Inturrisi, C. E., Renault, P., and Senay, E. C., 1976, Effects of acetylmethadol on plasma testosterone, *Clin. Pharmacol. Ther.* **19**:371–374.

Mendelson, J. H., Mello, N. K., and Ellingboe, J., 1977, Effects of acute alcohol intake on pituitary-gonadal hormones in normal human males, *J. Pharmacol. Exp. Ther.* **202**:676–682.

Mendelson, J. H., Ellingboe, J., Kuehnle, J. C., and Mello, N. K., 1978, Effects of chronic marihuana use on integrated plasma testosterone and luteinizing hormone levels, *J. Pharmacol. Exp. Ther.* **207**:611–617.

Merari, A., Barak, A., and Plaves, M., 1973, Effects of $\Delta^{1(2)}$-tetrahydrocannabinol on copulation in the male rat, *Psychopharmacologia* **28**:243–246.

Merry, J., and Marks, V., 1969, Plasma–hydroxycortisone response to ethanol in chronic alcoholics, *Lancet* **1**:921–923.

Merry, J., and Marks, V., 1972, The effect of alcohol, barbiturate, and diazepam on hypothalamic/pituitary/adrenal function in chronic alcoholics, *Lancet* **2**:990–991.

Miller, M., 1975, Inhibition of ADH release in the rat by narcotic antagonists, *Neuroendocrinology* **19**:241–251.

Mintz, J., O'Hare, K., O'Brien, C. P., and Goldschmidt, J., 1974, Sexual problems of heroin addicts, *Arch. Gen. Psychiatry* **31**:700–703.

Mirin, S. M., Mendelson, J. H., Ellingboe, J., and Meyer, R. E., 1976, Acute effects of heroin and naltrexone on testosterone and gonadotropin secretion: A pilot study, *Psychoneuroendocrinology* **1**:359–369.

Morita, Y., Koyama, K., and Nakao, T., 1974, Proceedings: Influence of morphine on ACTH secretion in the rat, *Jpn. J. Pharmacol.* **24**(Suppl.):126.

Mowat, N. A., Edwards, C. R. W., Fisher, R., McNeilly, A. S., Green, J. R. B., and Dawson, A M., 1976, Hypothalamic–pituitary–gonadal function in men with cirrhosis of the liver, *Gut* **17**:345–350.

Moyle, W. R., and Ramachandran, J., 1973, Effect of LH on steroidogenesis and cyclic-AMP accumulation in rat Leydig cell preparations and mouse tumor Leydig cells, *Endocrinology* **93**:127–134.

Muraki, T., and Tokunaga, Y., 1977, Inhibitory effect of morphine on serum gonadotropins and prolactin on proestrous rats, *Jpn. J. Pharmacol.* **27**:461–462.

Muraki, T., Tokunaga, Y., and Makino, T., 1977, Effects of morphine and naloxone on serum LH, FSH and prolactin levels and on hypothalamic content of LH–RF in proestrous rats, *Endocrinol Jpn.* **24**:313–315.

Murdock, H. R., 1967, Thyroidal effect of alcohol, *Q. J. Stud. Alcohol* **28**:419–423.

Nazar, B., Kairys, D. J., Fowler, R., and Harclerode, J., 1977, Effects of Δ^9-tetrahydrocannabinol on serum thyroxine concentrations in the rat, *J. Pharm. Pharmacol.* **29**:778–779.

Nir, I., Ayalon, D., Tsafriri, A., Cordova, T., and Lindner, H. R., 1973, Letter: Suppression of the cyclic surge of luteinizing hormone secretion and of ovulation in the rat by delta-1-tetrahydrocannabinol, *Nature* **234**:470–471.

Noble, E. P., 1971, Ethanol and adrenocortical stimulation in inbred mouse strains, in: *Recent Advances in Studies of Alcoholism* (N. K. Mello and J. H. Mendelson, eds.), pp. 77–106, U.S. Government Printing Office, Washington, D.C.

Nomura, S., Pittman, C. S., Chambers, J. B., Jr., Buck, M. W., and Shimizu, T., 1975, Reduced peripheral conversion of thyroxine to triiodothyronine in patients with hepatic cirrhosis, *J. Clin. Invest.* **56**:643–652.

Nutt, J. G., and Jasinski, D. R., 1974, Diuretic action of the narcotic antagonist oxilorphan, *Clin. Pharmacol. Ther.* **15**:361–367.

Okey, A. B., and Bondy, G. P., 1977, Letter: Is delta-9-tetrahydrocannabinol estrogenic? *Science* **195**:904–906.

Okey, A. B., and Truant, G. S., 1975, Cannabis demasculinizes rats but is not estrogenic, *Life Sci.* **17**:1113–1118.

Packman, P. M., and Rothchild, J. A., 1976, Morphine inhibition of ovulation: Reversal by naloxone, *Endocrinology* **99**:7–10.

Pang, C. N., and Zimmermann, E., 1975, Effects of morphine on plasma levels of luteinizing hormone (LH), thyroid stimulating hormone (THS) and prolactin in ovariectomized rats, *Anat. Rec.* **181**:444.

Pang, C. N., Zimmermann, E., and Sawyer, C. H., 1974, Effects of morphine on the proestrous surge of luteinizing hormone in the rat, *Anat. Rec.* **178**:434–435.

Pang, C. N., Zimmermann, E., and Sawyer, C. H., 1977, Morphine inhibition of the preovulatory surges of plasma luteinizing hormone and follicle-stimulating hormone in the rat, *Endocrinology* **101**:1726–1743.

Parkes, J. D., Debono, A. G., Jenner, P., and Walters, J., 1977, Amphetamines, growth hormone and narcolepsy, *Br. J. Clin. Pharmacol.* **4**:343–349.

Patel, D. G., Singh, S. P., Kabir, M., and Premachandra, B. N., 1978, Effects of chronic ethanol on thyroid function in rats, *Fed. Proc.* **37**:519.

Pelletier, G., Leclerc, R., Labrie, F., Côté, J., Chrétien, M., and Lis, M., 1977, Immunohistochemical localization of β-lipotropic hormone in the pituitary gland, *Endocrinology* **100**:770.

Pentikäinen, P. J., Pentikäinen, L. A., Azarnoff, D. L., and Dugovne, C. A., 1975, Plasma levels and excretion of estrogens in urine in chronic liver disease, *Gastroenterology* **69**:20–27.

Perman, E. S., 1960, Observations on the effect of ethanol on the urinary excretion of histamine, 5-hydroxyindole acetic acid, catecholamines and 17-hydroxycorticosteroids in man, *Acta Physio. Scand.* **51**:62–67.

Persky, H., O'Brien, C. P., Fine, E., Howard, W. J., Khan, M. A., and Beck, R. W., 1977, The effect of alcohol and smoking on testosterone function and aggression in chronic alcoholics, *Am. J. Psychiatry* **134**:621–625.

Pertwee, R. G., 1974, Tolerance to the effect of Δ^1-tetrahydrocannabinol on corticosterone levels in mouse plasma produced by repeated administration of cannabis extract or Δ^1-tetrahydrocannabinol, *Br. J. Pharmacol.* **51**:391–397.

Pohorecky, L. A., Newman, B., Sun, J., and Bailey, W. E., 1978, Acute and chronic ethanol and serotonin metabolism in rat brain, *J. Pharmacol. Exp. Ther.* **204**:424–432.

Priem, H. A., Shanley, B. C., and Malan, C., 1976, Effect of alcohol administration on plasma growth hormone response to insulin-induced hypoglycemia, *Metabolism* **25**:397–403.

Prieto, R., Varela, A., and Mardones, J., 1958, Influence of oral administration of thyroid powder on the voluntary alcohol intake by rats, *Acta Physiol. Lat. Am.* **8**:203.

Räihä, N., 1960, Effect of ethanol on cytological changes induced by salt load in nucleus supraopticus of rat, *Proc. Soc. Exp. Biol. Med.* **103**:387–389.

Ramakrishanan, S., Prasanna, C. V., and Balasubramanian, A., 1976, Effect of alcohol intake on rat hepatic enzymes and thyroid function, *Indian J. Biochem. Biophys.* **13**:49–51.

Ratcliffe, F., 1972, The effect of chronic ethanol administration on the growth of rats, *Arch. Intern. Pharmacodyn. Ther.* **197**:19–30.

Ravitz, A. J., and Moore, K. E., 1977, Effects of amphetamine, methylphenidate and cocaine on serum prolactin concentrations in the male rat, *Life Sci.* **21**:267–272.

Rawitch, A. B., Schultz, G. S., Ebner, K. E., and Vardaris, R. M., 1977, Competition of delta-9-tetrahydrocannabinol with estrogen in rat uterine estrogen receptor binding, *Science* **197**:1189–1191.

Rees, L., Butler, P. W. P., Gosling, C., and Besser, G. M., 1970, Adrenergic blockade and the corticosteroid and growth hormone responses to methylamphetamine, *Nature* **228**:565–566.

Rennels, E. G., 1961, Effect of morphine on pituitary cytology and gonadotrophic levels in the rat, *Tex. Rep. Biol. Med.* **19**:646–657.

Richter, C. P., 1956, Loss of appetite for alcohol and alcoholic beverages produced in rats by treatment with thyroid preparations, *Endocrinology* **59**:472–478.

Richter, C. P., 1957, Production and control of alcoholic cravings in rats, in: *Neuropharmacology* (H. A. Abramson, ed.), pp. 39–146, Josiah Macy Foundation, Princeton.

Riesco, J., Costamaillere, L., and Litvak, J., 1974, Growth hormone secretion in chronic alcoholics: Lack of response to L-dopa and glucagon, *Rev. Med. (Chile)* **102**:443–446.

Rivier, C., Vale, W., Ling, N., Brown, M., and Guillemin, R., 1977, Stimulation *in vivo* of the secretion of prolactin and growth hormone by β-endorphin, *Endocrinology* **100**:238–241.

Rosenkrantz, H., and Braude, M. C., 1976, Comparative chronic toxicities of Δ⁹-THC administered orally or by inhalation in rats, in: *The Pharmacology of Marihuana* (M. C. Braude and S. Szara, eds.), pp. 571–584, Raven, New York.

Rowe, P. H., Racey, P. A., Shenton, J. C., Ellwood, M., and Lehane, J., 1974, Proceedings: Effects of acute administration of alcohol and barbiturates on plasma luteinizing hormone and testosterone in man, *J. Endocrinol.* **63**:50–51.

Rubin, E., Lieber, C. S., Altman, K., Gordon, G. G., and Southren, A. L., 1976, Prolonged ethanol consumption increases testosterone metabolism in the liver, *Science* **191**:563564.

Santagostino, A., Cocchi, D., Giagnoni, G., Gori, E., Muller, E., and Ferri, S., 1978, Some relationships between endorphins and pituitary hormones, *Adv. Biochem. Psychopharmacol.* **18**:175–181.

Santen, F. J., Sofsky, J., Bilic, N., and Lippert, R., 1975, Mechanism of action of narcotics in the production of menstrual dysfunction in women, *Fertil. Steril.* **26**:538–548.

Sassin, J. F., Frantz, A. G., Weitzman, E. D., and Kapen, S., 1972, Human prolactin: 24-hour pattern with increased release during sleep, *Science* **177**:1205–1207.

Satterfield, J. H., and Guze, S. B., 1961, Treatment of alcoholic patients with triiodothyronine, *Dis. Nerv. Syst.* **22**:227–231.

Sawyer, C. H., Critchlow, B. V., and Barraclough, C. A., 1955, Mechanism of blockade of pituitary activation in the rat by morphine, atropine and barbiturates, *Endocrinology* **57**:345–354.

Schneiden, H., and Blackmore, E. K., 1955, The effect of nalorphine on the antidiuretic action of morphine in rats and mice, *Br. J. Pharmacol.* **10**:45–50.

Schreiber, V., Zbusek, V., and Zbuzková-Kmentová, V., 1968, Effect of codeine on thyroid function in the rat, *Physiol. Bohemoslov.* **17**:253–258.

Selzer, M. L., and Van Houten, N. H., 1964, Normal thyroid function in chronic alcoholism, *J. Clin. Endocrinol. Metab.* **24**:380–382.

Shaar, C. J., Frederickson, R. C. A., Dininger, N. B., and Jackson, L., 1977, Enkephalin analogues and naloxone modulate the release of growth hormone and prolactin—Evidence for regulation by an endogenous opioid peptide in brain, *Life Sci.* **21**:853–860.

Shenkman, L., Massie, B., Mitsuma, T., and Hollander, C. S., 1972, Effects of chronic methadone administration on the hypothalamic–pituitary–thyroid axis, *J. Clin. Endocrinol. Metab.* **35**:169–170.

Simionescu, L., Oprescu, M., Protici, M., and Dimitriu, V., 1977, The hormonal pattern in alcoholic disease, I. Luteinizing hormone (LH), follicle-stimulating hormone (FSH) and testosterone, *Endocrinologie* **15**:45–49.

Simon, M. L., George, R., and Garcia, J., 1975, Acute morphine effects on regional brain amines, growth hormone and corticosterone, *Eur. J. Pharmacol.* **34**:27–38.

Sloan, J. W., 1971, Corticosteroid hormones, in: *Narcotic Drugs, Biochemical Pharmacology* (D. H. Clouet, ed.), pp. 262–282, Plenum, New York.

Smith, C. G., Moore, C. E., Besch, N. F., and Besch, P. K., 1976, Effects of delta-9-tetrahydrocannabinol (THC) on the secretion of male sex hormone in the Rhesus Monkey, *Pharmacologist* **18**:248.

Smith, E. R., and Davidson, M. J., 1974, Location of feedback receptors: Effects of intracranially implanted steroids on plasma LH and LRF responses, *Endocrinology* **95**:1566–1573.

Smith, G. P., Russ, R. D., Stokes, P., Duckett, G. E., and Root, A. W., 1977, Plasma GH response to *d*- and *l*-amphetamine in monkeys, *Horm. Metab. Res.* **4**:339–340.

Solomon, J., and Cocchia, M. A., 1977, Is delta-9-tetrahydrocannabinol estrogenic? *Science* **195**:905–906.

Solomon, J., and Shattuck, D. X., 1974, Letter: Marijuana and sex, *N. Engl. J. Med.* **291**:309.

Solomon, J., Cocchia, M. A., Gray, R., Shattuck, D., and Vossmer, A., 1976, Uterotrophic effect of delta-9-tetrahydrocannabinol in ovariectomized rats, *Science* **192**:559–561.

Solomon, J., Cocchia, M. A., and DiMartino, R., 1977, Effect of delta-9-tetrahydrocannabinol on uterine and vaginal cytology of ovariectomized rats, *Science* **195**:875–877.

Southren, A. L., and Gordon, G. G., 1976, Effects of alcohol and alcoholic cirrhosis on sex hormone metabolism, *Fertil. Steril.* **27**:202.

Stoffer, S. S., 1968, A gynecologic study of drug addicts, *Am. J. Obstet. Gynecol.* **101**:779–783.

Stokes, P. E., 1973, Adrenocortical activation in alcoholics during chronic drinking, *Ann. N.Y. Acad. Sci.* **215**:77–83.

Strauss, M. B., Rosenbaum, J. D., and Nelson, W. P., III, 1950, The effect of alcohol on the renal excretion of water and electrolyte, *J. Clin. Invest.* **29**:1053–1058.

Suzuki, T., Higashi, R., Hirose, T., Iheda, H., and Tamura, K., 1972, Adrenal 17-hydroxycorticosteroid secretion in the dog in response to ethanol, *Acta Endocrinol.* **70**:736–740.

Symons, A. M., and Marks, V., 1975, The effects of alcohol on weight gain and the hypothalamic–pituitary–gonadotropin axis in the maturing male rat, *Biochem. Pharmacol.* **24**:955–958.

Symons, A. M., Teale, J. D., and Marks, V., 1976, Proceedings: Effect of Δ^9-tetrahydrocannabinol on the hypothalamic–pituitary–gonadal system in the maturing male rat, *J. Endocrinol.* **68**:43–44.

Sze, P. Y., Yanai, J., and Ginsburg, B. E., 1974, Adrenal glucocorticoids as a required factor in the development of ethanol withdrawal seizures in mice, *Brain Res.* **80**:155–159.

Thomas, J. A., and Dombrosky, J. T., 1975, Effect of methadone on the male reproductive system, *Arch. Int. Pharmacodyn. Ther.* **215**:215–221.

Thomas, J. A., Shahid-Salles, K. S., and Donovan, M. P., 1977, Effects of narcotics on the reproductive system, *Adv. Sex Horm. Res.* **3**:169–195.

Thompson, G. R., Mason, M. M., Rosenkrantz, H., and Braude, M. C., 1973, Chronic oral toxicity of cannabinoids in rats, *Appl. Pharmacol.* **25**:373–390.

Thorner, M. O., Kirk, C. R., and MacLeod, R. M., 1978, Alcohol stimulation of prolactin release from perfused isolated rat pituitary cells, *Fed. Proc.* **37**:637.

Tokunaga, Y., Muraki, T., and Hosoya, E., 1977, Effects of repeated morphine administration on copulation and on the hypothalamic–pituitary–gonadal axis of male rats, *Jpn. J. Pharmacol.* **27**:65–70.

Tolis, G., Hickey, J., and Guyda, H., 1975, Effects of morphine on serum growth hormone, cortisol, prolactin and thyroid stimulating hormone in man, *J. Clin. Endocrinol. Metab.* **41**:797–800.

Toro, G., Kolodny, R. C., Jacobs, L. S., Masters, W. H., and Daughaday, W. H., 1973, Failure of alcohol to alter pituitary and target organ hormone levels, *Clin. Res.* **21**:505.

Turkington, R. W., 1972, Serum prolactin levels in patients with gynecomastia, *J. Clin. Endocrinol. Metab.* **34**:62–66.

Van Thiel, D. H., and Lester, R., 1974, Editorial: Sex and alcohol, *N. Engl. J. Med.* **291**:251–253.

Van Thiel, D. H., and Lester, R., 1976a, Alcoholism: Its effect on hypothalamic–pituitary–gonadal function, *Gastroenterology* **71**:318–327.

Van Thiel, D. H., and Lester, R., 1976b, Editorial: Sex and alcohol: A second peek, *N. Engl. J. Med.* **295**:835–836.

Van Thiel, D. H., Gavaler, J., and Lester, R., 1974a, Ethanol inhibition of vitamin A metabolism in the testes: Possible mechanism for sterility in alcoholics, *Science* **186**:941–942.

Van Thiel, D. H., Lester, R., and Sherins, R. J., 1974b, Hypogonadism in alcoholic liver disease: Evidence for a double defect, *Gastroenterology* **67**:1188–1199.

Van Thiel, D. H., Gavaler, J. S., Lester, R., and Goodman, M. D., 1975a, Alcohol-induced testicular atrophy: An experimental model for hypogonadism occurring in chronic alcoholic men, *Gastroenterology* **69**:326–332.

Van Thiel, D. H., Gavaler, J. S., Lester, R., Loriaux, D. L., and Braunstein, G. D., 1975b, Plasma estrone, prolactin, neurophysin, and sex steroid-binding globulin in chronic alcoholic men, *Metabolism* **24**:1015–1019.

Van Thiel, D. H., Gavaler, J. S., and Lester, R., 1977, Ethanol: A gonadal toxin in the female *Drug Alcohol Depend.* **2**:373–380.

Vyas, D. K., and Singh, R., 1976, Effect of cannabis and opium on the testis of the pigeon Columba livia Gmelin, *Indian J. Exp. Biol.* **14**:22–25.

Wagner, G., and Fuchs, A. R., 1968, Effect of ethanol on uterine activity during suckling in post-partum women, *Acta Endocrinol.* **58**:133–141.

Wallgren, H., and Barry, H., 1971, *Actions of Alcohol,* Elsevier, New York.

Watson, S. J., Barchas, J. D., and Li, C. H., 1977, β-Lipotropin: Localization of cells and axons in rat brain by immunocytochemistry, *Proc. Natl. Acad. Sci. USA* **74**:5155–5158.

Weitzman, E. D., Fukushima, D., Nogeire, C., Roffwarg, H., Gallagher, T. F., and Hellman, L., 1971, Twenty-four hour pattern of the episodic secretion of cortisol in normal subjects, *J. Clin. Endocrinol. Metab.* **33**:14–22.

West, C. D., Mahajan, D. K., Chavré, V. J., Nabors, C. J., and Tyler, F. H., 1973, Simultaneous measurement of multiple plasma steroids by radioimmunoassay demonstrating episodic secretion, *J. Clin. Endocrinol. Metab.* **36**:1230–1236.

Wright, J., Merry, J., Fry, D., and Marks, V., 1975, Pituitary function in chronic alcoholism, *Adv. Exp. Med. Biol.* **59**:253–255.

Wright, J. W., Fry, D. E., Merry, J., and Marks, V., 1976, Abnormal hypothalamic–pituitary–gonadal function in chronic alcoholics, *Br. J. Addict.* **71**:211–215.

Yen, S. S. C., Ehara, Y., and Siler, T. M., 1974, Augmentation of prolactin secretion by estrogen in hypogonadal women, *J. Clin. Invest.* **53**:652–655.

Ylikahri, R., Huttunen, M., Härkönen, M., and Adlercreutz, H., 1974a, Letter: Hangover and testosterone, *Br. Med. J.* **2**:445.

Ylikahri, R., Huttunen, M., Härkönen, M., Seuderling, U., Onikki, S., Karonen, S. L., and Adlercreutz, H., 1974b, Low plasma testosterone values in men during hangover, *J. Steroid Biochem.* **5**:655–658.

Ylikahri, R. H., Huttunen, M. O., and Härkönen, M., 1976, Letter: Effect of alcohol on anterior-pituitary secretion of trophic hormones, *Lancet* **1**:1353.

Zanoboni, A., and Zanoboni-Muciacci, W., 1975, Gynaecomastia in alcoholic cirrhosis, *Lancet* **2**:876.

Zimmermann, E., and Pang, C. N., 1976, Acute effects of opiate administration on pituitary gonadotropin and prolactin release, in: *Tissue Responses to Addictive Drugs* (D. H. Ford and D. H. Clouet, eds.), pp. 517–526, Spectrum, New York.

Zimmermann, E., Sonderegger, T., and Bromley, B., 1977, Development and adult pituitary–adrenal function in female rats injected with morphine during different postnatal periods, *Life Sci.* **20**:639–646.

16

The Effects of Alcohol on the Fetus and Offspring

HENRY L. ROSETT

1. INTRODUCTION

During the years following the identification and description of the morphological characteristics now known as the *fetal alcohol syndrome* (FAS), there has been growing recognition of the adverse effects on offspring of heavy drinking during pregnancy. Within a relatively brief period, a body of new research findings has developed that supports research and clinical observations dating back to the 18th century. The scientific attitude toward these data has shifted from skepticism and ridicule to the recognition of a major health problem that should be preventable.

Few teratogens have been as thoroughly investigated as ethanol. Multiple biochemical and pathophysiological effects have been attributed to ethanol and its metabolites. Ethanol has the potential to alter the growth and development of the embryo and fetus differently at various stages of pregnancy. Prospective clinical studies together with experimental animal research now support the view that there may be a wide range of fetal ethanol effects in the absence of the full syndrome. These effects have usually been reported in offspring of women who drank heavily but sporadically during pregnancy.

Ethanol is our most widely used drug. The greatest increase in ethanol consumption during the past decade has occurred among young women of high school age. Some of these women will continue to drink heavily throughout their reproductive years. Protection of their offspring has become a public health goal of high priority. Both basic and clinical research are necessary to develop effective prevention strategies.

HENRY L. ROSETT • Departments of Psychiatry and Obstetrics and Gynecology, Boston University School of Medicine, Boston, Massachusetts.

2. HISTORICAL SURVEY

The belief that parental consumption of alcohol at the time of conception and during pregnancy could have adverse effects on the health of offspring has a long history. Both Carthage and Sparta had laws prohibiting the use of alcohol by newly married couples in order to prevent conception during intoxication. In 1621, Burton cited Aristotle's *Problemata,* "foolish, drunken, or hair-brain women for the most part bring forth children like unto themselves, *morosos et languidos*" (Burton, 1621/1906).

From 1720 to 1750, England lifted traditional restrictions on distillation; cheap gin flooded the country, creating the "gin epidemic" (Warner and Rosett, 1975). In 1726, the College of Physicians petitioned Parliament for control of the distilling trade, calling gin a "cause of weak, feeble, and distempered children." During these years, birthrates dropped, and there was a sharp rise in the mortality of children under five years of age (George, 1965; Coffey, 1966). While multiple factors must be considered, this was a period when crops and wages were good and epidemic disease relatively rare. Throughout the 19th century, there are reports of observations of offspring of alcoholics with a high frequency of mental retardation, epilepsy, stillbirths, and infant deaths. These findings were utilized by religious temperance leaders to prove that the sins of the parents could be visited on the children for several generations.

In 1899, William Sullivan, physician to a Liverpool prison, published a careful study of 600 offspring of 120 alcoholic women (Sullivan, 1899). He also located 28 nondrinking female relatives of the alcoholic women and found that the infant mortality and stillborn rate was 2½ times higher in the alcoholics' children than in the comparison population. Sullivan also observed that several alcoholic women who had infants with severe and often fatal complications later bore healthy children when, because of imprisonment, they were forced to abstain from alcohol during pregnancy.

In the American and British medical literature, interest in the effects of alcohol on offspring declined after 1920, following the institution of prohibition. The early research in this field was criticized by Haggard and Jellinek in 1942. They felt that while damage to the reproductive organs had been observed in chronic alcoholics, there was no evidence of damage to the human germ cells. They recognized the detrimental influence of poor nutrition in the alcoholic mother and the disturbance of home life created by parental alcoholism, but they did not differentiate between genetic damage and the possible intrauterine effects of alcohol.

The French and German literature continued to report much higher frequencies of neurologic disorders, together with delays in growth and development in the offspring of alcoholic parents (Heuyer et al., 1957; Christiaens et al., 1960).

3. DESCRIPTION OF THE FETAL ALCOHOL SYNDROME (FAS)

In 1968, Lemoine et al. described 127 offspring from 69 French families in which there was chronic alcoholism. In 29, both parents were alcoholics; in 25, only the mother; and in 15, only the father. The role of maternal alcoholism was considered essential whenever the infant was dystrophic. Of these children, 25 had malformations: 5 cleft palates; 3 micro-ophthalmia; 6 limb malformations; 7 congenital heart disease; and 4 visceral anomalies. Their facial profile was characteristic, including a protruding forehead; a sunken nasal bridge; a short, upturned nose; a retracted upper lip; a receding chin; and deformed ears. Many were hyperactive, with delayed psychomotor and language development. As they grew older, they had difficulty sustaining an activity for a period of time and had behavior problems in school. Intellectual retardation with an average IQ of 70 was described. (No data on the types of tests administered, the ages of children examined, or the range of scores were presented.)

In America awareness of this problem was stimulated in 1970 by observations by Ulleland et al. at the University of Washington in Seattle. After observing that six infants who failed to thrive had mothers who were chronic alcoholics, they made a retrospective review of clinic records to identify all undergrown infants during an 18-month period: 11 women alcoholics were identified, and 10 of their 12 children were small for gestational age. These 10 infants were tested with the Gesell or Denver developmental scales: 5 had retarded development, and 3 were borderline, even when their score was corrected for prematurity. Of these 10 infants, 8 failed to grow, with weight and head circumference remaining below the third percentile. Subsequently, Jones and Smith recognized a syndrome in 4 of these 8 infants. An additional 7 infants were located who showed similar features; all of their mothers were chronic alcoholics (Jones et al., 1973; Jones and Smith, 1973). The fetal alcohol syndrome includes prenatal and postnatal growth deficiency, developmental delay or mental deficiency, microcephaly, and fine motor dysfunction. Facial characteristics include short palpebral fissures with associated microophthalmia, midfacial hypoplasia, and epicanthal folds. In the limbs, abnormal palmar creases and minor joint anomalies have been observed. Cardiac defects, anomalies of the external genitalia, small hemangiomas, and minor ear anomalies have also been observed in a significant number of these children. The Seattle group subsequently reported observations on 41 infants demonstrating this syndrome, all born to chronic alcoholic women who drank heavily throughout their pregnancy (Hanson et al., 1976).

Streissguth et al. (1978) tested the IQ of 20 FAS patients, ranging from age 9 months to 21 years diagnosed at the University of Washington Dysmorphology Clinic. The average IQ was 65, with a range of 16–105. Sixty percent had an IQ more than 2 SD below the mean score for their age group. The children demonstrating the most severe dysmorphogenesis also tended to have the more severe intellectual handicaps. When 17 patients were retested one to four years later, the retest IQ score was within 1 SD of the original score in 77%. Variability may be due to the different IQ tests used as the child grows, which often measure different intellectual abilities.

4. FURTHER CASE REPORTS

The initial publications from Seattle identifying and describing the fetal alcohol syndrome stimulated many case reports from around the world (Ferrier et al., 1973; Hall and Orenstein, 1974; Saule, 1974; Palmer et al., 1975; Tenbrinck and Buchin, 1975; Barry and O'Nuallain, 1975; Root et al., 1975; Christoffel and Salafsky, 1975; Manzke and Grosse, 1975; Reinhold et al., 1975; Loiodice et al., 1975; Mulvihill et al., 1976; Mulvihill and Yeager, 1976; Bierich et al., 1976; Ijaiya et al., 1976; Noonan, 1976). Variability in the pattern of defects may be related to different patterns of chronic alcohol use at different stages of pregnancy, as well as to such issues as the maximum blood alcohol concentration, binge drinking versus relatively steady-state alcohol levels, type of beverage, general nutritional status, and so on. Another important factor seems to be genetic differences in the susceptibility to the dysmorphogenic influence of alcohol. This factor is demonstrated by a report describing a pair of fraternal twins born to a mother who consumed at least one quart of red wine and an unspecified amount of hard liquor daily throughout pregnancy (Christoffel and Salafsky, 1975). One boy was markedly affected, with weight and length below the 10th percentile and head circumference at the 10th percentile. The weight of his twin brother was at the 30th percentile, length at the 15th percentile, and head circumference at the 60th percentile. Both twins showed facial characteristics of the fetal alcohol syndrome and both were jittery. Both were retarded in postnatal growth and development. Differences in rate of development may make dizygotic twins susceptible to teratogens at different times. Differences in placental and fetal vasculature may also affect growth rates.

In the USSR, Shruygin (1974) studied the effects of maternal alcoholism in 42 children of 18 mothers. Of 23 children (ages 9 months to 20 years) born after the mother had developed full-fledged alcoholism, 14 were mentally retarded, and many had demonstrated signs of organic impairment of the CNS early in infancy. In contrast, 19 offspring (ages 12–32) born before their mothers had developed full-fledged alcoholism demonstrated mainly "vegetative, emotional, and behavioral" disorders. These developed around ages 9 or 10 and tended to remit following improvement in the social environment as a result of marriage or employment.

Majewski et al. (1976) described 68 cases of FAS seen in Germany. While there was variation in the severity of malformation, they observed intrauterine and postnatal growth retardation in 91%, microcephaly in 87%, psychomotor and mental retardation in 84%, cardiac defects in 31%, and anomalies of joints in 23% and of genitalia in 50%.

Clarren and Smith (1978) reviewed their findings from 65 patients evaluated in Seattle together with the characteristics described in 180 other cases reported from many different nations and including infants of most racial groups (see Tables 1 and 2). The principal features, those seen in over 80% and over 50% of patients, were grouped into three categories: CNS dysfunctions, growth deficiency, and facial characteristics. Associated features were classified as frequent (reported in 26–50% of patients) or occasional (reported in 1–25% of patients).

After reviewing these clinical reports, the Fetal Alcohol Study Group of the Research Society on Alcoholism recommended that the diagnosis of FAS be made only when the patient has signs in each of three categories: (1) prenatal and/or postnatal growth retardation (weight, length, and/or head circumference below the tenth percentile when corrected for gestational age); (2) central nervous system involvement (signs of neurologic abnormality, developmental delay, or intellectual impairment); (3) characteristic facial dysmorphology with at least these three signs: microcephaly (head circumference below the third percentile); microphthalmia, and/or short palpehral fissures, or poorly developed philtrum; thin upper lip and/or flattening of the maxillary area (Rosett, 1980).

5. RETROSPECTIVE EPIDEMIOLOGIC STUDIES

The Seattle group reviewed the charts of the Perinatal Project of the National Institute of Neurologic Disease and Stroke, a prospective study of 55,000 pregnant women and their offspring who had been observed up to seven years postnatally in 12 medical centers (Jones et al., 1974).

Table 1. Principal Features of the Fetal Alcohol Syndrome Observed in 245 Persons Affected[a]

Feature	Manifestation
Central nervous system	
dysfunction	Mild to moderate mental retardation[b]
Intellectual	Microcephaly[b]
Neurological	Poor coordination, hypotonia[c]
	Irritability in infancy[b]
Behavioral	Hyperactivity in childhood[c]
Growth deficiency	>2SD below mean for length and weight[b]
Prenatal	>2SD below mean for length and weight[b]
Postnatal	Disproportionately diminished adipose tissue[c]
Facial characteristics	Short palpebral fissures[b]
Eyes	Short, upturned[c]
Nose	Hypoplastic philtrum[b]
	Hypoplastic[c]
Maxilla	Thinned upper vermilion[b]
Mouth	Retrognathia in infancy[b]
	Micrognathia or relative prognathia in adolescence[c]

[a] From Clarren and Smith (1978).
[b] Feature seen in > 80% of patients.
[c] Feature seen in > 50% of patients.

Table 2. Associated Features of the Fetal Alcohol Syndrome Observed in 245 Persons Affected[a]

Area	Frequent[b]	Occasional[c]
Eyes	Ptosis, strabismus, epicanthal folds	Myopia, clinical microphthalmia, blepharophimosis
Ears	Posterior rotation	Poorly formed concha
Mouth	Prominent lateral palatine ridges	Cleft lip or cleft palate, small teeth with faulty enamel
Cardiac	Murmurs, especially in early childhood, usually atrial septal defect	Ventricular septal defect, great-vessel anomalies, tetralogy of Fallot
Renogenital	Labial hypoplasia	Hypospadias, small rotated kidneys, hydronephrosis
Cutaneous	Hemangiomas	Hirsutism in infancy
Skeletal	Aberrant palmar creases, pectus excavatum	Limited joint movements, especially fingers and elbows, nail hypoplasia, especially 5th, polydactyly, radioulnar synostosis, pectus carinatum, bifid xiphoid, Klippel–Feil anomaly, scoliosis
Muscular		Hernias of diaphragm, umbilicus or groin, diastasis recti

[a] From Clarren and Smith (1978).
[b] Reported in between 26% and 50% of patients.
[c] Reported in between 1% and 25% of patients.

Unfortunately, direct questions about alcohol use during pregnancy had not been included in the original research design. However, whenever alcoholism was mentioned in the clinical record, a retrospective entry had been made in the chart summary. These 69 charts were reviewed, and in 23 there was evidence of chronic alcoholism before and during the pregnancy. Each of these charts was compared with charts of two matched nonalcoholic control women. Charts of the offspring were reviewed by another investigator who had no information about the mothers' drinking status. Among the offspring of the alcoholic women, there were four who died in the perinatal period and six who had physical findings consistent with the fetal alcohol syndrome. This 43% rate of adverse outcome compared with a 2% rate in the control group. Offspring of the alcoholic women had smaller growth parameters in the newborn nursery as well as at age seven. IQ testing at age seven was available in 12 offspring of the alcoholic women. Of the 12, the 6 who had lived with their mothers had a mean IQ at age seven of 73, while the 6 who had spent some time with relatives had a mean IQ of 84. The frequency of adverse outcomes in the pregnancies of chronically alcoholic women was regarded as being of such magnitude that the authors suggested that serious consideration be given to early termination of pregnancy.

The sampling methodology and the conclusions of this review of the records from the Perinatal Project have been questioned (Rosett, 1974). On the basis of a national survey of drinking practices, one could estimate that among the 55,000 pregnant women, 5% (or 2750) may have been heavy drinkers. The 23 cases of chronic alcoholism selected were probably the most conspicuous in that population and represented extremes in terms of the physical, psychological, and sociological ravages of alcoholism.

Russell (1977) reviewed records of women attending a county hospital outpatient clinic and the birth certificates of their children. She hypothesized that women with an alcohol-related psychiatric diagnosis were more likely to have been drinking heavily during a prior pregnancy than either women selected at random from the general population or women with a psychiatric diagnosis that was not alcohol related. Birth weights of 223 offspring of 81 women with an alcohol-related diagnosis were obtained from birth certificates and compared with the birth weights of 276 offspring of 94 women with a non-alcohol-related diagnosis. The birth weight of each infant born to a study woman was subtracted from that of the matched control infant, and these differences were analyzed with respect to maternal drinking histories. The average birth weight of infants born to women with an alcohol-related psychiatric disorder was significantly lower than that of infants born to other women seen in the clinic. No congenital malformations were recorded on the birth certificates of the 499 study children, and only one malformation was recorded on those of 499 matched controls. Since the expected rate of malformation is 1.1 per 100 live births, there are clear limitations in reviewing birth certificates to obtain such data. Drinking histories could be estimated from clinical records for 95 women. When mothers started drinking more than 11 years before delivery, the mean birth weight was 898 g less than that of matched controls ($p < .01$); 6–10 years of maternal drinking, 403 g ($p < .01$); 0–5 years, 319 g ($p < .05$). Drinking by fathers was not associated with lower birth weights.

Russell's investigation of birth weights of infants born to women who had received alcohol-related diagnoses, as well as the data from the Perinatal Project (Jones et al., 1974), point to adverse effects associated with heavy alcohol consumption during pregnancy. However, further clarification requires prospective studies in which quantity, frequency, and variability of alcohol consumption during pregnancy, as well as the full range of effects on offspring, are examined in several populations.

6.   PROSPECTIVE STUDIES

The largest prospective study has been reported from Europe. Kaminski et al. (1976) examined the relationship between alcohol consumption among pregnant women and outcome from a prospective study of 9236 pregnancies at 13 French maternity centers between 1963 and 1969. Data were collected on wine, beer, and cider consumption, but no information was gathered on the consumption of aperitifs, after-dinner drinks, or other forms of distilled liquor. Alcohol consumption was calculated in terms of the equivalent volume of 11% wine. Offspring of women who drank more than the equivalent of 40 cl of wine (1.5 oz of absolute alcohol) daily were compared with those born to mothers who consumed less.

While there were significantly more stillbirths among the heavier drinkers, no significant variation in frequency of congenital malformations was observed. Infants born to the heavier drinkers had lower birth weight and their placentas were smaller. No data on the length, head circumference, or palpebral fissures were reported. Actual differences between groups in birth weight were relatively small even though they attained statistical significance. The difference in birth weight between infants born to the heavier drinkers and those born to the lighter drinkers was only 58 g. When the extremes are compared, the mean weight of 103 infants born to women who consumed over 60 cl was 106 g lighter than that of 4347 infants born to women who did not drink any alcoholic beverages. The 106-g difference could be significant if most of the growth retardation occurred in vital organs such as the brain, the kidneys, and the liver.

Women who consumed over 40 cl per day differed from the lighter drinkers in terms of other risk factors: maternal age, parity, smoking, previous low birth weight of children, marital status, and metrorrhagia. However, when each of these factors was taken into account through appropriate statistical techniques, the increased risk due to alcohol use remained significant in terms of perinatal mortality, birth weight, and placental weight.

When women who drank over 1.5 oz of alcohol per day were compared according to types of beverages consumed, the 158 women (1.7%) who drank only beer were found to have more severely affected infants than those mothers who drank only wine, or wine and beer together. Infants born to women who drank only beer had a lower mean birth weight ($p < .05$) and placental weight ($p < .001$). Their weight was more likely to be below the 10th percentile ($p < .001$). However, infants born to women who drank both beer and wine were more likely to be below the 3rd percentile in weight ($p < .001$). The greatest difference was 49 g between the offspring of women who drank wine and beer and those of women who drank beer only. While this difference attained statistical significance ($p < .05$), it may be of little clinical importance. In a nation where wine is fully integrated into dietary patterns, women who drink only beer probably differ on other significant parameters.

Mau and Netter (1974) compared data collected by questionnaires from 5200 women at 20 German hospitals during the first trimester with the outcome of pregnancy. They concluded that alcohol consumption was associated with shorter gestation, and heavy use of coffee with low birth weight. Unfortunately, this large study had serious methodological problems. Alcohol and coffee consumption were not evaluated quantitatively but only in vague subjective terms: "never," "rarely," or "frequently." Since only 0.1% of the women acknowledged frequent alcohol consumption, the authors tabulated alcohol use only in terms of "yes" (4.8%) and "no" (95.2%). The absence of quantification precludes investigation of the alcohol dose–effect relationship and renders the authors' conclusions questionable.

A program set up to study patterns of alcohol use prospectively by prenatal clinic patients and the effects on their offspring was initiated in May 1974 at the Boston City Hospital (BCH) (Ouellette et al., 1977; Rosett et al., 1978). Each year, about 1700 women are delivered at this municipal hospital, which serves a high-risk, inner-city population. About one-third choose to receive prenatal care at the BCH clinic; the others are patients of several affiliated neighborhood health centers.

At the time of registration at the BCH Prenatal Clinic, women were asked to participate voluntarily in a 15-min structured interview designed to determine the volume and variability of alcohol intake, the use of other drugs, smoking, nutritional status, and demographic data. Cahalan's Volume-Variability Index (Cahalan et al., 1969) was used to evaluate alcohol consumption. Separate inquiry was made about the use of wine, beer, and other liquors.

Patients were divided into three groups on the basis of their drinking practices. Heavy drinkers were defined according to Cahalan et al.'s (1969) criteria for "high-volume high-maximum": they consumed at least five or six drinks on some occasions with a minimum average of 1½ drinks per day. Rare drinkers used alcohol less than once a month and never consumed five or six drinks on any occasion. Moderate drinkers included all women who drank more than once a month but did not meet the criteria for heavy drinkers. For statistical analysis, each woman remained in the group assigned as a result of the initial survey even though some later reported a change in their drinking patterns. The survey was conducted by two female interviewers who possessed an objective and accepting attitude. The patient distribution by drinking category was the same for each of the interviewers.

All women who reported moderate or heavy alcohol use were informed that excessive drinking might be harmful to their unborn child. Heavy-drinking women were encouraged to participate in counseling sessions scheduled to coincide with their routine prenatal clinic appointments.

Detailed pediatric, neurological, and developmental examinations were administered in the newborn nursery to offspring of women who had participated in the survey. These were conducted by a pediatric neurologist who had no prior knowledge of the mother's drinking history nor any other details of the pregnancy.

A total of 322 newborns were examined, representing 94% of the live births at BCH to the women who had participated in this survey as of June 1, 1976. Of these 322 women, 42 (13%) were heavy drinkers; 128 (40%) were moderate drinkers; and 152 (47%) were rare drinkers. The heavy drinkers consumed an average of 174 ml (5.8 oz) of absolute alcohol per day; 31% of them drank between 240 and 480 ml (8 and 16 oz) of absolute alcohol per day; their mean dose was estimated at 2.2 g of absolute alcohol per kilogram per day. The relationship between the mothers' drinking classification and the findings of the newborn examination are presented in Table 3.

Offspring of the heavily drinking women, as compared with offspring of the moderately and rarely drinking women, demonstrated significantly more congenital malformation, growth retardation, and functional abnormalities. These components of the fetal alcohol syndrome were observed, but the complete syndrome was not seen in any individual.

Table 3. Relationships between Infant's Clinical Status and Mother's Drinking Classification[a]

Infant's clinical status[b]	Drinking classification at prenatal clinic registration						Significance of differences (p values from chi-square test)[c]
	Rare		Moderate		Heavy		
	N = 152	(47%)	N = 128	(40%)	N = 42	(13%)	
Normal	99	(65%)[f]	82	64%	12	29%	< .001
Congenital anomalies[d]							
Major	5	3%	3	2%	5	12% }	< .01
Minor	8	5%	15	12%	7	17% }	
Growth abnormalities[d]							
Small for gestational age[e]	14	9%	5	4%	10	24%	< .001
Premature[e]	7	5%	4	3%	7	17%	< .001
Postmature[e]	12	8%	12	9%	8	19%	NS
Head circumference below 10th percentile[e]	11	7%	7	5%	9	21%	< .05
Weight below 10th percentile[e]	17	11%	10	8%	11	26%	< .01
Length below 10th percentile[e]	5	4%	4	3%	4	10%	< .01
Functional Abnormalities[d]							
Jittery	15	10%	14	11%	12	29%	< .01
Hypotonic	19	13%	11	9%	7	17%	NS
Poor suck	9	6%	3	2%	5	12%	NS

[a] From Rosett et al. (1978).
[b] Total number of subjects = 322.
[c] Heavy versus rare and moderate combined.
[d] Abnormalities not mutually exclusive: infants with abnormality were tested against sum of all other infants in respective drinking classification.
[e] Based on University of Colorado Medical Center Classification of Newborns
[f] Percentage shown beside each number refers to the proportion relative to the number of cases indicated at the top of the corresponding column.

Several characteristics that may affect fetal outcome were also related to heavy drinking. The relationship of maternal age, parity, smoking, drug use, and marital status to several outcome measures was examined. These statistically significant relationships were found by use of chi-square analysis: maternal age and classification of abnormality (p < .01); parity greater than three and weight and head circumference (p < .01); heavy smoking and low birth weight (p < .001) and small head circumference (p < .01). There were no significant relationships between marital status and pregnancy outcome. Because of the small number of drug users, it was not possible to ascertain the effect of drugs. Some of these variables may account for a portion of the variance; however, none relates as strongly and consistently to outcome as heavy drinking.

Table 4 compares the characteristics of offspring of heavily drinking women who reduced alcohol consumption before the third trimester with characteristics of the offspring born to women who continued drinking. Of the 15 infants born to women who reduced alcohol use, 10 (67%) were diagnosed as normal, compared with only 2 of the 27 (7%) born to mothers who continued heavy drinking (chi-square p < .001). No differences were found between offspring of heavy drinkers who reported abstinence and those who reduced drinking to the moderate range. For

Table 4. Relationship between Clinical Status of Offspring of Heavy-Drinking Women and Change in Alcohol Consumption before Third Trimester[a]

Evaluation of newborn (total N = 42)	Abstinent or reduced drinking (N = 15)		Continued heavy drinking (N = 27)	
Normal	10	67%	2	7%
Congenital Anomalies[b]				
Major	1	7%	4	15%
Minor	0		7	26%
Growth Abnormalities[b]				
Small for gestational age[c]	0		10	37%
Premature	0		7	26%
Postmature	4	27%	3	11%
Head circumference below 10th percentile[c]	0		9	33%
Weight below 10th percentile[c]	0		11	41%
Length below 10th percentile[c]	0		4	15%
Functional Abnormalities[b]				
Jittery	2	13%	11	41%
Hypotonic	0		6	22%
Poor suck	0		5	18%

[a] From Rosett et al. (1978).
[b] Abnormalities not mutually exclusive: infants with abnormality were tested against sum of all other infants in respective drinking classification.
[c] Based on University of Colorado Medical Center Classification of Newborns.

those newborns whose mothers continued heavy drinking, prenatal care alone did not improve prognosis. There were no significant differences between offspring of heavy drinkers who did and did not receive prenatal care. Analysis of additional cases supported the initial findings (Rosett et al., 1980). The benefits to growth which are found with reduction of alcohol consumption in mid-pregnancy seem to persist even in the presence of heavy smoking. The implications of these findings for the development of prevention programs will be discussed in Section 11.

A prospective study in Seattle was conducted by interviewing 1529 mothers receiving prenatal care through a prepaid medical cooperative and the University of Washington Hospital and clinics (Hanson et al., 1978). The patients were from a higher socioeconomic group than the BCH prenatal patients and differed in many parameters. Within the large population, 82 heavy-drinking women were identified. They reported an average consumption of 30 ml or more of absolute alcohol per day or intoxication with five or more drinks on some occasions. When an infant was born to one of the heavy-drinking women, a control infant was randomly selected from among the other study infants born the same day to mothers who were abstainers or infrequent drinkers.

A total of 163 infants were examined by a pediatrician trained in dysmorphology who had no knowledge of the mother's drinking pattern. They were placed in one of three clinical categories on the basis of features suggestive of a prenatal effect of alcohol. Of the 11 infants demonstrating features compatible with FAS, 2 were judged clearly to have this disorder. Both were born to mothers who were clinically evaluated as alcoholics. Of the 9 other infants who showed features suggestive of fetal alcohol effects (FAE), 7 were born to mothers who consumed over 30 ml of absolute alcohol daily.

Those mothers whose infants showed some features compatible with FAS reported higher alcohol consumption prior to pregnancy and presumably during the early weeks before they realized that they had conceived. All three infants born to mothers who drank over 60 ml of absolute alcohol daily before pregnancy showed features consistent with the fetal alcohol syndrome, while they were seen in only 6 of 54 infants born to mothers who reported consumption between 30 and 60 ml of absolute alcohol per day before they knew they were pregnant.

The effects of moderate or light alcohol use on birth weight and motor development has been reported by Streissguth et al. (1980). All variables measured, including alcohol, nicotine, and caffeine use, only accounted for 5 or 6% of the total variance measured by the Bayley Scales of Infant Motor and Mental Development. Since moderate or light alcohol use accounted for less than 2% of the total variance in the Bayley Scores, the clinical significance of these findings is unclear.

Different patterns of alcohol use have been found in women of various ethnic and socioeconomic groups. Little et al. (1976) interviewed 162 obstetrical patients in a health maintenance organization serving a middle-class population. Of these patients, 7% were drinking over an ounce of absolute alcohol per day before pregnancy, but only 2% in early pregnancy and 2% in late pregnancy. The decrease in alcohol consumption during the first trimester was also paralleled by a decrease in heavy coffee consumption during pregnancy. Growth retardation was observed in offspring of 263 members of the same health maintenance organization. Ingestion of an average of 30 ml of absolute alcohol before pregnancy was associated with an average decrease in birth weight of 91 g. When the same amount was ingested late in pregnancy, mean weight was decreased by 160 g (Little, 1977).

Little's observation of decreasing alcohol consumption during the course of pregnancy has also been made for some women interviewed at Boston City Hospital. However, at Boston City Hospital, which serves a low-income group, 9% of women were drinking heavily early in pregnancy. Women who are physically or psychologically dependent on alcohol more often sustain their level of consumption throughout pregnancy. A wide spectrum of perinatal risk factors, including malnutrition, poor housing, and general stress, have been observed in this multiproblem group. It is likely that maternal drinking during pregnancy interacts with the other risk factors and compounds the adverse effects on the fetus. Therefore, it is important to collect information on drinking practices and living conditions from many different socioeconomic and cultural groups, so that the specific effects of the alcohol on offspring can be disentangled from the social and environmental matrix in which the baby develops.

The report by Sokol et al. (1980), based on a prospective cohort of over 12,000 pregnancies delivered at a single hospital during a four-year period, attempts to define the relative risk among heavy drinkers. Maternal alcohol abuse was identified clinically in 204 pregnancies; however, the amount of alcohol consumed was not tabulated. Pregnancies of the alcohol abusers were marked by a higher risk of premature placental separation and infection, fetal distress during labor, growth retardation, and fetal anomalies. These findings are consistent with earlier reports. Alcohol abuse was associated with other risk factors, including abuse of other drugs and cigarette smoking. It was determined that alcohol abuse and cigarette smoking each approximately double the risk of growth retardation; together they increase the risk about fourfold. The estimate of risk due to alcohol abuse for adverse perinatal outcome was 50%, twenty times the 2.5% risk for the full FAS.

In summary, the research on the impact of maternal alcohol consumption on human infants has demonstrated that fetal alcohol syndrome is a clinically observable syndrome. The morphological characteristics of fetal alcohol syndrome have been observed in 245 offspring of alcoholic mothers around the world. Typically, the fetal alcohol syndrome pattern of dysmorphology has been identified first, and maternal alcoholism has been documented subsequently. Retrospectively, accurate information about alcohol consumption during pregnancy and other risk factors is often difficult to obtain. Prospective studies are necessary to determine the incidence of the fetal alcohol syndrome and the range of symptoms, as well as the relationship between anomalies and the amount of alcohol consumed and the other risk factors shared by so many of these mothers.

Few infants clearly manifesting the morphological characteristics of FAS have been found in prospective studies. A high blood alcohol level during a critical time of embryonic development probably is necessary to produce the FAS. The average alcohol consumption may not be as important as the maximum concentrations obtained during binge drinking at critical periods. Undoubtedly, there are many more cases in which only part of the syndrome is found. These may be instances of single malformations or retarded growth and development or behavioral problems such as jitteriness or abnormal state regulation.

It is useful to consider the components of the FAS in terms of the characteristic pattern of malformation, retarded growth and development, and behavioral impairment involving activity and learning. Malformations are probably produced by high alcohol concentrations at critical periods during the first trimester when embryonic development is taking place. Growth may be most vulnerable to heavy drinking during the second and third trimester. Behavioral disturbances which are consequences of neurophysiological and structural disruption of the central nervous system may differ depending on blood ethanol concentrations (BECs) at critical developmental stages.

7. ANIMAL MODELS OF THE FETAL ALCOHOL SYNDROME

Animal models permit isolation of the effects of the multiple variables that are difficult to separate in studies of the effects of alcohol on human infants. Species differences in gestational time and similarity to human physiology are factors that determine the suitability of a given species to the study of a particular aspect of FAS. In 1888, Combemale reported mating two dogs and exposing the bitch to ethanol for the first 23 days of gestation. Of the six pups, three were stillborn, and three were of "weak intelligence." When they were mated with normal studs, the young were "defective."

In 1894, Féré exposed hens' eggs to alcohol vapors before incubation. Ethanol that penetrated the eggshell produced a broad range of
abnormalities. Similar effects were obtained by Stockard (1910) using
fish and chicken eggs. Anomalies of the eyes were most common,
followed by abnormal development of the central nervous system.
Experiments with mammals were stimulated by the demonstration by
Nicloux (1899, 1900) that alcohol crossed the placenta and could be
demonstrated in the fetus of the guinea pig, dog, and woman at concentrations close to that in the maternal circulation. Hodge (1903) treated
pregnant cocker spaniels with alcohol from 1895 to 1897 and observed in
1903 that there was a greater percentage of deformity as well as less
vigor and vitality in the offspring of the alcoholized dogs.

Pearl (1916) treated hens by inhalation and found that alcoholized
chicks were superior in viability and growth, and suggested that alcohol
"acts as a selective agent upon the germ cells of the alcoholized animals,
eliminating the weak and permitting the survival of the vigorous and
highly resistant." MacDowell (1923) studied maze behavior in alcoholized
white rats and found inferior learning ability in treated animals and their
offspring. For a review of the effects of ethanol on animal growth and
reproduction, including a tabular comparison of 33 experimental regi-
mens, see Wallgren and Barry (1970).

The many conflicting observations in the early literature can be
related to species differences, as well as to the amount of alcohol
administered, the route of administration, the stage of pregnancy when
alcohol was introduced, and lack of paired feeding (matching food intake
of the control animal with the amounts consumed by the experimental
animal). Some of these problems have been overcome in the experimental
design of recent animal research on the effects of prenatal ethanol
exposure.

Sandor and Elias (1968) studied the effects of ethanol, simulating in
the early stages of development in chick embryos the blood ethanol
levels found in human alcoholics. Early maldevelopment and mortality
occurred in a considerable portion of the embryos, and the remaining
specimens showed a significant loss of weight toward the end of the
incubation. The central nervous system was the most sensitive. Sandor
and Amels (1971) investigated the effects of ethanol on the prenatal
development of albino rats. Ethanol diluted by distilled water was
administered intravenously in order to obtain dosages of 1.5 g/kg and 2
g/kg. Some embryos were removed at 9.5 days. Fetuses were examined
at 19.5 days. Injections were made at Days 6, 7, and 8 of pregnancy with
one group and at Days 6 and 7 of gestation with another group. Alcohol,
in the concentration of 2 g/kg body weight, induced twice the number of
malformations that 1.5 g/kg induced. Two heavy intoxications were more

injurious than three lighter concentrations. Effects on the bones seemed to be most apparent in the extremities and the facial areas, the same regions observed in humans showing signs of the fetal alcohol syndrome.

Skosyreva (1973) administered by mouth 5 ml of 40% alcohol per kilogram of body weight to 13 rats between Day 8 and 14 of pregnancy. They were sacrificed on Day 21, and their 103 fetuses were compared with those of 10 control animals. Postimplantation mortality was 25% in the alcoholized animals compared with 2% in the controls. Mean fetal weight was 3 g in the alcoholized rats and 3.8 g in the controls ($p <$ .001). Hemorrhages were observed in the brain membranes and the serous cavities of fetuses born to mothers given alcohol, but no gross skeletal or organic anomalies were observed.

Tze and Lee (1975) fed a group of female rats water containing ethanol at 30 g/100 ml as their only available fluid, in a balanced powdered diet. After one month, their BEC was 61 ± 23 mg%. A pair-fed group received a diet isocaloric with that of the alcohol-fed group. A control group received food and water ad lib. All three groups gave birth at 21–22 days. Only 50% of the alcohol-fed mothers known to have copulated produced litters, compared with 88% and 91% of control and pair-fed females. The average litter size of the alcohol-fed mothers was significantly lower than the mean litter size of either pair-fed or control mothers. In addition to small size, the offspring of the alcohol-fed mothers exhibited microcephaly; cracked, dry, loose skin; reddened areas on the head and body; and a generally shriveled appearance. By studying only the fetuses born, the authors may have overlooked resorptions, since rodents tend to resorb rather than abort. Implantation sites can be quantified and compared with those of controls, but this procedure has rarely been done. Often rodents cannibalize their young, especially if visceral organs are exposed. Sacrifice of the animals prior to delivery can avert some of these sources of error.

Kronick (1976) developed a mouse model in which a 25% solution of ethyl alcohol in physiological saline was injected intraperitoneally at a dosage of 0.03 ml/g of body weight. Control animals received intraperitoneal injections of physiological saline in the same dosage. Three schedules of injections were utilized. One group of mice received injections on Gestation Days 8 and 9, another group on Gestation Days 10 and 11, and a third group received either alcohol or saline on only one gestational day, ranging from Day 7 through Day 12. Mice were sacrificed on Gestation Day 18, the uterus was removed, and the number and location of live fetuses, dead fetuses, and resorptions were recorded. Fetal mortality rate was substantially increased following alcohol treatment on Gestation Days 9–12. The incidence of fetal anomalies was significantly increased following alcohol treatment only on Days 8, 9, and 10. There was considerable time dependency of both the overall teratogenic response to alcohol and the genesis of specific malformations. Coloboma of the iris was most frequently observed in animals injected on Days 8 and 9; absence of the forepaw was seen only in offspring of mothers injected on Day 10. Critical periods for other anomalies were not apparent. The intraperitoneal route of administration of ethanol might have direct effects on the uterus; oral feedings are more similar to the conditions in human alcoholism.

Chernoff (1977) administered alcohol orally via a liquid diet to two highly inbred strains of mice that differed in ethanol preference, alcohol dehydrogenase activity, and ethanol sleep times. Blood alcohol levels were maintained in a range from 73 mg/dl to 398 mg/dl for at least 30 days before mating. Females were sacrificed on Day 18 and the uterine contents examined. Fetal resorptions increased with increasing ethanol concentrations. The dose–response curve suggested that the strain with the lower ADH activity was more sensitive to ethanol than the strain with the greater metabolic capacity. There was a definite growth deficiency due to ethanol, which was fatal at a critical dose. Fetuses were sacrificed, and anomalies affecting the skeleton, the brain, the heart, and the eyes were observed. The pattern of growth deficiency together with ocular, neural, cardiac, and skeletal anomalies was similar to that of the fetal alcohol syndrome in humans.

Randall et al. (1977) also administered a liquid diet with 25% of total daily calories supplied by ethanol to mice but administered it only from Gestation Day 5 through Gestation Day 10. Blood alcohol levels ranged between 70 and 120 mg/dl. A pair-fed control group was treated similarly except that sucrose was substituted isocalorically for ethanol. Gravid females were sacrificed on Gestation Day 19. Systematic external examination of the fetuses was followed by examination for internal malformations under a dissecting microscope. The alcohol-fed group implanted a larger number of ova, but twice as many of their fetuses were resorbed compared with the control group. The increase in resorptions decreased litter size so that the average number of fetuses and the fetal weight were similar between groups. Of the 16 experimental litters, 15 had at least one malformed fetus; of the 29 control litters, only 5 had any malformed fetuses. In both the alcohol and sucrose groups, defective fetuses weighed significantly less than their normal litter mates. In the ethanol-fed group, anomalies involved the limbs, including fusion or absence of digits, while no limb anomalies were observed in the control fetuses. Cardiovascular anomalies included abnormalities of the major branches of both the aorta and the vena caval system, as well as intracardiac anomalies such as atresia of the mitral valve and interventricular septal defects. Urogenital anomalies included hydronephrosis and/or hydroureter. Head anomalies included exencephaly, hydrocephalus, anophthalmia, and microophthalmia.

A beagle dog model of the FAS, developed by Ellis and Pick (1980), demonstrates a dose–response relationship when ethanol is administered by an intragastric tube throughout gestation. At a daily dose of 5.66 g/kg, fertilization and implantation occurred, but no fetal differentiation was observed. A daily dose of 4.71 g/kg resulted in spontaneous abortion of dead fetuses or uterine retention of immature fetuses. Bitches receiving a dose of 4.2 g/kg daily delivered 49 viable offspring with severe growth retardation. In addition, there was an absence of one kidney in three offspring, an opening of the penile urethra into the abdominal cavity in one offspring, cleft palate in four, and "kink" tail in seven. Growth retardation without anomalies was found when bitches were administered 3.0 and 3.6 g/kg daily. Bitches fed 2.4 g/kg daily delivered more stillbirths; however, their viable offspring were not smaller than those born to the controls.

Since ethanol pharmacokinetics in dogs and in human subjects are similar, the beagle model has several advantages over rodent models. The quantities of ethanol which produced the fetal anomalies are comparable to those consumed by alcoholic women and also result in comparable BECs. The longer gestation period of the dog as compared to the rodent will facilitate future investigations of dose–response relationships when ethanol is administered only at specific stages of pregnancy. The longer life span of dogs should also permit testing of recovery from any effects on learning and behavior which may be found in the absence of gross morphologic damage. Such research would have direct implications for clinical management of infants with analagous pathology.

Dexter et al. (1980) developed a miniature swine model of the FAS. Miniature swine have been used in alcoholism research because they consume ethanol voluntarily and continue heavy drinking for many years. Three groups of piglets were compared: those born to gilts delivering their first litter after having access to 20% alcohol and water for 18 months, those born to sows delivering their second litter after consuming ethanol for 2.5 years, and those born to control gilts and sows with no exposure to ethanol. Growth retardation, anomaly rates, and stillbirth rates were significantly higher among piglets born to ethanol-exposed dams as compared with controls. Second-litter piglets were more severely affected than those in the first litters. Further experiments are needed to separate the effects of duration of ethanol exposure, multiple pregnancies, maternal age, and long-term nutritional problems. The findings of these studies should have direct relevance to clinical issues.

An *in vitro* culture system which supports growth and development of rat embryos has been developed by Brown et al. (1979) These embryos are indistinguishable from those which develop *in utero*. This permits investigation of the direct effects of ethanol at concentrations of 150 or 300 mg/100 ml of culture medium. Embryos were exposed to ethanol from Day 9½ to Day 11½, equivalent to approximately 10 days of human development from Day 20 to Day 30 of gestation. Growth retardation was demonstrated, but no gross alteration in morphogenesis was induced. This model will facilitate study of effects of short-duration ethanol exposure early in pregnancy.

8.   BEHAVIORAL EFFECTS ON ANIMAL OFFSPRING

There are many inconsistencies and contradictions in the literature on the effects of ethanol during pregnancy on the behavior of offspring of rats (see Table 5). Several reasons become clear when the methodologies of different researchers are compared. Different results may be explained by a number of variables, including (1) types of behavior examined and tests used to observe this behavior; (2) differences in developmental stage during pregnancy and lactation at which ethanol exposure takes place; (3) differences in quantity of ethanol administered to the subjects; (4) nutritional differences between experimental animals and controls (e.g., only three used pair feeding); and (5) possible differences between various breeds of rats.

Activity level was measured in four studies (Bond and DiGiusto, 1976; Branchey and Friedhoff, 1976; Shaywitz et al., 1976; Martin et al., 1977). The first three studies showed increased activity level in the offspring of ethanol-fed mothers. Martin et al. found that the ethanol-exposed offspring moved significantly less on Day 15. However, it should be noted that on Day 16, the ethanol-fed group had significantly fewer eyes opened. Shaywitz et al. found that the ethanol-exposed offspring were more active when tested on Days 12 and 19, but there was no significant difference between the two groups on Day 26. Bond and DiGiusto, and Branchey and Friedhoff had similar methodology: in an open field box, they both measured ambulation, hind leg support, and defecation. Both found significantly more ambulation among the ethanol-exposed groups. Neither found a significant difference in defecation. However, Bond and DiGiusto found significantly more hind leg support in the ethanol-exposed group, while Branchey and Friedhoff found no significant difference on this parameter.

Ambulation, hind leg support, and defecation were also used by Abel (1974) as criteria for emotionality. He found that the ethanol-exposed females had less ambulation and greater defecation than the control females; there was no significant difference between the two male groups. There was no significant difference in hind leg support or in physical contact, which was also considered a criterion of emotionality.

Learning abilities were measured in three studies. Shaywitz et al. (1976) found that T-maze learning at 21 days and shuttle-box learning at 27 and 33 days were impaired in the ethanol-exposed group. Deficiency in learning was also found by Martin et al. (1977), determined in this case by an impaired ability to discriminate contingencies in a shock reinforcement punishment situation. In the study by Auroux (1973), males at 1.5 months were significantly less proficient in shuttle-box learning, although significant differences were not found in males or females tested at 3, 4.5, and 6 months of age. This finding contrasts with earlier work, where Auroux and Dehaupas (1970) found that the ethanol-exposed rats at the age of 1.5 months required significantly fewer trials to be conditioned in the same shuttle-box situation.

Alcohol preference was measured by Bond and DiGiusto (1976). At concentrations of alcohol between 3% and 6%, the ethanol-exposed rats consumed a significantly greater volume than the control group. At higher concentrations (7% and 8%), alcohol was consumed equally by both groups. Sze et al. (1976) demonstrated in mice that early ethanol exposure caused induction of alcohol dehydrogenase (ADH) and microsomal ethanol-oxidizing system (MEOS) enzymes.

Increased metabolic capacity in offspring exposed to ethanol throughout the nursing period may also account for the finding in Abel's study (1974). Rat pups exposed to ethanol for the first two weeks of the nursing period and a control group were both administered 4 g/kg of ethanol intraperitoneally on Day 21. Pups exposed to ethanol through Day 14 slept a significantly shorter time. At the time of awakening, the mean ethanol blood levels in the two groups were identical, and there was no significant difference in the ethanol levels in the brain. Thus, the shorter sleeping time seems to be related to a capacity that had been induced while nursing to metabolize ethanol more readily.

While most of the behavioral studies on rats show that the offspring of the ethanol-fed mothers have increased ambulation in open field tests, a developmental genetic study conducted with offspring of treated mice of two genotypes showed that the offspring of the alcohol-treated parents had lower ambulation scores (Ginsburg et al., 1975). The inbred strains chosen for the study were known to differ in their preference for alcohol, in their direct susceptibility to alcohol narcosis and withdrawal reactions, and in the activity of their alcohol-metabolizing enzymes.

The major effects, which were of long-term significance, consisted of a reduction in open field activity and a long-lasting increase in susceptibility to audiogenic seizures after *in utero* and neonatal exposure

Table 5. Effects of Ethanol *in Utero* on Animal Offspring Behavior

References	Breed	Ethanol (E) dates[a] and dose	Pair-fed	Test results
Bond and DiGiusto (1976)	Wistar	Days 0–21 6.5% E at 14 g/kg/day	No	Tested in open field box on 45–50 days, the E-fed had greater ambulation ($p < .05$), greater hind leg support ($p < .05$), but NSD in defecation. At 65–70 days, the E-fed had greater consumption of E up to 6% ($p < .05$), but for 7% and 8% there was NSD.
Branchey and Friedhoff (1976)	Not given	Days 10–21 Metrecal and E at 12 g/kg/day	Yes	At 23 days, in open field box, E-fed pups had greater ambulation ($p < .025$), but hind leg support and defecation had NSD.
Shaywitz et al. (1976)	Not given	Days 2–51 Sustacal and E (35% of calories)	No	E-fed were more active on Day 12 and 19 ($p < 0.001$) but not on Day 26 ($p < .05$). E-fed were impaired in learning in the T-maze on Day 21 and in shuttle box at Days 27 and 33. (Significance not given.)
Abel (1974)	Sprague–Dawley	Days 21–35 10% E ad lib	No	E-fed pups slept less ($p < .05$) after receiving 4 g/kg I.P.E. on Day 21.
Abel (1975)	Sprague–Dawley	Days 21–35 8.5% E	Yes	E-fed females ambulated and defecated less ($p < .05$) than control females. NSD in physical control or hind leg support.

Auroux and Dehaupas (1970)	Wistar	Days 0–42 15% E at 105ml/kg/day	No	At 1.5 months, E-fed needed fewer trials to be conditioned in shuttle box ($p < .0001$), but there was NSD in number conditioned.
Auroux (1973)	Wistar	E 120 days before conception; no E during gestation 18 ml of 15% E	Yes	At 1.5 months, E-fed males performed worse than controls ($p < .02$). Other tests had NSD.
Martin et al. (1977)	Sprague–Dawley	AGN[b]: Days 1–42 AN[c]: Days 21–42 1000 mg/kg/d I.P. AGN also had 20% E	Yes	AGN and AN moved less on Day 15 ($p < .00005$), but fewer had open eyes on Day 16 ($p < .0005$). AGN had poorest discrimination of contingencies on punishment schedule.

[a] For this column only, Day 0 = conception; Day 21 = delivery; and Day 42 starts weaning.
[b] AGN: Alcohol during gestation and nursing.
[c] AN: Alcohol during nursing only.

to ethanol. These effects were a direct result of ethanol, probably on the developing central nervous system, and not an indirect effect mediated by malnutrition, since pair-fed control mice had normal seizure susceptibility. Further studies indicated that this increase in susceptibility may have resulted from an ethanol-induced change in the level of serotonin. The discovery that low doses of alcohol tend to suppress genetically induced seizures in mice exposed to ethanol *in utero* suggests that the ethanol had a sedative normalizing effect on the central nervous systems of these animals (Yanai and Ginsburg, 1976).

While the ethanol-fed mothers had BECs in the range of 20–40 mg/dl, the physical development of their offspring was essentially normal, either because of the lower BECs maintained in these mothers or because of their cannibalizing any malformed pups on delivery.

While animal experiments offer the potential for controlling many of the uncertainties that necessarily exist in collecting data from humans, such as the precise amount of alcohol, the date of ingestion, the BEC, and genetic characteristics, the literature contains many inconsistencies. Often these are due to differences in technique. The route of administration may be oral by means of a liquid diet, with a proportion of the total calories supplied by ethanol, or by ethanol and water as the only source of liquid. In dogs, gastric intubation has been used. Intraperitoneal injection of ethanol may have direct effects on the ovaries and the uterus. There also is considerable variation among researchers in terms of the time period selected for the administration of ethanol. Some feed it to the mother throughout her pregnancy; others select a few critical days during embryonic development. Some continue the ethanol through lactation; others stop it at birth. Timing is critical in terms of producing morphological abnormalities during specific growth periods. In rats, pups fail to grow if alcohol is administered to the mother while nursing. This effect is probably secondary to alcohol's inhibiting action on the release of oxytocin, essential for milk ejection. Poor growth also may be related to altered maternal behavior or aversion of the offspring to ethanol-contaminated milk. Collard and Chen (1973) found that mouse pups weighed less than their controls at weaning when alcohol was injected into the nursing mother. When litters were raised in alcohol vapor chambers, pups weighed more at weaning and at seven weeks of age than did controls. The differences were presumably due to additional calories metabolically available from the inhaled ethanol.

Control animals should be pair-fed and should receive the same number of calories as the experimental animals. The all-liquid diet, with the experimental animals receiving ethanol in place of most of the carbohydrate and the pair-fed control animals receiving equicaloric sucrose in place of the ethanol, seems to be the model closest to human alcoholism.

Despite methodological differences, offspring exposed to ethanol *in utero* and during lactation generally show hyperactivity, impaired learning, and greater alcohol preferences. It has been suggested (Bond and DiGiusto, 1976; Shaywitz et al., 1976; Yanai and Ginsburg, 1976) that hyperactivity that abates with maturation and cognitive difficulties that persist also characterize hyperactive and minimal-brain-damaged (MBD) children. Evidence linking some cases of MBD to parental alcoholism is considered in Section 9.

9. MECHANISMS OF ETHANOL'S EFFECTS ON THE MATERNAL–PLACENTAL–FETAL SYSTEM

Ethanol has the capacity to cause a greater variety of adverse metabolic and physiological disturbances, with the potential for adversely affecting fetal development, than any other substance commonly ingested during pregnancy. While the mother, the placenta, and the fetus interact as a dynamic system, it is helpful to consider the effects of alcohol in terms of mechanisms that directly affect the fetus, those that have their primary effects on maternal metabolism and physiology and the associated maternal risk factors.

Direct Effects of Ethanol on Fetal Physiology and Metabolism

In 1900, Nicloux demonstrated that alcohol ingested by the mother crossed the placenta and reached the fetus in concentrations similar to those found in the maternal circulation. Placental transfer and tissue distribution have been studied employing ethanol labeled with radioactive carbon in the pregnant mouse, hamster, and monkey (Ho et al., 1972; Akesson, 1974). Radioactivity was shown to distribute very quickly throughout the body.

Acute Effects. The use of intravenous ethanol to prevent premature labor served to stimulate research on the acute effects of alcohol on the fetus and the mother close to term (Fuchs et al., 1967). Ethanol inhibits release of oxytocin by the pituitary; at concentrations equivalent to blood levels used to arrest premature labor (100–160 mg/dl) (Fuchs, 1966), there is no effect on the uterine muscle itself (Wagner and Fuchs, 1968; Wilson et al., 1969). Because of the immaturity of fetal hepatic enzymes, after delivery the newborn's blood alcohol concentration falls at only half the rate of that of the mother (Seppälä et al., 1971; Waltman and Iniquez, 1972).

The effect of ethanol infusion on maternal and fetal acid–base balance was investigated in pregnant ewes by Mann et al. (1975b). Ewes close to term were administered 15 ml/kg of body weight of 9.75%

solution of ethanol for 1 or 2 hr. The peak concentration in the maternal blood was 237 mg/dl at 90 min and in the fetal blood 222 mg/dl at 120 min. A significant maternal hyperlactacidemia and hyperglycemia were noted, but these did not result in significant alteration of the maternal acid–base balance. An initial fetal metabolic acidosis and, later, a mixed acidosis were observed during the alcohol infusion; this worsened during the postinfusion period. The authors also found that the fetal EEG showed a decrease in amplitude and a slowing of the dominant rhythm as the BEC increased (Mann et al., 1975a). The EEG became isoelectric on occasion during the postinfusion period associated with severe fetal acidosis. Fetal cerebral oxygen uptake was unaffected, while the cerebral uptake of glucose and the glucose–oxygen utilization ratio was significantly increased. Horiguchi et al. (1975) carried out similar investigations with 13 pregnant rhesus monkeys, with fetal ages ranging from 120 to 160 days (term is about 168 days). They were infused during 60 min with 2–4 g of ethanol per kilogram of body weight after a spontaneous onset of labor or following its induction by infusion of oxytocin. Maximum BECs were 237 mg/dl. The maternal respiratory rate was decreased, and there was increase in the fetal heart rate. The authors also observed a fetal acidosis and concluded that intravenous infusion of ethanol in doses sufficient to suppress labor may be hazardous because the fetus becomes progressively asphyxiated.

These experimental studies may demonstrate the probable physiological changes in the human fetus when the mother engages in binge drinking. Repeated episodes of severe acidosis and hypoxia may be important factors in the impaired neurological functioning of babies with the fetal alcohol syndrome.

Intravenous administration of alcohol during labor also increases obstetric risks by stimulating the acidity and volume of maternal gastric secretion. Subsequent anesthesia has been associated with aspirations of a highly acid secretion followed by pneumonitis (Greenhouse et al., 1969).

Chronic Effects on Fetal Metabolism.   The most fundamental effects of ethanol are on cellular metabolism. The concentration of ethanol and the duration of exposure determine whether ethanol is a rapidly metabolized nutrient or a toxic agent. At low concentrations, passive permeability of normal resting cell and capillary membranes is not influenced by ethanol. However, at higher concentrations of $0.1\,M$ there is a significant effect on membrane enzyme systems that employ energy derived from the cleavage of ATP to transport Na^+ to the outside of the cell and K^+ to the inside, against their respective concentration gradients. The variable effects of alcohol on mitochondrial membranes with alteration of permeability and swelling have been reviewed by Kalant (1971).

Cedarbaum (1975) demonstrated that chronic ethanol ingestion is associated with striking ultrastructural changes in the mitochondria, as well as with persistent impairment of mitochondrial oxidation of fatty acids to carbon dioxide.

Hepatic cells of five rat pups born to mothers fed 250 ml of 25% ethanol twice a day throughout gestation were compared with those of two control pups (Beskid et al., 1975). Electron microscopy demonstrated altered mitochondria in the liver cells of the experimental pups as compared with the controls. Mitochondria were described as "considerably elongated, monstrous, with an increased number of cristae."

Sze et al. (1976) found that ethanol exposure *in utero* induced increased activity of the ADH as well as the MEOS ethanol-metabolizing enzymes in mice. Pikkarainen and Räihä (1967) showed that ADH activity is present in two-month-old human fetal livers at an activity level of 3–4% of that of adult livers. ADH activity increases with maturation and reaches 18% of the adult capacity at birth, and by age five, it is comparable to that found in the adult liver.

Rawat (1976a) studied the effect of maternal ethanol consumption on fetal hepatic metabolism in the rat. The first measurable changes in the fetal hepatic redox state were observed after 18 days of pregnancy, when there was a steady linear increase in the cytoplasmic and mitochondrial NADH reduction in the ethanol-exposed group; adult hepatic redox levels were reached 12 days after birth. ADH seems to control hepatic ethanol oxidation capacity and is not affected by the sudden changes observed in neonatal hepatic redox state immediately upon birth.

Kesäniemi (1974) found that the elimination rate of ethanol was equal in pregnant and nonpregnant rats but that the acetaldehyde content of the peripheral blood after ethanol administration was higher in pregnant than in nonpregnant animals. Since no differences were found in the liver alcohol and acetaldehyde dehydrogenase, a difference in the extrahepatic metabolism of acetaldehyde was suggested. Kesäniemi and Sippel (1975) subsequently demonstrated that following the administration of ethanol to pregnant rats, the ethanol content of the maternal aortic blood was comparable to that of the intact placenta and the whole fetus. However, the acetaldehyde content of the placenta was only 25% of that present in the maternal blood, and no acetaldehyde was found in the intact fetal tissue. Since both ethanol and paraldehyde cross the placenta freely, it is improbable that the acetaldehyde should be unable to cross the placenta because of physicochemical properties. It is more likely that it is oxidized as it crosses the placenta. No acetaldehyde is found in the milk of lactating women who have consumed alcohol even when the maternal peripheral blood demonstrates a considerable amount of acetaldehyde. Thus, offspring seem to be protected from this toxic by-product of ethanol oxidation.

Alcohol has profound effects on carbohydrate, lipid, and protein metabolism in the adult (Kissin and Begleiter, 1971). Rawat (1976b) studied rates of protein synthesis by livers of fetal and neonatal rats born to mothers who had consumed ethanol during pregnancy. Rates of incorporation of labeled leucine into hepatic proteins was significantly lower in the offspring of the ethanol-fed rats compared with the control group. Maternal ethanol consumption resulted in a decrease in hepatic total RNA content, the RBA–DNA ratio, and the ribosomal protein content of the fetal liver. Inhibition of protein synthesis could be directly related to the retarded growth of the offspring of alcoholic mothers.

Henderson et al. (1980) concluded that, in pregnant rats, ethanol-induced hypothermia was the major contributor to the depression of net protein synthesis in maternal brain and heart and in fetal brain. At high ethanol levels, ethanol, directly and independent of hypothermia, also reduced net protein synthesis in maternal kidney, liver, and placenta and in fetal heart, kidney, and liver.

Henderson and Schenker (1977) investigated the effects of long-term maternal alcohol consumption by the rat on viability, growth, and development of brain, liver, kidney, and heart in three-day-old offspring. Both total body weight and organ weights were lower in the ethanol-exposed group. However, when the ratio of organ weight to body weight was compared, the weight of individual organs seemed to be preserved preferentially to other tissues. DNA concentration was decreased in the liver but not in the brain, heart, or kidney. The RNA concentration in all four organs was about 10–30% lower in the ethanol-exposed pups than in the control rats.

Thadani et al. (1977a) assessed the effects of maternal ethanol ingestion on the activity of ornithine decarboxylase in the brain and heart of rat pups. The enzyme catalyzes the conversion of ornithine to putrescine, the first and probable rate-limiting step in polyamine biosynthesis. Patterns of enzyme activity were different for the two organs and consistent with the hypothesis that ethanol *in utero* exerts significant effects on fetal polyamine metabolism and ultimately on the growth and development of these tissues. Further experiments demonstrated that the alterations of polyamine metabolism and growth of brain and heart are related to the duration of ethanol exposure and the developmental age of the fetus or pups (Thadani et al., 1977c). These biochemical findings support clinical observations that offspring of women who cease heavy drinking in mid-pregnancy have less growth retardation.

Stoewsand and Anderson (1974) exposed weanling mice to wine, 12% ethanol, or distilled water. After 10 weeks of gradually increased intake, the experimental mice were receiving exclusively wine or ethanol as their sole dietary liquid. They then were mated, and their offspring were studied in terms of cholesterol and triglyceride in blood plasma and liver. After weaning, the offspring were exposed to either wine, ethanol, or water. Liver cholesterols of the offspring from wine-fed parents were significantly higher than liver cholesterols of the offspring of water-drinking parents ($p < .05$). Data indicated that male mice born from water-fed parents and later fed wine had liver triglyceride and cholesterol levels that were 60% of the levels of mice fed a solution of the equivalent amount of ethanol ($p < .05$). No comparable effect was seen in female offspring. A complex interaction was demonstrated between the influence of parental treatment and sex on cholesterol and triglyceride metabolism. It also was shown that the physiological effects of wine are related to both its ethanol and its nonethanol components.

When pregnant rats were fed a liquid diet containing 6% alcohol, a retardation in the maturation of adrenal catecholamine stores was observed in the pups (Lau et al., 1976). Offspring of the ethanol-fed mothers showed a 20–30% deficit in adrenal catecholamines from Days 3 to 17 of postnatal development. Adrenal dopamine beta hydroxylase activity was significantly low after 10 days of age. The actual mechanism by which ethanol retards maturation of the adrenal stores has not been determined. The effects on the adrenals precede those on general growth and are fully reversible on withdrawal within the first week of postnatal life.

Effects on the Developing Central Nervous System. Exposure of the fetal central nervous system to moderate or high concentrations of ethanol probably has different effects at different stages of development. Malformations at the earliest stages of embryonic growth are probably incompatible with life. Clarren et al. (1978) presented neuropathological data on brains of four human neonates exposed *in utero* to high peak concentrations of ethanol. The most frequent finding was a sheet of aberrant neural and glial tissue covering part of the brain surface, termed *leptomeningeal neuroglial heterotopia*. Brain lesions were found in two infants who showed no external dysmorphic features of the FAS. In some infants, abnormal brain structure and function may be the only abnormality caused by ethanol *in utero*.

Bauer-Moffett and Altman (1975) studied morphological effects on the developing cerebellar cortex of rat pups who inhaled ethanol vapor from Days 3 to 20. Ethanol exposure during this period of cerebellar neurogenesis produced a greater reduction of cerebellar tissue, nearly twice that observed in parts of the brain that developed at an earlier time. The body weights of control and ethanol-treated animals did not differ significantly. In order to produce cerebellar stunting by undernutrition, the body weight had to be reduced by 42%. With undernutrition, stunting is limited to the postnatally acquired cells, while ethanol affected prenatally as well as postnatally forming elements.

Anderson (1978) placed one-day-old rats in an alcohol inhalation chamber for 1, 2, 6, or 8 days of continuous treatment. Animals were sacrificed at 10, 21, and 30 days of age. Brain weights were significantly decreased only in those exposed for 6–8 days. Cerebellar measurements revealed a significant decrease in the total area, the molecular area, and the internal granular area. Ten-day-old cerebellums showed regional destruction of the proliferative matrix, the external granular area, suggesting that ethanol may selectively destroy proliferating neuroblasts.

Jacobson et al. (1978) exposed female rats to a modified Freund diet with 30% of calories derived from ethanol for 30 days before mating and throughout pregnancy. Comparison of Nissl-stained cortex of the alcohol-exposed pups with that of controls of the same age showed a delay in cortical development. Nearly complete cortical lamination was seen in controls at 14 days postnatal but not until 23 days in the alcohol-exposed pups. Further studies are needed to determine if the retardation of cortical development persists throughout the life of the animal.

Rosman and Malone (1974) maintained pregnant rats on isocaloric liquid diets containing 10%, 21%, and 36% ethanol. Fetal loss was 100% when the mother was on the highest-level diet and 60% on the diets containing less ethanol. Pups were sacrificed between Postnatal Days 12 and 28. Starting at Day 24, brains of the experimental animals, as compared with pair-fed controls, showed delayed myelination affecting all fiber tracts.

Druse and Hofteig (1977) pair-fed female rats, using isocaloric control or 6.6% (v/v) ethanol liquid diets for one month prior to conception and throughout gestation. Ethanol pups had smaller brain and body weights but 18- and 25-day-old ethanol pups had more CNS myelin than controls. The increase was due to an excess of the chemically and morphologically immature heavy myelin fraction. At 18 and 25 days, the ethanol pups incorporated more [^{3}H]leucine and [^{14}C]glucose into the myelin subfractions; but by 54 days, they demonstrated decreased incorporation and they had a small deficit in total CNS myelin. In the ethanol pups, both the onset and the slowdown of active myelination occurred prematurely. Myelination abnormalities might have resulted from an effect of ethanol on either oligodendroglial or neuronal cells or possibly from metabolic or hormonal abnormalities in dams or pups.

Ethanol affects the CNS via multiple mechanisms. At physiological concentrations, ethanol has its primary effect on the neuronal membrane; active transport of sodium and potassium across the membrane is impaired (Grenell, 1972). Thiamine, pyridoxine, and folic acid, as well as calcium, magnesium, and zinc, all essential for CNS enzymes, frequently are depleted because of the malnutrition and diureses associated with chronic ethanol ingestion (Vitale and Coffey, 1971; Flink, 1971).

Tewari et al. (1975; Tewari and Noble, 1975) investigated the effects of chronic ethanol ingestion on brain RNA metabolism in mature mice. Changes in RNA metabolism were due to an alteration in the transcription and/or the processing of RNA in the nucleus. Similar studies of ethanol effects on fetal and neonatal brain are needed. Pilstrom and Kiessling (1967) administered ethanol to pregnant rats and studied the effects on liver and brain mitochondria of offspring. No significant effect could be found in the capacity to oxidize pyruvate, glutamate, and β-hydroxybutyrate or in oxidative phosphorylation.

Rawat (1975b) studied effects of long-term ethanol consumption by pregnant rats on the incorporation of [14C]leucine into fetal and neonatal brain ribosomes. He found a 30% decrease in the rate of [14C]leucine incorporation by the fetal cerebral ribosomes, while neonatal rats suckling on ethanol-fed mothers showed about 60% decrease as compared with a control group that had not been exposed to ethanol in utero but was cross-fostered by ethanol-fed mothers. A control group, cross-fostered by mothers not fed ethanol, was omitted.

Impaired learning, observed in animal behavior experiments as well as in the psychological evaluation of FAS children, may be related to altered RNA metabolism. Increased motor activity, another behavioral manifestation observed in animals exposed to ethanol in utero, may be due to an alteration in neurohumoral amine metabolism. Ethanol affects uptake, storage, and release of serotonin, catecholamines, acetylcholine, and γ-aminobutyric acid (Feldstein, 1971). Branchey and Friedhoff (1973) found that the activity of tyrosine hydroxylase, a rate-limiting enzyme in catecholamine biosynthesis, was increased at one, two, and three weeks of age in the caudates of rat pups exposed to ethanol in utero. They also observed increased activity in litter mates at 23 days. Rawat (1975a) studied the influence of prolonged ethanol consumption by pregnant and lactating rats on the activities of several neurotransmitters together with the activities of the enzymes in fetal and neonatal brains. An increase in the cerebral content of GABA was found in both fetal and suckling neonates' brains. Glutamate, serotonin, and norepinephrine are also increased while acetylcholine was decreased in the suckling neonates but was unchanged in the fetuses. The significance of early changes in the metabolism of neurotransmitters must await future studies investigating long-term effects on the developing organization of the CNS and on behavior.

Exposure to ethanol in utero can produce metabolic changes in the fetal rat brain that are not observed in the adult rat brain. Thadani et al. (1977b) studied pups exposed to ethanol from Day 13 of gestation and others exposed from Day 18 of gestation. In both groups, synaptosomal uptake of [³H]tyramine and its conversion to [³H]octopamine were increased. The increase persisted longer when the fetus was exposed on Day 18. Withdrawal from ethanol enhanced synaptosomal uptake and conversion, with the magnitude dependent on the time of exposure and age at which withdrawal was initiated.

At the cellular level, alterations of the membrane of the neuron and of neurotransmitters interfere with proper synaptic transduction. Heavy alcohol consumption alters physiological functions in many areas of the CNS, and sleep disturbances are common (Williams and Salamy, 1973). EEG studies have revealed marked disruption of the quantitative composition of rapid-eye-movement (REM) and slow-wave sleep (SWS), together with instability or fragmentation of the circadian rhythm of 24-hr cycles and the ultradian rhythms (shorter cycles occurring periodically). In adult alcoholics, continued disturbance of sleep rhythms persists months after abstinence has been attained.

Sander et al. (1977) investigated the extent to which the organization of sleep substates in the newborn are affected by exposure to high BECs during fetal life. Sleep states of infants in this study were observed for a 24-hr period on the third day of life by means of a continuous nonintrusive bassinet sleep monitor, as well as by standard sleep polygraphy for one interfeed interval on that same day. Infants born to heavy-drinking women who continued to drink throughout the pregnancy were compared with infants born to heavy-drinking women who were able to abstain or significantly reduce alcohol consumption for the third trimester. Measures of infant state obtained from the bassinet sleep monitor have a high correlation with standard polygraphic determination of REM and non-REM states. Fourteen infants born to mothers who drank heavily throughout pregnancy were more restless, with more frequent major body movements and more quiet sleep periods interrupted by awake states when compared with nine babies whose mothers never were heavy drinkers (Rosett et al., 1979). The 14 offspring of mothers who continued their heavy drinking slept less on the third day of life than did 8 infants born to women who were able to reduce alcohol consumption during the third trimester.

Havlicek et al. (1977) compared EEG-frequency-spectrum characteristics of sleep states in infants of alcoholic mothers with those of infants matched for postconceptual age born to healthy mothers. During 2-hr sleep polygraphy sessions, the infants of alcoholic mothers had more difficulty reaching quiet sleep and were more easily disturbed from this stage of sleep. They awoke more frequently during active sleep and were more restless during indeterminate sleep. Landesman-Dwyer et al. (1978) reported decreased body activity and more time with eyes open, but no differences in REM sleep during two hours of naturalistic observation after an early feeding among one-day-old infants born to moderate drinkers. Some implications of these findings for strategies of intervention with heavy drinking during pregnancy are discussed in Section 12.

Effects of Alcohol on Maternal Physiology and Metabolism

Metabolic Disturbances. Chronic heavy alcohol consumption adversely affects almost every organ system in the body. Nonspecific risk factors for the pregnancy are associated with disease of the liver and other parts of the gastrointestinal system, the cardiovascular system, and the hematopoietic system, as well as the body's defense mechanism against infectious disease (Seixas et al., 1975). Alcohol-induced metabolic disturbances in the mother—such as alcohol hypoglycemia; alcohol ketoacidosis; alterations in lactate, uric acid, and lipid metabolism; or changes in the metabolism of individual amino acids—may all have effects on the fetus.

Cooperman et al. (1974) described seven episodes of severe ketoacidosis in six nondiabetic patients. All were women who indulged both in heavy chronic alcohol use and in binges. One patient was admitted because of metabolic acidosis four times during two pregnancies. During her first episode in the 30th week of pregnancy, she delivered a premature fetus. During her second pregnancy, she was admitted at 8 weeks', 28 weeks', and 32 weeks' gestation. Each episode followed excessive drinking, and each time the metabolic acidosis was progressively more severe. After the second pregnancy, she gave birth to a normal term infant. It was suggested that ovarian and placental hormones together with the fetal drain on carbohydrate reserves may play a part in the pathogenesis of alcoholic ketoacidosis during pregnancy.

Withdrawal Syndrome. Acute alcohol withdrawal syndromes have been described in newborn infants delivered by severely alcoholic mothers (Schaefer, 1962; Nichols, 1967). Withdrawal symptoms were observed in six infants, all born to mothers with alcohol on their breath at the time of delivery (Pierog et al., 1977). All mothers admitted heavy alcohol use for several years, and all neonates showed signs of FAS. The most prominent symptoms of withdrawal were irritability and tremor, startle reaction to noise, abdominal distention, and spontaneous convulsions.

If a woman undergoes an acute withdrawal syndrome in mid-pregnancy it seems probable that the fetus would be subject to major metabolic and physiological disturbances. Two patients who had been consuming over a quart of vodka a day had been withdrawn during the second trimester on the Boston City Hospital Obstetrical Service (Rosett et al., 1977). Chlordiazepoxide was utilized for one week to modify withdrawal symptoms. No adverse effects were detected by monitoring fetal heart rate or on careful neurological examination in the newborn nursery.

Mineral Deficiencies.   Deficiencies of magnesium, zinc, and calcium occur in chronic alcoholism as a consequence of increased urinary excretion, loss due to vomiting and diarrhea, and inadequate intake (Flink, 1971). A 100% increase in urinary excretion of calcium and a 167% increase in magnesium excretion have been observed to begin within 20 min of the ingestion of 30 ml of ethanol by normal volunteers and to continue for about 2 hr. Magnesium has important roles in fetal development since it stabilizes DNA and RNA, binds sRNA to the ribosome, and is also involved in the activating and transfer system of all amino acids. Zinc is needed for a number of enzymes, including carbonic anhydrase and alcohol dehydrogenase, and is also necessary for RNA metabolism and DNA synthesis.

Female rats, maintained on a zinc deficient diet from the time of weaning (Hurley and Swenerton, 1966) or only for the period of pregnancy (Hurley et al., 1971), bore fetuses with abnormalities of the skull, the limbs, the heart, the eyes, and the urogenital system. Preschool children consuming diets deficient in zinc had significantly more height, weight, and head circumference measurements below the 3rd percentile (Hambidge et al., 1976). Recently, the low zinc content of certain infant diets has been shown to be growth-limiting (Walravens and Hambidge, 1975).

Vitamin Metabolism.   Chronic alcoholics have multiple disturbances of vitamin metabolism; dietary intake often is poor, intestinal absorption is impaired, storage is limited by hepatic damage, and urinary loss may be elevated (Vitale and Coffey, 1971). In a study of 120 indigent or low-income adult patients admitted to a general hospital, 59% had a significant reduction in circulating levels of two or more vitamins. The most common deficiency was of folate, measured by the serum folate level. Ethanol causes impaired intestinal absorption of folic acid. Sullivan and Herbert (1964) demonstrated that hematologic response to folic acid therapy was repeatedly prevented by the concomitant administration of whiskey, wine, or ethanol. When body stores are decreased and dietary intake is poor, ethanol may act as a weak folate antagonist. Folate antagonists have been shown to cause fetal resorption, stillbirths, and congenital malformations in the rat (Sullivan, 1967). There also have been reports suggesting that human fetal malformations may result from a dietary deficiency of folate (Lindenbaum, 1974).

Thiamine deficiency, frequently seen in chronic alcoholics, is due to decreased dietary intake during drinking episodes, impaired absorption, and possibly also acute liver injury, which lowers the response to administered thiamine (Vitale and Coffey, 1971). Magnesium deficiency concomitant with thiamine deficiency may interfere with response to thiamine. Central nervous system lesions produced by experimental thiamine deficiency are comparable to those observed in the Wernicke–Korsakoff syndrome. The effects of thiamine, pyridoxine, and folate deficiency on the developing fetal nervous system should be investigated.

Effects on Endocrine Function. Stokes (1974) reviewed alcohol–endocrine interrelationships and stressed the importance of differentiating the effects of ethanol on the anterior pituitary, on its trophic hormones, on their hypothalamic releasing factors, and on the target glands. Stokes found evidence of effects of alcohol on adrenal–medullary function and thyroid function but little systematic data on the effects of alcohol on gonadal function.

Van Thiel et al. (1977) demonstrated that in the Wistar rat, ethanol is toxic for the female gonad. When 28-day-old females were fed a diet in which ethanol accounted for 36% of total calories over a 56-day period, they developed smaller ovaries, uteri, and Fallopian tubes than the isocaloric pair-fed animals. Ovaries of the alcohol-fed rats showed evidence of ovulatory failure, since they lacked any recognizable corpus lutea and corpora hemorrhagica. The few follicles observed were small and showed no signs of follicular maturation. Histological examination of the cells lining the uterus and the Fallopian tubes revealed immature, flat, cuboidal epithelial cells. Plasma levels of estradiol and progesterone were markedly reduced, while levels of estrone and corticosterone were increased.

A link has been demonstrated between exposure to female sex hormones early in pregnancy and cardiovascular malformations (Heinonen et al., 1977). Heavy-drinking women with chronic liver disease might endogenously produce hormones that alter fetal cardiovascular and genital development.

Hypothalamic–pituitary function in four children ages 9–15 born to an alcoholic woman was studied in order to determine if hormonal abnormalities account for FAS aberrant growth patterns (Root et al., 1975). Biochemical and endocrine test values were all within normal limits.

The possible role of human growth hormone or somatomedin deficiency in the postnatal growth deficiency of FAS was investigated in five FAS children. Human growth hormone secretion was assessed after insulin-induced hypoglycemia and on a separate day after arginine infusion (Tze et al., 1976). The response was a normal or slightly hypernormal level of growth hormone and normal somatomedin activity. It was concluded that the FAS postnatal growth retardation was not caused by deficiencies of these hormones.

Effects on the Placenta. Placental growth and function may be affected by chronic alcohol use, but this problem has received little direct study. Kaminski et al. (1976) compared the mean weight of the placentas from 236 women who consumed over 1.5 oz of absolute alcohol per day with those from 4074 who drank less than that amount. Heavier drinkers had placentas that weighed 22 g less than those of lighter drinkers. This difference attained statistical significance ($p < .01$). However, the clinical significance of this small difference is unclear. Ethanol may have detrimental effects on active transport mechanisms across placental membranes. This is an important area that is yet to be investigated.

10. ASSOCIATED RISK FACTORS

Nutrition

Heavy drinking is often associated with other variables that contribute to reproductive risk, such as nutritional deficiency, heavy smoking, use of other drugs, and emotional stress. Each of these associated factors has been extensively studied; only brief reference to some of the more recent reviews will be cited here.

The relationship between alcoholism and malnutrition has been reviewed by Hillman (1974). Alcohol and vitamin metabolism have been reviewed by Vitale and Coffey (1971). The clinical stereotype of the malnourished alcoholic had been questioned by Neville et al. (1968). Thirty-four alcoholics were admitted to a research ward. A careful evaluation of nutrient intake for the month prior to admission was made, and excretion levels of various vitamins were studied. There was no significant difference between the mean excretion of vitamin metabolites by alcoholics and normal controls. These results did not support the view that the nutritional status of alcoholics is markedly inferior to that of nonalcoholics, particularly those of similar economic and health histories. At the Boston City Hospital Prenatal Clinic, few patients' diets met the minimum daily requirements of the National Research Council (Rosett et al., 1978). Heavy-drinking women did not ingest significantly poorer diets than the abstinent women. However, utilization may be impaired by the effects of alcohol on intestinal absorption, liver function, urinary excretion of vitamins and trace minerals, disturbances of intermediate metabolism, and gastrointestinal disturbances such as vomiting and diarrhea.

Naeye et al. (1973) have considered the effects of maternal nutrition on the human fetus and presented evidence that undernutrition has its greatest effect on fetal growth in late gestation. Dobbing (1974) emphasized that two growth spurts represent critical periods of vulnerability for the development of the human brain. In humans, the first period of vulnerability is between the 12th and 18th gestational weeks, the period of greatest neuronal multiplication. Neuronal multiplication is close to completion early in the second trimester. The late spurt of brain growth begins during the third trimester and continues during the first 18 months of life. During this time, there is an explosive increase in dendritic complexity with establishment of synaptic connections. This component may be as important in the development of brain function as the neuronal cell number. Growth restriction during only the first part of the brain growth spurt period may not be sufficient to produce lasting brain cell deficit. Rebound growth after birth may compensate if birth releases the infant from factors such as intrauterine ethanol exposure, which may have been disrupting normal growth processes.

Smoking

The association between heavy drinking and heavy cigarette smoking that has been repeatedly observed (U.S. Department of Health, Education, and Welfare, 1973) is confirmed by current epidemiologic data coming from the Boston and Seattle prospective studies. The relationship between maternal smoking, low birth weight, and reduced body length is well established. Longo (1977) has reviewed these as well as other relationships that have been less clear-cut. These include an increased perinatal mortality, congenital heart disease, and complications of pregnancy such as abruptio placentae, placenta previa, and premature rupture of fetal membranes. Epidemiologic studies of the effects of alcohol during pregnancy must also collect smoking information and account statistically for the effects of each separately as well as possible synergistic actions.

Other Drugs

The use of other drugs, such as heroin, methadone, LSD, and barbiturates, has also been associated with a higher incidence of low-birth-weight infants and increased perinatal mortality (Rothstein and Gould, 1974). Heavier drinkers are more likely to have tried other drugs in the past; however, in the Boston City Hospital Prenatal Clinic study, only 4% of the total group reported currently using drugs other than alcohol (Rosett et al., 1978). In the Loma Linda study, 6% reported illicit drug use (Kuzma and Phillip, 1977). In both populations, drugs were used by women with low, moderate, and high alcohol intake. Total abstainers from alcohol also avoided illicit drugs.

A pattern of congenital malformations, growth deficiency, and retarded mental development, which may resemble the fetal alcohol syndrome, has been observed in neonates exposed *in utero* to antiepileptic drugs (Hill et al., 1974). Janz (1975) reported that congenital anomalies had been observed in association with use during pregnancy of the following anticonvulsants, alone or in combination: barbiturates, hydantoins, oxazolidines, succinimides, benzodiazepines, acetylurea, or carbamazepine. Patients receiving long-term treatment with phenytoin, primidone, or phenobarbital have been found to have disturbances in the metabolism of calcium, corticosteroids, folic acid, and vitamin D, as well as alterations in connective tissue repair processes and prothrombin time (Hill, 1976). Effects of chronic ingestion of ethanol on maternal physiology and metabolism are comparable in several ways, as reviewed in Section 9. Hill (1976) suggested that the multiple deficiency states and alterations of metabolism that have been reported following the long-term use of anticonvulsants as well as following the consumption of large amounts of alcohol may contribute to some of the similarities in the abnormalities found in offspring.

Caffeine

Heavy coffee consumption is often associated with heavy alcohol use and smoking. While there have been animal studies of caffeine as a teratogen, the dosages employed ranged from the equivalent of 40 to 100 cups of coffee per day (Mulvihill, 1973). No human malformations have been attributed to caffeine, perhaps because man is protected by a rapid metabolism of caffeine, with only 1% secreted unchanged. Gilbert (1976) has extensively reviewed caffeine as a drug of abuse.

Disulfiram

Disulfiram (Antabuse), which may be useful as an adjunct to the treatment of alcoholism, should not be prescribed during pregnancy. A prospective cohort of five pregnancies in which there was maternal exposure to between 250 mg and 500 mg of disulfiram daily revealed one spontaneous abortion in the second month, two infants with club feet, and two normal babies (Tissot-Favre and Delatour, 1965). A teratogen surveillance program identified two infants with severe limb-reduction anomalies whose mothers had been maintained on disulfiram during the first trimester of pregnancy (Nora et al., 1977). Neither mother was exposed to alcohol or any other established teratogen during this trimester. One infant had multiple anomalies, including radial aplasia, vertebral fusion, and tracheoesophageal fistula (Vacterl syndrome), while the other had phocomelia of the lower extremities. A cohort of 1320 histories during the same time frame revealed no other exposures to disulfiram. Disulfiram inhibits several enzymes, including aldehyde dehydrogenase, needed for oxidation of acetaldehyde, and dopamine betahydroxylase, which catalyzes the conversion of dopamine to norepinephrine (Truitt and Walsh, 1971). In addition, the three major metabolites of disulfiram (carbon disulfide, diethylamine, and diethyldithiócarbamate) have been found to be neurotoxic (Rainey, 1977).

Paternal Drinking

The possibility that heavy alcohol consumption by the male can cause genetic damage has been the subject of speculation for over 200 years. The mutagenic role of ethanol in male mice was studied by Badr and Badr (1975), who administered ethanol in doses of 1.24 g/kg by gastric tube to male mice for three consecutive days. Each mouse was then caged with a virgin untreated female of the same strain. At weekly intervals, the males were transferred to cages with different virgins. Pregnant females were sacrificed 13–15 days after conception, and dead and live implants were scored for each pregnancy. Females mated 4–13 days after treatment of the male with alcohol had a two- to fourfold increase in the number of dead implants found. The conclusion was that ethanol in the doses used induced dominant lethal mutations in several different spermatogenic stages. Efficiency of induction was most pronounced in the epididymal spermatozoa and the late spermatid stage.

Klassen and Persaud (1976) fed six male rats a 6% ethanol Metrecal diet for one week and a 10% ethanol Metrecal diet the next four weeks. Six controls received Metrecal with an isocaloric amount of sucrose substituted for the alcohol; however, controls were not pair-fed. The alcohol-fed males became lethargic and ataxic, lost weight, and had ruffled, dull hair and small pale eyes. After five weeks, the alcohol-fed males had significantly lower blood sugar and testosterone levels than did the controls. After 15 days on the diet, each male was mated with two normally fed females on a nightly basis. Since no alcohol was provided during hours of mating, withdrawal symptoms were observed in the alcohol-fed males. All pregnancies were terminated on Gestational Day 20 by Cesarean section. Among 13 females mated with controls, there were 158 pups and 9 early resorptions, while among 6 mated with the alcohol-fed males, there were 21 pups and 28 early resorptions. No malformed pups were observed, but the early resorptions probably represented defective offspring. Pups of alcohol-fed fathers demonstrated significantly lower ($p < .01$) weight, length, and placental index and lower growth index ($p < 0.5$).

The effects of ethanol on spermatogonial cells in the rat have been directly investigated by giving rats a nutritionally adequate diet containing 10% ethanol as the only supply of liquid for 70 days (Kohila et al., 1976). Following this experiment, testicular tissue was directly examined for the frequency of aberrations such as chromosome breaks, chromatid breaks, and chromatid gaps. There was no significant difference between the experimental and the control groups. Subsequently, the experiment was repeated with male rats who received a thiamine-deficient diet as well as ethanol (Halkka and Eriksson, 1977). Combining thiamine deficiency with alcohol feeding did not lead to any significant increase in the frequency of chromosomal aberrations.

Ethanol has no damaging effects on human chromosomes *in vitro* (Obe et al., 1977). However, chromosomes of alcoholics show a significant increase in aberrations. One possible reason may be an inhibition of cellular RNA synthesis, which impedes cellular repair *in vivo*. The effects of alcohol administration on sex hormone metabolism in normal men include an augmented conversion of androgenic precursors to estrogens, a higher plasma concentration and production rate of estradiol, and an increased plasma concentration of estrone (Gordon et al., 1976). The alteration of metabolism of androgens has been shown to be coupled with direct effects of ethanol on hypothalamic–pituitary function, with changes in plasma luteinizing hormone. The effect of these changes on offspring is not known.

Further studies of the effects of alcohol administration to the male should include more complete evaluation of hormonal and nutritional status. Physiological abnormalities in the male may affect the motility, viability, and capacity of sperm to impregnate. Such variables might alter the outcome of conception in the absence of an increase in the frequency of chromosomal damage.

Maternal Psychological Stress

Emotional stress has been demonstrated to be related to perinatal complications (Sameroff and Chandler, 1975). Differences have not been found between various psychiatric diagnostic groups; however, when psychiatric patients are divided on a dimension of chronicity, those with the greatest number of psychiatric contacts and hospitalizations have had infants with the most perinatal complications. Heavy-drinking women frequently use alcohol to relieve symptoms of chronic anxiety and depression. Emotional stress data should be reexamined in terms of alcohol and other drug use, including tranquilizers, by the patients with the more severe and chronic diagnoses.

Sameroff and Chandler (1975) emphasized the importance of viewing the continuum between prenatal and newborn care. A number of studies of failure to thrive describe the infants as being irritable, difficult to manage, and unappealing and as having fussy eating habits, poor food intake, and frequent regurgitations. Traditionally, these symptoms were interpreted as the result of parental neglect. These characteristics may be part of the etiology of parental neglect, rather than the consequence of poor mothering.

There are almost no case studies of the management of the pregnant chronic alcoholic patient in the literature. There is one report of successful cooperation between the psychiatrist and the obstetrician following a patient jointly, enabling an alcoholic mother who had a potential for psychosis to deal successfully with the stress of pregnancy and also to control her alcohol use (Silber et al., 1960). The dire consequences of fragmentation of medical care are illustrated in another case report of a 37-year-old alcoholic woman who had a ruptured uterus at 32 weeks, which was not managed properly, resulting in her death (Jewett, 1976).

Offspring of alcoholics are a high-risk group for child abuse and neglect (Mayer and Black, 1977), hyperactivity, delinquency, and other behavioral disorders (Chafetz et al., 1971), and, as they mature, for alcoholism. This pessimistic prognosis undoubtedly is multidetermined. The family of an alcoholic has many crises in which the children's loyalties to each parent become tools in the struggle between mother and father (Jackson, 1954). Genetic predispositions to affective disorders or alcoholism itself have also been investigated (Goodwin, 1971). Several studies of the families of hyperactive children have indicated that the parents have a higher incidence of psychiatric illness and particularly alcoholism (Morrison and Stewart, 1971; Cantwell, 1972). Goodwin et al. (1973) reported a higher occurrence of alcohol problems in adoptees raised apart from their alcoholic biological parents, and they found a high incidence of hyperactive behavior in the childhood of a sample of these alcoholic adoptees (1975). Waldrop and Halverson (1971) described minor physical anomalies associated with hyperactive behavior in young children but did not investigate parental alcohol use. Rapoport et al. (1974) studied a similar group and also found a higher than normal mean plasma dopamine-β-hydroxylase activity. These observations resemble findings in rat offspring exposed to ethanol *in utero*. Intrauterine exposure of the developing central nervous system to alcohol may contribute to hyperactive behavior in children and to subsequent behavioral disturbances and development of alcoholism.

A critical review of the literature on the risk status of offspring of alcoholics over the past 25 years has been published recently (El-Guebaly and Offord, 1977). The need for more carefully controlled studies using blind data collection and clear operational definitions is emphasized. The importance of including detailed histories of life events that may be associated with increased infant morbidity is stressed. Many of these questions could be studied by long-term follow-up of the infants being observed in the FAS epidemiologic studies now under way.

11. PREVENTION OF THE FETAL ALCOHOL SYNDROME

Toward a Theory of Prevention

Hypotheses firmly grounded in theory are fundamental to basic research. However, prevention programs have frequently evolved pragmatically. Our theoretical understanding of the etiologic mechanisms of the fetal alcohol syndrome and of the psychological and environmental forces affecting the heavy-drinking woman must be incorporated in the design of programs for prevention.

One theory of FAS etiology is that alcohol functions as a teratogen, similarly to such drugs as thalidomide. Exposure of the embryo or the fetus at a critical developmental point can result in malformation. Since no safe level of such a teratogenic substance has been determined, total abstinence is the only safe strategy. Once the drug has been ingested during a vulnerable developmental period, the only option remaining for complete prevention is therapeutic termination of pregnancy. These strategies have been advocated by some FAS authorities (Jones et al., 1974; Hanson et al., 1976).

An alternative theory has been presented in this chapter. The effects on offspring of heavy drinking during pregnancy are multidetermined, the cumulative result of ethanol's actions on the maternal–placental–fetal system. This model recognizes that early damage may not be reversible; however, whenever heavy drinking ceases, an opportunity is created for physiological restitution and catch-up growth.

Another determinant of prevention strategy is our understanding of heavy drinking during pregnancy. The experimental model is derived from animal research where precise regular doses can be administered under conditions controlled to reduce confounding variables. A clinical perspective acknowledges variability in drinking patterns throughout pregnancy, as well as multiple associated stresses in the lives of those women. Reduction of alcohol consumption to lower risks to the fetus is the primary goal of therapy; assistance with the many stresses of pregnancy facilitates moderation. If other associated risk factors such as smoking and malnutrition can be modified, there will be reduction of possible hazards due to synergistic mechanisms that could potentiate the adverse effects of alcohol.

Therapy of Heavy Drinking in the Prenatal Clinic

A program focused on the reduction of alcohol consumption during pregnancy was initiated at the Boston City Hospital Prenatal Clinic in May 1974 (Rosett et al., 1978). At the initial registration, a drinking history was obtained from all patients. Women who reported moderate or heavy alcohol use were informed that excessive drinking might be harmful to their unborn child. Heavy-drinking women were encouraged to meet with the project psychiatrist. Information obtained in unstructured interviews with the psychiatrist was in close agreement with that gathered in the survey. The psychiatrist urged all heavy drinkers to participate in counseling sessions held in the clinic and scheduled to coincide with their routine appointments.

A male psychiatrist and a female counselor worked as a team. The women were generally seen individually, but on a few occasions, two to four patients met together. The variability of delivery dates and clinic appointments precluded the establishment of an ongoing therapy group. The sessions averaged 20 min. The therapists attempted to sustain a positive, supportive relationship. Abstinence was praised and direct criticism of drinking was avoided. Criticism often increases guilt and obstructs the therapeutic alliance.

The content of each session was determined by the problems presented by the patient. Most women were confronted with a variety of psychological and social difficulties that were intensified by the normal crises related to pregnancy. Many had trouble accepting their bodily changes and feared delivery. Confusion about sexual anatomy and the details of the birth process were alleviated through an educational approach. A diagram of the placental circulation helped explain how alcohol reached the fetus; the possible adverse effects of alcohol and other drugs were discussed. While similar information had been presented in childbirth classes conducted by the prenatal clinic staff, these patients needed more individual instruction. Many women were having troubles in their relationships with the father of the baby, their other children, or members of their extended families. Support and practical help in dealing with these difficult life situations were provided through liaison with obstetricians, public health nurses, and social service and alcoholism treatment agencies. Several women could not reduce their alcohol use until they received this direct assistance.

Careful evaluation of the total personality was necessary in planning a therapeutic program for pregnancy, delivery, and the newborn period. The ego strength of the pregnant woman was assessed in terms of her style of coping with anxiety and depression, her capacity to sustain relationships with family and friends, and her resourcefulness in times of adversity. Associations with family, friends, members of Alcoholics Anonymous, and other programs that have provided stability and supported sobriety were encouraged.

A three-phase classification based on drinking patterns proved useful in planning treatment. Women in the social phase use alcohol primarily to facilitate socialization. After they were informed that heavy drinking might harm their child, many were able to stop drinking for the duration of the pregnancy.

Women in the symptom relief phase were psychologically dependent on alcohol to alter mood and perception and to relieve a variety of symptoms, particularly depression. They required both counseling and assistance with the many problems they confronted during pregnancy before they could reduce drinking.

Women in the syndrome phase had developed a physiological tolerance and dependency on alcohol and demonstrated early signs of the withdrawal syndrome when they stopped drinking. Detoxification on an inpatient basis was indicated in order to reduce the risk of physiological disturbances that could adversely affect the pregnancy. Therapy should continue after delivery for women in the symptom relief and syndrome phases.

Psychotropic drugs were rarely prescribed because of uncertainties concerning harmful effects on the fetus. Chlordiazepoxide was utilized for one week to modify symptoms of alcohol withdrawal in two patients, with no adverse effects. Disulfiram (Antabuse) was not prescribed during pregnancy because of the hazards described in Section 10.

Our pilot observations, described in Section 6, suggested that abstinence or marked reduction of alcohol use during the third trimester of pregnancy lowers the risk to offspring. Programs established to assist pregnant women to reduce alcohol use can build on the strong concern that pregnant women have for their unborn children. There was great variability between heavy drinkers in patterns of alcohol use, in terms of types of beverages, rates of consumption, and intervals between drinking episodes. Some women also spontaneously varied alcohol use at different stages of their pregnancy. High blood alcohol concentrations probably have different pathogenic effects at different stages of pregnancy.

Heavy drinking was associated with a continuum of prenatal risk factors, including heavy smoking, age, multiparity, and emotional stress. Participation in a program that focused on the reduction of alcohol use encouraged utilization of other health and social service agencies with multiple benefits for the mother and the offspring. Since regular prenatal appointments were scheduled for the same days as counseling sessions, the women who sustained the counseling relationship were also more likely to have any obstetrical problems promptly diagnosed and treated. Conversely, women who rejected health advice concerning alcohol probably were less likely to follow prenatal instruction about nutrition and other health issues. Since late gestation is the period when adverse factors have the greatest effect on fetal growth, cessation or marked reduction of alcohol consumption may facilitate growth and functional development (Rosett et al., 1978). The reduction of morphological abnormalities (possibly an artifact of small numbers) will be investigated further as more data become available.

Strategies for Prevention

National awareness of the potential danger that heavy drinking during pregnancy may pose for the fetus has been one goal of the National Institute on Alcohol Abuse and Alcoholism. This educational campaign has been endorsed by the American Medical Association and the American College of Obstetricians and Gynecologists. A brochure, "Alcohol and Your Unborn Baby," and a poster have been distributed by the National Clearinghouse for Alcohol Information (Sandmaier, 1978). A proposal to place labels on containers of alcoholic beverages warning of possible hazards during pregnancy was considered at a U.S. Senate hearing and supported by many groups (Alcohol Labeling, 1978). The plan is currently undergoing evaluation by the Bureau of Alcohol, Tobacco, and Firearms of the U.S. Treasury Department, which has regulatory authority. While a warning label will not change the behavior of many chronic alcoholics, a great many heavy social drinkers should respond with decreased alcohol consumption during pregnancy. In addition, a health warning would heighten the awareness of family and professionals in contact with pregnant women, providing another opportunity for early intervention.

The education of physicians, nurses, social workers, and others treating pregnant women requires more than the mere presentation of didactic information and research reports. Professionals must develop new attitudes toward women who drink heavily. They must learn that they cannot recognize them by appearance or socioeconomic characteristics. A thorough drinking history is essential and should be obtained from all patients during their initial history.

Traditional pessimism about the treatment of alcoholics must be replaced by interest and hope derived from experience with heavy-drinking pregnant women. When professionals have the opportunity to identify a previously unsuspected heavy drinker and observe her response to counseling, they become involved and optimistic. This reaction, in turn, improves their effectiveness with other patients.

Doctors and nurses often have sufficient skills to provide supportive counseling focused on the reduction of alcohol use. These professionals can provide practical help in dealing with difficult life situations through liaison with social service and alcoholism treatment agencies. Some women cannot reduce alcohol use without this direct assistance. Pregnant women who do not respond promptly should be referred to specialized treatment programs.

The ideal plan would be to initiate therapy with heavy-drinking women during pregnancy and continue to assist them with their alcohol problem as well as the tasks of motherhood. Abstinence or moderation of alcohol consumption would be facilitated by a supportive and educational approach dealing with parenthood and continuing through the first years of the baby's life. Disturbances in 24-hour sleep–awake distribution identified in infants exposed to ethanol *in utero* suggest that facilitating caretaking procedures might be developed (Rosett et al., 1979). For example, infants with sleep cycle disturbances may require darker and more quiet sleeping areas or might respond to a soothing voice or swaddling. Parents of a newborn with a poorly developed circadian rhythm could be prepared for the necessity of a greater sharing of responsibilities so that all in the family will obtain enough sleep.

The "Pregnancy and Health Program" described by Little et al. (1980) offers an informal physical facility with a relaxed emphasis on health, designed to reduce the fear and shame which accompany drinking problems. They contrast this with the atmosphere of many medical and alcoholism treatment facilities. Each approach may appeal to different target groups. Long-term results of various strategies need to be evaluated in order to design more effective programs.

12.   DIRECTIONS FOR FUTURE RESEARCH

Experimental research utilizing the various animal models of the fetal alcohol syndrome should produce basic knowledge of the etiologic mechanisms. Now that the teratogenic changes in humans have been reproduced in animals, a specialized investigation of effects on cells in vital organs such as brain, liver, heart, and kidney should be productive. Ultimately, the effects of ethanol on individual enzyme systems and regulators of cell organization will be investigated. Basic research on the fetal alcohol syndrome may also lead to further understanding of the mechanisms that link the effects of ethanol to the malignancy, hepatic disease, and neurological complications observed in adult alcoholics.

Animal models could be modified to examine effects of abstinence occurring at different stages of pregnancy. Some functional damage may be reversible if alcohol is discontinued while the fetus is not yet fully developed. Other potential prevention techniques should be studied in animals. These include supplementing diets with essential vitamins and trace elements to facilitate catch-up growth after alcohol consumption is discontinued.

Epidemiologic research should be designed to provide the data needed for the development of prevention programs. Careful attention to information on changes in individual drinking patterns during pregnancy may help explain why some offspring of alcoholic women escape damage. Binges should be described as carefully as possible in terms of the types and amounts of alcohol ingested, the duration of drinking, and the precise stage of the pregnancy. The development of affected offspring should be followed as long as possible so that parents can have more facts about the prognosis for each component of the fetal alcohol syndrome.

The pessimistic prognosis for FAS infants has developed from observations of the most severely affected offspring of chronic alcoholic women. Frequently, multiple compounding risk factors exist. Initial experience with infants born to women able to abstain or significantly reduce alcohol use in mid-pregnancy suggests that in some instances, rebound growth and physiological adaptation can compensate for early disruption. Long-term follow-up of children impaired by perinatal risk factors such as anoxia and prematurity suggests that in the less severely damaged infants, a facilitating environment can effect relatively normal developmental outcomes. Deviant development may result from severe insult to the organism's integrative mechanism or severe familial or social abnormalities that can prevent the restoration of normal growth processes.

Prevention approaches must be developed to effect early identification and reduction of alcohol use by heavy-drinking pregnant women. Particular techniques may be more effective in different settings with various ethnic and socioeconomic groups. Improvement of social supports during pregnancy and assistance with caregiving should be provided to help parents with children who overtax their emotional resources. Educational programs for adolescents should present facts about the fetal alcohol syndrome together with information on the changes in drinking patterns among adolescents (*Families* . . . , 1978). The fact that choices within the woman's control can improve her chances of having a healthy baby is the strongest motivation for improving lifestyles.

13. SUMMARY AND CONCLUSIONS

The adverse effects on offspring of heavy maternal alcohol consumption during pregnancy have been investigated by clinical, epidemiologic, and experimental methods.

Clinical observations on over 245 cases of FAS have been reported from medical centers around the world. The diagnosis of FAS should be restricted to children demonstrating signs of CNS dysfunction and prenatal and postnatal growth deficiency, together with characteristic facial anomalies. Some offspring of alcoholic mothers showed several characteristics of the FAS but failed to demonstrate a sign in each of the three areas. Since these signs are not specific for FAS, it is suggested that in the absence of the complete syndrome, the term *possible fetal alcohol effects* (FAE) should be used to describe these children.

Prospective epidemiologic studies to date have differed greatly in terms of sample size, the demographic and socioeconomic characteristics of the population, the methodology used to estimate maternal alcohol consumption, and the type of newborn examination. A French study of 9236 pregnancies showed that the consumption of more than 40 ml of absolute alcohol daily was associated with decreased birth weight and placental weight and with increased perinatal mortality, but no increase in malformations. A Boston study of 332 women showed that the 42 offspring of heavy drinkers (consumption of 6 drinks on some occasions and at least 45 drinks per month), when compared with those born to moderate drinkers or abstainers, demonstrated two or three times more congenital malformations, growth retardation, and functional abnormalities. However, no cases of the complete FAS were observed among the infants examined on the third day of life. The Seattle study compared 81 neonates born to women who consumed an average of one ounce or more of absolute alcohol daily or ingested five or more drinks on some occasions, and 82 matched controls. When the 163 infants were examined by dysmorphologists, two cases of the FAS and seven cases of FAE were identified among the offspring born to the heavier drinkers and two cases of FAE among the control group.

There are many problems in comparing the results of epidemiologic studies carried out by different research groups. Central are the methodological difficulties in precise determination of alcohol exposure during pregnancy. The volume, variability, and frequency of alcohol consumption must be carefully evaluated. Attention must be paid to changes in drinking patterns that occur throughout pregnancy. Some women binge, while others abstain for varying periods. Data on associated risk factors have been collected in several studies; however, only the French sample was large enough to permit measurement by appropriate statistical techniques of the independent effects of the alcohol. The lifestyles and health habits of women who drink heavily during pregnancy often differ from those of other pregnant women on a number of parameters that could adversely affect outcome. Therefore, it is not likely that any single study will be able to examine and control for all relevant risk factors.

Clinical observations and epidemiologic studies on several populations will have to be combined with experimental evidence from animal models. These have been developed in several species and permit precise measurement of dose at specific times during pregnancy. Animal models also permit control of confounding variables, such as maternal health, nutrition, smoking, age, and parity.

There is also evidence from animal studies that exposure to ethanol *in utero* may be associated with hyperactivity and impaired learning in the absence of dysmorphology. Observations on three-day-old infants born to heavy-drinking women suggest a disturbance of 24-hr sleep–awake state regulation. This finding is consistent with naturalistic observations and EEG abnormalities reported by other centers. The long-term effects of these abnormalities on development and mother–infant adaptation need to be investigated prospectively.

Variability in the effects of alcohol on pregnancy outcome is probably related to the multiple alterations of biochemistry and physiology that occur as a consequence of chronic alcohol use. Variability of blood alcohol concentrations at critical stages of pregnancy and individual differences in metabolic susceptibility can also affect outcome. During the first trimester of pregnancy, alcohol may affect the cell membrane and cell migration and alter the embryonic organization of tissue. During the second trimester, disturbances in the metabolism of carbohydrates, lipids, and proteins probably retard cell growth and division. At any particular time, the organ systems with the most rapid growth probably are most susceptible. During the third trimester, the brain may be the most sensitive organ, since this is the time of its rapid growth. Neurophysiological functioning in preparation for regulation of the neonate is also vulnerable.

Additional research is needed to delineate specific mechanisms and to develop specific prevention and treatment strategies. The present state of knowledge is sufficient to warrant general health advice. Physicians and other health professionals should be educated about the hazards of heavy drinking during pregnancy so that they can give appropriate advice to their patients. Professionals should be trained to obtain an adequate drinking history from all women of childbearing age. Women who report heavy drinking should be counseled and supported in their attempts to reduce alcohol consumption. Those who do not respond to counseling within a few weeks should be referred to more comprehensive therapeutic programs. On the basis of present knowledge, patients can be advised that the consumption of over 3 oz of absolute alcohol at any one time (six drinks) places the fetus at risk. While an occasional drink probably is of little consequence, we do not know if there is a safe level. Preliminary experience suggests that the reduction of alcohol consumption during pregnancy will improve a woman's chances of having a healthy baby. This knowledge, together with the interest and concern of those to whom the pregnant woman has turned for health care, is a powerful force for improving her health and that of her unborn child.

ACKNOWLEDGMENTS

This review is based on an earlier paper prepared under contract NIA 76-25 (P). Initial research was supported by ADAMHA Career Teacher Awards #TO1DA00031 (NIDA) and PHSAA07008 (NIAAA). Further research was supported in part by NIAAA Grant AA02446-01, the National Council on Alcoholism, the Massachusetts Developmental Disabilities Council, the United States Brewers Association, Inc., and both University Hospital and Boston City Hospital General Research Support Awards. I thank all my colleagues in the Maternal Health and Child Development Program at Boston City Hospital for continued support and sharing of ideas. Lyn Weiner has worked most closely and effectively on the prenatal clinic programs. I also wish to acknowledge the editorial assistance of Jill Marcus and Amy Rosett.

REFERENCES

Abel, E. L., 1974, Alcohol ingestion in lactating rats: Effects on mothers and offspring, *Arch. Int. Pharmacodyn. Ther.* **210**:121–217.
Abel, E. L., 1975, Emotionality in offspring of rats fed alcohol while nursing, *J. Stud. Alcohol* **36**:654–658.
Akesson, C., 1974, Autoradiographic studies on the distribution of ^{14}C-2-ethanol and its non-volatile metabolites in the pregnant mouse, *Arch. Int. Pharmacodyn. Ther.* **209**:296–304.
Alcohol Labeling and Fetal Alcohol Syndrome, 1978, Hearing before the Subcommittee on Alcoholism and Drug Abuse of the Committee on Human Resources, U.S. Senate, Jan. 31, 1978, U.S. Government Printing Office, Washington, D.C.
Anderson, W. J., 1978, Alcohol-induced effects in cerebellar development in the rat, *Alcoholism Clin. Exp. Res.* **2**:192.
Auroux, M., 1973, Influence, chez le rat, de la nutrition de la mère sur le développment tardif du système nerveux central de la progéniture. (Influence in the rat of the mother's nutrition on the late development of the central nervous system of the offspring) *C. R. Soc. Biol.* **167**:626–629.
Auroux, M., and Dehaupas, M., 1970, Influence de la nutrition de la mère sur le développement tardif du système nerveux central de la progéniture. (The influence of the mother's nutrition on the late development of the central nervous system in the offspring) *C. R. Soc. Biol.* **164**:1432–1436.
Badr, F. M., and Badr, R. S., 1975, Induction of dominant lethal mutation in male mice by ethyl alcohol, *Nature* **253**:134–136.
Barry, R. G. G., and O'Nuallain, S., 1975, Foetal alcoholism, *Ir. J. Med. Sci.* **144**:286–288.
Bauer-Moffett, C., and Altman, J., 1975, Ethanol-induced reductions in cerebellar growth of infant rats, *Exp. Neurol.* **48**:378–382.

Beskid, M., Majdecki, T., and Skladzinski, J., 1975, The effect of ethanol applied during gestation on the mitochondria of the hepatic cells of pups, *Folia Histochem. Cytochem.* 13:175–180.

Bierich, J. R., Majewski, F., Michaelis, R., and Tillner, I., 1976, Über das embryo-fetal Alkoholsyndrom. (On the embryo-fetal alcohol syndrome.) *Eur. J. Pediatr.* 121:155–177.

Bond, N. W., and DiGiusto, E. L., 1976, Effects of prenatal alcohol consumption on open-field behavior and alcohol preference in rats, *Psychopharmacologia* 46:163–168.

Branchey, L., and Friedhoff, A. J., 1973, The influence of ethanol administered to pregnant rats on tyrosine hydroxylase activity of their offspring, *Psychopharmacologia* 32:151–156.

Branchey, L., and Friedhoff, A. J., 1976, Biochemical and behavioral changes in rats exposed to ethanol in utero, *Ann. N.Y. Acad. Sci.* 273:328–330.

Brown, N. A., Goulding, E. H., and Fabro, S., 1979, Ethanol embryotoxicity: Direct effects on mammalian embryos *in vitro*, *Science* 206:573–575.

Burton, R., 1906 (*Democritus Junior*) *The Anatomy of Melancholy*, Vol. 1, Part I, Section 2, *Causes of Melancholy*, William Tegg, London. (Originally published, 1621.)

Cahalan, D., Cisin, I. H., and Crossley, H. M., 1969, *American Drinking Practices, A National Study of Drinking Behavior and Attitudes*, Rutgers Center of Alcohol Studies, New Brunswick, N.J.

Cantwell, D. P., 1972, Psychiatric illness in the families of hyperactive children, *Arch. Gen. Psychiatry* 27:414–417.

Cederbaum, A. I., Lieber, C. S., Beattie, D. S., and Rubin, E., 1975, Effect of chronic ethanol ingestion of fatty acid oxidation of hepatic mitochondria, *J. Biochem.* 250:5122–5129.

Chafetz, M. E., Blane, H. T., and Hill, M. J., 1971, Children of alcoholics: Observations in a child guidance clinic, *Q. J. Stud. Alcohol* 32:687–698.

Chernoff, G., 1977, A mouse model of the fetal alcohol syndrome, *Teratology* 15:223–230.

Christiaens, L., Mizon, J. P., and Delmarle, G., 1960, Sur la descendance des alcooliques. (On the offspring of alcoholics.) *Ann. Pediatr. (Paris)* 36:257–262.

Christoffel, K. K., and Salafsky, I., 1975, Fetal alcohol syndrome in dizygotic twins, *J. Pediatr.* 87:963–967.

Clarren, S. K., and Smith, D. W., 1978, The fetal alcohol syndrome, *N. Engl. J. Med.* 298:1063–1067.

Clarren, S. K., Alvord, E. C., Jr., Sumi, S. M., Streissguth, A. P., and Smith, D. W., 1978, Brain malformations related to prenatal exposure to ethanol, *J. Pediatr.* 92:64–67.

Coffey, T. G., 1966, Beer Street: Gin Lane; Some views of 18th-century drinking, *Q. J. Stud. Alcohol* 27:669–692.

Collard, M. E., and Chen, C. S., 1973, Effect of ethanol on growth of neonate mice as a function of modes of ethanol administration, *Q. J. Stud. Alcohol* 34:1323–1326.

Combemale, F., 1888, *La descendance des alcooliques*. (Offspring of alcoholics.) Thèse de Montpellier.

Cooperman, M. T., Davidoff, F., Spark, R., and Pallotta, J., 1974, Clinical studies of alcoholic ketoacidosis, *Diabetes* 23:433–439.

Dexter, J. D., Tumbleson, M. E., Decker, J. D., and Middleton, C. C., 1980, Fetal alcohol syndrome in Sinclair (S-1) miniature swine, *Alcohol Clin. Exp. Res.* 4:146–157.

Dobbing, J., 1974, The later growth of the brain and its vulnerability, *Pediatrics* 53:2–6.

Druse, M. J., and Hofteig, J. H., 1977, The effect of chronic maternal alcohol consumption on the development of central nervous system myelin subfractions in rat offspring, *Drug Alcohol Depend.* 2:421–429.

El-Guebaly, N., and Offord, D. R., 1977, The offspring of alcoholics: A critical review, *Am. J. Psychiatr.* 134:357–365.

Ellis, F. W., and Pick, J. R., 1976, Beagle model of the fetal alcohol syndrome (abstract), *Pharmacologist* **18:**190.

Ellis, F. W., and Pick, J. R., 1980, An animal model of fetal alcohol syndrome in beagles, *Alcohol Clin. Exp. Res.* **4:**123–134.

Families and Futures: Helping Self and Others, 1978 (Curriculum for high school students), Education Development Center, Newton, Mass.

Feldstein, A., 1971, Effect of ethanol on neurohumoral amine metabolism, in: *The Biology of Alcoholism,* Vol. 1, *Biochemistry* (B. Kissin and H. Begleiter, eds.), pp. 127–159, Plenum, New York.

Féré, C., 1894, Presentation de poulets vivants provenant d'oeufs ayant subi des injections d'alcool ethylique dans l'albumen. (Presentation of living chicks from eggs which had undergone ethanol injections in the albumen.) *C. R. Soc. Biol.* **46:**646.

Ferrier, P. E., Nicod, I., and Ferrier, S., 1973, Fetal alcohol syndrome, *Lancet* **2:**1496.

Flink, E. B., 1971, Mineral metabolism in alcoholism, in: *The Biology of Alcoholism,* Vol. 1, *Biochemistry* (B. Kissin and H. Begleiter, eds.), pp. 377–395, Plenum, New York.

Fuchs, A. R., 1966, The inhibitory effect of ethanol on the release of oxytocin during parturition in the rabbit, *J. Endocrinol.* **35:**125–134.

Fuchs, F., Fuchs, A. R., Poblete, V. F., Jr., and Risk, A., 1967, Effect of alcohol on threatened premature labor, *Am. J. Obstet. Gynecol.* **99:**627–637.

George, M. D., 1965, *London Life in the Eighteenth Century,* pp. 21–61, Capricorn, New York. (Originally published, 1925).

Gilbert, R. M., 1976, Caffeine as a drug of abuse, in: *Research Advances in Alcohol and Drug Problems,* Vol. 3 (R. J. Gibbins, Y. Israel, H. Kalant, R. E. Popham, W. Schmidt, and R. G. Smart, eds.), pp. 49–176, Wiley, New York.

Ginsburg, B. E., Yanai, J., and Sze, P. Y., 1975, A developmental genetic study of the effects of alcohol consumed by parent mice on the behavior and development of their offspring, Proc. 4th Annual Alcoholism Conference, NIAAA, pp. 183–204.

Goodwin, D. W., 1971, Is alcoholism hereditary? A review and critique, *Arch. Gen. Psychiatry* **25:**545–549.

Goodwin, D. W., Schulsinger, F., Hermansen, L., Guze, S. B., and Winokur, G., 1973, Alcohol problems in adoptees raised apart from alcoholic biological parents, *Arch. Gen. Psychiatry* **28:**238–243.

Goodwin, D. W., Schulsinger, F., Hermansen, L., Guze, S. B., and Winokur, G., 1975, Alcoholism and the hyperactive child syndrome, *J. Nerv. Ment. Dis.* **160:**349–353.

Gordon, G. G., Altman, K., Southren, A. L., Rubin, E., and Lieber, C. S., 1976, Effect of alcohol (ethanol) administration on sex-hormone metabolism in normal men, *N. Engl. J. Med.* **295:**793–836.

Greenhouse, B. S., Hook, R., and Hehre, F. W., 1969, Aspiration pneumonia following intravenous administration of alcohol during labor, *J. Am. Med. Assoc.* **210:**2393–2395.

Grenell, R. G., 1972, Effects of alcohol on the neuron, in: *The Biology of Alcoholism,* Vol. 2, *Physiology and Behavior* (B. Kissin and H. Begleiter, eds.), pp. 1–19, Plenum, New York.

Haggard, H. W., and Jellinek, E. M., 1942, *Alcohol Explored,* Doubleday, Garden City, N.Y.

Halkka, O., and Eriksson, K., 1977, The effects of chronic ethanol consumption on goniomitosis in the rat, in: *Alcohol Intoxication and Withdrawal: Experimental Studies,* Vol. 3 (M. M. Gross, ed.), pp. 1–6, Plenum, New York.

Hall, B. D., and Orenstein, W. A., 1974, Noonan's phenotype in an offspring of an alcoholic mother, *Lancet* **1:**680–681.

Hambidge, K. M., Walravens, P. A., Brown, R. M., Webster, J., White, S., Anthony, M., and Roth, M. L., 1976, Zinc nutrition of preschool children in the Denver Head Start program, *Am. J. Clin. Nutr.* **29:**734–738.

Hanson, J. W., Jones, K. L., and Smith, D. W., 1976, Fetal alcohol syndrome, experience with 41 patients, *J. Am. Med. Assoc.* **235:**1458.

Hanson, J. W., Streissguth, A. P., and Smith, D. W., 1978, The effects of moderate alcohol consumption during pregnancy on fetal growth and morphogenesis, *J. Pediatr.* **92:**457–460.

Havlicek, V., Childiaeva, R., and Chernick, V., 1977, EEG frequency spectrum characteristics of sleep states in infants of alcoholic mothers, *Neuropädiatrie* **8:**360–373.

Heinonen, O. P., Slone, D., Monson, R. R., Hook, E. B., and Shapiro, S., 1977, Cardiovascular birth defects and antenatal exposure to female sex hormones, *N. Engl. J. Med* **296:**67–70.

Henderson, G. I., and Schenker, S., 1977, The effect of maternal alcohol consumption on the viability and visceral development of the newborn rat, *Res. Comm. Chem. Pathol. Pharmacol.* **16:**15–32.

Henderson, G. I., Hoyumpa, A. M., Rothschild, M. A. and Schenker, S., 1980, Effect of ethanol and ethanol-induced hypothermia on protein synthesis in pregnant and fetal rats, *Alcohol Clin. Exp. Res.* **4:**165–177.

Heuyer, O., Misès, R., and Dereux, J. F., 1957, La descendance des alcooliques. (The offspring of alcoholics.) *Presse Méd.* **29:**657–658.

Hill, R. H., 1976, Fetal malformations and antiepileptic drugs, *Am. J. Dis. Child.* **130:**923–925.

Hill, R. H., Verniaud, W. M., Horning, M. G., McCulley, L. B., Morgan, N. F., and Houston, R. N., 1974, Infants exposed in utero to antiepileptic drugs, *Am. J. Dis. Child.* **127:**645–653.

Hillman, R. W., 1974, Alcoholism and malnutrition, in: *The Biology of Alcohol,* Vol. 3, *Clinical Pathology* (B. Kissin and H. Begleiter, eds.), pp. 513–581, Plenum, New York.

Ho, B. T., Fritchie, G. E., Idänpään-Heikkila, J. E., and McIsaac, W. M., 1972, Placental transfer and tissue distribution of ethanol-1-^{14}C: A radioautographic study in monkeys and hamsters, *Q. J. Stud. Alcohol* **33:**485–493.

Hodge, C. F., 1903, The influence of alcohol on growth and development, in: *Physiological Aspects of the Liquor Problem,* Vol. 1 (W. O. Atwater, J. S. Billings, H. P. Bowditch, R. H. Chittenden, and W. H. Welch, eds.), pp. 359–375, Houghton Mifflin, Boston.

Horiguchi, T., Suzuki, K., Comas-Urrutia, A. C., Mueller-Heubach, E., Boyer-Milic, A. M., Baratz, R. A., Morishima, H. O., James, L. S., and Adamsons, K., 1975, Effect of ethanol upon uterine activity and fetal acid-base state of the rhesus monkey, *Am. J. Obstet. Gynecol.* **122:**910–917.

Hurley, L. S., and Swenerton, H., 1966, Congenital malformations resulting from zinc deficiency in rats, *Proc. Soc. Exp. Biol. Med.* **123:**692–696.

Hurley, L. S., Gowan, J., and Swenerton, H., 1971, Teratogenic effects of short-term and transitory zinc deficiency in rats, *Teratology* **4:**199–204.

Ijaiya, K., Schwenk, A., and Gladtke, E., 1976, Fetales Alkoholsyndrom. (Fetal alcohol syndrome.) *Dtsch. Med. Wochenschr.* **101:**1563–1568.

Jackson, J. K., 1954, The adjustment of the family to the crisis of alcoholism, *Q. J. Stud. Alcohol* **15:**562–586.

Jacobson, S., Rich, J., and Tovsky, N., 1978, Retardation of cerebral cortical development as a consequence of the fetal alcoholic syndrome, *Alcohol. Clin. Exp. Res.* **2:**193.

Janz, D., 1975, The teratogenic risk of antiepileptic drugs, *Epilepsia* **16:**159–169.

Jewett, J. F., 1976, Alcoholism and ruptured uterus, *N. Engl. J. Med.* **294:**335–336.

Jones, K. L., and Smith, D. W., 1973, Recognition of the fetal alcohol syndrome in early infancy, *Lancet* **2:**999–1001.

Jones, K. L., Smith, D. W., Ulleland, C. N., and Streissguth, A. P., 1973, Pattern of malformation in offspring of chronic alcoholic mothers, *Lancet* **1:**1267–1271.

Jones, K. L., Smith, D. W., Streissguth, A. P., and Myrianthopoulos, N. C., 1974, Outcome in offspring of chronic alcoholic women, *Lancet* **1**:1076–1078.

Kalant, H., 1971, Absorption, diffusion, distribution, and elimination of ethanol: Effects on biological membranes, in: *The Biology of Alcoholism,* Vol. 1, *Biochemistry* (B. Kissin and H. Begleiter, eds.), pp. 1–62, Plenum, New York.

Kaminski, M., Rumeau-Rouquette, C., and Schwartz, D., 1976, Consommation d'alcool chez les femmes enceintes et issue de la grossesse. (Alcohol consumption among pregnant women and outcome of pregnancy.) *Rev. Epidémiol. Santé Publique* **24**:27–40.

Kesäniemi, Y. A., 1974, Metabolism of ethanol and acetaldehyde in intact rats during pregnancy, *Biochem. Pharmacol.* **23**:1157–1162.

Kesäniemi, Y. A., and Sippel, H. W., 1975, Placental and foetal metabolism of acetaldehyde in rat, *Acta. Pharmacol. Toxicol.* **37**:43–48.

Kissin, B., and Begleiter, H. (eds.), 1971, *The Biology of Alcoholism,* Vol. 1, *Biochemistry,* Plenum, New York.

Klassen, R. W., and Persaud, T. V. N., 1976, Experimental studies on the influence of male alcoholism on pregnancy and progeny, *Exp. Pathol.* **12**:38–45.

Kohila, T., Eriksson, K., and Halkka, O., 1976, Goniomitosis in rats subjected to ethanol, *Med. Biol.* **54**:150–151.

Kronick, J. B., 1976, Teratogenic effects of ethyl alcohol administered to pregnant mice, *Am. J. Obstet. Gynecol.* **124**:676–680.

Kuzma, J. W., and Phillip, R. L., 1977, Characteristics of drinking and non-drinking mothers, Presented at Fetal Alcohol Syndrome Workshop, San Diego, February 1977.

Landesman-Dwyer, S., Keller, L. S., and Streissguth, A. P., 1978, Naturalistic observations of newborns: Effects of maternal alcohol intake, *Alcohol. Clin. Exp. Res.* **2**:171–177.

Lau, C., Thadani, P. V., Schanberg, S. M., and Slotkin, T. A., 1976, Effects of maternal ethanol ingestion on development of adrenal catecholamines and dopamine-β-hydroxylase in the offspring, *Neuropharmacology* **15**:505–507.

Lemoine, P., Haronsseau, H., Borteryu, J.-P., and Menuet, J.-C., 1968, Les enfants de parents alcooliques: Anomalies observées à propos de 127 cas. (Children of alcoholic parents: anomalies observed in 127 cases.) *Ouest Med.* **25**:476–482.

Lindenbaum, J., 1974, Hematologic effects of alcohol, in: *The Biology of Alcohol,* Vol. 3, *Clinical Pathology* (B. Kissin and H. Begleiter, eds.), pp. 461–480, Plenum, New York.

Little, R. E., 1977, Moderate alcohol use during pregnancy and decreased infant birth weight, *Am. J. Public Health* **67**:1154–1156.

Little, R. E., Schultz, F. A., and Mandell, W., 1976, Drinking during pregnancy, *J. Stud. Alcohol* **37**:375–379.

Little, R. E., Streissguth, A. P., and Guzinski, G. M., 1980, Prevention of fetal alcohol syndrome: A model program, *Alcohol Clin. Exp. Res.* **4**:185–189.

Loiodice, G., Fortuna, G., Guidetti, A., Ria, N., and D'Elia, R., 1975, Considerazioni cliniche intorno a due casi de malformazioni congenite in bambini nati da madri affette da alcolismo cronico. (Clinical notes on two cases of congenital deformity in children born of chronic alcoholic mothers.) *Minerva Pediatr.* **27**:1891–1893.

Longo, L. D., 1977, The biologic effects of carbon monoxide on the pregnant woman, fetus, and newborn infant. *Am. J. Obstet. Gynecol.* **129**:69–103.

MacDowell, E. C., 1923, Alcoholism and the behavior of white rats, II, The maze behavior of treated rats and their offspring, *J. Exp. Zool.* **37**:417–456.

Majewski, F., Bierich, J. R., Loser, H., Michaelis, R., Leiber, B., and Bettecken, F., 1976, Zur Klinik and Pathogenese der Alkoholembryopathie. (Clinical aspects and pathogenesis of alcohol embryopathy.) *Münch. Med. Wochenschr.* **118**:1635–1642.

Mann, L. I., Bhakthavathsalan, A., Lui, M., and Makowski, P., 1975a, Effect of alcohol on fetal cerebral function and metabolism, *Am. J. Obstet. Gynecol.* **122**:845–851.

Mann, L. I., Bhakthavathsalan, A., Lui, M., and Makowski, P., 1975b, Placental transport of alcohol and its effect on maternal and fetal acid-base balance, *Am. J. Obstet. Gynecol.* **122**:837–844.

Manzke, H., and Grosse, F. R., 1975, Inkomplettes und komplettes des Alkohol-Syndrom: Bei drei Kindern einer Trinkerin. (Incomplete and complete alcohol syndrome: Three children of an alcoholic mother.) *Med. Welt* **26**:709–712.

Martin, J. C., Martin, D. C., Sigman, P., and Redow, B., 1977, Offspring survival, development, and operant performance following maternal ethanol consumption, *Dev. Psychobiol.* **10**:435–446.

Mau, G., and Netter, P., 1974, Kaffee- und Alkoholkonsum—Riskfactoren in der Schwangerschaft? (Are coffee and alcohol consumption risk factors in pregnancy?) *Geburtshilfe Frauenheilkd.* **34**:1018–1022.

Mayer, J., and Black, R., 1977, The relationship between alcoholism and child abuse/neglect, in: *Currents in Alcoholism,* Vol. 2 (F. A. Seixas, ed.), pp. 429–444, Grune & Stratton, New York.

Morrison, J. R., and Stewart, M. A., 1971, A family study of the hyperactive child syndrome, *Biol. Psychiatry* **3**:189–195.

Mulvihill, J. J., 1973, Caffeine as teratogen and mutagen, *Teratology* **8**:68–72.

Mulvihill, J. J., and Yeager, A. M., 1976, Fetal alcohol syndrome, *Teratology* **13**:345–348.

Mulvihill, J. J., Klimas, J. T., Stokes, D. C., and Risemberg, H. M., 1976, Fetal alcohol syndrome: Seven new cases, *Am. J. Obstet. Gynecol.* **125**:937–941.

Naeye, R. L., Blanc, W., and Paul, C., 1973, Effects of maternal nutrition on the human fetus, *Pediatrics* **52**:494–503.

Neville, J. N., Eagles, J. A., Samson, G., and Olson, R. E., 1968, Nutritional status of alcoholics, *Am. J. Clin. Nutr.* **21**:1329–1340.

Nichols, M. M., 1967, Acute alcohol withdrawal syndrome in a newborn, *Am. J. Dis. Child.* **113**:714–715.

Nicloux, M., 1899, Sur le passage de l'alcool ingéré de la mère au foetus, en particulier chez la femme. (Passage of alcohol ingested by the mother to the fetus, particularly in women.) *C. R. Soc. Biol.* **51**:980–982.

Nicloux, M., 1900, Passage de l'alcool ingéré de la mère au foetus et passage de l'alcool ingéré dans le lait, en particulier chez la femme. (Passage of alcohol ingested by the mother to the fetus and passage of alcohol ingested in milk, particularly in women.) *Obstétrique* **5**:97–132.

Noonan, J. A., 1976, Congenital heart disease in the fetal alcohol syndrome, *Am. J. Cardiol.* **37**:160.

Nora, A. H., Nora, J. J., and Blu, J., 1977, Limb-reduction anomalies in infants born to disulfiram-treated alcoholic mothers, *Lancet* **2**:664.

Obe, G., Jurgen-Ristow, H., and Herha, J., 1977, Chromosomal damage by alcohol in vitro and in vivo, in: *Alcohol Intoxication and Withdrawal: Experimental Studies,* Vol. 3 (M. M. Gross, ed.), pp. 47–70, Plenum, New York.

Ouellette, E. M., Rosett, H. L., Rosman, N. P., and Weiner, L., 1977, Adverse effects on offspring of maternal alcohol abuse during pregnancy, *N. Engl. J. Med.* **297**:528–530.

Palmer, H. P., Ouellette, E. M., Warner, L., and Leichtman, S. R., 1975, Congenital malformations in offspring of a chronic alcoholic mother, *Pediatrics* **53**:490–494.

Pearl, R., 1916, The effect of parental alcoholism (and certain other drug intoxications) upon the progeny in the domestic fowl, *Proc. Natl. Acad. Sci. USA* **2**:380–384.

Pierog, S., Chandavasu, O., and Wexler, I., 1977, Withdrawal syndrome in infants with the fetal alcohol syndrome, *J. Pediatr.* **90**:630–633.

Pikkarainen, P. H., and Räihä, N. C., 1967, Development of alcohol dehydrogenase activity in the human liver, *Pediatr. Res.* **1**:165–168.

Pilstrom, L., and Kiessling, K.-H., 1967, Effect of ethanol on the growth and on the liver and brain mitochondrial functions of the offspring of rats, *Acta Pharmacol. Toxicol.* **25**:225–232.

Rainey, J. M., Jr., 1977, Disulfiram toxicity and carbon disulfide poisoning, *Am. J. Psychiatry* **134**:371–378.

Randall, C. L., Taylor, W. J., and Walker, D. W., 1977, Ethanol-induced malformations in mice, *Alcohol. Clin. Exp. Res.* **1**:219–224.

Rapoport, J. L., Quinn, P. O., and Lamprecht, F., 1974, Minor physical anomalies and plasma dopamine-beta-hydroxylase activity in hyperactive boys, *Am. J. Psychiatry* **131**:386–409.

Rawat, A., 1975a, Effects of maternal ethanol consumption on the fetal and neonatal cerebral neurotransmitters, in: *The Role of Acetaldehyde in the Actions of Ethanol, Satellite Symposium, 6th International Congress of Pharmacology, Helsinki, 1975* (K. O. Lindros and C. J. P. Eriksson, eds.), The Finnish Foundation for Alcohol Studies, **23**:159–176.

Rawat, A., 1975b, Ribosomal protein synthesis in the fetal and neonatal rat brain as influenced by maternal ethanol consumption, *Res. Comm. Chem. Pathol. Pharmacol.* **12**:723–732.

Rawat, A. K., 1976a, Effect of maternal ethanol consumption on fetal hepatic metabolism in the rat, *Ann. N.Y. Acad. Sci.* **273**:175–187.

Rawat, A. K., 1976b, Effect of maternal ethanol consumption on foetal and neonatal rat hepatic protein synthesis, *Biochem. J.* **160**:653–661.

Reinhold, L., Hütteroth, H., and Schulte-Wisserman, H., 1975, Das fetale Alkohol-Syndrom: Fallbericht über 2 Geschwister. (The fetal alcohol syndrome: Case of two siblings.) *Münch Med. Wochenschr.* **117**:1731–1734.

Root, A. W., Reiter, E. O., Andriola, M., and Duckett, G., 1975, Hypothalamic–pituitary function in the fetal alcohol syndrome, *J. Pediatr.* **87**:585–587.

Rosett, H. L., 1974, Maternal alcoholism and intellectual development of offspring, *Lancet* **2**:218.

Rosett, H. L., 1980, A clinical perspective of the fetal alcohol syndrome, *Alcohol and Clin. Exp. Res.* **4**:119–122.

Rosett, H. L., Ouellette, E. M., Weiner, L., and Owens, E., 1977, The prenatal clinic: A site for alcoholism prevention and treatment, in: *Currents in Alcoholism,* Vol. 1 (F. A. Seixas, ed.), pp. 419–430, Grune & Stratton, New York.

Rosett, H. L., Ouellette, E. M., Weiner, L., and Owens, E., 1978, Therapy of heavy drinking during pregnancy, *Obstet. Gynecol.* **51**:41–46.

Rosett, H. L., Snyder, P., Sander, L. W., Lee, A., Cook, P., Weiner, L., and Gould, J., 1979, Effects of maternal drinking on neonate state regulation, *Dev. Med. Child Neurol.* **21**:464–473.

Rosett, H. L., Weiner, L., Zuckerman, B., McKinlay, S., and Edelin, K. C., 1980, Reduction of alcohol consumption during pregnancy with benefits to the newborn, *Alcohol Clin. Exp. Res.* **4**:172–184.

Rosman, N. P., and Malone, M. J., 1974, An experimental study of the fetal alcohol syndrome, *Abstr. Neurology (Minneapolis)* **24**:377.

Rothstein, P., and Gould, J. B., 1974, Born with a habit: Infants of drug-addicted mothers, *Pediatr. Clin. North Am.* **21**:307–321.

Russell, M., 1977, Intrauterine growth in infants born to women with alcohol-related psychiatric diagnoses, *Alcohol. Clin. Exp. Res.* **1**:225–231.

Sameroff, A. J., and Chandler, M. J., 1975, Reproductive risk and the continuum of caretaking casuality, in: *Review of Child Development Research,* Vol. 4 (F. D. Horowitz, ed.), pp. 187–243, University of Chicago Press, Chicago.

Sander, L. W., Snyder, P. A., Rosett, H. L., Lee, A., Gould, J. B., and Ouellette, E. M., 1977, Effects of alcohol intake during pregnancy on newborn state regulation: A progress report, *Alcohol. Clin. Exp. Res.* **1**:233–241.

Sandmaier, M., 1978, *Alcohol and Your Unborn Baby*, U.S. Department of Health, Education, and Welfare, DHEW Pub. No. (ADM)78-521.

Sandor, S., and Amels, D., 1971, The action of ethanol on the prenatal development of albino rats, *Rev. Roum. Embryol. Cytol. Ser. Embryol.* **8**:105–118.

Sandor, S., and Elias, S., 1968, The influence of aethyl-alcohol on the development of the chick embryo, *Rev. Roum. Embryol. Cytol. Ser. Embryol.* **5**:51–76.

Saule, H., 1974, Fetales Alkohol-Syndrom: Ein Fallbericht. (Fetal alcohol syndrome: One case.) *Klin. Paediatr.* **186**:452–455.

Schaefer, O., 1962, Alcohol withdrawal syndrome in a newborn infant of a Yukon Indian mother, *Can. Med. Assoc. J.* **87**:1333–1334.

Seixas, F. A., Williams, K., and Eggleston, S. (eds.), 1975, Medical consequences of alcoholism, *Ann. N.Y. Acad. Sci.* **252**:399.

Seppälä, M., Räihä, N. C., and Tamminen, V., 1971, Ethanol elimination in a mother and her premature twins, *Lancet* **1**:1188–1189.

Shaywitz, B. A., Klopper, J. H., and Gordon, J. W., 1976, A syndrome resembling minimal brain dysfunction (MBD) in rat pups born to alcoholic mothers, *Pediatr. Res.* **10**:451.

Shruygin, G. I., 1974, Ob osobennostyakh psikhicheskogo razvitiya detei ot materie, stradayushchikh khronicheskim alkogolizmom. (Characteristics of the mental development of children of alcoholic mothers.) *Pediatriya (Moscow)* **11**:71–73.

Silber, A., Gottschalk, W., and Sarnoff, C., 1960, Alcoholism in pregnancy, *Psychiatr. Q.* **34**:461–471.

Skosyreva, A. M., 1973, Vliyaniye etilovogo spirta na razvitiye embrionov stadii organogeneza. (Effect of ethyl alcohol on the development of embryos at the organogenesis stage.) *Akush. Ginekol. (Moscow)* **4**:15–18.

Sokol, R. J., Miller, S. I., and Reed, G., 1980, Alcohol abuse during pregnancy: An epidemiological model, *Alcohol Clin. Exp. Res.* **4**:135–145.

Stockard, C. R., 1910, Influence of alcohol and other anaesthetics on embryonic development, *Am. J. Anat.* **10**:369–392.

Stoewsand, G. S., and Anderson, J. L., 1974, Influence of wine intake on mouse growth, reproduction and changes in triglyceride and cholesterol metabolism in offspring, *J. Food Sci.* **39**:957–961.

Stokes, P. E., 1974, Alcohol-endocrine interrelationships, in: *The Biology of Alcohol*, Vol. 1, *Biochemistry* (B. Kissin and H. Begleiter, eds.), pp. 397–436, Plenum, New York.

Streissguth, A. P., Herman, C. S., and Smith, D. W., 1978, Intelligence, behavior and dysmorphogenesis in the fetal alcohol syndrome: Report on 20 patients, *J. Pediatr.* **92**:363–367.

Streissguth, A. P., Barr, H. M., Martin, D. C., and Herman, C. S., 1980, Effects of maternal alcohol, nicotine and caffeine use during pregnancy on infant mental and motor development at eight months, *Alcohol Clin. Exp. Res.* **4**:152–164.

Sullivan, L. W., and Herbert, V., 1964, Suppression of hematopoiesis by ethanol, *J. Clin. Invest.* **43**:2048–2062.

Sullivan, L. W., 1967, Folates in human nutrition, in: *Newer Methods of Nutritional Biochemistry*, Vol. 3 (A. A. Albanese, ed.), pp. 365–406, Academic, New York.

Sullivan, W. C., 1899, A note on the influence of maternal inebriety on the offspring, *J. Ment. Sci.* **45**:489–503.

Sze, P. Y., Yanai, J., and Ginsburg, B. E., 1976, Effects of early ethanol input on the activities of ethanol metabolizing enzymes in mice, *Biochem. Pharmacol.* **25**:215–217.

Tenbrinck, M. S., and Buchin, S. Y., 1975, Fetal alcohol syndrome: A report of a case, *J. Am. Med. Assoc.* **232**:1144–1147.

Tewari, S., and Noble, E. P., 1975, Chronic ethanol ingestion by rodents: Effects on brain RNA, in: *Alcohol and Abnormal Protein Biosynthesis: Biochemical and Clinical* (M. A. Rothschild, M. Oratz, and S. S. Schreiber, eds.), pp. 421–448, Pergamon, New York.

Tewari, S., Fleming, E. W., and Noble, E. P., 1975, Alterations in brain RNA metabolism following chronic ethanol ingestion, *J. Neurochem.* **24**:561–569.

Thadani, P. V., Lau, C., Slotkin, T. A., and Schanberg, S. M., 1977a, Effect of maternal ethanol ingestion on neonatal rat brain and heart ornithine decarboxylase, *Biochem. Pharmacol.* **26**:523–527.

Thadani, P. V., Lau, C., Slotkin, T. A., and Schanberg, S. M., 1977b, Effects of maternal ethanol ingestion on amine uptake into synaptosomes of fetal and neonatal rat brain, *J. Pharmacol. Exp. Ther.* **200**:292–297.

Thadani, P. V., Slotkin, T. A., and Schanberg, S. M., 1977c, Effects of late prenatal or early postnatal ethanol exposure on ornithine decarboxylase activity in brain and heart of developing rats, *Neuropharmacology* **16**:289–293.

Tissot-Favre, M., and Delatour, P., 1965, Psychopharmacologie et teratogenèse à propos du disulfirame: Essai expérimental. (Psychopharmacology and teratogenicity of disulfiram: An experimental study.) *Ann. Méd. Psychol.* **1**:735–740.

Truitt, E. B., and Walsh, M. J., 1971, The role of acetaldehyde in the actions of ethanol, in: *The Biology of Alcohol,* Vol. 1, *Biochemistry* (B. Kissin and H. Begleiter, eds.), pp. 161–195, Plenum, New York.

Tze, W. J., and Lee, M., 1975, Adverse effects of maternal alcohol consumption on pregnancy and foetal growth in rats, *Nature* **257**:479–480.

Tze, W. J., Friesen, H. G., and MacLeod, P. M., 1976, Growth hormone response in fetal alcohol syndrome, *Arch. Dis. Child.* **51**:703–706.

Ulleland, C., Wennberg, R. P., Igo, R. P., and Smith, N. J., 1970, The offspring of alcoholic mothers, *Pediatr. Res.* **4**:474.

U.S. Department of Health, Education, and Welfare, 1973, *The health consequences of smoking,* January 1973, DHEW Pub. No. (HSM)73-8704.

Van Thiel, D. H., Gavaler, J. S., and Lester, R., 1977, Ethanol: A gonadal toxin in the female, *Drug Alcohol Depend.* **2**:373–380.

Vitale, J. J., and Coffey, J., 1971, Alcohol and vitamin metabolism, in: *The Biology of Alcoholism,* Vol. 1, *Biochemistry* (B. Kissin and H. Begleiter, eds.), pp. 327–352, Plenum, New York.

Wagner, G., and Fuchs, A. R., 1968, Effect of ethanol on uterine activity during suckling in post-partum women, *Acta Endocrinol. (Copenhagen)* **58**:133–141.

Waldrop, M. F., and Halverson, C. F., 1971, Minor physical anomalies and hyperactive behavior in young children, in: *The Exceptional Infant,* Vol. 2 (J. Hellmuth, ed.), pp. 343–380, Brunner/Mazel, New York.

Wallgren, H., and Barry, H., 1970, *Actions of Alcohol,* Vol. 2, Elsevier, Amsterdam, pp. 482–489.

Walravens, P. A., and Hambidge, K. M., 1975, Growth of infants fed a zinc supplemented formula, *Pediatr. Res.* **9**:310.

Waltman, R., and Iniquez, E. S., 1972, Placental transfer of ethanol and its elimination at term, *Obstet. Gynecol.* **40**:180–185.

Warner, R., and Rosett, H. L., 1975, The effects of drinking on offspring: An historical survey of the American and British literature, *J. Stud. Alcohol* **36**:1395–1420.

Williams, H. L., and Salamy, A., 1973, in: *The Biology of Alcoholism,* Vol. 2, *Physiology and Behavior* (B. Kissin and H. Begleiter, eds.), pp. 436–483, Plenum, New York.

Wilson, K. H., Landesman, R., Fuchs, A. R., and Fuchs, F., 1969, The effect of ethyl alcohol on isolated human myometrium, *Am. J. Obstet. Gynecol.* **104**:436–439.

Yanai, J., and Ginsburg, B. E., 1976, Audiogenic seizures in mice whose parents drank alcohol, *J. Stud. Alcohol* **37**:1564–1571.

17

The Effects of Opiates, Sedative–Hypnotics, Amphetamines, Cannabis, and Other Psychoactive Drugs on the Fetus and Newborn

LORETTA P. FINNEGAN and KEVIN O'BRIEN FEHR

1. INTRODUCTION

Over the past 20 years, the medical and nonmedical use of psychoactive agents has markedly increased in the United States as well as in other countries. Sir William Osler's statement, made in the 19th century, still seems applicable: "The desire to take medicine is, perhaps, the greatest feature which distinguishes man from animals" (Cushing, 1925).

Since the 1960s, the nonmedical use of opiates and other psychoactive drugs has reached epidemic proportions. The medical use of psychotropic drugs, which are frequently prescribed for the treatment of emotional and other disorders, is also increasing. Balter and Levine (1973) reported that during the year 1970 a total of 214 million prescriptions for psychotropics was filled in U.S. pharmacies, at a retail cost of $972 million. These prescriptions accounted for approximately 17% of the total of 1.3 billion prescriptions for all drugs used in the United States in that year. In 1973, the total of all prescriptions amounted to 2.8 billion (Rucker, 1974); therefore, psychoactive drug use may also have doubled between 1970 and 1973 to at least 450 million prescriptions, if the ratio of psychoactive drug prescriptions to total prescriptions has remained constant.

Twice as many women as men use prescribed psychotropics in the

LORETTA P. FINNEGAN ● Department of Pediatrics, Thomas Jefferson University, Philadelphia, Pennsylvania.   KEVIN O'BRIEN FEHR ● Addiction Research Foundation, Toronto, Ontario.

United States and Canada as well as in other countries (Cooperstock, 1976). Several factors may account for this trend. Women tend to seek help from doctors more frequently than men (Parry, 1968; Cooperstock, 1976) and present with symptoms of anxiety and generalized discomfort (Cooperstock, 1976). Parry (1968) also suggested that women make less use of alternative substances such as alcohol in dealing with stress.

Over-the-counter (i.e., nonprescription) drug use is also prevalent. The National Marijuana Commission survey in the United States revealed that 56% of adults and 20% of youth experienced the effects of one or more psychoactive over-the-counter drugs within the period of the survey. In addition, the use of tobacco, an agent recognized as a major health hazard and known to produce dependence, remains prevalent in the United States despite legally restricted advertising. Gritz (this volume) states that in 1975 approximately 28% of married women were tobacco smokers.

With this growing drug use, many investigators and clinicians have become interested in the hazard of exposing the human fetus to drugs. Most clinicians have advocated the avoidance of all but essential medications in pregnancy and in the potentially pregnant woman, even though it has been difficult to prove that certain commonly used drugs can directly cause fetal disorders or malformations. Although many drugs continue to be prescribed by physicians, the vast majority of pharmacologic agents used in pregnancy are self-prescribed by the obstetrical patient. A recent study of 67 private patients in the last trimester of pregnancy revealed that each mother took an average of 4.5 drug preparations (including combinations) for a total of 8.7 different drug entities during the period of study. Of these drugs, 80% were taken without a doctor's supervision or knowledge. The remaining 20% were prescribed by a physician. The drugs included vitamin preparations (86% of the patients), aspirin (69%), antacids (60%), diuretics (30%), cathartics (26%), antibiotics (16%), antihistamines (14%), and barbiturates (12%) (Bleyer and Breckenridge, 1970).

Peckham and King (1963) reported that a series of pregnant women received an average of 3.6 drugs during pregnancy, and 4% received 10 or more drugs. In another series (Nora et al., 1967), the average rose to 6.3 per patient. Hill (1973) reported that gravid women from a middle socioeconomic population received 10.3 drugs, with a range from 3 to 29 drugs. These did not include vitamins, iron, intravenous fluids, anesthetic agents, or tobacco, or exposure to pesticides, paints, chemicals, radiation, or alcohol. The greatest incidence of fetal drug exposure occurred between 24 and 36 weeks' gestation and again during labor and delivery. Multiple drugs frequently were ingested concomitantly. Forfar and Nelson

(1973) in Edinburgh found from a survey of 911 pregnant women that, excluding iron, drugs were prescribed for 82% of women during pregnancy with an average of four drugs each; 65% took drugs not prescribed by their doctor. The drugs most often used were those for analgesia and relief of anxiety.

During pregnancy, emotional disturbances occur that are related to the mother's physical or psychological condition. A factor such as an undesirable pregnancy will obviously strongly influence the mother's state of mind. With the widespread medical use of psychoactive drugs reported by Balter and Levine (1973), it can be assumed that many pregnant women receive these agents.

In Baltimore, the nonmedical use of drugs was studied in a group of 100 adolescents of a low socioeconomic class who were entering prenatal care (Young et al., 1977). Careful histories revealed the following incidence of drug intake: heroin or methadone —3%; barbiturates–depressants —8%; marijuana—10%; tobacco—50%; and alcohol—25% (Young et al., 1977).

Schardein (1976) discussed the many ways in which drugs could affect reproduction and development. These include drug-induced alterations of sexual behavior, infertility due to inhibition of ovulation or prevention of implantation, impaired parturition, lactation failure, maternal neglect of the offspring, and direct embryotoxicity. The latter may be reflected by an increase in the incidence of fetal or neonatal deaths, growth retardation, malformations, or functional deficits. In addition, many psychoactive drugs can produce passive physical dependence in the fetus, with the subsequent appearance of an abstinence syndrome in the newborn.

This chapter reviews the effects of psychoactive agents on the fetus and the neonate, with emphasis on the effects of nonmedically used drugs. The opiates, the amphetamines, cannabis, and the hallucinogens are discussed in detail, and the nonopiate depressants, the tranquilizers, the antihistamines, nicotine, and caffeine are also mentioned. The fetal alcohol syndrome is discussed by Rosett in this volume. The relationship between the use of these agents during pregnancy and congenital malformations has been reviewed in detail elsewhere (Schardein, 1976), and therefore, it is discussed only briefly here. Since the possibility of drug-induced chromosomal aberrations has recently been the subject of much concern, the chromosome studies are also discussed. The review also focuses on some of the pharmacologic factors affecting the response of the fetus to psychoactive drugs, the clinical management of the opiate-dependent mother and her child, the neonatal abstinence syndrome, and the long-term effects of *in utero* drug exposure on development and behavior.

2. GENERAL PHARMACOLOGY

Response of the Pregnant Woman to Drugs

In the gravid female, metabolic and functional parameters undergo considerable change, and therefore drug disposition is modified (Eriksson et al., 1973). Unfortunately, information about the nature of this modification is minimal despite the high intake of drugs throughout gestation. Tetracycline in high doses has been reported to cause hepatic dysfunction, azotemia, and even death when used for the treatment of pyelonephritis in pregnant and early postpartum patients.

Very little is known about the absorption of drugs, although the absorption of certain nutrients seems to be enhanced during pregnancy. Total serum protein concentrations, especially albumin, decrease in pregnancy. The binding capacity for sulfisoxazole and Congo red is also lower in pregnant women at term. Eriksson et al. (1973) suggested that this reduction is due to both hypoalbuminemia and an increased occupation of binding sites by endogenous material. Decreased drug binding would lead to an increase in the proportion of free to total drug, tending to increase the risk of drug toxicity. This change, however, would tend to be counterbalanced by the increase in total body water (Eriksson et al., 1973), which would increase the volume of distribution and therefore lower the drug concentration. The increase in glomular filtration rate of up to 40% (Lindheimer and Katz, 1977) would also be expected to lower free drug concentration by enhancing the rate of renal excretion of drugs.

Studies of drug biotransformation capacity *in vitro* by tissue from pregnant rats have shown a decrease in oxidative and reductive pathways, whereas sulfatation is increased. The mechanism behind these changes during pregnancy is not fully understood, though it may be related to the known hormonal changes. Increased levels of reduced progesterone derivatives may inhibit the activities of certain drug hydroxylases in the maternal liver. Although the effects are not completely clear, results of the administration of exogenous estrogens and progesterones have varied according to the structure of the compound under consideration and the duration of treatment (Eriksson et al., 1973). Inhibition of drug biotransformation would tend to delay excretion and thus increase the drug exposure and risk of toxicity. It is clear that pharmacokinetics are altered during pregnancy in a complex manner. The pharmacokinetics and the dose–response relationship of each drug must be reevaluated separately in pregnant and nonpregnant women before any conclusions regarding increased risk of toxicity can be drawn.

Response of the Placenta to Drugs

Many of the rate-limiting processes that modulate the transplacental passage of pharmacologic agents are poorly understood, and some have probably not been identified. Relevant characteristics of the placenta and the drugs passing through it include lipid solubility, degree of drug ionization, molecular weight, placental blood flow, placental metabolism of drugs, protein binding of drugs, and aging of the placenta (Mirkin, 1973b).

The membranes of placental cells are generally assumed to be similar to other mammalian cell membranes, in which lipids and lipoproteins are important constituents that largely determine membrane permeability to drugs. Compounds possessing a high degree of lipid solubility, or those with large lipid:water partition coefficients, generally permeate the placenta readily. Psychoactive drugs, which usually possess enough lipid solubility to reach the brain rapidly, belong to this class. Drugs penetrate biological membranes more rapidly when in their un-ionized state and much less rapidly when highly ionized. Compounds whose molecular weights are less than 600 readily traverse the placenta, whereas those exceeding 1000 do not. Most therapeutically effective agents have molecular weights ranging from 250 to 400 and thus would appear to meet this criterion (Mirkin, 1973b).

The mechanisms involved in the transfer of both exogenous and endogenous substances across the placenta include simple diffusion, facilitated diffusion, active transport, and special processes. In simple diffusion, substances cross the placenta from a region of higher to one of lower concentration at a rate that depends on molecular size, ionic dissociation, and lipid solubility. In this case, drugs with high lipid solubility and low ionic strength diffuse rapidly, as in the case of several barbituric acid derivatives. Facilitated diffusion occurs in proportion to the concentration gradient but is accelerated by a carrier system, such as that for glucose and other sugars. With active transport, the movement takes place against an electrochemical gradient and requires energy in the form of adenosine triphosphate (ATP). Other substances are transferred across the placenta only after metabolic conversion by it. Generally, though, any substance, if present in sufficient concentration on the maternal side, eventually reaches the fetus (Ginsburg, 1971).

The transfer of highly lipid soluble drugs is proportional to placental blood flow in a manner analogous to the relationship between alveolar ventilation and the uptake of volatile anesthetic agents. The effect of fetal circulation on drug transfer must also be considered. If circulation is impaired secondary to heart failure, erythroblastosis fetalis, or drug intoxication (e.g., local anesthetics), it will significantly decrease drug transfer rates between the maternal and fetal compartments. Placental circulation may be impaired by the vasoconstricting effects of some drugs. *In vitro,* the opiates (such as meperidine, morphine, and codeine) and hallucinogens (such as LSD) have this effect (Ciuchta and Gautieri, 1964). If vasoconstriction occurs *in vivo,* it could restrict the amount of nutrients and oxygen reaching the fetus and thus adversely affect development.

Many therapeutic agents can be metabolized by placental homogenates *in vitro.* The overall significance of these reactions in the intact maternal–fetal placental unit still remains to be defined (Mirkin, 1973b).

Agents that are tenaciously bound to plasma proteins are probably transferred less rapidly across the placenta than those less tightly bound, because the proportion of free to total drug present at any time is significantly lower. Other types of binding may affect the transfer of drugs across biological membranes, particularly if the agent in question has a relatively high affinity for components present within a specific tissue. Thus drug binding may lead to unusual and unanticipated drug distribution patterns (Mirkin, 1973b).

As the placenta matures, the thickness of its trophoblastic epithelium decreases. This decrease should lead to an increase in the rate of diffusion of drug molecules. Unfortunately, there is little information in this area, although several studies suggest that drugs cross the rodent placenta more rapidly in early than in late pregnancy (Mirkin, 1973b).

Response of the Fetus to Drugs

Disposition of pharmacologic agents in the maternal–fetal placental unit represents a complex series of pharmacodynamic processes. These processes operate in an integrated manner so that multiple kinetic events occur simultaneously in both the maternal and fetal environment. The major part of the blood in the umbilical vein of the fetus appears to pass directly through the liver rather than into the vena cava through the ductus venosus. The fetal brain receives a much greater proportion of the cardiac output than the infant brain. Consequently, tissue concentrations of a drug in the fetus may vary from those observed in the newborn infant. The distribution of a drug is also dependent on the extent of its binding to protein (Krasner et al., 1973).

The pharmacologic effect of a drug depends on its interaction with the active site of the tissue i.e., the receptor. McMurphy and Boréus (1968) used isolated ileums from human fetuses (12–24 weeks old) and showed that autonomic receptors are present and functional during the second trimester.

The effect of drug metabolism is to render nonpolar substances more water-soluble, facilitating their excretion into the urine and/or feces. Oxidation, reduction, or hydrolysis, sometimes followed by conjugation to different substrates, is involved in this biotransformation. Metabolism of most compounds takes place in the microsomal fraction of the liver, though other tissues have some activity when tested *in vitro*. Human fetal tissues in mid-gestation have the capacity to oxidize as well as to reduce several drug substrates. Recent observations have shown that human fetal liver microsomes contain the necessary electron transport components (NADPH-specific cytochrome P-450 reductase and cytochrome P-450) for drug hydroxylation reactions. Oxidation of several drugs and endogenous substrates such as testosterone and laurate has been demonstrated in human fetal liver preparations *in vitro*. These results are in marked contrast to the reported lack of cytochrome P-450 or P-450-dependent drug hydroxylation reactions in liver microsomes from fetuses of a wide variety of animal species, even at comparatively late stages of gestation. Rane and Sjökvist (1972) suggested that this discrepancy might be due either to species differences or to induction of the human fetal liver enzymes by exposure to exogenous compounds during the long period of gestation. Evidence of hydroxylation and of drug conjugation reactions (acetylation, glycine conjugation, sulfate transfer) has been found in the placenta and in tissues of the human fetus other than the liver, including the adrenal gland, although the significance of this finding remains unclear. Several highly active sulfatase enzymes are present in the placenta, and these, together with sulfurylation capability, may represent an extremely important mechanism for regulating fetal drug distribution as well as placental drug movement (Yaffe, 1974).

The Response of the Neonate to Drugs

Prior to delivery, the fetus is frequently exposed to drugs that are administered to the mother for the treatment of preexisting diseases, pregnancy-related disorders, or labor pains. No assistance is given to the infant in the metabolism and excretion of drugs once the umbilical cord is cut. Burmeister (1970) reviewed several factors that affect the response of the newborn to drugs. These include absorption, volume of distribution, plasma binding, receptor sensitivity, biotransformation, and excretion. Differences in drug absorption between the neonate and the adult are not consistent, and they depend on the route of administration and the physicochemical properties of the drug (Morselli, 1977). For example, the absorption of phenobarbital from the gastrointestinal tract is delayed in the newborn, while diazepam is absorbed rapidly after oral or intra-muscular administration.

In the newborn infant, total body water is much greater than in an adult and varies from 85% of body weight in small premature infants to 70% in full-term infants. The extracellular volume is approximately 40% of the body weight in comparison with 15–20% in the adult. Fat content is lower in the premature (1%) than in the normal full-term infant (15%). These variations in body composition cause differences in drug distri-bution (Burmeister, 1970).

Neonatal and adult plasma show considerable differences in the protein binding of drugs, due not only to a lower concentration of plasma protein in the neonate but also to qualitative differences in the binding properties. During the first few days of life, endogenous substances, such as hormones and free fatty acids, may occupy binding sites, thus reducing drug-binding capacity. Drugs with a high protein affinity, such as salicy-lates or phenytoin, may displace bilirubin from plasma albumin. This effect is important to the neonate, since the unbound fraction of drugs or of endogenous substances is free to cross membranes and therefore exert its action.

Receptors in the newborn infant do seem to be functionally active, and there is an apparent positive correlation between the degree of function and the gestational age and birth weight (Burmeister, 1970). Studies of drug metabolism in newborn animals suggest a low or absent activity for most pathways, with certain exceptions such as reduction, sulfatation, and hydroxylation of steroids. In human newborns, there is generally a lower elimination rate than in adults and older children (Vest and Rossier, 1963). In addition, the conjugating and oxidizing capacities of the neonate seem to be somewhat immature, although greater than in newborn animals. The low biotransformation activity is not due to insufficient cofactor availability and may be stimulated by induction during gestation (Klinger, 1977).

The majority of drugs, whether biotransformed or not, are removed from the body by renal excretion. Kidney function has not yet reached its full development in the newborn infant. The glomerular filtration rate of the neonate, as indicated by inulin clearance, is significantly lower than in adults. Their active tubular secretion rate of many substances is also lower than in adults. In addition, the renal excretion mechanisms for water and electrolytes are not fully developed, and acid base balance is not fully efficient during the newborn period (Braunlich, 1977).

From the above, one can see that the newborn infant who has been exposed to pharmacologic agents at or prior to birth is somewhat at a disadvantage in regard to the utilization, metabolism, and excretion of these substances.

Fetal Developmental Anomalies

Birth defects, which may be manifested by morphological, biochemical, or behavioral abnormalities, have a variety of causes. Yaffe (1974) estimated that 25% of human malformations can be attributed to genetic factors, 3% to chromosomal aberrations, and 3% to environmental factors such as maternal infection, radiation, and drug administration. The etiology of the remaining 69% is still unknown. Drugs and other environmental agents could potentially induce these anomalies in several ways. Genetic damage in either the parental germinal cells or in the fetus could occur as a result of drug exposure prior to or during pregnancy. Drug administration during pregnancy can interfere with the development of the fetus (teratogenicity) or produce signs of toxicity in the fetus similar to those observed in the adult (fetal toxicity).

Chromosomal Damage. The observations of chromatid- and chromosome-type aberrations in the peripheral leukocytes of street drug users have recently become a matter of considerable concern. Underlying this concern is the speculation that chromosome damage in peripheral leukocytes may reflect aberrations in the chromosomes of the germ cells, which may lead to increased incidences of fetal wastage or congenital malformations. Before the significance of these observations can be estimated, the following questions must be answered: Are drug-induced chromosomal aberrations in peripheral leukocytes reversible? Are they correlated with damage to the germinal chromosomes? If they are correlated, is germinal chromosome damage manifested by fetal development anomalies?

Although the biological significance of the chromosome studies is unclear, they have been included in this review because of their potential importance.

Teratology. *Teratogenicity* refers to a drug's ability to induce a birth defect when administered during gestation. These abnormalities may be detected at birth or later. The teratogenic potential of a drug depends on the following four principles: the nature of the agent and its access to the fetus; the time of its action; the level and duration of its dosage; and the genetic constitution of the fetus. During the preimplantation period, which, in the human, comprises the first two weeks following conception, the developing embryo is generally considered relatively resistant to environmental influences. If damage occurs during this period, it will probably be severe and cause the death of the embryo with subsequent abortion. There will also be an increased incidence of abnormalities in the aborted fetuses (Eriksson et al., 1973). In man, approximately Days 13–56 of gestation are considered the organ-forming period, and the type of malformation observed at this time will be closely related to the state of development at the time of drug exposure. Sensitivity periods for various organ systems in humans include: nervous system, 15–25 days; heart, 20–40 days; limbs, 24–46 days (Eriksson et al., 1973).

Maturation continues in all organs after the first trimester, but most extensively in the genital apparatus, the teeth, and the central nervous system. For this reason, drug effects on the CNS may be induced prenatally following the first trimester and may not become apparent until much later during postnatal life or adulthood. For example, behavioral changes of various types have been observed in animals following treatment *in utero* during middle and late pregnancy with tranquilizers and sex hormones (Joffe, 1969). During this period, most adverse drug effects observed in other organs are similar to those observed in adults and are usually termed *fetal toxicity*.

When different results are obtained under identical environmental influences, one must consider genetic makeup as an important factor. Drug sensitivity varies among species, strains, and individuals. For example, a significant percentage of mothers who took thalidomide during the susceptible period did not give birth to children with malformations (Eriksson et al., 1973).

Dosage is important when considering the teratogenicity of a specific drug. The teratogenic dose lies between two extremes: a low one, which may cause temporary impairment, and a high one producing fetal death. However, in most cases, the teratogenic zone is narrow and the dose–effect curve has a steep slope. If the drug is given more than once, the total drug exposure (i.e., both dose and treatment duration) must be considered. Repeated dosage can result in enzyme induction or inhibition with consequent alteration of the plasma concentration and therefore changes in effect (Eriksson et al., 1973). Also, drugs with a long half-life can accumulate in body tissues if administration is repeated at short intervals.

Drug Interactions

It was previously stated that many individuals are currently using a variety of drugs simultaneously. These include prescription drugs, illicit street drugs, and self-administered over-the-counter medications. The failure to make periodic reviews of the drugs currently being taken by patients, the use of multicomponent preparations, and the administration of two or more drugs simultaneously for the treatment of a single disorder all contribute to multiple drug use. In clinical practice as well as in the field of addiction, there has therefore been a growing awareness of the occurrence of drug interactions and their consequences.

The term *drug interaction* refers to the modification of the effects of one drug by the prior or concurrent administration of another drug or drugs. This definition may be expanded to include the interaction of drugs with endogenous hormones or other body constituents, components of the diet, substances present in the environment (such as pesticides), and the interference of drugs with diagnostic tests (Mallov, 1977).

When drug interactions occur in the pregnant woman, one must be concerned about the potential effects on the growing fetus and, if they occur at term, on the neonate. The expected result of a given drug regimen may be altered quantitatively and sometimes qualitatively by administration or withdrawal of another agent, so that optimal therapy does not occur. Also, drug toxicity that was not previously present may occur when the second medication is added or removed, with possible harm to the patient. It has been estimated that 20% of all adverse drug reactions are due to drug interactions (Mallov, 1977).

Mallov (1977) has reviewed in detail a host of interactions that have been identified among medications administered in the field of obstetrics. Some of the interactions involving psychoactive drugs are described here because of their significance not only for the pregnant woman but also for the fetus and the neonate.

Psychoactive drugs may interact by means of one or more of several different mechanisms. A drug can either change the sensitivity of the CNS to another drug, or it can alter the pharmacokinetics, and thus the resulting brain levels, of another drug by affecting such processes as biotransformation or protein binding.

Drugs with similar effects tend to potentiate each other. Thus, severe CNS depression can occur when two or more of the central depressants (barbiturates, opiates, alcohol, general anesthetics, tranquilizers, antihistamines, cannabis, and other sedatives) are administered simultaneously. For example, opiate analgesics potentiate the central nervous system depression produced by other classes of drugs, and this synergism may lead to severe respiratory depression, hypothermia, coma, and death. Severe respiratory depression and atelectasis may occur if an opiate and a skeletal muscle relaxant are administered at the same time, for example, morphine and *d*-tubocurarine; the central respiratory depression produced by the opiate adds to the neuromuscular blocking action of the skeletal muscle relaxant. Some phenothiazines reduce the amount of opiate required to produce a given level of analgesia, while others do the opposite, although they enhance the sedative effects (Mallov, 1977).

The opiate antagonists interact with the opiates by interfering with the binding of the opiate with the opiate receptor. This interference can lead to the precipitation of severe withdrawal symptoms in the opiate-addicted mother or newborn. Physicians must be cautioned that in the truly opiate-dependent pregnant woman, narcotic antagonists are contraindicated at the time of birth regardless of how large an amount of opiates she may be using. Only if the mother has overdosed (i.e., taken more than the amount of drug to which she is tolerant) will the fetus manifest depression from opiates. In this case, opiate antagonists are helpful, but the physician must be aware that immediately on administration, the newborn infant will begin prompt and severe withdrawal symptoms that will need treatment.

As stated previously, a drug may affect the blood level of a second drug by enhancing or inhibiting its biotransformation. For example, acute intake of alcohol inhibits pentobarbital biotransformation in humans, while chronic ethanol ingestion enhances it as a result of enzyme induction (Pirola, 1977). The administration of a metabolizable barbiturate to a patient who has recently consumed an alcoholic beverage may result in unexpectedly severe depression of the central nervous system, both because of the direct effect of the two agents on the system and because the metabolism of the barbiturate is inhibited. These effects are especially detrimental to the fetus, who will suffer distress because of the depressant effects of the drug interaction (Mallov, 1977). On the other hand, the administration of a barbiturate to a chronic alcoholic may produce less sedation than anticipated because of the development of cross-tolerance in the central nervous system itself, as well as an enhanced rate of barbiturate biotransformation. Many other psychoactive drugs, including the barbiturates, the tranquilizers, and the antihistaminics, can induce hepatic enzymes and thus increase the rate of metabolism of a variety of endogenous and exogenous compounds. These include the oral anticoagulants, steroids, griseofulvin, and phenylbutazone.

In general, then, because of the tendency of pregnant women to ingest multiple drugs, it is not enough merely to consider the effects of a specific agent. One must also be aware of *interactions* between those agents that have been prescribed for health reasons and those nonprescribed psychoactive drugs that the woman may be taking.

3. EFFECTS OF CNS DEPRESSANTS

In view of the multitude of drugs used in general therapeutics, as well as those in common illicit use, this review is focused on those agents most commonly self-prescribed or used nonmedically. CNS depressants in this class include the opiate and nonopiate analgesics, the antinauseants and antihistaminics, and the sedative–hypnotics and minor tranquilizers.

The Opiates

Medical Complications.   The therapeutic use of the opiate analgesics in pregnancy, mainly for the relief of pain during labor, may increase the incidence of neonatal morbidity. Currently, morphine is not as frequently used as meperidine hydrochloride, a potent synthetic analgesic. The newborn may have respiratory depression and apnea following the administration of meperidine to the mother two to four hours prior to delivery (Campbell et al., 1961). Pentazocine, another synthetic analgesic, produces a degree of pain relief similar to that produced by meperidine, but it also causes an equal respiratory depression in the newborn. One must always consider the drug interactions previously mentioned when these analgesics are used during labor concomitantly with street drugs or other prescribed medications given to the mother. As previously mentioned, additive effects may cause severe depression in the newly born infant (Mallov, 1977).

Opiate dependence in the pregnant woman has an overwhelming effect not only on her own physical condition but also on that of the fetus and eventually the newborn infant. The vast majority of opiate-dependent women neglect health care in general, and nearly three-quarters of heroin addicts never see a physician during their pregnancy. Therefore, these women are predisposed to a host of medical and obstetrical complications that affect their well-being as well as that of the unborn fetus. Frequently encountered medical complications include anemia, cardiac disease (often secondary to subacute bacterial endocarditis), cellulitis, poor dental hygiene, diabetes mellitus, edema, hepatitis, hypertension, phlebitis, pneumonia, and tuberculosis. Urinary tract infection is common, including cystitis, urethritis, and pyelonephritis. Because a considerable number of women use prostitution as a means of supporting their drug habit, venereal disease is common, including condyloma acuminatum, gonorrhea, herpes simplex, and syphilis. Therefore, nearly 40–50% of drug-dependent women observed in the prenatal period demonstrate medical complications (Connaughton et al., 1977).

Malnutrition presents another complication to the maternal–fetal unit. The lack of proper food intake that leads to nutritional deficiencies in alcoholics and drug addicts is largely due to drug inhibition of the central mechanism that controls appetite and hunger. Furthermore, toxic responses to alcohol, barbiturates, or opiates may contribute to malnutrition by interfering with the absorption or utilization of ingested nutrients. Lack of adequate nutrition, or possibly malabsorption, may lead to iron and folic acid deficiency and thereby result in anemia (Jones, 1974).

Obstetrical Complications.   The obstetrical complications associated with heroin addiction include abortion, abruptio placentae, amnionitis, breech presentation, increased need for Cesarean section, chorioamnionitis, eclampsia, intrauterine death, gestational diabetes, placental insufficiency, postpartum hemorrhage, preeclampsia, premature labor, premature rupture of membranes, and septic thrombophlebitis. One or more of these complications occurred during the pregnancies of 33% of 63 heroin-dependent women who had had no prenatal care. About 10–15% of these women had toxemia of pregnancy and 50% delivered prematurely (Connaughton et al., 1977). The authors suggested that uterine irritability secondary to drug withdrawal due to the intermittent supply of heroin may have accounted for the increased incidence of prematurity. Methadone maintenance and prenatal care in a second group of patients reduced the incidence of obstetrical complications and prematurity to about 23% and 16%, respectively, essentially the same as in a group of 75 non-drug-exposed women receiving adequate prenatal care.

Chromosome Studies.   Many investigators have been concerned that drug abuse may possibly produce irreversible chromosome damage that could be deleterious to the fetus. Amarose and Norusis (1976) studied the cytogenetics of methadone-managed and heroin-addicted pregnant women and their newborn infants. They assessed chromosomal damage in cultured leukocytes obtained prenatally and at delivery from 99 addicted pregnant women (80 from a methadone maintenance program and 19 heroin addicts) and their 101 offspring at delivery. About 10% of the 27,907 cells scored showed some type of chromosomal aberration excluding gaps. Chromosome damage was observed randomly in any chromosome of any particular cell and was mainly of the acentric fragment type. The percentage of hypodiploidy was significantly higher than the percentage of hyperdiploidy. The dosage and duration of methadone treatment or the years of heroin abuse did not affect chromosomal aberration rates in either the mother or the infant. Although the authors implied that the 10% aberration rate was higher than normal, no data from a matched group of control subjects were reported. This is an important point, since in various laboratories the percentage of chromosome breaks in control unexposed subjects ranged from 0–12% (Dishotsky et al., 1971). In an earlier study, the same group (Amarose and Shuster, 1971) observed an aberration rate of 7.8% in 22 male control subjects, and it is unclear whether the 10% rate in the former study is significantly higher.

Abrams (1975) studied chromosomal aberrations in the peripheral lymphocytes of infants exposed *in utero* to heroin or methadone and of infants exposed to no drug at all. The infants exposed predominantly to heroin showed a significant increase in the frequency of aberrations. About 10% of the cells demonstrated abnormalities as opposed to 1.6% in the control group. The methadone-exposed infants demonstrated no significant increase in the percentage of aberrant cells as compared with controls. However, in both drug-exposed groups, chromosomal rearrangements were detected that led the author to suspect that heroin and methadone can induce chromosome damage *in vivo*.

In both of these studies, the opiate use was compounded by the presence of poor nutrition; lack of rest; stress; increased incidence of tuberculosis, hepatitis, and syphilis; and a lack of early and consistent prenatal care. These compounding factors together with simultaneous polydrug abuse make it impossible to isolate either methadone or heroin as a causative agent. In addition, and as stated previously, the biological significance of opiate-induced chromosome damage, if it does occur, is not really understood.

Fetal Complications. Since the quality control of illicit drugs is obviously very poor, the dose consumed by the street drug user is usually unknown. For this and other reasons, these users frequently experience repeated episodes of withdrawal and overdose. In the pregnant user, opiate withdrawal has been associated with the occurrence of stillbirth. Severe withdrawal is associated with increased muscular activity, which in its turn increases the metabolic rate and oxygen consumption of the pregnant woman. Since fetal activity also increases during maternal withdrawal, the oxygen needs of the fetus can be assumed to increase. The oxygen reserve in the intervillous space of the placenta may not be able to supply the extra oxygen needed by the fetus. During labor, contractions compromise the blood flow through the uterus and consequently have an effect on the oxygen reserve in the intervillous space. The longer and stronger the contractions, the more compromised the circulation through the uterus. If labor coincides with abstinence symptoms in the mother, the increased oxygen needs of the withdrawing fetus will coincide with a period of variable uterine blood flow. Hypoxia and possibly death may occur in the fetus if it is exposed to an environment of insufficient oxygen for any length of time. As the fetus grows older, the metabolic rate and oxygen consumption are greater; therefore, a pregnant woman undergoing severe abstinence symptoms during the latter part of pregnancy is less likely to supply the withdrawing fetus with the oxygen it needs than an addict in the first trimester of pregnancy (Rementería and Nunag, 1973).

Naeye (1965) studied other fetal complications of maternal heroin addiction and found that nearly 60% of the mothers or their newborn infants showed evidence of acute infection. Most of the infected mothers were delivered prematurely, whereas those not affected went to term. The placentas of the heroin-exposed infants commonly revealed meconium histiocytosis, suggesting that they had experienced episodes of distress during fetal life, perhaps related to episodes of heroin withdrawal.

Many investigators have noted that infants born to heroin-addicted mothers are, as a group, small for gestational age (Gruenwald, 1963; Sussman, 1963; Naeye, 1965; Zelson et al., 1971; Finnegan et al., 1972; Glass, 1974; Newman, 1974), with all of their organs affected. Naeye suggested that periodic episodes of heroin withdrawal during pregnancy might restrict fetal growth by reducing uterine or placental blood flow. However, this explanation is unlikely since the organ and cell growth pattern associated with fetal growth retardation in uteroplacental disorders is quite different from that observed in the offspring of heroin addicts. Others have suspected that the low birth weights are due to poor maternal nutrition and health. While these factors may play a role, they do not provide a full explanation. In nonaddicted women, undernutrition restricts both the size and the number of cells in many fetal organs, especially the adrenal glands, the liver, and adipose tissue, during the last trimester. In contrast, the smallness of these organs in infants exposed to heroin in the third trimester is due mainly to a subnormal number of cells. Moreover, growth retardation is still evident in the offspring of addicts even when the mothers are matched with nonaddicts in the same nutritional categories.

Indeed, there is some laboratory evidence that heroin itself may be a factor in growth retardation (Taeusch et al., 1973; Smith et al., 1974; Hutchings et al., 1976; Zagon and McLaughlin, 1977). However, the mechanism for inhibition of growth by heroin is not known. Several investigators have noted that infants born to women who have used methadone have somewhat higher birth weights than infants born to women using heroin (Zelson, 1973; Connaughton et al., 1975; Kandall et al., 1976).

An analysis of birth weights of 337 neonates in relation to history of maternal opiate use was undertaken by Kandall et al. (1976). The mean birth weight of infants born to mothers abusing heroin during the pregnancy was 2490 g, an effect primarily of intrauterine growth retardation. Low mean birth weight (2615 g) was also seen in infants born to mothers who had abused heroin only prior to this pregnancy and mothers who had used both heroin and methadone during the pregnancy (2535 g). It is unclear how heroin use prior to conception could affect fetal weight. Infants born to mothers on methadone maintenance during the pregnancy had significantly higher mean birth weights (2961 g) than the heroin-exposed infants, but lower than the control group (3176 g). A highly significant relationship was observed between maternal methadone dosage in the first trimester and birth weight: the higher the dosage, the larger the infant. In addition to the fact that heroin has been found to cause fetal growth retardation that may persist beyond the period of addiction, this study has shown that methadone may promote fetal growth in a dose-related fashion after maternal use of heroin. The authors suggested that methadone may act by producing hormone-mediated alterations in carbohydrate metabolism either in the mother or in the fetus.

In contrast to the opiate-induced effects on fetal growth, the incidence of congenital abnormalities does not appear to be significantly higher among the infants exposed *in utero* to opiates than among unexposed infants (Schardein, 1976). A few sporadic cases of malformation have been observed after prenatal exposure to heroin, morphine, or propoxyphene, but there has been no discernible pattern of defects. Eleven larger studies reviewed by Schardein (1976) reported no significant increase in the incidence of congenital anomalies in infants exposed *in utero* to either heroin or methadone.

Neonatal Morbidity. Because of the extremely high risk situation in which the pregnant heroin-dependent woman is placed, her infant is predisposed to a host of neonatal problems. The majority of medical complications seen in these neonates reflect the fact that they are prematurely born, and therefore such conditions as asphyxia neonatorum, intracranial hemorrhage, hyaline membrane disease, intrauterine growth retardation, hypoglycemia, hypocalcemia, septicemia, and hyperbilirubinemia are seen in more than 80% of these infants. In contrast, infants born to women who receive methadone maintenance are more apt to have higher birth weights and a decreased incidence of premature birth, and their medical complications generally reflect (1) the amount of prenatal care that the mother has had; (2) whether she has suffered any particular obstetrical or medical complications, including toxemia of pregnancy, Rh hemolytic disease, hypertension, and infection; and, most importantly, (3) multiple drug use, which may have contributed to an unstable intrauterine milieu complicated by withdrawal and overdose. The latter situation is extremely hazardous in that it predisposes to fetal meconium staining and subsequent aspiration pneumonia in the newborn, which in itself causes a marked morbidity and increased mortality (Connaughton et al., 1977). Over three-quarters of infants born to heroin addicts without prenatal care, as well as those born to methadone-dependent women with insignificant prenatal care, suffered neonatal morbidity. This morbidity was somewhat decreased in infants born to methadone-dependent women who had significant prenatal care. Mean duration of hospitalization varied in these two groups of infants between 17 days (methadone-exposed infants) and 27 days (heroin-exposed infants).

The majority of infants born to drug-dependent women undergo abstinence symptoms of varying degree and duration. Over the past decade, drugs other than the opiate analgesics have been shown to produce abstinence symptoms in newborns. The neonatal abstinence syndrome is described later in this chapter, and the drugs involved are considered.

Neonatal Mortality. With the increase in obstetrical and medical complications, the lack of prenatal care, and the increase in low-birth-weight infants, it is not surprising to find a marked increase in mortality among infants born to opiate-dependent women. Twenty years ago, when neonatologists lacked the techniques to care for the very-low-birth-weight infant, the majority of infants born to opiate-dependent women were reported not to survive. With the advent of newer techniques for the care of sick newborn infants, mortality rates have markedly decreased to about 3–4.5% (Zelson et al., 1971).

Available data on 278 infants born to opiate-dependent women and 1586 control infants from the general population born at the same hospital revealed an increased incidence of low birth weight and neonatal mortality in the former (Finnegan et al., 1977a). Among the offspring of heroin- and methadone-dependent mothers (the latter a stratified group of women having inadequate and adequate prenatal care), there was an overall mortality incidence of 5.4%, while in controls it was 1.6%. For low-birth-weight infants, mortality in the opiate-dependent population was 13.3% and in the controls, 10.0%. There was a marked difference between the methadone-dependent groups with and without adequate prenatal care, revealing a significantly higher neonatal mortality in the latter. Overall mortality in the two groups was 3% and 10%, respectively, versus 4.8% in the heroin-dependent group. The same trend was found in the mortality rates seen in the low-birth-weight infants. In general, the causes of neonatal mortality can be ascribed to the overall lack of health care that the pregnant opiate-dependent woman undergoes, with the subsequent onset of premature labor, resulting in the birth of a low-weight infant and all of the initial sequelae secondary to premature birth. In this study, causes of mortality included those that were seen in low-birth-weight infants as well as those seen when perinatal asphyxia occurs. These data revealed that comprehensive care for pregnant opiate-dependent women significantly reduced the morbidity and mortality in both the mother and the infant.

Specific neuropathological studies were done on 10 of the infants in the previous study (Rorke et al., 1977). Detailed neuropathological examination revealed eight categories of lesions, three of which were thought to bear some relationship to the maternal drug dependence. (These latter lesions have not been seen in severely ill control infants of similar gestational ages.) These included gliosis (5/10), foci of old infarction (4/10), and retardation of brain development (3/10). Only minor microscopic brain malformations were found in three cases. Other lesions identified included those common to high-risk neonates: germinal plate hemorrhage (7/10), acute brain necrosis with and without hemorrhage (5/10), germinal plate cysts (4/10), and focal subarachnoid hemorrhages (3/10). Single instances of vascular and arachnoidal proliferation (1/10) and a posterior poliomyelitis (1/10) completed the spectrum of abnormalities in these infants. This evidence suggests that the majority of the adverse effects resulting from opiate addiction may be due to nonspecific secondary gestational complications. Nevertheless, several aspects of neuropathological findings suggest that there are, in addition, primary and specific effects of the addictive drugs on the developing nervous system. Further studies, including those that utilize an animal model, are necessary to define the effect of maternal opiate addiction on the nervous system of the neonate.

Sudden Infant Death Syndrome. Sudden unexpected death in infancy, otherwise known as crib death, has been defined as "the sudden death of an infant or a young child unexpected by history in which a thorough post mortem examination fails to demonstrate an adequate cause for death" (Valdes-Dapena et al., 1973). A review of the literature (Pierson et al., 1972; Harper et al., 1973; Rajegowda et al., 1976; Finnegan et al., 1977a) suggests an association between methadone and sudden infant death syndrome. However, whether the effect is direct or indirect is not yet clear. Various hypotheses suggesting drug effect on the autonomic nervous system, neonatal abstinence syndrome and its subsequent treatment, chronic fetal hypoxia, and infection are strongly supported by the findings in these cases. The incidence of sudden infant death syndrome in infants of opiate-dependent women is further detailed in Table 1. Kahn et al. (1969) reported one case of the sudden infant death syndrome among 38 infants born to heroin-dependent mothers. A more careful study of the previous cases as well as future cases is essential in order to clarify the causal or contributory role of opiate use during pregnancy.

Care of the Pregnant Opiate Addict. Many authors have reported the previously described effects of perinatal addiction (Finnegan and MacNew, 1974; Strauss et al., 1974; Fraser, 1976; Yacavone et al., 1976; Connaughton et al., 1977; Kandall et al., 1977). These, and many others not listed here, have made recommendations as to the care of the pregnant opiate-dependent woman. The majority recommend methadone

Table 1. Incidence of Sudden Infant Death Syndrome (SIDS) in
Infants of Opiate Dependent Women

Investigator	Total infants (N)	SIDS (N)	Incidence of SIDS (%)
Kahn et al. (1969)	38	1	2.6
Pierson et al. (1972)	14	3	21.4
Harper et al. (1973)	244	4	1.6
Rajegowda et al. (1976)	383	8	2.1
Finnegan and Reeser (1978)	349	5	1.4
Total	1024	21	2.1

maintenance and adequate prenatal care. Connaughton et al. (1977) described a comprehensive approach in the care of 278 pregnant opiate-dependent women and their infants in the Family Center Program at Thomas Jefferson University in Philadelphia. This program—encompassing medical, psychosocial, obstetrical, and addiction management, including methadone maintenance—significantly reduced maternal and infant morbidity theretofore associated with pregnancies complicated by opiate addiction. Most significantly, the incidence of low birth weight was reduced to 20%, and there was a decrease in the incidence of severe withdrawal syndrome in the infants born to mothers in the comprehensive care program.

Kandall et al. (1977) studied 230 infants born to opiate-dependent women and 33 infants born to ex-addicts between the years 1971 and 1974. They found that heroin abuse declined, while methadone use increased during those years. Methadone maintenance treatment during pregnancy was associated with more consistent prenatal care, more normal fetal growth, and reduced fetal mortality, compared with continued heroin abuse. Meconium staining of amniotic fluid was increased in the heroin and the heroin–methadone groups, but this increase was not associated with an increase in meconium aspiration or a reduction in Apgar scores. Infants born to former heroin addicts who were free of narcotic use during pregnancy also showed severe intrauterine growth retardation. In this study, the neonatal withdrawal syndrome from methadone appeared to be more severe than that of heroin, but the severity of the withdrawal syndrome did not correlate with late pregnancy maternal methadone dosage. Of particular interest in the study was that neonatal seizures occurred in 1.5% of the heroin group and 10% of the methadone group.

Additional findings concerning various groups of methadone-maintained women and heroin-dependent women in comparison to control

populations have been described (Finnegan, 1976), showir
that methadone maintenance with adequate prenatal car
improve the prognosis of the unborn fetus as well as the ne

Experimental Studies

Teratology. With the use of animal models, several investigators
have attempted to clarify the relationship between maternal opiate
exposure, teratogenesis, and perinatal development.

Teratogenic effects of opiates have been reported in hamsters after
prenatal treatment with heroin (Geber and Schramm, 1969b) and morphine (Geber, 1970) and in mice after treatment with morphine (Harpel
and Gautieri, 1968; Iuliucci and Gautieri, 1971). The anomalies most
commonly observed were exencephaly and other brain abnormalities,
but doses in the order of 200 mg/kg were necessary to produce these
effects. The teratogenic actions of morphine could be blocked by nalorphine and cyclazocine (Harpel and Gautieri, 1968) and potentiated by
antihistaminics (Iuliucci and Gautieri, 1971). Increases in infant mortality
and decreases in fetal size and rates of postnatal growth have been
reported by a number of groups after prenatal treatment with lower
doses of morphine ($<$ 50 mg/kg) (Davis and Lin, 1972; Friedler and
Cochin, 1972; Sobrian, 1977). Treatment of male rats with morphine or
methadone prior to mating can produce similar effects in the offspring
(Smith and Joffe, 1975).

Hutchings et al. (1976) administered methadone hydrochloride orally
to four groups of pregnant rats on Days 8–22 of gestation. Methadone,
particularly at higher dose levels, reduced maternal weight gain during
pregnancy and increased both maternal mortality and total mortality
among the young (resorptions plus stillbirths). Birth weight covaried with
dose level and litter size: the 5-, 10-, and 15-mg/kg dosage yielded litter
sizes comparable to, or somewhat smaller than, controls, but with lower
birth weights; the 20-mg dosage yielded the smallest litter sizes, but with
birth weights greater than any other treated or control group. Blood
levels were dose-related and corresponded to those found in human
subjects receiving daily maintenance doses of approximately 30, 60, and
100 mg respectively.

It therefore appears that large doses of the opiates are necessary to
induce congenital abnormalities in animal models. Smaller doses that
produce blood levels comparable to those observed in human users can
produce symptoms of fetal toxicity, such as decreased birth weights and
increased perinatal mortality. These observations are in good agreement
with the clinical findings.

Behavioral Teratology. The offspring of pregnant rats treated with
morphine demonstrate postnatal hyperactivity manifested by transient

increases in spontaneous motor activity. This effect has been observed at 15–25 days of age (Sobrian, 1977) and at 70 days of age (Davis and Lin, 1972).

Zagon and McLaughlin (1977) studied the effects of pre- and perinatal exposure to methadone on body growth and brain development in the rat. Body weights were reduced in drug-treated mothers during gestation and the first two weeks of lactation. At birth, no differences in gestation time, weight of offspring, litter size, or infant mortality were recorded. However, methadone-treated offspring grew more slowly than controls. From birth to Day 21, brain weight and length, cerebral width, and cerebellar weight and width were generally smaller in methadone-exposed rats. It appeared from these results that maternal methadone treatment retards the growth of young rats and affects brain development.

These studies, therefore, suggest adverse effects of prenatal opiate exposure on the growth and development of young rats. Much further work is needed in this area.

Nonopiate Analgesics

Salicylates. Aspirin (acetylsalicylic acid) is the most frequently used nonopiate analgesic. Up to 80% of all women have been said to take aspirin sometime during pregnancy (Eriksson et al., 1973). In addition, in a study of 272 consecutive deliveries, 10% of all newborns had measurable amounts of salicylate in cord blood (Palmisano and Cassady, 1969).

Experimental Studies. The teratology of the salicylates has been reviewed by Schardein (1976). Most salicylates are embryotoxic and teratogenic in mice and rats, at high doses (250 mg/kg), giving rise primarily to skeletal defects. Observations in other species are inconsistent. It has been demonstrated that the metabolite salicylic acid is responsible for the teratogenic effects.

In a developmental study, Butcher et al. (1972) observed that the offspring of rats treated with 250 mg/kg aspirin on Days 8–10 of gestation made more errors than control offspring in a water-filled multiple T-maze when tested at 50 days of age. This deficit was not accompanied by anatomical abnormalities of the CNS, although minor skeletal anomalies and a significant reduction in fetal weight were observed in the treated group.

Clinical Studies. In an Australian survey, Collins and Turner (1975) found that 6.6% of all patients attending an antenatal clinic were taking salicylate preparations regularly. This group had an increased incidence of anemia, antepartum and postpartum hemorrhage, complicated deliveries, and perinatal mortality. Turner and Collins (1975) observed no increase in the incidence of congenital abnormalities in the infants of 144 mothers who took salicylates regularly during pregnancy. However, the birth weights of the exposed infants were reduced, and the incidence of perinatal mortality was increased. Retrospective studies in England have shown an increase in the number of minor congenital anomalies when mothers took aspirin during the first trimester of pregnancy (Richards, 1969; Nelson and Forfar, 1971). In the perinatal period, some aspirin-exposed infants demonstrated platelet dysfunction and a decrease of clotting factor XII. Hemorrhagic phenomena, though of the less serious type, occurred in 3 of 14 exposed infants (Bleyer and Breckenridge, 1970).

Schardein (1976) concluded that evidence of defects is sufficiently small to suggest that the salicylates, despite their widespread use over many years, have little teratogenic potential in man. However, the increased risk of hemorrhage and increased perinatal mortality among chronic users should not be ignored.

Antinauseants and Antihistaminics

On the basis of substantial numbers (1169 mother–child pairs exposed), there has been no evidence to suggest that exposure to antihistaminics and antinauseants is related to overall incidence of malformations or to large categories of major or minor malformations (Heinonen et al., 1977). There is some suggestion of drug-specific association (for example, between respiratory malformations and pheniramine, between genitourinary malformations and diphenhydramine, or between inguinal hernia and both meclizine and diphenhydramine), but there has been little in the way of consistently discernible patterns. Animal data favor the hypothesis that cyclizine and meclizine may produce a variety of defects, particularly cleft anomalies. However, contradictory findings have been reported in humans (Heinonen et al., 1977).

Sedative–Hypnotics and Minor Tranquilizers

Barbiturates
Teratology. The teratogenic potential of the barbiturates and other sedative–hypnotics has been reviewed by Schardein (1976). Barbital sodium and pentobarbital have induced a variety of defects in mice but not in other species. Several reports have associated the use of sedative–hypnotics during pregnancy with congenital defects (Crombie et al., 1970; Nelson and Forfar, 1971; Richards, 1972), while another found no such correlation (Meyer, 1973). Isolated cases have been reported of infants born with a variety of abnormalities after *in utero* exposure to

one of several barbiturates, including amobarbital, secobarbital, or hep-tabarbital, or to nonbarbiturate sedative–hypnotics such as glutethimide or methaqualone. Concurrent use of other drugs, however, makes evaluation of many of these cases difficult.

Phenobarbital, in combination with other anticonvulsive agents, has been associated with congenital anomalies, as well as with an increased incidence of coagulation defects noted in the neonate at birth (Schardein, 1976).

Seip (1976) reported a case in which developmental anomalies followed massive exposure to phenobarbitone *in utero*. A woman received phenobarbitone 0.2 g and primidone (which is in part oxidized to phenobarbitone in the body) 0.5 g daily. A syndrome of facial dysmorphism, pre- and postnatal growth deficiency, developmental delay, and minor malformations was noted in two siblings. The facial anomalies consisted of short nose with low nasal bridge, hypertelorism, epicanthal folds, ptosis of the eyelids, low-set ears, wide mouth with protruding lips, and relative prognathism. In addition, one of the infants had a cleft soft palate and a hypoplastic phalanx of his fifth finger. Both siblings were exposed to extraordinarily high levels of phenobarbitone *in utero*. This syndrome is similar to the clinical picture reported to be produced by the use of phenytoin in pregnancy and dubbed the *fetal hydantoin syndrome* (Smith, 1977). Both these drugs may have a similar mechanism of action on the development of the fetus. In contrast, a beneficial effect of phenobarbital has been to lower the serum bilirubin levels in newborns of epileptic mothers, probably as a result of its ability to induce liver enzymes.

Behavioral Teratology. Phenobarbital treatment during pregnancy has also been associated with altered behavior in the offspring. The offspring of rats treated with 8 mg/kg on Days 5–8 of gestation demonstrated impaired performance in the Hebb–Williams maze and elevated electroshock seizure thresholds (Murai, 1966).

Chronic use of phenobarbital, as well as acute use in labor, has been associated with a decreased sucking response in human newborn infants (Kron et al., 1966). Furthermore, Brazelton (1970) has shown a depressed neurophysiological response in the neonate after the use of phenobarbital in the mother. The phenobarbital-induced abstinence syndrome is described below. Although a need for further studies is indicated on the pre- and perinatal effects of barbiturates on growth and morphogenesis, especially on the development and function of the brain, the available evidence indicates that barbiturates do cause substantial problems and that adverse effects may be related to relatively high dosages (> 50 mg).

In light of the hazards outlined above, the use of barbiturates should be avoided in pregnancy whenever possible, and, if the drug is necessary, efforts should be made to monitor any toxic levels in the mother.

Minor Tranquilizers. Among the tranquilizers that are currently used most commonly are those in the benzodiazepine category (chlordiazepoxide, diazepam, oxazepam). Most of the information available in regard to pregnancy and the newborn stems from studies of diazepam, which has been recognized as an excellent general anticonvulsant (Gladstone et al., 1975).

Pharmacokinetics. Mirkin (1973a) reviewed the pharmacokinetics of diazepam during pregnancy. Investigations utilizing [^{14}C]diazepam in the pregnant monkey have demonstrated a rapid transfer across the placenta, as well as significant uptake and prolonged retention of this compound and its metabolites in the fetal cerebellum, spinal cord, and peripheral nerves. Recent studies in humans have shown that [^{14}C]diazepam and its metabolites are rapidly transferred across the placenta, much greater concentrations being present in cord blood than in maternal blood one hour after administration. Fetal tissue concentrations of diazepam and metabolites peak at this time. The highest levels were observed in the fetal liver, brain, and gastrointestinal tract. No metabolism of diazepam has been observed in homogenates prepared from human placenta, fetal brain, or fetal small intestine, and the rate of metabolism in homogenates of fetal liver was much lower than in adult liver homogenates. Because of the long half-life of diazepam, and its active metabolites oxazepam and desmethyl-diazepam, their blood levels in the fetus remain high for considerable periods. Kanto et al. (1974) treated mothers with a daily dose of 10–15 mg diazepam per day for the last 6–21 days before labor. The blood levels of drug and metabolites remained high enough in the newborns to be pharmacologically active for up to 10 days after birth.

Teratology. Schardein (1976), Goldberg and Di Mascio (1978), and Cooper (1978) have discussed the teratogenic effects of the minor tranquilizers. Diazepam, chlordiazepoxide, and meprobamate have induced abnormalities such as cleft palate and digital defects in mice, but not in the rat or the rabbit. Isolated human cases of malformations associated with the use of diazepam or meprobamate during pregnancy have been reported, but in almost every case, other drugs were taken at the same time.

Safra and Oakley (1975) have shown an association between cleft anomalies and prenatal exposure to diazepam. The investigators interviewed 278 women who bore infants with selected major malformations. In these women, diazepam ingestion during the first trimester of pregnancy was found to be four times more frequent among mothers of children with cleft lip, with or without cleft palate, than among mothers of children with other defects. This association was one of many examined in the analysis and quite possibly may simply be due to chance; the investigators stated that it requires further investigation. They suggested that if a causal relationship does exist, the risk of having a child with cleft lip with or without cleft palate is about 0.4% if diazepam is used in the first trimester. Two other studies (Aarskog, 1975; Saxén and Saxén, 1975) reported a similar association between the use of benzodiazepine during the first trimester and increased risk of oral clefts. On the other hand, Czeizel (1976) was unable to replicate these findings.

In a prospective study of 19,044 live births, Milkovich and van den Berg (1974) found that exposure to meprobamate or chlordiazepoxide during the first trimester of pregnancy increased the number of individuals showing severe abnormalities to 12.1 and 11.4 per 100 births, respectively, compared with an incidence of 2.6% in offspring of mothers who took neither drug, despite experiencing symptoms of anxiety during pregnancy. Five of the meprobamate-exposed babies had cardiac defects. Exposure to the drugs in late pregnancy did not appear to affect the frequency of malformations. In a combined English and French survey of over 20,000 pregnancies, Crombie et al. (1975) found that meprobamate use during early pregnancy was again associated with a significantly increased incidence of malformations (5% versus 2% in the drug-free controls). Chlordiazepoxide and diazepam appeared to have no effect. In a follow-up study of 50,282 pregnancies in the Collaborative Perinatal Project, Hartz et al. (1975) found that chlordiazepoxide exposure during pregnancy did not increase the incidence of mortality or serious congenital malformations among the offspring. Meprobamate exposure did not affect the mortality rate, but a small increase in the frequency of abnormalities was observed when use occurred in early pregnancy. On the basis of these observations, Cooper (1978) concluded that the use of these drugs should not be recommended for women in early pregnancy.

Fetal and Neonatal Toxicity. The use of diazepam has been advocated (Leinzinger, 1970; Joyce and Kenyon, 1972) in the management of eclamptic convulsions because the diazepam-treated patient can be cared for much more easily than the patient who is treated with other anticonvulsants. She can be easily awakened, responds to questions, and can clear her throat, thus maintaining a clear airway. Unfortunately, certain disadvantages appear to be present for the fetus when the total dose to the mother exceeds 30 mg (Cree et al., 1973). Sucking ability is definitely decreased in babies whose mothers have received diazepam, and they have been noted to have hypotonia. The vehicle (caffeine sodium benzoate) in injectable diazepam combines with albumin in the neonate, predisposing the infant to the serious effects of hyperbilirubinemia. It has been found to cause a loss of beat-to-beat variability in the fetal heart rate, which is a parameter important in the evaluation of fetal oxygenation. This drug-induced flattening of the baseline could interfere with a physician's ability to assess fetal well-being in a high-risk situation. The drug causes a drop in the newborn's temperature, indicating an interference with the infant's thermoregulatory system. The decrease in respiratory rate, as well as neonatal depression, has been profound in some infants who have received diazepam. A "floppy infant" syndrome has been reported by Gillberg (1977). It includes hypotonia, sucking difficulties, hypothermia, and attacks of cyanosis following chronic maternal use of low doses of diazepam. For these reasons, diazepam has not been highly recommended in the initial management of eclamptic convulsions (Owen et al., 1972; Scher et al., 1972; Mandelli et al., 1975; Kron et al., 1976; Kelly, 1977). Similar symptoms have been reported in the infant of a mother treated acutely with 500 mg of chlordiazepoxide 4 hr before delivery (Stirrat et al., 1974).

Behavioral Teratology. Information regarding the effects of these drugs on the behavior and development of exposed offspring is scanty. The offspring of rats treated with 60 mg/kg meprobamate during pregnancy were less active and had lower emotionality scores on the open field test than nontreated offspring. They were also slower on the inclined-plane test, made more errors on the Lashley III maze, and were more susceptible to audiogenic seizures than controls (Werboff and Havlena, 1962; Werboff and Kesner, 1963). Murai (1966) also found that prenatal treatment with the same dose of meprobamate produced decreased activity in the offspring as measured in a revolving-drum test and impaired performance in the Hebb–Williams maze. However, attempts to replicate these observations with similar or lower doses of meprobamate were unsuccessful (Kletzkin et al., 1964; Hoffeld and Webster, 1965). In none of these experiments were any of the litters cross-fostered. Differences in treatment protocols and in ages of offspring at testing also make these studies difficult to compare, but it appears that under certain conditions, meprobamate can cause behavioral deficits. It is not known whether the benzodiazepines produce similar effects.

4. CNS STIMULANTS

Amphetamines

The use of the amphetamines during pregnancy is of particular interest since drugs of this class have frequently been prescribed for the purpose of controlling excess prenatal weight gain. In 1947, Finch advocated the use of *d*-amphetamine and, more recently, methylphenidate (Notter and Delande, 1962) and diethylpropion (Silverman and Okun, 1971) have been suggested for the same purpose. Lately, however, the anorexiants have been used less often, first, since there is a tendency toward less stringent control of weight gain during pregnancy, and second, since the therapeutic efficacy of these compounds has been questioned (Milkovich and van den Berg, 1977). However, self-administration of the amphetamines for their stimulant effects still remains a significant problem in some areas. For example, Eriksson et al. (1978) stated that there are approximately 3000 young female methamphetamine users in Sweden, mostly in the metropolitan Stockholm area. However, the total extent of illicit amphetamine use among pregnant women is still unknown.

Chromosome Studies.   The effects of the amphetamines on human chromosomes have not been determined, although Fu et al. (1978) presented preliminary results suggesting that *in vivo,* a single therapeutic dose of d-amphetamine did not increase the incidence of chromosome abnormalities in samples of cultured male human leukocytes. Further work in this area is necessary.

Teratology.   Dextroamphetamine is known to cross the placenta in mice, peak concentrations in the fetal tissues occurring 60 min after i.p. administration of 5 mg/kg [^{3}H]dextroamphetamine to the mother on the 16th day of gestation (Shah and Yates, 1978). Drug concentrations in the fetal brain and liver were one-sixth as high as those in the corresponding maternal tissues. The consequences of prenatal exposure to amphetamines have been the subject of many recent investigations.

Experimental Studies.   The teratogenic potential of the amphetamines and other CNS stimulants has been reviewed by Schardein (1976) and appears to depend on the species and route of administration. Dextroamphetamine has produced a significantly higher incidence of fetal resorptions and of heart, eye, and skeletal abnormalities in two strains of mice after i.p. administration of 50 mg/kg (Nora et al., 1965, 1968). Prenatal intravenous administration of methamphetamine in doses of up to 10 mg/kg in mice and 1.5 mg/kg in rabbits produced a 15% incidence of fetal anomalies, including exencephaly, cleft palate, and eye abnormalities. Schardein (1976) stated that teratogenic effects have never been demonstrated in mice treated orally with comparable doses, or in rats or monkeys. It is possible that differences in the rate of drug metabolism dependent on the route of administration, or in metabolic pathways dependent on species, may explain why parenterally treated mice are most susceptible to drug effects.

Clinical Studies.   Several retrospective studies in humans have reported that amphetamine use during pregnancy is associated with an increased incidence of congenital abnormalities (Nelson and Forfar,

1971), particularly cardiac defects (Nora et al., 1970; Forrest, 1976). Isolated cases of cardiac abnormalities (Gilbert and Khoury, 1970) and exencephaly (Matera et al., 1968) have also been reported after the use of this drug. Schardein (1976) cited a total of seven isolated cases of visceral abnormalities reported in infants of mothers receiving phenmetrazine between the 3rd and 12th weeks of gestation.

Other defects including biliary atresia (Levin, 1971), and microcephaly and mental retardation (McIntire, 1966) have been described in infants of mothers who received various amphetamines, and a variety of other drugs including CNS depressants. Thus, the teratogenic role of amphetamines in the latter cases in unclear.

In two prospective studies of pregnancy and child development, the anorectic drugs (amphetamines and phenmetrazine) prescribed to gravid women during different stages of pregnancy were evaluated for their teratogenicity. Notter and Delande (1962) found no abnormalities in 192 offspring of mothers for whom phenmetrazine had been prescribed during pregnancy. In a larger study, Milkovich and van den Berg (1977) studied 1824 children of mothers with known prepregnancy weight and gestation of 37 weeks or greater, who had anorectic drugs prescribed during pregnancy, and they compared them with 8989 children of mothers who did not receive these drugs. The rate of severe congenital anomalies per 100 live-born children, examined at age five years, did not differ from the rate seen in the group of children whose mothers did not use these drugs. There was, however, an excess of oral cleft anomalies in the offspring of mothers who had amphetamines prescribed in the first 56 days after the last menstrual period. This association may not have been apparent in the Notter and Delande (1962) study because of the smaller sample size. The risk does not appear to be justified by the therapeutic benefit; a rough test of the efficacy of anorectic drugs, comparing mean weight gains in four-week periods before and after the prescription, showed only short-term and limited reduction of weight gain in the mothers.

Because of the growth retardation observed in methylphenidate-treated children (Greenhill et al., 1977), it could be expected that *in utero* amphetamine exposure would increase the incidence of small-for-date fetuses. Unfortunately, the Notter and Delande (1962) and Milkovich and van den Berg (1977) studies did not report birth weights. Eriksson et al. (1978), in a retrospective study of 23 infants of amphetamine-dependent mothers, reported only three that were small for gestational age. An additional six, however, were born prematurely. Although obstetrical complications were few, the occurrence of premature and low-birth-weight infants is probably related to the inadequate prenatal care obtained by these women.

Behavioral Teratology.   The effects of prenatal treatment with amphetamines on the postnatal development and behavior of experimental animals have been the subject of several studies. While not all findings agree, most of the observations in rats and mice are consistent with the theory that prenatal treatment with amphetamines increases the excitability of the offspring. This excitability is manifested by increased nondirected locomotion (Middaugh et al., 1974), hyperactivity (Seliger, 1973), a reduced ability to adapt to new surroundings in the open-field test (Hitzemann et al., 1976), increased ability to learn a conditioned avoidance response (Nasello et al., 1974; Martin, 1975), a reduced hippocampal seizure threshold (Nasello et al., 1974), and more errors in the Lashley III maze on the first four days of testing, probably due to increased locomotor activity (Nasello and Ramirez, 1978).

These effects have resulted from a dose as low as 0.5 mg/kg/day throughout pregnancy (Nasello et al., 1974; Nasello and Ramirez, 1978). This dose is comparatively much lower than the 10- to 50-mg/kg dose needed to produce structural anomalies in the same species. Increased excitability has not been confirmed by all authors. Clark et al. (1970) and Seliger (1975) have reported either hypoactivity or no changes at all. These differences can probably be accounted for by the inconsistent experimental protocols employed.

Three groups have attempted to correlate the observed hyperexcitability of experimental animals with brain catecholamine levels. Hitzemann et al. (1976) reported decreased norepinephrine and dopamine levels up to 84 days of age. Wender (1972) reported increased levels at 30 days, and Middaugh et al. (1974) found that the levels were either increased or decreased depending on the age of the offspring. It is probable that whole brain catecholamine levels do not reflect subtle differences in the localized areas of the brain that govern specific behaviors. Catecholamine turnover studies in specific brain sites may prove to be more valuable in correlating prenatal amphetamine treatment and behavioral alterations with a possible biochemical lesion.

From the above discussion, it would appear that the risk of amphetamine-induced alterations of postnatal behavior is at least as great as, if not greater than, the risk of congenital anomalies. To date, however, no systematic developmental and behavioral study of human infants or children exposed to amphetamines *in utero* has been performed.

Cocaine

Although cocaine is known to cross the placenta (Evans and Harbison, 1977), virtually nothing is known about its effects on the fetus. In the light of the present popularity of this drug in North America, it is obvious that research in this area is necessary.

Tobacco

The prevalence of tobacco use among North American women of childbearing age has been rising over the past few decades to a plateau of 28% (Gritz, this volume). Meanwhile, a large number of investigators have been delineating the adverse effects of tobacco smoke on the fetus, the neonate, and the developing child. The report of the Surgeon General (U.S. Public Health Service, 1979) reviewed in detail the observations and conclusions of over 200 clinical and experimental studies. The conclusions of the report are summarized briefly here.

Tobacco smoke contains many potentially toxic agents, including nicotine, a large number of carcinogenic polycyclic hydrocarbons, carbon monoxide, and cyanide. Many as yet unidentified components of the particulate and vapor phases may also be toxic. Therefore, the effects of both whole smoke and some of the isolated components have been investigated.

Effects on Birth Weight.   Over 45 studies of more than 500,000 births have demonstrated conclusively that tobacco smoking by pregnant women is associated with a smaller birth weight of their infants. This decrease in birth weight, which averages 200 g, is dose-related and is independent of all other factors that influence birth weight, such as race, parity, maternal size and weight gain, socioeconomic status, and sex of child. The reduction in fetal size is not related to a significant decrease in the average duration of gestation, and thus, the infants were small-for-date rather than preterm. A few authors (Rush, 1974; Davies et al., 1976) have suggested that this effect may be secondary to reduced maternal appetite and low weight gain during pregnancy. Miller et al. (1976), however, found that smoking mothers were more likely to have infants with unduly short body lengths and decreases in chest and head circumferences, whereas mothers who had a low weight gain during pregnancy were more likely to have infants with low ponderal indices (light babies with a normal crown–heel length). Thus, maternal smoking appears to be the direct cause of the retardation of fetal growth. Yerushalmy (1971) and Silverman (1977) attempted to correlate differences between the psychological characteristics or life-styles of smokers and nonsmokers with the reduction in birth weights. Their studies suggested that these factors may also contribute to the inhibition of growth. Follow-up studies of growth and development at 1 year (Russell et al., 1968), 5 years (Wingerd and Schoen, 1974), 6½ years (Dunn et al., 1976), and 7 years

(Davie et al., 1972) demonstrated that the children of smoking mothers remain lighter and 1–2 cm shorter than the children of nonsmokers.

Fetal and Perinatal Mortality. The offspring of smoking women have, in addition to a decrease in birth weight, a dose-related increase in the risk of spontaneous abortion, of fetal death, and of neonatal death (U.S. Public Health Service, 1979). When correction is made for the effects of other important variables that influence perinatal mortality, such as race, socioeconomic status, age, and parity, the risk of perinatal death is increased by about 35% for smokers of a pack a day or more. Maternal smoking is associated with a dose-dependent increase in the risk of abruptio placentae, placenta previa, bleeding early or late in pregnancy, premature and prolonged rupture of the membranes, and premature delivery. In fact, most of the perinatal deaths are related to complications of labor or prematurity, rather than to abnormalities of the fetus. The U.S. Public Health Service (1979) report concluded that the immediate cause of most tobacco-induced fetal deaths is probably anoxia, which may be related to placental complications, or to the reduced oxygen-carrying capacity of maternal and fetal hemoglobin caused by the presence of carbon monoxide.

Effects on Placental Function. The ratio of placenta weight to birth weight increases with increasing levels of maternal smoking (U.S. Public Health Service, 1979). The authors of this report suggested that this increase could be a response to a reduced oxygen availability to the fetus mediated by both nicotine and carbon monoxide.

Many clinical and experimental studies of fetal levels of carboxyhemoglobin have demonstrated that the affinity of fetal hemoglobin for carbon monoxide is at least as high as if not higher than the affinity of maternal hemoglobin (U.S. Public Health Service, 1979). An elevated fetal blood carboxyhemoglobin level of 10% would reduce oxygen tension to the point where normal oxygen exchange in the placenta could not be maintained. Carbon monoxide may therefore play a major role in the development of fetal anoxia.

Manning and Feyerabend (1976) found that cigarette smoking caused a reduction in the incidence of fetal breathing movements (an index that appears to reflect fetal condition) in normal and abnormal pregnancies. The size of the reduction varied and was greatest in small-for-date infants and pregnancies complicated by fetal distress in labor. The fall in the amount of fetal breathing movements was significantly related to the rise in the maternal plasma nicotine after smoking, but it was unrelated to the rise in carboxyhemoglobin. Nicotine, which can cause a sympathomimetic response in humans, may cause uterine vasoconstriction and a reduction in uterine blood flow. This would also contribute to fetal anoxia. The greater effect of smoking in pregnancies with clinical evidence of impaired placental function (the small-for-date pregnancies with limited placental reserve and the pregnancies complicated by fetal distress in labor) suggests that the reduction in fetal breathing movements may be related to reduced maternoplacental perfusion.

The U.S. Public Health Service report (1979) also summarized other effects of tobacco smoke on the placenta. In addition to the nicotine-induced vasoconstriction leading to decreased placental blood flow, there is a carbon-monoxide-mediated reduction in *in vitro* placental oxygen consumption. This, however, is countered by a benzo[a]pyrene-related induction of placental oxidative enzyme pathways. These factors could alter in a complex manner the metabolism and transport of various compounds by the trophoblast cells.

Electron-microscopic comparison of full-term placentas from smokers and nonsmokers revealed pronounced changes in those of the smoking group (Asmussen, 1977). Characteristic findings included a broadening of the basement membrane of the placental villus, an increase in the collagen content of the villus, a decrease in vascularization, and intimal changes in the villous capillaries and arterioles, with pronounced intimal edema. Similar changes have been reported from human umbilical arteries. Changes similar to the above can be induced in animal arteries by exposure to carbon monoxide or perfusion with nicotine. Consequently, this study supports the concept that tobacco smoking is harmful to the human vascular system and tissues, aside from the detrimental effect that placentas with this pathology may have on the developing fetus. The toxic effects of other smoke components have not as yet been studied in detail. There is evidence that a single dose of benzo[a]pyrene administered to pregnant mice on Day 18 of gestation produced a significant increase in the incidence of neoplasms of the lungs, the liver, and the mammary glands of the offspring (Nikonova, 1977). McGarry and Andrews (1972) suggested that a dose-related decrease in serum vitamin B_{12} levels in women smoking during pregnancy may reflect a disorder of cyanide detoxification.

Sudden Infant Death Syndrome.   Maternal postpartum smoking may also affect infant mortality. The smoking habits of 56 families who lost babies to the sudden infant death syndrome (SIDS) were compared with those of 86 control families (Bergman and Wiesner, 1976). A higher proportion of the mothers of victims smoked both during pregnancy (61% versus 42%) and after their babies were born (59% versus 37%). The SIDS mothers also smoked a significantly greater number of cigarettes than controls. Therefore, exposure to cigarette smoke may enhance the risk of sudden infant death syndrome for reasons that are not known at this time.

Since there does not seem to be any question that smoking has a detrimental effect on the developing fetus and the newborn, physicians should encourage pregnant women to stop smoking as soon as possible. Stopping is especially important in mothers at high risk, such as those of low socioeconomic class or with a poor obstetrical performance.

Caffeine

Caffeine, a xanthine present in coffee, tea, cola drinks, chocolate, and many over-the-counter analgesics, is one of the most widely used psychoactive drugs (Gilbert, 1976). The effects of caffeine on reproduction have been reviewed by Gilbert (1976) and Weathersbee and Lodge (1977).

Chromosomal Studies.   The mutagenic properties of caffeine have been well defined *in vitro,* although the relevance of the concentrations used to those found in blood serum *in vivo* remains in doubt. This action appears to be related to caffeine-induced disruption of DNA replication (Weathersbee and Lodge, 1977). In humans, however, caffeine does not appear to cause a significant amount of chromosome damage in peripheral leukocytes (Gilbert, 1976; Weathersbee and Lodge, 1977).

Teratology.   Caffeine does produce teratogenic effects in animals. Bertrand et al. (1970) and Nishimura and Nakai (1960) reported cleft palate and digital defects in mice, rats, and rabbits treated orally and parenterally with doses on the order of 50–100 mg/kg per day. These abnormalities can be prevented by pretreatment with propranolol (Fujii and Nishimura, 1974), suggesting that they may arise indirectly as a result of caffeine-induced increases in catecholamine levels in fetal circulation (Gilbert, 1976). There is additional evidence of caffeine-induced fetal toxicity. Rats treated with intraperitoneal administration of up to 80 mg/kg caffeine per day showed a dose-related increase in resorptions, smaller litters, and lower fetal and placental weights, compared with saline-treated controls (Gilbert and Pistey, 1973).

In humans, the use of caffeine does not appear to be associated with a marked increase in the risk of congenital abnormalities (Mulvihill, 1973; Weathersbee et al., 1977). In a prospective study, however, caffeine consumption has been associated with an increased risk of prematurity and deaths of premature infants (Mau, 1974) and lower birth weights (Mau and Netter, 1974) irrespective of age, parity, socioeconomic status, body weight, or the use of tobacco or beer. The results of this study are difficult to interpret, however, since the levels of coffee, tea, and cola consumption were poorly specified.

Fetal and Perinatal Mortality.   In a retrospective study, Weathersbee et al. (1977) examined the outcomes of the pregnancies of 489 women selected at random from the obstetrical records of seven Utah hospitals. This population was predominantly Mormon, and therefore, their consumption of alcohol, tobacco, and illicit drugs would be expected to be low. A subpopulation of 16 women was identified whose mean daily caffeine consumption was 600 mg (8 cups of coffee) or more, while their husbands' intake averaged 566 mg. Of these 16 pregnancies, 8 ended in spontaneous abortion during the first trimester, 5 ended in stillbirth, and 2 ended in the premature birth of a live infant. There was one normal delivery. A second subpopulation of 23 households in which the male mean daily consumption exceeded 600 mg, while the female consumption was less than 400 mg, was also studied. Of 23 pregnancies, 4 ended in spontaneous abortion, 2 in stillbirth, and 2 in premature delivery. In 104 households where the male and female daily caffeine consumption did not exceed 450 mg/day, the percentage of uncomplicated deliveries was similar to that of "control households" whose members drank large amounts of decaffeinated coffee, and to that of 345 control households in which no caffeine-containing beverages were consumed. The authors suggested that a daily caffeine intake of 600 mg or more may predispose women to an increased risk of fetal loss. They also speculated, on the basis of the observations cited above, that much of the toxicity may be male mediated.

Weathersbee et al. (1977) speculated that the fetal wastage may be related to caffeine-induced inhibition of the phosphodiesterases responsible for the hydrolysis of cyclic AMP and cyclic GMP. This could alter both cell division processes and the hormone balances in the mother and in the fetus. Because of the widespread consumption of caffeine, these striking findings, although observed in a small number of subjects, underline the need for further study in this area.

5.   CANNABIS AND HALLUCINOGENS

Cannabis

Traditionally, cannabis was used almost exclusively by males in Eastern countries (Chopra and Chopra, 1939). However, the recent increase in the number of women using this drug in Western countries has caused serious concern that cannabis-induced genetic damage or fetal toxicity may become a significant problem. Like tobacco, cannabis presents a complex problem, since humans are usually exposed in the form of smoke, which contains, along with the main psychoactive ingredient Δ^9-tetrahydrocannabinol (Δ^9-THC), many other cannabinoids that may interact with Δ^9-THC (Karniol et al., 1975), carbon monoxide, polycyclic hydrocarbons, and a host of other largely uncharacterized components in the particulate and vapor phases.

Chromosome Studies

In Vitro Studies. The cytogenetic studies designed to assess the effects of cannabinoids on chromosomes have been reviewed by Falek (1975). In most studies performed *in vitro,* cannabis does not appear to be a potent mutagen. Human leukocytes exposed to rather high concentrations of Δ^9-THC (0.1–100 μM culture medium) do not show an increase in chromosomal abnormalities (Neu et al., 1969; Stenchever and Allen, 1972; Martin et al., 1974). Pace et al. (1971) and Martin et al. (1974) reported similar results in rat leukocytes incubated *in vitro* with cannabis resin. Likewise, no mutagenic activity could be demonstrated when Δ^9-THC was tested *in vivo* and *in vitro* in a variety of microbial and eukaryotic test systems, including the dominant lethal test, the micronucleus test, and the host-mediated assay (Legator et al., 1976; Van Went, 1978; Zimmerman et al., 1978).

On the other hand, cultures of mammalian lung explants consisting mainly of fibroblasts that were exposed *in vitro* to whole cannabis smoke, and to the gas vapor phase alone, demonstrated a decrease in the mitotic index, alterations in DNA content and numbers of chromosomes, and malignant changes (Leuchtenberger et al., 1976).

Experimental Studies in Vivo. In vivo, the administration of up to 100 mg/kg Δ^9-THC for 10 consecutive days to golden hamsters did not produce an increase in the number of chromosome breaks in cultured leukocytes (Nicholson et al., 1973). Likewise, the daily administration of cannabis smoke to beagle dogs for 30 months did not produce an increase in the number of chromosome abnormalities in cultured leukocytes, although a decrease in the mitotic index and an increase in the number of aneuploid cells were observed (Genest et al., 1976).

Staab and de Paul Lynch (1977) reported impaired fetal growth and increased perinatal mortality in the F_2 generation of mice treated with cannabis smoke during pregnancy. These observations, suggestive of genetically transmitted toxicity, indicate that the previously reported negative results must be considered with caution.

Clinical Studies. Cytogenetic studies of cannabis smokers have also been inconclusive. Of seven retrospective comparisons between cannabis users and controls, five groups reported an increased frequency of chromosomal breaks in cultured lymphocytes (Gilmour et al., 1971; Kumar and Kunwar, 1971; Herha and Obe, 1974; Nahas et al., 1974; Stenchever et al., 1974) or an increased number of micronuclei (Morishima et al., 1976). The latter authors considered the micronuclei suggestive of errors in chromosomal segregation during meiosis. This could arise from a THC-induced impairment of protein synthesis, which may lead to a disturbance in the formation of microtubules and spindles. Two groups (Dorrance et al., 1970; Rubin and Comitas, 1972) reported negative results. The interpretation of these retrospective studies is confounded by such variables as multiple drug use (Gilmour et al., 1971), a history of hepatitis among many of the users (Herha and Obe, 1974), and the variety of cell culture techniques and criteria of chromosome damage used.

Three prospective studies (Matsuyama et al., 1973, 1976; Nichols et al., 1974) showed no evidence that daily cannabis smoking for up to 72 days produced chromosomal damage, although all of the subjects in these studies were experienced cannabis users, and the actual predrug frequency of chromosome breakage among these subjects is unknown. There is also no independent basis for estimating how long or how intensive an exposure *in vivo* would be required to produce chromosome damage if it did occur, and it may be that 72 days or less is insufficient exposure.

Stenchever (1975) pointed out that toxicity may be significant even if only a small number of cells are damaged. Newer and more sensitive techniques, such as chromosome banding, that screen for chromatid exchanges may prove valuable in determining whether cannabis causes an increase in the frequency of chromosome breaks.

At this time, therefore, the question is still unresolved. It appears, however, that, despite the lack of a significant mutagenic activity of Δ^9-THC *in vitro, in vivo* exposure to cannabis smoke may increase the hazard of genetic damage and that smoke components other than Δ^9-THC may be either directly responsible for these actions or may potentiate the effects of Δ^9-THC.

Teratology. Exposure to cannabis during pregnancy could affect fetal development either directly by actions on the fetus or indirectly by effects on the mother. Radiolabeled Δ^9-THC is known to cross the placental barrier (Idänpään-Heikkilä, 1969; Harbison and Mantilla-Plata, 1972). Fetal levels are low, however, and the only fetal tissue to show increased affinity for Δ^9-THC or metabolites compared to maternal tissue is the fetal central nervous system (Kennedy and Waddell, 1972). The subcellular distribution of Δ^9-THC in fetal dog brain differs from that in maternal brain (Martin et al., 1977) and appears to be related to differing phospholipid contents of the respective fractions. The authors suggested that this difference was due to the deficiency of myelin in the fetal brain. Placental transfer is higher in early pregnancy than in late pregnancy (Idänpään-Heikkilä, 1969).

Experimental Studies.   The teratogenicity of cannabis extracts and Δ^9-THC has been reviewed by Fleischman et al. (1975) and is summarized briefly here. In early experiments, crude cannabis extracts with an unknown Δ^9-THC content produced an increased incidence of resorptions, stunting, and abnormalities in mice and rats when administered between Days 1 and 6 of gestation (Persaud and Ellington, 1967, 1968). Similar effects occurred in hamsters and rabbits when the drug was given between Days 6 and 8 and Days 7 and 10, respectively (Geber and Schramm, 1969a,c). The potency of these extracts varied with the time of year and the origin of the plant material. The abnormalities most commonly observed included syndactyly, encephalocele, eventration of viscera, and phocomelia. Attempts to replicate these experiments with pure Δ^9-THC in mice, rats, and hamsters have generally been unsuccessful, except at doses high enough to be directly toxic to the mothers (Borgen et al., 1971; Pace et al., 1971; Banerjee et al., 1975; Fleischman et al., 1975; Mantilla-Plata et al., 1975; Joneja, 1976, 1977a,b; Harbison et al., 1977). Doses of 50 mg/kg or greater, however, have produced retardation of maternal weight gain, reduction in fetal size, increased incidence of oral clefts, and increased perinatal mortality due to insufficient maternal lactation (Borgen et al., 1971). Harbison et al. (1977) demonstrated that the teratogenic effects of high doses of Δ^9-THC could be potentiated in mice by pretreatment with a metabolic inhibitor (SKF 525A) or an inducer (phenobarbital). They postulated that this potentiation was due to an alteration of metabolic pathways, possibly producing an increased formation of reactive metabolites, such as epoxides. The relevance of these high doses in terms of human consumption, however, remains in doubt.

Wright et al. (1976) reported a comprehensive study using rats and rabbits in which Δ^9-THC was administered at doses that were considerably lower than previously and more relevant behaviorally. The animals were treated with Δ^9-THC either in pure form or in cannabis extract at doses up to 50 mg/kg prior to mating and throughout pregnancy and lactation. No significant differences with respect to controls in the number of corpora lutea, implantation sites, resorption sites, viable fetuses, or abnormalities were observed. In the rabbits, fetal and pup survival was reduced at the highest dose of cannabis extract. On the other hand, Δ^9-THC administered in the form of cannabis smoke to rats and mice at doses as low as 3.5 mg/kg has produced an increased number of fetal resorptions, reduction in fetal weight, and enhanced perinatal mortality in comparison with controls exposed to cannabinoid-free smoke (Staab and de Paul Lynch, 1977; Rosenkrantz et al., 1978).

Therefore, it seems that cannabis administered in the form of smoke or extract is more likely to produce fetal toxicity than pure Δ^9-THC.

This increased risk is again probably associated with components other than Δ^9-THC. The smoke appears to be even more potent than the extract in this respect. This point is particularly important when human use is considered, since users of illicit cannabis are exposed to all the components of the plant or its smoke, in addition to Δ^9-THC.

Clinical Studies. A variety of anomalies have been reported retrospectively in offspring of pregnant women who were chronic users of marijuana (Hecht et al., 1968; Carakushansky et al., 1969; Gelehrter, 1970; Jacobson and Berlin, 1972; Bogdanoff et al., 1972). However, since all of the women had used LSD and other drugs at some time during pregnancy, the etiology of these anomalies is unclear. A large prospective study would be necessary to quantify the risk of cannabis-induced teratogenesis in humans.

Other Manifestations of Fetal Toxicity. In addition to the more obvious manifestations of fetal toxicity, some of the specific pharmacological properties of cannabis could possibly compromise some of the developing fetal systems in a more subtle manner. For example, impaired cellular-mediated immunity related to the altered function of the thymus-derived lymphocytes has been demonstrated in young male subjects who were using cannabis at least three times per week (Nahas et al., 1974; Cushman et al., 1976). Cannabis could affect the immunological development of the fetus, predisposing it to an increased risk of perinatal infection. The developing rat fetus is also exposed to the effects of Δ^9-THC-induced alterations in maternal luteinizing hormone (LH), follicle-stimulating hormone (FSH), and estrogen levels (Esber et al., 1975). These changes during pregnancy have not so far been demonstrated in humans.

Behavioral Teratology. The fetal CNS is another potential target for the actions of cannabis. Δ^9-THC has high lipid solubility, a long half-life, and a known affinity for the fetal brain. Singer et al. (1973) reported changes in fetal EEG *in utero* when cannabis smoke was administered to guinea pig mothers. There was, however, no control for the effects of carbon monoxide in this investigation. There have been a few studies exploring the possibility of postnatal developmental and behavioral deficits induced by prenatal cannabis treatment. The wide variations in species, dose, methods of drug administration, time and duration of treatment, fostering techniques, age at testing, and behaviors observed make these experiments difficult to compare. Some of the observed deficits included retarded development of cliff avoidance and visual placing reflexes, hyperactivity at 9 days of age, and decrements in grooming behavior at 17 days of age in offspring of rats treated with 10 mg/kg Δ^9-THC on Days 10–12 of gestation (Borgen et al., 1973). These animals also demonstrated delayed incisor eruption and retarded growth until weaning, despite the fact that they were cross-fostered by control mothers that were presumably lactating normally.

Gianutsos and Abbatiello (1972) reported impaired performance in the Lashley III maze in 65-day-old rats exposed to an unquantified amount of Δ^9-THC in cannabis extract during Days 8–11 of gestation. Uyeno (1973) found that spontaneous activity levels and Y-maze performance of 16- to 20-day-old rat pups were unaffected after prenatal treatment with up to 120 mg/kg Δ^9-THC on Days 10–12 of gestation. However, an unspecified amount of alcohol used as a vehicle in this experiment may have masked subtle cannabis-induced changes. Vardaris et al. (1976) found an impairment in acquisition of a passive avoidance response and increased aggression in 21-day-old rat pups exposed to a low dose (2 mg/kg *per os*) of Δ^9-THC throughout pregnancy. These behavioral changes, however, became less evident as the animals grew older. Fried (1976) reported reduced activity and delayed incisor eruption and eye opening in the offspring of rats that were exposed to cannabis smoke on Days 1–19 of gestation. These differences were observed in all cannabis-exposed pups, including those cross-fostered by control mothers. Sassenrath and Chapman (1975) treated a group of macaques daily for a year with 2–4 mg/kg Δ^9-THC *per os*. During the course of the experiment, two offspring were born. One female infant died at birth with "neurohistopathology of hydrocephalus," and the surviving male demonstrated normal postweaning social interaction with peers, but persistent hyperactivity. It is apparent that with one exception, behavioral changes have occurred consistently, even in those experiments that by the use of cross-fostering have controlled for residual effects of cannabis on maternal behavior or lactation. These changes should be more precisely defined and, if possible, correlated with structural, biochemical, or EEG alterations.

These behavioral alterations could be related to the Δ^9-THC-induced impairment of macromolecular synthesis observed by Nahas et al. (1976), or they may possibly result from prenatal hormonal changes, which can affect subsequent behavior (Reinisch, 1977). In addition, Siegel et al. (1977) have demonstrated stressful effects in rat pups exposed to as little as 5 mg/kg Δ^9-THC from Day 9 of gestation until parturition. Fluctuating dental asymmetry, known to be sensitive to such stressing agents as noise and cold, was increased in the drug-exposed offspring. Offspring behavior can also be affected by an increase in prenatal stress (Archer and Blackman, 1971).

Behavioral and developmental follow-ups in the children of cannabis smokers are lacking, but it would seem prudent, on the basis of the animal evidence alone, to advocate abstinence from cannabis during pregnancy.

Hallucinogens

LSD. Since Cohen et al. (1967b) first described chromosomal abnormalities in cultures of human leukocytes exposed *in vitro* to lysergic acid diethylamide (LSD), there has been much debate about the potential reproductive hazards of this drug and other hallucinogens. The rapidly escalating use of these agents by young men and women in the late 1960s and the early 1970s, mainly for illicit but also for therapeutic purposes, raised concern that LSD-induced chromosome breakage or direct fetal toxicity could become a serious problem.

Chromosome Studies. The effect of LSD on chromosomes has been reviewed by many authors, including Dishotsky et al. (1971), Egozcue and Escude (1972), and Titus (1972). Dishotsky et al. reviewed 68 studies and case reports and concluded that prolonged *in vitro* exposure to high concentrations of LSD could cause increased rates of chromosome damage. These high concentrations, however, are not achieved *in vivo* at customary doses. Most studies *in vivo* have demonstrated that treatment with moderate doses of pure LSD does not break human chromosomes. Studies in which LSD-exposed subjects were compared with a control group yielded similar findings to those in which each subject was tested both prior to and after treatment, thus serving as his own control. Irwin and Egozcue (1967) and Cohen et al. (1967a) reported significantly increased breakage rates in users of illicit LSD. LSD sold on the street may contain, in addition to or instead of LSD, a variety of synthetic byproducts and other impurities (Marshman and Gibbins, 1970). Nine other investigators, however, were unable to confirm these findings. Dishotsky et al. (1971) concluded that the positive results, when found, were more related to the general hazards of drug abuse, which include impure preparations, infection, and malnutrition, than to the effects of LSD *per se*.

Teratology. The teratogenic potential of LSD has been reviewed by Dishotsky et al. (1971) and by Schardein (1976). Placental transfer of [^{14}C]-LSD, first demonstrated in mice by Idänpään-Heikkilä and Schoolar (1969), has since been confirmed by many other groups. In the mouse, a higher percentage of the administered dose (2–4%) is distributed to the fetus during early than during late gestation.

The results of the teratogenic studies in animals are inconclusive. Abnormalities have been reported in a variety of species, including mice, rats, hamsters, and rhesus monkeys, after as little as a single dose of 5 μg/kg early in gestation (Alexander et al., 1970) and have consisted of stunting, CNS malformations, and lens abnormalities. Auerbach (1970) suggested that the drug potentiates the spontaneous occurrence of defects in inbred strains of mice. In a multigenerational study, Alexander et al.

(1968) found an increased incidence of LSD-induced fetal mortality that persisted for four generations. A number of other investigators, however, have not observed any teratogenic effects of LSD in mice, rats, hamsters, and rabbits at doses as high as 500 μg/kg administered during the mid-pregnancy. Dishotsky et al. (1971) concluded that the studies in animals indicate a wide variation in individual, strain, and species susceptibility and that an effect, when found, was at a highly specific time in early gestation.

The information on humans is scanty. Dishotsky et al. (1971) cited three studies in which cultured leukocytes of children of illicit LSD users had elevated numbers of chromosome breaks. All of the children were in good health and had no birth defects.

McGlothlin et al. (1970) reported an increased frequency of spontaneous abortions, premature births, and birth defects in 148 pregnancies studied retrospectively, when one parent or both parents were exposed to pure and illicit LSD or pure LSD alone. Illicit LSD exposure appeared to account for these effects, which were less marked among users of pure LSD. One woman, however, accounted for 5 of the 10 abortions observed in the pure plus illicit group. Jacobson and Berlin (1972) studied 148 pregnancies of 140 illicit LSD users. Of the pregnancies identified during the first trimester, 43% ended in spontaneous abortion. In addition, 4 of 14 embryos from therapeutic abortions showed gross anomalies, mainly of the CNS. Of 83 live-born infants, 8 also had serious congenital anomalies, including 5 with limb abnormalities. Since the patients in this study had also been taking other drugs, including cannabis, and the incidence of infectious disease and poor nutrition was high, a definitive correlation of increased reproductive risk with the use of illicit LSD is precluded. However, Jacobson and Berlin (1972) suggested that LSD might be hazardous to human reproduction.

Dishotsky et al. (1971) reviewed six cases of malformed infants born to women who used illicit LSD and other drugs prior to and during pregnancy. The defects consisted mainly of a variety of limb abnormalities, including syndactyly and amputation defects. At that time (1971), no case of malformation in infants exposed *in utero* to pure LSD had been reported. Subsequent cases reviewed by Schardein (1976) confirm the occurrence of limb defects. He concluded that although there is no strong evidence of teratogenetic action of LSD in man, the 11 reported cases of limb defects (including those reported by Jacobson and Berlin, 1972) underline the need for continued surveillance. Recently, Chan et al. (1978) reported the case of a premature infant with severe ocular malformations whose mother had ingested illicit LSD during the first trimester. On the basis of a comparison of this infant with two similar cases, they suggested that there may be a relationship between LSD and ocular abnormalities. Thus, the use of illicit LSD appears to be associated with an increased risk of spontaneous abortion and may be related to an increased incidence of congenital abnormalities. As mentioned previously, other factors associated with illicit drug use confound the interpretation of the published reports. Almost all of the abnormal children of LSD users were also exposed to cannabis, and one group (Stenchever et al., 1974) has suggested that this drug, rather than LSD, may account for the observed toxicity. This question remains unanswered.

Behavioral Teratology. LSD effects on the subsequent behavior of exposed offspring have been the subject of only one study. Uyeno (1970) treated rats on Day 4 of pregnancy with a rather low dose (2.5–10 μg/kg) and observed no changes in the behavior of the pups with respect to untreated controls as ascertained from performance on tests of spontaneous activity, Lashley III maze running, shock avoidance, and food competition.

Other Hallucinogens. Little is known about the teratogenic potential of other hallucinogens. Mescaline was found to increase the incidence of resorptions, stillbirth, runting, and congenital abnormalities in hamsters, but it was much less potent than LSD in this regard (Geber, 1967). Dimethoxyamphetamine was teratogenic in the developing chick embryo (Spindler and Garcia Monge, 1970). Obviously, more work is necessary in this area.

6. NEONATAL ABSTINENCE SYNDROMES FROM PRENATAL DRUG EXPOSURE

CNS Depressants

It has been well documented over the years that infants born to heroin- or methadone-dependent mothers have a high incidence of neonatal abstinence reactions. Recently, less potent opiates have been identified as also precipitating the neonatal opiate abstinence syndrome. These include propoxyphene hydrochloride (Darvon) (Tyson, 1974; Quillian and Dunn, 1976), codeine (Van Leeuwen et al., 1965), and pentazocine (Talwin) (Goetz and Bain, 1974; Preis et al., 1977). In addition, a number of nonopiate CNS depressants have been implicated. These have been reviewed by Ostrea et al. (1977) and include alcohol (Nichols, 1967), barbiturates (Bleyer and Marshall, 1972; Desmond et al., 1972; Blumenthal and Lindsay, 1977), bromide (Rossiter and Rendle-Short, 1972), chlordiazepoxide (Athinarayanan et al., 1976), diazepam (Rementería and Bhatt, 1977), ethchlorvynol (Rumack and Walravens, 1973), diphenhydramine (Parkin, 1974), and imipramine (Webster, 1973).

Neonatal opiate or CNS depressant abstinence syndrome is described as a generalized disorder characterized by signs and symptoms of central nervous system hyperirritability, gastrointestinal dysfunction, respiratory distress, and vague autonomic symptoms, which include yawning, sneezing, mottling, and fever (Table 2). Infants that are afflicted generally develop tremors, which are initially mild and occur only when the infants are disturbed, but which progress to the point where they occur spontaneously without any stimulation of the infant. A high-pitched cry, increased muscle tone, and irritability develop. The infants tend to have increased deep tendon reflexes and an exaggerated Moro reflex. The rooting reflex is increased, and the infants are frequently seen sucking their fists or thumbs, yet when feedings are administered, they have extreme difficulty and regurgitate frequently. The feeding difficulty occurs because of an uncoordinated and ineffectual sucking reflex. The infants may develop loose stools and therefore are susceptible to dehydration and electrolyte imbalance.

The origin of the neonatal abstinence syndrome lies in the abnormal intrauterine environment. A series of steps appears to be necessary for its genesis and for the infant's recovery. The growth and survival of the fetus in the intrauterine environment are endangered by the continuing or episodic transfer of drugs of addictive potential from the maternal to the fetal circulation. The fetus undergoes a biochemical adaptation to the presence of the abnormal agent in its tissues. Abrupt removal of the drug at delivery precipitates the onset of symptoms. The newborn infant continues to metabolize and excrete the drug, and withdrawal or abstinence signs occur when critically low tissue levels have been reached. Recovery from the abstinence syndrome is gradual and occurs as the infant's metabolism is reprogrammed to adjust to the absence of the dependence-producing agent (Desmond and Wilson, 1975).

These infants' respiratory systems are also affected during the withdrawal stage, causing excessive nasal secretions, stuffy nose, and rapid respirations, sometimes accompanied by chest retractions, intermittent cyanosis, and apnea. Severe respiratory embarrassment occurs most often when the infant regurgitates, aspirates, and develops aspiration pneumonia. The high-pitched cry is similar to that of infants with central nervous system hyperirritability. Sucking reflexes are ineffectual and uncoordinated, causing extreme difficulties in feeding behavior. Sleep patterns are disturbed, and infants have spontaneous generalized sweating to an excessive degree.

The above symptoms are found secondary to abstinence from the opiate as well as the nonopiate CNS depressants listed previously. Although infants born to barbiturate addicts may manifest symptoms similar to those of infants passively addicted to opiates, their symptoms

Table 2. Abstinence Symptoms in the Neonatal Period:
Frequency Seen in 138 Newborns at Family Center Program
in Philadelphia

Symptoms	Frequency (percentage)
Common	
Tremors	
Mild/disturbed	96
Mild/undisturbed	95
Marked/disturbed	77
Marked/undisturbed	67
High-pitched cry	95
Continuous high-pitched cry	54
Sneezing	83
Increased muscle tone	82
Frantic sucking of fists	79
Regurgitation	74
Sleeps less than 3 hr after feeding	65
Sleeps less than 2 hr after feeding	66
Sleeps less than 1 hr after feeding	58
Respiratory rate greater than 60/min	66
Poor feeding	65
Hyperactive Moro reflex	62
Loose stools	51
Less common	
Sweating	49
Excoriation	43
Mottling	33
Nasal stuffiness	33
Frequent yawning	30
Fever less than 101°F (38.3°C)	29
Respiratory rate greater than 60/min and retractions	28
Markedly hyperactive Moro reflex	15
Projectile vomiting	12
Watery stools	12
Fever higher than 101°F (38.3°C)	3
Dehydration	1
Generalized convulsions	1

tend to begin at a later age, and undernutrition at birth has not been a usual feature. Since the barbiturate withdrawal syndrome may not develop until an infant has been discharged from the nursery, it may not be treated unless suspicion has been aroused by the mother's symptoms or actions. Furthermore, there is a greater risk of seizure activity in infants withdrawing from barbiturates than in those withdrawing from opiates.

At birth, most dependent infants, whether born to heroin- or methadone-dependent mothers, appear physically and behaviorally normal. The time of onset of withdrawal signs ranges from shortly after birth to two weeks of age, but for the majority, signs appear within 72 hrs. The type of drug used by the mother, her dosage, the timing of the last dose before delivery, the character of the labor, the type and amount of anesthesia and analgesia given during labor, and the maturity, nutrition, and presence of intrinsic disease in the infant may all play a role in determining the time of onset in the individual infant. Because of the variation in time of onset and in severity, a range of types of clinical courses may be delineated. The withdrawal syndrome may be mild and transient, may be delayed in onset, may have a stepwise increase in severity, may be intermittently present, or may have a biphasic course that includes acute neonatal withdrawal signs followed by improvement and then the onset of a subacute withdrawal reaction (Desmond and Wilson, 1975).

The occurrence of neonatal seizures associated with the opiate abstinence syndrome is also a problem causing concern. Goddard and Wilson (1977) reported only one seizure that they could attribute to the opiate abstinence syndrome in over 150 infants born to heroin- or methadone-dependent mothers. On the other hand, other authors have reported a higher incidence of seizures, especially among those infants exposed *in utero* to methadone (Zelson et al., 1971; Kandall, 1977). Herzlinger et al. (1977) found that 18 (5.9%) of 302 neonates passively exposed to opiates during pregnancy had seizures that were attributable to withdrawal. Again, the percentage experiencing seizures was higher in the group exposed to methadone alone than in the group exposed to both heroin and methadone. However, there was no apparent relationship between maternal methadone dosage and the frequency or severity of the seizures. In addition, no significant differences were found between neonates with and those without seizures in birth weight, gestational age, occurrence of other withdrawal symptoms, day of onset of withdrawal symptoms, or the need for specific pharmacologic treatment. All infants with seizures manifested other withdrawal symptoms prior to the initial seizure, and the mean age of seizure onset was 10 days. Generalized motor seizures or rhythmic myoclonic jerks, each of which occurred in seven infants, were the principal seizure manifestations, although in some, the seizure manifestations were complex. Abnormal EEG tended to occur only during the active seizure phenomenon, with normal interictal tracings, and the myoclonic jerks observed during neonatal abstinence reactions by many authors (Kahn et al., 1969; Harper et al., 1974; Lipsitz and Blatman, 1974) may be true seizures.

Controversy has existed over the past few years in regard to the severity of heroin and methadone abstinence reactions in the neonate. Initially, the majority of infants seen in neonatal units suffering from the abstinence syndrome were born to heroin-dependent mothers. Currently, the majority of infants treated are those born to methadone-maintained women. It is virtually impossible to compare the quantity and quality of drug presented to the infant of the heroin-dependent mother with that of the drug presented to the infant of the methadone-maintained mother. Furthermore, methadone-dependent women frequently augment their maintenance methadone dosage with street drugs, barbiturates, and tranquilizers. Therefore, comparisons between the heroin and methadone abstinence syndromes in neonates have been fraught with numerous difficulties of interpretation. It appears that methadone is responsible for a moderate to severe abstinence reaction in the neonate that can be readily treated by experienced individuals. The withdrawal syndrome may be prolonged and may be complicated with seizures in a small percentage of cases. Even though the infant born to the methadone-maintained mother has a good chance of developing the abstinence syndrome to a moderate or severe degree, the stabilization of the maternal lifestyle with increased prenatal care has decreased other medical problems in the infant. It is surely better to have a full-term newborn with moderate to severe methadone withdrawal signs but otherwise healthy than to have a prematurely born and infected infant with mild to moderate heroin withdrawal.

Concern still exists about the reported late withdrawal symptoms in infants born to methadone-dependent women, as well as the somewhat increased incidence of seizure activity. These reported problems need further definition and evaluation (Challis and Scopes, 1977; Harper et al., 1977; Ostrea et al., 1976).

CNS Stimulants

Amphetamines.   The recognition of a distinct amphetamine-induced abstinence syndrome in adults has been impeded by a common tendency to expect all drug withdrawal reactions to resemble those caused by the CNS depressants. It is now well recognized, however, that a syndrome of depression, prolonged sleep, and voracious appetite is characteristic of amphetamine withdrawal (Kalant, 1973). These effects would be expected as rebound phenomena of physical dependence on stimulant and anorexiant drugs.

Four investigators have reported a neonatal abstinence syndrome in infants born to mothers dependent on amphetamines during their pregnancies. Sussman (1963) described two infants who exhibited symptoms so similar to those observed in the opiate abstinence syndrome that he suspected that the mothers were using opiates as well as methamphetamine. Two additional infants, however, showed no symptoms. Ramer (1974) reported the case of an infant whose mother had taken up to 1 g of methamphetamine a day throughout pregnancy, with the "occasional" use of opiates, other CNS depressants, and hallucinogens. Six hours after birth, the infant experienced episodes of sweating, restlessness, hyperirritability, and brief seizures, alternating with periods of listlessness and decreased muscle tone. These symptoms subsided by the sixth postnatal day, and the subsequent development of the child was normal. One infant described by Neuberg (1970) and two by Eriksson et al. (1978), whose mothers had received an unreported amount of amphetamines throughout pregnancy, demonstrated extreme drowsiness persisting up to four days after birth. This drowsiness was so severe in the two reported by Eriksson et al. that they had to be tube-fed. This drowsiness is characteristic of the amphetamine abstinence syndrome in adults and would therefore also be expected to occur in the newborn (Eriksson et al., 1978). It is possible, however, that the observed depression occurs as a result of a direct effect of amphetamines remaining in the newborn after delivery. Amphetamines can reduce motor activity in hyperactive children (Cantwell and Carlson, 1978), although it is unlikely that this effect would be of sufficient magnitude to account for the depression observed by Eriksson et al. (1978). Probably, the hyperirritability observed by Sussman (1963) and Ramer (1974) could be accounted for by the simultaneous withdrawal from CNS depressants.

Caffeine.   Although a caffeine-induced neonatal abstinence syndrome *per se* has never been described, Deutsch (1976) suggested that the therapeutic effect of caffeine in reducing the incidence of apneic episodes in premature babies might be a result of a passively acquired caffeine dependence (i.e., that the apnea might be the result of the withdrawal of caffeine at birth). There is no evidence to deny or support this hypothesis (Aranda, 1976), although there is a coincidence of the usual onset of apnea (2–3 days) and the rate of elimination of caffeine in premature infants.

7. PSYCHOACTIVE DRUGS AND LACTATION

An important aspect of psychoactive drug use among women who wish to breast-feed during the postpartum period is the question of adverse drug effects on the infant's health or on the maternal milk supply.

The rate of drug excretion from the plasma into breast milk is dependent on the plasma concentration of free drug and on the degree of ionization, lipid:water partition coefficient, and molecular weight of the substance (Vorherr, 1974). Because under normal conditions human breast milk is more acid than plasma, the concentration of weakly acidic compounds such as the barbiturates and the salicylates is lower in milk than in plasma. Conversely, the concentration of weakly alkaline drugs (alkaloids, amphetamines, caffeine, opiates) often equals or exceeds plasma levels. Water-soluble drugs of low molecular weight, such as ethanol, are normally present in milk and plasma at equal concentrations. Most drugs enter the mammary alveolar cells by diffusion or by active transport through the basement lamina and the plasma membrane. The plasma membrane is most permeable during the colostral phase of secretion (first week postpartum) (Vorherr, 1974).

Infant Morbidity

Ananth (1978) has reviewed the side effects observed in the neonate from some of the commonly prescribed psychotropic drugs secreted in breast milk. All of the opiates, including morphine, heroin, methadone, and propoxyphene, are detectable in breast milk after maternal use, but the total amounts secreted are small. Blinick et al. (1975) concluded on the basis of quantitative assays of methadone in maternal milk that breast-feeding should be permitted in methadone-maintained mothers if desired. However, it was recommended that since the levels in milk reach a peak shortly after the methadone administration each day, a supplementary bottle be given at this time. Heroin, however, is administered several times per day, in amounts that may exceed the maintenance doses of methadone. There are several reported cases of breast-fed babies that suffered abstinence symptoms when their mothers were deprived of heroin (Ananth, 1978).

The barbiturates are also excreted in breast milk in small amounts. It appears that when given to the nursing mother in therapeutic doses, phenobarbital has little or no effect on the infant, although very high doses may produce toxicity. In animals, the small quantities of phenobarbital excreted in breast milk have been sufficient to induce hepatic enzymes, thus altering the rates of metabolism of many other compounds passed through breast milk or present endogenously (Ananth, 1978).

The benzodiazepines are also excreted in breast milk. At therapeutic doses, drug effects in the infant are minimal, although occasional cases of CNS depression and weight loss have been reported (Ananth, 1978).

Erkkola and Kanto (1972) noted that diazepam, like bilirubin, is conjugated with glucuronic acid. Therefore, the administration of diazepam to nursing mothers is contraindicated, since it may inhibit the metabolism of bilirubin competitively and thus contribute to the development of hyperbilirubinemia.

Although it can be assumed that small amounts of other psychoactive drugs, such as the stimulants, the hallucinogens, and cannabis, are also excreted in breast milk, virtually nothing is known about the effects of these maternally administered compounds on the infant.

Maternal Milk Supply

There is experimental evidence in the rat that Δ^9-THC can impair lactation (Borgen et al., 1971). Several investigators have observed similar trends in women tobacco smokers (U.S. Public Health Service, 1979). It is obvious that further epidemiological studies of tobacco smokers and users of other drugs are necessary to clarify the relationship between psychoactive drug use and milk supply.

8. CLINICAL FOLLOW-UP STUDIES OF GROWTH, DEVELOPMENT, AND BEHAVIOR

Despite the fact that a newborn may be free of physical, behavioral, or neurological deficits at the time of birth after intrauterine exposure to pharmacologic agents, one cannot assume that no effect has occurred. It has long been known that the effects of pharmacologic agents may not become apparent for many months or years. Therefore, the follow-up of infants prenatally exposed to pharmacologic agents is extremely important. A few such studies have been reported or are now in progress.

Hartz et al. (1975) obtained the scores of a mental and motor evaluation at eight months and intelligence scores at four years of 1870 children exposed *in utero* to meprobamate or chlordiazepoxide. These scores were not different from those of 48,412 children who had not been exposed to minor tranquilizers. The authors concluded that these drugs do not cause brain damage.

Tobacco

On the other hand, Dunn et al. (1976,1977) have studied the effect of maternal cigarette smoking during pregnancy and the child's subsequent physical growth, neurological status, and intellectual maturation.

At the age of 6.5 years, children born to smokers, in comparison with a control group, demonstrated significant deficits in physical growth and neurological and intellectual status, even when the observations were corrected for such variables as socioeconomic status. Similar observations have been reported by other groups (Hardy and Mellits, 1972; Davie et al., 1972), but the differences were not always significant. In addition, Denson et al. (1975) found that mothers of 20 methylphenidate-sensitive hyperactive children had smoked significantly more tobacco during pregnancy than the mothers of 20 dyslexic children matched for sex, age, and social class. The authors suggested that this observation may be related to carbon-monoxide-induced anoxia during pregnancy.

The Opiates

Evaluations of infants born to women who have taken licit drugs or smoked cigarettes are somewhat easier than those involving the maternal use of illicit drugs. Therefore, few studies in regard to maternal drug addiction are available, and the numbers of patients involved in those that have been done are small.

Wilson et al. (1973) observed 14 infants of heroin addicts for one year or longer. All of these children were cared for in "stable foster homes" and were presumably not exposed to adverse environments. Of these infants, 7 demonstrated "behavioral disturbances," which included hyperactivity, brief attention span, and temper outbursts. Two others had abnormal neurological findings. Growth impairment was associated with the behavioral abnormalities in 4 infants. All children, however, performed within normal ranges on the Gesell developmental evaluation. It is impossible to conclude from this study whether the behavioral disruption was actually due to the residual effects of prenatal heroin exposure or whether it was correlated with the fact that all of the children in this study were adopted.

McCreary (1976) studied the development, intellectual functioning, and behavior of 22 children prenatally exposed to heroin, ranging in age from three to six years, and compared the results with those of 20 unexposed children also in contact with the drug culture, 15 unexposed children of low birth weight, and 20 unexposed children of normal birth weight. The heroin-exposed children were significantly smaller than those of the other groups according to several growth indices, including height, weight, and head circumference. The parents' response to the Cassel Child Behavior Rating Scale suggested that these children had more behavioral problems during the preschool years. The heroin-exposed group also performed significantly more poorly on a battery of tests designed to assess short-term memory, concentration, and organizational ability. All children, however, had similar scores on the Minnesota Child Development Inventory, a test of general development.

There has also been great concern about the effect of methadone maintenance treatment, given to pregnant women, on the fetus and the neonate. The initial physical condition of the methadone-exposed neonate seems to be somewhat better than that of the heroin-exposed infant, although concern exists about the severity of the abstinence syndrome. It was unknown until recently what possible effects or irreversible damage methadone might cause in the future for these newborns. The literature (Strauss et al., 1974; Ramer and Lodge, 1975) has indicated that as early as three months of age and throughout the first year of life, infants born to methadone-dependent women do function within the normal range in their mental and motor development. In addition, Blinick et al. (1973), Ting et al. (1974), and Green and Zarin-Ackerman (1977) have reported normal psychometric test findings in a total of 54 such children observed up to the age of four years.

In Philadelphia, in a specially designed comprehensive program for pregnant drug-dependent women (Family Center), a follow-up study on infants born to methadone-maintained women has been in progress. A total of 59 infants born to women maintained on methadone during pregnancy were evaluated periodically in regard to development and physical growth and were compared with a control group of 42 infants, randomly selected from the same socioeconomic class and born at the hospital. No drug use was evident in the control group. All were evaluated by the Gesell Developmental Schedule. The data indicated that children of mothers maintained on methadone during pregnancy were lighter in weight and shorter in stature than controls, from birth through 89 weeks of age. Statistical analysis of measurements from birth through 38 weeks showed that, though the study group was consistently below the 50th percentile for weight and height, they did not demonstrate growth lag in comparison with the control group. Furthermore, the study group did not have any unusual or significant health problems as compared with the control group, and there were no abnormal neurolog-

Table 3. Results of Weschler Preschool and Primary Scale of Intelligence

	Children of methadone-dependent women ($N = 10$)		Control children ($N = 12$)	
	Mean	Standard deviation	Mean	Standard deviation
Verbal scale	94.44	11.32	97.75	20.78
Performance scale	86.11	12.81	88.25	13.76
Full scale IQ	89.33	12.97	92.66	18.05

Table 4. Results of Perception and Language Assessment

	Children of methadone-dependent women			Control children		
	N	Mean	Standard deviation	N	Mean	Standard deviation
Imitation of gestures	9	13.77	2.48	13	12.76	4.14
Test of language development	7	81.00	6.16	11	81.81	6.96
Motor-free visual perception test	6	83.33	11.23	10	82.50	10.55

ical findings. There was no correlation between maternal drug intake, degree of neonatal withdrawal, and Gesell behavioral profiles (developmental schedules were accomplished through 24 months of age) (Finnegan et al., 1977b).

Additional studies in progress in Philadelphia include assessments of a present total of 50 four-year-old children. A total of 25 study children were born to women who received methadone maintenance during pregnancy, as well as prenatal care while enrolled in the Family Center Program. The 25 control children were randomly selected from a stratified population of comparable socioeconomic, race, and medical background from a pediatric outpatient clinic. In the preliminary evaluations, 22 children (10 males and 12 females) have been studied. The mean age of the methadone-exposed group is 4 years, 4 months, and the mean age of the control group is 4 years, 4.5 months. Children are assessed by means of a neurological examination, the Weschler Preschool and Primary Scale of Intelligence, the Test of Language Development, Imitation of Gestures, and the Motor-Free Visual Perception Test. Table 3 describes the group means and standard deviations for the Weschler Preschool and Primary Scale of Intelligence. The differences between children born to women maintained on methadone and the controls are very small and not statistically significant, for both subscales and the full-scale IQs. Both groups performed better on the verbal scale than on the performance scale. Table 4 describes the group means and standard deviations for the Imitation of Gestures, the Test of Language Development, and the Motor-Free Visual Perception Test. The data also show no differences between the groups. All neurological findings were within the normal range, and there was no relationship between severity of withdrawal reaction and the IQ scores (Kaltenbach et al., 1978).

These data suggest that at four years of age, children who were born to women maintained on methadone and who underwent neonatal abstinence reactions are functioning within the normal range in their mental development and do not appear to differ in language and perceptual skills from children of comparable backgrounds whose mothers were not involved with drugs. It is encouraging that these observations support the findings of other investigators. However, the question of differences in behavioral patterns still requires extensive investigation, as does the question of the possible existence of learning disability.

9. CONCLUSIONS

It is quite clear from the preceding discussion that the occurrence of fetal and neonatal toxicity induced by the CNS drugs is by no means fully delineated. Conflicting evidence exists in almost every aspect of this field, and data interpretation is very often confounded by such factors as poor maternal nutrition, maternal infections, and polydrug use. From the available evidence, however, many conclusions can be drawn and additional questions raised.

The illicit use of several street drugs has been reported to be associated with signs of toxicity, such as an increased frequency of chromosome breaks in peripheral leukocytes, increased obstetrical complications, and increased fetal morbidity and mortality. It has been difficult to separate the direct pharmacological actions of these agents from each other and from effects mediated by the unfavorable street environment. In some cases, however, limited evidence permits such a distinction to be made.

Since the first reports of chromosome damage in the leukocytes of users of illicit LSD, there has been intense concern that drug-induced genetic damage may become apparent in succeeding generations in the form of congenital abnormalities or other defects. This fear persists, although the biological significance of chromosome damage in peripheral leukocytes is unknown (Gilmour et al., 1971). Use of heroin, cannabis, and illicit LSD has been reported to be associated with an increased incidence of chromosome breaks, while the risk is less to users of methadone only or of pure LSD. This finding suggests that the damage may occur as a result of the adverse street environment or that it may be the result of the administration of only one agent, such as cannabis, that is common to almost all street drug users. In any case, more advanced experimental techniques, such as chromosome banding, may assist in the elucidation of drug effects on chromosomes. The use of animal models may define the biological significance of chromosomal damage observed in the peripheral leukocytes or in the germ cells. Additional multigenerational studies may be useful in this respect. The question of male-mediated toxicity observed with methadone (Smith and Joffe, 1975) and caffeine (Weathersbee and Lodge, 1977) should also be investigated further.

It is also apparent that the teratogenic potential of the CNS agents reviewed is not strikingly dramatic in humans. With most of these compounds, the evidence is conflicting, and no clear pattern of abnormalities has emerged. None of these drugs can begin to match the effects of thalidomide in this respect. There is some indication that some of these agents, when given in the first trimester, can interact with environment and genotype to increase slightly the risk of teratogenesis. The minor tranquilizers, particularly meprobamate, have been associated with an increased incidence of oral clefts and other malformations, the amphetamines with oral clefts and cardiovascular abnormalities, and LSD with amputation defects and ocular abnormalities. It is obvious that continued surveillance in this area is necessary.

The increased incidence of spontaneous abortion associated with some drugs (LSD, caffeine, and nicotine) may occur as a result of the genetic damage described above, as a result of direct fetal toxicity, or both. In humans, these effects are difficult to separate, since drug use generally occurs both prior to and during early pregnancy. This question could best be resolved by the use of animal models.

Illicit drug use has also been associated frequently with an increased risk of prematurity. Prematurity is often the result of infections and other untreated obstetrical complications, and indeed, in heroin and methadone users, this risk is inversely correlated with the extent of prenatal care. This relationship is also true of amphetamine users. With tobacco, however, the increased risk of prematurity is more closely related to the amount smoked than to the degree of prenatal care. Medical complications related to this prematurity, such as asphyxia neonatorum and hyaline membrane disease, rather than direct drug toxicity, appear to account for the increased neonatal morbidity and mortality observed in these infants.

In utero growth retardation has been the most consistent sign of fetal toxicity in both humans and animals. In humans, small-for-date infants have been observed after the maternal use of heroin, tobacco, salicylates, barbiturates, amphetamines, and alcohol (see Chapter 16). This effect appears to be largely independent of maternal food intake, and it probably occurs as a result of fetal anoxia or of alterations in hormonal balance. It is unclear whether all of these agents act by the same mechanism, and until the patterns of impaired fetal growth are more consistently reported (ponderal indices, head circumferences, organ cell counts and weights, etc.), their actions cannot be compared.

A neonatal abstinence syndrome has been associated with almost every drug capable of producing withdrawal symptoms in adults. As in adults, the CNS depressants produce a syndrome characterized by hyperexcitability, while the stimulants, although less well studied, appear to produce depression. These symptoms are often severe enough to require medical intervention. Treatment of the opiate abstinence symptoms with CNS depressants is generally successful, although there is little consensus as to the optimal therapy.

The increased incidence of sudden infant death syndrome in the infants of smokers and opiate users is also worthy of note. It is not known whether infection, fetal hypoxia, prolonged abstinence symptoms, or other factors are responsible for this finding. The occurrence of SIDS should be monitored in the infants of users of other drugs as well, in order to determine whether this effect is common to other psychoactive drugs.

Great concern is sparked by the experimental observations of behavioral alterations in the offspring of animals treated during pregnancy with psychoactive drugs. Behavioral teratology is a new field in which experimental design and techniques were largely unstandardized until recently. Faced with the impossibility of comparing studies from different laboratories, and the difficulty of defining the relevance of such tasks as open field behavior or avoidance learning in terms of human behavior, one is inclined to overlook the fact that a great many laboratories have observed behavioral changes at doses often much lower than those required to produce congenital abnormalities. The changes are almost always quite subtle, and they require quantitative behavioral techniques, rather than simple observations, to become apparent. These effects, not limited to treatment during early pregnancy or to the period of closure of the neural tube, can occur after treatment even during late pregnancy, when CNS development is rapid. Some of the changes appear to be reversible, while others are not.

Attempts to correlate these findings with histological or neurochemical changes have, at present, met with little success. This situation, similar to that found in behavioral toxicity studies in adult animals, probably reflects the relative insensitivity of histological or neurochemical techniques to subtle changes in localized areas of the brain. There is little doubt, however, that behavioral changes are one of the most sensitive indices of CNS toxicity. The standardization of experimental design with respect to treatment schedules, dose, species, fostering and cross-fostering, age at testing, and behaviors monitored will be of great benefit in the interpretation of these results.

Human follow-up studies with observations extending past the first few months are ongoing. Here again, a lack of standardized techniques makes the results difficult to interpret. It is clear that additional studies are still necessary to define further the physical, developmental, and social effects of many of the illicit drugs on the fetus and the neonate and on the future of the children.

As a general observation, it is interesting that the most intensively studied drug, tobacco, has emerged with the most consistent, broad, and dose-dependent pattern of toxicity. It is probable that if some of the other drugs were studied in such a huge number of subjects, the observations would also be more clear-cut.

What, then, should be the approach of the clinician when handling the pregnant woman, and especially the drug-dependent pregnant woman? It is obvious that since no absolutely safe dosage level of any psychoactive drug can be set with respect to the fetus, the benefits of the drug that is to be taken by the pregnant woman must be carefully weighed against the potential hazards to which the fetus may be exposed. The use of recreational drugs, such as tobacco, cannabis, hallucinogens, and alcohol, should be entirely discouraged, and caffeine consumption should be kept within moderation.

Heroin dependence, however, presents an interesting problem. First, the pregnant heroin addict is almost impossible to detoxify, and second, maternal abstinence may produce fetal distress that may be more harmful than passive dependence. On the other hand, a comprehensive methadone maintenance program with adequate prenatal care reduces the incidence of obstetrical and fetal complications, *in utero* growth retardation, and neonatal morbidity and mortality and is associated with a better long-term prognosis than heroin dependence. For these reasons, it is recommended that the pregnant heroin addict be maintained on methadone rather than detoxified.

The pharmacokinetics of the psychoactive drugs in the pregnant woman and her fetus must also be considered when these agents are administered. Psychoactive drugs are all lipid-soluble, and those that have been studied cross the placenta rapidly. Since the metabolism and excretion of most drugs are slow in the neonate, blood levels, if elevated at birth, may remain high for several days. For this reason, prolonged drug effects and delayed onset of neonatal abstinence symptoms may be observed after the administration of those drugs with a long half-life. Drug interactions may compound the total effect on the fetus. In addition, the excretion of drugs in the milk must be considered in those mothers who wish to nurse their infants.

It is especially important, when dealing with drug dependence during pregnancy, that the approach of the physician should not be so critical that it discourages the mother from prenatal care. Instead, the physician should strive to show compassion and understanding with regard to the mother's habit while helping her to protect the developing fetus.

710 LORETTA P. FINNEGAN AND KEVIN O'BRIEN FEHR

In conclusion, adverse initial neonatal effects, as well as the long-term sequelae of psychoactive drug use during pregnancy, have been described in the past and continue to be delineated further. In view of the widespread use of these agents, it is essential, for the protection of future generations, to obtain as broad an understanding of this problem as possible.

ACKNOWLEDGMENTS

The authors wish to express their gratitude to Ms. Kathy Gibbons, to Ms. Dian Reeser, and to Miss Lise Anglin for their assistance in the compilation of data and the preparation of this chapter, and to Mrs. Deborah Lindholm for the typing of the final manuscript. The authors would especially like to thank the editor, Dr. Oriana J. Kalant, for her patience, understanding, and valuable critical comments.

REFERENCES

Aarskog, D., 1975, Association between maternal intake of diazepam and oral clefts, *Lancet* **2**:921.
Abrams, C. A. L., 1975, Cytogenetic risks to the offspring of pregnant addicts, *Addict. Dis.* **2**:63–77.
Alexander, G. J., Machiz, S., and Alexander, R. B., 1968, Inherited abnormalities in three generations of offspring of LSD-treated rats, *Fed. Proc.***27**:220.
Alexander, G. J., Gold, G. M., Miles, B. E., and Alexander, R. B., 1970, Lysergic acid diethylamide intake in pregnancy: Fetal damage in rats, *J. Pharmacol. Exp. Ther.* **173**:48–59.
Amarose, A. P., and Norusis, M. J., 1976, Cytogenetics of methadone-managed and heroin-addicted pregnant women and their newborn infants, *Am. J. Obstet. Gynecol.* **124**:635–640.
Amarose, A. P., and Schuster, C. R., 1971, Chromosomal analyses of bone marrow and peripheral blood in subjects with a history of illicit drug use, *Arch. Gen. Psychiatry* **25**:181–186.
Ananth, J., 1978, Side effects in the neonate from psychotropic agents excreted through breast-feeding, *Am. J. Psychiatry* **135**:801–805.
Aranda, J. V., 1976, Coffee, tea, and apnea—reply, *J. Am. Med. Assoc.***236**:823.
Archer, J. E., and Blackman, D. E., 1971, Prenatal psychological stress and offspring behavior in rats and mice, *Dev. Psychobiol.* **4**:193–248.
Asmussen, I., 1977, Ultrastructure of the human placenta at term: Observations on placentas from newborn children of smoking and nonsmoking mothers, *Acta Obstet. Gynecol. Scand.* **56**:119–126.
Athinarayanan, P., Pierog, S. H., Nigam, S. K., and Glass, L., 1976, Chlordiazepoxide withdrawal in the neonate, *Am. J. Obstet. Gynecol.* **124**:212–213.
Auerbach, R., 1970, LSD: Teratogenicity in mice, *Science* **170**:558.
Balter, M., and Levine, J., 1973, Character and extent of psychotherapeutic drug usage in the United States, in: *Psychiatry,* Part 1, *Proceedings of the Fifth World Congress of*

Psychiatry (R. de la Fuente and M. N. Weisman, eds.), pp. 80–81, American Elsevier, New York.

Banerjee, B. N., Galbreath, C., and Sofia, R. D., 1975, Teratologic evaluation of synthetic Δ⁹-tetrahydrocannabinol in rats, *Teratology* 11:99–101.

Bergman, A. B., and Wiesner, L. A., 1976, Relationship of passive cigarette-smoking to sudden infant death syndrome, *Pediatrics* 58:665–668.

Bertrand, M., Girod, J., and Rigaud, M. F., 1970, Ectrodactylie provoquée par la caféine chez les rongeurs. Rôle des facteurs spécifiques et génétiques, *C. R. Séances Soc. Biol. (Paris)* 164:1488–1489.

Bleyer, W. A., and Breckenridge, R. T., 1970, Studies on the detection of adverse drug reactions in the newborn, II, The effects of prenatal aspirin on newborn hemostasis, *J. Am. Med. Assoc.* 213:2049–2053.

Bleyer, W. A., and Marshall, R. E., 1972, Barbiturate withdrawal syndrome in a passively addicted infant, *J. Am. Med. Assoc.* 221:185–186.

Blinick, G., Jerez, E., and Wallach, R. C., 1973, Methadone maintenance, pregnancy and progeny, *J. Am. Med. Assoc.* 225:477–479.

Blinick, G., Inturrisi, C. E., Jerez, E., and Wallach, M. D., 1975, Methadone assays in pregnant women and progeny, *Am. J. Obstet. Gynecol.* 121:617–621.

Blumenthal, I., and Lindsay, S., 1977, Neonatal barbiturate withdrawal, *Postgrad. Med. J.* 53:157–158.

Bogdanoff, B., Rorke, L. B., Yanoff, M., and Warren, W. S., 1972, Brain and eye abnormalities: Possible sequelae to prenatal use of multiple drugs including LSD, *Am. J. Dis. Child.* 123:145–148.

Borgen, L. A., Davis, W. M., and Pace, H. B., 1971, Effects of synthetic Δ⁹-tetrahydrocannabinol on pregnancy and offspring in the rat, *Toxicol. Appl. Pharmacol.* 20:480–486.

Borgen, L. A., Davis, W. M., and Pace, H. B., 1973, Effects of prenatal Δ⁹-tetrahydrocannabinol on the development of rat offspring, *Pharmacol. Biochem. Behav.* 1:203–206.

Brazelton, T. B., 1970, Effect of prenatal drugs on the behavior of the neonate, *Am. J. Psychiatry* 126:1261–1266.

Braunlich, H., 1977, Kidney development: Drug elimination mechanisms, in: *Drug Disposition During Development* (P. L. Morselli, ed.), pp. 89–100, Spectrum Publications, New York.

Burmeister, W., 1970, Clinical pharmacology in paediatrics, *Int. Z. Klin. Pharmakol. Ther. Toxikol.* 4:32–36.

Butcher, R. E., Vorhees, C. V., and Kimmel, C. A., 1972, Learning impairment from maternal salicylate treatment in rats, *Nature* 236:211–212.

Campbell, C., Phillips, O. C., and Frazier, T. M., 1961, Analgesia during labor: A comparison of pentobarbital, meperidine and morphine, *Obstet. Gynecol.* 17:714–718.

Cantwell, D. P., and Carlson, G. A., 1978, Stimulants in: *Pediatric Psychopharmacology: The Use of Behavior Modifying Drugs in Children* (J. Werry, ed.), pp. 171–207, Brunner/Mazel, New York.

Carakushansky, G., Neu, R. L., and Goudner, L. I., 1969, Lysergide and cannabis as possible teratogens in man, *Lancet* 1:150–151.

Challis, R. E., and Scopes, J. W., 1977, Letter: Late withdrawal symptoms in babies born to methadone addicts, *Lancet* 2:1230.

Chan, C. C., Fishman, M., and Egbert, P. R., 1978, Multiple ocular anomalies associated with maternal LSD ingestion, *Arch. Ophthalmol.* 96:282–284.

Chopra, R. N., and Chopra, G. S., 1939, The present position of hemp-drug addiction in India, *Indian J. Med. Res.*, Supplementary Series, Memoir No. 31:1–119.

Ciuchta, H. P., and Gautieri, R. F., 1964, Effect of certain drugs on perfused human placenta, III, Sympathomimetics, acetylcholine, and histamine, *J. Pharm. Sci.* **53**:184–188.

Clark, C. V. H., Gorman, D., and Vernadakis, A., 1970, Effects of prenatal administration of psychotropic drugs on behavior of developing rats, *Dev. Psychobiol.***3**:225–235.

Cohen, M. M., Hirschhorn, K., and Frosch, W. A., 1967a, *In vivo* and *in vitro* chromosomal damage induced by LSD-25, *N. Engl. J. Med.* **277**:1043–1049.

Cohen, M. M., Marinello, M. J., and Back, N., 1967b, Chromosomal damage in human leukocytes induced by lysergic acid diethylamide, *Science* **155**:1417–1419.

Collins, E., and Turner, G., 1975, Maternal effects of regular salicylate ingestion in pregnancy, *Lancet* **2**:335–337.

Connaughton, J. F., Jr., Finnegan, L. P., Schut, J., and Emich, J. P., 1975, Current concepts in the management of the pregnant opiate addict, *Addict. Dis.* **2**:21–35.

Connaughton, J. F., Jr., Reeser, D., Schut, J., and Finnegan, L. P., 1977, Perinatal addiction: Outcome and management, *Am. J. Obstet. Gynecol.* **129**:679–686.

Cooper, S. J., 1978, Psychotropic drugs in pregnancy: Morphological and psychological adverse effects on offspring, *J. Biosocial Sci.* **10**:321–334.

Cooperstock, R., 1976, Psychotropic drug use among women, *Can. Med. Assoc. J.* **115**:760–763.

Cree, J. E., Meyer, J., and Hailey, D. M., 1973, Diazepam in labour: Its metabolism and effect on the clinical condition and thermogenesis of the newborn, *Br. Med. J.* **4**:251–255.

Crombie, D. L., Pinsent, R. J. F. H., Slater, B. C., Fleming, D., and Cross, K. W., 1970, Teratogenic drugs—RCGP survey, *Br. Med. J.* **4**:178–179.

Crombie, D. L., Pinsent, R. J., Fleming, D. M., Rumeau-Rouquette, C., Goujard, J., and Huel, G., 1975, Fetal effects of tranquilizers in pregnancy, *N. Engl. J. Med.* **293**:198–199.

Cushing, H. W., 1925, *The Life of Sir William Osler,* Vol. 1, Clarendon Press, Oxford, England.

Cushman, P., Khurana, R., and Hashim, G., 1976, Tetrahydrocannabinol: Evidence for reduced rosette formation by normal T lymphocytes, in: *Pharmacology of Marihuana* (M. C. Braude and S. Szara, eds.), pp. 207–209, Raven, New York.

Czeizel, A., 1976, Diazepam, phenytoin, and aetiology of cleft lip and/or cleft palate, *Lancet* **1**:810.

Davie, R., Butler, N., and Goldstein, H., 1972, *From Birth to Seven,* The second report of the National Child Development Study (1958 Cohort), London, Longman, in association with the National Children's Bureau, 198 pp.

Davies, D. P., Gray, O. P., Ellwood, P. C., and Abernethy, M., 1976, Cigarette smoking in pregnancy: Associations with maternal weight gain and fetal growth, *Lancet* **1**:385–387.

Davis, W. M., and Lin, C. H., 1972, Prenatal morphine effects on survival and behavior of rat offspring, *Res. Commun. Chem. Pathol. Pharmacol.* **3**:205–214.

Denson, R., Nanson, L. L., and McWatters, M. A., 1975, Hyperkinesis and maternal smoking, *Can. Psychiatr. Assoc. J.* **20**:183–187.

Desmond, M. M., Schwanecke, R. P., Wilson, G. S., Yasunaga, S., and Burgdorff, I., 1972, Maternal barbiturate utilization and neonatal withdrawal symptomatology, *J. Pediatr.* **80**:190–197.

Desmond, M. M., and Wilson, G. S., 1975, Neonatal abstinence syndrome: Recognition and diagnosis, *Addict. Dis.* **2**:113–121.

Deutsch, M. E., 1976, Letter, Coffee, tea, and apnea, *J. Am. Med. Assoc.* **236**:823.

Dishotsky, N. I., Loughman, W. D., Mogar, R. E., and Lipscomb, W. R., 1971, LSD and genetic damage, *Science* **172**:431–440.

Dorrance, P., Janiger, O., and Teplitz, R. L., 1970, In vivo effects of illicit hallucinogens on human lymphocyte chromosomes, *J. Am. Med. Assoc.* **212**:1488–1491.

Dunn, H. G., McBurney, A. K., Ingram, S., and Hunter, C. M., 1976, Maternal cigarette smoking during pregnancy and the child's subsequent development, I, Physical growth to the age of 6 1/2 years, *Can. J. Public Health* **67**:499–505.

Dunn, H. G., McBurney, A. K., Ingram, S., and Hunter, C. M., 1977, Maternal cigarette smoking during pregnancy and the child's subsequent development, II, Neurological and intellectual maturation to the age of 6 1/2 years, *Can. J. Public Health* **68**:43–50.

Egozcue, J., and Escude, D., 1972, LSD and chromosomes, *Int. Pharmacopsychiatry* **7**:237–243.

Eriksson, M., Catz, C. S., and Yaffe, S. J., 1973, Drugs and pregnancy, *Clin. Obstet. Gynecol.* **16**:199–224.

Eriksson, M., Larsson, G., Winbladh, and Zetterström, R., 1978, The influence of amphetamine addiction on pregnancy and the newborn infant, *Acta Paediatr. Scand.* **67**:95–99.

Erkkola, R., and Kanto, J., 1972, Diazepam and breast-feeding, *Lancet* **1**:1235–1236.

Esber, H. J., Kuo, E. H., Rosenkrantz, H., and Braude, M. C., 1975, Serum hormone levels in non-pregnant and pregnant rats after chronic oral treatment with Δ^9-tetrahydrocannabinol, *Fed. Proc.* **34**:783.

Evans, M. A., and Harbison, R. D., 1977, Cocaine, marihuana and LSD: Pharmacological effects in the fetus and newborn, in: *Drug Abuse in Pregnancy and Neonatal Effects* (J. L. Rementería, ed.), pp. 195–208, Mosby, St. Louis.

Falek, A., 1975, Genetic studies of marijuana: Current findings and future directions, in: *Marijuana and Health Hazards* (J. R. Tinklenberg, ed.), pp. 1–16, Academic, New York.

Finch, J. W., 1947, The overweight obstetric patient with special reference to the use of dexadrine sulfate, *J. Okla. State Med. Assoc.* **40**:119–122.

Finnegan, L., 1976, Clinical effects of pharmacologic agents on pregnancy, the fetus, and the neonate, *Ann. N.Y. Acad. Sci.* **281**:74–89.

Finnegan, L. P., and MacNew, B. A., 1974, Care of the addicted infant, *Am. J. Nurs.* **74**:685–693.

Finnegan, L. P., Connaughton, J. F., Emich, J. P., and Wieland, W. F., 1972, Comprehensive care of the pregnant addict and its effect on maternal and infant outcome, *Contemp. Drug Probl.* **1**:795–809.

Finnegan, L. P., and Reeser, D. S., 1978, Opiate use in pregnancy: A possible causative factor in the sudden infant death syndrome, in: *Proceedings of the 40th Annual Scientific Meeting of the Committee on Problems of Drug Dependence*, pp. 340–349, Baltimore.

Finnegan, L. P., Reeser, D. S., and Connaughton, J. F., Jr., 1977a, The effects of maternal drug dependence on neonatal mortality, *Drug Alcohol Depend.* **2**:131–140.

Finnegan, L. P., Reeser, D. S., and Ting, R. Y., 1977b, Methadone use during pregnancy: Effects on growth and development, *Pediatr. Res.* **11**:377.

Fleischman, R. W., Hayden, D. W., Rosenkrantz, H., and Braude, M. C., 1975, Teratologic evaluation of Δ^9-tetrahydrocannabinol in mice, including a review of the literature, *Teratology* **12**:47–50.

Forfar, J. O., and Nelson, M. M., 1973, Epidemiology of drugs taken by pregnant women: Drugs that may affect the fetus adversely, *Clin. Pharmacol. Ther.* **14**:632–642.

Forrest, J. M., 1976, Drugs in pregnancy and lactation, *Med. J. Aust.* **2**:138–141.

Fraser, A. C., 1976, Drug addiction in pregnancy, *Lancet* **2**:896–899.

Fried, P. A., 1976, Short and long-term effects of pre-natal cannabis inhalation upon rat offspring, *Psychopharmacology* **50**:285–291.

Friedler, G., and Cochin, J., 1972, Growth retardation in offspring of female rats treated with morphine prior to conception, *Science* **175**:645–656.

Fu, T. K., Jarvik, L. F., and Matsuyama, S. S., 1978, Amphetamine and human chromosomes, *Mutat. Res.* **53**:127–128.

Fujii, T., and Nishimura, H., 1974, Reduction in frequency of fetopathic effects of caffeine in mice by treatment with propranolol, *Teratology* **10**:149–152.

Geber, W. F., 1967, Congenital malformations induced by mescaline, lysergic acid diethylamide and bromolysergic acid in the hamster, *Science* **158**:265–267.

Geber, W. F., 1970, Blockade of teratogenic effect of morphine and dehydromorphinone by nalorphine and cyclazocine, *Pharmacologist* **12**:296.

Geber, W. F., and Schramm, L. C., 1969a, Effect of marihuana extract on fetal hamsters and rabbits, *Toxicol. Appl. Pharmacol.* **14**:276–282.

Geber, W. F., and Schramm, L. C., 1969b, Heroin teratogenic and behavioral activity in hamsters, *Fed. Proc.* **28**:262.

Geber, W. F., and Schramm, L. C., 1969c, Teratogenicity of marihuana extract as influenced by plant origin and seasonal variation, *Arch. Int. Pharmacodyn. Ther.* **177**: 224–230.

Gelehrter, T. D., 1970, Lysergic acid diethylamide (LSD) and exstrophy of the bladder, *J. Pediatr.* **77**:1065–1066.

Genest, P., Huy, N. D., and Roy, P. E., 1976, Toxicity study of marijuana in dogs: Effects on the mitotic index and the chromosomes, *Res. Commun. Psychol. Psychiatr. Behav.* **1**:283–290.

Gianutsos, G., and Abbatiello, E. R., 1972, The effect of pre-natal *cannabis sativa* on maze learning ability in the rat, *Psychopharmacologia* **27**:117–122.

Gilbert, E. F., and Khoury, G. H., 1970, Letter, Dextroamphetamine and congenital cardiac malformations, *J. Pediatr.* **76**:638.

Gilbert, E. F., and Pistey, W. R., 1973, Effect on the offspring of repeated caffeine administration to pregnant rats, *J. Reprod. Fertil.* **34**:495–499.

Gilbert, R. M., 1976, Caffeine as a drug of abuse, in: *Research Advances in Alcohol and Drug Problems,* Vol. 3 (R. J. Gibbins, Y. Israel, H. Kalant, R. E. Popham, W. Schmidt, and R. G. Smart, eds.), pp. 49–176, Wiley, New York.

Gillberg, C., 1977, Letter, "Floppy infant syndrome" and maternal diazepam, *Lancet* **2**:244.

Gilmour, D. G., Bloom, A. D., Lele, K. P., Robbins, E. S., and Maximilian, C., 1971, Chromosomal aberrations in users of psychoactive drugs, *Arch. Gen. Psychiatry* **24**:268–272.

Ginsburg, J., 1971, Placental drug transfer, *Annu. Rev. Pharmacol.* **11**:387–408.

Gladstone, G. R., Hordof, A., and Gersony, W. M., 1975, Propanolol administration during pregnancy: Effects on the fetus, *J. Pediatr.* **86**:962–964.

Glass, L., 1974, Narcotic withdrawal in the newborn infant, *J. Natl. Med. Assoc.* **66**:117–120.

Goddard, J., and Wilson, G. S., 1977, Management of neonatal drug withdrawal, *J. Pediatr.* **92**:861.

Goetz, R. L., and Bain, R. V., 1974, Neonatal withdrawal symptoms associated with maternal use of pentazocine, *J. Pediatr.* **84**:887–888.

Goldberg, H. L., and Di Mascio, A., 1978, Psychotropic drugs in pregnancy, in: *Psychopharmacology: A Generation of Progress* (M. A. Lipton, A. Di Mascio, and K. F. Killam, eds.) pp. 1047–1055, Raven, New York.

Green, M., and Zarin-Ackerman, J., 1977, Effect of prenatal exposure to narcotics on central nervous system function of the child, in: *Drug Abuse in Pregnancy and Neonatal Effects* (J. L. Rementería, ed.), pp. 145–154, Mosby, St. Louis.

Greenhill, L. L., Puig-Antich, J., Sassin, J., and Sachar, E. J., 1977, Hormone and growth responses in hyperkinetic children on stimulant medication, *Psychopharmacol. Bull.* 13:33–36.

Gruenwald, P., 1963, Chronic fetal distress and placental insufficiency, *Biol. Neonate* 5:215–265.

Harbison, R. D., and Mantilla-Plata, B., 1972, Prenatal toxicity, maternal distribution and placental transfer of tetrahydrocannabinol, *J. Pharmacol. Exp. Ther.* 180:446–453.

Harbison, R. D., Mantilla-Plata, B., and Rubin, D. J., 1977, Alteration of Δ^9-tetrahydro-cannabinol-induced teratogenicity by stimulation and inhibition of its metabolism, *J. Pharmacol. Exp. Ther.* 202:455–465.

Hardy, J. B., and Mellits, E. D., 1972, Does maternal smoking during pregnancy have a long-term effect on the child? *Lancet* 2:1332–1336.

Harpel, H. S., Jr., and Gautieri, R. F., 1968, Morphine-induced fetal malformations. 1. Exencephaly and axial skeletal fusions, *J. Pharm. Sci.* 57:1590–1597.

Harper, R., Concepcion, G. S., and Blenman, S., 1973, Observations on the sudden death of infants born to addicted mothers, in: *Proceedings Fifth National Conference on Methadone Treatment*, pp. 1122–1126, National Association for the Prevention of Addiction to Narcotics, New York.

Harper, R. G., Solish, G. I., Purow, H. M., Sang, E., and Panepinto, W. C., 1974, The effect of a methadone treatment program upon pregnant heroin addicts and their newborn infants, *Pediatrics* 54:300–305.

Harper, R. G., Solish, G., Feingold, E., Gersten-Woolf, N. B., and Sokal, M. M., 1977, Maternal ingested methadone, body fluid methadone, and the neonatal withdrawal syndrome, *Am. J. Obstet. Gynecol.* 129:417–424.

Hartz, S. C., Heinonen, O. P., Shapiro, S., Siskind, V., and Slone, D., 1975, Antenatal exposure to meprobamate and chlordiazepoxide in relation to malformations, mental development, and childhood mortality, *N. Engl. J. Med.* 292:726–728.

Hecht, F., Beals, R. K., Lees, M. H., Jolly, H., and Roberts, P., 1968, Lysergic-acid-diethylamide and cannabis as possible teratogens in man, *Lancet* 2:1087.

Heinonen, O. P., Slone, D., and Shapiro, S., 1977, Antinauseants, antihistamines, and phenothiazines, in: *Birth Defects and Drugs in Pregnancy*, pp. 322–334, Publishing Sciences Group Inc., Littleton, Mass.

Herha, J., and Obe, G., 1974, Chromosomal damage in chronical users of cannabis—*In vivo* investigation with two-day leukocyte cultures, *Pharmakopsychiatr. Neuropsychopharmakol.* 7:328–337.

Herzlinger, R. A., Kandall, S. R., and Vaughan, H. G., Jr., 1977, Neonatal seizures associated with narcotic withdrawal, *J. Pediatr.* 91:638–641.

Hill, R. M., 1973, Drugs ingested by pregnant woman, *Clin. Pharmacol. Ther.* 14:654–659.

Hitzemann, B. A., Hitzemann, R. J., Brase, D. A., and Loh, H. H., 1976, Influence of prenatal *d*-amphetamine administration on development and behavior of rats, *Life Sci.* 18:605–612.

Hoffeld, D. R., and Webster, R. L., 1965, Effect of injection of tranquilizing drugs during pregnancy on offspring, *Nature* 205:1070–1072.

Hutchings, D. E., Hunt, H. F., Towey, J. P., Rosen, T. S., and Gorinson, H. S., 1976, Methadone during pregnancy in the rat: Dose level effects on maternal and perinatal mortality and growth in the offspring, *J. Pharmacol. Exp. Ther.* 197:171–179.

Idänpään-Heikkilä, J., 1969, Placental transfer of tritiated-1-Δ^9-tetrahydrocannabinol, *N. Engl. J. Med.* 281:330.

Idänpään-Heikkilä, J. E., and Schoolar, J. C., 1969, LSD: Autoradiographic study on the placental transfer and tissue distribution in mice, *Science* **164**:1295–1297.

Irwin, S., and Egozcue, J., 1967, Chromosomal abnormalities in leukocytes from LSD-25 users, *Science* **157**:313–314.

Iuliucci, J. D., and Gautieri, R. F., 1971, Morphine-induced fetal malformations. II: Influence of histamine and diphenhydramine, *J. Pharm. Sci.* **60**:420–425.

Jacobson, C. B., and Berlin, C. M., 1972, Possible reproductive detriment in LSD users, *J. Am. Med., Assoc.* **222**:1367–1373.

Joffe, J. M., 1969, Environmental agents. II. Drugs, in: *Prenatal Determinants of Behavior,* pp. 61–94, Pergamon, New York.

Joneja, M. G., 1976, A study of teratological effects of intravenous, subcutaneous, and intragastric administration of Δ^9-tetrahydrocannabinol in mice, *Toxicol. Appl. Pharmacol.* **36**:151–162.

Joneja, M. G., 1977a, Effects of Δ^9-tetrahydrocannabinol on hamster fetuses, *J. Toxicol. Environ. Health* **2**:1031–1040.

Joneja, M. G., 1977b, Experimental teratological studies with Δ^9-tetrahydrocannabinol in rodents, *Teratology* **16**:110.

Jones, J., 1974, Nutrition, drugs and their interrelations, *Pa. Health* **35**:6–8.

Joyce, D. N., and Kenyon, V. G., 1972, The use of diazepam and hydrallazine in the treatment of severe pre-eclampsia, *J. Obstet. Gynaecol. Br. Commonw.* **79**:250–254.

Kahn, E. J., Neumann, L. L., and Polk, G. A., 1969, The course of the heroin withdrawal syndrome in newborn infants treated with phenobarbital or chlorpromazine, *J. Pediatr.* **75**:495–500.

Kalant, O. J., 1973, *The Amphetamines: Toxicity and Addiction* (2nd ed.), University of Toronto Press, Toronto.

Kaltenbach, K., Graziani, L. J., and Finnegan, L. P., 1978, Development of children born to women who received methadone during pregnancy, *Pediatr. Res.* **12**:372.

Kandall, S. R., Albin, S., Lowinson, J., Berle, B., Eidelman, A. I., and Gartner, L. M., 1976, Differential effects of maternal heroin and methadone use on birthweight, *Pediatrics* **58**:681–685.

Kandall, S. R., Albin, S., Gartner, L. M., Lee, K. S., Eidelman, A., and Lowinson, J., 1977, The narcotic dependent mother: Fetal and meonatal consequences, *Early Human Development* **1**:159–169.

Kanto, J., Erkkola, R., and Sellman, R., 1974, Perinatal metabolism of diazepam, *Br. Med. J.* **1**:641–642.

Karniol, I. G., Shirakawa, I., Takahashi, R. N., Knobel, E., and Musty, R. E., 1975, Effects of Δ^9-tetrahydrocannabinol and cannabinol in man, *Pharmacology* **13**:502–512.

Kelly, J. V., 1977, Drugs used in the management of toxemia of pregnancy, *Clin. Obstet. Gynecol.* **20**:395–410.

Kennedy, J. S., and Waddell, W. J., 1972, Whole-body autoradiography of the pregnant mouse after administration of ^{14}C-Δ^9-THC, *Toxicol. Appl. Pharmacol.* **22**:252–258.

Kletzkin, M., Wojciechowski, H., and Margolin, S., 1964, Postnatal behavioral effects of meprobamate injected into the gravid rat, *Nature* **204**:1206.

Klinger, W., 1977, Development of drug metabolizing enzymes, in: *Drug Disposition during Development* (P. L., Morselli, ed.), pp. 71–88, Spectrum, New York.

Krasner, J., Giacoia, G. P., and Yaffe, S. J., 1973, Drug-protein binding in the newborn infant, *Ann. N.Y. Acad. Sci.* **226**:101–114.

Kron, R. E., Stein, M., and Goddard, K. E., 1966, Newborn sucking behavior affected by obstetric sedation, *Pediatrics* **37**:1012–1016.

Kron, R. E., Litt, M., Eng, D., Phoenix, M. D., and Finnegan, L. P., 1976, Neonatal narcotic abstinence: Effects of pharmacotherapeutic agents and maternal drug usage on nutritive sucking behavior, *J. Pediatr.* **88**:637–641.

Kumar, S., and Kunwar, K. B., 1971, Chromosome abnormalities in cannabis addicts, *J. Assoc. Physicians India* **19:**193–195.

Legator, M. S., Weber, E., Connor, T., and Stoeckel, M., 1976, Failure to detect mutagenic effects of Δ^9-tetrahydrocannabinol in the dominant lethal test, host-mediated assay, blood-urine studies, and cytogenetic evaluation with mice, in: *Pharmacology of Marihuana*, Vol. 2 (M. C. Braude and S. Szara, eds.), pp. 699–709, Raven, New York.

Leinzinger, E., 1970, Prophylaxe und Behandlung des eklamptischen Symptomenkomplexes, *Wien. Klin. Wochenschr.* **82:**584–588.

Leuchtenberger, C., Leuchtenberger, R., Zbinden, J., and Schleh, E., 1976, Cytological and cytochemical effects of whole smoke and of the gas vapor phase from marihuana cigarettes on growth and DNA metabolism of cultured mammalian cells, in: *Marihuana: Chemistry, Biochemistry and Cellular Effects*, pp. 243–256, Springer-Verlag, New York.

Levin, J. N., 1971, Amphetamine ingestion with biliary atresia, *J. Pediatr.* **79:**130–131.

Lindheimer, M. D., and Katz, A. I., 1977, *Kidney Function and Disease in Pregnancy,* Lea and Febiger, Philadelphia.

Lipsitz, P. J., and Blatman, S., 1974, Newborn infants of mothers on methadone maintenance, *N.Y. State J. Med.* **74:**994–999.

Mallov, S., 1977, Drug interactions, *Clin. Obstet. Gynecol.* **20:**483–498.

Mandelli, M., Morselli, P. L., Nordio, S., Pardi, G., Principi, N., Sereni, F., and Tognoni, G., 1975, Placental transfer of diazepam and its disposition in the newborn, *Clin. Pharmacol. Ther.* **17:**564–572.

Manning, F. A., and Feyerabend, C., 1976, Cigarette smoking and fetal breathing movements, *Br. J. Obstet. Gynaecol.* **83:**262–270.

Mantilla-Plata, B., Clewe, G. L., and Harbison, R. D., 1975, Δ^9-tetrahydrocannabinol-induced changes in prenatal growth and development of mice, *Toxicol. Appl. Pharmacol.* **33:**333–340.

Marshman, J. A., and Gibbins, R. J., 1970, A note on the composition of illicit drugs, *Ont. Med. Rev.* September: 1–3.

Martin, B. R., Dewey, W. L., Harris, L. S., and Beckner, J. S., 1977, ^{3}H-Δ^9-tetrahydrocannabinol distribution in pregnant dogs and their fetuses, *Res. Commun. Chem. Pathol. Pharmacol.* **17:**457–470.

Martin, J. C., 1975, Effects on offspring of chronic maternal methamphetamine exposure, *Develop. Psychobiol.* **8:**397–404.

Martin, P. A., Thorburn, M. J., and Bryant, S. A., 1974, *In vivo* and *in vitro* studies of the cytogenetic effects of *Cannabis sativa* in rats and men, *Teratology* **9:**81–85.

Matera, R. F., Zabala, H., and Jimenez, A. P., 1968, Bifid exencephalia. Teratogen action of amphetamine, *Int. Surg.* **50:**79–85.

Matsuyama, S., Yen, F. S., Jarvik, L. F., and Fu, T. K., 1973, Marijuana and human chromosomes, *Genetics* **74:**175.

Matsuyama, S. S., Jarvik, L. F., Fu, T.-K., and Yen, F.-S., 1976, Chromosome studies before and after supervised marijuana smoking, in: *Pharmacology of Marihuana,* Vol. 2 (M. C. Braude and S. Szara, eds.), pp. 723–729, Raven, New York.

Mau, G., 1974, Nahrungs und Genussmittelkonsum in der Schwangerschaft und seine Auswirkungen auf perinatale Sterblichkeit, Frühgeburtlichkeit und andere perinatale Faktoren, *Monatsschr. Kinderheilkd.* **122:**539–540.

Mau, G., and Netter, P., 1974, Kaffee—und Alkoholkonsum—Riskfaktoren in der Schwangerschaft, *Geburtshilfe Frauenheilkd.* **34:**1018–1022.

McCreary, R., 1976, An evaluation of pre-school children born to heroin addicted mothers, Paper presented to the American Psychological Association, Washington, D.C., September.

McGarry, J. M., and Andrews, J., 1972, Smoking in pregnancy and vitamin B_{12} metabolism, *Br. Med. J.* **2:**74–77.

McGlothlin, W. H., Sparkes, R. S., and Arnold, D. O., 1970, Effect of LSD on human pregnancy, *J. Am. Med. Assoc.* **212:**1483–1487.

McIntire, M. S., 1966, Letter, Possible adverse drug reaction, *J. Am. Med. Assoc.* **197:** 62–63.

McMurphy, D. M., and Boréus, L. O., 1968, Pharmacology of the human fetus: Adrenergic receptor function in the small intestine, *Biol. Neonate* **13:**325–339.

Meyer, J. G., 1973, The teratological effects of anticonvulsants and the effects on pregnancy and birth, *Eur. Neurol.* **10:**179–190.

Middaugh, L. D., Blackwell, L. A., Santos, C. A., and Zemp, J. W., 1974, Effects of d-amphetamine sulfate given to pregnant mice on activity and on catecholamines in the brains of offspring, *Dev. Psychobiol.* **7:**429–438.

Milkovich, L., and van den Berg, B. J., 1974, Effects of prenatal meprobamate and chlordiazepoxide hydrochloride on human embryonic and fetal development, *N. Engl. J. Med.* **291:**1268–1271.

Milkovich, L., and van den Berg, B. J., 1977, Effects of antenatal exposure to anorectic drugs, *Am. J. Obstet. Gynecol.* **129:**637–642.

Miller, H. C., Hassanein, K., and Hensleigh, P. A., 1976, Fetal growth retardation in relation to maternal smoking and weight gain in pregnancy, *Am. J. Obstet. Gynecol.* **125:**55–60.

Mirkin, B. L., 1973a, Drug distribution in pregnancy, in: *Fetal Pharmacology* (L. Boréus, ed.), pp. 1–27, Raven, New York.

Mirkin, B. L., 1973b, Maternal and fetal distribution of drugs in pregnancy, *Clin. Pharmacol. Ther.* **14:**643–647.

Morishima, A., Milstein, M., Henrich, R. T., and Nahas, G. G., 1976, Effects of marihuana smoking, cannabinoids, and olivetol on replication of human lymphocytes: Formation of micronuclei, in: *Pharmacology of Marihuana,* Vol. 2 (M. C. Braude and S. Szara, eds.), pp. 711–722, Raven, New York.

Morselli, P. L., 1977, Drug absorption, in: *Drug Disposition During Development* (P. L., Morselli, ed.), pp. 51–60, Spectrum, New York.

Mulvihill, J. J., 1973, Caffeine as a teratogen and mutagen, *Teratology* **8:**69–72.

Murai, N., 1966, Effect of maternal medication during pregnancy upon behavioral development of offspring, *Tohoku J. Exp. Med.* **89:**265–272.

Naeye, R. L., 1965, Malnutrition: Probable cause of fetal growth retardation, *Arch. Pathol.* **79:**284–291.

Nahas, G. G., Suciu-Foca, N., Armand, J. P., and Morishima, A., 1974, Inhibition of cellular mediated immunity in marihuana smokers, *Science* **183:**419–420.

Nahas, G. G., Desoize, B., Hsu, J., and Morishima, A., 1976, Inhibitory effects of Δ^9-tetrahydrocannabinol on nucleic acid synthesis and proteins in cultured lymphocytes, in: *Marihuana: Chemistry, Biochemistry and Cellular Effects* (G. G. Nahas, ed.), pp. 299–312, Springer-Verlag, New York.

Nasello, A. G., and Ramirez, O. A., 1978, Open-field and Lashley III maze behaviour of the offspring of amphetamine-treated rats, *Psychopharmacology* **58:**171–173.

Nasello, A. G., Astrada, C. A., and Ramirez, O. A., 1974, Effects on the acquisition of conditioned avoidance responses and seizure threshold in the offspring of amphetamine treated gravid rats, *Psychopharmacologia* **40:**25–31.

Nelson, M. M., and Forfar, J. O., 1971, Associations between drugs administered during pregnancy and congenital abnormalities of the fetus, *Br. Med. J.* **1:**523–527.

Neu, R. L., Powers, H. O., King, S., and Gardner, L. I., 1969, Cannabis and chromosomes, *Lancet* **1:**675.

Neuberg, R., 1970, Drug dependence and pregnancy: A review of the problems and their management, *J. Obstet. Gynaecol. Br. Commonw.* **77**:1117–1122.

Newman, R. G., 1974, Pregnancies of methadone patients: Findings in New York City Methadone Maintenance Treatment Program, *N.Y. State J. Med.* **74**:52–54.

Nichols, M. M., 1967, Acute alcohol withdrawal syndrome in a newborn, *Am. J. Dis. Child.* **113**:714–715.

Nichols, W. W., Miller, R. C., Heneen, W., Bradt, C., Hollister, L., and Kanter, S., 1974, Cytogenetic studies on human subjects receiving marihuana and delta-9-tetrahydrocannabinol, *Mutat. Res.* **26**:413–417.

Nicholson, M. T., Pace, H. B., and Davis, W. M., 1973, Effects of marihuana and lysergic acid diethylamide on leukocyte chromosomes of the golden hamster, *Res. Commun. Chem. Pathol. Pharmacol.* **6**:427–434.

Nikonova, T. V., 1977, Transplacental action of benzo[a]pyrene and pyrene, *Bull. Exp. Biol. Med.* **84**:1025–1027.

Nishimura, H., and Nakai, K., 1960, Congenital malformations in offspring of mice treated with caffeine, *Proc. Soc. Exp. Biol. Med.* **104**:140–142.

Nora, J. J., Trasler, D. G., and Fraser, F. C., 1965. Malformations in mice induced by dexamphetamine sulfate, *Lancet* **2**:1021–1022.

Nora, J. J., Nora, A. H., Sommerville, R. J., Hill, R, M., and McNamara, D. G., 1967, Maternal exposure to potential teratogens, *J. Am. Med. Assoc.* **202**:1065–1069.

Nora, J. J., Sommerville, R. J., and Fraser, F. C., 1968, Homologies for congenital heart diseases: Murine models, influenced by dextroamphetamine, *Teratology* **1**:413–416.

Nora, J. J., Vargo, T. A., Nora, A. H., Love, K. F., and McNamara, D. G., 1970, Dexamphetamine: A possible environmental trigger in cardiovascular malformations, *Lancet* **1**:1290–1291.

Notter, A., and Delande, M. F., 1962, Prophylaxie des excès de poids chez les gestantes d'apparence normale (À propos de 192 observations réunies en série continue). *Gynecol. Obstet.* **61**:359–377.

Ostrea, E. M., Chavez, C. J., and Strauss, M. E., 1976, A study of factors that influence the severity of neonatal narcotic withdrawal, *J. Pediatr.* **88**:642–645.

Ostrea, E. M., Jr., Ting, E. C., and Cohen, S. N., 1977, Neonatal withdrawal from non-narcotic drugs, in: *Drug Abuse in Pregnancy and Neonatal Effects* (J. L. Rementería, ed.), pp. 165–178. C. V. Mosby, St. Louis.

Owen, J. R., Irani, S. F., and Blair, A. W., 1972, Effect of diazepam administered to mothers during labour on temperature regulation of neonate, *Arch. Dis. Child.* **47**:107–110.

Pace, H. B., Davis, W. M., and Borgen, L. A., 1971, Teratogenesis and marijuana, *Ann. N.Y. Acad. Sci.* **191**:123–131.

Palmisano, P. A., and Cassady, G., 1969, Salicylate exposure in the perinate, *J. Am. Med. Assoc.* **209**:556–558.

Parkin, D. E., 1974, Probable Benadryl withdrawal manifestations in a newborn infant, *J. Pediatr.* **85**:580.

Parry, H., 1968, The use of psychotropic drugs by U.S. adults, *Public Health Service Report* **83**:799–810.

Peckham, C. H., and King, R. W., 1963, A study of intercurrent conditions observed during pregnancy, *Am. J. Obstet. Gynecol.* **87**:609–624.

Persaud, T. V. N., and Ellington, A. C., 1967, Letter, Cannabis in early pregnancy, *Lancet* **2**:1306.

Persaud, T. V. N., and Ellington, A. C., 1968, Teratogenic activity of cannabis resin, *Lancet* **2**:406–407.

Pierson, P. S., Howard, P., and Kleber, H. D., 1972, Sudden deaths in infants born to methadone-maintained addicts, *J. Am. Med. Assoc.* **220:**1733–1734.

Pirola, R. C., 1977, *Drug Metabolism and Alcohol,* University Park Press, Baltimore.

Preis, O., Choi, S. J., and Rudolph, N., 1977, Pentazocine withdrawal syndrome in the newborn infant, *Am. J. Obstet. Gynecol.* **127:**205–206.

Quillian, W. W., II, and Dunn, C. A., 1976, Neonatal drug withdrawal from propoxyphene, *J. Am. Med. Assoc.* **235:**2128.

Rajegowda, B. K., Kandall, S. R., and Falciglia, H., 1976, Sudden infant death (SIDS) in infants of narcotic-addicted mothers, *Pediatr. Res.* **10:**334.

Ramer, C. M., 1974, The case history of an infant born to an amphetamine-addicted mother, *Clin. Pediatr.* **13:**596–597.

Ramer, C. M., and Lodge, A., 1975, Clinical and developmental characteristics of infants of mothers on methadone maintenance, *Addict. Dis.* **2:**227–233.

Rane, A., and Sjöqvist, F., 1972, Drug metabolism in the human fetus and newborn infant, *Pediatr. Clin. North Am.* **19:**37–49.

Reinisch, J. M., 1977, Prenatal exposure of human foetuses to synthetic progestin and oestrogen affects personality, *Nature* **266:**561–562.

Rementería, J. L., and Bhatt, K., 1977, Withdrawal symptoms in neonates from intrauterine exposure to diazepam, *J. Pediatr.* **90:**123–126.

Rementería, J. L., and Nunag, N. N., 1973, Narcotic withdrawal in pregnancy: Stillbirth incidence with a case report, *Am. J. Obstet. Gynecol.* **116:**152–156.

Richards, I. D., 1969, Congenital malformations and environmental influences in pregnancy, *Br. J. Prev. Soc. Med.* **23:**218–225.

Richards, I. D. G., 1972, A retrospective enquiry into possible teratogenic effects of drugs in pregnancy, in: *Drugs and Fetal Development* (M. A. Klingberg, A. Abramovici, and J. Chemke, eds.), pp. 441–455, Plenum, New York.

Rorke, L. B., Reeser, D. S., and Finnegan, L. P., 1977, Nervous system lesions in infants of opiate dependent mothers, *Pediatr. Res.* **11:**565.

Rosenkrantz, H., Fleischman, R. W., and Baker, J. R., 1978, Embryotoxicity of marihuana by inhalation, *Fed. Proc.* **37:**737.

Rossiter, E. J. R., and Rendle-Short, T. J., 1972, Letter, Congenital effects of bromism, *Lancet* **2:**705.

Rubin, V., and Comitas, L., 1972, A study of the effects of chronic ganja smoking in Jamaica, NIMH Contract #42-70:97.

Rucker, T. D., 1974, Drug use. Data, sources, and limitations, *J. Am. Med. Assoc.* **230:**888–890.

Rumack, B. H., and Walravens, P. A., 1973, Neonatal withdrawal following maternal ingestion of ethchlorvynol (Placidyl), *Pediatrics* **52:**714–716.

Rush, D., 1974, Examination of the relationship between birth weight, cigarette smoking during pregnancy and maternal weight gain, *J. Obstet. Gynaecol. Br. Commonw.* **81:**746–752.

Russell, C. S., Taylor, R., and Law, C. E., 1968, Smoking in pregnancy, maternal blood pressure, pregnancy outcome, baby weight and growth, and other related factors: A prospective study, *Br. J. Prev. Soc. Med.* **22:**119–126.

Safra, M. J., and Oakley, G. P., 1975, Association between cleft lip with or without cleft palate and prenatal exposure to diazepam, *Lancet* **2:**478–480.

Sassenrath, E. N., and Chapman, L. F., 1975, Tetrahydrocannabinol-induced manifestations of the "marihuana-syndrome" in group-living macaques, *Fed. Proc.* **34:**1666–1670.

Saxén, I., and Saxén, L., 1975, Association between maternal intake of diazepam and oral clefts, *Lancet* **2:**498.

Schardein, J. L., 1976, *Drugs as Teratogens,* CRC Press, Cleveland.

Scher, J., Hailey, D. M., and Beard, R. W., 1972, The effects of diazepam on the fetus, *J. Obstet. Gynaecol. Br. Commonw.* **79:**635–638.

Seip, M., 1976, Growth retardation, dysmorphic facies, and minor malformations following massive exposure to phenobarbitone *in utero, Acta Paediatr. Scand.* **65:**617–621.

Seliger, D. L., 1973, Effect of prenatal maternal administration of *d*-amphetamine on rat offspring activity and passive avoidance learning, *Physiol. Psychol.* **1:**273–280.

Seliger, D. L., 1975, Prenatal maternal *d*-amphetamine effects on emotionality and audiogenic seizure susceptibility of rat offspring, *Dev. Psychobiol.* **8:**261–268.

Shah, N. S., and Yates, J. D., 1978, Placental transfer and tissue distribution of dextroamphetamine in the mouse, *Arch. Int. Pharmacodyn. Ther.* **233:**200–208.

Siegel, P., Siegel, M. I., Krimmer, E. C., Doyle, W. J., and Barry, H., III, 1977, Fluctuating dental asymmetry as an indicator of the stressful prenatal effects of Δ^9-tetrahydrocannabinol in the laboratory rat, *Toxicol. Appl. Pharmacol.* **42:**339–344.

Silverman, D. T., 1977, Maternal smoking and birth weight, *Am. J. Epidemiol.* **105:**513–521.

Silverman, M., and Okun, R., 1971, The use of an appetite suppressant (diethylpropion hydrochloride) during pregnancy, *Curr. Ther. Res.* **13:**648–653.

Singer, P. R., Scibetta, J. J., and Rosen, M. G., 1973, Simulated marihuana smoking in the maternal and fetal guinea pig, *Am. J. Obstet. Gynecol.* **117:**331–340.

Smith, A. A., Hui, F. W., and Crofford, M., 1974, Retardation of growth by opioids, in: *Perinatal Pharmacology: Problems and Priorities* (J. Dancis and J. C. Hwang, eds.), pp. 195–201, Raven, New York.

Smith, D. J., and Joffe, J. M., 1975, Increased neonatal mortality in offspring of male rats treated with methadone or morphine before mating, *Nature* **253:**202–203.

Smith, D. W., 1977, Teratogenicity of anticonvulsive medications, *Am. J. Dis. Child.* **131:**1337–1339.

Sobrian, S. K., 1977, Prenatal morphine administration alters behavioral development in the rat, *Pharmacol. Biochem. Behav.* **7:**285–288.

Spindler, J. S., and Garcia Monge, M. T., 1970, Effects of DOM (STP) on the chick embryo, *Bull. Narc.* **22(1):**55–60.

Staab, R. J., and de Paul Lynch, V., 1977, Cannabis induced teratogenesis in the CF_1 mouse, *Pharmacologist* **19:**179.

Stenchever, M. A., 1975, Observations on the cytogenetic effects of marijuana, in: *Marijuana and Health Hazards* (J. R. Tinklenberg, ed.), pp. 25–29, Academic, New York.

Stenchever, M. A., and Allen, M., 1972, The effect of delta-9-tetrahydrocannabinol on the chromosomes of human lymphocytes *in vitro, Am. J. Obstet. Gynecol.* **114:**819–821.

Stenchever, M. A., Kunysz, T. J., and Allen, M. A., 1974, Chromosome breakage in users of marihuana, *Am. J. Obstet. Gynecol.* **118:**106–113.

Stirrat, G. M., Edington, P. T., and Berry, D. J., 1974, Transplacental passage of chlordiazepoxide, *Br. Med. J.* **2:**729.

Strauss, M. E., Andresko, M., Stryker, J. C., Wardell, J. N., and Dunkel, L. D., 1974, Methadone maintenance during pregnancy: Pregnancy, birth and neonate characteristics, *Am. J. Obstet. Gynecol.* **120:**895–900.

Sussman, S., 1963, Narcotic and methamphetamine use during pregnancy: Effect on newborn infants, *Am. J. Dis. Child.* **106:**325–330.

Taeusch, H. W., Jr., Carson, S. H., Wang, N. S., and Avery, M. E., 1973, Heroin induction of lung maturation and growth retardation in fetal rabbits, *J. Pediatr.* **82:**869–875.

Ting, R., Keller, A., Berman, P., and Finnegan, L. P., 1974, Follow-up studies of infants born to methadone dependent mothers, *Pediatr. Res.* **8:**346.

Titus, R. J., 1972, Lysergic acid diethylamide: Its effects on human chromosomes and the human organism *in utero*. A review of current findings, *Int. J. Addict.* **7**:701–714.

Turner, G., and Collins, E., 1975, Fetal effects of regular salicylate ingestion in pregnancy, *Lancet* **2**:338–339.

Tyson, H. K., 1974, Neonatal withdrawal symptoms associated with maternal use of propoxyphene hydrochloride (Darvon), *J. Pediatr.* **85**:684–685.

U.S. Public Health Service, 1979, Pregnancy and infant health, in: *The Health Consequences of Smoking: A Report of the Surgeon General*, U.S. Department of Health, Education and Welfare, Washington, D.C.

Uyeno, E. T., 1970, Lysergic acid diethylamide in gravid rats, *Proc. West. Pharmacol. Soc.* **13**:200–203.

Uyeno, E. T., 1973, Δ⁹-Tetrahydrocannabinol administration during pregnancy of the rat, *Proc. West. Pharmacol. Soc.* **16**:64–67.

Valdes-Dapena, M. A., Greene, M., Basavanand, N., Catherman, R., and Treux, R. C., 1973, The myocardial conduction system in sudden death in infancy, *N. Engl. J. Med.* **289**:1179–1180.

Van Leeuwen, G., Guthrie, R., and Stange, F., 1965, Narcotic withdrawal reaction in a newborn infant due to codeine, *Pediatrics* **36**:635–636.

Van Went, G. F., 1978, Mutagenicity testing of 3 hallucinogens: LSD, psilocybin and Δ⁹-THC, using the micronucleus test, *Experientia* **34**:324–325.

Vardaris, R. M., Weisz, D. J., Fazel, A., and Rawitch, A. B., 1976, Chronic administration of delta-9-tetrahydrocannabinol to pregnant rats: Studies of pup behavior and placental transfer, *Pharmacol. Biochem. Behav.* **4**:249–254.

Vest, M. F., and Rossier, R., 1963, Detoxification in the newborn: The ability of the newborn infant to form conjugates with glucuronic acid, glycine, acetate and glutathione, *Ann. N.Y. Acad. Sci.* **111**:183–198.

Vorherr, H., 1974, Drug excretion in breast milk, *Postgrad. Med.* **56**:97–104.

Weathersbee, P. S., and Lodge, J. R., 1977, Caffeine: Its direct and indirect influence on reproduction, *J. Reprod. Med.* **19**:55–63.

Weathersbee, P. S., Olsen, L. K., and Lodge, J. R., 1977, Caffeine and pregnancy: A retrospective survey, *Postgrad. Med.* **62**:64–69.

Webster, P. A. C., 1973, Letter: Withdrawal symptoms in neonates associated with maternal antidepressant therapy, *Lancet* **2**:318–319.

Wender, P. H., 1972, The minimal brain dysfunction syndrome in children, *J. Nerv. Ment. Dis.* **155**:55–71.

Werboff, J., and Havlena, J., 1962, Postnatal behavioral effects of tranquilizers administered to the gravid rat, *Exp. Neurol.* **6**:263–269.

Werboff, J., Kesner, R., 1963, Learning deficits of offspring after administration of tranquilizing drugs to mothers, *Nature* **197**:106–107.

Wilson, G. S., Desmond, M. M., and Verniaud, W. M., 1973, Early development of infants of heroin-addicted mothers, *Am. J. Dis. Child.* **126**:457–462.

Wingerd, J., and Schoen, E. J., 1974, Factors influencing length at birth and height at five years, *Pediatrics* **53**:737–741.

Wright, P. L., Smith, S. H., Keplinger, M. L., Calandra, J. C., and Braude, M. C., 1976, Reproductive and teratologic studies with Δ⁹-tetrahydrocannabinol and crude marijuana extract, *Toxicol. Appl. Pharmacol.* **38**:223–235.

Yacavone, D., Scher, J., Kim, Y. R., Schwitz, B., and O'Connor, H., 1976, Heroin addiction, methadone maintenance, and pregnancy, *J. Am. Osteopath. Assoc.* **75**:826–829.

Yaffe, S. J., 1974, Fetal and neonatal pharmacology, *Clin. Perinatol.* **1**:39–46.

Yerushalmy, J., 1971, The relationship of parents' cigarette smoking to outcome of pregnancy. Implications as to the problem of inferring causation from observed associations, *Am. J. Epidemiol.* **93**:443–456.

Young, D. D., Niebyl, J. R., Blake, D. A., Shipp, D. A., Stanley, J., and King, T. M., 1977, Experience with an adolescent pregnancy program: A preliminary report, *Obstet. Gynecol.* **50**:212–216.

Zagon, I. S., and McLaughlin, P. J., 1977, Effect of chronic maternal methadone exposure on perinatal development, *Biol. Neonate* **31**:271–282.

Zelson, C., 1973, Infant of the addicted mother, *N. Engl. J. Med.* **288**:1393–1395.

Zelson, C., Rubio, E., and Wasserman, E., 1971, Neonatal narcotic addiction: 10 year observation, *Pediatrics* **48**:178–189.

Zimmerman, A. M., Stich, H., and San, R., 1978, Nonmutagenic action of cannabinoids *in vitro*, *Pharmacology* **16**:333–343.

287

Author Index

Subject Index

Bacterial endocarditis, 665
Barbital, 437
  sodium, 675
Barbiturate(s), 11, 12, 18, 137, 174, 181, 193,
    343, 424, 428, 435, 437–438, 439, 440, 449,
    455, 480, 654, 663, 664, 665, 675–677, 695,
    696, 697, 698, 699, 701, 707
  addiction, 266, 267
  use, 174, 186, 303, 338, 358, 376, 378, 434,
    442, 631, 632, 655, 676
    illicit, 140, 169, 173
    licit, 173
Bavaria, 366
Bayley Scales of Infant Motor and Mental
    Development, 607
Beer, 30, 76, 78, 206, 218, 305, 337, 602, 603,
    604, 686
Behavior, 226, 229, 237, 274, 277, 283, 290, 521,
    535, 613, 655, 682, 691, 702, 708
  aggressive, 287, 431
  alcoholic, 12, 305, 312, 639
  antisocial, 206, 224, 226, 227, 228, 242, 313,
    430, 431, 434, 447, 450, 452, 467–470
  consumer, 504
  coping, 430
  criminal, 24, 113
  delinquent, 434, 447
  deviant, 112, 134, 188, 191, 214, 216, 223, 307
  disorder, 22, 268, 609, 635, 703
  drinking. See Drinking, behavior
  drug-using. See Drug(s), using behavior
  economic, 191
  liberal, 492
  maternal, 23, 618, 692
  maze, 610, 676, 679, 682, 692, 695
  modification, 528, 532, 533, 534
  motor, 284
  neurotic, 310
  nondeviant, 127
  political, 192
  problem, 205, 597, 609, 703
  sexual, 125, 205, 453, 655
  smoking, 20, 182, 191, 366, 367, 371, 381, 496,
    502, 503, 505, 533, 534, 537
  social, 10, 129, 286
  sociopathic, 477, 480
  unlawful, 126, 127
  verbal, 286
  women's, 304, 312
Benzedrine, 448
Benzedrine inhaler, 446
Benzo[a]pyrene, 685
Benzodiazepines, 18, 435, 439, 455, 632, 677,
    678, 679, 701
Bereavement, 428
Betel nut, 448, 450
Beverage, 20, 236, 345, 357, 392, 409, 598, 602,
    603, 638, 639, 664, 687
  preference, 115, 334, 409
Bias, 8, 70, 101, 132, 211, 222, 236, 245, 303,
    400, 401, 402
  reporting, 133–136
  sampling, 131–133, 337, 338, 387
  sex, 71, 74, 111, 113
    sources of, 71, 135

Bilirubin, 660, 676, 702
Blackouts, 78
  male, 78
  female, 78
Blacks, 179, 208, 213, 214, 222, 271, 467, 515
Blood alcohol concentration (BAC), 86, 89, 101,
    104, 112, 598, 611, 613, 618, 619, 620, 623,
    626, 638, 643
Blood alcohol level (BAL), 13, 72, 73, 101, 270,
    280, 281, 282, 283, 285, 287, 291, 357, 358,
    563, 609, 610, 612, 615
Brain, 254, 475, 490, 501, 535, 565, 603, 611, 640,
    643, 657, 682, 708
  abnormalities, 612, 623, 624, 673
  damage, 338, 352, 358, 550, 619, 702
  development, 631, 674, 676
  drug levels, 663
  ethanol levels, 615
  fetal, 622, 625, 658, 677, 680, 689, 691
  infant, 658, 671
  maternal, 622, 689
  pathology, 547
Brain Committee, 449
Breast-feeding, 701
Breath test, 104
Breech presentation, 475, 666
Brief Psychiatric Rating Scale, 307
Bromides, 435–437, 444, 455, 695
Bromureides, 434, 435, 436, 437
Bronchitis, 17, 334, 351, 371, 443, 506, 508, 514,
    520
Butorphanol, 572, 573

Cactus, 424, 452, 489
Caffeine, 19, 441, 607, 632, 655, 686–687, 700,
    707, 709
  sodium benzoate, 678
Calcium, 624, 628, 632
California, 53, 140, 186, 207, 208, 447
Canada, 81, 84, 96, 100, 101, 132, 141, 354, 445
  death rates in, 92, 331
  drug use in, 9, 136, 137, 138, 187, 445, 654
  heavy drinking in, 86
  impaired driving in, female, 101
  problem drinking in, 112
  tobacco use in, 145, 488
Cancer, 15, 314, 354–355, 357, 358, 376, 466,
    508–513
  bladder, 509, 536
  breast, 512
  bronchus, 379
  cervix uteri, 512
  corpus uteri, 512
  esophagus, 354, 374, 379, 509
  gastrointestinal tract, 357
  head, 354, 371, 374
  large intestine, 512
  larynx, 354, 509, 536
  liver, 354
  lung, 17, 91, 92, 95, 116, 371, 374, 379, 381,
    506, 508, 509, 510, 513, 514, 536
    among men, 381, 511, 512
    among women, 190, 381, 511, 512
  mouth, 354, 374, 379
  neck, 355, 371, 374

Fish, 610
Floppy infant syndrome, 679
Folate, 348, 349, 356, 628, 629
France, 302, 343, 490
French, 271
Freons, 446
Frigidity, 310

Gambling, 41
Gas, 446, 513, 519, 688
Gasoline, 172, 447
Gastritis, 409
Genetic damage, 596, 633, 661, 687, 689, 706,
    707
Genetic endowment, 234, 235, 662
Genetic factors, 12, 13, 233, 236, 237, 240, 246,
    256, 259, 269–270, 598, 618, 661
Genetic markers, 235–236, 247–254, 258
Genetic predisposition, 635
Genetics, 242, 244, 245, 247, 256, 258, 315, 367,
    505
  of alcoholism, 237
  cyto-, 666
Georgia, 399
Germany, 440, 455, 599
Gesell Developmental Scale, 597, 703, 704
Gin, 596
"Gin epidemic," 596
Gliosis, 671
Glue, 168, 172, 181
  sniffing, 141, 169, 447
Glutamate, 625
Glutethimide, 676
Gonad(s), 554, 561, 629
Gonadotropins, 470, 472, 556, 558, 562
  human chorionic (hCG), 551, 552, 554, 555
Gonorrhea, 665. See also Venereal disease
Gottschalk Verbal Anxiety Scale, 273
Great Britain, 306, 441, 455
Greeks, 271
Griseofulvin, 664
Guinea pig, 610, 691
Gynecomastia, 548, 553, 574

Habit(s), 18, 442, 447, 497, 517, 535
  drinking, 207, 337, 357, 366, 367, 441
    surveys of, 337
  drug, 468, 665, 709
  health, 642
  prescribing, 128
  smoking, 338, 351, 357, 366, 367, 494, 499,
    503, 505, 508, 511, 524, 685
Halfway house, 400
Hallucinations, 239
Hallucinogens, 9, 134, 136, 137, 138, 168, 177,
    179, 180, 424, 451–453, 456, 489, 490, 655,
    658, 693–695, 702, 709
Halothane, 471
Hamster, 673, 688, 690, 693, 694, 695
Hardy Rand Rittler (HRR), pseudoisochromatic
    plates, 250, 251
Harrison Narcotic Act, 127, 466, 467
Hashish, 424

Health, 22, 208, 367, 393, 505, 596, 640, 694, 701
  attitudes, 21, 514
  mental, 118, 502, 505
  physical, 118
  problems, 110, 117, 208, 514, 595, 704
  risk, 19, 176, 188, 190, 220, 367, 487, 488, 507,
    508, 514, 521, 536, 654
  of women, 22, 193, 400, 643, 644, 664, 665,
    668, 670
Heart, 350, 612, 620, 622, 628, 640, 662, 678, 680
Heart disease, 15, 91, 116, 349, 350, 371, 374,
    443, 505, 506, 514, 596, 631
  death from, 116, 349, 381
  among women, 17, 190, 339, 536
Heart failure, 290
Hedonism, 290
Hematopoiesis, 348, 350
Hemoglobin, 519, 684
  carboxy-, 684
Hemorrhage, 348, 475, 508, 611, 666, 669, 671,
    674, 675
Hemp, 446
Hens, 610, 695
Hepatitis, 161, 339–343, 376, 475, 477, 665, 667,
    689
Hepatocytes, 343
Hepatoma, 343, 354
Heptabarbital, 676
Hereditary component, 235
Hereditary effect, 238
Heredity, 301
Heritability, 237
Hernia, 675
Heroin, 130, 136, 138, 140, 174, 179, 210, 215,
    219, 220, 221, 222, 224, 228, 446, 452, 470,
    472, 475, 476, 478, 556, 571, 655, 666, 667,
    668, 669, 670, 672, 673, 695, 698, 699, 701,
    703, 704, 707
  addiction, 216, 227, 267, 527, 666, 667, 709
  use, 131, 135, 140, 168, 174, 177, 180, 182,
    185, 214, 218, 221, 222, 223, 440, 445, 631,
    706
    intravenous, 129
    rates, 213
  users, 222, 227, 453, 477, 556
Herpes simplex, 665. See also Venereal disease
"Hidden housewife" hypothesis, 107, 115
"High," 443
Hippie, 451
Hippocampus, 501
"Home protection," 55
  manual, 56
Homeless men, 304, 305
Homeless women, 304, 305
Homosexuality, 310, 468
Hormone(s), 277, 283, 284, 291, 470–472, 514,
    546, 547, 567, 568, 576, 578, 627, 660, 663,
    669, 687
  adrenocorticotropic (ACTH), 17, 471, 546, 563,
    565, 566, 569, 575
  anterior pituitary, 567, 568–570, 629
  antidiuretic (ADH), 573–574, 575, 577
  follicle-stimulating (FSH), 470, 546, 547, 552,
    557, 558, 560, 562, 577, 691